DONALD E. KNUTH *Stanford University*

ADDISON–WESLEY

Volume 1 / **Fundamental Algorithms**

THE ART OF
COMPUTER PROGRAMMING

THIRD EDITION

Boston · Columbus · New York · San Francisco · Amsterdam · Cape Town
Dubai · London · Madrid · Milan · Munich · Paris · Montréal · Toronto · Delhi · Mexico City
São Paulo · Sydney · Hong Kong · Seoul · Singapore · Taipei · Tokyo

TEX is a trademark of the American Mathematical Society

METAFONT is a trademark of Addison–Wesley

The author and publisher have taken care in the preparation of this book, but make no expressed or implied warranty of any kind and assume no responsibility for errors or omissions. No liability is assumed for incidental or consequential damages in connection with or arising out of the use of the information or programs contained herein.

For government sales inquiries, please contact governmentsales@pearsoned.com
For questions about sales outside the U.S., please contact intlcs@pearson.com

Visit us on the Web: informit.com/aw

Library of Congress Cataloging-in-Publication Data

```
Knuth, Donald Ervin, 1938-
   The art of computer programming / Donald Ervin Knuth.
   xx,652 p.   24 cm.
   Includes bibliographical references and index.
   Contents: v. 1. Fundamental algorithms. -- v. 2. Seminumerical
algorithms. -- v. 3. Sorting and searching. -- v. 4a. Combinatorial
algorithms, part 1.
   Contents: v. 1. Fundamental algorithms. -- 3rd ed.
   ISBN 978-0-201-89683-1 (v. 1, 3rd ed.)
   ISBN 978-0-201-89684-8 (v. 2, 3rd ed.)
   ISBN 978-0-201-89685-5 (v. 3, 2nd ed.)
   ISBN 978-0-201-03804-0 (v. 4a)
   1. Electronic digital computers--Programming.  2. Computer
algorithms.   I. Title.
QA76.6.K64  1997
005.1--DC21                                              97-2147
```

Internet page https://www-cs-faculty.stanford.edu/~knuth/taocp.html contains current information about this book and related books.

ISBN-13   978-0-201-89683-1
ISBN-10   0-201-89683-4

Fifty-second printing, February 2024
52 2024

PREFACE

*Here is your book, the one your thousands of letters have asked us
to publish. It has taken us years to do, checking and rechecking countless
recipes to bring you only the best, only the interesting, only the perfect.
Now we can say, without a shadow of a doubt, that every single one of them,
if you follow the directions to the letter, will work for you exactly as well
as it did for us, even if you have never cooked before.*

— *McCall's Cook Book* (1963)

THE PROCESS of preparing programs for a digital computer is especially attractive, not only because it can be economically and scientifically rewarding, but also because it can be an aesthetic experience much like composing poetry or music. This book is the first volume of a multi-volume set of books that has been designed to train the reader in various skills that go into a programmer's craft.

The following chapters are *not* meant to serve as an introduction to computer programming; the reader is supposed to have had some previous experience. The prerequisites are actually very simple, but a beginner requires time and practice in order to understand the concept of a digital computer. The reader should possess:

a) Some idea of how a stored-program digital computer works; not necessarily the electronics, rather the manner in which instructions can be kept in the machine's memory and successively executed.

b) An ability to put the solutions to problems into such explicit terms that a computer can "understand" them. (These machines have no common sense; they do exactly as they are told, no more and no less. This fact is the hardest concept to grasp when one first tries to use a computer.)

c) Some knowledge of the most elementary computer techniques, such as looping (performing a set of instructions repeatedly), the use of subroutines, and the use of indexed variables.

d) A little knowledge of common computer jargon — "memory," "registers," "bits," "floating point," "overflow," "software." Most words not defined in the text are given brief definitions in the index at the close of each volume.

These four prerequisites can perhaps be summed up into the single requirement that the reader should have already written and tested at least, say, four programs for at least one computer.

I have tried to write this set of books in such a way that it will fill several needs. In the first place, these books are reference works that summarize the knowledge that has been acquired in several important fields. In the second place, they can be used as textbooks for self-study or for college courses in the computer and information sciences. To meet both of these objectives, I have incorporated a large number of exercises into the text and have furnished answers for most of them. I have also made an effort to fill the pages with facts rather than with vague, general commentary.

This set of books is intended for people who will be more than just casually interested in computers, yet it is by no means only for the computer specialist. Indeed, one of my main goals has been to make these programming techniques more accessible to the many people working in other fields who can make fruitful use of computers, yet who cannot afford the time to locate all of the necessary information that is buried in technical journals.

We might call the subject of these books "nonnumerical analysis." Computers have traditionally been associated with the solution of numerical problems such as the calculation of the roots of an equation, numerical interpolation and integration, etc., but such topics are not treated here except in passing. Numerical computer programming is an extremely interesting and rapidly expanding field, and many books have been written about it. Since the early 1960s, however, computers have been used even more often for problems in which numbers occur only by coincidence; the computer's decision-making capabilities are being used, rather than its ability to do arithmetic. We have some use for addition and subtraction in nonnumerical problems, but we rarely feel any need for multiplication and division. Of course, even a person who is primarily concerned with numerical computer programming will benefit from a study of the nonnumerical techniques, for they are present in the background of numerical programs as well.

The results of research in nonnumerical analysis are scattered throughout numerous technical journals. My approach has been to try to distill this vast literature by studying the techniques that are most basic, in the sense that they can be applied to many types of programming situations. I have attempted to coordinate the ideas into more or less of a "theory," as well as to show how the theory applies to a wide variety of practical problems.

Of course, "nonnumerical analysis" is a terribly negative name for this field of study; it is much better to have a positive, descriptive term that characterizes the subject. "Information processing" is too broad a designation for the material I am considering, and "programming techniques" is too narrow. Therefore I wish to propose *analysis of algorithms* as an appropriate name for the subject matter covered in these books. This name is meant to imply "the theory of the properties of particular computer algorithms."

The complete set of books, entitled *The Art of Computer Programming*, has the following general outline:

> *Volume 1. Fundamental Algorithms*
>> Chapter 1. Basic Concepts
>> Chapter 2. Information Structures

Volume 2. Seminumerical Algorithms

   Chapter 3. Random Numbers
   Chapter 4. Arithmetic

Volume 3. Sorting and Searching

   Chapter 5. Sorting
   Chapter 6. Searching

Volume 4. Combinatorial Algorithms

   Chapter 7. Combinatorial Searching
   Chapter 8. Recursion

Volume 5. Syntactical Algorithms

   Chapter 9. Lexical Scanning
   Chapter 10. Parsing

Volume 4 deals with such a large topic, it actually represents several separate books (Volumes 4A, 4B, and so on). Two additional volumes on more specialized topics are also planned: Volume 6, *The Theory of Languages* (Chapter 11); Volume 7, *Compilers* (Chapter 12).

I started out in 1962 to write a single book with this sequence of chapters, but I soon found that it was more important to treat the subjects in depth rather than to skim over them lightly. The resulting length of the text has meant that each chapter by itself contains more than enough material for a one-semester college course; so it has become sensible to publish the series in separate volumes. I know that it is strange to have only one or two chapters in an entire book, but I have decided to retain the original chapter numbering in order to facilitate cross references. A shorter version of Volumes 1 through 5 is planned, intended specifically to serve as a more general reference and/or text for undergraduate computer courses; its contents will be a subset of the material in these books, with the more specialized information omitted. The same chapter numbering will be used in the abridged edition as in the complete work.

The present volume may be considered as the "intersection" of the entire set, in the sense that it contains basic material that is used in all the other books. Volumes 2 through 5, on the other hand, may be read independently of each other. Volume 1 is not only a reference book to be used in connection with the remaining volumes; it may also be used in college courses or for self-study as a text on the subject of *data structures* (emphasizing the material of Chapter 2), or as a text on the subject of *discrete mathematics* (emphasizing the material of Sections 1.1, 1.2, 1.3.3, and 2.3.4), or as a text on the subject of *machine-language programming* (emphasizing the material of Sections 1.3 and 1.4).

The point of view I have adopted while writing these chapters differs from that taken in most contemporary books about computer programming in that I am not trying to teach the reader how to use somebody else's software. I am concerned rather with teaching people how to write better software themselves.

My original goal was to bring readers to the frontiers of knowledge in every subject that was treated. But it is extremely difficult to keep up with a field that is economically profitable, and the rapid rise of computer science has made such a dream impossible. The subject has become a vast tapestry with tens of thousands of subtle results contributed by tens of thousands of talented people all over the world. Therefore my new goal has been to concentrate on "classic" techniques that are likely to remain important for many more decades, and to describe them as well as I can. In particular, I have tried to trace the history of each subject, and to provide a solid foundation for future progress. I have attempted to choose terminology that is concise and consistent with current usage. I have tried to include all of the known ideas about sequential computer programming that are both beautiful and easy to state.

A few words are in order about the mathematical content of this set of books. The material has been organized so that persons with no more than a knowledge of high-school algebra may read it, skimming briefly over the more mathematical portions; yet a reader who is mathematically inclined will learn about many interesting mathematical techniques related to discrete mathematics. This dual level of presentation has been achieved in part by assigning ratings to each of the exercises so that the primarily mathematical ones are marked specifically as such, and also by arranging most sections so that the main mathematical results are stated *before* their proofs. The proofs are either left as exercises (with answers to be found in a separate section) or they are given at the end of a section.

A reader who is interested primarily in programming rather than in the associated mathematics may stop reading most sections as soon as the mathematics becomes recognizably difficult. On the other hand, a mathematically oriented reader will find a wealth of interesting material collected here. Much of the published mathematics about computer programming has been faulty, and one of the purposes of this book is to instruct readers in proper mathematical approaches to this subject. Since I profess to be a mathematician, it is my duty to maintain mathematical integrity as well as I can.

A knowledge of elementary calculus will suffice for most of the mathematics in these books, since most of the other theory that is needed is developed herein. However, I do need to use deeper theorems of complex variable theory, probability theory, number theory, etc., at times, and in such cases I refer to appropriate textbooks where those subjects are developed.

The hardest decision that I had to make while preparing these books concerned the manner in which to present the various techniques. The advantages of flow charts and of an informal step-by-step description of an algorithm are well known; for a discussion of this, see the article "Computer-Drawn Flowcharts" in the ACM *Communications*, Vol. 6 (September 1963), pages 555–563. Yet a formal, precise language is also necessary to specify any computer algorithm, and I needed to decide whether to use an algebraic language, such as ALGOL or FORTRAN, or to use a machine-oriented language for this purpose. Perhaps many of today's computer experts will disagree with my decision to use a machine-oriented language, but I have become convinced that it was definitely the correct choice, for the following reasons:

a) A programmer is greatly influenced by the language in which programs are written; there is an overwhelming tendency to prefer constructions that are simplest in that language, rather than those that are best for the machine. By understanding a machine-oriented language, the programmer will tend to use a much more efficient method; it is much closer to reality.

b) The programs we require are, with a few exceptions, all rather short, so with a suitable computer there will be no trouble understanding the programs.

c) High-level languages are inadequate for discussing important low-level details such as coroutine linkage, random number generation, multi-precision arithmetic, and many problems involving the efficient usage of memory.

d) A person who is more than casually interested in computers should be well schooled in machine language, since it is a fundamental part of a computer.

e) Some machine language would be necessary anyway as output of the software programs described in many of the examples.

f) New algebraic languages go in and out of fashion every five years or so, while I am trying to emphasize concepts that are timeless.

From the other point of view, I admit that it is somewhat easier to write programs in higher-level programming languages, and it is considerably easier to debug the programs. Indeed, I have rarely used low-level machine language for my own programs since 1970, now that computers are so large and so fast. Many of the problems of interest to us in this book, however, are those for which the programmer's art is most important. For example, some combinatorial calculations need to be repeated a trillion times, and we save about 11.6 days of computation for every microsecond we can squeeze out of their inner loop. Similarly, it is worthwhile to put an additional effort into the writing of software that will be used many times each day in many computer installations, since the software needs to be written only once.

Given the decision to use a machine-oriented language, which language should be used? I could have chosen the language of a particular machine X, but then those people who do not possess machine X would think this book is only for X-people. Furthermore, machine X probably has a lot of idiosyncrasies that are completely irrelevant to the material in this book yet which must be explained; and in two years the manufacturer of machine X will put out machine $X + 1$ or machine $10X$, and machine X will no longer be of interest to anyone.

To avoid this dilemma, I have attempted to design an "ideal" computer with very simple rules of operation (requiring, say, only an hour to learn), which also resembles actual machines very closely. There is no reason why a student should be afraid of learning the characteristics of more than one computer; once one machine language has been mastered, others are easily assimilated. Indeed, serious programmers may expect to meet many different machine languages in the course of their careers. So the only remaining disadvantage of a mythical machine is the difficulty of executing any programs written for it. Fortunately, that is not really a problem, because many volunteers have come forward to write simulators for the hypothetical machine. Such simulators are ideal for instructional purposes, since they are even easier to use than a real computer would be.

I have attempted to cite the best early papers in each subject, together with a sampling of more recent work. When referring to the literature, I use standard abbreviations for the names of periodicals, except that the most commonly cited journals are abbreviated as follows:

CACM = Communications of the Association for Computing Machinery

JACM = Journal of the Association for Computing Machinery

Comp. J. = The Computer Journal (British Computer Society)

Math. Comp. = Mathematics of Computation

AMM = The American Mathematical Monthly

SICOMP = SIAM Journal on Computing

FOCS = IEEE Symposium on Foundations of Computer Science

SODA = ACM–SIAM Symposium on Discrete Algorithms

STOC = ACM Symposium on Theory of Computing

Crelle = Journal für die reine und angewandte Mathematik

As an example, "*CACM* **6** (1963), 555–563" stands for the reference given in a preceding paragraph of this preface. I also use "*CMath*" to stand for the book *Concrete Mathematics*, which is cited in the introduction to Section 1.2.

Much of the technical content of these books appears in the exercises. When the idea behind a nontrivial exercise is not my own, I have attempted to give credit to the person who originated that idea. Corresponding references to the literature are usually given in the accompanying text of that section, or in the answer to that exercise, but in many cases the exercises are based on unpublished material for which no further reference can be given.

I have, of course, received assistance from a great many people during the years I have been preparing these books, and for this I am extremely thankful. Acknowledgments are due, first, to my wife, Jill, for her infinite patience, for preparing several of the illustrations, and for untold further assistance of all kinds; secondly, to Robert W. Floyd, who contributed a great deal of his time towards the enhancement of this material during the 1960s. Thousands of other people have also provided significant help — it would take another book just to list their names! Many of them have kindly allowed me to make use of hitherto unpublished work. My research at Caltech and Stanford was generously supported for many years by the National Science Foundation and the Office of Naval Research. Addison–Wesley has provided excellent assistance and cooperation ever since I began this project in 1962. The best way I know how to thank everyone is to demonstrate by this publication that their input has led to books that resemble what I think they wanted me to write.

Preface to the Third Edition

After having spent ten years developing the TEX and METAFONT systems for computer typesetting, I am now able to fulfill the dream that I had when I began that work, by applying those systems to *The Art of Computer Programming*. At last the entire text of this book has been captured inside my personal computer, in an electronic form that will make it readily adaptable to future changes in printing and display technology. The new setup has allowed me to make literally thousands of improvements that I've been wanting to incorporate for a long time.

In this new edition I have gone over every word of the text, trying to retain the youthful exuberance of my original sentences while perhaps adding some more mature judgment. Dozens of new exercises have been added; dozens of old exercises have been given new and improved answers.

The Art of Computer Programming is, however, still a work in progress. Therefore some parts of this book are headed by an "under construction" icon, to apologize for the fact that the material is not up-to-date. My files are bursting with important material that I plan to include in the final, glorious, fourth edition of Volume 1, perhaps 15 years from now; but I must finish Volumes 4 and 5 first, and I do not want to delay their publication any more than absolutely necessary.

My efforts to extend and enhance these volumes have been enormously enhanced since 1980 by the wise guidance of Addison–Wesley's editor Peter Gordon. He has become not only my "publishing partner" but also a close friend, while continually nudging me to move in fruitful directions. Indeed, my interactions with dozens of Addison–Wesley people during more than three decades have been much better than any author deserves. The tireless support of managing editor John Fuller, whose meticulous attention to detail has maintained the highest standards of production quality in spite of frequent updates, has been particularly praiseworthy.

Most of the hard work of preparing the new edition was accomplished by Phyllis Winkler and Silvio Levy, who expertly keyboarded and edited the text of the second edition, and by Jeffrey Oldham, who converted nearly all of the original illustrations to METAPOST format. I have corrected every error that alert readers detected in the second edition (as well as some mistakes that, alas, nobody else noticed); and I have tried to avoid introducing new errors in the new material. However, I suppose some defects still remain, and I want to fix them as soon as possible. Therefore I will cheerfully award \$2.56 to the first finder of each technical, typographical, or historical error. The webpage cited on page iv contains a current listing of all corrections that have been reported to me.

Stanford, California   D. E. K.
April 1997

> *Things have changed in the past two decades.*
> — BILL GATES (1995)

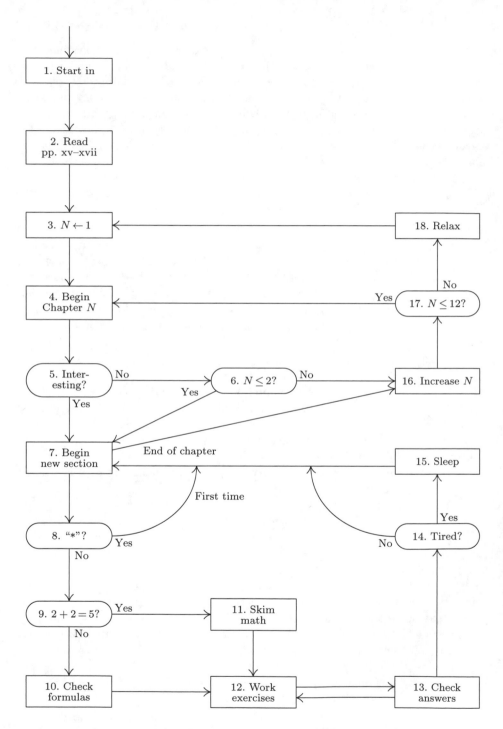

Flow chart for reading this set of books.

Procedure for Reading This Set of Books

1. Begin reading this procedure, unless you have already begun to read it. *Continue to follow the steps faithfully.* (The general form of this procedure and its accompanying flow chart will be used throughout this book.)

2. Read the Notes on the Exercises, on pages xv–xvii.

3. Set N equal to 1.

4. Begin reading Chapter N. Do *not* read the quotations that appear at the beginning of the chapter.

5. Is the subject of the chapter interesting to you? If so, go to step 7; if not, go to step 6.

6. Is $N \leq 2$? If not, go to step 16; if so, scan through the chapter anyway. (Chapters 1 and 2 contain important introductory material and also a review of basic programming techniques. You should at least skim over the sections on notation and about MIX.)

7. Begin reading the next section of the chapter; if you have already reached the end of the chapter, however, go to step 16.

8. Is section number marked with "*"? If so, you may omit this section on first reading (it covers a rather specialized topic that is interesting but not essential); go back to step 7.

9. Are you mathematically inclined? If math is all Greek to you, go to step 11; otherwise proceed to step 10.

10. Check the mathematical derivations made in this section (and report errors to the author). Go to step 12.

11. If the current section is full of mathematical computations, you had better omit reading the derivations. However, you should become familiar with the basic results of the section; they are usually stated near the beginning, or in *slanted type* right at the very end of the hard parts.

12. Work the recommended exercises in this section in accordance with the hints given in the Notes on the Exercises (which you read in step 2).

13. After you have worked on the exercises to your satisfaction, check your answers with the answer printed in the corresponding answer section at the

rear of the book (if any answer appears for that problem). Also read the answers to the exercises you did not have time to work. *Note:* In most cases it is reasonable to read the answer to exercise n before working on exercise $n + 1$, so steps 12–13 are usually done simultaneously.

14. Are you tired? If not, go back to step 7.

15. Go to sleep. Then, wake up, and go back to step 7.

16. Increase N by one. If $N = 3$, 5, 7, 9, 11, or 12, begin the next volume of this set of books.

17. If N is less than or equal to 12, go back to step 4.

18. Congratulations. Now try to get your friends to purchase a copy of Volume 1 and to start reading it. Also, go back to step 3.

Woe be to him that reads but one book.
— GEORGE HERBERT, *Jacula Prudentum*, 1144 (1651)

Les meilleurs auteurs parlent trop.
— VAUVENARGUES, *Paradoxes, mêlés de Réflexions et Maximes*, 115 (1746)

Books are a triviality. Life alone is great.
— THOMAS CARLYLE, *Journal* (1839)

NOTES ON THE EXERCISES

THE EXERCISES in this set of books have been designed for self-study as well as for classroom study. It is difficult, if not impossible, for anyone to learn a subject purely by reading about it, without applying the information to specific problems and thereby being encouraged to think about what has been read. Furthermore, we all learn best the things that we have discovered for ourselves. Therefore the exercises form a major part of this work; a definite attempt has been made to keep them as informative as possible and to select problems that are enjoyable as well as instructive.

In many books, easy exercises are found mixed randomly among extremely difficult ones. A motley mixture is, however, often unfortunate because readers like to know in advance how long a problem ought to take — otherwise they may just skip over all the problems. A classic example of such a situation is the book *Dynamic Programming* by Richard Bellman; this is an important, pioneering work in which a group of problems is collected together at the end of some chapters under the heading "Exercises and Research Problems," with extremely trivial questions appearing in the midst of deep, unsolved problems. It is rumored that someone once asked Dr. Bellman how to tell the exercises apart from the research problems, and he replied, "If you can solve it, it is an exercise; otherwise it's a research problem."

Good arguments can be made for including both research problems and very easy exercises in a book of this kind; therefore, to save the reader from the possible dilemma of determining which are which, *rating numbers* have been provided to indicate the level of difficulty. These numbers have the following general significance:

Rating   Interpretation

   00 An extremely easy exercise that can be answered immediately if the material of the text has been understood; such an exercise can almost always be worked "in your head."

   10 A simple problem that makes you think over the material just read, but is by no means difficult. You should be able to do this in one minute at most; pencil and paper may be useful in obtaining the solution.

   20 An average problem that tests basic understanding of the text material, but you may need about fifteen or twenty minutes to answer it completely.

30 A problem of moderate difficulty and/or complexity; this one may involve more than two hours' work to solve satisfactorily, or even more if the TV is on.

40 Quite a difficult or lengthy problem that would be suitable for a term project in classroom situations. A student should be able to solve the problem in a reasonable amount of time, but the solution is not trivial.

50 A research problem that has not yet been solved satisfactorily, as far as the author knew at the time of writing, although many people have tried. If you have found an answer to such a problem, you ought to write it up for publication; furthermore, the author of this book would appreciate hearing about the solution as soon as possible (provided that it is correct).

By interpolation in this "logarithmic" scale, the significance of other rating numbers becomes clear. For example, a rating of *17* would indicate an exercise that is a bit simpler than average. Problems with a rating of *50* that are subsequently solved by some reader may appear with a *40* rating in later editions of the book, and in the errata posted on the Internet (see page iv).

The remainder of the rating number divided by 5 indicates the amount of detailed work required. Thus, an exercise rated *24* may take longer to solve than an exercise that is rated *25*, but the latter will require more creativity. All exercises with ratings of *46* or more are open problems for future research, rated according to the number of different attacks that they've resisted so far.

The author has tried earnestly to assign accurate rating numbers, but it is difficult for the person who makes up a problem to know just how formidable it will be for someone else to find a solution; and everyone has more aptitude for certain types of problems than for others. It is hoped that the rating numbers represent a good guess at the level of difficulty, but they should be taken as general guidelines, not as absolute indicators.

This book has been written for readers with varying degrees of mathematical training and sophistication; as a result, some of the exercises are intended only for the use of more mathematically inclined readers. The rating is preceded by an *M* if the exercise involves mathematical concepts or motivation to a greater extent than necessary for someone who is primarily interested only in programming the algorithms themselves. An exercise is marked with the letters "*HM*" if its solution necessarily involves a knowledge of calculus or other higher mathematics not developed in this book. An "*HM*" designation does *not* necessarily imply difficulty.

Some exercises are preceded by an arrowhead, "▶"; this designates problems that are especially instructive and especially recommended. Of course, no reader/student is expected to work *all* of the exercises, so those that seem to be the most valuable have been singled out. (This distinction is not meant to detract from the other exercises!) Each reader should at least make an attempt to solve all of the problems whose rating is *10* or less; and the arrows may help to indicate which of the problems with a higher rating should be given priority.

Solutions to most of the exercises appear in the answer section. Please use them wisely; do not turn to the answer until you have made a genuine effort to solve the problem by yourself, or unless you absolutely do not have time to work this particular problem. *After* getting your own solution or giving the problem a decent try, you may find the answer instructive and helpful. The solution given will often be quite short, and it will sketch the details under the assumption that you have earnestly tried to solve it by your own means first. Sometimes the solution gives less information than was asked; often it gives more. It is quite possible that you may have a better answer than the one published here, or you may have found an error in the published solution; in such a case, the author will be pleased to know the details. Later printings of this book will give the improved solutions together with the solver's name where appropriate.

When working an exercise you may generally use the answers to previous exercises, unless specifically forbidden from doing so. The rating numbers have been assigned with this in mind; thus it is possible for exercise $n + 1$ to have a lower rating than exercise n, even though it includes the result of exercise n as a special case.

Summary of codes:		*00*	Immediate
		10	Simple (one minute)
		20	Medium (quarter hour)
▶	Recommended	*30*	Moderately hard
M	Mathematically oriented	*40*	Term project
HM	Requiring "higher math"	*50*	Research problem

EXERCISES

▶ **1.** [*00*] What does the rating "*M20*" mean?

2. [*10*] Of what value can the exercises in a textbook be to the reader?

3. [*14*] Prove that $13^3 = 2197$. Generalize your answer. [This is an example of a horrible kind of problem that the author has tried to avoid.]

4. [*HM45*] Prove that when n is an integer, $n > 2$, the equation $x^n + y^n = z^n$ has no solution in positive integers x, y, z.

We can face our problem.
We can arrange such facts as we have
with order and method.
— HERCULE POIROT, in *Murder on the Orient Express* (1934)

CONTENTS

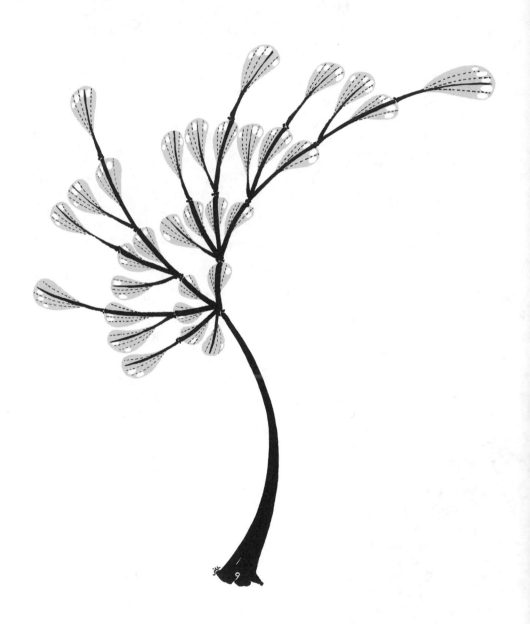

CHAPTER ONE

BASIC CONCEPTS

Practice yourself, for heaven's sake, in little things;
and thence proceed to greater.

— EPICTETUS, *Discourses* IV.i (C. A.D. 110)

Many persons who are not conversant with mathematical studies
imagine that because the business of [Babbage's Analytical Engine] is to
give its results in numerical notation, the nature of its processes must
consequently be arithmetical and numerical, rather than algebraical and
analytical. This is an error. The engine can arrange and combine its
numerical quantities exactly as if they were letters or any other general
symbols; and in fact it might bring out its results in algebraical notation,
were provisions made accordingly.

— AUGUSTA ADA, Countess of Lovelace (1843)

1.1. ALGORITHMS

THE NOTION of an *algorithm* is basic to all of computer programming, so we should begin with a careful analysis of this concept.

The word "algorithm" itself is quite interesting; at first glance it may look as though someone intended to write "logarithm" but jumbled up the first four letters. The word did not appear in *Webster's New World Dictionary* as late as 1957; we find only the older form "algorism" with its ancient meaning, the process of doing arithmetic using Arabic numerals. During the Middle Ages, abacists computed on the abacus and algorists computed by algorism. By the time of the Renaissance, the origin of this word was in doubt, and early linguists attempted to guess at its derivation by making combinations like *algiros* [painful]+*arithmos* [number]; others said no, the word comes from "King Algor of Castile." Finally, historians of mathematics found the true origin of the word algorism: It comes from the name of a famous Persian textbook author, Abū 'Abd Allāh Muḥammad ibn Mūsā al-Khwārizmī (c. 825)—literally, "Father of Abdullah, Mohammed, son of Moses, native of Khwārizm." The Aral Sea in Central Asia was once known as Lake Khwārizm, and the Khwārizm region is located in the Amu River basin just south of that sea. Al-Khwārizmī wrote the celebrated Arabic text *Kitāb al-jabr wa'l-muqābala* ("Rules of restoring and equating"); another word, "algebra," stems from the title of that book, which was a systematic study of the solution of linear and quadratic equations. [For notes on al-Khwārizmī's life and work, see H. Zemanek, *Lecture Notes in Computer Science* **122** (1981), 1–81.]

1

Gradually the form and meaning of *algorism* became corrupted; as explained by the *Oxford English Dictionary*, the word "passed through many pseudo-etymological perversions, including a recent *algorithm*, in which it is learnedly confused" with the Greek root of the word *arithmetic*. This change from "algorism" to "algorithm" is not hard to understand in view of the fact that people had forgotten the original derivation of the word. An early German mathematical dictionary, *Vollständiges mathematisches Lexicon* (Leipzig: 1747), gave the following definition for the word *Algorithmus*: "Under this designation are combined the notions of the four types of arithmetic calculations, namely addition, multiplication, subtraction, and division." The Latin phrase *algorithmus infinitesimalis* was at that time used to denote "ways of calculation with infinitely small quantities, as invented by Leibniz."

By 1950, the word algorithm was most frequently associated with Euclid's algorithm, a process for finding the greatest common divisor of two numbers that appears in Euclid's *Elements* (Book 7, Propositions 1 and 2). It will be instructive to exhibit Euclid's algorithm here:

Algorithm E (*Euclid's algorithm*). Given two positive integers m and n, find their *greatest common divisor*, that is, the largest positive integer that evenly divides both m and n.

E1. [Find remainder.] Divide m by n and let r be the remainder. (We will have $0 \leq r < n$.)

E2. [Is it zero?] If $r = 0$, the algorithm terminates; n is the answer.

E3. [Reduce.] Set $m \leftarrow n$, $n \leftarrow r$, and go back to step E1. ▮

Of course, Euclid did not present his algorithm in just this manner. The format above illustrates the style in which all of the algorithms throughout this book will be presented.

Each algorithm we consider has been given an identifying letter (E in the preceding example), and the steps of the algorithm are identified by this letter followed by a number (E1, E2, E3). The chapters are divided into numbered sections; within a section the algorithms are designated by letter only, but when algorithms are referred to in other sections, the appropriate section number is attached. For example, we are now in Section 1.1; within this section Euclid's algorithm is called Algorithm E, while in later sections it is referred to as Algorithm 1.1E.

Each step of an algorithm, such as step E1 above, begins with a phrase in brackets that sums up as briefly as possible the principal content of that step. This phrase often appears also in an accompanying *flow chart*, such as Fig. 1, so that the reader will be able to picture the algorithm more readily.

After the summarizing phrase comes a description in words and symbols of some *action* to be performed or some decision to be made. Parenthesized *comments*, like the second sentence in step E1, may also appear. Comments are included as explanatory information about that step, often indicating certain invariant characteristics of the variables or the current goals. They do not specify

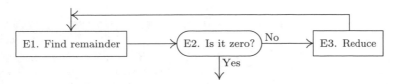

Fig. 1. Flow chart for Algorithm E.

actions that belong to the algorithm, but are meant only for the reader's benefit
as possible aids to comprehension.

The arrow "$\leftarrow$" in step E3 is the all-important *replacement* operation, sometimes called *assignment* or *substitution*: "$m \leftarrow n$" means that the value of
variable m is to be replaced by the current value of variable n. When Algorithm E
begins, the values of m and n are the originally given numbers; but when it
ends, those variables will have, in general, different values. An arrow is used
to distinguish the replacement operation from the equality relation: We will
not say, "Set $m = n$," but we will perhaps ask, "Does $m = n$?" The "$=$"
sign denotes a condition that can be tested, the "$\leftarrow$" sign denotes an action
that can be performed. The operation of *increasing n by one* is denoted by
"$n \leftarrow n + 1$" (read "n is replaced by $n + 1$" or "n gets $n + 1$"). In general,
"variable $\leftarrow$ formula" means that the formula is to be computed using the present
values of any variables appearing within it; then the result should replace the
previous value of the variable at the left of the arrow. Persons untrained in
computer work sometimes have a tendency to say "n becomes $n + 1$" and to
write "$n \rightarrow n + 1$" for the operation of increasing n by one; this symbolism can
only lead to confusion because of its conflict with standard conventions, and it
should be avoided.

Notice that the order of actions in step E3 is important: "Set $m \leftarrow n$,
$n \leftarrow r$" is quite different from "Set $n \leftarrow r$, $m \leftarrow n$," since the latter would imply
that the previous value of n is lost before it can be used to set m. Thus the
latter sequence is equivalent to "Set $n \leftarrow r$, $m \leftarrow r$." When several variables
are all to be set equal to the same quantity, we can use multiple arrows; for
example, "$n \leftarrow r$, $m \leftarrow r$" may be written "$n \leftarrow m \leftarrow r$." To interchange the
values of two variables, we can write "Exchange $m \leftrightarrow n$"; this action could also
be specified by using a new variable t and writing "Set $t \leftarrow m$, $m \leftarrow n$, $n \leftarrow t$."

An algorithm starts at the lowest-numbered step, usually step 1, and it
performs subsequent steps in sequential order unless otherwise specified. In step
E3, the imperative "go back to step E1" specifies the computational order in an
obvious fashion. In step E2, the action is prefaced by the condition "If $r = 0$";
so if $r \neq 0$, the rest of that sentence does not apply and no action is specified.
We might have added the redundant sentence, "If $r \neq 0$, go on to step E3."

The heavy vertical line "$\blacksquare$" appearing at the end of step E3 is used to
indicate the end of an algorithm and the resumption of text.

We have now discussed virtually all the notational conventions used in the
algorithms of this book, except for a notation used to denote "subscripted" or

"indexed" items that are elements of an ordered array. Suppose we have n quantities, $v_1, v_2, \ldots, v_n$; instead of writing v_j for the jth element, the notation $v[j]$ is often used. Similarly, $a[i, j]$ is sometimes used in preference to a doubly subscripted notation like a_{ij}. Sometimes multiple-letter names are used for variables, usually set in capital letters; thus TEMP might be the name of a variable used for temporarily holding a computed value, PRIME[K] might denote the Kth prime number, and so on.

So much for the *form* of algorithms; now let us *perform* one. It should be mentioned immediately that the reader should *not* expect to read an algorithm as if it were part of a novel; such an attempt would make it pretty difficult to understand what is going on. An algorithm must be seen to be believed, and the best way to learn what an algorithm is all about is to try it. The reader should always take pencil and paper and work through an example of each algorithm immediately upon encountering it in the text. Usually the outline of a worked example will be given, or else the reader can easily conjure one up. This is a simple and painless way to gain an understanding of a given algorithm, and all other approaches are generally unsuccessful.

Let us therefore work out an example of Algorithm E. Suppose that we are given $m = 119$ and $n = 544$; we are ready to begin, at step E1. (The reader should now follow the algorithm as we give a play-by-play account.) Dividing m by n in this case is quite simple, almost too simple, since the quotient is zero and the remainder is 119. Thus, $r \leftarrow 119$. We proceed to step E2, and since $r \neq 0$ no action occurs. In step E3 we set $m \leftarrow 544$, $n \leftarrow 119$. It is clear that if $m < n$ originally, the quotient in step E1 will always be zero and the algorithm will always proceed to interchange m and n in this rather cumbersome fashion. We could insert a new step at the beginning:

E0. [Ensure $m \geq n$.] If $m < n$, exchange $m \leftrightarrow n$.

This would make no essential change in the algorithm, except to increase its length slightly, and to decrease its running time in about one-half of all cases.

Back at step E1, we find that $544/119 = 4 + 68/119$, so $r \leftarrow 68$. Again E2 is inapplicable, and at E3 we set $m \leftarrow 119$, $n \leftarrow 68$. The next round sets $r \leftarrow 51$, and ultimately $m \leftarrow 68$, $n \leftarrow 51$. Next $r \leftarrow 17$, and $m \leftarrow 51$, $n \leftarrow 17$. Finally, when 51 is divided by 17, we set $r \leftarrow 0$, so at step E2 the algorithm terminates. The greatest common divisor of 119 and 544 is 17.

So this is an algorithm. The modern meaning for algorithm is quite similar to that of *recipe, process, method, technique, procedure, routine, rigmarole*, except that the word "algorithm" connotes something just a little different. Besides merely being a finite set of rules that gives a sequence of operations for solving a specific type of problem, an algorithm has five important features:

1) *Finiteness.* An algorithm must always terminate after a finite number of steps. Algorithm E satisfies this condition, because after step E1 the value of r is *less* than n; so if $r \neq 0$, the value of n *decreases* the next time step E1 is encountered. A decreasing sequence of positive integers must eventually terminate, so step E1 is executed only a finite number of times for any given original

value of n. Note, however, that the number of steps can become arbitrarily large; certain huge choices of m and n will cause step E1 to be executed more than a million times.

(A procedure that has all of the characteristics of an algorithm except that it possibly lacks finiteness may be called a *computational method*. Euclid originally presented not only an algorithm for the greatest common divisor of numbers, but also a very similar geometrical construction for the "greatest common measure" of the lengths of two line segments; this is a computational method that does not terminate if the given lengths are incommensurable. Another example of a nonterminating computational method is a *reactive process*, which continually interacts with its environment.)

2) *Definiteness.* Each step of an algorithm must be precisely defined; the actions to be carried out must be rigorously and unambiguously specified for each case. The algorithms of this book will hopefully meet this criterion, but they are specified in the English language, so there is a possibility that the reader might not understand exactly what the author intended. To get around this difficulty, formally defined *programming languages* or *computer languages* are designed for specifying algorithms, in which every statement has a very definite meaning. Many of the algorithms of this book will be given both in English and in a computer language. An expression of a computational method in a computer language is called a *program*.

In Algorithm E, the criterion of definiteness as applied to step E1 means that the reader is supposed to understand exactly what it means to divide m by n and what the remainder is. In actual fact, there is no universal agreement about what this means if m and n are not positive integers; what is the remainder of -8 divided by $-\pi$? What is the remainder of $59/13$ divided by zero? Therefore the criterion of definiteness means we must make sure that the values of m and n are always positive integers whenever step E1 is to be executed. This is initially true, by hypothesis; and after step E1, r is a nonnegative integer that must be nonzero if we get to step E3. So m and n are indeed positive integers as required.

3) *Input.* An algorithm has zero or more *inputs*: quantities that are given to it initially before the algorithm begins, or dynamically as the algorithm runs. These inputs are taken from specified sets of objects. In Algorithm E, for example, there are two inputs, namely m and n, both taken from the set of *positive integers*.

4) *Output.* An algorithm has one or more *outputs*: quantities that have a specified relation to the inputs. Algorithm E has one output, namely n in step E2, the greatest common divisor of the two inputs.

(We can easily *prove* that this number is indeed the greatest common divisor, as follows. After step E1, we have

$$m = qn + r,$$

for some integer q. If $r = 0$, then m is a multiple of n, and clearly in such a case n is the greatest common divisor of m and n. If $r \neq 0$, note that any number that divides both m and n must divide $m - qn = r$, and any number that divides both n and r must divide $qn + r = m$; so the set of common divisors of m and n is the same as the set of common divisors of n and r. In particular, the *greatest* common divisor of m and n is the same as the greatest common divisor of n and r. Therefore step E3 does not change the answer to the original problem.)

5) *Effectiveness.* An algorithm is also generally expected to be *effective*, in the sense that its operations must all be sufficiently basic that they can in principle be done exactly and in a finite length of time by someone using pencil and paper. Algorithm E uses only the operations of dividing one positive integer by another, testing if an integer is zero, and setting the value of one variable equal to the value of another. Those operations are effective, because integers can be represented on paper in a finite manner, and because there is at least one method (the "division algorithm") for dividing one by another. But the same operations would *not* be effective if the values involved were arbitrary real numbers specified by an infinite decimal expansion, nor if the values were the lengths of physical line segments (which cannot be specified exactly). Another example of a noneffective step is, "If 4 is the largest integer n for which there is a solution to the equation $w^n + x^n + y^n = z^n$ in positive integers w, x, y, and z, then go to step E4." Such a statement would not be an effective operation until someone successfully constructs an algorithm to determine whether 4 is or is not the largest integer with the stated property.

Let us try to compare the concept of an algorithm with that of a cookbook recipe. A recipe presumably has the qualities of finiteness (although it is said that a watched pot never boils), input (eggs, flour, etc.), and output (TV dinner, etc.), but it notoriously lacks definiteness. There are frequent cases in which a cook's instructions are indefinite: "Add a dash of salt." A "dash" is defined to be "less than $1/8$ teaspoon," and salt is perhaps well enough defined; but where should the salt be added — on top? on the side? Instructions like "toss lightly until mixture is crumbly" or "warm cognac in small saucepan" are quite adequate as explanations to a trained chef, but an algorithm must be specified to such a degree that even a computer can follow the directions. Nevertheless, a computer programmer can learn much by studying a good recipe book. (The author has in fact barely resisted the temptation to name the present volume "The Programmer's Cookbook." Perhaps someday he will attempt a book called "Algorithms for the Kitchen.")

We should remark that the finiteness restriction is not really strong enough for practical use. A useful algorithm should require not only a finite number of steps, but a *very* finite number, a reasonable number. For example, there is an algorithm that determines whether or not the game of chess can always be won by White if no mistakes are made (see exercise 2.2.3–28). That algorithm can solve a problem of intense interest to thousands of people, yet it is a safe bet that we will never in our lifetimes know the answer; the algorithm requires fantastically large amounts of time for its execution, even though it is finite. See also Chapter 8 for a discussion of some finite numbers that are so large as to actually be beyond comprehension.

In practice we not only want algorithms, we want algorithms that are *good* in some loosely defined aesthetic sense. One criterion of goodness is the length of time taken to perform the algorithm; this can be expressed in terms of the number of times each step is executed. Other criteria are the adaptability of the algorithm to different kinds of computers, its simplicity and elegance, etc.

We often are faced with several algorithms for the same problem, and we must decide which is best. This leads us to the extremely interesting and all-important field of *algorithmic analysis*: Given an algorithm, we want to determine its performance characteristics.

For example, let's consider Euclid's algorithm from this point of view. Suppose we ask the question, "Assuming that the value of n is known but m is allowed to range over all positive integers, what is the *average* number of times, T_n, that step E1 of Algorithm E will be performed?" In the first place, we need to check that this question does have a meaningful answer, since we are trying to take an average over infinitely many choices for m. But it is evident that after the first execution of step E1 only the remainder of m after division by n is relevant. So all we must do to find T_n is to try the algorithm for $m = 1$, $m = 2$, ..., $m = n$, count the total number of times step E1 has been executed, and divide by n.

Now the important question is to determine the *nature* of T_n; is it approximately equal to $\frac{1}{3}n$, or $\sqrt{n}$, for instance? As a matter of fact, the answer to this question is an extremely difficult and fascinating mathematical problem, not yet completely resolved, which is examined in more detail in Section 4.5.3. For large values of n it is possible to prove that T_n is approximately $\left(12(\ln 2)/\pi^2\right)\ln n$, that is, proportional to the *natural logarithm* of n, with a constant of proportionality that might not have been guessed offhand! For further details about Euclid's algorithm, and other ways to calculate the greatest common divisor, see Section 4.5.2.

Analysis of algorithms is the name the author likes to use to describe investigations such as this. The general idea is to take a particular algorithm and to determine its quantitative behavior; occasionally we also study whether or not an algorithm is optimal in some sense. The *theory of algorithms* is another subject entirely, dealing primarily with the existence or nonexistence of effective algorithms to compute particular quantities.

So far our discussion of algorithms has been rather imprecise, and a mathematically oriented reader is justified in thinking that the preceding commentary makes a very shaky foundation on which to erect any theory about algorithms. We therefore close this section with a brief indication of one method by which the concept of algorithm can be firmly grounded in terms of mathematical set theory. Let us formally define a *computational method* to be a quadruple (Q, I, Ω, f), in which Q is a set, I and Ω are subsets of Q, and f is a function from Q into itself. Furthermore f should leave Ω pointwise fixed; that is, $f(q)$ should equal q for all elements q of Ω. The four quantities Q, I, Ω, f are intended to represent respectively the states of the computation, the input, the output, and the computational rule. Each input x in the set I defines a *computational sequence,* $x_0, x_1, x_2, \ldots$, as follows:

$$x_0 = x \quad \text{and} \quad x_{k+1} = f(x_k) \quad \text{for} \quad k \geq 0. \tag{1}$$

The computational sequence is said to *terminate in k steps* if k is the smallest integer for which x_k is in Ω, and in this case it is said to produce the output x_k from x. (Notice that if x_k is in Ω, so is x_{k+1}, because $x_{k+1} = x_k$ in such a case.) Some computational sequences may never terminate; an *algorithm* is a computational method that terminates in finitely many steps for all x in I.

Algorithm E may, for example, be formalized in these terms as follows: Let Q be the set of all singletons (n), all ordered pairs (m, n), and all ordered quadruples $(m, n, r, 1)$, $(m, n, r, 2)$, and $(m, n, p, 3)$, where m, n, and p are positive integers and r is a nonnegative integer. Let I be the subset of all pairs (m, n) and let Ω be the subset of all singletons (n). Let f be defined as follows:

$$
\begin{aligned}
f\big((m, n)\big) &= (m, n, 0, 1); \qquad f\big((n)\big) = (n); \\
f\big((m, n, r, 1)\big) &= (m,\ n,\ \text{remainder of } m \text{ divided by } n,\ 2); \\
f\big((m, n, r, 2)\big) &= (n) \quad \text{if} \quad r = 0, \qquad (m, n, r, 3) \quad \text{otherwise;} \\
f\big((m, n, p, 3)\big) &= (n, p, p, 1).
\end{aligned}
\tag{2}
$$

The correspondence between this notation and Algorithm E is evident.

This formulation of the concept of an algorithm does not include the restriction of effectiveness mentioned earlier. For example, Q might denote infinite sequences that are not computable by pencil and paper methods, or f might involve operations that mere mortals cannot always perform. If we wish to restrict the notion of algorithm so that only elementary operations are involved, we can place restrictions on Q, I, Ω, and f, for example as follows: Let A be a finite set of letters, and let A^* be the set of all strings on A (the set of all ordered sequences $x_1 x_2 \ldots x_n$, where $n \geq 0$ and x_j is in A for $1 \leq j \leq n$). The idea is to encode the states of the computation so that they are represented by strings of A^*. Now let N be a nonnegative integer and let Q be the set of all (σ, j), where σ is in A^* and j is an integer, $0 \leq j \leq N$; let I be the subset of Q with $j = 0$; and let Ω be the subset with $j = N$. If θ and σ are strings in A^*, we say that θ occurs in σ if σ has the form $\alpha\theta\omega$ for some strings α and ω in A^*. To complete our definition, let f be a function of the following type, defined by the strings θ_j, ϕ_j and the integers a_j, b_j for $0 \leq j < N$:

$$
\begin{aligned}
f\big((\sigma, j)\big) &= (\sigma, a_j) && \text{if } \theta_j \text{ does not occur in } \sigma; \\
f\big((\sigma, j)\big) &= (\alpha\phi_j\omega, b_j) && \text{if } \alpha \text{ is the shortest possible string for which } \sigma = \alpha\theta_j\omega; \\
f\big((\sigma, N)\big) &= (\sigma, N).
\end{aligned}
\tag{3}
$$

Every step of such a computational method is clearly effective, and experience shows that pattern-matching rules of this kind are also powerful enough to do anything we can do by hand. There are many other essentially equivalent ways to formulate the concept of an effective computational method (for example, using Turing machines). The formulation above is virtually the same as that given by A. A. Markov in his book *The Theory of Algorithms* [*Trudy Mat. Inst. Akad. Nauk* **42** (1954), 1–376], later revised and enlarged by N. M. Nagorny (Moscow: Nauka, 1984; English edition, Dordrecht: Kluwer, 1988).

EXERCISES

1. [*10*] The text showed how to interchange the values of variables m and n, using the replacement notation, by setting $t \leftarrow m$, $m \leftarrow n$, $n \leftarrow t$. Show how the values of *four* variables (a, b, c, d) can be rearranged to (b, c, d, a) by a sequence of replacements. In other words, the new value of a is to be the original value of b, etc. Try to use the minimum number of replacements.

2. [*15*] Prove that m is always greater than n at the beginning of step E1, except possibly the first time this step occurs.

3. [*20*] Change Algorithm E (for the sake of efficiency) so that all trivial replacement operations such as "$m \leftarrow n$" are avoided. Write this new algorithm in the style of Algorithm E, and call it Algorithm F.

4. [*16*] What is the greatest common divisor of 2166 and 6099?

▶ **5.** [*12*] Show that the "Procedure for Reading This Set of Books" that appears after the preface actually fails to be a genuine algorithm on at least three of our five counts! Also mention some differences in format between it and Algorithm E.

6. [*20*] What is T_5, the average number of times step E1 is performed when $n = 5$?

▶ **7.** [*HM21*] Let U_m be the average number of times that step E1 is executed in Algorithm E, if m is known and n is allowed to range over all positive integers. Show that U_m is well defined. Is U_m in any way related to T_m?

8. [*M25*] Give an "effective" formal algorithm for computing the greatest common divisor of positive integers m and n, by specifying θ_j, ϕ_j, a_j, b_j as in Eqs. (3). Let the input be represented by the string $a^m b^n$, that is, m a's followed by n b's. Try to make your solution as simple as possible. [*Hint:* Use Algorithm E, but instead of division in step E1, set $r \leftarrow |m - n|$, $n \leftarrow \min(m, n)$.]

▶ **9.** [*M30*] Suppose that $C_1 = (Q_1, I_1, \Omega_1, f_1)$ and $C_2 = (Q_2, I_2, \Omega_2, f_2)$ are computational methods. For example, C_1 might stand for Algorithm E as in Eqs. (2), except that m and n are restricted in magnitude, and C_2 might stand for a computer program implementation of Algorithm E. (Thus Q_2 might be the set of all states of the machine, i.e., all possible configurations of its memory and registers; f_2 might be the definition of single machine actions; and I_2 might be the set of initial states, each including the program that determines the greatest common divisor as well as the particular values of m and n.)

Formulate a set-theoretic definition for the concept "C_2 is a representation of C_1" or "C_2 simulates C_1." This is to mean intuitively that any computation sequence of C_1 is mimicked by C_2, except that C_2 might take more steps in which to do the computation and it might retain more information in its states. (We thereby obtain a rigorous interpretation of the statement, "Program X is an implementation of Algorithm Y.")

1.2. MATHEMATICAL PRELIMINARIES

IN THIS SECTION we shall investigate the mathematical notations that occur throughout *The Art of Computer Programming*, and we'll derive several basic formulas that will be used repeatedly. Even a reader not concerned with the more complex mathematical derivations should at least become familiar with the *meanings* of the various formulas, so as to be able to use the results of the derivations.

Mathematical notation is used for two main purposes in this book: to describe portions of an algorithm, and to analyze the performance characteristics of an algorithm. The notation used in descriptions of algorithms is quite simple, as explained in the previous section. When analyzing the performance of algorithms, we need to use other more specialized notations.

Most of the algorithms we will discuss are accompanied by mathematical calculations that determine the speed at which the algorithm may be expected to run. These calculations draw on nearly every branch of mathematics, and a separate book would be necessary to develop all of the mathematical concepts that are used in one place or another. However, the majority of the calculations can be carried out with a knowledge of college algebra, and the reader with a knowledge of elementary calculus will be able to understand nearly all of the mathematics that appears. Sometimes we will need to use deeper results of complex variable theory, group theory, number theory, probability theory, etc.; in such cases the topic will be explained in an elementary manner, if possible, or a reference to other sources of information will be given.

The mathematical techniques involved in the analysis of algorithms usually have a distinctive flavor. For example, we will quite often find ourselves working with finite summations of rational numbers, or with the solutions to recurrence relations. Such topics are traditionally given only a light treatment in mathematics courses, and so the following subsections are designed not only to give a thorough drilling in the use of the notations to be defined but also to illustrate in depth the types of calculations and techniques that will be most useful to us.

Important note: Although the following subsections provide a rather extensive training in the mathematical skills needed in connection with the study of computer algorithms, most readers will not see at first any very strong connections between this material and computer programming (except in Section 1.2.1). The reader may choose to read the following subsections carefully, with implicit faith in the author's assertion that the topics treated here are indeed very relevant; but it is probably preferable, for motivation, to *skim over this section lightly at first, and* (after seeing numerous applications of the techniques in future chapters) *return to it later for more intensive study.* If too much time is spent studying this material when first reading the book, a person might never get on to the computer programming topics! However, each reader should at least become familiar with the general contents of these subsections, and should try to solve a few of the exercises, even on first reading. Section 1.2.10 should receive particular attention, since it is the point of departure for most of the theoretical material

developed later. Section 1.3, which follows 1.2, abruptly leaves the realm of
"pure mathematics" and enters into "pure computer programming."

A more leisurely presentation of much of the following material, together
with related concepts, can be found in the book *Concrete Mathematics* by
R. L. Graham, D. E. Knuth, and O. Patashnik, second edition (Reading, Mass.:
Addison–Wesley, 1994). That book will be called simply *CMath* when we need
to refer to it later.

1.2.1. Mathematical Induction

Let $P(n)$ be some statement about the integer n; for example, $P(n)$ might be
"n times $(n + 3)$ is an even number," or "if $n \geq 10$, then $2^n > n^3$." Suppose we
want to prove that $P(n)$ is true for all positive integers n. An important way to
do this is:

a) Give a proof that $P(1)$ is true.

b) Give a proof that "if all of $P(1), P(2), \ldots, P(n)$ are true, then $P(n + 1)$ is
also true"; this proof should be valid for any positive integer n.

As an example, consider the following series of equations, which many people
have discovered independently since ancient times:

$$1 = 1^2,$$
$$1 + 3 = 2^2,$$
$$1 + 3 + 5 = 3^2,$$
$$1 + 3 + 5 + 7 = 4^2,$$
$$1 + 3 + 5 + 7 + 9 = 5^2. \tag{1}$$

We can formulate the general property as follows:

$$1 + 3 + \cdots + (2n - 1) = n^2. \tag{2}$$

Let us, for the moment, call this equation $P(n)$; we wish to prove that $P(n)$ is
true for all positive n. Following the procedure outlined above, we have:

a) "$P(1)$ is true, since $1 = 1^2$."

b) "If all of $P(1), \ldots, P(n)$ are true, then, in particular, $P(n)$ is true, so Eq. (2)
holds; adding $2n + 1$ to both sides we obtain

$$1 + 3 + \cdots + (2n - 1) + (2n + 1) = n^2 + 2n + 1 = (n + 1)^2,$$

which proves that $P(n + 1)$ is also true."

We can regard this method as an *algorithmic proof procedure.* In fact, the
following algorithm produces a proof of $P(n)$ for any positive integer n, assuming
that steps (a) and (b) above have been worked out:

Algorithm I (*Construct a proof*). Given a positive integer n, this algorithm
will output a proof that $P(n)$ is true.

I1. [Prove $P(1)$.] Set $k \leftarrow 1$, and, according to (a), output a proof of $P(1)$.

I2. $[k = n?]$ If $k = n$, terminate the algorithm; the required proof has been output.

I3. [Prove $P(k+1)$.] According to (b), output a proof that "If all of $P(1), \ldots,$ $P(k)$ are true, then $P(k+1)$ is true." Also output "We have already proved $P(1), \ldots, P(k)$; hence $P(k+1)$ is true."

I4. [Increase k.] Increase k by 1 and go to step I2. ∎

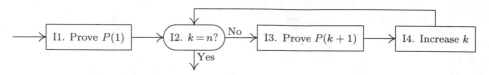

Fig. 2. Algorithm I: Mathematical induction.

Since this algorithm clearly presents a proof of $P(n)$, for any given n, the proof technique consisting of steps (a) and (b) is logically valid. It is called *proof by mathematical induction*.

The concept of mathematical induction should be distinguished from what is usually called inductive reasoning in science. A scientist takes specific observations and creates, by "induction," a general theory or hypothesis that accounts for these facts; for example, we might observe the five relations in (1), above, and formulate (2). In this sense, induction is no more than our best guess about the situation; mathematicians would call it an empirical result or a conjecture.

Another example will be helpful. Let $p(n)$ denote the number of *partitions* of n, that is, the number of different ways to write n as a sum of positive integers, disregarding order. Since 5 can be partitioned in exactly seven ways,

$$1+1+1+1+1 = 2+1+1+1 = 2+2+1 = 3+1+1 = 3+2 = 4+1 = 5,$$

we have $p(5) = 7$. In fact, it is easy to establish the first few values,

$$p(0) = 1, \quad p(1) = 1, \quad p(2) = 2, \quad p(3) = 3, \quad p(4) = 5, \quad p(5) = 7.$$

At this point we might tentatively formulate, by induction, the hypothesis that the sequence $p(2)$, $p(3)$, ... runs through the *prime numbers*. To test this hypothesis, we proceed to calculate $p(6)$ and behold! $p(6) = 11$, confirming our conjecture.

[Unfortunately, $p(7)$ turns out to be 15, spoiling everything, and we must try again. The numbers $p(n)$ are known to be quite complicated, although S. Ramanujan succeeded in guessing and proving many remarkable things about them. For further information, see G. H. Hardy, *Ramanujan* (London: Cambridge University Press, 1940), Chapters 6 and 8. See also Section 7.2.1.4.]

Mathematical induction is quite different from induction in the sense just explained. It is not just guesswork, but a conclusive proof of a statement; indeed, it is a proof of infinitely many statements, one for each n. It has been called "induction" only because one must first decide somehow *what* is to be proved, *before* one can apply the technique of mathematical induction. Henceforth in this book we shall use the word induction only when we wish to imply proof by mathematical induction.

There is a geometrical way to prove Eq. (2). Figure 3 shows, for $n = 6$, n^2 cells broken into groups of $1 + 3 + \cdots + (2n - 1)$ cells. However, in the final analysis, this picture can be regarded as a "proof" only if we show that the construction can be carried out for all n, and such a demonstration is essentially the same as a proof by induction.

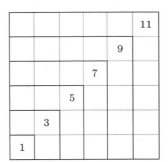

Our proof of Eq. (2) used only a special case of (b); we merely showed that the truth of $P(n)$ implies the truth of $P(n+1)$. This is an important simple case that arises frequently, but our next example illustrates the power of the method a little more. We define the *Fibonacci sequence* F_0, F_1, F_2, ... by the rule that $F_0 = 0$, $F_1 = 1$, and every further term is the sum of the preceding two. Thus the sequence begins 0, 1, 1, 2, 3, 5, 8, 13, ...; we will investigate it in detail in Section 1.2.8. We will now prove that if ϕ is the number $(1 + \sqrt{5})/2$ we have

$$F_n \le \phi^{n-1} \tag{3}$$

Fig. 3. The sum of odd numbers is a square.

for all positive integers n. Call this formula $P(n)$.

If $n = 1$, then $F_1 = 1 = \phi^0 = \phi^{1-1}$, so step (a) has been done. For step (b) we notice first that $P(2)$ is also true, since $F_2 = 1 < \phi^1 = \phi^{2-1}$. Now, if all of $P(1)$, $P(2)$, ..., $P(n)$ are true and $n > 1$, we know in particular that $P(n-1)$ and $P(n)$ are true; so $F_{n-1} \le \phi^{n-2}$ and $F_n \le \phi^{n-1}$. Adding these inequalities, we get

$$F_{n+1} = F_{n-1} + F_n \le \phi^{n-2} + \phi^{n-1} = \phi^{n-2}(1 + \phi). \tag{4}$$

The important property of the number ϕ, indeed the reason we chose this number for this problem in the first place, is that

$$1 + \phi = \phi^2. \tag{5}$$

Plugging (5) into (4) gives $F_{n+1} \le \phi^n$, which is $P(n+1)$. So step (b) has been done, and (3) has been proved by mathematical induction.

Notice that we approached step (b) in two different ways here: We proved $P(n+1)$ *directly* when $n = 1$, and we used an *inductive* method when $n > 1$. This was necessary, since when $n = 1$ our reference to $P(n-1) = P(0)$ would not have been legitimate. [Actually $P(0)$ does happen to be true, in this particular context; but we weren't asked to prove it. So we didn't.]

Mathematical induction can also be used to prove things about *algorithms*. Consider the following generalization of Euclid's algorithm.

Algorithm E (*Extended Euclid's algorithm*). Given two positive integers m and n, we compute their greatest common divisor d, and we also compute two not-necessarily-positive integers a and b such that $am + bn = d$.

E1. [Initialize.] Set $a' \leftarrow b \leftarrow 1$, $a \leftarrow b' \leftarrow 0$, $c \leftarrow m$, $d \leftarrow n$.

E2. [Divide.]   Let q and r be the quotient and remainder, respectively, of c divided by d. (We have $c = qd + r$ and $0 \le r < d$.)

E3. [Remainder zero?] If $r = 0$, the algorithm terminates; we have in this case $am + bn = d$ as desired.

E4. [Recycle.]   Set $c \leftarrow d$, $d \leftarrow r$, $t \leftarrow a'$, $a' \leftarrow a$, $a \leftarrow t - qa$, $t \leftarrow b'$, $b' \leftarrow b$, $b \leftarrow t - qb$, and go back to E2.   ∎

If we suppress the variables a, b, a', and b' from this algorithm and use m and n for the auxiliary variables c and d, we have our old algorithm, 1.1E. The new version does a little more, by determining the coefficients a and b. Suppose that $m = 1769$ and $n = 551$; we have successively (after step E2):

a'	a	b'	b	c	d	q	r
1	0	0	1	1769	551	3	116
0	1	1	-3	551	116	4	87
1	-4	-3	13	116	87	1	29
-4	5	13	-16	87	29	3	0

The answer is correct: $5 \times 1769 - 16 \times 551 = 8845 - 8816 = 29$, the greatest common divisor of 1769 and 551.

The problem is to *prove* that this algorithm works properly, for all m and n. We can try to apply the method of mathematical induction by letting $P(n)$ be the statement "Algorithm E works for n and all integers m." However, that approach doesn't work out so easily, and we need to prove some extra facts. After a little study, we find that something must be proved about a, b, a', and b', and the appropriate fact is that the equalities

$$a'm + b'n = c, \qquad am + bn = d \tag{6}$$

always hold whenever step E2 is executed. We may prove these equalities directly by observing that they are certainly true the first time we get to E2, and that step E4 does not change their validity. (See exercise 6.)

Now we are ready to show that Algorithm E is valid, by induction on n: If m is a multiple of n, the algorithm obviously works properly, since we are done immediately at E3 the first time. This case always occurs when $n = 1$. The only case remaining is when $n > 1$ and m is not a multiple of n. In such a case, the algorithm proceeds to set $c \leftarrow n$, $d \leftarrow r$ after the first execution, and since $r < n$, *we may assume by induction* that the final value of d is the gcd of n and r. By the argument given in Section 1.1, the pairs $\{m, n\}$ and $\{n, r\}$ have the same common divisors, and, in particular, they have the same greatest common divisor. Hence d is the gcd of m and n, and $am + bn = d$ by (6).

The italicized phrase in the proof above illustrates the conventional language that is so often used in an inductive proof: When doing part (b) of the construction, rather than saying "We will now assume $P(1), P(2), \ldots, P(n)$, and with this assumption we will prove $P(n+1)$," we often say simply "We will now prove $P(n)$; *we may assume by induction* that $P(k)$ is true whenever $1 \le k < n$."

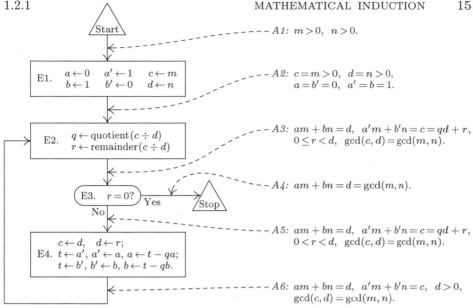

Fig. 4. Flow chart for Algorithm E, labeled with assertions that prove its validity.

If we examine this argument very closely and change our viewpoint slightly, we can envision a general method applicable to proving the validity of *any* algorithm. The idea is to take a flow chart for some algorithm and to label each of the arrows with an assertion about the current state of affairs at the time the computation traverses that arrow. See Fig. 4, where the assertions have been labeled $A1$, $A2$, ..., $A6$. (All of these assertions have the additional stipulation that the variables are integers; this stipulation has been omitted to save space.) $A1$ gives the initial assumptions upon entry to the algorithm, and $A4$ states what we hope to prove about the output values a, b, and d.

The general method constructs a proof, for each box in the flow chart, that

> if an assertion attached to any arrow leading into the box is true
> before the operation in that box is performed, then all of the
> assertions on relevant arrows leading away from the box are true
> after the operation.   (7)

Thus, for example, we must prove that either $A2$ or $A6$ before E2 implies $A3$ after E2. (In this case $A2$ is a stronger statement than $A6$; that is, $A2$ implies $A6$. So we need only prove that $A6$ before E2 implies $A3$ after. Notice that the condition $d > 0$ is necessary in $A6$ just to prove that operation E2 even makes sense.) It is also necessary to show that $A3$ and $r = 0$ implies $A4$; that $A3$ and $r \neq 0$ implies $A5$; etc. Each of the required proofs is very straightforward.

Once statement (7) has been proved for each box, it follows that all assertions are true during any execution of the algorithm. For we can now use induction on the number of steps of the computation, in the sense of the number of arrows traversed in the flow chart. While traversing the first arrow, the one leading from "Start", the assertion $A1$ is true since we always assume that our input values meet the specifications; so the assertion on the first arrow traversed is correct. If the assertion that labels the nth arrow is true, then by (7) the assertion that labels the $(n + 1)$st arrow is also true.

Using this general method, the problem of proving that a given algorithm is valid evidently consists mostly of inventing the right assertions to put in the flow chart. Once this inductive leap has been made, it is pretty much routine to carry out the proofs that each assertion leading into a box logically implies each assertion leading out. In fact, it is pretty much routine to invent the assertions themselves, once a few of the difficult ones have been discovered; thus it is very simple in our example to write out essentially what $A2$, $A3$, and $A5$ must be, if only $A1$, $A4$, and $A6$ are given. In our example, assertion $A6$ is the creative part of the proof; all the rest could, in principle, be supplied mechanically. Hence no attempt has been made to give detailed formal proofs of the algorithms that follow in this book, at the level of detail found in Fig. 4. It suffices to state the key assertions. Those assertions — which are often called "inductive assertions" because we prove them by induction on the length of computation — either appear in the discussion following an algorithm or they are given as parenthetical remarks in the text of the algorithm itself.

This approach to proving the correctness of algorithms has another aspect that is even more important: *It mirrors the way we understand an algorithm.* Recall that in Section 1.1 the reader was cautioned not to expect to read an algorithm like part of a novel; one or two trials of the algorithm on some sample data were recommended. This was done expressly because an example run-through of the algorithm helps a person formulate the various assertions mentally. It is the contention of the author that we really understand why an algorithm is valid only when we reach the point that our minds have implicitly filled in all the assertions, as was done in Fig. 4. This point of view has important psychological consequences for the proper communication of algorithms from one person to another: It implies that the key assertions, those that cannot easily be derived by an automaton, should always be stated explicitly when an algorithm is being explained to someone else. When Algorithm E is being put forward, assertion $A6$ should be mentioned too.

An alert reader will have noticed a gaping hole in our last proof of Algorithm E, however. We never showed that the algorithm terminates; all we have proved is that *if* it terminates, it gives the right answer!

(Notice, for example, that Algorithm E still makes sense if we allow its variables m, n, c, d, and r to assume values of the form $u + v\sqrt{2}$, where u and v are integers. The variables q, a, b, a', b' are to remain integer-valued. If we start the method with $m = 12 - 6\sqrt{2}$ and $n = 20 - 10\sqrt{2}$, say, it will compute a "greatest common divisor" $d = 4 - 2\sqrt{2}$ with $a = +2$, $b = -1$. Even under this extension of the assumptions, the proofs of assertions $A1$ through $A6$ remain valid; therefore all assertions are true throughout any execution of the procedure. But if we start out with $m = 1$ and $n = \sqrt{2}$, the computation never terminates (see exercise 12). Hence a proof of assertions $A1$ through $A6$ does *not* logically prove that the algorithm is finite.)

Proofs of termination are usually handled separately. But exercise 13 shows that it *is* possible to extend the method above in many important cases so that a proof of termination is included as a by-product.

We have now twice proved the validity of Algorithm E. To be strictly logical, we should also try to prove that the first algorithm in this section, Algorithm I, is valid; in fact, we have used Algorithm I to establish the correctness of any proof by induction. If we attempt to *prove* that Algorithm I works properly, however, we are confronted with a dilemma — we can't really prove it without using induction again! The argument would be circular.

In the last analysis, *every* property of the integers must be proved using induction somewhere along the line, because if we get down to basic concepts, the integers are essentially *defined* by induction. Therefore we may take as axiomatic the idea that any positive integer n either equals 1 or can be reached by starting with 1 and repetitively adding 1; this suffices to prove that Algorithm I is valid. [For a rigorous study of fundamental concepts about the integers, see the article "On Mathematical Induction" by Leon Henkin, *AMM* **67** (1960), 323–338.]

The idea behind mathematical induction is thus intimately related to the concept of number. Noteworthy early examples of inductive reasoning can be found in *Sefer Maasei Hoshev* by Levi ben Gershon in France (1321), and in *Arithmeticorum libri duo* by Francesco Maurolico in Italy (1557). Pierre de Fermat made further improvements, in the early 17th century; he called it the "method of infinite descent." The notion also appears clearly in the later writings of Blaise Pascal (1653).

The phrase "mathematical induction" was apparently coined by A. De Morgan in the early nineteenth century. [See *The Penny Cyclopædia* **12** (1838), 465–466; *AMM* **24** (1917), 199–207; **25** (1918), 197–201; *Arch. Hist. Exact Sci.* **9** (1972), 1–21.] Further discussion of mathematical induction can be found in G. Pólya's book *Induction and Analogy in Mathematics* (Princeton, N.J.: Princeton University Press, 1954), Chapter 7.

The formulation of algorithm-proving in terms of assertions and induction, as given above, is essentially due to R. W. Floyd. He pointed out that a semantic definition of each operation in a programming language can be formulated as a logical rule that tells exactly what assertions can be proved after the operation, based on what assertions are true beforehand [see "Assigning Meanings to Programs," *Proc. Symp. Appl. Math.*, Amer. Math. Soc., **19** (1967), 19–32]. Similar ideas were voiced independently by Peter Naur, *BIT* **6** (1966), 310–316, who called the assertions "general snapshots." An important refinement, the notion of "invariants," was introduced by C. A. R. Hoare; see, for example, *CACM* **14** (1971), 39–45.

Later authors found it advantageous to reverse Floyd's direction, going from an assertion that should hold *after* an operation to the "weakest precondition" that must hold *before* the operation is done; such an approach makes it possible to discover new algorithms that are guaranteed to be correct, if we start from the specifications of the desired output and work backwards. [See E. W. Dijkstra, *CACM* **18** (1975), 453–457; *A Discipline of Programming* (Prentice–Hall, 1976).]

The concept of inductive assertions actually appeared in embryonic form in 1946, at the same time as flow charts were introduced by H. H. Goldstine and J. von Neumann. Their original flow charts included "assertion boxes" that are in close analogy with the assertions in Fig. 4. [See John von Neumann, *Collected Works* **5** (New York: Macmillan, 1963), 91–99. See also A. M. Turing's early comments about verification in *Report of a Conference on High Speed Automatic Calculating Machines* (Cambridge Univ., 1949), 67–68 and figures; reprinted with commentary by F. L. Morris and C. B. Jones in *Annals of the History of Computing* **6** (1984), 139–143.]

> *The understanding of the theory of a routine*
> *may be greatly aided by providing, at the time of construction*
> *one or two statements concerning the state of the machine*
> *at well chosen points. ...*
> *In the extreme form of the theoretical method*
> *a watertight mathematical proof is provided for the assertions.*
> *In the extreme form of the experimental method*
> *the routine is tried out on the machine with a variety of initial*
> *conditions and is pronounced fit if the assertions hold in each case.*
> *Both methods have their weaknesses.*
> — A. M. TURING, Ferranti Mark I Programming Manual (1950)

EXERCISES

1. [*05*] Explain how to modify the idea of proof by mathematical induction, in case we want to prove some statement $P(n)$ for all *nonnegative* integers — that is, for $n = 0$, 1, 2, ... instead of for $n = 1, 2, 3, \ldots$.

▶ **2.** [*15*] There must be something wrong with the following proof. What is it? "**Theorem.** Let a be any positive number. For all positive integers n we have $a^{n-1} = 1$. *Proof.* If $n = 1$, $a^{n-1} = a^{1-1} = a^0 = 1$. And by induction, assuming that the theorem is true for $1, 2, \ldots, n$, we have

$$a^{(n+1)-1} = a^n = \frac{a^{n-1} \times a^{n-1}}{b^{n-1}} = \frac{1 \times 1}{1} = 1, \quad \text{where } b = a^{(n-2)/(n-1)};$$

so the theorem is true for $n + 1$ as well."

3. [*18*] The following proof by induction seems correct, but for some reason the equation for $n = 6$ gives $\frac{1}{2} + \frac{1}{6} + \frac{1}{12} + \frac{1}{20} + \frac{1}{30} = \frac{5}{6}$ on the left-hand side, and $\frac{3}{2} - \frac{1}{6} = \frac{4}{3}$ on the right-hand side. Can you find a mistake? "**Theorem.**

$$\frac{1}{1 \times 2} + \frac{1}{2 \times 3} + \cdots + \frac{1}{(n-1) \times n} = \frac{3}{2} - \frac{1}{n}.$$

Proof. We use induction on n. For $n = 1$, clearly $3/2 - 1/n = 1/(1 \times 2)$; and, assuming that the theorem is true for n,

$$\frac{1}{1 \times 2} + \cdots + \frac{1}{(n-1) \times n} + \frac{1}{n \times (n+1)}$$
$$= \frac{3}{2} - \frac{1}{n} + \frac{1}{n(n+1)} = \frac{3}{2} - \frac{1}{n} + \left(\frac{1}{n} - \frac{1}{n+1}\right) = \frac{3}{2} - \frac{1}{n+1}.\text{"}$$

4. [*20*] Prove that, in addition to Eq. (3), Fibonacci numbers satisfy $F_n \geq \phi^{n-2}$ for all positive integers n.

5. [*21*] A *prime number* is an integer > 1 that has no positive integer divisors other than 1 and itself. Using this definition and mathematical induction, prove that every integer $n > 1$ may be written as a product of one or more prime numbers, namely in the form $n = p_1 \ldots p_k$ for some $k \geq 1$, where each of $p_1, \ldots, p_k$ is prime. (A prime number is considered to be the "product" of a single prime, namely itself.)

6. [*20*] Prove that if Eqs. (6) hold just before step E4, they hold afterwards also.

7. [*23*] Formulate and prove by induction a rule for the sums 1^2, $2^2 - 1^2$, $3^2 - 2^2 + 1^2$, $4^2 - 3^2 + 2^2 - 1^2$, $5^2 - 4^2 + 3^2 - 2^2 + 1^2$, etc.

▶ **8.** [*25*] (a) Prove the following theorem of Nicomachus (A.D. c. 100) by induction: $1^3 = 1$, $2^3 = 3 + 5$, $3^3 = 7 + 9 + 11$, $4^3 = 13 + 15 + 17 + 19$, etc. (b) Use this result to prove the remarkable formula $1^3 + 2^3 + \cdots + n^3 = (1 + 2 + \cdots + n)^2$.

[*Note:* An attractive geometric interpretation of this formula, suggested by Warren Lushbaugh, is shown in Fig. 5; see *Math. Gazette* **49** (1965), 200. The idea is related to Nicomachus's theorem and Fig. 3. Other "look-see" proofs can be found in books by Martin Gardner, *Knotted Doughnuts* (New York: Freeman, 1986), Chapter 16; J. H. Conway and R. K. Guy, *The Book of Numbers* (New York: Copernicus, 1996), Chapter 2.]

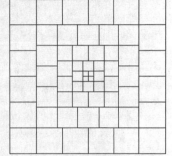

$$\text{Side} = 5+5+5+5+5+5 = 5 \cdot (5+1)$$

$$\begin{aligned}\text{Side} &= 5+4+3+2+1+1+2+3+4+5\\ &= 2 \cdot (1+2+ \cdots +5)\end{aligned}$$

$$\begin{aligned}\text{Area} &= 4 \cdot 1^2 + 4 \cdot 2 \cdot 2^2 + 4 \cdot 3 \cdot 3^2 + 4 \cdot 4 \cdot 4^2 + 4 \cdot 5 \cdot 5^2\\ &= 4 \cdot (1^3 + 2^3 + \cdots + 5^3)\end{aligned}$$

Fig. 5. Geometric version of exercise 8(b).

9. [*20*] Prove by induction that if $0 < a < 1$, then $(1-a)^n \geq 1 - na$ for all integers n.

10. [*M22*] Prove by induction that if $n \geq 10$, then $2^n > n^3$.

11. [*M30*] Find and prove a simple formula for the sum

$$\frac{1^3}{1^4 + 4} - \frac{3^3}{3^4 + 4} + \frac{5^3}{5^4 + 4} - \cdots + \frac{(-1)^n (2n + 1)^3}{(2n + 1)^4 + 4}.$$

12. [*M25*] Show how Algorithm E can be generalized as stated in the text so that it will accept input values of the form $u + v\sqrt{2}$, where u and v are integers, and the computations can still be done in an elementary way (that is, without using the infinite decimal expansion of $\sqrt{2}$). Prove that the computation will not terminate, however, if $m = 1$ and $n = \sqrt{2}$.

▶ **13.** [*M23*] Extend Algorithm E by adding a new variable T and adding the operation "$T \leftarrow T+1$" at the beginning of each step. (Thus, T is like a clock, counting the number of steps executed.) Assume that T is initially zero, so that assertion A1 in Fig. 4 becomes "$m > 0, n > 0, T = 0$." The additional condition "$T = 1$" should similarly be appended to A2. Show how to append additional conditions to the assertions in such a way that any one of A1, A2, ..., A6 implies $T \leq 3n$, and such that the inductive proof can still be carried out. (Hence the computation must terminate in at most $3n$ steps.)

14. [*50*] (R. W. Floyd.) Prepare a computer program that accepts, as input, programs in some programming language together with optional assertions, and that attempts to fill in the remaining assertions necessary to make a proof that the computer program is valid. (For example, strive to get a program that is able to prove the validity of Algorithm E, given only assertions *A1*, *A4*, and *A6*. See the papers by R. W. Floyd and J. C. King in the IFIP Congress proceedings, 1971, for further discussion.)

▶ **15.** [*HM28*] (*Generalized induction.*) The text shows how to prove statements $P(n)$ that depend on a single integer n, but it does not describe how to prove statements $P(m, n)$ depending on two integers. In these circumstances a proof is often given by some sort of "double induction," which frequently seems confusing. Actually, there is an important principle more general than simple induction that applies not only to this case but also to situations in which statements are to be proved about uncountable sets — for example, $P(x)$ for all real x. This general principle is called *well-ordering*.

Let "$\prec$" be a relation on a set S, satisfying the following properties:

i) Given x, y, and z in S, if $x \prec y$ and $y \prec z$, then $x \prec z$.

ii) Given x and y in S, exactly one of the following three possibilities is true: $x \prec y$, $x = y$, or $y \prec x$.

iii) If A is any nonempty subset of S, there is an element x in A with $x \preceq y$ (that is, $x \prec y$ or $x = y$) for all y in A.

This relation is said to be a well-ordering of S. For example, it is clear that the positive integers are well-ordered by the ordinary "less than" relation, $<$.

a) Show that the set of *all* integers is not well-ordered by $<$.

b) Define a well-ordering relation on the set of all integers.

c) Is the set of all nonnegative real numbers well-ordered by $<$?

d) (*Lexicographic order.*) Let S be well-ordered by $\prec$, and for $n > 0$ let T_n be the set of all n-tuples $(x_1, x_2, \ldots, x_n)$ of elements x_j in S. Define $(x_1, x_2, \ldots, x_n) \prec (y_1, y_2, \ldots, y_n)$ if there is some k, $1 \leq k \leq n$, such that $x_j = y_j$ for $1 \leq j < k$, but $x_k \prec y_k$ in S. Is $\prec$ a well-ordering of T_n?

e) Continuing part (d), let $T = \bigcup_{n \geq 1} T_n$; define $(x_1, x_2, \ldots, x_m) \prec (y_1, y_2, \ldots, y_n)$ if $x_j = y_j$ for $1 \leq j < k$ and $x_k \prec y_k$, for some $k \leq \min(m, n)$, or if $m < n$ and $x_j = y_j$ for $1 \leq j \leq m$. Is $\prec$ a well-ordering of T?

f) Show that $\prec$ is a well-ordering of S if and only if it satisfies (i) and (ii) above and there is no infinite sequence x_1, x_2, x_3, $\ldots$ with $x_{j+1} \prec x_j$ for all $j \geq 1$.

g) Let S be well-ordered by $\prec$, and let $P(x)$ be a statement about the element x of S. Show that if $P(x)$ can be proved under the assumption that $P(y)$ is true for all $y \prec x$, then $P(x)$ is true for *all* x in S.

[*Notes:* Part (g) is the generalization of simple induction that was promised; in the case $S =$ positive integers, it is just the simple case of mathematical induction treated in the text. In that case we are asked to prove that $P(1)$ is true if $P(y)$ is true for all positive integers $y < 1$; this is the same as saying we should prove $P(1)$, since $P(y)$ certainly is (vacuously) true for all such y. Consequently, one finds that in many situations $P(1)$ need not be proved using a special argument.

Part (d), in connection with part (g), gives us a powerful method of n-tuple induction for proving statements $P(m_1, \ldots, m_n)$ about n positive integers $m_1, \ldots, m_n$.

Part (f) has further application to computer algorithms: If we can map each state x of a computation into an element $f(x)$ belonging to a well-ordered set S, in such a way that every step of the computation takes a state x into a state y with $f(y) \prec f(x)$, then

the algorithm must terminate. This principle generalizes the argument about strictly
decreasing values of n, by which we proved the termination of Algorithm 1.1E.]

1.2.2. Numbers, Powers, and Logarithms

Let us now begin our study of numerical mathematics by taking a good look at
the numbers we are dealing with. The *integers* are the whole numbers

$$\ldots, -3, -2, -1, 0, 1, 2, 3, \ldots$$

(negative, zero, or positive). A *rational number* is the ratio (quotient) of two
integers, p/q, where q is positive. A *real number* is a quantity x that has a
decimal expansion

$$x = n + 0.d_1 d_2 d_3 \ldots, \tag{1}$$

where n is an integer, each d_i is a digit between 0 and 9, and the sequence of
digits doesn't end with infinitely many 9s. (Instead of $999\ldots$, we can use $000\ldots$
and add 1 to the digit at the left.) The representation (1) means that

$$n + \frac{d_1}{10} + \frac{d_2}{100} + \cdots + \frac{d_k}{10^k} \le x < n + \frac{d_1}{10} + \frac{d_2}{100} + \cdots + \frac{d_k}{10^k} + \frac{1}{10^k}, \tag{2}$$

for all positive integers k. Examples of real numbers that are not rational are

$$\pi = 3.14159265358979\ldots, \quad \text{the ratio of circumference to diameter in a circle;}$$

$$\phi = 1.61803398874989\ldots, \quad \text{the } golden \ ratio \ (1 + \sqrt{5})/2 \ (\text{see Section 1.2.8}).$$

A table of important constants, to forty decimal places of accuracy, appears in
Appendix A. We need not discuss the familiar properties of addition, subtraction, multiplication, division, and comparison of real numbers.

Difficult problems about integers are often solved by working with real
numbers, and difficult problems about real numbers are often solved by working
with a still more general class of values called complex numbers. A *complex
number* is a quantity z of the form $z = x + iy$, where x and y are real and i is
a special quantity that satisfies the equation $i^2 = -1$. We call x and y the *real
part* and *imaginary part* of z, and we define the absolute value of z to be

$$|z| = \sqrt{x^2 + y^2}. \tag{3}$$

The *complex conjugate* of z is $\bar{z} = x - iy$, and we have $z\bar{z} = x^2 + y^2 = |z|^2$. The
theory of complex numbers is in many ways simpler and more beautiful than
the theory of real numbers, but it is usually considered to be an advanced topic.
Therefore we shall concentrate on real numbers in this book, except when real
numbers turn out to be unnecessarily complicated.

If u and v are real numbers with $u \le v$, the *closed interval* $[u \mathrel{..} v]$ is the set
of real numbers x such that $u \le x \le v$. The *open interval* $(u \mathrel{..} v)$ is, similarly,
the set of x such that $u < x < v$. And *half-open intervals* $[u \mathrel{..} v)$ or $(u \mathrel{..} v]$ are
defined in an analogous way. We also allow u to be $-\infty$ or v to be ∞ at an
open endpoint, meaning that there is no lower or upper bound; thus $(-\infty \mathrel{..} \infty)$
stands for the set of all real numbers, and $[0 \mathrel{..} \infty)$ denotes the nonnegative reals.

Throughout this section, let the letter b stand for a positive real number. If n is an integer, then b^n and 0^n and $(-b)^n$ are defined by the familiar rules

$$b^0 = 1, \qquad b^n = b^{n-1}b \text{ if } n > 0, \qquad b^n = b^{n+1}/b \text{ if } n < 0; \qquad (4)$$

$$0^0 = 1, \qquad 0^n = 0 \text{ if } n > 0; \qquad (-b)^n = (-1)^n b^n. \qquad (5)$$

It is easy to prove by induction that the *laws of exponents* are valid:

$$b^{x+y} = b^x b^y, \qquad (b^x)^y = b^{xy}, \qquad (6)$$

whenever x and y are integers.

If u is a positive real number and if m is a positive integer, there is always a unique positive real number v such that $v^m = u$; it is called the *mth root* of u, and denoted $v = \sqrt[m]{u}$.

We now define b^r for rational numbers $r = p/q$ as follows:

$$b^{p/q} = \sqrt[q]{b^p}. \qquad (7)$$

This definition, due to Oresme (c. 1360), is a good one, since $b^{ap/aq} = b^{p/q}$, and since the laws of exponents are still correct even when x and y are arbitrary rational numbers (see exercise 9).

Finally, we define b^x for all real values of x. Suppose first that $b > 1$; if x is given by Eq. (1), we want

$$b^{n+d_1/10+\cdots+d_k/10^k} \le b^x < b^{n+d_1/10+\cdots+d_k/10^k+1/10^k}. \qquad (8)$$

This *defines* b^x as a unique positive real number, since the difference between the right and left extremes in Eq. (8) is $b^{n+d_1/10+\cdots+d_k/10^k}(b^{1/10^k} - 1)$; by exercise 13 below, this difference is less than $b^{n+1}(b-1)/10^k$, and if we take k large enough, we can therefore get any desired accuracy for b^x.

For example, we find that

$$10^{0.30102999} = 1.9999999739\ldots, \qquad 10^{0.30103000} = 2.0000000199\ldots; \qquad (9)$$

therefore if $b = 10$ and $x = 0.30102999\ldots$, we know the value of b^x with an accuracy of better than one part in 10 million (although we still don't even know whether the decimal expansion of b^x begins with $1.999\ldots$ or $2.000\ldots$).

When $b < 1$, we define $b^x = (1/b)^{-x}$; and when $b = 1$, $b^x = 1$. With these definitions, it can be proved that the laws of exponents (6) hold for any *real* values of x and y. These ideas for defining b^x were first formulated by John Wallis (1655) and Isaac Newton (1669).

Now we come to an important question. Suppose that a positive real number y is given; can we find a real number x such that $y = b^x$? The answer is "yes" (provided that $b \ne 1$), for we simply use Eq. (8) *in reverse* to determine n and $d_1, d_2, \ldots$ when $b^x = y$ is given. The resulting number x is called the *logarithm of y to the base b*, and we write this as $x = \log_b y$. By this definition we have

$$x = b^{\log_b x} = \log_b(b^x). \qquad (10)$$

As an example, Eqs. (9) show that

$$\log_{10} 2 = 0.30102999\ldots. \qquad (11)$$

From the laws of exponents it follows that

$$\log_b(xy) = \log_b x + \log_b y, \quad \text{if} \quad x > 0, \ y > 0 \tag{12}$$

and

$$\log_b(c^y) = y \log_b c, \quad \text{if} \quad c > 0. \tag{13}$$

Equation (11) illustrates the so-called *common logarithms*, which we get when the base is 10. One might expect that in computer work *binary logarithms* (to the base 2) would be more useful, since most computers do binary arithmetic. Actually, we will see that binary logarithms are indeed very useful, but not only for that reason; the reason is primarily that a computer algorithm often makes two-way branches. Binary logarithms arise so frequently, it is wise to have a shorter notation for them. Therefore we shall write

$$\lg x = \log_2 x, \tag{14}$$

following a suggestion of Ernesto Trucco [*Bull. Math. Biophysics* **18** (1956), 130].

The question now arises as to whether or not there is any relationship between $\lg x$ and $\log_{10} x$; fortunately there is,

$$\log_{10} x = \log_{10}(2^{\lg x}) = (\lg x)(\log_{10} 2),$$

by Eqs. (10) and (13). Hence $\lg x = \log_{10} x / \log_{10} 2$, and in general we find that

$$\log_c x = \frac{\log_b x}{\log_b c}. \tag{15}$$

Equations (12), (13), and (15) are the fundamental rules for manipulating logarithms.

It turns out that neither base 10 nor base 2 is really the most convenient base to work with in most cases. There is a real number, denoted by $e = 2.718281828459045\ldots$, for which the logarithms have simpler properties. Logarithms to the base e are conventionally called *natural logarithms*, and we write

$$\ln x = \log_e x. \tag{16}$$

This rather arbitrary definition (in fact, we haven't really defined e) probably doesn't strike the reader as being a very "natural" logarithm; yet we'll find that $\ln x$ seems more and more natural, the more we work with it. John Napier actually discovered natural logarithms (with slight modifications, and without connecting them with powers) before the year 1590, many years before any other kind of logarithm was known. The following two examples, proved in every calculus text, shed some light on why Napier's logarithms deserve to be called "natural": (a) In Fig. 6 the area of the shaded portion is $\ln x$. (b) If a bank pays compound interest at rate r, compounded semiannually, the annual return on each dollar is

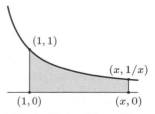

Fig. 6. Natural logarithm.

$(1 + r/2)^2$ dollars; if it is compounded quarterly, you get $(1 + r/4)^4$ dollars; and if it is compounded daily you probably get $(1 + r/365)^{365}$ dollars. Now if the interest were compounded *continuously*, you would get exactly e^r dollars for every dollar (ignoring roundoff error). In this age of computers, many bankers have now actually reached the limiting formula.

The interesting history of the concepts of logarithm and exponential has been told in a series of articles by F. Cajori, *AMM* **20** (1913), 5–14, 35–47, 75–84, 107–117, 148–151, 173–182, 205–210.

We conclude this section by considering how to *compute* logarithms. One method is suggested immediately by Eq. (8): If we let $b^x = y$ and raise all parts of that equation to the 10^k-th power, we find that

$$b^m \leq y^{10^k} < b^{m+1},\tag{17}$$

for some integer m. All we have to do to get the logarithm of y is to raise y to this huge power and find which powers $(m, m + 1)$ of b the result lies between; then $m/10^k$ is the answer to k decimal places.

A slight modification of this apparently impractical method leads to a simple and reasonable procedure. We will show how to calculate $\log_{10} x$ and to express the answer in the *binary* system, as

$$\log_{10} x = n + b_1/2 + b_2/4 + b_3/8 + \cdots.\tag{18}$$

First we shift the decimal point of x to the left or to the right so that we have $1 \leq x/10^n < 10$; this determines the integer part, n. To obtain $b_1, b_2, \ldots$, we now set $x_0 = x/10^n$ and, for $k \geq 1$,

$$\begin{aligned} b_k = 0, \quad & x_k = x_{k-1}^2, & \text{if} \quad x_{k-1}^2 < 10; \\ b_k = 1, \quad & x_k = x_{k-1}^2/10, & \text{if} \quad x_{k-1}^2 \geq 10. \end{aligned}\tag{19}$$

The validity of this procedure follows from the fact that

$$1 \leq x_k = x^{2^k}/10^{2^k(n+b_1/2+\cdots+b_k/2^k)} < 10,\tag{20}$$

for $k = 0, 1, 2, \ldots$, as is easily proved by induction.

In practice, of course, we must work with only finite accuracy, so we cannot set $x_k = x_{k-1}^2$ exactly. Instead, we set $x_k = x_{k-1}^2$ *rounded* or *truncated* to a certain number of decimal places. For example, here is the evaluation of $\log_{10} 2$ rounded to four significant figures:

$$\begin{aligned} x_0 &= 2.000; \\ x_1 &= 4.000, & b_1 &= 0; & x_6 &= 1.845, & b_6 &= 1; \\ x_2 &= 1.600, & b_2 &= 1; & x_7 &= 3.404, & b_7 &= 0; \\ x_3 &= 2.560, & b_3 &= 0; & x_8 &= 1.159, & b_8 &= 1; \\ x_4 &= 6.554, & b_4 &= 0; & x_9 &= 1.343, & b_9 &= 0; \\ x_5 &= 4.295, & b_5 &= 1; & x_{10} &= 1.804, & b_{10} &= 0; & \text{etc.} \end{aligned}$$

Computational error has caused errors to propagate; the true rounded value of x_{10} is 1.798. This will eventually cause b_{19} to be computed incorrectly, and we get the binary value $(0.0100110100010000011\ldots)_2$, which corresponds to the decimal equivalent $0.301031\ldots$ rather than the true value given in Eq. (11).

With any method such as this it is necessary to examine the amount of computational error due to the limitations imposed. Exercise 27 derives an upper bound for the error; working to four figures as above, we find that the error in the value of the logarithm is guaranteed to be less than 0.00044. Our answer above was more accurate than this primarily because x_0, x_1, x_2, and x_3 were obtained *exactly*.

This method is simple and quite interesting, but it is probably not the best way to calculate logarithms on a computer. Another method is given in exercise 25.

EXERCISES

1. [*00*] What is the smallest positive rational number?

2. [*00*] Is $1 + 0.239999999\ldots$ a decimal expansion?

3. [*02*] What is $(-3)^{-3}$?

▶ **4.** [*05*] What is $(0.125)^{-2/3}$?

5. [*05*] We defined real numbers in terms of a decimal expansion. Discuss how we could have defined them in terms of a binary expansion instead, and give a definition to replace Eq. (2).

6. [*10*] Let $x = m + 0.d_1 d_2 \ldots$ and $y = n + 0.e_1 e_2 \ldots$ be real numbers. Give a rule for determining whether $x = y$, $x < y$, or $x > y$, based on the decimal representation.

7. [*M23*] Given that x and y are integers, prove the laws of exponents, starting from the definition given by Eq. (4).

8. [*25*] Let m be a positive integer. *Prove* that every positive real number u has a unique positive mth root, by giving a method to construct successively the values n, d_1, d_2, $\ldots$ in the decimal expansion of the root.

9. [*M23*] Given that x and y are rational, prove the laws of exponents under the assumption that the laws hold when x and y are integers.

10. [*18*] Prove that $\log_{10} 2$ is not a rational number.

▶ **11.** [*10*] If $b = 10$ and x is approximately equal to $\log_{10} 2$, how many decimal places of x's value will guarantee that we can determine the first three places of the decimal expansion of b^x? [*Note:* You may use the result of exercise 10 in your discussion.]

12. [*02*] Explain why Eq. (11) follows from Eqs. (9).

▶ **13.** [*M23*] (a) Given that x is a positive real number and n is a positive integer, prove the inequality $\sqrt[n]{1+x} - 1 \le x/n$. (b) Use this fact to justify the remarks following (8).

14. [*15*] Prove Eq. (13).

15. [*10*] Prove or disprove: $\log_b x/y = \log_b x - \log_b y$, for all real $x, y > 0$.

16. [*00*] How can $\log_{10} x$ be expressed in terms of $\ln x$ and $\ln 10$?

▶ **17.** [*05*] What is $\lg 32$? $\log_\pi \pi$? $\ln e$? $\log_b 1$? $\log_b(-1)$?

18. [*10*] Prove or disprove: $\log_8 x = \frac{1}{2} \lg x$, for all real $x > 0$.

▶ **19.** [*20*] If n is an integer whose decimal representation is 14 digits long, will the value of n fit in a computer word with a capacity of 47 bits and a sign bit?

20. [*10*] Is there any simple relation between $\log_{10} 2$ and $\log_2 10$?

21. [*15*] (*Logs of logs.*) Express $\log_b \log_b x$ in terms of $\ln \ln x$, $\ln \ln b$, and $\ln b$.

▶ **22.** [*20*] (R. W. Hamming.) Prove that

$$\lg x \approx \ln x + \log_{10} x,$$

with less than 1% error! (Thus a table of natural logarithms and of common logarithms can be used to get approximate values of binary logarithms as well.)

23. [*M25*] Give a *geometric* proof that $\ln xy = \ln x + \ln y$, based on Fig. 6.

24. [*15*] Explain how the method used for calculating logarithms to the base 10 at the end of this section can be modified to produce logarithms to base 2.

25. [*22*] Suppose that we have a binary computer and a number x, $1 \le x < 2$. Show that the following algorithm, which uses only shifting, addition, and subtraction operations proportional to the number of places of accuracy desired, may be used to calculate an approximation to $y = \log_b x$:

L1. [Initialize.] Set $y \leftarrow 0$, $z \leftarrow x$ shifted right 1, $k \leftarrow 1$.

L2. [Test for end.] If $x = 1$, stop.

L3. [Compare.] If $x - z < 1$, set $z \leftarrow z$ shifted right 1, $k \leftarrow k + 1$, and repeat this step.

L4. [Reduce values.] Set $x \leftarrow x - z$, $z \leftarrow x$ shifted right k, $y \leftarrow y + \log_b(2^k/(2^k - 1))$, and go to L2. ▮

[*Notes:* This method is very similar to the method used for division in computer hardware. The idea goes back in essence to Henry Briggs, who used it (in decimal rather than binary form) to compute logarithm tables, published in 1624. We need an auxiliary table of the constants $\log_b 2$, $\log_b(4/3)$, $\log_b(8/7)$, etc., to as many values as the precision of the computer. The algorithm involves intentional computational errors, as numbers are shifted to the right, so that eventually x will be reduced to 1 and the algorithm will terminate. The purpose of this exercise is to explain why it will terminate and why it computes an approximation to $\log_b x$.]

26. [*M27*] Find a rigorous upper bound on the error made by the algorithm in the previous exercise, based on the precision used in the arithmetic operations.

▶ **27.** [*M25*] Consider the method for calculating $\log_{10} x$ discussed in the text. Let x'_k denote the computed approximation to x_k, determined as follows: $x(1 - \delta) \le 10^n x'_0 \le x(1 + \epsilon)$; and in the determination of x'_k by Eqs. (19), the quantity y_k is used in place of $(x'_{k-1})^2$, where $(x'_{k-1})^2(1 - \delta) \le y_k \le (x'_{k-1})^2(1 + \epsilon)$ and $1 \le y_k < 100$. Here δ and ϵ are small constants that reflect the upper and lower errors due to rounding or truncation. If $\log' x$ denotes the result of the calculations, show that after k steps we have

$$\log_{10} x + 2\log_{10}(1 - \delta) - 1/2^k < \log' x \le \log_{10} x + 2\log_{10}(1 + \epsilon).$$

28. [*M30*] (R. Feynman.) Develop a method for computing b^x when $0 \le x < 1$, using only shifting, addition, and subtraction (similar to the algorithm in exercise 25), and analyze its accuracy.

29. [*HM20*] Let x be a real number greater than 1. (a) For what real number $b > 1$ is $b \log_b x$ a minimum? (b) For what *integer* $b > 1$ is it a minimum? (c) For what integer $b > 1$ is $(b + 1) \log_b x$ a minimum?

30. [*12*] Simplify the expression $(\ln x)^{\ln x / \ln \ln x}$, assuming that $x > 1$ and $x \neq e$.

1.2.3. Sums and Products

Let $a_1, a_2, \ldots$ be any sequence of numbers. We are often interested in sums such as $a_1 + a_2 + \cdots + a_n$, and this sum is more compactly written using either of the following essentially equivalent notations:

$$\sum_{j=1}^{n} a_j \qquad \text{or} \qquad \sum_{1 \leq j \leq n} a_j. \qquad (1)$$

If n is zero, the value of $a_1 + a_2 + \cdots + a_n = \sum_{j=1}^{n} a_j = \sum_{1 \leq j \leq n} a_j$ is defined to be zero. Our convention of using "three dots" in sums such as $a_1 + a_2 + \cdots + a_n$ therefore has some slightly peculiar, but sensible, behavior in borderline cases (see exercise 1).

In general, if $R(j)$ is any relation involving j, the symbol

$$\sum_{R(j)} a_j \qquad (2)$$

means the sum of all a_j where j is an integer satisfying the condition $R(j)$. If no such integers exist, notation (2) denotes zero. The letter j in (1) and (2) is a *dummy index* or *index variable*, introduced just for the purposes of the notation. Symbols used as index variables are usually the letters i, j, k, m, n, r, s, t (occasionally with subscripts or accent marks). Large summation signs like those in (1) and (2) can also be rendered more compactly as $\sum_{j=1}^{n} a_j$ or $\sum_{R(j)} a_j$. The use of a $\sum$ and index variables to indicate summation with definite limits was introduced by J. Fourier in 1820.

Strictly speaking, the notation $\sum_{1 \leq j \leq n} a_j$ is ambiguous, since it does not clarify whether the summation is taken with respect to j or to n. In this particular case it would be rather silly to interpret it as a sum $a_j + a_j + a_j + \cdots$ over all indices n that satisfy $n \geq j$! But meaningful examples can be constructed in which the index variable is not clearly specified, as in $\sum_{j \leq k} \binom{j+k}{2j-k}$. In such cases the context must make clear which variable is a dummy variable and which variable has a significance that extends beyond its appearance in the sum. A sum such as $\sum_{j \leq k} \binom{j+k}{2j-k}$ would presumably be used only if either j or k (not both) has exterior significance.

In most cases we will use notation (2) only when the sum is *finite* — that is, when only a finite number of values j satisfy $R(j)$ and have $a_j \neq 0$. If an infinite sum is required, for example

$$\sum_{j=1}^{\infty} a_j = \sum_{j \geq 1} a_j = a_1 + a_2 + a_3 + \cdots$$

with infinitely many nonzero terms, the techniques of calculus must be employed; the precise meaning of (2) is then

$$\sum_{R(j)} a_j = \left(\lim_{n \to \infty} \sum_{\substack{R(j) \\ 0 \leq j < n}} a_j \right) + \left(\lim_{n \to \infty} \sum_{\substack{R(j) \\ -n \leq j < 0}} a_j \right), \qquad (3)$$

provided that both limits exist. If either limit fails to exist, the infinite sum is *divergent*; it does not exist. Otherwise it is *convergent*.

When two or more conditions are placed under the $\sum$ sign, as in (3), we mean that *all* conditions must hold.

Four simple algebraic operations on sums are very important, and familiarity with them makes the solution of many problems possible. We shall now discuss these four operations.

a) *The distributive law*, for products of sums:

$$\left(\sum_{R(i)} a_i\right)\left(\sum_{S(j)} b_j\right) = \sum_{R(i)}\left(\sum_{S(j)} a_i b_j\right). \tag{4}$$

To understand this law, consider for example the special case

$$\left(\sum_{i=1}^{2} a_i\right)\left(\sum_{j=1}^{3} b_j\right) = (a_1 + a_2)(b_1 + b_2 + b_3)$$

$$= (a_1 b_1 + a_1 b_2 + a_1 b_3) + (a_2 b_1 + a_2 b_2 + a_2 b_3)$$

$$= \sum_{i=1}^{2}\left(\sum_{j=1}^{3} a_i b_j\right).$$

It is customary to drop the parentheses on the right-hand side of (4); a double summation such as $\sum_{R(i)}\left(\sum_{S(j)} a_{ij}\right)$ is written simply $\sum_{R(i)} \sum_{S(j)} a_{ij}$.

b) *Change of variable:*

$$\sum_{R(i)} a_i = \sum_{R(j)} a_j = \sum_{R(p(j))} a_{p(j)}. \tag{5}$$

This equation represents two kinds of transformations. In the first case we are simply changing the name of the index variable from i to j. The second case is more interesting: Here $p(j)$ is a function of j that represents a *permutation* of the relevant values; more precisely, for each integer i satisfying the relation $R(i)$, there must be exactly one integer j satisfying the relation $p(j) = i$. This condition is always satisfied in the important cases $p(j) = c + j$ and $p(j) = c - j$, where c is an integer not depending on j, and these are the cases used most frequently in applications. For example,

$$\sum_{1 \le j \le n} a_j = \sum_{1 \le j-1 \le n} a_{j-1} = \sum_{2 \le j \le n+1} a_{j-1}. \tag{6}$$

The reader should study this example carefully.

The replacement of j by $p(j)$ cannot be done for all *infinite* sums. The operation is always valid if $p(j) = c \pm j$, as above, but in other cases some care must be used. [For example, see T. M. Apostol, *Mathematical Analysis* (Reading, Mass.: Addison–Wesley, 1957), Chapter 12. A sufficient condition to guarantee the validity of (5) for any permutation of the integers, $p(j)$, is that $\sum_{R(j)} |a_j|$ exists.]

c) *Interchanging order of summation:*

$$\sum_{R(i)} \sum_{S(j)} a_{ij} = \sum_{S(j)} \sum_{R(i)} a_{ij}. \tag{7}$$

Let us consider a very simple special case of this equation:

$$\sum_{R(i)} \sum_{j=1}^{2} a_{ij} = \sum_{R(i)} (a_{i1} + a_{i2}),$$

$$\sum_{j=1}^{2} \sum_{R(i)} a_{ij} = \sum_{R(i)} a_{i1} + \sum_{R(i)} a_{i2}.$$

By Eq. (7), these two are equal; this says no more than

$$\sum_{R(i)} (b_i + c_i) = \sum_{R(i)} b_i + \sum_{R(i)} c_i, \tag{8}$$

where we let $b_i = a_{i1}$ and $c_i = a_{i2}$.

The operation of interchanging the order of summation is extremely useful, since it often happens that we know a simple form for $\sum_{R(i)} a_{ij}$, but not for $\sum_{S(j)} a_{ij}$. We frequently need to interchange the summation order also in a more general situation, where the relation $S(j)$ depends on i as well as j. In such a case we can denote the relation by "$S(i,j)$." The interchange of summation can always be carried out, in theory at least, as follows:

$$\sum_{R(i)} \sum_{S(i,j)} a_{ij} = \sum_{S'(j)} \sum_{R'(i,j)} a_{ij}, \tag{9}$$

where $S'(j)$ specifies summing over all j such that "there is an integer i such that both $R(i)$ and $S(i,j)$ are true"; and $R'(i,j)$ specifies summing over all i such that "both $R(i)$ and $S(i,j)$ are true." For example, if the summation is $\sum_{i=1}^{n} \sum_{j=1}^{i} a_{ij}$, then $S'(j)$ sums over j where "there is an integer i such that $1 \le i \le n$ and $1 \le j \le i$," that is, $1 \le j \le n$; and $R'(i,j)$ sums over i where "$1 \le i \le n$ and $1 \le j \le i$," that is, $j \le i \le n$. Thus,

$$\sum_{i=1}^{n} \sum_{j=1}^{i} a_{ij} = \sum_{j=1}^{n} \sum_{i=j}^{n} a_{ij}. \tag{10}$$

[*Note:* As in case (b), the operation of interchanging order of summation is *not always valid for infinite series.* If the series is *absolutely convergent* — that is, if $\sum_{R(i)} \sum_{S(j)} |a_{ij}|$ exists — it can be shown that Eqs. (7) and (9) are valid. Also if *either one* of $R(i)$ or $S(j)$ specifies a *finite* sum in Eq. (7), and if each infinite sum that appears is convergent, then the interchange is justified. In particular, Eq. (8) is always true for convergent infinite sums.]

d) *Manipulating the domain.* If $R(j)$ and $S(j)$ are arbitrary relations, we have

$$\sum_{R(j)} a_j + \sum_{S(j)} a_j = \sum_{R(j) \text{ or } S(j)} a_j + \sum_{R(j) \text{ and } S(j)} a_j. \tag{11}$$

For example,

$$\sum_{1 \le j \le m} a_j + \sum_{m \le j \le n} a_j = \left(\sum_{1 \le j \le n} a_j \right) + a_m, \tag{12}$$

assuming that $1 \le m \le n$. In this case "$R(j)$ and $S(j)$" is simply "$j = m$," so we have reduced the second sum to simply "a_m." In most applications of Eq. (11), either $R(j)$ and $S(j)$ are simultaneously satisfied for only one or two values of j, or else it is impossible to have both $R(j)$ and $S(j)$ true for the same j. In the latter case, the second sum on the right-hand side of Eq. (11) simply disappears.

Now that we have seen the four basic rules for manipulating sums, let's study some further illustrations of how to apply these techniques.

Example 1.

$$\sum_{0 \le j \le n} a_j = \sum_{\substack{0 \le j \le n \\ j \text{ even}}} a_j + \sum_{\substack{0 \le j \le n \\ j \text{ odd}}} a_j \qquad \text{by rule (d)}$$

$$= \sum_{\substack{0 \le 2j \le n \\ 2j \text{ even}}} a_{2j} + \sum_{\substack{0 \le 2j+1 \le n \\ 2j+1 \text{ odd}}} a_{2j+1} \qquad \text{by rule (b)}$$

$$= \sum_{0 \le j \le n/2} a_{2j} + \sum_{0 \le j < n/2} a_{2j+1}.$$

The last step merely simplifies the relations below the $\sum$'s.

Example 2. Let

$$S_1 = \sum_{i=0}^{n} \sum_{j=0}^{i} a_i a_j = \sum_{j=0}^{n} \sum_{i=j}^{n} a_i a_j \qquad \text{by rule (c) [see Eq. (10)]}$$

$$= \sum_{i=0}^{n} \sum_{j=i}^{n} a_i a_j \qquad \text{by rule (b),}$$

interchanging the names i and j and recognizing that $a_j a_i = a_i a_j$. If we denote the latter sum by S_2, we have

$$2S_1 = S_1 + S_2 = \sum_{i=0}^{n} \left(\sum_{j=0}^{i} a_i a_j + \sum_{j=i}^{n} a_i a_j \right) \qquad \text{by Eq. (8)}$$

$$= \sum_{i=0}^{n} \left(\left(\sum_{j=0}^{n} a_i a_j \right) + a_i a_i \right) \qquad \begin{array}{l} \text{by rule (d)} \\ \text{[see Eq. (12)]} \end{array}$$

$$= \sum_{i=0}^{n} \sum_{j=0}^{n} a_i a_j + \sum_{i=0}^{n} a_i a_i \qquad \text{by Eq. (8)}$$

$$= \left(\sum_{i=0}^{n} a_i \right) \left(\sum_{j=0}^{n} a_j \right) + \left(\sum_{i=0}^{n} a_i^2 \right) \qquad \text{by rule (a)}$$

$$= \left(\sum_{i=0}^{n} a_i \right)^2 + \left(\sum_{i=0}^{n} a_i^2 \right) \qquad \text{by rule (b).}$$

Thus we have derived the important identity

$$\sum_{i=0}^{n} \sum_{j=0}^{i} a_i a_j = \frac{1}{2} \left(\left(\sum_{i=0}^{n} a_i \right)^2 + \left(\sum_{i=0}^{n} a_i^2 \right) \right). \qquad (13)$$

Example 3 (*The sum of a geometric progression*). Assume that $x \neq 1$ and that $n \geq 0$. Then

$$a + ax + \cdots + ax^n = \sum_{0 \leq j \leq n} ax^j \qquad \text{by definition (2)}$$

$$= a + \sum_{1 \leq j \leq n} ax^j \qquad \text{by rule (d)}$$

$$= a + x \sum_{1 \leq j \leq n} ax^{j-1} \qquad \text{by a very special case of (a)}$$

$$= a + x \sum_{0 \leq j \leq n-1} ax^j \qquad \text{by rule (b) [see Eq. (6)]}$$

$$= a + x \sum_{0 \leq j \leq n} ax^j - ax^{n+1} \qquad \text{by rule (d).}$$

Comparing the first relation with the last, we have

$$(1 - x) \sum_{0 \leq j \leq n} ax^j = a - ax^{n+1};$$

hence we obtain the basic formula

$$\sum_{0 \leq j \leq n} ax^j = a \left(\frac{1 - x^{n+1}}{1 - x} \right). \qquad (14)$$

Example 4 (*The sum of an arithmetic progression*). Assume that $n \geq 0$. Then

$$a + (a+b) + \cdots + (a + nb)$$

$$= \sum_{0 \leq j \leq n} (a + bj) \qquad \text{by definition (2)}$$

$$= \sum_{0 \leq n-j \leq n} \left(a + b(n - j)\right) \qquad \text{by rule (b)}$$

$$= \sum_{0 \leq j \leq n} (a + bn - bj) \qquad \text{by simplification}$$

$$= \sum_{0 \leq j \leq n} (2a + bn) - \sum_{0 \leq j \leq n} (a + bj) \qquad \text{by Eq. (8)}$$

$$= (n + 1)(2a + bn) - \sum_{0 \leq j \leq n} (a + bj),$$

since the first sum simply adds together $(n + 1)$ terms that do not depend on j. Now by equating the first and last expressions and dividing by 2, we obtain

$$\sum_{0 \leq j \leq n} (a + bj) = a(n + 1) + \tfrac{1}{2}bn(n + 1). \qquad (15)$$

This is $n + 1$ times $\tfrac{1}{2}\left(a + (a + bn)\right)$, which can be understood as the number of terms times the average of the first and last terms.

Notice that we have derived the important equations (13), (14), and (15) purely by using simple manipulations of sums. Most textbooks would simply *state* those formulas, and prove them by *induction*. Induction is, of course, a perfectly valid procedure; but it does not give any insight into how on earth a person would ever have dreamed the formula up in the first place, except by some lucky guess. In the analysis of algorithms we are confronted with hundreds of sums that do not conform to any apparent pattern; by manipulating those sums, as above, we can often get the answer without the need for ingenious guesses.

Many manipulations of sums and other formulas become considerably simpler if we adopt the following *bracket notation*:

$$[\text{statement}] = \begin{cases} 1, & \text{if the statement is true;} \\ 0, & \text{if the statement is false.} \end{cases} \qquad (16)$$

Then we can write, for example,

$$\sum_{R(j)} a_j = \sum_j a_j \left[R(j)\right], \qquad (17)$$

where the sum on the right is over *all* integers j, because the terms of that infinite sum are zero when $R(j)$ is false. (We assume that a_j is defined for all j.)

With bracket notation we can derive rule (b) from rules (a) and (c) in an interesting way:

$$\sum_{R(p(j))} a_{p(j)} = \sum_j a_{p(j)} \left[R(p(j))\right]$$

$$= \sum_j \sum_i a_i \left[R(i)\right] \left[i = p(j)\right]$$

$$= \sum_i a_i \big[R(i) \big] \sum_j [i = p(j)] \, . \tag{18}$$

The remaining sum on j is equal to 1 when $R(i)$ is true, if we assume that p is a permutation of the relevant values as required in (5); hence we are left with $\sum_i a_i[R(i)]$, which is $\sum_{R(i)} a_i$. This proves (5). If p is *not* such a permutation, (18) tells us the true value of $\sum_{R(p(j))} a_{p(j)}$.

The most famous special case of bracket notation is the so-called *Kronecker delta* symbol,

$$\delta_{ij} \;=\; [i = j] \;=\; \begin{cases} 1, & \text{if } i = j, \\ 0, & \text{if } i \neq j, \end{cases} \tag{19}$$

introduced by Leopold Kronecker in 1868. More general notations such as (16) were introduced by K. E. Iverson in 1962; therefore (16) is often called *Iverson's convention*. [See D. E. Knuth, *AMM* **99** (1992), 403–422.]

There is a notation for products, analogous to our notation for sums: The symbols

$$\prod_{R(j)} a_j \tag{20}$$

stand for the product of all a_j for which the integer j satisfies $R(j)$. If no such integer j exists, the product is defined to have the value 1 (*not* 0).

Operations (b), (c), and (d) are valid for the $\prod$-notation as well as for the $\sum$-notation, with suitable simple modifications. The exercises at the end of this section give a number of examples of product notation in use.

We conclude this section by mentioning another notation for multiple summation that is often convenient: A single $\sum$-sign may be used with one or more relations in *several* index variables, meaning that the sum is taken over all combinations of variables that meet the conditions. For example,

$$\sum_{0 \leq i \leq n} \sum_{0 \leq j \leq n} a_{ij} = \sum_{0 \leq i,j \leq n} a_{ij}; \quad \sum_{0 \leq i \leq n} \sum_{0 \leq j \leq i} a_{ij} = \sum_{0 \leq j \leq i \leq n} a_{ij}.$$

This notation gives no preference to one index of summation over any other, so it allows us to derive (10) in a new way:

$$\sum_{i=1}^{n} \sum_{j=1}^{i} a_{ij} = \sum_{i,j} a_{ij}[1 \leq i \leq n][1 \leq j \leq i] = \sum_{i,j} a_{ij}[1 \leq j \leq n][j \leq i \leq n]$$

$$= \sum_{j=1}^{n} \sum_{i=j}^{n} a_{ij} \, ,$$

using the fact that $[1 \leq i \leq n][1 \leq j \leq i] = [1 \leq j \leq i \leq n] = [1 \leq j \leq n][j \leq i \leq n]$. The more general equation (9) follows in a similar way from the identity

$$\big[R(i) \big] \big[S(i,j) \big] \;=\; \big[R(i) \text{ and } S(i,j) \big] \;=\; \big[S'(j) \big] \big[R'(i,j) \big] \, . \tag{21}$$

A further example that demonstrates the usefulness of summation with several indices is

$$\sum_{\substack{j_1+\cdots+j_n=n \\ j_1\geq\cdots\geq j_n\geq 0}} a_{j_1\ldots j_n}, \tag{22}$$

where a is an n-tuply subscripted variable; for example, if $n = 5$ this notation stands for

$$a_{11111} + a_{21110} + a_{22100} + a_{31100} + a_{32000} + a_{41000} + a_{50000}.$$

(See the remarks on partitions of a number in Section 1.2.1.)

EXERCISES — First Set

▶ **1.** [*10*] The text says that $a_1 + a_2 + \cdots + a_0 = 0$. What, then, is $a_2 + \cdots + a_0$?

2. [*01*] What does the notation $\sum_{1\leq j\leq n} a_j$ mean, if $n = 3.14$?

▶ **3.** [*13*] Without using the $\sum$-notation, write out the equivalent of

$$\sum_{0\leq n\leq 5} \frac{1}{2n+1},$$

and also the equivalent of

$$\sum_{0\leq n^2\leq 5} \frac{1}{2n^2+1}.$$

Explain why the two results are different, in spite of rule (b).

4. [*10*] Without using the $\sum$-notation, write out the equivalent of each side of Eq. (10) as a sum of sums for the case $n = 3$.

▶ **5.** [*HM20*] Prove that rule (a) is valid for arbitrary infinite series, provided that the series converge.

6. [*HM20*] Prove that rule (d) is valid for an arbitrary infinite series, provided that any three of the four sums exist.

7. [*HM23*] Given that c is an integer, show that $\sum_{R(j)} a_j = \sum_{R(c-j)} a_{c-j}$, even if both series are infinite.

8. [*HM25*] Find an example of a doubly infinite sequence of integers $\langle a_{ij}\rangle$ for which Eq. (7) is false.

▶ **9.** [*05*] Is the derivation of Eq. (14) valid even if $n = -1$?

10. [*05*] Is the derivation of Eq. (14) valid even if $n = -2$?

11. [*03*] What should the right-hand side of Eq. (14) be if $x = 1$?

12. [*10*] What is $1 + \frac{1}{7} + \frac{1}{49} + \frac{1}{343} + \cdots + \left(\frac{1}{7}\right)^n$?

13. [*10*] Using Eq. (15) and assuming that $m \leq n$, evaluate $\sum_{j=m}^{n} j$.

14. [*11*] Using the result of the previous exercise, evaluate $\sum_{j=m}^{n}\sum_{k=r}^{s} jk$.

▶ **15.** [*M22*] Compute the sum $1\times 2 + 2\times 2^2 + 3\times 2^3 + \cdots + n\times 2^n$ for small values of n. Do you see the pattern developing in these numbers? If not, discover it by manipulations similar to those leading up to Eq. (14).

16. [*M22*] Prove that

$$\sum_{j=0}^{n} j x^j = \frac{n x^{n+2} - (n+1) x^{n+1} + x}{(x-1)^2},$$

if $x \neq 1$, without using mathematical induction.

▶ **17.** [*M00*] Let S be a set of integers. What is $\sum_{j \in S} 1$?

18. [*M20*] Show how to interchange the order of summation as in Eq. (9) given that $R(i)$ specifies summing over all i such that "n is a multiple of i" and $S(i,j)$ specifies summing over all j such that "$1 \leq j < i$."

19. [*20*] What is $\sum_{j=m}^{n} (a_j - a_{j-1})$?

▶ **20.** [*25*] Dr. I. J. Matrix has observed a remarkable sequence of formulas:

$$9 \times 1 + 2 = 11, \ 9 \times 12 + 3 = 111, \ 9 \times 123 + 4 = 1111, \ 9 \times 1234 + 5 = 11111.$$

a) Write the good doctor's great discovery in terms of the $\sum$-notation.

b) Your answer to part (a) undoubtedly involves the number 10 as base of the decimal system; generalize this formula so that you get a formula that will perhaps work in any base b.

c) Prove your formula from part (b) by using formulas derived in the text or in exercise 16 above.

▶ **21.** [*M25*] Derive rule (d) from (8) and (17).

▶ **22.** [*20*] State the appropriate analogs of Eqs. (5), (7), (8), and (11) for *products* instead of sums.

23. [*10*] Explain why it is a good idea to define $\sum_{R(j)} a_j$ and $\prod_{R(j)} a_j$ as zero and one, respectively, when no integers satisfy $R(j)$.

24. [*20*] Suppose that $R(j)$ is true for only finitely many j. By induction on the number of integers satisfying $R(j)$, prove that $\log_b \prod_{R(j)} a_j = \sum_{R(j)} (\log_b a_j)$, assuming that all $a_j > 0$.

▶ **25.** [*15*] Consider the following derivation; is anything amiss?

$$\left(\sum_{i=1}^{n} a_i \right) \left(\sum_{j=1}^{n} \frac{1}{a_j} \right) = \sum_{1 \leq i \leq n} \sum_{1 \leq j \leq n} \frac{a_i}{a_j} = \sum_{1 \leq i \leq n} \sum_{1 \leq i \leq n} \frac{a_i}{a_i} = \sum_{i=1}^{n} 1 = n.$$

26. [*25*] Show that $\prod_{i=0}^{n} \prod_{j=0}^{i} a_i a_j$ may be expressed in terms of $\prod_{i=0}^{n} a_i$ by manipulating the $\prod$-notation as stated in exercise 22.

27. [*M20*] Generalize the result of exercise 1.2.1–9 by proving that

$$\prod_{j=1}^{n} (1 - a_j) \geq 1 - \sum_{j=1}^{n} a_j,$$

assuming that $0 < a_j < 1$.

28. [*M22*] Find a simple formula for $\prod_{j=2}^{n} (1 - 1/j^2)$.

▶ **29.** [*M30*] (a) Express $\sum_{i=0}^{n} \sum_{j=0}^{i} \sum_{k=0}^{j} a_i a_j a_k$ in terms of the multiple-sum notation explained at the end of the section. (b) Express the same sum in terms of $\sum_{i=0}^{n} a_i$, $\sum_{i=0}^{n} a_i^2$, and $\sum_{i=0}^{n} a_i^3$ [see Eq. (13)].

▶ **30.** [*M23*] (J. Binet, 1812.) Without using induction, prove the identity

$$\left(\sum_{j=1}^{n} a_j x_j\right)\left(\sum_{j=1}^{n} b_j y_j\right) = \left(\sum_{j=1}^{n} a_j y_j\right)\left(\sum_{j=1}^{n} b_j x_j\right) + \sum_{1 \le j < k \le n} (a_j b_k - a_k b_j)(x_j y_k - x_k y_j).$$

[An important special case arises when $w_1, \ldots, w_n, z_1, \ldots, z_n$ are arbitrary complex numbers and we set $a_j = w_j$, $b_j = \bar{z}_j$, $x_j = \bar{w}_j$, $y_j = z_j$:

$$\left(\sum_{j=1}^{n} |w_j|^2\right)\left(\sum_{j=1}^{n} |z_j|^2\right) = \left|\sum_{j=1}^{n} w_j z_j\right|^2 + \sum_{1 \le j < k \le n} |w_j \bar{z}_k - w_k \bar{z}_j|^2.$$

The terms $|w_j \bar{z}_k - w_k \bar{z}_j|^2$ are nonnegative, so the famous *Cauchy–Schwarz inequality*

$$\left(\sum_{j=1}^{n} |w_j|^2\right)\left(\sum_{j=1}^{n} |z_j|^2\right) \ge \left|\sum_{j=1}^{n} w_j z_j\right|^2$$

is a consequence of Binet's formula.]

31. [*M20*] Use Binet's formula to express the sum $\sum_{1 \le j < k \le n}(u_j - u_k)(v_j - v_k)$ in terms of $\sum_{j=1}^{n} u_j v_j$, $\sum_{j=1}^{n} u_j$, and $\sum_{j=1}^{n} v_j$.

32. [*M20*] Prove that

$$\prod_{j=1}^{n} \sum_{i=1}^{m} a_{ij} = \sum_{1 \le i_1, \ldots, i_n \le m} a_{i_1 1} \ldots a_{i_n n}.$$

▶ **33.** [*M30*] One evening Dr. Matrix discovered some formulas that might even be classed as more remarkable than those of exercise 20:

$$\frac{1}{(a-b)(a-c)} + \frac{1}{(b-a)(b-c)} + \frac{1}{(c-a)(c-b)} = 0,$$

$$\frac{a}{(a-b)(a-c)} + \frac{b}{(b-a)(b-c)} + \frac{c}{(c-a)(c-b)} = 0,$$

$$\frac{a^2}{(a-b)(a-c)} + \frac{b^2}{(b-a)(b-c)} + \frac{c^2}{(c-a)(c-b)} = 1,$$

$$\frac{a^3}{(a-b)(a-c)} + \frac{b^3}{(b-a)(b-c)} + \frac{c^3}{(c-a)(c-b)} = a+b+c.$$

Prove that these formulas are a special case of a general law; let $x_1, x_2, \ldots, x_n$ be distinct numbers, and show that

$$\sum_{j=1}^{n} \left(x_j^r \bigg/ \prod_{\substack{1 \le k \le n \\ k \ne j}} (x_j - x_k)\right) = \begin{cases} 0, & \text{if } 0 \le r < n-1; \\ 1, & \text{if } r = n-1; \\ \sum_{j=1}^{n} x_j, & \text{if } r = n. \end{cases}$$

34. [*M25*] Prove that

$$\sum_{k=1}^{n} \frac{\prod_{1 \le r \le n, r \ne m}(x + k - r)}{\prod_{1 \le r \le n, r \ne k}(k - r)} = 1,$$

provided that $1 \leq m \leq n$ and x is arbitrary. For example, if $n = 4$ and $m = 2$, then

$$\frac{x(x-2)(x-3)}{(-1)(-2)(-3)} + \frac{(x+1)(x-1)(x-2)}{(1)(-1)(-2)} + \frac{(x+2)x(x-1)}{(2)(1)(-1)} + \frac{(x+3)(x+1)x}{(3)(2)(1)} = 1.$$

35. [*HM20*] The notation $\sup_{R(j)} a_j$ is used to denote the least upper bound of the elements a_j, in a manner exactly analogous to the $\sum$- and $\prod$-notations. (When $R(j)$ is satisfied for only finitely many j, the notation $\max_{R(j)} a_j$ is often used to denote the same quantity.) Show how rules (a), (b), (c), and (d) can be adapted for manipulation of *this* notation. In particular discuss the following analog of rule (a):

$$(\sup_{R(i)} a_i) + (\sup_{S(j)} b_j) = \sup_{R(i)} (\sup_{S(j)} (a_i + b_j)),$$

and give a suitable definition for the notation when $R(j)$ is satisfied for *no* j.

EXERCISES — Second Set

Determinants and matrices. The following interesting problems are for the reader who has experienced at least an introduction to determinants and elementary matrix theory. A determinant may be evaluated by astutely combining the operations of: (a) factoring a quantity out of a row or column; (b) adding a multiple of one row (or column) to another row (or column); (c) expanding by cofactors. The simplest and most often used version of operation (c) is to simply delete the entire first row and column, provided that the element in the upper left corner is $+1$ and the remaining elements in either the entire first row or the entire first column are zero; then evaluate the resulting smaller determinant. In general, the cofactor of an element a_{ij} in an $n \times n$ determinant is 1 if $n = 1$, otherwise it's $(-1)^{i+j}$ times the $(n-1) \times (n-1)$ determinant obtained by deleting the row and column in which a_{ij} appeared. The value of a determinant is equal to $\sum a_{ij} \cdot \text{cofactor}(a_{ij})$ summed with either i or j held constant and with the other subscript varying from 1 to n.

If (b_{ij}) is the *inverse* of matrix (a_{ij}), then b_{ij} equals the cofactor of a_{ji} (*not* a_{ij}), divided by the determinant of the whole matrix.

The following types of matrices are of special importance:

Vandermonde's matrix,   Combinatorial matrix,

$$a_{ij} = x_j^i \qquad\qquad\qquad\qquad\qquad a_{ij} = y + \delta_{ij} x$$

$$\begin{pmatrix} x_1 & x_2 & \cdots & x_n \\ x_1^2 & x_2^2 & \cdots & x_n^2 \\ \vdots & \vdots & \ddots & \vdots \\ x_1^n & x_2^n & \cdots & x_n^n \end{pmatrix} \qquad\qquad \begin{pmatrix} x+y & y & \cdots & y \\ y & x+y & \cdots & y \\ \vdots & \vdots & \ddots & \vdots \\ y & y & \cdots & x+y \end{pmatrix}$$

Cauchy's matrix,

$$a_{ij} = 1/(x_i + y_j)$$

$$\begin{pmatrix} 1/(x_1+y_1) & 1/(x_1+y_2) & \cdots & 1/(x_1+y_n) \\ 1/(x_2+y_1) & 1/(x_2+y_2) & \cdots & 1/(x_2+y_n) \\ \vdots & \vdots & \ddots & \vdots \\ 1/(x_n+y_1) & 1/(x_n+y_2) & \cdots & 1/(x_n+y_n) \end{pmatrix}$$

36. [*M23*] Show that the determinant of the combinatorial matrix is $x^{n-1}(x+ny)$.

▶ **37.** [*M24*] Show that the determinant of Vandermonde's matrix is

$$\prod_{1\le j\le n} x_j \prod_{1\le i<j\le n} (x_j - x_i).$$

▶ **38.** [*M25*] Show that the determinant of Cauchy's matrix is

$$\prod_{1\le i<j\le n} (x_j - x_i)(y_j - y_i) \Big/ \prod_{1\le i,j\le n} (x_i + y_j).$$

39. [*M23*] Show that the inverse of a combinatorial matrix is a combinatorial matrix with the entries $b_{ij} = (-y + \delta_{ij}(x+ny))/x(x+ny)$.

40. [*M24*] Show that the inverse of Vandermonde's matrix is given by

$$b_{ij} = \left(\sum_{\substack{1\le k_1<\cdots<k_{n-j}\le n \\ k_1,\dots,k_{n-j}\ne i}} (-1)^{j-1} x_{k_1}\dots x_{k_{n-j}} \right) \Big/ x_i \prod_{\substack{1\le k\le n \\ k\ne i}} (x_k - x_i).$$

Don't be dismayed by the complicated sum in the numerator — it's just the coefficient of x^{j-1} in the polynomial $(x_1-x)\dots(x_n-x)/(x_i-x)$. (It equals $(-1)^{n-1}$ when $j=n$.)

41. [*M26*] Show that the inverse of Cauchy's matrix is given by

$$b_{ij} = \left(\prod_{1\le k\le n} (x_j+y_k)(x_k+y_i) \right) \Big/ (x_j+y_i)\left(\prod_{\substack{1\le k\le n \\ k\ne j}} (x_j-x_k) \right)\left(\prod_{\substack{1\le k\le n \\ k\ne i}} (y_i-y_k) \right).$$

42. [*M18*] What is the sum of all n^2 elements in the inverse of the combinatorial matrix?

43. [*M24*] What is the sum of all n^2 elements in the inverse of Vandermonde's matrix? [*Hint:* Use exercise 33.]

▶ **44.** [*M26*] What is the sum of all n^2 elements in the inverse of Cauchy's matrix?

▶ **45.** [*M25*] A *Hilbert matrix*, sometimes called an $n\times n$ segment of *the* (infinite) Hilbert matrix, is a matrix for which $a_{ij} = 1/(i+j-1)$. Show that this is a special case of Cauchy's matrix, find its inverse, show that each element of the inverse is an integer, and show that the sum of all elements of the inverse is n^2. [*Note:* Hilbert matrices have often been used to test various matrix manipulation algorithms, because they are numerically unstable, and they have known inverses. However, it is a mistake to compare the *known* inverse, given in this exercise, to the *computed* inverse of a Hilbert matrix, since the matrix to be inverted must be expressed in rounded numbers beforehand; the inverse of an approximate Hilbert matrix will be somewhat different from the inverse of an exact one, due to the instability present. Since the elements of the inverse are integers, and since the inverse matrix is just as unstable as the original, the inverse can be specified exactly, and one could try to invert the inverse. The integers that appear in the inverse are, however, quite large.] The solution to this problem requires an elementary knowledge of factorials and binomial coefficients, which are discussed in Sections 1.2.5 and 1.2.6.

▶ **46.** [*M30*] Let A be an $m \times n$ matrix, and let B be an $n \times m$ matrix. Given that $1 \le j_1, j_2, \dots, j_m \le n$, let $A_{j_1 j_2\dots j_m}$ denote the $m \times m$ matrix consisting of columns

$j_1, \ldots, j_m$ of A, and let $B_{j_1 j_2 \ldots j_m}$ denote the $m \times m$ matrix consisting of rows $j_1, \ldots, j_m$ of B. Prove the *Binet–Cauchy identity*

$$\det(AB) = \sum_{1 \le j_1 < j_2 < \cdots < j_m \le n} \det(A_{j_1 j_2 \ldots j_m}) \det(B_{j_1 j_2 \ldots j_m}).$$

(Note the special cases: (i) $m = n$, (ii) $m = 1$, (iii) $B = A^T$, (iv) $m > n$, (v) $m = 2$.)

47. [*M27*] (C. Krattenthaler.) Prove that

$$\det \begin{pmatrix} (x+q_2)(x+q_3) & (x+p_1)(x+q_3) & (x+p_1)(x+p_2) \\ (y+q_2)(y+q_3) & (y+p_1)(y+q_3) & (y+p_1)(y+p_2) \\ (z+q_2)(z+q_3) & (z+p_1)(z+q_3) & (z+p_1)(z+p_2) \end{pmatrix}$$
$$= (x-y)(x-z)(y-z)(p_1-q_2)(p_1-q_3)(p_2-q_3),$$

and generalize this equation to an identity for an $n \times n$ determinant in $3n - 2$ variables $x_1, \ldots, x_n, p_1, \ldots, p_{n-1}, q_2, \ldots, q_n$. Compare your formula to the result of exercise 38.

1.2.4. Integer Functions and Elementary Number Theory

If x is any real number, we write

$\lfloor x \rfloor$ = the greatest integer less than or equal to x (the *floor* of x);

$\lceil x \rceil$ = the least integer greater than or equal to x (the *ceiling* of x).

The notation $[x]$ was often used before 1970 for one or the other of these functions, usually the former; but the notations above, introduced by K. E. Iverson in the 1960s, are more useful, because $\lfloor x \rfloor$ and $\lceil x \rceil$ occur about equally often in practice. The function $\lfloor x \rfloor$ is sometimes called the *entier* function, from the French word for "integer."

The following formulas and examples are easily verified:

$$\lfloor \sqrt{2} \rfloor = 1, \quad \lceil \sqrt{2} \rceil = 2, \quad \left\lfloor +\frac{1}{2} \right\rfloor = 0, \quad \left\lceil -\frac{1}{2} \right\rceil = 0, \quad \left\lfloor -\frac{1}{2} \right\rfloor = -1 \ (not \ \text{zero!});$$

$$\lceil x \rceil = \lfloor x \rfloor \qquad \text{if and only if } x \text{ is an integer,}$$
$$\lceil x \rceil = \lfloor x \rfloor + 1 \quad \text{if and only if } x \text{ is not an integer;}$$

$$\lfloor -x \rfloor = -\lceil x \rceil; \qquad x - 1 < \lfloor x \rfloor \le x \le \lceil x \rceil < x + 1.$$

Exercises at the end of this section list other important formulas involving the floor and ceiling operations.

If x and y are any real numbers, we define the following binary operation:

$$x \bmod y = x - y \lfloor x/y \rfloor, \quad \text{if } y \ne 0; \qquad x \bmod 0 = x. \qquad (1)$$

From this definition we can see that, when $y \ne 0$,

$$0 \le \frac{x}{y} - \left\lfloor \frac{x}{y} \right\rfloor = \frac{x \bmod y}{y} < 1. \qquad (2)$$

Consequently

a) if $y > 0$, then $0 \le x \bmod y < y$;

b) if $y < 0$, then $0 \ge x \bmod y > y$;

c) the quantity $x - (x \bmod y)$ is an integral multiple of y.

We call $x \bmod y$ the *remainder* when x is divided by y; similarly, we call $\lfloor x/y \rfloor$ the *quotient*.

When x and y are integers, "mod" is therefore a familiar operation:

$$5 \bmod 3 = 2, \qquad 18 \bmod 3 = 0, \qquad -2 \bmod 3 = 1. \tag{3}$$

We have $x \bmod y = 0$ if and only if x is a multiple of y, that is, if and only if x is divisible by y. The notation $y \backslash x$, read "y divides x," means that y is a positive integer and $x \bmod y = 0$.

The "mod" operation is useful also when x and y take arbitrary real values. For example, with trigonometric functions we can write

$$\tan x = \tan (x \bmod \pi).$$

The quantity $x \bmod 1$ is the *fractional part* of x; we have, by Eq. (1),

$$x = \lfloor x \rfloor + (x \bmod 1). \tag{4}$$

Writers on number theory often use the abbreviation "mod" in a different but closely related sense. We will use the following form to express the number-theoretical concept of *congruence*: The statement

$$x \equiv y \pmod{z} \tag{5}$$

means that $x \bmod z = y \bmod z$; it is the same as saying that $x - y$ is an integral multiple of z. Expression (5) is read, "x is congruent to y modulo z."

Let's turn now to the basic elementary properties of congruences that will be used in the number-theoretical arguments of this book. All variables in the following formulas are assumed to be integers. Two integers x and y are said to be *relatively prime* if they have no common factor, that is, if their greatest common divisor is 1; in such a case we write $x \perp y$. The concept of relatively prime integers is a familiar one, since it is customary to say that a fraction is in "lowest terms" when the numerator is relatively prime to the denominator.

Law A. If $a \equiv b$ and $x \equiv y$, then $a \pm x \equiv b \pm y$ and $ax \equiv by \pmod{m}$.

Law B. If $ax \equiv by$ and $a \equiv b$, and if $a \perp m$, then $x \equiv y \pmod{m}$.

Law C. $a \equiv b \pmod{m}$ if and only if $an \equiv bn \pmod{mn}$, when $n \neq 0$.

Law D. If $r \perp s$, then $a \equiv b \pmod{rs}$ if and only if $a \equiv b \pmod{r}$ and $a \equiv b \pmod{s}$.

Law A states that we can do addition, subtraction, and multiplication modulo m just as we do ordinary addition, subtraction, and multiplication. Law B considers the operation of division and shows that, when the divisor is relatively prime to the modulus, we can also divide out common factors. Laws C and D consider what happens when the modulus is changed. These laws are proved in the exercises below.

The following important theorem is a consequence of Laws A and B.

Theorem F (*Fermat's theorem, 1640*). *If p is a prime number, then $a^p \equiv a$ (modulo p) for all integers a.*

Proof. If a is a multiple of p, obviously $a^p \equiv 0 \equiv a$ (modulo p). So we need only consider the case $a \bmod p \neq 0$. Since p is a prime number, this means that $a \perp p$. Consider the numbers

$$0 \bmod p, \quad a \bmod p, \quad 2a \bmod p, \quad \ldots, \quad (p-1)a \bmod p. \tag{6}$$

These p numbers are all *distinct*, for if $ax \bmod p = ay \bmod p$, then by definition (5) $ax \equiv ay$ (modulo p); hence by Law B, $x \equiv y$ (modulo p).

Since (6) gives p distinct numbers, all nonnegative and less than p, we see that the first number is zero and the rest are the integers $1, 2, \ldots, p-1$ in some order. Therefore by Law A,

$$(a)(2a) \ldots \big((p-1)a\big) \equiv 1 \cdot 2 \ldots (p-1) \pmod{p}. \tag{7}$$

Multiplying each side of this congruence by a, we obtain

$$a^p\big(1 \cdot 2 \ldots (p-1)\big) = a\big(1 \cdot 2 \ldots (p-1)\big) \pmod{p}; \tag{8}$$

and this proves the theorem, since each of the factors $1, 2, \ldots, p-1$ is relatively prime to p and can be canceled by Law B. ∎

EXERCISES

1. [*00*] What are $\lfloor 1.1 \rfloor$, $\lfloor -1.1 \rfloor$, $\lceil -1.1 \rceil$, $\lfloor 0.99999 \rfloor$, and $\lfloor \lg 35 \rfloor$?

▶ **2.** [*01*] What is $\lceil \lfloor x \rfloor \rceil$?

3. [*M10*] Let n be an integer, and let x be a real number. Prove that
a) $\lfloor x \rfloor < n$ if and only if $x < n$;   b) $n \leq \lfloor x \rfloor$ if and only if $n \leq x$;
c) $\lceil x \rceil \leq n$ if and only if $x \leq n$;   d) $n < \lceil x \rceil$ if and only if $n < x$;
e) $\lfloor x \rfloor = n$ if and only if $x - 1 < n \leq x$, and if and only if $n \leq x < n+1$;
f) $\lceil x \rceil = n$ if and only if $x \leq n < x+1$, and if and only if $n-1 < x \leq n$.

[*These formulas are the most important tools for proving facts about $\lfloor x \rfloor$ and $\lceil x \rceil$.*]

▶ **4.** [*M10*] Using the previous exercise, prove that $\lfloor -x \rfloor = -\lceil x \rceil$.

5. [*16*] Given that x is a positive real number, state a simple formula that expresses x *rounded to the nearest integer*. The desired rounding rule is to produce $\lfloor x \rfloor$ when $x \bmod 1 < \frac{1}{2}$, and to produce $\lceil x \rceil$ when $x \bmod 1 \geq \frac{1}{2}$. Your answer should be a single formula that covers both cases. Discuss the rounding that would be obtained by your formula when x is negative.

▶ **6.** [*20*] Which of the following equations are true for all positive real numbers x?
(a) $\lfloor \sqrt{\lfloor x \rfloor} \rfloor = \lfloor \sqrt{x} \rfloor$; (b) $\lceil \sqrt{\lceil x \rceil} \rceil = \lceil \sqrt{x} \rceil$; (c) $\lceil \sqrt{\lfloor x \rfloor} \rceil = \lceil \sqrt{x} \rceil$.

7. [*M15*] Show that $\lfloor x \rfloor + \lfloor y \rfloor \leq \lfloor x + y \rfloor$ and that equality holds if and only if $x \bmod 1 + y \bmod 1 < 1$. Does a similar formula hold for ceilings?

8. [*00*] What are 100 mod 3, 100 mod 7, -100 mod 7, -100 mod 0?

9. [*05*] What are 5 mod -3, 18 mod -3, -2 mod -3?

▶ **10.** [*10*] What are 1.1 mod 1, 0.11 mod .1, 0.11 mod $-.1$?

11. [*00*] What does "$x \equiv y$ (modulo 0)" mean by our conventions?

12. [*00*] What integers are relatively prime to 1?

13. [*M00*] By convention, we say that the greatest common divisor of 0 and n is $|n|$. What integers are relatively prime to 0?

▶ **14.** [*12*] If $x \bmod 3 = 2$ and $x \bmod 5 = 3$, what is $x \bmod 15$?

15. [*10*] Prove that $z(x \bmod y) = (zx) \bmod (zy)$. [Law C is an immediate consequence of this distributive law.]

16. [*M10*] Assume that $y > 0$. Show that if $(x - z)/y$ is an integer and if $0 \le z < y$, then $z = x \bmod y$.

17. [*M15*] Prove Law A directly from the definition of congruence, and also prove half of Law D: If $a \equiv b$ (modulo rs), then $a \equiv b$ (modulo r) and $a \equiv b$ (modulo s). (Here r and s are arbitrary integers.)

18. [*M15*] Using Law B, prove the other half of Law D: If $a \equiv b$ (modulo r) and $a \equiv b$ (modulo s), then $a \equiv b$ (modulo rs), provided that $r \perp s$.

▶ **19.** [*M10*] (*Law of inverses.*) If $n \perp m$, there is an integer n' such that $nn' \equiv 1$ (modulo m). Prove this, using the extension of Euclid's algorithm (Algorithm 1.2.1E).

20. [*M15*] Use the law of inverses and Law A to prove Law B.

21. [*M22*] (*Fundamental theorem of arithmetic.*) Use Law B and exercise 1.2.1–5 to prove that every integer $n > 1$ has a *unique* representation as a product of primes (except for the order of the factors). In other words, show that there is exactly one way to write $n = p_1 p_2 \ldots p_k$, where each p_j is prime and $p_1 \le p_2 \le \cdots \le p_k$.

▶ **22.** [*M10*] Give an example to show that Law B is not always true if a is not relatively prime to m.

23. [*M10*] Give an example to show that Law D is not always true if r is not relatively prime to s.

▶ **24.** [*M20*] To what extent can Laws A, B, C, and D be generalized to apply to arbitrary real numbers instead of integers?

25. [*M02*] Show that, according to Theorem F, $a^{p-1} \bmod p = [a$ is not a multiple of $p]$, whenever p is a prime number.

26. [*M15*] Let p be an odd prime number, let a be any integer, and let $b = a^{(p-1)/2}$. Show that $b \bmod p$ is either 0 or 1 or $p - 1$. [*Hint:* Consider $(b+1)(b-1)$.]

27. [*M15*] Given that n is a positive integer, let $\varphi(n)$ be the number of values among $\{0, 1, \ldots, n - 1\}$ that are relatively prime to n. Thus $\varphi(1) = 1$, $\varphi(2) = 1$, $\varphi(3) = 2$, $\varphi(4) = 2$, etc. Show that $\varphi(p) = p - 1$ if p is a prime number; and evaluate $\varphi(p^e)$, when e is a positive integer.

▶ **28.** [*M25*] Show that the method used to prove Theorem F can be used to prove the following extension, called *Euler's theorem*: $a^{\varphi(m)} \equiv 1$ (modulo m), for *any* positive integer m, when $a \perp m$. (In particular, the number n' in exercise 19 may be taken to be $n^{\varphi(m)-1} \bmod m$.)

29. [*M22*] A function $f(n)$ of positive integers n is called *multiplicative* if $f(rs) = f(r)f(s)$ whenever $r \perp s$. Show that each of the following functions is multiplicative: (a) $f(n) = n^c$, where c is any constant; (b) $f(n) = [n$ is not divisible by k^2 for any integer $k > 1]$; (c) $f(n) = c^k$, where k is the number of distinct primes that divide n; (d) the product of any two multiplicative functions.

30. [*M30*] Prove that the function $\varphi(n)$ of exercise 27 is multiplicative. Using this fact, evaluate $\varphi(1000000)$, and give a method for evaluating $\varphi(n)$ in a simple way once n has been factored into primes.

31. [*M22*] Prove that if $f(n)$ is multiplicative, so is $g(n) = \sum_{d\backslash n} f(d)$.

32. [*M18*] Prove the double-summation identity

$$\sum_{d\backslash n} \sum_{c\backslash d} f(c,d) = \sum_{c\backslash n} \sum_{d\backslash(n/c)} f(c,cd),$$

for any function $f(x,y)$.

33. [*M18*] Given that m and n are integers, evaluate (a) $\lfloor \frac{1}{2}(n+m)\rfloor + \lfloor \frac{1}{2}(n-m+1)\rfloor$; (b) $\lceil \frac{1}{2}(n+m)\rceil + \lceil \frac{1}{2}(n-m+1)\rceil$. (The special case $m=0$ is worth noting.)

▸ **34.** [*M21*] What conditions on the real number $b > 1$ are necessary and sufficient to guarantee that $\lfloor \log_b x \rfloor = \lfloor \log_b \lfloor x \rfloor \rfloor$ for all real $x \geq 1$?

▸ **35.** [*M20*] Given that m and n are integers and $n > 0$, prove that

$$\lfloor (x+m)/n \rfloor = \lfloor (\lfloor x \rfloor + m)/n \rfloor$$

for all real x. (When $m = 0$, we have an important special case.) Does an analogous result hold for the ceiling function?

36. [*M23*] Prove that $\sum_{k=1}^n \lfloor k/2 \rfloor = \lfloor n^2/4 \rfloor$; also evaluate $\sum_{k=1}^n \lceil k/2 \rceil$.

▸ **37.** [*M30*] Let m and n be integers, $n > 0$. Show that

$$\sum_{0 \leq k < n} \left\lfloor \frac{mk+x}{n} \right\rfloor = \frac{(m-1)(n-1)}{2} + \frac{d-1}{2} + d\lfloor x/d \rfloor,$$

where d is the greatest common divisor of m and n, and x is any real number.

38. [*M26*] (E. Busche, 1909.) Prove that, for all real x and y with $y > 0$,

$$\sum_{0 \leq k < y} \left\lfloor x + \frac{k}{y} \right\rfloor = \lfloor xy + \lfloor x+1 \rfloor (\lceil y \rceil - y) \rfloor.$$

In particular, when y is a positive integer n, we have the important formula

$$\lfloor x \rfloor + \left\lfloor x + \frac{1}{n} \right\rfloor + \cdots + \left\lfloor x + \frac{n-1}{n} \right\rfloor = \lfloor nx \rfloor.$$

39. [*HM35*] A function f for which $f(x) + f(x + \frac{1}{n}) + \cdots + f(x + \frac{n-1}{n}) = f(nx)$, whenever n is a positive integer, is called a *replicative function*. The previous exercise establishes the fact that $\lfloor x \rfloor$ is replicative. Show that the following functions are replicative:

a) $f(x) = x - \frac{1}{2}$;
b) $f(x) = [x$ is an integer$]$;
c) $f(x) = [x$ is a positive integer$]$;
d) $f(x) = [$there exists a rational number r and an integer m such that $x = r\pi + m]$;
e) three other functions like the one in (d), with r and/or m restricted to positive values;
f) $f(x) = \log|2\sin \pi x|$, if the value $f(x) = -\infty$ is allowed;
g) the sum of any two replicative functions;
h) a constant multiple of a replicative function;
i) the function $g(x) = f(x - \lfloor x \rfloor)$, where $f(x)$ is replicative.

40. [*HM46*] Study the class of replicative functions; determine all replicative functions of a special type. For example, is the function in (a) of exercise 39 the only continuous replicative function? It may be interesting to study also the more general class of functions for which

$$f(x) + f\left(x + \frac{1}{n}\right) + \cdots + f\left(x + \frac{n-1}{n}\right) = a_n f(nx) + b_n.$$

Here a_n and b_n are numbers that depend on n but not on x. Derivatives and (if $b_n = 0$) integrals of these functions are of the same type. If we require that $b_n = 0$, we have, for example, the Bernoulli polynomials, the trigonometric functions $\cot \pi x$ and $\csc^2 \pi x$, as well as Hurwitz's generalized zeta function $\zeta(s, x) = \sum_{k \geq 0} 1/(k + x)^s$ for fixed s. With $b_n \neq 0$ we have still other well-known functions, such as the psi function.

41. [*M23*] Let a_1, a_2, a_3, ... be the sequence 1, 2, 2, 3, 3, 3, 4, 4, 4, 4, ...; find an expression for a_n in terms of n, using the floor and/or ceiling function.

42. [*M24*] (a) Prove that

$$\sum_{k=1}^{n} a_k = n a_n - \sum_{k=1}^{n-1} k(a_{k+1} - a_k), \qquad \text{if } n > 0.$$

(b) The preceding formula is useful for evaluating certain sums involving the floor function. Prove that, if b is an integer ≥ 2,

$$\sum_{k=1}^{n} \lfloor \log_b k \rfloor = (n+1)\lfloor \log_b n \rfloor - (b^{\lfloor \log_b n \rfloor + 1} - b)/(b - 1).$$

43. [*M23*] Evaluate $\sum_{k=1}^{n} \lfloor \sqrt{k} \rfloor$.

44. [*M24*] Show that $\sum_{k \geq 0} \sum_{1 \leq j < b} \lfloor (n + jb^k)/b^{k+1} \rfloor = n$, if b and n are integers, $n \geq 0$, and $b \geq 2$. What is the value of this sum when $n < 0$?

▶ **45.** [*M28*] The result of exercise 37 is somewhat surprising, since it implies that

$$\sum_{0 \leq k < n} \left\lfloor \frac{mk + x}{n} \right\rfloor = \sum_{0 \leq k < m} \left\lfloor \frac{nk + x}{m} \right\rfloor$$

when m and n are positive integers and x is arbitrary. This "reciprocity relationship" is one of many similar formulas (see Section 3.3.3). Show that in general we have

$$\sum_{0 \leq j < n} f\left(\left\lfloor \frac{mj}{n} \right\rfloor\right) = \sum_{0 \leq r < m} \left\lceil \frac{rn}{m} \right\rceil (f(r - 1) - f(r)) + n f(m - 1)$$

for any function f and all integers $m, n > 0$. In particular, prove that

$$\sum_{0 \leq j < n} \binom{\lfloor mj/n \rfloor + 1}{k} + \sum_{0 \leq j < m} \left\lceil \frac{jn}{m} \right\rceil \binom{j}{k - 1} = n \binom{m}{k}.$$

[*Hint:* Consider the change of variable $r = \lfloor mj/n \rfloor$. Binomial coefficients $\binom{m}{k}$ are discussed in Section 1.2.6.]

46. [*M29*] (*General reciprocity law.*) Extend the formula of exercise 45 to obtain an expression for $\sum_{0 \leq j < \alpha n} f(\lfloor mj/n \rfloor)$, where α is *any* positive real number.

▶ **47.** [*M31*] When p is an odd prime number, the *Legendre symbol* $\left(\frac{q}{p}\right)$ is defined to be $+1$, 0, or -1, depending on whether $q^{(p-1)/2} \bmod p$ is 1, 0, or $p-1$. (Exercise 26 proves that these are the only possible values.)

a) Given that q is not a multiple of p, show that the numbers

$$(-1)^{\lfloor 2kq/p \rfloor}(2kq \bmod p), \qquad 0 < k < p/2,$$

are congruent in some order to the numbers $2, 4, \ldots, p-1$ (modulo p). Hence $\left(\frac{q}{p}\right) = (-1)^\sigma$ where $\sigma = \sum_{0 \le k < p/2} \lfloor 2kq/p \rfloor$.

b) Use the result of (a) to calculate $\left(\frac{2}{p}\right)$.

c) Given that q is odd, show that $\sum_{0 \le k < p/2} \lfloor 2kq/p \rfloor \equiv \sum_{0 \le k < p/2} \lfloor kq/p \rfloor$ (modulo 2), unless q is a multiple of p. [*Hint:* Consider the quantity $\lfloor (p-1-2k)q/p \rfloor$.]

d) Use the general reciprocity formula of exercise 46 to obtain the *law of quadratic reciprocity*, $\left(\frac{q}{p}\right)\left(\frac{p}{q}\right) = (-1)^{(p-1)(q-1)/4}$, given that p and q are distinct odd primes.

48. [*M26*] Prove or disprove the following identities, for integers m and n:

(a) $\left\lfloor \dfrac{m+n-1}{n} \right\rfloor = \left\lceil \dfrac{m}{n} \right\rceil$, if $n \ne 0$;   (b) $\left\lfloor \dfrac{n+2-\lfloor n/25 \rfloor}{3} \right\rfloor = \left\lfloor \dfrac{8n+24}{25} \right\rfloor$.

49. [*M30*] Suppose the integer-valued function $f(x)$ satisfies the two simple laws (i) $f(x+1) = f(x) + 1$; (ii) $f(x) = f(f(nx)/n)$ for all positive integers n. Prove that either $f(x) = \lfloor x \rfloor$ for all rational x, or $f(x) = \lceil x \rceil$ for all rational x.

50. [*M20*] J. H. Quick noticed that $\lceil 1000\pi \rceil = 3142$ and $\lfloor 3142/\pi \rfloor = 1000$. Is it true that $\lceil m\pi \rceil = n \iff \lfloor n/\pi \rfloor = m$, for all integers m and n?

1.2.5. Permutations and Factorials

A *permutation of n objects* is an arrangement of n distinct objects in a row. There are six permutations of three objects $\{a, b, c\}$:

$$a\,b\,c, \qquad a\,c\,b, \qquad b\,a\,c, \qquad b\,c\,a, \qquad c\,a\,b, \qquad c\,b\,a. \tag{1}$$

The properties of permutations are of great importance in the analysis of algorithms, and we will deduce many interesting facts about them later in this book.* Our first task is simply to *count* them: How many permutations of n objects are possible? There are n ways to choose the leftmost object, and once this choice has been made there are $n-1$ ways to select a different object to place next to it; this gives us $n(n-1)$ choices for the first two positions. Similarly, we find that there are $n-2$ choices for the third object distinct from the first two, and a total of $n(n-1)(n-2)$ possible ways to choose the first three objects. In general, if p_{nk} denotes the number of ways to choose k objects out of n and to arrange them in a row, we see that

$$p_{nk} = n(n-1)\ldots(n-k+1). \tag{2}$$

The total number of permutations is therefore $p_{nn} = n(n-1) \ldots (1)$.

The process of *constructing* all permutations of n objects in an inductive manner, assuming that all permutations of $n-1$ objects have been constructed,

---

* In fact, permutations are so important, Vaughan Pratt has suggested calling them "perms." As soon as Pratt's convention is established, textbooks of computer science will be somewhat shorter (and perhaps less expensive).

is very important in our applications. Let us rewrite (1) using the numbers $\{1,2,3\}$ instead of the letters $\{a, b, c\}$; the permutations are then

$$1\,2\,3, \qquad 1\,3\,2, \qquad 2\,1\,3, \qquad 2\,3\,1, \qquad 3\,1\,2, \qquad 3\,2\,1. \qquad (3)$$

Consider how to get from this array to the permutations of $\{1,2,3,4\}$. There are two principal ways to go from $n-1$ objects to n objects.

Method 1. For each permutation $a_1 a_2 \ldots a_{n-1}$ of $\{1,2,\ldots,n-1\}$, form n others by inserting the number n in all possible places, obtaining

$$n\,a_1 a_2 \ldots a_{n-1}, \quad a_1\, n\, a_2 \ldots a_{n-1}, \quad \ldots, \quad a_1 a_2 \ldots n\, a_{n-1}, \quad a_1 a_2 \ldots a_{n-1}\, n.$$

For example, from the permutation 2 3 1 in (3), we get 4 2 3 1, 2 4 3 1, 2 3 4 1, 2 3 1 4. It is clear that all permutations of n objects are obtained in this manner and that no permutation is obtained more than once.

Method 2. For each permutation $a_1 a_2 \ldots a_{n-1}$ of $\{1,2,\ldots,n-1\}$, form n others as follows: First construct the array

$$a_1 a_2 \ldots a_{n-1} \tfrac{1}{2}, \quad a_1 a_2 \ldots a_{n-1} \tfrac{3}{2}, \quad \ldots, \quad a_1 a_2 \ldots a_{n-1} \left(n - \tfrac{1}{2}\right).$$

Then rename the elements of each permutation using the numbers $\{1,2,\ldots,n\}$, *preserving order*. For example, from the permutation 2 3 1 in (3) we get

$$2\,3\,1\tfrac{1}{2}, \quad 2\,3\,1\tfrac{3}{2}, \quad 2\,3\,1\tfrac{5}{2}, \quad 2\,3\,1\tfrac{7}{2}$$

and, renaming, we get

$$3\,4\,2\,1, \quad 3\,4\,1\,2, \quad 2\,4\,1\,3, \quad 2\,3\,1\,4.$$

Another way to describe this process is to take the permutation $a_1 a_2 \ldots a_{n-1}$ and a number k, $1 \le k \le n$; add one to each a_j whose value is $\ge k$, thus obtaining a permutation $b_1 b_2 \ldots b_{n-1}$ of the elements $\{1, \ldots, k-1, k+1, \ldots, n\}$; then $b_1 b_2 \ldots b_{n-1} k$ is a permutation of $\{1, \ldots, n\}$.

Again it is clear that we obtain each permutation of n elements exactly once by this construction. Putting k at the left instead of the right, or putting k in any other fixed position, would obviously work just as well.

If p_n is the number of permutations of n objects, both of these methods show that $p_n = np_{n-1}$; this offers us two further proofs that $p_n = n(n-1) \ldots (1)$, as we already established in Eq. (2).

The important quantity p_n is called n *factorial* and it is written

$$n! = 1 \cdot 2 \cdot \ldots \cdot n = \prod_{k=1}^{n} k. \qquad (4)$$

Our convention for vacuous products (Section 1.2.3) gives us the value

$$0! = 1, \qquad (5)$$

and with this convention the basic identity

$$n! = (n-1)!\, n \qquad (6)$$

is valid for all positive integers n.

Factorials come up sufficiently often in computer work that the reader is advised to memorize the values of the first few:

$$0! = 1, \quad 1! = 1, \quad 2! = 2, \quad 3! = 6, \quad 4! = 24, \quad 5! = 120.$$

The factorials increase very rapidly; for example, 1000! is an integer with more than 2500 decimal digits.

It is helpful to keep the value $10! = 3{,}628{,}800$ in mind; one should remember that 10! is about $3\frac{1}{2}$ million. In a sense, this number represents an approximate dividing line between things that are practical to compute and things that are not. If an algorithm requires the testing of more than 10! cases, it may consume too much computer time to be practical. On the other hand, if we decide to test 10! cases and each case requires, say, one millisecond of computer time, then the entire run will take about an hour. These comments are very vague, of course, but they can be useful to give an intuitive idea of what is computationally feasible.

It is only natural to wonder what relation $n!$ bears to other quantities in mathematics. Is there any way to tell how large 1000! is, without laboriously carrying out the multiplications implied in Eq. (4)? The answer was found by James Stirling in his famous work *Methodus Differentialis* (1730), page 137; we have

$$n! \approx \sqrt{2\pi} \left(\frac{n + 1/2}{e} \right)^{n+1/2} \approx \sqrt{2\pi n} \left(\frac{n}{e} \right)^n. \tag{7}$$

The "$\approx$" sign that appears here denotes "approximately equal"; and "e" is the base of natural logarithms introduced in Section 1.2.2. We will prove Stirling's approximation (7) in Section 1.2.11.2. Exercise 24 gives a simple proof of a less precise result.

As an example of the use of this formula, we may compute

$$40320 = 8! \approx 4\sqrt{\pi} \left(\frac{8}{e} \right)^8 = 2^{26} \sqrt{\pi}\, e^{-8} \approx 67108864 \cdot 1.77245 \cdot 0.00033546 \approx 39902.$$

In this case the error is about 1%; we will see later that the relative error is approximately $1/(12n)$.

In addition to the approximate value given by Eq. (7), we can also rather easily obtain the exact value of $n!$ factored into primes. In fact, the prime p is a divisor of $n!$ with the multiplicity

$$\mu = \left\lfloor \frac{n}{p} \right\rfloor + \left\lfloor \frac{n}{p^2} \right\rfloor + \left\lfloor \frac{n}{p^3} \right\rfloor + \cdots = \sum_{k>0} \left\lfloor \frac{n}{p^k} \right\rfloor. \tag{8}$$

For example, if $n = 1000$ and $p = 3$, we have

$$\mu = \left\lfloor \frac{1000}{3} \right\rfloor + \left\lfloor \frac{1000}{9} \right\rfloor + \left\lfloor \frac{1000}{27} \right\rfloor + \left\lfloor \frac{1000}{81} \right\rfloor + \left\lfloor \frac{1000}{243} \right\rfloor + \left\lfloor \frac{1000}{729} \right\rfloor$$

$$= 333 + 111 + 37 + 12 + 4 + 1 = 498,$$

so 1000! is divisible by 3^{498} but not by 3^{499}. Although formula (8) is written as an infinite sum, it is really finite for any particular values of n and p, because all of the terms are eventually zero. It follows from exercise 1.2.4–35 that $\lfloor n/p^{k+1} \rfloor = \lfloor \lfloor n/p^k \rfloor /p \rfloor$; this fact facilitates the calculation in Eq. (8), since we can just divide the value of the previous term by p and discard the remainder.

Equation (8) follows from the fact that $\lfloor n/p^k \rfloor$ is the number of integers among $\{1, 2, \ldots, n\}$ that are multiples of p^k. If we study the integers in the product (4), any integer that is divisible by p^j but not by p^{j+1} is counted exactly j times: once in $\lfloor n/p \rfloor$, once in $\lfloor n/p^2 \rfloor$, $\ldots$, once in $\lfloor n/p^j \rfloor$. This accounts for all occurrences of p as a factor of $n!$. [See A. M. Legendre, *Essai sur la Théorie des Nombres*, second edition (Paris: 1808), page 8.]

Another natural question arises: Now that we have defined $n!$ for non-negative integers n, perhaps the factorial function is meaningful also for rational values of n, and even for real values. What is $\left(\frac{1}{2}\right)!$, for example? Let us illustrate this point by introducing the "termial" function

$$n? = 1 + 2 + \cdots + n = \sum_{k=1}^{n} k, \qquad (9)$$

which is analogous to the factorial function except that we are adding instead of multiplying. We already know the sum of this arithmetic progression from Eq. 1.2.3–(15):

$$n? = \tfrac{1}{2}n(n+1). \qquad (10)$$

This suggests a good way to generalize the "termial" function to arbitrary n, by using (10) instead of (9). We have $\left(\frac{1}{2}\right)? = \frac{3}{8}$.

Stirling himself made several attempts to generalize $n!$ to noninteger n. He extended the approximation (7) into an infinite sum, but unfortunately the sum did not converge for any value of n; his method gave extremely good approximations, but it couldn't be extended to give an *exact* value. [For a discussion of this somewhat unusual situation, see K. Knopp, *Theory and Application of Infinite Series*, 2nd ed. (Glasgow: Blackie, 1951), 518–520, 527, 534.]

Stirling tried again, by noticing that

$$n! = 1 + \left(1 - \frac{1}{1!}\right)n + \left(1 - \frac{1}{1!} + \frac{1}{2!}\right)n(n-1)$$
$$+ \left(1 - \frac{1}{1!} + \frac{1}{2!} - \frac{1}{3!}\right)n(n-1)(n-2) + \cdots. \qquad (11)$$

(We will prove this formula in the next section.) The apparently infinite sum in Eq. (11) is in reality finite for any nonnegative integer n; however, it does not provide the desired generalization of $n!$, since the infinite sum does not exist *except* when n is a nonnegative integer. (See exercise 16.)

Still undaunted, Stirling found a sequence $a_1, a_2, \ldots$ such that

$$\ln n! = a_1 n + a_2 n(n-1) + \cdots = \sum_{k \geq 0} a_{k+1} \prod_{0 \leq j \leq k} (n-j). \qquad (12)$$

He was unable to *prove* that this sum defined $n!$ for all fractional values of n, although he was able to deduce the value of $\left(\frac{1}{2}\right)! = \sqrt{\pi}/2$.

At about the same time, Leonhard Euler considered the same problem, and he was the first to find the appropriate generalization:

$$n! = \lim_{m \to \infty} \frac{m^n m!}{(n+1)(n+2)\ldots(n+m)}. \tag{13}$$

Euler communicated this idea in a letter to Christian Goldbach on October 13, 1729. His formula defines $n!$ for any value of n except negative integers (when the denominator becomes zero); in such cases $n!$ is taken to be infinite. Exercises 8 and 22 explain why Eq. (13) is a reasonable definition.

Nearly two centuries later, in 1900, C. Hermite proved that Stirling's idea (12) actually does define $n!$ successfully for nonintegers n, and that in fact Euler's and Stirling's generalizations are identical.

Many notations were used for factorials in the early days. Euler actually wrote $[n]$, Gauss wrote Πn, and the symbols $\lfloor n$ and $n \rfloor$ were popular in England and Italy. The notation $n!$, which is universally used today when n is an integer, was introduced by a comparatively little known mathematician, Christian Kramp, in an algebra text [*Élémens d'Arithmétique Universelle* (Cologne: 1808), page 219].

When n is *not* an integer, however, the notation $n!$ is less common; instead we customarily employ a notation due to A. M. Legendre:

$$n! - \Gamma(n+1) = n\Gamma(n). \tag{14}$$

This function $\Gamma(x)$ is called the *gamma function*, and by Eq. (13) we have the definition

$$\Gamma(x) = \frac{x!}{x} = \lim_{m \to \infty} \frac{m^x m!}{x(x+1)(x+2)\ldots(x+m)}. \tag{15}$$

A graph of $\Gamma(x)$ is shown in Fig. 7.

Equations (13) and (15) define factorials and the gamma function for complex values as well as real values; but we generally use the letter z, instead of n or x, when thinking of a variable that has both real and imaginary parts. The factorial and gamma functions are related not only by the rule $z! = \Gamma(z+1)$ but also by

$$(-z)! \, \Gamma(z) = \frac{\pi}{\sin \pi z}, \tag{16}$$

which holds whenever z is not an integer. (See exercise 23.)

Although $\Gamma(z)$ is infinite when z is zero or a negative integer, the function $1/\Gamma(z)$ is well defined for all complex z. (See exercise 1.2.7–24.) Advanced applications of the gamma function often make use of an important contour integral formula due to Hermann Hankel:

$$\frac{1}{\Gamma(z)} = \frac{1}{2\pi i} \oint \frac{e^t \, dt}{t^z}; \tag{17}$$

the path of complex integration starts at $-\infty$, then circles the origin in a counterclockwise direction and returns to $-\infty$. [*Zeitschrift für Math. und Physik* **9** (1864), 1–21.]

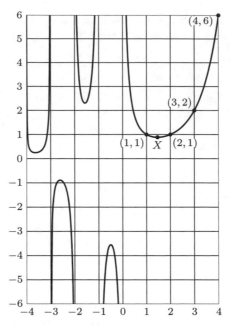

Fig. 7. The function $\Gamma(x) = (x - 1)!$. The local minimum at X has the coordinates $(1.46163\,21449\,68362\,34126\,26595, 0.88560\,31944\,10888\,70027\,88159)$.

Many formulas of discrete mathematics involve factorial-like products known as *factorial powers*. The quantities $x^{\underline{k}}$ and $x^{\overline{k}}$ (read, "x to the k falling" and "x to the k rising") are defined as follows, when k is a positive integer:

$$x^{\underline{k}} = x(x - 1)\ldots(x - k + 1) = \prod_{j=0}^{k-1}(x - j); \qquad (18)$$

$$x^{\overline{k}} = x(x + 1)\ldots(x + k - 1) = \prod_{j=0}^{k-1}(x + j). \qquad (19)$$

Thus, for example, the number p_{nk} of (2) is just $n^{\underline{k}}$. Notice that we have

$$x^{\overline{k}} = (x + k - 1)^{\underline{k}} = (-1)^k(-x)^{\underline{k}}. \qquad (20)$$

The general formulas

$$x^{\underline{k}} = \frac{x!}{(x - k)!}, \qquad x^{\overline{k}} = \frac{\Gamma(x + k)}{\Gamma(x)} \qquad (21)$$

can be used to define factorial powers for other values of k. [The notations $x^{\overline{k}}$ and $x^{\underline{k}}$ are due respectively to A. Capelli, *Giornale di Mat. di Battaglini* **31** (1893), 291–313, and L. Toscano, *Comment. Accademia delle Scienze* **3** (1939), 721–757.]

The interesting history of factorials from the time of Stirling to the present day is traced in an article by P. J. Davis, "Leonhard Euler's integral: A historical profile of the gamma function," *AMM* **66** (1959), 849–869. See also J. Dutka, *Archive for History of Exact Sciences* **31** (1984), 15–34.

EXERCISES

1. [00] How many ways are there to shuffle a 52-card deck?

2. [10] In the notation of Eq. (2), show that $p_{n(n-1)} = p_{nn}$, and explain why this happens.

3. [10] What permutations of $\{1, 2, 3, 4, 5\}$ would be constructed from the permutation 3 1 2 4 using Methods 1 and 2, respectively?

▶ **4.** [13] Given the fact that $\log_{10} 1000! = 2567.60464\ldots$, determine exactly how many decimal digits are present in the number 1000!. What is the *most significant* digit? What is the *least significant* digit?

5. [15] Estimate 8! using the following more exact version of Stirling's approximation:

$$n! \approx \sqrt{2\pi n} \left(\frac{n}{e}\right)^n \left(1 + \frac{1}{12n}\right).$$

▶ **6.** [17] Using Eq. (8), write 20! as a product of prime factors.

7. [M10] Show that the "generalized termial" function in Eq. (10) satisfies the identity $x? = x + (x - 1)?$ for all real numbers x.

8. [HM15] Show that the limit in Eq. (13) does equal $n!$ when n is a nonnegative integer.

9. [M10] Determine the values of $\Gamma(\frac{1}{2})$ and $\Gamma(-\frac{1}{2})$, given that $(\frac{1}{2})! = \sqrt{\pi}/2$.

▶ **10.** [HM20] Does the identity $\Gamma(x + 1) = x\Gamma(x)$ hold for all real numbers x? (See exercise 7.)

11. [M15] Let the representation of n in the binary system be $n = 2^{e_1} + 2^{e_2} + \cdots + 2^{e_r}$, where $e_1 > e_2 > \cdots > e_r \geq 0$. Show that $n!$ is divisible by 2^{n-r} but not by 2^{n-r+1}.

▶ **12.** [M22] (A. Legendre, 1808.) Generalizing the result of the previous exercise, let p be a prime number, and let the representation of n in the p-ary number system be $n = a_k p^k + a_{k-1} p^{k-1} + \cdots + a_1 p + a_0$. Express the number μ of Eq. (8) in a simple formula involving n, p, and a's.

13. [M23] (*Wilson's theorem*, actually due to Leibniz, 1682.) If p is prime, then $(p - 1)! \bmod p = p - 1$. Prove this, by pairing off numbers among $\{1, 2, \ldots, p - 1\}$ whose product modulo p is 1.

▶ **14.** [M28] (L. Stickelberger, 1890.) In the notation of exercise 12, we can determine $n! \bmod p$ in terms of the p-ary representation, for *any* positive integer n, thus generalizing Wilson's theorem. In fact, prove that $n!/p^\mu \equiv (-1)^\mu a_0! \, a_1! \ldots a_k! \pmod{p}$.

15. [HM15] The *permanent* of a square matrix is defined by the same expansion as the determinant except that each term of the permanent is given a plus sign while the determinant alternates between plus and minus. Thus the permanent of

$$\begin{pmatrix} a & b & c \\ d & e & f \\ g & h & i \end{pmatrix}$$

is $aei + bfg + cdh + gec + hfa + idb$. What is the permanent of

$$\begin{pmatrix} 1 \times 1 & 1 \times 2 & \cdots & 1 \times n \\ 2 \times 1 & 2 \times 2 & \cdots & 2 \times n \\ \vdots & \vdots & \ddots & \vdots \\ n \times 1 & n \times 2 & \cdots & n \times n \end{pmatrix} ?$$

16. [*HM15*] Show that the infinite sum in Eq. (11) does not converge unless n is a nonnegative integer.

17. [*HM20*] Prove that the infinite product

$$\prod_{n\geq 1} \frac{(n+\alpha_1)\,\ldots\,(n+\alpha_k)}{(n+\beta_1)\,\ldots\,(n+\beta_k)}$$

equals $\Gamma(1+\beta_1)\,\ldots\,\Gamma(1+\beta_k)/\Gamma(1+\alpha_1)\,\ldots\,\Gamma(1+\alpha_k)$, if $\alpha_1+\cdots+\alpha_k = \beta_1+\cdots+\beta_k$ and if none of the β's is a negative integer.

18. [*M20*] Assume that $\pi/2 = \frac{2}{1}\cdot\frac{2}{3}\cdot\frac{4}{3}\cdot\frac{4}{5}\cdot\frac{6}{5}\cdot\frac{6}{7}\cdot\ldots$. (This is "Wallis's product," obtained by J. Wallis in 1655, and we will prove it in exercise 1.2.6–43.) Using the previous exercise, prove that $(\frac{1}{2})! = \sqrt{\pi}/2$.

19. [*HM22*] Denote the quantity appearing after "$\lim_{m\to\infty}$" in Eq. (15) by $\Gamma_m(x)$. Show that

$$\Gamma_m(x) = \int_0^m \left(1-\frac{t}{m}\right)^m t^{x-1}\,dt = m^x \int_0^1 (1-t)^m t^{x-1}\,dt, \quad \text{if } x > 0.$$

20. [*HM21*] Using the fact that $0 \leq e^{-t} - (1-t/m)^m \leq t^2 e^{-t}/m$, if $0 \leq t \leq m$, and the previous exercise, show that $\Gamma(x) = \int_0^\infty e^{-t} t^{x-1}\,dt$, if $x > 0$.

21. [*HM25*] (L. F. A. Arbogast, 1800.) Let $D_x^k u$ represent the kth derivative of a function u with respect to x. The chain rule states that $D_x^1 w = D_u^1 w\, D_x^1 u$. If we apply this to second derivatives, we find $D_x^2 w = D_u^2 w (D_x^1 u)^2 + D_u^1 w\, D_x^2 u$. Show that the *general formula* is

$$D_x^n w = \sum_{j=0}^n \sum_{\substack{k_1+k_2+\cdots+k_n=j \\ k_1+2k_2+\cdots+nk_n=n \\ k_1,k_2,\ldots,k_n\geq 0}} D_u^j w \frac{n!}{k_1!\,(1!)^{k_1}\ldots k_n!\,(n!)^{k_n}} (D_x^1 u)^{k_1}\ldots(D_x^n u)^{k_n}.$$

▶ **22.** [*HM20*] Try to put yourself in Euler's place, looking for a way to generalize $n!$ to noninteger values of n. Since $(n+\frac{1}{2})!/n!$ times $((n+\frac{1}{2})+\frac{1}{2})!/(n+\frac{1}{2})!$ equals $(n+1)!/n! = n+1$, it seems natural that $(n+\frac{1}{2})!/n!$ should be approximately $\sqrt{n}$. Similarly, $(n+\frac{1}{3})!/n!$ should be $\approx \sqrt[3]{n}$. Invent a hypothesis about the ratio $(n+x)!/n!$ as n approaches infinity. Is your hypothesis correct when x is an integer? Does it tell anything about the appropriate value of $x!$ when x is not an integer?

23. [*HM20*] Prove (16), given that $\pi z \prod_{n=1}^\infty (1 - z^2/n^2) = \sin\pi z$.

▶ **24.** [*HM21*] Prove the handy inequalities

$$\frac{n^n}{e^{n-1}} \leq n! \leq \frac{n^{n+1}}{e^{n-1}}, \qquad \text{integer } n \geq 1.$$

[*Hint:* $1+x \leq e^x$ for all real x; hence $(k+1)/k \leq e^{1/k} \leq k/(k-1)$ when $k > 1$.]

25. [*M20*] Do factorial powers satisfy a law analogous to the ordinary law of exponents, $x^{m+n} = x^m x^n$?

1.2.6. Binomial Coefficients

The *combinations of n objects taken k at a time* are the possible choices of k different elements from a collection of n objects, disregarding order. The combinations of the five objects $\{a, b, c, d, e\}$ taken three at a time are

$$abc, \quad abd, \quad abe, \quad acd, \quad ace, \quad ade, \quad bcd, \quad bce, \quad bde, \quad cde. \qquad (1)$$

It is a simple matter to count the total number of k-combinations of n objects: Equation (2) of the previous section told us that there are $n(n-1)\ldots(n-k+1)$ ways to choose the first k objects for a permutation; and every k-combination appears exactly $k!$ times in these arrangements, since each combination appears in all its permutations. Therefore the number of combinations, which we denote by $\binom{n}{k}$, is

$$\binom{n}{k} = \frac{n(n-1)\ldots(n-k+1)}{k(k-1)\ldots(1)}. \qquad (2)$$

For example,

$$\binom{5}{3} = \frac{5 \cdot 4 \cdot 3}{3 \cdot 2 \cdot 1} = 10,$$

which is the number of combinations we found in (1).

The quantity $\binom{n}{k}$, read "n choose k," is called a *binomial coefficient*; these numbers have an extraordinary number of applications. They are probably the most important quantities entering into the analysis of algorithms, so the reader is urged to become familiar with them.

Equation (2) may be used to define $\binom{n}{k}$ even when n is not an integer. To be precise, we define the symbol $\binom{r}{k}$ for all real numbers r and all integers k as follows:

$$\binom{r}{k} = \frac{r(r-1)\ldots(r-k+1)}{k(k-1)\ldots(1)} = \frac{r^{\underline{k}}}{k!} = \prod_{j=1}^{k} \frac{r+1-j}{j}, \qquad \text{integer } k \geq 0;$$

$$\binom{r}{k} = 0, \qquad \text{integer } k < 0.$$

$$(3)$$

In particular cases we have

$$\binom{r}{0} = 1, \qquad \binom{r}{1} = r, \qquad \binom{r}{2} = \frac{r(r-1)}{2}. \qquad (4)$$

Table 1 gives values of the binomial coefficients for small integer values of r and k; the values for $0 \leq r \leq 4$ should be memorized.

Binomial coefficients have a long and interesting history. Table 1 is called "Pascal's triangle" because it appeared in Blaise Pascal's *Traité du Triangle Arithmétique* in 1653. This treatise was significant because it was one of the first works on probability theory, but Pascal did not invent the binomial coefficients (which were well-known in Europe at that time). Table 1 also appeared in the treatise *Szu-yüan Yü-chien* ("The Precious Mirror of the Four Elements") by the Chinese mathematician Chu Shih-Chieh in 1303, where they were said to be an old invention. Yang Hui, in 1261, credited them to Chia Hsien (c. 1100), whose work is now lost. Long before that (c. 700), in India, Virahänka had explained two ways to compute them in his *Vṛttajātisamuccaya* ("Manual of prosody"), slokas 6.7–6.11; we'll see those two ways below in Eqs. (9) and (11).

Table 1

TABLE OF BINOMIAL COEFFICIENTS (PASCAL'S TRIANGLE)

r	$\binom{r}{0}$	$\binom{r}{1}$	$\binom{r}{2}$	$\binom{r}{3}$	$\binom{r}{4}$	$\binom{r}{5}$	$\binom{r}{6}$	$\binom{r}{7}$	$\binom{r}{8}$	$\binom{r}{9}$
0	1	0	0	0	0	0	0	0	0	0
1	1	1	0	0	0	0	0	0	0	0
2	1	2	1	0	0	0	0	0	0	0
3	1	3	3	1	0	0	0	0	0	0
4	1	4	6	4	1	0	0	0	0	0
5	1	5	10	10	5	1	0	0	0	0
6	1	6	15	20	15	6	1	0	0	0
7	1	7	21	35	35	21	7	1	0	0
8	1	8	28	56	70	56	28	8	1	0
9	1	9	36	84	126	126	84	36	9	1

Virahāṅka was inspired by an ancient Hindu classic, Piṅgala's
Chandaḥśāstra. The earliest known detailed discussion of binomial coefficients is in Halāyudha's tenth-century commentary on Piṅgala's work; see G. Chakravarti, *Bull. Calcutta
Math. Soc.* **24** (1932), 79–88. Another Indian mathematician,
Mahāvīra, had previously explained rule (3) for computing $\binom{r}{k}$
in Chapter 6 of his *Gaṇita Sāra Saṅgraha*, written about 850;
and in 1150 Bhāskara repeated Mahāvīra's rule near the end of
his famous book *Līlāvatī*. For small values of k, binomial coefficients were known much earlier; they appeared in Greek and
Roman writings with a geometric interpretation (see Fig. 8).
The notation $\binom{r}{k}$ was introduced by Andreas von Ettingshausen
in §31 of his book *Die combinatorische Analysis* (Vienna: 1826).

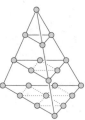

Fig. 8.
A geometric
interpretation
of $\binom{n+2}{3}$, $n = 4$.

The reader has probably noticed several interesting patterns in Table 1.
Binomial coefficients satisfy literally thousands of identities, and for centuries
their amazing properties have been continually explored. In fact, there are so
many relations present that when someone finds a new identity, not many people
get excited about it any more, except the discoverer.

In order to manipulate the formulas that arise in the analysis of algorithms,
a facility for handling binomial coefficients is a must, and so an attempt has
been made in this section to explain in a simple way how to maneuver with
these numbers. Mark Twain once tried to reduce all jokes to a dozen or so
primitive kinds (farmer's daughter, mother-in-law, etc.); we will try to condense
the thousands of identities into a small set of basic operations with which we can
solve nearly every problem involving binomial coefficients that we will meet.

In most applications, both of the numbers r and k that appear in $\binom{r}{k}$ will
be integers, and some of the techniques we will describe are applicable only in
such cases. Therefore we will be careful to list, at the right of each numbered
equation, any restrictions on the variables that appear. For example, Eq. (3)

mentions the requirement that k is an integer; there is no restriction on r. The identities with fewest restrictions are the most useful.

Now let us study the basic techniques for operating on binomial coefficients:

A. Representation by factorials. From Eq. (3) we have immediately

$$\binom{r}{k} = \frac{r!}{k!\,(r-k)!}, \qquad r \geq \text{integer } k \geq 0. \tag{5}$$

This allows combinations of factorials to be represented as binomial coefficients and conversely.

B. Symmetry condition. From Eqs. (3) and (5), we have

$$\binom{n}{k} = \binom{n}{n-k}, \qquad \text{integer } n \geq 0, \text{ integer } k. \tag{6}$$

This formula holds for all integers k. When k is negative or greater than n, the binomial coefficient is zero (provided that n is a nonnegative integer).

C. Moving in and out of parentheses. From the definition (3), we have

$$\binom{r}{k} = \frac{r}{k}\binom{r-1}{k-1}, \qquad \text{integer } k \neq 0. \tag{7}$$

This formula is very useful for combining a binomial coefficient with other parts of an expression. By elementary transformation we have the rules

$$k\binom{r}{k} = r\binom{r-1}{k-1}, \qquad \frac{1}{r}\binom{r}{k} = \frac{1}{k}\binom{r-1}{k-1},$$

the first of which is valid for all integers k, and the second when no division by zero has been performed. We also have a similar relation:

$$\binom{r}{k} = \frac{r}{r-k}\binom{r-1}{k}, \qquad \text{integer } k \neq r. \tag{8}$$

Let us illustrate these transformations, by proving Eq. (8) using Eqs. (6) and (7) alternately:

$$\binom{r}{k} = \binom{r}{r-k} = \frac{r}{r-k}\binom{r-1}{r-1-k} = \frac{r}{r-k}\binom{r-1}{k}.$$

[*Note:* This derivation is valid only when r is a positive integer $\neq k$, because of the constraints involved in Eqs. (6) and (7); yet Eq. (8) claims to be valid for *arbitrary* $r \neq k$. This can be proved in a simple and important manner: We have verified that

$$r\binom{r-1}{k} = (r-k)\binom{r}{k}$$

for *infinitely many values* of r. Both sides of this equation are *polynomials* in r. A nonzero polynomial of degree n can have at most n distinct zeros; so (by subtraction) *if two polynomials of degree $\leq n$ agree at $n+1$ or more different points, the polynomials are identically equal.* This principle may be used to extend the validity of many identities from integers to all real numbers.]

D. Addition formula. The basic relation

$$\binom{r}{k} = \binom{r-1}{k} + \binom{r-1}{k-1}, \quad \text{integer } k, \tag{9}$$

is clearly valid in Table 1 (every value is the sum of the two values above and to the left) and we may easily verify it in general from Eq. (3). Alternatively, Eqs. (7) and (8) tell us that

$$r\binom{r-1}{k} + r\binom{r-1}{k-1} = (r-k)\binom{r}{k} + k\binom{r}{k} = r\binom{r}{k}.$$

Equation (9) is often useful in obtaining proofs by induction on r, when r is an integer.

E. Summation formulas. Repeated application of (9) gives

$$\binom{r}{k} = \binom{r-1}{k} + \binom{r-1}{k-1} = \binom{r-1}{k} + \binom{r-2}{k-1} + \binom{r-2}{k-2} = \cdots;$$

or

$$\binom{r}{k} = \binom{r-1}{k-1} + \binom{r-1}{k} = \binom{r-1}{k-1} + \binom{r-2}{k-1} + \binom{r-2}{k} = \cdots.$$

Thus we are led to two important summation formulas that can be expressed as follows:

$$\sum_{k=0}^{n}\binom{r+k}{k} = \binom{r}{0} + \binom{r+1}{1} + \cdots + \binom{r+n}{n} = \binom{r+n+1}{n},$$

$$\text{integer } n. \tag{10}$$

$$\sum_{k=0}^{n}\binom{k}{m} = \binom{0}{m} + \binom{1}{m} + \cdots + \binom{n}{m} = \binom{n+1}{m+1},$$

$$\text{integer } m \geq 0, \text{ integer } n \geq 0. \tag{11}$$

Equation (11) can be proved easily by induction on n, but it is interesting to see how it can also be derived from Eq. (10) and Eq. (6):

$$\sum_{0 \leq k \leq n}\binom{k}{m} = \sum_{0 \leq m+k \leq n}\binom{m+k}{m} = \sum_{-m \leq k < 0}\binom{m+k}{m} + \sum_{0 \leq k \leq n-m}\binom{m+k}{k}$$

$$= 0 + \binom{m+(n-m)+1}{n-m} = \binom{n+1}{m+1},$$

assuming that $n \geq m$. If $n < m$, Eq. (11) is obvious.

Equation (11) occurs very frequently in applications; in fact, we have already derived special cases of it in previous sections. For example, when $m = 1$, we have our old friend, the sum of an arithmetic progression:

$$\binom{0}{1} + \binom{1}{1} + \cdots + \binom{n}{1} = 0 + 1 + \cdots + n = \binom{n+1}{2} = \frac{(n+1)n}{2}.$$

Suppose that we want a simple formula for the sum $1^2 + 2^2 + \cdots + n^2$. This can be obtained by observing that $k^2 = 2\binom{k}{2} + \binom{k}{1}$; hence

$$\sum_{k=0}^{n} k^2 = \sum_{k=0}^{n} \left(2\binom{k}{2} + \binom{k}{1} \right) = 2\binom{n+1}{3} + \binom{n+1}{2}.$$

And this answer, obtained in terms of binomial coefficients, can be put back into polynomial notation if desired:

$$1^2 + 2^2 + \cdots + n^2 = 2\frac{(n+1)n(n-1)}{6} + \frac{(n+1)n}{2} = \tfrac{1}{3}n(n+\tfrac{1}{2})(n+1). \quad (12)$$

The sum $1^3 + 2^3 + \cdots + n^3$ can be obtained in a similar way; *any* polynomial $a_0 + a_1 k + a_2 k^2 + \cdots + a_m k^m$ can be expressed as $b_0 \binom{k}{0} + b_1 \binom{k}{1} + \cdots + b_m \binom{k}{m}$ for suitably chosen coefficients $b_0, \ldots, b_m$. We will return to this subject later.

F. The binomial theorem. Of course, the binomial theorem is one of our principal tools:

$$(x + y)^r = \sum_k \binom{r}{k} x^k y^{r-k}, \quad \text{integer } r \geq 0. \quad (13)$$

For example, $(x + y)^4 = x^4 + 4x^3 y + 6x^2 y^2 + 4xy^3 + y^4$. (At last we are able to justify the name "binomial coefficient" for the numbers $\binom{r}{k}$.)

It is important to notice that we have written $\sum_k$ in Eq. (13), rather than $\sum_{k=0}^{r}$ as might have been expected. If no restriction is placed on k, we are summing over *all* integers, $-\infty < k < +\infty$; but the two notations are exactly equivalent in this case, since we consider $\binom{r}{k}$ to be "strongly zero" when $k < 0$ or $k > r = \lfloor r \rfloor$ — strong enough to cancel negative powers of 0. The simpler form $\sum_k$ is to be preferred, since all manipulations with sums are simpler when the conditions of summation are simpler. We save a good deal of tedious effort if we do not need to keep track of the lower and/or upper limits of summation, so the limits should be left unspecified whenever possible. Our notation has another advantage also: If r is not a nonnegative integer, Eq. (13) becomes an *infinite* sum, and the *binomial theorem* of calculus states that *Eq. (13) is valid for all r, if $|x/y| < 1$*.

It should be noted that formula (13) gives

$$0^0 = 1. \quad (14)$$

We will use this convention consistently.

The special case $y = 1$ in Eq. (13) is so important, we state it specially:

$$\sum_k \binom{r}{k} x^k = (1 + x)^r, \quad \text{integer } r \geq 0 \text{ or } |x| < 1. \quad (15)$$

The discovery of the binomial theorem was announced by Isaac Newton in letters to Oldenburg on June 13, 1676 and October 24, 1676. [See D. Struik, *Source Book in Mathematics* (Harvard Univ. Press, 1969), 284–291.] But he apparently had no real proof of the formula; at that time the necessity for rigorous proof was not fully realized. The first attempted proof was given by L. Euler in 1774, although his effort was incomplete. Finally, C. F. Gauss gave the first actual proof in 1812. In fact, Gauss's work represented the first time *anything* about infinite sums was proved satisfactorily.

Early in the nineteenth century, N. H. Abel found a surprising generalization of the binomial formula (13):

$$(x+y)^n = \sum_k \binom{n}{k} x(x - kz)^{k-1}(y + kz)^{n-k}, \quad \text{integer } n \geq 0, \; x \neq 0. \quad (16)$$

This is an identity in *three* variables, x, y, and z (see exercises 50 through 52). Abel published and proved this formula in Volume 1 of A. L. Crelle's soon-to-be-famous *Journal für die reine und angewandte Mathematik* (1826), pages 159–160. It is interesting to note that Abel contributed many other papers to the same Volume 1, including his famous memoirs on the unsolvability of algebraic equations of degree 5 or more by radicals, and on the binomial theorem. See H. W. Gould, *AMM* **69** (1962), 572, for a number of references to Eq. (16).

G. Negating the upper index. The basic identity

$$\binom{r}{k} = (-1)^k \binom{k - r - 1}{k}, \quad \text{integer } k, \quad (17)$$

follows immediately from the definition (3) when each term of the numerator is negated. This is often a useful transformation on the upper index.

One easy consequence of Eq. (17) is the summation formula

$$\sum_{k \leq n} \binom{r}{k}(-1)^k = \binom{r}{0} - \binom{r}{1} + \cdots + (-1)^n \binom{r}{n} = (-1)^n \binom{r-1}{n}, \quad \text{integer } n. \quad (18)$$

This identity could be proved by induction using Eq. (9), but we can use Eqs. (17) and (10) directly:

$$\sum_{k \leq n} \binom{r}{k}(-1)^k = \sum_{k \leq n} \binom{k - r - 1}{k} = \binom{-r + n}{n} = (-1)^n \binom{r - 1}{n}.$$

Another important application of Eq. (17) can be made when r is an integer:

$$\binom{n}{m} = (-1)^{n-m} \binom{-(m + 1)}{n - m}, \quad \text{integer } n \geq 0, \text{ integer } m. \quad (19)$$

(Set $r = n$ and $k = n - m$ in Eq. (17) and use (6).) We have moved n from the upper position to the lower.

H. Simplifying products. When products of binomial coefficients appear, they can usually be reexpressed in several different ways by expanding into factorials and out again using Eq. (5). For example,

$$\binom{r}{m}\binom{m}{k} = \binom{r}{k}\binom{r - k}{m - k}, \quad \text{integer } m, \quad \text{integer } k. \quad (20)$$

It suffices to prove Eq. (20) when r is an integer $\geq m$ (see the remarks after Eq. (8)), and when $0 \leq k \leq m$. Then

$$\binom{r}{m}\binom{m}{k} = \frac{r!\,m!}{m!\,(r-m)!\,k!\,(m-k)!} = \frac{r!\,(r-k)!}{k!\,(r-k)!\,(m-k)!\,(r-m)!} = \binom{r}{k}\binom{r-k}{m-k}.$$

Equation (20) is very useful when an index (namely m) appears in both the upper and the lower position, and we wish to have it appear in one place rather than two. Notice that Eq. (7) is the special case of Eq. (20) when $k = 1$.

I. Sums of products. To complete our set of binomial-coefficient manipulations, we present the following very general identities, which are proved in the exercises at the end of this section. These formulas show how to sum over a product of two binomial coefficients, considering various places where the running variable k might appear:

$$\sum_k \binom{r}{k}\binom{s}{n-k} = \binom{r+s}{n}, \quad \text{integer } n. \tag{21}$$

$$\sum_k \binom{r}{m+k}\binom{s}{n+k} = \binom{r+s}{r-m+n},$$
$$\text{integer } m, \text{ integer } n, \text{ integer } r \geq 0. \tag{22}$$

$$\sum_k \binom{r}{k}\binom{s+k}{n}(-1)^{r-k} = \binom{s}{n-r}, \quad \text{integer } n, \text{ integer } r \geq 0. \tag{23}$$

$$\sum_{k=0}^{r} \binom{r-k}{m}\binom{s}{k-t}(-1)^{k-t} = \binom{r-t-s}{r-t-m},$$
$$\text{integer } t \geq 0, \text{ integer } r \geq 0, \text{ integer } m \geq 0. \tag{24}$$

$$\sum_{k=0}^{r} \binom{r-k}{m}\binom{s+k}{n} = \binom{r+s+1}{m+n+1},$$
$$\text{integer } n \geq \text{integer } s \geq 0, \text{ integer } m \geq 0, \text{ integer } r \geq 0. \tag{25}$$

$$\sum_{k\geq 0} \binom{r-tk}{k}\binom{s-t(n-k)}{n-k}\frac{r}{r-tk} = \binom{r+s-tn}{n}, \quad \text{integer } n. \tag{26}$$

Of these identities, Eq. (21) is by far the most important, and it should be memorized. One way to remember it is to interpret the right-hand side as the number of ways to select n people from among r men and s women; each term on the left is the number of ways to choose k of the men and $n - k$ of the women. Equation (21) is commonly called Vandermonde's convolution, since A. Vandermonde published it in *Mém. Acad. Roy. Sciences* (Paris, 1772), part 1, 489–498. However, it had appeared already in Chu Shih-Chieh's 1303 treatise mentioned earlier [see J. Needham, *Science and Civilisation in China* **3** (Cambridge University Press, 1959), 138–139].

If $r = tk$ in Eq. (26), we avoid the zero denominator by canceling with a factor in the numerator; therefore Eq. (26) is a polynomial identity in the variables r, s, t. Obviously Eq. (21) is a special case of Eq. (26) with $t = 0$.

We should point out a nonobvious use of Eqs. (23) and (25): It is often helpful to replace the simple binomial coefficient on the right-hand side by the more complicated expression on the left, interchange the order of summation, and simplify. We may regard the left-hand sides as expansions of

$$\binom{s}{n+a} \quad \text{in terms of} \quad \binom{s+k}{n}.$$

Formula (23) is used for negative a, formula (25) for positive a.

This completes our study of binomial-coefficientology. The reader is advised to learn especially Eqs. (5), (6), (7), (9), (13), (17), (20), and (21) — frame them with your favorite highlighter pen!

With all these methods at our disposal, we should be able to solve almost any problem that comes along, in at least three different ways. The following examples illustrate the techniques.

Example 1. If r is a nonnegative integer, what is the value of $\sum_{k} \binom{r}{k}\binom{s}{k}k$?

Solution. Formula (7) is useful for disposing of the outside k:

$$\sum_{k}\binom{r}{k}\binom{s}{k}k = \sum_{k}\binom{r}{k}\binom{s-1}{k-1}s = s\sum_{k}\binom{r}{k}\binom{s-1}{k-1}.$$

Now formula (22) applies, with $m = 0$ and $n = -1$. The answer is therefore

$$\sum_{k}\binom{r}{k}\binom{s}{k}k = \binom{r+s-1}{r-1}s, \quad \text{integer } r \geq 0.$$

Example 2. What is the value of $\sum_{k\geq 0}\binom{n+k}{2k}\binom{2k}{k}\frac{(-1)^k}{k+1}$, if n is a nonnegative integer?

Solution. This problem is tougher; the summation index k appears in six places! First we apply Eq. (20), and we obtain

$$\sum_{k\geq 0}\binom{n+k}{k}\binom{n}{k}\frac{(-1)^k}{k+1}.$$

We can now breathe more easily, since several of the menacing characteristics of the original formula have disappeared. The next step should be obvious; we apply Eq. (7) in a manner similar to the technique used in Example 1:

$$\sum_{k\geq 0}\binom{n+k}{k}\binom{n+1}{k+1}\frac{(-1)^k}{n+1}. \tag{27}$$

Good, another k has vanished. At this point there are two equally promising lines of attack. We can replace the $\binom{n+k}{k}$ by $\binom{n+k}{n}$, because $k \geq 0$, and evaluate the sum with Eq. (23):

$$\sum_{k\geq 0}\binom{n+k}{n}\binom{n+1}{k+1}\frac{(-1)^k}{n+1}$$

$$= -\frac{1}{n+1}\sum_{k\geq 1}\binom{n-1+k}{n}\binom{n+1}{k}(-1)^k$$

$$= -\frac{1}{n+1}\sum_{k\geq 0}\binom{n-1+k}{n}\binom{n+1}{k}(-1)^k + \frac{1}{n+1}\binom{n-1}{n}$$

$$= -\frac{1}{n+1}(-1)^{n+1}\binom{n-1}{-1} + \frac{1}{n+1}\binom{n-1}{n} = \frac{1}{n+1}\binom{n-1}{n}.$$

The binomial coefficient $\binom{n-1}{n}$ equals zero except when $n = 0$, in which case it equals one. So we can conveniently state the answer to our problem as $[n=0]$, using Iverson's convention $\big($Eq. 1.2.3–(16)$\big)$, or as δ_{n0}, using the Kronecker delta $\big($Eq. 1.2.3–(19)$\big)$.

Another way to proceed from Eq. (27) is to use Eq. (17), obtaining

$$\sum_{k\geq 0}\binom{-(n+1)}{k}\binom{n+1}{k+1}\frac{1}{n+1}.$$

We can now apply Eq. (22), which yields the sum

$$\binom{n+1-(n+1)}{n+1-1+0}\frac{1}{n+1} = \binom{0}{n}\frac{1}{n+1}.$$

Once again we have derived the answer:

$$\sum_{k\geq 0}\binom{n+k}{2k}\binom{2k}{k}\frac{(-1)^k}{k+1} = \delta_{n0}, \qquad \text{integer } n \geq 0. \qquad (28)$$

Example 3. What is the value of $\displaystyle\sum_{k\geq 0}\binom{n+k}{m+2k}\binom{2k}{k}\frac{(-1)^k}{k+1}$, for positive integers m and n?

Solution. If m were zero, we would have the same formula to work with that we had in Example 2. However, the presence of m means that we cannot even begin to use the method of the previous solution, since the first step there was to use Eq. (20) — which no longer applies.

In this situation it pays to complicate things even *more*, by replacing the unwanted $\binom{n+k}{m+2k}$ by a sum of terms of the form $\binom{x+k}{2k}$, since our problem will then become a sum of problems that we know how to solve. Accordingly, we use Eq. (25) with

$$k \mapsto j, \quad r \mapsto n-1, \quad m \mapsto m-1, \quad s \mapsto k, \quad n \mapsto 2k;$$

all of the conditions required for (25) are satisfied, because m and n are positive.

The sum to be solved now takes the form

$$\sum_{k \geq 0} \sum_{j=0}^{n-1} \binom{n-1-j}{m-1} \binom{k+j}{2k} \binom{2k}{k} \frac{(-1)^k}{k+1}; \tag{29}$$

and the rest is easy, by interchanging the order of summation: Equation (28) tells us how to sum on k, and all the complications melt away. Everything reduces to just

$$\sum_{j=0}^{n-1} \binom{n-1-j}{m-1} \delta_{j0},$$

so our final answer is

$$\binom{n-1}{m-1}.$$

The solution to this problem was fairly complicated, but not really mysterious; there was a good reason for each step. The derivation should be studied closely, because the use of (25) illustrates some delicate maneuvering with the conditions in our equations.

There is actually a better way to attack this problem, however! The reader is invited to figure out how to transform the given sum so that Eq. (26) applies (see exercise 30).

Example 4. Prove that

$$\sum_{k} A_k(r,t) A_{n-k}(s,t) = A_n(r+s,t), \quad \text{integer } n \geq 0, \tag{30}$$

where $A_n(x,t)$ is the nth degree polynomial in x that satisfies

$$A_n(x,t) = \binom{x-nt}{n} \frac{x}{x-nt}, \quad \text{for } x \neq nt.$$

Solution. We may assume that $r \neq kt \neq s$ for $0 \leq k \leq n$, since both sides of (30) are polynomials in r, s, t. Our problem is to evaluate

$$\sum_{k} \binom{r-kt}{k} \binom{s-(n-k)t}{n-k} \frac{r}{r-kt} \frac{s}{s-(n-k)t},$$

which, if anything, looks much worse than our previous horrible problems! Notice the strong similarity to Eq. (26), however, and also note the case $t = 0$.

We are tempted to change

$$\binom{r-kt}{k} \frac{r}{r-kt} \qquad \text{to} \qquad \binom{r-kt-1}{k-1} \frac{r}{k},$$

except that the latter tends to lose the analogy with Eq. (26) and it fails when $k = 0$. A better way to proceed is to use the technique of *partial fractions*, whereby a fraction with a complicated denominator can often be replaced by a sum of fractions with simpler denominators. Indeed, we have

$$\frac{1}{r-kt}\,\frac{1}{s-(n-k)t} = \frac{1}{r+s-nt}\left(\frac{1}{r-kt}+\frac{1}{s-(n-k)t}\right),$$

assuming, as we may, that $nt \neq r+s$. Putting this into our sum we get

$$\frac{s}{r+s-nt}\sum_{k}\binom{r-kt}{k}\binom{s-(n-k)t}{n-k}\frac{r}{r-kt}$$

$$+\frac{r}{r+s-nt}\sum_{k}\binom{r-kt}{k}\binom{s-(n-k)t}{n-k}\frac{s}{s-(n-k)t},$$

and Eq. (26) evaluates both of these formulas if we change k to $n-k$ in the second; the desired result follows immediately. Identities (26) and (30) are due to H. A. Rothe, *Formulæ de Serierum Reversione* (Leipzig: 1793); special cases of these formulas are still being "discovered" frequently. For the interesting history of these identities and some generalizations, see H. W. Gould and J. Kaucký, *Journal of Combinatorial Theory* **1** (1966), 233–247.

Example 5. Determine the values of a_0, a_1, a_2, ... such that

$$n! = a_0 + a_1 n + a_2 n(n-1) + a_3 n(n-1)(n-2) + \cdots \qquad (31)$$

for all nonnegative integers n.

Solution. Equation 1.2.5–(11), which was presented without proof in the previous section, gives the answer. Let us pretend that we don't know it yet. It is clear that the problem does have a solution, since we can set $n=0$ and determine a_0, then set $n=1$ and determine a_1, etc.

First we would like to write Eq. (31) in terms of binomial coefficients:

$$n! = \sum_{k\geq 0}\binom{n}{k}k!\,a_k. \qquad (32)$$

The problem of solving implicit equations like this for a_k is called the *inversion problem*, and the technique we shall use applies to similar problems as well.

The idea is based on the special case $s=0$ of Eq. (23):

$$\sum_{k}\binom{r}{k}\binom{k}{n}(-1)^{r-k} = \binom{0}{n-r} = \delta_{nr}, \quad \text{integer } n,\ \text{integer } r\geq 0. \qquad (33)$$

The importance of this formula is that when $n \neq r$, the sum is zero; this enables us to solve our problem since a lot of terms cancel out as they did in Example 3:

$$\sum_{n\geq 0}n!\binom{m}{n}(-1)^{m-n} = \sum_{n\geq 0}\sum_{k\geq 0}\binom{n}{k}k!\,a_k\binom{m}{n}(-1)^{m-n}$$

$$= \sum_{k\geq 0}k!\,a_k\sum_{n\geq 0}\binom{n}{k}\binom{m}{n}(-1)^{m-n}$$

$$= \sum_{k\geq 0}k!\,a_k\delta_{km} = m!\,a_m, \quad \text{when } m\geq 0.$$

Notice how we were able to get an equation in which only one value a_m appears, by adding together suitable multiples of Eq. (32) for $n = 0, 1, \ldots$. We have now

$$a_m = \sum_{n \geq 0} (-1)^{m-n} \frac{n!}{m!} \binom{m}{n} = \sum_{0 \leq n \leq m} \frac{(-1)^{m-n}}{(m-n)!} = \sum_{0 \leq n \leq m} \frac{(-1)^n}{n!}.$$

This completes the solution to Example 5. Let us now take a closer look at the implications of Eq. (33): When r and m are nonnegative integers we have

$$\sum_k \binom{r}{k} (-1)^{r-k} \left(c_0 \binom{k}{0} + c_1 \binom{k}{1} + \cdots + c_m \binom{k}{m} \right) = c_r,$$

since the other terms vanish after summation. By properly choosing the coefficients c_i, we can represent *any* polynomial in k as a sum of binomial coefficients with upper index k. We find therefore that

$$\sum_k \binom{r}{k} (-1)^{r-k} (b_0 + b_1 k + \cdots + b_r k^r) = r! \, b_r, \quad \text{integer } r \geq 0, \qquad (34)$$

where $b_0 + \cdots + b_r k^r$ represents any polynomial whatever of degree r or less. (This formula will be of no great surprise to students of numerical analysis, since $\sum_k \binom{r}{k} (-1)^{r-k} f(x+k)$ is the "rth difference" of the function $f(x)$.)

Using Eq. (34), we can immediately obtain many other relations that appear complicated at first and that are often given very lengthy proofs, such as

$$\sum_k \binom{r}{k} \binom{s - kt}{r} (-1)^k = t^r, \quad \text{integer } r \geq 0. \qquad (35)$$

It is customary in textbooks such as this to give a lot of impressive examples of neat tricks, etc., but never to mention simple-looking problems where the techniques fail. The examples above may have given the impression that all things are possible with binomial coefficients; it should be mentioned, however, that in spite of Eqs. (10), (11), and (18), there seems to be no simple formula for the analogous sum

$$\sum_{k=0}^{n} \binom{m}{k} = \binom{m}{0} + \binom{m}{1} + \cdots + \binom{m}{n}, \qquad (36)$$

when $n < m$. (For $n = m$ the answer is simple; what is it? See exercise 36.)

On the other hand this sum does have a closed form as a function of n when m is an explicit negative integer; for example,

$$\sum_{k=0}^{n} \binom{-2}{k} = (-1)^n \left\lceil \frac{n+1}{2} \right\rceil. \qquad (37)$$

There is also a simple formula

$$\sum_{k=0}^{n} \binom{m}{k} \left(k - \frac{m}{2} \right) = -\frac{m}{2} \binom{m-1}{n} \qquad (38)$$

for a sum that looks as though it should be harder, not easier.

How can we decide when to stop working on a sum that resists simplification? Fortunately, there is now a good way to answer that question in many important cases: An algorithm due to R. W. Gosper and D. Zeilberger will discover closed forms in binomial coefficients when they exist, and will prove the impossibility when they do not exist. The Gosper–Zeilberger algorithm is beyond the scope of this book, but it is explained in *CMath* §5.8. See also the book $A = B$ by Petkovšek, Wilf, and Zeilberger (Wellesley, Mass.: A K Peters, 1996).

The principal tool for dealing with sums of binomial coefficients in a systematic, mechanical way is to exploit the properties of *hypergeometric functions*, which are infinite series defined as follows in terms of rising factorial powers:

$$F\left(\begin{matrix} a_1, \ \ldots, \ a_m \\ b_1, \ \ldots, \ b_n \end{matrix} \,\middle|\, z\right) = \sum_{k \geq 0} \frac{a_1^{\overline{k}} \ldots a_m^{\overline{k}}}{b_1^{\overline{k}} \ldots b_n^{\overline{k}}} \frac{z^k}{k!}. \tag{39}$$

An introduction to these important functions can be found in Sections 5.5 and 5.6 of *CMath*. See also J. Dutka, *Archive for History of Exact Sciences* **31** (1984), 15–34, for historical references.

The concept of binomial coefficients has several significant generalizations, which we should discuss briefly. First, we can consider arbitrary real values of the lower index k in $\binom{r}{k}$; see exercises 40 through 45. We also have the generalization

$$\binom{r}{k}_q = \frac{(1 - q^r)(1 - q^{r-1}) \ldots (1 - q^{r-k+1})}{(1 - q^k)(1 - q^{k-1}) \ldots (1 - q^1)}, \quad \text{integer } k \geq 0, \tag{40}$$

which becomes the ordinary binomial coefficient $\binom{r}{k}_1 = \binom{r}{k}$ when q approaches the limiting value 1; this can be seen by dividing each factor in numerator and denominator by $1 - q$. The basic properties of such "q-nomial coefficients" are discussed in exercise 58.

However, for our purposes the most important generalization is the *multinomial coefficient*

$$\binom{k_1 + k_2 + \cdots + k_m}{k_1, k_2, \ldots, k_m} = \frac{(k_1 + k_2 + \cdots + k_m)!}{k_1! \, k_2! \ldots k_m!}, \quad \text{integer } k_i \geq 0. \tag{41}$$

The chief property of multinomial coefficients is the generalization of Eq. (13):

$$(x_1 + x_2 + \cdots + x_m)^n = \sum_{k_1 + k_2 + \cdots + k_m = n} \binom{n}{k_1, k_2, \ldots, k_m} x_1^{k_1} x_2^{k_2} \ldots x_m^{k_m}. \tag{42}$$

It is important to observe that any multinomial coefficient can be expressed in terms of binomial coefficients:

$$\binom{k_1 + k_2 + \cdots + k_m}{k_1, k_2, \ldots, k_m} = \binom{k_1 + k_2}{k_1} \binom{k_1 + k_2 + k_3}{k_1 + k_2} \cdots \binom{k_1 + k_2 + \cdots + k_m}{k_1 + \cdots + k_{m-1}}, \tag{43}$$

so we may apply the techniques that we already know for manipulating binomial coefficients. Both sides of Eq. (20) are the trinomial coefficient

$$\binom{r}{k, \ m - k, \ r - m}.$$

Table 2

STIRLING NUMBERS OF BOTH KINDS

n	$\begin{bmatrix} n \\ 0 \end{bmatrix}$	$\begin{bmatrix} n \\ 1 \end{bmatrix}$	$\begin{bmatrix} n \\ 2 \end{bmatrix}$	$\begin{bmatrix} n \\ 3 \end{bmatrix}$	$\begin{bmatrix} n \\ 4 \end{bmatrix}$	$\begin{bmatrix} n \\ 5 \end{bmatrix}$	$\begin{bmatrix} n \\ 6 \end{bmatrix}$	$\begin{bmatrix} n \\ 7 \end{bmatrix}$	$\begin{bmatrix} n \\ 8 \end{bmatrix}$
0	1	0	0	0	0	0	0	0	0
1	0	1	0	0	0	0	0	0	0
2	0	1	1	0	0	0	0	0	0
3	0	2	3	1	0	0	0	0	0
4	0	6	11	6	1	0	0	0	0
5	0	24	50	35	10	1	0	0	0
6	0	120	274	225	85	15	1	0	0
7	0	720	1764	1624	735	175	21	1	0
8	0	5040	13068	13132	6769	1960	322	28	1

n	$\begin{Bmatrix} n \\ 0 \end{Bmatrix}$	$\begin{Bmatrix} n \\ 1 \end{Bmatrix}$	$\begin{Bmatrix} n \\ 2 \end{Bmatrix}$	$\begin{Bmatrix} n \\ 3 \end{Bmatrix}$	$\begin{Bmatrix} n \\ 4 \end{Bmatrix}$	$\begin{Bmatrix} n \\ 5 \end{Bmatrix}$	$\begin{Bmatrix} n \\ 6 \end{Bmatrix}$	$\begin{Bmatrix} n \\ 7 \end{Bmatrix}$	$\begin{Bmatrix} n \\ 8 \end{Bmatrix}$
0	1	0	0	0	0	0	0	0	0
1	0	1	0	0	0	0	0	0	0
2	0	1	1	0	0	0	0	0	0
3	0	1	3	1	0	0	0	0	0
4	0	1	7	6	1	0	0	0	0
5	0	1	15	25	10	1	0	0	0
6	0	1	31	90	65	15	1	0	0
7	0	1	63	301	350	140	21	1	0
8	0	1	127	966	1701	1050	266	28	1

For approximations valid when n is large, see L. Moser and M. Wyman, *J. London Math. Soc.* (2) **33** (1958), 133–146; *Duke Math. J.* **25** (1958), 29–43; D. E. Barton, F. N. David, and M. Merrington, *Biometrika* **47** (1960), 439–445; **50** (1963), 169–176; N. M. Temme, *Studies in Applied Math.* **89** (1993), 233–243; H. S. Wilf, *J. Combinatorial Theory* **A64** (1993), 344–349; H.-K. Hwang, *J. Combinatorial Theory* **A71** (1995), 343–351.

We conclude this section with a brief analysis of the transformation from a polynomial expressed in powers of x to a polynomial expressed in binomial coefficients. The coefficients involved in this transformation are called *Stirling numbers*, and these numbers arise in the study of numerous algorithms.

Stirling numbers come in two flavors: We denote Stirling numbers of the first kind by $\begin{bmatrix} n \\ k \end{bmatrix}$, and those of the second kind by $\begin{Bmatrix} n \\ k \end{Bmatrix}$. These notations, due to Jovan Karamata [*Mathematica* (Cluj) **9** (1935), 164–178], have compelling advantages over the many other symbolisms that have been tried [see D. E. Knuth, *AMM* **99** (1992), 403–422]. We can remember the curly braces in $\begin{Bmatrix} n \\ k \end{Bmatrix}$ because curly braces denote sets, and $\begin{Bmatrix} n \\ k \end{Bmatrix}$ is the number of ways to partition a set of n elements into k disjoint subsets (exercise 64). The other Stirling numbers $\begin{bmatrix} n \\ k \end{bmatrix}$ also have a combinatorial interpretation, which we will study in Section 1.3.3: $\begin{bmatrix} n \\ k \end{bmatrix}$ is the number of permutations on n letters having k cycles.

Table 2 displays Stirling's triangles, which are in some ways analogous to Pascal's triangle.

Stirling numbers of the first kind are used to convert from factorial powers to ordinary powers:

$$x^{\underline{n}} = x(x-1)\ldots(x-n+1)$$

$$= \left[\begin{matrix} n \\ n \end{matrix}\right]x^n - \left[\begin{matrix} n \\ n-1 \end{matrix}\right]x^{n-1} + \cdots + (-1)^n\left[\begin{matrix} n \\ 0 \end{matrix}\right]$$

$$= \sum_k (-1)^{n-k}\left[\begin{matrix} n \\ k \end{matrix}\right]x^k. \tag{44}$$

For example, from Table 2,

$$\binom{x}{5} = \frac{x^{\underline{5}}}{5!} = \frac{1}{120}(x^5 - 10x^4 + 35x^3 - 50x^2 + 24x).$$

Stirling numbers of the second kind are used to convert from ordinary powers to factorial powers:

$$x^n = \left\{\begin{matrix} n \\ n \end{matrix}\right\}x^{\underline{n}} + \cdots + \left\{\begin{matrix} n \\ 1 \end{matrix}\right\}x^{\underline{1}} + \left\{\begin{matrix} n \\ 0 \end{matrix}\right\}x^{\underline{0}} = \sum_k \left\{\begin{matrix} n \\ k \end{matrix}\right\}x^{\underline{k}}. \tag{45}$$

This formula was, in fact, Stirling's original reason for studying the numbers $\left\{\begin{smallmatrix} n \\ k \end{smallmatrix}\right\}$ in his *Methodus Differentialis* (London: 1730). From Table 2 we have, for example,

$$x^5 = x^{\underline{5}} + 10x^{\underline{4}} + 25x^{\underline{3}} + 15x^{\underline{2}} + x^{\underline{1}}$$

$$= 120\binom{x}{5} + 240\binom{x}{4} + 150\binom{x}{3} + 30\binom{x}{2} + \binom{x}{1}.$$

We shall now list the most important identities involving Stirling numbers. In these equations, the variables m and n always denote nonnegative integers.

Addition formulas:

$$\left[\begin{matrix} n+1 \\ m \end{matrix}\right] = n\left[\begin{matrix} n \\ m \end{matrix}\right] + \left[\begin{matrix} n \\ m-1 \end{matrix}\right];$$

$$\left\{\begin{matrix} n+1 \\ m \end{matrix}\right\} = m\left\{\begin{matrix} n \\ m \end{matrix}\right\} + \left\{\begin{matrix} n \\ m-1 \end{matrix}\right\}. \tag{46}$$

Inversion formulas (compare with Eq. (33)):

$$\sum_k \left[\begin{matrix} n \\ k \end{matrix}\right]\left\{\begin{matrix} k \\ m \end{matrix}\right\}(-1)^{n-k} = \delta_{mn}, \quad \sum_k \left\{\begin{matrix} n \\ k \end{matrix}\right\}\left[\begin{matrix} k \\ m \end{matrix}\right](-1)^{n-k} = \delta_{mn}. \tag{47}$$

Special values:

$$\binom{0}{n} = \left[\begin{matrix} 0 \\ n \end{matrix}\right] = \left\{\begin{matrix} 0 \\ n \end{matrix}\right\} = \delta_{n0}, \qquad \binom{n}{n} = \left[\begin{matrix} n \\ n \end{matrix}\right] = \left\{\begin{matrix} n \\ n \end{matrix}\right\} = 1; \tag{48}$$

$$\left[\begin{matrix} n \\ n-1 \end{matrix}\right] = \left\{\begin{matrix} n \\ n-1 \end{matrix}\right\} = \binom{n}{2}; \tag{49}$$

$$\begin{bmatrix} n+1 \\ 0 \end{bmatrix} = \left\{ \begin{matrix} n+1 \\ 0 \end{matrix} \right\} = 0, \quad \begin{bmatrix} n+1 \\ 1 \end{bmatrix} = n!, \quad \left\{ \begin{matrix} n+1 \\ 1 \end{matrix} \right\} = 1, \quad \left\{ \begin{matrix} n+1 \\ 2 \end{matrix} \right\} = 2^n - 1.$$
(50)

Expansion formulas:

$$\sum_k \begin{bmatrix} n \\ k \end{bmatrix} \binom{k}{m} = \begin{bmatrix} n+1 \\ m+1 \end{bmatrix}, \quad \sum_k \begin{bmatrix} n+1 \\ k+1 \end{bmatrix} \binom{k}{m} (-1)^{k-m} = \begin{bmatrix} n \\ m \end{bmatrix};$$
(51)

$$\sum_k \left\{ \begin{matrix} k \\ m \end{matrix} \right\} \binom{n}{k} = \left\{ \begin{matrix} n+1 \\ m+1 \end{matrix} \right\}, \quad \sum_k \left\{ \begin{matrix} k+1 \\ m+1 \end{matrix} \right\} \binom{n}{k} (-1)^{n-k} = \left\{ \begin{matrix} n \\ m \end{matrix} \right\};$$
(52)

$$\sum_k \binom{m}{k} (-1)^{m-k} k^n = m! \left\{ \begin{matrix} n \\ m \end{matrix} \right\};$$
(53)

$$\sum_k \binom{m-n}{m+k} \binom{m+n}{n+k} \left\{ \begin{matrix} m+k \\ k \end{matrix} \right\} = \begin{bmatrix} n \\ n-m \end{bmatrix},$$

$$\sum_k \binom{m-n}{m+k} \binom{m+n}{n+k} \begin{bmatrix} m+k \\ k \end{bmatrix} = \left\{ \begin{matrix} n \\ n-m \end{matrix} \right\};$$
(54)

$$\sum_k \left\{ \begin{matrix} n+1 \\ k+1 \end{matrix} \right\} \begin{bmatrix} k \\ m \end{bmatrix} (-1)^{k-m} = \binom{n}{m};$$
(55)

$$\sum_{k \leq n} \begin{bmatrix} k \\ m \end{bmatrix} \frac{n!}{k!} = \begin{bmatrix} n+1 \\ m+1 \end{bmatrix}, \quad \sum_{k \leq n} \left\{ \begin{matrix} k \\ m \end{matrix} \right\} (m+1)^{n-k} = \left\{ \begin{matrix} n+1 \\ m+1 \end{matrix} \right\}.$$
(56)

Some other fundamental Stirling number identities appear in exercises 1.2.6–61 and 1.2.7–6, and in Eqs. (23), (26), (27), and (28) of Section 1.2.9.

Eq. (49) is just one instance of a general phenomenon: Both kinds of Stirling numbers $\begin{bmatrix} n \\ n-m \end{bmatrix}$ and $\left\{ \begin{matrix} n \\ n-m \end{matrix} \right\}$ are polynomials in n of degree $2m$, whenever m is a nonnegative integer. For example, the formulas for $m = 2$ and $m = 3$ are

$$\begin{bmatrix} n \\ n-2 \end{bmatrix} = \binom{n}{4} + 2\binom{n+1}{4}, \qquad \left\{ \begin{matrix} n \\ n-2 \end{matrix} \right\} = \binom{n+1}{4} + 2\binom{n}{4};$$

$$\begin{bmatrix} n \\ n-3 \end{bmatrix} = \binom{n}{6} + 8\binom{n+1}{6} + 6\binom{n+2}{6}, \quad \left\{ \begin{matrix} n \\ n-3 \end{matrix} \right\} = \binom{n+2}{6} + 8\binom{n+1}{6} + 6\binom{n}{6}.$$
(57)

Therefore it makes sense to define the numbers $\begin{bmatrix} r \\ r-m \end{bmatrix}$ and $\left\{ \begin{matrix} r \\ r-m \end{matrix} \right\}$ for arbitrary real (or complex) values of r. With this generalization, the two kinds of Stirling numbers are united by an interesting duality law

$$\left\{ \begin{matrix} n \\ m \end{matrix} \right\} = \begin{bmatrix} -m \\ -n \end{bmatrix},$$
(58)

which was implicit in Stirling's original discussion. Moreover, Eq. (45) remains true in general, in the sense that the infinite series

$$z^r = \sum_k \left\{ {r \atop r-k} \right\} z^{\underline{r-k}} \qquad (59)$$

converges whenever the real part of z is positive. The companion formula, Eq. (44), generalizes in a similar way to an asymptotic (but not convergent) series:

$$z^{\underline{r}} = \sum_{k=0}^{m} \left[{r \atop r-k} \right] (-1)^k z^{r-k} + O(z^{r-m-1}). \qquad (60)$$

(See exercise 65.) Sections 6.1, 6.2, and 6.5 of *CMath* contain additional information about Stirling numbers and how to manipulate them in formulas. See also exercise 4.7–21 for a general family of triangles that includes Stirling numbers as a very special case.

EXERCISES

1. [*00*] How many combinations of n things taken $n-1$ at a time are possible?

2. [*00*] What is $\binom{0}{0}$?

3. [*00*] How many bridge hands (13 cards out of a 52-card deck) are possible?

4. [*10*] Give the answer to exercise 3 as a product of prime numbers.

▶ **5.** [*05*] Use Pascal's triangle to explain the fact that $11^4 = 14641$.

▶ **6.** [*10*] Pascal's triangle (Table 1) can be extended in all directions by use of the addition formula, Eq. (9). Find the three rows that go on *top* of Table 1 (i.e., for $r = -1, -2$, and -3).

7. [*12*] If n is a fixed positive integer, what value of k makes $\binom{n}{k}$ a maximum?

8. [*00*] What property of Pascal's triangle is reflected in the "symmetry condition," Eq. (6)?

9. [*01*] What is the value of $\binom{n}{n}$? (Consider all integers n.)

▶ **10.** [*M25*] If p is prime and n is an integer, show that:

a) $\binom{n}{p} \equiv \left\lfloor \frac{n}{p} \right\rfloor$ (modulo p).

b) $\binom{p}{k} \equiv 0$ (modulo p), for $1 \le k \le p-1$.

c) $\binom{p-1}{k} \equiv (-1)^k$ (modulo p), for $0 \le k \le p-1$.

d) $\binom{p+1}{k} \equiv 0$ (modulo p), for $2 \le k \le p-1$.

e) (É. Lucas, 1877.)

$$\binom{n}{k} \equiv \binom{\lfloor n/p \rfloor}{\lfloor k/p \rfloor} \binom{n \bmod p}{k \bmod p} \text{ (modulo } p\text{).}$$

f) If the representations of n and k in the p-ary number system are

$$n = a_r p^r + \cdots + a_1 p + a_0, \qquad \text{then} \qquad \binom{n}{k} \equiv \binom{a_r}{b_r} \cdots \binom{a_1}{b_1} \binom{a_0}{b_0} \text{ (modulo } p\text{).}$$
$$k = b_r p^r + \cdots + b_1 p + b_0,$$

▶ **11.** [*M20*] (E. Kummer, 1852.) Let p be prime. Show that if p^n divides

$$\binom{a+b}{a}$$

but p^{n+1} does not, then n is equal to the number of *carries* that occur when a is added to b in the p-ary number system. [*Hint:* See exercise 1.2.5–12.]

12. [*M22*] Are there any positive integers n for which all the nonzero entries in the nth row of Pascal's triangle are *odd*? If so, find all such n.

13. [*M13*] Prove the summation formula, Eq. (10).

14. [*M21*] Evaluate $\sum_{k=0}^{n} k^4$.

15. [*M15*] Prove the binomial formula, Eq. (13).

16. [*M15*] Given that n and k are positive integers, prove the symmetrical identity

$$(-1)^n \binom{-n}{k-1} = (-1)^k \binom{-k}{n-1}.$$

▶ **17.** [*M18*] Prove the Chu–Vandermonde formula (21) from Eq. (15), using the idea that $(1+x)^{r+s} = (1+x)^r (1+x)^s$.

18. [*M15*] Prove Eq. (22) using Eqs. (21) and (6).

19. [*M18*] Prove Eq. (23) by induction.

20. [*M20*] Prove Eq. (24) by using Eqs. (21) and (19), then show that another use of Eq. (19) yields Eq. (25).

▶ **21.** [*M05*] Both sides of Eq. (25) are polynomials in s; why isn't that equation an identity in s?

22. [*M20*] Prove Eq. (26) for the special case $s = n - 1 - r + nt$.

23. [*M13*] Assuming that Eq. (26) holds for (r, s, t, n) and $(r, s - t, t, n - 1)$, prove it for $(r, s + 1, t, n)$.

24. [*M15*] Explain why the results of the previous two exercises combine to give a proof of Eq. (26).

25. [*HM30*] Let the polynomial $A_n(x,t)$ be defined as in Example 4 (see Eq. (30)). Let $z = x^{t+1} - x^t$. Prove that $\sum_k A_k(r,t)z^k = x^r$, provided that x is close enough to 1. [*Note:* If $t = 0$, this result is essentially the binomial theorem, and this equation is an important generalization of that theorem. The binomial theorem (15) may be assumed in the proof.] *Hint:* Start with multiples of a special case of (34),

$$\sum_j (-1)^j \binom{k}{j} \binom{r - jt}{k} \frac{r}{r - jt} = \delta_{k0},$$

where again the left-hand side is considered to be a polynomial in r.

26. [*HM25*] Using the assumptions of the previous exercise, prove that

$$\sum_k \binom{r - tk}{k} z^k = \frac{x^{r+1}}{(t+1)x - t}.$$

27. [*HM21*] Solve Example 4 in the text by using the result of exercise 25; and prove Eq. (26) from the preceding two exercises. [*Hint:* See exercise 17.]

28. [*M25*] Prove that

$$\sum_k \binom{r+tk}{k}\binom{s-tk}{n-k} = \sum_{k\geq 0}\binom{r+s-k}{n-k}t^k,$$

if n is a nonnegative integer.

29. [*M20*] Show that Eq. (34) is just a special case of the general identity proved in exercise 1.2.3–33.

▶ **30.** [*M24*] Show that there is a better way to solve Example 3 than the way used in the text, by manipulating the sum so that Eq. (26) applies.

▶ **31.** [*M20*] Evaluate

$$\sum_k \binom{m-r+s}{k}\binom{n+r-s}{n-k}\binom{r+k}{m+n}$$

in terms of r, s, m, and n, given that m and n are integers. Begin by replacing

$$\binom{r+k}{m+n}\qquad \text{by}\qquad \sum_j\binom{r}{m+n-j}\binom{k}{j}.$$

32. [*M20*] Show that $\sum_k \left[\begin{smallmatrix}n\\k\end{smallmatrix}\right]x^k = x^{\bar{n}}$, where $x^{\bar{n}}$ is the rising factorial power defined in Eq. 1.2.5–(19).

33. [*M20*] (A. Vandermonde, 1772.) Show that the binomial formula is valid also when it involves factorial powers instead of the ordinary powers. In other words, prove that

$$(x+y)^{\underline{n}} = \sum_k \binom{n}{k}x^{\underline{k}}y^{\underline{n-k}}; \qquad (x+y)^{\overline{n}} = \sum_k \binom{n}{k}x^{\overline{k}}y^{\overline{n-k}}.$$

34. [*M23*] (*Torelli's sum.*) In the light of the previous exercise, show that Abel's generalization, Eq. (16), of the binomial formula is true also for rising powers:

$$(x+y)^{\overline{n}} = \sum_k \binom{n}{k}x(x-kz+1)^{\overline{k-1}}(y+kz)^{\overline{n-k}}.$$

35. [*M23*] Prove the addition formulas (46) for Stirling numbers directly from the definitions, Eqs. (44) and (45).

36. [*M10*] What is the sum $\sum_k \binom{n}{k}$ of the numbers in each row of Pascal's triangle? What is the sum of those numbers with alternating signs, $\sum_k \binom{n}{k}(-1)^k$?

37. [*M10*] From the answers to the preceding exercise, deduce the value of the sum of every other entry in a row, $\binom{n}{0} + \binom{n}{2} + \binom{n}{4} + \cdots$.

38. [*HM30*] (C. Ramus, 1834.) Generalizing the result of the preceding exercise, show that we have the following formula, given that $0 \leq k < m$:

$$\binom{n}{k} + \binom{n}{m+k} + \binom{n}{2m+k} + \cdots = \frac{1}{m}\sum_{0\leq j<m}\left(2\cos\frac{j\pi}{m}\right)^n\cos\frac{j(n-2k)\pi}{m}.$$

For example,

$$\binom{n}{1} + \binom{n}{4} + \binom{n}{7} + \cdots = \frac{1}{3}\left(2^n + 2\cos\frac{(n-2)\pi}{3}\right).$$

[*Hint:* Find the right combinations of these coefficients multiplied by mth roots of unity.] This identity is particularly remarkable when $m \geq n$.

39. [*M10*] What is the sum $\sum_k \left[{n \atop k}\right]$ of the numbers in each row of Stirling's first triangle? What is the sum of those numbers with alternating signs? (See exercise 36.)

40. [*HM17*] The *beta function* $\mathrm{B}(x, y)$ is defined for positive real numbers x, y by the formula $\mathrm{B}(x, y) = \int_0^1 t^{x-1}(1 - t)^{y-1}\, dt$.

a) Show that $\mathrm{B}(x, 1) = \mathrm{B}(1, x) = 1/x$.
b) Show that $\mathrm{B}(x + 1,\, y) + \mathrm{B}(x,\, y + 1) = \mathrm{B}(x, y)$.
c) Show that $\mathrm{B}(x, y) = ((x + y)/y)\,\mathrm{B}(x,\, y + 1)$.

41. [*HM22*] We proved a relation between the gamma function and the beta function in exercise 1.2.5–19, by showing that $\Gamma_m(x) = m^x\,\mathrm{B}(x, m+1)$, if m is a positive integer.

a) Prove that
$$\mathrm{B}(x, y) = \frac{\Gamma_m(y)m^x}{\Gamma_m(x + y)}\mathrm{B}(x,\, y + m + 1).$$

b) Show that
$$\mathrm{B}(x, y) = \frac{\Gamma(x)\Gamma(y)}{\Gamma(x + y)}.$$

42. [*HM10*] Express the binomial coefficient $\binom{r}{k}$ in terms of the beta function defined above. (This gives us a way to extend the definition to all complex numbers r and k.)

43. [*HM20*] Show that $\mathrm{B}(1/2, 1/2) = \pi$. (From exercise 41 we may now conclude that $\Gamma(1/2) = \sqrt{\pi}$.)

44. [*HM20*] Using the generalized binomial coefficient suggested in exercise 42, show that
$$\binom{r}{1/2} = 2^{2r+1}\bigg/\binom{2r}{r}\,\pi.$$

45. [*HM21*] Using the generalized binomial coefficient suggested in exercise 42, find $\lim_{r \to \infty} \binom{r}{k}/r^k$.

▸ **46.** [*M21*] Using Stirling's approximation, Eq. 1.2.5–(7), find an approximate value of $\binom{x+y}{y}$, assuming that both x and y are large. In particular, find the approximate size of $\binom{2n}{n}$ when n is large.

47. [*M21*] Given that k is an integer, show that
$$\binom{r}{k}\binom{r - 1/2}{k} = \binom{2r}{k}\binom{2r - k}{k}\bigg/4^k = \binom{2r}{2k}\binom{2k}{k}\bigg/4^k.$$

Give a simpler formula for the special case $r = -1/2$.

▸ **48.** [*M25*] Show that
$$\sum_{k \geq 0} \binom{n}{k}\frac{(-1)^k}{k + x} = \frac{n!}{x(x + 1)\ldots(x + n)} = \frac{1}{x\binom{n+x}{n}},$$

if the denominators are not zero. [Note that this formula gives us the reciprocal of a binomial coefficient, as well as the partial fraction expansion of $1/x(x + 1)\ldots(x + n)$.]

49. [*M20*] Show that the identity $(1 + x)^r = (1 - x^2)^r(1 - x)^{-r}$ implies a relation on binomial coefficients.

50. [*M20*] Prove Abel's formula, Eq. (16), in the special case $x + y = 0$.

51. [*M21*] Prove Abel's formula, Eq. (16), by writing $y = (x + y) - x$, expanding the right-hand side in powers of $(x + y)$, and applying the result of the previous exercise.

52. [*HM11*] Prove that Abel's binomial formula (16) is not always valid when n is not a nonnegative integer, by evaluating the right-hand side when $n = x = -1$, $y = z = 1$.

53. [*M25*] (a) Prove the following identity by induction on m, where m and n are integers:

$$\sum_{k=0}^{m} \binom{r}{k}\binom{s}{n-k}(nr - (r+s)k) = (m+1)(n-m)\binom{r}{m+1}\binom{s}{n-m}.$$

(b) Making use of important relations from exercise 47,

$$\binom{-1/2}{n} = \frac{(-1)^n}{2^{2n}}\binom{2n}{n}, \quad \binom{1/2}{n} = \frac{(-1)^{n-1}}{2^{2n}(2n-1)}\binom{2n}{n} = \frac{(-1)^{n-1}}{2^{2n-1}(2n-1)}\binom{2n-1}{n} - \delta_{n0},$$

show that the following formula can be obtained as a special case of the identity in part (a):

$$\sum_{k=0}^{m}\binom{2k-1}{k}\binom{2n-2k}{n-k}\frac{-1}{2k-1} = \frac{n-m}{2n}\binom{2m}{m}\binom{2n-2m}{n-m} + \frac{1}{2}\binom{2n}{n}.$$

(This result is considerably more general than Eq. (26) in the case $r = -1$, $s = 0$, $t = -2$.)

54. [*M21*] Consider Pascal's triangle (as shown in Table 1) as a matrix. What is the *inverse* of that matrix?

55. [*M21*] Considering each of Stirling's triangles (Table 2) as matrices, determine their inverses.

56. [*20*] (*The combinatorial number system.*) For each integer $n = 0, 1, 2, \ldots, 20$, find three integers a, b, c for which $n = \binom{a}{3} + \binom{b}{2} + \binom{c}{1}$ and $a > b > c \geq 0$. Can you see how this pattern can be continued for higher values of n?

▸ **57.** [*M22*] Show that the coefficient a_m in Stirling's attempt at generalizing the factorial function, Eq. 1.2.5–(12), is

$$\frac{(-1)^m}{m!}\sum_{k\geq 1}(-1)^k\binom{m-1}{k-1}\ln k.$$

58. [*M23*] (H. A. Rothe, 1811.) In the notation of Eq. (40), prove the "q-nomial theorem":

$$(1+x)(1+qx)\ldots(1+q^{n-1}x) = \sum_{k}\binom{n}{k}_q q^{k(k-1)/2}x^k.$$

Also find q-nomial generalizations of the fundamental identities (17) and (21).

59. [*M25*] A sequence of numbers A_{nk}, $n \geq 0$, $k \geq 0$, satisfies the relations $A_{n0} = 1$, $A_{0k} = \delta_{0k}$, $A_{nk} = A_{(n-1)k} + A_{(n-1)(k-1)} + \binom{n}{k}$ for $nk > 0$. Find A_{nk}.

▸ **60.** [*M23*] We have seen that $\binom{n}{k}$ is the number of combinations of n things, k at a time, namely the number of ways to choose k different things out of a set of n. The *combinations with repetitions* are similar to ordinary combinations, except that we may choose each object any number of times. Thus, the list (1) would be extended to include also aaa, aab, aac, aad, aae, abb, etc., if we were considering combinations with repetition. How many k-combinations of n objects are there, if repetition is allowed?

61. [*M25*] Evaluate the sum

$$\sum_k \begin{bmatrix} n+1 \\ k+1 \end{bmatrix} \begin{Bmatrix} k \\ m \end{Bmatrix} (-1)^{k-m},$$

thereby obtaining a companion formula for Eq. (55).

▶ **62.** [*M23*] The text gives formulas for sums involving a product of two binomial coefficients. Of the sums involving a product of three binomial coefficients, the following one and the identity of exercise 31 seem to be most useful:

$$\sum_k (-1)^k \binom{l+m}{l+k} \binom{m+n}{m+k} \binom{n+l}{n+k} = \frac{(l+m+n)!}{l!\, m!\, n!}, \quad \text{integer } l, m, n \geq 0.$$

(The sum includes both positive and negative values of k.) Prove this identity.
[*Hint:* There is a very short proof, which begins by applying the result of exercise 31.]

63. [*M30*] If l, m, and n are integers and $n \geq 0$, prove that

$$\sum_{j,k} (-1)^{j+k} \binom{j+k}{k+l} \binom{r}{j} \binom{n}{k} \binom{s+n-j-k}{m-j} = (-1)^l \binom{n+r}{n+l} \binom{s-r}{m-n-l}.$$

▶ **64.** [*M20*] Show that $\begin{Bmatrix} n \\ m \end{Bmatrix}$ is the number of ways to partition a set of n elements into m nonempty disjoint subsets. For example, the set $\{1, 2, 3, 4\}$ can be partitioned into two subsets in $\begin{Bmatrix} 4 \\ 2 \end{Bmatrix} = 7$ ways: $\{1, 2, 3\}\{4\}$; $\{1, 2, 4\}\{3\}$; $\{1, 3, 4\}\{2\}$; $\{2, 3, 4\}\{1\}$; $\{1, 2\}\{3, 4\}$; $\{1, 3\}\{2, 4\}$; $\{1, 4\}\{2, 3\}$. *Hint:* Use Eq. (46).

65. [*HM35*] (B. F. Logan.) Prove Eqs. (59) and (60).

66. [*HM30*] Suppose x, y, and z are real numbers satisfying

$$\binom{x}{n} = \binom{y}{n} + \binom{z}{n-1},$$

where $x \geq n-1$, $y \geq n-1$, $z > n-2$, and n is an integer ≥ 2. Prove that

$$\binom{x}{n-1} \leq \binom{y}{n-1} + \binom{z}{n-2} \qquad \text{if and only if} \qquad y \geq z;$$

$$\binom{x}{n+1} \leq \binom{y}{n+1} + \binom{z}{n} \qquad \text{if and only if} \qquad y \leq z.$$

▶ **67.** [*M20*] We often need to know that binomial coefficients aren't too large. Prove the easy-to-remember upper bound

$$\binom{n}{k} \leq \left(\frac{ne}{k}\right)^k, \qquad \text{when } n \geq k > 0.$$

68. [*M25*] (A. de Moivre.) Prove that, if n is a nonnegative integer,

$$\sum_k \binom{n}{k} p^k (1-p)^{n-k} |k - np| = 2\lceil np \rceil \binom{n}{\lceil np \rceil} p^{\lceil np \rceil} (1-p)^{n+1-\lceil np \rceil}.$$

1.2.7. Harmonic Numbers

The following sum will be of great importance in our later work:

$$H_n = 1 + \frac{1}{2} + \frac{1}{3} + \cdots + \frac{1}{n} = \sum_{k=1}^{n} \frac{1}{k}, \quad n \geq 0. \tag{1}$$

This sum does not occur very frequently in classical mathematics, and there is no standard notation for it; but in the analysis of algorithms it pops up nearly every time we turn around, and we will consistently call it H_n. Besides H_n, the notations h_n and S_n and $\psi(n+1) + \gamma$ are found in mathematical literature. The letter H stands for "harmonic," and we speak of H_n as a *harmonic number* because (1) is customarily called the harmonic series. Chinese bamboo strips written before 186 B.C. already explained how to compute $H_{10} = 7381/2520$, as an exercise in arithmetic. [See C. Cullen, *Historia Math.* **34** (2007), 10–44.]

It may seem at first that H_n does not get too large when n has a large value, since we are always adding smaller and smaller numbers. But actually it is not hard to see that H_n will get as large as we please if we take n to be big enough, because

$$H_{2^m} \geq 1 + \frac{m}{2}. \tag{2}$$

This lower bound follows from the observation that, for $m \geq 0$, we have

$$H_{2^{m+1}} = H_{2^m} + \frac{1}{2^m + 1} + \frac{1}{2^m + 2} + \cdots + \frac{1}{2^{m+1}}$$

$$\geq H_{2^m} + \frac{1}{2^{m+1}} + \frac{1}{2^{m+1}} + \cdots + \frac{1}{2^{m+1}} = H_{2^m} + \tfrac{1}{2}.$$

So as m increases by 1, the left-hand side of (2) increases by at least $\frac{1}{2}$.

It is important to have more detailed information about the value of H_n than is given in Eq. (2). The approximate size of H_n is a well-known quantity (at least in mathematical circles) that may be expressed as follows:

$$H_n = \ln n + \gamma + \frac{1}{2n} - \frac{1}{12n^2} + \frac{1}{120n^4} - \epsilon, \quad 0 < \epsilon < \frac{1}{252n^6}. \tag{3}$$

Here $\gamma = 0.5772156649\ldots$ is *Euler's constant*, introduced by Leonhard Euler in *Commentarii Acad. Sci. Imp. Pet.* **7** (1734), 150–161. Exact values of H_n for small n, and a 40-place value for γ, are given in the tables in Appendix A. We shall derive Eq. (3) in Section 1.2.11.2.

Thus H_n is reasonably close to the natural logarithm of n. Exercise 7(a) demonstrates in a simple way that H_n has a somewhat logarithmic behavior.

In a sense, H_n just barely goes to infinity as n gets large, because the similar sum

$$1 + \frac{1}{2^r} + \frac{1}{3^r} + \cdots + \frac{1}{n^r} \tag{4}$$

stays bounded for all n, when r is any real-valued exponent *greater* than unity. (See exercise 3.) We denote the sum in Eq. (4) by $H_n^{(r)}$.

When the exponent r in Eq. (4) is at least 2, the value of $H_n^{(r)}$ is fairly close to its maximum value $H_\infty^{(r)}$, except for very small n. The quantity $H_\infty^{(r)}$ is very well known in mathematics as *Riemann's zeta function*:

$$H_\infty^{(r)} = \zeta(r) = \sum_{k \geq 1} \frac{1}{k^r}. \tag{5}$$

If r is an even integer, the value of $\zeta(r)$ is known to be equal to

$$H_\infty^{(r)} = \frac{1}{2} |B_r| \frac{(2\pi)^r}{r!}, \qquad \text{integer } r/2 \geq 1, \tag{6}$$

where B_r is a Bernoulli number (see Section 1.2.11.2 and Appendix A). In particular,

$$H_\infty^{(2)} = \frac{\pi^2}{6}, \quad H_\infty^{(4)} = \frac{\pi^4}{90}, \quad H_\infty^{(6)} = \frac{\pi^6}{945}, \quad H_\infty^{(8)} = \frac{\pi^8}{9450}. \tag{7}$$

These results are due to Euler; for discussion and proof, see *CMath*, §6.5.

Now we will consider a few important sums that involve harmonic numbers. First,

$$\sum_{k=1}^{n} H_k = (n+1)H_n - n. \tag{8}$$

This follows from a simple interchange of summation:

$$\sum_{k=1}^{n} \sum_{j=1}^{k} \frac{1}{j} = \sum_{j=1}^{n} \sum_{k=j}^{n} \frac{1}{j} = \sum_{j=1}^{n} \frac{n+1-j}{j}.$$

Formula (8) is a special case of the sum $\sum_{k=1}^{n} \binom{k}{m} H_k$, which we will now determine using an important technique called summation by parts (see exercise 10). Summation by parts is a useful way to evaluate $\sum a_k b_k$ whenever the quantities $\sum a_k$ and $(b_{k+1} - b_k)$ have simple forms. We observe in this case that

$$\binom{k}{m} = \binom{k+1}{m+1} - \binom{k}{m+1},$$

and therefore

$$\binom{k}{m} H_k = \binom{k+1}{m+1} \left(H_{k+1} - \frac{1}{k+1} \right) - \binom{k}{m+1} H_k;$$

hence

$$\sum_{k=1}^{n} \binom{k}{m} H_k = \left(\binom{2}{m+1} H_2 - \binom{1}{m+1} H_1 \right) + \cdots$$

$$+ \left(\binom{n+1}{m+1} H_{n+1} - \binom{n}{m+1} H_n \right) - \sum_{k=1}^{n} \binom{k+1}{m+1} \frac{1}{k+1}$$

$$= \binom{n+1}{m+1} H_{n+1} - \binom{1}{m+1} H_1 - \frac{1}{m+1} \sum_{k=0}^{n} \binom{k}{m} + \frac{1}{m+1} \binom{0}{m}.$$

Applying Eq. 1.2.6–(11) yields the desired formula:

$$\sum_{k=1}^{n}\binom{k}{m}H_k = \binom{n+1}{m+1}\left(H_{n+1} - \frac{1}{m+1}\right). \tag{9}$$

(This derivation and its final result are analogous to the evaluation of

$$\int_{1}^{n} x^m \ln x \, dx = \frac{n^{m+1}}{m+1}\left(\ln n - \frac{1}{m+1}\right) + \frac{1}{(m+1)^2}$$

using what calculus books call integration by parts.)

We conclude this section by considering a different kind of sum, $\sum_k \binom{n}{k}x^k H_k$, which we will temporarily denote by S_n for brevity. We find that

$$S_{n+1} = \sum_{k}\left(\binom{n}{k} + \binom{n}{k-1}\right)x^k H_k = S_n + x\sum_{k\geq 1}\binom{n}{k-1}x^{k-1}\left(H_{k-1} + \frac{1}{k}\right)$$

$$= S_n + x\,S_n + \frac{1}{n+1}\sum_{k\geq 1}\binom{n+1}{k}x^k.$$

Hence $S_{n+1} = (x+1)S_n + ((x+1)^{n+1} - 1)/(n+1)$, and we have

$$\frac{S_{n+1}}{(x+1)^{n+1}} = \frac{S_n}{(x+1)^n} + \frac{1}{n+1} - \frac{1}{(n+1)(x+1)^{n+1}}.$$

This equation, together with the fact that $S_0 = 0$, shows us that

$$\frac{S_n}{(x+1)^n} = H_n - \sum_{k=1}^{n}\frac{1}{k(x+1)^k}. \tag{10}$$

The new sum is part of the infinite series 1.2.9–(17) for $\ln\big(1/(1 - 1/(x+1))\big) = \ln(1 + 1/x)$, and when $x > 0$, the series is convergent; the difference is

$$\sum_{k>n}\frac{1}{k(x+1)^k} < \frac{1}{(n+1)(x+1)^{n+1}}\sum_{k\geq 0}\frac{1}{(x+1)^k} = \frac{1}{(n+1)(x+1)^n x}.$$

This proves the following theorem:

Theorem A. *If $x > 0$ and $n \geq 0$, then*

$$\sum_{k=1}^{n}\binom{n}{k}x^k H_k = (x+1)^n\left(H_n - \ln\left(1 + \frac{1}{x}\right)\right) + \epsilon,$$

where $0 < \epsilon < 1/(x(n+1))$. ∎

EXERCISES

1. [*01*] What are H_0, H_1, and H_2?

2. [*13*] Show that the simple argument used in the text to prove that $H_{2^m} \geq 1 + m/2$ can be slightly modified to prove that $H_{2^m} \leq 1 + m$.

3. [*M21*] Generalize the argument used in the previous exercise to show that, for $r > 1$, the sum $H_n^{(r)}$ remains bounded for all n. Find an upper bound.

▶ **4.** [*10*] Decide which of the following statements are true for all positive integers n:
(a) $H_n < \ln n$. (b) $H_n > \ln n$. (c) $H_n > \ln n + \gamma$.

5. [*15*] Give the value of H_{10000} to 15 decimal places, using the tables in Appendix A.

6. [*M15*] Prove that the harmonic numbers are directly related to Stirling's numbers, which were introduced in the previous section; in fact,

$$ H_n = \begin{bmatrix} n+1 \\ 2 \end{bmatrix} \Big/ n!. $$

7. [*M21*] Let $T(m,n) = H_m + H_n - H_{mn}$. (a) Show that when m or n increases, $T(m,n)$ never increases (assuming that m and n are positive). (b) Compute the minimum and maximum values of $T(m,n)$ for $m,n > 0$.

8. [*HM18*] Compare Eq. (8) with $\sum_{k=1}^{n} \ln k$; estimate the difference as a function of n.

▶ **9.** [*M18*] Theorem A applies only when $x > 0$. What is the value of the sum considered when $x = -1$?

10. [*M20*] (*Summation by parts.*) We have used special cases of the general method of summation by parts in exercise 1.2.4–42 and in the derivation of Eq. (9). Prove the general formula

$$ \sum_{1 \le k < n} (a_{k+1} - a_k) b_k = a_n b_n - a_1 b_1 - \sum_{1 \le k < n} a_{k+1}(b_{k+1} - b_k). $$

▶ **11.** [*M21*] Using summation by parts, evaluate

$$ \sum_{1 < k \le n} \frac{1}{k(k-1)} H_k. $$

▶ **12.** [*M10*] Evaluate $H_\infty^{(1000)}$ correct to at least 100 decimal places.

13. [*M22*] Prove the identity

$$ \sum_{k=1}^{n} \frac{x^k}{k} = H_n + \sum_{k=1}^{n} \binom{n}{k} \frac{(x-1)^k}{k}. $$

(Note in particular the special case $x = 0$, which gives us an identity related to exercise 1.2.6–48.)

14. [*M22*] Show that $\sum_{k=1}^{n} H_k/k = \frac{1}{2}(H_n^2 + H_n^{(2)})$, and evaluate $\sum_{k=1}^{n} H_k/(k+1)$.

▶ **15.** [*M23*] Express $\sum_{k=1}^{n} H_k^2$ in terms of n and H_n.

16. [*18*] Express the sum $1 + \frac{1}{3} + \cdots + \frac{1}{2n-1}$ in terms of harmonic numbers.

17. [*M24*] (E. Waring, 1782.) Let p be an odd prime. Show that the numerator of H_{p-1} is divisible by p.

18. [*M33*] (J. Selfridge.) What is the highest power of 2 that divides the numerator of $1 + \frac{1}{3} + \cdots + \frac{1}{2n-1}$?

▶ **19.** [*M30*] List all nonnegative integers n for which H_n is an integer. [*Hint:* If H_n has odd numerator and even denominator, it cannot be an integer.]

20. [*HM22*] There is an analytic way to approach summation problems such as the one leading to Theorem A in this section: If $f(x) = \sum_{k \geq 0} a_k x^k$, and this series converges for $x = x_0$, prove that

$$\sum_{k \geq 0} a_k x_0^k H_k = \int_0^1 \frac{f(x_0) - f(x_0 y)}{1 - y} \, dy.$$

21. [*M24*] Evaluate $\sum_{k=1}^n H_k / (n + 1 - k)$.

22. [*M28*] Evaluate $\sum_{k=0}^n H_k H_{n-k}$.

▶ **23.** [*HM20*] By considering the function $\Gamma'(x)/\Gamma(x)$, generalize H_n to noninteger values of n. You may use the fact that $\Gamma'(1) = -\gamma$, anticipating the next exercise.

24. [*HM21*] Show that

$$xe^{\gamma x} \prod_{k \geq 1} \left(\left(1 + \frac{x}{k} \right) e^{-x/k} \right) = \frac{1}{\Gamma(x)}.$$

(Consider the partial products of this infinite product.)

25. [*M21*] Let $H_n^{(u,v)} = \sum_{1 \leq j \leq k \leq n} 1/(j^u k^v)$. What are $H_n^{(0,v)}$ and $H_n^{(u,0)}$? Prove the general identity $H_n^{(u,v)} + H_n^{(v,u)} = H_n^{(u)} H_n^{(v)} + H_n^{(u+v)}$.

1.2.8. Fibonacci Numbers

The sequence

$$0, \ 1, \ 1, \ 2, \ 3, \ 5, \ 8, \ 13, \ 21, \ 34, \ \ldots, \tag{1}$$

in which each number is the sum of the preceding two, plays an important role in at least a dozen seemingly unrelated algorithms that we will study later. The numbers in the sequence are denoted by F_n, and we formally define them as

$$F_0 = 0; \qquad F_1 = 1; \qquad F_{n+2} = F_{n+1} + F_n, \quad n \geq 0. \tag{2}$$

This famous sequence was published in 1202 by Leonardo Pisano (Leonardo of Pisa), who is sometimes called Leonardo Fibonacci (*Filius Bonaccii*, son of Bonaccio). His *Liber Abaci* (Book of Calculation) contains the following exercise: "How many pairs of rabbits can be produced from a single pair in a year's time?" To solve this problem, we are told to assume that each pair produces a new pair of offspring every month, and that each new pair becomes fertile at the age of one month. Furthermore, the rabbits never die. After one month there will be 2 pairs of rabbits; after two months, there will be 3; the following month the original pair and the pair born during the first month will both usher in a new pair and there will be 5 in all; and so on.

Fibonacci was by far the greatest European mathematician of the Middle Ages. He studied the work of al-Khwārizmī (after whom "algorithm" is named, see Section 1.1) and he added numerous original contributions to arithmetic and geometry. The writings of Fibonacci were reprinted in 1857 [B. Boncompagni, *Scritti di Leonardo Pisano* (Rome, 1857–1862), 2 vols.; F_n appears in Vol. 1, 283–284]. His rabbit problem was, of course, not posed as a practical application to biology and the population explosion; it was an exercise in addition. In fact, it still makes a rather good computer exercise about addition (see exercise 3);

Fibonacci wrote: "It is possible to do [the addition] in this order for an infinite number of months."

Before Fibonacci wrote his work, the sequence $\langle F_n \rangle$ had already been discussed by Indian scholars, who had long been interested in rhythmic patterns that are formed from one-beat and two-beat notes or syllables. The number of such rhythms having n beats altogether is F_{n+1}; and the rule for computing those numbers was stated by Virahāṅka (c. 700) in his work Vṛttajātisamuccaya, sloka 6.49. Therefore both Gopāla (before 1135) and Hemacandra (c. 1150) mentioned the numbers 1, 2, 3, 5, 8, 13, 21, 34, ... explicitly. [See P. Singh, Historia Math. **12** (1985), 229–244; see also exercise 4.5.3–32.]

The same sequence also appears in the work of Johannes Kepler, 1611, who was musing about the numbers he saw around him [J. Kepler, The Six-Cornered Snowflake (Oxford: Clarendon Press, 1966), 21]. Kepler was presumably unaware of Fibonacci's brief mention of the sequence. Fibonacci numbers have often been observed in nature, probably for reasons similar to the original assumptions of the rabbit problem. [See Conway and Guy, The Book of Numbers (New York: Copernicus, 1996), 113–124, for an especially lucid explanation.]

A first indication of the intimate connections between F_n and algorithms came to light in 1837, when É. Léger used Fibonacci's sequence to study the efficiency of Euclid's algorithm. He observed that if the numbers m and n in Algorithm 1.1E are not greater than F_k, and $k > 1$, step E2 will be executed at most $k - 1$ times. This was the first practical application of Fibonacci's sequence. (See Theorem 4.5.3F.) During the 1870s the mathematician É. Lucas obtained very profound results about the Fibonacci numbers, and in particular he used them to prove that the 39-digit number $2^{127} - 1$ is prime. Lucas gave the name "Fibonacci numbers" to the sequence $\langle F_n \rangle$, and that name has been used ever since.

We already have examined the Fibonacci sequence briefly in Section 1.2.1 (Eq. (3) and exercise 4), where we found that $\phi^{n-2} \leq F_n \leq \phi^{n-1}$ if n is a positive integer and if

$$\phi = \tfrac{1}{2}(1 + \sqrt{5}). \tag{3}$$

We will see shortly that this quantity, ϕ, is intimately connected with the Fibonacci numbers.

The number ϕ itself has a very interesting history. Euclid called it the "extreme and mean ratio"; the ratio of A to B is the ratio of $A + B$ to A, if the ratio of A to B is ϕ. Renaissance writers called it the "divine proportion"; and in the last century it has commonly been called the "golden ratio." Many artists and writers have said that the ratio of ϕ to 1 is the most aesthetically pleasing proportion, and their opinion is confirmed from the standpoint of computer programming aesthetics as well. For the story of ϕ, see the excellent article "The Golden Section, Phyllotaxis, and Wythoff's Game," by H. S. M. Coxeter, Scripta Math. **19** (1953), 135–143; see also Chapter 8 of The 2nd Scientific American Book of Mathematical Puzzles and Diversions, by Martin Gardner (New York: Simon and Schuster, 1961). Several popular myths about ϕ have been debunked by George Markowsky in College Math. J. **23** (1992), 2–19. The fact that the ratio

F_{n+1}/F_n approaches ϕ was known to the early European reckoning master Simon Jacob, who died in 1564 [see P. Schreiber, *Historia Math.* **22** (1995), 422–424].

The notations we are using in this section are a little undignified. In much of the sophisticated mathematical literature, F_n is called u_n instead, and ϕ is called τ. Our notations are almost universally used in recreational mathematics (and some crank literature!) and they are rapidly coming into wider use. The designation ϕ comes from the name of the Greek artist Phidias who is said to have used the golden ratio in his sculpture. [See T. A. Cook, *The Curves of Life* (1914), 420.] The notation F_n is in accordance with that used in the *Fibonacci Quarterly*, where the reader may find numerous facts about the Fibonacci sequence. A good reference to the classical literature about F_n is Chapter 17 of L. E. Dickson's *History of the Theory of Numbers* **1** (Carnegie Inst. of Washington, 1919).

The Fibonacci numbers satisfy many interesting identities, some of which appear in the exercises at the end of this section. One of the most commonly discovered relations, mentioned by Kepler in a letter he wrote in 1608 but first published by J. D. Cassini [*Histoire Acad. Roy. Paris* **1** (1680), 201], is

$$F_{n+1}F_{n-1} - F_n^2 = (-1)^n, \tag{4}$$

which is easily proved by induction. A more esoteric way to prove the same formula starts with a simple inductive proof of the matrix identity

$$\begin{pmatrix} F_{n+1} & F_n \\ F_n & F_{n-1} \end{pmatrix} = \begin{pmatrix} 1 & 1 \\ 1 & 0 \end{pmatrix}^n. \tag{5}$$

We can then take the determinant of both sides of this equation.

Relation (4) shows that F_n and F_{n+1} are relatively prime, since any common divisor would have to be a divisor of $(-1)^n$.

From the definition (2) we find immediately that

$$F_{n+3} = F_{n+2} + F_{n+1} = 2F_{n+1} + F_n; \quad F_{n+4} = 3F_{n+1} + 2F_n;$$

and, in general, by induction that

$$F_{n+m} = F_m F_{n+1} + F_{m-1} F_n \tag{6}$$

for any positive integer m.

If we take m to be a multiple of n in Eq. (6), we find inductively that

$$F_{nk} \text{ is a multiple of } F_n.$$

Thus every third number is even, every fourth number is a multiple of 3, every fifth is a multiple of 5, and so on.

In fact, much more than this is true. If we write $\gcd(m, n)$ to stand for the greatest common divisor of m and n, a rather surprising theorem emerges:

Theorem A (É. Lucas, 1876). *A number divides both F_m and F_n if and only if it is a divisor of F_d, where $d = \gcd(m, n)$; in particular,*

$$\gcd(F_m, F_n) = F_{\gcd(m,n)}. \tag{7}$$

Proof. This result is proved by using Euclid's algorithm. We observe that because of Eq. (6) any common divisor of F_m and F_n is also a divisor of F_{n+m}; and, conversely, any common divisor of F_{n+m} and F_n is a divisor of $F_m F_{n+1}$. Since F_{n+1} is relatively prime to F_n, a common divisor of F_{n+m} and F_n also divides F_m. Thus we have proved that, for any number d,

$$d \text{ divides } F_m \text{ and } F_n \text{ if and only if } d \text{ divides } F_{m+n} \text{ and } F_n. \tag{8}$$

We will now show that *any* sequence $\langle F_n \rangle$ for which statement (8) holds, and for which $F_0 = 0$, satisfies Theorem A.

First it is clear that statement (8) may be extended by induction on k to the rule

$$d \text{ divides } F_m \text{ and } F_n \text{ if and only if } d \text{ divides } F_{m+kn} \text{ and } F_n,$$

where k is any nonnegative integer. This result may be stated more succinctly:

$$d \text{ divides } F_{m \bmod n} \text{ and } F_n \text{ if and only if } d \text{ divides } F_m \text{ and } F_n. \tag{9}$$

Now if r is the remainder after division of m by n, that is, if $r = m \bmod n$, then the common divisors of $\{F_m, F_n\}$ are the common divisors of $\{F_n, F_r\}$. It follows that throughout the manipulations of Algorithm 1.1E the set of common divisors of $\{F_m, F_n\}$ remains unchanged as m and n change; finally, when $r = 0$, the common divisors are simply the divisors of $F_0 = 0$ and $F_{\gcd(m,n)}$. ∎

Most of the important results involving Fibonacci numbers can be deduced from the representation of F_n in terms of ϕ, which we now proceed to derive. The method we shall use in the following derivation is extremely important, and the mathematically oriented reader should study it carefully; we will study the same method in detail in the next section.

We start by setting up the infinite series

$$\begin{aligned} G(z) &= F_0 + F_1 z + F_2 z^2 + F_3 z^3 + F_4 z^4 + \cdots \\ &= z + z^2 + 2z^3 + 3z^4 + \cdots. \end{aligned} \tag{10}$$

We have no *a priori* reason to expect that this infinite sum exists or that the function $G(z)$ is at all interesting—but let us be optimistic and see what we can conclude about the function $G(z)$ if it does exist. The advantage of such a procedure is that $G(z)$ is a single quantity that represents the *entire* Fibonacci sequence at once; and if we find out that $G(z)$ is a "known" function, its coefficients can be determined. We call $G(z)$ the *generating function* for the sequence $\langle F_n \rangle$.

We can now proceed to investigate $G(z)$ as follows:

$$\begin{aligned} zG(z) &= F_0 z + F_1 z^2 + F_2 z^3 + F_3 z^4 + \cdots, \\ z^2 G(z) &= \quad\quad\; F_0 z^2 + F_1 z^3 + F_2 z^4 + \cdots; \end{aligned}$$

by subtraction, therefore,

$$\begin{aligned} (1 - z - z^2)G(z) = F_0 + (F_1 - F_0)z &+ (F_2 - F_1 - F_0)z^2 \\ &+ (F_3 - F_2 - F_1)z^3 + (F_4 - F_3 - F_2)z^4 + \cdots. \end{aligned}$$

All terms but the second vanish because of the definition of F_n, so this expression equals z. Therefore we see that, if $G(z)$ exists,

$$G(z) = z/(1 - z - z^2).$$

(11)

In fact, this function *can* be expanded in an infinite series in z (a Taylor series); working backwards we find that the coefficients of the power series expansion of Eq. (11) must be the Fibonacci numbers.

We can now manipulate $G(z)$ and find out more about the Fibonacci sequence. The denominator $1 - z - z^2$ is a quadratic polynomial with the two roots $\frac{1}{2}(-1 \pm \sqrt{5})$; after a little calculation we find that $G(z)$ can be expanded by the method of partial fractions into the form

$$G(z) = \frac{1}{\sqrt{5}} \left(\frac{1}{1 - \phi z} - \frac{1}{1 - \hat{\phi} z} \right),$$

(12)

where

$$\hat{\phi} = 1 - \phi = -1/\phi = \tfrac{1}{2}(1 - \sqrt{5}).$$

(13)

The quantity $1/(1 - \phi z)$ is the sum of the infinite geometric series $1 + \phi z + \phi^2 z^2 + \cdots$, so we have

$$G(z) = \frac{1}{\sqrt{5}} (1 + \phi z + \phi^2 z^2 + \cdots - 1 - \hat{\phi} z - \hat{\phi}^2 z^2 - \cdots).$$

We now look at the coefficient of z^n, which must be equal to F_n; hence

$$F_n = \frac{1}{\sqrt{5}} (\phi^n - \hat{\phi}^n).$$

(14)

This is an important closed form expression for the Fibonacci numbers, first discovered early in the eighteenth century. (See D. Bernoulli, *Comment. Acad. Sci. Petrop.* **3** (1728), 85–100, §7; see also A. de Moivre, *Philos. Trans.* **32** (1722), 162–178, who showed how to solve general linear recurrences in essentially the way we have derived (14).)

We could have merely stated Eq. (14) and proved it by induction. However, the point of the rather long derivation above was to show how it would be possible to *discover* the equation in the first place, using the important method of generating functions, which is a valuable technique for solving a wide variety of problems.

Many things can be proved from Eq. (14). First we observe that $\hat{\phi}$ is a *negative* number $(-0.61803\ldots)$ whose magnitude is less than unity, so $\hat{\phi}^n$ gets very small as n gets large. In fact, the quantity $\hat{\phi}^n/\sqrt{5}$ is always small enough so that we have

$$F_n = \phi^n/\sqrt{5} \text{ rounded to the nearest integer,} \quad \text{for all integers } n \geq 0.$$

(15)

Other results can be obtained directly from $G(z)$; for example,

$$G(z)^2 = \frac{1}{5} \left(\frac{1}{(1 - \phi z)^2} + \frac{1}{(1 - \hat{\phi} z)^2} - \frac{2}{1 - z - z^2} \right),$$

(16)

and the coefficient of z^n in $G(z)^2$ is $\sum_{k=0}^{n} F_k F_{n-k}$. We deduce therefore that

$$\sum_{k=0}^{n} F_k F_{n-k} = \tfrac{1}{5}\big((n+1)(\phi^n + \hat{\phi}^n) - 2F_{n+1}\big)$$

$$= \tfrac{1}{5}\big((n+1)(F_n + 2F_{n-1}) - 2F_{n+1}\big)$$

$$= \tfrac{1}{5}(n-1)F_n + \tfrac{2}{5}nF_{n-1}. \tag{17}$$

(The second step in this derivation follows from the result of exercise 11.)

EXERCISES

1. [*10*] What is the answer to Leonardo Fibonacci's original problem: How many pairs of rabbits are present after a year?

▶ **2.** [*20*] In view of Eq. (15), what is the approximate value of F_{1000}? (Use logarithms found in Appendix A.)

3. [*25*] Write a computer program that calculates and prints F_1 through F_{1000} in decimal notation. (The previous exercise determines the size of numbers that must be handled.)

▶ **4.** [*14*] Find all n for which $F_n = n$.

5. [*20*] Find all n for which $F_n = n^2$.

6. [*HM10*] Prove Eq. (5).

▶ **7.** [*15*] If n is not a prime number, F_n is not a prime number (with one exception). Prove this and find the exception.

8. [*15*] In many cases it is convenient to define F_n for *negative* n, by assuming that $F_{n+2} = F_{n+1} + F_n$ for *all* integers n. Explore this possibility: What is F_{-1}? What is F_{-2}? Can F_{-n} be expressed in a simple way in terms of F_n?

9. [*M20*] Using the conventions of exercise 8, determine whether Eqs. (4), (6), (14), and (15) still hold when the subscripts are allowed to be *any* integers.

10. [*15*] Is $\phi^n/\sqrt{5}$ greater than F_n or less than F_n?

11. [*M20*] Show that $\phi^n = F_n\phi + F_{n-1}$ and $\hat{\phi}^n = F_n\hat{\phi} + F_{n-1}$, for *all* integers n.

▶ **12.** [*M26*] The "second order" Fibonacci sequence is defined by the rule

$$\mathcal{F}_0 = 0, \quad \mathcal{F}_1 = 1, \quad \mathcal{F}_{n+2} = \mathcal{F}_{n+1} + \mathcal{F}_n + F_n.$$

Express $\mathcal{F}_n$ in terms of F_n and F_{n+1}. [*Hint:* Use generating functions.]

▶ **13.** [*M22*] Express the following sequences in terms of the Fibonacci numbers, when r, s, and c are given constants:

a) $a_0 = r$, $a_1 = s$; $a_{n+2} = a_{n+1} + a_n$, for $n \geq 0$.
b) $b_0 = 0$, $b_1 = 1$; $b_{n+2} = b_{n+1} + b_n + c$, for $n \geq 0$.

14. [*M28*] Let m be a fixed positive integer. Find a_n, given that

$$a_0 = 0, \quad a_1 = 1; \quad a_{n+2} = a_{n+1} + a_n + \binom{n}{m}, \quad \text{for } n \geq 0.$$

15. [*M22*] Let $f(n)$ and $g(n)$ be arbitrary functions, and for $n \geq 0$ let

$$\begin{aligned}
a_0 &= 0, \quad a_1 = 1, \quad a_{n+2} = a_{n+1} + a_n + f(n); \\
b_0 &= 0, \quad b_1 = 1, \quad b_{n+2} = b_{n+1} + b_n + g(n); \\
c_0 &= 0, \quad c_1 = 1, \quad c_{n+2} = c_{n+1} + c_n + xf(n) + yg(n).
\end{aligned}$$

Express c_n in terms of x, y, a_n, b_n, and F_n.

▶ **16.** [*M20*] Fibonacci numbers appear implicitly in Pascal's triangle if it is viewed from the right angle. Show that the following sum of binomial coefficients is a Fibonacci number:

$$\sum_{k=0}^{n} \binom{n-k}{k}.$$

17. [*M24*] Using the conventions of exercise 8, prove the following generalization of Eq. (4): $F_{n+k}F_{m-k} - F_n F_m = (-1)^n F_{m-n-k} F_k$.

18. [*20*] Is $F_n^2 + F_{n+1}^2$ always a Fibonacci number?

▶ **19.** [*M27*] What is $\cos 36°$?

20. [*M16*] Express $\sum_{k=0}^{n} F_k$ in terms of Fibonacci numbers.

21. [*M25*] What is $\sum_{k=0}^{n} F_k x^k$?

▶ **22.** [*M20*] Show that $\sum_k \binom{n}{k} F_{m+k}$ is a Fibonacci number when $n \geq 0$.

23. [*M23*] Generalizing the preceding exercise, show that $\sum_k \binom{n}{k} F_t^k F_{t-1}^{n-k} F_{m+k}$ is always a Fibonacci number when $n \geq 0$.

24. [*HM20*] Evaluate the $n \times n$ determinant

$$\det \begin{pmatrix} 1 & -1 & 0 & 0 & \cdots & 0 & 0 & 0 \\ 1 & 1 & -1 & 0 & \cdots & 0 & 0 & 0 \\ 0 & 1 & 1 & -1 & \cdots & 0 & 0 & 0 \\ \vdots & \vdots & \vdots & \vdots & \ddots & \vdots & \vdots & \vdots \\ 0 & 0 & 0 & 0 & \cdots & 1 & 1 & -1 \\ 0 & 0 & 0 & 0 & \cdots & 0 & 1 & 1 \end{pmatrix}.$$

25. [*M21*] Show that

$$2^n F_n = 2 \sum_{k \text{ odd}} \binom{n}{k} 5^{(k-1)/2}, \quad \text{when } n \geq 0.$$

▶ **26.** [*M20*] Using the previous exercise, show that $F_p \equiv 5^{(p-1)/2}$ (modulo p) if p is an odd prime.

27. [*M20*] Using the previous exercise, show that if p is a prime different from 5, then either F_{p-1} or F_{p+1} (not both) is a multiple of p.

28. [*M21*] What is $F_{n+1} - \phi F_n$?

▶ **29.** [*M23*] (*Fibonomial coefficients.*) Édouard Lucas defined the quantities

$$\binom{n}{k}_{\mathcal{F}} = \frac{F_n F_{n-1} \cdots F_{n-k+1}}{F_k F_{k-1} \cdots F_1} = \prod_{j=1}^{k} \left(\frac{F_{n-k+j}}{F_j} \right)$$

in a manner analogous to binomial coefficients.

a) Make a table of $\binom{n}{k}_{\mathcal{F}}$ for $0 \leq k, n \leq 6$.

b) Show that $\binom{n}{k}_{\mathcal{F}}$ is always an integer because we have

$$\binom{n}{k}_{\mathcal{F}} = F_{k-1} \binom{n-1}{k}_{\mathcal{F}} + F_{n-k+1} \binom{n-1}{k-1}_{\mathcal{F}}.$$

▶ **30.** [*M38*] (D. Jarden, T. Motzkin.) The sequence of mth powers of Fibonacci numbers satisfies a recurrence relation in which each term depends on the preceding $m+1$ terms. Show that

$$\sum_k \binom{m}{k}_{\mathcal{F}} (-1)^{\lceil (m-k)/2 \rceil} F_{n+k}^{m-1} = 0, \quad \text{if } m > 0.$$

For example, when $m = 3$ we get the identity $F_n^2 - 2F_{n+1}^2 - 2F_{n+2}^2 + F_{n+3}^2 = 0$.

31. [*M20*] Show that $F_{2n}\phi \bmod 1 = 1 - \phi^{-2n}$ and $F_{2n+1}\phi \bmod 1 = \phi^{-2n-1}$, when $n \geq 0$.

32. [*M24*] The remainder of one Fibonacci number divided by another is $\pm$ a Fibonacci number: Show that, modulo F_n,

$$F_{mn+r} \equiv \begin{cases} F_r, & \text{if } m \bmod 4 = 0; \\ (-1)^{r+1} F_{n-r}, & \text{if } m \bmod 4 = 1; \\ (-1)^n F_r, & \text{if } m \bmod 4 = 2; \\ (-1)^{r+1+n} F_{n-r}, & \text{if } m \bmod 4 = 3. \end{cases}$$

33. [*HM24*] Given that $z = \pi/2 + i \ln \phi$, show that $\sin nz / \sin z = i^{1-n} F_n$.

▶ **34.** [*M24*] (*The Fibonacci number system.*) Let the notation $k \gg m$ mean that $k \geq m + 2$. Show that every positive integer n has a *unique* representation $n = F_{k_1} + F_{k_2} + \cdots + F_{k_r}$, where $k_1 \gg k_2 \gg \cdots \gg k_r \gg 0$.

35. [*M24*] (*A phi number system.*) Consider real numbers written with the digits 0 and 1 using base ϕ; thus $(100.1)_\phi = \phi^2 + \phi^{-1}$. Show that there are infinitely many ways to represent the number 1; for example, $1 = (.11)_\phi = (.011111\ldots)_\phi$. But if we require that no two adjacent 1s occur and that the representation does not end with the infinite sequence $01010101\ldots$, then every nonnegative number has a unique representation. What are the representations of integers?

▶ **36.** [*M32*] (*Fibonacci strings.*) Let $S_1 = $ "a", $S_2 = $ "b", and $S_{n+2} = S_{n+1}S_n$, $n > 0$; in other words, S_{n+2} is formed by placing S_n at the right of S_{n+1}. We have $S_3 = $ "ba", $S_4 = $ "bab", $S_5 = $ "babba", etc. Clearly S_n has F_n letters. Explore the properties of S_n. (Where do double letters occur? Can you predict the value of the kth letter of S_n? What is the density of the b's? And so on.)

▶ **37.** [*M35*] (R. E. Gaskell, M. J. Whinihan.) Two players compete in the following game: There is a pile containing n chips; the first player removes any number of chips except that he cannot take the whole pile. From then on, the players alternate moves, each person removing one or more chips but *not more than twice as many chips as the preceding player has taken*. The player who removes the last chip wins. (For example, suppose that $n = 11$; player A removes 3 chips; player B may remove up to 6 chips, and he takes 1. There remain 7 chips; player A may take 1 or 2 chips, and he takes 2; player B may remove up to 4, and he picks up 1. There remain 4 chips; player A now takes 1; player B must take at least one chip and player A wins in the following turn.)

What is the best move for the first player to make if there are initially 1000 chips?

38. [*35*] Write a computer program that plays the game described in the previous exercise, and plays it optimally.

39. [*M24*] Find a closed form expression for a_n, given that $a_0 = 0$, $a_1 = 1$, and $a_{n+2} = a_{n+1} + 6a_n$ for $n \geq 0$.

40. [*M25*] Solve the recurrence

$$f(1) = 0; \quad f(n) = \min_{0 < k < n} \max(1 + f(k), 2 + f(n - k)), \quad \text{for } n > 1.$$

▶ **41.** [*M25*] (Yuri Matiyasevich, 1990.) Let $f(x) = \lfloor x + \phi^{-1} \rfloor$. Prove that if $n = F_{k_1} + \cdots + F_{k_r}$ is the representation of n in the Fibonacci number system of exercise 34, then $F_{k_1+1} + \cdots + F_{k_r+1} = f(\phi n)$. Find a similar formula for $F_{k_1-1} + \cdots + F_{k_r-1}$.

42. [*M26*] (D. A. Klarner.) Show that if m and n are nonnegative integers, there is a unique sequence of indices $k_1 \gg k_2 \gg \cdots \gg k_r$ such that

$$m = F_{k_1} + F_{k_2} + \cdots + F_{k_r}, \qquad n = F_{k_1+1} + F_{k_2+1} + \cdots + F_{k_r+1}.$$

(See exercise 34. The k's may be negative, and r may be zero.)

1.2.9. Generating Functions

Whenever we want to obtain information about a sequence of numbers $\langle a_n \rangle = a_0, a_1, a_2, \ldots$, we can set up an infinite sum in terms of a "parameter" z,

$$G(z) = a_0 + a_1 z + a_2 z^2 + \cdots = \sum_{n \geq 0} a_n z^n. \tag{1}$$

We can then try to obtain information about the function G. This function is a single quantity that represents the whole sequence; if the sequence $\langle a_n \rangle$ has been defined inductively (that is, if a_n has been defined in terms of $a_0, a_1, \ldots, a_{n-1}$) this is an important advantage. Furthermore, we can recover the individual values of a_0, a_1, ... from the function $G(z)$, assuming that the infinite sum in Eq. (1) exists for some nonzero value of z, by using techniques of differential calculus.

We call $G(z)$ the *generating function* for the sequence a_0, a_1, a_2, ... The use of generating functions opens up a whole new range of techniques, and it broadly increases our capacity for problem solving. As mentioned in the previous section, A. de Moivre introduced generating functions in order to solve the general linear recurrence problem. De Moivre's theory was extended to slightly more complicated recurrences by James Stirling, who showed how to apply differentiation and integration as well as arithmetic operations [*Methodus Differentialis* (London: 1730), Proposition 15]. A few years later, L. Euler began to use generating functions in several new ways, for example in his papers on partitions [*Commentarii Acad. Sci. Pet.* **13** (1741), 64–93; *Novi Comment. Acad. Sci. Pet.* **3** (1750), 125–169]. Pierre S. Laplace developed the techniques further in his classic work *Théorie Analytique des Probabilités* (Paris: 1812).

The question of convergence of the infinite sum (1) is of some importance. Any textbook about the theory of infinite series will prove that:

a) If the series converges for a particular value of $z = z_0$, then it converges for all values of z with $|z| < |z_0|$.

b) The series converges for some $z \neq 0$ if and only if the sequence $\langle \sqrt[n]{|a_n|} \rangle$ is bounded. (If this condition is not satisfied, we may be able to get a convergent series for the sequence $\langle a_n/n! \rangle$ or for some other related sequence.)

On the other hand, it often does not pay to worry about convergence of the series when we work with generating functions, since we are only exploring possible approaches to the solution of some problem. When we discover the solution by *any* means, however sloppy, we may be able to justify the solution independently. For example, in the previous section we used a generating function to deduce Eq. (14); yet once such an equation has been found, it is a simple matter to prove it by induction, and we need not even mention that we used generating functions to discover it. Furthermore one can show that most (if not all) of the operations we do with generating functions can be rigorously justified without regard to the convergence of the series. See, for example, E. T. Bell, *Trans. Amer. Math. Soc.* **25** (1923), 135–154; Ivan Niven, *AMM* **76** (1969),

871–889; Peter Henrici, *Applied and Computational Complex Analysis* **1** (Wiley, 1974), Chapter 1.

Let us now study the principal techniques used with generating functions.

A. Addition. If $G(z)$ is the generating function for $\langle a_n \rangle = a_0, a_1, \ldots$ and $H(z)$ is the generating function for $\langle b_n \rangle = b_0, b_1, \ldots$, then $\alpha G(z) + \beta H(z)$ is the generating function for $\langle \alpha a_n + \beta b_n \rangle = \alpha a_0 + \beta b_0, \alpha a_1 + \beta b_1, \ldots$:

$$\alpha \sum_{n\geq 0} a_n z^n + \beta \sum_{n\geq 0} b_n z^n = \sum_{n\geq 0} (\alpha a_n + \beta b_n) z^n. \tag{2}$$

B. Shifting. If $G(z)$ is the generating function for $\langle a_n \rangle = a_0, a_1, \ldots$ then $z^m G(z)$ is the generating function for $\langle a_{n-m} \rangle = 0, \ldots, 0, a_0, a_1, \ldots$:

$$z^m \sum_{n\geq 0} a_n z^n = \sum_{n\geq m} a_{n-m} z^n. \tag{3}$$

The last summation may be extended over all $n \geq 0$ if we regard $a_n = 0$ for any negative value of n.

Similarly, $\left(G(z) - a_0 - a_1 z - \cdots - a_{m-1} z^{m-1}\right)/z^m$ is the generating function for $\langle a_{n+m} \rangle = a_m, a_{m+1}, \ldots$:

$$z^{-m} \sum_{n\geq m} a_n z^n = \sum_{n\geq 0} a_{n+m} z^n. \tag{4}$$

We combined operations A and B to solve the Fibonacci problem in the previous section: $G(z)$ was the generating function for $\langle F_n \rangle$, $zG(z)$ for $\langle F_{n-1} \rangle$, $z^2 G(z)$ for $\langle F_{n-2} \rangle$, and $(1 - z - z^2)G(z)$ for $\langle F_n - F_{n-1} - F_{n-2} \rangle$. Then, since $F_n - F_{n-1} - F_{n-2}$ is zero when $n \geq 2$, we found that $(1 - z - z^2)G(z)$ is a polynomial. Similarly, given any *linearly recurrent* sequence, that is, a sequence where $a_n = c_1 a_{n-1} + \cdots + c_m a_{n-m}$, the generating function will be a polynomial divided by $(1 - c_1 z - \cdots - c_m z^m)$.

Let us consider the simplest nontrivial example of all: If $G(z)$ is the generating function for the *constant* sequence $1, 1, 1, \ldots$, then $zG(z)$ generates the sequence $0, 1, 1, \ldots$; so $(1 - z)G(z) = 1$. This gives us the simple but very important formula

$$\frac{1}{1 - z} = 1 + z + z^2 + \cdots. \tag{5}$$

C. Multiplication. If $G(z)$ is the generating function for $a_0, a_1, \ldots$ and $H(z)$ is the generating function for $b_0, b_1, \ldots$, then

$$G(z)H(z) = (a_0 + a_1 z + a_2 z^2 + \cdots)(b_0 + b_1 z + b_2 z^2 + \cdots)$$
$$= (a_0 b_0) + (a_0 b_1 + a_1 b_0)z + (a_0 b_2 + a_1 b_1 + a_2 b_0)z^2 + \cdots;$$

thus $G(z)H(z)$ is the generating function for the sequence $c_0, c_1, \ldots$, where

$$c_n = \sum_{k=0}^{n} a_k b_{n-k}. \tag{6}$$

Equation (3) is a very special case of this. Another important special case occurs when each b_n is equal to unity:

$$\frac{1}{1-z}G(z) = a_0 + (a_0 + a_1)z + (a_0 + a_1 + a_2)z^2 + \cdots. \tag{7}$$

Here we have the generating function for the sums of the original sequence.

The rule for a product of *three* functions follows from (6); $F(z)G(z)H(z)$ generates $d_0, d_1, d_2, \ldots$, where

$$d_n = \sum_{\substack{i,j,k \geq 0 \\ i+j+k=n}} a_i b_j c_k. \tag{8}$$

The general rule for products of *any number* of functions (whenever this is meaningful) is

$$\prod_{j \geq 0} \sum_{k \geq 0} a_{jk} z^k = \sum_{n \geq 0} z^n \sum_{\substack{k_0, k_1, \ldots \geq 0 \\ k_0 + k_1 + \cdots = n}} a_{0k_0} a_{1k_1} \cdots . \tag{9}$$

When the recurrence relation for some sequence involves binomial coefficients, we often want to get a generating function for a sequence $c_0, c_1, \ldots$ defined by

$$c_n = \sum_k \binom{n}{k} a_k b_{n-k}. \tag{10}$$

In this case it is usually better to use generating functions for the sequences $\langle a_n/n! \rangle$, $\langle b_n/n! \rangle$, $\langle c_n/n! \rangle$, since we have

$$\left(\frac{a_0}{0!} + \frac{a_1}{1!}z + \frac{a_2}{2!}z^2 + \cdots \right) \left(\frac{b_0}{0!} + \frac{b_1}{1!}z + \frac{b_2}{2!}z^2 + \cdots \right) = \left(\frac{c_0}{0!} + \frac{c_1}{1!}z + \frac{c_2}{2!}z^2 + \cdots \right), \tag{11}$$

where c_n is given by Eq. (10).

D. Change of z. Clearly $G(cz)$ is the generating function for the sequence $a_0, ca_1, c^2 a_2, \ldots$. As a particular case, the generating function for $1, c, c^2, c^3, \ldots$ is $1/(1-cz)$.

There is a familiar trick for extracting alternate terms of a series:

$$\begin{aligned} \tfrac{1}{2}(G(z) + G(-z)) &= a_0 \ + \ a_2 z^2 \ + \ a_4 z^4 \ + \ \cdots, \\ \tfrac{1}{2}(G(z) - G(-z)) &= \ a_1 z \ + \ a_3 z^3 \ + \ a_5 z^5 \ + \ \cdots. \end{aligned} \tag{12}$$

Using complex roots of unity, we can extend this idea and extract every mth term: Let $\omega = e^{2\pi i/m} = \cos(2\pi/m) + i\sin(2\pi/m)$; we have

$$\sum_{n \geq 0, \, n \bmod m = r} a_n z^n = \frac{1}{m} \sum_{0 \leq k < m} \omega^{-kr} G(\omega^k z), \quad 0 \leq r < m. \tag{13}$$

(See exercise 14.) For example, if $m = 3$ and $r = 1$, we have $\omega = -\frac{1}{2} + \frac{\sqrt{3}}{2}i$, a complex cube root of unity; it follows that

$$a_1 z + a_4 z^4 + a_7 z^7 + \cdots = \tfrac{1}{3}(G(z) + \omega^{-1}G(\omega z) + \omega^{-2}G(\omega^2 z)).$$

E. Differentiation and integration. The techniques of calculus give us further operations. If $G(z)$ is given by Eq. (1), the derivative is

$$G'(z) = a_1 + 2a_2 z + 3a_3 z^2 + \cdots = \sum_{k \geq 0} (k+1)a_{k+1} z^k. \tag{14}$$

The generating function for the sequence $\langle na_n \rangle$ is $zG'(z)$. Hence we can combine the nth term of a sequence with polynomials in n by manipulating the generating function.

Reversing the process, integration gives another useful operation:

$$\int_0^z G(t)\, dt = a_0 z + \frac{1}{2}a_1 z^2 + \frac{1}{3}a_2 z^3 + \cdots = \sum_{k \geq 1} \frac{1}{k} a_{k-1} z^k. \tag{15}$$

As special cases, we have the derivative and integral of (5):

$$\frac{1}{(1-z)^2} = 1 + 2z + 3z^2 + \cdots = \sum_{k \geq 0} (k+1)z^k. \tag{16}$$

$$\ln \frac{1}{1-z} = z + \frac{1}{2}z^2 + \frac{1}{3}z^3 + \cdots = \sum_{k \geq 1} \frac{1}{k} z^k. \tag{17}$$

We can combine the second formula with Eq. (7) to get the generating function for the harmonic numbers:

$$\frac{1}{1-z} \ln \frac{1}{1-z} = z + \frac{3}{2}z^2 + \frac{11}{6}z^3 + \cdots = \sum_{k \geq 0} H_k z^k. \tag{18}$$

F. Known generating functions. Whenever it is possible to determine the power series expansion of a function, we have implicitly found the generating function for a particular sequence. These special functions can be quite useful in conjunction with the operations described above. The most important power series expansions are given in the following list.

i) *Binomial theorem.*

$$(1+z)^r = 1 + rz + \frac{r(r-1)}{2}z^2 + \cdots = \sum_{k \geq 0} \binom{r}{k} z^k. \tag{19}$$

When r is a negative integer, we get a special case already reflected in Eqs. (5) and (16):

$$\frac{1}{(1-z)^{n+1}} = \sum_{k \geq 0} \binom{-n-1}{k}(-z)^k = \sum_{k \geq 0} \binom{n+k}{n} z^k. \tag{20}$$

There is also a generalization, which was proved in exercise 1.2.6–25:

$$x^r = 1 + rz + \frac{r(r-2t-1)}{2}z^2 + \cdots = \sum_{k \geq 0} \binom{r-kt}{k} \frac{r}{r-kt} z^k, \tag{21}$$

if x is the continuous function of z that solves the equation $x^{t+1} = x^t + z$, where $x = 1$ when $z = 0$.

ii) *Exponential series.*

$$\exp z = e^z = 1 + z + \frac{1}{2!}z^2 + \cdots = \sum_{k \geq 0} \frac{1}{k!}z^k. \tag{22}$$

In general, we have the following formula involving Stirling numbers:

$$(e^z - 1)^n = z^n + \frac{1}{n+1}\left\{\begin{matrix}n+1\\n\end{matrix}\right\}z^{n+1} + \cdots = n!\sum_k \left\{\begin{matrix}k\\n\end{matrix}\right\}\frac{z^k}{k!}. \tag{23}$$

iii) *Logarithm series* (see (17) and (18)).

$$\ln(1+z) = z - \frac{1}{2}z^2 + \frac{1}{3}z^3 - \cdots = \sum_{k \geq 1}\frac{(-1)^{k+1}}{k}z^k, \tag{24}$$

$$\frac{1}{(1-z)^{m+1}}\ln\left(\frac{1}{1-z}\right) = \sum_{k \geq 1}(H_{m+k} - H_m)\binom{m+k}{k}z^k. \tag{25}$$

Stirling numbers, as in (23), give us a more general equation:

$$\left(\ln\frac{1}{1-z}\right)^n = z^n + \frac{1}{n+1}\left[\begin{matrix}n+1\\n\end{matrix}\right]z^{n+1} + \cdots = n!\sum_k\left[\begin{matrix}k\\n\end{matrix}\right]\frac{z^k}{k!}. \tag{26}$$

Further generalizations, including many sums of harmonic numbers, appear in papers by D. A. Zave, *Inf. Proc. Letters* **5** (1976), 75–77; J. Spieß, *Math. Comp.* **55** (1990), 839–863.

iv) *Miscellaneous.*

$$z(z+1)\ldots(z+n-1) = \sum_k\left[\begin{matrix}n\\k\end{matrix}\right]z^k, \tag{27}$$

$$\frac{z^n}{(1-z)(1-2z)\ldots(1-nz)} = \sum_k\left\{\begin{matrix}k\\n\end{matrix}\right\}z^k, \tag{28}$$

$$\frac{z}{1-e^{-z}} = 1 + \frac{1}{2}z + \frac{1}{12}z^2 + \cdots = \sum_{k \geq 0}\frac{B_k z^k}{k!}. \tag{29}$$

The coefficients B_k that appear in the last formula are the *Bernoulli numbers*; they will be examined further in Section 1.2.11.2. A table of Bernoulli numbers appears in Appendix A.

The next identity, analogous to (21), will be proved in exercise 2.3.4.4–29:

$$x^r = 1 + rz + \frac{r(r+2t)}{2}z^2 + \cdots = \sum_{k \geq 0}\frac{r(r+kt)^{k-1}}{k!}z^k, \tag{30}$$

if x is the continuous function of z that solves the equation $x = e^{zx^t}$, where $x = 1$ when $z = 0$. Significant generalizations of (21) and (30) are discussed in exercise 4.7–22.

G. Extracting a coefficient. It is often convenient to use the notation

$$[z^n] \, G(z) \tag{31}$$

for the coefficient of z^n in $G(z)$. For example, if $G(z)$ is the generating function in (1) we have $[z^n] \, G(z) = a_n$ and $[z^n] \, G(z)/(1 - z) = \sum_{k=0}^{n} a_k$. One of the most fundamental results in the theory of complex variables is a formula of A. L. Cauchy [*Exercices de Math.* **1** (1826), 95–113 = Œuvres (2) **6**, 124–145, Eq. (11)], by which we can extract any desired coefficient with the help of a contour integral:

$$[z^n] \, G(z) = \frac{1}{2\pi i} \oint_{|z|=r} \frac{G(z) \, dz}{z^{n+1}}, \tag{32}$$

if $G(z)$ converges for $z = z_0$ and $0 < r < |z_0|$. The basic idea is that $\oint_{|z|=r} z^m \, dz$ is zero for all integers m except $m = -1$, when the integral is

$$\int_{-\pi}^{\pi} (re^{i\theta})^{-1} \, d(re^{i\theta}) = i \int_{-\pi}^{\pi} d\theta = 2\pi i.$$

Equation (32) is of importance primarily when we want to study the approximate value of a coefficient.

We conclude this section by returning to a problem that was only partially solved in Section 1.2.3. We saw in Eq. 1.2.3–(13) and exercise 1.2.3–29 that

$$\sum_{1 \le i \le j \le n} x_i x_j = \frac{1}{2} \left(\sum_{k=1}^{n} x_k \right)^2 + \frac{1}{2} \left(\sum_{k=1}^{n} x_k^2 \right);$$

$$\sum_{1 \le i \le j \le k \le n} x_i x_j x_k = \frac{1}{6} \left(\sum_{k=1}^{n} x_k \right)^3 + \frac{1}{2} \left(\sum_{k=1}^{n} x_k \right) \left(\sum_{k=1}^{n} x_k^2 \right) + \frac{1}{3} \left(\sum_{k=1}^{n} x_k^3 \right).$$

In general, suppose that we have n numbers $x_1, x_2, \ldots, x_n$ and we want the sum

$$h_m = \sum_{1 \le j_1 \le \cdots \le j_m \le n} x_{j_1} \ldots x_{j_m}; \qquad h_0 = 1. \tag{33}$$

If possible, this sum should be expressed in terms of $S_1, S_2, \ldots, S_m$, where

$$S_j = \sum_{k=1}^{n} x_k^j, \tag{34}$$

the sum of jth powers. Using this more compact notation, the formulas above become $h_2 = \frac{1}{2} S_1^2 + \frac{1}{2} S_2$; $h_3 = \frac{1}{6} S_1^3 + \frac{1}{2} S_1 S_2 + \frac{1}{3} S_3$.

We can attack this problem by setting up the generating function

$$G(z) = 1 + h_1 z + h_2 z^2 + \cdots = \sum_{k \ge 0} h_k z^k. \tag{35}$$

By our rules for multiplying series, we find that

$$G(z) = (1 + x_1 z + x_1^2 z^2 + \cdots)(1 + x_2 z + x_2^2 z^2 + \cdots) \ldots (1 + x_n z + x_n^2 z^2 + \cdots)$$

$$= \frac{1}{(1 - x_1 z)(1 - x_2 z) \ldots (1 - x_n z)}. \tag{36}$$

So $G(z)$ is the reciprocal of a polynomial. It often helps to take the logarithm of a product, and we find from (17) that

$$\ln G(z) = \ln \frac{1}{1 - x_1 z} + \cdots + \ln \frac{1}{1 - x_n z}$$

$$= \left(\sum_{k \geq 1} \frac{x_1^k z^k}{k} \right) + \cdots + \left(\sum_{k \geq 1} \frac{x_n^k z^k}{k} \right) = \sum_{k \geq 1} \frac{S_k z^k}{k}. \tag{37}$$

Now $\ln G(z)$ has been expressed in terms of the S's; so all we must do to obtain the answer to our problem is to compute the power series expansion of $G(z)$ again, with the help of (22) and (9):

$$G(z) = e^{\ln G(z)} = \exp\left(\sum_{k \geq 1} \frac{S_k z^k}{k} \right) = \prod_{k \geq 1} e^{S_k z^k / k}$$

$$= \left(1 + S_1 z + \frac{S_1^2 z^2}{2!} + \cdots \right) \left(1 + \frac{S_2 z^2}{2} + \frac{S_2^2 z^4}{2^2 \cdot 2!} + \cdots \right) \cdots$$

$$= \sum_{m \geq 0} \left(\sum_{\substack{k_1, k_2, \ldots, k_m \geq 0 \\ k_1 + 2k_2 + \cdots + mk_m = m}} \frac{S_1^{k_1}}{1^{k_1} k_1!} \frac{S_2^{k_2}}{2^{k_2} k_2!} \cdots \frac{S_m^{k_m}}{m^{k_m} k_m!} \right) z^m. \tag{38}$$

The parenthesized quantity is h_m. This rather imposing sum is really not complicated when it is examined carefully. The number of terms for a particular value of m is $p(m)$, the number of partitions of m (Section 1.2.1). For example, one partition of 12 is

$$12 = 5 + 2 + 2 + 2 + 1;$$

this corresponds to a solution of the equation $k_1 + 2k_2 + \cdots + 12k_{12} = 12$, where k_j is the number of j's in the partition. In our example $k_1 = 1$, $k_2 = 3$, $k_5 = 1$, and the other k's are zero; so we get the term

$$\frac{S_1}{1^1 1!} \frac{S_2^3}{2^3 3!} \frac{S_5}{5^1 1!} = \frac{1}{240} S_1 S_2^3 S_5$$

as part of the expression for h_{12}. By differentiating (37) it is not difficult to derive the recurrence

$$h_m = \frac{1}{m}(S_1 h_{m-1} + S_2 h_{m-2} + \cdots + S_m h_0), \qquad m \geq 1. \tag{39}$$

An enjoyable introduction to the applications of generating functions has been given by G. Pólya, "On picture-writing," *AMM* **63** (1956), 689–697; his approach is continued in *CMath*, Chapter 7. See also the book *generating-functionology* by H. S. Wilf, second edition (Academic Press, 1994).

A generating function is a clothesline
on which we hang up a sequence of numbers for display.

— H. S. WILF (1989)

EXERCISES

1. [*M12*] What is the generating function for the sequence $2, 5, 13, 35, \ldots = \langle 2^n + 3^n \rangle$?

▶ **2.** [*M13*] Prove Eq. (11).

3. [*HM21*] Differentiate the generating function (18) for $\langle H_n \rangle$, and compare this with the generating function for $\langle \sum_{k=0}^{n} H_k \rangle$. What relation can you deduce?

4. [*M01*] Explain why Eq. (19) is a special case of Eq. (21).

5. [*M20*] Prove Eq. (23) by induction on n.

▶ **6.** [*HM15*] Find the generating function for

$$\left\langle \sum_{0 < k < n} \frac{1}{k(n-k)} \right\rangle;$$

differentiate it and express the coefficients in terms of harmonic numbers.

7. [*M15*] Verify all the steps leading to Eq. (38).

8. [*M23*] Find the generating function for $p(n)$, the number of partitions of n.

9. [*M11*] In the notation of Eqs. (34) and (35), what is h_4 in terms of S_1, S_2, S_3, and S_4?

▶ **10.** [*M25*] An *elementary symmetric function* is defined by the formulas

$$e_m = \sum_{1 \le j_1 < \cdots < j_m \le n} x_{j_1} \ldots x_{j_m}; \qquad e_0 = 1.$$

(This is the same as h_m of Eq. (33), except that equal subscripts are not allowed.) Find the generating function for e_m, and express e_m in terms of the S_j in Eq. (34). Write out the formulas for e_1, e_2, e_3, and e_4.

▶ **11.** [*M25*] Equation (39) can also be used to express the S's in terms of the h's: We find $S_1 = h_1$, $S_2 = 2h_2 - h_1^2$, $S_3 = 3h_3 - 3h_1 h_2 + h_1^3$, etc. What is the coefficient of $h_1^{k_1} h_2^{k_2} \ldots h_m^{k_m}$ in this representation of S_m, when $k_1 + 2k_2 + \cdots + mk_m = m$?

▶ **12.** [*M20*] Suppose we have a doubly subscripted sequence $\langle a_{mn} \rangle$ for $m, n = 0, 1, \ldots$; show how this double sequence can be represented by a *single* generating function of two variables, and determine the generating function for $\langle \binom{n}{m} \rangle$.

13. [*HM22*] The *Laplace transform* of a function $f(x)$ is the function

$$\mathbf{L}f(s) = \int_0^\infty e^{-st} f(t) \, dt.$$

Given that $a_0, a_1, a_2, \ldots$ is an infinite sequence having a convergent generating function, let $f(x)$ be the step function $\sum_k a_k \, [0 \le k \le x]$. Express the Laplace transform of $f(x)$ in terms of the generating function G for this sequence. (Assume that the real part of s is positive, so that the integral exists.)

14. [*HM21*] Prove Eq. (13).

15. [*M28*] By considering $H(w) = \sum_{n \geq 0} G_n(z) w^n$, find a closed form for the generating function

$$G_n(z) = \sum_{k=0}^{n} \binom{n-k}{k} z^k = \sum_{k=0}^{n} \binom{2k-n-1}{k} (-z)^k.$$

16. [*M22*] Give a simple formula for the generating function $G_{nr}(z) = \sum_k a_{nkr} z^k$, where a_{nkr} is the number of ways to choose k out of n objects, subject to the condition that each object may be chosen at most r times. (If $r = 1$, we have $\binom{n}{k}$ ways, and if $r \geq k$, we have the number of combinations with repetitions as in exercise 1.2.6–60.)

17. [*M25*] What are the coefficients of $1/(1-z)^w$ if this function is expanded into a *double* power series in terms of both z and w?

▶ **18.** [*M25*] Given positive integers n and r, find a simple formula for the value of the following sums: (a) $\sum_{1 \leq k_1 < k_2 < \cdots < k_r \leq n} k_1 k_2 \ldots k_r$; (b) $\sum_{1 \leq k_1 \leq k_2 \leq \cdots \leq k_r \leq n} k_1 k_2 \ldots k_r$. (For example, when $n = 3$ and $r = 2$ the sums are, respectively, $1 \cdot 2 + 1 \cdot 3 + 2 \cdot 3$ and $1 \cdot 1 + 1 \cdot 2 + 1 \cdot 3 + 2 \cdot 2 + 2 \cdot 3 + 3 \cdot 3$.)

19. [*HM32*] (C. F. Gauss, 1812.) The sums of the following infinite series are well known:

$$1 - \frac{1}{2} + \frac{1}{3} - \frac{1}{4} + \cdots = \ln 2; \quad 1 - \frac{1}{3} + \frac{1}{5} - \frac{1}{7} + \cdots = \frac{\pi}{4};$$

$$1 - \frac{1}{4} + \frac{1}{7} - \frac{1}{10} + \cdots = \frac{\pi\sqrt{3}}{9} + \frac{1}{3} \ln 2.$$

Using the definition

$$H_x = \sum_{n \geq 1} \left(\frac{1}{n} - \frac{1}{n+x} \right)$$

found in the answer to exercise 1.2.7–24, these series may be written respectively as

$$1 - \frac{1}{2} H_{1/2}; \quad \frac{2}{3} - \frac{1}{4} H_{1/4} + \frac{1}{4} H_{3/4}; \quad \frac{3}{4} - \frac{1}{6} H_{1/6} + \frac{1}{6} H_{2/3}.$$

Prove that, in general, $H_{p/q}$ has the value

$$\frac{q}{p} - \frac{\pi}{2} \cot \frac{p}{q} \pi - \ln 2q + 2 \sum_{0 < k < q/2} \cos \frac{2pk}{q} \pi \cdot \ln \sin \frac{k}{q} \pi,$$

when p and q are integers with $0 < p < q$. [*Hint:* By Abel's limit theorem the sum is

$$\lim_{x \to 1-} \sum_{n \geq 1} \left(\frac{1}{n} - \frac{1}{n+p/q} \right) x^{p+nq}.$$

Use Eq. (13) to express this power series in such a way that the limit can be evaluated.]

20. [*M21*] For what coefficients c_{mk} is $\sum_{n \geq 0} n^m z^n = \sum_{k=0}^{m} c_{mk} z^k / (1-z)^{k+1}$?

21. [*HM30*] Set up the generating function for the sequence $\langle n! \rangle$ and study properties of this function.

22. [*M21*] Find a generating function $G(z)$ for which

$$[z^n] G(z) = \sum_{k_0 + 2k_1 + 4k_2 + 8k_3 + \cdots = n} \binom{r}{k_0} \binom{r}{k_1} \binom{r}{k_2} \binom{r}{k_3} \cdots.$$

23. [*M33*] (L. Carlitz.) (a) Prove that for all integers $m \geq 1$ there are polynomials $f_m(z_1, \ldots, z_m)$ and $g_m(z_1, \ldots, z_m)$ such that the formula

$$\sum_{k_1, \ldots, k_m \geq 0} \binom{r}{n - k_1} \binom{k_1}{n - k_2} \cdots \binom{k_{m-1}}{n - k_m} z_1^{k_1} \ldots z_m^{k_m}$$
$$= f_m(z_1, \ldots, z_m)^{n-r} g_m(z_1, \ldots, z_m)^r$$

is an identity for all integers $n \geq r \geq 0$.

(b) Generalizing exercise 15, find a closed form for the sum

$$S_n(z_1, \ldots, z_m) = \sum_{k_1, \ldots, k_m \geq 0} \binom{k_1}{n - k_2} \binom{k_2}{n - k_3} \cdots \binom{k_m}{n - k_1} z_1^{k_1} \ldots z_m^{k_m}$$

in terms of the functions f_m and g_m in part (a).

(c) Find a simple expression for $S_n(z_1, \ldots, z_m)$ when $z_1 = \cdots = z_m = z$.

24. [*M22*] Prove that, if $G(z)$ is any generating function, we have

$$\sum_k \binom{m}{k} [z^{n-k}] G(z)^k = [z^n] (1 + zG(z))^m.$$

Evaluate both sides of this identity when $G(z)$ is (a) $1/(1 - z)$; (b) $(e^z - 1)/z$.

▶ **25.** [*M23*] Evaluate the sum $\sum_k \binom{n}{k} \binom{2n-2k}{n-k} (-2)^k$ by simplifying the equivalent formula $\sum_k [w^k] (1 - 2w)^n [z^{n-k}] (1 + z)^{2n-2k}$.

26. [*M40*] Explore a generalization of the notation (31) according to which we might write, for example, $[z^2 - 2z^5] G(z) = a_2 - 2a_5$ when $G(z)$ is given by (1).

1.2.10. Analysis of an Algorithm

Let us now apply some of the techniques of the preceding sections to the study of a typical algorithm.

Algorithm M (*Find the maximum*). Given n elements $X[1], X[2], \ldots, X[n]$, we will find m and j such that $m = X[j] = \max_{1 \leq i \leq n} X[i]$, where j is the largest index that satisfies this relation.

M1. [Initialize.] Set $j \leftarrow n$, $k \leftarrow n - 1$, $m \leftarrow X[n]$. (During this algorithm we will have $m = X[j] = \max_{k < i \leq n} X[i]$.)

M2. [All tested?] If $k = 0$, the algorithm terminates.

M3. [Compare.] If $X[k] \leq m$, go to M5.

M4. [Change m.] Set $j \leftarrow k$, $m \leftarrow X[k]$. (This value of m is a new current maximum.)

M5. [Decrease k.] Decrease k by one and return to M2. ▮

This rather obvious algorithm may seem so trivial that we shouldn't bother to analyze it in detail; but it actually makes a good demonstration of the way in which more complicated algorithms may be studied. Analysis of algorithms is quite important in computer programming, because there are usually several algorithms available for a particular application and we would like to know which is best.

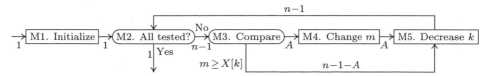

Fig. 9. Algorithm M. Labels on the arrows indicate the number of times each path is taken. Note that "Kirchhoff's first law" must be satisfied: The amount of flow into each node must equal the amount of flow going out.

Algorithm M requires a fixed amount of storage, so we will analyze only the time required to perform it. To do this, we will count the number of times each step is executed (see Fig. 9):

Step number	Number of times
M1	1
M2	n
M3	$n - 1$
M4	A
M5	$n - 1$

Knowing the number of times each step is executed gives us the information necessary to determine the running time on a particular computer.

In the table above we know everything except the quantity A, which is the number of times we must change the value of the current maximum. To complete the analysis, we shall study this interesting quantity A.

The analysis usually consists of finding the *minimum* value of A (for optimistic people), the *maximum* value of A (for pessimistic people), the *average* value of A (for probabilistic people), and the *standard deviation* of A (a quantitative indication of how close to the average we may expect the value to be).

The *minimum* value of A is zero; this happens if

$$X[n] = \max_{1 \leq k \leq n} X[k].$$

The *maximum* value is $n - 1$; this happens in case

$$X[1] > X[2] > \cdots > X[n].$$

Thus the average value lies between 0 and $n - 1$. Is it $\frac{1}{2}n$? Is it $\sqrt{n}$? To answer this question we need to define what we mean by the average; and to define the average properly, we must make some assumptions about the characteristics of the input data $X[1], X[2], \ldots, X[n]$. *We will assume that the $X[k]$ are distinct values, and that each of the $n!$ permutations of these values is equally likely.* (This is a reasonable assumption to make in most situations, but the analysis can be carried out under other assumptions, as shown in the exercises at the end of this section.)

The performance of Algorithm M does not depend on the precise values of the $X[k]$; only the relative order is involved. For example, if $n = 3$ we are assuming that each of the following six possibilities is equally probable:

Situation	Value of A		Situation	Value of A
$X[1] < X[2] < X[3]$	0		$X[2] < X[3] < X[1]$	1
$X[1] < X[3] < X[2]$	1		$X[3] < X[1] < X[2]$	1
$X[2] < X[1] < X[3]$	0		$X[3] < X[2] < X[1]$	2

The average value of A when $n = 3$ comes to $(0+1+0+1+1+2)/6 = 5/6$.

It is clear that we may take $X[1], X[2], \ldots, X[n]$ to be the numbers $1, 2, \ldots, n$ in some order; under our assumption we regard each of the $n!$ permutations as equally likely. The *probability* that A has the value k will be

$$p_{nk} = (\text{number of permutations of } n \text{ objects for which } A = k)/n!. \qquad (1)$$

For example, from our table above, $p_{30} = \frac{1}{3}$, $p_{31} = \frac{1}{2}$, $p_{32} = \frac{1}{6}$.

The *average* ("mean" or "expected") value is defined, as usual, to be

$$A_n = \sum_k k p_{nk}. \qquad (2)$$

The *variance* V_n is defined to be the average value of $(A - A_n)^2$; we have therefore

$$V_n = \sum_k (k - A_n)^2 p_{nk} = \sum_k k^2 p_{nk} - 2 A_n \sum_k k p_{nk} + A_n^2 \sum_k p_{nk}$$

$$= \sum_k k^2 p_{nk} - 2 A_n A_n + A_n^2 = \sum_k k^2 p_{nk} - A_n^2. \qquad (3)$$

Finally, the *standard deviation* σ_n is defined to be $\sqrt{V_n}$.

The significance of σ_n can perhaps best be understood by noting that, for all $r \geq 1$, the probability that A fails to lie within $r\sigma_n$ of its average value is less than $1/r^2$. For example, $|A - A_n| > 2\sigma_n$ with probability $< 1/4$. (*Proof:* Let p be the stated probability. Then if $p > 0$, the average value of $(A - A_n)^2$ is more than $p \cdot (r\sigma_n)^2 + (1 - p) \cdot 0$; that is, $V_n > pr^2 V_n$.) This is usually called *Chebyshev's inequality*, although it was actually discovered first by J. Bienaymé [*Comptes Rendus Acad. Sci.* **37** (Paris, 1853), 320–321].

We can determine the behavior of A by determining the probabilities p_{nk}. It is not hard to do this inductively: By Eq. (1) we want to count the number of permutations on n elements that have $A = k$. Let this number be $P_{nk} = n! \, p_{nk}$.

Consider the permutations $x_1 x_2 \ldots x_n$ on $\{1, 2, \ldots, n\}$, as in Section 1.2.5. If $x_1 = n$, the value of A is *one higher* than the value obtained on $x_2 \ldots x_n$; if $x_1 \neq n$, the value of A is *exactly the same* as its value on $x_2 \ldots x_n$. Therefore we find that $P_{nk} = P_{(n-1)(k-1)} + (n-1)P_{(n-1)k}$, or equivalently

$$p_{nk} = \frac{1}{n} P_{(n-1)(k-1)} + \frac{n-1}{n} P_{(n-1)k}. \qquad (4)$$

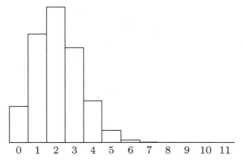

0 1 2 3 4 5 6 7 8 9 10 11

Fig. 10. Probability distribution for step M4, when $n = 12$. The mean is $58301/27720$, or approximately 2.10. The variance is approximately 1.54.

This equation will determine p_{nk} if we provide the initial conditions

$$p_{1k} = \delta_{0k}; \qquad p_{nk} = 0 \quad \text{if } k < 0. \tag{5}$$

We can now get information about the quantities p_{nk} by using generating functions. Let

$$G_n(z) = p_{n0} + p_{n1}z + \cdots = \sum_k p_{nk} z^k. \tag{6}$$

We know that $A \leq n - 1$, so $p_{nk} = 0$ for large values of k; thus $G_n(z)$ is actually a polynomial, even though an infinite sum has been specified for convenience.

From Eq. (5) we have $G_1(z) = 1$; and from Eq. (4) we have

$$G_n(z) = \frac{z}{n} G'_{n-1}(z) + \frac{n-1}{n} G_{n-1}(z) = \frac{z+n-1}{n} G_{n-1}(z). \tag{7}$$

(The reader should study the relation between Eqs. (4) and (7) carefully.) We can now see that

$$G_n(z) = \frac{z+n-1}{n} G_{n-1}(z) = \frac{z+n-1}{n} \frac{z+n-2}{n-1} G_{n-2}(z) = \cdots$$

$$= \frac{1}{n!}(z+n-1)(z+n-2)\ldots(z+1)$$

$$= \frac{1}{z+n}\binom{z+n}{n}. \tag{8}$$

So $G_n(z)$ is essentially a binomial coefficient!

This function appears in the previous section, Eq. 1.2.9–(27), where we have

$$G_n(z) = \frac{1}{n!} \sum_k \begin{bmatrix} n \\ k \end{bmatrix} z^{k-1}.$$

Therefore p_{nk} can be expressed in terms of Stirling numbers:

$$p_{nk} = \begin{bmatrix} n \\ k+1 \end{bmatrix} \Big/ n!. \tag{9}$$

Figure 10 shows the approximate sizes of p_{nk} when $n = 12$.

Now all we must do is plug this value of p_{nk} into Eqs. (2) and (3) and we have the desired average value. But this is easier said than done. It is, in fact, unusual to be able to determine the probabilities p_{nk} explicitly; in most problems we will know the generating function $G_n(z)$, but we will not have any special knowledge about the actual probabilities. The important fact is that *we can determine the mean and variance easily from the generating function itself.*

To see this, let's suppose that we have a generating function whose coefficients represent probabilities:

$$G(z) = p_0 + p_1 z + p_2 z^2 + \cdots.$$

Here p_k is the probability that some random nonnegative integer has the value k. We wish to calculate the quantities

$$\operatorname{mean}(G) = \sum_k k p_k, \quad \operatorname{var}(G) = \sum_k k^2 p_k - \big(\operatorname{mean}(G)\big)^2. \qquad (10)$$

Using differentiation, it is not hard to discover how to do this. Note that

$$G(1) = 1, \qquad (11)$$

since $G(1) = p_0 + p_1 + p_2 + \cdots$ is the sum of all possible probabilities. Similarly, since $G'(z) = \sum_k k p_k z^{k-1}$, we have

$$\operatorname{mean}(G) = \sum_k k p_k = G'(1). \qquad (12)$$

Finally, we apply differentiation again and we obtain (see exercise 2)

$$\operatorname{var}(G) = G''(1) + G'(1) - G'(1)^2. \qquad (13)$$

Equations (12) and (13) give the desired expressions of the mean and variance in terms of the generating function.

In our case, we wish to calculate $G'_n(1) = A_n$. From Eq. (7) we have

$$G'_n(z) = \frac{1}{n} G_{n-1}(z) + \frac{z+n-1}{n} G'_{n-1}(z);$$

$$G'_n(1) = \frac{1}{n} + G'_{n-1}(1).$$

From the initial condition $G'_1(1) = 0$, we find therefore

$$A_n = G'_n(1) = H_n - 1. \qquad (14)$$

This is the desired average number of times step M4 is executed; it is approximately $\ln n$ when n is large. [*Note:* The rth moment of $A+1$, namely the quantity $\sum_k (k+1)^r p_{nk}$, is $[z^n](1-z)^{-1} \sum_k \left\{ {r \atop k} \right\} (\ln \frac{1}{1-z})^k$, and it has the approximate value $(\ln n)^r$; see P. B. M. Roes, *CACM* **9** (1966), 342. The distribution of A was first studied by F. G. Foster and A. Stuart, *J. Roy. Stat. Soc.* **B16** (1954), 1–22.]

We can proceed similarly to calculate the variance V_n. Before doing this, let us state an important simplification:

Theorem A. *Let G and H be two generating functions with $G(1) = H(1) = 1$. If the quantities $\mathrm{mean}(G)$ and $\mathrm{var}(G)$ are defined by Eqs. (12) and (13), we have*

$$\mathrm{mean}(GH) = \mathrm{mean}(G) + \mathrm{mean}(H); \qquad \mathrm{var}(GH) = \mathrm{var}(G) + \mathrm{var}(H). \quad (15)$$

We will prove this theorem later. It tells us that the mean and variance of a product of generating functions may be reduced to a sum. ∎

Letting $Q_n(z) = (z + n - 1)/n$, we have $Q'_n(1) = 1/n$, $Q''_n(1) = 0$; hence

$$\mathrm{mean}(Q_n) = \frac{1}{n}, \quad \mathrm{var}(Q_n) = \frac{1}{n} - \frac{1}{n^2}.$$

Finally, since $G_n(z) = \prod_{k=2}^{n} Q_k(z)$, it follows that

$$\mathrm{mean}(G_n) = \sum_{k=2}^{n} \mathrm{mean}(Q_k) = \sum_{k=2}^{n} \frac{1}{k} = H_n - 1;$$

$$\mathrm{var}(G_n) = \sum_{k=2}^{n} \mathrm{var}(Q_k) = \sum_{k=1}^{n} \left(\frac{1}{k} - \frac{1}{k^2} \right) = H_n - H_n^{(2)}.$$

Summing up, we have found the desired statistics related to quantity A:

$$A = \left(\min\; 0, \quad \mathrm{ave}\; H_n - 1, \quad \max\; n - 1, \quad \mathrm{dev}\; \sqrt{H_n - H_n^{(2)}} \right). \quad (16)$$

The notation used in Eq. (16) will be used to describe the statistical characteristics of other probabilistic quantities throughout this book.

We have completed the analysis of Algorithm M; the new feature that has appeared in this analysis is the introduction of probability theory. Elementary probability theory is sufficient for most of the applications in this book: The simple counting techniques and the definitions of mean, variance, and standard deviation already given will answer most of the questions we want to ask. More complicated algorithms will help us develop an ability to reason fluently about probabilities.

Let us consider some simple probability problems, to get a little more practice using these methods. In all probability the first question that comes to mind is a coin-tossing problem: Suppose we flip a coin n times and there is a probability p that heads turns up after any particular toss; what is the average number of heads that will occur? What is the standard deviation?

We will consider our coin to be biased; that is, we will not assume that $p = \frac{1}{2}$. This makes the problem more interesting, and, furthermore, every real coin is biased (or we could not tell one side from the other).

Proceeding as before, we let p_{nk} be the probability that k heads will occur, and let $G_n(z)$ be the corresponding generating function. We have clearly

$$p_{nk} = p\, p_{(n-1)(k-1)} + q\, p_{(n-1)k}, \qquad (17)$$

where $q = 1 - p$ is the probability that tails turns up. As before, we argue from Eq. (17) that $G_n(z) = (q + pz)G_{n-1}(z)$; and from the obvious initial condition

$G_0(z) = 1$ we have

$$G_n(z) = (q + pz)^n. \tag{18}$$

Hence, by Theorem A,

$$\text{mean}(G_n) = n\ \text{mean}(G_1) = pn;$$
$$\text{var}(G_n) = n\ \text{var}(G_1) = (p - p^2)n = pqn.$$

For the number of heads, we have therefore

$$(\text{min } 0, \quad \text{ave } pn, \quad \text{max } n, \quad \text{dev } \sqrt{pqn}). \tag{19}$$

Figure 11 shows the values of p_{nk} when $p = \frac{3}{5}$, $n = 12$. When the standard deviation is proportional to $\sqrt{n}$ and the difference between maximum and minimum is proportional to n, we may consider the situation "stable" about the average.

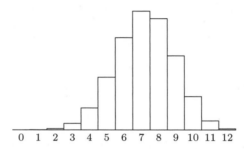

Fig. 11. Probability distribution for coin-tossing: 12 independent tosses with a chance of success equal to 3/5 at each toss.

Let us work one more simple problem. Suppose that in some process there is *equal* probability of obtaining the values $1, 2, \dots, n$. The generating function for this situation is

$$G(z) = \frac{1}{n}z + \frac{1}{n}z^2 + \cdots + \frac{1}{n}z^n = \frac{1}{n}\frac{z^{n+1} - z}{z - 1}. \tag{20}$$

We find after some rather laborious calculation that

$$G'(z) = \frac{nz^{n+1} - (n+1)z^n + 1}{n(z - 1)^2};$$

$$G''(z) = \frac{n(n-1)z^{n+1} - 2(n+1)(n-1)z^n + n(n+1)z^{n-1} - 2}{n(z - 1)^3}.$$

Now to calculate the mean and variance, we need to know $G'(1)$ and $G''(1)$; but the form in which we have expressed these equations reduces to $0/0$ when we substitute $z = 1$. This makes it necessary to find the limit as z approaches unity, and that is a nontrivial task.

Fortunately there is a much simpler way to proceed. By Taylor's theorem we have

$$G(1 + z) = G(1) + G'(1)z + \frac{G''(1)}{2!}z^2 + \cdots; \tag{21}$$

therefore we merely have to replace z by $1+z$ in (20) and read off the coefficients:

$$G(1+z) = \frac{1}{n}\frac{(1+z)^{n+1}-1-z}{z} = 1 + \frac{n+1}{2}z + \frac{(n+1)(n-1)}{6}z^2 + \cdots.$$

It follows that $G'(1) = \frac{1}{2}(n+1)$, $G''(1) = \frac{1}{3}(n+1)(n-1)$, and the statistics for the uniform distribution are

$$\left(\text{min } 1, \quad \text{ave } \frac{n+1}{2}, \quad \text{max } n, \quad \text{dev }\sqrt{\frac{(n+1)(n-1)}{12}}\right). \qquad (22)$$

In this case the deviation of approximately $0.289n$ gives us a recognizably *unstable* situation.

We conclude this section by proving Theorem A and relating our notions to classical probability theory. Suppose X is a random variable that takes on only nonnegative integer values, where $X = k$ with probability p_k. Then $G(z) = p_0 + p_1 z + p_2 z^2 + \cdots$ is called the *probability generating function* for X, and the quantity $G(e^{it}) = p_0 + p_1 e^{it} + p_2 e^{2it} + \cdots$ is conventionally called the *characteristic function* of this distribution. The distribution given by the product of two such generating functions is called the *convolution* of the two distributions, and it represents the sum of two independent random variables belonging to those respective distributions.

The mean or average value of a random quantity X is often called its *expected value*, and denoted by $\text{E}\,X$. The variance of X is then $\text{E}\,X^2 - (\text{E}\,X)^2$. Using this notation, the probability generating function for X is $G(z) = \text{E}\,z^X$, the expected value of z^X, in cases when X takes only nonnegative integer values. Similarly, if X is a statement that is either true or false, the probability that X is true is $\Pr(X) = \text{E}\,[X]$, using Iverson's convention $\bigl(\text{Eq. 1.2.3--}(16)\bigr)$.

The mean and variance are just two of the so-called *semi-invariants* or *cumulants* introduced by T. N. Thiele in 1889 [see A. Hald, *International Statistical Review* **68** (2000), 137–153]. The semi-invariants $\kappa_1, \kappa_2, \kappa_3, \ldots$ are defined by the rule

$$\frac{\kappa_1 t}{1!} + \frac{\kappa_2 t^2}{2!} + \frac{\kappa_3 t^3}{3!} + \cdots = \ln G(e^t). \qquad (23)$$

We have

$$\kappa_n = \frac{d^n}{dt^n}\ln G(e^t)\Big|_{t=0};$$

in particular,

$$\kappa_1 = \frac{e^t G'(e^t)}{G(e^t)}\Big|_{t=0} = G'(1)$$

because $G(1) = \sum_k p_k = 1$, and

$$\kappa_2 = \frac{e^{2t}G''(e^t)}{G(e^t)} + \frac{e^t G'(e^t)}{G(e^t)} - \frac{e^{2t}G'(e^t)^2}{G(e^t)^2}\Big|_{t=0} = G''(1) + G'(1) - G'(1)^2.$$

Since the semi-invariants are defined in terms of the *logarithm* of a generating function, Theorem A is obvious, and, in fact, it can be generalized to apply to all of the semi-invariants.

A *normal distribution* is one for which all semi-invariants are zero except possibly the mean and variance. In a normal distribution, we can improve significantly on Chebyshev's inequality: The probability that a normally distributed random value differs from the mean by less than the standard deviation is

$$\frac{1}{\sqrt{2\pi}} \int_{-1}^{+1} e^{-t^2/2}\, dt,$$

that is, about 68.268949213709% of the time. The difference is less than twice the standard deviation about 95.449973610364% of the time, and it is less than three times the standard deviation about 99.730020393674% of the time. The distributions specified by Eqs. (8) and (18) are *approximately* normal when n is large (see exercises 13 and 14).

We often need to know that a random nonnegative integer is unlikely to be much larger or smaller than its mean value. Two extremely simple yet powerful formulas, called the *tail inequalities*, provide convenient estimates of such probabilities. If X has the probability generating function $G(z)$, then

$$\Pr(X \le r) \le x^{-r} G(x) \qquad \text{for } 0 < x \le 1; \tag{24}$$
$$\Pr(X \ge r) \le x^{-r} G(x) \qquad \text{for } x \ge 1. \tag{25}$$

The proofs are easy: If $G(z) = p_0 + p_1 z + p_2 z^2 + \cdots$, we have

$$\Pr(X \le r) = p_0 + p_1 + \cdots + p_{\lfloor r \rfloor} \le x^{-r} p_0 + x^{1-r} p_1 + \cdots + x^{\lfloor r \rfloor - r} p_{\lfloor r \rfloor} \le x^{-r} G(x)$$

when $0 < x \le 1$; and

$$\Pr(X \ge r) = p_{\lceil r \rceil} + p_{\lceil r \rceil + 1} + \cdots \le x^{\lceil r \rceil - r} p_{\lceil r \rceil} + x^{\lceil r \rceil + 1 - r} p_{\lceil r \rceil + 1} + \cdots \le x^{-r} G(x)$$

when $x \ge 1$. By choosing values of x that minimize or approximately minimize the right-hand sides of (24) and (25), we often obtain upper bounds that are fairly close to the true tail probabilities on the left-hand sides.

Exercises 21–23 illustrate the tail inequalities in several important cases. These inequalities are special cases of a general principle pointed out by A. N. Kolmogorov in his book *Grundbegriffe der Wahrscheinlichkeitsrechnung* (1933): If $f(t) \ge s > 0$ for all $t \ge r$, and if $f(t) \ge 0$ for all t in the domain of the random variable X, then $\Pr(X \ge r) \le s^{-1} \operatorname{E} f(X)$ whenever $\operatorname{E} f(X)$ exists. We obtain (25) when $f(t) = x^t$ and $s = x^r$. [S. Bernstein had contributed key ideas in *Uchenye zapiski Nauchno-Issledovatel'skikh kafedr Ukrainy* **1** (1924), 38–48.]

EXERCISES

1. [*10*] Determine the value of p_{n0} from Eqs. (4) and (5) and interpret this result from the standpoint of Algorithm M.

2. [*HM16*] Derive Eq. (13) from Eq. (10).

3. [*M15*] What are the minimum, maximum, average, and standard deviation of the number of times step M4 is executed, if we are using Algorithm M to find the maximum of 1000 randomly ordered, distinct items? (Give your answer as decimal approximations to these quantities.)

4. [*M10*] Give an explicit, closed formula for the values of p_{nk} in the coin-tossing experiment, Eq. (17).

5. [*M13*] What are the mean and standard deviation of the distribution in Fig. 11?

6. [*HM27*] We've computed the mean and the variance of the important probability distributions (8), (18), (20). What is the *third* semi-invariant, κ_3, in each of those cases?

▶ **7.** [*M27*] In our analysis of Algorithm M, we assumed that all the $X[k]$ were distinct. Suppose, instead, that we make only the weaker assumption that $X[1], X[2], \ldots, X[n]$ contain precisely m distinct values; the values are otherwise random, subject to this constraint. What is the probability distribution of A in this case?

▶ **8.** [*M20*] Suppose that each $X[k]$ is taken at random from a set of M distinct elements, so that each of the M^n possible choices for $X[1], X[2], \ldots, X[n]$ is considered equally likely. What is the probability that all the $X[k]$ will be distinct?

9. [*M25*] Generalize the result of the preceding exercise to find a formula for the probability that exactly m distinct values occur among the X's. Express your answer in terms of Stirling numbers.

10. [*M20*] Combine the results of the preceding three exercises to obtain a formula for the probability that $A = k$ under the assumption that each X is selected at random from a set of M objects.

▶ **11.** [*M15*] What happens to the semi-invariants of a distribution if we change $G(z)$ to $F(z) = z^n G(z)$?

12. [*HM21*] When $G(z) = p_0 + p_1 z + p_2 z^2 + \cdots$ represents a probability distribution, the quantities $M_n = \sum_k k^n p_k$ and $m_n = \sum_k (k - M_1)^n p_k$ are called the "nth moment" and "nth central moment," respectively. Show that $G(e^t) = 1 + M_1 t + M_2 t^2/2! + \cdots$; then use Arbogast's formula (exercise 1.2.5–21) to show that

$$\kappa_n = \sum_{\substack{k_1, k_2, \ldots, k_n \geq 0 \\ k_1 + 2k_2 + \cdots = n}} \frac{(-1)^{k_1 + k_2 + \cdots + k_n - 1} n! \, (k_1 + k_2 + \cdots + k_n - 1)!}{k_1! \, 1!^{k_1} k_2! \, 2!^{k_2} \ldots k_n! \, n!^{k_n}} M_1^{k_1} M_2^{k_2} \ldots M_n^{k_n}.$$

In particular, $\kappa_1 = M_1$, $\kappa_2 = M_2 - M_1^2$ (as we already knew), $\kappa_3 = M_3 - 3M_1 M_2 + 2M_1^3$, and $\kappa_4 = M_4 - 4M_1 M_3 + 12 M_1^2 M_2 - 3 M_2^2 - 6 M_1^4$. What are the analogous expressions for κ_n in terms of the central moments m_2, m_3, $\ldots$, when $n \geq 2$?

13. [*HM38*] A sequence of probability generating functions $G_n(z)$ with means μ_n and deviations σ_n is said to *approach a normal distribution* if

$$\lim_{n \to \infty} e^{-it\mu_n/\sigma_n} G_n(e^{it/\sigma_n}) = e^{-t^2/2}$$

for all real values of t. Using $G_n(z)$ as given by Eq. (8), show that $G_n(z)$ approaches a normal distribution.

Note: "Approaching the normal distribution," as defined here, can be shown to be equivalent to the fact that

$$\lim_{n \to \infty} \Pr\left(\frac{X_n - \mu_n}{\sigma_n} \leq x \right) = \frac{1}{\sqrt{2\pi}} \int_{-\infty}^{x} e^{-t^2/2} \, dt,$$

where X_n is a random quantity whose probabilities are specified by $G_n(z)$. This is a special case of P. Lévy's important "continuity theorem," a basic result in mathematical probability theory. A proof of Lévy's theorem would take us rather far afield, although it is not extremely difficult [for example, see *Limit Distributions for Sums of Independent Random Variables* by B. V. Gnedenko and A. N. Kolmogorov, translated by K. L. Chung (Cambridge, Mass.: Addison–Wesley, 1954)].

14. [*HM30*] (A. de Moivre.) Using the conventions of the previous exercise, show that the binomial distribution $G_n(z)$ given by Eq. (18) approaches the normal distribution.

15. [*HM23*] When the probability that some quantity has the value k is $e^{-\mu}(\mu^k/k!)$, it is said to have the *Poisson distribution with mean* μ.

  a) What is the generating function for this set of probabilities?

  b) What are the values of the semi-invariants?

  c) Show that as $n \to \infty$ the Poisson distribution with mean np approaches the normal distribution in the sense of exercise 13.

16. [*M25*] Suppose X is a random variable whose values are a *mixture* of the probability distributions generated by $g_1(z)$, $g_2(z)$, ..., $g_r(z)$, in the sense that it uses $g_k(z)$ with probability p_k, where $p_1 + p_2 + \cdots + p_r = 1$. What is the generating function for X? Express the mean and variance of X in terms of the means and variances of g_1, g_2, ..., g_r.

▶ **17.** [*M27*] Let $f(z)$ and $g(z)$ be generating functions that represent probability distributions.

  a) Show that $h(z) = g(f(z))$ is also a generating function representing a probability distribution.

  b) Interpret the significance of $h(z)$ in terms of $f(z)$ and $g(z)$. (What is the *meaning* of the probabilities represented by the coefficients of $h(z)$?)

  c) Give formulas for the mean and variance of h in terms of those for f and g.

18. [*M28*] Suppose that the values taken on by $X[1]$, $X[2]$, ..., $X[n]$ in Algorithm M include exactly k_1 ones, k_2 twos, ..., k_n n's, arranged in random order. (Here

$$k_1 + k_2 + \cdots + k_n = n.$$

The assumption in the text is that $k_1 = k_2 = \cdots = k_n = 1$.) Show that in this generalized situation, the generating function (8) becomes

$$\left(\frac{k_n z}{k_n}\right) \left(\frac{k_{n-1} z + k_n}{k_{n-1} + k_n}\right) \left(\frac{k_{n-2} z + k_{n-1} + k_n}{k_{n-2} + k_{n-1} + k_n}\right) \cdots \left(\frac{k_1 z + k_2 + \cdots + k_n}{k_1 + k_2 + \cdots + k_n}\right) \Big/ z,$$

using the convention $0/0 = 1$.

19. [*M21*] If $a_k > a_j$ for $1 \le j < k$, we say that a_k is a *left-to-right maximum* of the sequence $a_1 a_2 \ldots a_n$. Suppose $a_1 a_2 \ldots a_n$ is a permutation of $\{1, 2, \ldots, n\}$, and let $b_1 b_2 \ldots b_n$ be the inverse permutation, so that $a_k = l$ if and only if $b_l = k$. Show that a_k is a left-to-right maximum of $a_1 a_2 \ldots a_n$ if and only if k is a right-to-left minimum of $b_1 b_2 \ldots b_n$.

▶ **20.** [*M22*] Suppose we want to calculate $\max\{|a_1 - b_1|, |a_2 - b_2|, \ldots, |a_n - b_n|\}$ when $b_1 \le b_2 \le \cdots \le b_n$. Show that it is sufficient to calculate $\max\{m_L, m_R\}$, where

$$m_L = \max\{a_k - b_k \mid a_k \text{ is a left-to-right maximum of } a_1 a_2 \ldots a_n\},$$
$$m_R = \max\{b_k - a_k \mid a_k \text{ is a right-to-left minimum of } a_1 a_2 \ldots a_n\}.$$

(Thus, if the a's are in random order, the number of k's for which a subtraction must be performed is only about $2 \ln n$.)

▶ **21.** [*HM21*] Let X be the number of heads that occur when a random coin is flipped n times, with generating function (18). Use (25) to prove that

$$\Pr(X \ge n(p + \epsilon)) \le e^{-\epsilon^2 n/(2q)}$$

when $q = 1 - p$ and $\epsilon \ge 0$. Also obtain a similar estimate for $\Pr(X \le n(p - \epsilon))$.

▶ **22.** [*HM22*] Suppose X has the generating function $(q_1 + p_1 z)(q_2 + p_2 z) \ldots (q_n + p_n z)$, where $p_k + q_k = 1$ and $0 \le p_k \le 1$ for $1 \le k \le n$. Let $\mu = E\,X = p_1 + p_2 + \cdots + p_n$.

a) Prove that

$$\Pr(X \le \mu r) \le (r^{-r} e^{r-1})^\mu, \quad \text{when } 0 < r \le 1;$$

$$\Pr(X \ge \mu r) \le (r^{-r} e^{r-1})^\mu, \quad \text{when } r \ge 1.$$

b) Express the right-hand sides of these estimates in convenient form when $r \approx 1$.

c) Show that if r is sufficiently large we have $\Pr(X \ge \mu r) \le 2^{-\mu r}$.

23. [*HM23*] Estimate the tail probabilities for a random variable that has the *negative binomial distribution* generated by $(q - pz)^{-n}$, where $q = p + 1$.

*1.2.11. Asymptotic Representations

We often want to know a quantity approximately, instead of exactly, in order to compare it to another. For example, Stirling's approximation to $n!$ is a useful representation of this type, when n is large, and we have also made use of the fact that $H_n \approx \ln n + \gamma$. The derivations of such *asymptotic formulas* generally involve higher mathematics, although in the following subsections we will use nothing more than elementary calculus to get the results we need.

*1.2.11.1. The O-notation.

Paul Bachmann introduced a very convenient notation for approximations in his book *Analytische Zahlentheorie* (1894). It is the O-notation, which allows us to replace the "$\approx$" sign by "=" and to quantify the degree of accuracy; for example,

$$H_n = \ln n + \gamma + O\left(\frac{1}{n}\right). \tag{1}$$

(Read, "H sub n equals the natural log of n plus Euler's constant [pronounced 'Oiler's constant'] plus big-oh of one over n.")

In general, the notation $O(f(n))$ may be used whenever $f(n)$ is a function of the positive integer n; it stands for a *quantity that is not explicitly known*, except that its magnitude isn't too large. Every appearance of $O(f(n))$ means precisely this: There are positive constants M and n_0 such that the number x_n represented by $O(f(n))$ satisfies the condition $|x_n| \le M\,|f(n)|$, for all integers $n \ge n_0$. We do not say *what* the constants M and n_0 are, and indeed those constants are usually different for each appearance of O.

For example, Eq. (1) means that $|H_n - \ln n - \gamma| \le M/n$ when $n \ge n_0$. Although the constants M and n_0 are not stated, we can be sure that the quantity $O(1/n)$ will be arbitrarily small if n is large enough.

Let's look at some more examples. We know that

$$1^2 + 2^2 + \cdots + n^2 = \tfrac{1}{3}n(n + \tfrac{1}{2})(n + 1) = \tfrac{1}{3}n^3 + \tfrac{1}{2}n^2 + \tfrac{1}{6}n;$$

so it follows that

$$1^2 + 2^2 + \cdots + n^2 = O(n^4), \tag{2}$$

$$1^2 + 2^2 + \cdots + n^2 = O(n^3), \tag{3}$$

$$1^2 + 2^2 + \cdots + n^2 = \tfrac{1}{3}n^3 + O(n^2). \tag{4}$$

Equation (2) is rather crude, but not incorrect; Eq. (3) is a stronger statement; and Eq. (4) is stronger yet. To justify these equations we shall prove that *if* $P(n) = a_0 + a_1 n + \cdots + a_m n^m$ *is any polynomial of degree m or less, then we have* $P(n) = O(n^m)$. This follows because

$$|P(n)| \leq |a_0| + |a_1| n + \cdots + |a_m| n^m = \left(|a_0|/n^m + |a_1|/n^{m-1} + \cdots + |a_m|\right) n^m$$
$$\leq \left(|a_0| + |a_1| + \cdots + |a_m|\right) n^m,$$

when $n \geq 1$. So we may take $M = |a_0| + |a_1| + \cdots + |a_m|$ and $n_0 = 1$. Or we could take, say, $M = |a_0|/2^m + |a_1|/2^{m-1} + \cdots + |a_m|$ and $n_0 = 2$.

The O-notation is a big help in approximation work, since it describes briefly a concept that occurs often and it suppresses detailed information that is usually irrelevant. Furthermore, it can be manipulated algebraically in familiar ways, although certain important differences need to be kept in mind. The most important consideration is the idea of *one-way equalities*: We write $\frac{1}{2}n^2 + n = O(n^2)$, but we *never* write $O(n^2) = \frac{1}{2}n^2 + n$. (Or else, since $\frac{1}{4}n^2 = O(n^2)$, we might come up with the absurd relation $\frac{1}{4}n^2 = \frac{1}{2}n^2 + n$.) We always use the convention that *the right-hand side of an equation does not give more information than the left-hand side*; the right-hand side is a "crudification" of the left.

This convention about the use of "=" may be stated more precisely as follows: Formulas that involve the $O\big(f(n)\big)$-notation may be regarded as sets of functions of n. The symbol $O\big(f(n)\big)$ stands for the set of all functions g of integers such that there exist constants M and n_0 with $|g(n)| \leq M\,|f(n)|$ for all integers $n \geq n_0$. If S and T are sets of functions, then $S + T$ denotes the set $\{g + h \mid g \in S \text{ and } h \in T\}$; we define $S + c$, $S - T$, $S \cdot T$, $\log S$, etc., in a similar way. If $\alpha(n)$ and $\beta(n)$ are formulas that involve the O-notation, then the notation $\alpha(n) = \beta(n)$ means that the set of functions denoted by $\alpha(n)$ is *contained in* the set denoted by $\beta(n)$.

Consequently we may perform most of the operations we are accustomed to doing with the "=" sign: If $\alpha(n) = \beta(n)$ and $\beta(n) = \gamma(n)$, then $\alpha(n) = \gamma(n)$. Also, if $\alpha(n) = \beta(n)$ and if $\delta(n)$ is a formula resulting from the substitution of $\beta(n)$ for some occurrence of $\alpha(n)$ in a formula $\gamma(n)$, then $\gamma(n) = \delta(n)$. These two statements imply, for example, that if $g(x_1, x_2, \ldots, x_m)$ is any real function whatever, and if $\alpha_k(n) = \beta_k(n)$ for $1 \leq k \leq m$, then $g\big(\alpha_1(n), \alpha_2(n), \ldots, \alpha_m(n)\big) = g\big(\beta_1(n), \beta_2(n), \ldots, \beta_m(n)\big)$.

Here are some of the simple operations we can do with the O-notation:

$$f(n) = O\big(f(n)\big), \tag{5}$$

$$c \cdot O\big(f(n)\big) = O\big(f(n)\big), \qquad \text{if } c \text{ is a constant}, \tag{6}$$

$$O\big(f(n)\big) + O\big(f(n)\big) = O\big(f(n)\big), \tag{7}$$

$$O\big(O(f(n))\big) = O\big(f(n)\big), \tag{8}$$

$$O\big(f(n)\big) O\big(g(n)\big) = O\big(f(n)g(n)\big), \tag{9}$$

$$O\big(f(n)g(n)\big) = f(n)O\big(g(n)\big), \quad \text{if } f(n) \text{ is never zero}. \tag{10}$$

The O-notation is also frequently used with functions of a complex variable z, in the neighborhood of $z = 0$. We write $O\bigl(f(z)\bigr)$ to stand for any quantity $g(z)$ such that $|g(z)| \le M\,|f(z)|$ whenever $|z| < r$. (As before, M and r are unspecified constants, although we could specify them if we wanted to.) The context of O-notation should always identify the variable that is involved and the range of that variable. When the variable is called n, we implicitly assume that $O\bigl(f(n)\bigr)$ refers to functions of a large integer n; when the variable is called z, we implicitly assume that $O\bigl(f(z)\bigr)$ refers to functions of a small complex number z.

Suppose that $g(z)$ is a function given by an infinite power series

$$g(z) = \sum_{k \ge 0} a_k z^k$$

that converges for $z = z_0$. Then the sum of absolute values $\sum_{k \ge 0} |a_k z^k|$ also converges whenever $|z| < |z_0|$. If $z_0 \ne 0$, we can therefore always write

$$g(z) = a_0 + a_1 z + \cdots + a_m z^m + O(z^{m+1}). \tag{11}$$

For we have $g(z) = a_0 + a_1 z + \cdots + a_m z^m + z^{m+1}(a_{m+1} + a_{m+2}z + \cdots)$; we need only show that the parenthesized quantity is bounded when $|z| \le r$, for some positive r, and it is easy to see that $|a_{m+1}| + |a_{m+2}|\,r + |a_{m+3}|\,r^2 + \cdots$ is an upper bound whenever $|z| \le r < |z_0|$.

For example, the generating functions listed in Section 1.2.9 give us many important asymptotic formulas valid when z is sufficiently small, including

$$e^z = 1 + z + \frac{1}{2!}z^2 + \cdots + \frac{1}{m!}z^m + O(z^{m+1}), \tag{12}$$

$$\ln(1+z) = z - \frac{1}{2}z^2 + \cdots + \frac{(-1)^{m+1}}{m}z^m + O(z^{m+1}), \tag{13}$$

$$(1+z)^\alpha = 1 + \alpha z + \binom{\alpha}{2}z^2 + \cdots + \binom{\alpha}{m}z^m + O(z^{m+1}), \tag{14}$$

$$\frac{1}{1-z}\ln\frac{1}{1-z} = z + H_2 z^2 + \cdots + H_m z^m + O(z^{m+1}), \tag{15}$$

for all nonnegative integers m. It is important to note that the hidden constants M and r implied by any particular O are related to each other. For example, the function e^z is obviously $O(1)$ when $|z| \le r$, for any fixed r, since $|e^z| \le e^{|z|}$; but there is no constant M such that $|e^z| \le M$ for all values of z. Therefore we need to use larger and larger bounds M as the range r increases.

Sometimes an asymptotic series is correct although it does not correspond to a convergent infinite series. For example, the basic formulas that express factorial powers in terms of ordinary powers,

$$n^{\bar{r}} = \sum_{k=0}^{m} \left[\begin{matrix} r \\ r-k \end{matrix} \right] n^{r-k} + O(n^{r-m-1}), \tag{16}$$

$$n^{\underline{r}} = \sum_{k=0}^{m} (-1)^k \left[\begin{matrix} r \\ r-k \end{matrix} \right] n^{r-k} + O(n^{r-m-1}), \tag{17}$$

are asymptotically valid for any real r and any fixed integer $m \geq 0$, yet the sum

$$\sum_{k=0}^{\infty} \begin{bmatrix} 1/2 \\ 1/2 - k \end{bmatrix} n^{1/2-k}$$

diverges for all n. (See exercise 12.) Of course, when r is a nonnegative integer, $n^{\bar{r}}$ and $n^{\underline{r}}$ are simply polynomials of degree r, and (17) is essentially the same as 1.2.6–(44). When r is a negative integer and $|n| > |r|$, the infinite sum $\sum_{k=0}^{\infty} \begin{bmatrix} r \\ r-k \end{bmatrix} n^{r-k}$ does converge to $n^{\bar{r}} = 1/(n-1)^{\underline{-r}}$; this sum can also be written in the more natural form $\sum_{k=0}^{\infty} \begin{Bmatrix} k-r \\ -r \end{Bmatrix} n^{r-k}$, using Eq. 1.2.6–(58).

Let us give one simple example of the concepts we have introduced so far. Consider the quantity $\sqrt[n]{n}$; as n gets large, the operation of taking an nth root tends to decrease the value, but it is not immediately obvious whether $\sqrt[n]{n}$ decreases or increases. It turns out that $\sqrt[n]{n}$ decreases to unity. Let us consider the slightly more complicated quantity $n(\sqrt[n]{n} - 1)$. Now $(\sqrt[n]{n} - 1)$ gets smaller as n gets bigger; what happens to $n(\sqrt[n]{n} - 1)$?

This problem is easily solved by applying the formulas above. We have

$$\sqrt[n]{n} = e^{\ln n / n} = 1 + (\ln n / n) + O\big((\log n / n)^2\big), \tag{18}$$

because $\log n / n \to 0$ as $n \to \infty$; see exercises 8 and 11. (Notice that we needn't specify the base of 'log' inside O-notation, where constants are ignored.) This equation proves our previous contention that $\sqrt[n]{n} \to 1$. It also tells us that

$$n(\sqrt[n]{n} - 1) = n\big(\ln n / n + O((\log n / n)^2)\big) = \ln n + O\big((\log n)^2/n\big). \tag{19}$$

In other words, $n(\sqrt[n]{n} - 1)$ is approximately equal to $\ln n$; the difference is $O\big((\log n)^2/n\big)$, which approaches zero as n approaches infinity.

People often abuse O-notation by assuming that it gives an exact order of growth; they use it as if it specifies a lower bound as well as an upper bound. For example, an algorithm to sort n numbers might be called inefficient "because its running time is $O(n^2)$." But a running time of $O(n^2)$ does not necessarily imply that the running time is not also $O(n)$. There's another notation, Big Omega, for lower bounds: The statement

$$g(n) = \Omega\big(f(n)\big) \tag{20}$$

means that there are positive constants L and n_0 such that

$$\big|g(n)\big| \geq L\big|f(n)\big| \quad \text{for all } n \geq n_0.$$

Using this notation we can correctly conclude that a sorting algorithm whose running time is $\Omega(n^2)$ will not be as efficient as one whose running time is $O(n \log n)$, if n is large enough. However, without knowing the constant factors implied by O and Ω, we cannot say anything about how large n must be before the $O(n \log n)$ method will begin to win.

Finally, if we want to state an exact order of growth without being precise about constant factors, we can use Big Theta:

$$g(n) = \Theta\big(f(n)\big) \quad \Longleftrightarrow \quad g(n) = O\big(f(n)\big) \text{ and } g(n) = \Omega\big(f(n)\big). \tag{21}$$

EXERCISES

1. [*HM01*] What is $\lim_{n\to\infty} O(n^{-1/3})$?

▶ **2.** [*M10*] Mr. B. C. Dull obtained astonishing results by using the "self-evident" formula $O(f(n)) - O(f(n)) = 0$. What was his mistake, and what should the right-hand side of his formula have been?

3. [*M15*] Multiply $(\ln n + \gamma + O(1/n))$ by $(n + O(\sqrt{n}))$, and express your answer in O-notation.

▶ **4.** [*M15*] Give an asymptotic expansion of $n(\sqrt[n]{a} - 1)$, if $a > 0$, to terms $O(1/n^3)$.

5. [*M20*] Prove or disprove: $O(f(n) + g(n)) = f(n) + O(g(n))$, if $f(n)$ and $g(n)$ are positive for all n. (Compare with (10).)

▶ **6.** [*M20*] What is wrong with the following argument? "Since $n = O(n)$, and $2n = O(n)$, ..., we have

$$\sum_{k=1}^{n} kn = \sum_{k=1}^{n} O(n) = O(n^2)."$$

7. [*HM15*] Prove that if m is any integer, there is no M such that $e^x \le Mx^m$ for arbitrarily large values of x.

8. [*HM20*] Prove that as $n \to \infty$, $(\ln n)^m/n \to 0$.

9. [*HM20*] Show that $e^{O(z^m)} = 1 + O(z^m)$, for all fixed $m \ge 0$.

10. [*HM22*] Make a statement similar to that in exercise 9 about $\ln(1 + O(z^m))$.

▶ **11.** [*M11*] Explain why Eq. (18) is true.

12. [*HM25*] Prove that $\left[\begin{smallmatrix}1/2\\1/2-k\end{smallmatrix}\right] n^{-k}$ does not approach zero as $k \to \infty$ for any integer n, using the fact that $\left[\begin{smallmatrix}1/2\\1/2-k\end{smallmatrix}\right] = (-\frac{1}{2})^k [z^k] (ze^z/(e^z - 1))^{1/2}$.

▶ **13.** [*M10*] Prove or disprove: $g(n) = \Omega(f(n))$ if and only if $f(n) = O(g(n))$.

***1.2.11.2. Euler's summation formula.** One of the most useful ways to obtain good approximations to a sum is an approach due to Leonhard Euler. His method approximates a finite sum by an integral, and gives us a means to get better and better approximations in many cases. [*Commentarii Academiæ Scientiarum Imperialis Petropolitanæ* **6** (1732), 68–69; **8** (1735), 9–22.]

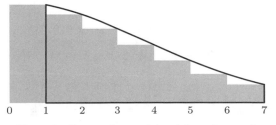

Fig. 12. Comparing a sum with an integral.

Figure 12 shows a comparison of $\int_1^n f(x)\,dx$ and $\sum_{k=1}^{n} f(k)$, when $n = 7$. Euler's strategy leads to a useful formula for the difference between these two quantities, assuming that $f(x)$ is a differentiable function.

For convenience we shall use the notation

$$\{x\} = x \bmod 1 = x - \lfloor x \rfloor. \tag{1}$$

Our derivation starts with the following identity:

$$\int_k^{k+1} \left(\{x\} - \tfrac{1}{2}\right) f'(x)\, dx = (x - k - \tfrac{1}{2}) f(x)\Big|_k^{k+1} - \int_k^{k+1} f(x)\, dx$$

$$= \tfrac{1}{2}\left(f(k+1) + f(k)\right) - \int_k^{k+1} f(x)\, dx. \tag{2}$$

(This follows from integration by parts.) Adding both sides of this equation for $1 \le k < n$, we find that

$$\int_1^n \left(\{x\} - \tfrac{1}{2}\right) f'(x)\, dx = \sum_{1 \le k < n} f(k) + \tfrac{1}{2}\left(f(n) - f(1)\right) - \int_1^n f(x)\, dx;$$

that is,

$$\sum_{1 \le k \le n} f(k) = \int_1^n f(x)\, dx + \tfrac{1}{2}\left(f(n) + f(1)\right) + \int_1^n B_1(\{x\}) f'(x)\, dx, \tag{3}$$

where $B_1(x)$ is the polynomial $x - \tfrac{1}{2}$. This is the desired connection between the sum and the integral.

The approximation can be carried further if we continue to integrate by parts. Before doing this, however, we shall discuss the *Bernoulli numbers*, which are the coefficients in the following infinite series:*

$$\frac{z}{1 - e^{-z}} = B_0 + B_1 z + \frac{B_2 z^2}{2!} + \cdots = \sum_{k \ge 0} \frac{B_k z^k}{k!}. \tag{4}$$

The coefficients of this series, which occur in a wide variety of problems, were introduced to European mathematicians in James Bernoulli's *Ars Conjectandi*, published posthumously in 1713. Curiously, they were also discovered at about the same time by Takakazu Seki in Japan — and first published in 1712, shortly after *his* death. [See *Takakazu Seki's Collected Works* (Osaka: 1974), 39–42.]

We have

$$B_0 = 1, \quad B_1 = \tfrac{1}{2}, \quad B_2 = \tfrac{1}{6}, \quad B_3 = 0, \quad B_4 = -\tfrac{1}{30}; \tag{5}$$

further values appear in Appendix A. Since

$$\frac{z}{1 - e^{-z}} - \frac{z}{2} = \frac{z}{2}\frac{1 + e^{-z}}{1 - e^{-z}} = -\frac{z}{2}\frac{1 + e^z}{1 - e^z}$$

is an even function, we see that

$$B_3 = B_5 = B_7 = B_9 = \cdots = 0. \tag{6}$$

---

* *Warning:* Many books, including earlier printings of The Art of Computer Programming, have used the formula $z/(e^z - 1)$ instead of $z/(1 - e^{-z})$ to define the Bernoulli numbers, thereby making $B_1 = -\tfrac{1}{2}$. But Peter Luschny published an online "Bernoulli Manifesto" in 2013, with compelling arguments that B_1 should be $+\tfrac{1}{2}$, as in the original works of Seki and Bernoulli.

If we multiply both sides of the defining equation (4) by $1 - e^{-z}$, and equate coefficients of equal powers of z, we obtain the formula

$$\sum_k \binom{n}{k}(-1)^{n-k} B_k = B_n - \delta_{n1}. \tag{7}$$

(See exercise 1.) We now define the *Bernoulli polynomial*

$$B_m(x) = \sum_k B_k \binom{m}{k}(x-1)^{m-k} = \sum_k \binom{m}{k}(-1)^k B_k x^{m-k}. \tag{8}$$

If $m = 1$, then $B_1(x) = B_0 x - B_1 = x - \frac{1}{2}$, corresponding to the polynomial used above in Eq. (3). If $m > 1$, we have $B_m(1) = B_m = B_m(0)$, by (6) and (7); in other words, $B_m(\{x\})$ has no discontinuities at integer points x.

The relevance of Bernoulli polynomials and Bernoulli numbers to our problem will soon be clear. We find by differentiating Eq. (8) that

$$B'_m(x) = \sum_k \binom{m}{k}(m-k)(-1)^k B_k x^{m-k-1}$$

$$= m \sum_k \binom{m-1}{k}(-1)^k B_k x^{m-1-k}$$

$$= m B_{m-1}(x); \tag{9}$$

and therefore when $m \geq 1$, we can integrate by parts as follows:

$$\frac{1}{m!} \int_1^n B_m(\{x\}) f^{(m)}(x)\, dx = \frac{1}{(m+1)!}\left(B_{m+1}(1) f^{(m)}(n) - B_{m+1}(0) f^{(m)}(1)\right)$$

$$- \frac{1}{(m+1)!} \int_1^n B_{m+1}(\{x\}) f^{(m+1)}(x)\, dx.$$

From this result we can continue to improve the approximation, Eq. (3), and we obtain Euler's general formula:

$$\sum_{k=1}^n f(k) = \int_1^n f(x)\, dx + f(1) + \frac{B_1}{1!}\left(f(n) - f(1)\right) + \frac{B_2}{2!}\left(f'(n) - f'(1)\right) + \cdots$$

$$+ \frac{B_m}{m!}\left(f^{(m-1)}(n) - f^{(m-1)}(1)\right) + R_{mn}$$

$$= \int_1^n f(x)\, dx + f(1) + \sum_{k=1}^m \frac{B_k}{k!}\left(f^{(k-1)}(n) - f^{(k-1)}(1)\right) + R_{mn}, \tag{10}$$

using (6), where

$$R_{mn} = \frac{(-1)^{m+1}}{m!} \int_1^n B_m(\{x\}) f^{(m)}(x)\, dx. \tag{11}$$

The remainder R_{mn} will be small when $B_m(\{x\}) f^{(m)}(x)/m!$ is very small, and in fact, one can show that

$$\left|\frac{B_m(\{x\})}{m!}\right| \leq \frac{|B_m|}{m!} < \frac{4}{(2\pi)^m} \tag{12}$$

when m is even. [See *CMath*, §9.5.] On the other hand, it usually turns out that the magnitude of $f^{(m)}(x)$ gets large as m increases, so there is a "best" value of m at which $|R_{mn}|$ has its least value when n is given.

It is known that, when m is even, there is a number θ such that

$$R_{mn} = \theta \frac{B_{m+2}}{(m+2)!}\left(f^{(m+1)}(n) - f^{(m+1)}(1)\right), \quad 0 < \theta < 1, \qquad (13)$$

provided that $f^{(m+2)}(x)\,f^{(m+4)}(x) > 0$ for $1 < x < n$. So in these circumstances the remainder has the same sign as, and is less in absolute value than, the first discarded term. A simpler version of this result is proved in exercise 3.

Let us now apply Euler's formula to some important examples. First, we set $f(x) = 1/x$. The derivatives are $f^{(m)}(x) = (-1)^m m!/x^{m+1}$, so we have, by Eq. (10),

$$H_n = \ln n + 1 + \sum_{k=1}^{m} \frac{B_k}{k}(-1)^{k-1}\left(\frac{1}{n^k} - 1\right) + R_{mn}. \qquad (14)$$

Now we find

$$\gamma = \lim_{n\to\infty}(H_n - \ln n) = 1 + \sum_{k=1}^{m} \frac{B_k}{k}(-1)^k + \lim_{n\to\infty} R_{mn}. \qquad (15)$$

The fact that $\lim_{n\to\infty} R_{mn} = -\int_1^\infty B_m(\{x\})\,dx/x^{m+1}$ exists proves that the constant γ does in fact exist. We can therefore put Eqs. (14) and (15) together, to deduce a general approximation for the harmonic numbers:

$$H_n = \ln n + \gamma + \sum_{k=1}^{m} \frac{(-1)^{k-1}B_k}{kn^k} + \int_n^\infty \frac{B_m(\{x\})\,dx}{x^{m+1}}$$

$$= \ln n + \gamma + \sum_{k=1}^{m-1} \frac{(-1)^{k-1}B_k}{kn^k} + O\left(\frac{1}{n^m}\right).$$

Replacing m by $m+1$ yields

$$H_n = \ln n + \gamma + \sum_{k=1}^{m} \frac{(-1)^{k-1}B_k}{kn^k} + O\left(\frac{1}{n^{m+1}}\right). \qquad (16)$$

Furthermore, by Eq. (13) we see that the error is less than the first term discarded. As a particular case we have

$$H_n = \ln n + \gamma + \frac{1}{2n} - \frac{1}{12n^2} + \frac{1}{120n^4} - \epsilon, \quad 0 < \epsilon < \frac{B_6}{6n^6} = \frac{1}{252n^6}.$$

This is Eq. 1.2.7–(3). The Bernoulli numbers B_k for large k get very large (approximately $(-1)^{1+k/2}2\big(k!/(2\pi)^k\big)$ when k is even), so Eq. (16) cannot be extended to a convergent infinite series for any fixed value of n.

The same technique can be applied to deduce Stirling's approximation. This time we set $f(x) = \ln x$, and Eq. (10) yields

$$\ln n! = n \ln n - n + 1 + \tfrac{1}{2} \ln n + \sum_{1 < k \leq m} \frac{B_k (-1)^k}{k(k-1)} \left(\frac{1}{n^{k-1}} - 1 \right) + R_{mn}. \quad (17)$$

Proceeding as above, we find that the limit

$$\lim_{n \to \infty} \left(\ln n! - n \ln n + n - \tfrac{1}{2} \ln n \right) = 1 + \sum_{1 < k \leq m} \frac{B_k (-1)^{k+1}}{k(k-1)} + \lim_{n \to \infty} R_{mn}$$

exists; let it be called σ ("Stirling's constant") temporarily. We get Stirling's result

$$\ln n! = (n + \tfrac{1}{2}) \ln n - n + \sigma + \sum_{1 < k \leq m} \frac{B_k (-1)^k}{k(k-1)n^{k-1}} + O\left(\frac{1}{n^m} \right). \quad (18)$$

In particular, let $m = 5$; we have

$$\ln n! = (n + \tfrac{1}{2}) \ln n - n + \sigma + \frac{1}{12n} - \frac{1}{360n^3} + O\left(\frac{1}{n^5} \right).$$

Now we can take the exponential of both sides:

$$n! = e^\sigma \sqrt{n} \left(\frac{n}{e} \right)^n \exp\left(\frac{1}{12n} - \frac{1}{360n^3} + O\left(\frac{1}{n^5} \right) \right).$$

Using the fact that $e^\sigma = \sqrt{2\pi}$ (see exercise 5), and expanding the exponential, we get our final result:

$$n! = \sqrt{2\pi n} \left(\frac{n}{e} \right)^n \left(1 + \frac{1}{12n} + \frac{1}{288n^2} - \frac{139}{51840n^3} - \frac{571}{2488320n^4} + O\left(\frac{1}{n^5} \right) \right). \quad (19)$$

EXERCISES

1. [*M18*] Prove Eq. (7).

2. [*HM20*] Note that Eq. (9) follows from Eq. (8) for *any* sequence B_n, not only for the sequence defined by Eq. (4). Explain why the latter sequence is necessary for the validity of Eq. (10).

3. [*HM20*] Let $C_{mn} = (B_m/m!)(f^{(m-1)}(n) - f^{(m-1)}(1))$ be the mth correction term in Euler's summation formula. Assuming that $f^{(m)}(x)$ has a constant sign for all x in the range $1 \leq x \leq n$, prove that $|R_{mn}| \leq |C_{mn}|$ when $m = 2k > 0$; in other words, show that the remainder is not larger in absolute value than the last term computed.

▶ **4.** [*HM20*] (*Sums of powers.*) When $f(x) = x^m$, the high-order derivatives of f are all zero, so Euler's summation formula gives an *exact* value for the sum

$$S_m(n) = \sum_{k=0}^{n} k^m$$

in terms of Bernoulli numbers. (It was the study of $S_m(n)$ for $m = 1, 2, 3, \ldots$ that led Bernoulli and Seki to discover those numbers in the first place.) Express $S_m(n)$ in terms of Bernoulli *polynomials*. Check your answer for $m = 0$, 1, and 2. (Note that the desired sum is performed for $0 \leq k \leq n$ instead of $1 \leq k \leq n$; Euler's summation formula may be applied with 0 replacing 1 throughout.)

5. [*HM30*] Given that

$$n! = \kappa \sqrt{n} \left(\frac{n}{e}\right)^n \left(1 + O\left(\frac{1}{n}\right)\right),$$

show that $\kappa = \sqrt{2\pi}$ by using Wallis's product (exercise 1.2.5–18). [*Hint:* Consider $\binom{2n}{n}$ for large values of n.]

▶ **6.** [*HM30*] Show that Stirling's approximation holds for noninteger n as well:

$$\Gamma(x+1) = \sqrt{2\pi x} \left(\frac{x}{e}\right)^x \left(1 + O\left(\frac{1}{x}\right)\right), \qquad x \geq a > 0.$$

[*Hint:* Let $f(x) = \ln(x + c)$ in Euler's summation formula, and apply the definition of $\Gamma(x)$ given in Eq. 1.2.5–(15).]

▶ **7.** [*HM32*] What is the approximate value of $1^1 2^2 3^3 \ldots n^n$?

8. [*M23*] Find the asymptotic value of $\ln(an^2 + bn)!$ with absolute error $O(n^{-2})$. Use it to compute the asymptotic value of $\binom{cn^2}{n} / (c^n \binom{n^2}{n})$ with relative error $O(n^{-2})$, when c is a positive constant. Here *absolute error* ϵ means that (truth) = (approximation)$+\epsilon$; *relative error* ϵ means that (truth) = (approximation)$(1 + \epsilon)$.

▶ **9.** [*M25*] Find the asymptotic value of $\binom{2n}{n}$ with a relative error of $O(n^{-3})$, in two ways: (a) via Stirling's approximation; (b) via exercise 1.2.6–47 and Eq. 1.2.11.1–(16).

*1.2.11.3. Some asymptotic calculations. In this subsection we shall investigate the following three intriguing sums, in order to deduce their approximate values:

$$P(n) = 1 + \frac{n-1}{n} + \frac{n-2}{n} \frac{n-2}{n-1} + \cdots = \sum_{k=0}^{n} \frac{(n-k)^k (n-k)!}{n!}, \qquad (1)$$

$$Q(n) = 1 + \frac{n-1}{n} + \frac{n-1}{n} \frac{n-2}{n} + \cdots = \sum_{k=1}^{n} \frac{n!}{(n-k)! \, n^k}, \qquad (2)$$

$$R(n) = 1 + \frac{n}{n+1} + \frac{n}{n+1} \frac{n}{n+2} + \cdots = \sum_{k \geq 0} \frac{n! \, n^k}{(n+k)!}. \qquad (3)$$

These functions, which are similar in appearance yet intrinsically different, arise in several algorithms that we shall encounter later. Both $P(n)$ and $Q(n)$ are finite sums, while $R(n)$ is an infinite sum. It seems that when n is large, all three sums will be nearly equal, although it is not obvious what the approximate value of *any* of them will be. Our quest for approximate values of these functions will lead us through a number of very instructive side results. (You may wish to stop reading temporarily and try your hand at studying these functions before going on to see how they are attacked here.)

First, we observe an important connection between $Q(n)$ and $R(n)$:

$$Q(n) + R(n) = \frac{n!}{n^n} \left(\left(1 + n + \cdots + \frac{n^{n-1}}{(n-1)!}\right) + \left(\frac{n^n}{n!} + \frac{n^{n+1}}{(n+1)!} + \cdots\right) \right)$$

$$= \frac{n! \, e^n}{n^n}. \qquad (4)$$

Stirling's formula tells us that $n!\,e^n/n^n$ is approximately $\sqrt{2\pi n}$, so we can guess that $Q(n)$ and $R(n)$ will each turn out to be roughly equal to $\sqrt{\pi n/2}$.

To get any further we must consider the partial sums of the series for e^n. By using Taylor's formula with remainder,

$$f(x) = f(0) + f'(0)x + \cdots + \frac{f^{(n)}(0)x^n}{n!} + \int_0^x \frac{t^n}{n!} f^{(n+1)}(x-t)\,dt, \qquad (5)$$

we are soon led to an important function known as the *incomplete gamma function:*

$$\gamma(a, x) = \int_0^x e^{-t} t^{a-1}\,dt. \qquad (6)$$

We shall assume that $a > 0$. By exercise 1.2.5–20, we have $\gamma(a, \infty) = \Gamma(a)$; this accounts for the name "incomplete gamma function." It has two useful series expansions in powers of x (see exercises 2 and 3):

$$\gamma(a, x) = \frac{x^a}{a} - \frac{x^{a+1}}{a+1} + \frac{x^{a+2}}{2!\,(a+2)} - \cdots = \sum_{k \geq 0} \frac{(-1)^k x^{k+a}}{k!\,(k+a)}, \qquad (7)$$

$$e^x \gamma(a, x) = \frac{x^a}{a} + \frac{x^{a+1}}{a(a+1)} + \frac{x^{a+2}}{a(a+1)(a+2)} + \cdots = \sum_{k \geq 0} \frac{x^{k+a}}{a(a+1)\dots(a+k)}. \qquad (8)$$

From the second formula we see the connection with $R(n)$:

$$R(n) = \frac{n!\,e^n}{n^n}\left(\frac{\gamma(n, n)}{(n-1)!}\right). \qquad (9)$$

This equation has purposely been written in a more complicated form than necessary, since $\gamma(n, n)$ is a fraction of $\gamma(n, \infty) = \Gamma(n) = (n-1)!$, and $n!\,e^n/n^n$ is the quantity in (4).

The problem boils down to getting good estimates of $\gamma(n, n)/(n-1)!$. We shall now determine the approximate value of $\gamma(x+1, x+y)/\Gamma(x+1)$, when y is fixed and x is large. The methods to be used here are more important than the results, so the reader should study the following derivation carefully.

By definition, we have

$$\frac{\gamma(x+1, x+y)}{\Gamma(x+1)} = \frac{1}{\Gamma(x+1)} \int_0^{x+y} e^{-t} t^x\,dt$$

$$= 1 - \frac{1}{\Gamma(x+1)} \int_x^\infty e^{-t} t^x\,dt + \frac{1}{\Gamma(x+1)} \int_x^{x+y} e^{-t} t^x\,dt. \qquad (10)$$

Let us set

$$I_1 = \int_x^\infty e^{-t} t^x\,dt,$$

$$I_2 = \int_x^{x+y} e^{-t} t^x\,dt,$$

and consider each integral in turn.

Estimate of I_1: We convert I_1 to an integral from 0 to infinity by substituting $t = x(1 + u)$; we further substitute $v = u - \ln(1 + u)$, $dv = \left(1 - 1/(1 + u)\right) du$, which is legitimate since v is a monotone function of u:

$$I_1 = e^{-x} x^x \int_0^\infty x e^{-xu} (1 + u)^x \, du = e^{-x} x^x \int_0^\infty x e^{-xv} \left(1 + \frac{1}{u}\right) dv. \qquad (11)$$

In the last integral we will replace $1 + 1/u$ by a power series in v. We have

$$v = \tfrac{1}{2} u^2 - \tfrac{1}{3} u^3 + \tfrac{1}{4} u^4 - \tfrac{1}{5} u^5 + \cdots = (u^2/2)(1 - \tfrac{2}{3} u + \tfrac{1}{2} u^2 - \tfrac{2}{5} u^3 + \cdots).$$

Setting $w = \sqrt{2v}$, we have therefore

$$w = u(1 - \tfrac{2}{3} u + \tfrac{1}{2} u^2 - \tfrac{2}{5} u^3 + \cdots)^{1/2} = u - \tfrac{1}{3} u^2 + \tfrac{7}{36} u^3 - \tfrac{73}{540} u^4 + \tfrac{1331}{12960} u^5 + O(u^6).$$

(This expansion may be obtained by the binomial theorem; efficient methods for performing such transformations, and for doing the other power series manipulations needed below, are considered in Section 4.7.) We can now solve for u as a power series in w:

$$u = w + \frac{1}{3} w^2 + \frac{1}{36} w^3 - \frac{1}{270} w^4 + \frac{1}{4320} w^5 + O(w^6);$$

$$1 + \frac{1}{u} = 1 + \frac{1}{w} - \frac{1}{3} + \frac{1}{12} w - \frac{2}{135} w^2 + \frac{1}{864} w^3 + O(w^4)$$

$$= \frac{1}{\sqrt{2}} v^{-1/2} + \frac{2}{3} + \frac{\sqrt{2}}{12} v^{1/2} - \frac{4}{135} v + \frac{\sqrt{2}}{432} v^{3/2} + O(v^2). \qquad (12)$$

In all of these formulas, the O-notation refers to small values of the argument, that is, $|u| \le r$, $|v| \le r$, $|w| \le r$ for sufficiently small positive r. Is this good enough? The substitution of $1 + 1/u$ in terms of v in Eq. (11) is supposed to be valid for $0 \le v < \infty$, not only for $|v| \le r$. Fortunately, it turns out that the value of the integral from 0 to ∞ depends almost entirely on the values of the integrand near zero. In fact, we have (see exercise 4)

$$\int_r^\infty x e^{-xv} \left(1 + \frac{1}{u}\right) dv = O(e^{-rx}) \qquad (13)$$

for any fixed $r > 0$ and for large x. We are interested in an approximation up to terms $O(x^{-m})$, and since $O\left((1/e^r)^x\right)$ is much smaller than $O(x^{-m})$ for any positive r and m, we need integrate only from 0 to r, for any fixed positive r. We therefore take r to be small enough so that all the power series manipulations done above are justified (see Eqs. 1.2.11.1–(11) and 1.2.11.1–(13)).

Now

$$\int_0^\infty x e^{-xv} v^\alpha \, dv = \frac{1}{x^\alpha} \int_0^\infty e^{-q} q^\alpha \, dq = \frac{1}{x^\alpha} \Gamma(\alpha + 1), \quad \text{if } \alpha > -1; \qquad (14)$$

so by plugging the series (12) into the integral (11) we have finally

$$I_1 = e^{-x} x^x \left(\sqrt{\frac{\pi}{2}} x^{1/2} + \frac{2}{3} + \frac{\sqrt{2\pi}}{24} x^{-1/2} - \frac{4}{135} x^{-1} + \frac{\sqrt{2\pi}}{576} x^{-3/2} + O(x^{-2}) \right). \qquad (15)$$

Estimate of I_2: In the integral I_2, we substitute $t = u + x$ and obtain

$$I_2 = e^{-x}x^x \int_0^y e^{-u}\left(1 + \frac{u}{x}\right)^x du. \tag{16}$$

Now

$$e^{-u}\left(1 + \frac{u}{x}\right)^x = \exp\left(-u + x\ln\left(1 + \frac{u}{x}\right)\right) = \exp\left(\frac{-u^2}{2x} + \frac{u^3}{3x^2} + O(x^{-3})\right)$$

$$= 1 - \frac{u^2}{2x} + \frac{u^4}{8x^2} + \frac{u^3}{3x^2} + O(x^{-3})$$

for $0 \le u \le y$ and large x. Therefore we find that

$$I_2 = e^{-x}x^x\left(y - \frac{y^3}{6}x^{-1} + \left(\frac{y^4}{12} + \frac{y^5}{40}\right)x^{-2} + O(x^{-3})\right). \tag{17}$$

Finally, we analyze the coefficient $e^{-x}x^x/\Gamma(x+1)$ that appears when we multiply Eqs. (15) and (17) by the factor $1/\Gamma(x+1)$ in (10). By Stirling's approximation, which is valid for the gamma function by exercise 1.2.11.2–6, we have

$$\frac{e^{-x}x^x}{\Gamma(x+1)} = \frac{e^{-1/12x+O(x^{-3})}}{\sqrt{2\pi x}}$$

$$= \frac{1}{\sqrt{2\pi}}x^{-1/2} - \frac{1}{12\sqrt{2\pi}}x^{-3/2} + \frac{1}{288\sqrt{2\pi}}x^{-5/2} + O(x^{-7/2}). \tag{18}$$

And now the grand summing up: Equations (10), (15), (17), and (18) yield

Theorem A. *For large values of x, and fixed y,*

$$\frac{\gamma(x+1, x+y)}{\Gamma(x+1)} = \frac{1}{2} + \left(\frac{y - 2/3}{\sqrt{2\pi}}\right)x^{-1/2} + \frac{1}{\sqrt{2\pi}}\left(\frac{23}{270} - \frac{y}{12} - \frac{y^3}{6}\right)x^{-3/2}$$

$$+ O(x^{-5/2}). \quad \blacksquare \tag{19}$$

The method we have used shows how this approximation could be extended to further powers of x as far as we please.

Theorem A can be used to obtain the approximate values of $R(n)$ and $Q(n)$, by using Eqs. (4) and (9), but we shall defer that calculation until later. Let us now turn to $P(n)$, for which somewhat different methods seem to be required. We have

$$P(n) = \sum_{k=0}^{n} \frac{k^{n-k}k!}{n!} = \frac{\sqrt{2\pi}}{n!}\sum_{k=0}^{n} k^{n+1/2}e^{-k}\left(1 + \frac{1}{12k} + O(k^{-2})\right). \tag{20}$$

Thus to get the values of $P(n)$, we must study sums of the form

$$\sum_{k=0}^{n} k^{n+1/2}e^{-k}.$$

Let $f(x) = x^{n+1/2}e^{-x}$ and apply Euler's summation formula:

$$\sum_{k=0}^{n} k^{n+1/2}e^{-k} = \int_{0}^{n} x^{n+1/2}e^{-x}\,dx + \tfrac{1}{2}n^{n+1/2}e^{-n} + \tfrac{1}{24}n^{n-1/2}e^{-n} - R. \quad (21)$$

A crude analysis of the remainder (see exercise 5) shows that $R = O(n^n e^{-n})$; and since the integral is an incomplete gamma function, we have

$$\sum_{k=0}^{n} k^{n+1/2}e^{-k} = \gamma(n + \tfrac{3}{2},\, n) + \tfrac{1}{2}n^{n+1/2}e^{-n} + O(n^n e^{-n}). \quad (22)$$

Our formula, Eq. (20), also requires an estimate of the sum

$$\sum_{k=0}^{n} k^{n-1/2}e^{-k} = \sum_{0 \le k \le n-1} k^{(n-1)+1/2}e^{-k} + n^{n-1/2}e^{-n},$$

and this can also be obtained by Eq. (22).

We now have enough formulas at our disposal to determine the approximate values of $P(n)$, $Q(n)$, and $R(n)$, and it is only a matter of substituting and multiplying, etc. In this process we shall have occasion to use the expansion

$$(n + \alpha)^{n+\beta} = n^{n+\beta}e^{\alpha}\left(1 + \alpha\left(\beta - \frac{\alpha}{2}\right)\frac{1}{n} + O(n^{-2})\right), \quad (23)$$

which is proved in exercise 6. The method of (21) yields only the first two terms in the asymptotic series for $P(n)$; further terms can be obtained by using the instructive technique described in exercise 14.

The result of all these calculations gives us the desired asymptotic formulas:

$$P(n) = \sqrt{\frac{\pi n}{2}} - \frac{2}{3} + \frac{11}{24}\sqrt{\frac{\pi}{2n}} + \frac{4}{135n} - \frac{71}{1152}\sqrt{\frac{\pi}{2n^3}} + O(n^{-2}), \quad (24)$$

$$Q(n) = \sqrt{\frac{\pi n}{2}} - \frac{1}{3} + \frac{1}{12}\sqrt{\frac{\pi}{2n}} - \frac{4}{135n} + \frac{1}{288}\sqrt{\frac{\pi}{2n^3}} + O(n^{-2}), \quad (25)$$

$$R(n) = \sqrt{\frac{\pi n}{2}} + \frac{1}{3} + \frac{1}{12}\sqrt{\frac{\pi}{2n}} + \frac{4}{135n} + \frac{1}{288}\sqrt{\frac{\pi}{2n^3}} + O(n^{-2}). \quad (26)$$

The functions studied here have received only light treatment in the published literature. The first term $\sqrt{\pi n/2}$ in the expansion of $P(n)$ was given by H. B. Demuth [Ph.D. thesis (Stanford University, October 1956), 67–68]. Using this result, a table of $P(n)$ for $n \le 2000$, and a good slide rule, the author proceeded in 1963 to deduce the empirical estimate $P(n) \approx \sqrt{\pi n/2} - 0.6667 + 0.575/\sqrt{n}$. It was natural to conjecture that 0.6667 was really an approximation to $2/3$, and that 0.575 would perhaps turn out to be an approximation to $\gamma = 0.57721\ldots$ (why not be optimistic?). Later, as this section was being written, the correct expansion of $P(n)$ was developed, and the conjecture $2/3$ was verified; for the other coefficient 0.575 we have not γ but $\frac{11}{24}\sqrt{\pi/2} \approx 0.5744$. This nicely confirms both the theory and the empirical estimates.

Formulas equivalent to the asymptotic values of $Q(n)$ and $R(n)$ were first determined by the brilliant self-taught Indian mathematician S. Ramanujan, who posed the problem of estimating $n!\,e^n/2n^n - Q(n)$ in *J. Indian Math. Soc.* **3** (1911), 128; **4** (1912), 151–152. In his answer to the problem, he gave the asymptotic series $\frac{1}{3} + \frac{4}{135}n^{-1} - \frac{8}{2835}n^{-2} - \frac{16}{8505}n^{-3} + \cdots$, which goes considerably beyond Eq. (25). His derivation was somewhat more elegant than the method described above; to estimate I_1, he substituted $t = x + u\sqrt{2x}$, and expressed the integrand as a sum of terms of the form $c_{jk}\int_0^\infty \exp(-u^2)u^j x^{-k/2}\,du$. The integral I_2 can be avoided completely, since $a\gamma(a, x) = x^a e^{-x} + \gamma(a+1, x)$ when $a > 0$; see (8). An even simpler approach to the asymptotics of $Q(n)$, perhaps the simplest possible, appears in exercise 20. The derivation we have used, which is instructive in spite of its unnecessary complications, is due to R. Furch [*Zeitschrift für Physik* **112** (1939), 92–95], who was primarily interested in the value of y that makes $\gamma(x+1, x+y) = \Gamma(x+1)/2$. The asymptotic properties of the incomplete gamma function were later extended to complex arguments by F. G. Tricomi [*Math. Zeitschrift* **53** (1950), 136–148]. See also N. M. Temme, *Math. Comp.* **29** (1975), 1109–1114; *SIAM J. Math. Anal.* **10** (1979), 757–766. H. W. Gould has listed references to several other investigations of $Q(n)$ in *AMM* **75** (1968), 1019–1021.

Our derivations of the asymptotic series for $P(n)$, $Q(n)$, and $R(n)$ use only simple techniques of elementary calculus; notice that we have used different methods for each function! Actually we could have solved all three problems using the techniques of exercise 14, which are explained further in Sections 5.1.4 and 5.2.2. That would have been more elegant but less instructive.

For additional information, interested readers should consult the beautiful book *Asymptotic Methods in Analysis* by N. G. de Bruijn (Amsterdam: North-Holland, 1958). See also the more recent survey by A. M. Odlyzko [*Handbook of Combinatorics* **2** (MIT Press, 1995), 1063–1229], which includes 65 detailed examples and an extensive bibliography.

EXERCISES

1. [*HM20*] Prove Eq. (5) by induction on n.

2. [*HM20*] Obtain Eq. (7) from Eq. (6).

3. [*M20*] Derive Eq. (8) from Eq. (7).

▸ **4.** [*HM10*] Prove Eq. (13).

5. [*HM24*] Show that R in Eq. (21) is $O(n^n e^{-n})$.

▸ **6.** [*HM20*] Prove Eq. (23).

▸ **7.** [*HM30*] In the evaluation of I_2, we had to consider $\int_0^y e^{-u}\left(1 + \dfrac{u}{x}\right)^x du$. Give an asymptotic representation of

$$\int_0^{yx^{1/4}} e^{-u}\left(1 + \frac{u}{x}\right)^x du$$

to terms of order $O(x^{-2})$, when y is fixed and x is large.

8. [*HM30*] If $f(x) = O(x^r)$ as $x \to \infty$ and $0 \le r < 1$, show that

$$\int_0^{f(x)} e^{-u} \left(1 + \frac{u}{x}\right)^x du = \int_0^{f(x)} \exp\left(\frac{-u^2}{2x} + \frac{u^3}{3x^2} - \cdots + \frac{(-1)^{m-1}u^m}{mx^{m-1}}\right) du + O(x^{-s})$$

if $m = \lceil (s + 2r)/(1 - r) \rceil$. [This proves in particular a result due to Tricomi: If $f(x) = O(\sqrt{x})$, then

$$\int_0^{f(x)} e^{-u} \left(1 + \frac{u}{x}\right)^x du = \sqrt{2x} \int_0^{f(x)/\sqrt{2x}} e^{-t^2} dt + O(1).]$$

▶ **9.** [*HM36*] What is the behavior of $\gamma(x + 1, px)/\Gamma(x + 1)$ for large x? (Here p is a real constant; and if $p < 0$, we assume that x is an integer, so that t^x is well defined for negative t.) Obtain at least two terms of the asymptotic expansion, before resorting to O-terms.

10. [*HM34*] Under the assumptions of the preceding problem, with $p \ne 1$, obtain the asymptotic expansion of $\gamma(x + 1, px + py/(p - 1)) - \gamma(x + 1, px)$, for fixed y, to terms of the same order as obtained in the previous exercise.

▶ **11.** [*HM35*] Let us generalize the functions $Q(n)$ and $R(n)$ by introducing a parameter x:

$$Q_x(n) = 1 + \frac{n-1}{n}x + \frac{n-1}{n}\frac{n-2}{n}x^2 + \cdots,$$

$$R_x(n) = 1 + \frac{n}{n+1}x + \frac{n}{n+1}\frac{n}{n+2}x^2 + \cdots.$$

Explore this situation and find asymptotic formulas when $x \ne 1$.

12. [*HM20*] The function $\int_0^x e^{-t^2/2} dt$ that appeared in connection with the normal distribution (see Section 1.2.10) can be expressed as a special case of the incomplete gamma function. Find values of a, b, and y such that $b\gamma(a, y)$ equals $\int_0^x e^{-t^2/2} dt$.

13. [*HM42*] (S. Ramanujan.) Prove that $R(n) - Q(n) = \frac{2}{3} + 8/(135(n + \theta(n)))$, where $\frac{2}{21} \le \theta(n) \le \frac{8}{45}$. (This implies the much weaker result $R(n + 1) - Q(n + 1) < R(n) - Q(n)$.)

▶ **14.** [*HM39*] (N. G. de Bruijn.) The purpose of this exercise is to find the asymptotic expansion of $\sum_{k=0}^n k^{n+\alpha} e^{-k}$ for fixed α, as $n \to \infty$.

a) Replacing k by $n-k$, show that the given sum equals $n^{n+\alpha}e^{-n} \sum_{k=0}^n e^{-k^2/2n} f(k, n)$, where

$$f(k, n) = \left(1 - \frac{k}{n}\right)^\alpha \exp\left(-\frac{k^3}{3n^2} - \frac{k^4}{4n^3} - \cdots\right).$$

b) Show that for all $m \ge 0$ and $\epsilon > 0$, the quantity $f(k, n)$ can be written in the form

$$\sum_{0 \le i \le j \le m} c_{ij} k^{2i+j} n^{-i-j} + O(n^{(m+1)(-1/2+3\epsilon)}), \quad \text{if } 0 \le k \le n^{1/2+\epsilon}.$$

c) Prove that as a consequence of (b), we have

$$\sum_{k=0}^n e^{-k^2/2n} f(k, n) = \sum_{0 \le i \le j \le m} c_{ij} n^{-i-j} \sum_{k \ge 0} k^{2i+j} e^{-k^2/2n} + O(n^{-m/2+\delta}),$$

for all $\delta > 0$. [*Hint:* The sums over the range $n^{1/2+\epsilon} < k < \infty$ are $O(n^{-r})$ for all r.]

d) Show that the asymptotic expansion of $\sum_{k\geq 0} k^t e^{-k^2/2n}$ for fixed $t \geq 0$ can be obtained by Euler's summation formula.

e) Finally therefore

$$\sum_{k=0}^{n} k^{n+\alpha} e^{-k} = n^{n+\alpha} e^{-n} \left(\sqrt{\frac{\pi n}{2}} - \frac{1}{6} - \alpha + \left(\frac{1}{12} + \frac{1}{2}\alpha + \frac{1}{2}\alpha^2 \right) \sqrt{\frac{\pi}{2n}} + O(n^{-1}) \right);$$

this computation can in principle be extended to $O(n^{-r})$ for any desired r.

15. [*HM20*] Show that the following integral is related to $Q(n)$:

$$\int_0^\infty \left(1 + \frac{z}{n} \right)^n e^{-z} \, dz.$$

16. [*M24*] Prove the identity

$$\sum_k (-1)^k \binom{n}{k} k^{n-1} Q(k) = (-1)^n (n-1)!, \quad \text{when } n > 0.$$

17. [*HM29*] (K. W. Miller.) Symmetry demands that we consider also a fourth series, which is to $P(n)$ as $R(n)$ is to $Q(n)$:

$$S(n) = 1 + \frac{n}{n+1} + \frac{n}{n+2}\frac{n+1}{n+2} + \cdots = \sum_{k\geq 0} \frac{(n+k-1)!}{(n-1)!\,(n+k)^k}.$$

What is the asymptotic behavior of this function?

18. [*M25*] Show that the sums $\sum \binom{n}{k} k^k (n-k)^{n-k}$ and $\sum \binom{n}{k} (k+1)^k (n-k)^{n-k}$ can be expressed very simply in terms of the Q function.

19. [*HM30*] (*Watson's lemma.*) Show that if the integral $C_n = \int_0^\infty e^{-nx} f(x) \, dx$ exists for all large n, and if $f(x) = O(x^\alpha)$ for $0 \leq x \leq r$, where $r > 0$ and $\alpha > -1$, then $C_n = O(n^{-1-\alpha})$.

▶ **20.** [*HM30*] Let $u = w + \frac{1}{3}w^2 + \frac{1}{36}w^3 - \frac{1}{270}w^4 + \cdots = \sum_{k=1}^\infty c_k w^k$ be the power series solution to the equation $w = (u^2 - \frac{2}{3}u^3 + \frac{2}{4}u^4 - \frac{2}{5}u^5 + \cdots)^{1/2}$, as in (12). Show that

$$Q(n) + 1 = \sum_{k=1}^{m-1} k c_k \Gamma(k/2) \left(\frac{n}{2} \right)^{1-k/2} + O(n^{1-m/2})$$

for all $m \geq 1$. [*Hint:* Apply Watson's lemma to the identity of exercise 15.]

> *I feel as if I should succeed in doing something in mathematics,*
> *although I cannot see why it is so very important.*
>
> — HELEN KELLER (1898)

1.3. MIX

IN MANY PLACES throughout this book we will have occasion to refer to a computer's internal machine language. The machine we use is a mythical computer called "MIX." MIX is very much like nearly every computer of the 1960s and 1970s, except that it is, perhaps, nicer. The language of MIX has been designed to be powerful enough to allow brief programs to be written for most algorithms, yet simple enough so that its operations are easily learned.

The reader is urged to study this section carefully, since MIX language appears in so many parts of this book. There should be no hesitation about learning a machine language; indeed, the author once found it not uncommon to be writing programs in a half dozen different machine languages during the same week! Everyone with more than a casual interest in computers will probably get to know at least one machine language sooner or later. MIX has been specially designed to preserve the simplest aspects of historic computers, so that its characteristics are easy to assimilate.

However, it must be admitted that MIX is now quite obsolete. Therefore MIX will be replaced in subsequent editions of this book by a new machine called MMIX, the 2009. MMIX will be a so-called reduced instruction set computer (RISC), which will do arithmetic on 64-bit words. It will be even nicer than MIX, and it will be similar to machines that have become dominant during the 1990s.

The task of converting everything in this book from MIX to MMIX will take a long time; volunteers are solicited to help with that conversion process. Meanwhile, the author hopes that people will be content to live for a few more years with the old-fashioned MIX architecture — which is still worth knowing, because it helps to provide a context for subsequent developments.

1.3.1. Description of MIX

MIX is the world's first polyunsaturated computer. Like most machines, it has an identifying number — the 1009. This number was found by taking 16 actual computers very similar to MIX and on which MIX could easily be simulated, then averaging their numbers with equal weight:

$$\lfloor (360 + 650 + 709 + 7070 + U3 + SS80 + 1107 + 1604 + G20 + B220$$
$$+ S2000 + 920 + 601 + H800 + PDP\text{-}4 + II)/16 \rfloor = 1009. \quad (1)$$

The same number may also be obtained in a simpler way by taking Roman numerals.

MIX has a peculiar property in that it is both binary and decimal at the same time. *MIX programmers don't actually know whether they are programming a machine with base 2 or base 10 arithmetic.* Therefore algorithms written in MIX can be used on either type of machine with little change, and MIX can be simulated easily on either type of machine. Programmers who are accustomed to a binary machine can think of MIX as binary; those accustomed to decimal may regard MIX as decimal. Programmers from another planet might choose to think of MIX as a ternary computer.

Words. The basic unit of MIX data is a *byte*. Each byte contains an *unspecified* amount of information, but it must be capable of holding at least 64 distinct values. That is, we know that any number between 0 and 63, inclusive, can be contained in one byte. Furthermore, each byte contains *at most* 100 distinct values. On a binary computer a byte must therefore be composed of six bits; on a decimal computer we have two digits per byte.*

Programs expressed in MIX's language should be written so that no more than sixty-four values are ever assumed for a byte. If we wish to treat the number 80, we should always leave two adjacent bytes for expressing it, even though one byte is sufficient on a decimal computer. *An algorithm in MIX should work properly regardless of how big a byte is.* Although it is quite possible to write programs that depend on the byte size, such actions are anathema to the spirit of this book; the only legitimate programs are those that would give correct results with all byte sizes. It is usually not hard to abide by this ground rule, and we will thereby find that programming a decimal computer isn't so different from programming a binary one after all.

Two adjacent bytes can express the numbers 0 through 4,095.

Three adjacent bytes can express the numbers 0 through 262,143.

Four adjacent bytes can express the numbers 0 through 16,777,215.

Five adjacent bytes can express the numbers 0 through 1,073,741,823.

A computer word consists of five bytes and a sign. The sign portion has only two possible values, + and −.

Registers. There are nine registers in MIX (see Fig. 13):

The A-register (Accumulator) consists of five bytes and a sign.

The X-register (Extension), likewise, comprises five bytes and a sign.

The I-registers (Index registers) I1, I2, I3, I4, I5, and I6 each hold two bytes together with a sign.

The J-register (Jump address) holds two bytes; it behaves as if its sign is always +.

We shall use a small letter "r", prefixed to the name, to identify a MIX register. Thus, "rA" means "register A."

The A-register has many uses, especially for arithmetic and for operating on data. The X-register is an extension on the "right-hand side" of rA, and it is used in connection with rA to hold ten bytes of a product or dividend, or it can be used to hold information shifted to the right out of rA. The index registers rI1, rI2, rI3, rI4, rI5, and rI6 are used primarily for counting and for referencing variable memory addresses. The J-register always holds the address of the instruction following the most recent "jump" operation, and it is primarily used in connection with subroutines.

---

* Since 1975 or so, the word "byte" has come to mean a sequence of precisely eight binary digits, capable of representing the numbers 0 to 255. Real-world bytes are therefore larger than the bytes of the hypothetical MIX machine; indeed, MIX's old-style bytes are just barely bigger than nybbles. When we speak of bytes in connection with MIX we shall confine ourselves to the former sense of the word, harking back to the days when bytes were not yet standardized.

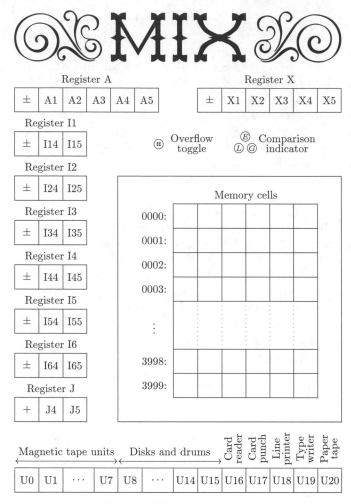

Fig. 13. The MIX computer.

Besides its registers, MIX contains

an *overflow toggle* (a single bit that is either "on" or "off");
a *comparison indicator* (having three values: LESS, EQUAL, or GREATER);
memory (4000 words of storage, each word with five bytes and a sign);
and *input-output devices* (cards, tapes, disks, etc.).

Partial fields of words. The five bytes and sign of a computer word are numbered as follows:

0	1	2	3	4	5
±	Byte	Byte	Byte	Byte	Byte

(2)

Most of the instructions allow a programmer to use only part of a word if desired. In such cases a nonstandard "field specification" can be given. The allowable fields are those that are adjacent in a computer word, and they are represented by (L:R), where L is the number of the left-hand part and R is the number of the right-hand part of the field. Examples of field specifications are:

(0:0), the sign only.

(0:2), the sign and the first two bytes.

(0:5), the whole word; this is the most common field specification.

(1:5), the whole word except for the sign.

(4:4), the fourth byte only.

(4:5), the two least significant bytes.

The use of field specifications varies slightly from instruction to instruction, and it will be explained in detail for each instruction where it applies. Each field specification (L:R) is actually represented inside the machine by the single number $8L + R$; notice that this number fits easily in one byte.

Instruction format. Computer words used for instructions have the following form:

0	1	2	3	4	5
±	A	A	I	F	C

$$(3)$$

The rightmost byte, C, is the *operation code* telling what operation is to be performed. For example, $C = 8$ specifies the operation LDA, "load the A-register."

The F-byte holds a *modification* of the operation code. It is usually a field specification $(L:R) = 8L + R$; for example, if $C = 8$ and $F = 11$, the operation is "load the A-register with the (1:3) field." Sometimes F is used for other purposes; on input-output instructions, for example, F is the number of the relevant input or output unit.

The left-hand portion of the instruction, ±AA, is the *address*. (Notice that the sign is part of the address.) The I-field, which comes next to the address, is the *index specification*, which may be used to modify the effective address. If $I = 0$, the address ±AA is used without change; otherwise I should contain a number i between 1 and 6, and the contents of index register Ii are added algebraically to ±AA before the instruction is carried out; the result is used as the address. This indexing process takes place on *every* instruction. We will use the letter M to indicate the address after any specified indexing has occurred. (If the addition of the index register to the address ±AA yields a result that does not fit in two bytes, the value of M is undefined.)

In most instructions, M will refer to a memory cell. The terms "memory cell" and "memory location" are used almost interchangeably in this book. We assume that there are 4000 memory cells, numbered from 0 to 3999; hence every memory location can be addressed with two bytes. For every instruction in which M refers to a memory cell we must have $0 \le M \le 3999$, and in this case we will write CONTENTS(M) to denote the value stored in memory location M.

On certain instructions, the "address" M has another significance, and it may even be negative. Thus, one instruction adds M to an index register, and such an operation takes account of the sign of M.

Notation. To discuss instructions in a readable manner, we will use the notation

$$\text{OP} \quad \text{ADDRESS,I(F)} \tag{4}$$

to denote an instruction like (3). Here OP is a symbolic name given to the operation code (the C-part) of the instruction; ADDRESS is the $\pm$AA portion; I and F represent the I- and F-fields, respectively.

If I is zero, the ',I' is omitted. If F is the *normal* F-specification for this particular operator, the '(F)' need not be written. The normal F-specification for almost all operators is (0:5), representing a whole word. If a different F is normal, it will be mentioned explicitly when we discuss a particular operator.

For example, the instruction to load a number into the accumulator is called LDA and it is operation code number 8. We have

Conventional representation		Actual numeric instruction				
LDA	2000,2(0:3)	+	2000	2	3	8
LDA	2000,2(1:3)	+	2000	2	11	8
LDA	2000(1:3)	+	2000	0	11	8
LDA	2000	+	2000	0	5	8
LDA	-2000,4	-	2000	4	5	8

$$(5)$$

The instruction 'LDA 2000,2(0:3)' may be read "Load A with the contents of location 2000 indexed by 2, the zero-three field."

To represent the numerical contents of a MIX word, we will always use a box notation like that above. Notice that in the word

+	2000	2	3	8

the number +2000 is shown filling two adjacent bytes and sign; the actual contents of byte (1:1) and of byte (2:2) will vary from one MIX computer to another, since byte size is variable. As a further example of this notation for MIX words, the diagram

-	10000	3000

represents a word with two fields, a three-byte-plus-sign field containing -10000 and a two-byte field containing 3000. When a word is split into more than one field, it is said to be "packed."

Rules for each instruction. The remarks following (3) above have defined the quantities M, F, and C for every word used as an instruction. We will now define the actions corresponding to each instruction.

Loading operators.

• LDA (load A). C = 8; F = field.
The specified field of CONTENTS (M) replaces the previous contents of register A.

On all operations where a partial field is used as an input, the sign is used if it is a part of the field, otherwise the sign + is understood. The field is shifted over to the right-hand part of the register as it is loaded.

Examples: If F is the normal field specification (0:5), everything in location M is copied into rA. If F is (1:5), the absolute value of CONTENTS (M) is loaded with a plus sign. If M contains an *instruction* word and if F is (0:2), the "±AA" field is loaded as

$$\pm \boxed{0 \mid 0 \mid 0 \mid A \mid A} .$$

Suppose location 2000 contains the word

$$\boxed{- \mid 80 \mid 3 \mid 5 \mid 4} ; \qquad\qquad (6)$$

then we get the following results from loading various partial fields:

Instruction	Contents of rA afterwards
LDA 2000	$-$ 80 $\mid$ 3 $\mid$ 5 $\mid$ 4
LDA 2000(1:5)	$+$ 80 $\mid$ 3 $\mid$ 5 $\mid$ 4
LDA 2000(3:5)	$+$ 0 $\mid$ 0 $\mid$ 3 $\mid$ 5 $\mid$ 4
LDA 2000(0:3)	$-$ 0 $\mid$ 0 $\mid$ 80 $\mid$ 3
LDA 2000(4:4)	$+$ 0 $\mid$ 0 $\mid$ 0 $\mid$ 0 $\mid$ 5
LDA 2000(0:0)	$-$ 0 $\mid$ 0 $\mid$ 0 $\mid$ 0 $\mid$ 0
LDA 2000(1:1)	$+$ 0 $\mid$ 0 $\mid$ 0 $\mid$ 0 $\mid$?

(The last example has a partially unknown effect, since byte size is variable.)

• LDX (load X). C = 15; F = field.
This is the same as LDA, except that rX is loaded instead of rA.

• LDi (load i). C = 8 + i; F = field.
This is the same as LDA, except that rIi is loaded instead of rA. An index register contains only two bytes (not five) and a sign; bytes 1, 2, 3 are always assumed to be zero. The LDi instruction is undefined if it would result in setting bytes 1, 2, or 3 to anything but zero.

In the description of all instructions, "i" stands for an integer, $1 \le i \le 6$. Thus, LDi stands for six different instructions: LD1, LD2, ..., LD6.

• LDAN (load A negative). C = 16; F = field.
• LDXN (load X negative). C = 23; F = field.
• LDiN (load i negative). C = 16 + i; F = field.
These eight instructions are the same as LDA, LDX, LDi, respectively, except that the *opposite* sign is loaded.

Storing operators.

• **STA** (store A). C = 24; F = field.

A portion of the contents of rA replaces the field of CONTENTS(M) specified by F. The other parts of CONTENTS(M) are unchanged.

On a *store* operation the field F has the opposite significance from the *load* operation: The number of bytes in the field is taken from the right-hand portion of the register and shifted *left* if necessary to be inserted in the proper field of CONTENTS(M). The sign is not altered unless it is part of the field. The contents of the register are not affected.

Examples: Suppose that location 2000 contains

$$\boxed{-\ |\ 1\ |\ 2\ |\ 3\ |\ 4\ |\ 5}$$

and register A contains

$$\boxed{+\ |\ 6\ |\ 7\ |\ 8\ |\ 9\ |\ 0}\ .$$

Then:

Instruction	Contents of location 2000 afterwards
STA 2000	+ 6 7 8 9 0
STA 2000(1:5)	− 6 7 8 9 0
STA 2000(5:5)	− 1 2 3 4 0
STA 2000(2:2)	− 1 0 3 4 5
STA 2000(2:3)	− 1 9 0 4 5
STA 2000(0:1)	+ 0 2 3 4 5

• **STX** (store X). C = 31; F = field.
Same as STA, except that rX is stored rather than rA.

• **STi** (store i). C = 24 + i; F = field.
Same as STA, except that rIi is stored rather than rA. Bytes 1, 2, 3 of an index register are zero; thus if rI1 contains

$$\boxed{\pm\ |\ m\ |\ n}\ ,$$

it behaves as though it were

$$\boxed{\pm\ |\ 0\ |\ 0\ |\ 0\ |\ m\ |\ n}\ .$$

• **STJ** (store J). C = 32; F = field.
Same as STi, except that rJ is stored and its sign is always +.

With STJ the normal field specification for F is (0:2), *not* (0:5). This is natural, since STJ is almost always done into the address field of an instruction.

• **STZ** (store zero). C = 33; F = field.
Same as STA, except that plus zero is stored. In other words, the specified field of CONTENTS(M) is cleared to zero.

Arithmetic operators. On the add, subtract, multiply, and divide operations, a field specification is allowed. A field specification of "(0:6)" can be used to indicate a "floating point" operation (see Section 4.2), but few of the programs we will write for MIX will use this feature, since we will primarily be concerned with algorithms on integers.

The standard field specification is, as usual, (0:5). Other fields are treated as in LDA. We will use the letter V to indicate the specified field of CONTENTS(M); thus, V is the value that would have been loaded into register A if the operation code were LDA.

• ADD. C = 1; F = field.

V is added to rA. If the magnitude of the result is too large for register A, the overflow toggle is set on, and the remainder of the addition appearing in rA is as though a "1" had been carried into another register to the left of rA. (Otherwise the setting of the overflow toggle is unchanged.) If the result is zero, the sign of rA is unchanged.

Example: The sequence of instructions below computes the sum of the five bytes of register A.

```
                        STA    2000
                        LDA    2000(5:5)
                        ADD    2000(4:4)
                        ADD    2000(3:3)
                        ADD    2000(2:2)
                        ADD    2000(1:1)
```

This is sometimes called "sideways addition."

Overflow will occur in some MIX computers when it would not occur in others, because of the variable definition of byte size. We have not said that overflow will occur definitely if the value is greater than 1073741823; overflow occurs when the magnitude of the result is greater than the contents of five bytes, depending on the byte size. One can still write programs that work properly and that give the same final answers, regardless of the byte size.

• SUB (subtract). C = 2; F = field.

V is subtracted from rA. (Equivalent to ADD but with −V in place of V.)

• MUL (multiply). C = 3; F = field.

The 10-byte product, V times rA, replaces registers A and X. The signs of rA and rX are both set to the algebraic sign of the product (namely, + if the signs of V and rA were the same, − if they were different).

• DIV (divide). C = 4; F = field.

The value of rA and rX, treated as a 10-byte number rAX with the sign of rA, is divided by the value V. If V = 0 or if the quotient is more than five bytes in magnitude (this is equivalent to the condition that $|rA| \geq |V|$), registers A and X are filled with undefined information and the overflow toggle is set on. Otherwise the quotient $\pm\lfloor|rAX/V|\rfloor$ is placed in rA and the remainder $\pm(|rAX| \bmod |V|)$ is placed in rX. The sign of rA afterwards is the algebraic sign of the quotient (namely, + if the signs of V and rA were the same, − if they were different). The sign of rX afterwards is the previous sign of rA.

Examples of arithmetic instructions: In most cases, arithmetic is done only with MIX words that are single five-byte numbers, not packed with several fields. It is, however, possible to operate arithmetically on packed MIX words, if some caution is used. The following examples should be studied carefully. (As before, ? designates an unknown value.)

		+	1234	1	150		rA before
		+	100	5	50		Cell 1000
ADD	1000	+	1334	6	200		rA after

		−	1234	0	0	9	rA before
		−	2000	150	0	Cell 1000
SUB	1000	+	766	149	?	rA after

		+	1	1	1	1	1	rA before
		+	1	1	1	1	1	Cell 1000
MUL	1000	+	0	1	2	3	4	rA after
		+	5	4	3	2	1	rX after

		−					112	rA before
		?	2	?	?	?	?	Cell 1000
MUL	1000(1:1)	−					0	rA after
		−					224	rX after

		−	50	0	112	4	rA before
		−	2	0	0	0	0	Cell 1000
MUL	1000	+	100	0	224	rA after
		+	8	0	0	0	0	rX after

		+	0	rA before
		?	17	rX before
		+	3	Cell 1000
DIV	1000	+	5	rA after
		+	2	rX after

−					0	rA before
+	1235	0	3	1		rX before
−	0	0	0	2	0	Cell 1000
+	0	617	?	?		rA after
−	0	0	0	?	1	rX after

DIV 1000

(These examples have been prepared with the philosophy that it is better to give a complete, baffling description than an incomplete, straightforward one.)

Address transfer operators. In the following operations, the (possibly indexed) "address" M is used as a signed number, not as the address of a cell in memory.

- **ENTA** (enter A). C = 48; F = 2.

The quantity M is loaded into rA. The action is equivalent to 'LDA' from a memory word containing the signed value of M. If M = 0, the sign of the instruction is loaded.

Examples: 'ENTA 0' sets rA to zeros, with a + sign. 'ENTA 0,1' sets rA to the current contents of index register 1, except that −0 is changed to +0. 'ENTA -0,1' is similar, except that +0 is changed to −0.

- **ENTX** (enter X). C = 55; F = 2.
- **ENTi** (enter i). C = 48 + i; F = 2.

Analogous to **ENTA**, loading the appropriate register.

- **ENNA** (enter negative A). C = 48; F = 3.
- **ENNX** (enter negative X). C = 55; F = 3.
- **ENNi** (enter negative i). C = 48 + i; F = 3.

Same as **ENTA**, **ENTX**, and **ENTi**, except that the opposite sign is loaded.

Example: 'ENN3 0,3' replaces rI3 by its negative, although −0 remains −0.

- **INCA** (increase A). C = 48; F = 0.

The quantity M is added to rA; the action is equivalent to 'ADD' from a memory word containing the value of M. Overflow is possible and it is treated just as in **ADD**.

Example: 'INCA 1' increases the value of rA by one.

- **INCX** (increase X). C = 55; F = 0.

The quantity M is added to rX. If overflow occurs, the action is equivalent to **ADD**, except that rX is used instead of rA. Register A is never affected by this instruction.

- **INCi** (increase i). C = 48 + i; F = 0.

Add M to rIi. Overflow must not occur; if M + rIi doesn't fit in two bytes, the result of this instruction is undefined.

- **DECA** (decrease A). C = 48; F = 1.
- **DECX** (decrease X). C = 55; F = 1.
- **DEC*i*** (decrease *i*). C = 48 + *i*; F = 1.

These eight instructions are the same as **INCA**, **INCX**, and **INC*i***, respectively, except that M is subtracted from the register rather than added.

Notice that the operation code C is the same for **ENTA**, **ENNA**, **INCA**, and **DECA**; the F-field is used to distinguish the various operations from each other.

Comparison operators. MIX's comparison operators all compare the value contained in a register with a value contained in memory. The comparison indicator is then set to **LESS**, **EQUAL**, or **GREATER** according to whether the value of the register is less than, equal to, or greater than the value of the memory cell. A minus zero is *equal to* a plus zero.

- **CMPA** (compare A). C = 56; F = field.

The specified field of rA is compared with the *same* field of **CONTENTS(M)**. If F does not include the sign position, the fields are both considered nonnegative; otherwise the sign is taken into account in the comparison. (An equal comparison always occurs when F is (0:0), since minus zero equals plus zero.)

- **CMPX** (compare X). C = 63; F = field.

This is analogous to **CMPA**.

- **CMP*i*** (compare *i*). C = 56 + *i*; F = field.

Analogous to **CMPA**. Bytes 1, 2, and 3 of the index register are treated as zero in the comparison. (Thus if F = (1:2), the result cannot be **GREATER**.)

Jump operators. Instructions are ordinarily executed in sequential order; in other words, the command that is performed after the command in location P is usually the one found in location P + 1. But several "jump" instructions allow this sequence to be interrupted. When a typical jump takes place, the J-register is set to the address of the next instruction (that is, to the address of the instruction that would have been next if we hadn't jumped). A "store J" instruction then can be used by the programmer, if desired, to set the address field of another command that will later be used to return to the original place in the program. The J-register is changed whenever a jump actually occurs in a program, except when the jump operator is **JSJ**, and it is never changed by non-jumps.

- **JMP** (jump). C = 39; F = 0.

Unconditional jump: The next instruction is taken from location M.

- **JSJ** (jump, save J). C = 39; F = 1.

Same as **JMP** except that the contents of rJ are unchanged.

- **JOV** (jump on overflow). C = 39; F = 2.

If the overflow toggle is on, it is turned off and a **JMP** occurs; otherwise nothing happens.

- **JNOV** (jump on no overflow). C = 39; F = 3.

If the overflow toggle is off, a **JMP** occurs; otherwise it is turned off.

• JL, JE, JG, JGE, JNE, JLE (jump on less, equal, greater, greater-or-equal, unequal, less-or-equal). C = 39; F = 4, 5, 6, 7, 8, 9, respectively.
Jump if the comparison indicator is set to the condition indicated. For example, JNE will jump if the comparison indicator is LESS or GREATER. The comparison indicator is not changed by these instructions.

• JAN, JAZ, JAP, JANN, JANZ, JANP (jump A negative, zero, positive, nonnegative, nonzero, nonpositive). C = 40; F = 0, 1, 2, 3, 4, 5, respectively.
If the contents of rA satisfy the stated condition, a JMP occurs, otherwise nothing happens. "Positive" means *greater* than zero (not zero); "nonpositive" means the opposite, namely zero or negative.

• JXN, JXZ, JXP, JXNN, JXNZ, JXNP (jump X negative, zero, positive, nonnegative, nonzero, nonpositive). C = 47; F = 0, 1, 2, 3, 4, 5, respectively.

• JiN, JiZ, JiP, JiNN, JiNZ, JiNP (jump i negative, zero, positive, nonnegative, nonzero, nonpositive). C = 40 + i; F = 0, 1, 2, 3, 4, 5, respectively. These 42 instructions for rX and rIi are analogous to the corresponding operations for rA.

Miscellaneous operators.

• SLA, SRA, SLAX, SRAX, SLC, SRC (shift left A, shift right A, shift left AX, shift right AX, shift left AX circularly, shift right AX circularly). C = 6; F = 0, 1, 2, 3, 4, 5, respectively.
These six are the "shift" commands, in which M specifies a number of MIX bytes to be shifted left or right; M must be nonnegative. SLA and SRA do not affect rX; the other shifts affect both registers A and X as though they were a single 10-byte register. With SLA, SRA, SLAX, and SRAX, zeros are shifted into the register at one side, and bytes disappear at the other side. The instructions SLC and SRC call for a "circulating" shift, in which the bytes that leave one end enter in at the other end. Both rA and rX participate in a circulating shift. The signs of registers A and X are not affected in any way by any of the shift commands.

Examples:	Register A						Register X				
Initial contents	+	1	2	3	4	5	−	6	7	8	9	10
SRAX 1	+	0	1	2	3	4	−	5	6	7	8	9
SLA 2	+	2	3	4	0	0	−	5	6	7	8	9
SRC 4	+	6	7	8	9	2	−	3	4	0	0	5
SRA 2	+	0	0	6	7	8	−	3	4	0	0	5
SLC 501	+	0	6	7	8	3	−	4	0	0	5	0

• MOVE. C = 7; F = number, normally 1.
The number of words specified by F is moved, starting from location M to the location specified by the contents of index register 1. The transfer occurs one word at a time, and rI1 is increased by the value of F at the end of the operation. If F = 0, nothing happens.

Care must be taken when there's overlap between the locations involved; for example, suppose that F = 3 and M = 1000. Then if rI1 = 999, we transfer

CONTENTS(1000) to CONTENTS(999), CONTENTS(1001) to CONTENTS(1000), and CONTENTS(1002) to CONTENTS(1001); nothing unusual occurred here. But if rI1 were 1001 instead, we would move CONTENTS(1000) to CONTENTS(1001), then CONTENTS(1001) to CONTENTS(1002), then CONTENTS(1002) to CONTENTS(1003), so we would have moved the *same* word CONTENTS(1000) into three places.

• NOP (no operation). C = 0.

No operation occurs, and this instruction is bypassed. F and M are ignored.

• HLT (halt). C = 5; F = 2.

The machine stops. When the computer operator restarts it, the net effect is equivalent to NOP.

Input-output operators. MIX has a fair amount of input-output equipment (all of which is optional at extra cost). Each device is given a number as follows:

Unit number	Peripheral device	Block size
t	Tape unit number t ($0 \le t \le 7$)	100 words
d	Disk or drum unit number d ($8 \le d \le 15$)	100 words
16	Card reader	16 words
17	Card punch	16 words
18	Line printer	24 words
19	Typewriter terminal	14 words
20	Paper tape	14 words

Not every MIX installation will have all of this equipment available; we will occasionally make appropriate assumptions about the presence of certain devices. Some devices may not be used both for input and for output. The number of words mentioned in the table above is a fixed block size associated with each unit.

Input or output with magnetic tape, disk, or drum units reads or writes full words (five bytes and a sign). Input or output with units 16 through 20, however, is always done in a *character code* where each byte represents one alphameric character. Thus, five characters per MIX word are transmitted. The character code is given at the top of Table 1, which appears at the close of this section and on the end papers of this book. The code 00 corresponds to '␣', which denotes a *blank space*. Codes 01–29 are for the letters A through Z with a few Greek letters thrown in; codes 30–39 represent the digits 0, 1, ..., 9; and further codes 40, 41, ... represent punctuation marks and other special characters. (MIX's character set harks back to the days before computers could cope with lowercase letters.) We cannot use character code to read in or write out all possible values that a byte may have, since certain combinations are undefined. Moreover, some input-output devices may be unable to handle all the symbols in the character set; for example, the symbols Σ and Π that appear amid the letters will perhaps not be acceptable to the card reader. When character-code input is being done, the signs of all words are set to +; on output, signs are ignored. If a typewriter is used for input, the "carriage return" that is typed at the end of each line causes the remainder of that line to be filled with blanks.

The disk and drum units are external memory devices each containing 100-word blocks. On every IN, OUT, or IOC instruction as defined below, the particular 100-word block referred to by the instruction is specified by the current contents of rX, which should not exceed the capacity of the disk or drum involved.

• **IN** (input). C = 36; F = unit.
This instruction initiates the transfer of information from the input unit specified into consecutive locations starting with M. The number of locations transferred is the block size for this unit (see the table above). The machine will wait at this point if a preceding operation for the same unit is not yet complete. The transfer of information that starts with this instruction will not be complete until an unknown future time, depending on the speed of the input device, so a program must not refer to the information in memory until then. It is improper to attempt to read any block from magnetic tape that follows the latest block written on that tape.

• **OUT** (output). C = 37; F = unit.
This instruction starts the transfer of information from memory locations starting at M to the output unit specified. The machine waits until the unit is ready, if it is not initially ready. The transfer will not be complete until an unknown future time, depending on the speed of the output device, so a program must not alter the information in memory until then.

• **IOC** (input-output control). C = 35; F = unit.
The machine waits, if necessary, until the specified unit is not busy. Then a control operation is performed, depending on the particular device being used. The following examples are used in various parts of this book:

Magnetic tape: If M = 0, the tape is rewound. If M < 0 the tape is skipped backward $-$M blocks, or to the beginning of the tape, whichever comes first. If M > 0, the tape is skipped forward; it is improper to skip forward over any blocks following the one last written on that tape.

For example, the sequence 'OUT 1000(3); IOC -1(3); IN 2000(3)' writes out one hundred words onto tape 3, then reads it back in again. Unless the tape reliability is questioned, the last two instructions of that sequence are only a slow way to move words 1000–1099 to locations 2000–2099. The sequence 'OUT 1000(3); IOC +1(3)' is improper.

Disk or drum: M should be zero. The effect is to position the device according to rX so that the next IN or OUT operation on this unit will take less time if it uses the same rX setting.

Line printer: M should be zero. 'IOC 0(18)' skips the printer to the top of the following page.

Paper tape: M should be zero. 'IOC 0(20)' rewinds the tape.

• **JRED** (jump ready). C = 38; F = unit.
A jump occurs if the specified unit is ready, that is, finished with the preceding operation initiated by IN, OUT, or IOC.

• **JBUS** (jump busy). C = 34; F = unit.
Analogous to JRED, but the jump occurs when the specified unit is *not* ready.

Example: In location 1000, the instruction 'JBUS 1000(16)' will be executed repeatedly until unit 16 is ready.

The simple operations above complete MIX's repertoire of input-output instructions. There is no "tape check" indicator, etc., to cover exceptional conditions on the peripheral devices. Any such condition (e.g., paper jam, unit turned off, out of tape, etc.) causes the unit to remain busy, a bell rings, and the skilled computer operator fixes things manually using ordinary maintenance procedures. Some more complicated peripheral units, which are more expensive and more representative of contemporary equipment than the fixed-block-size tapes, drums, and disks described here, are discussed in Sections 5.4.6 and 5.4.9.

Conversion Operators.

• NUM (convert to numeric). $C = 5$; $F = 0$.
This operation is used to change the character code into numeric code. M is ignored. Registers A and X are assumed to contain a 10-byte number in character code; the NUM instruction sets the magnitude of rA equal to the numerical value of this number (treated as a decimal number). The value of rX and the sign of rA are unchanged. Bytes 00, 10, 20, 30, 40, ... convert to the digit zero; bytes 01, 11, 21, ... convert to the digit one; etc. Overflow is possible, and in this case the remainder modulo b^5 is retained, where b is the byte size.

• CHAR (convert to characters). $C = 5$; $F = 1$.
This operation is used to change numeric code into character code suitable for output to punched cards or tape or the line printer. The value in rA is converted into a 10-byte decimal number that is put into registers A and X in character code. The signs of rA and rX are unchanged. M is ignored.

Examples:		Register A						Register X				
Initial contents	−	00	00	31	32	39	+	37	57	47	30	30
NUM 0	−			12977700			+	37	57	47	30	30
INCA 1	−			12977699			+	37	57	47	30	30
CHAR 0	−	30	30	31	32	39	+	37	37	36	39	39

Timing. To give quantitative information about the efficiency of MIX programs, each of MIX's operations is assigned an *execution time* typical of vintage-1970 computers.

ADD, SUB, all LOAD operations, all STORE operations (including STZ), all shift commands, and all comparison operations take *two units* of time. MOVE requires one unit plus two for each word moved. MUL, NUM, CHAR each require 10 units and DIV requires 12. The execution time for floating point operations is specified in Section 4.2.1. All remaining operations take one unit of time, plus the time the computer may be idle on the IN, OUT, IOC, or HLT instructions.

Notice in particular that ENTA takes one unit of time, while LDA takes two units. The timing rules are easily remembered because of the fact that, except for shifts, conversions, MUL, and DIV, the number of time units equals the number of references to memory (including the reference to the instruction itself).

MIX's basic unit of time is a relative measure that we will denote simply by u. It may be regarded as, say, 10 microseconds (for a relatively inexpensive computer) or as 10 nanoseconds (for a relatively high-priced machine).

Example: The sequence LDA 1000; INCA 1; STA 1000 takes exactly $5u$.

> *And now I see with eye serene*
> *The very pulse of the machine.*
> — WILLIAM WORDSWORTH,
> *She Was a Phantom of Delight* (1804)

Summary. We have now discussed all the features of MIX, except for its "GO button," which is discussed in exercise 26. Although MIX has nearly 150 different operations, they fit into a few simple patterns so that they can easily be remembered. Table 1 summarizes the operations for each C-setting. The name of each operator is followed in parentheses by its default F-field.

The following exercises give a quick review of the material in this section. They are mostly quite simple, and the reader should try to do nearly all of them.

EXERCISES

1. [*00*] If MIX were a ternary (base 3) computer, how many "trits" would there be per byte?

2. [*02*] If a value to be represented within MIX may get as large as 99999999, how many adjacent bytes should be used to contain this quantity?

3. [*02*] Give the partial field specifications, (L:R), for the (a) address field, (b) index field, (c) field field, and (d) operation code field of a MIX instruction.

4. [*00*] The last example in (5) is 'LDA -2000,4'. How can this be legitimate, in view of the fact that memory addresses should not be negative?

5. [*10*] What symbolic notation, analogous to (4), corresponds to (6) if (6) is regarded as a MIX instruction?

▶ **6.** [*10*] Assume that location 3000 contains

$$\boxed{+ \;|\; 5 \;|\; 1 \;|\; 200 \;|\; 15} \; .$$

What is the result of the following instructions? (State if any of them are undefined or only partially defined.) (a) LDAN 3000; (b) LD2N 3000(3:4); (c) LDX 3000(1:3); (d) LD6 3000; (e) LDXN 3000(0:0).

7. [*M15*] Give a precise definition of the results of the DIV instruction for all cases in which overflow does not occur, using the algebraic operations $X \bmod Y$ and $\lfloor X/Y \rfloor$.

8. [*15*] The last example of the DIV instruction that appears on page 133 has "rX before" equal to $\boxed{+ \;|\; 1235 \;|\; 0 \;|\; 3 \;|\; 1}$. If this were $\boxed{- \;|\; 1234 \;|\; 0 \;|\; 3 \;|\; 1}$ instead, but other parts of that example were unchanged, what would registers A and X contain after the DIV instruction?

Table 1

Character code:

00	01	02	03	04	05	06	07	08	09	10	11	12	13	14	15	16	17	18	19	20	21	22	23	24
␣	A	B	C	D	E	F	G	H	I	Δ	J	K	L	M	N	O	P	Q	R	Σ	Π	S	T	U

00	*1*	**01**	*2*	**02**	*2*	**03**	*10*
No operation		$rA \leftarrow rA + V$		$rA \leftarrow rA - V$		$rAX \leftarrow rA \times V$	
NOP(0)		ADD(0:5) FADD(6)		SUB(0:5) FSUB(6)		MUL(0:5) FMUL(6)	
08	*2*	**09**	*2*	**10**	*2*	**11**	*2*
$rA \leftarrow V$		$rI1 \leftarrow V$		$rI2 \leftarrow V$		$rI3 \leftarrow V$	
LDA(0:5)		LD1(0:5)		LD2(0:5)		LD3(0:5)	
16	*2*	**17**	*2*	**18**	*2*	**19**	*2*
$rA \leftarrow -V$		$rI1 \leftarrow -V$		$rI2 \leftarrow -V$		$rI3 \leftarrow -V$	
LDAN(0:5)		LD1N(0:5)		LD2N(0:5)		LD3N(0:5)	
24	*2*	**25**	*2*	**26**	*2*	**27**	*2*
$M(F) \leftarrow rA$		$M(F) \leftarrow rI1$		$M(F) \leftarrow rI2$		$M(F) \leftarrow rI3$	
STA(0:5)		ST1(0:5)		ST2(0:5)		ST3(0:5)	
32	*2*	**33**	*2*	**34**	*1*	**35**	*1 + T*
$M(F) \leftarrow rJ$		$M(F) \leftarrow 0$		Unit F busy?		Control, unit F	
STJ(0:2)		STZ(0:5)		JBUS(0)		IOC(0)	
40	*1*	**41**	*1*	**42**	*1*	**43**	*1*
$rA:0$, jump		$rI1:0$, jump		$rI2:0$, jump		$rI3:0$, jump	
JA[+]		J1[+]		J2[+]		J3[+]	
48	*1*	**49**	*1*	**50**	*1*	**51**	*1*
$rA \leftarrow [rA]? \pm M$		$rI1 \leftarrow [rI1]? \pm M$		$rI2 \leftarrow [rI2]? \pm M$		$rI3 \leftarrow [rI3]? \pm M$	
INCA(0) DECA(1) ENTA(2) ENNA(3)		INC1(0) DEC1(1) ENT1(2) ENN1(3)		INC2(0) DEC2(1) ENT2(2) ENN2(3)		INC3(0) DEC3(1) ENT3(2) ENN3(3)	
56	*2*	**57**	*2*	**58**	*2*	**59**	*2*
$CI \leftarrow rA(F):V$		$CI \leftarrow rI1(F):V$		$CI \leftarrow rI2(F):V$		$CI \leftarrow rI3(F):V$	
CMPA(0:5) FCMP(6)		CMP1(0:5)		CMP2(0:5)		CMP3(0:5)	

General form:

C		*t*
Description		
OP(F)		

C = operation code, (5:5) field of instruction
F = op variant, (4:4) field of instruction
M = address of instruction after indexing
$V = M(F)$ = contents of F field of location M
OP = symbolic name for operation
(F) = normal F setting
t = execution time; T = interlock time

25 26 27 28 29 30 31 32 33 34 35 36 37 38 39 40 41 42 43 44 45 46 47 48 49 50 51 52 53 54 55
V W X Y Z 0 1 2 3 4 5 6 7 8 9 . , ( ) + - * / = $ < > @ ; : '

04	12	05	10	06	2	07	$1 + 2F$
rA ← rAX/V rX ← remainder DIV(0:5) FDIV(6)		Special NUM(0) CHAR(1) HLT(2)		Shift M bytes SLA(0) SRA(1) SLAX(2) SRAX(3) SLC(4) SRC(5)		Move F words from M to rI1 MOVE(1)	
12	2	**13**	2	**14**	2	**15**	2
rI4 ← V LD4(0:5)		rI5 ← V LD5(0:5)		rI6 ← V LD6(0:5)		rX ← V LDX(0:5)	
20	2	**21**	2	**22**	2	**23**	2
rI4 ← −V LD4N(0:5)		rI5 ← −V LD5N(0:5)		rI6 ← −V LD6N(0:5)		rX ← −V LDXN(0:5)	
28	2	**29**	2	**30**	2	**31**	2
M(F) ← rI4 ST4(0:5)		M(F) ← rI5 ST5(0:5)		M(F) ← rI6 ST6(0:5)		M(F) ← rX STX(0:5)	
36	$1 + T$	**37**	$1 + T$	**38**	1	**39**	1
Input, unit F IN(0)		Output, unit F OUT(0)		Unit F ready? JRED(0)		Jumps JMP(0) JSJ(1) JOV(2) JNOV(3) also [*] below	
44	1	**45**	1	**46**	1	**47**	1
rI4 : 0, jump J4[+]		rI5 : 0, jump J5[+]		rI6 : 0, jump J6[+]		rX : 0, jump JX[+]	
52	1	**53**	1	**54**	1	**55**	1
rI4 ← [rI4]? ± M INC4(0) DEC4(1) ENT4(2) ENN4(3)		rI5 ← [rI5]? ± M INC5(0) DEC5(1) ENT5(2) ENN5(3)		rI6 ← [rI6]? ± M INC6(0) DEC6(1) ENT6(2) ENN6(3)		rX ← [rX]? ± M INCX(0) DECX(1) ENTX(2) ENNX(3)	
60	2	**61**	2	**62**	2	**63**	2
CI ← rI4(F) : V CMP4(0:5)		CI ← rI5(F) : V CMP5(0:5)		CI ← rI6(F) : V CMP6(0:5)		CI ← rX(F) : V CMPX(0:5)	

rA = register A
rX = register X
rAX = registers A and X as one
rIi = index register i, $1 \le i \le 6$
rJ = register J
CI = comparison indicator

[*]:		[+]:	
JL(4)	<	N(0)	
JE(5)	=	Z(1)	
JG(6)	>	P(2)	
JGE(7)	≥	NN(3)	
JNE(8)	≠	NZ(4)	
JLE(9)	≤	NP(5)	

▶ **9.** [*15*] List all the MIX operators that can possibly affect the setting of the overflow toggle. (Do not include floating point operators.)

10. [*15*] List all the MIX operators that can possibly affect the setting of the comparison indicator.

▶ **11.** [*15*] List all the MIX operators that can possibly affect the setting of rI1.

12. [*10*] Find a single instruction that has the effect of multiplying the current contents of rI3 by two and leaving the result in rI3.

▶ **13.** [*10*] Suppose location 1000 contains the instruction 'JOV 1001'. This instruction turns off the overflow toggle if it is on (and the next instruction executed will be in location 1001, in any case). If this instruction were changed to 'JNOV 1001', would there be any difference? What if it were changed to 'JOV 1000' or 'JNOV 1000'?

14. [*20*] For each MIX operation, consider whether there is a way to set the $\pm$AA, I, and F portions so that the result of the instruction is precisely equivalent to NOP (except that the execution time may be longer). Assume that nothing is known about the contents of any registers or any memory locations. Whenever it is possible to produce a NOP, state how it can be done. *Examples:* INCA is a no-op if the address and index parts are zero. JMP can never be a no-op, since it affects rJ.

15. [*10*] How many *alphameric characters* are there in a typewriter or paper-tape block? in a card-reader or card-punch block? in a line-printer block?

16. [*20*] Write a program that sets memory cells 0000–0099 all to zero and is (a) as short a program as possible; (b) as fast a program as possible. [*Hint:* Consider using the MOVE command.]

17. [*26*] This is the same as the previous exercise, except that locations 0000 through N, inclusive, are to be set to zero, where N is the current contents of rI2. Your programs (a) and (b) should work for any value $0 \le N \le 2999$; they should start in location 3000.

▶ **18.** [*22*] After the following "number one" program has been executed, what changes to registers, memory, and other aspects of MIX's state have taken place? (For example, what is the final setting of rI1? of rX? of the overflow and comparison indicators?)

```
STZ  1
ENNX 1
STX  1(0:1)
SLAX 1
ENNA 1
INCX 1
ENT1 1
SRC  1
ADD  1
DEC1 -1
STZ  1
CMPA 1
MOVE -1,1(1)
NUM  1
CHAR 1
HLT  1  ▮
```

▶ **19.** [*14*] What is the execution time of the program in the preceding exercise, not counting the HLT instruction?

20. [*20*] Write a program that sets *all* 4000 memory cells equal to a 'HLT' instruction, and then stops.

▶ **21.** [*24*] (a) Can the J-register ever be zero? (b) Write a program that, given a number *N* in rI4, sets register J equal to *N*, assuming that $0 < N \leq 3000$. Your program should start in location 3000. When your program has finished its execution, the contents of all memory cells must be unchanged.

▶ **22.** [*28*] Location 2000 contains an integer number, *X*. Write two programs that compute X^{13} and halt with the result in register A. One program should use the minimum number of MIX memory locations; the other should require the minimum execution time possible. Assume that X^{13} fits into a single word.

23. [*27*] Location 0200 contains a word

$$\boxed{\;+\;|\;a\;|\;b\;|\;c\;|\;d\;|\;e\;}\;;$$

write two programs that compute the "reflected" word

$$\boxed{\;+\;|\;e\;|\;d\;|\;c\;|\;b\;|\;a\;}$$

and halt with the result in register A. One program should do this without using MIX's ability to load and store partial fields of words. Both programs should take the minimum possible number of memory locations under the stated conditions (including all locations used for the program and for temporary storage of intermediate results).

24. [*21*] Assuming that registers A and X contain

$$\boxed{\;+\;|\;0\;|\;a\;|\;b\;|\;c\;|\;d\;}\qquad\text{and}\qquad\boxed{\;+\;|\;e\;|\;f\;|\;g\;|\;h\;|\;i\;}\;,$$

respectively, write two programs that change the contents of these registers to

$$\boxed{\;+\;|\;a\;|\;b\;|\;c\;|\;d\;|\;e\;}\qquad\text{and}\qquad\boxed{\;+\;|\;0\;|\;f\;|\;g\;|\;h\;|\;i\;}\;,$$

respectively, using (a) minimum memory space and (b) minimum execution time.

▶ **25.** [*30*] Suppose that the manufacturer of MIX wishes to come out with a more powerful computer ("Mixmaster"?), and he wants to convince as many as possible of those people now owning a MIX computer to invest in the more expensive machine. He wants to design this new hardware to be an *extension* of MIX, in the sense that all programs correctly written for MIX will work on the new machines without change. Suggest desirable things that could be incorporated in this extension. (For example, can you make better use of the I-field of an instruction?)

▶ **26.** [*32*] This problem is to write a card-loading routine. Every computer has its own peculiar "bootstrapping" problems for getting information initially into the machine and for starting a job correctly. In MIX's case, the contents of a card can be read only in character code, and the cards that contain the loading program itself must meet this restriction. Not all possible byte values can be read from a card, and each word read in from cards is positive.

MIX has one feature that has not been explained in the text: There is a "GO button," which is used to get the computer started from scratch when its memory contains arbitrary information. When this button is pushed by the computer operator, the following actions take place:

1) A single card is read into locations 0000–0015; this is essentially equivalent to the instruction 'IN 0(16)'.

2) When the card has been completely read and the card reader is no longer busy, a JMP to location 0000 occurs. The J-register is also set to zero, and the overflow toggle is cleared.

3) The machine now begins to execute the program it has read from the card.

Note: MIX computers without card readers have their GO-button attached to another input device. But in this problem we will assume the presence of a card reader, unit 16.

The loading routine to be written must satisfy the following conditions:

i) The input deck should begin with the loading routine, followed by information cards containing the numbers to be loaded, followed by a "transfer card" that shuts down the loading routine and jumps to the beginning of the program. The loading routine should fit onto two cards.

ii) The information cards have the following format:

> Columns 1–5, ignored by the loading routine.
> Column 6, the number of consecutive words to be loaded on this card (a number between 1 and 7, inclusive).
> Columns 7–10, the location of word 1, which is always 0100 or more (so that it does not overlay the loading routine).
> Columns 11–20, word 1.
> Columns 21–30, word 2 (if column 6 ≥ 2).
> ...
> Columns 71–80, word 7 (if column 6 = 7).

The contents of words 1, 2, ... are punched numerically as decimal numbers. If a word is to be negative, a minus ("11-punch") is *overpunched* over the least significant digit, e.g., in column 20. Assume that this causes the character code input to be 10, 11, 12, ..., 19 rather than 30, 31, 32, ..., 39. For example, a card that has

$$\text{ABCDE3100000123456789000000000010000000010}\overline{0}$$

punched in columns 1–40 should cause the following data to be loaded:

> 1000:   +0123456789;   1001:   +0000000001;   1002:   −0000000100.

iii) The transfer card has the format TRANSOnnnn in columns 1–10, where nnnn is the place where execution should start.

iv) The loading routine should work for all byte sizes without any changes to the cards bearing the loading routine. No card should contain any of the characters corresponding to bytes 20, 21, 48, 49, 50, ... (namely, the characters Σ, Π, =, $, <, ...), since these characters cannot be read by all card readers. In particular, the ENT, INC, and CMP instructions cannot be used; they can't necessarily be punched on a card.

1.3.2. The MIX Assembly Language

A symbolic language is used to make MIX programs considerably easier to read and to write, and to save the programmer from worrying about tedious clerical details that often lead to unnecessary errors. This language, MIXAL ("MIX Assembly Language"), is an extension of the notation used for instructions in the previous section. Its main features are the optional use of alphabetic names to stand for numbers, and a location field to associate names with memory locations.

MIXAL can readily be comprehended if we consider first a simple example. The following code is part of a larger program; it is a subroutine to find the maximum of n elements $X[1], \ldots, X[n]$, according to Algorithm 1.2.10M.

Program M (*Find the maximum*). Register assignments: $rA \equiv m$, $rI1 \equiv n$, $rI2 \equiv j$, $rI3 \equiv k$, CONTENTS$(X + i) \equiv X[i]$.

Assembled instructions	Line no.	LOC	OP	ADDRESS	Times	Remarks
	01	X	EQU	1000		
	02		ORIG	3000		
3000: + 3009 0 2 32	03	MAXIMUM	STJ	EXIT	1	Subroutine linkage
3001: + 0 1 2 51	04	INIT	ENT3	0,1	1	*M1. Initialize.* $k \leftarrow n$.
3002: + 3005 0 0 39	05		JMP	CHANGEM	1	$j \leftarrow n, m \leftarrow X[n], k \leftarrow n-1$.
3003: + 1000 3 5 56	06	LOOP	CMPA	X,3	$n-1$	*M3. Compare.*
3004: + 3007 0 7 39	07		JGE	*+3	$n-1$	To M5 if $m \geq X[k]$.
3005: + 0 3 2 50	08	CHANGEM	ENT2	0,3	$A+1$	*M4. Change m.* $j \leftarrow k$.
3006: + 1000 3 5 08	09		LDA	X,3	$A+1$	$m \leftarrow X[k]$.
3007: + 1 0 1 51	10		DEC3	1	n	*M5. Decrease k.*
3008: + 3003 0 2 43	11		J3P	LOOP	n	*M2. All tested?* To M3 if $k > 0$.
3009: + 3009 0 0 39	12	EXIT	JMP	*	1	Return to main program. ∎

This program is an example of several things simultaneously:

a) The columns headed "LOC", "OP", and "ADDRESS" are of principal interest; they contain a program in the MIXAL symbolic machine language, and we shall explain the details of this program below.

b) The column headed "Assembled instructions" shows the actual numeric machine language that corresponds to the MIXAL program. MIXAL has been designed so that any MIXAL program can easily be translated into numeric machine language; the translation is usually carried out by another computer program called an *assembly program* or *assembler*. Thus, programmers may do all of their machine language programming in MIXAL, never bothering to determine the equivalent numeric codes by hand. Virtually all MIX programs in this book are written in MIXAL.

c) The column headed "Line no." is not an essential part of the MIXAL program; it is merely included with MIXAL examples in this book so that we can readily refer to parts of the program.

d) The column headed "Remarks" gives explanatory information about the program, and it is cross-referenced to the steps of Algorithm 1.2.10M. The reader should compare that algorithm (page 96) with the program above. Notice that a little "programmer's license" was used during the transcription into MIX code; for example, step M2 has been put last. The "register assignments" stated at the beginning of Program M show what components of MIX correspond to the variables in the algorithm.

e) The column headed "Times" will be instructive in many of the MIX programs we will be studying in this book; it represents the *profile*, the number of times the instruction on that line will be executed during the course of the program. Thus, line 06 will be performed $n-1$ times, etc. From this information we can determine the length of time required to perform the subroutine; it is $(5+5n+3A)u$, where A is the quantity that was carefully analyzed in Section 1.2.10.

Now let's discuss the MIXAL part of Program M. Line 01,

X EQU 1000,

says that symbol X is to be *equivalent* to the number 1000. The effect of this may be seen on line 06, where the numeric equivalent of the instruction 'CMPA X,3' appears as

$$\boxed{+\ |\ 1000\ |\ 3\ |\ 5\ |\ 56}\ ,$$

that is, 'CMPA 1000,3'.

Line 02 says that the locations for succeeding lines should be chosen sequentially, originating with 3000. Therefore the symbol MAXIMUM that appears in the LOC field of line 03 becomes equivalent to the number 3000, INIT is equivalent to 3001, LOOP is equivalent to 3003, etc.

On lines 03 through 12 the OP field contains the symbolic names of MIX instructions: STJ, ENT3, etc. But the symbolic names EQU and ORIG, which appear in the OP column of lines 01 and 02, are somewhat different; EQU and ORIG are called *pseudo-operations*, because they are operators of MIXAL but not of MIX. Pseudo-operations provide special information about a symbolic program, without being instructions of the program itself. Thus the line

X EQU 1000

only talks *about* Program M, it does not signify that any variable is to be set equal to 1000 when the program is run. Notice that no instructions are assembled for lines 01 and 02.

Line 03 is a "store J" instruction that stores the contents of register J into the (0:2) field of location EXIT. In other words, it stores rJ into the address part of the instruction found on line 12.

As mentioned earlier, Program M is intended to be part of a larger program; elsewhere the sequence

ENT1 100
JMP MAXIMUM
STA MAX

would, for example, jump to Program M with n set to 100. Program M would then find the largest of the elements $X[1], \ldots, X[100]$ and would return to the instruction 'STA MAX' with the maximum value in rA and with its position, j, in rI2. (See exercise 3.)

Line 05 jumps the control to line 08. Lines 04, 05, 06 need no further explanation. Line 07 introduces a new notation: An asterisk (read "self") refers to the location of the line on which it appears; '*+3' ("self plus three") therefore refers to three locations past the current line. Since line 07 is an instruction that corresponds to location 3004, the '*+3' appearing there refers to location 3007.

The rest of the symbolic code is self-explanatory. Notice the appearance of an asterisk again on line 12 (see exercise 2).

Our next example introduces a few more features of the assembly language. The object is to compute and print a table of the first 500 prime numbers, with 10 columns of 50 numbers each. The table should appear as follows on the line printer:

```
FIRST FIVE HUNDRED PRIMES
      0002 0233 0547 0877 1229 1597 1993 2371 2749 3187
      0003 0239 0557 0881 1231 1601 1997 2377 2753 3191
      0005 0241 0563 0883 1237 1607 1999 2381 2767 3203
      0007 0251 0569 0887 1249 1609 2003 2383 2777 3209
      0011 0257 0571 0907 1259 1613 2011 2389 2789 3217
       ⋮                                            ⋮
      0229 0541 0863 1223 1583 1987 2357 2741 3181 3571
```

We will use the following method.

Algorithm P (*Print table of 500 primes*). This algorithm has two distinct parts: Steps P1–P8 prepare an internal table of 500 primes, and steps P9–P11 print the answer in the form shown above. The latter part uses two "buffers," in which line images are formed; while one buffer is being printed, the other one is being filled.

P1. [Start table.] Set PRIME[1] ← 2, N ← 3, J ← 1. (In the following steps, N will run through the odd numbers that are candidates for primes; J will keep track of how many primes have been found so far.)

P2. [N is prime.] Set J ← J + 1, PRIME[J] ← N.

P3. [500 found?] If J = 500, go to step P9.

P4. [Advance N.] Set N ← N + 2.

P5. [K ← 2.] Set K ← 2. (PRIME[K] will run through the possible prime divisors of N.)

P6. [PRIME[K]\N?] Divide N by PRIME[K]; let Q be the quotient and R the remainder. If R = 0 (hence N is not prime), go to P4.

P7. [PRIME[K] large?] If Q ≤ PRIME[K], go to P2. (In such a case, N must be prime; the proof of this fact is interesting and a little unusual — see exercise 6.)

P8. [Advance K.] Increase K by 1, and go to P6.

P9. [Print title.] Now we are ready to print the table. Advance the printer to the next page. Set BUFFER[0] to the title line and print this line. Set B ← 1, M ← 1.

P10. [Set up line.] Put PRIME[M], PRIME[50 + M], ..., PRIME[450 + M] into BUFFER[B] in the proper format.

P11. [Print line.] Print BUFFER[B]; set B ← 1 − B (thereby switching to the other buffer); and increase M by 1. If M ≤ 50, return to P10; otherwise the algorithm terminates. ∎

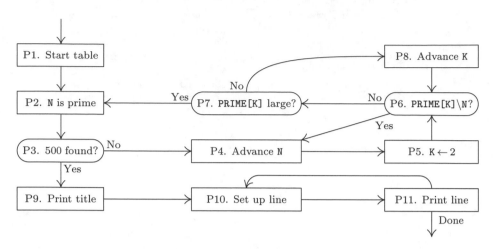

Fig. 14. Algorithm P.

Program P (*Print table of 500 primes*). This program has deliberately been written in a slightly clumsy fashion in order to illustrate most of the features of **MIXAL** in a single program. rI1 $\equiv$ J − 500; rI2 $\equiv$ N; rI3 $\equiv$ K; rI4 indicates B; rI5 is M plus multiples of 50.

```
01  * EXAMPLE PROGRAM   ...   TABLE OF PRIMES
02  *
03  L       EQU   500           The number of primes to find
04  PRINTER EQU   18            Unit number of the line printer
05  PRIME   EQU   99            Memory area for table of primes
06  BUF0    EQU   2000          Memory area for BUFFER[0]
07  BUF1    EQU   BUF0+25       Memory area for BUFFER[1]
08          ORIG  3000
09  START   IOC   0(PRINTER)    Skip to new page.
10          LD1   =1-L=         P1. Start table. J ← 1.
11          LD2   =3=               N ← 3.
12  2H      INC1  1             P2. N is prime. J ← J + 1.
13          ST2   PRIME+L,1         PRIME[J] ← N.
14          J1Z   2F            P3. 500 found?
15  4H      INC2  2             P4. Advance N.
16          ENT3  2             P5. K ← 2.
17  6H      ENTA  0             P6. PRIME[K]\N?
18          ENTX  0,2               rAX ← N.
19          DIV   PRIME,3           rA ← Q,  rX ← R.
20          JXZ   4B                To P4 if R = 0.
21          CMPA  PRIME,3       P7. PRIME[K] large?
22          INC3  1             P8. Advance K.
23          JG    6B                To P6 if Q > PRIME[K].
24          JMP   2B                Otherwise N is prime.
```

```
25  2H        OUT   TITLE(PRINTER)    P9. Print title.
26            ENT4  BUF1+10               Set B ← 1.
27            ENT5  -50                   Set M ← 0.
28  2H        INC5  L+1                   Advance M.
29  4H        LDA   PRIME,5            P10. Set up line. (Right to left)
30            CHAR                        Convert PRIME[M] to decimal.
31            STX   0,4(1:4)
32            DEC4  1
33            DEC5  50                    (rI5 goes down by 50 until
34            J5P   4B                        it becomes nonpositive)
35            OUT   0,4(PRINTER)      P11. Print line.
36            LD4   24,4                  Switch buffers.
37            J5N   2B                    If rI5 = 0, we are done.
38            HLT
39  * INITIAL CONTENTS OF TABLES AND BUFFERS
40            ORIG  PRIME+1
41            CON   2                     The first prime is 2.
42            ORIG  BUF0-5
43  TITLE     ALF   FIRST                 Alphabetic information for
44            ALF    FIVE                     title line
45            ALF    HUND
46            ALF   RED P
47            ALF   RIMES
48            ORIG  BUF0+24
49            CON   BUF1+10               Each buffer refers to the other.
50            ORIG  BUF1+24
51            CON   BUF0+10
52            END   START                 End of routine.   ▌
```

The following points of interest should be noted about this program:

1. Lines 01, 02, and 39 begin with an asterisk: This signifies a "comment" line that is merely explanatory, having no actual effect on the assembled program.

2. As in Program M, the pseudo-operation EQU in line 03 sets the equivalent of a symbol; in this case, the equivalent of L is set to 500. (In the program of lines 10–24, L represents the number of primes to be computed.) Notice that in line 05 the symbol PRIME gets a *negative* equivalent; the equivalent of a symbol may be any signed five-byte number. In line 07 the equivalent of BUF1 is calculated as BUF0+25, namely 2025. MIXAL provides a limited amount of arithmetic on numbers; another example appears on line 13, where the value of PRIME+L (in this case, 499) is calculated by the assembly program.

3. The symbol PRINTER has been used in the F-part on lines 09, 25, and 35. The F-part, which is always enclosed in parentheses, may be numeric or symbolic, just as the other portions of the ADDRESS field are. Line 31 illustrates the partial field specification '(1:4)', using a colon.

4. MIXAL provides several ways to specify non-instruction words. Line 41 uses the pseudo-operation CON to specify an ordinary constant, '2'; the result of

line 41 is to assemble the word

$$\boxed{+ \quad | \quad | \quad | \quad | \quad 2} \;.$$

Line 49 shows a slightly more complicated constant, 'BUF1+10', which assembles as the word

$$\boxed{+ \quad | \quad | \quad | \quad 2035} \;.$$

A constant may be enclosed in equal signs, in which case we call it a *literal constant* (see lines 10 and 11). The assembler automatically creates internal names and inserts 'CON' lines for literal constants. For example, lines 10 and 11 of Program P are effectively changed to

10	LD1	con1
11	LD2	con2

and then at the end of the program, between lines 51 and 52, the lines

51a	con1	CON	1-L
51b	con2	CON	3

are effectively inserted as part of the assembly procedure (possibly with con2 first). Line 51a will assemble into the word

$$\boxed{- \quad | \quad | \quad | \quad 499} \;.$$

The use of literal constants is a decided convenience, because it means that programmers do not have to invent symbolic names for trivial constants, nor do they have to remember to insert constants at the end of each program. Programmers can keep their minds on the central problems and not worry about such routine details. (However, the literal constants in Program P aren't especially good examples, because we would have had a slightly better program if we had replaced lines 10 and 11 by the more efficient commands 'ENT1 1-L' and 'ENT2 3'.)

5. A good assembly language should mimic the way a programmer *thinks* about machine programs. One example of this philosophy is the use of literal constants, as we have just mentioned; another example is the use of '*', which was explained in Program M. A third example is the idea of *local symbols* such as the symbol 2H, which appears in the location field of lines 12, 25, and 28.

Local symbols are special symbols whose equivalents can be *redefined* as many times as desired. A global symbol like PRIME has but one significance throughout a program, and if it were to appear in the location field of more than one line an error would be indicated by the assembler. But local symbols have a different nature; we write, for example, 2H ("2 here") in the location field, and 2F ("2 forward") or 2B ("2 backward") in the address field of a MIXAL line:

2B means the closest *previous* location 2H;
2F means the closest *following* location 2H.

Thus the '2F' in line 14 refers to line 25; the '2B' in line 24 refers back to line 12; and the '2B' in line 37 refers to line 28. An address of 2F or 2B never refers to its *own* line; for example, the three lines of MIXAL code

```
2H      EQU     10
2H      MOVE    2F(2B)
2H      EQU     2B-3
```

are virtually equivalent to the single line

$$\text{MOVE } *-3(10).$$

The symbols 2F and 2B should never be used in the location field; the symbol 2H should never be used in the address field. There are ten local symbols, which can be obtained by replacing '2' in these examples by any digit from 0 to 9.

The idea of local symbols was introduced by M. E. Conway in 1958, in connection with an assembly program for the UNIVAC I. Local symbols relieve programmers from the necessity of choosing symbolic names for every address, when all they want to do is refer to an instruction a few lines away. There often is no appropriate name for nearby locations, so programmers have tended to introduce meaningless symbols like X1, X2, X3, etc., with the potential danger of duplication. Local symbols are therefore quite useful and natural in an assembly language.

6. The address part of lines 30 and 38 is blank. This means that the assembled address will be zero. We could have left the address blank in line 17 as well, but the program would have been less readable without the redundant 0.

7. Lines 43–47 use the pseudo-operation ALF, which creates a five-byte constant in MIX alphameric character code. For example, line 45 causes the word

+	00	08	24	15	04

to be assembled, representing '⎵HUND' — part of the title line in Program P's output.

All locations whose contents are not specified in the MIXAL program are ordinarily set to positive zero (except the locations that are used by the loading routine, usually 3700–3999). Thus there is no need to set the other words of the title line to blanks, after line 47.

8. Arithmetic may be used together with ORIG: See lines 40, 42, 48, and 50.

9. The last line of a complete MIXAL program always has the OP-code 'END'. The address on this line is the location at which the program is to begin, once it has been loaded into memory.

10. As a final note about Program P, we can observe that the instructions have been organized so that index registers are counted towards zero, and tested against zero, whenever possible. For example, the quantity J–500, not J, is kept in rI1. Lines 26–34 are particularly noteworthy, although perhaps a bit tricky.

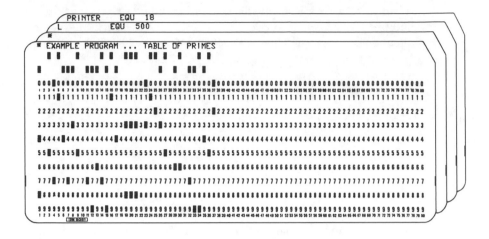

```
* EXAMPLE PROGRAM ...   TABLE OF PRIMES
*
L EQU 500
PRINTER EQU 18
PRIME EQU -1
BUF0 EQU 2000
BUF1 EQU BUF0+25
 ORIG 3000
START IOC 0(PRINTER)
 LD1 =1-L=
```

Fig. 15. The first lines of Program P punched onto cards, or typed on a terminal.

It may be of interest to note a few of the statistics observed when Program P was actually run. The division instruction in line 19 was executed 9538 times; the time to perform lines 10–24 was 182144u.

MIXAL programs can be punched onto cards or typed on a computer terminal, as shown in Fig. 15. The following format is used in the case of punched cards:

Columns 1–10	LOC (location) field;
Columns 12–15	OP field;
Columns 17–80	ADDRESS field and optional remarks;
Columns 11, 16	blank.

However, if column 1 contains an asterisk, the entire card is treated as a comment. The ADDRESS field ends with the first blank column following column 16; any explanatory information may be punched to the right of this first blank column with no effect on the assembled program. (*Exception:* When the OP field is ALF, the remarks always start in column 22.)

When the input comes from a terminal, a less restrictive format is used: The LOC field ends with the first blank space, while the OP and ADDRESS fields (if present) begin with a nonblank character and continue to the next blank; the special OP-code ALF is, however, followed either by two blank spaces and five characters of alphameric data, or by a single blank space and five alphameric characters, the first of which is nonblank. The remainder of each line contains optional remarks.

The MIX assembly program accepts input files prepared in this manner and converts them to machine language programs in loadable form. Under favorable circumstances the reader will have access to a MIX assembler and MIX simulator, on which various exercises in this book can be worked out.

Now we have seen what can be done in MIXAL. We conclude this section by describing the rules more carefully, and in particular we shall observe what is *not* allowed in MIXAL. The following comparatively few rules define the language.

1. A *symbol* is a string of one to ten letters and/or digits, containing at least one letter. *Examples:* PRIME, TEMP, 20BY20. The special symbols dH, dF, and dB, where d is a single digit, will for the purposes of this definition be replaced by other unique symbols according to the "local symbol" convention described earlier.

2. A *number* is a string of one to ten digits. *Example:* 00052.

3. Each appearance of a symbol in a MIXAL program is said to be either a "defined symbol" or a "future reference." A *defined symbol* is a symbol that has appeared in the LOC field of a preceding line of this MIXAL program. A *future reference* is a symbol that has not yet been defined in this way.

4. An *atomic expression* is either

a) a number, or

b) a defined symbol (denoting the numerical equivalent of that symbol, see rule 13), or

c) an asterisk (denoting the value of ⊛; see rules 10 and 11).

5. An *expression* is either

a) an atomic expression, or

b) a plus or minus sign followed by an atomic expression, or

c) an expression followed by a binary operation followed by an atomic expression.

The six admissible binary operations are +, -, *, /, //, and :. They are defined on numeric MIX words as follows:

```
C = A+B      LDA AA; ADD BB; STA CC.
C = A-B      LDA AA; SUB BB; STA CC.
C = A*B      LDA AA; MUL BB; STX CC.
C = A/B      LDA AA; SRAX 5; DIV BB; STA CC.
C = A//B     LDA AA; ENTX 0; DIV BB; STA CC.
C = A:B      LDA AA; MUL =8=; SLAX 5; ADD BB; STA CC.
```

Here AA, BB, and CC denote locations containing the respective values of the symbols A, B, and C. Operations within an expression are carried out from left to right. *Examples:*

-1+5	equals 4.
-1+5*20/6	equals 4*20/6 equals 80/6 equals 13 (going from left to right).
1//3	equals a MIX word whose value is approximately $b^5/3$ where b is the byte size; that is, a word representing the fraction $\frac{1}{3}$ with an assumed radix point at the left.
1:3	equals 11 (usually used in partial field specification).
*-3	equals ⊛ minus three.
***	equals ⊛ times ⊛.

6. An *A-part* (which is used to describe the address field of a MIX instruction) is either

a) vacuous (denoting the value zero), or

b) an expression, or

c) a future reference (denoting the eventual equivalent of the symbol; see rule 13), or

d) a literal constant (denoting a reference to an internally created symbol; see rule 12).

7. An *index part* (which is used to describe the index field of a MIX instruction) is either

a) vacuous (denoting the value zero), or

b) a comma followed by an expression (denoting the value of that expression).

8. An *F-part* (which is used to describe the F-field of a MIX instruction) is either

a) vacuous (denoting the normal F-setting, based on the OP field as shown in Table 1.3.1–1), or

b) a left parenthesis followed by an expression followed by a right parenthesis (denoting the value of the expression).

9. A *W-value* (which is used to describe a *full-word* MIX constant) is either

a) an expression followed by an F-part $\big($in which case a vacuous F-part denotes $(0:5)\big)$, or

b) a W-value followed by a comma followed by a W-value of the form (a).

A W-value denotes the value of a numeric MIX word determined as follows: Let the W-value have the form "$E_1(F_1),E_2(F_2),\ \ldots\ ,E_n(F_n)$", where $n \geq 1$, the E's are expressions, and the F's are fields. The desired result is the final value that would appear in memory location WVAL if the following hypothetical program were executed:

STZ WVAL; LDA C$_1$; STA WVAL(F$_1$); ...; LDA C$_n$; STA WVAL(F$_n$).

Here $C_1, \ldots, C_n$ denote locations containing the values of expressions $E_1, \ldots, E_n$. Each F_i must have the form $8L_i + R_i$ where $0 \le L_i \le R_i \le 5$. *Examples:*

1		is the word	+			1
1,-1000(0:2)		is the word	−	1000		1
-1000(0:2),1		is the word	+			1

10. The assembly process makes use of a value denoted by ⊛ (called the *location counter*), which is initially zero. The value of ⊛ should always be a nonnegative number that can fit in two bytes. When the location field of a line is not blank, it must contain a symbol that has not been previously defined. The equivalent of that symbol is then defined to be the current value of ⊛.

11. After processing the LOC field as described in rule 10, the assembly process depends on the value of the OP field. There are six possibilities for OP:

a) OP is a symbolic MIX operator (see Table 1 at the end of the previous section). The chart defines the normal C and F values for each MIX operator. In this case the ADDRESS should be an A-part (rule 6), followed by an index part (rule 7), followed by an F-part (rule 8). We thereby obtain four values: C, F, A, and I. The effect is to assemble the word determined by the sequence 'LDA C; STA WORD; LDA F; STA WORD(4:4); LDA I; STA WORD(3:3); LDA A; STA WORD(0:2)' into the location specified by ⊛, and to advance ⊛ by 1.

b) OP is 'EQU'. The ADDRESS should be a W-value (see rule 9). If the LOC field is nonblank, the equivalent of the symbol appearing there is set equal to the value specified in ADDRESS. This rule takes precedence over rule 10. The value of ⊛ is unchanged. (As a nontrivial example, consider the line

BYTESIZE EQU 1(4:4)

which allows the programmer to have a symbol whose value depends on the byte size. This is an acceptable situation so long as the resulting program is meaningful with each possible byte size.)

c) OP is 'ORIG'. The ADDRESS should be a W-value (see rule 9); the location counter, ⊛, is set to this value. (Notice that because of rule 10, a symbol appearing in the LOC field of an ORIG line gets as its equivalent the value of ⊛ *before* it has changed. For example,

TABLE   ORIG *+100

sets the equivalent of TABLE to the *first* of 100 locations.)

d) OP is 'CON'. The ADDRESS should be a W-value; the effect is to assemble a word, having this value, into the location specified by ⊛, and to advance ⊛ by 1.

e) OP is 'ALF'. The effect is to assemble the word of character codes formed by the first five characters of the address field, otherwise behaving like CON.

f) OP is 'END'. The ADDRESS should be a W-value, which specifies in its (4:5) field the location of the instruction at which the program begins. The END line signals the end of a MIXAL program. The assembler effectively inserts additional lines just before the END line, in arbitrary order, corresponding to all undefined symbols and literal constants (see rules 12 and 13). Thus a symbol in the LOC field of the END line will denote the first location following the inserted words.

12. Literal constants: A W-value that is less than 10 characters long may be enclosed between '=' signs and used as a future reference. The effect is to create a new symbol internally and to insert a CON line defining that symbol, just before the END line (see remark 4 following Program P).

13. Every symbol has one and only one equivalent value; this is a full-word MIX number that is normally determined by the symbol's appearance in LOC according to rule 10 or rule 11(b). If the symbol never appears in LOC, a new line is effectively inserted before the END line, having OP = 'CON' and ADDRESS = '0' and the name of the symbol in LOC.

Note: The most significant consequence of the rules above is the restriction on future references. A symbol that has not yet been defined in the LOC field of a previous line may not be used except as the A-part of an instruction. In particular, it may not be used (a) in connection with arithmetic operations; or (b) in the ADDRESS field of EQU, ORIG, or CON. For example,

                    LDA   2F+1

and

                    CON   3F

are both illegal. This restriction has been imposed in order to allow more efficient assembly of programs, and the experience gained in writing this set of books has shown that it is a mild limitation that rarely makes much difference.

Actually MIX has two symbolic languages for low-level programming: MIXAL,* a machine-oriented language that is designed to facilitate one-pass translation by a very simple assembly program; and PL/MIX, which more adequately reflects data and control structures and which looks rather like the Remarks field of MIXAL programs.

EXERCISES — First set

1. [*00*] The text remarked that 'X EQU 1000' does not assemble any instruction that sets the value of a variable. Suppose that you are writing a MIX program in which the algorithm is supposed to set the value contained in a certain memory cell (whose symbolic name is X) equal to 1000. How could you express this in MIXAL?

▶ **2.** [*10*] Line 12 of Program M says 'JMP *', where * denotes the location of that line. Why doesn't the program go into an infinite loop, endlessly repeating this instruction?

---

* The author was astonished to learn in 1971 that MIXAL is also the name of a laundry detergent in Yugoslavia, developed for use with *avtomate* [automatics].

▶ **3.** [*23*] What is the effect of the following program, if it is used in conjunction with Program M?

```
START IN    X+1(0)
      JBUS  *(0)
      ENT1  100
1H    JMP   MAXIMUM
      LDX   X,1
      STA   X,1
      STX   X,2
      DEC1  1
      J1P   1B
      OUT   X+1(1)
      HLT
      END   START
```

▶ **4.** [*25*] Assemble Program P by hand. (It won't take as long as you think.) What are the actual numerical contents of memory, corresponding to that symbolic program?

5. [*11*] Why doesn't Program P need a JBUS instruction to determine when the line printer is ready?

6. [*HM20*] (a) Show that if n is not prime, n has a divisor d with $1 < d \leq \sqrt{n}$. (b) Use this fact to show that the test in step P7 of Algorithm P proves that N is prime.

7. [*10*] (a) What is the meaning of '4B' in line 34 of Program P? (b) What effect, if any, would be caused if the location of line 15 were changed to '2H' and the address of line 20 were changed to '2B'?

▶ **8.** [*24*] What does the following program do? (Do not run it on a computer, figure it out by hand!)

```
* MYSTERY PROGRAM
BUF ORIG *+3000
1H  ENT1  1
    ENT2  0
    LDX   4F
2H  ENT3  0,1
3H  STZ   BUF,2
    INC2  1
    DEC3  1
    J3P   3B
    STX   BUF,2
    INC2  1
    INC1  1
    CMP1  =75=
    JL    2B
    ENN2  2400
    OUT   BUF+2400,2(18)
    INC2  24
    J2N   *-2
    HLT
4H  ALF   AAAAA
    END   1B
```

EXERCISES — Second set

These exercises are short programming problems, representing typical computer applications and covering a wide range of techniques. Every reader is encouraged to choose a few of these problems, in order to get some experience using MIX as well as a good review of basic programming skills. If desired, these exercises may be worked concurrently as the rest of Chapter 1 is being read.

The following list indicates the types of programming techniques that are involved:

The use of switching tables for multiway decisions: exercises 9, 13, and 23.

The use of index registers with two-dimensional arrays: exercises 10, 21, and 23.

Unpacking characters: exercises 13 and 23.

Integer and scaled decimal arithmetic: exercises 14, 16, and 18.

The use of subroutines: exercises 14 and 20.

Input buffering: exercise 13.

Output buffering: exercises 21 and 23.

List processing: exercise 22.

Real-time control: exercise 20.

Graphical display: exercise 23.

Whenever an exercise in this book says, "write a MIX program" or "write a MIX subroutine," you need only write symbolic MIXAL code for what is asked. This code will not be complete in itself, it will merely be a fragment of a (hypothetical) complete program. No input or output need be done in a code fragment, if the data is to be supplied externally; one need write only LOC, OP, and ADDRESS fields of MIXAL lines, together with appropriate remarks. The numeric machine language, line number, and "times" columns (see Program M) are not required unless specifically requested, nor will there be an END line.

On the other hand, if an exercise says, "write a *complete* MIX program," it implies that an executable program should be written in MIXAL, including in particular the final END line. Assemblers and MIX simulators on which such complete programs can be tested are widely available.

▶ **9.** [*25*] Location INST contains a MIX word that purportedly is a MIX instruction. Write a MIX program that jumps to location GOOD if the word has a valid C-field, valid ±AA-field, valid I-field, and valid F-field, according to Table 1.3.1–1; your program should jump to location BAD otherwise. Remember that the test for a valid F-field depends on the C-field; for example, if C = 7 (MOVE), any F-field is acceptable, but if C = 8 (LDA), the F-field must have the form $8L + R$ where $0 \le L \le R \le 5$. The "±AA"-field is to be considered valid *unless* C specifies an instruction requiring a memory address and I = 0 and ±AA is not a valid memory address.

Note: Inexperienced programmers tend to tackle a problem like this by writing a long series of tests on the C-field, such as 'LDA C; JAZ 1F; DECA 5; JAN 2F; JAZ 3F; DECA 2; JAN 4F; ...'. This is *not* good practice! The best way to make multiway decisions is to prepare an auxiliary *table* containing information that encapsulates the desired logic. If there were, for example, a table of 64 entries, we could write 'LD1 C; LD1 TABLE,1; JMP 0,1'—thereby jumping very speedily to the desired routine. Other useful information can also be kept in such a table. A tabular approach to the present problem makes the program only a little bit longer (including the table) and greatly increases its speed and flexibility.

▶ **10.** [*31*] Assume that we have a 9×8 matrix

$$\begin{pmatrix} a_{11} & a_{12} & a_{13} & \cdots & a_{18} \\ a_{21} & a_{22} & a_{23} & \cdots & a_{28} \\ \vdots & \vdots & \vdots & \ddots & \vdots \\ a_{91} & a_{92} & a_{93} & \cdots & a_{98} \end{pmatrix}$$

stored in memory so that a_{ij} is in location $1000+8i+j$. In memory the matrix therefore appears as follows:

$$\begin{pmatrix} (1009) & (1010) & (1011) & \cdots & (1016) \\ (1017) & (1018) & (1019) & \cdots & (1024) \\ \vdots & \vdots & \vdots & \ddots & \vdots \\ (1073) & (1074) & (1075) & \cdots & (1080) \end{pmatrix}.$$

A matrix is said to have a "saddle point" if some position is the smallest value in its row and the largest value in its column. In symbols, a_{ij} is a saddle point if

$$a_{ij} = \min_{1 \le k \le 8} a_{ik} = \max_{1 \le k \le 9} a_{kj}.$$

Write a MIX program that computes the location of a saddle point (if there is at least one) or zero (if there is no saddle point), and stops with this value in rI1.

11. [*M29*] What is the *probability* that the matrix in the preceding exercise has a saddle point, assuming that the 72 elements are distinct and assuming that all 72! arrangements are equally probable? What is the corresponding probability if we assume instead that the elements of the matrix are zeros and ones, and that all 2^{72} such matrices are equally probable?

12. [*HM42*] Two solutions are given for exercise 10 (see page 512), and a third is suggested; it is not clear which of them is better. Analyze the algorithms, using each of the assumptions of exercise 11, and decide which is the better method.

13. [*28*] A cryptanalyst wants a frequency count of the letters in a certain code. The code has been punched on paper tape; the end is signaled by an asterisk. Write a complete MIX program that reads in the tape, counts the frequency of each character up to the first asterisk, and then types out the results in the form

```
A     0010257
B     0000179
D     0794301
```

etc., one character per line. The number of blanks should not be counted, nor should characters for which the count is zero (like C in the above) be printed. For efficiency, "buffer" the input: While reading a block into one area of memory you can be counting characters from another area. You may assume that an extra block (following the one that contains the terminating asterisk) is present on the input tape.

▶ **14.** [*31*] The following algorithm, due to the Neapolitan astronomer Aloysius Lilius and the German Jesuit mathematician Christopher Clavius in the late 16th century, is used by most Western churches to determine the date of Easter Sunday for any year after 1582.

Algorithm E (*Date of Easter*). Let Y be the year for which the date of Easter is desired.

E1. [Golden number.] Set $G \leftarrow (Y \bmod 19) + 1$. ($G$ is the so-called "golden number" of the year in the 19-year Metonic cycle.)

E2. [Century.] Set $C \leftarrow \lfloor Y/100 \rfloor + 1$. (When Y is not a multiple of 100, C is the century number; for example, 1984 is in the twentieth century.)

E3. [Corrections.] Set $X \leftarrow \lfloor 3C/4 \rfloor - 12$, $Z \leftarrow \lfloor (8C + 5)/25 \rfloor - 5$. (Here X is the number of years, such as 1900, in which leap year was dropped in order to keep in step with the sun; Z is a special correction designed to synchronize Easter with the moon's orbit.)

E4. [Find Sunday.] Set $D \leftarrow \lfloor 5Y/4 \rfloor - X - 10$. (March $((-D) \bmod 7)$ will actually be a Sunday.)

E5. [Epact.] Set $E \leftarrow (11G + 20 + Z - X) \bmod 30$. If $E = 25$ and the golden number G is greater than 11, or if $E = 24$, then increase E by 1. (This number E is the *epact*, which specifies when a full moon occurs.)

E6. [Find full moon.] Set $N \leftarrow 44 - E$. If $N < 21$ then set $N \leftarrow N + 30$. (Easter is supposedly the first Sunday following the first full moon that occurs on or after March 21. Actually perturbations in the moon's orbit do not make this strictly true, but we are concerned here with the "calendar moon" rather than the actual moon. The Nth of March is a calendar full moon.)

E7. [Advance to Sunday.] Set $N \leftarrow N + 7 - ((D + N) \bmod 7)$.

E8. [Get month.] If $N > 31$, the date is $(N - 31)$ APRIL; otherwise the date is N MARCH. ▮

Write a subroutine to calculate and print Easter date given the year, assuming that the year is less than 100000. The output should have the form '*dd* MONTH, *yyyyy*' where *dd* is the day and *yyyyy* is the year. Write a complete MIX program that uses this subroutine to prepare a table of the dates of Easter from 1950 through 2000.

15. [*M30*] A fairly common error in the coding of the previous exercise is to fail to realize that the quantity $(11G + 20 + Z - X)$ in step E5 may be negative; therefore the positive remainder mod 30 might not be computed properly. (See *CACM* **5** (1962), 556.) For example, in the year 14250 we would find $G = 1$, $X = 95$, $Z = 40$; so if we had $E = -24$ instead of $E = +6$ we would get the ridiculous answer '**42 APRIL**'. Write a complete MIX program that finds the *earliest* year for which this error would actually cause the wrong date to be calculated for Easter.

16. [*31*] We showed in Section 1.2.7 that the sum $1 + \frac{1}{2} + \frac{1}{3} + \cdots$ becomes infinitely large. But if it is calculated with finite accuracy by a computer, the sum actually exists, in some sense, because the terms eventually get so small that they contribute nothing to the sum if added one by one. For example, suppose we calculate the sum by rounding to one decimal place; then we have $1 + 0.5 + 0.3 + 0.3 + 0.2 + 0.2 + 0.1 + 0.1 + 0.1 + 0.1 + 0.1 + 0.1 + 0.1 + 0.1 + 0.1 + 0.1 + 0.1 + 0.1 + 0.1 = 3.9$.

More precisely, let $r_n(x)$ be the number x rounded to n decimal places; we define $r_n(x) = \lfloor 10^n x + \frac{1}{2} \rfloor / 10^n$. Then we wish to find

$$S_n = r_n(1) + r_n(\tfrac{1}{2}) + r_n(\tfrac{1}{3}) + \cdots;$$

we know that $S_1 = 3.9$, and the problem is to write a complete MIX program that calculates and prints S_n for $n = 2, 3, 4,$ and 5.

Note: There is a much faster way to do this than the simple procedure of adding $r_n(1/m)$, one number at a time, until $r_n(1/m)$ becomes zero. For example, we have $r_5(1/m) = 0.00001$ for all values of m from 66667 to 200000; it's wise to avoid calculating $1/m$ all 133334 times! An algorithm along the following lines should rather be used:

A. Start with $m_h = 1$, $S = 1$.

B. Set $m_e = m_h + 1$ and calculate $r_n(1/m_e) = r$. Stop if $r = 0$.

C. Find m_h, the largest m for which $r_n(1/m) = r$.

D. Add $(m_h - m_e + 1)r$ to S and return to Step B.

17. [*HM30*] Using the notation of the preceding exercise, prove or disprove the formula

$$\lim_{n \to \infty}(S_{n+1} - S_n) = \ln 10.$$

18. [*25*] The ascending sequence of all reduced fractions between 0 and 1 that have denominators $\leq n$ is called the "Farey series of order n." For example, the Farey series of order 7 is

$$\frac{0}{1}, \frac{1}{7}, \frac{1}{6}, \frac{1}{5}, \frac{1}{4}, \frac{2}{7}, \frac{1}{3}, \frac{2}{5}, \frac{3}{7}, \frac{1}{2}, \frac{4}{7}, \frac{3}{5}, \frac{2}{3}, \frac{5}{7}, \frac{3}{4}, \frac{4}{5}, \frac{5}{6}, \frac{6}{7}, \frac{1}{1}.$$

If we denote this series by x_0/y_0, x_1/y_1, x_2/y_2, $\ldots$, exercise 19 proves that

$$x_0 = 0, \quad y_0 = 1; \qquad x_1 = 1, \quad y_1 = n;$$
$$x_{k+2} = \lfloor (y_k + n)/y_{k+1} \rfloor x_{k+1} - x_k;$$
$$y_{k+2} = \lfloor (y_k + n)/y_{k+1} \rfloor y_{k+1} - y_k.$$

Write a MIX subroutine that computes the Farey series of order n, by storing the values of x_k and y_k in locations $X + k$, $Y + k$, respectively. (The total number of terms in the series is approximately $3n^2/\pi^2$, so you may assume that n is rather small.)

19. [*M30*] (a) Show that the numbers x_k and y_k defined by the recurrence in the preceding exercise satisfy the relation $x_{k+1}y_k - x_k y_{k+1} = 1$. (b) Show that the fractions x_k/y_k are indeed the Farey series of order n, using the fact proved in (a).

▶ **20.** [*33*] Assume that MIX's overflow toggle and X-register have been wired up to the traffic signals at the corner of Del Mar Boulevard and Berkeley Avenue, as follows:

$$\left.\begin{array}{l} \text{rX}(2{:}2) = \text{Del Mar traffic light} \\ \text{rX}(3{:}3) = \text{Berkeley traffic light} \end{array}\right\} \text{ 0 off, 1 green, 2 amber, 3 red;}$$

$$\left.\begin{array}{l} \text{rX}(4{:}4) = \text{Del Mar pedestrian light} \\ \text{rX}(5{:}5) = \text{Berkeley pedestrian light} \end{array}\right\} \text{ 0 off, 1 "WALK", 2 "DON'T WALK".}$$

Cars or pedestrians wishing to travel on Berkeley across the boulevard must trip a switch that causes the overflow toggle of MIX to go on. If this condition never occurs, the light for Del Mar should remain green.

Cycle times are as follows:

> Del Mar traffic light is green $\geq$ 30 sec, amber 8 sec;
> Berkeley traffic light is green 20 sec, amber 5 sec.

When a traffic light is green or amber for one direction, the other direction has a red light. When the traffic light is green, the corresponding WALK light is on, except that

22	47	16	41	10	35	04
05	23	48	17	42	11	29
30	06	24	49	18	36	12
13	31	07	25	43	19	37
38	14	32	01	26	44	20
21	39	08	33	02	27	45
46	15	40	09	34	03	28

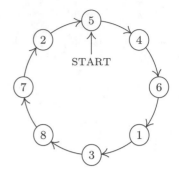

Fig. 16. A magic square.   **Fig. 17.** Josephus's problem, $n = 8$, $m = 4$.

DON'T WALK flashes for 12 sec just before a green light turns to amber, as follows:

$$
\left.\begin{array}{ll}
\text{DON'T WALK} & \tfrac{1}{2}\ \text{sec}\\[2pt]
\text{off} & \tfrac{1}{2}\ \text{sec}
\end{array}\right\}\ \text{repeat 8 times;}
$$

DON'T WALK   4 sec (and remains on through amber and red cycles).

If the overflow is tripped while the Berkeley light is green, the car or pedestrian will pass on that cycle, but if it is tripped during the amber or red portions, another cycle will be necessary after the Del Mar traffic has passed.

Assume that one MIX time unit equals 10 μsec. Write a complete MIX program that controls these lights by manipulating rX, according to the input given by the overflow toggle. The stated times are to be followed exactly unless it is impossible to do so. *Note:* The setting of rX changes precisely at the *completion* of a LDX or INCX instruction.

21. [*28*] A *magic square of order n* is an arrangement of the numbers 1 through n^2 in a square array in such a way that the sum of each row and column is $n(n^2+1)/2$, and so is the sum of the two main diagonals. Figure 16 shows a magic square of order 7. The rule for generating it is easily seen: Start with 1 just below the middle square, then go down and to the right diagonally — when running off the edge imagine an entire plane tiled with squares — until reaching a filled square; then drop down two spaces from the most-recently-filled square and continue. This method works whenever n is odd.

Using memory allocated in a fashion like that of exercise 10, write a complete MIX program to generate the 23×23 magic square by the method above, and to print the result. [This algorithm is due to Ibn al-Haytham, who was born in Basra about 965 and died in Cairo about 1040. Many other magic square constructions make good programming exercises; see W. W. Rouse Ball, *Mathematical Recreations and Essays*, revised by H. S. M. Coxeter (New York: Macmillan, 1939), Chapter 7.]

22. [*31*] (*The Josephus problem.*) There are n men arranged in a circle. Beginning at a particular position, we count around the circle and brutally execute every mth man; the circle closes as men die. For example, the execution order when $n = 8$ and $m = 4$ is 54613872, as shown in Fig. 17: The first man is fifth to go, the second man is fourth, etc. Write a complete MIX program that prints out the order of execution when $n = 24$, $m = 11$. Try to design a clever algorithm that works at high speed when n and m are large (it may save your life). *Reference:* W. Ahrens, *Mathematische Unterhaltungen und Spiele* **2** (Leipzig: Teubner, 1918), Chapter 15.

23. [*37*] This is an exercise designed to give some experience in the many applications of computers for which the output is to be displayed graphically rather than in the usual tabular form. In this case, the object is to "draw" a crossword puzzle diagram.

You are given as input a matrix of zeros and ones. An entry of zero indicates a white square; a one indicates a black square. The output should be a diagram of the puzzle, with the appropriate squares numbered for words across and down.

For example, given the matrix

$$\begin{pmatrix} 1 & 0 & 0 & 0 & 0 & 1 \\ 0 & 0 & 1 & 0 & 0 & 0 \\ 0 & 0 & 0 & 0 & 1 & 0 \\ 0 & 1 & 0 & 0 & 0 & 0 \\ 0 & 0 & 0 & 1 & 0 & 0 \\ 1 & 0 & 0 & 0 & 0 & 1 \end{pmatrix},$$

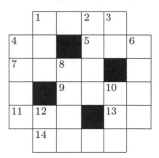

Fig. 18. Diagram corresponding to the matrix in exercise 23.

the corresponding puzzle diagram would be as shown in Fig. 18. A square is numbered if it is a white square and either (a) the square below it is white and there is no white square immediately above, or (b) the square to its right is white and there is no white square immediately to its left. If black squares occur at the edges, they should be removed from the diagram. This is illustrated in Fig. 18, where the black squares at the corners were dropped. A simple way to accomplish this is to artificially insert rows and columns of -1's at the top, bottom, and sides of the given input matrix, then to change every $+1$ that is adjacent to a -1 into a -1 until no $+1$ remains next to any -1.

The following method should be used to print the final diagram on a line printer: Each box of the puzzle should correspond to 5 columns and 3 rows of the output page, where the 15 positions are filled as follows:

Unnumbered white squares:	⊔⊔⊔⊔+ ⊔⊔⊔⊔+ +++++	Number **nn** white squares:	**nn**⊔⊔+ ⊔⊔⊔⊔+ +++++	Black squares:	+++++ +++++ +++++

"−1" squares, depending on whether there are −1's to the right or below:

⊔⊔⊔⊔+ ⊔⊔⊔⊔+ +++++	⊔⊔⊔⊔+ ⊔⊔⊔⊔+ ⊔⊔⊔⊔+	⊔⊔⊔⊔⊔ ⊔⊔⊔⊔⊔ +++++	⊔⊔⊔⊔⊔ ⊔⊔⊔⊔⊔ ⊔⊔⊔⊔+	⊔⊔⊔⊔⊔ ⊔⊔⊔⊔⊔ ⊔⊔⊔⊔⊔

The diagram shown in Fig. 18 would then be printed as shown in Fig. 19.

The width of a printer line — 120 characters — is enough to allow up to 23 columns in the crossword puzzle. The data supplied as input to your program will be a 23 × 23 matrix of zeros and ones, where each row is punched in columns 1–23 of an input card. For example, the card corresponding to the top row of the matrix above would be punched '10000111111111111111111'. The diagram will not necessarily be symmetrical, and it might have long paths of black squares that are connected to the outside in strange ways.

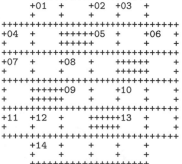

Fig. 19. Representation of Fig. 18 on a line printer.

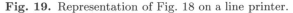

1.3.3. Applications to Permutations

In this section we shall give several more examples of MIX programs, and at the same time introduce some important properties of permutations. These investigations will also bring out some interesting aspects of computer programming in general.

Permutations were discussed earlier in Section 1.2.5; we treated the permutation $c\,d\,f\,b\,e\,a$ as an *arrangement* of the six objects a, b, c, d, e, f in a straight line. Another viewpoint is also possible: We may think of a permutation as a *rearrangement* or renaming of the objects. With this interpretation it is customary to use a two-line notation, for example,

$$\begin{pmatrix} a & b & c & d & e & f \\ c & d & f & b & e & a \end{pmatrix}, \tag{1}$$

to mean "a becomes c, b becomes d, c becomes f, d becomes b, e becomes e, f becomes a." Considered as a rearrangement, this means that object c moves to the place formerly occupied by object a; considered as a renaming, it means that object a is renamed c. The two-line notation is unaffected by changes in the order of the columns; for example, the permutation (1) could also be written

$$\begin{pmatrix} c & d & f & b & a & e \\ f & b & a & d & c & e \end{pmatrix}$$

and in 718 other ways.

A *cycle notation* is often used in connection with this interpretation. Permutation (1) could be written

$$(a\,c\,f)\,(b\,d), \tag{2}$$

again meaning "a becomes c, c becomes f, f becomes a, b becomes d, d becomes b." A cycle $(x_1\,x_2\,\ldots\,x_n)$ means "x_1 becomes x_2, $\ldots$, x_{n-1} becomes x_n, x_n becomes x_1." Since e is fixed under the permutation, it does not appear in the cycle notation; that is, singleton cycles like "(e)" are conventionally not written. If a permutation fixes *all* elements, so that there are only singleton cycles present, it is called the *identity permutation*, and we denote it by "$()$".

The cycle notation is not unique. For example,

$$(b\,d)\,(a\,c\,f), \qquad (c\,f\,a)\,(b\,d), \qquad (d\,b)\,(f\,a\,c), \tag{3}$$

etc., are all equivalent to (2). However, "$(a\,f\,c)\,(b\,d)$" is not the same, since it says that a goes to f.

It is easy to see why the cycle notation is always possible. Starting with any element x_1, the permutation takes x_1 into x_2, say, and x_2 into x_3, etc., until finally (since there are only finitely many elements) we get to some element x_{n+1} that has already appeared among $x_1, \ldots, x_n$. Now x_{n+1} must equal x_1. For if it were equal to, say, x_3, we already know that x_2 goes into x_3; but by assumption, $x_n \neq x_2$ goes to x_{n+1}. So $x_{n+1} = x_1$, and we have a cycle $(x_1\,x_2\,\ldots\,x_n)$ as part of our permutation, for some $n \geq 1$. If this does not account for the entire permutation, we can find another element y_1 and get another cycle $(y_1\,y_2\,\ldots\,y_m)$

in the same way. None of the y's can equal any of the x's, since $x_i = y_j$ implies that $x_{i+1} = y_{j+1}$, etc., and we would ultimately find $x_k = y_1$ for some k, contradicting the choice of y_1. All cycles will eventually be found.

One application of these concepts to programming comes up whenever some set of n objects is to be put into a different order. If we want to rearrange the objects without moving them elsewhere, we must essentially follow the cycle structure. For example, to do the rearrangement (1), namely to set

$$(a, b, c, d, e, f) \leftarrow (c, d, f, b, e, a),$$

we would essentially follow the cycle structure (2) and successively set

$$t \leftarrow a, \quad a \leftarrow c, \quad c \leftarrow f, \quad f \leftarrow t; \quad t \leftarrow b, \quad b \leftarrow d, \quad d \leftarrow t.$$

It is frequently useful to realize that any such transformation takes place in disjoint cycles.

Products of permutations. We can multiply two permutations together, with the understanding that multiplication means the application of one permutation after the other. For example, if permutation (1) is followed by the permutation

$$\begin{pmatrix} a & b & c & d & e & f \\ b & d & c & a & f & e \end{pmatrix},$$

we have a becomes c, which then becomes c; b becomes d, which becomes a; etc.:

$$\begin{pmatrix} a & b & c & d & e & f \\ c & d & f & b & e & a \end{pmatrix} \times \begin{pmatrix} a & b & c & d & e & f \\ b & d & c & a & f & e \end{pmatrix}$$

$$= \begin{pmatrix} a & b & c & d & e & f \\ c & d & f & b & e & a \end{pmatrix} \times \begin{pmatrix} c & d & f & b & e & a \\ c & a & e & d & f & b \end{pmatrix}$$

$$= \begin{pmatrix} a & b & c & d & e & f \\ c & a & e & d & f & b \end{pmatrix}. \tag{4}$$

It should be clear that multiplication of permutations is not commutative; in other words, $\pi_1 \times \pi_2$ is not necessarily equal to $\pi_2 \times \pi_1$ when π_1 and π_2 are permutations. The reader may verify that the product in (4) gives a different result if the two factors are interchanged (see exercise 3).

Some people multiply permutations from right to left rather than the somewhat more natural left-to-right order shown in (4). In fact, mathematicians are divided into two camps in this regard; should the result of applying transformation T_1, then T_2, be denoted by $T_1 T_2$ or by $T_2 T_1$? Here we use $T_1 T_2$.

Equation (4) would be written as follows, using the cycle notation:

$$(a\,c\,f)\,(b\,d)\,(a\,b\,d)\,(e\,f) = (a\,c\,e\,f\,b). \tag{5}$$

Note that the multiplication sign "$\times$" is conventionally dropped; this does not conflict with the cycle notation since it is easy to see that the permutation $(a\,c\,f)(b\,d)$ is really the product of the permutations $(a\,c\,f)$ and $(b\,d)$.

Multiplication of permutations can be done directly in terms of the cycle notation. For example, to compute the product of several permutations

$$(a\,c\,f\,g)\,(b\,c\,d)\,(a\,e\,d)\,(f\,a\,d\,e)\,(b\,g\,f\,a\,e), \tag{6}$$

we find (proceeding from left to right) that "a goes to c, then c goes to d, then d goes to a, then a goes to d, then d is unchanged"; so the net result is that a goes to d under (6), and we write down "$(a\,d$" as the partial answer. Now we consider the effect on d: "d goes to b goes to g"; we have the partial result "$(a\,d\,g$". Considering g, we find that "g goes to a, to e, to f, to a", and so the first cycle is closed: "$(a\,d\,g)$". Now we pick a new element that hasn't appeared yet, say c; we find that c goes to e, and the reader may verify that ultimately the answer "$(a\,d\,g)(c\,e\,b)$" is obtained for (6).

Let us now try to do this process by computer. The following algorithm formalizes the method described in the preceding paragraph, in a way that is amenable to machine calculation.

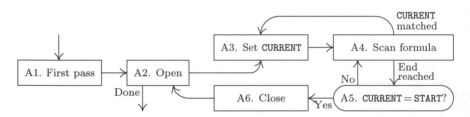

Fig. 20. Algorithm A for multiplying permutations.

Algorithm A (*Multiply permutations in cycle form*). This algorithm takes a product of cycles, such as (6), and computes the resulting permutation in the form of a product of disjoint cycles. For simplicity, the removal of singleton cycles is not described here; that would be a fairly simple extension of the algorithm. As this algorithm is performed, we successively "tag" the elements of the input formula; that is, we mark somehow those symbols of the input formula that have been processed.

A1. [First pass.] Tag all left parentheses, and replace each right parenthesis by a tagged copy of the input symbol that follows its matching left parenthesis. (See the example in Table 1.)

A2. [Open.] Searching from left to right, find the first untagged element of the input. (If all elements are tagged, the algorithm terminates.) Set START equal to it; output a left parenthesis; output the element; and tag it.

A3. [Set CURRENT.] Set CURRENT equal to the next element of the formula.

A4. [Scan formula.] Proceed to the right until either reaching the end of the formula, or finding an element equal to CURRENT; in the latter case, tag it and go back to step A3.

Table 1

ALGORITHM A APPLIED TO (6)

After step	START	CURRENT	$(\,a\,c\,f\,g\,)\,(\,b\,c\,d\,)\,(\,a\,e\,d\,)\,(\,f\,a\,d\,e\,)\,(\,b\,g\,f\,a\,e\,)$	Output
A1			$(\,a\,c\,f\,g\,a\,(\,b\,c\,d\,b\,(\,a\,e\,d\,a\,(\,f\,a\,d\,e\,f\,(\,b\,g\,f\,a\,e\,b$	
A2	a		$(\,a\,c\,f\,g\,a\,(\,b\,c\,d\,b\,(\,a\,e\,d\,a\,(\,f\,a\,d\,e\,f\,(\,b\,g\,f\,a\,e\,b$	$(a$
A3	a	c	$(\,a\,c\,f\,g\,a\,(\,b\,c\,d\,b\,(\,a\,e\,d\,a\,(\,f\,a\,d\,e\,f\,(\,b\,g\,f\,a\,e\,b$	
A4 ...	a	c	$(\,a\,c\,f\,g\,a\,(\,b\,c\,d\,b\,(\,a\,e\,d\,a\,(\,f\,a\,d\,e\,f\,(\,b\,g\,f\,a\,e\,b$	
A4 ...	a	d	$(\,a\,c\,f\,g\,a\,(\,b\,c\,d\,b\,(\,a\,e\,d\,a\,(\,f\,a\,d\,e\,f\,(\,b\,g\,f\,a\,e\,b$	
A4 ...	a	a	$(\,a\,c\,f\,g\,a\,(\,b\,c\,d\,b\,(\,a\,e\,d\,a\,(\,f\,a\,d\,e\,f\,(\,b\,g\,f\,a\,e\,b$	
A5 ...	a	d	$(\,a\,c\,f\,g\,a\,(\,b\,c\,d\,b\,(\,a\,e\,d\,a\,(\,f\,a\,d\,e\,f\,(\,b\,g\,f\,a\,e\,b$	d
A5 ...	a	g	$(\,a\,c\,f\,g\,a\,(\,b\,c\,d\,b\,(\,a\,e\,d\,a\,(\,f\,a\,d\,e\,f\,(\,b\,g\,f\,a\,e\,b$	g
A5 ...	a	a	$(\,a\,c\,f\,g\,a\,(\,b\,c\,d\,b\,(\,a\,e\,d\,a\,(\,f\,a\,d\,e\,f\,(\,b\,g\,f\,a\,e\,b$	
A6 ...	a	a	$(\,a\,c\,f\,g\,a\,(\,b\,c\,d\,b\,(\,a\,e\,d\,a\,(\,f\,a\,d\,e\,f\,(\,b\,g\,f\,a\,e\,b$	$)$
A2 ...	c	a	$(\,a\,c\,f\,g\,a\,(\,b\,c\,d\,b\,(\,a\,e\,d\,a\,(\,f\,a\,d\,e\,f\,(\,b\,g\,f\,a\,e\,b$	$(c$
A5 ...	c	e	$(\,a\,c\,f\,g\,a\,(\,b\,c\,d\,b\,(\,a\,e\,d\,a\,(\,f\,a\,d\,e\,f\,(\,b\,g\,f\,a\,e\,b$	e
A5 ...	c	b	$(\,a\,c\,f\,g\,a\,(\,b\,c\,d\,b\,(\,a\,e\,d\,a\,(\,f\,a\,d\,e\,f\,(\,b\,g\,f\,a\,e\,b$	b
A6 ...	c	c	$(\,a\,c\,f\,g\,a\,(\,b\,c\,d\,b\,(\,a\,e\,d\,a\,(\,f\,a\,d\,e\,f\,(\,b\,g\,f\,a\,e\,b$	$)$
A6	f	f	$(\,a\,c\,f\,g\,a\,(\,b\,c\,d\,b\,(\,a\,e\,d\,a\,(\,f\,a\,d\,e\,f\,(\,b\,g\,f\,a\,e\,b$	(f)

Here ⌶ represents a cursor following the element just scanned; tagged elements are light gray.

A5. [CURRENT = START?] If CURRENT ≠ START, output CURRENT and go back to step A4 starting again at the left of the formula (thereby continuing the development of a cycle in the output).

A6. [Close.] (A complete cycle in the output has been found.) Output a right parenthesis, and go back to step A2. ∎

For example, consider formula (6); Table 1 shows successive stages in its processing. The first line of that table shows the formula after right parentheses have been replaced by the leading element of the corresponding cycle; succeeding lines show the progress that is made as more and more elements are tagged. A cursor shows the current point of interest in the formula. The output is "$(a\,d\,g)\,(c\,e\,b)\,(f)$"; notice that singleton cycles will appear in the output.

A MIX program. To implement this algorithm for MIX, the "tagging" can be done by using the sign of a word. Suppose our input is punched onto cards in the following format: An 80-column card is divided into 16 five-character fields. Each field is either (a) '␣␣␣␣(', representing the left parenthesis beginning a cycle; (b) ')␣␣␣␣', representing the right parenthesis ending a cycle; (c) '␣␣␣␣␣', all blanks, which may be inserted anywhere to fill space; or (d) anything else, representing an element to be permuted. The last card of the input is recognized by having columns 76–80 equal to '␣␣␣␣='. For example, (6) might be punched on two cards as follows:

(A	C	F	G	)	(B	C	D	)	(A	E	D	)
(F	A	D	E	)	(B	G	F	A	E	)		=

The output of our program will consist of a verbatim copy of the input, followed by the answer in essentially the same format.

Program A (*Multiply permutations in cycle form*). This program implements Algorithm A, and it also includes provision for input, output, and the removing of singleton cycles. But it doesn't catch errors in the input.

```
01  MAXWDS   EQU   1200                  Maximum length of input
02  PERM     ORIG  *+MAXWDS              The input permutation
03  ANS      ORIG  *+MAXWDS              Place for answer
04  OUTBUF   ORIG  *+24                  Place for printing
05  CARDS    EQU   16                    Unit number for card reader
06  PRINTER  EQU   18                    Unit number for printer
07  BEGIN    IN    PERM(CARDS)           Read first card.
08           ENT2  0
09           LDA   EQUALS
10  1H       JBUS  *(CARDS)              Wait for cycle complete.
11           CMPA  PERM+15,2
12           JE    *+2                   Is it the last card?
13           IN    PERM+16,2(CARDS)      No, read another.
14           ENT1  OUTBUF
15           JBUS  *(PRINTER)            Print a copy of
16           MOVE  PERM,2(16)                the input card.
17           OUT   OUTBUF(PRINTER)
18           JE    1F
19           INC2  16
20           CMP2  =MAXWDS-16=
21           JLE   1B                    Repeat until input is complete.
22           HLT   666                   Too much input!
23  1H       INC2  15              1     At this point, rI2 words of
24           ST2   SIZE            1        input are in PERM, PERM + 1, ...
25           ENT3  0               1     A1. First pass.
26  2H       LDAN  PERM,3          A     Get next element of input.
27           CMPA  LPREN(1:5)      A     Is it '('?
28           JNE   1F              A
29           STA   PERM,3          B     If so, tag it.
30           INC3  1               B     Put the next nonblank input symbol
31           LDXN  PERM,3          B        into rX.
32           JXZ   *-2             B
33  1H       CMPA  RPREN(1:5)      C
34           JNE   *+2             C
35           STX   PERM,3          D     Replace ')' by tagged rX.
36           INC3  1               C
37           CMP3  SIZE            C     Have all elements been processed?
38           JL    2B              C
```

```
39              LDA  LPREN              1   Prepare for main program.
40              ENT1 ANS               1   rI1 = place to store next answer
41   OPEN       ENT3 0                 E   A2. Open.
42   1H         LDXN PERM,3            F   Look for untagged element.
43              JXN  GO                F
44              INC3 1                 G
45              CMP3 SIZE              G
46              JL   1B                G
47   *                                     All are tagged. Now comes the output.
48   DONE       CMP1 =ANS=
49              JNE  *+2                   Is answer the identity permutation?
50              MOVE LPREN(2)              If so, change to '()'.
51              MOVE =0=                   Put 23 words of blanks after answer.
52              MOVE -1,1(22)
53              ENT3 0
54              OUT  ANS,3(PRINTER)
55              INC3 24
56              LDX  ANS,3                 Print as many lines as necessary.
57              JXNZ *-3
58              HLT
59   *
60   LPREN      ALF       (               Constants used in the program
61   RPREN      ALF  )
62   EQUALS     ALF       =
63   *
64   GO         MOVE LPREN             H   Open a cycle in the output.
65              MOVE PERM,3            H
66              STX  START             H
67   SUCC       STX  PERM,3            J   Tag an element.
68              INC3 1                 J   Move one step to the right.
69              LDXN PERM,3(1:5)       J   A3. Set CURRENT (namely rX).
70              JXN  1F                J   Skip past blanks.
71              JMP  *-3               0
72   5H         STX  0,1               Q   Output CURRENT.
73              INC1 1                 Q
74              ENT3 0                 Q   Scan formula again.
75   4H         CMPX PERM,3(1:5)       K   A4. Scan formula.
76              JE   SUCC              K   Element = CURRENT?
77   1H         INC3 1                 L   Move to right.
78              CMP3 SIZE              L   End of formula?
79              JL   4B                L
80              CMPX START(1:5)        P   A5. CURRENT = START?
81              JNE  5B                P
82   CLOSE      MOVE RPREN             R   A6. Close.
83              CMPA -3,1              R   Note: rA = '('.
84              JNE  OPEN              R
85              INC1 -3                S   Suppress singleton cycles.
86              JMP  OPEN              S
87              END  BEGIN
```

This program of approximately 75 instructions is quite a bit longer than the programs of the previous section, and indeed it is longer than most of the programs we will meet in this book. Its length is not formidable, however, since it divides into several small parts that are fairly independent. Lines 07–22 read in the input cards and print a copy of each card; lines 23–38 accomplish step A1 of the algorithm, the preconditioning of the input; lines 39–46 and 64–86 do the main business of Algorithm A; and lines 48–57 output the answer.

The reader will find it instructive to study as many of the MIX programs given in this book as possible. An ability to read and to understand computer programs that you haven't written yourself is exceedingly important; yet such training has been sadly neglected in too many computer courses, and some horribly inefficient uses of computing machinery have arisen as a result.

Timing. The parts of Program A that are not concerned with input-output have been decorated with frequency counts, as we did for Program 1.3.2M. Thus, for example, line 30 is supposedly executed B times. For convenience we shall assume that no blank words appear in the input except at the extreme right end; under this assumption, line 71 is never executed and the jump in line 32 never occurs.

By simple addition the total time to execute the program is

$$(7 + 5A + 6B + 7C + 2D + E + 3F + 4G + 8H + 6J$$
$$+ 3K + 4L + 3P + 4Q + 6R + 2S)u, \quad (7)$$

plus the time for input and output. In order to understand the meaning of formula (7), we need to examine the fifteen unknowns A, B, C, D, E, F, G, H, J, K, L, P, Q, R, S and we must relate them to pertinent characteristics of the input. Let's look at some general principles of attack for problems of this kind.

First we can apply "Kirchhoff's first law" of electrical circuit theory: The number of times an instruction is executed must equal the number of times we transfer to that instruction. This seemingly obvious rule often relates several quantities in a nonobvious way. Analyzing the flow of Program A, we get the following equations.

From lines	We deduce
26, 38, 39	$A = 1 + (C - 1)$
33, 28, 29	$C = B + (A - B)$
41, 84, 86	$E = 1 + R$
42, 46, 48	$F = E + (G - 1)$
64, 43, 44	$H = F - G$
67, 70, 76	$J = H + (K - (L - J))$
75, 79, 80	$K = Q + (L - P)$
82, 72, 81	$R = P - Q$

The equations given by Kirchhoff's law will not all be independent; in the present case, for example, we see that the first and second equations are obviously equivalent. Furthermore, the last equation can be deduced from the others, since the third, fourth, and fifth imply that $H = R$; hence the sixth says that $K = L - R$. At any rate we have already eliminated six of our fifteen unknowns:

$$A = C, \quad E = R + 1, \quad F = R + G, \quad H = R, \quad K = L - R, \quad Q = P - R. \quad (8)$$

Kirchhoff's first law is an effective tool that is analyzed more closely in Section 2.3.4.1.

The next step is to try to match up the variables with important characteristics of the data. We find from lines 24, 25, 30, and 36 that

$$B + C = \text{number of words of input} = 16X - 1, \quad (9)$$

where X is the number of input cards. From line 28,

$$B = \text{number of "(" in input} = \text{number of cycles in input.} \quad (10)$$

Similarly, from line 34,

$$D = \text{number of ")" in input} = \text{number of cycles in input.} \quad (11)$$

Now (10) and (11) give us a fact that could not be deduced by Kirchhoff's law:

$$B = D. \quad (12)$$

From line 64,

$$H = \text{number of cycles in output (including singletons).} \quad (13)$$

Line 82 says R is equal to this same quantity; the fact that $H = R$ *was* in this case deducible from Kirchhoff's law, since it already appears in (8).

Using the fact that each nonblank word is ultimately tagged, and lines 29, 35, and 67, we find that

$$J = Y - 2B, \quad (14)$$

where Y is the number of nonblank words appearing in the input permutations. From the fact that every *distinct* element appearing in the input permutation is written into the output just once, either at line 65 or line 72, we have

$$P = H + Q = \text{number of distinct elements in input.} \quad (15)$$

(See Eqs. (8).) A moment's reflection makes this clear from line 80 as well. Finally, we see from line 85 that

$$S = \text{number of singleton cycles in output.} \quad (16)$$

Clearly the quantities B, C, H, J, P, and S that we have now interpreted are essentially independent parameters that may be expected to enter into the timing of Program A.

The results we have obtained so far leave us with only the unknowns G and L to be analyzed. For these we must use a little more ingenuity. The scans of the input that start at lines 41 and 74 always terminate either at line 47 (the last time) or at line 80. During each one of these $P + 1$ loops, the instruction

'INC3 1' is performed $B + C$ times; this takes place only at lines 44, 68, and 77, so we get the nontrivial relation

$$G + J + L = (B + C)(P + 1) \qquad (17)$$

connecting our unknowns G and L. Fortunately, the running time (7) is a function of $G + L$ (it involves $\cdots + 3F + 4G + \cdots + 3K + 4L + \cdots = \cdots + 7G + 7L + \cdots$), so we need not try to analyze the individual quantities G and L any further.

Summing up all these results, we find that the total time exclusive of input-output comes to

$$(112NX + 304X - 2M - Y + 11U + 2V - 11)u; \qquad (18)$$

in this formula, new names for the data characteristics have been used as follows:

$$\begin{aligned} &X = \text{number of cards of input,} \\ &Y = \text{number of nonblank fields in input (excluding final ``='),} \\ &M = \text{number of cycles in input,} \\ &N = \text{number of distinct element names in input,} \\ &U = \text{number of cycles in output (including singletons),} \\ &V = \text{number of singleton cycles in output.} \end{aligned} \qquad (19)$$

In this way we have found that analysis of a program like Program A is in many respects like solving an amusing puzzle.

We will show below that, if the output permutation is assumed to be random, the quantities U and V will be H_N and 1, respectively, on the average.

Another approach. Algorithm A multiplies permutations together much as people ordinarily do the same job. Quite often we find that problems to be solved by computer are very similar to problems that have confronted humans for many years; therefore time-honored methods of solution, which have evolved for use by mortals such as we, are also appropriate procedures for computer algorithms.

Just as often, however, we encounter new methods that turn out to be superior for computers, although they are quite unsuitable for human use. The central reason is that a computer "thinks" differently; it has a different kind of memory for facts. An instance of this difference may be seen in our permutation-multiplication problem: Using the algorithm below, a computer can do the multiplication in one sweep over the formula, remembering the entire current state of the permutation as its cycles are being multiplied. The human-oriented Algorithm A scans the formula many times, once for each element of the output, but the new algorithm handles everything in one scan. This is a feat that could not be done reliably by *Homo sapiens*.

What is this computer-oriented method for permutation multiplication? Table 2 illustrates the basic idea. The column below each character of the cycle form in that table says what permutation is represented by the partial cycles *to the right*. For example, the fragmentary formula "$\ldots\ d\ e)(b\ g\ f\ a\ e)$" represents

Table 2

MULTIPLYING PERMUTATIONS IN ONE PASS

$$(\, a \, c \, f \, g \,) \, (\, b \, c \, d \,) \, (\, a \, e \, d \,) \, (\, f \, a \, d \, e \,) \, (\, b \, g \, f \, a \, e \,)$$

$a \rightarrow d \, d \, a \, a \, a \, a \, a \, a \, a \, a \, a \, a \, a \, d \, d \, d \, d \, d \, d \, e \, e \, e \, e \, e \, e \, e \, a \, a$

$b \rightarrow c \, c \, c \, c \, c \, c \, c \, c \, g \, g \, g \, g \, g \, g \, g \, g \, g \, g \, g \, g \, g \, g \, g \, g \, b \, b \, b \, b \, b$

$c \rightarrow e \, e \, e \, d \, d \, d \, d \, d \, d \, c \, c \, c \, c \, c \, c \, c \, c \, c \, c \, c \, c \, c \, c \, c \, c \, c \, c \, c \, c$

$d \rightarrow g \, g \, g \, g \, g \, g \, g \,) \,) \,) \, d \, d \,) \,) \,) \, b \, b \, b \, b \, b \, d \, d \, d \, d \, d \, d \, d \, d$

$e \rightarrow b \, b \, b \, b \, b \, b \, b \, b \, b \, b \, b \, b \, b \, a \, a \, a \,) \,) \,) \,) \, b \, b \,) \,) \,) \,) \,) \, e$

$f \rightarrow f \, f \, f \, f \, e \, e \, e \, e \, e \, e \, e \, e \, e \, e \, e \, e \, e \, a \, a \, a \, a \, a \, a \, a \, a \, f \, f \, f$

$g \rightarrow a \,) \,) \,) \,) \, f \, f \, f \, f \, f \, f \, f \, f \, f \, f \, f \, f \, f \, f \, f \, f \, f \, f \, f \, f \, g \, g \, g \, g$

the permutation

$$\begin{pmatrix} a & b & c & d & e & f & g \\ e & g & c & b & ? & a & f \end{pmatrix},$$

which appears under the rightmost d of the table, except that the unknown
destination of e is represented there by ')' not '?'.

Inspection of Table 2 shows that it can be created systematically, if we
start with the identity permutation on the right and work backward from right
to left. The column below letter x differs from the column to its right (which
records the previous status) only in row x; and the new value in row x is the one
that disappeared in the preceding change. More precisely, we have the following
algorithm:

Algorithm B (*Multiply permutations in cycle form*). This algorithm accom-
plishes essentially the same result as Algorithm A. Assume that the elements permuted are named $x_1, x_2, \ldots, x_n$. We use an auxiliary table $T[1], T[2], \ldots, T[n]$;
upon termination of this algorithm, x_i goes to x_j under the input permutation
if and only if $T[i] = j$.

B1. [Initialize.] Set $T[k] \leftarrow k$ for $1 \leq k \leq n$. Also, prepare to scan the input
from right to left.

B2. [Next element.] Examine the next element of the input (right to left). If
the input has been exhausted, the algorithm terminates. If the element is
a ')', set $Z \leftarrow 0$ and repeat step B2; if it is a '(', go to B4. Otherwise the
element is x_i for some i; go on to B3.

B3. [Change $T[i]$.] Exchange $Z \leftrightarrow T[i]$. If this makes $T[i] = 0$, set $j \leftarrow i$. Return
to step B2.

B4. [Change $T[j]$.] Set $T[j] \leftarrow Z$. (At this point, j is the row that shows a ')'
entry in the notation of Table 2, corresponding to the right parenthesis that
matches the left parenthesis just scanned.) Return to step B2. ∎

Of course, after this algorithm has been performed, we still must output the
contents of table T in cycle form; this is easily done by a "tagging" method, as
we shall see below.

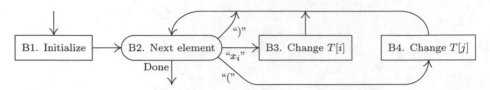

Fig. 21. Algorithm B for multiplying permutations.

Let us now write a MIX program based on the new algorithm. We wish to use the same ground rules as those in Program A, with input and output in the same format as before. A slight problem presents itself; namely, how can we implement Algorithm B without knowing in advance what the elements $x_1, x_2, \ldots, x_n$ are? We don't know n, and we don't know whether the element named b is to be x_1, or x_2, etc. A simple way to solve this problem is to maintain a table of the element names that have been encountered so far, and to search for the current name each time (see lines 35–44 in the program below).

Program B (*Same effect as Program A*). $rX \equiv Z$; $rI4 \equiv i$; $rI1 \equiv j$; $rI3 = n$, the number of distinct names seen.

01	MAXWDS	EQU	1200	Maximum length of input
02	X	ORIG	*+MAXWDS	The table of names
03	T	ORIG	*+MAXWDS	The auxiliary state table
04	PERM	ORIG	*+MAXWDS	The input permutation
05	ANS	EQU	PERM	Place for answer
06	OUTBUF	ORIG	*+24	Place for printing
07	CARDS	EQU	16	
	...			Same as lines 05–22 of Program A
24		HLT	666	At this point, rI2 words of
25	1H	INC2	15	1 input are in PERM, PERM + 1, ...
26		ENT3	0	1 and we haven't seen any names yet.
27	RIGHT	ENTX	0	A Set $Z \leftarrow 0$.
28	SCAN	DEC2	1	B _B2. Next element._
29		LDA	PERM,2	B
30		JAZ	CYCLE	B Skip over blanks.
31		CMPA	RPREN	C
32		JE	RIGHT	C Is the next element ')'?
33		CMPA	LPREN	D
34		JE	LEFT	D Is it '('?
35		ENT4	1,3	E Prepare for the search.
36		STA	X	E Store at beginning of table.
37	2H	DEC4	1	F Search through names table.
38		CMPA	X,4	F
39		JNE	2B	F Repeat until match found.
40		J4P	FOUND	G Has the name appeared before?
41		INC3	1	H No; increase the table size.
42		STA	X,3	H Insert the new name x_n.

43		ST3	T,3	H	Set $T[n] \leftarrow n$,
44		ENT4	0,3	H	$i \leftarrow n$.
45	FOUND	LDA	T,4	J	B3. Change $T[i]$.
46		STX	T,4	J	Store Z.
47		SRC	5	J	Set Z.
48		JANZ	SCAN	J	
49		ENT1	0,4	K	If Z was zero, set $j \leftarrow i$.
50		JMP	SCAN	K	
51	LEFT	STX	T,1	L	B4. Change $T[j]$.
52	CYCLE	J2P	SCAN	P	Return to B2, unless finished.
53	*				
54	OUTPUT	ENT1	ANS	1	All input has been scanned.
55		J3Z	DONE	1	The x and T tables contain the answer.
56	1H	LDAN	X,3	Q	Now we construct cycle notation.
57		JAP	SKIP	Q	Has name been tagged?
58		CMP3	T,3	R	Is there a singleton cycle?
59		JE	SKIP	R	
60		MOVE	LPREN	S	Open a cycle.
61	2H	MOVE	X,3	T	
62		STA	X,3	T	Tag the name.
63		LD3	T,3	T	Find successor of element.
64		LDAN	X,3	T	
65		JAN	2B	T	Is it already tagged?
66		MOVE	RPREN	W	Yes, cycle closes.
67	SKIP	DEC3	1	Z	Move to next name.
68		J3P	1B	Z	
69	*				
70	DONE	CMP1	=ANS=		
	...				} Same as lines 48–62 of Program A
84	EQUALS	ALF	=		
85		END	BEGIN	▌	

Lines 54–68, which construct the cycle notation from the T table and the table of names, make a rather pretty little algorithm that merits some study. The quantities A, B, ..., R, S, T, W, Z that enter into the timing of this program are, of course, different from the quantities of the same name in the analysis of Program A. The reader will find it an interesting exercise to analyze these times (see exercise 10).

Experience shows that the main portion of the execution time of Program B will be spent in searching the names table — this is quantity F in the timing. Much better algorithms for searching and building dictionaries of names are available; they are called *symbol table algorithms*, and they are of great importance in computer applications. Chapter 6 contains a thorough discussion of efficient symbol table algorithms.

Inverses. The inverse π^- of a permutation π is the rearrangement that undoes the effect of π; if i goes to j under π, then j goes to i under π^-. Thus the product $\pi\pi^-$ equals the identity permutation, and so does the product $\pi^-\pi$.

People often denote the inverse by π^{-1} instead of π^-, but the superscript 1 is redundant (for the same reason that $x^1 = x$).

Every permutation has an inverse. For example, the inverse of

$$\begin{pmatrix} a & b & c & d & e & f \\ c & d & f & b & e & a \end{pmatrix} \quad \text{is} \quad \begin{pmatrix} c & d & f & b & e & a \\ a & b & c & d & e & f \end{pmatrix} = \begin{pmatrix} a & b & c & d & e & f \\ f & d & a & b & e & c \end{pmatrix}.$$

We will now consider some simple algorithms for computing the inverse of a permutation.

In the rest of this section, let us assume that we are dealing with permutations of the numbers $\{1, 2, \ldots, n\}$. If $X[1]\,X[2] \ldots X[n]$ is such a permutation, there is a simple method to compute its inverse: Set $Y[X[k]] \leftarrow k$ for $1 \leq k \leq n$. Then $Y[1]\,Y[2] \ldots Y[n]$ is the desired inverse. This method uses $2n$ memory cells, namely n for X and n for Y.

Just for fun, however, let's suppose that n is very large and suppose also that we wish to compute the inverse of $X[1]\,X[2] \ldots X[n]$ without using much additional memory space. We want to compute the inverse "in place," so that after our algorithm is finished the array $X[1]\,X[2] \ldots X[n]$ will be the inverse of the original permutation. Merely setting $X[X[k]] \leftarrow k$ for $1 \leq k \leq n$ will certainly fail, but by considering the cycle structure we can derive the following simple algorithm:

Algorithm I (*Inverse in place*). Replace $X[1]X[2] \ldots X[n]$, a permutation of $\{1, 2, \ldots, n\}$, by its inverse. This algorithm is due to Bing-Chao Huang [*Inf. Proc. Letters* **12** (1981), 237–238].

I1. [Initialize.] Set $m \leftarrow n$, $j \leftarrow -1$.

I2. [Next element.] Set $i \leftarrow X[m]$. If $i < 0$, go to step I5 (the element has already been processed).

I3. [Invert one.] (At this point $j < 0$ and $i = X[m]$. If m is not the largest element of its cycle, the original permutation had $X[-j] = m$.) Set $X[m] \leftarrow j$, $j \leftarrow -m$, $m \leftarrow i$, $i \leftarrow X[m]$.

I4. [End of cycle?] If $i > 0$, go back to I3 (the cycle has not ended); otherwise set $i \leftarrow j$. (In the latter case, the original permutation had $X[-j] = m$, and m is largest in its cycle.)

I5. [Store final value.] Set $X[m] \leftarrow -i$. (Originally $X[-i]$ was equal to m.)

I6. [Loop on m.] Decrease m by 1. If $m > 0$, go back to I2; otherwise the algorithm terminates. ∎

See Table 3 for an example of this algorithm. The method is based on inversion of successive cycles of the permutation, tagging the inverted elements by making them negative, afterwards restoring the correct sign.

Algorithm I resembles parts of Algorithm A, and it very strongly resembles the cycle-finding algorithm in Program B (lines 54–68). Thus it is typical of a number of algorithms involving rearrangements. When preparing a MIX implementation, we find that it is most convenient to keep the value of $-i$ in a register instead of i itself:

Table 3

COMPUTING THE INVERSE OF 6 2 1 5 4 3 BY ALGORITHM I

After step:	I2	I3	I3	I3	I5*	I2	I3	I3	I5	I2	I5	I5	I3	I5	I5
$X[1]$	6	6	6	−3	−3	−3	−3	−3	−3	−3	−3	−3	−3	−3	3
$X[2]$	2	2	2	2	2	2	2	2	2	2	2	2	−4	2	2
$X[3]$	1	1	−6	−6	−6	−6	−6	−6	−6	−6	6	6	6	6	6
$X[4]$	5	5	5	5	5	5	5	−5	−5	−5	5	5	5	5	5
$X[5]$	4	4	4	4	4	4	−1	−1	4	4	4	4	4	4	4
$X[6]$	3	−1	−1	−1	1	1	1	1	1	1	1	1	1	1	1
m	6	3	1	6	6	5	4	5	5	4	4	3	2	2	1
j	−1	−6	−3	−1	−1	−1	−5	−4	−4	−4	−4	−4	−2	−2	−2
i	3	1	6	−1	−1	4	5	−1	−4	−5	−5	−6	−4	−2	−3

Read the columns from left to right. At point *, the cycle (1 6 3) has been inverted.

Program I (*Inverse in place*). $rI1 \equiv m$; $rI2 \equiv -i$; $rI3 \equiv j$; and $n = \mathbb{N}$, a symbol to be defined when this program is assembled as part of a larger routine.

```
01  INVERT  ENT1 N     1   I1. Initialize. m ← n.
02          ENT3 -1    1   j ← -1.
03  2H      LD2N X,1   N   I2. Next element. i ← X[m].
04          J2P  5F    N   To I5 if i < 0.
05  3H      ST3  X,1   N   I3. Invert one. X[m] ← j.
06          ENN3 0,1   N   j ← -m.
07          ENN1 0,2   N   m ← i.
08          LD2N X,1   N   i ← X[m].
09  4H      J2N  3B    N   I4. End of cycle? To I3 if i > 0.
10          ENN2 0,3   C   Otherwise set i ← j.
11  5H      ST2  X,1   N   I5. Store final value. X[m] ← -i.
12  6H      DEC1 1     N   I6. Loop on m.
13          J1P  2B    N   To I2 if m > 0.  ▮
```

The timing for this program is easily worked out in the manner shown earlier; every element $X[m]$ is set first to a negative value in step I3 and later to a positive value in step I5. The total time comes to $(14N + C + 2)u$, where N is the size of the array and C is the total number of cycles. The behavior of C in a random permutation is analyzed below.

There is almost always more than one algorithm to do any given task, so we would expect that there may be another way to invert a permutation. The following ingenious algorithm is due to J. Boothroyd:

Algorithm J (*Inverse in place*). This algorithm has the same effect as Algorithm I but uses a different method.

J1. [Negate all.] Set $X[k] \leftarrow -X[k]$, for $1 \le k \le n$. Also set $m \leftarrow n$.

J2. [Initialize j.] Set $j \leftarrow m$.

J3. [Find negative entry.] Set $i \leftarrow X[j]$. If $i > 0$, set $j \leftarrow i$ and repeat this step.

J4. [Invert.] Set $X[j] \leftarrow X[-i]$, $X[-i] \leftarrow m$.

J5. [Loop on m.] Decrease m by 1; if $m > 0$, go back to J2. Otherwise the algorithm terminates. ▮

Table 4

COMPUTING THE INVERSE OF 6 2 1 5 4 3 BY ALGORITHM J

After step:	J2	J3	J5	J3	J5	J3	J5	J3	J5	J3	J5	J3	J5
$X[1]$	-6	-6	-6	-6	-6	-6	-6	-6	3	3	3	3	3
$X[2]$	-2	-2	-2	-2	-2	-2	-2	-2	-2	-2	2	2	2
$X[3]$	-1	-1	6	6	6	6	6	6	6	6	6	6	6
$X[4]$	-5	-5	-5	-5	5	5	5	5	5	5	5	5	5
$X[5]$	-4	-4	-4	-4	-5	-5	4	4	4	4	4	4	4
$X[6]$	-3	-3	-1	-1	-1	-1	-1	-1	-6	-6	-6	-6	1
m	6	6	5	5	4	4	3	3	2	2	1	1	0
i		-3	-3	-4	-4	-5	-5	-1	-1	-2	-2	-6	-6
j	6	6	6	5	5	5	5	6	6	2	2	6	6

See Table 4 for an example of Boothroyd's algorithm. Again the method is essentially based on the cycle structure, but this time it is less obvious that the algorithm really works! Verification is left to the reader (see exercise 13).

Program J (*Analogous to Program I*). rI1 $\equiv m$; rI2 $\equiv j$; rI3 $\equiv -i$.

01	INVERT	ENN1	N	1	*J1. Negate all.*
02		ST1	X+N+1,1(0:0)	N	Set sign negative.
03		INC1	1	N	
04		J1N	*-2	N	More?
05		ENT1	N	1	$m \leftarrow n$.
06	2H	ENN3	0,1	N	*J2. Initialize j.* $i \leftarrow m$.
07		ENN2	0,3	A	$j \leftarrow i$.
08		LD3N	X,2	A	*J3. Find negative entry.*
09		J3N	*-2	A	$i > 0$?
10		LDA	X,3	N	*J4. Invert.*
11		STA	X,2	N	$X[j] \leftarrow X[-i]$.
12		ST1	X,3	N	$X[-i] \leftarrow m$.
13		DEC1	1	N	*J5. Loop on m.*
14		J1P	2B	N	To J2 if $m > 0$. ∎

To decide how fast this program runs, we need to know the quantity A; this quantity is so interesting and instructive, it has been left as an exercise (see exercise 14).

Although Algorithm J is deucedly clever, analysis shows that Algorithm I is definitely superior. In fact, the average running time of Algorithm J turns out to be essentially proportional to $n \ln n$, while that of Algorithm I is essentially proportional to n. Maybe some day someone will find a use for Algorithm J (or some related modification); it is a bit too pretty to be forgotten altogether.

An unusual correspondence. We have already remarked that the cycle notation for a permutation is not unique; the six-element permutation (1 6 3)(4 5) may be written (5 4)(3 1 6), etc. It will be useful to consider a *canonical form* for the cyclic notation; the canonical form *is* unique. To get the canonical form, proceed as follows:

a) Write all singleton cycles explicitly.

b) Within each cycle, put the smallest number first.

c) Order the cycles in *decreasing* order of the first number in the cycle.

For example, starting with (3 1 6)(5 4) we would get

$$\text{(a): } (3\ 1\ 6)\ (5\ 4)\ (2); \quad \text{(b): } (1\ 6\ 3)\ (4\ 5)\ (2); \quad \text{(c): } (4\ 5)\ (2)\ (1\ 6\ 3). \qquad (20)$$

The important property of this canonical form is that the parentheses may be dropped and uniquely reconstructed again. Thus there is only one way to insert parentheses in "4 5 2 1 6 3" to get a canonical cycle form: One must insert a left parenthesis just before each *left-to-right minimum* (namely, just before each element that is preceded by no smaller elements).

This insertion and removal of parentheses gives us an unusual one-to-one correspondence between the set of all permutations expressed in cycle form and the set of all permutations expressed in linear form. For example, the permutation 6 2 1 5 4 3 in canonical cycle form is (4 5) (2) (1 6 3); remove parentheses to get 4 5 2 1 6 3, which in cycle form is (2 5 6 3) (1 4); remove parentheses to get 2 5 6 3 1 4, which in cycle form is (3 6 4) (1 2 5); etc.

This correspondence has numerous applications to the study of permutations of different types. For example, let us ask "How many cycles does a permutation of n elements have, on the average?" To answer this question we consider the set of all $n!$ permutations expressed in canonical form, and drop the parentheses; we are left with the set of all $n!$ permutations in some order. Our original question is therefore equivalent to, "How many left-to-right minima does a permutation of n elements have, on the average?" We have already answered the latter question in Section 1.2.10; this was the quantity $(A + 1)$ in the analysis of Algorithm 1.2.10M, for which we found the statistics

$$\min 1, \quad \text{ave } H_n, \quad \max n, \quad \text{dev } \sqrt{H_n - H_n^{(2)}}. \qquad (21)$$

(Actually, we discussed the average number of right-to-left maxima, but that's clearly the same as the number of left-to-right minima.) Furthermore, we proved in essence that a permutation of n objects has k left-to-right minima with probability $\left[{n \atop k}\right]/n!$; therefore *a permutation of n objects has k cycles with probability* $\left[{n \atop k}\right]/n!$.

We can also ask about the average distance *between* left-to-right minima, which becomes equivalent to the average length of a cycle. By (21), the *total* number of cycles among all the $n!$ permutations is $n!\,H_n$, since it is $n!$ times the *average* number of cycles. If we pick one of these cycles at random, what is its average length?

Imagine all $n!$ permutations of $\{1, 2, \ldots, n\}$ written down in cycle notation; how many three-cycles are present? To answer this question, let us consider how many times a particular three-cycle $(x\ y\ z)$ appears: It clearly appears in exactly $(n - 3)!$ of the permutations, since this is the number of ways the remaining $n - 3$ elements may be permuted. Now the number of different possible three-cycles $(x\ y\ z)$ is $n(n - 1)(n - 2)/3$, since there are n choices for x, $(n - 1)$ for y, $(n - 2)$ for z, and among these $n(n - 1)(n - 2)$ choices each different three-cycle has appeared in three forms $(x\,y\,z)$, $(y\,z\,x)$, $(z\,x\,y)$. Therefore the total number of three-cycles among all $n!$ permutations is $n(n-1)(n-2)/3$ times $(n-3)!$, namely $n!/3$. Similarly, the total number of m-cycles is $n!/m$, for $1 \le m \le n$. (This provides another simple proof of the fact that the total number of cycles is $n!\,H_n$; hence the average number of cycles in a random permutation is H_n, as we already knew.) Exercise 17 shows that the average length of a randomly chosen cycle is n/H_n, if we consider the $n!\,H_n$ *cycles* to be equally probable; but if we choose an *element* at random in a random permutation, the average length of the cycle containing that element is somewhat greater than n/H_n.

To complete our analyses of Algorithms A and B, we would like to know the average number of *singleton cycles* in a random permutation. This is an interesting problem. Suppose we write down the $n!$ permutations, listing first those with no singleton cycles, then those with just one, etc.; for example, if $n = 4$,

no fixed elements:	2143 2341 2413 3142 3412 3421 4123 4312 4321
one fixed element:	$\bar{1}$342 $\bar{1}$423 3$\bar{2}$41 4$\bar{2}$13 24$\bar{3}$1 41$\bar{3}$2 231$\bar{4}$ 312$\bar{4}$
two fixed elements:	$\bar{1}\bar{2}$43 $\bar{1}$4$\bar{3}$2 $\bar{1}$3$\bar{2}\bar{4}$ 4$\bar{2}\bar{3}$1 3$\bar{2}\bar{1}\bar{4}$ 21$\bar{3}\bar{4}$
three fixed elements:	
four fixed elements:	$\bar{1}\bar{2}\bar{3}\bar{4}$

(Singleton cycles, which are the elements that remain fixed by a permutation, have been specially marked in this list.) Permutations with no fixed elements are called *derangements*; the number of derangements is the number of ways to put n letters into n envelopes, getting them all wrong.

Let P_{nk} be the number of permutations of n objects having exactly k fixed elements, so that for example,

$$P_{40} = 9, \quad P_{41} = 8, \quad P_{42} = 6, \quad P_{43} = 0, \quad P_{44} = 1.$$

An examination of the list above reveals the principal relationship between these numbers: We can get all permutations with k fixed elements by first choosing the k that are to be fixed (this can be done in $\binom{n}{k}$ ways) and then permuting the remaining $n-k$ elements in all $P_{(n-k)0}$ ways that leave no further elements fixed. Hence

$$P_{nk} = \binom{n}{k} P_{(n-k)0}. \tag{22}$$

We also have the rule that "the whole is the sum of its parts":

$$n! = P_{nn} + P_{n(n-1)} + P_{n(n-2)} + P_{n(n-3)} + \cdots. \tag{23}$$

Combining Eqs. (22) and (23) and rewriting the result slightly, we find that

$$n! = \frac{P_{00}}{0!} + n\frac{P_{10}}{1!} + n(n-1)\frac{P_{20}}{2!} + n(n-1)(n-2)\frac{P_{30}}{3!} + \cdots, \tag{24}$$

an equation that must be true for all positive integers n. This equation has already confronted us before—it appears in Section 1.2.5 in connection with

Stirling's attempt to generalize the factorial function — and we found a simple derivation of its coefficients in Section 1.2.6 (Example 5). We conclude that

$$\frac{P_{m0}}{m!} = 1 - \frac{1}{1!} + \frac{1}{2!} - \cdots + (-1)^m \frac{1}{m!}. \tag{25}$$

Now let p_{nk} be the probability that a permutation of n objects has exactly k singleton cycles. Since $p_{nk} = P_{nk}/n!$, we have from Eqs. (22) and (25)

$$p_{nk} = \frac{1}{k!} \left(1 - \frac{1}{1!} + \frac{1}{2!} - \cdots + (-1)^{n-k} \frac{1}{(n-k)!} \right). \tag{26}$$

The generating function $G_n(z) = p_{n0} + p_{n1}z + p_{n2}z^2 + \cdots$ is therefore

$$G_n(z) = 1 + \frac{1}{1!}(z-1) + \cdots + \frac{1}{n!}(z-1)^n = \sum_{0 \le j \le n} \frac{1}{j!}(z-1)^j. \tag{27}$$

From this formula it follows that $G'_n(z) = G_{n-1}(z)$, and with the methods of Section 1.2.10 we obtain the following statistics on the number of singleton cycles:

$$(\text{min } 0, \quad \text{ave } 1, \quad \text{max } n, \quad \text{dev } 1), \quad \text{if } n \ge 2. \tag{28}$$

A somewhat more direct way to count the number of permutations having no singleton cycles follows from the *principle of inclusion and exclusion*, which is an important method for many enumeration problems. The general principle of inclusion and exclusion may be formulated as follows: We are given N elements, and M subsets, $S_1, S_2, \ldots, S_M$, of these elements; and our goal is to count how many of the elements lie in none of the subsets. Let $|S|$ denote the number of elements in a set S; then the desired number of objects in none of the sets S_j is

$$N - \sum_{1 \le j \le M} |S_j| + \sum_{1 \le j < k \le M} |S_j \cap S_k| - \sum_{1 \le i < j < k \le M} |S_i \cap S_j \cap S_k| + \cdots$$
$$+ (-1)^M |S_1 \cap \cdots \cap S_M|. \tag{29}$$

(Thus we first subtract the number of elements in $S_1, \ldots, S_M$ from the total number, N; but this underestimates the desired total. So we add back the number of elements that are common to pairs of sets, $S_j \cap S_k$, for each pair S_j and S_k; this, however, gives an overestimate. So we subtract the elements common to triples of sets, etc.) There are several ways to prove this formula, and the reader is invited to discover one of them. (See exercise 25.)

To count the number of permutations on n elements having no singleton cycles, we consider the $N = n!$ permutations and let S_j be the set of permutations in which element j forms a singleton cycle. If $1 \le j_1 < j_2 < \cdots < j_k \le n$, the number of elements in $S_{j_1} \cap S_{j_2} \cap \cdots \cap S_{j_k}$ is the number of permutations in which $j_1, \ldots, j_k$ are singleton cycles, and this is clearly $(n-k)!$. Thus formula (29) becomes

$$n! - \binom{n}{1}(n-1)! + \binom{n}{2}(n-2)! - \binom{n}{3}(n-3)! + \cdots + (-1)^n \binom{n}{n} 0!,$$

in agreement with (25).

The principle of inclusion and exclusion is due to A. de Moivre [see his *Doctrine of Chances* (London: 1718), 61–63; 3rd ed. (1756, reprinted by Chelsea, 1967), 110–112], but its significance was not generally appreciated until it was popularized and developed further by I. Todhunter in his *Algebra* (second edition, 1860), §762, and by W. A. Whitworth in the well-known book *Choice and Chance* (Cambridge: 1867).

Combinatorial properties of permutations are explored further in Section 5.1.

EXERCISES

1. [*02*] Consider the transformation of $\{0, 1, 2, 3, 4, 5, 6\}$ that replaces x by $2x$ mod 7. Show that this transformation is a permutation, and write it in cycle form.

2. [*10*] The text shows how we might set $(a, b, c, d, e, f) \leftarrow (c, d, f, b, e, a)$ by using a series of replacement operations $(x \leftarrow y)$ and one auxiliary variable t. Show how to do the job by using a series of *exchange* operations $(x \leftrightarrow y)$ and no auxiliary variables.

3. [*03*] Compute the product $\left(\begin{smallmatrix} a & b & c & d & e & f \\ b & d & c & a & f & e \end{smallmatrix} \right) \times \left(\begin{smallmatrix} a & b & c & d & e & f \\ c & d & f & b & e & a \end{smallmatrix} \right)$, and express the answer in two-line notation. (Compare with Eq. (4).)

4. [*10*] Express $(a\,b\,d)(e\,f)(a\,c\,f)(b\,d)$ as a product of disjoint cycles.

▶ **5.** [*M10*] Equation (3) shows several equivalent ways to express the same permutation in cycle form. How many different ways of writing that permutation are possible, if all singleton cycles are suppressed?

6. [*M28*] What changes are made to the timing of Program A if we remove the assumption that all blank words occur at the extreme right?

7. [*10*] If Program A is presented with the input (6), what are the quantities X, Y, M, N, U, and V of (19)? What is the time required by Program A, excluding input-output?

▶ **8.** [*23*] Would it be feasible to modify Algorithm B to go from left to right instead of from right to left through the input?

9. [*10*] Both Programs A and B accept the same input and give the answer in essentially the same form. Is the output *exactly* the same under both programs?

▶ **10.** [*M28*] Examine the timing characteristics of Program B, namely, the quantities A, B, ..., Z shown there; express the total time in terms of the quantities X, Y, M, N, U, V defined in (19), and of F. Compare the total time for Program B with the total time for Program A on the input (6), as computed in exercise 7.

11. [*15*] Find a simple rule for writing π^- in cycle form, if the permutation π is given in cycle form.

12. [*M27*] (*Transposing a rectangular matrix.*) Suppose an $m \times n$ matrix (a_{ij}), $m \neq n$, is stored in memory in a fashion like that of exercise 1.3.2–10, so that the value of a_{ij} appears in location $L + n(i-1) + (j-1)$, where L is the location of a_{11}. The problem is to find a way to *transpose* this matrix, obtaining an $n \times m$ matrix (b_{ij}), where $b_{ij} = a_{ji}$ is stored in location $L + m(i-1) + (j-1)$. Thus the matrix is to be transposed "on itself." (a) Show that the transposition transformation moves the value that appears in cell $L + x$ to cell $L + (mx \bmod N)$, for all x in the range $0 \le x < N = mn - 1$. (b) Discuss methods for doing this transposition by computer.

▶ **13.** [*M24*] Prove that Algorithm J is valid.

▶ **14.** [*M34*] Find the average value of the quantity A in the timing of Algorithm J.

15. [*M12*] Is there a permutation that represents exactly the same transformation both in the canonical cycle form without parentheses and in the linear form?

16. [*M15*] Start with the permutation 1324 in linear notation; convert it to canonical cycle form and then remove the parentheses; repeat this process until arriving at the original permutation. What permutations occur during this process?

17. [*M24*] (a) The text demonstrates that there are $n! \, H_n$ cycles altogether, among all the permutations on n elements. If these cycles (including singleton cycles) are individually written on $n! \, H_n$ slips of paper, and if one of these slips of paper is chosen at random, what is the average length of the cycle that is thereby picked? (b) If we write the $n!$ permutations on $n!$ slips of paper, and if we choose a number k at random and also choose one of the slips of paper, what is the probability that the cycle containing k on that slip is an m-cycle? What is the average length of the cycle containing k?

▶ **18.** [*M27*] What is p_{nkm}, the probability that a permutation of n objects has exactly k cycles of length m? What is the corresponding generating function $G_{nm}(z)$? What is the average number of m-cycles and what is the standard deviation? (The text considers only the case $m = 1$.)

19. [*HM21*] Show that, in the notation of Eq. (25), the number P_{n0} of derangements is exactly equal to $n!/e$ *rounded to the nearest integer*, for all $n \geq 1$.

20. [*M20*] Given that all singleton cycles are written out explicitly, how many different ways are there to write the cycle notation of a permutation that has α_1 one-cycles, α_2 two-cycles, ...? (See exercise 5.)

21. [*M22*] What is the probability $P(n; \alpha_1, \alpha_2, \dots)$ that a permutation of n objects has exactly α_1 one-cycles, α_2 two-cycles, etc.?

▶ **22.** [*HM34*] (The following approach, due to L. Shepp and S. P. Lloyd, gives a convenient and powerful method for solving problems related to the cycle structure of random permutations.) Instead of regarding the number, n, of objects as fixed, and the permutation variable, let us assume instead that we independently choose the quantities $\alpha_1, \alpha_2, \alpha_3, \dots$ appearing in exercises 20 and 21 according to some probability distribution. Let w be any real number between 0 and 1.

   a) Suppose that we choose the random variables $\alpha_1, \alpha_2, \alpha_3, \dots$ according to the rule that "the probability that $\alpha_m = k$ is $f(w, m, k)$," for some function $f(w, m, k)$. Determine the value of $f(w, m, k)$ so that the following two conditions hold: (i) $\sum_{k \geq 0} f(w, m, k) = 1$, for $0 < w < 1$ and $m \geq 1$; (ii) the probability that $\alpha_1 + 2\alpha_2 + 3\alpha_3 + \cdots = n$ *and that* $\alpha_1 = k_1$, $\alpha_2 = k_2$, $\alpha_3 = k_3$, ... equals $(1 - w) w^n P(n; k_1, k_2, k_3, \dots)$, where $P(n; k_1, k_2, k_3, \dots)$ is defined in exercise 21.

   b) A permutation whose cycle structure is $\alpha_1, \alpha_2, \alpha_3, \dots$ clearly permutes exactly $\alpha_1 + 2\alpha_2 + 3\alpha_3 + \cdots$ objects. Show that if the α's are randomly chosen according to the probability distribution in part (a), the probability that $\alpha_1 + 2\alpha_2 + 3\alpha_3 + \cdots = n$ is $(1 - w) w^n$; the probability that $\alpha_1 + 2\alpha_2 + 3\alpha_3 + \cdots$ is *infinite* is zero.

   c) Let $\phi(\alpha_1, \alpha_2, \dots)$ be any function of the infinitely many numbers $\alpha_1, \alpha_2, \dots$. Show that if the α's are chosen according to the probability distribution in (a), the average value of ϕ is $(1 - w) \sum_{n \geq 0} w^n \phi_n$; here ϕ_n denotes the average value of ϕ taken over all permutations of n objects, where the variable α_j represents the number of j-cycles of a permutation. [For example, if $\phi(\alpha_1, \alpha_2, \dots) = \alpha_1$, the value of ϕ_n is the average number of singleton cycles in a random permutation of n objects; we showed in (28) that $\phi_n = 1$ for all $n \geq 1$.]

   d) Use this method to find the average number of cycles of *even* length in a random permutation of n objects.

   e) Use this method to solve exercise 18.

23. [*HM42*] (Golomb, Shepp, Lloyd.) If l_n denotes the average length of the *longest* cycle in a permutation of n objects, show that $l_n \approx \lambda n + \frac{1}{2}\lambda$, where $\lambda \approx 0.62433$ is a constant. Prove in fact that $\lim_{n\to\infty}(l_n - \lambda n - \frac{1}{2}\lambda) = 0$.

24. [*M41*] Find the variance of the quantity A that enters into the timing of Algorithm J. (See exercise 14.)

25. [*M22*] Prove Eq. (29).

▶ **26.** [*M24*] Extend the principle of inclusion and exclusion to obtain a formula for the number of elements that are in exactly r of the subsets $S_1, S_2, \ldots, S_M$. (The text considers only the case $r = 0$.)

27. [*M20*] Use the principle of inclusion and exclusion to count the number of integers n in the range $0 \le n < am_1m_2 \ldots m_t$ that are not divisible by any of $m_1, m_2, \ldots, m_t$. Here $m_1, m_2, \ldots, m_t$, and a are positive integers, with $m_j \perp m_k$ when $j \ne k$.

28. [*M21*] (I. Kaplansky.) If the "Josephus permutation" defined in exercise 1.3.2–22 is expressed in cycle form, we obtain $(1\ 5\ 3\ 6\ 8\ 2\ 4)(7)$ when $n = 8$ and $m = 4$. Show that this permutation in the general case is the product $(n\ n{-}1\ \ldots\ 2\ 1)^{m-1} \times (n\ n{-}1\ \ldots\ 2)^{m-1} \ldots (n\ n{-}1)^{m-1}$.

29. [*M25*] Prove that the cycle form of the Josephus permutation when $m = 2$ can be obtained by first expressing the "perfect shuffle" permutation of $\{1, 2, \ldots, 2n\}$, which takes $(1, 2, \ldots, 2n)$ into $(2, 4, \ldots, 2n, 1, 3, \ldots, 2n{-}1)$, in cycle form, then reversing left and right and erasing all the numbers greater than n. For example, when $n = 11$ the perfect shuffle is $(1\ 2\ 4\ 8\ 16\ 9\ 18\ 13\ 3\ 6\ 12)(5\ 10\ 20\ 17\ 11\ 22\ 21\ 19\ 15\ 7\ 14)$ and the Josephus permutation is $(7\ 11\ 10\ 5)(6\ 3\ 9\ 8\ 4\ 2\ 1)$.

30. [*M24*] Use exercise 29 to show that the fixed elements of the Josephus permutation when $m = 2$ are precisely the numbers $(2^d - 1)(2n + 1)/(2^{d+1} - 1)$ for all positive integers d such that this is an integer.

31. [*HM38*] Generalizing exercises 29 and 30, prove that the jth man to be executed, for general m and n, is in position x, where x may be computed as follows: Set $x \leftarrow jm$; then, while $x > n$, set $x \leftarrow \lfloor (m(x - n) - 1)/(m - 1) \rfloor$. Consequently the average number of fixed elements, for $1 \le n \le N$ and fixed $m > 1$ as $N \to \infty$, approaches $\sum_{k\ge 1}(m-1)^k/(m^{k+1} - (m-1)^k)$. [Since this value lies between $(m-1)/m$ and 1, the Josephus permutations have slightly fewer fixed elements than random ones do.]

32. [*M25*] (a) Prove that any permutation $\pi = \pi_1\pi_2 \ldots \pi_{2m+1}$ of the form

$$\pi = (2\ 3)^{e_2}(4\ 5)^{e_4} \ldots (2m\ 2m{+}1)^{e_{2m}}(1\ 2)^{e_1}(3\ 4)^{e_3} \ldots (2m{-}1\ 2m)^{e_{2m-1}},$$

where each e_k is 0 or 1, has $|\pi_k - k| \le 2$ for $1 \le k \le 2m + 1$.

(b) Given any permutation ρ of $\{1, 2, \ldots, n\}$, construct a permutation π of the stated form such that $\rho\pi$ is a single cycle. Thus every permutation is "near" a cycle.

33. [*M33*] If $m = 2^{2^l}$ and $n = 2^{2l+1}$, show how to construct sequences of permutations $(\alpha_{j1}, \alpha_{j2}, \ldots, \alpha_{jn}; \beta_{j1}, \beta_{j2}, \ldots, \beta_{jn})$ for $0 \le j < m$ with the following "orthogonality" property:

$$\alpha_{i1}\beta_{j1}\alpha_{i2}\beta_{j2} \ldots \alpha_{in}\beta_{jn} = \begin{cases} (1\ 2\ 3\ 4\ 5), & \text{if } i = j; \\ (), & \text{if } i \ne j. \end{cases}$$

Each α_{jk} and β_{jk} should be a permutation of $\{1, 2, 3, 4, 5\}$.

▶ **34.** [*M25*] (*Transposing blocks of data.*) One of the most common permutations needed in practice is the change from $\alpha\beta$ to $\beta\alpha$, where α and β are substrings of an array.

In other words, if $x_0 x_1 \ldots x_{m-1} = \alpha$ and $x_m x_{m+1} \ldots x_{m+n-1} = \beta$, we want to change the array $x_0 x_1 \ldots x_{m+n-1} = \alpha\beta$ to the array $x_m x_{m+1} \ldots x_{m+n-1} x_0 x_1 \ldots x_{m-1} = \beta\alpha$; each element x_k should be replaced by $x_{p(k)}$ for $0 \leq k < m + n$, where $p(k) = (k + m) \bmod (m + n)$. Show that every such "cyclic-shift" permutation has a simple cycle structure, and exploit that structure to devise a simple algorithm for the desired rearrangement.

35. [*M30*] Continuing the previous exercise, let $x_0 x_1 \ldots x_{l+m+n-1} = \alpha\beta\gamma$ where α, β, and γ are strings of respective lengths l, m, and n, and suppose that we want to change $\alpha\beta\gamma$ to $\gamma\beta\alpha$. Show that the corresponding permutation has a convenient cycle structure that leads to an efficient algorithm. [Exercise 34 considered the special case $m = 0$.] *Hint:* Consider changing $(\alpha\beta)(\gamma\beta)$ to $(\gamma\beta)(\alpha\beta)$.

36. [*27*] Write a MIX subroutine for the algorithm in the answer to exercise 35, and analyze its running time. Compare it with the simpler method that goes from $\alpha\beta\gamma$ to $(\alpha\beta\gamma)^R = \gamma^R \beta^R \alpha^R$ to $\gamma\beta\alpha$, where σ^R denotes the left-right reversal of the string σ.

37. [*M26*] (*Even permutations.*) Let π be a permutation of $\{1, \ldots, n\}$. Prove that π can be written as the product of an even number of 2-cycles if and only if π can be written as the product of exactly two n-cycles.

▶ **38.** [*M22*] (*Conjugate permutations.*) When π and τ are arbitrary permutations, the permutation

$$\pi^\tau = \tau^- \pi \tau$$

is called "the conjugate of π by τ."

a) Prove that $\pi = \pi^\tau$ if and only if π commutes with τ.
b) Suppose π has the cycle form $(a_{11} \ldots a_{1l_1}) \ldots (a_{k1} \ldots a_{kl_k})$. Prove that π^τ has the cycle form $(b_{11} \ldots b_{1l_1}) \ldots (b_{k1} \ldots b_{kl_k})$, where τ takes $a_{ij} \mapsto b_{ij}$.
c) Find all τ for which $((1\,2\,3)(4\,5)(6\,7\,8))^\tau = (8\,7\,6)(5\,4)(3\,2\,1)$.
d) Find all τ for which $((1\,2\,3)(4\,5)(6\,7\,8))^\tau = (8\,7\,6\,5)(4\,3\,2\,1)$.
e) True or false: Every permutation π is conjugate to its inverse, π^-.
f) True or false: $(\pi\sigma)^\tau = \pi^\tau \sigma^\tau$ and $\pi^{(\sigma\tau)} = (\pi^\sigma)^\tau$, for all π, σ, and τ.

1.4. SOME FUNDAMENTAL PROGRAMMING TECHNIQUES

1.4.1. Subroutines

WHEN A CERTAIN task is to be performed at several different places in a program, it is usually undesirable to repeat the coding in each place. To avoid this situation, the coding (called a *subroutine*) can be put into one place only, and a few extra instructions can be added to restart the outer program properly after the subroutine is finished. Transfer of control between subroutines and main programs is called *subroutine linkage*.

Each machine has its own peculiar manner for achieving efficient subroutine linkage, usually involving special instructions. In MIX, the J-register is used for this purpose; our discussion will be based on MIX machine language, but similar remarks will apply to subroutine linkage on other computers.

Subroutines are used to save space in a program; they do not save any time, other than the time implicitly saved by occupying less space — for example, less time to load the program, or fewer passes necessary in the program, or better use of high-speed memory on machines with several grades of memory. The extra time taken to enter and leave a subroutine is usually negligible.

Subroutines have several other advantages. They make it easier to visualize the structure of a large and complex program; they form a logical segmentation of the entire problem, and this usually makes debugging of the program easier. Many subroutines have additional value because they can be used by people other than the programmer of the subroutine.

Most computer installations have built up a large library of useful subroutines, and such a library greatly facilitates the programming of standard computer applications that arise. A programmer should not think of this as the *only* purpose of subroutines, however; subroutines should not always be regarded as general-purpose programs to be used by the community. Special-purpose subroutines are just as important, even when they are intended to appear in only one program. Section 1.4.3.1 contains several typical examples.

The simplest subroutines are those that have only one entrance and one exit, such as the MAXIMUM subroutine we have already considered (see Section 1.3.2, Program M). For reference, we will recopy that program here, changing it so that a fixed number of cells, 100, is searched for the maximum:

```
* MAXIMUM OF X[1..100]
MAX100  STJ   EXIT    Subroutine linkage
        ENT3  100     M1. Initialize.
        JMP   2F
1H      CMPA  X,3     M3. Compare.
        JGE   *+3
2H      ENT2  0,3     M4. Change m.
        LDA   X,3     New maximum found
        DEC3  1       M5. Decrease k.
        J3P   1B      M2. All tested?
EXIT    JMP   *       Return to main program.   ∎
```

(1)

In a larger program containing this coding as a subroutine, the single instruction
'JMP MAX100' would cause register A to be set to the current maximum value
of locations $X + 1$ through $X + 100$, and the position of the maximum would
appear in rI2. Subroutine linkage in this case is achieved by the instructions
'MAX100 STJ EXIT' and, later, 'EXIT JMP *'. Because of the way the J-register
operates, the exit instruction will then jump to the location following the place
where the original reference to MAX100 was made.

*Newer computers, such as the machine MMIX that is destined to replace MIX,
have better ways to remember return addresses. The main difference is that
program instructions are no longer modified in memory; the relevant information
is kept in registers or in a special array, not within the program itself. (See
exercise 7.) The next edition of this book will adopt the modern view, but for
now we will stick to the old-time practice of self-modifying code.*

It is not hard to obtain *quantitative* statements about the amount of code
saved and the amount of time lost when subroutines are used. Suppose that
a piece of coding requires k locations and that it appears in m places in the
program. Rewriting this as a subroutine, we need an extra instruction STJ and
an exit line for the subroutine, plus a single JMP instruction in each of the m
places where the subroutine is called. This gives a total of $m + k + 2$ locations,
rather than mk, so the amount saved is

$$(m - 1)(k - 1) - 3. \tag{2}$$

If k is 1 or m is 1 we cannot possibly save any space by using subroutines; this,
of course, is obvious. If k is 2, m must be greater than 4 in order to gain, etc.

The amount of time lost is the time taken for the extra JMP, STJ, and JMP
instructions, which are not present if the subroutine is not used; therefore if the
subroutine is used t times during a run of the program, $4t$ extra cycles of time
are required.

These estimates must be taken with a grain of salt, because they were given
for an idealized situation. Many subroutines cannot be called simply with a
single JMP instruction. Furthermore, if the coding is repeated in many parts of a
program, without using a subroutine approach, the coding for each part can be
customized to take advantage of special characteristics of the particular part of
the program in which it lies. With a subroutine, on the other hand, the coding
must be written for the most general case, not a specific case, and this will often
add several additional instructions.

When a subroutine is written to handle a general case, it is expressed in
terms of *parameters*. Parameters are values that govern the subroutine's actions;
they are subject to change from one call of the subroutine to another.

The coding in the outside program that transfers control to the subroutine
and gets it properly started is known as the *calling sequence*. Particular values
of parameters, supplied when the subroutine is called, are known as *arguments*.
With our MAX100 subroutine, the calling sequence is simply 'JMP MAX100', but

a longer calling sequence is generally necessary when arguments must be supplied. For example, Program 1.3.2M is a generalization of MAX100 that finds the maximum of the first n elements of the table. The parameter n appears in index register 1, and its calling sequence

$$
\begin{array}{ccc}
\texttt{LD1} \quad \texttt{=}n\texttt{=} & & \texttt{ENT1} \quad n \\
& \text{or} & \\
\texttt{JMP} \quad \texttt{MAXIMUM} & & \texttt{JMP} \quad \texttt{MAXIMUM}
\end{array}
$$

involves two steps.

If the calling sequence takes c memory locations, formula (2) for the amount of space saved changes to

$$(m - 1)\,(k - c) - \text{constant} \tag{3}$$

and the time lost for subroutine linkage is slightly increased.

A further correction to the formulas above can be necessary because certain registers might need to be saved and restored. For example, in the MAX100 subroutine, we must remember that by writing 'JMP MAX100' we are not only getting the maximum value in register A and its position in register I2; we are also setting register I3 to zero. A subroutine may destroy register contents, and this must be kept in mind. In order to prevent MAX100 from changing the setting of rI3, it would be necessary to include additional instructions. The shortest and fastest way to do this with MIX would be to insert the instruction 'ST3 3F(0:2)' just after MAX100 and then '3H ENT3 *' just before EXIT. The net cost would be an extra two lines of code, plus three machine cycles on every call of the subroutine.

A subroutine may be regarded as an *extension* of the computer's machine language. With the MAX100 subroutine in memory, we now have a single instruction (namely, 'JMP MAX100') that is a maximum-finder. It is important to define the effect of each subroutine just as carefully as the machine language operators themselves have been defined; a programmer should therefore be sure to write down the characteristics of each subroutine, even though nobody else will be making use of the routine or its specification. In the case of MAXIMUM as given in Section 1.3.2, the characteristics are as follows:

$$
\left.
\begin{array}{l}
\text{Calling sequence: } \texttt{JMP MAXIMUM}. \\
\text{Entry conditions: } \text{rI1} = n; \quad \text{assume that } n \geq 1. \\
\text{Exit conditions: } \quad \text{rA} = \max_{1 \leq k \leq n} \texttt{CONTENTS(X} + k) = \texttt{CONTENTS(X} + \text{rI2}); \\
\qquad\qquad\qquad \text{rI3} = 0; \text{ rJ and CI are also affected.}
\end{array}
\right\} \tag{4}
$$

(We will customarily omit mention of the fact that register J and the comparison indicator are affected by a subroutine; it has been mentioned here only for completeness.) Note that rX and rI1 are unaffected by the action of the subroutine, for otherwise these registers would have been mentioned in the exit conditions. A specification should also mention all memory locations external to the subroutine that might be affected; in this case the specification allows us to conclude that nothing has been stored, since (4) doesn't say anything about changes to memory.

Now let's consider *multiple entrances* to subroutines. Suppose we have a program that requires the general subroutine MAXIMUM, but it usually wants to use the special case MAX100 in which $n = 100$. The two can be combined as follows:

```
MAX100 ENT3 100     First entrance
MAXN    STJ  EXIT   Second entrance
        JMP  2F     Continue as in (1).                    (5)
. . .
EXIT    JMP  *      Return to main program.  ▌
```

Subroutine (5) is essentially the same as (1), with the first two instructions interchanged; we have used the fact that 'ENT3' does not change the setting of the J-register. If we wanted to add a *third* entrance, MAX50, to this subroutine, we could insert the code

```
MAX50  ENT3 50
       JSJ  MAXN                                            (6)
```

at the beginning. (Recall that 'JSJ' means jump without changing register J.)

When the number of parameters is small, it is often desirable to transmit them to a subroutine either by having them in convenient registers (as we have used rI3 to hold the parameter n in MAXN and as we used rI1 to hold the parameter n in MAXIMUM), or by storing them in fixed memory cells.

Another convenient way to supply arguments is simply to list them *after* the JMP instruction; the subroutine can refer to its parameters because it knows the J-register setting. For example, if we wanted to make the calling sequence for MAXN be

```
       JMP  MAXN
       CON  n                                               (7)
```

then the subroutine could be written as follows:

```
MAXN  STJ  *+1
      ENT1 *      rI1 ← rJ.
      LD3  0,1    rI3 ← n.
      JMP  2F     Continue as in (1).                       (8)
. . .
      J3P  1B
      JMP  1,1    Return.  ▌
```

On machines like System/360, for which linkage is ordinarily done by putting the exit location in an index register, a convention like this is particularly convenient. It is also useful when a subroutine needs many arguments, or when a program has been written by a compiler. The technique of multiple entrances that we used above often fails in this case, however. We could "fake it" by writing

```
MAX100 STJ  1F
       JMP  MAXN
       CON  100
1H     JMP  *    ▌
```

but this is not as attractive as (5).

A technique similar to that of listing arguments after the jump is normally used for subroutines with *multiple exits*. Multiple exit means that we want the subroutine to return to one of several different locations, depending on conditions detected by the subroutine. In the strictest sense, the location to which a subroutine exits is a parameter; so if there are several places to which it might exit, depending on the circumstances, they should be supplied as arguments. Our final example of the "maximum" subroutine will have two entrances and two exits. The calling sequence is:

For general n

```
ENT3   n
JMP    MAXN
```
Exit here if max ≤ 0 or max $\geq$ rX.
Exit here if $0 <$ max $<$ rX.

For $n = 100$

```
JMP    MAX100
```
Exit here if max ≤ 0 or max $\geq$ rX.
Exit here if $0 <$ max $<$ rX.

(In other words, exit is made to the location *two* past the jump when the maximum value is positive and less than the contents of register X.) The subroutine for these conditions is easily written:

```
MAX100 ENT3 100     Entrance for n = 100
MAXN   STJ  EXIT    Entrance for general n
       JMP  2F      Continue as in (1).
...
       J3P  1B
       JANP EXIT    Take normal exit if the max is ≤ 0.          (9)
       STX  TEMP
       CMPA TEMP
       JGE  EXIT    Take normal exit if the max is ≥ rX.
       ENT3 1       Otherwise take the second exit.
EXIT   JMP  *,3     Return to proper place.  ▌
```

Subroutines may call on other subroutines; in complicated programs it is not unusual to have subroutine calls nested more than five deep. The only restriction that must be followed when using linkage as described here is that no subroutine may call on any other subroutine that is (directly or indirectly) calling on it. For example, consider the following scenario:

[Main program]	[Subroutine A]	[Subroutine B]	[Subroutine C]
	A STJ EXITA	B STJ EXITB	C STJ EXITC
⋮	⋮	⋮	⋮
JMP A	JMP B	JMP C	JMP A
⋮	⋮	⋮	⋮
	EXITA JMP *	EXITB JMP *	EXITC JMP * (10)

If the main program calls on A, which calls B, which calls C, and then C calls on A, the address in EXITA referring to the main program is destroyed, and there is no way to return to that program. A similar remark applies to all temporary storage cells and registers used by each subroutine. It is not difficult to devise subroutine linkage conventions that will handle such recursive situations properly; Chapter 8 considers recursion in detail.

We conclude this section by discussing briefly how we might go about writing a complex and lengthy program. How can we decide what kind of subroutines we will need, and what calling sequences should be used? One successful way to determine this is to use an iterative procedure:

Step 0 (Initial idea). First we decide vaguely upon the general plan of attack that the program will use.

Step 1 (A rough sketch of the program). We start now by writing the "outer levels" of the program, in any convenient language. A somewhat systematic way to go about this has been described very nicely by E. W. Dijkstra, *Structured Programming* (Academic Press, 1972), Chapter 1, and by N. Wirth, *CACM* **14** (1971), 221–227. We may begin by breaking the whole program into a small number of pieces, which might be thought of temporarily as subroutines, although they are called only once. These pieces are successively refined into smaller and smaller parts, having correspondingly simpler jobs to do. Whenever some computational task arises that seems likely to occur elsewhere or that has already occurred elsewhere, we define a subroutine (a real one) to do that job. We do not write the subroutine at this point; we continue writing the main program, assuming that the subroutine has performed its task. Finally, when the main program has been sketched, we tackle the subroutines in turn, trying to take the most complex subroutines first and then their sub-subroutines, etc. In this manner we will come up with a list of subroutines. The actual function of each subroutine has probably already changed several times, so that the first parts of our sketch will by now be incorrect; but that is no problem, it is merely a sketch. For each subroutine we now have a reasonably good idea about how it will be called and how general-purpose it should be. It usually pays to extend the generality of each subroutine a little.

Step 2 (First working program). This step goes in the opposite direction from step 1. We now write in computer language, say MIXAL or PL/MIX or a higher-level language; we start this time with the lowest level subroutines, and do the main program last. As far as possible, we try never to write any instructions that call a subroutine before the subroutine itself has been coded. (In step 1, we tried the opposite, never considering a subroutine until all of its calls had been written.)

As more and more subroutines are written during this process, our confidence gradually grows, since we are continually extending the power of the machine we are programming. After an individual subroutine is coded, we should immediately prepare a complete description of what it does, and what its calling sequences are, as in (4). It is also important not to overlay temporary storage cells; it may very well be disastrous if every subroutine refers to location TEMP, although when preparing the sketch in step 1, it was convenient not to worry about such problems. An obvious way to overcome overlay worries is to have each subroutine use only its own temporary storage, but if this is too wasteful of space, another scheme that does fairly well is to name the cells TEMP1, TEMP2, etc.; the numbering within a subroutine starts with TEMPj, where j is one higher than the greatest number used by any of the sub-subroutines of this subroutine.

Step 3 (Reexamination). The result of step 2 should be very nearly a working program, but it may be possible to improve on it. A good way is to reverse direction again, studying for each subroutine *all* of the calls made on it. It may well be that the subroutine should be enlarged to do some of the more common things that are always done by the outside routine just before or after it uses the subroutine. Perhaps several subroutines should be merged into one; or perhaps a subroutine is called only once and should not be a subroutine at all. (Perhaps a subroutine is never called and can be dispensed with entirely.)

At this point, it is often a good idea to scrap everything and start over again at step 1! This is not intended to be a facetious remark; the time spent in getting this far has not been wasted, for we have learned a great deal about the problem. With hindsight, we will probably have discovered several improvements that could be made to the program's overall organization. There's no reason to be afraid to go back to step 1 — it will be much easier to go through steps 2 and 3 again, now that a similar program has been done already. Moreover, we will quite probably save as much debugging time later on as it will take to rewrite everything. Some of the best computer programs ever written owe much of their success to the fact that all the work was unintentionally lost, at about this stage, and the authors had to begin again.

On the other hand, there is probably never a point when a complex computer program cannot be improved somehow, so steps 1 and 2 should not be repeated indefinitely. When significant improvement can clearly be made, it is well worth the additional time required to start over, but eventually a point of diminishing returns is reached.

Step 4 (Debugging). After a final polishing of the program, including perhaps the allocation of storage and other last-minute details, it is time to look at it in still another direction from the three that were used in steps 1, 2, and 3 — now we study the program in the order in which the computer will *perform* it. This may be done by hand or, of course, by machine. The author has found it quite helpful at this point to make use of system routines that trace each instruction the first two times it is executed; it is important to rethink the ideas underlying the program and to check that everything is actually taking place as expected.

Debugging is an art that needs much further study, and the way to approach it is highly dependent on the facilities available at each computer installation. A good start towards effective debugging is often the preparation of appropriate test data. The most effective debugging techniques seem to be those that are designed and built into the program itself — many of today's best programmers will devote nearly half of their programs to facilitating the debugging process in the other half; the first half, which usually consists of fairly straightforward routines that display relevant information in a readable format, will eventually be thrown away, but the net result is a surprising gain in productivity.

Another good debugging practice is to keep a record of every mistake made. Even though this will probably be quite embarrassing, such information is invaluable to anyone doing research on the debugging problem, and it will also help you learn how to reduce the number of future errors.

Note: The author wrote most of the preceding comments in 1964, after he had successfully completed several medium-sized software projects but before he had developed a mature programming style. Later, during the 1980s, he learned that an additional technique, called *structured documentation* or *literate programming*, is probably even more important. A summary of his current beliefs about the best way to write programs of all kinds appears in the book *Literate Programming* (Cambridge Univ. Press, first published in 1992). Incidentally, Chapter 11 of that book contains a detailed record of all bugs removed from the TEX program during the period 1978–1991.

> *Up to a point it is better to let the snags [bugs] be there*
> *than to spend such time in design that there are none*
> *(how many decades would this course take?).*
> — A. M. TURING, Proposals for ACE (1945)

EXERCISES

1. [*10*] State the characteristics of subroutine (5), just as (4) gives the characteristics of Subroutine 1.3.2M.

2. [*10*] Suggest code to substitute for (6) without using the JSJ instruction.

3. [*M15*] Complete the information in (4) by stating precisely what happens to register J and the comparison indicator as a result of the subroutine; state also what happens if register I1 is not positive.

▶ **4.** [*21*] Write a subroutine that generalizes MAXN by finding the maximum value of $X[a], X[a+r], X[a+2r], \ldots, X[n]$, where r and n are parameters and a is the smallest positive number with $a \equiv n$ (modulo r), namely $a = 1 + (n-1) \bmod r$. Give a special entrance for the case $r = 1$. List the characteristics of your subroutine, as in (4).

5. [*21*] Suppose MIX did not have a J-register. Invent a means for subroutine linkage that does not use register J, and give an example of your invention by writing a MAX100 subroutine effectively equivalent to (1). State the characteristics of this subroutine in a fashion similar to (4). (Retain MIX's conventions of self-modifying code.)

▶ **6.** [*26*] Suppose MIX did not have a MOVE operator. Write a subroutine entitled MOVE such that the calling sequence 'JMP MOVE; NOP A,I(F)' has an effect just the same as 'MOVE A,I(F)' if the latter were admissible. The only differences should be the effect on register J and the fact that a subroutine naturally consumes more time and space than a hardware instruction does.

▶ **7.** [*20*] Why is self-modifying code now frowned on?

1.4.2. Coroutines

Subroutines are special cases of more general program components, called *coroutines*. In contrast to the unsymmetric relationship between a main routine and a subroutine, there is complete symmetry between coroutines, which *call on each other*.

To understand the coroutine concept, let us consider another way of thinking about subroutines. The viewpoint adopted in the previous section was that a subroutine merely was an extension of the computer hardware, introduced to save lines of coding. This may be true, but another point of view is possible: We may consider the main program and the subroutine as a *team* of programs, each member of the team having a certain job to do. The main program, in the course of doing its job, will activate the subprogram; the subprogram will perform its own function and then activate the main program. We might stretch our imagination to believe that, from the subroutine's point of view, when it exits *it* is calling the *main* routine; the main routine continues to perform its duty, then "exits" to the subroutine. The subroutine acts, then calls the main routine again.

This somewhat far-fetched philosophy actually takes place with coroutines, for which it is impossible to distinguish which is a subroutine of the other. Suppose we have coroutines A and B; when programming A, we may think of B as our subroutine, but when programming B, we may think of A as our subroutine. That is, in coroutine A, the instruction 'JMP B' is used to activate coroutine B. In coroutine B the instruction 'JMP A' is used to activate coroutine A again. Whenever a coroutine is activated, it resumes execution of its program at the point where the action was last suspended.

The coroutines A and B might, for example, be two programs that play chess. We can combine them so that they will play against each other.

With MIX, such linkage between coroutines A and B is done by including the following four instructions in the program:

$$
\begin{array}{llll}
\text{A} & \text{STJ} & \text{BX} & \\
\text{AX} & \text{JMP} & \text{A1} &
\end{array}
\qquad
\begin{array}{lll}
\text{B} & \text{STJ} & \text{AX} \\
\text{BX} & \text{JMP} & \text{B1}
\end{array}
\qquad (1)
$$

This requires four machine cycles for transfer of control each way. Initially AX and BX are set to jump to the starting places of each coroutine, A1 and B1. Suppose we start up coroutine A first, at location A1. When it executes 'JMP B' from location A2, say, the instruction in location B stores rJ in AX, which then says 'JMP A2+1'. The instruction in BX gets us to location B1, and after coroutine B begins its execution, it will eventually get to an instruction 'JMP A' in location B2, say. We store rJ in BX and jump to location A2+1, continuing the execution of coroutine A until it again jumps to B, which stores rJ in AX and jumps to B2+1, etc.

The essential difference between routine-subroutine and coroutine-coroutine linkage, as can be seen by studying the example above, is that a subroutine is always initiated *at its beginning*, which is usually a fixed place; the main routine or a coroutine is always initiated *at the place following* where it last terminated.

Coroutines arise most naturally in practice when they are connected with algorithms for input and output. For example, suppose it is the duty of coroutine A to read cards and to perform some transformation on the input, reducing it to a sequence of items. Another coroutine, which we will call B, does further processing of these items, and prints the answers; B will periodically call for the successive input items found by A. Thus, coroutine B jumps to A whenever it wants the next input item, and coroutine A jumps to B whenever an input item has been found. The reader may say, "Well, B is the main program and A is merely a *subroutine* for doing the input." This, however, becomes less true when the process A is very complicated; indeed, we can imagine A as the main routine and B as a subroutine for doing the output, and the above description remains valid. The usefulness of the coroutine idea emerges midway between these two extremes, when both A and B are complicated and each one calls the other in numerous places. It is rather difficult to find short, simple examples of coroutines that illustrate the importance of the idea; the most useful coroutine applications are generally quite lengthy.

In order to study coroutines in action, let us consider a contrived example. Suppose we want to write a program that translates one code into another. The input code to be translated is a sequence of alphameric characters terminated by a period, such as

$$\text{A2B5E3426FG0ZYW3210PQ89R.} \qquad (2)$$

This has been punched onto cards; blank columns appearing on these cards are to be ignored. The input is to be understood as follows, from left to right: If the next character is a digit $0, 1, \ldots, 9$, say n, it indicates $(n+1)$ repetitions of the following character, whether the following character is a digit or not. A nondigit simply denotes itself. The output of our program is to consist of the sequence indicated in this manner and separated into groups of three characters each, until a period appears; the last group may have fewer than three characters. For example, (2) should be translated by our program into

$$\text{ABB BEE EEE E44 446 66F GZY W22 220 0PQ 999 999 999 R.} \qquad (3)$$

Note that 3426F does not mean 3427 repetitions of the letter F; it means 4 fours and 3 sixes followed by F. If the input sequence is '1.', the output is simply '.', not '..', because the first period terminates the output. Our program should punch the output onto cards, with sixteen groups of three on each card except possibly the last.

To accomplish this translation, we will write two coroutines and a subroutine. The subroutine, called NEXTCHAR, is designed to find nonblank characters of the input, and to put the next such character into register A:

```
01  * SUBROUTINE FOR CHARACTER INPUT
02  READER    EQU  16              Unit number of card reader
03  INPUT     ORIG *+16            Place for input cards
04  NEXTCHAR STJ  9F               Entrance to subroutine
05            JXNZ 3F              Initially rX = 0
06  1H        J6N  2F              Initially rI6 = 0
07            IN   INPUT(READER)   Read next card.
08            JBUS *(READER)       Wait for completion.
09            ENN6 16              Let rI6 point to the first word.
10  2H        LDX  INPUT+16,6      Get the next word of input.
11            INC6 1               Advance pointer.
```

```
12  3H        ENTA 0
13            SLAX 1                    Next character → rA.
14  9H        JANZ *                    Skip blanks.
15            JMP  NEXTCHAR+1     ▮
```

This subroutine has the following characteristics:

Calling sequence: JMP NEXTCHAR.

Entry conditions: rX = characters yet to be used; rI6 points to next word, or rI6 = 0 indicating that a new card must be read.

Exit conditions: rA = next nonblank character of input; rX and rI6 are set for next entry to NEXTCHAR.

Our first coroutine, called IN, finds the characters of the input code with the proper replication. It begins initially at location IN1:

```
16  * FIRST COROUTINE
17  2H        INCA 30                   Nondigit found
18            JMP  OUT                  Send it to OUT coroutine.
19  IN1       JMP  NEXTCHAR             Get character.
20            DECA 30
21            JAN  2B                   Is it a letter?
22            CMPA =10=
23            JGE  2B                   Is it a special character?
24            STA  *+1(0:2)             Digit n found
25            ENT5 *                    rI5 ← n.
26            JMP  NEXTCHAR             Get next character.
27            JMP  OUT                  Send it to OUT coroutine.
28            DEC5 1                    Decrease n by 1.
29            J5NN *-2                  Repeat if necessary.
30            JMP  IN1                  Begin new cycle.  ▮
```

(Recall that in MIX's character code, the digits 0–9 have codes 30–39.) This coroutine has the following characteristics:

Calling sequence: JMP IN.

Exit conditions (when
    jumping to OUT):   rA = next character of input with proper replication; rI4 unchanged from its value at entry.

Entry conditions
    (upon return):   rA, rX, rI5, rI6 should be unchanged from their values at the last exit.

The other coroutine, called OUT, puts the code into three-character groups and punches the cards. It begins initially at OUT1:

```
31  * SECOND COROUTINE
32            ALF  ␣␣␣␣␣               Constant used for blanking
33  OUTPUT    ORIG *+16                 Buffer area for answers
34  PUNCH     EQU  17                   Unit number for card punch
35  OUT1      ENT4 -16                  Start new output card.
```

```
36              ENT1 OUTPUT
37              MOVE -1,1(16)         Set output area to blanks.
38   1H         JMP  IN              Get next translated character.
39              STA  OUTPUT+16,4(1:1) Store it in the (1:1) field.
40              CMPA PERIOD           Is it '.'?
41              JE   9F
42              JMP  IN              If not, get another character.
43              STA  OUTPUT+16,4(2:2) Store it in the (2:2) field.
44              CMPA PERIOD           Is it '.'?
45              JE   9F
46              JMP  IN              If not, get another character.
47              STA  OUTPUT+16,4(3:3) Store it in the (3:3) field.
48              CMPA PERIOD           Is it '.'?
49              JE   9F
50              INC4 1               Move to next word in output buffer.
51              J4N  1B              End of card?
52   9H         OUT  OUTPUT(PUNCH)    If so, punch it.
53              JBUS *(PUNCH)         Wait for completion.
54              JNE  OUT1            Return for more, unless
55              HLT                      '.' was sensed.
56   PERIOD ALF  ␣␣␣␣.               ▮
```

This coroutine has the following characteristics:

Calling sequence: JMP OUT.

Exit conditions (when
    jumping to IN):   rA, rX, rI5, rI6 unchanged from their value at entry; rI1,
                        rI4 possibly affected; previous character has been output.

Entry conditions
    (upon return):   rA = next character of input with proper replication; rI4
                        unchanged from its value at the last exit.

To complete the program, we need to write the coroutine linkage (see (1))
and to provide the proper initialization. Initialization of coroutines tends to be
a little tricky, although not really difficult.

```
57   * INITIALIZATION AND LINKAGE
58   START    ENT6 0         Initialize rI6 for NEXTCHAR.
59            ENTX 0         Initialize rX for NEXTCHAR.
60            JMP  OUT1       Start with OUT (see exercise 2).
61   OUT      STJ  INX        Coroutine linkage
62   OUTX     JMP  OUT1
63   IN       STJ  OUTX
64   INX      JMP  IN1
65            END  START      ▮
```

This completes the program. The reader should study it carefully, noting in
particular how each coroutine can be written independently as though the other
coroutine were its subroutine.

The entry and exit conditions for the IN and OUT coroutines mesh perfectly in the program above. In general, we would not be so fortunate, and the coroutine linkage would also include instructions for loading and storing appropriate registers. For example, if OUT would destroy the contents of register A, the coroutine linkage would become

```
OUT   STJ  INX
      STA  HOLDA    Store A when leaving IN.
OUTX  JMP  OUT1
IN    STJ  OUTX
      LDA  HOLDA    Restore A when leaving OUT.
INX   JMP  IN1      ▌
```

$$(4)$$

There is an important relation between coroutines and *multipass algorithms*. For example, the translation process we have just described could have been done in two distinct passes: We could first have done just the IN coroutine, applying it to the entire input and writing each character with the proper amount of replication onto magnetic tape. After this was finished, we could rewind the tape and then do just the OUT coroutine, taking the characters from tape in groups of three. This would be called a "two-pass" process. (Intuitively, a "pass" denotes a complete scan of the input. This definition is not precise, and in many algorithms the number of passes taken is not at all clear; but the intuitive concept of "pass" is useful in spite of its vagueness.)

Figure 22(a) illustrates a four-pass process. Quite often we will find that the same process can be done in just one pass, as shown in part (b) of the figure, if we substitute four coroutines A, B, C, D for the respective passes A, B, C, D. Coroutine A will jump to B when pass A would have written an item of output on tape 1; coroutine B will jump to A when pass B would have read an item of input from tape 1, and B will jump to C when pass B would have written an item of output on tape 2; etc. UNIX® users will recognize this as a "pipe," denoted by 'PassA | PassB | PassC | PassD'. The programs for passes B, C, and D are sometimes referred to as "filters."

Conversely, a process done by n coroutines can often be transformed into an n-pass process. Due to this correspondence it is worthwhile to compare multipass algorithms with one-pass algorithms.

a) *Psychological difference.* A multipass algorithm is generally easier to create and to understand than a one-pass algorithm for the same problem. Breaking a process down into a sequence of small steps that happen one after the other is easier to comprehend than an involved process in which many transformations take place simultaneously.

Also, if a very large problem is being tackled and if many people are to co-operate in producing a computer program, a multipass algorithm provides a natural way to divide up the job.

These advantages of a multipass algorithm are present in coroutines as well, since each coroutine can be written essentially separate from the others, and the linkage makes an apparently multipass algorithm into a single-pass process.

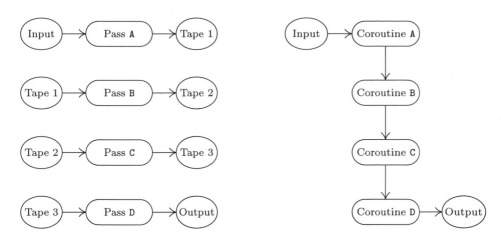

Fig. 22. Passes: (a) a four-pass algorithm, and (b) a one-pass algorithm.

b) *Time difference.* The time required to pack, write, read, and unpack the intermediate data that flows between passes (for example, the information on tapes in Fig. 22) is avoided in a one-pass algorithm. For this reason, a one-pass algorithm will be faster.

c) *Space difference.* The one-pass algorithm requires space to hold all the programs in memory simultaneously, while a multipass algorithm requires space for only one at a time. This requirement may affect the speed, even to a greater extent than indicated in statement (b). For example, many computers have a limited amount of "fast memory" and a larger amount of slower memory; if each pass just barely fits into the fast memory, the result will be considerably faster than if we use coroutines in a single pass (since the use of coroutines would presumably force most of the program to appear in the slower memory or to be repeatedly swapped in and out of fast memory).

Occasionally there is a need to design algorithms for several computer configurations at once, some of which have larger memory capacity than others. In such cases it is possible to write the program in terms of coroutines, and to let the memory size govern the number of passes: Load together as many coroutines as feasible, and supply input or output subroutines for the missing links.

Although this relationship between coroutines and passes is important, we should keep in mind that coroutine applications cannot always be split into multipass algorithms. If coroutine B gets input from A and also sends back crucial information to A, as in the example of chess play mentioned earlier, the sequence of actions can't be converted into pass A followed by pass B.

Conversely, it is clear that some multipass algorithms cannot be converted to coroutines. Some algorithms are inherently multipass; for example, the second pass may require cumulative information from the first pass (like the total number of occurrences of a certain word in the input). There is an old joke worth noting in this regard:

> *Little old lady, riding a bus.* "Little boy, can you tell me how to get off at Pasadena Street?"
>
> *Little boy.* "Just watch me, and get off two stops before I do."

(The joke is that the little boy gives a two-pass algorithm.)

So much for multipass algorithms. We will see further examples of coroutines in numerous places throughout this book, for example, as part of the buffering schemes in Section 1.4.4. Coroutines also play an important role in discrete system simulation; see Section 2.2.5. The important idea of *replicated coroutines* is discussed in Chapter 8, and some interesting applications of this idea may be found in Chapter 10.

EXERCISES

1. [*10*] Explain why short, simple examples of coroutines are hard for the author of a textbook to find.

▶ **2.** [*20*] The program in the text starts up the OUT coroutine first. What would happen if IN were the first to be executed — that is, if line 60 were changed from 'JMP OUT1' to 'JMP IN1'?

3. [*20*] True or false: The three 'CMPA PERIOD' instructions within OUT may all be omitted, and the program would still work. (Look carefully.)

4. [*20*] Show how coroutine linkage analogous to (1) can be given for real-life computers you are familiar with.

5. [*15*] Suppose both coroutines IN and OUT want the contents of register A to remain untouched between exit and entry; in other words, assume that wherever the instruction 'JMP IN' occurs within OUT, the contents of register A are to be unchanged when control returns to the next line, and make a similar assumption about 'JMP OUT' within IN. What coroutine linkage is needed? (Compare with (4).)

▶ **6.** [*22*] Give coroutine linkage analogous to (1) for the case of *three* coroutines, A, B, and C, each of which can jump to either of the other two. (Whenever a coroutine is activated, it begins where it last left off.)

▶ **7.** [*30*] Write a MIX program that *reverses* the translation done by the program in the text; that is, your program should convert cards punched like (3) into cards punched like (2). The output should be as short a string of characters as possible, so that the zero before the Z in (2) would not really be produced from (3).

1.4.3. Interpretive Routines

In this section we will investigate a common type of computer program, the *interpretive routine* (which will be called *interpreter* for short). An interpretive routine is a computer program that performs the instructions of another program, where the other program is written in some machine-like language. By a machine-like language, we mean a way of representing instructions, where the instructions typically have operation codes, addresses, etc. (This definition, like most definitions of today's computer terms, is not precise, nor should it be; we cannot draw the line exactly and say just which programs are interpreters and which are not.)

Historically, the first interpreters were built around machine-like languages designed specially for simple programming; such languages were easier to use than a real machine language. The rise of symbolic languages for programming soon eliminated the need for interpretive routines of that kind, but interpreters have by no means begun to die out. On the contrary, their use has continued to grow, to the extent that an effective use of interpretive routines may be regarded as one of the essential characteristics of modern programming. The new applications of interpreters are made chiefly for the following reasons:

a) a machine-like language is able to represent a complicated sequence of decisions and actions in a compact, efficient manner; and

b) such a representation provides an excellent way to communicate between passes of a multipass process.

In such cases, special purpose machine-like languages are developed for use in a particular program, and programs in those languages are often generated only by computers. (Today's expert programmers are also good machine designers, as they not only create an interpretive routine, they also define a *virtual machine* whose language is to be interpreted.)

The interpretive technique has the further advantage of being relatively machine-independent — only the interpreter must be rewritten when changing computers. Furthermore, helpful debugging aids can readily be built into an interpretive system.

Examples of interpreters of type (a) appear in several places later in this series of books; see, for example, the recursive interpreter in Chapter 8 and the "Parsing Machine" in Chapter 10. We typically need to deal with a situation in which a great many special cases arise, all similar, but having no really simple pattern.

For example, consider writing an algebraic compiler in which we want to generate efficient machine-language instructions that add two quantities together. There might be ten classes of quantities (constants, simple variables, temporary storage locations, subscripted variables, the contents of an accumulator or index register, fixed or floating point, etc.) and the combination of all pairs yields 100 different cases. A long program would be required to do the proper thing in each case. The interpretive solution to this problem is to make up an ad hoc language whose "instructions" fit in one byte. Then we simply prepare a table of 100 "programs" in this language, where each program ideally fits in a single word. The idea is then to pick out the appropriate table entry and to perform the program found there. This technique is simple and efficient.

An example interpreter of type (b) appears in the article "Computer-Drawn Flowcharts" by D. E. Knuth, *CACM* **6** (1963), 555–563. In a multipass program, the earlier passes must transmit information to the later passes. This information is often transmitted most efficiently in a machine-like language, as a set of instructions for the later pass; the later pass is then nothing but a special purpose interpretive routine, and the earlier pass is a special purpose "compiler." This philosophy of multipass operation may be characterized as *telling* the later pass what to do, whenever possible, rather than simply presenting it with a lot of facts and asking it to *figure out* what to do.

Another example of a type-(b) interpreter occurs in connection with compilers for special languages. If the language includes many features that are not easily done on the machine except by subroutine, the resulting object programs will be very long sequences of subroutine calls. This would happen, for example, if the language were concerned primarily with multiple-precision arithmetic. In such a case the object program would be considerably shorter if it were expressed in an interpretive language. See, for example, the book *ALGOL 60 Implementation*, by B. Randell and L. J. Russell (New York: Academic Press, 1964), which describes a compiler to translate from ALGOL 60 into an interpretive language, and which also describes the interpreter for that language; and see "An ALGOL 60 Compiler," by Arthur Evans, Jr., *Ann. Rev. Auto. Programming* **4** (1964), 87–124, for examples of interpretive routines used *within* a compiler. The rise of microprogrammed machines and of special-purpose integrated circuit chips has made this interpretive approach even more valuable.

The TeX program, which produced the pages of the book you are now reading, converted a file that contained the text of this section into an interpretive language called DVI format, designed by D. R. Fuchs in 1979. [See D. E. Knuth, *TeX: The Program* (Reading, Mass.: Addison–Wesley, 1986), Part 31.] The DVI file that TeX produced was then processed by an interpreter called dvips, written by T. G. Rokicki, and converted to a file of instructions in another interpretive language called PostScript® [Adobe Systems Inc., *PostScript Language Reference Manual*, 2nd edition (Reading, Mass.: Addison–Wesley, 1990)]. The PostScript file was sent to the publisher, who sent it to a commercial printer, who used a PostScript interpreter to produce printing plates. This three-pass operation illustrates interpreters of type (b); TeX itself also includes a small interpreter of type (a) to process the so-called ligature and kerning information for characters of each font of type [*TeX: The Program*, §545].

There is another way to look at a program written in interpretive language: It may be regarded as a series of subroutine calls, one after another. Such a program may in fact be expanded into a long sequence of calls on subroutines, and, conversely, such a sequence can usually be packed into a coded form that is readily interpreted. The advantages of interpretive techniques are the compactness of representation, the machine independence, and the increased diagnostic capability. An interpreter can often be written so that the amount of time spent in interpretation of the code itself and branching to the appropriate routine is negligible.

1.4.3.1. A MIX simulator. When the language presented to an interpretive routine is the machine language of another computer, the interpreter is often called a *simulator* (or sometimes an *emulator*).

In the author's opinion, entirely too much programmers' time has been spent in writing such simulators and entirely too much computer time has been wasted in using them. The motivation for simulators is simple: A computer installation buys a new machine and still wants to run programs written for the old machine (rather than rewriting the programs). However, this usually costs more and gives poorer results than if a special task force of programmers were given temporary employment to do the reprogramming. For example, the author once participated in such a reprogramming project, and a serious error was discovered in the original program, which had been in use for several years; the new program worked at five times the speed of the old, besides giving the right answers for a change! (Not all simulators are bad; for example, it is usually advantageous for a computer manufacturer to simulate a new machine before it has been built, so that software for the new machine may be developed as soon as possible. But that is a very specialized application.) An extreme example of the inefficient use of computer simulators is the true story of machine A simulating machine B running a program that simulates machine C! This is the way to make a large, expensive computer give poorer results than its cheaper cousin.

In view of all this, why should such a simulator rear its ugly head in this book? There are two reasons:

a) The simulator we will describe below is a good example of a typical interpretive routine; the basic techniques employed in interpreters are illustrated here. It also illustrates the use of subroutines in a moderately long program.

b) We will describe a simulator of the MIX computer, written in (of all things) the MIX language. This will facilitate the writing of MIX simulators for most computers, which are similar; the coding of our program intentionally avoids making heavy use of MIX-oriented features. A MIX simulator will be of advantage as a teaching aid in conjunction with this book and possibly others.

Computer simulators as described in this section should be distinguished from *discrete system simulators*. Discrete system simulators are important programs that will be discussed in Section 2.2.5.

Now let's turn to the task of writing a MIX simulator. The input to our program will be a sequence of MIX instructions and data, stored in locations 0000–3499. We want to mimic the precise behavior of MIX's hardware, pretending that MIX itself is interpreting those instructions; thus, we want to implement the specifications that were laid down in Section 1.3.1. Our program will, for example, maintain a variable called AREG that will hold the magnitude of the simulated A-register; another variable, SIGNA, will hold the corresponding sign. A variable called CLOCK will record how many MIX units of simulated time have elapsed during the simulated program execution.

The numbering of MIX's instructions LDA, LD1, ..., LDX and other similar commands suggests that we keep the simulated contents of these registers in consecutive locations, as follows:

AREG, I1REG, I2REG, I3REG, I4REG, I5REG, I6REG, XREG, JREG, ZERO.

Here ZERO is a "register" filled with zeros at all times. The positions of JREG and ZERO are suggested by the op-code numbers of the instructions STJ and STZ.

In keeping with our philosophy of writing the simulator as though it were not really done with MIX hardware, we will treat the signs as independent parts of a register. For example, many computers cannot represent the number "minus zero," while MIX definitely can; therefore we will always treat signs specially in this program. The locations AREG, I1REG, ..., ZERO will always contain the absolute values of the corresponding register contents; another set of locations in our program, called SIGNA, SIGN1, ..., SIGNZ will contain +1 or −1, depending on whether the sign of the corresponding register is plus or minus.

An interpretive routine generally has a central control section that is called into action between interpreted instructions. In our case, the program transfers to location CYCLE at the end of each simulated instruction.

The control routine does the things common to all instructions, unpacks the instruction into its various parts, and puts the parts into convenient places for later use. The program below sets

rI6 = location of the next instruction;
rI5 = M (address of the present instruction, plus indexing);
rI4 = operation code of the present instruction;
rI3 = F-field of the present instruction;
INST = the present instruction.

Program M.

```
001  * MIX SIMULATOR
002          ORIG 3500            Simulated memory is in locations 0000 up.
003  BEGIN   STZ  TIME(0:2)
004          STZ  OVTOG           OVTOG is the simulated overflow toggle.
005          STZ  COMPI           COMPI, ±1 or 0, is comparison indicator.
006          ENT6 0               Take first instruction from location zero.
007  CYCLE   LDA  CLOCK           Beginning of control routine:
008  TIME    INCA 0               This address is set to the execution time
009          STA  CLOCK              of the previous instruction (see line 033).
010          LDA  0,6             rA ← instruction to simulate.
011          STA  INST
012          INC6 1               Advance the location counter.
013          LDX  INST(1:2)       Get absolute value of the address.
014          SLAX 5               Attach sign to the address.
015          STA  M
016          LD2  INST(3:3)       Examine the index field.
017          J2Z  1F              Is it zero?
018          DEC2 6
019          J2P  INDEXERROR      Illegal index specified?
020          LDA  SIGN6,2         Get sign of the index register.
021          LDX  I6REG,2         Get magnitude of the index register.
022          SLAX 5               Attach the sign.
023          ADD  M               Do signed addition for indexing.
024          CMPA ZERO(1:3)       Is the result too large?
025          JNE  ADDRERROR       If so, simulate an error.
026          STA  M               Otherwise the address has been found.
```

```
027  1H       LD3   INST(4:4)      rI3 ← F-field.
028          LD5   M              rI5 ← M.
029          LD4   INST(5:5)      rI4 ← C-field.
030          DEC4  63
031          J4P   OPERROR        Is the op code ≥ 64?
032          LDA   OPTABLE,4(4:4) Get execution time from the table.
033          STA   TIME(0:2)
034          LD2   OPTABLE,4(0:2) Get address of the proper routine.
035          JNOV  0,2            Jump to operator.
036          JMP   0,2            (Protect against overflows.)   ▌
```

The reader's attention is called particularly to lines 034–036: A "switching table" of the 64 operators is part of the simulator, allowing it to jump rapidly to the correct routine for the current instruction. This is an important time-saving technique (see exercise 1.3.2–9).

The 64-word switching table, called OPTABLE, gives also the execution time for the various operators; the following lines indicate the contents of that table:

```
037       '   NOP   CYCLE(1)       Operation code table;
038          ADD   ADD(2)             typical entry is
039          SUB   SUB(2)             "OP routine(time)"
040          MUL   MUL(10)
041          DIV   DIV(12)
042          HLT   SPEC(10)
043          SLA   SHIFT(2)
044          MOVE  MOVE(1)
045          LDA   LOAD(2)
046          LD1   LOAD,1(2)
              . . .
051          LD6   LOAD,1(2)
052          LDX   LOAD(2)
053          LDAN  LOADN(2)
054          LD1N  LOADN,1(2)
              . . .
060          LDXN  LOADN(2)
061          STA   STORE(2)
              . . .
069          STJ   STORE(2)
070          STZ   STORE(2)
071          JBUS  JBUS(1)
072          IOC   IOC(1)
073          IN    IN(1)
074          OUT   OUT(1)
075          JRED  JRED(1)
076          JMP   JUMP(1)
077          JAP   REGJUMP(1)
              . . .
084          JXP   REGJUMP(1)
085          INCA  ADDROP(1)
```

```
086            INC1 ADDROP,1(1)
               . . .
092            INCX ADDROP(1)
093            CMPA COMPARE(2)
               . . .
100 OPTABLE    CMPX COMPARE(2)   ▌
```

(The entries for operators LD*i*, LD*i*N, and INC*i* have an additional ',1' to set the (3:3) field nonzero; this is used below in lines 289–290 to indicate the fact that the size of the quantity within the corresponding index register must be checked after simulating these operations.)

The next part of our simulator program merely lists the locations used to contain the contents of the simulated registers:

```
101 AREG    CON   0   Magnitude of A-register
102 I1REG   CON   0   Magnitude of index registers
            . . .
107 I6REG   CON   0
108 XREG    CON   0   Magnitude of X-register
109 JREG    CON   0   Magnitude of J-register
110 ZERO    CON   0   Constant zero, for 'STZ'
111 SIGNA   CON   1   Sign of A-register
112 SIGN1   CON   1   Sign of index registers
            . . .
117 SIGN6   CON   1
118 SIGNX   CON   1   Sign of X-register
119 SIGNJ   CON   1   Sign of J-register
120 SIGNZ   CON   1   Sign stored by 'STZ'
121 INST    CON   0   Instruction being simulated
122 COMPI   CON   0   Comparison indicator
123 OVTOG   CON   0   Overflow toggle
124 CLOCK   CON   0   Simulated execution time   ▌
```

Now we will consider three subroutines used by the simulator. First comes the MEMORY subroutine:

Calling sequence: JMP MEMORY.

Entry conditions: rI5 = valid memory address (otherwise the subroutine will jump to MEMERROR).

Exit conditions: rX = sign of word in memory location rI5; rA = magnitude of word in memory location rI5.

```
125 * SUBROUTINES
126 MEMORY   STJ   9F          Memory fetch subroutine:
127          J5N   MEMERROR
128          CMP5  =BEGIN=     The simulated memory is in
129          JGE   MEMERROR        locations 0000 to BEGIN − 1.
130          LDX   0,5
131          ENTA  1
132          SRAX  5           rX ← sign of word.
```

133		LDA	0,5(1:5)	rA ← magnitude of word.
134	9H	JMP	*	Exit. ▮

The FCHECK subroutine processes a partial field specification, making sure that it has the form 8L + R with L ≤ R ≤ 5.

Calling sequence: JMP FCHECK.
Entry conditions: rI3 = valid field specification (otherwise the subroutine will jump to FERROR).
Exit conditions: rA = rI1 = L, rX = R.

135	FCHECK	STJ	9F	Field check subroutine:
136		ENTA	0	
137		ENTX	0,3	rAX ← field specification.
138		DIV	=8=	rA ← L, rX ← R.
139		CMPX	=5=	Is R > 5?
140		JG	FERROR	
141		STX	R	
142		STA	L	
143		LD1	L	rI1 ← L.
144		CMPA	R	
145	9H	JLE	*	Exit unless L > R.
146		JMP	FERROR ▮	

The last subroutine, GETV, finds the quantity V (namely, the appropriate field of location M) used in various MIX operators, as defined in Section 1.3.1.

Calling sequence: JMP GETV.
Entry conditions: rI5 = valid memory address; rI3 = valid field. (If invalid, an error will be detected as above.)
Exit conditions: rA = magnitude of V; rX = sign of V; rI1 = L; rI2 = −R.
Second entrance: JMP GETAV, used only in comparison operators to extract a field from a register.

147	GETAV	STJ	9F	Special entrance, see line 300.
148		JMP	1F	
149	GETV	STJ	9F	Subroutine to find V:
150		JMP	FCHECK	Process the field and set rI1 ← L.
151		JMP	MEMORY	rA ← memory magnitude, rX ← sign.
152	1H	J1Z	2F	Is the sign included in the field?
153		ENTX	1	If not, set the sign positive.
154		SLA	-1,1	Zero out all bytes to the left
155		SRA	-1,1	of the field.
156	2H	LD2N	R	Shift right into the
157		SRA	5,2	proper position.
158	9H	JMP	*	Exit. ▮

Now we come to the routines for each individual operator. These routines are given here for completeness, but the reader should study only a few of them unless there's a compelling reason to look closer; the SUB and JUMP operators are recommended as typical examples for study. Notice the way in which routines

for similar operations can be neatly combined, and notice how the JUMP routine
uses another switching table to govern the type of jump.

```
159  * INDIVIDUAL OPERATORS
160  ADD      JMP   GETV        Get the value of V in rA and rX.
161           ENT1  0           rI1 ← index of simulated rA.
162           JMP   INC         Go to the "increase" routine.
163  SUB      JMP   GETV        Get the value of V in rA and rX.
164           ENT1  0           rI1 ← index of simulated rA.
165           JMP   DEC         Go to the "decrease" routine.
166  *
167  MUL      JMP   GETV        Get the value of V in rA and rX.
168           CMPX  SIGNA       Are signs the same?
169           ENTX  1
170           JE    *+2         Set rX to the result sign.
171           ENNX  1
172           STX   SIGNA       Put it in both simulated registers.
173           STX   SIGNX
174           MUL   AREG        Multiply the operands.
175           JMP   STOREAX     Store the magnitudes.
176  *
177  DIV      LDA   SIGNA       Set the sign of the remainder.
178           STA   SIGNX
179           JMP   GETV        Get the value of V in rA and rX.
180           CMPX  SIGNA       Are signs the same?
181           ENTX  1
182           JE    *+2         Set rX to the result sign.
183           ENNX  1
184           STX   SIGNA       Put it in the simulated rA.
185           STA   TEMP
186           LDA   AREG        Divide the operands.
187           LDX   XREG
188           DIV   TEMP
189  STOREAX  STA   AREG        Store the magnitudes.
190           STX   XREG
191  OVCHECK  JNOV  CYCLE       Did overflow just occur?
192           ENTX  1           If so, set the simulated
193           STX   OVTOG          overflow toggle on.
194           JMP   CYCLE       Return to control routine.
195  *
196  LOADN    JMP   GETV        Get the value of V in rA and rX.
197           ENT1  47,4        rI1 ← C − 16; indicates register.
198  LOADN1   STX   TEMP        Negate the sign.
199           LDXN  TEMP
200           JMP   LOAD1       Change LOADN to LOAD.
201  LOAD     JMP   GETV        Get the value of V in rA and rX.
202           ENT1  55,4        rI1 ← C − 8, indicates register.
203  LOAD1    STA   AREG,1      Store the magnitude.
204           STX   SIGNA,1     Store the sign.
```

205		JMP	SIZECHK	Check if the magnitude is too large.
206	*			
207	STORE	JMP	FCHECK	rI1 ← L.
208		JMP	MEMORY	Get contents of memory location.
209		J1P	1F	Is the sign included in the field?
210		ENT1	1	If so, change L to 1
211		LDX	SIGNA+39,4	and "store" the register's sign.
212	1H	LD2N	R	rI2 ← −R.
213		SRAX	5,2	Save the area to the field's right.
214		LDA	AREG+39,4	Insert register in the field.
215		SLAX	5,2	
216		ENN2	0,1	rI2 ← −L.
217		SRAX	6,2	
218		LDA	0,5	Restore the area to the field's left.
219		SRA	6,2	
220		SRAX	−1,1	Attach the sign.
221		STX	0,5	Store in memory.
222		JMP	CYCLE	Return to control routine.
223	*			
224	JUMP	DEC3	9	Jump operators:
225		J3P	FERROR	Is F too large?
226		LDA	COMPI	rA ← comparison indicator.
227		JMP	JTABLE,3	Jump to appropriate routine.
228	JMP	ST6	JREG	Set the simulated J-register.
229		JMP	JSJ	
230		JMP	JOV	
231		JMP	JNOV	
232		JMP	LS	
233		JMP	EQ	
234		JMP	GR	
235		JMP	GE	
236		JMP	NE	
237	JTABLE	JMP	LE	End of the jump table
238	JOV	LDX	OVTOG	Check whether to jump on
239		JMP	*+3	overflow.
240	JNOV	LDX	OVTOG	
241		DECX	1	Get complement of overflow toggle.
242		STZ	OVTOG	Shut off overflow toggle.
243		JXNZ	JMP	Jump.
244		JMP	CYCLE	Don't jump.
245	LE	JAZ	JMP	Jump if rA zero or negative.
246	LS	JAN	JMP	Jump if rA negative.
247		JMP	CYCLE	Don't jump.
248	NE	JAN	JMP	Jump if rA negative or positive.
249	GR	JAP	JMP	Jump if rA positive.
250		JMP	CYCLE	Don't jump.
251	GE	JAP	JMP	Jump if rA positive or zero.
252	EQ	JAZ	JMP	Jump if rA zero.
253		JMP	CYCLE	Don't jump.

254	JSJ	JMP	MEMORY	Check for valid memory address.
255		ENT6	0,5	Simulate a jump.
256		JMP	CYCLE	Return to main control routine.
257	*			
258	REGJUMP	LDA	AREG+23,4	Register jumps:
259		JAZ	*+2	Is register zero?
260		LDA	SIGNA+23,4	If not, put sign into rA.
261		DEC3	5	
262		J3NP	JTABLE,3	Change to a conditional JMP, unless
263		JMP	FERROR	the F-specification is too large.
264	*			
265	ADDROP	DEC3	3	Address transfer operators:
266		J3P	FERROR	Is F too large?
267		ENTX	0,5	
268		JXNZ	*+2	Find the sign of M.
269		LDX	INST	
270		ENTA	1	
271		SRAX	5	rX ← sign of M.
272		LDA	M(1:5)	rA ← magnitude of M.
273		ENT1	15,4	rI1 indicates the register.
274		JMP	1F,3	Four-way jump.
275		JMP	INC	Increase.
276		JMP	DEC	Decrease.
277		JMP	LOAD1	Enter.
278	1H	JMP	LOADN1	Enter negative.
279	DEC	STX	TEMP	Reverse the sign.
280		LDXN	TEMP	Reduce DEC to INC.
281	INC	CMPX	SIGNA,1	Addition routine:
282		JE	1F	Are signs the same?
283		SUB	AREG,1	No; subtract magnitudes.
284		JANP	2F	Sign change needed?
285		STX	SIGNA,1	Change the register's sign.
286		JMP	2F	
287	1H	ADD	AREG,1	Add magnitudes.
288	2H	STA	AREG,1(1:5)	Store magnitude of the result.
289	SIZECHK	LD1	OPTABLE,4(3:3)	Have we just loaded an
290		J1Z	OVCHECK	index register?
291		CMPA	ZERO(1:3)	If so, make sure that the result
292		JE	CYCLE	fits in two bytes.
293		JMP	SIZEERROR	
294	*			
295	COMPARE	JMP	GETV	Get the value of V in rA and rX.
296		SRAX	5	Attach the sign.
297		STX	V	
298		LDA	XREG,4	Get field F of the appropriate register.
299		LDX	SIGNX,4	
300		JMP	GETAV	
301		SRAX	5	Attach the sign.
302		CMPX	V	Compare (note that −0 = +0).

```
303              STZ  COMPI          Set comparison indicator to
304              JE   CYCLE              either zero, plus one,
305              ENTA 1                  or minus one.
306              JG   *+2
307              ENNA 1
308              STA  COMPI
309              JMP  CYCLE          Return to control routine.
310    *
311              END  BEGIN ▌
```

The code above adheres to a subtle rule that was stated in Section 1.3.1: The instruction 'ENTA -0' loads minus zero into register A, as does 'ENTA -5,1' when index register 1 contains +5. In general, when M is zero, ENTA loads the sign of the instruction and ENNA loads the opposite sign. The need to specify this condition was overlooked when the author prepared his first draft of Section 1.3.1; such questions usually come to light only when a computer program is being written to follow the rules.

In spite of its length, the program above is incomplete in several respects:

a) It does not recognize floating point operations.
b) The coding for operation codes 5, 6, and 7 has been left as an exercise.
c) The coding for input-output operators has been left as an exercise.
d) No provision has been made for loading simulated programs (see exercise 4).
e) The error routines

      INDEXERROR, ADDRERROR, OPERROR, MEMERROR, FERROR, SIZEERROR

have not been included; they handle error conditions that are detected in the simulated program.

f) There is no provision for diagnostic facilities. (A useful simulator should, for example, make it possible to print out the register contents as a program is being executed.)

EXERCISES

1. [14] Study all the uses of the FCHECK subroutine in the simulator program. Can you suggest a better way to organize the code? (See step 3 in the discussion at the end of Section 1.4.1.)

2. [20] Write the SHIFT routine, which is missing from the program in the text (operation code 6).

▶ **3.** [22] Write the MOVE routine, which is missing from the program in the text (operation code 7).

4. [14] Change the program in the text so that it begins as though MIX's "GO button" had been pushed (see exercise 1.3.1–26).

▶ **5.** [24] Determine the time required to simulate the LDA and ENTA operators, compared with the actual time for MIX to execute these operators directly.

6. [28] Write programs for the input-output operators JBUS, IOC, IN, OUT, and JRED, which are missing from the program in the text, allowing only units 16 and 18. Assume that the operations "read-card" and "skip-to-new-page" take $T = 10000u$, while "print-line" takes $T = 7500u$. [*Note:* Experience shows that the JBUS instruction should be simulated by treating 'JBUS *' as a special case; otherwise the simulator seems to stop!]

▶ **7.** [*32*] Modify the solutions of the previous exercise in such a way that execution of IN or OUT does not cause I/O transmission immediately; the transmission should take place after approximately half of the time required by the simulated devices has elapsed. (This will prevent a frequent student error, in which IN and OUT are used improperly.)

8. [*20*] True or false: Whenever line 010 of the simulator program is executed, we have $0 \le \text{rI6} < \text{BEGIN}$.

*1.4.3.2. Trace routines. When a machine is being simulated on itself (as MIX was simulated on MIX in the previous section) we have the special case of a simulator called a *trace* or *monitor* routine. Such programs are occasionally used to help in debugging, since they print out a step-by-step account of how the simulated program behaves.

The program in the preceding section was written as though another computer were simulating MIX. A quite different approach is used for trace programs; we generally let registers represent themselves and let the operators perform themselves. In fact, we usually contrive to let the machine execute most of the instructions by itself. The chief exception is a jump or conditional jump instruction, which must not be executed without modification, since the trace program must remain in control. Each machine also has idiosyncratic features that make tracing more of a challenge; in MIX's case, the J-register presents the most interesting problem.

The trace routine given below is initiated when the main program jumps to location ENTER, with register J set to the address for *starting* to trace and register X set to the address where tracing should *stop*. The program is interesting and merits careful study.

```
01   * TRACE ROUTINE
02   ENTER   STX   TEST(0:2)     Set the exit location.
03           STX   LEAVEX(0:2)
04           STA   AREG          Save the contents of rA.
05           STJ   JREG          Save the contents of rJ.
06           LDA   JREG(0:2)     Get the start location for tracing.
07   CYCLE   STA   PREG(0:2)     Store the location of the next instruction.
08   TEST    DECA  *             Is it the exit location?
09           JAZ   LEAVE
10   PREG    LDA   *             Get the next instruction.
11           STA   INST          Copy it.
12           SRA   2
13           STA   INST1(0:3)    Store the address and index parts.
14           LDA   INST(5:5)     Get the operation code, C.
15           DECA  38
16           JANN  1F            Is C ≥ 38 (JRED)?
17           INCA  6
```

18		JANZ	2F	Is C ≠ 32 (STJ)?
19		LDA	INST(0:4)	
20		STA	*+2(0:4)	Change STJ to STA.
21	JREG	ENTA	*	rA ← simulated rJ contents.
22		STA	*	
23		JMP	INCP	
24	2H	DECA	2	
25		JANZ	2F	Is C ≠ 34 (JBUS)?
26		JMP	3F	
27	1H	DECA	9	Test for jump instructions.
28		JAP	2F	Is C > 47 (JXNP)?
29	3H	LDA	8F(0:3)	We detected a jump instruction;
30		STA	INST(0:3)	change its address to 'JUMP'.
31	2H	LDA	AREG	Restore register A.
32	*			All registers except J now have proper
33	*			values with respect to the external program.
34	INST	NOP	*	The instruction is executed.
35		STA	AREG	Store register A again.
36	INCP	LDA	PREG(0:2)	Move to the next instruction.
37		INCA	1	
38		JMP	CYCLE	
39	8H	JSJ	JUMP	Constant for lines 29 and 40
40	JUMP	LDA	8B(4:5)	A jump has occurred.
41		SUB	INST(4:5)	Was it JSJ?
42		JAZ	*+4	
43		LDA	PREG(0:2)	If not, update the simulated
44		INCA	1	J-register.
45		STA	JREG(0:2)	
46	INST1	ENTA	*	
47		JMP	CYCLE	Move to the address of the jump.
48	LEAVE	LDA	AREG	Restore register A.
49	LEAVEX	JMP	*	Stop tracing.
50	AREG	CON	0	Simulated rA contents ▌

The following things should be noted about trace routines in general and this one in particular.

1) We have presented only the most interesting part of a trace program, the part that retains control while executing another program. For a trace to be useful, there must also be a routine for writing out the contents of registers, and this has not been included. Such a routine distracts from the more subtle features of a trace program, although it certainly is important; the necessary modifications are left as an exercise (see exercise 2).

2) Space is generally more important than time; that is, the program should be written to be as short as possible. Then the trace routine will be able to coexist with extremely large programs. The running time is consumed by output anyway.

3) Care was taken to avoid destroying the contents of most registers; in fact, the program uses only MIX's A-register. Neither the comparison indicator nor

the overflow toggle are affected by the trace routine. (The less we use, the less we need to restore.)

4) When a jump to location JUMP occurs, it is not necessary to 'STA AREG', since rA cannot have changed.

5) After leaving the trace routine, the J-register is not reset properly. Exercise 1 shows how to remedy this.

6) The program being traced is subject to only three restrictions:

a) It must not store anything into the locations used by the trace program.

b) It must not use the output device on which tracing information is being recorded (for example, JBUS would give an improper indication).

c) It will run at a slower speed while being traced.

EXERCISES

1. [22] Modify the trace routine of the text so that it restores register J when leaving. (You may assume that register J is not zero.)

2. [26] Modify the trace routine of the text so that before executing each program step it writes the following information on tape unit 0.

Word 1, (0:2) field: location.

Word 1, (4:5) field: register J (before execution).

Word 1, (3:3) field: 2 if comparison is greater, 1 if equal, 0 if less; plus 8 if overflow is not on before execution.

Word 2: instruction.

Word 3: register A (before execution).

Words 4–9: registers I1–I6 (before execution).

Word 10: register X (before execution).

Words 11–100 of each 100-word tape block should contain nine more ten-word groups, in the same format.

3. [10] The previous exercise suggests having the trace program write its output onto tape. Discuss why this would be preferable to printing directly.

▶ **4.** [25] What would happen if the trace routine were tracing *itself*? Specifically, consider the behavior if the two instructions ENTX LEAVEX; JMP *+1 were placed just before ENTER.

5. [28] In a manner similar to that used to solve the previous exercise, consider the situation in which two copies of the trace routine are placed in different places in memory, and each is set up to trace the other. What would happen?

▶ **6.** [40] Write a trace routine that is capable of tracing itself, in the sense of exercise 4: It should print out the steps of its own program at slower speed, and *that* program will be tracing itself at still *slower* speed, ad infinitum, until memory capacity is exceeded.

▶ **7.** [25] Discuss how to write an efficient *jump trace* routine, which emits much less output than a normal trace. Instead of displaying the register contents, a jump trace simply records the jumps that occur. It outputs a sequence of pairs (x_1, y_1), (x_2, y_2), ..., meaning that the program jumped from location x_1 to y_1, then (after performing the instructions in locations y_1, $y_1 + 1$, ..., x_2) it jumped from x_2 to y_2, etc. [From this information it is possible for a subsequent routine to reconstruct the flow of the program and to deduce how frequently each instruction was performed.]

1.4.4. Input and Output

Perhaps the most outstanding differences between one computer and the next are the facilities available for doing input and output, and the computer instructions that govern those peripheral devices. We cannot hope to discuss in a single book all of the problems and techniques that arise in this area, so we will confine ourselves to a study of typical input-output methods that apply to most computers. The input-output operators of MIX represent a compromise between the widely varying facilities available in actual machines; to give an example of how to think about input-output, let us discuss in this section the problem of getting the best MIX input-output.

> *Once again the reader is asked to be indulgent about the anachronistic MIX computer with its punched cards, etc. Although such old-fashioned devices are now quite obsolete, they still can teach important lessons. The MMIX computer, when it comes, will of course teach those lessons even better.*

Many computer users feel that input and output are not actually part of "real" programming; input and output are considered to be tedious tasks that people must perform only because they need to get information in and out of a machine. For this reason, the input and output facilities of a computer are usually not learned until after all other features have been examined, and it frequently happens that only a small fraction of the programmers of a particular machine ever know much about the details of input and output. This attitude is somewhat natural, because the input-output facilities of machines have never been especially pretty. However, the situation cannot be expected to improve until more people give serious thought to the subject. We shall see in this section and elsewhere (for example, in Section 5.4.6) that some very interesting issues arise in connection with input-output, and some pleasant algorithms do exist.

A brief digression about terminology is perhaps appropriate here. Although dictionaries of English formerly listed the words "input" and "output" only as nouns ("What kind of input are we getting?"), it is now customary to use them grammatically as adjectives ("Don't drop the input tape.") and as transitive verbs ("Why did the program output this garbage?"). The combined term "input-output" is most frequently referred to by the abbreviation "I/O". Inputting is often called *reading*, and outputting is, similarly, called *writing*. The stuff that is input or output is generally known as "data" — this word is, strictly speaking, a plural form of the word "datum," but it is used collectively as if it were singular ("The data has not been read."), just as the word "information" is both singular and plural. This completes today's English lesson.

Suppose now that we wish to read from magnetic tape. The IN operator of MIX, as defined in Section 1.3.1, merely *initiates* the input process, and the computer ·continues to execute further instructions while the input is taking place. Thus the instruction 'IN 1000(5)' will begin to read 100 words from tape unit number 5 into memory cells 1000–1099, but the ensuing program must not refer to these memory cells until later. The program can assume that input is complete only after (a) another I/O operation (IN, OUT, or IOC) referring to unit 5 has been initiated, or (b) a conditional jump instruction JBUS(5) or JRED(5) indicates that unit 5 is no longer "busy."

The simplest way to read a tape block into locations 1000–1099 and to have the information present is therefore the sequence of two instructions

$$\text{IN } 1000(5); \text{ JBUS } *(5). \tag{1}$$

We have used this rudimentary method in the program of Section 1.4.2 (see lines 07–08 and 52–53). The method is generally wasteful of computer time, however, because a very large amount of potentially useful calculating time, say $1000u$ or even $10000u$, is consumed by repeated execution of the 'JBUS' instruction. The program's running speed can be as much as doubled if this additional time is utilized for calculation. (See exercises 4 and 5.)

One way to avoid such a "busy wait" is to use two areas of memory for the input: We can read into one area while computing with the data in the other. For example, we could begin our program with the instruction

$$\text{IN}\quad 2000(5)\qquad \text{Begin reading first block.} \tag{2}$$

Subsequently, we may give the following five commands whenever a tape block is desired:

ENT1	1000	Prepare for MOVE operator.
JBUS	*(5)	Wait until unit 5 is ready.
MOVE	2000(50)	(2000–2049) → (1000–1049).
MOVE	2050(50)	(2050–2099) → (1050–1099).
IN	2000(5)	Begin reading next block.

$$\tag{3}$$

This has the same overall effect as (1), but it keeps the input tape busy while the program works on the data in locations 1000–1099.

The last instruction of (3) begins to read a tape block into locations 2000–2099 before the preceding block has been examined. This is called "reading ahead" or *anticipated input*— it is done on faith that the block will eventually be needed. In fact, however, we might discover that no more input is really required, after we begin to examine the block in 1000–1099. For example, consider the analogous situation in the coroutine program of Section 1.4.2, where the input was coming from punched cards instead of tape: A '.' appearing anywhere in the card meant that it was the final card of the deck. Such a situation would make anticipated input impossible, unless we could assume that either (a) a blank card or special trailer card of some other sort would follow the input deck, or (b) an identifying mark (e.g., '.') would appear in, say, column 80 of the final card of the deck. Some means for terminating the input properly at the end of the program must always be provided whenever input has been anticipated.

The technique of overlapping computation time and I/O time is known as *buffering*, while the rudimentary method (1) is called *unbuffered* input. The area of memory 2000–2099 used to hold the anticipated input in (3), as well as the area 1000–1099 to which the input was moved, is called a *buffer*. Webster's New World Dictionary defines "buffer" as "any person or thing that serves to lessen shock," and the term is appropriate because buffering tends to keep I/O devices running smoothly. (Computer engineers often use the word "buffer" in another sense, to denote a part of the I/O device that stores information during the transmission. In this book, however, "buffer" will signify an area of *memory* used by a programmer to hold I/O data.)

The sequence (3) is not always superior to (1), although the exceptions are rare. Let us compare the execution times: Suppose T is the time required to input 100 words, and suppose C is the computation time that intervenes between input requests. Method (1) requires a time of essentially $T + C$ per tape block, while method (3) takes essentially $\max(C, T) + 202u$. (The quantity $202u$ is the time required by the two MOVE instructions.) One way to look at this running time is to consider "critical path time" — in this case, the amount of time the I/O unit is idle between uses. Method (1) keeps the unit idle for C units of time, while method (3) keeps it idle for 202 units (assuming that $C < T$).

The relatively slow MOVE commands of (3) are undesirable, particularly because they take up critical path time when the tape unit must be inactive. An almost obvious improvement of the method allows us to avoid these MOVE instructions: The outside program can be revised so that it refers alternately to locations 1000–1099 and 2000–2099. While we are reading into one buffer area, we can be computing with the information in the other; then we can begin reading into the second buffer while computing with the information in the first. This is the important technique known as *buffer swapping*. The location of the current buffer of interest will be kept in an index register (or, if no index registers are available, in a memory location). We have already seen an example of buffer swapping applied to output in Algorithm 1.3.2P (see steps P9–P11) and the accompanying program.

As an example of buffer swapping on input, suppose that we have a computer application in which each tape block consists of 100 separate one-word items. The following program is a subroutine that gets the next word of input and begins to read in a new block if the current one is exhausted.

01	WORDIN	STJ	1F	Store the exit location.
02		INC6	1	Advance to the next word.
03	2H	LDA	0,6	Is it the end of the
04		CMPA	=SENTINEL=	buffer?
05	1H	JNE	*	If not, exit.
06		IN	-100,6(U)	Refill this buffer.
07		LD6	1,6	Switch to the other
08		JMP	2B	buffer and return.
09	INBUF1	ORIG	*+100	First buffer
10		CON	SENTINEL	Sentinel at end of buffer
11		CON	*+1	Address of other buffer
12	INBUF2	ORIG	*+100	Second buffer
13		CON	SENTINEL	Sentinel at end of buffer
14		CON	INBUF1	Address of other buffer

$$(4)$$

In this routine, index register 6 is used to address the last word of input; we assume that the calling program does not affect this register. The symbol U refers to a tape unit, and the symbol SENTINEL refers to a value that is known (from characteristics of the program) to be *absent* from all tape blocks.

Several things about this subroutine should be noted:

1) The sentinel constant appears as the 101st word of each buffer, and it makes a convenient test for the end of the buffer. In many applications, however, the sentinel technique will not be reliable, since any word may appear on tape. If we were doing card input, a similar method (with the 17th word of the buffer equal to a sentinel) could always be used without fear of failure; in that case, any negative word could serve as a sentinel, since MIX input from cards always gives nonnegative words.

2) Each buffer contains the address of the other buffer (see lines 07, 11, and 14). This "linking together" facilitates the swapping process.

3) No JBUS instruction was necessary, since the next input was initiated before any word of the previous block was accessed. If the quantities C and T refer as before to computation time and tape time, the execution time per tape block is now $\max(C, T)$; it is therefore possible to keep the tape going at full speed if $C \leq T$. (*Note:* MIX is an idealized computer in this regard, however, since no I/O errors must be treated by the program. On most machines some instructions to test the successful completion of the previous operation would be necessary just before the 'IN' instruction here.)

4) To make subroutine (4) work properly, it will be necessary to get things started out right when the program begins. Details are left to the reader (see exercise 6).

5) The WORDIN subroutine makes the tape unit appear to have a block length of 1 rather than 100 as far as the rest of the program is concerned. The idea of having several program-oriented records filling a single actual tape block is called *blocking of records*.

The techniques that we have illustrated for input apply, with minor changes, to output as well (see exercises 2 and 3).

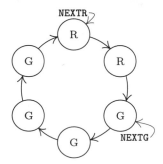

Fig. 23. A circle of buffers ($N = 6$).

Multiple buffers. Buffer swapping is just the special case $N = 2$ of a general method involving N buffers. In some applications it is desirable to have more than two buffers; for example, consider the following type of algorithm:

Step 1. Read five blocks in rapid succession.

Step 2. Perform a fairly long calculation based on this data.

Step 3. Return to step 1.

Here five or six buffers would be desirable, so that the next batch of five blocks could be read during step 2. This tendency for I/O activity to be "bunched" makes multiple buffering an improvement over buffer swapping.

Suppose we have N buffers for some input or output process using a single I/O device; we will imagine that the buffers are arranged in a circle, as in Fig. 23. The program external to the buffering process can be assumed to have the following general form with respect to the I/O unit of interest:

$$\vdots$$

```
ASSIGN
```

$$\vdots$$

```
RELEASE
```

$$\vdots$$

```
ASSIGN
```

$$\vdots$$

```
RELEASE
```

$$\vdots$$

in other words, we can assume that the program alternates between an action called "`ASSIGN`" and an action called "`RELEASE`", separated by other computations that do not affect the allocation of buffers.

> `ASSIGN` means that the program acquires the address of the next buffer area; this address is assigned as the value of some program variable.

> `RELEASE` means that the program is done with the current buffer area.

Between `ASSIGN` and `RELEASE` the program is communicating with one of the buffers, called the *current* buffer area; between `RELEASE` and `ASSIGN`, the program makes no reference to any buffer area.

Conceivably, `ASSIGN` could immediately follow `RELEASE`, and discussions of buffering have often been based on this assumption. However, if `RELEASE` is done as soon as possible, the buffering process has more freedom and will be more effective; by separating the two essentially different functions of `ASSIGN` and `RELEASE` we will find that the buffering technique remains easy to understand, and our discussion will be meaningful even if $N = 1$.

To be more explicit, let us consider the cases of input and output separately. For input, suppose we are dealing with a card reader. The action `ASSIGN` means that the program needs to see information from a new card; we would like to set an index register to the memory address at which the next card image is located. The action `RELEASE` occurs when the information in the current card image is no longer needed — it has somehow been digested by the program, perhaps copied to another part of memory, etc. The current buffer area may therefore be filled with further anticipated input.

For output, consider the case of a line printer. The action ASSIGN occurs when a free buffer area is needed, into which a line image is to be placed for printing. We wish to set an index register equal to the memory address of such an area. The action RELEASE occurs when this line image has been fully set up in the buffer area, in a form ready to be printed.

Example: To print the contents of locations 0800–0823, we might write

$$
\begin{array}{lll}
\texttt{JMP} & \texttt{ASSIGNP} & \text{(Sets rI5 to buffer location)} \\
\texttt{ENT1} & \texttt{0,5} & \\
\texttt{MOVE} & \texttt{800(24)} & \text{Move 24 words into the output buffer.} \\
\texttt{JMP} & \texttt{RELEASEP} &
\end{array} \tag{5}
$$

where ASSIGNP and RELEASEP represent subroutines to do the two buffering functions for the line printer.

In an optimal situation, from the standpoint of the computer, the ASSIGN operation will require virtually no execution time. This means, on input, that each card image will have been anticipated, so that the data is available when the program is ready for it; and on output, it means that there will always be a free place in memory to record the line image. In either case, no time will be spent waiting for the I/O device.

To help describe the buffering algorithm, and to make it more colorful, we will say that buffer areas are either green, yellow, or red (shown as G, Y, and R in Fig. 24).

Green means that the area is ready to be ASSIGNed; this means that it has been filled with anticipated information (in an input situation), or that it is a free area (in an output situation).

Yellow means that the area has been ASSIGNed, not RELEASEd; this means that it is the current buffer, and the program is communicating with it.

Red means that the area has been RELEASEd; thus it is a free area (in an input situation) or it has been filled with information (in an output situation).

Figure 23 shows two "pointers" associated with the circle of buffers. These are, conceptually, index registers in the program. NEXTG and NEXTR point to the "next green" and "next red" buffer, respectively. A third pointer, CURRENT (shown in Fig. 24), indicates the yellow buffer when one is present.

The algorithms below apply equally well to input or output, but for definiteness we will consider first the case of input from a card reader. Suppose that a program has reached the state shown in Fig. 23. This means that four card images have been anticipated by the buffering process, and they reside in the green buffers. At this moment, two things are happening *simultaneously*: (a) The program is computing, following a RELEASE operation; (b) a card is being read into the buffer indicated by NEXTR. This state of affairs will continue until the input cycle is completed (the unit will then go from "busy" to "ready"), or until the program does an ASSIGN operation. Suppose the latter occurs first; then the buffer indicated by NEXTG changes to yellow (it is assigned as the current buffer),

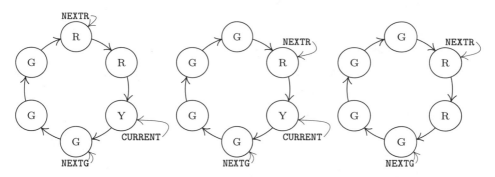

Fig. 24. Buffer transitions, (a) after `ASSIGN`, (b) after I/O complete, and (c) after `RELEASE`.

`NEXTG` moves clockwise, and we arrive at the position shown in Fig. 24(a). If now the input is completed, another anticipated block is present; so the buffer changes from red to green, and `NEXTR` moves over as shown in Fig. 24(b). If the `RELEASE` operation follows next, we obtain Fig. 24(c).

For an example concerning output, see Fig. 27 on page 226. That illustration shows the "colors" of buffer areas as a function of time, in a program that opens with four quick outputs, then produces four at a slow pace, and finally issues two in rapid succession as the program ends. Three buffers appear in that example.

The pointers `NEXTR` and `NEXTG` proceed merrily around the circle, each at an independent rate of speed, moving clockwise. It is a race between the program (which turns buffers from green to red) and the I/O buffering process (which turns them from red to green). Two situations of conflict can occur:

  a) if `NEXTG` tries to pass `NEXTR`, the program has gotten ahead of the I/O device and it must wait until the device is ready.

  b) if `NEXTR` tries to pass `NEXTG`, the I/O device has gotten ahead of the program and we must shut it down until the next `RELEASE` is given.

Both of these situations are depicted in Fig. 27. (See exercise 9.)

Fortunately, in spite of the rather lengthy explanation just given of the ideas behind a circle of buffers, the actual algorithms for handling the situation are quite simple. In the following description,

$$N = \text{total number of buffers};$$
$$n = \text{current number of red buffers}. \tag{6}$$

The variable n is used in the algorithm below to avoid interference between `NEXTG` and `NEXTR`.

Algorithm A (`ASSIGN`). This algorithm includes the steps implied by `ASSIGN` within a computational program, as described above.

A1. [Wait for $n < N$.] If $n = N$, stall the program until $n < N$. (If $n = N$, no buffers are ready to be assigned; but Algorithm B below, which runs in parallel with this one, will eventually succeed in producing a green buffer.)

A2. [CURRENT ← NEXTG.] Set CURRENT ← NEXTG (thereby assigning the current buffer).

A3. [Advance NEXTG.] Advance NEXTG to the next clockwise buffer. ∎

Algorithm R (RELEASE). This algorithm includes the steps implied by RELEASE within a computational program, as described above.

R1. [Increase n.] Increase n by one. ∎

Algorithm B (*Buffer control*). This algorithm performs the actual initiation of I/O operators in the machine; it is to be executed "simultaneously" with the main program, in the sense described below.

B1. [Compute.] Let the main program compute for a short period of time; step B2 will be executed after a certain time delay, at a time when the I/O device is ready for another operation.

B2. [$n = 0$?] If $n = 0$, go to B1. (Thus, if no buffers are red, no I/O action can be performed.)

B3. [Initiate I/O.] Initiate transmission between the buffer area designated by NEXTR and the I/O device.

B4. [Compute.] Let the main program run for a period of time; then go to step B5 when the I/O operation is completed.

B5. [Advance NEXTR.] Advance NEXTR to the next clockwise buffer.

B6. [Decrease n.] Decrease n by one, and go to B2. ∎

In these algorithms, we have two independent processes going on "simultaneously," the buffering control program and the computation program. These processes are, in fact, *coroutines*, which we will call CONTROL and COMPUTE. Coroutine CONTROL jumps to COMPUTE in steps B1 and B4; coroutine COMPUTE jumps to CONTROL by interspersing "jump ready" instructions at sporadic intervals in its program.

Coding this algorithm for MIX is extremely simple. For convenience, assume that the buffers are linked so that the word *preceding* each one is the address of the next; for example, with $N = 3$ buffers we have CONTENTS(BUF1 − 1) = BUF2, CONTENTS(BUF2 − 1) = BUF3, and CONTENTS(BUF3 − 1) = BUF1.

Program A (ASSIGN, *a subroutine within the* COMPUTE *coroutine*). rI4 ≡ CURRENT; rI6 ≡ n; calling sequence is JMP ASSIGN; on exit, rX contains NEXTG.

```
ASSIGN STJ  9F            Subroutine linkage
1H     JRED CONTROL(U)    A1. Wait for n < N.
       CMP6 =N=
       JE   1B
       LD4  NEXTG         A2. CURRENT ← NEXTG.
       LDX  -1,4          A3. Advance NEXTG.
       STX  NEXTG
9H     JMP  *             Exit. ∎
```

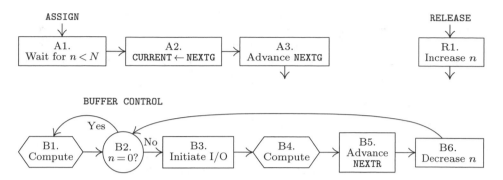

Fig. 25. Algorithms for multiple buffering.

Program R (RELEASE, *code used within the* COMPUTE *coroutine*). rI6 ≡ n. This short code is to be inserted wherever RELEASE is desired.

```
INC6 1              R1. Increase n.
JRED CONTROL(U)     Possible jump to CONTROL coroutine  ▌
```

Program B (*The* CONTROL *coroutine*). rI6 ≡ n, rI5 ≡ NEXTR.

```
CONT1   JMP   COMPUTE    B1. Compute.
1H      J6Z   *-1        B2. n = 0?
        IN    0,5(U)     B3. Initiate I/O.
        JMP   COMPUTE    B4. Compute.
        LD5   -1,5       B5. Advance NEXTR.
        DEC6  1          B6. Decrease n.
        JMP   1B  ▌
```

Besides the code above, we also have the usual coroutine linkage

```
CONTROL    STJ  COMPUTEX     COMPUTE    STJ  CONTROLX
CONTROLX   JMP  CONT1        COMPUTEX   JMP  COMP1
```

and the instruction 'JRED CONTROL(U)' should be placed within COMPUTE about once in every fifty instructions.

Thus the programs for multiple buffering essentially amount to only seven instructions for CONTROL, eight for ASSIGN, and two for RELEASE.

It is perhaps remarkable that *exactly* the same algorithm will work for both input and output. What is the difference—how does the control routine know whether to anticipate (for input) or to lag behind (for output)? The answer lies in the initial conditions: For input we start out with $n = N$ (all buffers red) and for output we start out with $n = 0$ (all buffers green). Once the routine has been started properly, it continues to behave as either an input process or an output process, respectively. The other initial condition is that NEXTR = NEXTG, both pointing at one of the buffers.

At the conclusion of the program, it is necessary to stop the I/O process (if it is input) or to wait until it is completed (for output); details are left to the reader (see exercises 12 and 13).

It is important to ask what is the best value of N to use. Certainly as N gets larger, the speed of the program will not decrease, but it will not increase indefinitely either and so we come to a point of diminishing returns. Let us refer again to the quantities C and T, representing computation time between I/O operators and the I/O time itself. More precisely, let C be the amount of time between successive ASSIGNs, and let T be the amount of time needed to transmit one block. If C is always *greater* than T, then $N = 2$ is adequate, for it is not hard to see that with two buffers we keep the computer busy at all times. If C is always *less* than T, then again $N = 2$ is adequate, for we keep the I/O device busy at all times (except when the device has special timing constraints as in exercise 19). Larger values of N are therefore useful chiefly when C varies between small values and large values; the average number of consecutive small values, plus 1, may be right for N, if the large values of C are significantly longer than T. (However, the advantage of buffering is virtually nullified if all input occurs at the beginning of the program and if all output occurs at the end.) If the time between ASSIGN and RELEASE is always quite small, the value of N may be decreased by 1 throughout the discussion above, with little effect on running time.

This approach to buffering can be adapted in many ways, and we will mention a few of them briefly. So far we have assumed that only one I/O device was being used; in practice, of course, several devices will be in use at the same time.

There are several ways to approach the subject of multiple units. In the simplest case, we can have a separate circle of buffers for each device. Each unit will have its own values of n, N, NEXTR, NEXTG, and CURRENT, and its own CONTROL coroutine. This will give efficient buffering action simultaneously on every I/O device.

It is also possible to "pool" buffer areas that are of the same size, so that two or more devices share buffers from a common list. This can be handled by using the linked memory techniques of Chapter 2, with all red input buffers linked together in one list and all green output buffers linked together in another. It becomes necessary to distinguish between input and output in this case, and to rewrite the algorithms without using n and N. The algorithm may get irrevocably stuck, if all buffers in the pool are filled with anticipated input; so a check should be made that there is always at least one buffer (preferably one for each device) that is not input-green; only if the COMPUTE routine is stalled at step A1 for some input device should we allow input into the final buffer of the pool from that device.

Some machines have additional constraints on the use of input-output units, so that it is impossible to be transmitting data from certain pairs of devices at the same time. (For example, several units might be attached to the computer by means of a single "channel.") This constraint also affects our buffering routine; when we must choose which I/O unit to initiate next, how is the choice to be made? This is called the problem of "forecasting." The best forecasting rule for the general case would seem to give preference to the unit whose buffer circle

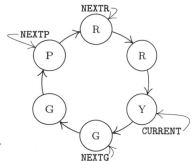

Fig. 26. Input and output from the same circle.

has the largest value of n/N, assuming that the number of buffers in the circles has been chosen wisely.

Let's conclude this discussion by taking note of a useful method for doing both input and output from the *same* buffer circle, under certain conditions. Figure 26 introduces a new kind of buffer, which has the color purple. In this situation, green buffers represent anticipated *input*; the program ASSIGNs and a green buffer becomes yellow, then upon **RELEASE** it turns red and represents a block to be *output*. The input and output processes follow around the circle independently as before, except that now we turn red buffers to purple after the output is done, and convert purple to green on input. It is necessary to ensure that none of the pointers NEXTG, NEXTR, NEXTP pass each other. At the instant shown in Fig. 26, the program is computing between ASSIGN and RELEASE, while accessing the yellow buffer; simultaneously, input is going into the buffer indicated by NEXTP; and output is coming from the buffer indicated by NEXTR.

EXERCISES

1. [*05*] (a) Would sequence (3) still be correct if the MOVE instructions were placed before the JBUS instruction instead of after it? (b) What if the MOVE instructions were placed after the IN command?

2. [*10*] The instructions 'OUT 1000(6); JBUS *(6)' may be used to output a tape block in an unbuffered fashion, just as the instructions (1) did this for input. Give a method analogous to (2) and (3) that buffers this output, by using MOVE instructions and an auxiliary buffer in locations 2000–2099.

▶ **3.** [*22*] Write a buffer-swapping output subroutine analogous to (4). The subroutine, called WORDOUT, should store the word in rA as the next word of output, and if a buffer is full it should write 100 words onto tape unit V. Index register 5 should be used to refer to the current buffer position. Show the layout of buffer areas and explain what instructions (if any) are necessary at the beginning and end of the program to ensure that the first and last blocks are properly written. The final block should be filled out with zeros if necessary.

4. [*M20*] Show that if a program refers to a single I/O device, we might be able to cut the running time in half by buffering the I/O, in favorable circumstances; but we can never decrease the running time by more than a factor of two, with respect to the time taken by unbuffered I/O.

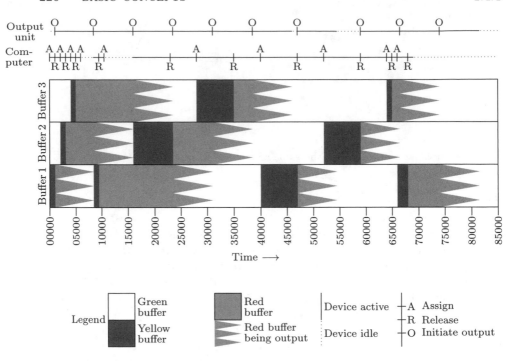

Fig. 27. Output with three buffers (see exercise 9).

▶ **5.** [*M21*] Generalize the situation of the preceding exercise to the case when the program refers to n I/O devices instead of just one.

6. [*12*] What instructions should be placed at the beginning of a program so that the WORDIN subroutine (4) gets off to the right start? (For example, index register 6 must be set to *something*.)

7. [*22*] Write a subroutine called WORDIN that is essentially like (4) except that it does not make use of a sentinel.

8. [*11*] The text describes a hypothetical input scenario that leads from Fig. 23 through parts (a), (b), and (c) of Fig. 24. Interpret the same scenario under the assumption that output to the line printer is being done, instead of input from cards. (For example, what things are happening at the time shown in Fig. 23?)

▶ **9.** [*21*] A program that leads to the buffer contents shown in Fig. 27 may be characterized by the following list of times:

> A, 1000, R, 1000, A, 1000, R, 1000, A, 1000, R, 1000, A, 1000, R, 1000,
> A, 7000, R, 5000, A, 7000, R, 5000, A, 7000, R, 5000, A, 7000, R, 5000,
> A, 1000, R, 1000, A, 2000, R, 1000.

This list means "assign, compute for $1000u$, release, compute for $1000u$, assign, ..., compute for $2000u$, release, compute for $1000u$." The computation times given do not include any intervals during which the computer might have to wait for the output device to catch up (as at the fourth "assign" in Fig. 27). The output device operates at a speed of $7500u$ per block.

The following chart specifies the actions shown in Fig. 27 as time passes:

Time	Action	Time	Action
0	ASSIGN(BUF1)	38500	OUT BUF3
1000	RELEASE, OUT BUF1	40000	ASSIGN(BUF1)
2000	ASSIGN(BUF2)	46000	Output stops.
3000	RELEASE	47000	RELEASE, OUT BUF1
4000	ASSIGN(BUF3)	52000	ASSIGN(BUF2)
5000	RELEASE	54500	Output stops.
6000	ASSIGN (wait)	59000	RELEASE, OUT BUF2
8500	BUF1 assigned, OUT BUF2	64000	ASSIGN(BUF3)
9500	RELEASE	65000	RELEASE
10500	ASSIGN (wait)	66000	ASSIGN(BUF1)
16000	BUF2 assigned, OUT BUF3	66500	OUT BUF3
23000	RELEASE	68000	RELEASE
23500	OUT BUF1	69000	Computation stops.
28000	ASSIGN(BUF3)	74000	OUT BUF1
31000	OUT BUF2	81500	Output stops.
35000	RELEASE		

The total time required was therefore $81500u$; the computer was idle from 6000–8500, 10500–16000, and 69000–81500, or $20500u$ altogether; the output unit was idle from 0–1000, 46000–47000, and 54500–59000, or $6500u$.

Make a time-action chart like the above for the same program, assuming that there are only *two* buffers.

10. [*21*] Repeat exercise 9, except with *four* buffers.

11. [*21*] Repeat exercise 9, except with just *one* buffer.

12. [*24*] Suppose that the multiple buffering algorithm in the text is being used for card input, and suppose the input is to terminate as soon as a card with "." in column 80 has been read. Show how the CONTROL coroutine (Algorithm B and Program B) should be changed so that input is shut off in this way.

13. [*20*] What instructions should be included at the end of the COMPUTE coroutine in the text, if the buffering algorithms are being applied to output, to ensure that all information has been output from the buffers?

▶ **14.** [*20*] Suppose the computational program does not alternate between ASSIGN and RELEASE, but instead gives the sequence of actions ...ASSIGN...ASSIGN...RELEASE... RELEASE. What effect does this have on the algorithms described in the text? Is it possibly useful?

▶ **15.** [*22*] Write a complete MIX program that copies 100 blocks from tape unit 0 to tape unit 1, using just three buffers. The program should be as fast as possible.

16. [*29*] Formulate the "green-yellow-red-purple" algorithm, suggested by Fig. 26, in the manner of the algorithms for multiple buffering given in the text, using three coroutines (one to control the input device, one for the output device, and one for the computation).

17. [*40*] Adapt the multiple-buffer algorithm to pooled buffers; build in methods that keep the process from slowing down, due to too much anticipated input. Try to make the algorithm as elegant as possible. Compare your method to nonpooling methods, applied to real-life problems.

▶ **18.** [*30*] A proposed extension of MIX allows its computations to be interrupted, as explained below. Your task in this exercise is to modify Algorithms and Programs A, R, and B of the text so that they use these interrupt facilities instead of the 'JRED' instructions.

The new MIX features include an additional 3999 memory cells, locations -3999 through -0001. The machine has two internal "states," *normal state* and *control state*. In normal state, locations -3999 through -0001 are not admissible memory locations and the MIX computer behaves as usual. When an "interrupt" occurs, due to conditions explained later, locations -0009 through -0001 are set equal to the contents of MIX's registers: rA in -0009; rI1 through rI6 in -0008 through -0003; rX in -0002; and rJ, the overflow toggle, the comparison indicator, and the location of the next instruction are stored in -0001 as

+	next inst.	OV, CI	rJ	;

the machine enters control state, at a location depending on the type of interrupt.

Location -0010 acts as a "clock": Every $1000u$ of time, the number appearing in this location is decreased by one, and if the result is zero an interrupt to location -0011 occurs.

The new MIX instruction 'INT' (C $= 5$, F $= 9$) works as follows: (a) In normal state, an interrupt occurs to location -0012. (Thus a programmer may force an interrupt, to communicate with a control routine; the address of INT has no effect, although the control routine may use it for information to distinguish between types of interrupt.) (b) In control state, all MIX registers are loaded from locations -0009 to -0001, the computer goes into normal state, and it resumes execution. The execution time for INT is $2u$ in each case.

An IN, OUT, or IOC instruction given in *control* state will cause an interrupt to occur as soon as the I/O operation is completed. The interrupt goes to location $-(0020+$ unit number).

No interrupts occur while in control state; any interrupt conditions are "saved" until after the next INT operation, and interrupt will occur after one instruction of the normal state program has been performed.

▶ **19.** [*M28*] Special considerations arise when input or output involves short blocks on a rotating device like a magnetic disk. Suppose a program works with $n \geq 2$ consecutive blocks of information in the following way: Block k begins to be input at time t_k, where $t_1 = 0$. It is assigned for processing at time $u_k \geq t_k + T$ and released from its buffer at time $v_k = u_k + C$. The disk rotates once every P units of time, and its reading head passes the start of a new block every L units; so we must have $t_k \equiv (k-1)L$ (modulo P). Since the processing is sequential, we must also have $u_k \geq v_{k-1}$ for $1 < k \leq n$. There are N buffers, hence $t_k \geq v_{k-N}$ for $N < k \leq n$.

How large does N have to be so that the finishing time v_n has its minimum possible value, $T + C + (n-1)\max(L, C)$? Give a general rule for determining the smallest such N. Illustrate your rule when $L = 1$, $P = 100$, $T = .5$, $n = 100$, and (a) $C = .5$; (b) $C = 1.0$; (c) $C = 1.01$; (d) $C = 1.5$; (e) $C = 2.0$; (f) $C = 2.5$; (g) $C = 10.0$; (h) $C = 50.0$; (i) $C = 200.0$.

1.4.5. History and Bibliography

Most of the fundamental techniques described in Section 1.4 have been developed independently by a number of different people, and the exact history of the ideas will probably never be known. An attempt has been made to record here the most important contributions to the history, and to put them in perspective.

Subroutines were the first labor-saving devices invented for programmers. In the 19th century, Charles Babbage envisioned a library of routines for his Analytical Engine [see *Charles Babbage and His Calculating Engines*, edited by Philip and Emily Morrison (Dover, 1961), 56]; and we might say that his dream came true in 1944 when Grace M. Hopper wrote a subroutine for computing $\sin x$ on the Harvard Mark I calculator [see *Mechanisation of Thought Processes* (London: Nat. Phys. Lab., 1959), 164]. However, these were essentially "open subroutines," meant to be inserted into a program where needed instead of being linked up dynamically. Babbage's planned machine was controlled by sequences of punched cards, as on the Jacquard loom; the Mark I was controlled by a number of paper tapes. Thus they were quite different from today's stored-program computers.

Subroutine linkage appropriate to stored-program machines, with the return address supplied as a parameter, was discussed by Herman H. Goldstine and John von Neumann in their widely circulated monograph on programming, written during 1946 and 1947; see von Neumann's *Collected Works* **5** (New York: Macmillan, 1963), 215–235. The main routine of their programs was responsible for storing parameters into the body of the subroutine, instead of passing the necessary information in registers. In England, A. M. Turing had designed hardware and software for subroutine linkage as early as 1945; see B. E. Carpenter and R. W. Doran, editors, *A. M. Turing's ACE Report of 1946 and Other Papers* (Cambridge, Mass.: MIT Press, 1986), 35–36, 76, 78–79. See also H. D. Huskey's remarks on "reversion storage" in *Proceedings of a Second Symposium on Large-Scale Digital Calculating Machinery* (Harvard University, 1949), 87–90. The use and construction of a very versatile subroutine library is the principal topic of the first textbook of computer programming, *The Preparation of Programs for an Electronic Digital Computer*, by M. V. Wilkes, D. J. Wheeler, and S. Gill, 1st ed. (Cambridge, Mass.: Addison–Wesley, 1951).

The word "coroutine" was coined by M. E. Conway in 1958, after he had developed the concept, and he first applied it to the construction of an assembly program. Coroutines were independently studied by J. Erdwinn and J. Merner, at about the same time; they wrote a paper entitled "Bilateral Linkage," which was not then considered sufficiently interesting to merit publication, and unfortunately no copies of that paper seem to exist today. The first published explanation of the coroutine concept appeared much later in Conway's article "Design of a Separable Transition-Diagram Compiler," *CACM* **6** (1963), 396–408. Actually a primitive form of coroutine linkage had already been noted briefly as a "programming tip" in an early UNIVAC publication [*The Programmer* **1**, 2 (February 1954), 4]. A suitable notation for coroutines in ALGOL-like languages was introduced in Dahl and Nygaard's SIMULA I [*CACM* **9** (1966), 671–678], and several excellent examples of coroutines (including replicated coroutines) appear in the book *Structured Programming* by O.-J. Dahl, E. W. Dijkstra, and C. A. R. Hoare, Chapter 3.

The first interpretive routine may be said to be the "Universal Turing Machine," a Turing machine capable of simulating any other Turing machines. Turing machines are not actual computers; they are theoretical constructions used to prove that certain problems are unsolvable by algorithms. Interpretive routines in the conventional sense were mentioned by John Mauchly in his lectures at the Moore School in 1946. The most notable early interpreters, chiefly intended to provide a convenient means of doing floating point arithmetic, were certain routines for the Whirlwind I (by C. W. Adams and others) and for the ILLIAC I (by D. J. Wheeler and others). Turing took a part in this development also; interpretive systems for the Pilot ACE computer were written under his direction. For references to the state of interpreters in the early fifties, see the article "Interpretative Sub-routines" by J. M. Bennett, D. G. Prinz, and M. L. Woods, *Proc. ACM* (Toronto: 1952), 81–87; see also various papers in the *Proceedings of the Symposium on Automatic Programming for Digital Computers* (1954), published by the Office of Naval Research, Washington, D.C.

The most extensively used early interpretive routine was probably John Backus's "IBM 701 Speedcoding system" [see *JACM* **1** (1954), 4–6]. This interpreter was slightly modified and skillfully rewritten for the IBM 650 by V. M. Wolontis and others of the Bell Telephone Laboratories; their routine, called the "Bell Interpretive System," became extremely popular. The IPL interpretive systems, which were designed beginning in 1956 by A. Newell, J. C. Shaw, and H. A. Simon for applications to quite different problems (see Section 2.6), were used extensively for list processing. Modern uses of interpreters, as mentioned in the introduction to Section 1.4.3, are often mentioned in passing in the computer literature; see the references listed in that section for articles that discuss interpreters in somewhat more detail.

The first tracing routine was developed by Stanley Gill in 1950; see his interesting article in *Proceedings of the Royal Society of London*, series A, **206** (1951), 538–554. The text by Wilkes, Wheeler, and Gill mentioned above includes several programs for tracing. Perhaps the most interesting of them is subroutine C-10 by D. J. Wheeler, which includes a provision for suppressing the trace upon entry to a library subroutine, executing the subroutine at full speed, then continuing the trace. Published information about trace routines is quite rare in the general computer literature, primarily because the methods are inherently oriented to a particular machine. The only other early reference known to the author is H. V. Meek, "An Experimental Monitoring Routine for the IBM 705," *Proc. Western Joint Computer Conf.* (1956), 68–70, which discusses a trace routine for a machine on which the problem was particularly difficult. See also the trace routine for IBM's System/360 architecture, presented in *A Compiler Generator* by W. M. McKeeman, J. J. Horning, and D. B. Wortman (Prentice–Hall, 1970), 305–363. Nowadays the emphasis on trace routines has shifted to software that provides selective symbolic output and measurements of program performance; one of the best such systems was developed by E. Satterthwaite, and described in *Software Practice & Experience* **2** (1972), 197–217.

Buffering was originally performed by computer hardware, in a manner analogous to the code 1.4.4–(3); an internal buffer area inaccessible to the programmer played the role of locations 2000–2099, and the instructions 1.4.4–(3) were implicitly performed behind the scenes when an input command was given. During the late 1940s, software buffering techniques that are especially useful for sorting were developed by early programmers of the UNIVAC (see Section 5.5). For a good survey of the prevailing philosophy towards I/O in 1952, see the proceedings of the Eastern Joint Computer Conference held in that year.

The DYSEAC computer [Alan L. Leiner, *JACM* **1** (1954), 57–81] introduced the idea of input-output devices communicating directly with memory while a program is running, then interrupting the program upon completion. Such a system implies that buffering algorithms had been developed, but the details went unpublished. The first published reference to buffering techniques in the sense we have described gives a highly sophisticated approach; see O. Mock and C. J. Swift, "Programmed Input-Output Buffering," *Proc. ACM Nat. Meeting* **13** (1958), paper 19, and *JACM* **6** (1959), 145–151. (The reader is cautioned that both articles contain a good deal of local jargon, which may take some time to understand, but neighboring articles in *JACM* **6** will help.) An interrupt system that enabled buffering of input and output was independently developed by E. W. Dijkstra in 1957 and 1958, in connection with B. J. Loopstra's and C. S. Scholten's X1 computer [see *Comp. J.* **2** (1959), 39–43]. Dijkstra's doctoral thesis, "Communication with an Automatic Computer" (1959), discussed primitive synchronization operations by which users could create long chains of buffers with respect to paper tape and typewriter I/O; each buffer contained either a single character or a single number. He later developed the ideas into the important general notion of *semaphores*, which are basic to the control of all sorts of concurrent processes, not just input-output [see *Programming Languages*, ed. by F. Genuys (Academic Press, 1968), 43–112; *BIT* **8** (1968), 174–186; *Acta Informatica* **1** (1971), 115–138]. The paper "Input-Output Buffering and FORTRAN" by David E. Ferguson, *JACM* **7** (1960), 1–9, describes buffer circles and gives a detailed description of simple buffering with many units at once.

> *About 1,000 instructions is a reasonable upper limit*
> *for the complexity of problems now envisioned.*
> — HERMAN GOLDSTINE and JOHN VON NEUMANN (1946)

CHAPTER TWO

INFORMATION STRUCTURES

I think that I shall never see
A poem lovely as a tree.
— JOYCE KILMER (1913)

Yea, from the table of my memory
I'll wipe away all trivial fond records.
— HAMLET (Act I, Scene 5, Line 98)

2.1. INTRODUCTION

COMPUTER PROGRAMS usually operate on tables of information. In most cases these tables are not simply amorphous masses of numerical values; they involve important *structural relationships* between the data elements.

In its simplest form, a table might be a linear list of elements, when its relevant structural properties might include the answers to such questions as: Which element is first in the list? Which is last? Which elements precede and follow a given one? How many elements are in the list? A lot can be said about structure even in this apparently simple case (see Section 2.2).

In more complicated situations, the table might be a two-dimensional array (a matrix or grid, having both a row and a column structure), or it might be an *n*-dimensional array for higher values of *n*; it might be a tree structure, representing hierarchical or branching relationships; or it might be a complex multilinked structure with a great many interconnections, such as we may find in a human brain.

In order to use a computer properly, we need to understand the structural relationships present within data, as well as the basic techniques for representing and manipulating such structure within a computer.

The present chapter summarizes the most important facts about information structures: the static and dynamic properties of different kinds of structure; means for storage allocation and representation of structured data; and efficient algorithms for creating, altering, accessing, and destroying structural information. In the course of this study, we will also work out several important examples that illustrate the application of such methods to a wide variety of problems. The examples include topological sorting, polynomial arithmetic, discrete system simulation, sparse matrix transformation, algebraic formula manipulation, and applications to the writing of compilers and operating systems. Our concern will be almost entirely with structure as represented *inside* a computer; the

232

conversion from external to internal representations is the subject of Chapters 9 and 10.

Much of the material we will discuss is often called "List processing," since a number of programming systems such as LISP have been designed to facilitate working with general kinds of structures called *Lists*. (When the word "list" is capitalized in this chapter, it is being used in a technical sense to denote a particular type of structure that is highlighted in Section 2.3.5.) Although List processing systems are useful in a large number of situations, they impose constraints on the programmer that are often unnecessary; it is usually better to use the methods of this chapter directly in one's own programs, tailoring the data format and the processing algorithms to the particular application. Many people unfortunately still feel that List processing techniques are quite complicated (so that it is necessary to use someone else's carefully written interpretive system or a prefabricated set of subroutines), and that List processing must be done only in a certain fixed way. We will see that there is nothing magic, mysterious, or difficult about the methods for dealing with complex structures; these techniques are an important part of every programmer's repertoire, and we can use them easily whether we are writing a program in assembly language or in an algebraic language like FORTRAN, C, or Java.

We will illustrate methods of dealing with information structures in terms of the MIX computer. A reader who does not care to look through detailed MIX programs should at least study the ways in which structural information is represented in MIX's memory.

It is important at this point to define several terms and notations that we will be using frequently from now on. The information in a table consists of a set of *nodes* (called "records," "entities," or "beads" by some authors); we will occasionally say "item" or "element" instead of "node." Each node consists of one or more consecutive words of the computer memory, divided into named parts called *fields*. In the simplest case, a node is just one word of memory, and it has just one field comprising that whole word. As a more interesting example, suppose the elements of our table are intended to represent playing cards; we might have two-word nodes broken into five fields, TAG, SUIT, RANK, NEXT, and TITLE:

+	TAG	SUIT	RANK	NEXT
+			TITLE	

(1)

(This format reflects the contents of two MIX words. Recall that a MIX word consists of five bytes and a sign; see Section 1.3.1. In this example we assume that the signs are + in each word.) The *address* of a node, also called a *link*, *pointer*, or *reference* to that node, is the memory location of its first word. The address is often taken relative to some base location, but in this chapter for simplicity we will take the address to be an absolute memory location.

The contents of any field within a node may represent numbers, alphabetic characters, links, or anything else the programmer may desire. In connection with the example above, we might wish to represent a pile of cards that might appear in a game of solitaire: TAG = 1 means that the card is face down, TAG = 0 means that it is face up; SUIT = 1, 2, 3, or 4 for clubs, diamonds, hearts, or spades, respectively; RANK = 1, 2, ..., 13 for ace, deuce, ..., king; NEXT is a *link* to the card *below* this one in the pile; and TITLE is a five-character alphabetic name of this card, for use in printouts. A typical pile might look like this:

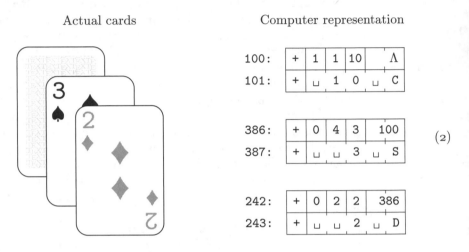

The memory locations in the computer representation are shown here as 100, 386, and 242; they could have been any other numbers as far as this example is concerned, since each card links to the one below it. Notice the special link "Λ" in node 100; *we use the capital Greek letter Lambda to denote the null link,* the link to no node. The null link Λ appears in node 100 since the 10 of clubs is the bottom card of the pile. Within the machine, Λ is represented by some easily recognizable value that cannot be the address of a node. We will generally assume that no node appears in location 0; consequently, Λ will almost always be represented as the link value 0 in MIX programs.

The introduction of links to other elements of data is an extremely important idea in computer programming; links are the key to the representation of complex structures. When displaying computer representations of nodes it is usually convenient to represent links by arrows, so that example (2) would appear thus:

The actual locations 242, 386, and 100 (which are irrelevant anyway) no longer appear in representation (3). Electrical circuit notation for a "grounded" wire is used to indicate a null link, shown here at the right of the diagram. Notice also that (3) indicates the top card by an arrow from "TOP"; here TOP is a *link variable,* often called a pointer variable, namely a variable whose value is a link. All references to nodes in a program are made directly through link variables (or link constants), or indirectly through link fields in other nodes.

Now we come to the most important part of the notation, the means of referring to fields within nodes. This is done simply by giving the name of the field followed by a link to the desired node in parentheses; for example, in (2) and (3) with the fields of (1) we have

$$\text{RANK(100)} = 10; \qquad \text{SUIT(TOP)} = 2;$$
$$\text{TITLE(TOP)} = \text{``}\llcorner\llcorner 2\llcorner D\text{''}; \qquad \text{RANK(NEXT(TOP))} = 3. \tag{4}$$

The reader should study these examples carefully, since such field notations will be used in many algorithms of this chapter and the following chapters. To make the ideas clearer, we will now state a simple algorithm for placing a new card face up on top of the pile, assuming that NEWCARD is a link variable whose value is a link to the new card:

A1. Set NEXT(NEWCARD) ← TOP. (This puts the appropriate link into the new card node.)

A2. Set TOP ← NEWCARD. (This keeps TOP pointing to the top of the pile.)

A3. Set TAG(TOP) ← 0. (This marks the card as "face up.") ▌

Another example is the following algorithm, which counts the number of cards currently in the pile:

B1. Set N ← 0, X ← TOP. (Here N is an integer variable, X is a link variable.)

B2. If X = Λ, stop; N is the number of cards in the pile.

B3. Set N ← N + 1, X ← NEXT(X), and go back to step B2. ▌

Notice that we are using symbolic names for two quite different things in these algorithms: as names of *variables* (TOP, NEWCARD, N, X) and as names of *fields* (TAG, NEXT). These two usages must not be confused. If F is a field name and L ≠ Λ is a link, then F(L) is a variable; but F itself is not a variable — it does not possess a value unless it is qualified by a nonnull link.

Two further notations are used, to convert between addresses and the values stored there, when we are discussing low-level machine details:

a) CONTENTS always denotes a full-word field of a one-word node. Thus CONTENTS(1000) denotes the value stored in memory location 1000; it is a variable having this value. If V is a link variable, CONTENTS(V) denotes the value pointed to by V (not the value V itself).

b) If V is the name of some value held in a memory cell, LOC(V) denotes the address of that cell. Consequently, if V is a variable whose value is stored in a full word of memory, we have CONTENTS(LOC(V)) = V.

It is easy to transform this notation into MIXAL assembly language code, although MIXAL's notation is somewhat backwards. The values of link variables are put into index registers, and the partial-field capability of MIX is used to refer to the desired field. For example, Algorithm A above could be written thus:

```
NEXT EQU  4:5          Definition of the NEXT
TAG  EQU  1:1             and TAG fields for the assembler
     LD1  NEWCARD     A1. rI1 ← NEWCARD.
     LDA  TOP             rA ← TOP.
     STA  0,1(NEXT)       NEXT(rI1) ← rA.
     ST1  TOP         A2. TOP ← rI1.
     STZ  0,1(TAG)    A3. TAG(rI1) ← 0.  ▮
```
(5)

The ease and efficiency with which these operations can be carried out in a computer is the primary reason for the importance of the "linked memory" concept.

Sometimes we have a single variable that denotes a whole node; its value is a sequence of fields instead of just one field. Thus we might write

$$CARD ← NODE(TOP),$$
(6)

where NODE is a field specification just like CONTENTS, except that it refers to an entire node, and where CARD is a variable that assumes structured values like those in (1). If there are c words in a node, the notation (6) is an abbreviation for the c low-level assignments

$$CONTENTS(LOC(CARD) + j) ← CONTENTS(TOP + j), \quad 0 \le j < c.$$
(7)

There is an important distinction between assembly language and the notation used in algorithms. Since assembly language is close to the machine's internal language, the symbols used in MIXAL programs stand for addresses instead of values. Thus in the left-hand columns of (5), the symbol TOP actually denotes the *address* where the pointer to the top card appears in memory; but in (6) and (7) and in the remarks at the right of (5), it denotes the *value* of TOP, namely the address of the top card node. This difference between assembly language and higher-level language is a frequent source of confusion for beginning programmers, so the reader is urged to work exercise 7. The other exercises also provide useful drills on the notational conventions introduced in this section.

EXERCISES

1. [04] In the situation depicted in (3), what is the value of (a) SUIT(NEXT(TOP)); (b) NEXT(NEXT(NEXT(TOP)))?

2. [10] The text points out that in many cases CONTENTS(LOC(V)) = V. Under what conditions do we have LOC(CONTENTS(V)) = V?

3. [11] Give an algorithm that essentially undoes the effect of Algorithm A: It removes the top card of the pile (if the pile is not empty) and sets NEWCARD to the address of this card.

4. [18] Give an algorithm analogous to Algorithm A, except that it puts the new card *face down* at the *bottom* of the pile. (The pile may be empty.)

▶ **5.** [21] Give an algorithm that essentially undoes the effect of exercise 4: Assuming that the pile is not empty and that its bottom card is face down, your algorithm should remove the bottom card and make `NEWCARD` link to it. (This algorithm is sometimes called "cheating" in solitaire games.)

6. [*06*] In the playing card example, suppose that `CARD` is the name of a variable whose value is an entire node as in (6). The operation `CARD ← NODE(TOP)` sets the fields of `CARD` respectively equal to those of the top of the pile. After this operation, which of the following notations stands for the suit of the top card? (a) `SUIT(CARD)`; (b) `SUIT(LOC(CARD))`; (c) `SUIT(CONTENTS(CARD))`; (d) `SUIT(TOP)` ?

▶ **7.** [*04*] In the text's example `MIX` program, (5), the link variable `TOP` is stored in the `MIX` computer word whose assembly language name is `TOP`. Given the field structure (1), which of the following sequences of code brings the quantity `NEXT(TOP)` into register A? Explain why the other sequence is incorrect.

         a) `LDA  TOP(NEXT)`   b) `LD1  TOP`
                                                  `LDA  0,1(NEXT)`

▶ **8.** [*18*] Write a `MIX` program corresponding to steps B1–B3.

9. [*23*] Write a `MIX` program that prints out the alphabetic names of the current contents of the card pile, starting at the top card, with one card per line, and with parentheses around cards that are face down.

2.2. LINEAR LISTS

2.2.1. Stacks, Queues, and Deques

DATA USUALLY HAS much more structural information than we actually want to represent directly in a computer. For example, each "playing card" node in the preceding section had a NEXT field to specify what card was beneath it in the pile, but we provided no direct way to find what card, if any, was *above* a given card, or to find what pile a given card was in. And of course we totally suppressed most of the characteristic features of *real* playing cards: the details of the design on the back, the relation to other objects in the room where the game was being played, the individual molecules within the cards, etc. It is conceivable that such structural information would be relevant in certain computer applications, but obviously we never want to store *all* of the structure that is present in every situation. Indeed, for most card-playing situations we would not need all of the facts retained in the earlier example; the TAG field, which tells whether a card is face up or face down, will often be unnecessary.

We must decide in each case how much structure to represent in our tables, and how accessible to make each piece of information. To make such decisions, we need to know what operations are to be performed on the data. For each problem considered in this chapter, therefore, *we consider not only the data structure but also the class of operations to be done on the data*; the design of computer representations depends on the desired function of the data as well as on its intrinsic properties. Indeed, an emphasis on function as well as form is basic to design problems in general.

In order to illustrate this point further, let's consider a related aspect of computer hardware design. A computer memory is often classified as a "random access memory," like MIX's main memory; or as a "read-only memory," which is supposed to contain essentially constant information; or a "secondary bulk memory," like MIX's disk units, which cannot be accessed at high speed although large quantities of information can be stored; or an "associative memory," more properly called a "content-addressed memory," for which information is addressed by its value rather than by its location; and so on. The intended function of each kind of memory is so important that it enters into the name of the particular memory type; all of these devices are "memory" units, but the purposes to which they are put profoundly influence their design and their cost.

A *linear list* is a sequence of $n \geq 0$ nodes X[1], X[2], ..., X[n] whose essential structural properties involve only the relative positions between items as they appear in a line. The only things we care about in such structures are the facts that, if $n > 0$, X[1] is the first node and X[n] is the last; and if $1 < k < n$, the kth node X[k] is preceded by X[k − 1] and followed by X[k + 1].

The operations we might want to perform on linear lists include, for example, the following.

i) Gain access to the kth node of the list to examine and/or to change the contents of its fields.

  ii) Insert a new node just before or after the kth node.

 iii) Delete the kth node.

 iv) Combine two or more linear lists into a single list.

  v) Split a linear list into two or more lists.

 vi) Make a copy of a linear list.

vii) Determine the number of nodes in a list.

viii) Sort the nodes of the list into ascending order based on certain fields of the nodes.

 ix) Search the list for the occurrence of a node with a particular value in some field.

In operations (i), (ii), and (iii) the special cases $k = 1$ and $k = n$ are of principal importance, since the first and last items of a linear list may be easier to get at than a general element is. We will not discuss operations (viii) and (ix) in this chapter, since those topics are the subjects of Chapters 5 and 6, respectively.

A computer application rarely calls for all nine of these operations in their full generality, so we find that there are many ways to represent linear lists depending on the class of operations that are to be done most frequently. It is difficult to design a single representation method for linear lists in which all of these operations are efficient; for example, the ability to gain access to the kth node of a long list for random k is comparatively hard to do if at the same time we are inserting and deleting items in the middle of the list. Therefore we distinguish between types of linear lists depending on the principal operations to be performed, just as we have noted that computer memories are distinguished by their intended applications.

Linear lists in which insertions, deletions, and accesses to values occur almost always at the first or the last node are very frequently encountered, and we give them special names:

    A *stack* is a linear list for which all insertions and deletions (and usually all accesses) are made at one end of the list.

    A *queue* is a linear list for which all insertions are made at one end of the list; all deletions (and usually all accesses) are made at the other end.

    A *deque* ("double-ended queue") is a linear list for which all insertions and deletions (and usually all accesses) are made at the ends of the list.

A deque is therefore more general than a stack or a queue; it has some properties in common with a deck of cards, and it is pronounced the same way. We also distinguish *output-restricted* or *input-restricted* deques, in which deletions or insertions, respectively, are allowed to take place at only one end.

In some disciplines the word "queue" has been used in a much broader sense, to describe any kind of list that is subject to insertions and deletions; the special cases identified above are then called various "queuing disciplines." Only the restricted use of the term "queue" is intended in this book, however, by analogy with orderly queues of people waiting in line for service.

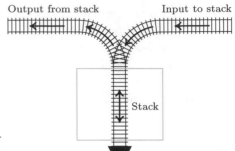

Fig. 1. A stack represented as a rail-way switching network.

Sometimes it helps to understand the mechanism of a stack in terms of an analogy from the switching of railroad cars, as suggested by E. W. Dijkstra (see Fig. 1). A corresponding picture for deques is shown in Fig. 2.

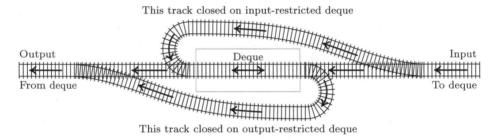

Fig. 2. A deque represented as a railway switching network.

With a stack we always remove the "youngest" item currently in the list, namely the one that has been inserted more recently than any other. With a queue just the opposite is true: The "oldest" item is always removed; the nodes leave the list in the same order as they entered it.

Many people who have independently realized the importance of stacks and queues have given them other names: Stacks have been called push-down lists, reversion storages, cellars, nesting stores, piles, last-in-first-out ("LIFO") lists, and even yo-yo lists. Queues are sometimes called circular stores or first-in-first-out ("FIFO") lists. The terms LIFO and FIFO have been used for many years by accountants, as names of methods for pricing inventories. Still another term, "shelf," has been applied to output-restricted deques, and input-restricted deques have been called "scrolls" or "rolls." This multiplicity of names is interesting in itself, since it is evidence for the importance of the concepts. The words stack and queue are gradually becoming standard terminology; of all the other words listed above, only "push-down list" is still reasonably common, particularly in connection with automata theory.

Stacks arise quite frequently in practice. We might, for example, go through a set of data and keep a list of exceptional conditions or things to do later; after we're done with the original set, we can then do the rest of the processing by coming back to the list, removing entries until it becomes empty. (The "saddle point" problem, exercise 1.3.2–10, is an instance of this situation.) Either a stack or a queue will be suitable for such a list, but a stack is generally more convenient. We all have "stacks" in our minds when we are solving problems: One problem leads to another and this leads to another; we stack up problems and subproblems and remove them as they are solved. Similarly, the process of entering and leaving subroutines during the execution of a computer program has a stack-like behavior. Stacks are particularly useful for the processing of languages with a nested structure, like programming languages, arithmetic expressions, and the literary German "Schachtelsätze." In general, stacks occur most frequently in connection with explicitly or implicitly recursive algorithms, and we will discuss this connection thoroughly in Chapter 8.

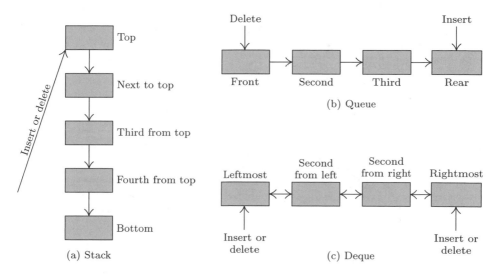

Fig. 3. Three important classes of linear lists.

Special terminology is generally used when algorithms refer to these structures: We put an item onto the *top* of a stack, or take the top item off (see Fig. 3(a)). The *bottom* of the stack is the least accessible item, and it will not be removed until all other items have been deleted. (People often say that they *push* an item *down* onto a stack, and *pop* the stack *up* when the top item is deleted. This terminology comes from an analogy with the stacks of plates often found in cafeterias. The brevity of the words "push" and "pop" has its advantages, but those terms falsely imply a motion of the whole list within computer memory. Nothing is physically pushed down; items are added onto the top, as in haystacks or stacks of boxes.) With queues, we speak of the *front* and the *rear* of the queue; things enter at the rear and are removed when they ultimately reach the front position (see Fig. 3(b)). When referring to deques, we speak of the *left* and *right* ends (Fig. 3(c)). The concepts of top, bottom, front, and rear are sometimes applied to deques that are being used as stacks or queues, with no standard conventions as to whether top, bottom, front, and rear should appear at the left or at the right.

Thus we find it easy to use a rich variety of descriptive words from English in our algorithms: "up-down" terminology for stacks, "waiting in line" terminology for queues, and "left-right" terminology for deques.

A little bit of additional notation has proved to be convenient for dealing with stacks and queues: We write

$$A \Leftarrow x \qquad (1)$$

(when A is a stack) to mean that the value x is *inserted* on top of stack A, or (when A is a queue) to mean that x is *inserted* at the rear of the queue. Similarly, the notation

$$x \Leftarrow A \qquad (2)$$

is used to mean that the variable x is set equal to the value at the top of stack A or at the front of queue A, and this value is *deleted* from A. Notation (2) is meaningless when A is empty — that is, when A contains no values.

If A is a nonempty stack, we may write

$$\mathrm{top}(A) \qquad (3)$$

to denote its top element.

EXERCISES

1. [*06*] An input-restricted deque is a linear list in which items may be inserted at one end but removed from either end; clearly an input-restricted deque can operate either as a stack or as a queue, if we consistently remove all items from one of the two ends. Can an output-restricted deque also be operated either as a stack or as a queue?

▶ **2.** [*15*] Imagine four railroad cars positioned on the input side of the track in Fig. 1, numbered 1, 2, 3, and 4, from left to right. Suppose we perform the following sequence of operations (which is compatible with the direction of the arrows in the diagram and does not require cars to "jump over" other cars): (i) move car 1 into the stack; (ii) move car 2 into the stack; (iii) move car 2 into the output; (iv) move car 3 into the stack; (v) move car 4 into the stack; (vi) move car 4 into the output; (vii) move car 3 into the output; (viii) move car 1 into the output.

As a result of these operations the original order of the cars, 1234, has been changed into 2431. *It is the purpose of this exercise and the following exercises to examine what permutations are obtainable in such a manner from stacks, queues, or deques.*

If there are six railroad cars numbered 123456, can they be permuted into the order 325641? Can they be permuted into the order 154623? (In case it is possible, show how to do it.)

3. [*25*] The operations (i) through (viii) in the previous exercise can be much more concisely described by the code SSXSSXXX, where S stands for "move a car from the input into the stack," and X stands for "move a car from the stack into the output." Some sequences of S's and X's specify meaningless operations, since there may be no cars available on the specified track; for example, the sequence SXXSSXXS cannot be carried out, since we assume that the stack is initially empty.

Let us call a sequence of S's and X's *admissible* if it contains n S's and n X's, and if it specifies no operations that cannot be performed. Formulate a rule by which it is easy to distinguish between admissible and inadmissible sequences; show furthermore that no two different admissible sequences give the same output permutation.

4. [*M34*] Find a simple formula for a_n, the number of permutations on n elements that can be obtained with a stack like that in exercise 2.

▶ **5.** [*M28*] Show that it is possible to obtain a permutation $p_1 p_2 \ldots p_n$ from $12 \ldots n$ using a stack if and only if there are no indices $i < j < k$ such that $p_j < p_k < p_i$.

6. [*00*] Consider the problem of exercise 2, with a queue substituted for a stack. What permutations of $12 \ldots n$ can be obtained with use of a queue?

▶ **7.** [*25*] Consider the problem of exercise 2, with a deque substituted for a stack. (a) Find a permutation of 1234 that can be obtained with an input-restricted deque, but it cannot be obtained with an output-restricted deque. (b) Find a permutation of 1234 that can be obtained with an output-restricted deque but not with an input-restricted deque. [As a consequence of (a) and (b), there is definitely a difference between input-restricted and output-restricted deques.] (c) Find a permutation of 1234 that cannot be obtained with either an input-restricted or an output-restricted deque.

8. [*22*] Are there any permutations of $12 \ldots n$ that cannot be obtained with the use of a deque that is neither input- nor output-restricted?

9. [*M20*] Let b_n be the number of permutations on n elements obtainable by the use of an input-restricted deque. (Note that $b_4 = 22$, as shown in exercise 7.) Show that b_n is also the number of permutations on n elements with an *output*-restricted deque.

10. [*M25*] (See exercise 3.) Let S, Q, and X denote respectively the operations of inserting an element at the left, inserting an element at the right, and emitting an element from the left, of an output-restricted deque. For example, the sequence QQXSXSXX will transform the input sequence 1234 into 1342. The sequence SXQSXSXX gives the same transformation.

Find a way to define the concept of an *admissible* sequence of the symbols S, Q, and X, so that the following property holds: Every permutation of n elements that is attainable with an output-restricted deque corresponds to precisely one admissible sequence.

▶ **11.** [*M40*] As a consequence of exercises 9 and 10, the number b_n is the number of admissible sequences of length $2n$. Find a closed form for the generating function $\sum_{n \geq 0} b_n z^n$.

12. [*HM34*] Compute the asymptotic values of the quantities a_n and b_n in exercises 4 and 11.

13. [*M48*] How many permutations of n elements are obtainable with the use of a general deque? [See Rosenstiehl and Tarjan, *J. Algorithms* **5** (1984), 389–390, for an algorithm that decides in $O(n)$ steps whether or not a given permutation is obtainable.]

▶ **14.** [*26*] Suppose you are allowed to use only stacks as data structures. How can you implement a queue efficiently with two stacks?

2.2.2. Sequential Allocation

The simplest and most natural way to keep a linear list inside a computer is to put the list items in consecutive locations, one node after the other. Then we will have

$$\text{LOC}(\text{X}[j+1]) = \text{LOC}(\text{X}[j]) + c,$$

where c is the number of words per node. (Usually $c = 1$. When $c > 1$, it is sometimes more convenient to split a single list into c "parallel" lists, so that the kth word of node $\text{X}[j]$ is stored a fixed distance from the location of the first word of $\text{X}[j]$, depending on k. We will continually assume, however, that adjacent groups of c words form a single node.) In general,

$$\text{LOC}(\text{X}[j]) = \text{L}_0 + cj, \tag{1}$$

where L_0 is a constant called the *base address*, the location of an artificially assumed node $\text{X}[0]$.

This technique for representing a linear list is so obvious and well-known that there seems to be no need to dwell on it at any length. But we will be seeing many other "more sophisticated" methods of representation later on in this chapter, and it is a good idea to examine the simple case first to see just how far we can go with it. It is important to understand the limitations as well as the power of the use of sequential allocation.

Sequential allocation is quite convenient for dealing with a *stack*. We simply have a variable T called the *stack pointer*. When the stack is empty, we let $\text{T} = 0$. To place a new element Y on top of the stack, we set

$$\text{T} \leftarrow \text{T} + 1; \qquad \text{X}[\text{T}] \leftarrow \text{Y}. \tag{2}$$

And when the stack is not empty, we can set Y equal to the top node and delete that node by reversing the actions of (2):

$$\text{Y} \leftarrow \text{X}[\text{T}]; \qquad \text{T} \leftarrow \text{T} - 1. \tag{3}$$

(Inside a computer it is usually most efficient to maintain the value $c\text{T}$ instead of T, because of (1). Such modifications are easily made, so we will continue our discussion as though $c = 1$.)

The representation of a *queue* or a more general *deque* is a little trickier. An obvious solution is to keep two pointers, say F and R (for the front and rear of the queue), with $\text{F} = \text{R} = 0$ when the queue is empty. Then inserting an element at the rear of the queue would be

$$\text{R} \leftarrow \text{R} + 1; \qquad \text{X}[\text{R}] \leftarrow \text{Y}. \tag{4}$$

Removing the front node (F points just below the front) would be

$$\text{F} \leftarrow \text{F} + 1; \qquad \text{Y} \leftarrow \text{X}[\text{F}]; \qquad \text{if } \text{F} = \text{R}, \text{ then set } \text{F} \leftarrow \text{R} \leftarrow 0. \tag{5}$$

But note what can happen: If R always stays ahead of F (so that there is always at least one node in the queue) the table entries used are $\text{X}[1]$, $\text{X}[2]$, $\dots$, $\text{X}[1000]$, $\dots$, ad infinitum, and this is terribly wasteful of storage space. The simple method of (4) and (5) should therefore be used only in the situation when F is known to catch up to R quite regularly — for example, if all deletions come in spurts that empty the queue.

To circumvent the problem of the queue overrunning memory, we can set aside M nodes X[1], ..., X[M] arranged implicitly in a circle with X[1] following X[M]. Then processes (4) and (5) above become

$$\text{if } R = M \text{ then } R \leftarrow 1, \quad \text{otherwise } R \leftarrow R + 1; \qquad X[R] \leftarrow Y. \qquad (6)$$

$$\text{if } F = M \text{ then } F \leftarrow 1, \quad \text{otherwise } F \leftarrow F + 1; \qquad Y \leftarrow X[F]. \qquad (7)$$

We have, in fact, already seen circular queuing action like this, when we looked at input-output buffering in Section 1.4.4.

Our discussion so far has been very unrealistic, because we have tacitly assumed that nothing could go wrong. When we deleted a node from a stack or queue, we assumed that there was at least one node present. When we inserted a node into a stack or queue, we assumed that there was room for it in memory. But clearly the method of (6) and (7) allows at most M nodes in the entire queue, and methods (2), (3), (4), (5) allow T and R to reach only a certain maximum amount within any given computer program. The following specifications show how the actions should be rewritten for the common case where we do not assume that these restrictions are automatically satisfied:

$$X \Leftarrow Y \text{ (insert into stack):} \quad \begin{cases} T \leftarrow T + 1; \\ \text{if } T > M, \text{ then OVERFLOW;} \\ X[T] \leftarrow Y. \end{cases} \qquad (2a)$$

$$Y \Leftarrow X \text{ (delete from stack):} \quad \begin{cases} \text{if } T = 0, \text{ then UNDERFLOW;} \\ Y \leftarrow X[T]; \\ T \leftarrow T - 1. \end{cases} \qquad (3a)$$

$$X \Leftarrow Y \text{ (insert into queue):} \quad \begin{cases} \text{if } R = M, \text{ then } R \leftarrow 1, \text{ otherwise } R \leftarrow R + 1; \\ \text{if } R = F, \text{ then OVERFLOW;} \\ X[R] \leftarrow Y. \end{cases} \qquad (6a)$$

$$Y \Leftarrow X \text{ (delete from queue):} \quad \begin{cases} \text{if } F = R, \text{ then UNDERFLOW;} \\ \text{if } F = M, \text{ then } F \leftarrow 1, \text{ otherwise } F \leftarrow F + 1; \\ Y \leftarrow X[F]. \end{cases} \qquad (7a)$$

Here we assume that X[1], ..., X[M] is the total amount of space allowed for the list; OVERFLOW and UNDERFLOW mean an excess or deficiency of items. The initial setting F = R = 0 for the queue pointers is no longer valid when we use (6a) and (7a), because overflow will not be detected when F = 0; we should start with F = R = 1, say.

The reader is urged to work exercise 1, which discusses a nontrivial aspect of this simple queuing mechanism.

The next question is, "What do we do when UNDERFLOW or OVERFLOW occurs?" In the case of UNDERFLOW, we have tried to remove a nonexistent item; this is usually a meaningful condition — not an error situation — that can be used to govern the flow of a program. For example, we might want to delete items repeatedly until UNDERFLOW occurs. An OVERFLOW situation, however, is usually an error; it means that the table is full already, yet there is still more information waiting to be put in. The usual policy in case of OVERFLOW is to report reluctantly that the program cannot go on because its storage capacity has been exceeded; then the program terminates.

Of course we hate to give up in an OVERFLOW situation when only one list has gotten too large, while other lists of the same program may very well have plenty of room remaining. In the discussion above we were primarily thinking of a program with only one list. However, we frequently encounter programs that involve several stacks, each of which has a dynamically varying size. In such a situation we don't want to impose a maximum size on each stack, since the size is usually unpredictable; and even if a maximum size has been determined for each stack, we will rarely find *all* stacks simultaneously filling their maximum capacity.

When there are just two variable-size lists, they can coexist together very nicely if we let the lists grow toward each other:

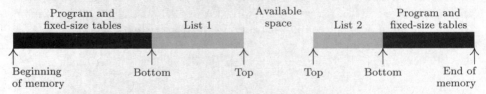

Here list 1 expands to the right, and list 2 (stored in reverse order) expands to the left. OVERFLOW will not occur unless the total size of both lists exhausts all memory space. The lists may independently expand and contract so that the effective maximum size of each one could be significantly more than half of the available space. This layout of memory space is used very frequently.

We can easily convince ourselves, however, that there is no way to store three or more variable-size sequential lists in memory so that (a) OVERFLOW will occur only when the total size of all lists exceeds the total space, and (b) each list has a fixed location for its "bottom" element. When there are, say, ten or more variable-size lists — and this is not unusual — the storage allocation problem becomes very significant. If we wish to satisfy condition (a), we must give up condition (b); that is, we must allow the "bottom" elements of the lists to change their positions. This means that the location L_0 of Eq. (1) is not constant any longer; no reference to the table may be made to an absolute memory address, since all references must be relative to the base address L_0. In the case of MIX, the coding to bring the Ith one-word node into register A is changed from

$$
\begin{array}{lll}
\texttt{LD1}\ \ \texttt{I} & & \texttt{LD1}\ \ \texttt{I} \\
\texttt{LDA}\ \ \texttt{L}_0\texttt{,1} & \text{to, for example,} & \texttt{LDA}\ \ \texttt{BASE(0:2)} \\
& & \texttt{STA}\ \ \texttt{*+1(0:2)} \\
& & \texttt{LDA}\ \ \texttt{*,1}
\end{array}
\qquad (8)
$$

where BASE contains $\boxed{\ \ L_0\ \ |\ 0\ |\ 0\ |\ 0\ }$. Such relative addressing evidently takes longer than fixed-base addressing, although it would be only slightly slower if MIX had an "indirect addressing" feature (see exercise 3).

An important special case occurs when each of the variable-size lists is a stack. Then, since only the top element of each stack is relevant at any time, we can proceed almost as efficiently as before. Suppose that we have n stacks; the insertion and deletion algorithms above become the following, if BASE[i] and TOP[i] are link variables for the ith stack, and if each node is one word long:

Insertion: TOP[i] $\leftarrow$ TOP[i] $+ 1$; if TOP[i] $>$ BASE[$i + 1$], then

  OVERFLOW; otherwise set CONTENTS(TOP[i]) $\leftarrow$ Y.   (9)

Deletion: if TOP[i] $=$ BASE[i], then UNDERFLOW; otherwise

  set Y $\leftarrow$ CONTENTS(TOP[i]), TOP[i] $\leftarrow$ TOP[i] $- 1$.   (10)

Here BASE[$i + 1$] is the base location of the $(i + 1)$st stack. The condition TOP[i] $=$ BASE[i] means that stack i is empty.

In (9), OVERFLOW is no longer such a crisis as it was before; we can "repack memory," making room for the table that overflowed by taking some away from tables that aren't yet filled. Several ways to do the repacking suggest themselves; we will now consider some of them in detail, since they can be quite important when linear lists are allocated sequentially. We will start by giving the simplest of the methods, and will then consider some of the alternatives.

Assume that there are n stacks, and that the values BASE[i] and TOP[i] are to be treated as in (9) and (10). These stacks are all supposed to share a common memory area consisting of all locations L with $L_0 < L \le L_\infty$. (Here L_0 and L_∞ are constants that specify the total number of words available for use.) We might start out with all stacks empty, and

$$\text{BASE}[j] = \text{TOP}[j] = L_0 \qquad \text{for } 1 \le j \le n. \qquad (11)$$

We also set BASE[$n + 1$] $= L_\infty$ so that (9) will work properly for $i = n$.

When OVERFLOW occurs with respect to stack i, there are three possibilities:

a) We find the smallest k for which $i < k \le n$ and TOP[k] $<$ BASE[$k + 1$], if any such k exist. Now move things *up* one notch:

  Set CONTENTS(L + 1) $\leftarrow$ CONTENTS(L),   for TOP[k] $\ge$ L $>$ BASE[$i + 1$].

(This must be done for decreasing, not increasing, values of L to avoid losing information. It is possible that TOP[k] $=$ BASE[$i + 1$], in which case nothing needs to be moved.) Finally we set BASE[j] $\leftarrow$ BASE[j] $+ 1$ and TOP[j] $\leftarrow$ TOP[j] $+ 1$, for $i < j \le k$.

b) No k can be found as in (a), but we find the largest k for which $1 \le k < i$ and TOP[k] $<$ BASE[$k + 1$]. Now move things *down* one notch:

  Set CONTENTS(L − 1) $\leftarrow$ CONTENTS(L),   for BASE[$k + 1$] $<$ L $<$ TOP[i].

(This must be done for increasing values of L.) Then set BASE[j] $\leftarrow$ BASE[j] $- 1$ and TOP[j] $\leftarrow$ TOP[j] $- 1$, for $k < j \le i$.

c) We have TOP[k] $=$ BASE[$k + 1$] for all $k \ne i$. Then obviously we cannot find room for the new stack entry, and we must give up.

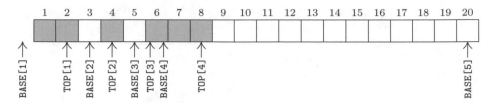

Fig. 4. Example of memory configuration after several insertions and deletions.

Figure 4 illustrates the configuration of memory for the case $n = 4$, $L_0 = 0$, $L_\infty = 20$, after the successive actions

$$I_1^* \; I_1^* \; I_4 \; I_2^* \; D_1 \; I_3^* \; I_1 \; I_1^* \; I_2^* \; I_4 \; D_2 \; D_1. \tag{12}$$

(Here I_j and D_j refer to insertion and deletion in stack j, and an asterisk refers to an occurrence of OVERFLOW, assuming that no space is initially allocated to stacks 1, 2, and 3.)

It is clear that many of the first stack overflows that occur with this method could be eliminated if we chose our initial conditions wisely, instead of allocating all space initially to the nth stack as suggested in (11). For example, if we expect each stack to be of the same size, we can start out with

$$\texttt{BASE}[j] = \texttt{TOP}[j] = \left\lfloor \left(\frac{j-1}{n}\right)(L_\infty - L_0) \right\rfloor + L_0, \qquad \text{for } 1 \leq j \leq n. \tag{13}$$

Operating experience with a particular program may suggest better starting values; however, no matter how well the initial allocation is set up, it can save at most a fixed number of overflows, and the effect is noticeable only in the early stages of a program run. (See exercise 17.)

Another possible way to improve the method above would be to make room for more than one new entry each time memory is repacked. This idea has been exploited by J. Garwick, who suggests a complete repacking of memory when overflow occurs, based on the change in size of each stack since the last repacking. His algorithm uses an additional array, called OLDTOP[j], $1 \leq j \leq n$, which retains the value that TOP[j] had just after the previous allocation of memory. Initially, the tables are set as before, with OLDTOP[j] = TOP[j]. The algorithm proceeds as follows:

Algorithm G (*Reallocate sequential tables*). Assume that OVERFLOW has occurred in stack i, according to (9). After Algorithm G has been performed, either we will find the memory capacity exceeded or the memory will have been rearranged so that the action CONTENTS(TOP[i]) $\leftarrow$ Y may be done. (Notice that TOP[i] has already been increased in (9) before Algorithm G takes place.)

G1. [Initialize.] Set SUM $\leftarrow$ $L_\infty - L_0$, INC $\leftarrow$ 0. Then do step G2 for $1 \leq j \leq n$. (The effect will be to make SUM equal to the total amount of memory space left, and INC equal to the total amount of increases in table sizes since the last allocation.) After this has been done, go on to step G3.

G2. [Gather statistics.] Set SUM ← SUM − (TOP[j] − BASE[j]). If TOP[j] > OLDTOP[j], set D[j] ← TOP[j] − OLDTOP[j] and INC ← INC + D[j]; otherwise set D[j] ← 0.

G3. [Is memory full?] If SUM < 0, we cannot proceed.

G4. [Compute allocation factors.] Set α ← 0.1 × SUM/n, β ← 0.9 × SUM/INC. (Here α and β are fractions, not integers, which are to be computed to reasonable accuracy. The following step awards the available space to individual lists as follows: Approximately 10 percent of the memory presently available will be shared equally among the n lists, and the other 90 percent will be divided proportionally to the amount of increase in table size since the previous allocation.)

G5. [Compute new base addresses.] Set NEWBASE[1] ← BASE[1] and σ ← 0; then for j = 2, 3, ..., n set τ ← $\sigma + \alpha +$ D[$j-1$]β, NEWBASE[j] ← NEWBASE[$j-1$] + TOP[$j-1$] − BASE[$j-1$] + $\lfloor \tau \rfloor - \lfloor \sigma \rfloor$, and $\sigma \leftarrow \tau$.

G6. [Repack.] Set TOP[i] ← TOP[i] − 1. (This reflects the true size of the ith list, so that no attempt will be made to move information from beyond the list boundary.) Perform Algorithm R below, and then reset TOP[i] ← TOP[i] + 1. Finally set OLDTOP[j] ← TOP[j] for $1 \le j \le n$. ∎

Perhaps the most interesting part of this whole algorithm is the general repacking process, which we shall now describe. Repacking is not trivial, since some portions of memory shift up and others shift down; it is obviously important not to overwrite any of the good information in memory while it is being moved.

Algorithm R (*Relocate sequential tables*). For $1 \le j \le n$, the information specified by BASE[j] and TOP[j] in accord with the conventions stated above is moved to new positions specified by NEWBASE[j], and the values of BASE[j] and TOP[j] are suitably adjusted. This algorithm is based on the easily verified fact that the data to be moved downward cannot overlap with any data that is to be moved upward, nor with any data that is supposed to stay put.

R1. [Initialize.] Set j ← 1.

R2. [Find start of shift.] (Now all lists from 1 to j that were to be moved down have been shifted into the desired position.) Increase j in steps of 1 until finding either

a) NEWBASE[j] < BASE[j]: Go to R3; or

b) $j > n$: Go to R4.

R3. [Shift list down.] Set δ ← BASE[j] − NEWBASE[j]. Set CONTENTS(L − δ) ← CONTENTS(L), for L = BASE[j] +1, BASE[j] +2, ..., TOP[j]. (It is possible for BASE[j] to equal TOP[j], in which case no action is required.) Set BASE[j] ← NEWBASE[j], TOP[j] ← TOP[j] − δ. Go back to R2.

R4. [Find start of shift.] (Now all lists from j to n that were to be moved up have been shifted into the desired position.) Decrease j in steps of 1 until finding either

a) NEWBASE[j] > BASE[j]: Go to R5; or

b) $j = 1$: The algorithm terminates.

R5. [Shift list up.] Set $\delta \leftarrow$ NEWBASE[j] $-$ BASE[j]. Set CONTENTS(L $+ \delta$) $\leftarrow$ CONTENTS(L), for L $=$ TOP[j], TOP[j] -1, ..., BASE[j] $+1$. (As in step R3, no action may actually be needed here.) Set BASE[j] $\leftarrow$ NEWBASE[j], TOP[j] $\leftarrow$ TOP[j] $+ \delta$. Go back to R4. ▌

Notice that stack 1 never needs to be moved. Therefore we should put the largest stack first, if we know which one will be largest.

In Algorithms G and R we have purposely made it possible to have

$$\text{OLDTOP}[j] \equiv \text{D}[j] \equiv \text{NEWBASE}[j+1]$$

for $1 \le j \le n$; that is, these three tables can share common memory locations since their values are never needed at conflicting times.

We have described these repacking algorithms for stacks, but it is clear that they can be adapted to any relatively addressed tables in which the current information is contained between BASE[j] and TOP[j]. Other pointers (for example, FRONT[j] and REAR[j]) could also be attached to the lists, making them serve as a queue or deque. See exercise 8, which considers the case of a queue in detail.

The mathematical analysis of dynamic storage-allocation algorithms like those above is extremely difficult. Some interesting results appear in the exercises below, although they only begin to scratch the surface as far as the general behavior is concerned.

As an example of the theory that *can* be derived, suppose we consider the case when the tables grow only by insertion; deletions and subsequent insertions that cancel their effect are ignored. Let us assume further that each table is expected to fill at the same rate. This situation can be modeled by imagining a sequence of m insertion operations $a_1, a_2, \ldots, a_m$, where each a_i is an integer between 1 and n (representing an insertion on top of stack a_i). For example, the sequence 1, 1, 2, 2, 1 means two insertions to stack 1, followed by two to stack 2, followed by another onto stack 1. We can regard each of the n^m possible specifications $a_1, a_2, \ldots, a_m$ as equally likely, and then we can ask for the average number of times it is necessary to move a word from one location to another during the repacking operations as the entire table is built. For the first algorithm, starting with all available space given to the nth stack, this question is analyzed in exercise 9. We find that the average number of move operations required is

$$\frac{1}{2}\left(1 - \frac{1}{n}\right)\binom{m}{2}. \tag{14}$$

Thus, as we might expect, the number of moves is essentially proportional to the *square* of the number of times the tables grow. The same is true if the individual stacks aren't equally likely (see exercise 10).

The moral of the story seems to be that a very large number of moves will be made if a reasonably large number of items is put into the tables. This is the price we must pay for the ability to pack a large number of sequential tables together tightly. No theory has been developed to analyze the average behavior of Algorithm G, and it is unlikely that any simple model will be able to describe the characteristics of real-life tables in such an environment. However, exercise 18 provides a worst-case guarantee that the running time will not be too bad if the memory doesn't get too full.

Experience shows that when memory is only half loaded (that is, when the available space equals half the total space), we need very little rearranging of the tables with Algorithm G. The important thing is perhaps that the algorithm behaves well in the half-full case and that it at least delivers the right answers in the almost-full case.

But let us think about the almost-full case more carefully. When the tables nearly fill memory, Algorithm R takes rather long to perform its job. And to make matters worse, OVERFLOW is much more frequent just before the memory space is used up. There are very few programs that will come *close* to filling memory without soon thereafter completely overflowing it; and those that do overflow memory will probably waste enormous amounts of time in Algorithms G and R just before memory is overrun. Unfortunately, undebugged programs will frequently overflow memory capacity. To avoid wasting all this time, a possible suggestion would be to stop Algorithm G in step G3 if SUM is less than $S_{\min}$, where the latter is chosen by the programmer to prevent excessive repacking. When there are many variable-size sequential tables, we should *not* expect to make use of 100 percent of the memory space before storage is exceeded.

Further study of Algorithm G has been made by D. S. Wise and D. C. Watson, *BIT* **16** (1976), 442–450. See also A. S. Fraenkel, *Inf. Proc. Letters* **8** (1979), 9–10, who suggests working with pairs of stacks that grow towards each other.

EXERCISES

▶ **1.** [*15*] In the queue operations given by (6a) and (7a), how many items can be in the queue at one time without OVERFLOW occurring?

▶ **2.** [*22*] Generalize the method of (6a) and (7a) so that it will apply to any deque with fewer than M elements. In other words, give specifications for the other two operations, "delete from rear" and "insert at front."

3. [*21*] Suppose that MIX is extended as follows: The I-field of each instruction is to have the form $8I_1 + I_2$, where $0 \le I_1 < 8$, $0 \le I_2 < 8$. In assembly language one writes 'OP ADDRESS,I_1:I_2' or (as presently) 'OP ADDRESS,I_2' if $I_1 = 0$. The meaning is to perform first the "address modification" I_1 on ADDRESS, then to perform the "address modification" I_2 on the resulting address, and finally to perform the OP with the new address. The address modifications are defined as follows:

0: M = A
1: M = A + rI1
2: M = A + rI2
   $\cdots$
6: M = A + rI6
7: M = resulting address defined from the 'ADDRESS,I_1:I_2' fields found in location A. The case $I_1 = I_2 = 7$ in location A is not allowed. (The reason for the latter restriction is discussed in exercise 5.)

Here A denotes the address before the operation, and M denotes the resulting address after the address modification. In all cases the result is undefined if the value of M does not fit in two bytes and a sign. The execution time is increased by one unit for each "indirect-addressing" (modification 7) operation performed.

As a nontrivial example, suppose that location 1000 contains 'NOP 1000,1:7'; location 1001 contains 'NOP 1000,2'; and index registers 1 and 2 respectively contain 1 and 2. Then the command 'LDA 1000,7:2' is equivalent to 'LDA 1004', because

$$1000,7:2 = (1000,1:7),2 = (1001,7),2 = (1000,2),2 = 1002,2 = 1004.$$

a) Using this indirect addressing feature (if necessary), show how to simplify the coding on the right-hand side of (8) so that two instructions are saved per reference to the table. How much faster is your code than (8)?

b) Suppose there are several tables whose base addresses are stored in locations BASE + 1, BASE + 2, BASE + 3, ...; how can the indirect addressing feature be used to bring the Ith element of the Jth table into register A in one instruction, assuming that I is in rI1 and J is in rI2?

c) What is the effect of the instruction 'ENT4 X,7', assuming that the (3:3)-field in location X is zero?

4. [*25*] Assume that MIX has been extended as in exercise 3. Show how to give a *single instruction* (plus auxiliary constants) for each of the following actions:

a) To loop indefinitely because indirect addressing never terminates.

b) To bring into register A the value LINK(LINK(x)), where the value of link variable x is stored in the (0:2) field of the location whose symbolic address is X, the value of LINK(x) is stored in the (0:2) field of location x, etc., assuming that the (3:3) fields in these locations are zero.

c) To bring into register A the value LINK(LINK(LINK(x))), under assumptions like those in (b).

d) To bring into register A the contents of location rI1 + rI2 + rI3 + rI4 + rI5 + rI6.

e) To quadruple the current value of rI6.

▸ **5.** [*35*] The extension of MIX suggested in exercise 3 has an unfortunate restriction that "7:7" is not allowed in an indirectly addressed location.

a) Give an example to indicate that, without this restriction, it would probably be necessary for the MIX hardware to be capable of maintaining a long internal stack of three-bit items. (This would be prohibitively expensive hardware, even for a mythical computer like MIX.)

b) Explain why such a stack is not needed under the present restriction; in other words, design an algorithm with which the hardware of a computer could perform the desired address modifications without much additional register capacity.

c) Give a milder restriction than that of exercise 3 on the use of 7:7 that alleviates the difficulties of exercise 4(c), yet can be cheaply implemented in computer hardware.

6. [*10*] Starting with the memory configuration shown in Fig. 4, determine which of the following sequences of operations causes overflow or underflow:
(a) I_1; (b) I_2; (c) I_3; (d) $I_4I_4I_4I_4I_4$; (e) $D_2D_2I_2I_2I_2$.

7. [*12*] Step G4 of Algorithm G indicates a division by the quantity INC. Can INC ever be zero at that point in the algorithm?

▸ **8.** [*26*] Explain how to modify (9), (10), and the repacking algorithms for the case that one or more of the lists is a queue being handled circularly as in (6a) and (7a).

▶ **9.** [*M27*] Using the mathematical model described near the end of the text, prove that Eq. (14) is the expected number of moves. (Note that the sequence 1, 1, 4, 2, 3, 1, 2, 4, 2, 1 specifies $0 + 0 + 0 + 1 + 1 + 3 + 2 + 0 + 3 + 6 = 16$ moves.)

10. [*M28*] Modify the mathematical model of exercise 9 so that some tables are expected to be larger than others: Let p_k be the probability that $a_j = k$, for $1 \leq j \leq m$, $1 \leq k \leq n$. Thus $p_1 + p_2 + \cdots + p_n = 1$; the previous exercise considered the special case $p_k = 1/n$ for all k. Determine the expected number of moves, as in Eq. (14), for this more general case. It is possible to rearrange the relative order of the n lists so that the lists expected to be longer are put to the right (or to the left) of the lists that are expected to be shorter; what relative order for the n lists will minimize the expected number of moves, based on $p_1, p_2, \ldots, p_n$?

11. [*M30*] Generalize the argument of exercise 9 so that the first t insertions in any stack cause no movement, while subsequent insertions are unaffected. Thus if $t = 2$, the sequence in exercise 9 specifies $0+0+0+0+0+3+0+0+3+6 = 12$ moves. What is the average total number of moves under this assumption? [This is an approximation to the behavior of the algorithm when each stack starts with t available spaces.]

12. [*M28*] The advantage of having two tables coexist in memory by growing towards each other, rather than by having them kept in separate independently bounded areas, may be quantitatively estimated (to a certain extent) as follows. Use the model of exercise 9 with $n = 2$; for each of the 2^m equally probable sequences $a_1, a_2, \ldots, a_m$, let there be k_1 1s and k_2 2s. (Here k_1 and k_2 are the respective sizes of the two tables after the memory is full. We are able to run the algorithm with $m = k_1 + k_2$ locations when the tables are adjacent, instead of $2 \max(k_1, k_2)$ locations to get the same effect with separate tables.)

What is the average value of $\max(k_1, k_2)$?

13. [*HM42*] The value $\max(k_1, k_2)$ investigated in exercise 12 will be even greater if larger fluctuations in the tables are introduced by allowing random *deletions* as well as random insertions. Suppose we alter the model so that with probability p the sequence value a_j is interpreted as a deletion instead of an insertion; the process continues until $k_1 + k_2$ (the total number of table locations in use) equals m. A deletion from an empty list causes no effect.

For example, if $m = 4$ it can be shown that we get the following probability distribution when the process stops:

$(k_1, k_2) =$	$(0,4)$	$(1,3)$	$(2,2)$	$(3,1)$	$(4,0)$
with probability	$\dfrac{1}{16-12p+4p^2}$,	$\dfrac{1}{4}$,	$\dfrac{6-6p+2p^2}{16-12p+4p^2}$,	$\dfrac{1}{4}$,	$\dfrac{1}{16-12p+4p^2}$.

Thus as p increases, the difference between k_1 and k_2 tends to increase. It is not difficult to show that in the limit as p approaches unity, the distribution of k_1 becomes essentially uniform, and the limiting expected value of $\max(k_1, k_2)$ is exactly $\frac{3}{4}m + \frac{1}{4m}$ [m odd]. This behavior is quite different from that in the previous exercise (when $p = 0$); however, it may not be extremely significant, since when p approaches unity, the amount of time taken to terminate the process rapidly approaches infinity. The problem posed in this exercise is to examine the dependence of $\max(k_1, k_2)$ on p and m, and to determine asymptotic formulas for fixed p (like $p = \frac{1}{3}$) as m approaches infinity. The case $p = \frac{1}{2}$ is particularly interesting.

14. [*HM43*] Generalize the result of exercise 12 to arbitrary $n \geq 2$, by showing that, when n is fixed and m approaches infinity, the quantity

$$\frac{m!}{n^m} \sum_{\substack{k_1+k_2+\cdots+k_n=m \\ k_1,k_2,\ldots,k_n \geq 0}} \frac{\max(k_1,k_2,\ldots,k_n)}{k_1!\,k_2!\ldots k_n!}$$

has the asymptotic form $m/n+c_n\sqrt{m}+O(1)$. Determine the constants c_2, c_3, c_4, and c_5.

15. [*40*] Using a Monte Carlo method, simulate the behavior of Algorithm G under varying distributions of insertions and deletions. What do your experiments imply about the efficiency of Algorithm G? Compare its performance with the algorithm given earlier that shifts up and down one node at a time.

16. [*20*] The text illustrates how two stacks can be located so they grow towards each other, thereby making efficient use of a common memory area. Can two *queues*, or a stack and a queue, make use of a common memory area with the same efficiency?

17. [*30*] If σ is any sequence of insertions and deletions such as (12), let $s_0(\sigma)$ be the number of stack overflows that occur when the simple method of Fig. 4 is applied to σ with initial conditions (11), and let $s_1(\sigma)$ be the corresponding number of overflows with respect to other initial conditions such as (13). Prove that $s_0(\sigma) \leq s_1(\sigma)+\mathrm{L}_\infty-\mathrm{L}_0$.

▶ **18.** [*M30*] Show that the total running time for any sequence of m insertions and/or deletions by Algorithms G and R is $O\big(m+n\sum_{k=1}^{m}\alpha_k/(1-\alpha_k)\big)$, where α_k is the fraction of memory occupied on the most recent repacking previous to the kth operation; $\alpha_k = 0$ before the first repacking. (Therefore if the memory never gets more than, say, 90% full, each operation takes at most $O(n)$ units of time in an amortized sense, regardless of the total memory size.) Assume that $\mathrm{L}_\infty - \mathrm{L}_0 \geq n^2$.

▶ **19.** [*16*] (*0-origin indexing.*) Experienced programmers learn that it is generally wise to denote the elements of a linear list by X[0], X[1], ..., X[$n - 1$], instead of using the more traditional notation X[1], X[2], ..., X[n]. Then, for example, the base address L_0 in (1) points to the smallest cell of the array.

Revise the insertion and deletion methods (2a), (3a), (6a), and (7a) for stacks and queues so that they conform to this convention. In other words, change them so that the list elements will appear in the array X[0], X[1], ..., X[$M - 1$], instead of X[1], X[2], ..., X[M].

2.2.3. Linked Allocation

Instead of keeping a linear list in sequential memory locations, we can make use of a much more flexible scheme in which each node contains a link to the next node of the list.

Sequential allocation:		Linked allocation:	
Address	Contents	Address	Contents
$L_0 + c$:	Item 1	A:	Item 1 · B
$L_0 + 2c$:	Item 2	B:	Item 2 · C
$L_0 + 3c$:	Item 3	C:	Item 3 · D
$L_0 + 4c$:	Item 4	D:	Item 4 · E
$L_0 + 5c$:	Item 5	E:	Item 5 · Λ

Here A, B, C, D, and E are arbitrary locations in the memory, and Λ is the null link (see Section 2.1). The program that uses this table in the case of sequential allocation would have an additional variable or constant whose value indicates that the table is five items in length, or else this information would be specified by a sentinel code within item 5 or in the following location. A program for linked allocation would have a link variable or link constant that points to A; all the other items of the list can be found from address A.

Recall from Section 2.1 that links are often shown simply by arrows, since the actual memory locations occupied are usually irrelevant. The linked table above might therefore be shown as follows:

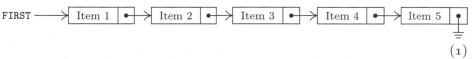

$$(1)$$

Here FIRST is a link variable pointing to the first node of the list.

We can make several obvious comparisons between these two basic forms of storage:

1) Linked allocation takes up additional memory space for the links. This can be the dominating factor in some situations. However, we frequently find that the information in a node does not take up a whole word anyway, so there is already space for a link field present. Also, it is possible in many applications to combine several items into one node so that there is only one link for several items of information (see exercise 2.5–2). But even more importantly, there is often an implicit *gain* in storage by the linked memory approach, since tables can overlap, sharing common parts; and in many cases, sequential allocation will not be as efficient as linked allocation unless a rather large number of additional memory locations are left vacant anyway. For example, the discussion at the end of the previous section explains why the systems described there are necessarily inefficient when memory is densely loaded.

2) It is easy to delete an item from within a linked list. For example, to delete item 3 we need only change the link associated with item 2. But with sequential allocation such a deletion generally implies moving a large part of the list up into different locations.

3) It is easy to insert an item into the midst of a list when the linked scheme is being used. For example, to insert an item $2\frac{1}{2}$ into (1) we need to change only two links:

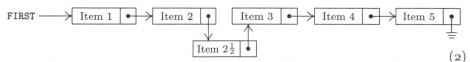

$$(2)$$

By comparison, this operation would be extremely time-consuming in a long sequential table.

4) References to random parts of the list are much faster in the sequential case. To gain access to the kth item in the list, when k is a variable, takes a fixed time in the sequential case, but we need k iterations to march down to the right

place in the linked case. Thus the usefulness of linked memory is predicated on the fact that in the large majority of applications we want to walk through lists sequentially, not randomly; if items in the middle or at the bottom of the list are needed, we try to keep an additional link variable or list of link variables pointing to the proper places.

5) The linked scheme makes it easier to join two lists together, or to break one apart into two that will grow independently.

6) The linked scheme lends itself immediately to more intricate structures than simple linear lists. We can have a variable number of variable-size lists; any node of the list may be a starting point for another list; the nodes may simultaneously be linked together in several orders corresponding to different lists; and so on.

7) Simple operations, like proceeding sequentially through a list, are slightly faster for sequential lists on many computers. For MIX, the comparison is between 'INC1 c' and 'LD1 0,1(LINK)', which is only one cycle different, but many machines do not enjoy the property of being able to load an index register from an indexed location. If the elements of a linked list belong to different pages in a bulk memory, the memory accesses might take significantly longer.

Thus we see that the linking technique, which frees us from any constraints imposed by the consecutive nature of computer memory, gives us a good deal more efficiency in some operations, while we lose some capabilities in other cases. It is usually clear which allocation technique will be most appropriate in a given situation, and both methods are often used in different lists of the same program.

In the next few examples we will assume for convenience that a node has one word and that it is broken into the two fields INFO and LINK:

$$\boxed{\text{INFO} \quad \text{LINK}} \ . \tag{3}$$

The use of linked allocation generally implies the existence of some mechanism for finding empty space available for a new node, when we wish to insert some newly created information onto a list. This is usually done by having a special list called the *list of available space*. We will call it the AVAIL list (or the AVAIL stack, since it is usually treated in a last-in-first-out manner). The set of all nodes not currently in use is linked together in a list just like any other list; the link variable AVAIL refers to the top element of this list. Thus, if we want to set link variable X to the address of a new node, and to reserve that node for future use, we can proceed as follows:

$$\text{X} \leftarrow \text{AVAIL}, \quad \text{AVAIL} \leftarrow \text{LINK(AVAIL)}. \tag{4}$$

This effectively removes the top of the AVAIL stack and makes X point to the node just removed. *Operation (4) occurs so often that we have a special notation for it:* "X $\Leftarrow$ AVAIL" will mean X is set to point to a new node.

When a node is deleted and no longer needed, process (4) can be reversed:

$$\text{LINK(X)} \leftarrow \text{AVAIL}, \quad \text{AVAIL} \leftarrow \text{X}. \tag{5}$$

This operation puts the node addressed by X back onto the list of raw material; we denote (5) by "$\text{AVAIL} \Leftarrow \text{X}$".

Several important things have been omitted from this discussion of the AVAIL stack. We did not say how to set it up at the beginning of a program; clearly this can be done by (a) linking together all nodes that are to be used for linked memory, (b) setting AVAIL to the address of the first of these nodes, and (c) making the last node link to Λ. The set of all nodes that can be allocated is called the *storage pool*.

A more important omission in our discussion was the test for overflow: We neglected to check in (4) if all available memory space has been taken. The operation $\text{X} \Leftarrow \text{AVAIL}$ should really be defined as follows:

if $\text{AVAIL} = \Lambda$, then OVERFLOW;

otherwise $\text{X} \leftarrow \text{AVAIL}, \text{AVAIL} \leftarrow \text{LINK(AVAIL)}$.   (6)

The possibility of overflow must always be considered. Here OVERFLOW generally means that we terminate the program with regrets; or else we can go into a "garbage collection" routine that attempts to find more available space. Garbage collection is discussed in Section 2.3.5.

There is another important technique for handling the AVAIL stack: We often do not know in advance how much memory space should be used for the storage pool. There may be a sequential table of variable size that wants to coexist in memory with the linked tables; in such a case we do not want the linked memory area to take any more space than is absolutely necessary. So suppose that we wish to place the linked memory area in ascending locations beginning with L_0 and that this area is never to extend past the value of variable SEQMIN (which represents the current lower bound of the sequential table). Then we can proceed as follows, using a new variable POOLMAX:

a) Initially set $\text{AVAIL} \leftarrow \Lambda$ and $\text{POOLMAX} \leftarrow L_0$.
b) The operation $\text{X} \Leftarrow \text{AVAIL}$ becomes the following:

"If $\text{AVAIL} \neq \Lambda$, then $\text{X} \leftarrow \text{AVAIL}, \text{AVAIL} \leftarrow \text{LINK(AVAIL)}$.
Otherwise set $\text{X} \leftarrow \text{POOLMAX}$ and $\text{POOLMAX} \leftarrow \text{X} + c$, where c is the   (7)
node size; OVERFLOW now occurs if $\text{POOLMAX} > \text{SEQMIN}$."

c) When other parts of the program attempt to decrease the value of SEQMIN, they should sound the OVERFLOW alarm if $\text{SEQMIN} < \text{POOLMAX}$.
d) The operation $\text{AVAIL} \Leftarrow \text{X}$ is unchanged from (5).

This idea actually represents little more than the previous method with a special recovery procedure substituted for the OVERFLOW situation in (6). The net effect is to keep the storage pool as small as possible. Many people like to use this idea even when *all* lists occupy the storage pool area (so that SEQMIN is constant), since it avoids the rather time-consuming operation of initially linking all available cells together and it facilitates debugging. We could, of course, put the sequential list on the bottom and the pool on the top, having POOLMIN and SEQMAX instead of POOLMAX and SEQMIN.

Thus it is quite easy to maintain a pool of available nodes, in such a way that free nodes can efficiently be found and later returned. These methods give us a source of raw material to use in linked tables. Our discussion was predicated on the implicit assumption that all nodes have a fixed size, c; the cases that arise when different sizes of nodes are present are very important, but we will defer that discussion until Section 2.5. Now we will consider a few of the most common list operations in the special case where stacks and queues are involved.

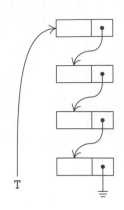

The simplest kind of linked list is a stack. Figure 5 shows a typical stack, with a pointer T to the top of the stack. When the stack is empty, this pointer will have the value Λ.

Fig. 5. A linked stack.

It is clear how to insert ("push down") new information Y onto the top of such a stack, using an auxiliary pointer variable P.

$$P \Leftarrow \text{AVAIL}, \quad \text{INFO}(P) \leftarrow Y, \quad \text{LINK}(P) \leftarrow T, \quad T \leftarrow P. \quad (8)$$

Conversely, to set Y equal to the information at the top of the stack and to "pop up" the stack:

If $T = \Lambda$, then UNDERFLOW;

otherwise set $P \leftarrow T$, $T \leftarrow \text{LINK}(P)$, $Y \leftarrow \text{INFO}(P)$, $\text{AVAIL} \Leftarrow P$.   (9)

These operations should be compared with the analogous mechanisms for sequentially allocated stacks, (2a) and (3a) in Section 2.2.2. The reader should study (8) and (9) carefully, since they are extremely important operations.

Before looking at the case of queues, let us see how the stack operations can be expressed conveniently in programs for MIX. A program for insertion, with $P \equiv \text{rI1}$, can be written as follows:

```
INFO EQU  0:3          Definition of the INFO field
LINK EQU  4:5          Definition of the LINK field
     LD1  AVAIL        P ← AVAIL.          ⎫
     J1Z  OVERFLOW     Is AVAIL = Λ?       ⎪  P ⇐ AVAIL
     LDA  0,1(LINK)                        ⎬
     STA  AVAIL        AVAIL ← LINK(P).    ⎭              (10)
     LDA  Y
     STA  0,1(INFO)    INFO(P) ← Y.
     LDA  T
     STA  0,1(LINK)    LINK(P) ← T.
     ST1  T            T ← P.           ∎
```

This takes 17 units of time, compared to 12 units for the comparable operation with a sequential table (although OVERFLOW in the sequential case would in many cases take considerably longer). In this program, as in others to follow in this chapter, OVERFLOW denotes either an ending routine or a subroutine that finds more space and returns to location $rJ - 2$.

A program for deletion is equally simple:

```
LD1   T            P ← T.
J1Z   UNDERFLOW    Is T = Λ?
LDA   0,1(LINK)
STA   T            T ← LINK(P).
LDA   0,1(INFO)
STA   Y            Y ← INFO(P).                    (11)
LDA   AVAIL
STA   0,1(LINK)    LINK(P) ← AVAIL. ⎫ AVAIL ⇐ P
ST1   AVAIL        AVAIL ← P.       ⎭  ∎
```

It is interesting to observe that each of these operations involves a cyclic permutation of three links. For example, in the insertion operation let P be the value of AVAIL before the insertion; if $P \neq \Lambda$, we find that after the operation

the value of AVAIL has become the previous value of LINK(P),
the value of LINK(P) has become the previous value of T, and
the value of T has become the previous value of AVAIL.

So the insertion process (except for setting INFO(P) ← Y) is the cyclic permutation

Similarly in the case of deletion, where P has the value of T before the operation and we assume that $P \neq \Lambda$, we have Y ← INFO(P) and

The fact that the permutation is cyclic is not really a relevant issue, since *any* permutation of three elements that moves every element is cyclic. The important point is rather that precisely three links are permuted in these operations.

The insertion and deletion algorithms of (8) and (9) have been described for stacks, but they apply much more generally to insertion and deletion in *any* linear list. Insertion, for example, is performed just before the node pointed to by link variable T. The insertion of item $2\frac{1}{2}$ in (2) above would be done by using operation (8) with T = LINK(LINK(FIRST)).

Linked allocation applies in a particularly convenient way to queues. In this case it is easy to see that the links should run from the front of the queue towards the rear, so that when a node is removed from the front, the new front node is directly specified. We will make use of pointers F and R, to the front and rear:

$$F \longrightarrow \boxed{|\bullet} \rightarrow \boxed{|\bullet} \rightarrow \boxed{|\bullet} \rightarrow \boxed{|\bullet} \leftarrow R \qquad (12)$$

Except for R, this diagram is abstractly identical to Fig. 5 on page 258.

Whenever the layout of a list is designed, it is important to specify all conditions carefully, particularly for the case when the list is empty. One of the most common programming errors connected with linked allocation is the failure to handle empty lists properly; the other common error is to forget about changing some of the links when a structure is being manipulated. In order to avoid the first type of error, we should always examine the "boundary conditions" carefully. To avoid making the second type of error, it is helpful to draw "before and after" diagrams and to compare them, in order to see which links must change.

Let's illustrate the remarks of the preceding paragraph by applying them to the case of queues. First consider the insertion operation: If (12) is the situation before insertion, the picture after insertion at the rear of the queue should be

$$\text{(13)}$$

(The notation used here implies that a new node has been obtained from the AVAIL list.) Comparing (12) and (13) shows us how to proceed when inserting the information Y at the rear of the queue:

$$P \Leftarrow \text{AVAIL}, \quad \text{INFO}(P) \leftarrow Y, \quad \text{LINK}(P) \leftarrow \Lambda, \quad \text{LINK}(R) \leftarrow P, \quad R \leftarrow P. \quad \text{(14)}$$

Let us now consider the "boundary" situation when the queue is empty: In this case the situation before insertion is yet to be determined, and the situation "after" is

$$\text{(15)}$$

It is desirable to have operations (14) apply in this case also, even if insertion into an empty queue means that we must change *both* F and R, not only R. We find that (14) will work properly if $R = \text{LOC}(F)$ when the queue is empty, *assuming that* $F \equiv \text{LINK}(\text{LOC}(F))$; the value of variable F must be *stored in the* LINK *field of its location* if this idea is to work. In order to make the testing for an empty queue as efficient as possible, we will let $F = \Lambda$ in this case. Our policy is therefore that

an empty queue is represented by $F = \Lambda$ *and* $R = \text{LOC}(F)$.

If the operations (14) are applied under these circumstances, we obtain (15).

The deletion operation for queues is derived in a similar fashion. If (12) is the situation before deletion, the situation afterwards is

$$\text{(16)}$$

For the boundary conditions we must make sure that the deletion operation works when the queue is empty either before or after the operation. These considerations lead us to the following way to do queue deletion in general:

> If F = Λ, then UNDERFLOW;
> otherwise set P ← F, F ← LINK(P), Y ← INFO(P), AVAIL ⇐ P,   (17)
>   and if F = Λ, then set R ← LOC(F).

Notice that R must be changed when the queue becomes empty; this is precisely the type of "boundary condition" we should always be watching for.

These suggestions are not the only way to represent queues in a linearly linked fashion; exercise 30 describes a more efficient alternative, and we will discuss other methods later in this chapter. Indeed, none of the operations above are meant to be prescribed as the only way to do something; they are intended as examples of the basic means of operating with linked lists. The reader who has had only a little previous experience with such techniques will find it helpful to reread the present section up to this point before going on.

So far in this chapter we have discussed how to perform certain operations on tables, but our discussions have always been "abstract," in the sense that we never exhibited actual programs in which the particular techniques were useful. People aren't generally motivated to study abstractions of a problem until they've seen enough special instances of the problem to arouse their interest. The operations discussed so far — manipulations of variable-size lists of information by insertion and deletion, and the use of tables as stacks or queues — are of such wide application, it is hoped that the reader will have encountered them often enough already to grant their importance. But now we will leave the realm of the abstract as we begin to study a series of significant practical examples of the techniques of this chapter.

Our first example is a problem called *topological sorting*, which is an important process needed in connection with network problems, with so-called PERT charts, and even with linguistics; in fact, it is of potential use whenever we have a problem involving a *partial ordering*. A partial ordering of a set S is a relation between the objects of S, which we may denote by the symbol "$\preceq$", satisfying the following properties for any objects x, y, and z (not necessarily distinct) in S:

i) If $x \preceq y$ and $y \preceq z$, then $x \preceq z$. (Transitivity.)

ii) If $x \preceq y$ and $y \preceq x$, then $x = y$. (Antisymmetry.)

iii) $x \preceq x$. (Reflexivity.)

The notation $x \preceq y$ may be read "x precedes or equals y." If $x \preceq y$ and $x \neq y$, we write $x \prec y$ and say "x precedes y." It is easy to see from (i), (ii), and (iii) that we always have

i') If $x \prec y$ and $y \prec z$, then $x \prec z$. (Transitivity.)

ii') If $x \prec y$, then $y \nprec x$. (Asymmetry.)

iii') $x \nprec x$. (Irreflexivity.)

The relation denoted by $y \not\prec x$ means "y does not precede x." If we start with a relation $\prec$ satisfying properties (i'), (ii'), and (iii'), we can reverse the process above and define $x \preceq y$ if $x \prec y$ or $x = y$; then properties (i), (ii), and (iii) are true. Therefore we may regard either properties (i), (ii), (iii) or properties (i'), (ii'), (iii') as the definition of partial order. Notice that property (ii') is actually a consequence of (i') and (iii'), although (ii) does not follow from (i) and (iii).

Partial orderings occur quite frequently in everyday life as well as in mathematics. As examples from mathematics we can mention the relation $x \leq y$ between real numbers x and y; the relation $x \subseteq y$ between sets of objects; the relation $x \backslash y$ (x divides y) between positive integers. In the case of PERT networks, S is a set of jobs that must be done, and the relation "$x \prec y$" means "x must be done before y."

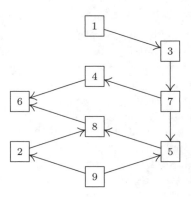

Fig. 6. A partial ordering.

We will naturally assume that S is a finite set, since we want to work with S inside a computer. A partial ordering on a finite set can always be illustrated by drawing a diagram such as Fig. 6, in which the objects are represented by small boxes and the relation is represented by arrows between these boxes; $x \prec y$ means there is a path from the box labeled x to box y that follows the direction of the arrows. Property (ii) of partial ordering means there are *no closed loops* (no paths that close on themselves) in the diagram. If an arrow were drawn from 4 to 1 in Fig. 6, we would no longer have a partial ordering.

The problem of topological sorting is to *embed the partial order in a linear order*; that is, to arrange the objects into a linear sequence $a_1 a_2 \ldots a_n$ such that whenever $a_j \prec a_k$, we have $j < k$. Graphically, this means that the boxes are to be rearranged into a line so that all arrows go towards the right (see Fig. 7). It is not immediately obvious that such a rearrangement is possible in every case, although such a rearrangement certainly could not be done if any loops were present. Therefore the algorithm we will give is interesting not only because it does a useful operation, but also because it proves that this operation is *possible* for every partial ordering.

As an example of topological sorting, imagine a large glossary containing definitions of technical terms. We can write $w_2 \prec w_1$ if the definition of word w_1

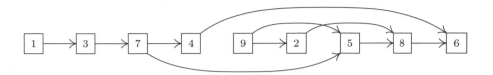

Fig. 7. The ordering relation of Fig. 6 after topological sorting.

depends directly or indirectly on that of word w_2. This relation is a partial ordering provided that there are no "circular" definitions. The problem of topological sorting in this case is to *find a way to arrange the words in the glossary so that no term is used before it has been defined.* Analogous problems arise in writing programs to process the declarations in certain assembly and compiler languages; they also arise in writing a user's manual describing a computer language or in writing textbooks about information structures.

There is a very simple way to do topological sorting: We start by taking an object that is not preceded by any other object in the ordering. This object may be placed first in the output. Now we remove this object from the set S; the resulting set is again partially ordered, and the process can be repeated until the whole set has been sorted. For example, in Fig. 6 we could start by removing 1 or 9; after 1 has been removed, 3 can be taken, and so on. The only way in which this algorithm could fail would be if there were a nonempty partially ordered set in which every element was preceded by another; for in such a case the algorithm would find nothing to do. But if every element is preceded by another, we could construct an arbitrarily long sequence $b_1, b_2, b_3, \ldots$ in which $b_{j+1} \prec b_j$. Since S is finite, we must have $b_j = b_k$ for some $j < k$; but $j < k$ implies that $b_k \preceq b_{j+1}$, hence $b_j = b_k$ contradicts (ii).

In order to implement this process efficiently by computer, we need to be ready to perform the actions described above, namely to locate objects that are not preceded by any others, and to remove them from the set. Our implementation is also influenced by the desired input and output characteristics. The most general program would accept alphabetic names for the objects and would allow gigantic sets of objects to be sorted — more than could possibly fit in the computer memory at once. Such complications would obscure the main points we are trying to make here, however; the handling of alphabetic data can be done efficiently by using the methods of Chapter 6, and the handling of large networks is left as an interesting project for the reader.

Therefore we will assume that the objects to be sorted are numbered from 1 to n in any order. The input of the program will be on tape unit 1: Each tape record contains 50 pairs of numbers, where the pair (j, k) means that object j precedes object k. The first pair, however, is $(0, n)$, where n is the number of objects. The pair $(0, 0)$ terminates the input. We shall assume that n plus the number of relation pairs will fit comfortably in memory; and we shall assume that it is not necessary to check the input for validity. The output is to be the numbers of the objects in sorted order, followed by the number 0, on tape unit 2.

As an example of the input, we might have the relations

$$9 \prec 2, \quad 3 \prec 7, \quad 7 \prec 5, \quad 5 \prec 8, \quad 8 \prec 6, \quad 4 \prec 6, \quad 1 \prec 3, \quad 7 \prec 4, \quad 9 \prec 5, \quad 2 \prec 8. \quad (18)$$

It is not necessary to give any more relations than are needed to characterize the desired partial ordering. Thus, additional relations like $9 \prec 8$ (which can be deduced from $9 \prec 5$ and $5 \prec 8$) may be omitted from or added to the input without harm. In general, it is necessary to give only the relations corresponding to arrows on a diagram such as Fig. 6.

The algorithm that follows uses a sequential table $\mathtt{X[1]}, \mathtt{X[2]}, \ldots, \mathtt{X}[n]$, and each node $\mathtt{X}[k]$ has the form

$$\boxed{\; + \;\mid\; 0 \;\mid\; \mathtt{COUNT}[k] \;\mid\; \mathtt{TOP}[k] \;} \; .$$

Here $\mathtt{COUNT}[k]$ is the *number of direct predecessors* of object k (the number of relations $j \prec k$ that have appeared in the input), and $\mathtt{TOP}[k]$ is a link to the beginning of the *list of direct successors* of object k. The latter list contains entries in the format

$$\boxed{\; + \;\mid\; 0 \;\mid\; \mathtt{SUC} \;\mid\; \mathtt{NEXT} \;} \; ,$$

where $\mathtt{SUC}$ is a direct successor of k and $\mathtt{NEXT}$ is the next item of the list. As an example of these conventions, Fig. 8 shows the schematic contents of memory corresponding to the input (18).

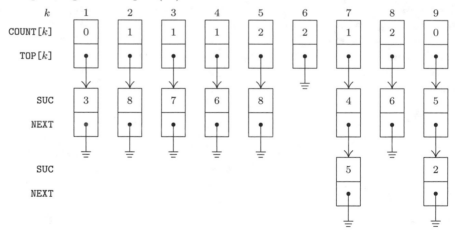

Fig. 8. Computer representation of Fig. 6 corresponding to the relations (18).

Using this memory layout, it is not difficult to work out the algorithm. We want to output the nodes whose $\mathtt{COUNT}$ field is zero, then to decrease the $\mathtt{COUNT}$ fields of all successors of those nodes by one. The trick is to avoid doing any "searching" for nodes whose $\mathtt{COUNT}$ field is zero, and this can be done by maintaining a queue containing those nodes. The links for this queue are kept in the $\mathtt{COUNT}$ field, which by now has served its previous purpose; for clarity in the algorithm below, we use the notation $\mathtt{QLINK}[k]$ to stand for $\mathtt{COUNT}[k]$ when that field is no longer being used to keep a count.

Algorithm T (*Topological sort*). This algorithm inputs a sequence of relations $j \prec k$, indicating that object j precedes object k in a certain partial ordering, assuming that $1 \le j, k \le n$. The output is the set of n objects embedded in a linear order. The internal tables used are: QLINK[0], COUNT[1] $=$ QLINK[1], COUNT[2] $=$ QLINK[2], ..., COUNT[n] $=$ QLINK[n]; TOP[1], TOP[2], ..., TOP[n]; a storage pool with one node for each input relation and with SUC and NEXT fields as shown above; P, a link variable used to refer to the nodes in the storage pool; F and R, integer-valued variables used to refer to the front and rear of a queue whose links are in the QLINK table; and N, a variable that counts how many objects have yet to be output.

T1. [Initialize.] Input the value of n. Set COUNT[k] $\leftarrow 0$ and TOP[k] $\leftarrow \Lambda$ for $1 \le k \le n$. Set N $\leftarrow n$.

T2. [Next relation.] Get the next relation "$j \prec k$" from the input; if the input has been exhausted, however, go to T4.

T3. [Record the relation.] Increase COUNT[k] by one. Set

$$\text{P} \Leftarrow \text{AVAIL}, \ \text{SUC(P)} \leftarrow k, \ \text{NEXT(P)} \leftarrow \text{TOP}[j], \ \text{TOP}[j] \leftarrow \text{P}.$$

(This is operation (8).) Go back to T2.

T4. [Scan for zeros.] (At this point we have completed the input phase; the input (18) would now have been transformed into the computer representation shown in Fig. 8. The next job is to initialize the queue of output, which is linked together in the QLINK field.) Set R $\leftarrow 0$ and QLINK[0] $\leftarrow 0$. For $1 \le k \le n$ examine COUNT[k], and if it is zero, set QLINK[R] $\leftarrow k$ and R $\leftarrow k$. After this has been done for all k, set F $\leftarrow$ QLINK[0] (which will contain the first value k encountered for which COUNT[k] was zero).

T5. [Output front of queue.] Output the value of F. If F $= 0$, go to T8; otherwise, set N $\leftarrow$ N $- 1$, and set P $\leftarrow$ TOP[F]. (Since the QLINK and COUNT tables overlap, we have QLINK[R] $= 0$; therefore the condition F $= 0$ occurs when the queue is empty.)

T6. [Erase relations.] If P $= \Lambda$, go to T7. Otherwise decrease COUNT[SUC(P)] by one, and if it has thereby gone down to zero, set QLINK[R] $\leftarrow$ SUC(P) and R $\leftarrow$ SUC(P). Set P $\leftarrow$ NEXT(P) and repeat this step. (We are removing all relations of the form "F $\prec k$" for some k from the system, and putting new nodes into the queue when all their predecessors have been output.)

T7. [Remove from queue.] Set F $\leftarrow$ QLINK[F] and go back to T5.

T8. [End of process.] The algorithm terminates. If N $= 0$, we have output all of the object numbers in the desired "topological order," followed by a zero. Otherwise the N object numbers not yet output contain a loop, in violation of the hypothesis of partial order. (See exercise 23 for an algorithm that prints out the contents of one such loop.) ▌

The reader will find it helpful to try this algorithm by hand on the input (18). Algorithm T shows a nice interplay between sequential memory and linked

memory techniques. Sequential memory is used for the main table X[1], ...,
X[n], which contains the COUNT[k] and TOP[k] entries, because we want to
make references to "random" parts of this table in step T3. (If the input were
alphabetic, however, another type of table would be used for speedier search, as
in Chapter 6.) Linked memory is used for the tables of "immediate successors,"
since those table entries have no particular order in the input. The queue of
nodes waiting to be output is kept in the midst of the sequential table by linking
the nodes together in output order. This linking is done by table index instead
of by address; in other words, when the front of the queue is X[k], we have
F = k instead of F = LOC(X[k]). The queue operations used in steps T4, T6,
and T7 are not identical to those in (14) and (17), since we are taking advantage
of special properties of the queue in this system; no nodes need to be created or
returned to available space during this part of the algorithm.

The coding of Algorithm T in MIX assembly language has a few additional
points of interest. Since no deletion from tables is made in the algorithm (because
no storage must be freed for later use), the operation P ⇐ AVAIL can be done
in an extremely simple way, as shown in lines 19 and 32 below; we need not
keep any linked pool of memory, and we can choose new nodes consecutively.
The program includes complete input and output with magnetic tape, according
to the conventions mentioned above, but buffering is omitted for the sake of
simplicity. The reader should not find it very difficult to follow the details of
the coding in this program, since it corresponds directly to Algorithm T but
with slight changes for efficiency. The efficient use of index registers, which is an
important aspect of linked memory processing, is illustrated here.

Program T (*Topological sort*). In this program, the following equivalences
should be noted: rI6 ≡ N, rI5 ≡ buffer pointer, rI4 ≡ k, rI3 ≡ j and R, rI2 ≡
AVAIL and P, rI1 ≡ F, TOP[j] ≡ X + j(4:5), COUNT[k] ≡ QLINK[k] ≡ X + k(2:3).

01	*	BUFFER AREA AND FIELD DEFINITIONS			
02	COUNT	EQU	2:3		Definition of symbolic
03	QLINK	EQU	2:3		names of fields
04	TOP	EQU	4:5		
05	SUC	EQU	2:3		
06	NEXT	EQU	4:5		
07	TAPEIN	EQU	1		Input is on tape unit 1
08	TAPEOUT	EQU	2		Output is on tape unit 2
09	BUFFER	ORIG	*+100		Tape buffer area
10		CON	-1		Sentinel at end of buffer
11	*	INPUT PHASE			
12	TOPSORT	IN	BUFFER(TAPEIN)	1	*T1. Initialize.* Read in the first
13		JBUS	*(TAPEIN)		tape block; wait for completion.
14	1H	LD6	BUFFER+1	1	N ← n.
15		ENT4	0,6	1	
16		STZ	X,4	$n+1$	Set COUNT[k] ← 0 and TOP[k] ← Λ,
17		DEC4	1	$n+1$	for $0 \le k \le n$.
18		J4NN	*-2	$n+1$	(Anticipate QLINK[0] ← 0 in step T4.)
19		ENT2	X,6	1	Available storage starts after X[n].

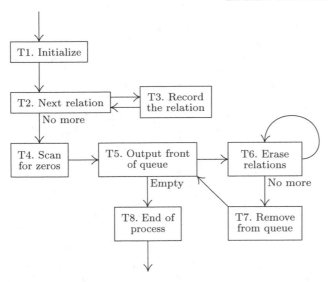

Fig. 9. Topological sorting.

20		ENT5	BUFFER+2	1	Prepare to read the first pair (j, k).
21	2H	LD3	0,5	$m + b$	_T2. Next relation._
22		J3P	3F	$m + b$	Is $j > 0$?
23		J3Z	4F	b	Is input exhausted?
24		IN	BUFFER(TAPEIN)	$b - 1$	Sentinel sensed; read another
25		JBUS	*(TAPEIN)		tape block, wait for completion.
26		ENT5	BUFFER	$b - 1$	Reset the buffer pointer.
27		JMP	2B	$b - 1$	
28	3H	LD4	1,5	m	_T3. Record the relation._
29		LDA	X,4(COUNT)	m	COUNT[k]
30		INCA	1	m	+1
31		STA	X,4(COUNT)	m	$\rightarrow$ COUNT[k].
32		INC2	1	m	AVAIL $\leftarrow$ AVAIL + 1.
33		LDA	X,3(TOP)	m	TOP[j]
34		STA	0,2(NEXT)	m	$\rightarrow$ NEXT(P).
35		ST4	0,2(SUC)	m	$k \rightarrow$ SUC(P).
36		ST2	X,3(TOP)	m	P $\rightarrow$ TOP[j].
37		INC5	2	m	Increase buffer pointer.
38		JMP	2B	m	
39	4H	IOC	0(TAPEIN)	1	Rewind the input tape.
40		ENT4	0,6	1	_T4. Scan for zeros._ $k \leftarrow n$.
41		ENT5	-100	1	Reset buffer pointer for output.
42		ENT3	0	1	R $\leftarrow$ 0.
43	4H	LDA	X,4(COUNT)	n	Examine COUNT[k].
44		JAP	*+3	n	Is it nonzero?
45		ST4	X,3(QLINK)	a	QLINK[R] $\leftarrow k$.
46		ENT3	0,4	a	R $\leftarrow k$.
47		DEC4	1	n	
48		J4P	4B	n	$n \geq k \geq 1$.

```
49  *   SORTING PHASE
50          LD1   X(QLINK)           1       F ← QLINK[0].
51  5H      JBUS  *(TAPEOUT)                 T5. Output front of queue.
52          ST1   BUFFER+100,5       n + 1   Store F in buffer area.
53          J1Z   8F                 n + 1   Is F zero?
54          INC5  1                  n       Advance buffer pointer.
55          J5N   *+3                n       Test if buffer is full.
56          OUT   BUFFER(TAPEOUT)    c − 1   If so, output a tape block.
57          ENT5  -100               c − 1   Reset the buffer pointer.
58          DEC6  1                  n       N ← N − 1.
59          LD2   X,1(TOP)           n       P ← TOP[F].
60          J2Z   7F                 n       T6. Erase relations.
61  6H      LD4   0,2(SUC)           m       rI4 ← SUC(P).
62          LDA   X,4(COUNT)         m       COUNT[rI4]
63          DECA  1                  m       −1
64          STA   X,4(COUNT)         m         → COUNT[rI4].
65          JAP   *+3                m       Has zero been reached?
66          ST4   X,3(QLINK)         n − a   If so, set QLINK[R] ← rI4.
67          ENT3  0,4                n − a   R ← rI4.
68          LD2   0,2(NEXT)          m       P ← NEXT(P).
69          J2P   6B                 m       If P ≠ Λ, repeat.
70  7H      LD1   X,1(QLINK)         n       T7. Remove from queue.
71          JMP   5B                 n       F ← QLINK[F], go to T5.
72  8H      OUT   BUFFER(TAPEOUT)    1       T8. End of process.
73          IOC   0(TAPEOUT)         1       Output last block and rewind.
74          HLT   0,6                1       Stop, displaying N on console.
75  X       END   TOPSORT                    Beginning of table area   ▮
```

The analysis of Algorithm T is quite simple with the aid of Kirchhoff's law; the execution time has the approximate form $c_1 m + c_2 n$, where m is the number of input relations, n is the number of objects, and c_1 and c_2 are constants. It is hard to imagine a faster algorithm for this problem! The exact quantities in the analysis are given with Program T above, where a = number of objects with no predecessor, b = number of tape records in input = $\lceil (m + 2)/50 \rceil$, and c = number of tape records in output = $\lceil (n + 1)/100 \rceil$. Exclusive of input-output operations, the total running time in this case is only $(32m + 24n + 7b + 2c + 16)u$.

A topological sorting technique similar to Algorithm T (but without the important feature of the queue links) was first published by A. B. Kahn, *CACM* **5** (1962), 558–562. The fact that topological sorting of a partial ordering is always possible was first proved in print by E. Szpilrajn, *Fundamenta Mathematicæ* **16** (1930), 386–389; he proved it for infinite sets as well as finite sets, and mentioned that the result was already known to several of his colleagues.

In Section 7.2.1.2 we will study an efficient way to find *all* of the topological sorts of a given partial order relation.

EXERCISES

▶ **1.** [*10*] Operation (9) for popping up a stack mentions the possibility of UNDERFLOW; why doesn't operation (8), pushing down a stack, mention the possibility of OVERFLOW?

2. [*22*] Write a "general purpose" MIX subroutine to do the insertion operation, (10). This subroutine should have the following specifications (as in Section 1.4.1):

Calling sequence: JMP   INSERT   Jump to subroutine.
                  NOP   T   Location of pointer variable
Entry conditions: rA = information to be put into the INFO field of a new node.
Exit conditions: The stack whose pointer is the link variable T has the new node on top; rI1 = T; rI2, rI3 are altered.

3. [*22*] Write a "general purpose" MIX subroutine to do the deletion operation, (11). This subroutine should have the following specifications:

Calling sequence: JMP   DELETE   Jump to subroutine.
                  NOP   T   Location of pointer variable
                  JMP   UNDERFLOW First exit, if UNDERFLOW sensed
Entry conditions: None
Exit conditions: If the stack whose pointer is the link variable T is empty, the first exit is taken; otherwise the top node of that stack is deleted, and exit is made to the third location following 'JMP DELETE'. In the latter case, rI1 = T and rA is the contents of the INFO field of the deleted node. In either case, rI2 and rI3 are used by this subroutine.

4. [*22*] The program in (10) is based on the operation P ⇐ AVAIL, as given in (6). Show how to write an OVERFLOW subroutine so that, without *any* change in the coding (10), the operation P ⇐ AVAIL makes use of SEQMIN, as given by (7). For general-purpose use, your subroutine should not change the contents of any registers, except rJ and possibly the comparison indicator. It should exit to location rJ − 2, instead of the usual rJ.

▶ **5.** [*24*] Operations (14) and (17) give the effect of a queue; show how to define the further operation "insert at front" so as to obtain all the actions of an output-restricted deque. How could the operation "delete from rear" be defined (so that we would have a general deque)?

6. [*21*] In operation (14) we set LINK(P) ← Λ, while the very next insertion at the rear of the queue will change the value of this same link field. Show how the setting of LINK(P) in (14) could be avoided if we make a change to the testing of "F = Λ" in (17).

▶ **7.** [*23*] Design an algorithm to "invert" a linked linear list such as (1), that is, to change its links so that the items appear in the opposite order. [If, for example, the list (1) were inverted, we would have FIRST linking to the node containing item 5; that node would link to the one containing item 4; etc.] Assume that the nodes have the form (3).

8. [*24*] Write a MIX program for the problem of exercise 7, attempting to design your program to operate as fast as possible.

9. [*20*] Which of the following relations is a partial ordering on the specified set S? [*Note:* If the relation "$x \prec y$" is defined below, the intent is to define the relation "$x \preceq y \equiv (x \prec y$ or $x = y)$," and then to determine whether $\preceq$ is a partial ordering.] (a) $S =$ all rational numbers, $x \prec y$ means $x > y$. (b) $S =$ all people, $x \prec y$ means x is an ancestor of y. (c) $S =$ all integers, $x \preceq y$ means x is a multiple of y (that is, $x \bmod y = 0$). (d) $S =$ all the mathematical results proved in this book, $x \prec y$ means the proof of y depends upon the truth of x. (e) $S =$ all positive integers, $x \preceq y$ means $x + y$ is even. (f) $S =$ a set of subroutines, $x \prec y$ means "x calls y," that is, y may be in operation while x is in operation, with recursion not allowed.

10. [*M21*] Given that "⊂" is a relation that satisfies properties (i) and (ii) of a partial ordering, prove that the relation "⪯", defined by the rule "$x \preceq y$ if and only if $x = y$ or $x \subset y$," satisfies all three properties of a partial ordering.

▶ **11.** [*24*] The result of topological sorting is not always completely determined, since there may be several ways to arrange the nodes and to satisfy the conditions of topological order. Find all possible ways to arrange the nodes of Fig. 6 into topological order.

12. [*M20*] There are 2^n subsets of a set of n elements, and these subsets are partially ordered by the set-inclusion relation. Give two interesting ways to arrange these subsets in topological order.

13. [*HM48*] How many ways are there to arrange the 2^n subsets described in exercise 12 into topological order? (Try for a "sharp" asymptotic estimate as $n \to \infty$.)

14. [*M21*] A *linear ordering* of a set S, also called a *total ordering*, is a partial ordering that satisfies the additional "comparability" condition

$$(iv) \qquad \text{For any two objects } x, y \text{ in } S, \text{ either } x \preceq y \text{ or } y \preceq x.$$

Prove directly from the definitions given that a topological sort can result in only one possible output if and only if the relation ⪯ is a linear ordering. (You may assume that the set S is finite.)

15. [*M25*] Show that for any partial ordering on a finite set S there is a *unique* set of irredundant relations that characterizes this ordering, as in (18) and Fig. 6. Is the same fact true also when S is an infinite set?

16. [*M22*] Given any partial ordering on a set $S = \{x_1, \ldots, x_n\}$, we can construct its *incidence matrix* (a_{ij}), where $a_{ij} = 1$ if $x_i \preceq x_j$, and $a_{ij} = 0$ otherwise. Show that there is a way to permute the rows and columns of this matrix so that all entries below the diagonal are zero.

▶ **17.** [*21*] What output does Algorithm T produce if it is presented with the input (18)?

18. [*20*] What, if anything, is the significance of the values of QLINK[0], QLINK[1], ..., QLINK[n] when Algorithm T terminates?

19. [*18*] In Algorithm T we examine the front position of the queue in step T5, but do not remove that element from the queue until step T7. What would happen if we set F ← QLINK[F] at the conclusion of step T5, instead of in T7?

▶ **20.** [*24*] Algorithm T uses F, R, and the QLINK table to obtain the effect of a queue that contains those nodes whose COUNT field has become zero but whose successor relations have not yet been removed. Could a stack be used for this purpose instead of a queue? If so, compare the resulting algorithm with Algorithm T.

21. [*21*] Would Algorithm T still perform a valid topological sort if one of the relations "$j \prec k$" were repeated several times in the input? What if the input contained a relation of the form "$j \prec j$"?

22. [*23*] Program T assumes that its input tape contains valid information, but a program that is intended for general use should always make careful tests on its input so that clerical errors can be detected, and so that the program cannot "destroy itself." For example, if one of the input relations for k were negative, Program T may erroneously change one of its own instructions when storing into X[k]. Suggest ways to modify Program T so that it is suitable for general use.

▶ **23.** [*27*] When the topological sort algorithm cannot proceed because it has detected a loop in the input (see step T8), it is usually of no use to stop and say, "There was a loop." It is helpful to print out one of the loops, thereby showing part of the input that was in error. Extend Algorithm T so that it will do this additional printing of a loop when necessary. [*Hint:* The text gives a proof for the existence of a loop when $N > 0$ in step T8; that proof suggests an algorithm.]

24. [*24*] Incorporate the extensions of Algorithm T made in exercise 23 into Program T.

25. [*47*] Design as efficient an algorithm as possible for doing a topological sort of very large sets S having considerably more nodes than the computer memory can contain. Assume that the input, output, and temporary working space are done with magnetic tape. [*Possible hint:* A conventional sort of the input allows us to assume that all relations for a given node appear together. But then what can be done? In particular, we must consider the worst case in which the given ordering is already a linear ordering that has been wildly permuted; exercise 24 in the introduction to Chapter 5 explains how to handle this case with $O(\log n)^2$ passes over the data.]

26. [*29*] (*Subroutine allocation.*) Suppose that we have a tape containing the main subroutine library in relocatable form, for a 1960s-style computer installation. The loading routine wants to determine the amount of relocation for each subroutine used, so that it can make one pass through the tape to load the necessary routines. The problem is that some subroutines require others to be present in memory. Infrequently used subroutines (which appear toward the end of the tape) may call on frequently used subroutines (which appear toward the beginning of the tape), and we want to know all of the subroutines that are required, before passing through the tape.

One way to tackle this problem is to have a "tape directory" that fits in memory. The loading routine has access to two tables:

a) The tape directory. This table is composed of variable-length nodes having the form

B	SPACE	LINK		B	SPACE	LINK
B	SUB1	SUB2		B	SUB1	SUB2
⋮			or	⋮		
B	SUBn	0		B	SUB$(n-1)$	SUBn

where SPACE is the number of words of memory required by the subroutine; LINK is a link to the directory entry for the subroutine that appears on the tape following this subroutine; SUB1, SUB2, ..., SUBn ($n \geq 0$) are links to the directory entries for any other subroutines required by this one; B = 0 on all words except the last, B = −1 on the last word of a node. The address of the directory entry for the first subroutine on the library tape is specified by the link variable FIRST.

b) The list of subroutines directly referred to by the program to be loaded. This is stored in consecutive locations X[1], X[2], ..., X[N], where N ≥ 0 is a variable known to the loading routine. Each entry in this list is a link to the directory entry for the subroutine desired.

The loading routine also knows MLOC, the amount of relocation to be used for the first subroutine loaded.

As a small example, consider the following configuration:

		Tape directory			List of subroutines needed
	B	SPACE	LINK		X[1] = 1003
1000:	0	20	1005		X[2] = 1010
1001:	−1	1002	0		
1002:	−1	30	1010		N = 2
1003:	0	200	1007		FIRST = 1002
1004:	−1	1000	1006		MLOC = 2400
1005:	−1	100	1003		
1006:	−1	60	1000		
1007:	0	200	0		
1008:	0	1005	1002		
1009:	−1	1006	0		
1010:	−1	20	1006		

The tape directory in this case shows that the subroutines on tape are 1002, 1010, 1006, 1000, 1005, 1003, and 1007 in that order. Subroutine 1007 takes 200 locations and implies the use of subroutines 1005, 1002, and 1006; etc. The program to be loaded requires subroutines 1003 and 1010, which are to be placed into locations ≥ 2400. These subroutines in turn imply that 1000, 1006, and 1002 must also be loaded.

The subroutine allocator is to change the X-table so that each entry X[1], X[2], X[3], ... has the form

+	0	BASE	SUB

(except the last entry, which is explained below), where SUB is a subroutine to be loaded, and BASE is the amount of relocation. These entries are to be in the order in which the subroutines appear on tape. One possible answer for the example above would be

	BASE	SUB		BASE	SUB
X[1]:	2400	1002	X[4]:	2510	1000
X[2]:	2430	1010	X[5]:	2530	1003
X[3]:	2450	1006	X[6]:	2730	0

The last entry contains the first unused memory address.

(Clearly, this is not the only way to treat a library of subroutines. The proper way to design a library is heavily dependent upon the computer used and the applications to be handled. Large modern computers require an entirely different approach to subroutine libraries. But this is a nice exercise anyway, because it involves interesting manipulations on both sequential and linked data.)

The problem in this exercise is to design an algorithm for the stated task. Your allocator may transform the tape directory in any way as it prepares its answer, since the tape directory can be read in anew by the subroutine allocator on its next assignment, and the tape directory is not needed by other parts of the loading routine.

27. [25] Write a MIX program for the subroutine allocation algorithm of exercise 26.

28. [40] The following construction shows how to "solve" a fairly general type of two-person game, including chess, nim, and many simpler games: Consider a finite set of nodes, each of which represents a possible position in the game. For each position there are zero or more moves that transform that position into some other position. We say that position x is a predecessor of position y (and y is a successor of x) if there is a move from x to y. Certain positions that have no successors are classified as *won* or *lost* positions. The player to move in position x is the opponent of the player to move in the successors of position x.

Given such a configuration of positions, we can compute the complete set of won positions (those in which the next player to move can force a victory) and the complete set of lost positions (those in which the player must lose against an expert opponent) by repeatedly doing the following operation until it yields no change: Mark a position "lost" if all its successors are marked "won"; mark a position "won" if at least one of its successors is marked "lost." (After this operation has been repeated as many times as possible, there may be some positions that have not been marked at all; a player in such a position can neither force a victory nor be compelled to lose.)

This procedure for obtaining the complete set of won and lost positions can be adapted to an efficient algorithm for computers that closely resembles Algorithm T. We may keep with each position a count of the number of its successors that have not been marked "won," and a list of all its predecessors.

The problem in this exercise is to work out the details of the algorithm that has just been so vaguely described, and to apply it to some interesting games that do not involve too many possible positions [like the "military game": É. Lucas, *Récréations Mathématiques* **3** (Paris: 1893) 105–116; E. R. Berlekamp, J. H. Conway, and R. K. Guy, *Winning Ways* **3** (A K Peters, 2003), Chapter 21].

▶ **29.** [*21*] (a) Give an algorithm to "erase" an entire list like (1), by putting all of its nodes on the AVAIL stack, given only the value of FIRST. The algorithm should operate as fast as possible. (b) Repeat part (a) for a list like (12), given the values of F and R.

30. [*20*] (X. Xie, 2021.) Suppose that queues are represented almost as in (12), but with R pointing to a "blank" node just *after* the rear. (The queue is empty if and only if F = R; the contents of INFO(R) are irrelevant.) What insertion and deletion procedures should replace (14) and (17)?

2.2.4. Circular Lists

A slight change in the manner of linking furnishes us with an important alternative to the methods of the preceding section.

A *circularly linked list* (briefly: a circular list) has the property that its last node links back to the first instead of to Λ. It is then possible to access all of the list starting at any given point; we also achieve an extra degree of symmetry, and if we choose we need not think of the list as having a last or first node.

The following situation is typical:

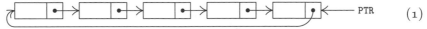

$$(1)$$

Assume that the nodes have two fields, INFO and LINK, as in the preceding section. There is a link variable PTR that points to the rightmost node of the list, and LINK(PTR) is the address of the leftmost node. The following primitive operations are most important:

a) Insert Y at left: P ⇐ AVAIL, INFO(P) ← Y, LINK(P) ← LINK(PTR), LINK(PTR) ← P.
b) Insert Y at right: Insert Y at left, then PTR ← P.
c) Set Y to left node and delete: P ← LINK(PTR), Y ← INFO(P), LINK(PTR) ← LINK(P), AVAIL ⇐ P.

Operation (b) is a little surprising at first glance; the operation PTR ← LINK(PTR) effectively moves the leftmost node to the right in the diagram (1), and this is quite easy to understand if the list is regarded as a circle instead of as a straight line with connected ends.

The alert reader will observe that we have made a serious mistake in operations (a), (b), and (c). What is it? *Answer:* We have forgotten to consider the possibility of an *empty* list. If, for example, operation (c) is applied five times to the list (1), we will have PTR pointing to a node in the AVAIL list, and this can lead to serious difficulties; for example, imagine applying operation (c) once more! If we take the position that PTR will equal Λ in the case of an empty list, we could remedy the operations by inserting the additional instructions "if PTR = Λ, then PTR ← LINK(P) ← P; otherwise ..." after "INFO(P) ← Y" in (a); preceding (c) by the test "if PTR = Λ, then UNDERFLOW"; and following (c) by "if PTR = P, then PTR ← Λ".

Notice that operations (a), (b), and (c) give us the actions of an output-restricted deque, in the sense of Section 2.2.1. Therefore we find in particular that a circular list can be used as either a stack or a queue. Operations (a) and (c) combined give us a stack; operations (b) and (c) give us a queue. These operations are only slightly less direct than their counterparts in the previous section, where we saw that operations (a), (b), and (c) can be performed on linear lists using two pointers F and R.

Other important operations become efficient with circular lists. For example, it is very convenient to "erase" a list, that is, to put an entire circular list onto the AVAIL stack at once:

$$\text{If PTR} \neq \Lambda, \text{ then AVAIL} \leftrightarrow \text{LINK(PTR)}. \tag{2}$$

[Recall that the "↔" operation denotes interchange: P ← AVAIL, AVAIL ← LINK(PTR), LINK(PTR) ← P.] Operation (2) is clearly valid if PTR points *anywhere* in the circular list. Afterwards we should of course set PTR ← Λ.

Using a similar technique, if PTR_1 and PTR_2 point to disjoint circular lists L_1 and L_2, respectively, we can insert the entire list L_2 at the right of L_1:

$$\begin{aligned}
&\text{If } PTR_2 \neq \Lambda, \text{ then}\\
&\quad (\text{if } PTR_1 \neq \Lambda, \text{ then LINK}(PTR_1) \leftrightarrow \text{LINK}(PTR_2);\\
&\quad \text{set } PTR_1 \leftarrow PTR_2, PTR_2 \leftarrow \Lambda).
\end{aligned} \tag{3}$$

Splitting one circular list into two, in various ways, is another simple operation that can be done. These operations correspond to the concatenation and deconcatenation of strings.

Thus we see that a circular list can be used not only to represent inherently circular structures, but also to represent linear structures; a circular list with one pointer to the rear node is essentially equivalent to a straight linear list with two pointers to the front and rear. The natural question to ask, in connection with this observation, is "How do we find the end of the list, when there is circular symmetry?" There is no Λ link to signal the end! The answer is that when we are operating on an entire list, moving from one node to the next, we should stop when we get back to our starting place (assuming, of course, that the starting place is still present in the list).

An alternative solution to the problem just posed is to put a special, recognizable node into each circular list, as a convenient stopping place. This special node is called the *list head*, and in applications we often find it is quite convenient to insist that every circular list must have exactly one node that is its list head. One advantage is that the circular list will then never be empty. With a list head, diagram (1) becomes

List head

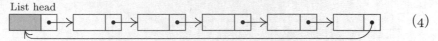

$$(4)$$

References to lists like (4) are usually made via the list head, which might occupy a fixed memory location. But a fixed list head leaves us without any pointer to the right end; so it forces us to sacrifice operation (b) stated above. Instead, we can retain (b) by letting the list head be mobile (see exercise 4).

Diagram (4) may be compared with 2.2.3–(1) at the beginning of the previous section, in which the link associated with "item 5" now points to LOC(FIRST) instead of to Λ; the variable FIRST is now thought of as a link within a node, namely the link that is in NODE(LOC(FIRST)). The principal difference between (4) and 2.2.3–(1) is that (4) makes it possible (though not necessarily efficient) to get to any point of the list from any other point.

As an example of the use of circular lists, we will discuss *arithmetic on polynomials* in the variables x, y, and z, with integer coefficients. There are many problems in which a scientist wants to manipulate polynomials instead of just numbers; we are thinking of operations like the multiplication of

$$(x^4 + 2x^3y + 3x^2y^2 + 4xy^3 + 5y^4) \qquad \text{by} \qquad (x^2 - 2xy + y^2)$$

to get

$$(x^6 - 6xy^5 + 5y^6).$$

Linked allocation is a natural tool for this purpose, since polynomials can grow to unpredictable sizes and we may want to represent many polynomials in memory at the same time.

We will consider here the two operations of addition and multiplication. Let us suppose that a polynomial is represented as a list in which each node stands for one nonzero term, and has the two-word form

COEF			
$\pm$ | A | B | C			LINK

$$(5)$$

Here COEF is the coefficient of the term in $x^A y^B z^C$. We will assume that the coefficients and exponents will always lie in the range allowed by this format, and that it is not necessary to check the ranges during our calculations. The notation ABC will be used to stand for the $\pm$ A B C fields of the node (5), treated as a single unit. The sign of ABC, namely the sign of the second word in (5), will always be

plus, except that there is a *special node* at the end of every polynomial that has
$ABC = -1$ and $COEF = 0$. This special node is a great convenience, analogous to
our discussion of a list head above, because it provides a convenient sentinel and
it avoids the problem of an empty list (corresponding to the polynomial 0). The
nodes of the list always appear in *decreasing order* of the ABC field, if we follow
the direction of the links, except that the special node (which has $ABC = -1$)
links to the largest value of ABC. For example, the polynomial $x^6 - 6xy^5 + 5y^6$
would be represented thus:

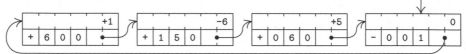

Algorithm A (*Addition of polynomials*). This algorithm adds polynomial(P)
to polynomial(Q), assuming that P and Q are pointer variables pointing to
polynomials having the form above. The list P will be unchanged; the list Q
will retain the sum. Pointer variables P and Q return to their starting points
at the conclusion of this algorithm; auxiliary pointer variables Q1 and Q2 are
also used.

A1. [Initialize.] Set $P \leftarrow LINK(P)$, $Q1 \leftarrow Q$, $Q \leftarrow LINK(Q)$. (Now both P and Q
point to the leading terms of their polynomials. Throughout most of this
algorithm the variable Q1 will be one step behind Q, in the sense that $Q =
LINK(Q1)$.)

A2. [ABC(P):ABC(Q).] If $ABC(P) < ABC(Q)$, set $Q1 \leftarrow Q$ and $Q \leftarrow LINK(Q)$ and
repeat this step. If $ABC(P) = ABC(Q)$, go to step A3. If $ABC(P) > ABC(Q)$,
go to step A5.

A3. [Add coefficients.] (We've found terms with equal exponents.) If $ABC(P) < 0$,
the algorithm terminates. Otherwise set $COEF(Q) \leftarrow COEF(Q) + COEF(P)$.
Now if $COEF(Q) = 0$, go to A4; otherwise, set $P \leftarrow LINK(P)$, $Q1 \leftarrow Q$,
$Q \leftarrow LINK(Q)$, and go to A2. (Curiously the latter operations are identical
to step A1.)

A4. [Delete zero term.] Set $Q2 \leftarrow Q$, $Q \leftarrow LINK(Q)$, $LINK(Q1) \leftarrow Q$, and $AVAIL \Leftarrow$
Q2. (A zero term created in step A3 has been removed from polynomial(Q).)
Set $P \leftarrow LINK(P)$ and go back to A2.

A5. [Insert new term.] (Polynomial(P) contains a term that is not present
in polynomial(Q), so we insert it in polynomial(Q).) Set $Q2 \Leftarrow AVAIL$,
$COEF(Q2) \leftarrow COEF(P)$, $ABC(Q2) \leftarrow ABC(P)$, $LINK(Q2) \leftarrow Q$, $LINK(Q1) \leftarrow Q2$,
$Q1 \leftarrow Q2$, $P \leftarrow LINK(P)$, and return to step A2. ∎

One of the most noteworthy features of Algorithm A is the manner in which
the pointer variable Q1 follows the pointer Q around the list. This is very typical
of list processing algorithms, and we will see a dozen more algorithms with the
same characteristic. Can the reader see why this idea was used in Algorithm A?

A reader who has little prior experience with linked lists will find it very
instructive to study Algorithm A carefully; as a test case, try adding $x + y + z$
to $x^2 - 2y - z$.

Given Algorithm A, the multiplication operation is surprisingly easy:

Algorithm M (*Multiplication of polynomials*). This algorithm, analogous to Algorithm A, replaces polynomial(Q) by

$$\text{polynomial(Q)} + \text{polynomial(M)} \times \text{polynomial(P)}.$$

M1. [Next multiplier.] Set M ← LINK(M). If ABC(M) < 0, the algorithm terminates.

M2. [Multiply cycle.] Perform Algorithm A, except that wherever the notation "ABC(P)" appears in that algorithm, replace it by "(if ABC(P) < 0 then −1, otherwise ABC(P) + ABC(M))"; wherever "COEF(P)" appears in that algorithm replace it by "COEF(P) × COEF(M)". Then go back to step M1. ∎

The programming of Algorithm A in MIX language shows again the ease with which linked lists are manipulated in a computer. In the following code we assume that OVERFLOW is a subroutine that either terminates the program (due to lack of memory space) or finds further available space and exits to rJ − 2.

Program A (*Addition of polynomials*). This is a subroutine written so that it can be used in conjunction with a multiplication subroutine (see exercise 15).

Calling sequence: JMP   ADD
Entry conditions: rI1 = P, rI2 = Q.
Exit conditions: polynomial(Q) has been replaced by polynomial(Q) + polynomial(P); rI1 and rI2 are unchanged; all other registers have undefined contents.

In the coding below, P ≡ rI1, Q ≡ rI2, Q1 ≡ rI3, and Q2 ≡ rI6, in the notation of Algorithm A.

01	LINK	EQU	4:5		Definition of LINK field
02	ABC	EQU	0:3		Definition of ABC field
03	ADD	STJ	3F	1	Entrance to subroutine
04	1H	ENT3	0,2	$1 + m''$	*A1. Initialize.* Set Q1 ← Q.
05		LD2	1,3(LINK)	$1 + m''$	Q ← LINK(Q1).
06	0H	LD1	1,1(LINK)	$1 + p$	P ← LINK(P).
07	SW1	LDA	1,1	$1 + p$	rA(0:3) ← ABC(P).
08	2H	CMPA	1,2(ABC)	x	*A2. ABC(P):ABC(Q).*
09		JE	3F	x	If equal, go to A3.
10		JG	5F	$p' + q'$	If greater, go to A5.
11		ENT3	0,2	q'	If less, set Q1 ← Q.
12		LD2	1,3(LINK)	q'	Q ← LINK(Q1).
13		JMP	2B	q'	Repeat.
14	3H	JAN	*	$m + 1$	*A3. Add coefficients.*
15	SW2	LDA	0,1	m	COEF(P)
16		ADD	0,2	m	+ COEF(Q)
17		STA	0,2	m	→ COEF(Q).
18		JANZ	1B	m	Jump if nonzero.

19		ENT6	0,2	m'	A4. Delete zero term. Q2 ← Q.
20		LD2	1,2(LINK)	m'	Q ← LINK(Q).
21		LDX	AVAIL	m'	⎫
22		STX	1,6(LINK)	m'	⎬ AVAIL ⇐ Q2.
23		ST6	AVAIL	m'	⎭
24		ST2	1,3(LINK)	m'	LINK(Q1) ← Q.
25		JMP	0B	m'	Go to advance P.
26	5H	LD6	AVAIL	p'	⎱ A5. Insert new term.
27		J6Z	OVERFLOW	p'	⎰
28		LDX	1,6(LINK)	p'	⎬ Q2 ⇐ AVAIL.
29		STX	AVAIL	p'	
30		STA	1,6	p'	ABC(Q2) ← ABC(P).
31	SW3	LDA	0,1	p'	rA ← COEF(P).
32		STA	0,6	p'	COEF(Q2) ← rA.
33		ST2	1,6(LINK)	p'	LINK(Q2) ← Q.
34		ST6	1,3(LINK)	p'	LINK(Q1) ← Q2.
35		ENT3	0,6	p'	Q1 ← Q2.
36		JMP	0B	p'	Go to advance P. ▮

Note that Algorithm A traverses each of the two lists just once; it is not necessary to loop around several times. Using Kirchhoff's law, we find that an analysis of the instruction counts presents no difficulties; the execution time depends on four quantities

m' = number of matching terms that cancel with each other;

m'' = number of matching terms that do not cancel;

p' = number of unmatched terms in polynomial(P);

q' = number of unmatched terms in polynomial(Q).

The analysis given with Program A uses the abbreviations

$$m = m' + m'', \quad p = m + p', \quad q = m + q', \quad x = 1 + m + p' + q';$$

the running time for MIX is $(27m' + 18m'' + 27p' + 8q' + 13)u$. The total number of nodes in the storage pool needed during the execution of the algorithm is at least $2 + p + q$, and at most $2 + p + q + p'$.

EXERCISES

1. [21] The text suggests at the beginning of this section that an empty circular list could be represented by PTR = Λ. It might be more consistent with the philosophy of circular lists to have PTR = LOC(PTR) indicate an empty list. Does this convention facilitate operations (a), (b), or (c) described at the beginning of this section?

2. [20] Draw "before and after" diagrams illustrating the effect of the concatenation operation (3), assuming that PTR₁ and PTR₂ are ≠ Λ.

▶ **3.** [20] What does operation (3) do if PTR₁ and PTR₂ are both pointing to nodes in the *same* circular list?

▶ **4.** [20] (X. Xie, 2021.) State insertion and deletion operations that give the effect of an output-restricted deque (in particular, of a stack and/or queue), using representation (4) with PTR pointing to the current list head.

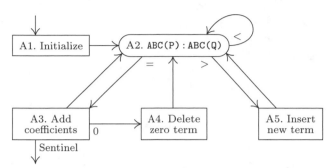

Fig. 10. Addition of polynomials.

▸ **5.** [*21*] Design an algorithm that takes a circular list such as (1) and reverses the direction of all the arrows.

6. [*18*] Give diagrams of the list representation for the polynomials (a) $xz - 3$; (b) 0.

7. [*10*] Why is it useful to assume that the ABC fields of a polynomial list appear in decreasing order?

▸ **8.** [*10*] Why is it useful to have Q1 trailing one step behind Q in Algorithm A?

▸ **9.** [*23*] Would Algorithm A work properly if P = Q (i.e., both pointer variables point at the same polynomial)? Would Algorithm M work properly if P = M, if P = Q, or if M = Q?

▸ **10.** [*20*] The algorithms in this section assume that we are using three variables x, y, and z in the polynomials, and that their exponents individually never exceed $b - 1$ (where b is the byte size in MIX's case). Suppose instead that we want to do addition and multiplication of polynomials in only one variable, x, and to let its exponent take on values up to $b^3 - 1$. What changes should be made to Algorithms A and M?

11. [*24*] (The purpose of this exercise and many of those following is to create a package of subroutines useful for polynomial arithmetic, in conjunction with Program A.) Since Algorithms A and M change the value of polynomial(Q), it is sometimes desirable to have a subroutine that makes a copy of a given polynomial. Write a MIX subroutine with the following specifications:

Calling sequence: JMP　COPY
Entry conditions: rI1 = P
Exit conditions:　rI2 points to a newly created polynomial equal to polynomial(P); rI1 is unchanged; other registers are undefined.

12. [*21*] Compare the running time of the program in exercise 11 with that of Program A when polynomial(Q) = 0.

13. [*20*] Write a MIX subroutine with the following specifications:

Calling sequence: JMP　ERASE
Entry conditions: rI1 = P
Exit conditions:　polynomial(P) has been added to the AVAIL list; all register contents are undefined.

[*Note:* This subroutine can be used in conjunction with the subroutine of exercise 11 in the sequence 'LD1 Q; JMP ERASE; LD1 P; JMP COPY; ST2 Q' to achieve the effect "polynomial(Q) ← polynomial(P)".]

14. [*22*] Write a MIX subroutine with the following specifications:

Calling sequence: JMP   ZERO
Entry conditions: None
Exit conditions: rI2 points to a newly created polynomial equal to 0; other register
contents are undefined.

15. [*24*] Write a MIX subroutine to perform Algorithm M, having the following specifications:

Calling sequence: JMP   MULT
Entry conditions: rI1 = P, rI2 = Q, rI4 = M.
Exit conditions: polynomial(Q) $\leftarrow$ polynomial(Q) + polynomial(M) × polynomial(P);
rI1, rI2, rI4 are unchanged; other registers undefined.

[*Note:* Use Program A as a subroutine, changing the settings of SW1, SW2, and SW3.]

16. [*M28*] Estimate the running time of the subroutine in exercise 15 in terms of some relevant parameters.

▶ **17.** [*22*] What advantage is there in representing polynomials with a circular list as in this section, instead of with a straight linear linked list terminated by Λ as in the previous section?

▶ **18.** [*25*] Devise a way to represent circular lists inside a computer in such a way that the list can be traversed efficiently in both directions, yet only one link field is used per node. [*Hint:* If we are given two pointers, to two successive nodes x_{i-1} and x_i, it should be possible to locate both x_{i+1} and x_{i-2}.]

2.2.5. Doubly Linked Lists

For even greater flexibility in the manipulation of linear lists, we can include *two* links in each node, pointing to the items on either side of that node:

$$(1)$$

Here LEFT and RIGHT are pointer variables to the left and right of the list. The two pointers in each node of the list are called, for example, LLINK and RLINK. The operations of a general deque are readily performed with such a representation; see exercise 1. However, manipulations of doubly linked lists almost always become much easier if a *list head* node is part of each list, as described in the preceding section. When a list head is present, we have the following typical diagram of a doubly linked list:

List head

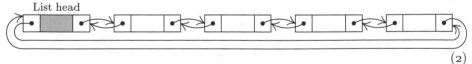

$$(2)$$

The RLINK and LLINK fields of the list head take the place of LEFT and RIGHT in (1). There is complete symmetry between left and right; the list head could equally well have been shown at the right of (2). If the list is empty, both link fields of the list head point to the head itself.

The list representation (2) clearly satisfies the condition

$$\text{RLINK}(\text{LLINK}(X)) = \text{LLINK}(\text{RLINK}(X)) = X \qquad (3)$$

if X is the location of any node in the list (including the head). This fact is the principal reason that representation (2) is preferable to (1).

A doubly linked list usually takes more memory space than a singly linked one does (although there is sometimes room for another link in a node that doesn't fill a complete computer word). But the additional operations that can be performed efficiently with two-way links are often more than ample compensation for the extra space requirement. Besides the obvious advantage of being able to go back and forth at will when examining a doubly linked list, one of the principal new abilities is the fact that *we can delete* NODE(X) *from the list it is in, given only the value of* X. This deletion operation is easy to derive from a "before and after" diagram (Fig. 11) and it is very simple:

$$\text{RLINK(LLINK(X))} \leftarrow \text{RLINK(X)}, \qquad \text{LLINK(RLINK(X))} \leftarrow \text{LLINK(X)},$$
$$\text{AVAIL} \Leftarrow \text{X}. \tag{4}$$

In a list that has only one-way links, we cannot delete NODE(X) without knowing which node precedes it in the chain, since the preceding node needs to have its link altered when NODE(X) is deleted. In all the algorithms considered in Sections 2.2.3 and 2.2.4 this additional knowledge was present whenever a node was to be deleted; see, in particular, Algorithm 2.2.4A, where we had pointer Q1 following pointer Q for just this purpose. But we will meet several algorithms that require removing random nodes from the middle of a list, and doubly linked lists are frequently used just for this reason. (We should point out that in a circular list it is possible to delete NODE(X), given X, if we go around the entire circle to find the predecessor of X. But this operation is clearly inefficient when the list is long, so it is rarely an acceptable substitute for doubly linking the list. See also the answer to exercise 2.2.4–8.)

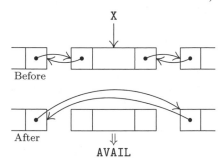

Fig. 11. Deletion from a doubly linked list.

Similarly, a doubly linked list permits the easy insertion of a node adjacent to NODE(X) at either the left or the right. The steps

$$\text{P} \Leftarrow \text{AVAIL}, \qquad \text{LLINK(P)} \leftarrow \text{X}, \qquad \text{RLINK(P)} \leftarrow \text{RLINK(X)},$$
$$\text{LLINK(RLINK(X))} \leftarrow \text{P}, \qquad \text{RLINK(X)} \leftarrow \text{P} \tag{5}$$

do such an insertion to the right of NODE(X); and by interchanging left and right we get the corresponding algorithm for insertion to the left. Operation (5) changes the settings of five links, so it is a little slower than an insertion operation in a one-way list where only three links need to be changed.

As an example of the use of doubly linked lists, we will now consider the writing of a *discrete simulation* program. "Discrete simulation" means the simulation of a system in which all changes in the state of the system may be assumed to happen at certain discrete instants of time. The "system" being simulated is usually a set of individual activities that are largely independent, although they interact with each other; examples are customers at a store, ships in a harbor, people in a corporation. In a discrete simulation, we proceed by doing whatever is to be done at a certain instant of simulated time, then advance the simulated clock to the next time when some action is scheduled to occur.

By contrast, a "continuous simulation" would be simulation of activities that are under continuous changes, such as traffic moving on a highway, spaceships traveling to other planets, etc. Continuous simulation can often be satisfactorily approximated by discrete simulation with very small time intervals between steps; however, in such a case we usually have "synchronous" discrete simulation, in which many parts of the system are slightly altered at each discrete time interval, and such an application generally calls for a somewhat different type of program organization than the kind considered here.

The program developed below simulates the elevator system in the Mathematics building of the California Institute of Technology. The results of such a simulation will perhaps be of use only to people who make reasonably frequent visits to Caltech; and even for them, it may be simpler just to try using the elevator several times instead of writing a computer program. But, as is usual with simulation studies, the methods we will use are of much more interest than the answers given by the program. The methods to be discussed below illustrate typical implementation techniques used with discrete simulation programs.

The Mathematics building has five floors: sub-basement, basement, first, second, and third. There is a single elevator, which has automatic controls and can stop at each floor. For convenience we will renumber the floors 0, 1, 2, 3, and 4.

On each floor there are two call buttons, one for UP and one for DOWN. (Actually floor 0 has only UP and floor 4 has only DOWN, but we may ignore that anomaly since the excess buttons will never be used.) Corresponding to these buttons, there are ten variables CALLUP[j] and CALLDOWN[j], $0 \leq j \leq 4$. There are also variables CALLCAR[j], $0 \leq j \leq 4$, representing buttons within the elevator car, which direct it to a destination floor. When a person presses a button, the appropriate variable is set to 1; the elevator clears the variable to 0 after the request has been fulfilled.

So far we have described the elevator from a user's point of view; the situation is more interesting as viewed by the elevator. The elevator is in one of three states: GOINGUP, GOINGDOWN, or NEUTRAL. (The current state is indicated to passengers by lighted arrows inside the elevator.) If it is in NEUTRAL state and not on floor 2, the machine will close its doors and (if no command is given by the time its doors are shut) it will change to GOINGUP or GOINGDOWN, heading for floor 2. (This is the "home floor," since most passengers get in there.) On floor 2 in NEUTRAL state, the doors will eventually close and the machine will wait silently for another command. The first command received for another floor sets the machine GOINGUP or GOINGDOWN as appropriate; it stays in this state until there are no commands waiting in the same direction, and then it switches direction or switches to NEUTRAL just before opening the doors, depending on what other commands are in the CALL variables. The elevator takes a certain amount of time to open and close its doors, to accelerate and decelerate, and to get from one floor to another. All of these quantities are indicated in the algorithm below, which is much more precise than an informal description can be. The algorithm we will now study may not reflect the elevator's true principles of operation, but it is believed to be the simplest set of rules that explain all the phenomena observed during several hours of experimentation by the author during the writing of this section.

The elevator system is simulated by using two coroutines, one for the passengers and one for the elevator; these routines specify all the actions to be performed, as well as various time delays that are to be used in the simulation. In the following description, the variable TIME represents the current value of the simulated time clock. All units of time are given in *tenths of seconds*. There arc also several other variables:

FLOOR, the current position of the elevator;

D1, a variable that is zero except during the time people are getting in or out of the elevator;

D2, a variable that becomes zero if the elevator has sat on one floor without moving for 30 sec or more;

D3, a variable that is zero except when the doors are open but nobody is getting in or out of the elevator;

STATE, the current state of the elevator (GOINGUP, GOINGDOWN, or NEUTRAL).

Initially FLOOR = 2, D1 = D2 = D3 = 0, and STATE = NEUTRAL.

Coroutine U (*Users*). Everyone who enters the system begins to perform the actions specified below, starting at step U1.

U1. [Enter, prepare for successor.] The following quantities are determined in some manner that will not be specified here:

IN, the floor on which the new user has entered the system;

OUT, the floor to which this user wants to go (OUT ≠ IN);

GIVEUPTIME, the amount of time this user will wait for the elevator before running out of patience and deciding to walk;

INTERTIME, the amount of time before another user will enter the system.

After these quantities have been computed, the simulation program sets things up so that another user enters the system at TIME + INTERTIME.

U2. [Signal and wait.] (The purpose of this step is to call for the elevator; some special cases arise if the elevator is already on the right floor.) If FLOOR = IN and if the elevator's next action is step E6 below (that is, if the elevator doors are now closing), send the elevator immediately to its step E3 and cancel its activity E6. (This means that the doors will open again before the elevator moves.) If FLOOR = IN and if D3 ≠ 0, set D3 ← 0, set D1 to a nonzero value, and start up the elevator's activity E4 again. (This means that the elevator doors are open on this floor, but everyone else has already gotten on or off. Elevator step E4 is a sequencing step that grants people permission to enter the elevator according to normal laws of courtesy; therefore, restarting E4 gives this user a chance to get in before the doors close.) In all other cases, the user sets CALLUP[IN] ← 1 or CALLDOWN[IN] ← 1, according as OUT > IN or OUT < IN; and if D2 = 0 or the elevator is in its "dormant" position E1, the DECISION subroutine specified below is performed. (The DECISION subroutine is used to take the elevator out of NEUTRAL state at certain critical times.)

U3. [Enter queue.] Insert this user at the rear of QUEUE[IN], which is a linear list representing the people waiting on this floor. Now the user waits patiently for GIVEUPTIME units of time, unless the elevator arrives first — more precisely, unless step E4 of the elevator routine below sends this user to U5 and cancels the scheduled activity U4.

U4. [Give up.] If FLOOR ≠ IN or D1 = 0, delete this user from QUEUE[IN] and from the simulated system. (The user has decided that the elevator is too slow, or that a bit of exercise will be better than an elevator ride.) If FLOOR = IN and D1 ≠ 0, the user stays and waits (knowing that the wait won't be long).

U5. [Get in.] This user now leaves QUEUE[IN] and enters ELEVATOR, which is a stack-like list representing the people now on board the elevator. Set CALLCAR[OUT] ← 1.

Now if STATE = NEUTRAL, set STATE ← GOINGUP or GOINGDOWN as appropriate, and set the elevator's activity E5 to be executed after 25 units of time. (This is a special feature of the elevator, allowing the doors to close faster than usual if the elevator is in NEUTRAL state when the user selects a destination floor. The 25-unit time interval gives step E4 the opportunity to make sure that D1 is properly set up by the time step E5, the door-closing action, occurs.)

Now the user waits until being sent to step U6 by step E4 below, when the elevator has reached the desired floor.

U6. [Get out.] Delete this user from the ELEVATOR list and from the simulated system. ∎

Coroutine E (*Elevator*). This coroutine represents the actions of the elevator; step E4 also handles the control of when people get in and out.

E1. [Wait for call.] (At this point the elevator is sitting at floor 2 with the doors closed, waiting for something to happen.) If someone presses a button, the DECISION subroutine will take us to step E3 or E6. Meanwhile, wait.

E2. [Change of state?] If STATE = GOINGUP and CALLUP[j] = CALLDOWN[j] = CALLCAR[j] = 0 for all j > FLOOR, then set STATE ← NEUTRAL or STATE ←

GOINGDOWN, according as CALLCAR[j] $= 0$ for all $j <$ FLOOR or not, and set all CALL variables for the current floor to zero. If STATE $=$ GOINGDOWN, do similar actions with directions reversed.

E3. [Open doors.] Set D1 and D2 to any nonzero values. Set elevator activity E9 to start up independently after 300 units of time. (This activity may be canceled in step E6 below before it occurs. If it has already been scheduled and not canceled, we cancel it and reschedule it.) Also set elevator activity E5 to start up independently after 76 units of time. Then wait 20 units of time (to simulate opening of the doors) and go to E4.

E4. [Let people out, in.] If anyone in the ELEVATOR list has OUT $=$ FLOOR, send the user of this type who has most recently entered immediately to step U6, wait 25 units, and repeat step E4. If no such users exist, but QUEUE[FLOOR] is not empty, send the front person of that queue immediately to step U5 instead of U4, wait 25 units, and repeat step E4. But if QUEUE[FLOOR] is empty, set D1 $\leftarrow 0$, make D3 nonzero, and wait for some other activity to initiate further action. (Step E5 will send us to E6, or step U2 will restart E4.)

E5. [Close doors.] If D1 $\neq 0$, wait 40 units and repeat this step (the doors flutter a little, but they spring open again, since someone is still getting out or in). Otherwise set D3 $\leftarrow 0$ and set the elevator to start at step E6 after 20 units of time. (This simulates closing the doors after people have finished getting in or out; but if a new user enters on this floor while the doors are closing, they will open again as stated in step U2.)

E6. [Prepare to move.] Set CALLCAR[FLOOR] to zero; also set CALLUP[FLOOR] to zero if STATE $\neq$ GOINGDOWN, and also set CALLDOWN[FLOOR] to zero if STATE $\neq$ GOINGUP. (*Note:* If STATE $=$ GOINGUP, the elevator does not clear out CALLDOWN, since it assumes that people who are going down will not have entered; but see exercise 6.) Now perform the DECISION subroutine.

     If STATE $=$ NEUTRAL even after the DECISION subroutine has acted, go to E1. Otherwise, if D2 $\neq 0$, cancel the elevator activity E9. Finally, if STATE $=$ GOINGUP, wait 15 units of time (for the elevator to build up speed) and go to E7; if STATE $=$ GOINGDOWN, wait 15 units and go to E8.

E7. [Go up a floor.] Set FLOOR $\leftarrow$ FLOOR $+ 1$ and wait 51 units of time. If now CALLCAR[FLOOR] $= 1$ or CALLUP[FLOOR] $= 1$, or if $\big($(FLOOR $= 2$ or CALLDOWN[FLOOR] $= 1$) and CALLUP[j] $=$ CALLDOWN[j] $=$ CALLCAR[j] $= 0$ for all $j >$ FLOOR$\big)$, wait 14 units (for deceleration) and go to E2. Otherwise, repeat this step.

E8. [Go down a floor.] This step is like E7 with directions reversed, and also the times 51 and 14 are changed to 61 and 23, respectively. (It takes the elevator longer to go down than up.)

E9. [Set inaction indicator.] Set D2 $\leftarrow 0$ and perform the DECISION subroutine. (This independent action is initiated in step E3 but it is almost always canceled in step E6. See exercise 4.) ∎

Table 1

SOME ACTIONS OF THE ELEVATOR SYSTEM

TIME	STATE	FLOOR	D1	D2	D3	step	action
0000	N	2	0	0	0	U1	User 1 arrives at floor 0, destination is 2.
0035	D	2	0	0	0	E8	Elevator moving down
0038	D	2	0	0	0	U1	User 2 arrives at floor 4, destination is 1.
0096	D	1	0	0	0	E8	Elevator moving down
0136	D	0	0	0	0	U1	User 3 arrives at floor 2, destination is 1.
0141	D	0	0	0	0	U1	User 4 arrives at floor 2, destination is 1.
0152	D	0	0	0	0	U4	User 1 decides to give up, leaves the system.
0180	D	0	0	0	0	E2	Elevator stops.
0180	N	0	0	0	0	E3	Elevator doors start to open.
0200	N	0	0	X	0	E4	Doors open, nobody is there.
0256	N	0	0	X	X	E5	Elevator doors start to close.
0291	U	0	0	X	0	U1	User 5 arrives at floor 3, destination is 1.
0291	U	0	0	X	0	E7	Elevator moving up
0342	U	1	0	X	0	E7	Elevator moving up
0364	U	2	0	X	0	U1	User 6 arrives at floor 2, destination is 1.
0393	U	2	0	X	0	E7	Elevator moving up
0444	U	3	0	X	0	E7	Elevator moving up
0509	U	4	0	X	0	E2	Elevator stops.
0509	N	4	0	X	0	E3	Elevator doors start to open.
0529	N	4	X	X	0	U5	User 2 gets in.
0540	D	4	X	X	0	U4	User 6 decides to give up, leaves the system.
0554	D	4	0	X	X	E5	Elevator doors start to close.
0589	D	4	0	X	0	E8	Elevator moving down
0602	D	3	0	X	0	U1	User 7 arrives at floor 1, destination is 2.
0673	D	3	0	X	0	E2	Elevator stops.
0673	D	3	0	X	0	E3	Elevator doors start to open.
0693	D	3	X	X	0	U5	User 5 gets in.
0749	D	3	0	X	X	E5	Elevator doors start to close.
0784	D	3	0	X	0	E8	Elevator moving down
0827	D	2	0	X	0	U1	User 8 arrives at floor 1, destination is 0.
0868	D	2	0	X	0	E2	Elevator stops.
0868	D	2	0	X	0	E3	Elevator doors start to open.
0876	D	2	X	X	0	U1	User 9 arrives at floor 1, destination is 3.
0888	D	2	X	X	0	U5	User 3 gets in.
0913	D	2	X	X	0	U5	User 4 gets in.
0944	D	2	0	X	0	E5	Elevator doors start to close.
0979	D	2	0	X	0	E8	Elevator moving down
1048	D	1	0	X	0	U1	User 10 arrives at floor 0, destination is 4.
1063	D	1	0	X	0	E2	Elevator stops.
1063	D	1	0	X	0	E3	Elevator doors start to open.
1083	D	1	X	X	0	U6	User 4 gets out, leaves the system.
1108	D	1	X	X	0	U6	User 3 gets out, leaves the system.
1133	D	1	X	X	0	U6	User 5 gets out, leaves the system.
1139	D	1	X	X	0	E5	Doors flutter.
1158	D	1	X	X	0	U6	User 2 gets out, leaves the system.
1179	D	1	X	X	0	E5	Doors flutter.
1183	D	1	X	X	0	U5	User 7 gets in.
1208	D	1	X	X	0	U5	User 8 gets in.
1219	D	1	X	X	0	E5	Doors flutter.
1233	D	1	X	X	0	U5	User 9 gets in.
1259	D	1	X	X	X	E5	Elevator doors start to close.
1294	D	0	0	X	0	E8	Elevator moving down
1378	D	0	0	X	0	E2	Elevator stops.
1378	U	0	0	X	0	E3	Elevator doors start to open.
1398	U	0	0	X	0	U6	User 8 gets out, leaves the system.
1423	U	0	0	X	0	U5	User 10 gets in.
1454	U	0	0	X	X	E5	Elevator doors start to close.
1489	U	0	0	X	0	E7	Elevator moving up
1554	U	1	0	X	0	E2	Elevator stops.
1554	U	1	0	X	0	E3	Elevator doors start to open.
1630	U	1	0	X	X	E5	Elevator doors start to close.
1665	U	1	0	X	0	E7	Elevator moving up
...							
4257	N	2	X	X	0	E1	Elevator dormant
4384	N	2	0	X	0	U1	User 17 arrives at floor 2, destination is 3.
4404	N	2	0	X	0	E3	Elevator doors start to open.
4424	N	2	X	X	0	U5	User 17 gets in.
4449	U	2	0	X	X	E5	Elevator doors start to close.
4484	U	2	0	X	0	E7	Elevator moving up
4549	U	3	0	X	0	E2	Elevator stops.
4549	N	3	0	X	0	E3	Elevator doors start to open.
4569	N	3	X	X	0	U6	User 17 gets out, leaves the system.
4625	D	3	0	X	X	E5	Elevator doors start to close.
4660	D	3	0	X	0	E8	Elevator moving down
4744	D	2	0	X	0	E2	Elevator stops.
4744	N	2	0	X	0	E3	Elevator doors start to open.
4764	D	2	0	X	0	E4	Doors open, nobody is there.
4820	D	2	0	X	X	E5	Elevator doors start to close.
4840	D	2	0	X	0	E1	Elevator dormant
...							

Subroutine D (DECISION *subroutine*). This subroutine is performed at certain critical times, as specified in the coroutines above, when a decision about the elevator's next direction is to be made.

D1. [Decision necessary?] If STATE ≠ NEUTRAL, exit from this subroutine.

D2. [Should doors open?] If the elevator is positioned at E1 and if CALLUP[2], CALLCAR[2], and CALLDOWN[2] are not all zero, cause the elevator to start its activity E3 after 20 units of time, and exit from this subroutine. (If the DECISION subroutine is currently being invoked by the independent activity E9, it is possible for the elevator coroutine to be positioned at E1.)

D3. [Any calls?] Find the smallest $j \neq$ FLOOR for which CALLUP[j], CALLCAR[j], or CALLDOWN[j] is nonzero, and go on to step D4. But if no such j exists, then set $j \leftarrow 2$ if the DECISION subroutine is currently being invoked by step E6; otherwise exit from this subroutine.

D4. [Set STATE.] If FLOOR $> j$, set STATE $\leftarrow$ GOINGDOWN; if FLOOR $< j$, set STATE $\leftarrow$ GOINGUP.

D5. [Elevator dormant?] If the elevator coroutine is positioned at step E1, and if $j \neq 2$, set the elevator to perform step E6 after 20 units of time. Exit from the subroutine. ∎

The elevator system described above is quite complicated by comparison with other algorithms we have seen in this book, but the choice of a real-life system is more typical of a simulation problem than any cooked-up "textbook example" would ever be.

To help understand the system, consider Table 1, which gives part of the history of one simulation. It is perhaps best to start by examining the simple case starting at time 4257: The elevator is sitting idly at floor 2 with its doors shut, when a user arrives (time 4384); let's say the user's name is Don. Two seconds later, the doors open, and Don gets in after two more seconds. By pushing button "3" he starts the elevator moving up; ultimately he gets off at floor 3 and the elevator returns to floor 2.

The first entries in Table 1 show a much more dramatic scenario: A user calls the elevator to floor 0, but loses patience and gives up after 15.2 sec. The elevator stops at floor 0 but finds nobody there; then it heads to floor 4, since there are several calls wanting to go downward; etc.

The programming of this system for a computer (in our case, MIX) merits careful study. At any given time during the simulation, we may have many simulated users in the system (in various queues and ready to "give up" at various times), and there is also the possibility of essentially simultaneous execution of steps E4, E5, and E9 if many people are trying to get out as the elevator is trying to close its doors. The passing of simulated time and the handling of "simultaneity" may be programmed by having each entity represented by a node that includes a NEXTTIME field (denoting the time when the next action for this entity is to take place) and a NEXTINST field (denoting the memory address where this entity is to start executing instructions, analogous to ordinary coroutine

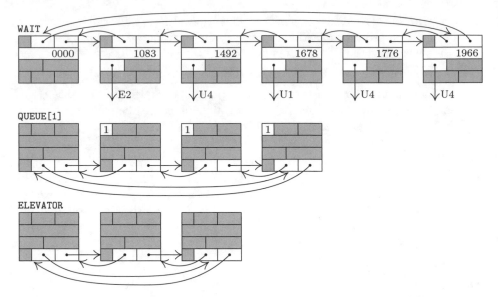

Fig. 12. Some lists used in the elevator simulation program. (List heads appear at the left.)

linkage). Each entity waiting for time to pass is placed in a doubly linked list called the WAIT list; this "agenda" is sorted on the NEXTTIME fields of its nodes, so that the actions may be processed in the correct sequence of simulated times. The program also uses doubly linked lists for the ELEVATOR and for the QUEUE lists.

Each node representing an activity (whether a user or an elevator action) has the form

+	IN	LLINK1		RLINK1	
+	NEXTTIME				
+	NEXTINST		0	0	39
+	OUT	LLINK2		RLINK2	

.   (6)

Here LLINK1 and RLINK1 are the links for the WAIT list; LLINK2 and RLINK2 are used as links in the QUEUE lists or the ELEVATOR. The latter two fields and the IN and OUT field are relevant when node (6) represents a user, but they are not relevant for nodes that represent elevator actions. The third word of the node is actually a MIX 'JMP' instruction.

Figure 12 shows typical contents of the WAIT list, ELEVATOR list, and one of the QUEUE lists; each node in the QUEUE list is simultaneously in the WAIT list with NEXTINST = U4, but this has not been indicated in the figure, since the complexity of the linking would obscure the basic idea.

Now let us consider the program itself. It is quite long, although (as with all long programs) it divides into small parts each of which is quite simple in itself.

First comes a number of lines of code that just serve to define the initial contents of the tables. There are several points of interest here: We have list heads for the WAIT list (lines 010–011), the QUEUE lists (lines 026–031), and the ELEVATOR list (lines 032–033). Each of them is a node of the form (6), but with unimportant words deleted; the WAIT list head contains only the first two words of a node, and the QUEUE and ELEVATOR list heads require only the last word of a node. We also have four nodes that are always present in the system (lines 012–023): USER1, a node that is always positioned at step U1 ready to enter a new user into the system; ELEV1, a node that governs the main actions of the elevator at steps E1, E2, E3, E4, E6, E7, and E8; and ELEV2 and ELEV3, nodes that are used for the elevator actions E5 and E9, which take place independently of other elevator actions with respect to simulated time. Each of these four nodes contains only three words, since they never appear in the QUEUE or ELEVATOR lists. The nodes representing each actual user in the system will appear in a storage pool following the main program.

```
001   * THE ELEVATOR SIMULATION
002   IN       EQU   1:1                        Definition of fields
003   LLINK1   EQU   2:3                           within nodes
004   RLINK1   EQU   4:5
005   NEXTINST EQU   0:2
006   OUT      EQU   1:1
007   LLINK2   EQU   2:3
008   RLINK2   EQU   4:5

009   * FIXED-SIZE TABLES AND LIST HEADS
010   WAIT     CON   *+2(LLINK1),*+2(RLINK1)     List head for WAIT list
011            CON   0                           NEXTTIME = 0 always
012   USER1    CON   *-2(LLINK1),*-2(RLINK1)     This node represents action
013            CON   0                           U1 and it is initially the
014            JMP   U1                          sole entry in the WAIT list.
015   ELEV1    CON   0                           This node represents the
016            CON   0                           elevator actions, except
017            JMP   E1                          for E5 and E9.
018   ELEV2    CON   0                           This node represents the
019            CON   0                           independent elevator
020            JMP   E5                          action at E5.
021   ELEV3    CON   0                           This node represents the
022            CON   0                           independent elevator
023            JMP   E9                          action at E9.
024   AVAIL    CON   0                           Link to available nodes
025   TIME     CON   0                           Current simulated time
026   QUEUE    EQU   *-3
027            CON   *-3(LLINK2),*-3(RLINK2)     List head for QUEUE[0]
028            CON   *-3(LLINK2),*-3(RLINK2)     List head for QUEUE[1]
029            CON   *-3(LLINK2),*-3(RLINK2)     All queues initially
030            CON   *-3(LLINK2),*-3(RLINK2)        are empty
031            CON   *-3(LLINK2),*-3(RLINK2)     List head for QUEUE[4]
```

```
032 ELEVATOR EQU  *-3
033          CON  *-3(LLINK2),*-3(RLINK2)   List head for ELEVATOR
034          CON  0                        ⎫
035          CON  0                        ⎪  "Padding" for CALL table
036          CON  0                        ⎬      (see lines 183–186)
037          CON  0                        ⎭
038 CALL     CON  0       CALLUP[0], CALLCAR[0], CALLDOWN[0]
039          CON  0       CALLUP[1], CALLCAR[1], CALLDOWN[1]
040          CON  0       CALLUP[2], CALLCAR[2], CALLDOWN[2]
041          CON  0       CALLUP[3], CALLCAR[3], CALLDOWN[3]
042          CON  0       CALLUP[4], CALLCAR[4], CALLDOWN[4]
043          CON  0                        ⎫
044          CON  0                        ⎪  "Padding" for CALL table
045          CON  0                        ⎬      (see lines 178–181)
046          CON  0                        ⎭
047 D1       CON  0             Indicates doors open, activity
048 D2       CON  0             Indicates no prolonged standstill
049 D3       CON  0             Indicates doors open, inactivity ▌
```

The next part of the program coding contains basic subroutines and the main control routines for the simulation process. Subroutines INSERT and DELETE perform typical manipulations on doubly linked lists; they put the current node into or take it out of a QUEUE or ELEVATOR list. (In the program, the "current node" C is always represented by index register 6.) There are also subroutines for the WAIT list: Subroutine SORTIN adds the current node to the WAIT list, sorting it into the right place based on its NEXTTIME field. Subroutine IMMED inserts the current node at the front of the WAIT list. Subroutine HOLD puts the current node into the WAIT list, with NEXTTIME equal to the current time plus the amount in register A. Subroutine DELETEW deletes the current node from the WAIT list.

The routine CYCLE is the heart of the simulation control: It decides which activity is to act next (namely, the first element of the WAIT list, which we know is nonempty), and jumps to it. There are two special entrances to CYCLE: CYCLE1 first sets NEXTINST in the current node, and HOLDC is the same with an additional call on the HOLD subroutine. Thus, the effect of the instruction 'JMP HOLDC' with amount t in register A is to suspend activity for t units of simulated time and then to return to the following location.

```
050 * SUBROUTINES AND CONTROL ROUTINE
051 INSERT  STJ  9F              Insert NODE(C) to left of NODE(rI1):
052         LD2  3,1(LLINK2)     rI2 ← LLINK2(rI1).
053         ST2  3,6(LLINK2)     LLINK2(C) ← rI2.
054         ST6  3,1(LLINK2)     LLINK2(rI1) ← C.
055         ST6  3,2(RLINK2)     RLINK2(rI2) ← C.
056         ST1  3,6(RLINK2)     RLINK2(C) ← rI1.
057 9H      JMP  *               Exit from subroutine.
058 DELETE  STJ  9F              Delete NODE(C) from its list:
059         LD1  3,6(LLINK2)     P ← LLINK2(C).
060         LD2  3,6(RLINK2)     Q ← RLINK2(C).
```

061		ST1	3,2(LLINK2)	LLINK2(Q) ← P.
062		ST2	3,1(RLINK2)	RLINK2(P) ← Q.
063	9H	JMP	*	Exit from subroutine.
064	IMMED	STJ	9F	Insert NODE(C) first in WAIT list:
065		LDA	TIME	
066		STA	1,6	Set NEXTTIME(C) ← TIME.
067		ENT1	WAIT	P ← LOC(WAIT).
068		JMP	2F	Insert NODE(C) to right of NODE(P).
069	HOLD	ADD	TIME	rA ← TIME + rA.
070	SORTIN	STJ	9F	Sort NODE(C) into WAIT list:
071		STA	1,6	Set NEXTTIME(C) ← rA.
072		ENT1	WAIT	P ← LOC(WAIT).
073		LD1	0,1(LLINK1)	P ← LLINK1(P).
074		CMPA	1,1	Compare NEXTTIME fields, right to left.
075		JL	*-2	Repeat until NEXTTIME(C) ≥ NEXTTIME(P).
076	2H	LD2	0,1(RLINK1)	Q ← RLINK1(P).
077		ST2	0,6(RLINK1)	RLINK1(C) ← Q.
078		ST1	0,6(LLINK1)	LLINK1(C) ← P.
079		ST6	0,1(RLINK1)	RLINK1(P) ← C.
080		ST6	0,2(LLINK1)	LLINK1(Q) ← C.
081	9H	JMP	*	Exit from subroutine.
082	DELETEW	STJ	9F	Delete NODE(C) from WAIT list:
083		LD1	0,6(LLINK1)	(This is same as lines 058–063
084		LD2	0,6(RLINK1)	except LLINK1, RLINK1 are used
085		ST1	0,2(LLINK1)	instead of LLINK2, RLINK2.)
086		ST2	0,1(RLINK1)	
087	9H	JMP	*	
088	CYCLE1	STJ	2,6(NEXTINST)	Set NEXTINST(C) ← rJ.
089		JMP	CYCLE	
090	HOLDC	STJ	2,6(NEXTINST)	Set NEXTINST(C) ← rJ.
091		JMP	HOLD	Insert NODE(C) in WAIT, delay rA.
092	CYCLE	LD6	WAIT(RLINK1)	Set current node C ← RLINK1(LOC(WAIT)).
093		LDA	1,6	
094		STA	TIME	TIME ← NEXTTIME(C).
095		JMP	DELETEW	Remove NODE(C) from WAIT list.
096		JMP	2,6	Jump to NEXTINST(C). ▮

Now comes the program for Coroutine U. At the beginning of step U1, the current node C is USER1 (see lines 012–014 above), and lines 099–100 of the program cause USER1 to be reinserted into the WAIT list so that the next user will be generated after INTERTIME units of simulated time. The following lines 101–114 take care of setting up a node for the newly generated user; the IN and OUT floors are recorded in this node position. The AVAIL stack is singly linked in the RLINK1 field of each node. Note that lines 101–108 perform the action "C ⇐ AVAIL" using the POOLMAX technique, 2.2.3–(7); no test for OVERFLOW is necessary here, since the total size of the storage pool (the number of users in the system at any one time) rarely exceeds 10 nodes (40 words). The return of a node to the AVAIL stack appears in lines 156–158.

Throughout the program, index register 4 equals the variable FLOOR, and index register 5 is positive, negative, or zero, depending on whether STATE = GOINGUP, GOINGDOWN, or NEUTRAL. The variables CALLUP[j], CALLCAR[j], and CALLDOWN[j] occupy the respective fields (1:1), (3:3), and (5:5) of location CALL + j.

097	* COROUTINE U		*U1. Enter, prepare for successor.*
098	U1	JMP VALUES	Set INFLOOR, OUTFLOOR, GIVEUPTIME, INTERTIME.
099		LDA INTERTIME	INTERTIME is computed by VALUES subroutine.
100		JMP HOLD	Put NODE(C) in WAIT, delay INTERTIME.
101		LD6 AVAIL	C ← AVAIL.
102		J6P 1F	If AVAIL ≠ Λ, jump.
103		LD6 POOLMAX(0:2)	
104		INC6 4	C ← POOLMAX + 4.
105		ST6 POOLMAX(0:2)	POOLMAX ← C.
106		JMP *+3	Assume that memory overflow won't happen.
107	1H	LDA 0,6(RLINK1)	
108		STA AVAIL	AVAIL ← RLINK1(AVAIL).
109		LD1 INFLOOR	rI1 ← INFLOOR (computed by VALUES above).
110		ST1 0,6(IN)	IN(C) ← rI1.
111		LD2 OUTFLOOR	rI2 ← OUTFLOOR (computed by VALUES).
112		ST2 3,6(OUT)	OUT(C) ← rI2.
113		ENTA 39	Put constant 39 (JMP operation code)
114		STA 2,6	into third word of node format (6).
115	U2	ENTA 0,4	*U2. Signal and wait.* Set rA ← FLOOR.
116		DECA 0,1	FLOOR − IN.
117		ST6 TEMP	Save value of C.
118		JANZ 2F	Jump if FLOOR ≠ IN.
119		ENT6 ELEV1	Set C ← LOC(ELEV1).
120		LDA 2,6(NEXTINST)	Is elevator positioned at E6?
121		DECA E6	
122		JANZ 3F	
123		ENTA E3	If so, reposition it at E3.
124		STA 2,6(NEXTINST)	
125		JMP DELETEW	Remove it from WAIT list
126		JMP 4F	and reinsert it at front of WAIT.
127	3H	LDA D3	
128		JAZ 2F	Jump if D3 = 0.
129		ST6 D1	Otherwise make D1 nonzero.
130		STZ D3	Set D3 ← 0.
131	4H	JMP IMMED	Insert ELEV1 at front of WAIT list.
132		JMP U3	(rI1 and rI2 have changed.)
133	2H	DEC2 0,1	rI2 ← OUT − IN.
134		ENTA 1	
135		J2P *+3	Jump if going up.
136		STA CALL,1(5:5)	Set CALLDOWN[IN] ← 1.
137		JMP *+2	
138		STA CALL,1(1:1)	Set CALLUP[IN] ← 1.
139		LDA D2	

140		JAZ	*+3	If D2 = 0, call the DECISION subroutine.
141		LDA	ELEV1+2(NEXTINST)	
142		DECA	E1	If the elevator is at E1, call
143		JAZ	DECISION	the DECISION subroutine.
144	U3	LD6	TEMP	*U3. Enter queue.*
145		LD1	0,6(IN)	
146		ENT1	QUEUE,1	rI1 ← LOC(QUEUE[IN]).
147		JMP	INSERT	Insert NODE(C) at right end of QUEUE[IN].
148	U4A	LDA	GIVEUPTIME	
149		JMP	HOLDC	Wait GIVEUPTIME units.
150	U4	LDA	0,6(IN)	*U4. Give up.*
151		DECA	0,4	IN(C) − FLOOR.
152		JANZ	*+3	
153		LDA	D1	FLOOR = IN(C).
154		JANZ	U4A	See exercise 7.
155	U6	JMP	DELETE	*U6. Get out.* NODE(C) is deleted
156		LDA	AVAIL	from QUEUE or ELEVATOR.
157		STA	0,6(RLINK1)	AVAIL ⇐ C.
158		ST6	AVAIL	
159		JMP	CYCLE	Continue simulation.
160	U5	JMP	DELETE	*U5. Get in.* NODE(C) is deleted
161		ENT1	ELEVATOR	from QUEUE.
162		JMP	INSERT	Insert it at right of ELEVATOR.
163		ENTA	1	
164		LD2	3,6(OUT)	
165		STA	CALL,2(3:3)	Set CALLCAR[OUT(C)] ← 1.
166		J5NZ	CYCLE	Jump if STATE ≠ NEUTRAL.
167		DEC2	0,4	rI2 ← OUT(C) − FLOOR.
168		ENT5	0,2	Set STATE to proper direction.
169		ENT6	ELEV2	Set C ← LOC(ELEV2).
170		JMP	DELETEW	Remove E5 action from WAIT list.
171		ENTA	25	
172		JMP	E5A	Restart E5 action 25 units from now. ▌

The program for Coroutine E is a rather straightforward rendition of the semiformal description given earlier. Perhaps the most interesting portion is the preparation for the elevator's independent actions in step E3, and the searching of the ELEVATOR and QUEUE lists in step E4.

173	* COROUTINE E		
174	E1A	JMP	CYCLE1	Set NEXTINST ← E1, go to CYCLE.
175	E1	EQU	*	*E1. Wait for call.* (no action)
176	E2A	JMP	HOLDC	
177	E2	J5N	1F	*E2. Change of state?*
178		LDA	CALL+1,4	State is GOINGUP.
179		ADD	CALL+2,4	
180		ADD	CALL+3,4	
181		ADD	CALL+4,4	
182		JAP	E3	Are there calls for higher floors?

```
183        LDA   CALL-1,4(3:3)        If not, have passengers in the
184        ADD   CALL-2,4(3:3)            elevator called for lower floors?
185        ADD   CALL-3,4(3:3)
186        ADD   CALL-4,4(3:3)
187        JMP   2F
188   1H   LDA   CALL-1,4             State is GOINGDOWN.
189        ADD   CALL-2,4             Actions are like lines 178-186.
      ⋮
196        ADD   CALL+4,4(3:3)
197   2H   ENN5  0,5                  Reverse direction of STATE.
198        STZ   CALL,4               Set CALL variables to zero.
199        JANZ  E3                   Jump if called to the opposite direction;
200        ENT5  0                        otherwise set STATE ← NEUTRAL.
201   E3   ENT6  ELEV3                E3. Open doors.
202        LDA   0,6                  If activity E9 is already scheduled,
203        JANZ  DELETEW                  remove it from the WAIT list.
204        ENTA  300
205        JMP   HOLD                 Schedule activity E9 after 300 units.
206        ENT6  ELEV2
207        ENTA  76
208        JMP   HOLD                 Schedule activity E5 after 76 units.
209        ST6   D2                   Set D2 nonzero.
210        ST6   D1                   Set D1 nonzero.
211        ENTA  20
212   E4A  ENT6  ELEV1
213        JMP   HOLDC
214   E4   ENTA  0,4                  E4. Let people out, in.
215        SLA   4                    Set OUT field of rA to FLOOR.
216        ENT6  ELEVATOR             C ← LOC(ELEVATOR).
217   1H   LD6   3,6(LLINK2)          C ← LLINK2(C).
218        CMP6  =ELEVATOR=           Search ELEVATOR list, right to left.
219        JE    1F                   If C = LOC(ELEVATOR), search is complete.
220        CMPA  3,6(OUT)             Compare OUT(C) with FLOOR.
221        JNE   1B                   If not equal, continue searching;
222        ENTA  U6                       otherwise prepare to send user to U6.
223        JMP   2F
224   1H   LD6   QUEUE+3,4(RLINK2)    Set C ← RLINK2(LOC(QUEUE[FLOOR])).
225        CMP6  3,6(RLINK2)          Is C = RLINK2(C)?
226        JE    1F                   If so, the queue is empty.
227        JMP   DELETEW              If not, cancel action U4 for this user.
228        ENTA  U5                   Prepare to replace U4 by U5.
229   2H   STA   2,6(NEXTINST)        Set NEXTINST(C).
230        JMP   IMMED                Put user at the front of the WAIT list.
231        ENTA  25
232        JMP   E4A                  Wait 25 units and repeat E4.
233   1H   STZ   D1                   Set D1 ← 0.
234        ST6   D3                   Set D3 nonzero.
235        JMP   CYCLE                Return to simulate other events.
```

236	E5A	JMP	HOLDC
237	E5	LDA	D1
238		JAZ	*+3
239		ENTA	40
240		JMP	E5A
241		STZ	D3
242		ENT6	ELEV1
243		ENTA	20
244		JMP	HOLDC
245	E6	J5N	*+2
246		STZ	CALL,4(1:3)
247		J5P	*+2
248		STZ	CALL,4(3:5)
249		J5Z	DECISION
250	E6B	J5Z	E1A
251		LDA	D2
252		JAZ	*+4
253		ENT6	ELEV3
254		JMP	DELETEW
255		STZ	ELEV3
256		ENT6	ELEV1
257		ENTA	15
258		J5N	E8A
259	E7A	JMP	HOLDC
260	E7	INC4	1
261		ENTA	51
262		JMP	HOLDC
263		LDA	CALL,4(1:3)
264		JAP	1F
265		ENT1	-2,4
266		J1Z	2F
267		LDA	CALL,4(5:5)
268		JAZ	E7
269	2H	LDA	CALL+1,4
270		ADD	CALL+2,4
271		ADD	CALL+3,4
272		ADD	CALL+4,4
273		JANZ	E7
274	1H	ENTA	14
275		JMP	E2A
276	E8A	JMP	HOLDC
⋮			
292		JMP	E2A
293	E9	STZ	0,6
294		STZ	D2
295		JMP	DECISION
296		JMP	CYCLE

E5. Close doors.
Is D1 = 0?
If not, people are still getting in or out.
Wait 40 units, repeat E5.
If D1 = 0, set D3 ← 0.

Wait 20 units, then go to E6.
E6. Prepare to move.
If STATE ≠ GOINGDOWN, CALLUP and CALLCAR
      on this floor are reset.
If ≠ GOINGUP, reset CALLCAR and CALLDOWN.
Perform DECISION subroutine.
If STATE = NEUTRAL, go to E1 and wait.

Otherwise, if D2 ≠ 0,
     cancel activity E9
     (see line 202).

Wait 15 units of time.
If STATE = GOINGDOWN, go to E8.

E7. Go up a floor.

Wait 51 units.
Is CALLCAR[FLOOR] or CALLUP[FLOOR] ≠ 0?
If not,
    is FLOOR = 2?
If not, is CALLDOWN[FLOOR] ≠ 0?
If not, repeat step E7.

Are there calls for higher floors?
It is time to stop the elevator.
Wait 14 units and go to E2.

(See exercise 8.)

E9. Set inaction indicator. (See line 202.)
D2 ← 0.
Perform DECISION subroutine.
Return to simulation of other events. ∎

We will not consider here the DECISION subroutine (see exercise 9), nor the VALUES subroutine that is used to specify the demands on the elevator. At the very end of the program comes the code

```
BEGIN     ENT4 2        Start with FLOOR = 2
          ENT5 0              and STATE = NEUTRAL.
          JMP  CYCLE    Begin simulation.
POOLMAX NOP  POOL
POOL      END  BEGIN    Storage pool follows literals, temp storage.  ▌
```

The program above does a fine job of simulating the elevator system, as it goes through its paces. But it would be useless to run this program, since there is no output! Actually, the author added a PRINT subroutine that was called at most of the critical steps in the program above, and this was used to prepare Table 1; the details have been omitted, since they are very straightforward but they only clutter up the code.

Several programming languages have been devised that make it quite easy to specify the actions in a discrete simulation, and to use a compiler to translate these specifications into machine language. Assembly language was used in this section, of course, since we are concerned here with the basic techniques of linked list manipulation, and we want to see the details of how discrete simulations can actually be performed by a computer that has a one-track mind. The technique of using a WAIT list or agenda to control the sequencing of coroutines, as we have done in this section, is called *quasiparallel processing*.

It is quite difficult to give a precise analysis of the running time of such a long program, because of the complex interactions involved; but large programs often spend most of their time in comparatively short routines doing comparatively simple things. Therefore we can usually get a good indication of the overall efficiency by using a special trace routine called a *profiler*, which executes the program and records how often each instruction is performed. This identifies the "bottlenecks," the places that should be given special attention. [See exercise 1.4.3.2–7. See also *Software Practice & Experience* 1 (1971), 105–133, for examples of such studies on randomly selected FORTRAN programs found in wastebaskets at the Stanford Computer Center.] The author made such an experiment with the elevator program above, running it for 10000 units of simulated elevator time; 26 users entered the simulated system. The instructions in the SORTIN loop, lines 073–075, were executed by far the most often, 1432 times, while the SORTIN subroutine itself was called 437 times. The CYCLE routine was performed 407 times; so we could gain a little speed by not calling the DELETEW subroutine at line 095: The four lines of that subroutine could be written out in full (to save $4u$ each time CYCLE is used). The profiler also showed that the DECISION subroutine was called only 32 times and the loop in E4 (lines 217–219) was executed only 142 times.

It is hoped that some reader will learn as much about simulation from the example above as the author learned about elevators while the example was being prepared.

EXERCISES

1. [*21*] Give specifications for the insertion and deletion of information at the left end of a doubly linked list represented as in (1). (With the dual operations at the right end, which are obtained by symmetry, we therefore have all the actions of a general deque.)

▶ **2.** [*22*] Explain why a list that is singly linked cannot allow efficient operation as a general deque; the deletion of items can be done efficiently at only one end of a singly linked list.

▶ **3.** [*22*] The elevator system described in the text uses three call variables, CALLUP, CALLCAR, and CALLDOWN, for each floor, representing buttons that have been pushed by the users in the system. It is conceivable that the elevator actually needs only one or two binary variables for the call buttons on each floor, instead of three. Explain how an experimenter could push buttons in a certain sequence with this elevator system to *prove* that there are three independent binary variables for each floor (except the top and bottom floors).

4. [*24*] Activity E9 in the elevator coroutine is usually canceled by step E6; and even when it hasn't been canceled, it doesn't do very much. Explain under what circumstances the elevator would behave differently if activity E9 were deleted from the system. Would it, for example, sometimes visit floors in a different order?

5. [*20*] In Table 1, user 10 arrived on floor 0 at time 1048. Show that if user 10 had arrived on floor 2 instead of floor 0, the elevator would have gone *up* after receiving its passengers on floor 1, instead of down, in spite of the fact that user 8 wants to go down to floor 0.

6. [*23*] During the time period 1183–1233 in Table 1, users 7, 8, and 9 all get in the elevator on floor 1; then the elevator goes down to floor 0 and only user 8 gets out. Now the elevator stops again on floor 1, presumably to pick up users 7 and 9 who are already aboard; nobody is actually on floor 1 waiting to get in. (This situation occurs not infrequently at Caltech; if you get on the elevator going the wrong way, you must wait for an extra stop as you go by your original floor again.) In many elevator systems, users 7 and 9 would not have boarded the elevator at time 1183, since lights outside the elevator would show that it was going down, not up; those users would have waited until the elevator came back up and stopped for them. On the system described, there are no such lights and it is impossible to tell which way the elevator is going to go until you are in it; hence Table 1 reflects the actual situation.

What changes should be made to coroutines U and E if we were to simulate the same elevator system, but with indicator lights, so that people do not get on the elevator when its state is contrary to their desired direction?

7. [*25*] Although bugs in programs are often embarrassing to a programmer, if we are to learn from our mistakes we should record them and tell other people about them instead of forgetting them. The following error (among others) was made by the author when he first wrote the program in this section: Line 154 said 'JANZ CYCLE' instead of 'JANZ U4A'. The reasoning was that if indeed the elevator had arrived at this user's floor, there was no need to perform the "give up" activity U4 any more, so we could simply go to CYCLE and continue simulating other activities. What was the error?

8. [*21*] Write the code for step E8, lines 277–292, which has been omitted from the program in the text.

9. [*23*] Write the code for the DECISION subroutine, which has been omitted from the program in the text.

10. [*40*] It is perhaps significant to note that although the author had used the elevator system for years and thought he knew it well, it wasn't until he attempted to write this section that he realized there were quite a few facts about the elevator's system of choosing directions that he did not know. He went back to experiment with the elevator six separate times, each time believing he had finally achieved a complete understanding of its *modus operandi*. (Now he is reluctant to ride it for fear that some new facet of its operation will appear, contradicting the algorithms given.) We often fail to realize how little we know about a thing until we attempt to simulate it on a computer.

Try to specify the actions of some elevator you are familiar with. Check the algorithm by experiments with the elevator itself (looking at its circuitry is not fair!); then design a discrete simulator for the system and run it on a computer.

▶ **11.** [*21*] (*A sparse-update memory.*) The following problem often arises in *synchronous* simulations: The system has n variables $V[1], \ldots, V[n]$, and at every simulated step new values for some of them are calculated from the old values. These calculations are assumed done "simultaneously" in the sense that the variables do not change to their new values until after all assignments have been made. Thus, the two statements

$$V[1] \leftarrow V[2] \qquad \text{and} \qquad V[2] \leftarrow V[1]$$

appearing at the same simulated time would interchange the values of $V[1]$ and $V[2]$; this is quite different from what would happen in a sequential calculation.

The desired action can of course be simulated by keeping an additional table $NEWV[1], \ldots, NEWV[n]$. Before each simulated step, we could set $NEWV[k] \leftarrow V[k]$ for $1 \le k \le n$, then record all changes of $V[k]$ in $NEWV[k]$, and finally, after the step we could set $V[k] \leftarrow NEWV[k]$, $1 \le k \le n$. But this "brute force" approach is not completely satisfactory, for the following reasons: (1) Often n is very large, but the number of variables changed per step is rather small. (2) The variables are often not arranged in a nice table $V[1], \ldots, V[n]$, but are scattered throughout memory in a rather chaotic fashion. (3) This method does not detect the situation (usually an error in the model) when one variable is given two values in the same simulated step.

Assuming that the number of variables changed per step is rather small, design an efficient algorithm that simulates the desired actions, using two auxiliary tables $NEWV[k]$ and $LINK[k]$, $1 \le k \le n$. If possible, your algorithm should give an error stop if the same variable is being given two different values in the same step.

▶ **12.** [*22*] Why is it a good idea to use doubly linked lists instead of singly linked or sequential lists in the simulation program of this section?

2.2.6. Arrays and Orthogonal Lists

One of the simplest generalizations of a linear list is a two-dimensional or higher-dimensional array of information. For example, consider the case of an $m \times n$ matrix

$$
\begin{pmatrix}
A[1,1] & A[1,2] & \ldots & A[1,n] \\
A[2,1] & A[2,2] & \ldots & A[2,n] \\
\vdots & \vdots & & \vdots \\
A[m,1] & A[m,2] & \ldots & A[m,n]
\end{pmatrix}. \tag{1}
$$

In this two-dimensional array, each node $A[j,k]$ belongs to two linear lists: the "row j" list $A[j,1]$, $A[j,2]$, ..., $A[j,n]$ and the "column k" list $A[1,k]$, $A[2,k]$, ..., $A[m,k]$. These orthogonal row and column lists essentially account for the two-dimensional structure of a matrix. Similar remarks apply to higher-dimensional arrays of information.

Sequential Allocation. When an array like (1) is stored in *sequential* memory locations, storage is usually allocated so that

$$\text{LOC}(A[J,K]) = a_0 + a_1 J + a_2 K, \tag{2}$$

where a_0, a_1, and a_2 are constants. Let us consider a more general case: Suppose we have a four-dimensional array with one-word elements $Q[I,J,K,L]$ for $0 \leq I \leq 2$, $0 \leq J \leq 4$, $0 \leq K \leq 10$, $0 \leq L \leq 2$. We would like to allocate storage so that

$$\text{LOC}(Q[I,J,K,L]) = a_0 + a_1 I + a_2 J + a_3 K + a_4 L. \tag{3}$$

This means that a change in I, J, K, or L leads to a readily calculated change in the location of $Q[I,J,K,L]$. The most natural (and most commonly used) way to allocate storage is to arrange the array elements according to the lexicographic order of their indices (exercise 1.2.1–15(d)), sometimes called "row major order":

$$Q[0,0,0,0], \; Q[0,0,0,1], \; Q[0,0,0,2], \; Q[0,0,1,0], \; Q[0,0,1,1], \; \ldots,$$
$$Q[0,0,10,2], \; Q[0,1,0,0], \; \ldots, \; Q[0,4,10,2], \; Q[1,0,0,0], \; \ldots,$$
$$Q[2,4,10,2].$$

It is easy to see that this order satisfies the requirements of (3), and we have

$$\text{LOC}(Q[I,J,K,L]) = \text{LOC}(Q[0,0,0,0]) + 165I + 33J + 3K + L. \tag{4}$$

In general, given a k-dimensional array with c-word elements $A[I_1, I_2, \ldots, I_k]$ for

$$0 \leq I_1 \leq d_1, \quad 0 \leq I_2 \leq d_2, \quad \ldots, \quad 0 \leq I_k \leq d_k,$$

we can store it in memory as

$$\begin{aligned}
\text{LOC}&(A[I_1, I_2, \ldots, I_k]) \\
&= \text{LOC}(A[0,0,\ldots,0]) + c(d_2+1)\ldots(d_k+1)I_1 + \cdots + c(d_k+1)I_{k-1} + cI_k \\
&= \text{LOC}(A[0,0,\ldots,0]) + \sum_{1 \leq r \leq k} a_r I_r,
\end{aligned} \tag{5}$$

where

$$a_r = c \prod_{r < s \leq k} (d_s + 1). \tag{6}$$

To see why this formula works, observe that a_r is the amount of memory needed to store the subarray $A[I_1, \ldots, I_r, J_{r+1}, \ldots, J_k]$ if $I_1, \ldots, I_r$ are constant and $J_{r+1}, \ldots, J_k$ vary through all values $0 \leq J_{r+1} \leq d_{r+1}, \ldots, 0 \leq J_k \leq d_k$; hence by the nature of lexicographic order the address of $A[I_1, \ldots, I_k]$ should change by precisely this amount when I_r changes by 1.

When $c = 1$, formulas (5) and (6) correspond to the value of the number $I_1 I_2 \ldots I_k$ in a mixed-radix number system. For example, if we had the array TIME[W,D,H,M,S] with $0 \leq W < 4$, $0 \leq D < 7$, $0 \leq H < 24$, $0 \leq M < 60$, and $0 \leq S < 60$, the location of TIME[W,D,H,M,S] would be the location of TIME[0,0,0,0,0] plus the quantity "W weeks + D days + H hours + M minutes + S seconds" converted to seconds. Of course, it takes a pretty fancy application to make use of an array that has 2,419,200 elements.

The normal method for storing arrays is generally suitable when the array has a complete rectangular structure, so that all elements $A[I_1, I_2, \ldots, I_k]$ are present for indices in the independent ranges $l_1 \leq I_1 \leq u_1$, $l_2 \leq I_2 \leq u_2$, $\ldots$, $l_k \leq I_k \leq u_k$. Exercise 2 shows how to adapt (5) and (6) to the case when the lower bounds $(l_1, l_2, \ldots, l_k)$ are not $(0, 0, \ldots, 0)$.

But there are many situations in which an array is not perfectly rectangular. Most common is the *triangular matrix*, where we want to store only the entries $A[j,k]$ for, say, $0 \leq k \leq j \leq n$:

$$
\begin{pmatrix}
A[0,0] & & & \\
A[1,0] & A[1,1] & & \\
\vdots & \vdots & \ddots & \\
A[n,0] & A[n,1] & \cdots & A[n,n]
\end{pmatrix}.
\tag{7}
$$

We may know that all other entries are zero, or that $A[j,k] = A[k,j]$, so that only half of the values need to be stored. If we want to store the lower triangular matrix (7) in $\frac{1}{2}(n+1)(n+2)$ consecutive memory positions, we are forced to give up the possibility of linear allocation as in Eq. (2), but we can ask instead for an allocation arrangement of the form

$$
\text{LOC}(A[J,K]) = a_0 + f_1(J) + f_2(K)
\tag{8}
$$

where f_1 and f_2 are functions of one variable. (The constant a_0 may be absorbed into either f_1 or f_2 if desired.) When the addressing has the form (8), a random element $A[j,k]$ can be quickly accessed if we keep two (rather short) auxiliary tables of the values of f_1 and f_2; therefore these functions need to be calculated only once.

It turns out that lexicographic order of indices for the array (7) satisfies condition (8), and with one-word entries we have in fact the simple formula

$$
\text{LOC}(A[J,K]) = \text{LOC}(A[0,0]) + \frac{J(J+1)}{2} + K.
\tag{9}
$$

But there is actually a far better way to store triangular matrices, if we are fortunate enough to have two of them with the same size. Suppose that we want to store both $A[j,k]$ and $B[j,k]$ for $0 \leq k \leq j \leq n$. Then we can fit them both into a single matrix $C[j,k]$ for $0 \leq j \leq n$, $0 \leq k \leq n+1$, using the convention

$$
A[j,k] = C[j,k], \qquad B[j,k] = C[k,j+1].
\tag{10}
$$

Thus

$$
\begin{pmatrix}
C[0,0] \; C[0,1] \; C[0,2] \ldots C[0,n{+}1] \\
C[1,0] \; C[1,1] \; C[1,2] \ldots C[1,n{+}1] \\
\vdots \qquad\quad \cdot \qquad\qquad\quad \vdots \\
C[n,0] \; C[n,1] \; C[n,2] \ldots C[n,n{+}1]
\end{pmatrix}
\equiv
\begin{pmatrix}
A[0,0] \; B[0,0] \; B[1,0] \ldots B[n,0] \\
A[1,0] \; A[1,1] \; B[1,1] \ldots B[n,1] \\
\vdots \qquad\qquad\qquad\qquad\quad \vdots \\
A[n,0] \; A[n,1] \; A[n,2] \ldots B[n,n]
\end{pmatrix}.
$$

The two triangular matrices are packed together tightly within the space of $(n+1)(n+2)$ locations, and we have linear addressing as in (2).

The generalization of triangular matrices to higher dimensions is called a *tetrahedral array*. This interesting topic is the subject of exercises 6 through 8.

As an example of typical programming techniques for use with sequentially stored arrays, see exercise 1.3.2–10 and the two answers given for that exercise. The fundamental techniques for efficient traversal of rows and columns, as well as the uses of sequential stacks, are of particular interest within those programs.

Linked Allocation. Linked memory allocation also applies to higher-dimensional arrays of information in a natural way. In general, our nodes can contain k link fields, one for each list the node belongs to. The use of linked memory is generally for cases in which the arrays are not strictly rectangular in character.

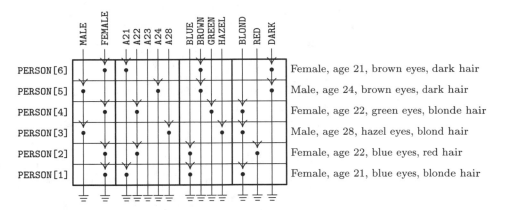

Fig. 13. Each node in four different lists.

As an example, we might have a list in which every node represents a person, with four link fields: SEX, AGE, EYES, and HAIR. In the EYES field we link together all nodes with the same eye color, etc. (See Fig. 13.) It is easy to visualize efficient algorithms for inserting new people into the list; deletion would, however, be much slower, unless we used double linking. We can also conceive of algorithms of varying degrees of efficiency for doing things like "Find all blue-eyed blonde women of ages 21 through 23"; see exercises 9 and 10. Problems in which each node of a list is to reside in several kinds of other lists at once arise rather frequently; indeed, the elevator system simulation described in the preceding section has nodes that are in both the QUEUE and WAIT lists simultaneously.

As a detailed example of the use of linked allocation for orthogonal lists, we will consider the case of *sparse matrices* (that is, matrices of large order in which most of the elements are zero). The goal is to operate on these matrices as though the entire matrix were present, but to save great amounts of time and space because the zero entries need not be represented. One way to do this, intended for random references to elements of the matrix, would be to use the storage and retrieval methods of Chapter 6, to find $A[j,k]$ from the key "$[j, k]$"; however, there is another way to deal with sparse matrices that is often preferable because it reflects the matrix structure more appropriately, and this is the method we will discuss here.

The representation we will discuss consists of circularly linked lists for each row and column. Every node of the matrix contains three words and five fields:

ROW	UP
COL	LEFT
VAL	

(11)

Here ROW and COL are the row and column indices of the node; VAL is the value stored at that part of the matrix; LEFT and UP are links to the next nonzero entry to the left in the row, or upward in the column, respectively. There are special list head nodes, BASEROW[i] and BASECOL[j], for every row and column. These nodes are identified by

$$\text{COL(LOC(BASEROW}[i])) < 0 \qquad \text{and} \qquad \text{ROW(LOC(BASECOL}[j])) < 0.$$

As usual in a circular list, the LEFT link in BASEROW[i] is the location of the rightmost value in that row, and UP in BASECOL[j] points to the bottom-most value in that column. For example, the matrix

$$\begin{pmatrix} 50 & 0 & 0 & 0 \\ 10 & 0 & 20 & 0 \\ 0 & 0 & 0 & 0 \\ -30 & 0 & -60 & 5 \end{pmatrix}$$

(12)

would be represented as shown in Fig. 14.

Using sequential allocation of storage, a 200×200 matrix would take 40000 words, and this is more memory than many computers used to have; but a suitably sparse 200×200 matrix can be represented as above even in MIX's 4000-word memory. (See exercise 11.) The amount of time taken to access a random element $A[j,k]$ is also quite reasonable, *if* there are but few elements in each row or column; and since most matrix algorithms proceed by walking sequentially through a matrix, instead of accessing elements at random, this linked representation often works faster than a sequential one.

As a typical example of a nontrivial algorithm dealing with sparse matrices in this form, we will consider the *pivot step* operation, which is an important part of algorithms for solving linear equations, for inverting matrices, and for solving

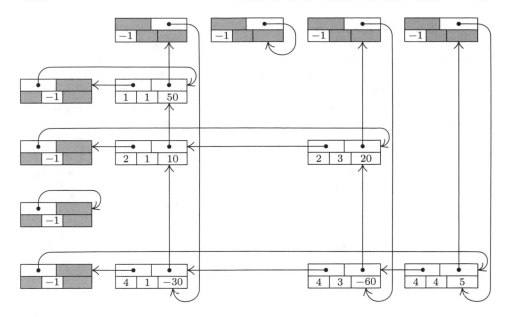

LEFT	UP
ROW	COL	VAL

Fig. 14. Representation of matrix (12), with nodes in the format [table above].
List heads appear at the left and at the top.

linear programming problems by the simplex method. A pivot step is the following matrix transformation (see M. H. Doolittle, *Report of the Superintendent of
the U.S. Coast and Geodetic Survey* (1878), 115–120):

<table>
<tr><td></td><td colspan="2">Before pivot step</td><td colspan="2">After pivot step</td></tr>
<tr><td></td><td>Pivot
column</td><td>Any
other
column</td><td>Pivot
column</td><td>Any
other
column</td></tr>
</table>

$$\begin{pmatrix} & \vdots & & \vdots & \\ \cdots & a & \cdots & b & \cdots \\ & \vdots & & \vdots & \\ \cdots & c & \cdots & d & \cdots \\ & \vdots & & \vdots & \end{pmatrix}, \quad \begin{pmatrix} & \vdots & & \vdots & \\ \cdots & 1/a & \cdots & b/a & \cdots \\ & \vdots & & \vdots & \\ \cdots & -c/a & \cdots & d - bc/a & \cdots \\ & \vdots & & \vdots & \end{pmatrix}$$

Pivot row ··· a ··· b ··· , ··· $1/a$ ··· b/a ···

Any other row ··· c ··· d ··· ··· $-c/a$ ··· $d - bc/a$ ···

$$(13)$$

It is assumed that the *pivot element*, a, is nonzero. For example, a pivot step
applied to matrix (12), with the element 10 in row 2 column 1 as pivot, leads to

$$\begin{pmatrix} -5 & 0 & -100 & 0 \\ 0.1 & 0 & 2 & 0 \\ 0 & 0 & 0 & 0 \\ 3 & 0 & 0 & 5 \end{pmatrix}. \tag{14}$$

Our goal is to design an algorithm that performs this pivot operation on sparse matrices that are represented as in Fig. 14. It is clear that the transformation (13) affects only those rows of a matrix for which there is a nonzero element in the pivot column, and it affects only those columns for which there is a nonzero entry in the pivot row.

The pivoting algorithm is in many ways a straightforward application of linking techniques we have already discussed; in particular, it bears strong resemblances to Algorithm 2.2.4A for addition of polynomials. There are two things, however, that make the problem a little tricky: If in (13) we have $b \neq 0$ and $c \neq 0$ but $d = 0$, the sparse matrix representation has no entry for d and we must insert a new entry; and if $b \neq 0$, $c \neq 0$, $d \neq 0$, but $d - bc/a = 0$, we must delete the entry that was formerly there. These insertion and deletion operations are more interesting in a two-dimensional array than in the one-dimensional case; to do them we must know what links are affected. Our algorithm processes the matrix rows successively from bottom to top. The efficient ability to insert and delete involves the introduction of a set of pointer variables $\texttt{PTR}[j]$, one for each column considered; these variables traverse the columns upwards, giving us the ability to update the proper links in both dimensions.

Algorithm S (*Pivot step in a sparse matrix*). Given a matrix represented as in Fig. 14, we perform the pivot operation (13). Assume that $\texttt{PIVOT}$ is a link variable pointing to the pivot element. The algorithm makes use of an auxiliary table of link variables $\texttt{PTR}[j]$, one for each column of the matrix. The variable $\texttt{ALPHA}$ and the $\texttt{VAL}$ field of each node are assumed to be floating point or rational quantities, while everything else in this algorithm has integer values.

S1. [Initialize.] Set $\texttt{ALPHA} \leftarrow 1.0/\texttt{VAL(PIVOT)}$, $\texttt{VAL(PIVOT)} \leftarrow 1.0$, and

$$\texttt{I0} \leftarrow \texttt{ROW(PIVOT)}, \quad \texttt{P0} \leftarrow \texttt{LOC(BASEROW[I0])};$$
$$\texttt{J0} \leftarrow \texttt{COL(PIVOT)}, \quad \texttt{Q0} \leftarrow \texttt{LOC(BASECOL[J0])}.$$

S2. [Process pivot row.] Set $\texttt{P0} \leftarrow \texttt{LEFT(P0)}$, $\texttt{J} \leftarrow \texttt{COL(P0)}$. If $\texttt{J} < 0$, go on to step S3 (the pivot row has been traversed). Otherwise set $\texttt{PTR[J]} \leftarrow \texttt{LOC(BASECOL[J])}$ and $\texttt{VAL(P0)} \leftarrow \texttt{ALPHA} \times \texttt{VAL(P0)}$, and repeat step S2.

S3. [Find new row.] Set $\texttt{Q0} \leftarrow \texttt{UP(Q0)}$. (The remainder of the algorithm deals successively with each row, from bottom to top, for which there is an entry in the pivot column.) Set $\texttt{I} \leftarrow \texttt{ROW(Q0)}$. If $\texttt{I} < 0$, the algorithm terminates. If $\texttt{I} = \texttt{I0}$, repeat step S3 (we have already done the pivot row). Otherwise set $\texttt{P} \leftarrow \texttt{LOC(BASEROW[I])}$, $\texttt{P1} \leftarrow \texttt{LEFT(P)}$. (The pointers P and P1 will now proceed across row I from right to left, as P0 goes in synchronization across row I0; Algorithm 2.2.4A is analogous. We have $\texttt{P0} = \texttt{LOC(BASEROW[I0])}$ at this point.)

S4. [Find new column.] Set $\texttt{P0} \leftarrow \texttt{LEFT(P0)}$, $\texttt{J} \leftarrow \texttt{COL(P0)}$. If $\texttt{J} < 0$, set $\texttt{VAL(Q0)} \leftarrow -\texttt{ALPHA} \times \texttt{VAL(Q0)}$ and return to S3. If $\texttt{J} = \texttt{J0}$, repeat step S4. (Thus we process the pivot column entry in row I *after* all other column entries have been processed; the reason is that $\texttt{VAL(Q0)}$ is needed in step S7.)

S5. [Find I, J element.] If COL(P1) > J, set P ← P1, P1 ← LEFT(P), and repeat step S5. If COL(P1) = J, go to step S7. Otherwise go to step S6 (we need to insert a new element in column J of row I).

S6. [Insert I, J element.] If ROW(UP(PTR[J])) > I, set PTR[J] ← UP(PTR[J]), and repeat step S6. (Otherwise, we will have ROW(UP(PTR[J])) < I; the new element is to be inserted just above NODE(PTR[J]) in the vertical dimension, and just left of NODE(P) in the horizontal dimension.) Otherwise set X ⇐ AVAIL, VAL(X) ← 0, ROW(X) ← I, COL(X) ← J, LEFT(X) ← P1, UP(X) ← UP(PTR[J]), LEFT(P) ← X, UP(PTR[J]) ← X, P1 ← X.

S7. [Pivot.] Set VAL(P1) ← VAL(P1) − VAL(Q0) × VAL(P0). If now VAL(P1) = 0, go to S8. (*Note:* When floating point arithmetic is being used, this test "VAL(P1) = 0" should be replaced by "|VAL(P1)| < EPSILON" or better yet by the condition "most of the significant figures of VAL(P1) were lost in the subtraction.") Otherwise, set PTR[J] ← P1, P ← P1, P1 ← LEFT(P), and go back to S4.

S8. [Delete I, J element.] If UP(PTR[J]) ≠ P1 (or, what is essentially the same thing, if ROW(UP(PTR[J])) > I), set PTR[J] ← UP(PTR[J]) and repeat step S8; otherwise, set UP(PTR[J]) ← UP(P1), LEFT(P) ← LEFT(P1), AVAIL ⇐ P1, P1 ← LEFT(P). Go back to S4. ∎

The programming of this algorithm is left as a very instructive exercise for the reader (see exercise 15). It is worth pointing out here that it is necessary to allocate only one word of memory to each of the nodes BASEROW[i], BASECOL[j], since most of their fields are irrelevant. (See the shaded areas in Fig. 14, and see the program of Section 2.2.5.) Furthermore, the value −PTR[j] can be stored as ROW(LOC(BASECOL[j])) for additional storage space economy. The running time of Algorithm S is very roughly proportional to the number of matrix elements affected by the pivot operation.

This representation of sparse matrices via orthogonal circular lists is instructive, but numerical analysts have developed better methods. See Fred G. Gustavson, *ACM Trans. on Math. Software* **4** (1978), 250–269; see also the graph and network algorithms in Chapter 7 (for example, Algorithm 7B).

EXERCISES

1. [*17*] Give a formula for LOC(A[J,K]) if A is the matrix of (1), and if each node of the array is two words long, assuming that the nodes are stored consecutively in lexicographic order of the indices.

▶ **2.** [*21*] Formulas (5) and (6) have been derived from the assumption that $0 \leq I_r \leq d_r$ for $1 \leq r \leq k$. Give a general formula that applies to the case $l_r \leq I_r \leq u_r$, where l_r and u_r are any lower and upper bounds on the dimensionality.

3. [*21*] The text considers lower triangular matrices A[j,k] for $0 \leq k \leq j \leq n$. How can the discussion of such matrices readily be modified for the case that subscripts start at 1 instead of 0, so that $1 \leq k \leq j \leq n$?

4. [*22*] Show that if we store the *upper* triangular array A[j,k] for $0 \leq j \leq k \leq n$ in lexicographic order of the indices, the allocation satisfies the condition of Eq. (8). Find a formula for LOC(A[J,K]) in this sense.

5. [*20*] Show that it is possible to bring the value of A[J,K] into register A in one MIX instruction, using the indirect addressing feature of exercise 2.2.2–3, even when A is a *triangular* matrix as in (9). (Assume that the values of J and K are in index registers.)

▶ **6.** [*M24*] Consider the "tetrahedral arrays" A[i,j,k], B[i,j,k], where $0 \le k \le j \le i \le n$ in A, and $0 \le i \le j \le k \le n$ in B. Suppose that both of these arrays are stored in consecutive memory locations in lexicographic order of the indices; show that LOC(A[I,J,K]) $= a_0 + f_1(\text{I}) + f_2(\text{J}) + f_3(\text{K})$ for certain functions f_1, f_2, f_3. Can LOC(B[I,J,K]) be expressed in a similar manner?

7. [*M23*] Find a general formula to allocate storage for the k-dimensional tetrahedral array A[$i_1,i_2,\ldots,i_k$], where $0 \le i_k \le \cdots \le i_2 \le i_1 \le n$.

8. [*33*] (P. Wegner.) Suppose we have six tetrahedral arrays A[I,J,K], B[I,J,K], C[I,J,K], D[I,J,K], E[I,J,K], and F[I,J,K] to store in memory, where $0 \le \text{K} \le \text{J} \le \text{I} \le n$. Is there a neat way to accomplish this, analogous to (10) in the two-dimensional case?

9. [*22*] Suppose a table, like that indicated in Fig. 13 but much larger, has been set up so that all links go in the same direction as shown there (namely, LINK(X) < X for all nodes and links). Design an algorithm that finds the addresses of all blue-eyed blonde women of ages 21 through 23, by going through the various link fields in such a way that upon completion of the algorithm at most one pass has been made through each of the lists FEMALE, A21, A22, A23, BLOND, and BLUE.

10. [*26*] Can you think of a better way to organize a personnel table so that searches as described in the previous exercise would be more efficient? (The answer to this exercise is *not* merely "yes" or "no.")

11. [*11*] Suppose that we have a 200 × 200 matrix in which there are at most four nonzero entries per row. How much storage is required to represent this matrix as in Fig. 14, if we use three words per node except for list heads, which will use one word?

▶ **12.** [*20*] What are VAL(Q0), VAL(P0), and VAL(P1) at the beginning of step S7, in terms of the notation a, b, c, d used in (13)?

▶ **13.** [*22*] Why were circular lists used in Fig. 14 instead of straight linear lists? Could Algorithm S be rewritten so that it does not make use of the circular linkage?

14. [*22*] Algorithm S actually saves pivoting time in a sparse matrix, since it avoids consideration of those columns in which the pivot row has a zero entry. Show that this savings in running time can be achieved in a large sparse matrix that is stored sequentially, with the help of an auxiliary table LINK[j], $1 \le j \le n$.

▶ **15.** [*29*] Write a MIXAL program for Algorithm S. Assume that the VAL field is a floating point number, and that MIX's floating point arithmetic operators FADD, FSUB, FMUL, and FDIV can be used for operations on this field. Assume for simplicity that FADD and FSUB return the answer zero when the operands added or subtracted cancel most of the significance, so that the test "VAL(P1) = 0" may safely be used in step S7. The floating point operations use only rA, not rX.

16. [*25*] Design an algorithm to *copy* a sparse matrix. (In other words, the algorithm is to yield two distinct representations of a matrix in memory, having the form of Fig. 14, given just one such representation initially.)

17. [*26*] Design an algorithm to *multiply* two sparse matrices; given matrices A and B, form a new matrix C, where C[i,j] $= \sum_k$ A[i,k]B[k,j]. The two input matrices and the output matrix should be represented as in Fig. 14.

18. [22] The following algorithm replaces a matrix by the inverse of that matrix, assuming that the entries are $A[i,j]$, for $1 \le i,j \le n$:

i) For $k = 1, 2, \ldots, n$ do the following: Search row k in all columns not yet used as a pivot column, to find an entry with the greatest absolute value; set $C[k]$ equal to the column in which this entry was found, and do a pivot step with this entry as pivot. (If all such entries are zero, the matrix is singular and has no inverse.)

ii) Permute rows and columns so that what was row k becomes row $C[k]$, and what was column $C[k]$ becomes column k.

The problem in this exercise is to use the stated algorithm to invert the matrix

$$\begin{pmatrix} 1 & 2 & 3 \\ 0 & 1 & 2 \\ 0 & 0 & 1 \end{pmatrix}$$

by hand calculation.

19. [31] Modify the algorithm described in exercise 18 so that it obtains the inverse of a sparse matrix that is represented in the form of Fig. 14. Pay special attention to making the row- and column-permutation operations of step (ii) efficient.

20. [20] A *tridiagonal matrix* has entries a_{ij} that are zero except when $|i - j| < 1$, for $1 \le i,j \le n$. Show that there is an allocation function of the form

$$\texttt{LOC}(\texttt{A[I,J]}) = a_0 + a_1 I + a_2 J, \quad |I - J| \le 1,$$

which represents all of the relevant elements of a tridiagonal matrix in $(3n - 2)$ consecutive locations.

21. [20] Suggest a storage allocation function for $n \times n$ matrices where n is variable. The elements $A[I,J]$ for $1 \le I, J \le n$ should occupy n^2 consecutive locations, regardless of the value of n.

22. [M25] (P. Chowla, 1961.) Find a polynomial $p(i_1,\ldots,i_k)$ that assumes each nonnegative integer value exactly once as the indices $(i_1,\ldots,i_k)$ run through all k-dimensional nonnegative integer vectors, with the additional property that $i_1 + \cdots + i_k < j_1 + \cdots + j_k$ implies $p(i_1,\ldots,i_k) < p(j_1,\ldots,j_k)$.

23. [23] An *extendible matrix* is initially 1×1, then it grows from size $m \times n$ either to size $(m+1) \times n$ or to size $m \times (n+1)$ by adding either a new row or a new column. Show that such a matrix can be given a simple allocation function in which the elements $A[I,J]$ occupy mn consecutive locations, for $0 \le I < m$ and $0 \le J < n$; no elements change location when the matrix grows.

▶ **24.** [25] (*The sparse array trick.*) Suppose you want to use a large array for random access, although you won't actually be referring to very many of its entries. You want $A[k]$ to be zero the first time you access it, yet you don't want to spend the time to set every location to zero. Explain how it is possible to read and write any desired elements $A[k]$ reliably, given k, without assuming anything about the actual initial memory contents, by doing only a small fixed number of additional operations per array access.

2.3. TREES

WE NOW TURN to a study of trees, the most important nonlinear structures that arise in computer algorithms. Generally speaking, tree structure means a "branching" relationship between nodes, much like that found in the trees of nature.

Let us define a *tree* formally as a finite set T of one or more nodes such that

a) there is one specially designated node called the *root* of the tree, root(T); and

b) the remaining nodes (excluding the root) are partitioned into $m \geq 0$ disjoint sets $T_1, \ldots, T_m$, and each of these sets in turn is a tree. The trees $T_1, \ldots, T_m$ are called the *subtrees* of the root.

The definition just given is recursive: We have defined a tree in terms of trees. Of course, there is no problem of circularity involved here, since trees with one node must consist of only the root, and trees with $n > 1$ nodes are defined in terms of trees with fewer than n nodes; hence the concept of a tree with two nodes, three nodes, or ultimately any number of nodes, is determined by the definition given. There are nonrecursive ways to define trees (for example, see exercises 10, 12, and 14, and Section 2.3.4), but a recursive definition seems most appropriate since recursion is an innate characteristic of tree structures. The recursive character of trees is present also in nature, since buds on young trees eventually grow into subtrees with buds of their own, and so on. Exercise 3 illustrates how to give rigorous proofs of important facts about trees based on a recursive definition such as the one above, by using induction on the number of nodes in a tree.

It follows from our definition that every node of a tree is the root of some subtree contained in the whole tree. The number of subtrees of a node is called the *degree* of that node. A node of degree zero is called a *terminal node*, or sometimes a *leaf*. A nonterminal node is often called a *branch node*. The *level* of a node with respect to T is defined recursively: The level of root(T) is zero, and the level of any other node is one higher than that node's level with respect to the subtree of root(T) containing it.

These concepts are illustrated in Fig. 15, which shows a tree with seven nodes. The root is A, and it has the two subtrees $\{B\}$ and $\{C, D, E, F, G\}$. The tree $\{C, D, E, F, G\}$ has node C as its root. Node C is on level 1 with respect to the whole tree, and it has three subtrees $\{D\}$, $\{E\}$, and $\{F, G\}$; therefore C has degree 3. The terminal nodes in Fig. 15 are B, D, E, and G; F is the only node with degree 1; G is the only node with level 3.

If the relative order of the subtrees $T_1, \ldots, T_m$ in (b) of the definition is important, we say that the tree is an *ordered tree*; when $m \geq 2$ in an ordered tree, it makes sense to call T_2 the "second subtree" of the root, etc. Ordered trees are also called "plane trees" by some authors, since the manner of embedding the tree in a plane is relevant. If we do not care to regard two trees as different when they differ only in the respective ordering of subtrees of nodes, the tree is said to be *oriented*, since only the relative orientation of the nodes, not their

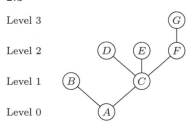

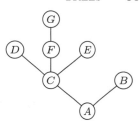

Level 3

Level 2

Level 1

Level 0

Fig. 15. A tree.

Fig. 16. Another tree.

order, is being considered. The very nature of computer representation defines an implicit ordering for any tree, so in most cases ordered trees are of greatest interest to us. We will therefore tacitly assume that *all trees we discuss are ordered, unless explicitly stated otherwise.* Accordingly, the trees of Figs. 15 and 16 will generally be considered to be different, although they would be the same as oriented trees.

A *forest* is a set (usually an ordered set) of zero or more disjoint trees. Another way to phrase part (b) of the definition of tree would be to say that *the nodes of a tree excluding the root form a forest.*

There is very little distinction between abstract forests and trees. If we delete the root of a tree, we have a forest; conversely, if we add just one node to any forest and regard the trees of the forest as subtrees of the new node, we get a tree. Therefore the words tree and forest are often used almost interchangeably during informal discussions about data structures.

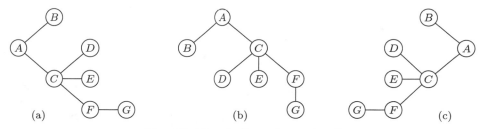

Fig. 17. How shall we draw a tree?

Trees can be drawn in many ways. Besides the diagram of Fig. 15, three of the principal alternatives are shown in Fig. 17, depending on where the root is placed. It is not a frivolous joke to worry about how tree structures are drawn in diagrams, since there are many occasions in which we want to say that one node is "above" or "higher than" another node, or to refer to the "rightmost" element, etc. Certain algorithms for dealing with tree structures have become known as "top down" methods, as opposed to "bottom up." Such terminology leads to confusion unless we adhere to a uniform convention for drawing trees.

It may seem that the form of Fig. 15 would be preferable simply because that is how trees grow in nature; in the absence of any compelling reason to adopt any of the other three forms, we might as well adopt nature's time-honored

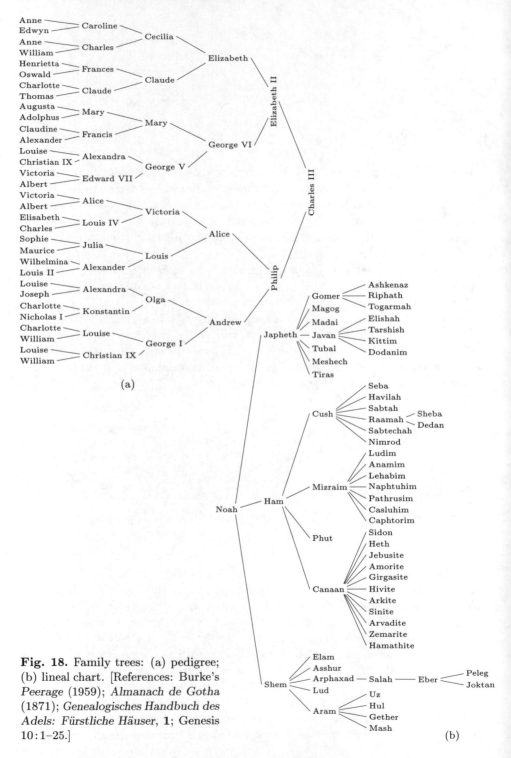

(a)

Fig. 18. Family trees: (a) pedigree; (b) lineal chart. [References: Burke's *Peerage* (1959); *Almanach de Gotha* (1871); *Genealogisches Handbuch des Adels: Fürstliche Häuser*, **1**; Genesis 10:1–25.]

(b)

tradition. With real trees in mind, the author consistently followed a root-at-the-bottom convention as the present set of books was first being prepared, but after two years of trial it was found to be a mistake: Observations of the computer literature and numerous informal discussions with computer scientists about a wide variety of algorithms showed that trees were drawn with the *root at the top* in more than 80 percent of the cases examined. There is an overwhelming tendency to make hand-drawn charts grow downwards instead of upwards (and this is easy to understand in view of the way we write); even the word "subtree," as opposed to "supertree," tends to connote a downward relationship. From these considerations we conclude that *Fig. 15 is upside down*. Henceforth we will almost always draw trees as in Fig. 17(b), with the root at the top and leaves at the bottom. Corresponding to this orientation, we should perhaps call the root node the *apex* of the tree, and speak of nodes at *shallow* and *deep* levels.

It is necessary to have good descriptive terminology for talking about trees. Instead of making somewhat ambiguous references to "above" and "below," we generally use genealogical words taken from the terminology of *family trees*. Figure 18 shows two common types of family trees. The two types are quite different: A *pedigree* shows the ancestors of a given individual, while a *lineal chart* shows the descendants.

If "cross-breeding" occurs, a pedigree is not really a tree, because different branches of a tree (as we have defined it) can never be joined together. To compensate for this discrepancy, Fig. 18(a) mentions Queen Victoria and Prince Albert twice in the sixth generation; King Christian IX and Queen Louise actually appear in both the fifth and sixth generations. A pedigree can be regarded as a true tree if each of its nodes represents "a person in the role of mother or father of so-and-so," not simply a person as an individual.

Standard terminology for tree structures is taken from the *second* form of family tree, the lineal chart: Each root is said to be the *parent* of the roots of its subtrees, and the latter are said to be *siblings*; they are *children* of their parent. The root of the entire tree has no parent. For example, in Fig. 19, C has three children, D, E, and F; E is the parent of G; B and C are siblings. Extension of this terminology — for example, A is the great-grandparent of G; B is an aunt or uncle of F; H and F are first cousins — is clearly possible. Some authors use the masculine designations "father, son, brother" instead of "parent, child, sibling"; others use "mother, daughter, sister." In any case a node has at most one parent or progenitor. We use the words *ancestor* and *descendant* to denote a relationship that may span several levels of the tree: The descendants of C in Fig. 19 are D, E, F, and G; the ancestors of G are E, C, and A. Sometimes, especially when talking

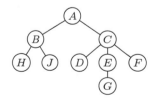

Fig. 19. Conventional tree diagram.

about "nearest common ancestors," we consider a node to be an ancestor of itself (and a descendant of itself); the *inclusive ancestors* of G are G, E, C, and A, while its *proper ancestors* are just E, C, and A.

The pedigree in Figure 18(a) is an example of a *binary tree*, which is another important type of tree structure. The reader has undoubtedly seen binary trees in connection with tennis tournaments or other sporting events. In a binary tree each node has at most two subtrees; and when only one subtree is present, we distinguish between the left and right subtree. More formally, let us define a binary tree as *a finite set of nodes that either is empty, or consists of a root and the elements of two disjoint binary trees* called the left and right subtrees of the root.

This recursive definition of binary tree should be studied carefully. Notice that a binary tree is *not* a special case of a tree; it is another concept entirely (although we will see many relations between the two concepts). For example, the binary trees

$$\overset{\textstyle\widehat{A}}{\underset{\textstyle\widehat{B}}{\diagup}} \qquad \text{and} \qquad \overset{\textstyle\widehat{A}}{\underset{\textstyle\widehat{B}}{\diagdown}} \tag{1}$$

are distinct — the root has an empty right subtree in one case and a nonempty right subtree in the other — although as trees these diagrams would represent identical structures. A binary tree can be empty; a tree cannot. Therefore we will always be careful to use the word "binary" to distinguish between binary trees and ordinary trees. Some authors define binary trees in a slightly different manner (see exercise 20).

Tree structure can be represented graphically in several other ways bearing no resemblance to actual trees. Figure 20 shows three diagrams that reflect the structure of Fig. 19: Figure 20(a) essentially represents Fig. 19 as an *oriented tree*; this diagram is a special case of the general idea of *nested sets*, namely a collection of sets in which any pair of sets is either disjoint or one contains the other. (See exercise 10.) Part (b) of the figure shows nested sets in a line, much as part (a) shows them in a plane; in part (b) the ordering of the tree is also indicated. Part (b) may also be regarded as an outline of an algebraic formula involving nested parentheses. Part (c) shows still another common way to represent tree structure, using *indentation*. The number of different representation methods in itself is ample evidence for the importance of tree structures in everyday life as well as in computer programming. Any hierarchical classification scheme leads to a tree structure.

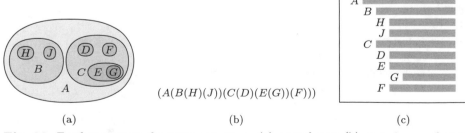

(a)   (b)   (c)

Fig. 20. Further ways to show tree structure: (a) nested sets; (b) nested parentheses; (c) indentation.

An algebraic formula defines an implicit tree structure that is often conveyed by other means instead of, or in addition to, the use of parentheses. For example, Figure 21 shows a tree corresponding to the arithmetic expression

$$a - b(c/d + e/f). \tag{2}$$

Standard mathematical conventions, according to which multiplication and division take precedence over addition and subtraction, allow us to use a simplified form like (2) instead of the fully parenthesized form "$a - \bigl(b \times \bigl((c/d) + (e/f)\bigr)\bigr)$". This connection between formulas and trees is very important in applications.

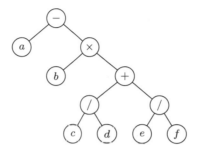

Fig. 21. Tree representation of formula (2).

Notice that the indented list in Fig. 20(c) looks very much like the table of contents in a book. Indeed, this book itself has a tree structure; the tree structure of Chapter 2 is shown in Fig. 22. Here we notice a significant idea: *The method used to number sections in this book is another way to specify tree structure.* Such a method is often called "Dewey decimal notation" for trees, by analogy with the similar classification scheme of this name used in libraries. The Dewey decimal notation for the tree of Fig. 19 is

$$1\ A; \quad 1.1\ B; \quad 1.1.1\ H; \quad 1.1.2\ J; \quad 1.2\ C;$$
$$1.2.1\ D; \quad 1.2.2\ E; \quad 1.2.2.1\ G; \quad 1.2.3\ F.$$

Dewey decimal notation applies to any forest: The root of the kth tree in the forest is given number k; and if α is the number of any node of degree m, its children are numbered $\alpha.1, \alpha.2, \ldots, \alpha.m$. The Dewey decimal notation satisfies many simple mathematical properties, and it is a useful tool in the analysis of trees. One example of this is the natural sequential ordering it gives to the nodes of an arbitrary tree, analogous to the ordering of sections within this book. Section 2.3 precedes Section 2.3.1, and follows Section 2.2.6.

There is an intimate relation between Dewey decimal notation and the notation for indexed variables that we have already been using extensively. If F is a forest of trees, we may let $F[1]$ denote the subtrees of the first tree, so that $F[1][2] \equiv F[1, 2]$ stands for the subtrees of the second subtree of $F[1]$, and $F[1, 2, 1]$ stands for the first subforest of the latter, and so on. Node $a.b.c.d$ in Dewey decimal notation is the parent of $F[a, b, c, d]$. This notation is an extension of ordinary index notation, because the admissible range of each index depends on the values in the preceding index positions.

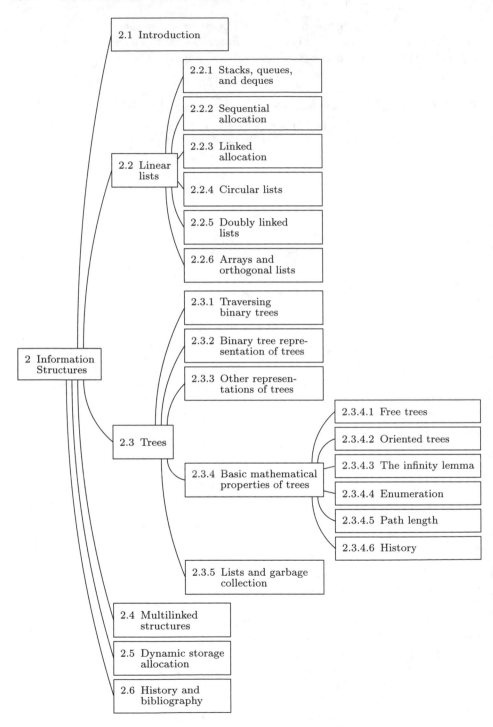

Fig. 22. The structure of Chapter 2.

Thus, in particular, we see that any rectangular array can be thought of as a special case of a tree or forest structure. For example, here are two representations of a 3×4 matrix:

$$\begin{pmatrix} A[1,1] & A[1,2] & A[1,3] & A[1,4] \\ A[2,1] & A[2,2] & A[2,3] & A[2,4] \\ A[3,1] & A[3,2] & A[3,3] & A[3,4] \end{pmatrix}$$

It is important to observe, however, that this tree structure does not faithfully reflect all of the matrix structure; the row relationships appear explicitly in the tree but the column relationships do not.

A forest can, in turn, be regarded as a special case of what is commonly called a *list structure*. The word "list" is being used here in a very technical sense, and to distinguish the technical use of the word we will always capitalize it: "List." A List is defined (recursively) as *a finite sequence of zero or more atoms or Lists*. Here "atom" is an undefined concept referring to elements from any universe of objects that might be desired, so long as it is possible to distinguish an atom from a List. By means of an obvious notational convention involving commas and parentheses, we can distinguish between atoms and Lists and we can conveniently display the ordering within a List. As an example, consider

$$L = (a,\ (b,a,b),\ (\ ),\ c,\ (((2)))), \tag{3}$$

which is a List with five elements: first the atom a, then the List (b,a,b), then the empty List $(\ )$, then the atom c, and finally the List $(((2)))$. The latter List consists of the List $((2))$, which consists of the List (2), which consists of the atom 2.

The following tree structure corresponds to L:

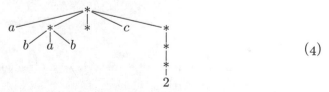

$$\tag{4}$$

The asterisks in this diagram indicate the definition and appearance of a List, as opposed to the appearance of an atom. Index notation applies to Lists as it does to forests; for example, $L[2] = (b,a,b)$, and $L[2,2] = a$.

No data is carried in the nodes for the Lists in (4) other than the fact that they are Lists. But it is possible to label the nonatomic elements of Lists with information, as we have done for trees and other structures; thus

$$A = (a{:}(b,c),\ d{:}(\ ))$$

would correspond to a tree that we can draw as follows:

The big difference between Lists and trees is that Lists may overlap (that is, sub-Lists need not be disjoint) and they may even be recursive (may contain themselves). The List

$$M = (M) \tag{5}$$

corresponds to no tree structure, nor does the List

$$N = (a:M, b:M, c, N). \tag{6}$$

(In these examples, capital letters refer to Lists, lowercase letters to labels and atoms.) We might diagram (5) and (6) as follows, using an asterisk to denote each place where a List is defined:

$$\tag{7}$$

Actually, Lists are not so complicated as the examples above might indicate. They are, in essence, a rather simple generalization of the linear lists that we have considered in Section 2.2, with the additional proviso that the elements of linear Lists may be link variables that point to other linear Lists (and possibly to themselves).

Summary: Four closely related kinds of information structures — trees, forests, binary trees, and Lists — arise from many sources, and they are therefore important in computer algorithms. We have seen various ways to diagram these structures, and we have considered some terminology and notations that are useful in talking about them. The following sections develop these ideas in greater detail.

EXERCISES

1. [*18*] How many different trees are there with three nodes, A, B, and C?

2. [*20*] How many different *oriented* trees are there with three nodes, A, B, and C?

3. [*M20*] Prove rigorously from the definitions that for every node X in a tree there is a unique path up to the root, namely a unique sequence of $k \geq 1$ nodes $X_1, X_2, \ldots, X_k$ such that X_1 is the root of the tree, $X_k = X$, and X_j is the parent of X_{j+1} for $1 \leq j < k$. (This proof will be typical of the proofs of nearly all the elementary facts about tree structures.) *Hint:* Use induction on the number of nodes in the tree.

4. [*01*] True or false: In a conventional tree diagram (root at the top), if node X has a *higher* level number than node Y, then node X appears *lower* in the diagram than node Y.

5. [*02*] If node A has three siblings and B is the parent of A, what is the degree of B?

▶ **6.** [*21*] Define the statement "X is an mth cousin of Y, n times removed" as a meaningful relation between nodes X and Y of a tree, by analogy with family trees, if $m > 0$ and $n \geq 0$. (See a dictionary for the meaning of these terms in regard to family trees.)

7. [*23*] Extend the definition given in the previous exercise to all $m \geq -1$ and to all integers $n \geq -(m+1)$ in such a way that for any two nodes X and Y of a tree there are unique m and n such that X is an mth cousin of Y, n times removed.

▶ **8.** [*03*] What binary tree is not a tree?

9. [*00*] In the two binary trees of (1), which node is the root (B or A)?

10. [*M20*] A collection of nonempty sets is said to be *nested* if, given any pair X, Y of the sets, either $X \subseteq Y$ or $X \supseteq Y$ or X and Y are disjoint. (In other words, $X \cap Y$ is either X, Y, or $\emptyset$.) Figure 20(a) indicates that any tree corresponds to a collection of nested sets; conversely, does every such collection correspond to a tree?

▶ **11.** [*HM32*] Extend the definition of tree to infinite trees by considering collections of nested sets as in exercise 10. Can the concepts of level, degree, parent, and child be defined for each node of an infinite tree? Give examples of nested sets of real numbers that correspond to a tree in which
   a) every node has uncountable degree and there are infinitely many levels;
   b) there are nodes with uncountable level;
   c) every node has degree at least 2 and there are uncountably many levels.

12. [*M23*] Under what conditions does a partially ordered set correspond to an unordered tree or forest? (Partially ordered sets are defined in Section 2.2.3.)

13. [*10*] Suppose that node X is numbered $a_1.a_2.\cdots.a_k$ in the Dewey decimal system; what are the Dewey numbers of the nodes in the path from X to the root (see exercise 3)?

14. [*M22*] Let S be any nonempty set of elements having the form "$1.a_1.\cdots.a_k$", where $k \geq 0$ and $a_1, \ldots, a_k$ are positive integers. Show that S specifies a tree when it is finite and satisfies the following condition: "If $\alpha.m$ is in the set, then so is $\alpha.(m-1)$ if $m > 1$, or α if $m = 1$." (This condition is clearly satisfied in the Dewey decimal notation for a tree; therefore it is another way to characterize tree structure.)

▶ **15.** [*20*] Invent a notation for the nodes of binary trees, analogous to the Dewey decimal notation for nodes of trees.

16. [*20*] Draw trees analogous to Fig. 21 corresponding to the arithmetic expressions (a) $2(a - b/c)$; (b) $a + b + 5c$.

17. [*01*] If Z stands for Fig. 19 regarded as a forest, what node is parent($Z[1,2,2]$)?

18. [*08*] In List (3), what is $L[5,1,1]$? What is $L[3,1]$?

19. [*15*] Draw a List diagram analogous to (7) for the List $L = (a, (L))$. What is $L[2]$ in this List? What is $L[2,1,1]$?

▶ **20.** [*M21*] Define a *0-2-tree* as a tree in which each node has exactly zero or two children. (Formally, a 0-2-tree consists of a single node, called its root, plus 0 or 2 disjoint 0-2-trees.) Show that every 0-2-tree has an odd number of nodes; and give a one-to-one correspondence between binary trees with n nodes and (ordered) 0-2-trees with $2n + 1$ nodes.

21. [*M22*] If a tree has n_1 nodes of degree 1, n_2 nodes of degree 2, ..., and n_m nodes of degree m, how many terminal nodes does it have?

▶ **22.** [*21*] Standard European paper sizes A0, A1, A2, ..., An, ... are rectangles whose sides are in the ratio $\sqrt{2}$ to 1 and whose areas are 2^{-n} square meters. Therefore if we cut a sheet of An paper in half, we get two sheets of A$(n+1)$ paper. Use this principle to design a graphic representation of binary trees, and illustrate your idea by drawing the representation of 2.3.1–(1) below.

2.3.1. Traversing Binary Trees

It is important to acquire a good understanding of the properties of binary trees before making further investigations of trees, since general trees are usually represented in terms of some equivalent binary tree inside a computer.

We have defined a binary tree as a finite set of nodes that either is empty, or consists of a root together with two binary trees. This definition suggests a natural way to represent binary trees within a computer: We can have two links, LLINK and RLINK, within each node, and a link variable T that is a "pointer to the tree." If the tree is empty, T = Λ; otherwise T is the address of the root node of the tree, and LLINK(T), RLINK(T) are pointers to the left and right subtrees of the root, respectively. These rules recursively define the memory representation of any binary tree; for example,

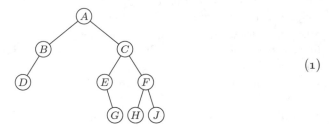

(1)

is represented by

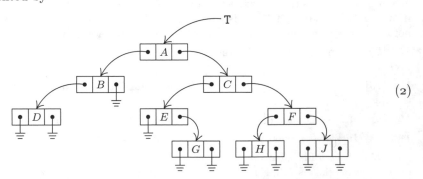

(2)

This simple and natural memory representation accounts for the special importance of binary tree structures. We will see in Section 2.3.2 that general trees can conveniently be represented as binary trees. Moreover, many trees that arise in applications are themselves inherently binary, so binary trees are of interest in their own right.

There are many algorithms for manipulation of tree structures, and one idea that occurs repeatedly in these algorithms is the notion of *traversing* or "walking through" a tree. This is a method of examining the nodes of the tree systematically so that each node is visited exactly once. A complete traversal of the tree gives us a linear arrangement of the nodes, and many algorithms are facilitated if we can talk about the "next" node following or preceding a given node in such a sequence.

Three principal ways may be used to traverse a binary tree: We can visit the nodes in *preorder*, *inorder*, or *postorder*. These three methods are defined recursively. When the binary tree is empty, it is "traversed" by doing nothing; otherwise the traversal proceeds in three steps:

<table>
<tr><td>Preorder traversal</td><td>Inorder traversal</td></tr>
<tr><td>Visit the root</td><td>Traverse the left subtree</td></tr>
<tr><td>Traverse the left subtree</td><td>Visit the root</td></tr>
<tr><td>Traverse the right subtree</td><td>Traverse the right subtree</td></tr>
</table>

Postorder traversal

Traverse the left subtree
Traverse the right subtree
Visit the root

If we apply these definitions to the binary tree of (1) and (2), we find that the nodes in preorder are

$$A \quad B \quad D \quad C \quad E \quad G \quad F \quad H \quad J. \tag{3}$$

(First comes the root A, then comes the left subtree

in preorder, and finally we traverse the right subtree in preorder.) For inorder we visit the root between visits to the nodes of each subtree, essentially as though the nodes were "projected" down onto a single horizontal line, and this gives the sequence

$$D \quad B \quad A \quad E \quad G \quad C \quad H \quad F \quad J. \tag{4}$$

The postorder for the nodes of this binary tree is, similarly,

$$D \quad B \quad G \quad E \quad H \quad J \quad F \quad C \quad A. \tag{5}$$

We will see that these three ways of arranging the nodes of a binary tree into a sequence are extremely important, as they are intimately connected with most of the computer methods for dealing with trees. The names *preorder*, *inorder*, and *postorder* come, of course, from the relative position of the root with respect to its subtrees. In many applications of binary trees, there is symmetry between the meanings of left subtrees and right subtrees, and in such cases the term *symmetric order* is used as a synonym for inorder. Inorder, which puts the root

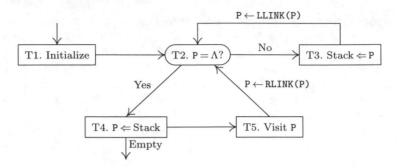

Fig. 23. Algorithm T for inorder traversal.

in the middle, is essentially symmetric between left and right: If the binary tree is reflected about a vertical axis, the symmetric order is simply reversed.

A recursively stated definition, such as the one just given for the three basic orders, must be reworked in order to make it directly applicable to computer implementation. General methods for doing this are discussed in Chapter 8; we usually make use of an auxiliary stack, as in the following algorithm:

Algorithm T (*Traverse binary tree in inorder*). Let T be a pointer to a binary tree having a representation as in (2); this algorithm visits all the nodes of the binary tree in inorder, making use of an auxiliary stack A.

T1. [Initialize.] Set stack A empty, and set the link variable P ← T.

T2. [P = Λ?] If P = Λ, go to step T4.

T3. [Stack ⇐ P.] (Now P points to a nonempty binary tree that is to be traversed.) Set A ⇐ P; that is, push the value of P onto stack A. (See Section 2.2.1.) Then set P ← LLINK(P) and return to step T2.

T4. [P ⇐ Stack.] If stack A is empty, the algorithm terminates; otherwise set P ⇐ A.

T5. [Visit P.] Visit NODE(P). Then set P ← RLINK(P) and return to step T2. ∎

In the final step of this algorithm, the word "visit" means that we do whatever activity is intended as the tree is being traversed. Algorithm T runs like a coroutine with respect to this other activity: The main program activates the coroutine whenever it wants P to move from one node to its inorder successor. Of course, since this coroutine calls the main routine in only one place, it is not much different from a subroutine (see Section 1.4.2). Algorithm T assumes that the external activity deletes neither NODE(P) nor any of its ancestors from the tree.

The reader should now attempt to play through Algorithm T using the binary tree (2) as a test case, in order to see the reasons behind the procedure. When we get to step T3, we want to traverse the binary tree whose root is indicated by pointer P. The idea is to save P on a stack and then to traverse the left subtree; when this has been done, we will get to step T4 and will find the old value of P on the stack again. After visiting the root, NODE(P), in step T5, the remaining job is to traverse the right subtree.

Algorithm T is typical of many other algorithms that we will see later, so it is instructive to look at a formal proof of the remarks made in the preceding paragraph. Let us now attempt to *prove* that Algorithm T traverses a binary tree of n nodes in inorder, by using induction on n. Our goal is readily established if we can prove a slightly more general result:

> *Starting at step T2 with* P *a pointer to a binary tree of n nodes and with the stack* A *containing* A[1] ... A[m] *for some $m \geq 0$, the procedure of steps T2–T5 will traverse the binary tree in question, in inorder, and will then arrive at step T4 with stack* A *returned to its original value* A[1] ... A[m].

This statement is obviously true when $n = 0$, because of step T2. If $n > 0$, let P_0 be the value of P upon entry to step T2. Since $P_0 \neq \Lambda$, we will perform step T3, which means that stack A is changed to A[1] ... A[m] P_0 and P is set to LLINK(P_0). Now the left subtree has fewer than n nodes, so by induction we will traverse the left subtree in inorder and will ultimately arrive at step T4 with A[1] ... A[m] P_0 on the stack. Step T4 returns the stack to A[1] ... A[m] and sets P $\leftarrow P_0$. Step T5 now visits NODE(P_0) and sets P $\leftarrow$ RLINK(P_0). Now the right subtree has fewer than n nodes, so by induction we will traverse the right subtree in inorder and arrive at step T4 as required. The tree has been traversed in inorder, by the definition of that order. This completes the proof.

An almost identical algorithm may be formulated that traverses binary trees in preorder (see exercise 12). It is slightly more difficult to achieve the traversal in postorder (see exercise 13), and for this reason postorder is not as important for binary trees as the others are.

It is convenient to define a new notation for the successors and predecessors of nodes in these various orders. If P points to a node of a binary tree, let

$$
\begin{aligned}
\text{P*} &= \text{ address of successor of NODE(P) in preorder;}\\
\text{P\$} &= \text{ address of successor of NODE(P) in inorder;}\\
\text{P\#} &= \text{ address of successor of NODE(P) in postorder;}\\
\text{*P} &= \text{ address of predecessor of NODE(P) in preorder;}\\
\text{\$P} &= \text{ address of predecessor of NODE(P) in inorder;}\\
\text{\#P} &= \text{ address of predecessor of NODE(P) in postorder.}
\end{aligned}
\tag{6}
$$

If there is no such successor or predecessor of NODE(P), the value LOC(T) is generally used, where T is an external pointer to the tree in question. We have *(P*) = (*P)* = P, \$(P\$) = (\$P)\$ = P, and #(P#) = (#P)# = P. As an example of this notation, let INFO(P) be the letter shown in NODE(P) in the tree (2); then if P points to the root, we have INFO(P) = A, INFO(P*) = B, INFO(P\$) = E, INFO(\$P) = B, INFO(#P) = C, and P# = *P = LOC(T).

At this point the reader will perhaps experience a feeling of insecurity about the intuitive meanings of P*, P\$, etc. As we proceed further, the ideas will gradually become clearer; exercise 16 at the end of this section may also be of help. The "\$" in "P\$" is meant to suggest the letter S, for "symmetric order."

There is an important alternative to the memory representation of binary trees given in (2), which is somewhat analogous to the difference between circular lists and straight one-way lists. Notice that there are more null links than other pointers in the tree (2), and indeed this is true of any binary tree represented by the conventional method (see exercise 14). But we don't really need to waste all that memory space. For example, we could store two "tag" indicators with each node, which would tell in just two bits of memory whether or not the LLINK or RLINK, or both, are null; the memory space for terminal links could then be used for other purposes.

An ingenious use of this extra space has been suggested by A. J. Perlis and C. Thornton, who devised the so-called *threaded* tree representation. In this method, terminal links are replaced by "threads" to other parts of the tree, as an aid to traversal. The threaded tree equivalent to (2) is

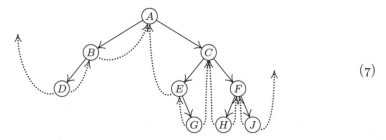

(7)

Here dotted lines represent the "threads," which always go to a higher node of the tree. *Every* node now has two links: Some nodes, like C, have two ordinary links to left and right subtrees; other nodes, like H, have two thread links; and some nodes have one link of each type. The special threads emanating from D and J will be explained later. They appear in the "leftmost" and "rightmost" nodes.

In the memory representation of a threaded binary tree it is necessary to distinguish between the dotted and solid links; this can be done as suggested above by two additional one-bit fields in each node, LTAG and RTAG. The threaded representation may be defined precisely as follows:

Unthreaded representation	Threaded representation
LLINK(P) = Λ	LTAG(P) = 1, LLINK(P) = \$P
LLINK(P) = Q $\neq \Lambda$	LTAG(P) = 0, LLINK(P) = Q
RLINK(P) = Λ	RTAG(P) = 1, RLINK(P) = P\$
RLINK(P) = Q $\neq \Lambda$	RTAG(P) = 0, RLINK(P) = Q

According to this definition, each new thread link points directly to the predecessor or successor of the node in question, in symmetric order (inorder). Figure 24 illustrates the general orientation of thread links in any binary tree.

In some algorithms it can be guaranteed that the root of any subtree always will appear in a lower memory location than the other nodes of the subtree. Then LTAG(P) will be 1 if and only if LLINK(P) < P, so LTAG will be redundant. The RTAG bit will be redundant for the same reason.

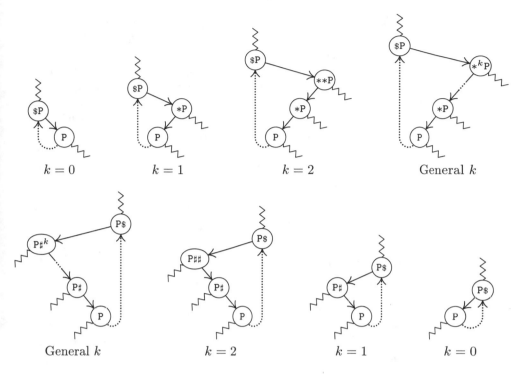

Fig. 24. General orientation of left and right thread links in a threaded binary tree. Wavy lines indicate links or threads to other parts of the tree.

The great advantage of threaded trees is that traversal algorithms become simpler. For example, the following algorithm calculates P\$, given P:

Algorithm S (*Symmetric (inorder) successor in a threaded binary tree*). If P points to a node of a threaded binary tree, this algorithm sets Q ← P\$.

S1. [RLINK(P) a thread?] Set Q ← RLINK(P). If RTAG(P) = 1, terminate the algorithm.

S2. [Search to left.] If LTAG(Q) = 0, set Q ← LLINK(Q) and repeat this step. Otherwise the algorithm terminates. ∎

Notice that no stack is needed here to accomplish what was done using a stack in Algorithm T. In fact, the ordinary representation (2) makes it impossible to find P\$ efficiently, given only the address of a random point P in the tree. Since no links point upward in an unthreaded representation, there is no clue to what nodes are above a given node, unless we retain a history of how we reached that point. The stack in Algorithm T provides the necessary history when threads are absent.

We claim that Algorithm S is "efficient," although this property is not immediately obvious, since step S2 can be executed any number of times. In view of the loop in step S2, would it perhaps be faster to use a stack after all, as Algorithm T does? To investigate this question, we will consider the average number of times that step S2 must be performed if P is a "random" point in the tree; or what is the same, we will determine the total number of times that step S2 is performed if Algorithm S is used repeatedly to traverse an entire tree.

At the same time as this analysis is being carried out, it will be instructive to study complete programs for both Algorithms S and T. As usual, we should be careful to set all of our algorithms up so that they work properly with empty binary trees; and if T is the pointer to the tree, we would like to have LOC(T)∗ and LOC(T)$ be the *first* nodes in preorder or symmetric order, respectively. For threaded trees, it turns out that things will work nicely if NODE(LOC(T)) is made into a "list head" for the tree, with

$$\text{LLINK(HEAD)} = \text{T}, \qquad \text{LTAG(HEAD)} = 0,$$
$$\text{RLINK(HEAD)} = \text{HEAD}, \qquad \text{RTAG(HEAD)} = 0. \tag{8}$$

(Here HEAD denotes LOC(T), the address of the list head.) An empty threaded tree will satisfy the conditions

$$\text{LLINK(HEAD)} = \text{HEAD}, \quad \text{LTAG(HEAD)} = 1. \tag{9}$$

The tree grows by having nodes inserted to the *left* of the list head. (These initial conditions are primarily dictated by the algorithm to compute P∗, which appears in exercise 17.) In accordance with these conventions, the computer representation for the binary tree (1), as a threaded tree, is

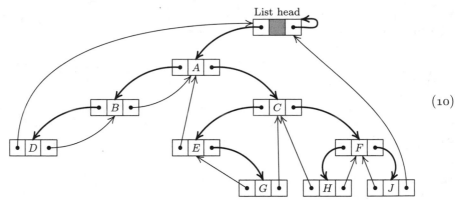

$$\tag{10}$$

With these preliminaries out of the way, we are now ready to consider MIX versions of Algorithms S and T. The following programs assume that binary tree nodes have the two-word form

LTAG	LLINK	INFO1
RTAG	RLINK	INFO2

In an unthreaded tree, LTAG and RTAG will always be "+" and terminal links will be represented by zero. In a threaded tree, we will use "+" for tags that are 0 and "−" for tags that are 1. The abbreviations LLINKT and RLINKT will be used to stand for the combined LTAG-LLINK and RTAG-RLINK fields, respectively.

The two tag bits occupy otherwise-unused sign positions of a MIX word, so they cost nothing in memory space. Similarly, with the MMIX computer we will be able to use the least significant bits of link fields as tag bits that come "for free," because pointer values will generally be even, and because MMIX will make it easy to ignore the low-order bits when addressing memory.

The following two programs traverse a binary tree in symmetric order (that is, inorder), jumping to location VISIT periodically with index register 5 pointing to the node that is currently of interest.

Program T. In this implementation of Algorithm T, the stack is kept in locations $A + 1$, $A + 2$, ..., $A + MAX$; rI6 is the stack pointer and rI5 $\equiv$ P. OVERFLOW occurs if the stack grows too large. The program has been rearranged slightly from Algorithm T (step T2 appears thrice), so that the test for an empty stack need not be made when going directly from T3 to T2 to T4.

```
01  LLINK EQU   1:2
02  RLINK EQU   1:2
03  T1    LD5   HEAD(LLINK)   1    T1. Initialize. Set P ← T.
04  T2A   J5Z   DONE          1    Stop if P = Λ.
05        ENT6  0             1
06  T3    DEC6  MAX           n    T3. Stack ⇐ P.
07        J6NN  OVERFLOW      n    Has that stack reached capacity?
08        INC6  MAX+1         n    If not, increase the stack pointer.
09        ST5   A,6           n    Store P in the stack.
10        LD5   0,5(LLINK)    n    P ← LLINK(P).
11  T2B   J5NZ  T3            n    To T3 if P ≠ Λ.
12  T4    LD5   A,6           n    T4. P ⇐ Stack.
13        DEC6  1             n    Decrease the stack pointer.
14  T5    JMP   VISIT         n    T5. Visit P.
15        LD5   1,5(RLINK)    n    P ← RLINK(P).
16  T2C   J5NZ  T3            n    T2. P = Λ?
17        J6NZ  T4            a    Test if the stack is empty.
18  DONE  ...
```

Program S. Algorithm S has been augmented with initialization and termination conditions to make this program comparable to Program T.

```
01  LLINKT EQU   0:2
02  RLINKT EQU   0:2
03  S0     ENT5  HEAD          1     S0. Initialize. Set P ← HEAD.
04         JMP   2F            1
05  S3     JMP   VISIT         n     S3. Visit P.
06  S1     LD5N  1,5(RLINKT)   n     S1. RLINK(P) a thread?
07         J5NN  1F            n     Jump if RTAG(P) = 1.
08         ENN6  0,5           n - a Otherwise set Q ← RLINK(P).
09  S2     ENT5  0,6           n     S2. Search to left. Set P ← Q.
10  2H     LD6   0,5(LLINKT)   n + 1 Q ← LLINKT(P).
11         J6P   S2            n + 1 If LTAG(P) = 0, repeat.
12  1H     ENT6  -HEAD,5       n + 1
13         J6NZ  S3            n + 1 Visit unless P = HEAD.
```

An analysis of the running time appears with the code above. These quantities are easy to determine, using Kirchhoff's law and the facts that

i) in Program T, the number of insertions onto the stack must equal the number of deletions;

ii) in Program S, the LLINK and RLINK of each node are examined precisely once;

iii) the number of "visits" is the number of nodes in the tree.

The analysis tells us Program T takes $15n + a + 4$ units of time, and Program S takes $11n - a + 7$ units, where n is the number of nodes in the tree and a is the number of terminal right links (nodes with no right subtree). The quantity a can be as low as 1, assuming that $n \neq 0$, and it can be as high as n. If left and right are symmetrical, the average value of a is $(n + 1)/2$, as a consequence of facts proved in exercise 14.

The principal conclusions we may reach on the basis of this analysis are:

i) Step S2 of Algorithm S is performed only *once* on the average per execution of that algorithm, if P is a random node of the tree.

ii) Traversal is slightly faster for threaded trees, because it requires no stack manipulation.

iii) Algorithm T needs more memory space than Algorithm S because of the auxiliary stack required. In Program T we kept the stack in consecutive memory locations; therefore we needed to put an arbitrary bound on its size. It would be very embarrassing if this bound were exceeded, so it must be set reasonably large (see exercise 10); thus the memory requirement of Program T is significantly more than Program S. Not infrequently a complex computer application will be independently traversing several trees at once, and a separate stack will be needed for each tree under Program T. This suggests that Program T might use linked allocation for its stack (see exercise 20); its execution time then becomes $30n + a + 4$ units, roughly twice as slow as before, although the traversal speed may not be terribly important when the execution time for the other coroutine is added in. Still another alternative is to keep the stack links within the tree itself in a tricky way, as discussed in exercise 21.

iv) Algorithm S is, of course, more general than Algorithm T, since it allows us to go from P to P$ when we are not necessarily traversing the entire binary tree.

So a threaded binary tree is decidedly superior to an unthreaded one, with respect to traversal. These advantages are offset in some applications by the slightly increased time needed to insert and delete nodes in a threaded tree. It is also sometimes possible to save memory space by "sharing" common subtrees with an unthreaded representation, while threaded trees require adherence to a strict tree structure with no overlapping of subtrees.

Thread links can also be used to compute P*, $P, and ♯P with efficiency comparable to that of Algorithm S. The functions *P and P♯ are slightly harder

to compute, just as they are for unthreaded tree representations. The reader is
urged to work exercise 17.

Most of the usefulness of threaded trees would disappear if it were hard to
set up the thread links in the first place. What makes the idea really work is that
threaded trees grow almost as easily as ordinary ones do. We have the following
algorithm:

Algorithm I (*Insertion into a threaded binary tree*). This algorithm attaches
a single node, NODE(Q), as the right subtree of NODE(P), if the right subtree is
empty (that is, if RTAG(P) = 1); otherwise it inserts NODE(Q) between NODE(P)
and NODE(RLINK(P)), making the latter node the right child of NODE(Q). The
binary tree in which the insertion takes place is assumed to be threaded as in
(10); for a modification, see exercise 23.

I1. [Adjust tags and links.] Set RLINK(Q) ← RLINK(P), RTAG(Q) ← RTAG(P),
RLINK(P) ← Q, RTAG(P) ← 0, LLINK(Q) ← P, LTAG(Q) ← 1.

I2. [Was RLINK(P) a thread?] If RTAG(Q) = 0, set LLINK(Q$) ← Q. (Here Q$ is
determined by Algorithm S, which will work properly even though LLINK(Q$)
now points to NODE(P) instead of NODE(Q). This step is necessary only when
inserting into the midst of a threaded tree instead of merely inserting a new
leaf.) ∎

By reversing the roles of left and right (in particular, by replacing Q$ by $Q
in step I2), we obtain an algorithm that inserts to the left in a similar way.

Our discussion of threaded binary trees so far has made use of thread links
both to the left and to the right. There is an important middle ground between
the completely unthreaded and completely threaded methods of representation:
A *right-threaded binary tree* combines the two approaches by making use of
threaded RLINKs, while representing empty left subtrees by LLINK = Λ. (Similarly, a left-threaded binary tree threads only the null LLINKs.) Algorithm S does
not make essential use of threaded LLINKs; if we change the test "LTAG = 0" in
step S2 to "LLINK ≠ Λ", we obtain an algorithm for traversing right-threaded
binary trees in symmetric order. Program S works without change in the right-
threaded case. A great many applications of binary tree structures require only
a left-to-right traversal of trees using the functions P$ and/or P*, and for these
applications there is no need to thread the LLINKs. We have described threading
in both the left and right directions in order to indicate the symmetry and
possibilities of the situation, but in practice one-sided threading is much more
common.

Let us now consider an important property of binary trees, and its connection to traversal. Two binary trees T and T' are said to be *similar* if they
have the same structure; formally, this means that (a) they are both empty, or
(b) they are both nonempty and their left and right subtrees are respectively
similar. Similarity means, informally, that the diagrams of T and T' have the
same "shape." Another way to phrase similarity is to say that there is a one-to-
one correspondence between the nodes of T and T' that preserves the structure:

If nodes u_1 and u_2 in T correspond respectively to u'_1 and u'_2 in T', then u_1 is in the left subtree of u_2 if and only if u'_1 is in the left subtree of u'_2, and the same is true for right subtrees.

The binary trees T and T' are said to be *equivalent* if they are similar and if corresponding nodes contain the same information. Formally, let info(u) denote the information contained in a node u; the trees are equivalent if and only if (a) they are both empty, or (b) they are both nonempty and $\text{info}(\text{root}(T)) = \text{info}(\text{root}(T'))$ and their left and right subtrees are respectively equivalent.

As examples of these definitions, consider the four binary trees

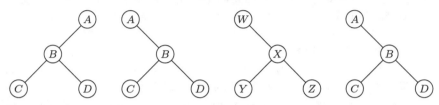

in which the first two are dissimilar. The second, third, and fourth are similar and, in fact, the second and fourth are equivalent.

Some computer applications involving tree structures require an algorithm to decide whether two binary trees are similar or equivalent. The following theorem is useful in this regard:

Theorem A. *Let the nodes of binary trees T and T' be respectively*

$$u_1, u_2, \ldots, u_n \qquad \text{and} \qquad u'_1, u'_2, \ldots, u'_{n'}$$

in preorder. For any node u let

$$
\begin{array}{llll}
l(u) = 1 & \text{if } u \text{ has a nonempty left subtree,} & l(u) = 0 & \text{otherwise;} \\
r(u) = 1 & \text{if } u \text{ has a nonempty right subtree,} & r(u) = 0 & \text{otherwise.}
\end{array}
\tag{11}
$$

Then T and T' are similar if and only if $n = n'$ and

$$l(u_j) = l(u'_j), \qquad r(u_j) = r(u'_j) \qquad \text{for } 1 \le j \le n. \tag{12}$$

Moreover, T and T' are equivalent if and only if in addition we have

$$\text{info}(u_j) = \text{info}(u'_j) \qquad \text{for } 1 \le j \le n. \tag{13}$$

Notice that l and r are the complements of the LTAG and RTAG bits in a threaded tree. This theorem characterizes any binary tree structure in terms of two sequences of 0s and 1s.

Proof. It is clear that the condition for equivalence of binary trees will follow immediately if we prove the condition for similarity; furthermore the conditions $n = n'$ and (12) are certainly necessary, since corresponding nodes of similar trees must have the same position in preorder. Therefore it suffices to prove that the conditions (12) and $n = n'$ are sufficient to guarantee the similarity of T and T'. The proof is by induction on n, using the following auxiliary result:

Lemma P. *Let the nodes of a nonempty binary tree be* $u_1, u_2, \ldots, u_n$ *in preorder, and let* $f(u) = l(u) + r(u) - 1$. *Then*

$$f(u_1) + f(u_2) + \cdots + f(u_n) = -1, \quad \text{and} \quad f(u_1) + \cdots + f(u_k) \geq 0, \ \ 1 \leq k < n. \quad (14)$$

Proof. The result is clear for $n = 1$. If $n > 1$, the binary tree consists of its root u_1 and further nodes. If $f(u_1) = 0$, then either the left subtree or the right subtree is empty, so the condition is obviously true by induction. If $f(u_1) = 1$, let the left subtree have n_l nodes; by induction we have

$$f(u_1) + \cdots + f(u_k) > 0 \quad \text{for } 1 \leq k \leq n_l, \quad f(u_1) + \cdots + f(u_{n_l+1}) = 0, \quad (15)$$

and the condition (14) is again evident. ∎

(For other theorems analogous to Lemma P, see the discussion of Polish notation in Chapter 10.)

To complete the proof of Theorem A, we note that the theorem is clearly true when $n = 0$. If $n > 0$, the definition of preorder implies that u_1 and u_1' are the respective roots of their trees, and there are integers n_l and n_l' (the sizes of the left subtrees) such that

$u_2, \ldots, u_{n_l+1}$ and $u_2', \ldots, u_{n_l'+1}'$ are the left subtrees of T and T';

$u_{n_l+2}, \ldots, u_n$ and $u_{n_l'+2}', \ldots, u_n'$ are the right subtrees of T and T'.

The proof by induction will be complete if we can show $n_l = n_l'$. There are three cases:

if $l(u_1) = 0$, then $n_l = 0 = n_l'$;

if $l(u_1) = 1$, $r(u_1) = 0$, then $n_l = n - 1 = n_l'$;

if $l(u_1) = r(u_1) = 1$, then by Lemma P we can find the least $k > 0$ such that $f(u_1) + \cdots + f(u_k) = 0$; and $n_l = k - 1 = n_l'$ $\big($see (15)$\big)$. ∎

As a consequence of Theorem A, we can test two threaded binary trees for equivalence or similarity by simply traversing them in preorder and checking the INFO and TAG fields. Some interesting extensions of Theorem A have been obtained by A. J. Blikle, *Bull. de l'Acad. Polonaise des Sciences*, Série des Sciences Math., Astr., Phys., **14** (1966), 203–208; he considered an infinite class of possible traversal orders, only six of which (including preorder) were called "addressless" because of their simple properties.

We conclude this section by giving a typical, yet basic, algorithm for binary trees, one that makes a copy of a binary tree into different memory locations.

Algorithm C (*Copy a binary tree*). Let HEAD be the address of the list head of a binary tree T; thus, T is the left subtree of HEAD, reached via LLINK(HEAD). Let NODE(U) be a node with an empty left subtree. This algorithm makes a copy of T and the copy becomes the left subtree of NODE(U). In particular, if NODE(U) is the list head of an empty binary tree, this algorithm changes the empty tree into a copy of T.

C1. [Initialize.] Set P ← HEAD, Q ← U. Go to C4.

C2. [Anything to right?] If NODE(P) has a nonempty right subtree, set R ⇐ AVAIL, and attach NODE(R) to the right of NODE(Q). (At the beginning of step C2, the right subtree of NODE(Q) was empty.)

C3. [Copy INFO.] Set INFO(Q) ← INFO(P). (Here INFO denotes all parts of the node that are to be copied, except for the links.)

C4. [Anything to left?] If NODE(P) has a nonempty left subtree, set R ⇐ AVAIL, and attach NODE(R) to the left of NODE(Q). (At the beginning of step C4, the left subtree of NODE(Q) was empty.)

C5. [Advance.] Set P ← P∗, Q ← Q∗.

C6. [Test if complete.] If P = HEAD (or equivalently if Q = RLINK(U), assuming that NODE(U) has a nonempty right subtree), the algorithm terminates; otherwise go to step C2. ∎

This simple algorithm shows a typical application of tree traversal. The description here applies to threaded, unthreaded, or partially threaded trees. Step C5 requires the calculation of preorder successors P∗ and Q∗; for unthreaded trees, this generally is done with an auxiliary stack. A proof of the validity of Algorithm C appears in exercise 29; a MIX program corresponding to this algorithm in the case of a right-threaded binary tree appears in exercise 2.3.2–13. For threaded trees, the "attaching" in steps C2 and C4 is done using Algorithm I.

The exercises that follow include quite a few topics of interest relating to the material of this section.

> *Binary or dichotomous systems, although regulated by a principle,*
> *are among the most artificial arrangements*
> *that have ever been invented.*
>
> — WILLIAM SWAINSON, *A Treatise on the Geography and*
> *Classification of Animals* (1835)

EXERCISES

1. [*01*] In the binary tree (2), let INFO(P) denote the letter stored in NODE(P). What is INFO(LLINK(RLINK(RLINK(T))))?

2. [*11*] List the nodes of the binary tree   in (a) preorder; (b) symmetric order; (c) postorder.

3. [*20*] Is the following statement true or false? "The terminal nodes of a binary tree occur in the same relative position in preorder, inorder, and postorder."

▶ **4.** [*20*] The text defines three basic orders for traversing a binary tree; another alternative would be to proceed in three steps as follows:

a) Visit the root,
b) traverse the right subtree,
c) traverse the left subtree,

using the same rule recursively on all nonempty subtrees. Does this new order bear any simple relation to the three orders already discussed?

5. [*22*] The nodes of a binary tree may be identified by a sequence of zeros and ones, in a notation analogous to "Dewey decimal notation" for trees, as follows: The root (if present) is represented by the sequence "1". Roots (if present) of the left and right subtrees of the node represented by α are respectively represented by $\alpha 0$ and $\alpha 1$. For example, the node H in (1) would have the representation "1110". (See exercise 2.3–15.)

Show that preorder, inorder, and postorder can be described conveniently in terms of this notation.

6. [*M22*] Suppose that a binary tree has n nodes that are $u_1 u_2 \ldots u_n$ in preorder and $u_{p_1} u_{p_2} \ldots u_{p_n}$ in inorder. Show that the permutation $p_1 p_2 \ldots p_n$ can be obtained by passing $12 \ldots n$ through a stack, in the sense of exercise 2.2.1–2. Conversely, show that any permutation $p_1 p_2 \ldots p_n$ obtainable with a stack corresponds to some binary tree in this way.

7. [*22*] Show that if we are given the preorder and the inorder of the nodes of a binary tree, the binary tree structure may be constructed. (Assume that the nodes are distinct.) Does the same result hold true if we are given the preorder and postorder, instead of preorder and inorder? Or if we are given the inorder and postorder?

8. [*20*] Find all binary trees whose nodes appear in exactly the same sequence in both (a) preorder and inorder; (b) preorder and postorder; (c) inorder and postorder. (As in the previous exercise, we assume that the nodes have distinct labels.)

9. [*M20*] When a binary tree having n nodes is traversed using Algorithm T, state how many times each of steps T1, T2, T3, T4, and T5 is performed (as a function of n).

▶ **10.** [*20*] What is the largest number of entries that can be in the stack at once, during the execution of Algorithm T, if the binary tree has n nodes? (The answer to this question is very important for storage allocation, if the stack is being stored consecutively.)

11. [*HM41*] Analyze the *average* value of the largest stack size occurring during the execution of Algorithm T as a function of n, given that all binary trees with n nodes are considered equally probable.

12. [*22*] Design an algorithm analogous to Algorithm T that traverses a binary tree in *preorder*, and prove that your algorithm is correct.

▶ **13.** [*24*] Design an algorithm analogous to Algorithm T that traverses a binary tree in *postorder*.

14. [*20*] Show that if a binary tree with n nodes is represented as in (2), the total number of Λ links in the representation can be expressed as a simple function of n; this quantity does not depend on the shape of the tree.

15. [*15*] In a threaded-tree representation like (10), each node except the list head has exactly one link pointing to it from above, namely the link from its parent. Some of the nodes also have links pointing to them from below; for example, the node containing C has two pointers coming up from below, while node E has just one. Is there any simple connection between the number of links pointing to a node and some other basic property of that node? (We need to know how many links point to a given node when we are changing the tree structure.)

▶ **16.** [*22*] The diagrams in Fig. 24 help to provide an intuitive characterization of the position of NODE(Q$) in a binary tree, in terms of the structure near NODE(Q): If NODE(Q) has a nonempty right subtree, consider Q = P, Q = P in the upper diagrams; NODE(Q$)

is the "leftmost" node of that right subtree. If NODE(Q) has an empty right subtree, consider Q = P in the lower diagrams; NODE(Q$) is located by proceeding upward in the tree until after the first upward step to the right.

Give a similar "intuitive" rule for finding the position of NODE(Q*) in a binary tree in terms of the structure near NODE(Q).

▶ **17.** [*22*] Give an algorithm analogous to Algorithm S for determining P* in a threaded binary tree. Assume that the tree has a list head as in (8), (9), and (10).

18. [*24*] Many algorithms dealing with trees like to visit each node *twice* instead of once, using a combination of preorder and inorder that we might call *double order*. Traversal of a binary tree in double order is defined as follows: If the binary tree is empty, do nothing; otherwise

a) visit the root, for the first time;
b) traverse the left subtree, in double order;
c) visit the root, for the second time;
d) traverse the right subtree, in double order.

For example, traversal of (1) in double order gives the sequence

$$A_1 B_1 D_1 D_2 B_2 A_2 C_1 E_1 E_2 G_1 G_2 C_2 F_1 H_1 H_2 F_2 J_1 J_2,$$

where A_1 means that A is being visited for the first time.

If P points to a node of the tree and if $d = 1$ or 2, define $(P, d)^\Delta = (Q, e)$ if the next step in double order after visiting NODE(P) the dth time is to visit NODE(Q) the eth time; or, if (P, d) is the last step in double order, we write $(P, d)^\Delta = (HEAD, 2)$, where HEAD is the address of the list head. We also define $(HEAD, 1)^\Delta$ as the first step in double order.

Design an algorithm analogous to Algorithm T that traverses a binary tree in double order, and also design an algorithm analogous to Algorithm S that computes $(P, d)^\Delta$. Discuss the relation between these algorithms and exercises 12 and 17.

▶ **19.** [*27*] Design an algorithm analogous to Algorithm S for the calculation of P♯ in (a) a right-threaded binary tree; (b) a fully threaded binary tree. If possible, the average running time of your algorithm should be at most a small constant, when P is a random node of the tree.

20. [*23*] Modify Program T so that it keeps the stack in a linked list, not in consecutive memory locations.

▶ **21.** [*33*] Design an algorithm that traverses an unthreaded binary tree in inorder *without using any auxiliary stack*. It is permissible to alter the LLINK and RLINK fields of the tree nodes in any manner whatsoever during the traversal, subject only to the condition that the binary tree should have the conventional representation illustrated in (2) both before and after your algorithm has traversed the tree. No other bits in the tree nodes are available for temporary storage.

22. [*25*] Write a MIX program for the algorithm given in exercise 21 and compare its execution time to Programs S and T.

23. [*22*] Design algorithms analogous to Algorithm I for insertion to the right and insertion to the left in a *right-threaded* binary tree. Assume that the nodes have the fields LLINK, RLINK, and RTAG.

24. [*M20*] Is Theorem A still valid if the nodes of T and T' are given in symmetric order instead of preorder?

25. [*M24*] Let $\mathcal{T}$ be a set of binary trees in which the value of each info field belongs to a given set S, where S is linearly ordered by a relation "$\preceq$" (see exercise 2.2.3–14). Given any trees T, T' in $\mathcal{T}$, let us now define $T \preceq T'$ if and only if

i) T is empty; or

ii) T and T' are not empty, and $\mathrm{info}(\mathrm{root}(T)) \prec \mathrm{info}(\mathrm{root}(T'))$; or

iii) T and T' are not empty, $\mathrm{info}(\mathrm{root}(T)) = \mathrm{info}(\mathrm{root}(T'))$, $\mathrm{left}(T) \preceq \mathrm{left}(T')$, and $\mathrm{left}(T)$ is not equivalent to $\mathrm{left}(T')$; or

iv) T and T' are not empty, $\mathrm{info}(\mathrm{root}(T)) = \mathrm{info}(\mathrm{root}(T'))$, $\mathrm{left}(T)$ is equivalent to $\mathrm{left}(T')$, and $\mathrm{right}(T) \preceq \mathrm{right}(T')$.

Here $\mathrm{left}(T)$ and $\mathrm{right}(T)$ denote the left and right subtrees of T. Prove that (a) $T \preceq T'$ and $T' \preceq T''$ implies $T \preceq T''$; (b) T is equivalent to T' if and only if $T \preceq T'$ and $T' \preceq T$; (c) for any T, T' in $\mathcal{T}$ we have either $T \preceq T'$ or $T' \preceq T$. [Thus, if equivalent trees in $\mathcal{T}$ are regarded as equal, the relation $\preceq$ induces a linear ordering on $\mathcal{T}$. This ordering has many applications (for example, in the simplification of algebraic expressions). When S has only one element, so that the "info" of each node is the same, we have the special case that equivalence is the same as similarity.]

26. [*M24*] Consider the ordering $T \preceq T'$ defined in the preceding exercise. Prove a theorem analogous to Theorem A, giving a necessary and sufficient condition that $T \preceq T'$, and making use of double order as defined in exercise 18.

▶ **27.** [*28*] Design an algorithm that tests two given trees T and T' to see whether $T \prec T'$, $T \succ T'$, or T is equivalent to T', in terms of the relation defined in exercise 25, assuming that both binary trees are right-threaded. Assume that each node has the fields LLINK, RLINK, RTAG, INFO; use no auxiliary stack.

28. [*00*] After Algorithm C has been used to make a copy of a tree, is the new binary tree *equivalent* to the original, or *similar* to it?

29. [*M25*] Prove as rigorously as possible that Algorithm C is valid.

▶ **30.** [*22*] Design an algorithm that threads an unthreaded tree; for example, it should transform (2) into (10). *Note:* Always use notations like P* and P$ when possible, instead of repeating the steps for traversal algorithms like Algorithm T.

31. [*23*] Design an algorithm that "erases" a right-threaded binary tree. Your algorithm should return all of the tree nodes except the list head to the AVAIL list, and it should make the list head signify an empty binary tree. Assume that each node has the fields LLINK, RLINK, RTAG; use no auxiliary stack.

32. [*21*] Suppose that each node of a binary tree has four link fields: LLINK and RLINK, which point to left and right subtrees or Λ, as in an unthreaded tree; SUC and PRED, which point to the successor and predecessor of the node in symmetric order. (Thus SUC(P) = P$ and PRED(P) = $P. Such a tree contains more information than a threaded tree.) Design an algorithm like Algorithm I for insertion into such a tree.

▶ **33.** [*30*] There is more than one way to thread a tree! Consider the following representation, using three fields LTAG, LLINK, RLINK in each node:

LTAG(P): defined the same as in a threaded binary tree;

LLINK(P): always equal to P*;

RLINK(P): defined the same as in an unthreaded binary tree.

Discuss insertion algorithms for such a representation, and write out the copying algorithm, Algorithm C, in detail for this representation.

34. [*22*] Let P point to a node in some binary tree, and let HEAD point to the list head of an empty binary tree. Give an algorithm that (i) removes NODE(P) and all of its subtrees from whatever tree it was in, and then (ii) attaches NODE(P) and its subtrees to NODE(HEAD). Assume that all the binary trees in question are right-threaded, with fields LLINK, RTAG, RLINK in each node.

35. [*40*] Define a *ternary tree* (and, more generally, a *t-ary tree* for any $t \geq 2$) in a manner analogous to our definition of a binary tree, and explore the topics discussed in this section (including topics found in the exercises above) that can be generalized to t-ary trees in a meaningful way.

36. [*M23*] Exercise 1.2.1–15 shows that lexicographic order extends a well-ordering of a set S to a well-ordering of the n-tuples of elements of S. Exercise 25 above shows that a linear ordering of the information in tree nodes can be extended to a linear ordering of trees, using a similar definition. If the relation $\prec$ well-orders S, is the extended relation of exercise 25 a well-ordering of $\mathcal{T}$?

▶ **37.** [*24*] (D. Ferguson.) If two computer words are necessary to contain two link fields and an INFO field, representation (2) requires $2n$ words of memory for a tree with n nodes. Design a representation scheme for binary trees that uses less space, assuming that *one* link and an INFO field will fit in a single computer word.

2.3.2. Binary Tree Representation of Trees

We turn now from binary trees to just plain trees. Let us recall the basic differences between trees and binary trees as we have defined them:

1) A tree always has a root node, so it is never empty; each node of a tree can have 0, 1, 2, 3, ... children.
2) A binary tree can be empty, and each of its nodes can have 0, 1, or 2 children; we distinguish between a "left" child and a "right" child.

Recall also that a forest is an ordered set of zero or more trees. The subtrees immediately below any node of a tree form a forest.

There is a natural way to represent any forest as a binary tree. Consider the following forest of two trees:

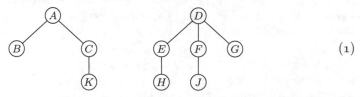

(1)

The corresponding binary tree is obtained by linking together the children of each family and removing vertical links except from a parent to a first child:

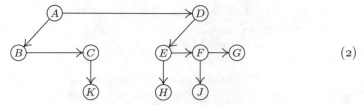

(2)

Then, tilt the diagram 45° clockwise and tweak it slightly, obtaining a binary tree:

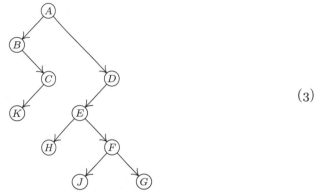

(3)

Conversely, it is easy to see that any binary tree corresponds to a unique forest of trees by reversing the process.

The transformation from (1) to (3) is extremely important; it is called the *natural correspondence* between forests and binary trees. In particular, it gives a correspondence between trees and a special class of binary trees, namely the binary trees that have a root but no right subtree. (We might also change our viewpoint slightly and let the root of a tree correspond to the list head of a binary tree, thus obtaining a one-to-one correspondence between trees with $n+1$ nodes and binary trees with n nodes.)

Let $F = (T_1, T_2, \ldots, T_n)$ be a forest of trees. The binary tree $B(F)$ corresponding to F can be defined rigorously as follows:

a) If $n = 0$, $B(F)$ is empty.

b) If $n > 0$, the root of $B(F)$ is root(T_1); the left subtree of $B(F)$ is $B(T_{11}, T_{12}, \ldots, T_{1m})$, where $T_{11}, T_{12}, \ldots, T_{1m}$ are the subtrees of root(T_1); and the right subtree of $B(F)$ is $B(T_2, \ldots, T_n)$.

These rules specify the transformation from (1) to (3) precisely.

It will occasionally be convenient to draw our binary tree diagram as in (2), without the 45° rotation. The *threaded* binary tree corresponding to (1) is

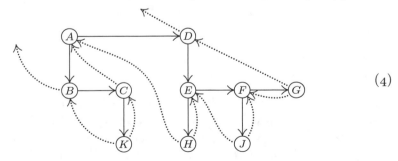

(4)

(compare with Fig. 24, giving the latter a 45° change in orientation). Notice that *right thread links go from the rightmost child of a family to the parent.*

Left thread links do not have such a natural interpretation, due to the lack of symmetry between left and right.

The ideas about traversal explored in the previous section can be recast in terms of forests (and, therefore, trees). There is no simple analog of the inorder sequence, since there is no obvious place to insert a root among its descendants; but preorder and postorder carry over in an obvious manner. Given any nonempty forest, the two basic ways to traverse it may be defined as follows:

Preorder traversal	Postorder traversal
Visit the root of the first tree	Traverse the subtrees of the first tree
Traverse the subtrees of the first tree	Visit the root of the first tree
Traverse the remaining trees	Traverse the remaining trees

In order to understand the significance of these two methods of traversal, consider the following notation for expressing tree structure by nested parentheses:

$$\big(A(B, C(K)), D(E(H), F(J), G)\big). \tag{5}$$

This notation corresponds to the forest (1): We represent a tree by the information written in its root, followed by a representation of its subtrees; we represent a nonempty forest by a parenthesized list of the representations of its trees, separated by commas.

If (1) is traversed in preorder, we visit the nodes in the sequence $A\,B\,C\,K\,D\,E\,H\,F\,J\,G$; this is simply (5) with the parentheses and commas removed. Preorder is a natural way to list the nodes of a tree: We list the root first, then the descendants. If a tree structure is represented by indentation as in Fig. 20(c), the rows appear in preorder. The section numbers of this book itself (see Fig. 22) appear in preorder; thus, for example, Section 2.3 is followed by Section 2.3.1, then come Sections 2.3.2, 2.3.3, 2.3.4, 2.3.4.1, ..., 2.3.4.6, 2.3.5, 2.4, etc.

It is interesting to note that preorder is a time-honored concept that might meaningfully be called *dynastic order*. At the death of a king, duke, or earl, the title passes to the first son, then to descendants of the first son, and finally if these all die out it passes to other sons of the family in the same way. (English custom also includes daughters in a family on the same basis as sons, except that they come after all the sons.) In theory, we could take a lineal chart of all the aristocracy and write out the nodes in preorder; then if we consider only the people presently living, we would obtain the *order of succession to the throne* (except as modified by Acts of Abdication).

Postorder for the nodes in (1) is $B\,K\,C\,A\,H\,E\,J\,F\,G\,D$; this is analogous to preorder, except that it corresponds to the similar parenthesis notation

$$((B, (K)C)A, ((H)E, (J)F, G)D), \tag{6}$$

in which a node appears just *after* its descendants instead of just before.

The definitions of preorder and postorder mesh very nicely with the natural correspondence between trees and binary trees, since the subtrees of the first tree correspond to the left binary subtree, and the remaining trees correspond to the right binary subtree. By comparing these definitions with the corresponding definitions on page 319, we find that traversing a forest in preorder is *exactly the same* as traversing the corresponding binary tree in preorder. Traversing a forest in postorder is exactly the same as traversing the corresponding binary tree in *inorder*. The algorithms developed in Section 2.3.1 may therefore be used without change. (Note that postorder for trees corresponds to inorder, *not* postorder, for binary trees. This is fortunate, since we have seen that it is comparatively hard to traverse binary trees in postorder.) Because of this equivalence, we use the notation P$ for the *postorder* successor of node P in a tree or forest, while it denotes the *inorder* successor in a binary tree.

As an example of the application of these methods to a practical problem, we will consider the manipulation of algebraic formulas. Such formulas are most properly regarded as representations of tree structures, not as one- or two-dimensional configurations of symbols, nor even as binary trees. For example, the formula $y = 3\ln(x + 1) - a/x^2$ has the tree representation

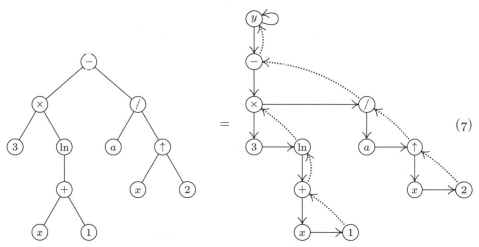

Here the illustration on the left is a conventional tree diagram like Fig. 21, in which the binary operators $+$, $-$, $\times$, $/$, and $\uparrow$ (the latter denotes exponentiation) have two subtrees corresponding to their operands; the unary operator "ln" has one subtree; variables and constants are terminal nodes. The illustration on the right shows the equivalent right-threaded binary tree, including an additional node y that is a list head for the tree. The list head has the form described in 2.3.1–(8).

It is important to note that, even though the left-hand tree in (7) bears a superficial resemblance to a binary tree, we are treating it here as a *tree*, and representing it by a quite different binary tree, shown at the right in (7). Although we could develop routines for algebraic manipulations based directly on binary tree structures — the so-called "three-address code" representations of algebraic formulas — several simplifications occur in practice if we use the general tree representation of algebraic formulas, as in (7), because postorder traversal is easier in a tree.

The nodes of the left-hand tree in (7) are

$$- \quad \times \quad 3 \quad \ln \quad + \quad x \quad 1 \quad / \quad a \quad \uparrow \quad x \quad 2 \qquad \text{in preorder;} \quad (8)$$

$$3 \quad x \quad 1 \quad + \quad \ln \quad \times \quad a \quad x \quad 2 \quad \uparrow \quad / \quad - \qquad \text{in postorder.} \quad (9)$$

Algebraic expressions like (8) and (9) are very important, and they are known as "Polish notations" because form (8) was introduced by the Polish logician, Jan Łukasiewicz. Expression (8) is the *prefix notation* for formula (7), and (9) is the corresponding *postfix notation*. We will return to the interesting topic of Polish notation in later chapters; for now let us be content with the knowledge that Polish notation is directly related to the basic orders of tree traversal.

We shall assume that tree structures for the algebraic formulas with which we will be dealing have nodes of the following form in MIX programs:

RTAG	RLINK	TYPE	LLINK
INFO			

(10)

Here RLINK and LLINK have the usual significance, and RTAG is negative for thread links (corresponding to RTAG = 1 in the statements of algorithms). The TYPE field is used to distinguish different kinds of nodes: TYPE = 0 means that the node represents a constant, and INFO is the value of the constant. TYPE = 1 means that the node represents a variable, and INFO is the five-letter alphabetic name of this variable. TYPE ≥ 2 means that the node represents an operator; INFO is the alphabetic name of the operator and the value TYPE = 2, 3, 4, ... is used to distinguish the different operators $+$, $-$, $\times$, $/$, etc. We will not concern ourselves here with how the tree structure has been set up inside the computer memory in the first place, since this topic is analyzed in great detail in Chapter 10; let us merely assume that the tree already appears in our computer memory, deferring questions of input and output until later.

We shall now discuss the classical example of algebraic manipulation, finding the *derivative* of a formula with respect to the variable x. Programs for algebraic differentiation were among the first symbol-manipulation routines ever written for computers; they were used as early as 1952. The process of differentiation illustrates many of the techniques of algebraic manipulation, and it is of significant practical value in scientific applications.

Readers who are not familiar with mathematical calculus may consider this problem as an abstract exercise in formula manipulation, defined by the following rules:

$$D(x) \quad = 1 \tag{11}$$

$$D(a) \quad = 0, \qquad \text{if } a \text{ is a constant or a variable} \neq x \tag{12}$$

$$D(\ln u) \quad = D(u)/u, \qquad \text{if } u \text{ is any formula} \tag{13}$$

$$D(-u) \quad = -D(u) \tag{14}$$

$$D(u + v) = D(u) + D(v) \tag{15}$$

$$D(u - v) = D(u) - D(v) \tag{16}$$

$$D(u \times v) = D(u) \times v + u \times D(v) \tag{17}$$

$$D(u \,/\, v) = D(u)/v - \big(u \times D(v)\big)/(v \uparrow 2) \qquad\qquad (18)$$
$$D(u \uparrow v) = D(u) \times \big(v \times (u \uparrow (v-1))\big) + \big((\ln u) \times D(v)\big) \times (u \uparrow v) \qquad (19)$$

These rules allow us to evaluate the derivative $D(y)$ for any formula y composed of the operators listed. The "$-$" sign in rule (14) is a unary operator, which is different from the binary "$-$" in (16); we will use "neg" to stand for unary negation in the tree nodes below.

Unfortunately rules (11)–(19) don't tell the whole story. If we apply them blindly to a rather simple formula like

$$y = 3\ln(x+1) - a/x^2,$$

we get

$$D(y) = 0 \cdot \ln(x+1) + 3\big((1+0)/(x+1)\big)$$
$$- \big(0/x^2 - \big(a(1(2x^{2-1}) + ((\ln x) \cdot 0)x^2)\big)/(x^2)^2\big), \qquad (20)$$

which is correct but totally unsatisfactory. To avoid so many redundant operations in the answer, we must recognize the special cases of adding or multiplying by zero, multiplying by one, or raising to the first power. These simplifications reduce (20) to

$$D(y) = 3\big(1/(x+1)\big) - \big(-(a(2x))/(x^2)^2\big), \qquad (21)$$

which is more acceptable but still not ideal. The concept of a really satisfactory answer is not well-defined, because different mathematicians will prefer formulas to be expressed in different ways; however, it is clear that (21) is not as simple as it could be. In order to make substantial progress over formula (21), it is necessary to develop algebraic simplification routines (see exercise 17), which would reduce (21) to, for example,

$$D(y) = 3(x+1)^{-1} + 2ax^{-3}. \qquad (22)$$

We will content ourselves here with routines that can produce (21), not (22).

Our main interest in this algorithm is, as usual, in the details of how the process is carried out inside a computer. Many higher-level languages and special routines are available at most computer installations, with built-in facilities to simplify algebraic manipulations like these; but the purpose of the present example is to gain more experience in fundamental tree operations.

The idea behind the following algorithm is to traverse the tree in postorder, forming the derivative of each node as we go, until eventually the entire derivative has been calculated. Using postorder means that we will arrive at an operator node (like "+") *after* its operands have been differentiated. Rules (11) through (19) imply that every subformula of the original formula will have to be differentiated, sooner or later, so we might as well do the differentiations in postorder.

By using a right-threaded tree, we avoid the need for a stack during the operation of the algorithm. On the other hand, a threaded tree representation has the disadvantage that we will need to make copies of subtrees; for example, in the rule for $D(u \uparrow v)$ we might need to copy u and v three times each. If we had chosen to use a List representation as in Section 2.3.5 instead of a tree, we could have avoided such copying.

Algorithm D (*Differentiation*). If Y is the address of a list head that points to a formula represented as described above, and if DY is the address of the list head for an empty tree, this algorithm makes NODE(DY) point to a tree representing the analytic derivative of Y with respect to the variable "X".

D1. [Initialize.] Set P ← Y$ (namely, the first node of the tree, in postorder, which is the first node of the corresponding binary tree in inorder).

D2. [Differentiate.] Set P1 ← LLINK(P); and if P1 ≠ Λ, also set Q1 ← RLINK(P1). Then perform the routine DIFF[TYPE(P)], described below. (The routines DIFF[0], DIFF[1], etc., will form the derivative of the tree with root P, and will set pointer variable Q to the address of the root of the derivative. The variables P1 and Q1 are set up first, in order to simplify the specification of the DIFF routines.)

D3. [Restore link.] If TYPE(P) denotes a binary operator, set RLINK(P1) ← P2. (See the next step for an explanation.)

D4. [Advance to P$.] Set P2 ← P, P ← P$. Now if RTAG(P2) = 0 (that is, if NODE(P2) has a sibling to the right), set RLINK(P2) ← Q. (This is the tricky part of the algorithm: We temporarily destroy the structure of tree Y, so that a link to the derivative of P2 is saved for future use. The missing link will be restored later in step D3. See exercise 21 for further discussion of this trick.)

D5. [Done?] If P ≠ Y, return to step D2. Otherwise set LLINK(DY) ← Q and RLINK(Q) ← DY, RTAG(Q) ← 1. ∎

The procedure described in Algorithm D is just the background routine for the differentiation operations that are performed by the processing routines DIFF[0], DIFF[1], ..., called in step D2. In many ways, Algorithm D is like the control routine for an interpretive system or machine simulator, as discussed in Section 1.4.3, but it traverses a tree instead of a simple sequence of instructions.

To complete Algorithm D we must define the routines that do the actual differentiation. In the following discussion, the statement "P points to a tree" means that NODE(P) is the root of a tree stored as a right-threaded binary tree, although both RLINK(P) and RTAG(P) will be meaningless so far as this tree is concerned. We will make use of a *tree construction function* that makes new trees by joining smaller ones together: Let x denote some kind of node, either a constant, variable, or operator, and let U and V denote pointers to trees; then

TREE(x,U,V) makes a new tree with x in its root node and with U and V the subtrees of the root: W ⇐ AVAIL, INFO(W) ← x, LLINK(W) ← U, RLINK(U) ← V, RTAG(U) ← 0, RLINK(V) ← W, RTAG(V) ← 1.

TREE(x,U) similarly makes a new tree with only one subtree: W ⇐ AVAIL, INFO(W) ← x, LLINK(W) ← U, RLINK(U) ← W, RTAG(U) ← 1.

TREE(x) makes a new tree with x as a terminal root node: W ⇐ AVAIL, INFO(W) ← x, LLINK(W) ← Λ.

Furthermore TYPE(W) is set appropriately, depending on x. In all cases, the value of TREE is W, that is, a pointer to the tree just constructed. The reader should study these three definitions carefully, since they illustrate the binary tree representation of trees. Another function, COPY(U), makes a copy of the tree pointed to by U and has as its value a pointer to the tree thereby created. The basic functions TREE and COPY make it easy to build up a tree for the derivative of a formula, step by step.

Nullary operators (*constants and variables*). For these operations, NODE(P) is a terminal node, and the values of P1, P2, Q1, and Q before the operation are irrelevant.

DIFF[0]: (NODE(P) is a constant.) Set Q ← TREE(0).

DIFF[1]: (NODE(P) is a variable.) If INFO(P) = "X", set Q ← TREE(1); otherwise set Q ← TREE(0).

Unary operators (*logarithm and negation*). For these operations, NODE(P) has one child, U, pointed to by P1, and Q points to $D(U)$. The values of P2 and Q1 before the operation are irrelevant.

DIFF[2]: (NODE(P) is "ln".) If INFO(Q) $\neq 0$, set Q ← TREE("/",Q,COPY(P1)).

DIFF[3]: (NODE(P) is "neg".) If INFO(Q) $\neq 0$, set Q ← TREE("neg",Q).

Binary operators (*addition, subtraction, multiplication, division, exponentiation*). For these operations, NODE(P) has two children, U and V, pointed to respectively by P1 and P2; Q1 and Q point respectively to $D(U)$, $D(V)$.

DIFF[4]: ("+" operation.) If INFO(Q1) $= 0$, set AVAIL $\Leftarrow$ Q1. Otherwise if INFO(Q) $= 0$, set AVAIL $\Leftarrow$ Q and Q ← Q1; otherwise set Q ← TREE("+",Q1,Q).

DIFF[5]: ("−" operation.) If INFO(Q) $= 0$, set AVAIL $\Leftarrow$ Q and Q ← Q1. Otherwise if INFO(Q1) $= 0$, set AVAIL $\Leftarrow$ Q1 and set Q ← TREE("neg",Q); otherwise set Q ← TREE("−",Q1,Q).

DIFF[6]: ("×" operation.) If INFO(Q1) $\neq 0$, set Q1 ← MULT(Q1,COPY(P2)). Then if INFO(Q) $\neq 0$, set Q ← MULT(COPY(P1),Q). Then go to DIFF[4].

Here MULT(U,V) is a new function that constructs a tree for U × V but also makes a test to see if U or V is equal to 1:

if INFO(U) = 1 and TYPE(U) = 0, set AVAIL $\Leftarrow$ U and MULT(U,V) ← V;
if INFO(V) = 1 and TYPE(V) = 0, set AVAIL $\Leftarrow$ V and MULT(U,V) ← U;
        otherwise set MULT(U,V) ← TREE("×",U,V).

DIFF[7]: ("/" operation.) If INFO(Q1) $\neq 0$, set

$$\text{Q1} \leftarrow \text{TREE("/",Q1,COPY(P2))}.$$

Then if INFO(Q) $\neq 0$, set

Q ← TREE("/",MULT(COPY(P1),Q),TREE("↑",COPY(P2),TREE(2))).

Then go to DIFF[5].

DIFF[8]: ("↑" operation.) See exercise 12.

We conclude this section by showing how all of the operations above are readily transformed into a computer program, starting "from scratch" with only MIX machine language as a basis.

Program D (*Differentiation*). The following MIXAL program performs Algorithm D, with rI2 ≡ P, rI3 ≡ P2, rI4 ≡ P1, rI5 ≡ Q, rI6 ≡ Q1. The order of computations has been rearranged a little, for convenience.

```
001  * DIFFERENTIATION IN A RIGHT-THREADED TREE
002  LLINK  EQU   4:5              Definition of fields, see (10)
003  RLINK  EQU   1:2
004  RLINKT EQU   0:2
005  TYPE   EQU   3:3
006  * MAIN CONTROL ROUTINE        D1. Initialize.
007  D1     STJ   9F               Treat the whole procedure as a subroutine.
008         LD4   Y(LLINK)         P1 ← LLINK(Y), prepare to find Y$.
009  1H     ENT2  0,4              P ← P1.
010  2H     LD4   0,2(LLINK)       P1 ← LLINK(P).
011         J4NZ  1B               If P1 ≠ Λ, repeat.
012  D2     LD1   0,2(TYPE)        D2. Differentiate.
013         JMP   *+1,1            Jump to DIFF[TYPE(P)].
014         JMP   CONSTANT         Switch to table entry for DIFF[0].
015         JMP   VARIABLE                                  DIFF[1].
016         JMP   LN                                        DIFF[2].
017         JMP   NEG                                       DIFF[3].
018         JMP   ADD                                       DIFF[4].
019         JMP   SUB                                       DIFF[5].
020         JMP   MUL                                       DIFF[6].
021         JMP   DIV                                       DIFF[7].
022         JMP   PWR                                       DIFF[8].
023  D3     ST3   0,4(RLINK)       D3. Restore link. RLINK(P1) ← P2.
024  D4     ENT3  0,2              D4. Advance to P$. P2 ← P.
025         LD2   0,2(RLINKT)      P ← RLINKT(P).
026         J2N   1F               Jump if RTAG(P) = 1;
027         ST5   0,3(RLINK)          otherwise set RLINK(P2) ← Q.
028         JMP   2B               Note that NODE(P$) will be terminal.
029  1H     ENN2  0,2
030  D5     ENT1  -Y,2             D5. Done?
031         LD4   0,2(LLINK)       P1 ← LLINK(P), prepare for step D2.
032         LD6   0,4(RLINK)       Q1 ← RLINK(P1).
033         J1NZ  D2               Jump to D2 if P ≠ Y;
034         ST5   DY(LLINK)           otherwise set LLINK(DY) ← Q.
035         ENNA  DY
036         STA   0,5(RLINKT)      RLINK(Q) ← DY, RTAG(Q) ← 1.
037  9H     JMP   *                Exit from differentiation subroutine.  ▮
```

The next part of the program contains the basic subroutines TREE and COPY. The former has three entrances TREE0, TREE1, and TREE2, according to the number of subtrees of the tree being constructed. Regardless of which entrance to the subroutine is used, rA will contain the address of a special constant indicating what type of node forms the root of the tree being constructed; these special constants appear in lines 105–124.

038		* BASIC SUBROUTINES FOR TREE CONSTRUCTION	
039	TREE0	STJ 9F	TREE(rA) function:
040		JMP 2F	
041	TREE1	ST1 3F(0:2)	TREE(rA,rI1) function:
042		JSJ 1F	
043	TREE2	STX 3F(0:2)	TREE(rA,rX,rI1) function:
044	3H	ST1 *(RLINKT)	RLINK(rX) ← rI1, RTAG(rX) ← 0.
045	1H	STJ 9F	
046		LDXN AVAIL	
047		JXZ OVERFLOW	
048		STX 0,1(RLINKT)	RLINK(rI1) ← AVAIL, RTAG(rI1) ← 1.
049		LDX 3B(0:2)	
050		STA *+1(0:2)	
051		STX *(LLINK)	Set LLINK of next root node.
052	2H	LD1 AVAIL	rI1 ⇐ AVAIL.
053		J1Z OVERFLOW	
054		LDX 0,1(LLINK)	
055		STX AVAIL	
056		STA *+1(0:2)	Copy root info to new node.
057		MOVE *(2)	
058		DEC1 2	Reset rI1 to point to the new root.
059	9H	JMP *	Exit from TREE, rI1 points to new tree.
060	COPYP1	ENT1 0,4	COPY(P1), special entrance to COPY
061		JSJ COPY	
062	COPYP2	ENT1 0,3	COPY(P2), special entrance to COPY
063	COPY	STJ 9F	COPY(rI1) function:
⋮		⋮	(see exercise 13)
104	9H	JMP *	Exit from COPY, rI1 points to new tree.
105	CON0	CON 0	Node representing the constant "0"
106		CON 0	
107	CON1	CON 0	Node representing "1"
108		CON 1	
109	CON2	CON 0	Node representing "2"
110		CON 2	
111	LOG	CON 2(TYPE)	Node representing "ln"
112		ALF LN	
113	NEGOP	CON 3(TYPE)	Node representing "neg"
114		ALF NEG	
115	PLUS	CON 4(TYPE)	Node representing "+"
116		ALF +	
117	MINUS	CON 5(TYPE)	Node representing "−"
118		ALF −	
119	TIMES	CON 6(TYPE)	Node representing "×"
120		ALF *	
121	SLASH	CON 7(TYPE)	Node representing "/"
122		ALF /	

123	UPARROW	CON	8(TYPE)	Node representing "↑"
124		ALF	**	▮

The remaining portion of the program corresponds to the differentiation routines
DIFF[0], DIFF[1], ...; these routines are written to return control to step D3
after processing a binary operator, otherwise they return to step D4.

125	* DIFFERENTIATION ROUTINES			
126	VARIABLE	LDX	1,2	
127		ENTA	CON1	
128		CMPX	2F	Is INFO(P) = "X"?
129		JE	*+2	If so, call TREE(1).
130	CONSTANT	ENTA	CON0	Call TREE(0).
131		JMP	TREE0	
132	1H	ENT5	0,1	Q ← location of new tree.
133		JMP	D4	Return to control routine.
134	2H	ALF	X	
135	LN	LDA	1,5	
136		JAZ	D4	Return to control routine if INFO(Q) = 0;
137		JMP	COPYP1	otherwise set rI1 ← COPY(P1).
138		ENTX	0,5	
139		ENTA	SLASH	
140		JMP	TREE2	rI1 ← TREE("/",Q,rI1).
141		JMP	1B	Q ← rI1, return to control.
142	NEG	LDA	1,5	
143		JAZ	D4	Return if INFO(Q) = 0.
144		ENTA	NEGOP	
145		ENT1	0,5	
146		JMP	TREE1	rI1 ← TREE("neg",Q).
147		JMP	1B	Q ← rI1, return to control.
148	ADD	LDA	1,6	
149		JANZ	1F	Jump unless INFO(Q1) = 0.
150	3H	LDA	AVAIL	AVAIL ⇐ Q1.
151		STA	0,6(LLINK)	
152		ST6	AVAIL	
153		JMP	D3	Return to control, binary operator.
154	1H	LDA	1,5	
155		JANZ	1F	Jump unless INFO(Q) = 0.
156	2H	LDA	AVAIL	AVAIL ⇐ Q.
157		STA	0,5(LLINK)	
158		ST5	AVAIL	
159		ENT5	0,6	Q ← Q1.
160		JMP	D3	Return to control.
161	1H	ENTA	PLUS	Prepare to call TREE("+",Q1,Q).
162	4H	ENTX	0,6	
163		ENT1	0,5	
164		JMP	TREE2	
165		ENT5	0,1	Q ← TREE("±",Q1,Q).
166		JMP	D3	Return to control.
167	SUB	LDA	1,5	
168		JAZ	2B	Jump if INFO(Q) = 0.

169		LDA	1,6	
170		JANZ	1F	Jump unless $\text{INFO(Q1)} = 0$.
171		ENTA	NEGOP	
172		ENT1	0,5	
173		JMP	TREE1	
174		ENT5	0,1	$Q \leftarrow \text{TREE}(\text{"neg"}, Q)$.
175		JMP	3B	$\text{AVAIL} \Leftarrow \text{Q1}$ and return.
176	1H	ENTA	MINUS	Prepare to call $\text{TREE}(\text{"}-\text{"}, \text{Q1}, Q)$.
177		JMP	4B	
178	MUL	LDA	1,6	
179		JAZ	1F	Jump if $\text{INFO(Q1)} = 0$;
180		JMP	COPYP2	otherwise set $\text{rI1} \leftarrow \text{COPY(P2)}$.
181		ENTA	0,6	
182		JMP	MULT	$\text{rI1} \leftarrow \text{MULT(Q1, COPY(P2))}$.
183		ENT6	0,1	$\text{Q1} \leftarrow \text{rI1}$.
184	1H	LDA	1,5	
185		JAZ	ADD	Jump if $\text{INFO(Q)} = 0$;
186		JMP	COPYP1	otherwise set $\text{rI1} \leftarrow \text{COPY(P1)}$.
187		ENTA	0,1	
188		ENT1	0,5	
189		JMP	MULT	$\text{rI1} \leftarrow \text{MULT(COPY(P1), Q)}$.
190		ENT5	0,1	$Q \leftarrow \text{rI1}$.
191		JMP	ADD	
192	MULT	STJ	9F	MULT(rA, rI1) subroutine:
193		STA	1F(0:2)	Let $\text{rA} \equiv U$, $\text{rI1} \equiv V$.
194		ST2	8F(0:2)	Save rI2.
195	1H	ENT2	*	$\text{rI2} \leftarrow U$.
196		LDA	1,2	Test if $\text{INFO(U)} = 1$
197		DECA	1	
198		JANZ	1F	
199		LDA	0,2(TYPE)	and if $\text{TYPE(U)} = 0$.
200		JAZ	2F	
201	1H	LDA	1,1	If not, test if $\text{INFO(V)} = 1$
202		DECA	1	
203		JANZ	1F	
204		LDA	0,1(TYPE)	and if $\text{TYPE(V)} = 0$.
205		JANZ	1F	
206		ST1	*+2(0:2)	If so, interchange $U \leftrightarrow V$.
207		ENT1	0,2	
208		ENT2	*	
209	2H	LDA	AVAIL	$\text{AVAIL} \Leftarrow U$.
210		STA	0,2(LLINK)	
211		ST2	AVAIL	
212		JMP	8F	Result is V.
213	1H	ENTA	TIMES	
214		ENTX	0,2	
215		JMP	TREE2	Result is $\text{TREE}(\text{"}\times\text{"}, U, V)$.
216	8H	ENT2	*	Restore rI2 setting.
217	9H	JMP	*	Exit MULT with result in rI1. ▌

The other two routines DIV and PWR are similar and they have been left as exercises (see exercises 15 and 16).

EXERCISES

▶ **1.** [*20*] The text gives a formal definition of $B(F)$, the binary tree corresponding to a forest F. Give a formal definition that reverses the process; in other words, define $F(B)$, the forest corresponding to a binary tree B.

▶ **2.** [*20*] We defined Dewey decimal notation for forests in Section 2.3, and for binary trees in exercise 2.3.1–5. Thus the node "J" in (1) is represented by "2.2.1", and in the equivalent binary tree (3) it is represented by "11010". If possible, give a rule that directly expresses the natural correspondence between trees and binary trees as a correspondence between the Dewey decimal notations.

3. [*22*] What is the relation between Dewey decimal notation for the nodes of a forest and the preorder and postorder of those nodes?

4. [*19*] Is the following statement true or false? "The terminal nodes of a tree occur in the same relative position in preorder and postorder."

5. [*23*] Another correspondence between forests and binary trees could be defined by letting RLINK(P) point to the rightmost child of NODE(P), and LLINK(P) to the nearest sibling on the left. Let F be a forest that corresponds in this way to a binary tree B. What order, on the nodes of B, corresponds to (a) preorder (b) postorder on F?

6. [*25*] Let T be a nonempty binary tree in which each node has 0 or 2 children. If we regard T as an ordinary tree, it corresponds (via the natural correspondence) to *another* binary tree T'. Is there any simple relation between preorder, inorder, and postorder of the nodes of T (as defined for binary trees) and the same three orders for the nodes of T'?

7. [*M20*] A forest may be regarded as a partial ordering, if we say that each node precedes its descendants in the tree. Are the nodes topologically sorted (as defined in Section 2.2.3) when they are listed in (a) preorder? (b) postorder? (c) reverse preorder? (d) reverse postorder?

8. [*M20*] Exercise 2.3.1–25 shows how an ordering between the information stored in the individual nodes of a binary tree may be extended to a linear ordering of all binary trees. The same construction leads to an ordering of all trees, under the natural correspondence. Reformulate the definition of that exercise, in terms of trees.

9. [*M21*] Show that the total number of nonterminal nodes in a forest has a simple relation to the total number of right links equal to Λ in the corresponding unthreaded binary tree.

10. [*M23*] Let F be a forest of trees whose nodes in preorder are $u_1, u_2, \ldots, u_n$, and let F' be a forest whose nodes in preorder are $u'_1, u'_2, \ldots, u'_{n'}$. Let $d(u)$ denote the degree (the number of children) of node u. In terms of these ideas, formulate and prove a theorem analogous to Theorem 2.3.1A.

11. [*15*] Draw trees analogous to those shown in (7), corresponding to the formula $y = e^{-x^2}$.

12. [*M21*] Give specifications for the routine DIFF[8] (the "↑" operation), which was omitted from the algorithm in the text.

▶ **13.** [*26*] Write a MIX program for the COPY subroutine (which fits in the program of the text between lines 063–104). [*Hint:* Adapt Algorithm 2.3.1C to the case of right-threaded binary trees, with suitable initial conditions.]

▶ **14.** [*M21*] How long does it take the program of exercise 13 to copy a tree with n nodes?

15. [*23*] Write a MIX program for the DIV routine, corresponding to DIFF[7] as specified in the text. (This routine should be added to the program in the text after line 217.)

16. [*24*] Write a MIX program for the PWR routine, corresponding to DIFF[8] as specified in exercise 12. (This routine should be added to the program in the text after the solution to exercise 15.)

17. [*M40*] Write a program to do algebraic simplification capable of reducing, for example, (20) or (21) to (22). [*Hints:* Include a new field with each node, representing its coefficient (for summands) or its exponent (for factors in a product). Apply algebraic identities, like replacing $\ln(u \uparrow v)$ by $v \ln u$; remove the operations $-$, $/$, $\uparrow$, and neg when possible by using equivalent addition or multiplication operations. Make $+$ and $\times$ into n-ary instead of binary operators; collect like terms by sorting their operands in tree order (exercise 8); some sums and products will now reduce to zero or unity, presenting perhaps further simplifications. Other adjustments, like replacing a sum of logarithms by the logarithm of a product, also suggest themselves.]

▶ **18.** [*25*] An oriented tree specified by n links PARENT[j] for $1 \le j \le n$ implicitly defines an ordered tree if the nodes in each family are ordered by their location. Design an efficient algorithm that constructs a doubly linked circular list containing the nodes of this ordered tree in preorder. For example, given

$$j = 1\ 2\ 3\ 4\ 5\ 6\ 7\ 8$$
$$\text{PARENT}[j] = 3\ 8\ 4\ 0\ 4\ 8\ 3\ 4$$

your algorithm should produce

$$\text{LLINK}[j] = 3\ 8\ 4\ 6\ 7\ 2\ 1\ 5$$
$$\text{RLINK}[j] = 7\ 6\ 1\ 3\ 8\ 4\ 5\ 2$$

and it should also report that the root node is 4.

19. [*M35*] A *free lattice* is a mathematical system, which (for the purposes of this exercise) can be simply defined as the set of all formulas composed of variables and two abstract binary operators "$\vee$" and "$\wedge$". A relation "$X \succeq Y$" is defined between certain formulas X and Y in the free lattice by the following rules:

i) $X \vee Y \succeq W \wedge Z$ if and only if $X \vee Y \succeq W$ or $X \vee Y \succeq Z$ or $X \succeq W \wedge Z$ or $Y \succeq W \wedge Z$;

ii) $X \wedge Y \succeq Z$ if and only if $X \succeq Z$ and $Y \succeq Z$;

iii) $X \succeq Y \vee Z$ if and only if $X \succeq Y$ and $X \succeq Z$;

iv) $x \succeq Y \wedge Z$ if and only if $x \succeq Y$ or $x \succeq Z$, when x is a variable;

v) $X \vee Y \succeq z$ if and only if $X \succeq z$ or $Y \succeq z$, when z is a variable;

vi) $x \succeq y$ if and only if $x = y$, when x and y are variables.

For example, we find $a \wedge (b \vee c) \succeq (a \wedge b) \vee (a \wedge c) \not\succeq a \wedge (b \vee c)$.

Design an algorithm that tests whether or not $X \succeq Y$, given two formulas X and Y in the free lattice.

▶ **20.** [*M22*] Prove that if u and v are nodes of a forest, u is a proper ancestor of v if and only if u precedes v in preorder and u follows v in postorder.

21. [*25*] Algorithm D controls the differentiation activity for binary operators, unary operators, and nullary operators, thus for trees whose nodes have degree 2, 1, and 0; but it does not indicate explicitly how the control would be handled for ternary operators and nodes of higher degree. (For example, exercise 17 suggests making addition and multiplication into operators with any number of operands.) Is it possible to extend Algorithm D in a simple way so that it will handle operators of degree more than 2?

▶ **22.** [*M26*] If T and T' are trees, let us say T *can be embedded in* T', written $T \subseteq T'$, if there is a one-to-one function f from the nodes of T into the nodes of T' such that f preserves both preorder and postorder. (In other words, u precedes v in preorder for T if and only if $f(u)$ precedes $f(v)$ in preorder for T', and the same holds for postorder. See Fig. 25.)

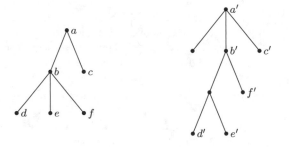

Fig. 25. One tree embedded in another (see exercise 22).

If T has more than one node, let $l(T)$ be the leftmost subtree of root(T) and let $r(T)$ be the rest of T, that is, T with $l(T)$ deleted. Prove that T can be embedded in T' if (i) T has just one node, or (ii) both T and T' have more than one node and either $T \subseteq l(T')$, or $T \subseteq r(T')$, or $\big(l(T) \subseteq l(T')$ and $r(T) \subseteq r(T')\big)$. Does the converse hold?

2.3.3. Other Representations of Trees

There are many ways to represent tree structures inside a computer besides the `LLINK-RLINK` (left child–right sibling) method given in the previous section. As usual, the proper choice of representation depends heavily on what kind of operations we want to perform on the trees. In this section we will consider a few of the tree representation methods that have proved to be especially useful.

First we can use *sequential* memory techniques. As in the case of linear lists, this mode of allocation is most suitable when we want a compact representation of a tree structure that is not going to be subject to radical dynamic changes in size or shape during program execution. There are many situations in which we need essentially constant tables of tree structures for reference within a program, and the desired form of these trees in memory depends on the way in which the tables are to be examined.

The most common sequential representation of trees (and forests) corresponds essentially to the omission of `LLINK` fields, by using consecutive addressing instead. For example, let us look again at the forest

$$\big(A(B,C(K)),\,D(E(H),F(J),G)\big) \qquad (1)$$

considered in the previous section, which has the tree diagrams

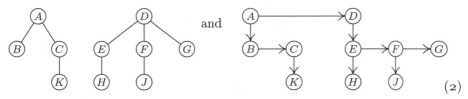

and

$$(2)$$

The *preorder sequential representation* has the nodes appearing in preorder, with the fields INFO, RLINK, and LTAG in each node:

$$\begin{array}{l} \text{RLINK}\\ \text{INFO}\\ \text{LTAG} \end{array} \qquad A \quad B \quad C \quad K \quad D \quad E \quad H \quad F \quad J \quad G \qquad (3)$$

Here nonnull RLINKs have been indicated by arrows, and LTAG = 1 (for terminal nodes) is indicated by "⌋". LLINK is unnecessary, since it would either be null or it would point to the next item in sequence. It is instructive to compare (1) with (3).

This representation has several interesting properties. In the first place, all subtrees of a node appear immediately after that node, so that all subtrees within the original forest appear in consecutive blocks. [Compare this with the "nested parentheses" in (1) and in Fig. 20(b).] In the second place, notice that the RLINK arrows never cross each other in (3); this will be true in general, for in a binary tree all nodes between X and RLINK(X) in preorder lie in the left subtree of X, hence no outward arrows will emerge from that part of the tree. In the third place, we may observe that the LTAG field, which indicates whether a node is terminal or not, is redundant, since "⌋" occurs only at the end of the forest and just *preceding* every downward pointing arrow.

Indeed, these remarks show that the RLINK field itself is almost redundant; all we really need to represent the structure is RTAG and LTAG. Thus it is possible to deduce (3) from much less data:

$$\begin{array}{l} \text{RTAG}\\ \text{INFO}\\ \text{LTAG} \end{array} \qquad A \quad B \quad C \quad K \quad D \quad E \quad H \quad F \quad J \quad G \qquad (4)$$

As we scan (4) from left to right, the positions with RTAG ≠ "⌉" correspond to nonnull RLINKs that must be filled in. Each time we pass an item with LTAG = "⌋", we should set the RLINK field of the most recent node whose RTAG was blank. (The locations of incomplete RLINKs can therefore be kept on a stack.) We have essentially proved Theorem 2.3.1A again.

The fact that RLINK or LTAG is redundant in (3) is of little or no help to us unless we are scanning the entire forest sequentially, since extra computation is required to deduce the missing information. Therefore we often need all of the data in (3). However, there is evidently some wasted space, since more than half of the RLINK fields are equal to Λ for this particular forest. There are two common ways to make use of the wasted space:

1) Fill the RLINK of each node with the address following the subtree below that node. The field is now often called "SCOPE" instead of RLINK, since it indicates the right boundary of the "influence" (descendants) of each node. Instead of (3), we would have

$$
\begin{array}{c}
\text{SCOPE} \\
\text{INFO} \qquad A \quad B \quad C \quad K \quad D \quad E \quad H \quad F \quad J \quad G
\end{array} \tag{5}
$$

The arrows still do not cross each other. Furthermore, LTAG(X) = "$\rfloor$" is characterized by the condition SCOPE(X) = X $+ c$, where c is the number of words per node. One example of the use of this SCOPE idea appears in exercise 2.4–12.

2) Decrease the size of each node by removing the RLINK field, and add special "link" nodes just before nodes that formerly had a nonnull RLINK:

$$
\begin{array}{c}
\text{INFO} \qquad * \quad A \quad * \quad B \quad C \quad K \quad D \quad * \quad E \quad H \quad * \quad F \quad J \quad G \\
\text{LTAG}
\end{array} \tag{6}
$$

Here "$*$" indicates the special link nodes, whose INFO somehow characterizes them as links pointing as shown by the arrows. If the INFO and RLINK fields of (3) occupy roughly the same amount of space, the net effect of the change to (6) is to consume less memory, since the number of "$*$" nodes is always less than the number of non-"$*$" nodes. Representation (6) is somewhat analogous to a sequence of instructions in a one-address computer like MIX, with the "$*$" nodes corresponding to conditional jump instructions.

Another sequential representation analogous to (3) may be devised by omitting RLINKs instead of LLINKs. In this case we list the nodes of the forest in a new order that may be called *family order* since the members of each family appear together. Family order for any forest may be defined recursively as follows:

Visit the root of the first tree.

Traverse the remaining trees (in family order).

Traverse the subtrees of the root of the first tree (in family order).

(Compare this with the definitions of preorder and postorder in the previous section. Family order is identical with the reverse of postorder in the corresponding binary tree.)

The *family order sequential representation* of the trees (2) is

$$
\begin{array}{c}
\text{LLINK} \\
\text{INFO} \qquad A \quad D \quad E \quad F \quad G \quad J \quad H \quad B \quad C \quad K \\
\text{RTAG}
\end{array} \tag{7}
$$

In this case the RTAG entries serve to delimit the families. Family order begins by listing the roots of all trees in the forest, then continues by listing individual families, successively choosing the family of the most recently appearing node whose family has not yet been listed. It follows that the LLINK arrows will never cross; and the other properties of preorder representation carry over in a similar way.

Instead of using family order, we could also simply list the nodes from left to right, one level at a time. This is called "level order" [see G. Salton, *CACM* **5** (1962), 103–114], and the *level order sequential representation* of (2) is

$$
\begin{array}{ll}
\text{LLINK} \\
\text{INFO} \quad A \;\; D \;\; B \;\; C \;\; E \;\; F \;\; G \;\; K \;\; H \;\; J \\
\text{RTAG}
\end{array}
\tag{8}
$$

This is like (7), but the families are chosen in first-in-first-out fashion rather than last-in-first-out. Either (7) or (8) may be regarded as a natural analog, for trees, of the sequential representation of linear lists.

The reader will easily see how to design algorithms that traverse and analyze trees represented sequentially as above, since the LLINK and RLINK information is essentially available just as though we had a fully linked tree structure.

Another sequential method, called *postorder with degrees*, is somewhat different from the techniques above. We list the nodes in postorder and give the degree of each node instead of links:

$$
\begin{array}{lllllllllll}
\text{DEGREE} & 0 & 0 & 1 & 2 & 0 & 1 & 0 & 1 & 0 & 3 \\
\text{INFO} & B & K & C & A & H & E & J & F & G & D
\end{array}
\tag{9}
$$

For a proof that this is sufficient to characterize the tree structure, see exercise 2.3.2–10. This order is useful for the "bottom-up" evaluation of functions defined on the nodes of a tree, as in the following algorithm.

Algorithm F (*Evaluate a locally defined function in a tree*). Suppose f is a function of the nodes of a tree, such that the value of f at a node x depends only on x and the values of f on the children of x. The following algorithm, using an auxiliary stack, evaluates f at each node of a nonempty forest.

F1. [Initialize.] Set the stack empty, and let P point to the first node of the forest in postorder.

F2. [Evaluate f.] Set $d \leftarrow$ DEGREE(P). (The first time this step is reached, d will be zero. In general, when we get to this point, it will always be true that the top d items of the stack are $f(x_d)$, ..., $f(x_1)$ — from the top of the stack downward — where x_1, ..., x_d are the children of NODE(P) from left to right.) Evaluate $f(\text{NODE(P)})$, using the values of $f(x_d)$, ..., $f(x_1)$ found on the stack.

F3. [Update the stack.] Remove the top d items of the stack; then put the value $f(\text{NODE(P)})$ on top of the stack.

F4. [Advance.] If P is the last node in postorder, terminate the algorithm. (The stack will then contain $f(\text{root}(T_m))$, ..., $f(\text{root}(T_1))$, from top to bottom, where T_1, ..., T_m are the trees of the given forest.) Otherwise set P to its successor in postorder (this would be simply $\text{P} \leftarrow \text{P} + c$ in the representation (9)), and return to step F2. ∎

The validity of Algorithm F follows by induction on the size of the trees processed (see exercise 16). This algorithm bears a striking similarity to the differentiation procedure of the previous section (Algorithm 2.3.2D), which evaluates a function of a closely related type; see exercise 3. The same idea is used in many interpretive routines in connection with the evaluation of arithmetic expressions in postfix notation; we will return to this topic in Chapter 8. See also exercise 17, which gives another important procedure similar to Algorithm F.

Thus we have seen various sequential representations of trees and forests. There are also a number of *linked* forms of representation, which we shall now consider.

The first idea is related to the transformation that takes (3) into (6): We remove the `INFO` fields from all nonterminal nodes and put this information as a new terminal node below the previous node. For example, the trees (2) would become

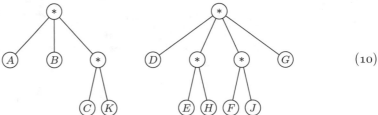

(10)

This new form shows that we may assume (without loss of generality) that all `INFO` in a tree structure appears in its terminal nodes. Therefore in the natural binary tree representation of Section 2.3.2, the `LLINK` and `INFO` fields are mutually exclusive and they can share the same field in each node. A node might have the fields

LTAG	LLINK or INFO	RLINK

where the sign `LTAG` tells whether the second field is a link or not. (Compare this representation with, for example, the two-word format of (10) in Section 2.3.2.) By cutting `INFO` down from 5 bytes to 3, we can fit each node into one word. However, notice that there are now 15 nodes instead of 10; the forest (10) takes 15 words of memory while (2) takes 20, yet the latter has 50 bytes of `INFO` compared to 30 in the other. There is no real gain in memory space in (10) unless the excess `INFO` space was going to waste; the `LLINK`s replaced in (10) are removed at the expense of about the same number of new `RLINK`s in the added nodes. Precise details of the differences between the two representations are discussed in exercise 4.

In the standard binary tree representation of a tree, the `LLINK` field might be more accurately called the `LCHILD` field, since it points from a parent node to its leftmost child. The leftmost child is usually the "youngest" of the children in the tree, since it is easier to insert a node at the left of a family than at the right; so the abbreviation `LCHILD` may also be thought of as the "last child" or "least child."

Many applications of tree structures require rather frequent references upward in the tree as well as downward. A threaded tree gives us the ability to go upward, but not with great speed; we can sometimes do better if we have a third link, PARENT, in each node. This leads to a *triply linked tree*, where each node has LCHILD, RLINK, and PARENT links. Figure 26 shows a triply linked tree representation of (2). For an example of the use of triply linked trees, see Section 2.4.

INFO	PARENT
LCHILD	RLINK

Fig. 26. A triply linked tree.

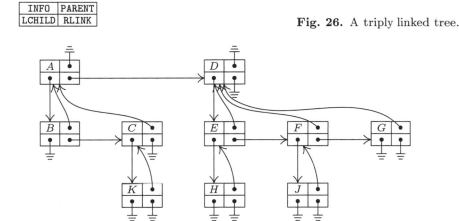

It is clear that the PARENT link all by itself is enough to specify any *oriented* tree (or forest) completely. For we can draw the diagram of the tree if we know all the upward links. Every node except the root has just one parent, but there may be several children; so it is simpler to give upward links than downward ones. Why then haven't we considered upward links much earlier in our discussion? The answer, of course, is that upward links by themselves are hardly adequate in most situations, since it is very difficult to tell quickly if a node is terminal or not, or to locate any of its children, etc. There is, however, a very important application in which upward links are sufficient by themselves: We now turn to a brief study of an elegant algorithm for dealing with equivalence relations, due to M. J. Fischer and B. A. Galler.

An *equivalence relation* "≡" is a relation between the elements of a set of objects S satisfying the following three properties for any objects x, y, and z (not necessarily distinct) in S:

i) If $x \equiv y$ and $y \equiv z$, then $x \equiv z$. (Transitivity.)
ii) If $x \equiv y$, then $y \equiv x$. (Symmetry.)
iii) $x \equiv x$. (Reflexivity.)

(Compare this with the definition of a partial ordering relation in Section 2.2.3; equivalence relations are quite different from partial orderings, in spite of the fact that two of the three defining properties are the same.) Examples of equivalence relations are the relation "=", the relation of congruence (modulo m) for integers, the relation of similarity between trees as defined in Section 2.3.1, etc.

The equivalence problem is to read in pairs of equivalent elements and to determine later whether two particular elements can be proved equivalent or not on the basis of the given pairs. For example, suppose that S is the set $\{1, 2, 3, 4, 5, 6, 7, 8, 9\}$ and suppose that we are given the pairs

$$1 \equiv 5, \quad 6 \equiv 8, \quad 7 \equiv 2, \quad 9 \equiv 8, \quad 3 \equiv 7, \quad 4 \equiv 2, \quad 9 \equiv 3. \tag{11}$$

It follows that, for example, $2 \equiv 6$, since $2 \equiv 7 \equiv 3 \equiv 9 \equiv 8 \equiv 6$. But we cannot show that $1 \equiv 6$. In fact, the pairs (11) divide S into two classes

$$\{1, 5\} \quad \text{and} \quad \{2, 3, 4, 6, 7, 8, 9\}, \tag{12}$$

such that two elements are equivalent if and only if they belong to the same class. It is not difficult to prove that *any* equivalence relation partitions its set S into disjoint classes (called the *equivalence classes*), such that two elements are equivalent if and only if they belong to the same class.

Therefore a solution to the equivalence problem is a matter of keeping track of equivalence classes like (12). We may start with each element alone in its class, thus:

$$\{1\} \ \{2\} \ \{3\} \ \{4\} \ \{5\} \ \{6\} \ \{7\} \ \{8\} \ \{9\} \tag{13}$$

Now if we are given the relation $1 \equiv 5$, we put $\{1, 5\}$ together in a class. After processing the first three relations $1 \equiv 5$, $6 \equiv 8$, and $7 \equiv 2$, we will have changed (13) to

$$\{1, 5\} \ \{2, 7\} \ \{3\} \ \{4\} \ \{6, 8\} \ \{9\}. \tag{14}$$

Now the pair $9 \equiv 8$ puts $\{6, 8, 9\}$ together, etc.

The problem is to find a good way to represent situations like (12), (13), and (14) within a computer so that we can efficiently perform the operations of merging classes together and of testing whether two given elements are in the same class. The algorithm below uses oriented tree structures for this purpose: The elements of S become nodes of an oriented forest; and two nodes are equivalent, as a consequence of the equivalent pairs read so far, *if and only if they belong to the same tree.* This test is easy to make, since two elements are in the same tree if and only if they are below the same root element. Furthermore, it is easy to merge two oriented trees together, by simply attaching one as a new subtree of the other's root.

Algorithm E (*Process equivalence relations*). Let S be the set of numbers $\{1, 2, \ldots, n\}$, and let PARENT[1], PARENT[2], ..., PARENT[n] be integer variables. This algorithm inputs a set of relations such as (11) and adjusts the PARENT table to represent a set of oriented trees, so that two elements are equivalent as a consequence of the given relations if and only if they belong to the same tree. (*Note:* In a more general situation, the elements of S would be symbolic names instead of simply the numbers from 1 to n; then a search routine, as in Chapter 6, would locate nodes corresponding to the elements of S, and PARENT would be a field in each node. The modifications for this more general case are straightforward.)

E1. [Initialize.] Set `PARENT[k] ← 0` for $1 \le k \le n$. (This means that all trees initially consist of a root alone, as in (13).)

E2. [Input new pair.] Get the next pair of equivalent elements "$j \equiv k$" from the input. If the input is exhausted, the algorithm terminates.

E3. [Find roots.] While `PARENT[j] > 0`, set $j \leftarrow$ `PARENT[j]`. Then, while `PARENT[k] > 0`, set $k \leftarrow$ `PARENT[k]`. (After these loops, j and k have moved up to the roots of two trees that are to be made equivalent. The input relation $j \equiv k$ was redundant if and only if we now have $j = k$.)

E4. [Merge trees.] If $j \ne k$, set `PARENT[j] ← k`. Go back to step E2. ∎

The reader should try this algorithm on the input (11). After processing $1 \equiv 5$, $6 \equiv 8$, $7 \equiv 2$, and $9 \equiv 8$, we will have

$$
\begin{array}{lccccccccc}
\texttt{PARENT[k]:} & 5 & 0 & 0 & 0 & 0 & 8 & 2 & 0 & 8 \\
k\;: & 1 & 2 & 3 & 4 & 5 & 6 & 7 & 8 & 9
\end{array}
\tag{15}
$$

which represents the trees

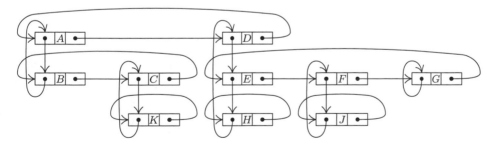

$$\tag{16}$$

After this point, the remaining relations of (11) are somewhat more interesting; see exercise 9.

This equivalence problem arises in many applications. We will discuss significant refinements of Algorithm E in Section 7.4.1.1, when we study the connectivity of graphs. A more general version of the problem, which arises when a compiler processes "equivalence declarations" in languages like FORTRAN, is discussed in exercise 11.

Fig. 27. A ring structure.

There are still more ways to represent trees in computer memory. Recall that we discussed three principal methods for representing linear lists in Section 2.2: the straight representation with terminal link Λ, the circularly linked lists, and the doubly linked lists. The representation of unthreaded binary trees described in Section 2.3.1 corresponds to a straight representation in both LLINKs and

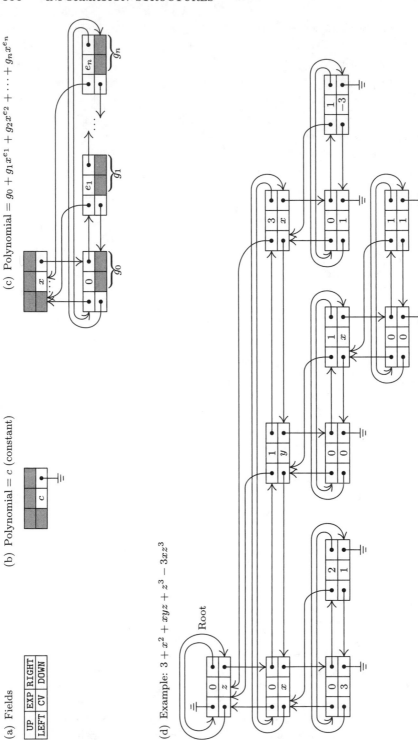

(a) Fields

(b) Polynomial = c (constant)

(c) Polynomial = $g_0 + g_1 x^{e_1} + g_2 x^{e_2} + \cdots + g_n x^{e_n}$

(d) Example: $3 + x^2 + xyz + z^3 - 3xz^3$

Fig. 28. Representation of polynomials using four-directional links. Shaded areas of nodes indicate information that is irrelevant in the context considered.

RLINKs. It is possible to get eight other binary tree representations by independently using any of these three methods in the LLINK and RLINK directions. For example, Fig. 27 shows what we get if circular linking is used in both directions. If circular links are used throughout as in the figure, we have what is called a *ring structure*; ring structures have proved to be quite flexible in a number of applications. The proper choice of representation depends, as always, on the types of insertions, deletions, and traversals that are needed in the algorithms that manipulate these structures. A reader who has looked over the examples given so far in this chapter should have no difficulty understanding how to deal with any of these memory representations.

We close this section with an example of modified doubly linked ring structures applied to a problem we have considered before: arithmetic on polynomials. Algorithm 2.2.4A performs the addition of one polynomial to another, given that the two polynomials are expressed as circular lists; various other algorithms in that section give other operations on polynomials. However, the polynomials of Section 2.2.4 are restricted to at most three variables. When multi-variable polynomials are involved, it is usually more appropriate to use a tree structure instead of a linear list.

A polynomial either is a constant or has the form

$$\sum_{0 \le j \le n} g_j x^{e_j},$$

where x is a variable, $n > 0$, $0 = e_0 < e_1 < \cdots < e_n$, and $g_0, \ldots, g_n$ are polynomials involving only variables alphabetically less than x; $g_1, \ldots, g_n$ are not zero. This recursive definition of polynomials lends itself to tree representation as indicated in Fig. 28. Nodes have six fields, which in the case of MIX might fit in three words:

+	0	LEFT	RIGHT
+	EXP	UP	DOWN
CV			

(17)

Here LEFT, RIGHT, UP, and DOWN are links; EXP is an integer representing an exponent; and CV is either a constant (coefficient) or the alphabetic name of a variable. The root node has UP = Λ, EXP = 0, LEFT = RIGHT = * (self).

The following algorithm illustrates traversal, insertion, and deletion in such a four-way-linked tree, so it bears careful study.

Algorithm A (*Addition of polynomials*). This algorithm adds polynomial(P) to polynomial(Q), assuming that P and Q are pointer variables that link to the roots of distinct polynomial trees having the form shown in Fig. 28. At the conclusion of the algorithm, polynomial(P) will be unchanged, and polynomial(Q) will contain the sum.

A1. [Test type of polynomial.] If DOWN(P) = Λ (that is, if P points to a constant), then set Q ← DOWN(Q) zero or more times until DOWN(Q) = Λ

and go to A3. If DOWN(P) $\neq$ Λ, then if DOWN(Q) = Λ or if CV(Q) < CV(P), go to A2. Otherwise if CV(Q) = CV(P), set P $\leftarrow$ DOWN(P), Q $\leftarrow$ DOWN(Q) and repeat this step; if CV(Q) > CV(P), set Q $\leftarrow$ DOWN(Q) and repeat this step. (Step A1 either finds two matching terms of the polynomials or else determines that an insertion of a new variable must be made into the current part of polynomial(Q).)

A2. [Downward insertion.] Set R $\Leftarrow$ AVAIL, S $\leftarrow$ DOWN(Q). If S $\neq$ Λ, set UP(S) $\leftarrow$ R, S $\leftarrow$ RIGHT(S) and if EXP(S) $\neq$ 0, repeat this operation until ultimately EXP(S) = 0. Set UP(R) $\leftarrow$ Q, DOWN(R) $\leftarrow$ DOWN(Q), LEFT(R) $\leftarrow$ R, RIGHT(R) $\leftarrow$ R, CV(R) $\leftarrow$ CV(Q) and EXP(R) $\leftarrow$ 0. Finally, set CV(Q) $\leftarrow$ CV(P) and DOWN(Q) $\leftarrow$ R, and return to A1. (We have inserted a "dummy" zero polynomial just below NODE(Q), to obtain a match with a corresponding polynomial found within P's tree. The link manipulations done in this step are straightforward and may be derived easily using "before-and-after" diagrams, as explained in Section 2.2.3.)

A3. [Match found.] (At this point, P and Q point to corresponding terms of the given polynomials, so addition is ready to proceed.) Set CV(Q) $\leftarrow$ CV(Q) + CV(P). If this sum is zero and if EXP(Q) $\neq$ 0, go to step A8. If EXP(Q) = 0, go to A7.

A4. [Advance to left.] (After successfully adding a term, we look for the next term to add.) Set P $\leftarrow$ LEFT(P). If EXP(P) = 0, go to A6. Otherwise set Q $\leftarrow$ LEFT(Q) one or more times until EXP(Q) $\leq$ EXP(P). If then EXP(Q) = EXP(P), return to step A1.

A5. [Insert to right.] Set R $\Leftarrow$ AVAIL. Set UP(R) $\leftarrow$ UP(Q), DOWN(R) $\leftarrow$ Λ, CV(R) $\leftarrow$ 0, LEFT(R) $\leftarrow$ Q, RIGHT(R) $\leftarrow$ RIGHT(Q), LEFT(RIGHT(R)) $\leftarrow$ R, RIGHT(Q) $\leftarrow$ R, EXP(R) $\leftarrow$ EXP(P), and Q $\leftarrow$ R. Return to step A1. (We needed to insert a new term in the current row, just to the right of NODE(Q), in order to match a corresponding exponent in polynomial(P). As in step A2, a "before-and-after" diagram makes the operations clear.)

A6. [Return upward.] (A row of polynomial(P) has now been completely traversed.) Set P $\leftarrow$ UP(P).

A7. [Move Q up to right level.] If UP(P) = Λ, go to A11; otherwise set Q $\leftarrow$ UP(Q) zero or more times until CV(UP(Q)) = CV(UP(P)). Return to step A4.

A8. [Delete zero term.] Set R $\leftarrow$ Q, Q $\leftarrow$ RIGHT(R), S $\leftarrow$ LEFT(R), LEFT(Q) $\leftarrow$ S, RIGHT(S) $\leftarrow$ Q, and AVAIL $\Leftarrow$ R. (Cancellation occurred, so a row element of polynomial(Q) is deleted.) If now EXP(LEFT(P)) = 0 and Q = S, go to A9; otherwise return to A4.

A9. [Delete constant polynomial.] (Cancellation has caused a polynomial to reduce to a constant, so a row of polynomial(Q) is deleted.) Set R $\leftarrow$ Q, Q $\leftarrow$ UP(Q), DOWN(Q) $\leftarrow$ DOWN(R), CV(Q) $\leftarrow$ CV(R), and AVAIL $\Leftarrow$ R. Set S $\leftarrow$ DOWN(Q); if S $\neq$ Λ, set UP(S) $\leftarrow$ Q, S $\leftarrow$ RIGHT(S), and if EXP(S) $\neq$ 0, repeat this operation until ultimately EXP(S) = 0.

A10. [Zero detected?] If DOWN(Q) = Λ, CV(Q) = 0, and EXP(Q) $\neq$ 0, set P $\leftarrow$ UP(P) and go to A8; otherwise go to A6.

A11. [Terminate.] Set Q $\leftarrow$ UP(Q) zero or more times until UP(Q) = Λ (thus bringing Q to the root of the tree). ∎

This algorithm will actually run much faster than Algorithm 2.2.4A if polynomial(P) has few terms and polynomial(Q) has many, since it is not necessary to pass over all of polynomial(Q) during the addition process. The reader will find it instructive to simulate Algorithm A by hand, adding the polynomial $xy - x^2 - xyz - z^3 + 3xz^3$ to the polynomial shown in Fig. 28. (This case does not demonstrate the efficiency of the algorithm, but it makes the algorithm go through all of its paces by showing the difficult situations that must be handled.) For further commentary on Algorithm A, see exercises 12 and 13.

No claim is being made here that the representation shown in Fig. 28 is the "best" for polynomials in several variables; in Chapter 8 we will consider another format for polynomial representation, together with arithmetic algorithms using an auxiliary stack, with significant advantages of conceptual simplicity when compared to Algorithm A. Our main interest in Algorithm A is the way it typifies manipulations on trees with many links.

EXERCISES

▶ **1.** [*20*] If we had only LTAG, INFO, and RTAG fields (not LLINK) in a level order sequential representation like (8), would it be possible to reconstruct the LLINKs? (In other words, are the LLINKs redundant in (8), as the RLINKs are in (3)?)

2. [*22*] (Burks, Warren, and Wright, *Math. Comp.* **8** (1954), 53–57.) The trees (2) stored in *preorder* with degrees would be

DEGREE	2	0	1	0	3	1	0	1	0	0
INFO	*A*	*B*	*C*	*K*	*D*	*E*	*H*	*F*	*J*	*G*

[compare with (9), where postorder was used]. Design an algorithm analogous to Algorithm F to evaluate a locally defined function of the nodes by going from right to left in this representation.

▶ **3.** [*24*] Modify Algorithm 2.3.2D so that it follows the ideas of Algorithm F, placing the derivatives it computes as intermediate results on a stack, instead of recording their locations in an anomalous fashion as is done in step D3. (See exercise 2.3.2–21.) The stack may be maintained by using the RLINK field in the root of each derivative.

4. [*18*] The trees (2) contain 10 nodes, five of which are terminal. Representation of these trees in the normal binary-tree fashion involves 10 LLINK fields and 10 RLINK fields (one for each node). Representation of these trees in the form (10), where LLINK and INFO share the same space in a node, requires 5 LLINKs and 15 RLINKs. There are 10 INFO fields in each case.

Given a forest with n nodes, m of which are terminal, compare the total number of LLINKs and RLINKs that must be stored using these two methods of tree representation.

5. [*16*] A triply linked tree, as shown in Fig. 26, contains PARENT, LCHILD, and RLINK fields in each node, with liberal use of Λ-links when there is no appropriate node to mention in the PARENT, LCHILD, or RLINK field. Would it be a good idea to extend this representation to a *threaded* tree, by putting "thread" links in place of the null LCHILD and RLINK entries, as we did in Section 2.3.1?

▶ **6.** [*24*] Suppose that the nodes of an *oriented* forest have three link fields, PARENT, LCHILD, and RLINK, but only the PARENT link has been set up to indicate the tree structure. The LCHILD field of each node is Λ and the RLINK fields are set as a linear list that simply links the nodes together in some order. The link variable FIRST points to the first node, and the last node has RLINK $= \Lambda$.

Design an algorithm that goes through these nodes and fills in the LCHILD and RLINK fields compatible with the PARENT links, so that a triply linked tree representation like that in Fig. 26 is obtained. Also, reset FIRST so that it now points to the root of the first tree in this representation.

7. [*15*] What classes would appear in (12) if the relation $9 \equiv 3$ had not been given in (11)?

8. [*15*] Algorithm E sets up a tree structure that represents the given pairs of equivalent elements, but the text does not mention explicitly how the result of Algorithm E can be used. Design an algorithm that answers the question, "Is $j \equiv k$?", assuming that $1 \le j \le n$, $1 \le k \le n$, and that Algorithm E has set up the PARENT table for some set of equivalences.

9. [*20*] Give a table analogous to (15) and a diagram analogous to (16) that shows the trees present after Algorithm E has processed all of the equivalences in (11) from left to right.

10. [*28*] In the worst case, Algorithm E may take order n^2 steps to process n equivalences. Show how to modify the algorithm so that the worst case is not this bad.

▶ **11.** [*24*] (*Equivalence declarations.*) Several compiler languages, notably FORTRAN, provide a facility for overlapping the memory locations assigned to sequentially stored tables. The programmer gives the compiler a set of relations of the form X[j] $\equiv$ Y[k], which means that variable X[$j + s$] is to be assigned to the same location as variable Y[$k + s$] for all s. Each variable is also given a range of allowable subscripts: "ARRAY X[l:u]" means that space is to be set aside in memory for the table entries X[l], X[$l + 1$], ..., X[u]. For each equivalence class of variables, the compiler reserves as small a block of consecutive memory locations as possible, to contain all the table entries for the allowable subscript values of these variables.

For example, suppose we have ARRAY X[0:10], ARRAY Y[3:10], ARRAY A[1:1], and ARRAY Z[−2:0], plus the equivalences X[7] $\equiv$ Y[3], Z[0] $\equiv$ A[0], and Y[1] $\equiv$ A[8]. We must set aside 20 consecutive locations

$$X_0 \ \ X_1 \ \ X_2 \ \ X_3 \ \ X_4 \ \ X_5 \ \ X_6 \ \ X_7 \ \ X_8 \ \ X_9 \ \ X_{10}$$

$\bullet \quad \bullet \quad \bullet \quad \bullet \quad \bullet \quad \bullet \quad \bullet \quad \bullet \quad \bullet \quad \bullet \quad \bullet \quad \bullet \quad \bullet \quad \bullet \quad \bullet \quad \bullet \quad \bullet \quad \bullet \quad \bullet \quad \bullet$

$$Z_{-2} \ Z_{-1} \ Z_0 \ \ A_1 \qquad\qquad\qquad\quad Y_3 \ \ Y_4 \ \ Y_5 \ \ Y_6 \ \ Y_7 \ \ Y_8 \ \ Y_9 \ \ Y_{10}$$

for these variables. (The location following A[1] is not an allowable subscript value for any of the arrays, but it must be reserved anyway.)

The object of this exercise is to modify Algorithm E so that it applies to the more general situation just described. Assume that we are writing a compiler for such a language, and the tables inside our compiler program itself have one node for each array, containing the fields NAME, PARENT, DELTA, LBD, and UBD. Assume that the compiler program has previously processed all the ARRAY declarations, so that if

ARRAY X[l:u] has appeared and if P points to the node for X, then

$$\text{NAME}(P) = \text{``X''}, \quad \text{PARENT}(P) = \Lambda, \quad \text{DELTA}(P) = 0,$$
$$\text{LBD}(P) = l, \quad \text{UBD}(P) = u.$$

The problem is to design an algorithm that processes the equivalence declarations, so that, after this algorithm has been performed,

PARENT(P) = Λ means that locations X[LBD(P)], ..., X[UBD(P)] are to be reserved in memory for this equivalence class;

PARENT(P) = $Q \neq \Lambda$ means that location X[k] equals location Y[k + DELTA(P)], where NAME(Q) = "Y".

For example, before the equivalences listed above we might have the nodes

P	NAME(P)	PARENT(P)	DELTA(P)	LBD(P)	UBD(P)
α	X	Λ	0	0	10
β	Y	Λ	0	3	10
γ	A	Λ	0	1	1
δ	Z	Λ	0	-2	0

After the equivalences are processed, the nodes might appear thus:

α	X	Λ	*	-5	14
β	Y	α	4	*	*
γ	A	δ	0	*	*
δ	Z	α	-3	*	*

("*" denotes irrelevant information.)

Design an algorithm that makes this transformation. Assume that inputs to your algorithm have the form (P, j, Q, k), denoting X[j] $\equiv$ Y[k], where NAME(P) = "X" and NAME(Q) = "Y". Be sure to check whether the equivalences are contradictory; for example, X[1] $\equiv$ Y[2] contradicts X[2] $\equiv$ Y[1].

12. [21] At the beginning of Algorithm A, the variables P and Q point to the roots of two trees. Let P_0 and Q_0 denote the values of P and Q before execution of Algorithm A. (a) After the algorithm terminates, is Q_0 always the address of the root of the sum of the two given polynomials? (b) After the algorithm terminates, have P and Q returned to their original values P_0 and Q_0?

▶ **13.** [M29] Give an informal proof that at the beginning of step A8 of Algorithm A we always have EXP(P) = EXP(Q) and CV(UP(P)) = CV(UP(Q)). (This fact is important to the proper understanding of that algorithm.)

14. [40] Give a formal proof (or disproof) of the validity of Algorithm A.

15. [40] Design an algorithm to compute the product of two polynomials represented as in Fig. 28.

16. [M24] Prove the validity of Algorithm F.

▶ **17.** [25] Algorithm F evaluates a "bottom-up" locally defined function, namely, one that should be evaluated at the children of a node before it is evaluated at the node. A "top-down" locally defined function f is one in which the value of f at a node x depends only on x and the value of f at the *parent* of x. Using an auxiliary stack, design an algorithm analogous to Algorithm F that evaluates a "top-down" function f at each node of a tree. (Like Algorithm F, your algorithm should work efficiently on trees that have been stored in *postorder* with degrees, as in (9).)

▶ **18.** [*28*] Design an algorithm that, given the two tables `INFO1[j]` and `RLINK[j]` for $1 \leq j \leq n$ corresponding to preorder sequential representation, forms tables `INFO2[j]` and `DEGREE[j]` for $1 \leq j \leq n$, corresponding to postorder with degrees. For example, according to (3) and (9), your algorithm should transform

j	1	2	3	4	5	6	7	8	9	10
`INFO1[j]`	A	B	C	K	D	E	H	F	J	G
`RLINK[j]`	5	3	0	0	0	8	0	10	0	0

into

`INFO2[j]`	B	K	C	A	H	E	J	F	G	D
`DEGREE[j]`	0	0	1	2	0	1	0	1	0	3

19. [*M27*] Instead of using `SCOPE` links in (5), we could simply list the number of descendants of each node, in preorder:

DESC	3	0	1	0	5	1	0	1	0	0
INFO	A	B	C	K	D	E	H	F	J	G

Let $d_1 d_2 \ldots d_n$ be the sequence of descendant numbers of a forest, obtained in this way.
  a) Show that $k + d_k \leq n$ for $1 \leq k \leq n$, and that $k \leq j \leq k + d_k$ implies $j + d_j \leq k + d_k$.
  b) Conversely, prove that if $d_1 d_2 \ldots d_n$ is a sequence of nonnegative integers satisfying the conditions of (a), it is the sequence of descendant numbers of a forest.
  c) Suppose $d_1 d_2 \ldots d_n$ and $d'_1 d'_2 \ldots d'_n$ are the descendant number sequences for two forests. Prove that there is a third forest whose descendant numbers are

$$\min(d_1, d'_1) \min(d_2, d'_2) \ldots \min(d_n, d'_n).$$

2.3.4. Basic Mathematical Properties of Trees

Tree structures have been the object of extensive mathematical investigations for many years, long before the advent of computers, and many interesting facts have been discovered about them. In this section we will survey the mathematical theory of trees, which not only gives us more insight into the nature of tree structures but also has important applications to computer algorithms.

Nonmathematical readers are advised to skip to subsection 2.3.4.5, which discusses several topics that arise frequently in the applications we shall study later.

The material that follows comes mostly from a larger area of mathematics known as the theory of graphs. Unfortunately, there will probably never be a standard terminology in this field, and so the author has followed the usual practice of contemporary books on graph theory, namely to use words that are similar but not identical to the terms used in any *other* books on graph theory. An attempt has been made in the following subsections (and, indeed, throughout this book) to choose short, descriptive words for the important concepts, selected from those that are in reasonably common use and that do not sharply conflict with other common terminology. The nomenclature used here is also biased towards computer applications. Thus, an electrical engineer may prefer to call a "tree" what we call a "free tree"; but we want the shorter term "tree" to stand for the concept that is generally used in the computer literature and that is so much

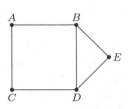

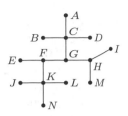

Fig. 29. A graph.   **Fig. 30.** A free tree.

more important in computer applications. If we were to follow the terminology of some authors on graph theory, we would have to say "finite labeled rooted ordered tree" instead of just "tree," and "topological bifurcating arborescence" instead of "binary tree"!

2.3.4.1. Free trees. A *graph* is generally defined to be a set of points (called *vertices*) together with a set of lines (called *edges*) joining certain pairs of distinct vertices. There is at most one edge joining any pair of vertices. Two vertices are called *adjacent* if there is an edge joining them. If V and V' are vertices and if $n \geq 0$, we say that $(V_0, V_1, \ldots, V_n)$ is a *walk* of length n from V to V' if $V = V_0$, V_k is adjacent to V_{k+1} for $0 \leq k < n$, and $V_n = V'$. The walk is a *path* if vertices $V_0, V_1, \ldots, V_n$ are distinct; it is a *cycle* if V_0 through V_{n-1} are distinct, $V_n = V_0$, and $n \geq 3$. Sometimes we are less precise, and refer to a cycle as "a path from a vertex to itself." We often speak of a "simple path" to emphasize the fact that we're talking about a path instead of an arbitrary walk. A graph is *connected* if there is a path between any two vertices of the graph.

These definitions are illustrated in Fig. 29, which shows a connected graph with five vertices and six edges. Vertex C is adjacent to A but not to B; there are two paths of length two from B to C, namely (B, A, C) and (B, D, C). There are several cycles, including (B, D, E, B).

A *free tree* or "unrooted tree" (Fig. 30) is defined to be a connected graph with no cycles. This definition applies to infinite graphs as well as to finite ones, although for computer applications we naturally are most concerned with finite trees. There are many equivalent ways to define a free tree; some of them appear in the following well-known theorem:

Theorem A. *If G is a graph, the following statements are equivalent:*

a) G *is a free tree.*

b) G *is connected, but if any edge is deleted, the resulting graph is no longer connected.*

c) *If V and V' are distinct vertices of G, there is exactly one simple path from V to V'.*

Furthermore, if G is finite, containing exactly $n > 0$ vertices, the following statements are also equivalent to (a), (b), *and* (c):

d) G *contains no cycles and has $n - 1$ edges.*

e) G *is connected and has $n - 1$ edges.*

Proof. (a) implies (b), for if the edge $V — V'$ is deleted but G is still connected, there must be a simple path $(V, V_1, \ldots, V')$ of length two or more — see exercise 2 — and then $(V, V_1, \ldots, V', V)$ would be a cycle in G.

(b) implies (c), for there is at least one simple path from V to V'. And if there were two such paths $(V_0, V_1, \ldots, V_s)$ and $(V'_0, V'_1, \ldots, V'_t)$, where $V_0 = V'_0 = V$ and $V_s = V'_t = V'$, we could find the smallest k for which $V_k \neq V'_k$; deleting the edge $V_{k-1} — V_k$ wouldn't disconnect G, since there would still be a path $(V_{k-1}, V'_k, \ldots, V'_{t-1}, V', V_{s-1}, \ldots, V_k)$ from V_{k-1} to V_k that avoids the deleted edge.

(c) implies (a), for if G contains a cycle $(V, V_1, \ldots, V)$, there are two simple paths from V to V_1.

To show that (d) and (e) are also equivalent to (a), (b), and (c), let us first prove an auxiliary result: If G is any finite graph that has no cycles and at least one edge, then there is at least one vertex that is adjacent to exactly one other vertex. This follows because we can find some vertex V_1 and an adjacent vertex V_2; for $k \geq 2$ either V_k is adjacent to V_{k-1} and no other, or it is adjacent to a vertex that we may call $V_{k+1} \neq V_{k-1}$. Since there are no cycles, $V_1, V_2, \ldots, V_{k+1}$ must be distinct vertices, so this process must ultimately terminate.

Now assume that G is a free tree with $n > 1$ vertices, and let V_n be a vertex that is adjacent to only one other vertex, namely V_{n-1}. If we delete V_n and the edge $V_{n-1} — V_n$, the remaining graph G' is a free tree, since V_n appears in no simple path of G except as the first or the last element. This argument proves (by induction on n) that G has $n - 1$ edges; hence (a) implies (d).

Assume that G satisfies (d) and let V_n, V_{n-1}, G' be as in the preceding paragraph. Then the graph G is connected, since V_n is connected to V_{n-1}, which (by induction on n) is connected to all other vertices of G'. Thus (d) implies (e).

Finally assume that G satisfies (e). If G contains a cycle, we can delete any edge appearing in that cycle and G would still be connected. We can therefore continue deleting edges in this way until we obtain a connected graph G' with $n - 1 - k$ edges and no cycles. But since (a) implies (d), we must have $k = 0$, that is, $G = G'$. ∎

The idea of a free tree can be applied directly to the analysis of computer algorithms. In Section 1.3.3, we discussed the application of Kirchhoff's first law to the problem of counting the number of times each step of an algorithm is performed; we found that Kirchhoff's law does not completely determine the number of times each step is executed, but it reduces the number of unknowns that must be specially interpreted. The theory of trees tells us how many independent unknowns will remain, and it gives us a systematic way to find them.

It is easier to understand the method that follows if an example is studied, so we will work an example as the theory is being developed. Figure 31 shows an abstracted flow chart for Program 1.3.3A, which was subjected to a "Kirchhoff's law" analysis in Section 1.3.3. Each box in Fig. 31 represents part of the computation, and the letter or number inside the box denotes the number of times that computation will be performed during one run of the program, using

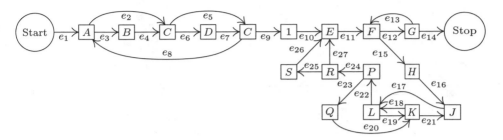

Fig. 31. Abstracted flow chart of Program 1.3.3A.

the notation of Section 1.3.3. An arrow between boxes represents a possible jump in the program. The arrows have been labeled $e_1, e_2, \ldots, e_{27}$. Our goal is to find all relations between the quantities A, B, C, D, E, F, G, H, J, K, L, P, Q, R, and S that are implied by Kirchhoff's law, and at the same time we hope to gain some insight into the general problem. (*Note:* Some simplifications have already been made in Fig. 31; for example, the box between C and E has been labeled "1", and this in fact is a consequence of Kirchhoff's law.)

Let E_j denote the number of times branch e_j is taken during the execution of the program being studied; Kirchhoff's law is

$$\text{sum of } E\text{'s into box} = \text{value in box} = \text{sum of } E\text{'s leaving box}; \qquad (1)$$

for example, in the case of the box marked K we have

$$E_{19} + E_{20} = K = E_{18} + E_{21}. \qquad (2)$$

In the discussion that follows, we will regard $E_1, E_2, \ldots, E_{27}$ as the unknowns, instead of $A, B, \ldots, S$.

The flow chart in Fig. 31 may be abstracted further so that it becomes a graph G as in Fig. 32. The boxes have shrunk to vertices, and the arrows $e_1, e_2, \ldots$ now represent edges of the graph. (A graph, strictly speaking, has no implied direction in its edges, and the direction of the arrows should be ignored when we refer to graph-theoretical properties of G. Our application to Kirchhoff's law, however, makes use of the arrows, as we will see shortly.) For convenience an extra edge e_0 has been drawn from the Stop vertex to the Start vertex, so that Kirchhoff's law applies uniformly to all parts of the graph. Figure 32 also includes some other minor changes from Fig. 31: An extra vertex and edge have been added to divide e_{13} into two parts e'_{13} and e''_{13}, so that the basic definition of a graph (no two edges join the same two vertices) is valid; e_{19} has also been split up in this way. A similar modification would have been made if we had any vertex with an arrow leading back to itself.

Some of the edges in Fig. 32 have been drawn much heavier than the others. These edges form a *free subtree* of the graph, connecting all the vertices. It is always possible to find a free subtree of the graphs arising from flow charts, because the graphs must be connected and, by part (b) of Theorem A, if G is connected and not a free tree, we can delete some edge and still have the

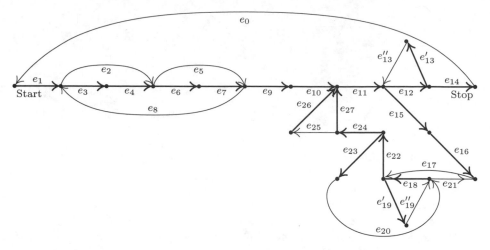

Fig. 32. Graph corresponding to Fig. 31, including a free subtree.

resulting graph connected; this process can be iterated until we reach a free subtree. Another algorithm for finding a free subtree appears in exercise 6. We can in fact always discard the edge e_0 (which went from the Stop to the Start vertex) first; thus we may assume that e_0 does not appear in the subtree chosen.

Let G' be a free subtree of the graph G found in this way, and consider any edge $V — V'$ of G that is *not* in G'. We may now note an important consequence of Theorem A: G' plus this new edge $V — V'$ contains a cycle; and in fact there is *exactly one* cycle, having the form $(V, V', \ldots, V)$, since there is a unique simple path from V' to V in G'. For example, if G' is the free subtree shown in Fig. 32, and if we add the edge e_2, we obtain a cycle that goes along e_2 and then (in the direction opposite to the arrows) along e_4 and e_3. This cycle may be written algebraically as "$e_2 - e_4 - e_3$", using plus signs and minus signs to indicate whether the cycle goes in the direction of the arrows or not.

If we carry out this process for each edge not in the free subtree, we obtain the so-called *fundamental cycles*, which in the case of Fig. 32 are

$$
\begin{aligned}
&C_0: \ e_0 + e_1 + e_3 + e_4 + e_6 + e_7 + e_9 + e_{10} + e_{11} + e_{12} + e_{14}, \\
&C_2: \ e_2 - e_4 - e_3, \\
&C_5: \ e_5 - e_7 - e_6, \\
&C_8: \ e_8 + e_3 + e_4 + e_6 + e_7, \\
&C''_{13}: e''_{13} + e_{12} + e'_{13}, \\
&C_{17}: e_{17} + e_{22} + e_{24} + e_{27} + e_{11} + e_{15} + e_{16}, \\
&C''_{19}: e''_{19} + e_{18} + e'_{19}, \\
&C_{20}: e_{20} + e_{18} + e_{22} + e_{23}, \\
&C_{21}: e_{21} - e_{16} - e_{15} - e_{11} - e_{27} - e_{24} - e_{22} - e_{18}, \\
&C_{25}: e_{25} + e_{26} - e_{27}.
\end{aligned}
\tag{3}
$$

Obviously an edge e_j that is not in the free subtree will appear in only one of the fundamental cycles, namely C_j.

We are now approaching the climax of this construction. Each fundamental cycle represents a solution to Kirchhoff's equations; for example, the solution corresponding to C_2 is to let $E_2 = +1$, $E_4 = -1$, $E_3 = -1$, and all other E's $= 0$. It is clear that flow around a cycle in a graph always satisfies the condition (1) of Kirchhoff's law. Moreover, Kirchhoff's equations are "homogeneous," so the sum or difference of solutions to (1) yields another solution. Therefore we may conclude that the values of $E_0, E_2, E_5, \ldots, E_{25}$ are *independent* in the following sense:

> If $x_0, x_2, \ldots, x_{25}$ are any real numbers (one x_j for each e_j not in the free subtree G'), there is a solution to Kirchhoff's equations (1) such that (4)
> $E_0 = x_0$, $E_2 = x_2$, $\ldots$, $E_{25} = x_{25}$.

Such a solution is found by going x_0 times around the cycle C_0, x_2 times around cycle C_2, etc. Furthermore, we find that the values of the remaining variables $E_1, E_3, E_4, \ldots$ are completely *dependent* on the values $E_0, E_2, \ldots, E_{25}$:

> The solution mentioned in statement (4) is unique. (5)

For if there are two solutions to Kirchhoff's equations such that $E_0 = x_0, \ldots,$ $E_{25} = x_{25}$, we can subtract one from the other and we thereby obtain a solution in which $E_0 = E_2 = E_5 = \cdots = E_{25} = 0$. But now *all* E_j must be zero, for it is easy to see that a nonzero solution to Kirchhoff's equations is impossible when the graph is a free tree (see exercise 4). Therefore the two assumed solutions must be identical. We have now proved that all solutions of Kirchhoff's equations may be obtained as sums of multiples of the fundamental cycles.

When these remarks are applied to the graph in Fig. 32, we obtain the following general solution of Kirchhoff's equations in terms of the independent variables $E_0, E_2, \ldots, E_{25}$:

$$
\begin{aligned}
E_1 &= E_0, & E_{14} &= E_0, \\
E_3 &= E_0 - E_2 + E_8, & E_{15} &= E_{17} - E_{21}, \\
E_4 &= E_0 - E_2 + E_8, & E_{16} &= E_{17} - E_{21}, \\
E_6 &= E_0 - E_5 + E_8, & E_{18} &= E_{19}'' + E_{20} - E_{21}, \\
E_7 &= E_0 - E_5 + E_8, & E_{19}' &= E_{19}'', \\
E_9 &= E_0, & E_{22} &= E_{17} + E_{20} - E_{21}, \\
E_{10} &= E_0, & E_{23} &= E_{20}, \\
E_{11} &= E_0 + E_{17} - E_{21}, & E_{24} &= E_{17} - E_{21}, \\
E_{12} &= E_0 + E_{13}'', & E_{26} &= E_{25}, \\
E_{13}' &= E_{13}'', & E_{27} &= E_{17} - E_{21} - E_{25}.
\end{aligned}
\tag{6}
$$

To obtain these equations, we merely list, for each edge e_j in the subtree, all E_k for which e_j appears in cycle C_k, with the appropriate sign. [Thus, the matrix of coefficients in (6) is just the transpose of the matrix of coefficients in (3).]

Strictly speaking, C_0 should not be called a fundamental cycle, since it involves the special edge e_0. We may call C_0 minus the edge e_0 a *fundamental path from Start to Stop*. Our boundary condition, that the Start and Stop boxes in the flow chart are performed exactly once, is equivalent to the relation

$$E_0 = 1. \tag{7}$$

The preceding discussion shows how to obtain all solutions to Kirchhoff's law; the same method may be applied (as Kirchhoff himself applied it) to electrical circuits instead of program flow charts. It is natural to ask at this point whether Kirchhoff's law is the strongest possible set of equations that can be given for the case of program flow charts, or whether more can be said: Any execution of a computer program that goes from Start to Stop gives us a set of values $E_1, E_2, \ldots, E_{27}$ for the number of times each edge is traversed, and these values obey Kirchhoff's law; but are there solutions to Kirchhoff's equations that do not correspond to any computer program execution? (In this question, we do not assume that we know anything about the given computer program, except its flow chart.) If there are solutions that meet Kirchhoff's conditions but do not correspond to actual program execution, we can give stronger conditions than Kirchhoff's law. For the case of electrical circuits Kirchhoff himself gave a second law [*Ann. Physik und Chemie* **64** (1845), 497–514]: The sum of the voltage drops around a fundamental cycle must be zero. This second law does not apply to our problem.

There is indeed an obvious further condition that the E's must satisfy, if they are to correspond to some actual walk in the flow chart from Start to Stop; they must be integers, and in fact they must be *nonnegative integers*. This is not a trivial condition, since we cannot simply assign any arbitrary nonnegative integer values to the independent variables $E_2, E_5, \ldots, E_{25}$; for example, if we take $E_2 = 2$ and $E_8 = 0$, we find from (6) and (7) that $E_3 = -1$. (Thus, no execution of the flow chart in Fig. 31 will take branch e_2 twice without taking branch e_8 at least once.) The condition that all the E's be nonnegative integers is not enough either; for example, consider the solution in which $E_{19}'' = 1$, $E_2 = E_5 = \cdots = E_{17} = E_{20} = E_{21} = E_{25} = 0$; there is no way to get to e_{18} except via e_{15}. The following condition is a necessary and sufficient condition that answers the problem raised in the previous paragraph: Let $E_2, E_5, \ldots, E_{25}$ be any given values, and determine $E_1, E_3, \ldots, E_{27}$ according to (6), (7). Assume that all the E's are nonnegative integers, and assume that the graph whose edges are those e_j for which $E_j > 0$, and whose vertices are those that touch such e_j, is *connected*. Then there is a walk from Start to Stop in which edge e_j is traversed exactly E_j times. This fact is proved in the next section (see exercise 2.3.4.2–24).

Let us now summarize the preceding discussion:

Theorem K. *If a flow chart (such as Fig. 31) contains n boxes (including Start and Stop) and m arrows, it is possible to find $m - n + 1$ fundamental cycles and a fundamental path from Start to Stop, such that any walk from Start to Stop is equivalent (in terms of the number of times each edge is traversed)* to one traversal of the fundamental path plus a uniquely determined number of traversals of each of the fundamental cycles. (The fundamental path and fundamental cycles may include some edges that are to be traversed in a direction *opposite* that shown by the arrow on the edge; we conventionally say that such edges are being traversed -1 times.)

Conversely, for any traversal of the fundamental path and the fundamental cycles in which the total number of times each edge is traversed is nonnegative, and in which the vertices and edges corresponding to a positive number of traversals form a connected graph, there is at least one equivalent walk from Start to Stop. ▮

The fundamental cycles are found by picking a free subtree as in Fig. 32; if we choose a different subtree we get, in general, a different set of fundamental cycles. The fact that there are $m - n + 1$ fundamental cycles follows from Theorem A. The modifications we made to get from Fig. 31 to Fig. 32, after adding e_0, do not change the value of $m - n + 1$, although they may increase both m and n; the construction could have been generalized so as to avoid these trivial modifications entirely (see exercise 9).

Theorem K is encouraging because it says that Kirchhoff's law (which consists of n equations in the m unknowns $E_1, E_2, \ldots, E_m$) has just one "redundancy": These n equations allow us to eliminate $n - 1$ unknowns. However, the unknown variables throughout this discussion have been the number of times the *edges* have been traversed, not the number of times each *box* of the flow chart has been entered. Exercise 8 shows how to construct another graph whose edges correspond to the boxes of the flow chart, so that the theory above can be used to deduce the true number of redundancies between the variables of interest.

Applications of Theorem K to software for measuring the performance of programs in high-level languages are discussed by Thomas Ball and James R. Larus in *ACM Trans. Prog. Languages and Systems* **16** (1994), 1319–1360.

EXERCISES

1. [*14*] List all cycles from B to B that are present in the graph of Fig. 29.

2. [*M20*] Prove that if V and V' are vertices of a graph and if there is a walk from V to V', then there is a (simple) path from V to V'.

3. [*15*] What walk from Start to Stop is equivalent (in the sense of Theorem K) to one traversal of the fundamental path plus one traversal of cycle C_2 in Fig. 32?

▶ **4.** [*M20*] Let G' be a finite free tree in which arrows have been drawn on its edges $e_1, \ldots, e_{n-1}$; let $E_1, \ldots, E_{n-1}$ be numbers satisfying Kirchhoff's law (1) in G'. Show that $E_1 = \cdots = E_{n-1} = 0$.

5. [*20*] Using Eqs. (6), express the quantities $A, B, \ldots, S$ that appear inside the boxes of Fig. 31 in terms of the independent variables $E_2, E_5, \ldots, E_{25}$.

▶ **6.** [*M27*] Suppose a graph has n vertices $V_1, \ldots, V_n$ and m edges $e_1, \ldots, e_m$. Each edge e is represented by a pair of integers (a, b) if it joins V_a to V_b. Design an algorithm that takes the input pairs (a_1, b_1), $\ldots$, (a_m, b_m) and prints out a subset of edges that forms a free tree; the algorithm reports failure if this is impossible. Strive for an efficient algorithm.

7. [*22*] Carry out the construction in the text for the flow chart

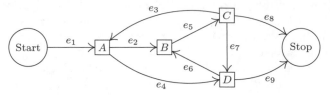

using the free subtree consisting of edges e_1, e_2, e_3, e_4, e_9. What are the fundamental cycles? Express E_1, E_2, E_3, E_4, E_9 in terms of E_5, E_6, E_7, and E_8.

▶ **8.** [*M25*] When applying Kirchhoff's first law to program flow charts, we usually are interested only in the *vertex flows* (the number of times each box of the flow chart is performed), not the edge flows analyzed in the text. For example, in the graph of exercise 7, the vertex flows are $A = E_2 + E_4$, $B = E_5$, $C = E_3 + E_7 + E_8$, $D = E_6 + E_9$.

If we group some vertices together, treating them as one "supervertex," we can combine edge flows that correspond to the same vertex flow. For example, edges e_2 and e_4 can be combined in the flow chart above if we also put B with D:

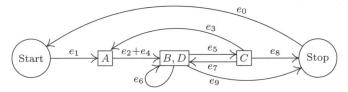

(Here e_0 has also been added from Stop to Start, as in the text.) Continuing this procedure, we can combine $e_3 + e_7$, then $(e_3 + e_7) + e_8$, then $e_6 + e_9$, until we obtain the *reduced flow chart* having edges $s = e_1$, $a = e_2 + e_4$, $b = e_5$, $c = e_3 + e_7 + e_8$, $d = e_6 + e_9$, $t = e_0$, precisely one edge for each vertex in the original flow chart:

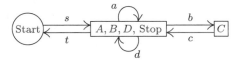

By construction, Kirchhoff's law holds in this reduced flow chart. The new edge flows are the vertex flows of the original; hence the analysis in the text, applied to the reduced flow chart, shows how the original vertex flows depend on each other.

Prove that this reduction process can be reversed, in the sense that any set of flows $\{a, b, \ldots\}$ satisfying Kirchhoff's law in the reduced flow chart can be "split up" into a set of edge flows $\{e_0, e_1, \ldots\}$ in the original flow chart. These flows e_j satisfy Kirchhoff's law and combine to yield the given flows $\{a, b, \ldots\}$; some of them might, however, be negative. (Although the reduction procedure has been illustrated here for only one particular flow chart, your proof should be valid in general.)

9. [*M22*] Edges e_{13} and e_{19} were split into two parts in Fig. 32, since a graph is not supposed to have two edges joining the same two vertices. However, if we look at the final result of the construction, this splitting into two parts seems quite artificial since $E'_{13} = E''_{13}$ and $E'_{19} = E''_{19}$ are two of the relations found in (6), while E''_{13} and E''_{19} are two of the independent variables. Explain how the construction could be generalized so that an artificial splitting of edges may be avoided.

10. [*16*] An electrical engineer, designing the circuitry for a computer, has n terminals $T_1, T_2, \ldots, T_n$ that should be at essentially the same voltage at all times. To achieve this, the engineer can solder wires between any pairs of terminals; the idea is to make enough wire connections so that there is a path through the wires from any terminal to any other. Show that the minimum number of wires needed to connect all the terminals is $n - 1$, and $n - 1$ wires achieve the desired connection if and only if they form a free tree (with terminals and wires standing for vertices and edges).

11. [*M27*] Consider the wire connection problem of exercise 10 with the additional proviso that a cost $c(i, j)$ is given for each $i < j$, denoting the expense of wiring terminal T_i to terminal T_j. Show that the following algorithm gives a connection tree of minimum cost: "If $n = 1$, do nothing. Otherwise, renumber terminals $\{1, \ldots, n-1\}$ and the associated costs so that $c(n - 1, n) = \min_{1 \leq i < n} c(i, n)$; connect terminal T_{n-1} to T_n; then change $c(j, n-1)$ to $\min(c(j, n-1), c(j, n))$ for $1 \leq j < n-1$, and repeat the algorithm for $n - 1$ terminals $T_1, \ldots, T_{n-1}$ using these new costs. (The algorithm is to be repeated with the understanding that whenever a connection is subsequently requested between the terminals now called T_j and T_{n-1}, the connection is actually made between terminals now called T_j and T_n if it is cheaper; thus T_{n-1} and T_n are being regarded as though they were one terminal in the remainder of the algorithm.)" This algorithm may also be paraphrased as follows: "Choose a particular terminal to start with; then repeatedly make the cheapest possible connection from an unchosen terminal to a chosen one, until all have been chosen."

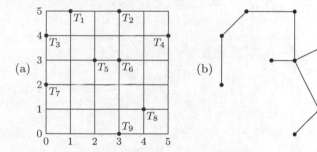

(a)

(b)

Fig. 33. Free tree of minimum cost. (See exercise 11.)

For example, consider Fig. 33(a), which shows nine terminals on a grid; let the cost of connecting two terminals be the wire length, namely the distance between them. (The reader may wish to try to find a minimum cost tree by hand, using intuition instead of the suggested algorithm.) The algorithm would first connect T_8 to T_9, then T_6 to T_8, T_5 to T_6, T_2 to T_6, T_1 to T_2, T_3 to T_1, T_7 to T_3, and finally T_4 to either T_2 or T_6. A minimum cost tree (wire length $7 + 2\sqrt{2} + 2\sqrt{5}$) is shown in Fig. 33(b).

▶ **12.** [*29*] The algorithm of exercise 11 is not stated in a fashion suitable for direct computer implementation. Reformulate that algorithm, specifying in more detail the operations that are to be done, in such a way that a computer program can carry out the process with reasonable efficiency.

13. [*M24*] Consider a graph with n vertices and m edges, in the notation of exercise 6. Show that it is possible to write any permutation of the integers $\{1, 2, \ldots, n\}$ as a product of transpositions $(a_{k_1} b_{k_1})(a_{k_2} b_{k_2}) \ldots (a_{k_t} b_{k_t})$ if and only if the graph is connected. (Hence there are sets of $n - 1$ transpositions that generate all permutations on n elements, but no set of $n - 2$ will do so.)

2.3.4.2. Oriented trees. In the previous section, we saw that an abstracted flow chart may be regarded as a graph, if we ignore the direction of the arrows on its edges; the graph-theoretic ideas of cycle, free subtree, etc., were shown to be relevant in the study of flow charts. There is a good deal more that can be said when the direction of each edge is given more significance, and in this case we have what is called a "directed graph" or "digraph."

Let us define a *directed graph* formally as a set of vertices and a set of *arcs*, each arc leading from a vertex V to a vertex V'. If e is an arc from V to V' we say V is the *initial* vertex of e, and V' is the *final* vertex, and we write $V = \text{init}(e)$, $V' = \text{fin}(e)$. The case that $\text{init}(e) = \text{fin}(e)$ is not excluded (although it was excluded from the definition of edge in an ordinary graph), and several different arcs may have the same initial and final vertices. The *out-degree* of a vertex V is the number of arcs leading out from it, namely the number of arcs e such that $\text{init}(e) = V$; similarly, the *in-degree* of V is defined to be the number of arcs with $\text{fin}(e) = V$.

The concepts of paths and cycles are defined for directed graphs in a manner similar to the corresponding definitions for ordinary graphs, but some important new technicalities must be considered. If $e_1, e_2, \ldots, e_n$ are arcs (with $n \geq 1$), we say that $(e_1, e_2, \ldots, e_n)$ is an *oriented walk* of length n from V to V' if $V = \text{init}(e_1)$, $V' = \text{fin}(e_n)$, and $\text{fin}(e_k) = \text{init}(e_{k+1})$ for $1 \leq k < n$. An oriented walk $(e_1, e_2, \ldots, e_n)$ is called *simple* if $\text{init}(e_1)$, $\ldots$, $\text{init}(e_n)$ are distinct and $\text{fin}(e_1)$, $\ldots$, $\text{fin}(e_n)$ are distinct; such a walk is an *oriented cycle* if $\text{fin}(e_n) = \text{init}(e_1)$, otherwise it's an *oriented path*. (An oriented cycle can have length 1 or 2, but such short cycles were excluded from our definition of "cycle" in the previous section. Can the reader see why this makes sense?)

As examples of these straightforward definitions, we may refer to Fig. 31 in the previous section. The box labeled "J" is a vertex with in-degree 2 (because of the arcs e_{16}, e_{21}) and out-degree 1. The sequence $(e_{17}, e_{19}, e_{18}, e_{22})$ is an oriented walk of length 4 from J to P; this walk is not simple since, for example, $\text{init}(e_{19}) = L = \text{init}(e_{22})$. The diagram contains no oriented cycles of length 1, but (e_{18}, e_{19}) is an oriented cycle of length 2.

A directed graph is said to be *strongly connected* if there is an oriented path from V to V' for any two vertices $V \neq V'$. It is said to be *rooted* if there is at least one *root*, that is, at least one vertex R such that there is an oriented path from V to R for all $V \neq R$. "Strongly connected" always implies "rooted," but the converse does not hold. A flow chart such as Fig. 31 in the previous section is an example of a rooted digraph, with R the Stop vertex; with the additional arc from Stop to Start (Fig. 32) it becomes strongly connected.

Every directed graph G corresponds in an obvious manner to an ordinary graph G_0, if we ignore orientations and discard duplicate edges or loops. Formally speaking, G_0 has an edge from V to V' if and only if $V \neq V'$ and G has an arc from V to V' or from V' to V. We can speak of (unoriented) *paths* and *cycles* in G with the understanding that these are paths and cycles of G_0; we can say that G is *connected* — this is a much weaker property than "strongly connected," even weaker than "rooted" — if the corresponding graph G_0 is connected.

An *oriented tree* (see Fig. 34), sometimes called a "rooted tree" by other authors, is a directed graph with a specified vertex R such that:

a) Each vertex $V \neq R$ is the initial vertex of exactly one arc, denoted by $e[V]$;

b) R is the initial vertex of no arc;

c) R is a root in the sense defined above (that is, for each vertex $V \neq R$ there is an oriented path from V to R).

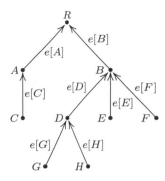

Fig. 34. An oriented tree.

It follows immediately that for each vertex $V \neq R$ there is a *unique* oriented path from V to R; and hence there are no oriented cycles.

Our previous definition of "oriented tree" (at the beginning of Section 2.3) is easily seen to be compatible with the new definition just given, when there are finitely many vertices. The vertices correspond to nodes, and the arc $e[V]$ is the link from V to `PARENT[V]`.

The (undirected) graph corresponding to an oriented tree is connected, because of property (c). Furthermore, it has no cycles. For if $(V_0, V_1, \ldots, V_n)$ is an undirected cycle with $n \geq 3$, and if the edge between V_0 and V_1 is $e[V_1]$, then the edge between V_1 and V_2 must be $e[V_2]$, and similarly the edge between V_{k-1} and V_k must be $e[V_k]$ for $1 \leq k \leq n$, contradicting the absence of oriented cycles. If the edge between V_0 and V_1 is not $e[V_1]$, it must be $e[V_0]$, and the same argument applies to the cycle

$$(V_1, V_0, V_{n-1}, \ldots, V_1),$$

because $V_n = V_0$. Therefore an oriented tree is a free tree when the direction of the arcs is neglected.

Conversely, it is important to note that we can reverse the process just described. If we start with any nonempty free tree, such as that in Fig. 30, we can choose *any* vertex as the root R, and assign directions to the edges. The intuitive idea is to "pick up" the graph at vertex R and shake it; then assign upward-pointing arrows. More formally, the rule is this:

Change the edge $V \longrightarrow V'$ to an arc from V to V' if and only if the simple path from V to R leads through V', that is, if it has the form $(V_0, V_1, \ldots, V_n)$, where $n > 0$, $V_0 = V$, $V_1 = V'$, $V_n = R$.

To verify that such a construction is valid, we need to prove that each edge $V \longrightarrow V'$ is assigned the direction $V \longleftarrow V'$ or the direction $V \longrightarrow V'$; and this is easy to prove, for if $(V, V_1, \ldots, R)$ and $(V', V_1', \ldots, R)$ are simple paths, there is a cycle unless $V = V_1'$ or $V_1 = V'$. This construction demonstrates that the directions of the arcs in an oriented tree are completely determined if we know which vertex is the root, so they need not be shown in diagrams when the root is explicitly indicated.

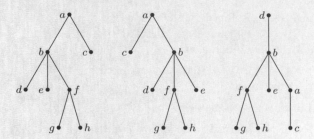

Fig. 35. Three tree structures.

We now see the relation between three types of trees: the (ordered) tree, which is of principal importance in computer programs, as defined at the beginning of Section 2.3; the oriented tree (or unordered tree); and the free tree. Both of the latter two types arise in the study of computer algorithms, but not as often as the first type. *The essential distinction between these types of tree structure is merely the amount of information that is taken to be relevant.* For example, Fig. 35 shows three trees that are distinct if they are considered as ordered trees (with root at the top). As oriented trees, the first and second are identical, since the left-to-right order of subtrees is immaterial; as free trees, all three graphs in Fig. 35 are identical, since the root is immaterial.

An *Eulerian trail* in a directed graph is an oriented walk $(e_1, e_2, \ldots, e_m)$ such that *every* arc in the directed graph occurs exactly once, and $\text{fin}(e_m) = \text{init}(e_1)$. This is a "complete traversal" of the arcs of the digraph. (Eulerian trails get their name from Leonhard Euler's famous discussion in 1736 of the impossibility of traversing each of the seven bridges in the city of Königsberg exactly once during a Sunday stroll. He treated the analogous problem for undirected graphs. Eulerian trails should be distinguished from "Hamiltonian cycles," which are oriented cycles that encounter each *vertex* exactly once; see Chapter 7.)

A directed graph is said to be *balanced* (see Fig. 36) if every vertex V has the same in-degree as its out-degree, that is, if there are just as many edges with V as their initial vertex as there are with V as their final vertex. This condition is closely related to Kirchhoff's law (see exercise 24). If a directed graph has an Eulerian trail, it must obviously be connected and balanced — unless it has *isolated vertices*, which are vertices with in-degree and out-degree both equal to zero.

So far in this section we've looked at quite a few definitions (directed graph, arc, initial vertex, final vertex, out-degree, in-degree, oriented walk, oriented path, oriented cycle, oriented tree, Eulerian trail, isolated vertex, and the properties of being strongly connected, rooted, and balanced), but there has been a scarcity of important results connecting these concepts. Now we are ready for meatier material. The first basic result is a theorem due to I. J. Good [*J. London Math. Soc.* (2) **21** (1946), 167–169], who showed that Eulerian trails are always possible unless they are obviously impossible:

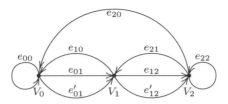

Fig. 36. A balanced directed graph.

Theorem G. *A finite, directed graph with no isolated vertices possesses an Eulerian trail if and only if it is connected and balanced.*

Proof. Assume that G is balanced, and let

$$P = (e_1, \ldots, e_m)$$

be an oriented walk of longest possible length that uses no arc twice. Then if $V = \text{fin}(e_m)$, and if k is the out-degree of V, all k arcs e with $\text{init}(e) = V$ must already appear in P; otherwise we could add e and get a longer walk. But if $\text{init}(e_j) = V$ and $j > 1$, then $\text{fin}(e_{j-1}) = V$. Hence, since G is balanced, we must have

$$\text{init}(e_1) = V = \text{fin}(e_m),$$

otherwise the in-degree of V would be at least $k + 1$.

Now by the cyclic permutation of P it follows that any arc e not in the walk has neither initial nor final vertex in common with any arc in the walk. So if P is not an Eulerian trail, G is not connected. ∎

There is an important connection between Eulerian trails and oriented trees:

Lemma E. *Let $(e_1, \ldots, e_m)$ be an Eulerian trail of a directed graph G having no isolated vertices. Let $R = \text{fin}(e_m) = \text{init}(e_1)$. For each vertex $V \neq R$ let $e[V]$ be the last exit from V in the trail; that is,*

$$e[V] = e_j \quad \text{if } \text{init}(e_j) = V \quad \text{and} \quad \text{init}(e_k) \neq V \quad \text{for } j < k \leq m. \qquad (1)$$

Then the vertices of G with the arcs $e[V]$ form an oriented tree with root R.

Proof. Properties (a) and (b) of the definition of oriented tree are evidently satisfied. By exercise 7 we need only show that there are no oriented cycles among the $e[V]$; but this is immediate, since if $\text{fin}(e[V]) = V' = \text{init}(e[V'])$, where $e[V] = e_j$ and $e[V'] = e_{j'}$, then $j < j'$. ∎

This lemma can perhaps be better understood if we turn things around and consider the "first entrances" to each vertex; the first entrances form an unordered tree with all arcs pointing *away* from R. Lemma E has a surprising and important converse, proved by T. van Aardenne-Ehrenfest and N. G. de Bruijn [*Simon Stevin* **28** (1951), 203–217]:

Theorem D. *Let G be a finite, balanced, directed graph, and let G′ be an oriented tree consisting of the vertices of G plus some of the arcs of G. Let R be the root of G′ and let e[V] be the arc of G′ with initial vertex V. Let e_1 be any arc of G with* $\text{init}(e_1) = R$. *Then* $P = (e_1, e_2, \ldots, e_m)$ *is an Eulerian trail if it is an oriented walk for which*

i) *no arc is used more than once; that is,* $e_j \neq e_k$ *when* $j \neq k$.

ii) *e[V] is not used in P unless it is the only choice consistent with rule* (i); *that is, if* $e_j = e[V]$ *and if e is an arc with* $\text{init}(e) = V$, *then* $e = e_k$ *for some* $k \leq j$.

iii) *P terminates only when it cannot be continued by rule* (i); *that is, if* $\text{init}(e) = \text{fin}(e_m)$, *then* $e = e_k$ *for some k.*

Proof. By (iii) and the argument in the proof of Theorem G, we must have $\text{fin}(e_m) = \text{init}(e_1) = R$. Now if e is an arc not appearing in P, let $V = \text{fin}(e)$. Since G is balanced, it follows that V is the initial vertex of some arc not in P; and if $V \neq R$, condition (ii) tells us that $e[V]$ is not in P. Now use the same argument with $e = e[V]$, and we ultimately find that R is the initial vertex of some arc not in the walk, contradicting (iii). ∎

The essence of Theorem D is that it shows us a simple way to construct an Eulerian trail in a balanced directed graph, given any oriented subtree of the graph. (See the example in exercise 14.) In fact, Theorem D allows us to count the exact number of Eulerian trails in a directed graph; this result and many other important consequences of the ideas developed in this section appear in the exercises that follow.

EXERCISES

1. [*M20*] Prove that if V and V' are vertices of a directed graph and if there is an oriented walk from V to V', then there is a simple oriented path or cycle from V to V'.

2. [*15*] Which of the ten "fundamental cycles" listed in (3) of Section 2.3.4.1 are *oriented* cycles in the directed graph (Fig. 32) of that section?

3. [*16*] Draw the diagram for a directed graph that is connected but not rooted.

▶ **4.** [*M20*] The concept of *topological sorting* can be defined for any finite directed graph G as a linear arrangement of the vertices $V_1 V_2 \ldots V_n$ such that $\text{init}(e)$ precedes $\text{fin}(e)$ in the ordering for all arcs e of G. (See Section 2.2.3, Figs. 6 and 7.) Not all finite directed graphs can be topologically sorted; which ones can be? (Use the terminology of this section to give the answer.)

5. [*M16*] Let G be a directed graph that contains an oriented walk $(e_1, \ldots, e_n)$ with $\text{fin}(e_n) = \text{init}(e_1)$. Give a proof that G is not an oriented tree, using the terminology defined in this section.

6. [*M21*] True or false: A directed graph that is rooted and contains no cycles and no oriented cycles is an oriented tree.

▶ **7.** [*M22*] True or false: A directed graph satisfying properties (a) and (b) of the definition of oriented tree, and having no oriented cycles, is an oriented tree.

8. [*HM40*] Study the properties of *automorphism groups* of oriented trees, namely the groups consisting of all permutations π of the vertices and arcs for which we have $\text{init}(e\pi) = \text{init}(e)\pi$, $\text{fin}(e\pi) = \text{fin}(e)\pi$.

9. [*18*] By assigning directions to the edges, draw the oriented tree corresponding to the free tree in Fig. 30 on page 363, with G as the root.

10. [*22*] An oriented tree with vertices $V_1, \ldots, V_n$ can be represented inside a computer by using a table $P[1], \ldots, P[n]$ as follows: If V_j is the root, $P[j] = 0$; otherwise $P[j] = k$, if the arc $e[V_j]$ goes from V_j to V_k. (Thus $P[1], \ldots, P[n]$ is the same as the "parent" table used in Algorithm 2.3.3E.)

The text shows how a free tree can be converted into an oriented tree by choosing any desired vertex to be the root. Consequently, it is possible to start with an oriented tree that has root R, then to convert this into a free tree by neglecting the orientation of the arcs, and finally to assign new orientations, obtaining an oriented tree with any specified vertex as the root. Design an algorithm that performs this transformation: Starting with a table $P[1], \ldots, P[n]$, representing an oriented tree, and given an integer j, $1 \le j \le n$, design the algorithm to transform the P table so that it represents the same free tree but with V_j as the root.

▶ **11.** [*28*] Using the assumptions of exercise 2.3.4.1–6, but with (a_k, b_k) representing an arc from V_{a_k} to V_{b_k}, design an algorithm that not only prints out a free subtree as in that algorithm, but also prints out the fundamental cycles. [*Hint:* The algorithm given in the solution to exercise 2.3.4.1–6 can be combined with the algorithm in the preceding exercise.]

12. [*M10*] In the correspondence between oriented trees as defined here and oriented trees as defined at the beginning of Section 2.3, is the *degree* of a tree node equal to the *in-degree* or the *out-degree* of the corresponding vertex?

▶ **13.** [*M24*] Prove that if R is a root of a (possibly infinite) directed graph G, then G contains an oriented subtree with the same vertices as G and with root R. (As a consequence, it is always possible to choose the free subtree in flow charts like Fig. 32 of Section 2.3.4.1 so that it is actually an *oriented* subtree; this would be the case in that diagram if we had selected e''_{13}, e''_{19}, e_{20}, and e_{17} instead of e'_{13}, e'_{19}, e_{23}, and e_{15}.)

14. [*21*] Let G be the balanced digraph shown in Fig. 36, and let G' be the oriented subtree with vertices V_0, V_1, V_2 and arcs e_{01}, e_{21}. Find all oriented walks P that meet the conditions of Theorem D, starting with arc e_{12}.

15. [*M20*] True or false: A directed graph that is connected and balanced is strongly connected.

▶ **16.** [*M24*] In a popular solitaire game called "clock," the 52 cards of an ordinary deck of playing cards are dealt face down into 13 piles of four each; 12 piles are arranged in a circle like the 12 hours of a clock and the thirteenth pile goes in the center. The solitaire game now proceeds by turning up the top card of the center pile, and then if its face value is k, by placing it next to the kth pile. (The numbers $1, 2, \ldots, 13$ are equivalent to $A, 2, \ldots, 10, J, Q, K$.) Play continues by turning up the top card of the kth pile and putting it next to *its* pile, etc., until we reach a point where we cannot continue since there are no more cards to turn up on the designated pile. (The player has no choice in the game, since the rules completely specify what to do.) The game is won if all cards are face up when play terminates. [*Reference:* E. D. Cheney, *Patience* (Boston: Lee & Shepard, 1870), 62–65; the game was called "Travellers' Patience" in

England, according to M. Whitmore Jones, *Games of Patience* (London: L. Upcott Gill, 1900), Chapter 7.]

Show that the game will be won if and only if the following directed graph is an oriented tree: The vertices are $V_1, V_2, \ldots, V_{13}$; the arcs are $e_1, e_2, \ldots, e_{12}$, where e_j goes from V_j to V_k if k is the *bottom* card in pile j after the deal.

(In particular, if the bottom card of pile j is a "j", for $j \neq 13$, it is easy to see that the game is certainly lost, since this card could never be turned up. The result proved in this exercise gives a much faster way to play the game!)

17. [*M32*] What is the probability of winning the solitaire game of clock (described in exercise 16), assuming the deck is randomly shuffled? What is the probability that exactly k cards are still face down when the game is over?

18. [*M30*] Let G be a graph with $n+1$ vertices $V_0, V_1, \ldots, V_n$ and m edges $e_1, \ldots, e_m$. Make G into a directed graph by assigning an arbitrary orientation to each edge; then construct the $m \times (n+1)$ matrix A with

$$a_{ij} = \begin{cases} +1, & \text{if } \mathrm{init}(e_i) = V_j\,; \\ -1, & \text{if } \mathrm{fin}(e_i) = V_j\,; \\ 0, & \text{otherwise.} \end{cases}$$

Let A_0 be the $m \times n$ matrix A with column 0 deleted.

a) If $m = n$, show that the determinant of A_0 is equal to 0 if G is not a free tree, and equal to ± 1 if G *is* a free tree.

b) Show that for general m the determinant of $A_0^T A_0$ is the number of free subtrees of G (namely the number of ways to choose n of the m edges so that the resulting graph is a free tree). [*Hint:* Use (a) and the result of exercise 1.2.3–46.]

19. [*M31*] (*The matrix tree theorem.*) Let G be a directed graph with $n+1$ vertices $V_0, V_1, \ldots, V_n$. Let A be the $(n+1) \times (n+1)$ matrix with

$$a_{ij} = \begin{cases} -k, & \text{if } i \neq j \text{ and there are } k \text{ arcs from } V_i \text{ to } V_j; \\ t, & \text{if } i = j \text{ and there are } t \text{ arcs from } V_j \text{ to other vertices.} \end{cases}$$

(It follows that $a_{i0} + a_{i1} + \cdots + a_{in} = 0$ for $0 \leq i \leq n$.) Let A_0 be the same matrix with row 0 and column 0 deleted. For example, if G is the directed graph of Fig. 36, we have

$$A = \begin{pmatrix} 2 & -2 & 0 \\ -1 & 3 & -2 \\ -1 & -1 & 2 \end{pmatrix}, \qquad A_0 = \begin{pmatrix} 3 & -2 \\ -1 & 2 \end{pmatrix}.$$

a) Show that if $a_{00} = 0$ and $a_{jj} = 1$ for $1 \leq j \leq n$, and if G contains no arcs from a vertex to itself, then $\det A_0 = [G$ is an oriented tree with root $V_0]$.

b) Show that in general, $\det A_0$ is the number of oriented subtrees of G rooted at V_0 (namely the number of ways to select n of the arcs of G so that the resulting directed graph is an oriented tree, with V_0 as the root). [*Hint:* Use induction on the number of arcs.]

20. [*M21*] If G is an undirected graph on $n+1$ vertices $V_0, \ldots, V_n$, let B be the $n \times n$ matrix defined as follows for $1 \leq i, j \leq n$:

$$b_{ij} = \begin{cases} t, & \text{if } i = j \text{ and there are } t \text{ edges touching } V_j; \\ -1, & \text{if } i \neq j \text{ and } V_i \text{ is adjacent to } V_j; \\ 0, & \text{otherwise.} \end{cases}$$

For example, if G is the graph of Fig. 29 on page 363, with $(V_0, V_1, V_2, V_3, V_4) = (A, B, C, D, E)$, we find that

$$B = \begin{pmatrix} 3 & 0 & -1 & -1 \\ 0 & 2 & -1 & 0 \\ -1 & -1 & 3 & -1 \\ -1 & 0 & -1 & 2 \end{pmatrix}.$$

Show that the number of free subtrees of G is $\det B$. [*Hint:* Use exercise 18 or 19.]

21. [*HM38*] (T. van Aardenne-Ehrenfest and N. G. de Bruijn.) Figure 36 is an example of a directed graph that is not only balanced, it is *regular*, which means that every vertex has the same in-degree and out-degree as every other vertex. Let G be a regular digraph with n vertices $V_0, V_1, \ldots, V_{n-1}$, in which every vertex has in-degree and out-degree equal to m. (Hence there are mn arcs in all.) Let G^* be the digraph with mn vertices corresponding to the arcs of G; let a vertex of G^* corresponding to an arc from V_j to V_k in G be denoted by V_{jk}. An arc goes from V_{jk} to $V_{j'k'}$ in G^* if and only if $k = j'$. For example, if G is the directed graph of Fig. 36, G^* is shown in Fig. 37. An Eulerian trail in G is a Hamiltonian cycle in G^* and conversely.

Prove that the number of oriented subtrees of G^* is $m^{(m-1)n}$ times the number of oriented subtrees of G. [*Hint:* Use exercise 19.]

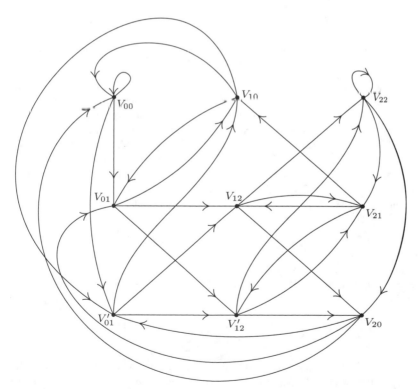

Fig. 37. Arc digraph corresponding to Fig. 36. (See exercise 21.)

▶ **22.** [*M26*] Let G be a balanced, directed graph with vertices $V_1, V_2, \ldots, V_n$ and no isolated vertices. Let σ_j be the out-degree of V_j. Show that the number of Eulerian trails of G is

$$(\sigma_1 + \sigma_2 + \cdots + \sigma_n)\, T \prod_{j=1}^{n}(\sigma_j - 1)!,$$

where T is the number of oriented subtrees of G with root V_1. [*Note:* The factor $(\sigma_1 + \cdots + \sigma_n)$, which is the number of arcs of G, may be omitted if the Eulerian trail $(e_1, \ldots, e_m)$ is regarded as equal to $(e_k, \ldots, e_m, e_1, \ldots, e_{k-1})$.]

▶ **23.** [*M33*] (N. G. de Bruijn.) For each sequence of nonnegative integers $x_1, \ldots, x_k$ less than m, let $f(x_1, \ldots, x_k)$ be a nonnegative integer less than m. Define an infinite sequence as follows: $X_1 = X_2 = \cdots = X_k = 0$; $X_{n+k+1} = f(X_{n+k}, \ldots, X_{n+1})$ when $n \geq 0$. For how many of the m^{m^k} possible functions f is this sequence periodic with a period of the maximum length m^k? [*Hint:* Construct a directed graph with vertices $(x_1, \ldots, x_{k-1})$ for all $0 \leq x_j < m$, and with arcs from $(x_1, x_2, \ldots, x_{k-1})$ to $(x_2, \ldots, x_{k-1}, x_k)$; apply exercises 21 and 22.]

▶ **24.** [*M20*] Let G be a connected digraph with arcs $e_0, e_1, \ldots, e_m$. Let $E_0, E_1, \ldots, E_m$ be a set of positive integers that satisfy Kirchhoff's law for G; that is, for each vertex V,

$$\sum_{\text{init}(e_j)=V} E_j = \sum_{\text{fin}(e_j)=V} E_j.$$

Assume further that $E_0 = 1$. Prove that there is an oriented walk in G from $\text{fin}(e_0)$ to $\text{init}(e_0)$ such that edge e_j appears exactly E_j times, for $1 \leq j \leq m$, while edge e_0 does not appear. [*Hint:* Apply Theorem G to a suitable directed graph.]

25. [*26*] Design a computer representation for directed graphs that generalizes the right-threaded binary tree representation of a tree. Use two link fields ALINK, BLINK and two one-bit fields ATAG, BTAG; and design the representation so that: (i) there is one node for each *arc* of the directed graph (*not* for each vertex); (ii) if the directed graph is an oriented tree with root R, and if we add an arc from R to a new vertex H, then the representation of this directed graph is essentially the same as a right-threaded representation of this oriented tree (with some order imposed on the children in each family), in the sense that ALINK, BLINK, BTAG are respectively the same as LLINK, RLINK, RTAG in Section 2.3.2; and (iii) the representation is symmetric in the sense that interchanging ALINK, ATAG, with BLINK, BTAG is equivalent to changing the direction on all the arcs of the directed graph.

▶ **26.** [*HM39*] (*Analysis of a random algorithm.*) Let G be a directed graph on the vertices $V_1, V_2, \ldots, V_n$. Assume that G represents the flow chart for an algorithm, where V_1 is the Start vertex and V_n is the Stop vertex. (Therefore V_n is a root of G.) Suppose each arc e of G has been assigned a probability $p(e)$, where the probabilities satisfy the conditions

$$0 < p(e) \leq 1; \qquad \sum_{\text{init}(e)=V_j} p(e) = 1 \quad \text{for } 1 \leq j < n.$$

Consider a random walk, which starts at V_1 and subsequently chooses branch e of G with probability $p(e)$, until V_n is reached; the choice of branch taken at each step is to be independent of all previous choices.

For example, consider the graph of exercise 2.3.4.1–7, and assign the respective probabilities $1, \frac{1}{2}, \frac{1}{2}, \frac{1}{2}, 1, \frac{3}{4}, \frac{1}{4}, \frac{1}{4}, \frac{1}{4}$ to arcs $e_1, e_2, \ldots, e_9$. Then the walk "Start–A–B–C–A–D–B–C–Stop" is chosen with probability $1 \cdot \frac{1}{2} \cdot 1 \cdot \frac{1}{2} \cdot \frac{1}{2} \cdot \frac{3}{4} \cdot 1 \cdot \frac{1}{4} = \frac{3}{128}$.

Such random walks are called *Markov chains*, after the Russian mathematician Andrei A. Markov, who first made extensive studies of stochastic processes of this kind. The situation serves as a model for certain algorithms, although our requirement that each choice must be independent of the others is a very strong assumption. The purpose of this exercise is to analyze the computation time for algorithms of this kind.

The analysis is facilitated by considering the $n \times n$ matrix $A = (a_{ij})$, where $a_{ij} = \sum p(e)$ summed over all arcs e that go from V_i to V_j. If there is no such arc, $a_{ij} = 0$. The matrix A for the example considered above is

$$\begin{pmatrix} 0 & 1 & 0 & 0 & 0 & 0 \\ 0 & 0 & \frac{1}{2} & 0 & \frac{1}{2} & 0 \\ 0 & 0 & 0 & 1 & 0 & 0 \\ 0 & \frac{1}{2} & 0 & 0 & \frac{1}{4} & \frac{1}{4} \\ 0 & 0 & \frac{3}{4} & 0 & 0 & \frac{1}{4} \\ 0 & 0 & 0 & 0 & 0 & 0 \end{pmatrix}.$$

It follows easily that $(A^k)_{ij}$ is the probability that a walk starting at V_i will be at V_j after k steps.

Prove the following facts, for an arbitrary directed graph G of the stated type:

a) The matrix $(I - A)$ is nonsingular. [*Hint:* Show that there is no nonzero vector x with $xA^n = x$.]

b) The average number of times that vertex V_j appears in the walk is

$$(I - A)_{1j}^{-1} = \text{cofactor}_{j1}(I - A)/\det(I - A), \qquad \text{for } 1 \le j \le n.$$

[Thus in the example considered we find that the vertices A, B, C, D are traversed respectively $\frac{12}{6}, \frac{7}{3}, \frac{7}{3}, \frac{5}{3}$ times, on the average.]

c) The probability that V_j occurs in the walk is

$$a_j = \text{cofactor}_{j1}(I - A)/\text{cofactor}_{jj}(I - A);$$

furthermore, $a_n = 1$, so the walk terminates in a finite number of steps with probability one.

d) The probability that a random walk starting at V_j will never return to V_j is $b_j = \det(I - A)/\text{cofactor}_{jj}(I - A)$.

e) The probability that V_j occurs exactly k times in the walk is $a_j(1 - b_j)^{k-1} b_j$, for $k \ge 1$, $1 \le j \le n$.

27. [*M30*] (*Steady states.*) Let G be a directed graph on vertices $V_1, \ldots, V_n$, whose arcs have been assigned probabilities $p(e)$ as in exercise 26. Instead of having Start and Stop vertices, however, assume that G is strongly connected; thus each vertex V_j is a root, and we assume that the probabilities $p(e)$ are positive and satisfy $\sum_{\text{init}(e)=V_j} p(e) = 1$ for all j. A random process of the kind described in exercise 26 is said to have a "steady state" $(x_1, \ldots, x_n)$ if

$$x_j = \sum_{\substack{\text{init}(e)=V_i \\ \text{fin}(e)=V_j}} p(e)\, x_i, \qquad \text{for } 1 \le j \le n.$$

Let t_j be the sum, over all oriented subtrees T_j of G that are rooted at V_j, of the products $\prod_{e \in T_j} p(e)$. Prove that $(t_1, \ldots, t_n)$ is a steady state of the random process.

▶ **28.** [*M35*] Consider the $(m+n) \times (m+n)$ determinant illustrated here for $m = 2$ and $n = 3$:

$$\det \begin{pmatrix} a_{10} + a_{11} + a_{12} + a_{13} & 0 & a_{11} & a_{12} & a_{13} \\ 0 & a_{20} + a_{21} + a_{22} + a_{23} & a_{21} & a_{22} & a_{23} \\ b_{11} & b_{12} & b_{10} + b_{11} + b_{12} & 0 & 0 \\ b_{21} & b_{22} & 0 & b_{20} + b_{21} + b_{22} & 0 \\ b_{31} & b_{32} & 0 & 0 & b_{30} + b_{31} + b_{32} \end{pmatrix}.$$

Show that when this determinant is expanded as a polynomial in the a's and b's, each nonzero term has coefficient $+1$. How many terms appear in the expansion? Give a rule, related to oriented trees, that characterizes exactly which terms are present.

*2.3.4.3. The "infinity lemma." Until now we have concentrated mainly on trees that have only finitely many vertices (nodes), but the definitions we have given for free trees and oriented trees apply to infinite graphs as well. Infinite *ordered* trees can be defined in several ways; we can, for example, extend the concept of "Dewey decimal notation" to infinite collections of numbers, as in exercise 2.3–14. Even in the study of computer algorithms there is occasionally a need to know the properties of infinite trees — for example, to prove by contradiction that a certain tree is *not* infinite. One of the most fundamental properties of infinite trees, first stated in its full generality by D. König, is the following:

Theorem K (*The "infinity lemma"*). *Every infinite oriented tree in which every vertex has finite degree has an infinite path to the root, that is, an infinite sequence of vertices $V_0, V_1, V_2, \ldots$ in which V_0 is the root and $\text{fin}(e[V_{j+1}]) = V_j$ for all $j \geq 0$.*

Proof. We define the path by starting with V_0, the root of the oriented tree. Assume that $j \geq 0$ and that V_j has been chosen having infinitely many descendants. The degree of V_j is finite by hypothesis, so V_j has finitely many children $U_1, \ldots, U_n$. At least one of these children must possess infinitely many descendants, so we take V_{j+1} to be such a child of V_j.

Now $V_0, V_1, V_2, \ldots$ is an infinite path to the root. ∎

Students of calculus may recognize that the argument used here is essentially like that used to prove the classical Bolzano–Weierstrass theorem, "A bounded infinite set of real numbers has an accumulation point." One way of stating Theorem K, as König observed, is this: "If the human race never dies out, somebody now living has a line of descendants that will never die out."

Most people think that Theorem K is completely obvious when they first encounter it, but after more thought and a consideration of further examples they realize that there is something profound about it. Although the degree of each node of the tree is finite, we have not assumed that the degrees are *bounded* (less than some number N for all vertices), so there may be nodes with higher and higher degrees. It is at least conceivable that everyone's descendants will ultimately die out although there will be some families that go on a million generations, others a billion, and so on. In fact, H. W. Watson once published a "proof" that under certain laws of biological probability carried out indefinitely, there will be infinitely many people born in the future but each family line will die out with probability one. His paper [*J. Anthropological Inst. Gt. Britain and Ireland* **4** (1874), 138–144] contains important and far-reaching theorems in spite of the minor slip that caused him to make this statement, and it is significant that he did not find his conclusions to be logically inconsistent.

The contrapositive of Theorem K is directly applicable to computer algorithms: *If we have an algorithm that periodically divides itself up into finitely many subalgorithms, and if each chain of subalgorithms ultimately terminates, then the algorithm itself terminates.*

Phrased yet another way, suppose we have a set S, finite or infinite, such that each element of S is a sequence $(x_1, x_2, \ldots, x_n)$ of positive integers of finite length $n \geq 0$. If we impose the conditions that

i) if $(x_1, \ldots, x_n)$ is in S, so is $(x_1, \ldots, x_k)$ for $0 \leq k \leq n$;

ii) if $(x_1, \ldots, x_n)$ is in S, only finitely many x_{n+1} exist for which $(x_1, \ldots, x_n, x_{n+1})$ is also in S;

iii) there is no infinite sequence $(x_1, x_2, \ldots)$ all of whose initial subsequences $(x_1, x_2, \ldots, x_n)$ lie in S;

then S is essentially an oriented tree, specified essentially in a Dewey decimal notation, and Theorem K tells us that S is *finite*.

One of the most convincing examples of the potency of Theorem K arises in connection with a family of interesting tiling problems introduced by Hao Wang. A *tetrad type* is a square divided into four parts, each part having a specified number in it, such as

$$\tag{1}$$

The problem of *tiling the plane* is to take a finite set of tetrad types, with an infinite supply of tetrads of each type, and to show how to place one in each square of an infinite plane (without rotating or reflecting the tetrad types) in such a way that two tetrads are adjacent only if they have equal numbers where they touch. For example, we can tile the plane using the six tetrad types

$$\tag{2}$$

in essentially only one way, by repeating the rectangle

$$\tag{3}$$

over and over. The reader may easily verify that there is no way to tile the plane
with the three tetrad types

   (4)

Wang's observation [*Scientific American* **213**, 5 (November 1965), 98–106] is
that *if it is possible to tile the upper right quadrant of the plane, it is possible to
tile the whole plane.* This is certainly unexpected, because a method for tiling
the upper right quadrant involves a "boundary" along the x and y axes, and it
would seem to give no hint as to how to tile the upper *left* quadrant of the plane
(since tetrad types may not be rotated or reflected). We cannot get rid of the
boundary merely by shifting the upper-quadrant solution down and to the left,
since it does not make sense to shift the solution by more than a finite amount.
But Wang's proof runs as follows: The existence of an upper-right-quadrant
solution implies that there is a way to tile a $2n \times 2n$ square, for all n. The set
of all solutions to the problem of tiling squares with an even number of cells on
each side forms an oriented tree, if the children of each $2n \times 2n$ solution x are
the possible $(2n + 2) \times (2n + 2)$ solutions that can be obtained by bordering x.
The root of this oriented tree is the 0×0 solution; its children are the 2×2
solutions, etc. Each node has only finitely many children, since the problem of
tiling the plane assumes that only finitely many tetrad types are given; hence by
the infinity lemma there is an infinite path to the root. This means that there
is a way to tile the whole plane (although we may be at a loss to find it)!

For later developments in tetrad tiling, see the beautiful book *Tilings and
Patterns* by B. Grünbaum and G. C. Shephard (Freeman, 1987), Chapter 11.

EXERCISES

1. [*M10*] The text refers to a set S containing finite sequences of positive integers,
and states that this set is "essentially an oriented tree." What is the root of this
oriented tree, and what are the arcs?

2. [*20*] Show that if rotation of tetrad types is allowed, it is always possible to tile
the plane.

▶ **3.** [*M23*] If it is possible to tile the upper right quadrant of the plane when given an
infinite set of tetrad types, is it always possible to tile the whole plane?

4. [*M25*] (H. Wang.) The six tetrad types (2) lead to a toroidal solution to the
tiling problem, that is, a solution in which some rectangular pattern — namely (3) —
is replicated throughout the entire plane.

Assume without proof that whenever it is possible to tile the plane with a finite
set of tetrad types, there is a toroidal solution using those tetrad types. Use this
assumption together with the infinity lemma to design an algorithm that, given the
specifications of any finite set of tetrad types, determines in a finite number of steps
whether or not there exists a way to tile the plane with these types.

5. [*M40*] Show that using the following 92 tetrad types it is possible to tile the plane,
but that there is no toroidal solution in the sense of exercise 4.

To simplify the specification of the 92 types, let us first introduce some notation. Define the following "basic codes":

$$\alpha = (\,1,\ 2,\ 1,\ 2) \quad \beta = (3,\ 4,\ 2,\ 1) \quad \gamma = (\,2,\ 1,\ 3,\ 4) \quad \delta = (\,4,\ 3,\ 4,\ 3)$$
$$a = (Q, D, P, R) \quad b = (\ ,\ \ ,\ L, P) \quad c = (U, Q, T, S) \quad d = (\ ,\ \ ,\ S, T)$$
$$J = (D, U,\ \ , X) \quad K = (\ , Y, R, L) \quad N = (Y,\ \ , X,\ \ ) \quad \epsilon = (\ ,\ \ ,\ \ ,\ \ )$$
$$R = (\ ,\ \ ,\ R, R) \quad L = (\ ,\ \ ,\ L, L) \quad P = (\ ,\ \ ,\ P, P) \quad S = (\ ,\ \ ,\ S, S)$$
$$T = (\ ,\ \ ,\ T, T) \quad X = (\ ,\ \ ,\ X, X)$$
$$Y = (Y, Y,\ \ ,\ \ ) \quad U = (U, U,\ \ ,\ \ ) \quad D = (D, D,\ \ ,\ \ ) \quad Q = (Q, Q,\ \ ,\ \ )$$

The tetrad types are now

$$\alpha\{a, b, c, d\} \qquad\qquad\qquad\qquad\qquad\qquad\qquad\qquad\qquad\qquad \text{[4 types]}$$
$$\beta\{Y\{\epsilon, U, Q\}\{P, T\},\ \{\epsilon, U, D, Q\}\{P, S, T\},\ K\{\epsilon, U, Q\}\} \qquad \text{[21 types]}$$
$$\gamma\{\{\{X, \epsilon\}\{L, P, S, T\}, R\}\{\epsilon, Q\},\ J\{L, P, S, T\}\} \qquad\quad \text{[22 types]}$$
$$\delta\{X\{L, P, S, T\}\{\epsilon, Q\},\ Y\{\epsilon, U, Q\}\{P, T\},\ N\{a, b, c, d\},$$
$$J\{L, P, S, T\},\ K\{\epsilon, U, Q\},\ \{R, L, P, S, T\}\{\epsilon, U, D, Q\}\} \quad \text{[45 types]}$$

These abbreviations mean that the basic codes are to be put together component by component and sorted into alphabetic order in each component; thus

$$\beta Y\{c, U, Q\}\{P, T\}$$

stands for six types βYP, βYUP, βYQP, βYT, βYUT, βYQT. The type βYQT is

$$(3, 4, 2, 1)(Y, Y,\ \ ,\ \ )(Q, Q,\ \ ,\ \ )(\ ,\ \ ,\ T, T) = (3QY, 4QY, 2T, 1T)$$

after multiplying corresponding components and sorting into order. This is intended to correspond to the tetrad type shown on the right, where we use strings of symbols instead of numbers in the four quarters of the type. Two tetrad types can be placed next to each other only if they have the same string of symbols at the place they touch.

A β-tetrad is one that has a β in its specification as given above. To get started on the solution to this exercise, note that any β-tetrad must have an α-tetrad to its left and to its right, and a δ-tetrad above and below. An αa-tetrad must have βK or βKU or βKQ to its right, and then must come an αb-tetrad, etc.

(This construction is a simplified version of a similar one given by Robert Berger, who went on to prove that the general problem in exercise 4, without the invalid assumption, cannot be solved. See *Memoirs Amer. Math. Soc.* **66** (1966).)

▶ **6.** [*M23*] (Otto Schreier.) In a famous paper [*Nieuw Archief voor Wiskunde* (2) **15** (1927), 212–216], B. L. van der Waerden proved the following theorem:

> If k and m are positive integers, and if we have k sets $S_1, \ldots, S_k$ of positive integers with every positive integer included in at least one of these sets, then at least one of the sets S_j contains an arithmetic progression of length m.

(The latter statement means there exist integers a and $\delta > 0$ such that $a + \delta$, $a + 2\delta$, $\ldots$, $a + m\delta$ are all in S_j.) If possible, use this result and the infinity lemma to prove the following stronger statement:

> If k and m are positive integers, there is a number N such that if we have k sets $S_1, \ldots, S_k$ of integers with every integer between 1 and N included in at least one of these sets, then at least one of the sets S_j contains an arithmetic progression of length m.

▶ **7.** [*M30*] If possible, use van der Waerden's theorem of exercise 6 and the infinity lemma to prove the following stronger statement:

> If k is a positive integer, and if we have k sets $S_1, \ldots, S_k$ of integers with every positive integer included in at least one of these sets, then at least one of the sets S_j contains an infinitely long arithmetic progression.

▶ **8.** [*M39*] (J. B. Kruskal.) If T and T' are (finite, ordered) trees, let the notation $T \subseteq T'$ signify that T can be embedded in T', as in exercise 2.3.2–22. Prove that if T_1, T_2, T_3, ... is any infinite sequence of trees, there exist integers $j < k$ such that $T_j \subseteq T_k$. (In other words, it is impossible to construct an infinite sequence of trees in which no tree contains any of the earlier trees of the sequence. This fact can be used to prove that certain algorithms must terminate.)

*2.3.4.4. Enumeration of trees. Some of the most instructive applications of the mathematical theory of trees to the analysis of algorithms are connected with formulas for counting how many different trees there are of various kinds. For example, if we want to know how many different oriented trees can be constructed having four indistinguishable vertices, we find that there are just 4 possibilities:

$$(1)$$

For our first enumeration problem, let us determine the number a_n of structurally different oriented trees with n vertices. Obviously, $a_1 = 1$. If $n > 1$, the tree has a root and various subtrees; suppose there are j_1 subtrees with 1 vertex, j_2 with 2 vertices, etc. Then we may choose j_k of the a_k possible k-vertex trees in

$$\binom{a_k + j_k - 1}{j_k}$$

ways, since repetitions are allowed (exercise 1.2.6–60), and so we see that

$$a_n = \sum_{j_1 + 2j_2 + \cdots = n-1} \binom{a_1 + j_1 - 1}{j_1} \cdots \binom{a_{n-1} + j_{n-1} - 1}{j_{n-1}}, \quad \text{for } n > 1. \quad (2)$$

If we consider the generating function $A(z) = \sum_n a_n z^n$, with $a_0 = 0$, we find that the identity

$$\frac{1}{(1 - z^r)^a} = \sum_j \binom{a + j - 1}{j} z^{rj}$$

together with (2) implies

$$A(z) = \frac{z}{(1 - z)^{a_1}(1 - z^2)^{a_2}(1 - z^3)^{a_3} \cdots}. \quad (3)$$

This is not an especially nice form for $A(z)$, since it involves an infinite product and the coefficients $a_1, a_2, \ldots$ appear on the right-hand side. A somewhat more aesthetic way to represent $A(z)$ is given in exercise 1; it leads to a reasonably efficient formula for calculating the values a_n (see exercise 2) and, in fact, it also can be used to deduce the asymptotic behavior of a_n for large n (see exercise 4). We find that

$$A(z) = z + z^2 + 2z^3 + 4z^4 + 9z^5 + 20z^6 + 48z^7 + 115z^8$$
$$+ 286z^9 + 719z^{10} + 1842z^{11} + \cdots. \quad (4)$$

Now that we have essentially found the number of oriented trees, it is quite interesting to determine the number of structurally different *free trees* with n vertices. There are just two distinct free trees with four vertices, namely

and (5)

because the first two and last two oriented trees of (1) become identical when the orientation is dropped.

We have seen that it is possible to select any vertex X of a free tree and to assign directions to the edges in a unique way so that it becomes an oriented tree with X as root. Once this has been done, for a given vertex X, suppose there are k subtrees of the root X, with $s_1, s_2, \ldots, s_k$ vertices in these respective subtrees. Clearly, k is the number of arcs touching X, and $s_1 + s_2 + \cdots + s_k = n - 1$. In these circumstances we say that the *weight* of X is $\max(s_1, s_2, \ldots, s_k)$. Thus in the tree

(6)

the vertex D has weight 3 (each of the subtrees leading from D has three of the nine remaining vertices), and vertex E has weight $\max(7, 2) = 7$. A vertex with minimum weight is called a *centroid* of the free tree.

Let X and $s_1, s_2, \ldots, s_k$ be as above, and let $Y_1, Y_2, \ldots, Y_k$ be the roots of the subtrees emanating from X. If Y is any node in the Y_1 subtree, its weight must be at least $n - s_1 = 1 + s_2 + \cdots + s_k$, since when Y is the assumed root there are at least $n - s_1$ vertices in its subtree containing X. Thus if Y is a centroid we have

$$\text{weight}\,(X) = \max\,(s_1, s_2, \ldots, s_k) \geq \text{weight}\,(Y) \geq 1 + s_2 + \cdots + s_k,$$

and this is possible only if $s_1 > s_2 + \cdots + s_k$. A similar result may be derived if we replace Y_1 by Y_j in this discussion. So *at most one of the subtrees at a vertex can contain a centroid.*

This is a strong condition, for it implies that *there are at most two centroids in a free tree, and if two centroids exist, they are adjacent.* (See exercise 9.)

Conversely, if $s_1 > s_2 + \cdots + s_k$, there *is* a centroid in the Y_1 subtree, since

$$\text{weight}\,(Y_1) \leq \max\,(s_1 - 1, 1 + s_2 + \cdots + s_k) \leq s_1 = \text{weight}\,(X),$$

and the weight of all nodes in the $Y_2, \ldots, Y_k$ subtrees is at least $s_1 + 1$. We have proved that *the vertex X is the only centroid of a free tree if and only if*

$$s_j \leq s_1 + \cdots + s_k - s_j, \qquad \text{for } 1 \leq j \leq k. \tag{7}$$

Therefore the number of free trees with n vertices, having only one centroid, is the number of oriented trees with n vertices minus the number of such oriented trees violating condition (7); the latter consist essentially of an oriented tree with s_j vertices and another oriented tree with $n - s_j \leq s_j = \max(s_1, s_2, \ldots, s_k)$ vertices. The number with one centroid therefore comes to

$$a_n - a_1 a_{n-1} - a_2 a_{n-2} - \cdots - a_{\lfloor n/2 \rfloor} a_{\lceil n/2 \rceil}. \tag{8}$$

A free tree with two centroids has an even number of vertices, and the weight of each centroid is $n/2$ (see exercise 10). So if $n = 2m$, the number of bicentroidal free trees is the number of choices of 2 things out of a_m with repetition, namely

$$\binom{a_m + 1}{2}.$$

To get the total number of free trees, we therefore add $\frac{1}{2} a_{n/2}(a_{n/2} + 1)$ to (8) when n is even. The form of Eq. (8) suggests a simple generating function, and indeed, we find without difficulty that *the generating function for the number of structurally different free trees is*

$$F(z) = A(z) - \frac{1}{2} A(z)^2 + \frac{1}{2} A(z^2)$$

$$= z + z^2 + z^3 + 2z^4 + 3z^5 + 6z^6 + 11z^7 + 23z^8$$

$$+ 47z^9 + 106z^{10} + 235z^{11} + \cdots. \tag{9}$$

This simple relation between $F(z)$ and $A(z)$ is due primarily to C. Jordan, who considered the problem in 1869.

Now let us turn to the question of enumerating *ordered trees*, which are our principal concern with respect to computer programming algorithms. There are five structurally different ordered trees with four vertices:

$$\tag{10}$$

The first two are identical as oriented trees, so only one of them appeared in (1) above.

Before we examine the number of different ordered tree structures, let us first consider the case of *binary trees*, since this is closer to the actual computer representation and it is easier to study. Let b_n be the number of different binary trees with n nodes. From the definition of binary tree it is apparent that $b_0 = 1$, and for $n > 0$ the number of possibilities is the number of ways to put a binary tree with k nodes to the left of the root and another with $n-1-k$ nodes to the right. So

$$b_n = b_0 b_{n-1} + b_1 b_{n-2} + \cdots + b_{n-1} b_0, \qquad n \geq 1. \tag{11}$$

From this relation it is clear that the generating function

$$B(z) = b_0 + b_1 z + b_2 z^2 + \cdots$$

satisfies the equation

$$z B(z)^2 = B(z) - 1. \tag{12}$$

Solving this quadratic equation and using the fact that $B(0) = 1$, we obtain

$$B(z) = \frac{1}{2z}\left(1 - \sqrt{1-4z}\right) = \frac{1}{2z}\left(1 - \sum_{k \geq 0}\binom{\frac{1}{2}}{k}(-4z)^k\right)$$

$$= 2\sum_{n \geq 0}\binom{\frac{1}{2}}{n+1}(-4z)^n = \sum_{n \geq 0}\binom{-\frac{1}{2}}{n}\frac{(-4z)^n}{n+1}$$

$$= \sum_{n \geq 0}\binom{2n}{n}\frac{z^n}{n+1}$$

$$= 1 + z + 2z^2 + 5z^3 + 14z^4 + 42z^5 + 132z^6 + 429z^7$$
$$+ 1430z^8 + 4862z^9 + 16796z^{10} + \cdots. \tag{13}$$

(See exercise 1.2.6–47.) The desired answer is therefore

$$b_n = \frac{1}{n+1}\binom{2n}{n}. \tag{14}$$

By Stirling's formula, this is asymptotically $4^n/n\sqrt{\pi n} + O(4^n n^{5/2})$. Some important generalizations of Eq. (14) appear in exercises 11 and 32.

Returning to our question about ordered trees with n nodes, we can see that this is essentially the same question as the number of binary trees, since we have a natural correspondence between binary trees and forests, and a tree minus its root is a forest. Hence *the number of (ordered) trees with n vertices is b_{n-1}, the number of binary trees with $n-1$ vertices.*

The enumerations performed above assume that the vertices are indistinguishable points. If we label the vertices 1, 2, 3, 4 in (1) and insist that 1 is to be the root, we now get 16 different oriented trees:

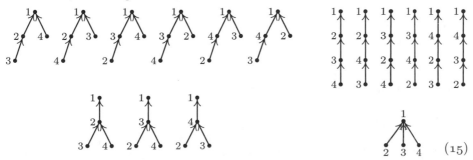

(15)

The question of enumeration for labeled trees is clearly quite different from the one solved above. In this case it can be rephrased as follows: "Consider drawing three lines, pointing from each of the vertices 2, 3, and 4 to another vertex; there are three choices of lines emanating from each vertex, so there are $3^3 = 27$ possibilities in all. How many of these 27 ways will yield oriented trees with 1 as the root?" The answer, as we have seen, is 16. A similar reformulation of the same problem, this time for the case of n vertices, is the following: "Let $f(x)$ be an integer-valued function such that $f(1) = 1$ and $1 \leq f(x) \leq n$ for all integers $1 \leq x \leq n$. We call f a *tree mapping* if $f^{[n]}(x)$, that is, $f\big(f(\cdots(f(x))\cdots)\big)$ iterated n times, equals 1, for all x. How many tree mappings are there?" This problem comes up, for example, in connection with random number generation. We will find, rather surprisingly, that on the average exactly one out of every n such functions f is a tree mapping.

The solution to this enumeration problem can readily be derived using the general formulas for counting subtrees of graphs that have been developed in previous sections (see exercise 12). But there is a much more informative way to solve the problem, one that gives us a new and compact manner to represent oriented tree structure.

Suppose that we've been given an oriented tree with vertices $\{1, 2, \ldots, n\}$ and with $n - 1$ arcs, where the arcs go from j to $f(j)$ for all j except the root. There is at least one terminal (leaf) vertex; let V_1 be the smallest number of a leaf. If $n > 1$, write down $f(V_1)$ and delete both V_1 and the arc $V_1 \to f(V_1)$ from the tree; then let V_2 be the smallest number whose vertex is terminal in the resulting tree. If $n > 2$, write down $f(V_2)$ and delete both V_2 and the arc $V_2 \to f(V_2)$ from the tree; and proceed in this way until all vertices have been deleted except the root. The resulting sequence of $n - 1$ numbers,

$$f(V_1), \ f(V_2), \ \ldots, \ f(V_{n-1}), \qquad 1 \leq f(V_j) \leq n, \qquad (16)$$

is called the *canonical representation* of the original oriented tree.

For example, the oriented tree

$$(17)$$

with 10 vertices has the canonical representation 1, 3, 10, 5, 10, 1, 3, 5, 3.

The important point here is that we can reverse this process and go from any sequence of $n - 1$ numbers (16) back to the oriented tree that produced it. For if we have any sequence $x_1, x_2, \ldots, x_{n-1}$ of numbers between 1 and n, let V_1 be the smallest number that does not appear in the sequence $x_1, \ldots, x_{n-1}$; then let V_2 be the smallest number $\neq V_1$ that does not appear in the sequence $x_2, \ldots, x_{n-1}$; and so on. After obtaining a permutation $V_1 V_2 \ldots V_n$ of the integers $\{1, 2, \ldots, n\}$ in this way, draw arcs from vertex V_j to vertex x_j, for $1 \leq j < n$. This gives a construction of a directed graph with no oriented cycles, and by exercise 2.3.4.2–7 it is an oriented tree. Clearly, the sequence $x_1, x_2, \ldots, x_{n-1}$ is the same as the sequence (16) for this oriented tree.

Since the process is reversible, we have obtained a one-to-one correspondence between $(n-1)$-tuples of numbers $\{1, 2, \ldots, n\}$ and oriented trees on these vertices. Hence *there are n^{n-1} distinct oriented trees with n labeled vertices.* If we specify that one vertex is to be the root, there is clearly no difference between one vertex and another, so there are n^{n-2} distinct oriented trees on $\{1, 2, \ldots, n\}$ having a given root. This accounts for the $16 = 4^{4-2}$ trees in (15). From this information it is easy to determine the number of *free trees* with labeled vertices (see exercise 22). The number of *ordered trees* with labeled vertices is also easy to determine, once we know the answer to that problem when no labels are involved (see exercise 23). So we have essentially solved the problems of enumerating the three fundamental classes of trees, with both labeled and unlabeled vertices.

It is interesting to see what would happen if we were to apply our usual method of generating functions to the problem of enumerating labeled oriented trees. For this purpose we would probably find it easiest to consider the quantity $r(n, q)$, the number of labeled directed graphs with n vertices, with no oriented cycles, and with one arc emanating from each of q designated vertices. The number of labeled oriented trees with a specified root is therefore $r(n, n-1)$. In this notation we find by simple counting arguments that, for any fixed integer m,

$$r(n, q) = \sum_k \binom{q}{k} r(m+k, k) r(n-m-k, q-k), \quad \text{if } 0 \le m \le n-q, \quad (18)$$

$$r(n, q) = \sum_k \binom{q}{k} r(n-1, q-k), \quad \text{if } q = n-1. \quad (19)$$

The first of these relations is obtained if we partition the undesignated vertices into two groups A and B, with m vertices in A and $n-q-m$ vertices in B; then the q designated vertices are partitioned into k vertices that begin paths leading into A, and $q-k$ vertices that begin paths leading into B. Relation (19) is obtained by considering oriented trees in which the root has degree k.

The form of these relations indicates that we can work profitably with the generating function

$$G_m(z) = r(m, 0) + r(m+1, 1)z + \frac{r(m+2, 2)z^2}{2!} + \cdots = \sum_k \frac{r(k+m, k)z^k}{k!}.$$

In these terms Eq. (18) says that $G_{n-q}(z) = G_m(z) G_{n-q-m}(z)$, and therefore by induction on m, we find that $G_m(z) = G_1(z)^m$. Now from Eq. (19), we obtain

$$G_1(z) = \sum_{n \ge 1} \frac{r(n, n-1)z^{n-1}}{(n-1)!} = \sum_{k \ge 0} \sum_{n \ge 1} \frac{r(n-1, n-1-k)z^{n-1}}{k!\,(n-1-k)!}$$

$$= \sum_{k \ge 0} \frac{z^k}{k!} G_k(z) = \sum_{k \ge 0} \frac{(zG_1(z))^k}{k!} = e^{zG_1(z)}.$$

In other words, putting $G_1(z) = w$, the solution to our problem comes from the coefficients of the solution to the transcendental equation

$$w = e^{zw}. \tag{20}$$

This equation can be solved with the use of Lagrange's inversion formula: $z = \zeta/f(\zeta)$ implies that

$$\zeta = \sum_{n \geq 1} \frac{z^n}{n!} g_n^{(n-1)}(0), \tag{21}$$

where $g_n(\zeta) = f(\zeta)^n$, when f is analytic in the neighborhood of the origin, and $f(0) \neq 0$ (see exercise 4.7–16). In this case, we may set $\zeta = zw$, $f(\zeta) = e^\zeta$, and we deduce the solution

$$w = \sum_{n \geq 0} \frac{(n+1)^{n-1}}{n!} z^n, \tag{22}$$

in agreement with the answer obtained above.

G. N. Raney has shown that we can extend this method in an important way to obtain an explicit power series for the solution to the considerably more general equation

$$w = y_1 e^{z_1 w} + y_2 e^{z_2 w} + \cdots + y_s e^{z_s w},$$

solving for w in terms of a power series in $y_1, \ldots, y_s$ and $z_1, \ldots, z_s$. For this generalization, let us consider s-dimensional vectors of integers

$$\mathbf{n} = (n_1, n_2, \ldots, n_s),$$

and let us write for convenience

$$\Sigma\mathbf{n} = n_1 + n_2 + \cdots + n_s.$$

Suppose that we have s colors $C_1, C_2, \ldots, C_s$, and consider directed graphs in which each vertex is assigned a color; for example,

(23)

Let $r(\mathbf{n}, \mathbf{q})$ be the number of ways to draw arcs and to assign colors to the vertices $\{1, 2, \ldots, n\}$, such that

i) for $1 \leq i \leq s$ there are exactly n_i vertices of color C_i (hence $n = \Sigma\mathbf{n}$);
ii) there are q arcs, one leading from each of the vertices $\{1, 2, \ldots, q\}$;
iii) for $1 \leq i \leq s$ there are exactly q_i arcs leading to vertices of color C_i (hence $q = \Sigma\mathbf{q}$);
iv) there are no oriented cycles (hence $q < n$, unless $q = n = 0$).

Let us call this an (**n**,**q**)-construction.

For example, if C_1 = red, C_2 = yellow, and C_3 = blue, then (23) shows a $((3, 2, 2), (1, 2, 2))$-construction. When there is only one color, we have the oriented tree problem that we have already solved. Raney's idea is to generalize the one-dimension construction to s dimensions.

Let $\mathbf{n}$ and $\mathbf{q}$ be fixed s-place vectors of nonnegative integers, and let $n = \Sigma\mathbf{n}$, $q = \Sigma\mathbf{q}$. For each $(\mathbf{n},\mathbf{q})$-construction and each number k, $1 \le k \le n$, we will define a *canonical representation* consisting of four things:

a) a number t, with $q < t \le n$;
b) a sequence of n colors, with n_i of color C_i;
c) a sequence of q colors, with q_i of color C_i;
d) for $1 \le i \le s$, a sequence of q_i elements of the set $\{1, 2, \ldots, n_i\}$.

The canonical representation is defined thus: First list the vertices $\{1, 2, \ldots, q\}$ in the order $V_1, V_2, \ldots, V_q$ of the canonical representation of oriented trees (as given above), and then write below vertex V_j the number $f(V_j)$ of the vertex on the arc leading from V_j. Let $t = f(V_q)$; and let the sequence (c) of colors be the respective colors of the vertices $f(V_1), \ldots, f(V_q)$. Let the sequence (b) of colors be the respective colors of the vertices k, $k + 1$, $\ldots$, n, 1, $\ldots$, $k - 1$. Finally, let the ith sequence in (d) be $x_{i1}, x_{i2}, \ldots, x_{iq_i}$, where $x_{ij} = m$ if the jth C_i-colored element of the sequence $f(V_1), \ldots, f(V_q)$ is the mth C_i-colored element of the sequence k, $k + 1$, $\ldots$, n, 1, $\ldots$, $k - 1$.

For example, consider construction (23) and let $k = 3$. We start by listing $V_1, \ldots, V_5$ and $f(V_1), \ldots, f(V_5)$ below them as follows:

$$1 \quad 2 \quad 4 \quad 5 \quad 3$$
$$7 \quad 6 \quad 3 \quad 3 \quad 6$$

Hence $t = 6$, and sequence (c) represents the respective colors of 7, 6, 3, 3, 6, namely red, yellow, blue, blue, yellow. Sequence (b) represents the respective colors of 3, 4, 5, 6, 7, 1, 2, namely blue, yellow, red, yellow, red, blue, red. Finally, to get the sequences in (d), proceed as follows:

color	elements this color in $3, 4, 5, 6, 7, 1, 2$	elements this color in $7, 6, 3, 3, 6$	encode column 3 by column 2
red	$5, 7, 2$	7	2
yellow	$4, 6$	$6, 6$	$2, 2$
blue	$3, 1$	$3, 3$	$1, 1$

Hence the (d) sequences are 2; 2, 2; and 1, 1.

From the canonical representation, we can recover both the original $(\mathbf{n},\mathbf{q})$-construction and the number k as follows: From (a) and (c) we know the color of vertex t. The last element of the (d) sequence for this color tells us, in conjunction with (b), the position of t in the sequence $k, \ldots, n, 1, \ldots, k - 1$; hence we know k and the colors of all vertices. Then the subsequences in (d) together with (b) and (c) determine $f(V_1), f(V_2), \ldots, f(V_q)$, and finally the directed graph is reconstructed by locating $V_1, \ldots, V_q$ as we did for oriented trees.

The reversibility of this canonical representation allows us to count the number of possible $(\mathbf{n},\mathbf{q})$-constructions, since there are $n - q$ choices for (a), and the multinomial coefficient

$$\binom{n}{n_1,\ldots,n_s}$$

choices for (b), and

$$\binom{q}{q_1,\ldots,q_s}$$

choices for (c), and $n_1^{q_1} n_2^{q_2} \ldots n_s^{q_s}$ choices for (d). Dividing by the n choices for k, we have the general result

$$r(\mathbf{n},\mathbf{q}) = \frac{n-q}{n}\, \frac{n!}{n_1!\ldots n_s!}\, \frac{q!}{q_1!\ldots q_s!}\, n_1^{q_1} n_2^{q_2} \ldots n_s^{q_s}. \qquad (24)$$

Furthermore, we can derive analogs of Eqs. (18) and (19):

$$r(\mathbf{n},\mathbf{q}) = \sum_{\substack{\mathbf{k},\mathbf{t} \\ \Sigma(\mathbf{t}-\mathbf{k})=m}} \binom{\Sigma\mathbf{q}}{\Sigma\mathbf{k}} r(\mathbf{t},\mathbf{k})\, r(\mathbf{n}-\mathbf{t},\mathbf{q}-\mathbf{k}) \quad \text{if } 0 \le m \le \Sigma(\mathbf{n}-\mathbf{q}), \quad (25)$$

with the convention that $r(\mathbf{0},\mathbf{0}) = 1$, and $r(\mathbf{n},\mathbf{q}) = 0$ if any n_i or q_i is negative or if $q > n$;

$$r(\mathbf{n},\mathbf{q}) = \sum_{i=1}^{s} \sum_{k} \binom{\Sigma\mathbf{q}}{k} r(\mathbf{n}-\mathbf{e}_i,\, \mathbf{q}-k\mathbf{e}_i) \quad \text{if } \Sigma\mathbf{n} = 1 + \Sigma\mathbf{q}, \qquad (26)$$

where $\mathbf{e}_i$ is the vector with 1 in position i and zeros elsewhere. Relation (25) is based on breaking the vertices $\{q + 1, \ldots, n\}$ into two parts having m and $n - q - m$ elements, respectively; the second relation is derived by removing the unique root and considering the remaining structure. We now obtain the following result:

Theorem R. [George N. Raney, *Canadian J. Math.* **16** (1964), 755–762.] *Let*

$$w = \sum_{\substack{\mathbf{n},\mathbf{q} \\ \Sigma(\mathbf{n}-\mathbf{q})=1}} \frac{r(\mathbf{n},\mathbf{q})}{(\Sigma\mathbf{q})!}\, y_1^{n_1} \ldots y_s^{n_s}\, z_1^{q_1} \ldots z_s^{q_s}, \qquad (27)$$

where $r(\mathbf{n},\mathbf{q})$ is defined by (24), and where $\mathbf{n}, \mathbf{q}$ are s-dimensional integer vectors. Then w satisfies the identity

$$w = y_1 e^{z_1 w} + y_2 e^{z_2 w} + \cdots + y_s e^{z_s w}. \qquad (28)$$

Proof. By (25) and induction on m, we find that

$$w^m = \sum_{\substack{\mathbf{n},\mathbf{q} \\ \Sigma(\mathbf{n}-\mathbf{q})=m}} \frac{r(\mathbf{n},\mathbf{q})}{(\Sigma\mathbf{q})!}\, y_1^{n_1} \ldots y_s^{n_s}\, z_1^{q_1} \ldots z_s^{q_s}. \qquad (29)$$

Now by (26),

$$
w = \sum_{i=1}^{s} \sum_{k} \sum_{\substack{\mathbf{n},\mathbf{q} \\ \Sigma(\mathbf{n}-\mathbf{q})=1}} \frac{r(\mathbf{n}-\mathbf{e}_i,\, \mathbf{q}-k\mathbf{e}_i)}{k!\,(\Sigma\mathbf{q}-k)!}\, y_1^{n_1} \dots y_s^{n_s}\, z_1^{q_1} \dots z_s^{q_s}
$$

$$
= \sum_{i=1}^{s} \sum_{k} \frac{1}{k!}\, y_i z_i^{k} \sum_{\substack{\mathbf{n},\mathbf{q} \\ \Sigma(\mathbf{n}-\mathbf{q})=k}} \frac{r(\mathbf{n},\mathbf{q})}{(\Sigma\mathbf{q})!}\, y_1^{n_1} \dots y_s^{n_s}\, z_1^{q_1} \dots z_s^{q_s}
$$

$$
= \sum_{i=1}^{s} \sum_{k} \frac{1}{k!}\, y_i z_i^{k} w^{k}. \quad \blacksquare
$$

The special case where $s = 1$ and $z_1 = 1$ in (27) and (28) is especially important in applications, so it has become known as the "tree function"

$$
T(y) = \sum_{n \geq 1} \frac{n^{n-1}}{n!} y^n = y e^{T(y)}. \tag{30}
$$

See Corless, Gonnet, Hare, Jeffrey, and Knuth, *Advances in Computational Math.* **5** (1996), 329–359, for a discussion of this function's history and some of its remarkable properties.

A survey of enumeration formulas for trees, based on skillful manipulations of generating functions, has been given by I. J. Good [*Proc. Cambridge Philos. Soc.* **61** (1965), 499–517; **64** (1968), 489]. More recently, a mathematical *theory of species* developed by André Joyal [*Advances in Math.* **42** (1981), 1–82] has led to a high-level viewpoint in which algebraic operations on generating functions correspond directly to combinatorial properties of structures. The book *Combinatorial Species and Tree-like Structures* by F. Bergeron, G. Labelle, and P. Leroux (Cambridge Univ. Press, 1998), presents numerous examples of this beautiful and instructive theory, generalizing many of the formulas derived above.

EXERCISES

1. [*M20*] (G. Pólya.) Show that

$$
A(z) = z \cdot \exp\left(A(z) + \tfrac{1}{2}A(z^2) + \tfrac{1}{3}A(z^3) + \cdots\right).
$$

[*Hint:* Take logarithms of (3).]

2. [*HM24*] (R. Otter.) Show that the numbers a_n satisfy the following condition:

$$
n a_{n+1} = a_1 s_{n1} + 2a_2 s_{n2} + \cdots + n a_n s_{nn},
$$

where

$$
s_{nk} = \sum_{1 \leq j \leq n/k} a_{n+1-jk}.
$$

(These formulas are useful for the calculation of the a_n, since $s_{nk} = s_{(n-k)k} + a_{n+1-k}$.)

3. [*M40*] Write a computer program that determines the number of (unlabeled) free trees and of oriented trees with n vertices, for $n \leq 100$. (Use the result of exercise 2.) Explore arithmetical properties of these numbers; can anything be said about their prime factors, or their residues modulo p?

▶ **4.** [*HM39*] (G. Pólya, 1937.) Using complex variable theory, determine the asymptotic value of the number of oriented trees as follows:

a) Show that there is a real number α between 0 and 1 for which $A(z)$ has radius of convergence α and $A(z)$ converges absolutely for all complex z such that $|z| \leq \alpha$, having maximum value $A(\alpha) = a < \infty$. [*Hint:* When a power series has nonnegative coefficients, it either is entire or has a positive real singularity; and show that $A(z)/z$ is bounded as $z \to \alpha-$, by using the identity in exercise 1.]

b) Let
$$F(z, w) = \exp\left(zw + \tfrac{1}{2}A(z^2) + \tfrac{1}{3}A(z^3) + \cdots\right) - w.$$
Show that in a neighborhood of $(z, w) = (\alpha, a/\alpha)$, $F(z, w)$ is analytic in each variable separately.

c) Show that at the point $(z, w) = (\alpha, a/\alpha)$, we have $\partial F/\partial w = 0$; hence $a = 1$.

d) At the point $(z, w) = (\alpha, 1/\alpha)$ show that
$$\frac{\partial F}{\partial z} = \beta = \alpha^{-2} + \sum_{k \geq 2} \alpha^{k-2} A'(\alpha^k), \quad \text{and} \quad \frac{\partial^2 F}{\partial w^2} = \alpha.$$

e) When $|z| = \alpha$ and $z \neq \alpha$, show that $\partial F/\partial w \neq 0$; hence $A(z)$ has only one singularity on $|z| = \alpha$.

f) Prove that there is a region larger than $|z| < \alpha$ in which
$$\frac{1}{z} A(z) = \frac{1}{\alpha} - \sqrt{2\beta(1 - z/\alpha)} + (1 - z/\alpha)R(z),$$
where $R(z)$ is an analytic function of $\sqrt{z - \alpha}$.

g) Prove that consequently
$$a_n = \frac{1}{\alpha^{n-1}n} \sqrt{\beta/2\pi n} + O(n^{-5/2}\alpha^{-n}).$$

[*Note:* $1/\alpha \approx 2.955765285652$, and $\alpha\sqrt{\beta/2\pi} \approx 0.439924012571$.]

▶ **5.** [*M25*] (A. Cayley.) Let c_n be the number of (unlabeled) oriented trees having n leaves (namely, vertices with in-degree zero) and having at least two subtrees at every other vertex. Thus $c_3 = 2$, by virtue of the two trees

Find a formula analogous to (3) for the generating function
$$C(z) = \sum_n c_n z^n.$$

6. [*M25*] Let an "oriented binary tree" be an oriented tree in which each vertex has in-degree two or less. Find a reasonably simple relation that defines the generating function $G(z)$ for the number of distinct oriented binary trees with n vertices, and find the first few values.

7. [*HM40*] Obtain asymptotic values for the numbers of exercise 6. (See exercise 4.)

8. [*20*] According to Eq. (9), there are six free trees with six vertices. Draw them, and indicate their centroids.

9. [*M20*] From the fact that at most one subtree of a vertex in a free tree can contain a centroid, prove that there are at most two centroids in a free tree; furthermore if there are two, then they must be adjacent.

▶ **10.** [*M22*] Prove that a free tree with n vertices and two centroids consists of two free trees with $n/2$ vertices, joined by an edge. Conversely, if two free trees with m vertices are joined by an edge, we obtain a free tree with $2m$ vertices and two centroids.

▶ **11.** [*M28*] The text derives the number of different binary trees with n nodes (14). Generalize this to find the number of different t-ary trees with n nodes. (See exercise 2.3.1–35; a t-ary tree is either empty or consists of a root and t disjoint t-ary trees.) *Hint:* Use Eq. (21) of Section 1.2.9.

12. [*M20*] Find the number of labeled oriented trees with n vertices by using determinants and the result of exercise 2.3.4.2–19. (See also exercise 1.2.3–36.)

13. [*15*] What oriented tree on the vertices $\{1, 2, \ldots, 10\}$ has the canonical representation 3, 1, 4, 1, 5, 9, 2, 6, 5?

14. [*10*] True or false: The last entry, $f(V_{n-1})$, in the canonical representation of an oriented tree is always the root of that tree.

15. [*21*] Discuss the relationships that exist (if any) between the topological sort algorithm of Section 2.2.3 and the canonical representation of an oriented tree.

16. [*25*] Design an algorithm (as efficient as possible) that converts from the canonical representation of an oriented tree to a conventional computer representation using **PARENT** links.

▶ **17.** [*M26*] Let $f(x)$ be an integer-valued function, where $1 \le f(x) \le m$ for all integers $1 \le x \le m$. Define $x \equiv y$ if $f^{[r]}(x) = f^{[s]}(y)$ for some $r, s \ge 0$, where $f^{[0]}(x) = x$ and $f^{[r+1]}(x) = f(f^{[r]}(x))$. By using methods of enumeration like those in this section, show that the number of functions such that $x \equiv y$ for all x and y is $m^{m-1}Q(m)$, where $Q(m)$ is the function defined in Section 1.2.11.3.

18. [*24*] Show that the following method is another way to define a one-to-one correspondence between $(n-1)$-tuples of numbers from 1 to n and oriented trees with n labeled vertices: Let the leaves of the tree be $V_1, \ldots, V_k$ in ascending order. Let $(V_1, V_{k+1}, V_{k+2}, \ldots, V_q)$ be the path from V_1 to the root, and write down the vertices $V_q, \ldots, V_{k+2}, V_{k+1}$. Then let $(V_2, V_{q+1}, V_{q+2}, \ldots, V_r)$ be the shortest oriented path from V_2 such that V_r has already been written down, and write down $V_r, \ldots, V_{q+2}, V_{q+1}$. Then let $(V_3, V_{r+1}, \ldots, V_s)$ be the shortest oriented path from V_3 such that V_s has already been written, and write $V_s, \ldots, V_{r+1}$; and so on. For example, the tree (17) would be encoded as 3, 1, 3, 3, 5, 10, 5, 10, 1. Show that this process is reversible, and in particular, draw the oriented tree with vertices $\{1, 2, \ldots, 10\}$ and representation 3, 1, 4, 1, 5, 9, 2, 6, 5.

19. [*M24*] How many different labeled, oriented trees are there having n vertices, k of which are leaves (have in-degree zero)?

20. [*M24*] (J. Riordan.) How many different labeled, oriented trees are there having n vertices, k_0 of which have in-degree 0, k_1 have in-degree 1, k_2 have in-degree 2, $\ldots$? (Note that necessarily $k_0 + k_1 + k_2 + \cdots = n$, and $k_1 + 2k_2 + 3k_3 + \cdots = n - 1$.)

▶ **21.** [*M21*] Enumerate the number of labeled oriented trees in which each vertex has in-degree zero or two. (See exercise 20 and exercise 2.3–20.)

22. [*M20*] How many *labeled* free trees are possible with n vertices? (In other words, if we are given n vertices, there are $2^{\binom{n}{2}}$ possible graphs having these vertices, depending on which of the $\binom{n}{2}$ possible edges are incorporated into the graph; how many of these graphs are free trees?)

23. [*M21*] How many ordered trees are possible with n labeled vertices? (Give a simple formula involving factorials.)

24. [*M16*] All labeled oriented trees with vertices 1, 2, 3, 4 and with root 1 are shown in (15). How many would there be if we listed all labeled *ordered* trees with these vertices and this root?

25. [*M20*] What is the value of the quantity $r(n, q)$ that appears in Eqs. (18) and (19)? (Give an explicit formula; the text only mentions that $r(n, n-1) = n^{n-2}$.)

26. [*20*] In terms of the notation at the end of this section, draw the $((3, 2, 4), (1, 4, 2))$-construction, analogous to (23), and find the number k that corresponds to the canonical representation having $t = 8$, the sequences of colors "red, yellow, blue, red, yellow, blue, red, blue, blue" and "red, yellow, blue, yellow, yellow, blue, yellow", and the index sequences 3; 1, 2, 2, 1; 2, 4.

▶ **27.** [*M28*] Let $U_1, U_2, \ldots, U_p, \ldots, U_q$; $V_1, V_2, \ldots, V_r$ be vertices of a directed graph, where $1 \le p \le q$. Let f be any function from the set $\{p+1, \ldots, q\}$ into the set $\{1, 2, \ldots, r\}$, and let the directed graph contain exactly $q - p$ arcs, from U_k to $V_{f(k)}$ for $p < k \le q$. Show that the number of ways to add r additional arcs, one from each of the V's to one of the U's, such that the resulting directed graph contains no oriented cycles, is $q^{r-1}p$. Prove this by generalizing the canonical representation method; that is, set up a one-to-one correspondence between all such ways of adding r further arcs and the set of all sequences of integers $a_1, a_2, \ldots, a_r$, where $1 \le a_k \le q$ for $1 \le k < r$, and $1 \le a_r \le p$.

28. [*M22*] (*Bipartite trees.*) Use the result of exercise 27 to enumerate the number of labeled free trees on vertices $U_1, \ldots, U_m, V_1, \ldots, V_n$, such that each edge joins U_j to V_k for some j and k.

29. [*HM26*] Prove that if $E_k(r, t) = r(r + kt)^{k-1}/k!$, and if $zx^t = \ln x$, then

$$x^r = \sum_{k \ge 0} E_k(r, t) z^k$$

for fixed t and for sufficiently small $|z|$ and $|x - 1|$. [Use the fact that $G_m(z) = G_1(z)^m$ in the discussion following Eq. (19).] In this formula, r stands for an arbitrary real number. [*Note:* As a consequence of this formula we have the identity

$$\sum_{k=0}^{n} E_k(r, t) E_{n-k}(s, t) = E_n(r + s, t);$$

this implies Abel's binomial theorem, Eq. (16) of Section 1.2.6. Compare also Eq. (30) of that section.]

30. [*M23*] Let $n, x, y, z_1, \ldots, z_n$ be positive integers. Consider a set of $x + y + z_1 + \cdots + z_n + n$ vertices r_i, s_{jk}, t_j ($1 \le i \le x + y$, $1 \le j \le n$, $1 \le k \le z_j$), in which arcs have been drawn from s_{jk} to t_j for all j and k. According to exercise 27, there are $(x + y)(x + y + z_1 + \cdots + z_n)^{n-1}$ ways to draw one arc from each of $t_1, \ldots, t_n$ to other vertices such that the resulting directed graph contains no oriented cycles. Use this fact to prove Hurwitz's generalization of the binomial theorem:

$$\sum x(x+\epsilon_1 z_1+\cdots+\epsilon_n z_n)^{\epsilon_1+\cdots+\epsilon_n-1} y(y+(1-\epsilon_1)z_1+\cdots+(1-\epsilon_n)z_n)^{n-1-\epsilon_1-\cdots-\epsilon_n}$$

$$= (x+y)(x+y+z_1+\cdots+z_n)^{n-1},$$

where the sum is over all 2^n choices of $\epsilon_1,\ldots,\epsilon_n$ equal to 0 or 1.

31. [*M24*] Solve exercise 5 for ordered trees; that is, derive the generating function for the number of unlabeled ordered trees with n terminal nodes and no nodes of degree 1.

32. [*M37*] (A. Erdélyi and I. M. H. Etherington, *Edinburgh Math. Notes* **32** (1941), 7–12.) How many (ordered, unlabeled) trees are there with n_0 nodes of degree 0, n_1 of degree 1, $\ldots$, n_m of degree m, and none of degree higher than m? (An explicit solution to this problem can be given in terms of factorials, thereby considerably generalizing the result of exercise 11.)

▸ **33.** [*M28*] The text gives an explicit power series solution for the equation $w = y_1 e^{z_1 w} + \cdots + y_r e^{z_r w}$, based on enumeration formulas for certain oriented forests. Similarly, show that the enumeration formula of exercise 32 leads to an explicit power series solution to the equation

$$w = z_1 w^{e_1} + z_2 w^{e_2} + \cdots + z_r w^{e_r},$$

expressing w as a power series in $z_1,\ldots,z_r$. (Here $e_1,\ldots,e_r$ are fixed nonnegative integers, at least one of which is zero.)

2.3.4.5. Path length. The concept of the "path length" of a tree is of great importance in the analysis of algorithms, since this quantity is often directly related to the execution time. Our primary concern is with binary trees, since they are so close to actual computer representations.

In the following discussion we will extend each binary tree diagram by adding special nodes wherever a null subtree was present in the original tree, so that

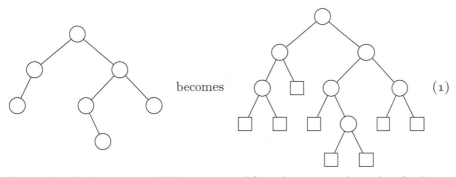

becomes (1)

The latter is called an *extended binary tree*. After the square-shaped nodes have been added in this way, the structure is sometimes more convenient to deal with, and we shall therefore meet extended binary trees frequently in later chapters. It is clear that every circular node has two children and every square node has none. (Compare with exercise 2.3–20.) If there are n circular nodes and s square nodes, we have $n+s-1$ edges (since the diagram is a free tree); counting another way, by the number of children, we see that there are $2n$ edges. Hence it is clear that

$$s = n + 1; \tag{2}$$

in other words, the number of "external" nodes just added is one more than the number of "internal" nodes we had originally. (For another proof, see exercise 2.3.1–14.) Formula (2) is correct even when $n = 0$.

Assume that a binary tree has been extended in this way. The *external path length of the tree*, E, is defined to be the sum — taken over all external (square) nodes — of the lengths of the paths from the root to each node. The *internal path length*, I, is the same quantity summed over the internal (circular) nodes. In (1) the external path length is

$$E = 3 + 3 + 2 + 3 + 4 + 4 + 3 + 3 = 25,$$

and the internal path length is

$$I = 2 + 1 + 0 + 2 + 3 + 1 + 2 = 11.$$

These two quantities are always related by the formula

$$E = I + 2n, \tag{3}$$

where n is the number of internal nodes.

To prove formula (3), consider deleting an internal node V at a distance k from the root, where both children of V are external. The quantity E goes down by $2(k + 1)$, since the children of V are removed, then it goes up by k, since V becomes external; so the net change in E is $-k - 2$. The net change in I is $-k$, so (3) follows by induction.

It is not hard to see that the internal path length (and hence the external path length also) is greatest when we have a degenerate tree with linear structure; in that case the internal path length is

$$(n - 1) + (n - 2) + \cdots + 1 + 0 = \frac{n^2 - n}{2}.$$

It can be shown that the "average" path length over all binary trees is essentially proportional to $n\sqrt{n}$ (see exercise 5).

Consider now the problem of constructing a binary tree with n nodes that has *minimum* path length. Such a tree will be important, since it will minimize the computation time for various algorithms. Clearly, only one node (the root) can be at zero distance from the root; at most two nodes can be at distance 1 from the root, at most four can be 2 away, and so on. Therefore *the internal path length is always at least as big as the sum of the first n terms of the series*

$$0, \ 1, \ 1, \ 2, \ 2, \ 2, \ 2, \ 3, \ 3, \ 3, \ 3, \ 3, \ 3, \ 3, \ 3, \ 4, \ 4, \ 4, \ 4, \ldots \ .$$

This is the sum $\sum_{k=1}^{n} \lfloor \lg k \rfloor$, which we know from exercise 1.2.4–42 is

$$(n + 1)q - 2^{q+1} + 2, \qquad q = \lfloor \lg(n + 1) \rfloor. \tag{4}$$

The optimum value (4) is $n \lg n + O(n)$, since $q = \lg n + O(1)$; it is clearly achieved in a tree that looks like this (illustrated for $n = 12$):

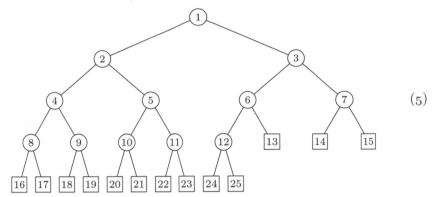

$$(5)$$

A tree such as (5) is called the *complete binary tree* with n internal nodes. In the general case we can number the internal nodes $1, 2, \ldots, n$; this numbering has the useful property that the parent of node k is node $\lfloor k/2 \rfloor$, and the children of node k are nodes $2k$ and $2k + 1$. The external nodes are numbered $n + 1$ through $2n + 1$, inclusive.

It follows that a complete binary tree may simply be represented in sequential memory locations, with the structure implicit in the locations of the nodes (not in links). The complete binary tree appears explicitly or implicitly in many important computer algorithms, so the reader should give it special attention.

These concepts have important generalizations to ternary, quaternary, and higher-order trees. We define a *t-ary tree* as a set of nodes that is either empty or consists of a root and t ordered, disjoint t-ary trees. (This generalizes the definition of binary tree in Section 2.3.) Here, for example, is the *complete ternary tree* with 12 internal nodes:

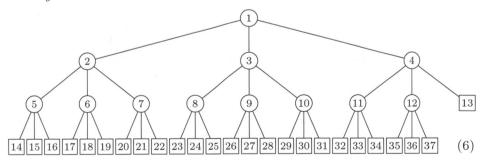

$$(6)$$

It is easy to see that the same construction works for any $t \geq 2$. In the complete t-ary tree with internal nodes $\{1, 2, \ldots, n\}$, the parent of node k is node

$$\lfloor (k + t - 2)/t \rfloor = \lceil (k - 1)/t \rceil,$$

and the children of node k are

$$t(k - 1) + 2, \quad t(k - 1) + 3, \quad \ldots, \quad tk + 1.$$

This tree has the minimum internal path length among all t-ary trees with n internal nodes; exercise 8 proves that its internal path length is

$$\left(n + \frac{1}{t-1}\right)q - \frac{(t^{q+1} - t)}{(t-1)^2}, \qquad q = \lfloor \log_t((t-1)n + 1) \rfloor. \tag{7}$$

These results have another important generalization if we shift our point of view slightly. Suppose that we are given m real numbers $w_1, w_2, \ldots, w_m$; the problem is to find an extended binary tree with m external nodes, and to associate the numbers $w_1, \ldots, w_m$ with these nodes in such a way that the sum $\sum w_j l_j$ is minimized, where l_j is the length of path from the root and the sum is taken over all external nodes. For example, if the given numbers are 2, 3, 4, 11, we can form extended binary trees such as these three:

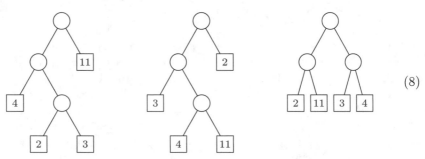

$$\tag{8}$$

Here the "weighted" path lengths $\sum w_j l_j$ are 34, 53, and 40, respectively. (Therefore a perfectly balanced tree does *not* give the minimum weighted path length when the weights are 2, 3, 4, and 11, although we have seen that it does give the minimum in the special case $w_1 = w_2 = \cdots = w_m = 1$.)

Several interpretations of weighted path length arise in connection with different computer algorithms; for example, we can apply it to the merging of sorted sequences of respective lengths $w_1, w_2, \ldots, w_m$ (see Chapter 5). One of the most straightforward applications of this idea is to consider a binary tree as a general search procedure, where we start at the root and then make some test; the outcome of the test sends us to one of the two branches, where we may make further tests, etc. For example, if we want to decide which of four different alternatives is true, and if these possibilities will be true with the respective probabilities $\frac{2}{20}, \frac{3}{20}, \frac{4}{20}$, and $\frac{11}{20}$, a tree that minimizes the weighted path length will constitute an *optimal search procedure*. [These are the weights shown in (8), times a scale factor.]

An elegant algorithm for finding a tree with minimum weighted path length was discovered by D. Huffman [*Proc. IRE* **40** (1952), 1098–1101]: First find the two w's of lowest value, say w_1 and w_2. Then solve the problem for $m-1$ weights $w_1 + w_2, w_3, \ldots, w_m$, and replace the node

$$\boxed{w_1 + w_2} \tag{9}$$

in this solution by

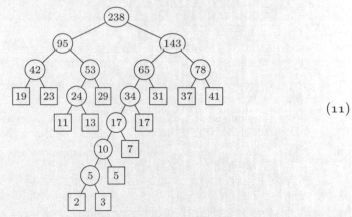

$$(10)$$

As an example of Huffman's method, let us find the optimal tree for the weights 2, 3, 5, 7, 11, 13, 17, 19, 23, 29, 31, 37, 41. First we combine $2 + 3$, and look for the solution to $5, 5, 7, \ldots, 41$; then we combine $5 + 5$, etc. The computation is summarized as follows:

2	3	5	7	11	13	17	19	23	29	31	37	41
	5	5	7	11	13	17	19	23	29	31	37	41
		10	7	11	13	17	19	23	29	31	37	41
			17	11	13	17	19	23	29	31	37	41
			17		24	17	19	23	29	31	37	41
					24	34	19	23	29	31	37	41
					24	34		42	29	31	37	41
						34		42	53	31	37	41
								42	53	65	37	41
								42	53	65		78
								95		65		78
								95				143
												238

Therefore the following tree corresponds to Huffman's construction:

(The numbers inside the circular nodes show the correspondence between this tree and our computation; see also exercise 9.)

It is not hard to prove that this method does in fact minimize the weighted path length, by induction on m. Suppose we have $w_1 \le w_2 \le w_3 \le \cdots \le w_m$, where $m \ge 2$, and suppose that we are given a tree that minimizes the weighted path length. (Such a tree certainly exists, since only finitely many binary trees with m terminal nodes are possible.) Let V be an internal node of maximum distance from the root. If w_1 and w_2 are not the weights already attached to the children of V, we can interchange them with the values that are already there;

such an interchange does not increase the weighted path length. Thus there is a tree that minimizes the weighted path length and contains the subtree (10). Now it is easy to prove that the weighted path length of a tree for the weights $w_1, \ldots, w_m$ that contains (10) as a subtree is minimized if and only if that tree with (10) replaced by (9) has minimum path length for the weights $w_1 + w_2$, w_3, $\ldots, w_m$. (See exercise 9.)

Every time this construction combines two weights, they are at least as big as the weights previously combined, if the given w_i were nonnegative. This means that there is a neat way to find Huffman's tree, provided that the given weights have been sorted into nondecreasing order: We simply maintain two queues, one containing the original weights and the other containing the combined weights. At each step the smallest unused weight will appear at the front of one of the queues, so we never have to search for it. See exercise 13, which shows that the same idea works even when the weights might be negative.

In general, there are many trees that minimize $\sum w_j l_j$. If the algorithm sketched in the preceding paragraph always uses an original weight instead of a combined weight in case of ties, then the tree it constructs has the smallest value of $\max l_j$ and of $\sum l_j$ among all trees that minimize $\sum w_j l_j$. If the weights are positive, this tree actually minimizes $\sum w_j f(l_j)$ for *any* convex function f, over all such trees. [See E. S. Schwartz, *Information and Control* **7** (1964), 37–44; G. Markowsky, *Acta Informatica* **16** (1981), 363–370.]

Huffman's method can be generalized to t-ary trees as well as binary trees. (See exercise 10.) Another important generalization of Huffman's method is discussed in Section 6.2.2. Further discussion of path length appears in Sections 5.3.1, 5.4.9, and 6.3.

EXERCISES

1. [*12*] Are there any other binary trees with 12 internal nodes and minimum path length, besides the complete binary tree (5)?

2. [*17*] Draw an extended binary tree with terminal nodes containing the weights 1, 4, 9, 16, 25, 36, 49, 64, 81, 100, having minimum weighted path length.

▶ **3.** [*M24*] An extended binary tree with m external nodes determines a set of path lengths $l_1, l_2, \ldots, l_m$ that describe the lengths of paths from the root to the respective external nodes. Conversely, if we are given a set of numbers $l_1, l_2, \ldots, l_m$, is it always possible to construct an extended binary tree in which these numbers are the path lengths in some order? Show that this is possible if and only if $\sum_{j=1}^{m} 2^{-l_j} = 1$.

▶ **4.** [*M25*] (E. S. Schwartz and B. Kallick.) Assume that $w_1 \le w_2 \le \cdots \le w_m$. Show that there is an extended binary tree that minimizes $\sum w_j l_j$ and for which the terminal nodes in left to right order contain the respective values $w_1, w_2, \ldots, w_m$. [For example, tree (11) does *not* meet this condition since the weights appear in the order 19, 23, 11, 13, 29, 2, 3, 5, 7, 17, 31, 37, 41. We seek a tree for which the weights appear in ascending order, and this does not always happen with Huffman's construction.]

5. [*HM26*] Let

$$B(w, z) = \sum_{n, p \ge 0} b_{np} w^p z^n,$$

where b_{np} is the number of binary trees with n nodes and internal path length p. [Thus,

$$B(w, z) = 1 + z + 2wz^2 + (w^2 + 4w^3)z^3 + (4w^4 + 2w^5 + 8w^6)z^4 + \cdots;$$

$B(1, z)$ is the function $B(z)$ of Eq. (13) in Section 2.3.4.4.]

    a) Find a functional relation that characterizes $B(w, z)$, generalizing 2.3.4.4–(12).

    b) Use the result of (a) to determine the *average internal path length* of a binary tree with n nodes, assuming that each of the $\frac{1}{n+1}\binom{2n}{n}$ trees is equally probable.

    c) Find the asymptotic value of this quantity.

    6. [*16*] If a t-ary tree is extended with square nodes as in (1), what is the relation between the number of square and circular nodes corresponding to Eq. (2)?

    7. [*M21*] What is the relation between external and internal path length in a t-ary tree? (See exercise 6; a generalization of Eq. (3) is desired.)

    8. [*M23*] Prove Eq. (7).

    9. [*M21*] The numbers that appear in the circular nodes of (11) are equal to the sums of the weights in the external nodes of the corresponding subtree. Show that the sum of all values in the circular nodes is equal to the weighted path length.

►   **10.** [*M26*] (D. Huffman.) Show how to construct a t-ary tree with minimum weighted path length, given nonnegative weights $w_1, w_2, \ldots, w_m$. Construct an optimal ternary tree for weights 1, 4, 9, 16, 25, 36, 49, 64, 81, 100.

    11. [*16*] Is there any connection between the complete binary tree (5) and the "Dewey decimal notation" for binary trees described in exercise 2.3.1–5?

►   **12.** [*M20*] Suppose that a node has been chosen at random in a binary tree, with each node equally likely. Show that the average size of the subtree rooted at that node is related to the path length of the tree.

    13. [*22*] Design an algorithm that begins with m weights $w_1 \leq w_2 \leq \cdots \leq w_m$ and constructs an extended binary tree having minimum weighted path length. Represent the final tree in three arrays

$$A[1] \ldots A[2m - 1], \quad L[1] \ldots L[m - 1], \quad R[1] \ldots R[m - 1];$$

here $L[i]$ and $R[i]$ point to the left and right children of internal node i, the root is node 1, and $A[i]$ is the weight of node i. The original weights should appear as the external node weights $A[m], \ldots, A[2m - 1]$. Your algorithm should make fewer than $2m$ weight-comparisons. *Caution:* Some or all of the given weights may be negative!

    14. [*25*] (T. C. Hu and A. C. Tucker.) After k steps of Huffman's algorithm, the nodes combined so far form a forest of $m - k$ extended binary trees. Prove that this forest has the smallest total weighted path length, among all forests of $m - k$ extended binary trees that have the given weights.

    15. [*M25*] Show that a Huffman-like algorithm will find an extended binary tree that minimizes (a) $\max(w_1 + l_1, \ldots, w_m + l_m)$; (b) $w_1 x^{l_1} + \cdots + w_m x^{l_m}$, given $x > 1$.

    16. [*M25*] (F. K. Hwang.) Let $w_1 \leq \cdots \leq w_m$ and $w_1' \leq \cdots \leq w_m'$ be two sets of weights with

$$\sum_{j=1}^{k} w_j \leq \sum_{j=1}^{k} w_j' \qquad \text{for } 1 \leq k \leq m.$$

Prove that the minimum weighted path lengths satisfy $\sum_{j=1}^{m} w_j l_j \leq \sum_{j=1}^{m} w_j' l_j'$.

17. [*HM30*] (C. R. Glassey and R. M. Karp.) Let $s_1, \ldots, s_{m-1}$ be the numbers inside the internal (circular) nodes of an extended binary tree formed by Huffman's algorithm, in the order of construction. Let $s'_1, \ldots, s'_{m-1}$ be the internal node weights of any extended binary tree on the same set of weights $\{w_1, \ldots, w_m\}$, listed in any order such that each nonroot internal node appears before its parent. (a) Prove that $\sum_{j=1}^{k} s_j \le \sum_{j=1}^{k} s'_j$ for $1 \le k < m$. (b) The result of (a) is equivalent to

$$\sum_{j=1}^{m-1} f(s_j) \le \sum_{j=1}^{m-1} f(s'_j)$$

for every nondecreasing concave function f, namely every function f with $f'(x) \ge 0$ and $f''(x) \le 0$. [See Hardy, Littlewood, and Pólya, *Messenger of Math.* **58** (1929), 145–152.] Use this fact to show that the minimum value in the recurrence

$$F(n) = f(n) + \min_{1 \le k < n} \left(F(k) + F(n-k) \right), \qquad F(1) = 0$$

always occurs when $k = 2^{\lceil \lg(n/3) \rceil}$, given any function $f(n)$ with the property that $\Delta f(n) = f(n+1) - f(n) \ge 0$ and $\Delta^2 f(n) = \Delta f(n+1) - \Delta f(n) \le 0$.

*2.3.4.6. History and bibliography. Trees have of course been in existence since the third day of creation, and through the ages tree structures (especially *family* trees) have been in common use. The concept of tree as a formally defined *mathematical* entity seems to have appeared first in the work of G. Kirchhoff [*Annalen der Physik und Chemie* **72** (1847), 497–508, English translation in *IRE Transactions* **CT-5** (1958), 4–7]; Kirchhoff used free trees to find a set of fundamental cycles in an electrical network in connection with the law that bears his name, essentially as we did in Section 2.3.4.1. The concept also appeared at about the same time in the book *Geometrie der Lage* (pages 20–21) by K. G. Chr. von Staudt. The name "tree" and many results dealing mostly with enumeration of trees began to appear ten years later in a series of papers by Arthur Cayley [see *Collected Mathematical Papers of A. Cayley* **3** (1857), 242–246; **4** (1859), 112–115; **9** (1874), 202–204; **9** (1875), 427–460; **10** (1877), 598–600; **11** (1881), 365–367; **13** (1889), 26–28]. Cayley was unaware of the previous work of Kirchhoff and von Staudt; his investigations began with studies of the structure of algebraic formulas, and they were later inspired chiefly by applications to the problem of isomers in chemistry. Tree structures were also studied independently by C. W. Borchardt [*Crelle* **57** (1860), 111–121]; J. B. Listing [*Göttinger Abhandlungen, Math. Classe,* **10** (1862), 137–139]; and C. Jordan [*Crelle* **70** (1869), 185–190].

The "infinity lemma" was formulated first by Dénes König [*Fundamenta Math.* **8** (1926), 114–134], and he gave it a prominent place in his classic book *Theorie der endlichen und unendlichen Graphen* (Leipzig: 1936), Chapter 6. A similar result called the "fan theorem" occurred slightly earlier in the work of L. E. J. Brouwer [*Verhandelingen Akad. Amsterdam* **12** (1919), 7:3–7:33], but this involved much stronger hypotheses; see A. Heyting, *Intuitionism* (1956), Section 3.4, for a discussion of Brouwer's work.

Formula (3) of Section 2.3.4.4 for enumerating unlabeled oriented trees was given by Cayley in his first paper on trees. In his second paper he enumerated unlabeled ordered trees; an equivalent problem in geometry (see exercise 1) had already been proposed and solved by L. Euler, who mentioned his results in a letter to C. Goldbach on 4 September 1751 [see J. von Segner and L. Euler, *Novi Commentarii Academiæ Scientiarum Petropolitanæ* **7** (1758–1759), summary 13–15, 203–210]. Euler's problem was the subject of seven papers by G. Lamé, E. Catalan, O. Rodrigues, and J. Binet in *Journal de mathématiques* **3, 4** (1838, 1839); additional references appear in the answer to exercise 2.2.1–4. The corresponding numbers are now commonly called "Catalan numbers." A Mongolian Chinese mathematician, An-T'u Ming, had actually encountered them before 1750 in his study of infinite series, but he did not relate them to trees or other combinatorial objects [see J. Luo, *Acta Scientiarum Naturalium Universitatis Intramongolicæ* **19** (1988), 239–245].

Catalan numbers occur in an enormous number of contexts: Richard Stanley's fascinating book *Catalan Numbers* (2015) features 214 different combinatorial interpretations, and also includes an appendix by Igor Pak that gives a definitive history of the subject. The most surprising of all these instances may well be the Catalan connection to certain arrangements of numbers that H. S. M. Coxeter has called "frieze patterns" because of their symmetry; see exercise 4.

The formula n^{n-2} for the number of *labeled* free trees was discovered by J. J. Sylvester [*Quart. J. Pure and Applied Math.* **1** (1857), 55–56], as a byproduct of his evaluation of a certain determinant (exercise 2.3.4.2–28). Cayley gave an independent derivation of the formula in 1889 [see the reference above]; his discussion, which was extremely vague, hinted at a connection between labeled oriented trees and $(n-1)$-tuples of numbers. An explicit correspondence demonstrating such a connection was first published by Heinz Prüfer [*Arch. Math. und Phys.* **27** (1918), 142–144], quite independently of Cayley's prior work. A large literature on this subject has developed, and the classical results are surveyed beautifully in J. W. Moon's book, *Counting Labelled Trees* (Montreal: Canadian Math. Congress, 1970).

A very important paper on the enumeration of trees and many other kinds of combinatorial structures was published by G. Pólya in *Acta Math.* **68** (1937), 145–253. For a discussion of enumeration problems for graphs and an excellent bibliography of the early literature, see the survey by Frank Harary in *Graph Theory and Theoretical Physics* (London: Academic Press, 1967), 1–41.

The principle of minimizing weighted path length by repeatedly combining the smallest weights was discovered by D. Huffman [*Proc. IRE* **40** (1952), 1098–1101], in connection with the design of codes for minimizing message lengths. The same idea was independently published by Seth Zimmerman [*AMM* **66** (1959), 690–693].

Several other noteworthy papers about the theory of tree structures have been cited in Sections 2.3.4.1 through 2.3.4.5 in connection with particular topics.

EXERCISES

▶ **1.** [*21*] Find a simple one-to-one correspondence between binary trees with n nodes and dissections of an $(n+2)$-sided convex polygon into n triangles, assuming that the sides of the polygon are distinct.

▶ **2.** [*M26*] T. P. Kirkman conjectured in 1857 that the number of ways to draw k non-overlapping diagonals in an r-sided convex polygon is $\binom{r+k}{k+1}\binom{r-3}{k}/(r+k)$.

    a) Extend the correspondence of exercise 1 to obtain an equivalent problem about the enumeration of trees.

    b) Prove Kirkman's conjecture by using the methods of exercise 2.3.4.4–32.

▶ **3.** [*M30*] Consider all ways of partitioning the vertices of a convex n-gon into k non-empty parts, in such a way that no diagonal between two vertices of one part crosses a diagonal between two vertices of another part.

    a) Find a one-to-one correspondence between noncrossing partitions and an interesting class of tree structures.

    b) Given n and k, how many ways are there to make such a partition?

▶ **4.** [*M38*] (Conway and Coxeter.) A *frieze pattern* is an infinite array such as

```
1  1  1  1  1  1  1  1  1  1  1  1  1  1  1  1  1  1  ...
  3  1  3  1  4  1  2  3  1  3  1  4  1  2  3  1  3  1  4   ...
5  2  2  2  3  3  1  5  2  2  2  3  3  1  5  2  2  2  3   ...
  3  3  1  5  2  2  2  3  3  1  5  2  2  2  3  3  1  5  2   ...
1  4  1  2  3  1  3  1  4  1  2  3  1  3  1  4  1  2  3   ...
  1  1  1  1  1  1  1  1  1  1  1  1  1  1  1  1  1  1   ...
```

in which the top and bottom rows consist entirely of 1s, and each diamond of adjacent values $a\ {}^{b}_{c}\ d$ satisfies $ad - bc = 1$. Find a one-to-one correspondence between n-node binary trees and $(n+1)$-rowed frieze patterns of positive integers.

2.3.5. Lists and Garbage Collection

Near the beginning of Section 2.3 we defined a List informally as "a finite sequence of zero or more atoms or Lists."

    Any forest is a List; for example,

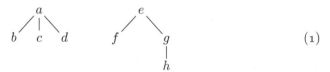

(1)

may be regarded as the List

$$\bigl(a\colon (b, c, d), e\colon (f, g\colon (h))\bigr), \tag{2}$$

and the corresponding List diagram would be

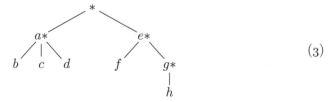

(3)

    The reader should review at this point the introduction to Lists given earlier, in particular (3), (4), (5), (6), (7) in the opening pages of Section 2.3. Recall that, in (2) above, the notation "$a\colon (b, c, d)$" means that (b, c, d) is a List of three atoms, which has been labeled with the attribute "a". This convention is compatible with our general policy that each node of a tree may contain information besides its structural connections. However, as was discussed for trees in Section 2.3.3, it is quite possible and sometimes desirable to insist that all Lists be unlabeled, so that all the information appears in the atoms.

Although any forest may be regarded as a List, the converse is not true. The following List is perhaps more typical than (2) and (3) since it shows how the restrictions of tree structure might be violated:

$$L = \bigl(a{:}\,N, b, c{:}\,(d{:}\,N), e{:}\,L\bigr), \qquad N = \bigl(f{:}\,(\,), g{:}\,(h{:}\,L, j{:}\,N)\bigr) \tag{4}$$

which may be diagrammed as

$$\begin{array}{c}
*[L]\\
\diagup \ \ | \ \ \diagdown\\
a*[N] \quad b \quad\ \ c* \quad\ e[L]\\
\diagup\ \diagdown \qquad\quad |\\
f* \quad g* \qquad d[N]\\
\diagup\ \diagdown\\
h[L]\ \ j[N]
\end{array} \tag{5}$$

[Compare with the example in 2.3 (7). The form of these diagrams need not be taken too seriously.]

As we might expect, there are many ways to represent List structures within a computer memory. These methods are usually variations on the same basic theme by which we have used binary trees to represent general forests of trees: One field, say RLINK, is used to point to the next element of a List, and another field DLINK may be used to point to the first element of a sub-List. By a natural extension of the memory representation described in Section 2.3.2, we would represent the List (5) as follows:

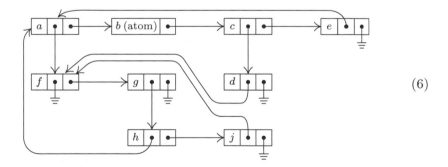

$$\tag{6}$$

Unfortunately, this simple idea is *not* quite adequate for the most common List processing applications. For example, suppose that we have the List $L = \bigl(A, a, (A, A)\bigr)$, which contains three references to another List $A = (b, c, d)$. One of the typical List processing operations is to remove the leftmost element of A, so that A becomes (c, d); but this requires *three* changes to the representation of L, if we are to use the technique shown in (6), since each pointer to A points to the element b that is being deleted. A moment's reflection will convince the reader that it is extremely undesirable to change the pointers in every reference to A just because the first element of A is being deleted. (In this example we could try to be tricky, assuming that there are no pointers to the element c, by copying the entire element c into the location formerly occupied by b and then deleting the old element c. But this trick fails to work when A loses its last element and becomes empty.)

For this reason the representation scheme (6) is generally replaced by another scheme that is similar, but uses a *List head* to begin each List, as was introduced in Section 2.2.4. Each List contains an additional node called its List head, so that the configuration (6) would, for example, be represented thus:

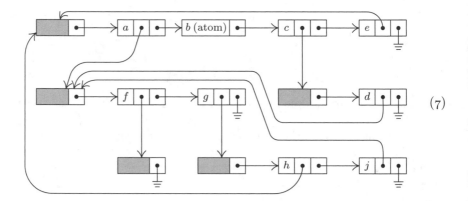

$$(7)$$

The introduction of such header nodes is not really a waste of memory space in practice, since many uses for the apparently unused fields — the shaded areas in diagram (7) — generally present themselves. For example, there is room for a reference count, or a pointer to the right end of the List, or an alphabetic name, or a "scratch" field that aids traversal algorithms, etc.

In our original diagram (6), the node containing b is an atom while the node containing f specifies an empty List. These two things are structurally identical, so the reader would be quite justified in asking why we bother to talk about "atoms" at all; with no loss of generality we could have defined Lists as merely "a finite sequence of zero or more Lists," with our usual convention that each node of a List may contain data besides its structural information. This point of view is certainly defensible and it makes the concept of an "atom" seem very artificial. There is, however, a good reason for singling out atoms as we have done, when efficient use of computer memory is taken into consideration, since atoms are not subject to the same sort of general-purpose manipulation that is desired for Lists. The memory representation (6) shows there is probably more room for information in an atomic node, b, than in a List node, f; and when List head nodes are also present as in (7), there is a dramatic difference between the storage requirements for the nodes b and f. Thus the concept of atoms is introduced primarily to aid in the effective use of computer memory. Typical

Lists contain many more atoms than our example would indicate; the example of (4)–(7) is intended to show the complexities that are possible, not the simplicities that are usual.

A List is in essence nothing more than a linear list whose elements may contain pointers to other Lists. The common operations we wish to perform on Lists are the usual ones desired for linear lists (creation, destruction, insertion, deletion, splitting, concatenation), plus further operations that are primarily of interest for tree structures (copying, traversal, input and output of nested information). For these purposes any of the three basic techniques for representing linked linear lists in memory — namely straight, circular, or double linkage — can be used, with varying degrees of efficiency depending on the algorithms being employed. For these three types of representation, diagram (7) might appear in memory as follows:

Memory location	Straight linkage INFO	DLINK	RLINK	Circular linkage INFO	DLINK	RLINK	Double linkage INFO	DLINK	LLINK	RLINK	
010:	—	head	020	—	head	020	—	head	050	020	
020:	a	060	030	a	060	030	a	060	010	030	
030:	b	atom	040	b	atom	040	b	atom	020	040	
040:	c	090	050	c	090	050	c	090	030	050	
050:	e	010	Λ	e	010	010	e	010	040	010	
060:	—	head	070	—	head	070	—	head	080	070	(8)
070:	f	110	080	f	110	080	f	110	060	080	
080:	g	120	Λ	g	120	060	g	120	070	060	
090:	—	head	100	—	head	100	—	head	100	100	
100:	d	060	Λ	d	060	090	d	060	090	090	
110:	—	head	Λ	—	head	110	—	head	110	110	
120:	—	head	130	—	head	130	—	head	140	130	
130:	h	010	140	h	010	140	h	010	120	140	
140:	j	060	Λ	j	060	120	j	060	130	120	

Here "LLINK" is used for a pointer to the left in a doubly linked representation. The INFO and DLINK fields are identical in all three forms.

There is no need to repeat here the algorithms for List manipulation in any of these three forms, since we have already discussed the ideas many times. The following important points about Lists, which distinguish them from the simpler special cases treated earlier, should however be noted:

1) It is implicit in the memory representation above that atomic nodes are distinguishable from nonatomic nodes; furthermore, when circular or doubly linked Lists are being used, it is desirable to distinguish header nodes from the other types, as an aid in traversing the Lists. Therefore each node generally contains a TYPE field that tells what kind of information the node represents. This TYPE field is often used also to distinguish between various types of atoms (for example, between alphabetic, integer, or floating point quantities, for use when manipulating or displaying the data).

2) The format of nodes for general List manipulation with the MIX computer might be designed in one of the following two ways.

a) Possible one-word format, assuming that all INFO appears in atoms:

$$\boxed{\text{S} \mid \text{T} \mid \text{REF} \mid \text{RLINK}} \tag{9}$$

S (sign):   Mark bit used in garbage collection (see below).

T (type):   T = 0 for List head; T = 1 for sub-List element; T > 1 for atoms.

REF: When T = 0, REF is a reference count (see below); when T = 1, REF points to the List head of the sub-List in question; when T > 1, REF points to a node containing a mark bit and five bytes of atomic information.

RLINK: Pointer for straight or circular linkage as in (8).

b) Possible two-word format:

$$\boxed{\begin{array}{c} \text{S} \mid \text{T} \mid \text{LLINK} \mid \text{RLINK} \\ \hline \text{INFO} \end{array}} \tag{10}$$

S, T: As in (9).

LLINK, RLINK: The usual pointers for double linkage as in (8).

INFO: A full word of information associated with this node; for a header node this may include a reference count, a running pointer to the interior of the List to facilitate linear traversal, an alphabetic name, etc.   When T = 1 this information includes DLINK.

3) It is clear that Lists are very general structures; indeed, it seems fair to state that any structure whatsoever can be represented as a List when appropriate conventions are made. Because of this universality of Lists, a large number of programming systems have been designed to facilitate List manipulation, and there are usually several such systems available at any computer installation. Such systems are based on a general-purpose format for nodes such as (9) or (10) above, designed for flexibility in List operations. Actually, it is clear that this general-purpose format is usually not the best format suited to a *particular* application, and the processing time using the general-purpose routines is noticeably slower than a person would achieve by hand-tailoring the system to a particular problem. For example, it is easy to see that nearly all of the applications we have worked out so far in this chapter would be encumbered by a general-List representation as in (9) or (10) instead of the node format that was given in each case. A List manipulation routine must often examine the T-field when it processes nodes, and that was not needed in any of our programs so far. This loss of efficiency is repaid in many instances by the comparative ease of programming and the reduction of debugging time when a general-purpose system is used.

4) There is also an extremely significant difference between algorithms for List processing and the algorithms given previously in this chapter. Since a single

List may be contained in many other Lists, it is by no means clear exactly when a List should be returned to the pool of available storage. Our algorithms so far have always said "AVAIL $\Leftarrow$ X", whenever NODE(X) was no longer needed. But since general Lists can grow and die in a completely unpredictable manner, it is often quite difficult to tell just when a particular node is superfluous. Therefore the problem of maintaining the list of available space is considerably more difficult with Lists than it was in the simple cases considered previously. We will devote the rest of this section to a discussion of the storage reclamation problem.

Let us imagine that we are designing a general-purpose List processing system that will be used by hundreds of other programmers. Two principal methods have been suggested for maintaining the available space list: the use of *reference counters*, and *garbage collection*. The reference-counter technique makes use of a new field in each node, which contains a count of how many arrows point to this node. Such a count is rather easy to maintain as a program runs, and whenever it drops to zero, the node in question becomes available. The garbage-collection technique, on the other hand, requires a new one-bit field in each node called the *mark bit*. The idea in this case is to write nearly all the algorithms so that they do not return any nodes to free storage, and to let the program run merrily along until all of the available storage is gone; then a "recycling" algorithm makes use of the mark bits to identify all nodes that are not currently accessible and to return them to available storage, after which the program can continue.

Neither of these two methods is completely satisfactory. The principal drawback of the reference-counter method is that it does not always free all the nodes that are available. It works fine for overlapped Lists (Lists that contain common sub-Lists); but recursive Lists, like our examples L and N in (4), will *never* be returned to storage by the reference-counter technique. Their counts will be nonzero (since they refer to themselves) even when no other List accessible to the running program points to them. Furthermore, the reference-counter method uses a good chunk of space in each node (although this space is sometimes available anyway due to the computer word size).

The difficulty with the garbage-collection technique, besides the annoying loss of a bit in each node, is that it runs very slowly when nearly all the memory space is in use; and in such cases the number of free storage cells found by the reclamation process is not worth the effort. Programs that exceed the capacity of storage (and many undebugged programs do!) often waste a good deal of time calling the garbage collector several almost fruitless times just before storage is finally exhausted. A partial solution to this problem is to let the programmer specify a number k, signifying that processing should not continue after a garbage collection run has found k or fewer free nodes.

Another problem is the occasional difficulty of determining exactly what Lists are not garbage at a given stage. If the programmer has been using any nonstandard techniques or keeping any pointer values in unusual places, chances are good that the garbage collector will go awry. Some of the greatest mysteries in the history of debugging have been caused by the fact that garbage collection suddenly took place at an unexpected time during the running of programs that had worked many times before. Garbage collection also requires that programmers keep valid information in all pointer fields at all times, although we often find it convenient to leave meaningless information in fields that the program doesn't use—for example, the link in the rear node of a queue; see exercise 2.2.3–6.

Although garbage collection requires one mark bit for each node, we could keep a separate table of all the mark bits packed together in another memory area, with a suitable correspondence between the location of a node and its mark bit. On some computers this idea can lead to a method of handling garbage collection that is more attractive than giving up a bit in each node.

J. Weizenbaum has suggested an interesting modification of the reference-counter technique. Using doubly linked List structures, he puts a reference counter only in the header of each List. Thus, when pointer variables traverse a List, they are not included in the reference counts for the individual nodes. If we know the rules by which reference counts are maintained for entire Lists, we know (in theory) how to avoid referring to any List that has a reference count of zero. We also have complete freedom to explicitly override reference counts and to return particular Lists to available storage. These ideas require careful handling; they prove to be somewhat dangerous in the hands of inexperienced programmers, and they've tended to make program debugging more difficult due to the consequences of referring to nodes that have been erased. The nicest part of Weizenbaum's approach is his treatment of Lists whose reference count has just gone to zero: Such a List is appended at the *end* of the current available list— this is easy to do with doubly linked Lists—and it is considered for available space only after all previously available cells are used up. Eventually, as the individual nodes of this List do become available, the reference counters of Lists *they* refer to are decreased by one. This delayed action of erasing Lists is quite efficient with respect to running time; but it tends to make incorrect programs run correctly for awhile! For further details see *CACM* **6** (1963), 524–544.

Algorithms for garbage collection are quite interesting for several reasons. In the first place, such algorithms are useful in other situations when we want to mark all nodes that are directly or indirectly referred to by a given node. (For example, we might want to find all subroutines called directly or indirectly by a certain subroutine, as in exercise 2.2.3–26.)

Garbage collection generally proceeds in two phases. We assume that the mark bits of all nodes are initially zero (or we set them all to zero). Now the first phase marks all the nongarbage nodes, starting from those that are immediately accessible to the main program. The second phase makes a sequential pass over the entire memory pool area, putting all unmarked nodes onto the list of free space. The marking phase is the most interesting, so we will concentrate our attention on it. Certain variations on the second phase can, however, make it nontrivial; see exercise 9.

When a garbage collection algorithm is running, only a very limited amount of storage is available to control the marking procedure. This intriguing problem will become clear in the following discussion; it is a difficulty that is not appreciated by most people when they first hear about the idea of garbage collection, and for several years there was no good solution to it.

The following marking algorithm is perhaps the most obvious.

Algorithm A (*Marking*). Let the entire memory used for List storage be NODE(1), NODE(2), ..., NODE(M), and suppose that these words either are atoms or contain two link fields ALINK and BLINK. Assume that all nodes are initially *unmarked*. The purpose of this algorithm is to *mark* all of the nodes that can be reached by a chain of ALINK and/or BLINK pointers in nonatomic nodes, starting from a set of "immediately accessible" nodes, that is, nodes pointed to by certain fixed locations in the main program; these fixed pointers are used as a source for all memory accesses.

A1. [Initialize.] Mark all nodes that are immediately accessible. Set $K \leftarrow 1$.

A2. [Does NODE(K) imply another?] Set $K1 \leftarrow K + 1$. If NODE(K) is an atom or unmarked, go to step A3. Otherwise, if NODE(ALINK(K)) is unmarked: Mark it and, if it is not an atom, set $K1 \leftarrow \min(K1, ALINK(K))$. Similarly, if NODE(BLINK(K)) is unmarked: Mark it and, if it is not an atom, set $K1 \leftarrow \min(K1, BLINK(K))$.

A3. [Done?] Set $K \leftarrow K1$. If $K \leq M$, return to step A2; otherwise the algorithm terminates. ∎

*Throughout this algorithm and the ones that follow in this section, we will assume for convenience that the nonexistent node "*NODE(Λ)*" is marked.* (For example, ALINK(K) or BLINK(K) may equal Λ in step A2.)

A variant of Algorithm A sets $K1 \leftarrow M + 1$ in step A1, removes the operation "$K1 \leftarrow K + 1$" from step A2, and instead changes step A3 to

A3′. [Done?] Set $K \leftarrow K + 1$. If $K \leq M$, return to step A2. Otherwise if $K1 \leq M$, set $K \leftarrow K1$ and $K1 \leftarrow M + 1$ and return to step A2. Otherwise the algorithm terminates. ∎

It is very difficult to give a precise analysis of Algorithm A, or to determine whether it is better or worse than the variant just described, since no meaningful way to describe the probability distribution of the input presents itself. We can say that it takes up time proportional to nM in the worst case, where n is the number of cells it marks; and, in general, we can be sure that it is very slow when n is large. Algorithm A is too slow to make garbage collection a usable technique.

Another fairly evident marking algorithm is to follow all paths and to record branch points on a stack as we go:

Algorithm B (*Marking*). This algorithm achieves the same effect as Algorithm A, using STACK[1], STACK[2], ... as auxiliary storage to keep track of all paths that have not yet been pursued to completion.

B1. [Initialize.] Let T be the number of immediately accessible nodes; mark them and place pointers to them in STACK[1], ..., STACK[T].

B2. [Stack empty?] If T = 0, the algorithm terminates.

B3. [Remove top entry.] Set K ← STACK[T], T ← T − 1.

B4. [Examine links.] If NODE(K) is an atom, return to step B2. Otherwise, if NODE(ALINK(K)) is unmarked, mark it and set T ← T + 1, STACK[T] ← ALINK(K); if NODE(BLINK(K)) is unmarked, mark it and set T ← T + 1, STACK[T] ← BLINK(K). Return to B2. ∎

Algorithm B clearly has an execution time essentially proportional to the number of cells it marks, and this is as good as we could possibly expect; but it is not really usable for garbage collection because there is no place to keep the stack! It does not seem unreasonable to assume that the stack in Algorithm B might grow up to, say, five percent of the size of memory; but when garbage collection is called, and all available space has been used up, there is only a fixed (rather small) number of cells to use for such a stack. Most of the early garbage collection procedures were essentially based on this algorithm. If the special stack space was used up, the entire program had to be terminated.

A somewhat better alternative is possible, using a fixed stack size, by combining Algorithms A and B:

Algorithm C (*Marking*). This algorithm achieves the same effect as Algorithms A and B, using an auxiliary table of H cells, STACK[0], STACK[1], ..., STACK[H − 1].

In this algorithm, the action "insert X on the stack" means the following: "Set T ← (T + 1) mod H, and STACK[T] ← X. If T = B, set B ← (B + 1) mod H and K1 ← min(K1, STACK[B])." (Note that T points to the current top of the stack, and B points one place below the current bottom; STACK essentially operates as an input-restricted deque.)

C1. [Initialize.] Set T ← H − 1, B ← H − 1, K1 ← M + 1. Mark all the immediately accessible nodes, and successively insert their locations onto the stack (as just described above).

C2. [Stack empty?] If T = B, go to C5.

C3. [Remove top entry.] Set K ← STACK[T], T ← (T − 1) mod H.

C4. [Examine links.] If NODE(K) is an atom, return to step C2. Otherwise, if NODE(ALINK(K)) is unmarked, mark it and insert ALINK(K) on the stack. Similarly, if NODE(BLINK(K)) is unmarked, mark it and insert BLINK(K) on the stack. Return to C2.

C5. [Sweep.] If K1 > M, the algorithm terminates. (The variable K1 represents the smallest location where there is a possibility of a new lead to a node that should be marked.) Otherwise, if NODE(K1) is an atom or unmarked, increase K1 by 1 and repeat this step. If NODE(K1) is marked, set K ← K1, increase K1 by 1, and go to C4. ∎

This algorithm and Algorithm B can be improved if X is never put on the stack when NODE(X) is an atom; moreover, steps B4 and C4 need not put items on the stack when they know that the items will immediately be removed. Such modifications are straightforward and they have been left out to avoid making the algorithms unnecessarily complicated.

Algorithm C is essentially equivalent to Algorithm A when $H = 1$, and to Algorithm B when $H = M$; it gradually becomes more efficient as H becomes larger. Unfortunately, Algorithm C defies a precise analysis for the same reason as Algorithm A, and we have no good idea how large H should be to make this method fast enough. It is plausible but uncomfortable to say that a value like $H = 50$ is sufficient to make Algorithm C usable for garbage collection in most applications.

Algorithms B and C use a stack kept in sequential memory locations; but we have seen earlier in this chapter that linked memory techniques are well suited to maintaining stacks that are not consecutive in memory. This suggests the idea that we might keep the stack of Algorithm B somehow scattered *through the same memory area in which we are collecting garbage*. This could be done easily if we were to give the garbage collection routine a little more room in which to breathe. Suppose, for example, we assume that all Lists are represented as in (9), except that the REF fields of List head nodes are used for garbage collection purposes instead of as reference counts. We can then redesign Algorithm B so that the stack is maintained in the REF fields of the header nodes:

Algorithm D (*Marking*). This algorithm achieves the same effect as Algorithms A, B, and C, but it assumes that the nodes have S, T, REF, and RLINK fields as described above, instead of ALINKs and BLINKs. The S field is used as the mark bit, so that $S(P) = 1$ means that NODE(P) is marked.

D1. [Initialize.] Set TOP $\leftarrow \Lambda$. Then for each pointer P to the head of an immediately accessible List (see step A1 of Algorithm A), if $S(P) = 0$, set $S(P) \leftarrow 1$, REF(P) $\leftarrow$ TOP, TOP $\leftarrow$ P.

D2. [Stack empty?] If TOP $= \Lambda$, the algorithm terminates.

D3. [Remove top entry.] Set P $\leftarrow$ TOP, TOP $\leftarrow$ REF(P).

D4. [Move through List.] Set P $\leftarrow$ RLINK(P); then if P $= \Lambda$, or if $T(P) = 0$, go to D2. Otherwise set $S(P) \leftarrow 1$. If $T(P) > 1$, set $S(REF(P)) \leftarrow 1$ (thereby marking the atomic information). Otherwise ($T(P) = 1$), set Q $\leftarrow$ REF(P); if Q $\neq \Lambda$ and $S(Q) = 0$, set $S(Q) \leftarrow 1$, REF(Q) $\leftarrow$ TOP, TOP $\leftarrow$ Q. Repeat step D4. ∎

Algorithm D may be compared to Algorithm B, which is quite similar, and its running time is essentially proportional to the number of nodes marked. However, Algorithm D is *not* recommended without qualification, because its seemingly rather mild restrictions are often too stringent for a general List-processing system. This algorithm essentially requires that all List structures be well-formed, as in (7), whenever garbage collection is called into action. But algorithms for List manipulations *momentarily* leave the List structures malformed, and a garbage collector such as Algorithm D must not be used during those momentary periods. Moreover, care must be taken in step D1 when the program contains pointers to the middle of a List.

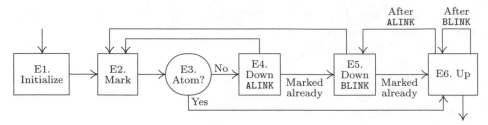

Fig. 38. Algorithm E for marking with no auxiliary stack space.

These considerations bring us to Algorithm E, which is an elegant marking method discovered independently by Peter Deutsch and by Herbert Schorr and W. M. Waite in 1965. The assumptions used in this algorithm are just a little different from those of Algorithms A through D.

Algorithm E (*Marking*). Assume that a collection of nodes is given having the following fields:

> MARK (a one-bit field),
> ATOM (another one-bit field),
> ALINK (a pointer field),
> BLINK (a pointer field).

When ATOM = 0, the ALINK and BLINK fields may contain Λ or a pointer to another node of the same format; when ATOM = 1, the contents of the ALINK and BLINK fields are irrelevant to this algorithm.

Given a nonnull pointer P0, this algorithm sets the MARK field equal to 1 in NODE(P0) and in every other node that can be reached from NODE(P0) by a chain of ALINK and BLINK pointers in nodes with ATOM = MARK = 0. The algorithm uses three pointer variables, T, Q, and P. It modifies the links and control bits in such a way that all ATOM, ALINK, and BLINK fields are restored to their original settings after completion, although they may be changed temporarily.

E1. [Initialize.] Set T $\leftarrow$ Λ, P $\leftarrow$ P0. (Throughout the remainder of this algorithm, the variable T has a dual significance: When T $\neq$ Λ, it points to the top of what is essentially a stack as in Algorithm D; and the node that T points to once contained a link equal to P in place of the "artificial" stack link that currently occupies NODE(T).)

E2. [Mark.] Set MARK(P) $\leftarrow$ 1.

E3. [Atom?] If ATOM(P) = 1, go to E6.

E4. [Down ALINK.] Set Q $\leftarrow$ ALINK(P). If Q $\neq$ Λ and MARK(Q) = 0, set ATOM(P) $\leftarrow$ 1, ALINK(P) $\leftarrow$ T, T $\leftarrow$ P, P $\leftarrow$ Q, and go to E2. (Here the ATOM field and ALINK fields are temporarily being altered, so that the List structure in certain marked nodes has been rather drastically changed. But these changes will be restored in step E6.)

E5. [Down BLINK.] Set Q $\leftarrow$ BLINK(P). If Q $\neq$ Λ and MARK(Q) = 0, set BLINK(P) $\leftarrow$ T, T $\leftarrow$ P, P $\leftarrow$ Q, and go to E2.

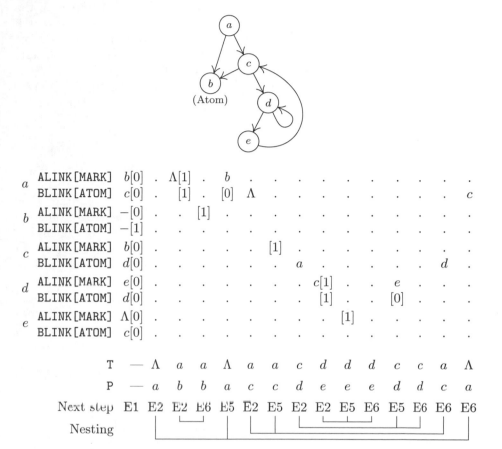

a ALINK[MARK]	$b[0]$	.	$\Lambda[1]$	.	b	.	.	.	.	.	.	.	.	.	.	.
BLINK[ATOM]	$c[0]$	.	$[1]$	.	$[0]$	Λ	.	.	.	.	.	.	.	.	.	c
b ALINK[MARK]	$-[0]$	.	.	$[1]$	.	.	.	.	.	.	.	.	.	.	.	.
BLINK[ATOM]	$-[1]$	.	.	.	.	.	.	.	.	.	.	.	.	.	.	.
c ALINK[MARK]	$b[0]$	.	.	.	.	$[1]$	.	.	.	.	.	.	.	.	.	.
BLINK[ATOM]	$d[0]$	.	.	.	.	.	a	.	.	.	.	.	d	.		
d ALINK[MARK]	$e[0]$	.	.	.	.	.	.	$c[1]$	.	.	e	.	.	.		
BLINK[ATOM]	$d[0]$	.	.	.	.	.	.	$[1]$	.	.	$[0]$	.	.	.		
e ALINK[MARK]	$\Lambda[0]$	.	.	.	.	.	.	.	$[1]$	.	.	.				
BLINK[ATOM]	$c[0]$	.	.	.	.	.	.	.	.	.	.	.				

T	—	Λ	a	a	Λ	a	a	c	d	d	d	c	c	a	Λ
P	—	a	b	b	a	c	c	d	e	e	e	d	d	c	a
Next step	E1	E2	E2	E6	E5	E2	E5	E2	E2	E5	E6	E5	E6	E6	E6
Nesting															

Fig. 39. A structure marked by Algorithm E. (The table shows only changes that have occurred since the previous step.)

E6. [Up.] (This step undoes the link switching made in step E4 or E5; the setting of ATOM(T) tells whether ALINK(T) or BLINK(T) is to be restored.) If T = Λ, the algorithm terminates. Otherwise set Q ← T. If ATOM(Q) = 1, set ATOM(Q) ← 0, T ← ALINK(Q), ALINK(Q) ← P, P ← Q, and return to E5. If ATOM(Q) = 0, set T ← BLINK(Q), BLINK(Q) ← P, P ← Q, and repeat E6. ∎

An example of this algorithm in action appears in Fig. 39, which shows the successive steps encountered for a simple List structure. The reader will find it worthwhile to study Algorithm E very carefully; notice how the linking structure is artificially changed in steps E4 and E5, in order to maintain a stack analogous to the stack in Algorithm D. When we return to a previous state, the ATOM field is used to tell whether ALINK or BLINK contains the artificial address. The "nesting" shown at the bottom of Fig. 39 illustrates how each nonatomic node is visited three times during Algorithm E: The same configuration (T, P) occurs at the beginning of steps E2, E5, and E6.

A proof that Algorithm E is valid can be formulated by induction on the number of nodes that are to be marked. We prove at the same time that P returns to its initial value PO at the conclusion of the algorithm; for details, see exercise 3. Algorithm E will run faster if step E3 is deleted and if special tests for "ATOM(Q) = 1" and appropriate actions are made in steps E4 and E5, as well as a test "ATOM(PO) = 1" in step E1. We have stated the algorithm in its present form for simplicity; the modifications just stated appear in the answer to exercise 4.

The idea used in Algorithm E can be applied to problems other than garbage collection; in fact, its use for tree traversal has already been mentioned in exercise 2.3.1–21. The reader may also find it useful to compare Algorithm E with the simpler problem solved in exercise 2.2.3–7.

Of all the marking algorithms we have discussed, only Algorithm D is directly applicable to Lists represented as in (9). The other algorithms all test whether or not a given node P is an atom, and the conventions of (9) are incompatible with such tests because they allow atomic information to fill an entire word except for the mark bit. However, each of the other algorithms can be modified so that they will work when atomic data is distinguished from pointer data in the word that links to it instead of by looking at the word itself. In Algorithms A or C we can simply avoid marking atomic words until all nonatomic words have been properly marked; then one further pass over all the data suffices to mark all the atomic words. Algorithm B is even easier to modify, since we need merely keep atomic words off the stack. The adaptation of Algorithm E is almost as simple, although if both ALINK and BLINK are allowed to point to atomic data it will be necessary to introduce another 1-bit field in nonatomic nodes. This is generally not hard to do. (For example, when there are two words per node, the least significant bit of each link field may be used to store temporary information.)

Although Algorithm E requires a time proportional to the number of nodes it marks, this constant of proportionality is not as small as in Algorithm B; the fastest garbage collection method known combines Algorithms B and E, as discussed in exercise 5.

Let us now try to make some quantitative estimates of the efficiency of garbage collection, as opposed to the philosophy of "AVAIL ⇐ X" that was used in most of the previous examples in this chapter. In each of the previous cases we could have omitted all specific mention of returning nodes to free space and we could have substituted a garbage collector instead. (In a special-purpose application, as opposed to a set of general-purpose List manipulation subroutines, the programming and debugging of a garbage collector is more difficult than the methods we have used, and, of course, garbage collection requires an extra bit reserved in each node; but we are interested here in the relative speed of the programs once they have been written and debugged.)

The best garbage collection routines known have an execution time essentially of the form $c_1 N + c_2 M$, where c_1 and c_2 are constants, N is the number of nodes marked, and M is the total number of nodes in the memory. Thus $M - N$ is the number of free nodes found, and the amount of time required to return these nodes to free storage is $(c_1 N + c_2 M)/(M - N)$ per node. Let $N = \rho M$; this figure becomes $(c_1\rho+c_2)/(1-\rho)$. So if $\rho = \frac{3}{4}$, that is, if the memory is three-fourths full, we spend $3c_1 + 4c_2$ units of time per free node returned to storage; when $\rho = \frac{1}{4}$, the corresponding cost is only $\frac{1}{3}c_1 + \frac{4}{3}c_2$. If we do not use the garbage collection technique, the amount of time per node returned is essentially a constant, c_3, and it is doubtful that c_3/c_1 will be very large. Hence we can see to what extent garbage collection is inefficient when the memory becomes full, and how it is correspondingly efficient when the demand on memory is light.

Many programs have the property that the ratio $\rho = N/M$ of good nodes to total memory is quite small. When the pool of memory becomes full in such cases, it might be best to move all the active List data to another memory pool of equal size, using a copying technique (see exercise 10) but without bothering to preserve the contents of the nodes being copied. Then when the second memory pool fills up, we can move the data back to the first one again. With this method more data can be kept in high-speed memory at once, because link fields tend to point to nearby nodes. Moreover, there's no need for a marking phase, and storage allocation is simply sequential.

It is possible to combine garbage collection with some of the other methods of returning cells to free storage; these ideas are not mutually exclusive, and some systems employ both the reference counter and the garbage collection schemes, besides allowing the programmer to erase nodes explicitly. The idea is to employ garbage collection only as a "last resort" whenever all other methods of returning cells have failed. An elaborate system, which implements this idea and also includes a mechanism for postponing operations on reference counts in order to achieve further efficiency, has been described by L. P. Deutsch and D. G. Bobrow in *CACM* **19** (1976), 522–526.

A sequential representation of Lists, which saves many of the link fields at the expense of more complicated storage management, is also possible. See N. E. Wiseman and J. O. Hiles, *Comp. J.* **10** (1968), 338–346; W. J. Hansen, *CACM* **12** (1969), 499–507; and C. J. Cheney, *CACM* **13** (1970), 677–678.

Daniel P. Friedman and David S. Wise have observed that the reference counter method can be employed satisfactorily in many cases even when Lists point to themselves, if certain link fields are not included in the counts [*Inf. Proc. Letters* **8** (1979), 41–45].

A great many variants and refinements of garbage collection algorithms have been proposed. Jacques Cohen, in *Computing Surveys* **13** (1981), 341–367, presents a detailed review of the literature prior to 1981, with important comments about the extra cost of memory accesses when pages of data are shuttled between slow memory and fast memory.

Garbage collection as we have described it is unsuitable for "real time" applications, where each basic List operation must be quick; even if the garbage collector goes into action infrequently, it requires large chunks of computer time on those occasions. Exercise 12 discusses some approaches by which real-time garbage collection is possible.

> *It is a very sad thing nowadays*
> *that there is so little useless information.*
> — OSCAR WILDE (1894)

EXERCISES

▶ **1.** [*M21*] In Section 2.3.4 we saw that trees are special cases of the "classical" mathematical concept of a directed graph. Can Lists be described in graph-theoretic terminology?

2. [*20*] In Section 2.3.1 we saw that tree traversal can be facilitated using a threaded representation inside the computer. Can List structures be threaded in an analogous way?

3. [*M26*] Prove the validity of Algorithm E. [*Hint:* See the proof of Algorithm 2.3.1T.]

4. [*28*] Write a MIX program for Algorithm E, assuming that nodes are represented as one MIX word, with MARK the (0:0) field ["+" = 0, "−" = 1], ATOM the (1:1) field, ALINK the (2:3) field, BLINK the (4:5) field, and $\Lambda = 0$. Also determine the execution time of your program in terms of relevant parameters. (In the MIX computer the problem of determining whether a memory location contains −0 or +0 is not quite trivial, and this can be a factor in your program.)

5. [*25*] (Schorr and Waite.) Give a marking algorithm that combines Algorithms B and E as follows: The assumptions of Algorithm E with regard to fields within the nodes, etc., are retained; but an auxiliary stack STACK[1], STACK[2], ..., STACK[N] is used as in Algorithm B, and the mechanism of Algorithm E is employed only when the stack is full.

6. [*00*] The quantitative discussion at the end of this section says that the cost of garbage collection is approximately $c_1 N + c_2 M$ units of time; where does the "$c_2 M$" term come from?

7. [*24*] (R. W. Floyd.) Design a marking algorithm that is similar to Algorithm E in using no auxiliary stack, except that (i) it has a more difficult task to do, because each node contains only MARK, ALINK, and BLINK fields — there is no ATOM field to provide additional control; yet (ii) it has a simpler task to do, because it marks only a binary tree instead of a general List. Here ALINK and BLINK are the usual LLINK and RLINK in a binary tree.

▶ **8.** [*27*] (L. P. Deutsch.) Design a marking algorithm similar to Algorithms D and E in that it uses no auxiliary memory for a stack, but modify the method so that it works with nodes of variable size and with a variable number of pointers having the following format: The first word of a node has two fields MARK and SIZE; the MARK field is to be treated as in Algorithm E, and the SIZE field contains a number $n \geq 0$. This means that there are n consecutive words after the first word, each containing two fields MARK (which is zero and should remain so) and LINK (which is Λ or points to the first word of another node). For example, a node with three pointers would comprise four consecutive words:

First word	MARK = 0 (will be set to 1)	SIZE = 3
Second word	MARK = 0	LINK = first pointer
Third word	MARK = 0	LINK = second pointer
Fourth word	MARK = 0	LINK = third pointer.

Your algorithm should mark all nodes reachable from a given node P0.

▶ **9.** [*28*] (D. Edwards.) Design an algorithm for the second phase of garbage collection that "compacts storage" in the following sense: Let NODE(1), ..., NODE(M) be one-word nodes with fields MARK, ATOM, ALINK, and BLINK, as described in Algorithm E. Assume that MARK = 1 in all nodes that are not garbage. The desired algorithm should relocate the marked nodes, if necessary, so that they all appear in consecutive locations NODE(1), ..., NODE(K), and at the same time the ALINK and BLINK fields of nonatomic nodes should be altered if necessary so that the List structure is preserved.

▶ **10.** [*28*] Design an algorithm that copies a List structure, assuming that an internal representation like that in (7) is being used. (Thus, if your procedure is asked to copy the List whose head is the node at the upper left corner of (7), a new set of Lists having 14 nodes, and with structure and information identical to that shown in (7), should be created.)

Assume that the List structure is stored in memory using S, T, REF, and RLINK fields as in (9), and that NODE(P0) is the head of the List to be copied. Assume further that the REF field in each List head node is Λ; to avoid the need for additional memory space, your copying procedure should make use of the REF fields (and reset them to Λ again afterwards).

11. [*M30*] Any List structure can be "fully expanded" into a tree structure by repeating all overlapping elements until none are left; when the List is recursive, this gives an infinite tree. For example, the List (5) would expand into an infinite tree whose first four levels are

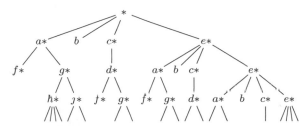

Design an algorithm to test the *equivalence* of two List structures, in the sense that they have the same diagram when fully expanded. For example, Lists A and B are equivalent in this sense, if

$$A = (a\!:\!C, b, a\!:\!(b\!:\!D))$$
$$B = (a\!:\!(b\!:\!D), b, a\!:\!E)$$
$$C = (b\!:\!(a\!:\!C))$$
$$D = (a\!:\!(b\!:\!D))$$
$$E = (b\!:\!(a\!:\!C)).$$

12. [*30*] (M. Minsky.) Show that it is possible to use a garbage collection method reliably in a "real time" application, for example when a computer is controlling some physical device, even when stringent upper bounds are placed on the maximum execution time required for each List operation performed. [*Hint:* Garbage collection can be arranged to work in parallel with the List operations, if appropriate care is taken.]

2.4. MULTILINKED STRUCTURES

NOW THAT WE have examined linear lists and tree structures in detail, the principles of representing structural information within a computer should be evident. In this section we will look at another application of these techniques, this time for the typical case in which the structural information is slightly more complicated: In higher-level applications, several types of structure are usually present simultaneously.

A "multilinked structure" involves nodes with several link fields in each node, not just one or two as in most of our previous examples. We have already seen some examples of multiple linkage, such as the simulated elevator system in Section 2.2.5 and the multivariate polynomials in Section 2.3.3.

We shall see that the presence of many different kinds of links per node does *not* necessarily make the accompanying algorithms any more difficult to write or to understand than the algorithms already studied. We will also discuss the important question, *"How much structural information ought to be explicitly recorded in memory?"*

The problem we will consider arises in connection with writing a compiler program for the translation of COBOL and related languages. A programmer who uses COBOL may give alphabetic names to program variables on several levels; for example, the program might refer to files of data for sales and purchases, having the following structure:

```
      1 SALES                1 PURCHASES
         2 DATE                 2 DATE
            3 MONTH               3 DAY
            3 DAY                 3 MONTH
            3 YEAR                3 YEAR
         2 TRANSACTION          2 TRANSACTION
            3 ITEM                3 ITEM            (1)
            3 QUANTITY            3 QUANTITY
            3 PRICE               3 PRICE
            3 TAX                 3 TAX
            3 BUYER               3 SHIPPER
               4 NAME               4 NAME
               4 ADDRESS            4 ADDRESS
```

This configuration indicates that each item in SALES consists of two parts, the DATE and the TRANSACTION; the DATE is further divided into three parts, and the TRANSACTION likewise has five subdivisions. Similar remarks apply to PURCHASES. The relative order of these names indicates the order in which the quantities appear in external representations of the file (for example, magnetic tape or printed forms); notice that in this example "DAY" and "MONTH" appear in opposite order in the two files. The programmer also gives further information, not shown in this illustration, that tells how much space each item of information occupies and in what format it appears; such considerations are not relevant to us in this section, so they will not be mentioned further.

A COBOL programmer first describes the file layout and the other program variables, then specifies the algorithms that manipulate those quantities. To refer to an individual variable in the example above, it would not be sufficient merely to give the name DAY, since there is no way of telling if the variable called DAY is in the SALES file or in the PURCHASES file. Therefore a COBOL programmer is given the ability to write "DAY OF SALES" to refer to the DAY part of a SALES item. The programmer could also write, more completely,

"DAY OF DATE OF SALES",

but in general there is no need to give more qualification than necessary to avoid ambiguity. Thus,

"NAME OF SHIPPER OF TRANSACTION OF PURCHASES"

may be abbreviated to
"NAME OF SHIPPER"

since only one part of the data has been called SHIPPER.

These rules of COBOL may be stated more precisely as follows:

a) Each name is immediately preceded by an associated positive integer called its *level number*. A name either refers to an *elementary item* or it is the name of a *group* of one or more items whose names follow. In the latter case, each item of the group must have the same level number, which must be greater than the level number of the group name. (For example, DATE and TRANSACTION above have level number 2, which is greater than the level number 1 of SALES.)

b) To refer to an elementary item or group of items named A_0, the general form is

$$A_0 \text{ OF } A_1 \text{ OF } \dots \text{ OF } A_n,$$

where $n \geq 0$ and where, for $0 \leq j < n$, A_j is the name of some item contained directly or indirectly within a group named A_{j+1}. There must be exactly one item A_0 satisfying this condition.

c) If the same name A_0 appears in several places, there must be a way to refer to each use of the name by using qualification.

As an example of rule (c), the data configuration

1 AA
  2 BB
    3 CC   (2)
    3 DD
  2 CC

would not be allowed, since there is no unambiguous way to refer to the second appearance of CC. (See exercise 4.)

COBOL has another feature that affects compiler writing and the application we are considering, namely an option in the language that makes it possible to refer to many items at once. A COBOL programmer may write

$$\text{MOVE CORRESPONDING } \alpha \text{ TO } \beta$$

which moves all items with corresponding names from data area α to data area β. For example, the COBOL statement

MOVE CORRESPONDING DATE OF SALES TO DATE OF PURCHASES

would mean that the values of MONTH, DAY, and YEAR from the SALES file are to be moved to the variables MONTH, DAY, and YEAR in the PURCHASES file. (The relative order of DAY and MONTH is thereby interchanged.)

The problem we will investigate in this section is to design three algorithms suitable for use in a COBOL compiler, which are to do the following things:

Operation 1. To process a description of names and level numbers such as (1), putting the relevant information into tables within the compiler for use in operations 2 and 3.

Operation 2. To determine if a given qualified reference, as in rule (b), is valid, and when it is valid to locate the corresponding data item.

Operation 3. To find all corresponding pairs of items indicated by a given CORRESPONDING statement.

We will assume that our compiler already has a "symbol table subroutine" that will convert an alphabetic name into a link that points to a table entry for that name. (Methods for constructing symbol table algorithms are discussed in detail in Chapter 6.) In addition to the Symbol Table, there is a larger table that contains one entry for each item of data in the COBOL source program that is being compiled; we will call this the *Data Table*.

Clearly, we cannot design an algorithm for operation 1 until we know what kind of information is to be stored in the Data Table, and the form of the Data Table depends on what information we need in order to perform operations 2 and 3; thus we look first at operations 2 and 3.

In order to determine the meaning of the COBOL reference

$$A_0 \text{ OF } A_1 \text{ OF } \ldots \text{ OF } A_n, \qquad n \geq 0, \tag{3}$$

we should first look up the name A_0 in the Symbol Table. There ought to be a series of links from the Symbol Table entry to all Data Table entries for this name. Then for each Data Table entry we will want a link to the entry for the group item that contains it. Now if there is a further link field from the Data Table items back to the Symbol Table, it is not hard to see how a reference like (3) can be processed. Furthermore, we will want some sort of links from the Data Table entries for group items to the items in the group, in order to locate the pairs indicated by "MOVE CORRESPONDING".

We have thereby found a potential need for five link fields in each Data Table entry:

PREV (a link to the previous entry with the same name, if any);
PARENT (a link to the smallest group, if any, containing this item);
NAME (a link to the Symbol Table entry for this item);
CHILD (a link to the first subitem of a group);
SIB (a link to the next subitem in the group containing this item).

It is clear that COBOL data structures like those for SALES and PURCHASES above are essentially trees; and the PARENT, CHILD, and SIB links that appear here are familiar from our previous study. (The conventional binary tree representation of a tree consists of the CHILD and SIB links; adding the PARENT link gives what we have called a "triply linked tree." The five links above consist of these three tree links together with PREV and NAME, which superimpose further information on the tree structure.)

Perhaps not all five of these links will turn out to be necessary, or sufficient, but we will try first to design our algorithms under the tentative assumption that Data Table entries will involve these five link fields (plus further information irrelevant to our problems). As an example of the multiple linking used, consider the two COBOL data structures

$$
\begin{array}{ll}
\begin{array}{ll}
1 & A \\
\quad 3 & B \\
\qquad 7 & C \\
\qquad 7 & D \\
\quad 3 & E \\
\quad 3 & F \\
\qquad 4 & G
\end{array}
&
\begin{array}{ll}
1 & H \\
\quad 5 & F \\
\qquad 8 & G \\
\quad 5 & B \\
\quad 5 & C \\
\qquad 9 & E \\
\qquad 9 & D \\
\qquad 9 & G
\end{array}
\end{array}
\tag{4}
$$

They would be represented as shown in (5) (with links indicated symbolically). The LINK field of each Symbol Table entry points to the most recently encountered Data Table entry for the symbolic name in question.

The first algorithm we require is one that builds the Data Table in such a form. Note the flexibility in choice of level numbers that is allowed by the COBOL rules; the left structure in (4) is completely equivalent to

$$
\begin{array}{ll}
1 & A \\
\quad 2 & B \\
\qquad 3 & C \\
\qquad 3 & D \\
\quad 2 & E \\
\quad 2 & F \\
\qquad 3 & G
\end{array}
$$

because level numbers do not have to be sequential.

Symbol Table   *Data Table*

Symbol Table (LINK)

	LINK
A:	A1
B:	B5
C:	C5
D:	D9
E:	E9
F:	F5
G:	G9
H:	H1

Empty boxes indicate additional information not relevant here

Data Table

	PREV	PARENT	NAME	CHILD	SIB	
A1:	Λ	Λ	A	B3	H1	
B3:	Λ	A1	B	C7	E3	
C7:	Λ	B3	C	Λ	D7	
D7:	Λ	B3	D	Λ	Λ	
E3:	Λ	A1	E	Λ	F3	
F3:	Λ	A1	F	G4	Λ	
G4:	Λ	F3	G	Λ	Λ	
H1:	Λ	Λ	H	F5	Λ	
F5:	F3	H1	F	G8	B5	
G8:	G4	F5	G	Λ	Λ	
B5:	B3	H1	B	Λ	C5	
C5:	C7	H1	C	E9	Λ	
E9:	E3	C5	E	Λ	D9	
D9:	D7	C5	D	Λ	G9	
G9:	G8	C5	G	Λ	Λ	

$$(5)$$

Some sequences of level numbers are illegal, however; for example, if the level number of D in (4) were changed to "**6**" (in either place) we would have a meaningless data configuration, violating the rule that all items of a group must have the same number. The following algorithm therefore makes sure that COBOL's rule (a) has not been broken.

Algorithm A (*Build Data Table*). This algorithm is given a sequence of pairs (L, P), where L is a positive integer "level number" and P points to a Symbol Table entry, corresponding to COBOL data structures such as (4) above. The algorithm builds a Data Table as in the example (5) above. When P points to a Symbol Table entry that has not appeared before, LINK(P) will equal Λ. This algorithm uses an auxiliary stack that is treated as usual (using either sequential memory allocation, as in Section 2.2.2, or linked allocation, as in Section 2.2.3).

A1. [Initialize.] Set the stack contents to the single entry (0, Λ). (The stack entries throughout this algorithm are pairs (L, P), where L is an integer and P is a pointer; as this algorithm proceeds, the stack contains the level numbers and pointers to the most recent data entries on all levels higher in the tree than the current level. For example, just before encountering the pair "**3 F**" in the example above, the stack would contain

$$(0, \Lambda) \qquad (1, A1) \qquad (3, E3)$$

from bottom to top.)

A2. [Next item.] Let (L, P) be the next data item from the input. If the input is exhausted, however, the algorithm terminates. Set $Q \Leftarrow \text{AVAIL}$ (that is, let Q be the location of a new node in which we can put the next Data Table entry).

A3. [Set name links.] Set

$$\text{PREV}(Q) \leftarrow \text{LINK}(P), \qquad \text{LINK}(P) \leftarrow Q, \qquad \text{NAME}(Q) \leftarrow P.$$

(This properly sets two of the five links in $\text{NODE}(Q)$. We now want to set PARENT, CHILD, and SIB appropriately.)

A4. [Compare levels.] Let the top entry of the stack be $(L1, P1)$. If $L1 < L$, set $\text{CHILD}(P1) \leftarrow Q$ (or, if $P1 = \Lambda$, set $\text{FIRST} \leftarrow Q$, where FIRST is a variable that will point to the first Data Table entry) and go to A6.

A5. [Remove top level.] If $L1 > L$, remove the top stack entry, let $(L1, P1)$ be the new entry that has just come to the top of the stack, and repeat step A5. If $L1 < L$, signal an error (mixed numbers have occurred on the same level). Otherwise, namely when $L1 = L$, set $\text{SIB}(P1) \leftarrow Q$, remove the top stack entry, and let $(L1, P1)$ be the pair that has just come to the top of the stack.

A6. [Set family links.] Set $\text{PARENT}(Q) \leftarrow P1$, $\text{CHILD}(Q) \leftarrow \Lambda$, $\text{SIB}(Q) \leftarrow \Lambda$.

A7. [Add to stack.] Place (L, Q) on top of the stack, and return to step A2.   ▮

The introduction of an auxiliary stack, as explained in step A1, makes this algorithm so transparent that it needs no further explanation.

The next problem is to locate the Data Table entry corresponding to a reference

$$A_0 \text{ OF } A_1 \text{ OF } \ldots \text{ OF } A_n, \qquad n \geq 0. \tag{6}$$

A good compiler will also check to ensure that such a reference is unambiguous. In this case, a suitable algorithm suggests itself immediately: All we need to do is to run through the list of Data Table entries for the name A_0 and make sure that exactly one of these entries matches the stated qualification $A_1, \ldots, A_n$.

Algorithm B (*Check a qualified reference*). Corresponding to reference (6), a Symbol Table subroutine will find pointers $P_0, P_1, \ldots, P_n$ to the Symbol Table entries for $A_0, A_1, \ldots, A_n$, respectively.

The purpose of this algorithm is to examine $P_0, P_1, \ldots, P_n$ and either to determine that reference (6) is in error, or to set variable Q to the address of the Data Table entry for the item referred to by (6).

B1. [Initialize.] Set $Q \leftarrow \Lambda$, $P \leftarrow \text{LINK}(P_0)$.

B2. [Done?] If $P = \Lambda$, the algorithm terminates; at this point Q will equal Λ if (6) does not correspond to any Data Table entry. But if $P \neq \Lambda$, set $S \leftarrow P$ and $k \leftarrow 0$. (S is a pointer variable that will run from P up the tree through PARENT links; k is an integer variable that goes from 0 to n. In practice, the pointers $P_0, \ldots, P_n$ would often be kept in a linked list, and instead of k, we would substitute a pointer variable that traverses this list; see exercise 5.)

B3. [Match complete?] If $k < n$ go on to B4. Otherwise we have found a matching Data Table entry; if $Q \neq \Lambda$, this is the second entry found, so an error condition is signaled. Set $Q \leftarrow P$, $P \leftarrow \text{PREV}(P)$, and go to B2.

B4. [Increase k.] Set $k \leftarrow k + 1$.

B5. [Move up tree.] Set $S \leftarrow \text{PARENT}(S)$. If $S = \Lambda$, we have failed to find a match; set $P \leftarrow \text{PREV}(P)$ and go to B2.

B6. [A_k match?] If $\text{NAME}(S) = P_k$, go to B3, otherwise go to B5. ∎

Note that the CHILD and SIB links are not needed by this algorithm.

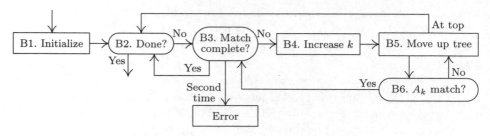

Fig. 40. Algorithm for checking a COBOL reference.

The third and final algorithm that we need concerns "MOVE CORRESPONDING"; before we design such an algorithm, we must have a precise definition of what is required. The COBOL statement

$$\text{MOVE CORRESPONDING } \alpha \text{ TO } \beta \tag{7}$$

where α and β are references such as (6) to data items, is an abbreviation for the set of all statements

$$\text{MOVE } \alpha' \text{ TO } \beta'$$

where there exists an integer $n \geq 0$ and n names $A_0, A_1, \ldots, A_{n-1}$ such that

$$\begin{aligned}
\alpha' &= A_0 \text{ OF } A_1 \text{ OF } \ldots \text{ OF } A_{n-1} \text{ OF } \alpha \\
\beta' &= A_0 \text{ OF } A_1 \text{ OF } \ldots \text{ OF } A_{n-1} \text{ OF } \beta
\end{aligned} \tag{8}$$

and either α' or β' is an elementary item (not a group item). Furthermore we require that the first levels of (8) show *complete* qualifications, namely that A_{j+1} be the parent of A_j for $0 \leq j < n - 1$ and that α and β are parents of A_{n-1}; α' and β' must be exactly n levels farther down in the tree than α and β are.

With respect to our example (4),

$$\text{MOVE CORRESPONDING A TO H}$$

is therefore an abbreviation for the statements

$$\text{MOVE B OF A TO B OF H}$$
$$\text{MOVE G OF F OF A TO G OF F OF H}$$

The algorithm to recognize all corresponding pairs α', β' is quite interesting although not difficult; we move through the tree whose root is α, in preorder, simultaneously looking in the β tree for matching names, and skipping over subtrees in which no corresponding elements can possibly occur. The names $A_0, \ldots, A_{n-1}$ of (8) are discovered in the opposite order $A_{n-1}, \ldots, A_0$.

Algorithm C (*Find* CORRESPONDING *pairs*). Given PO and QO, which point to Data Table entries for α and β, respectively, this algorithm successively finds all pairs (P, Q) of pointers to items (α', β') satisfying the constraints mentioned above.

C1. [Initialize.] Set P $\leftarrow$ PO, Q $\leftarrow$ QO. (In the remainder of this algorithm, the pointer variables P and Q will walk through trees having the respective roots α and β.)

C2. [Elementary?] If CHILD(P) $= \Lambda$ or CHILD(Q) $= \Lambda$, output (P, Q) as one of the desired pairs and go to C5. Otherwise set P $\leftarrow$ CHILD(P), Q $\leftarrow$ CHILD(Q). (In this step, P and Q point to items α' and β' satisfying (8), and we wish to MOVE α' TO β' if and only if either α' or β' (or both) is an elementary item.)

C3. [Match name.]　(Now P and Q point to data items that have respective complete qualifications of the forms

$$A_0 \text{ OF } A_1 \text{ OF } \ldots \text{ OF } A_{n-1} \text{ OF } \alpha$$

and

$$B_0 \text{ OF } A_1 \text{ OF } \ldots \text{ OF } A_{n-1} \text{ OF } \beta.$$

The object is to see if we can make $B_0 = A_0$ by examining all the names of the group $A_1 \text{ OF } \ldots \text{ OF } A_{n-1} \text{ OF } \beta$.) If NAME(P) $=$ NAME(Q), go to C2 (a match has been found). Otherwise, if SIB(Q) $\neq \Lambda$, set Q $\leftarrow$ SIB(Q) and repeat step C3. (If SIB(Q) $= \Lambda$, no matching name is present in the group, and we continue on to step C4.)

C4. [Move on.] If SIB(P) $\neq \Lambda$, set P $\leftarrow$ SIB(P) and Q $\leftarrow$ CHILD(PARENT(Q)), and go back to C3. If SIB(P) $= \Lambda$, set P $\leftarrow$ PARENT(P) and Q $\leftarrow$ PARENT(Q).

C5. [Done?] If P $=$ PO, the algorithm terminates; otherwise go to C4.　∎

A flow chart for this algorithm is shown in Fig. 41. A proof that this algorithm is valid can readily be constructed by induction on the size of the trees involved (see exercise 9).

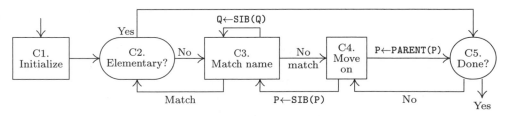

Fig. 41. Algorithm for "MOVE CORRESPONDING".

At this point it is worthwhile to study the ways in which the five link fields
PREV, PARENT, NAME, CHILD, and SIB are used by Algorithms B and C. The
striking feature is that these five links constitute a "complete set" in the sense
that Algorithms B and C do virtually the minimum amount of work as they
move through the Data Table. Whenever they need to refer to another Data
Table entry, its address is immediately available; there is no need to conduct a
search. It would be difficult to imagine how Algorithms B and C could possibly
be made any faster if any additional link information were present in the table.
(See exercise 11, however.)

Each link field may be viewed as a *clue* to the program, planted there in
order to make the algorithms run faster. (Of course, the algorithm that builds
the tables, Algorithm A, runs correspondingly slower, since it has more links to
fill in. But table-building is done only once.) It is clear, on the other hand, that
the Data Table constructed above contains much redundant information. Let us
consider what would happen if we were to *delete* certain of the link fields.

The PREV link, while not used in Algorithm C, is extremely important for
Algorithm B, and it seems to be an essential part of any COBOL compiler unless
lengthy searches are to be carried out. A field that links together all items of
the same name therefore seems essential for efficiency. We could perhaps modify
the strategy slightly and adopt circular linking instead of terminating each list
with Λ, but there is no reason to do this unless other link fields are changed or
eliminated.

The PARENT link is used in both Algorithms B and C, although its use in
Algorithm C could be avoided if we used an auxiliary stack in that algorithm, or
if we augmented SIB so that thread links are included (as in Section 2.3.2). So we
see that the PARENT link has been used in an essential way only in Algorithm B. If
the SIB link were threaded, so that the items that now have $\text{SIB} = \Lambda$ would have
$\text{SIB} = \text{PARENT}$ instead, it would be possible to locate the parent of any data item
by following the SIB links; the added thread links could be distinguished either
by having a new TAG field in each node that says whether the SIB link is a thread,
or by the condition "SIB(P) < P" if the Data Table entries are kept consecutively
in memory in order of appearance. This would mean a short search would be
necessary in step B5, and the algorithm would be correspondingly slower.

The NAME link is used by the algorithms only in steps B6 and C3. In both
cases we could make the tests "NAME(S) = P_k" and "NAME(P) = NAME(Q)" in
other ways if the NAME link were not present (see exercise 10), but this would
significantly slow down the inner loops of both Algorithms B and C. Here again
we see a tradeoff between the space for a link and the speed of the algorithms.
(The speed of Algorithm C is not especially significant in COBOL compilers, when
typical uses of MOVE CORRESPONDING are considered; but Algorithm B should be
fast.) Experience indicates that other important uses are found for the NAME link
within a COBOL compiler, especially in printing diagnostic information.

Algorithm A builds the Data Table step by step, and it never has occasion
to return a node to the pool of available storage; so we usually find that Data
Table entries take consecutive memory locations in the order of appearance of

the data items in the COBOL source program. Thus in our example (5), locations
A1, B3, ... would follow each other. This sequential nature of the Data Table
leads to certain simplifications; for example, the CHILD link of each node is
either Λ or it points to the node immediately following, so CHILD can be reduced
to a 1-bit field. Alternatively, CHILD could be removed in favor of a test if
PARENT$(P + c) = P$, where c is the node size in the Data Table.

Thus the five link fields are not all essential, although they are helpful from
the standpoint of speed in Algorithms B and C. This situation is fairly typical
of most multilinked structures.

It is interesting to note that at least half a dozen people writing COBOL
compilers in the early 1960s arrived independently at this same way to maintain
a Data Table using five links (or four of the five, usually with the CHILD link
missing). The first publication of such a technique was by H. W. Lawson, Jr.
[*ACM National Conference Digest* (Syracuse, N.Y.: 1962), 74–75]. But in 1965
an ingenious technique for achieving the effects of Algorithms B and C, using
only two link fields and sequential storage of the Data Table, without a very great
decrease in speed, was introduced by David Dahm; see exercises 12 through 14.

EXERCISES

1. [*00*] Considering COBOL data configurations as tree structures, are the data items
listed by a COBOL programmer in preorder, postorder, or neither of those orders?

2. [*10*] Comment about the running time of Algorithm A.

3. [*22*] The PL/I language accepts data structures like those in COBOL, except that
any sequence of level numbers is possible. For example, the sequence

1	A		1	A
3	B		2	B
5	C	is equivalent to	3	C
4	D		3	D
2	E		2	E

In general, rule (a) is modified to read, "The items of a group must have a sequence
of nonincreasing level numbers, all of which are greater than the level number of the
group name." What modifications to Algorithm A would change it from the COBOL
convention to this PL/I convention?

▶ **4.** [*26*] Algorithm A does not detect the error if a COBOL programmer violates rule
(c) stated in the text. How should Algorithm A be modified so that only data structures
satisfying rule (c) will be accepted?

5. [*20*] In practice, Algorithm B may be given a linked list of Symbol Table references
as input, instead of what we called "$P_0, P_1, \ldots, P_n$." Let T be a pointer variable such
that

$$\text{INFO(T)} \equiv P_0, \quad \text{INFO(RLINK(T))} \equiv P_1, \quad \ldots, \quad \text{INFO(RLINK}^{[n]}\text{(T))} \equiv P_n, \quad \text{RLINK}^{[n+1]}\text{(T)} = \Lambda.$$

Show how to modify Algorithm B so that it uses such a linked list as input.

6. [*23*] The PL/I language accepts data structures much like those in COBOL, but
does not make the restriction of rule (c); instead, we have the rule that a qualified
reference (3) is unambiguous if it shows "complete" qualification—that is, if A_{j+1} is

the parent of A_j for $0 \le j < n$, and if A_n has no parent. Rule (c) is now weakened to the simple condition that no two items of a group may have the same name. The second "CC" in (2) would be referred to as "CC OF AA" without ambiguity; the three data items

$$1 \ \text{A}$$
$$2 \ \text{A}$$
$$3 \ \text{A}$$

would be referred to as "A", "A OF A", "A OF A OF A" with respect to the PL/I convention just stated. [*Note:* Actually the word "OF" is replaced by a period in PL/I, and the order is reversed; "CC OF AA" is really written "AA.CC" in PL/I, but this is not important for the purposes of the present exercise.] Show how to modify Algorithm B so that it follows the PL/I convention.

7. [*15*] Given the data structures in (1), what does the COBOL statement "MOVE CORRESPONDING SALES TO PURCHASES" mean?

8. [*10*] Under what circumstances is "MOVE CORRESPONDING α TO β" exactly the same as "MOVE α TO β", according to the definition in the text?

9. [*M23*] Prove that Algorithm C is correct.

10. [*23*] (a) How could the test "NAME(S) = P_k" in step B6 be performed if there were no NAME link in the Data Table nodes? (b) How could the test "NAME(P) = NAME(Q)" in step C3 be performed if there were no NAME link in the Data Table entries? (Assume that all other links are present as in the text.)

▶ **11.** [*23*] What additional links or changes in the strategy of the algorithms of the text could make Algorithm B or Algorithm C faster?

12. [*25*] (D. M. Dahm.) Consider representing the Data Table in sequential locations with just two links for each item:

PREV (as in the text);

SCOPE (a link to the last elementary item in this group).

We have SCOPE(P) = P if and only if NODE(P) represents an elementary item. For example, the Data Table of (5) would be replaced by

	PREV	SCOPE		PREV	SCOPE		PREV	SCOPE
A1:	Λ	G4	F3:	Λ	G4	B5:	B3	B5
B3:	Λ	D7	G4:	Λ	G4	C5:	C7	G9
C7:	Λ	C7	H1:	Λ	G9	E9:	E3	E9
D7:	Λ	D7	F5:	F3	G8	D9:	D7	D9
E3:	Λ	E3	G8:	G4	G8	G9:	G8	G9

(Compare with (5) of Section 2.3.3.) Notice that NODE(P) is part of the tree below NODE(Q) if and only if $Q < P \le$ SCOPE(Q). Design an algorithm that performs the function of Algorithm B when the Data Table has this format.

▶ **13.** [*24*] Give an algorithm to substitute for Algorithm A when the Data Table is to have the format shown in exercise 12.

▶ **14.** [*28*] Give an algorithm to substitute for Algorithm C when the Data Table has the format shown in exercise 12.

15. [*25*] (David S. Wise.) Reformulate Algorithm A so that no extra storage is used for the stack. [*Hint:* The SIB fields of all nodes pointed to by the stack are Λ in the present formulation.]

2.5. DYNAMIC STORAGE ALLOCATION

WE HAVE SEEN how the use of links implies that data structures need not be sequentially located in memory; a number of tables may independently grow and shrink in a common pooled memory area. However, our discussions have always tacitly assumed that all nodes have the same size — that every node occupies a certain fixed number of memory cells.

For a great many applications, a suitable compromise can be found so that a uniform node size is indeed used for all structures (for example, see exercise 2). Instead of simply taking the maximum size that is needed and wasting space in smaller nodes, it is customary to pick a rather small node size and to employ what may be called the classical *linked-memory philosophy*: "If there isn't room for the information here, let's put it somewhere else and plant a link to it."

For a great many other applications, however, a single node size is not reasonable; we often wish to have nodes of varying sizes sharing a common memory area. Putting this another way, we want algorithms for reserving and freeing variable-size blocks of memory from a larger storage area, where these blocks are to consist of consecutive memory locations. Such techniques are generally called *dynamic storage allocation* algorithms.

Sometimes, often in simulation programs, we want dynamic storage allocation for nodes of rather small sizes (say one to ten words); and at other times, often in operating systems, we are dealing primarily with rather large blocks of information. These two points of view lead to slightly different approaches to dynamic storage allocation, although the methods have much in common. For uniformity in terminology between these two approaches, we will generally use the terms *block* and *area* rather than "node" in this section, to denote a set of contiguous memory locations.

In 1975 or so, several authors began to call the pool of available memory a "heap." But in the present series of books, we will use that word only in its more traditional sense related to priority queues (see Section 5.2.3).

A. Reservation. Figure 42 shows a typical *memory map* or "checkerboard," a chart showing the current state of some memory pool. In this case the memory is shown partitioned into 53 blocks of storage that are "reserved," or in use, mixed together with 21 "free" or "available" blocks that are not in use. After dynamic storage allocation has been in operation for awhile, the computer memory will perhaps look something like this. Our first problem is to answer two questions:

a) How is this partitioning of available space to be represented inside the computer?

b) Given such a representation of the available spaces, what is a good algorithm for finding a block of n consecutive free spaces and reserving them?

The answer to question (a) is, of course, to keep a *list* of the available space somewhere; this is almost always done best by using the available space *itself* to contain such a list. (An exception is the case when we are allocating storage for a disk file or other memory in which nonuniform access time makes it better to maintain a separate directory of available space.)

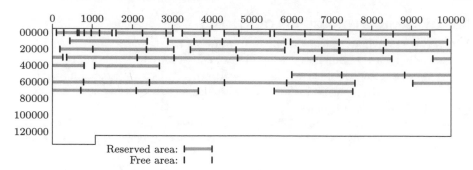

Fig. 42. A memory map.

Thus, we can *link together* the available segments: The first word of each free storage area can contain the size of that block and the address of the next free area. The free blocks can be linked together in increasing or decreasing order of size, or in order of memory address, or in essentially random order.

For example, consider Fig. 42, which illustrates a memory of 131,072 words, addressed from 0 to 131071. If we were to link together the available blocks in order of memory location, we would have one variable AVAIL pointing to the first free block (in this case AVAIL would equal 0), and the other blocks would be represented as follows:

location	SIZE	LINK	
0	101	632	
632	42	1488	
⋮	⋮	⋮	[17 similar entries]
73654	1909	77519	
77519	53553	Λ	[special marker for last link]

Thus locations 0 through 100 form the first available block; after the reserved areas 101–290 and 291–631 shown in Fig. 42, we have more free space in location 632–673; etc.

As for question (b), if we want n consecutive words, clearly we must locate some block of $m \geq n$ available words and reduce its size to $m - n$. (Furthermore, when $m = n$, we must also delete this block from the list.) There may be several blocks with n or more cells, and so the question becomes, *which* area should be chosen?

Two principal answers to this question suggest themselves: We can use the *best-fit method* or the *first-fit method*. In the former case, we decide to choose an area with m cells, where m is the smallest value present that is n or more. This might require searching the entire list of available space before a decision can be made. The first-fit method, on the other hand, simply chooses the first area encountered that has $\geq n$ words.

Historically, the best-fit method was widely used for several years; this naturally appears to be a good policy since it saves the larger available areas for a later time when they might be needed. But several objections to the best-fit technique can be raised: It is rather slow, since it involves a fairly long search; if best-fit is not substantially better than first-fit for other reasons, this extra searching time is not worthwhile. More importantly, the best-fit method tends to increase the number of very small blocks, and proliferation of small blocks is usually undesirable. There are certain situations in which the first-fit technique is demonstrably better than the best-fit method; for example, suppose we are given just two available areas of memory, of sizes 1300 and 1200, and suppose there are subsequent requests for blocks of sizes 1000, 1100, and 250:

memory request	available areas, first-fit	available areas, best-fit	
—	1300, 1200	1300, 1200	(1)
1000	300, 1200	1300, 200	
1100	300, 100	200, 200	
250	50, 100	stuck	

(A contrary example appears in exercise 7.) The point is that neither method clearly dominates the other, hence the simple first-fit method can be recommended.

Algorithm A (*First-fit method*). Let AVAIL point to the first available block of storage, and suppose that each available block with address P has two fields: SIZE(P), the number of words in the block; and LINK(P), a pointer to the next available block. The last pointer is Λ. This algorithm searches for and reserves a block of N words, or reports failure.

A1. [Initialize.] Set Q ← LOC(AVAIL). (Throughout the algorithm we use two pointers, Q and P, which are generally related by the condition P = LINK(Q). We assume that LINK(LOC(AVAIL)) = AVAIL.)

A2. [End of list?] Set P ← LINK(Q). If P = Λ, the algorithm terminates unsuccessfully; there is no room for a block of N consecutive words.

A3. [Is SIZE enough?] If SIZE(P) ≥ N, go to A4; otherwise set Q ← P and return to step A2.

A4. [Reserve N.] Set K ← SIZE(P) − N. If K = 0, set LINK(Q) ← LINK(P) (thereby removing an empty area from the list); otherwise set SIZE(P) ← K. The algorithm terminates successfully, having reserved an area of length N beginning with location P + K. ∎

This algorithm is certainly straightforward enough. However, a significant improvement in its running speed can be made with only a rather slight change in strategy. This improvement is quite important, and the reader will find it a pleasure to discover it without being told the secret (see exercise 6).

Algorithm A may be used whether storage allocation is desired for small N or large N. Let us assume temporarily, however, that we are primarily interested in *large* values of N. Then notice what happens when SIZE(P) is equal to N+1 in that algorithm: We get to step A4 and reduce SIZE(P) to 1. In other words, an available block of size 1 has just been created; this block is so small it is virtually useless, and it just clogs up the system. We would have been better off if we had reserved the whole block of N + 1 words, instead of saving the extra word; it is often better to expend a few words of memory to avoid handling unimportant details. Similar remarks apply to blocks of N + K words when K is very small.

If we allow the possibility of reserving slightly more than N words it will be necessary to remember how many words have been reserved, so that later when this block becomes available again the entire set of N + K words is freed. This added amount of bookkeeping means that we are tying up space in *every* block in order to make the system more efficient only in certain circumstances when a tight fit is found; so the strategy doesn't seem especially attractive. However, a special *control word* as the first word of each variable-size block often turns out to be desirable for other reasons, and so it is usually not unreasonable to expect the SIZE field to be present in the first word of all blocks, whether they are available or reserved.

In accordance with these conventions, we would modify step A4 above to read as follows:

A4′. [Reserve ≥ N.] Set K ← SIZE(P) − N. If K < c (where c is a small positive constant chosen to reflect an amount of storage we are willing to sacrifice in the interests of saving time), set LINK(Q) ← LINK(P) and L ← P. Otherwise set SIZE(P) ← K, L ← P + K, SIZE(L) ← N. The algorithm terminates successfully, having reserved an area of length N or more beginning with location L.

A value for the constant c of about 8 or 10 is suggested, although very little theory or empirical evidence exists to compare this with other choices. When the best-fit method is being used, the test of K < c is even *more* important than it is for the first-fit method, because tighter fits (smaller values of K) are much more likely to occur, and the number of available blocks should be kept as small as possible for that algorithm.

B. Liberation. Now let's consider the inverse problem: How should we return blocks to the available space list when they are no longer needed?

It is perhaps tempting to dismiss this problem by using garbage collection (see Section 2.3.5); we could follow a policy of simply doing nothing until space runs out, then searching for all the areas currently in use and fashioning a new AVAIL list.

The idea of garbage collection is not to be recommended, however, for all applications. In the first place, we need a fairly "disciplined" use of pointers if we are to be able to guarantee that all areas currently in use will be easy to locate, and this amount of discipline is often lacking in the applications considered here. Secondly, as we have seen before, garbage collection tends to be slow when the memory is nearly full.

There is another more important reason why garbage collection is not satisfactory, due to a phenomenon that did not confront us in our previous discussion of the technique: Suppose that there are two adjacent areas of memory, both of which are available, but because of the garbage-collection philosophy one of them (shown shaded) is not in the `AVAIL` list.

$$(2)$$

In this diagram, the heavily shaded areas at the extreme left and right are unavailable. We may now reserve a section of the area known to be available:

$$(3)$$

If garbage collection occurs at this point, we have two separate free areas,

$$(4)$$

Boundaries between available and reserved areas have a tendency to perpetuate themselves, and as time goes on the situation gets progressively worse. But if we had used a philosophy of returning blocks to the `AVAIL` list as soon as they become free, *and collapsing adjacent available areas together*, we would have collapsed (2) into

$$(5)$$

and we would have obtained

$$(6)$$

which is much better than (4). This phenomenon causes the garbage-collection technique to leave memory more broken up than it should be.

In order to remove this difficulty, we can use garbage collection together with the process of *compacting memory*, that is, moving all the reserved blocks into consecutive locations, so that all available blocks come together whenever garbage collection is done. The allocation algorithm now becomes completely trivial by contrast with Algorithm A, since there is only one available block at all times. Even though this technique takes time to recopy all the locations that are in use, and to change the value of the link fields therein, it can be applied with reasonable efficiency when there is a disciplined use of pointers, and when there is a spare link field in each block for use by the garbage collection algorithms. (See exercise 33.)

Since many applications do not meet the requirements for the feasibility of garbage collection, we shall now study methods for returning blocks of memory to the available space list. The only difficulty in these methods is the collapsing problem: Two adjacent free areas should be merged into one. In fact, when an area bounded by two available blocks becomes free, all three areas should be merged together into one. *In this way a good balance is obtained in memory even though storage areas are continually reserved and freed over a long period of time.* (For a proof of this fact, see the "fifty-percent rule" below.)

The problem is to determine whether the areas at either side of the returned block are currently available; and if they are, we want to update the `AVAIL` list properly. The latter operation is a little more difficult than it sounds.

The first solution to these problems is to maintain the AVAIL list in order of increasing memory locations.

Algorithm B (*Liberation with sorted list*). Under the assumptions of Algorithm A, with the additional assumption that the AVAIL list is sorted by memory location (that is, if P points to an available block and LINK(P) $\neq \Lambda$, then LINK(P) > P), this algorithm adds the block of N consecutive cells beginning at location P0 to the AVAIL list. We naturally assume that none of these N cells is already available.

B1. [Initialize.] Set Q ← LOC(AVAIL). (See the remarks in step A1 above.)

B2. [Advance P.] Set P ← LINK(Q). If P = Λ, or if P > P0, go to B3; otherwise set Q ← P and repeat step B2.

B3. [Check upper bound.] If P0 + N = P and P $\neq \Lambda$, set N ← N + SIZE(P) and set LINK(P0) ← LINK(P). Otherwise set LINK(P0) ← P.

B4. [Check lower bound.] If Q + SIZE(Q) = P0 (we assume that

$$SIZE(LOC(AVAIL)) = 0,$$

so this test always fails when Q = LOC(AVAIL)), set SIZE(Q) ← SIZE(Q) + N and LINK(Q) ← LINK(P0). Otherwise set LINK(Q) ← P0, SIZE(P0) ← N. $\blacksquare$

Steps B3 and B4 do the desired collapsing, based on the fact that the pointers Q < P0 < P are the beginning locations of three consecutive available areas.

If the AVAIL list is not maintained in order of locations, the reader can see that a "brute force" approach to the collapsing problem would require a complete search through the entire AVAIL list; Algorithm B reduces this to a search through about *half* of the AVAIL list (in step B2) on the average. Exercise 11 shows how Algorithm B can be modified so that, on the average, only about one-third of the AVAIL list must be searched. But obviously, when the AVAIL list is long, all of these methods are much slower than we want them to be. Isn't there some way to reserve and free storage areas so that we don't need to do extensive searching through the AVAIL list?

We will now consider a method that eliminates all searching when storage is returned and that can be modified, as in exercise 6, to avoid almost all of the searching when storage is reserved. The technique makes use of a TAG field at both ends of each block, and a SIZE field in the first word of each block; this overhead is negligible when reasonably large blocks are being used, although it is perhaps too much of a penalty to pay in situations when the blocks have a very small average size. Another method described in exercise 19 requires only one bit in the first word of each block, at the expense of a little more running time and a slightly more complicated program.

At any rate, let us now assume that we don't mind adding a little bit of control information, in order to save a good deal of time over Algorithm B when the AVAIL list is long. The method we will describe assumes that each block has the following form:

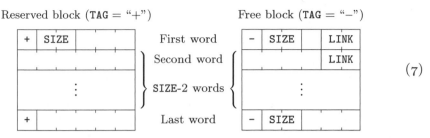

Reserved block (TAG = "+")   Free block (TAG = "−")

$$(7)$$

The idea in the following algorithm is to maintain a doubly linked AVAIL list, so that entries may conveniently be deleted from random parts of the list. The TAG field at either end of a block can be used to control the collapsing process, since we can tell easily whether or not both adjacent blocks are available.

Double linking is achieved in a familiar way, by letting the LINK in the first word point to the next free block in the list, and letting the LINK in the second word point back to the previous block; thus, if P is the address of an available block, we always have

$$\text{LINK}(\text{LINK}(P) + 1) = P = \text{LINK}(\text{LINK}(P + 1)). \qquad (8)$$

To ensure proper "boundary conditions," the list head is set up as follows:

LOC(AVAIL): | − | 0 | 0 | • —→ to first block in available space list
LOC(AVAIL)+1: | − | 0 | 0 | • —→ to last block in available space list (9)

A first-fit reservation algorithm for this technique may be designed very much like Algorithm A, so we shall not consider it here (see exercise 12). The principal new feature of this method is the way the block can be freed in essentially a fixed amount of time:

Algorithm C (*Liberation with boundary tags*). Assume that blocks of locations have the forms shown in (7), and assume that the AVAIL list is doubly linked, as described above. This algorithm puts the block of locations starting with address P0 into the AVAIL list. If the pool of available storage runs from locations m_0 through m_1, inclusive, the algorithm assumes for convenience that

$$\text{TAG}(m_0 - 1) = \text{TAG}(m_1 + 1) = \text{"+".}$$

C1. [Check lower bound.] If $\text{TAG}(P0 - 1) = $ "+", go to C3.

C2. [Delete lower area.] Set $P \leftarrow P0 - \text{SIZE}(P0 - 1)$, and then set $P1 \leftarrow \text{LINK}(P)$, $P2 \leftarrow \text{LINK}(P + 1)$, $\text{LINK}(P1 + 1) \leftarrow P2$, $\text{LINK}(P2) \leftarrow P1$, $\text{SIZE}(P) \leftarrow \text{SIZE}(P) + \text{SIZE}(P0)$, $P0 \leftarrow P$.

C3. [Check upper bound.] Set $P \leftarrow P0 + \text{SIZE}(P0)$. If $\text{TAG}(P) = $ "+", go to C5.

C4. [Delete upper area.] Set $P1 \leftarrow \text{LINK}(P)$, $P2 \leftarrow \text{LINK}(P+1)$, $\text{LINK}(P1+1) \leftarrow P2$, $\text{LINK}(P2) \leftarrow P1$, $\text{SIZE}(P0) \leftarrow \text{SIZE}(P0) + \text{SIZE}(P)$, $P \leftarrow P + \text{SIZE}(P)$.

C5. [Add to `AVAIL` list.] Set `SIZE(P − 1) ← SIZE(P0)`, `LINK(P0) ← AVAIL`, `LINK(P0 + 1) ← LOC(AVAIL)`, `LINK(AVAIL + 1) ← P0`, `AVAIL ← P0`, `TAG(P0) ← TAG(P − 1) ← "−"`. ∎

The steps of Algorithm C are straightforward consequences of the storage layout (7); a slightly longer algorithm that is a little faster appears in exercise 15. In step C5, `AVAIL` is an abbreviation for `LINK(LOC(AVAIL))`, as shown in (9).

C. The "buddy system." We will now study another approach to dynamic storage allocation, suitable for use with binary computers. This method uses just one bit of overhead in each block, and it requires all blocks to be of length 1, 2, 4, 8, or 16, etc. If a block is not 2^k words long for some integer k, the next higher power of 2 is chosen and extra unused space is allocated accordingly.

The idea of this method is to keep separate lists of available blocks of each size 2^k, $0 \le k \le m$. The entire pool of memory space under allocation consists of 2^m words, which can be assumed to have the addresses 0 through $2^m - 1$. Originally, the entire block of 2^m words is available. Later, when a block of 2^k words is desired, and if nothing of this size is available, a larger available block is *split* into two equal parts; ultimately, a block of the right size 2^k will appear. When one block splits into two (each of which is half as large as the original), these two blocks are called *buddies*. Later when both buddies are available again, they coalesce back into a single block; thus the process can be maintained indefinitely, unless we run out of space at some point.

The key fact underlying the practical usefulness of this method is that if we know the address of a block (the memory location of its first word), and if we also know the size of that block, we know the address of its buddy. For example, the buddy of the block of size 16 beginning in binary location 101110010110000 is a block starting in binary location 101110010100000. To see why this must be true, we first observe that as the algorithm proceeds, *the address of a block of size 2^k is a multiple of 2^k*. In other words, the address in binary notation has at least k zeros at the right. This observation is easily justified by induction: If it is true for all blocks of size 2^{k+1}, it is certainly true when such a block is halved.

Therefore a block of size, say, 32 has an address of the form $xx \ldots x00000$ (where the x's represent either 0 or 1); if it is split, the newly formed buddy blocks have the addresses $xx \ldots x00000$ and $xx \ldots x10000$. In general, let $\text{buddy}_k(x) =$ address of the buddy of the block of size 2^k whose address is x; we find that

$$\text{buddy}_k(x) = \begin{cases} x + 2^k, & \text{if } x \bmod 2^{k+1} = 0; \\ x - 2^k, & \text{if } x \bmod 2^{k+1} = 2^k. \end{cases} \tag{10}$$

This function is readily computed with the "exclusive or" instruction (sometimes called "selective complement" or "add without carry") usually found on binary computers; see exercise 28.

The buddy system makes use of a one-bit `TAG` field in each block:

$$\begin{aligned} \texttt{TAG(P)} = 0, &\quad \text{if the block with address P is reserved;} \\ \texttt{TAG(P)} = 1, &\quad \text{if the block with address P is available.} \end{aligned} \tag{11}$$

This TAG field is present in all blocks, and it must not be tampered with by the users who reserve blocks. The *available* blocks also have two link fields, LINKF and LINKB, which are the usual forward and backward links of a doubly linked list; and they also have a KVAL field to specify k when their size is 2^k. The algorithms below make use of the table locations AVAIL[0], AVAIL[1], ..., AVAIL[m], which serve respectively as the heads of the lists of available storage of sizes 1, 2, 4, ..., 2^m. These lists are doubly linked, so as usual the list heads contain two pointers (see Section 2.2.5):

$$\text{AVAILF}[k] = \text{LINKF}(\text{LOC}(\text{AVAIL}[k])) = \text{link to rear of AVAIL}[k] \text{ list;}$$
$$\text{AVAILB}[k] = \text{LINKB}(\text{LOC}(\text{AVAIL}[k])) = \text{link to front of AVAIL}[k] \text{ list.}$$
(12)

Initially, before any storage has been allocated, we have

$$\text{AVAILF}[m] = \text{AVAILB}[m] = 0,$$
$$\text{LINKF}(0) = \text{LINKB}(0) = \text{LOC}(\text{AVAIL}[m]),$$
$$\text{TAG}(0) = 1, \quad \text{KVAL}(0) = m$$
(13)

(indicating a single available block of length 2^m, beginning in location 0), and

$$\text{AVAILF}[k] = \text{AVAILB}[k] = \text{LOC}(\text{AVAIL}[k]), \quad \text{for } 0 \le k < m$$
(14)

(indicating empty lists for available blocks of lengths 2^k for all $k < m$).

From this description of the buddy system, the reader may find it enjoyable to design the necessary algorithms for reserving and freeing storage areas before looking at the algorithms given below. Notice the comparative ease with which blocks can be halved in the reservation algorithm.

Algorithm R (*Buddy system reservation*). This algorithm finds and reserves a block of 2^k locations, or reports failure, using the organization of the buddy system as explained above.

R1. [Find block.] Let j be the smallest integer in the range $k \le j \le m$ for which AVAILF[j] $\ne$ LOC(AVAIL[j]), that is, for which the list of available blocks of size 2^j is not empty. If no such j exists, the algorithm terminates unsuccessfully, since there are no known available blocks of sufficient size to meet the request.

R2. [Remove from list.] Set L $\leftarrow$ AVAILB[j], P $\leftarrow$ LINKB(L), AVAILB[j] $\leftarrow$ P, LINKF(P) $\leftarrow$ LOC(AVAIL[j]), and TAG(L) $\leftarrow$ 0.

R3. [Split required?] If $j = k$, the algorithm terminates (we have found and reserved an available block starting at address L).

R4. [Split.] Decrease j by 1. Then set P $\leftarrow$ L + 2^j, TAG(P) $\leftarrow$ 1, KVAL(P) $\leftarrow$ j, LINKF(P) $\leftarrow$ LINKB(P) $\leftarrow$ LOC(AVAIL[j]), AVAILF[j] $\leftarrow$ AVAILB[j] $\leftarrow$ P. (This splits a large block and enters the unused half in the AVAIL[j] list, which was empty.) Go back to step R3. ∎

Algorithm S (*Buddy system liberation*). This algorithm returns a block of 2^k locations, starting in address L, to free storage, using the organization of the buddy system as explained above. (The user is supposed to know the value of k, from the current context, because a reserved block has no KVAL field.)

S1. [Is buddy available?] Set P ← buddy_k(L). (See Eq. (10).) If $k = m$ or if TAG(P) = 0, or if TAG(P) = 1 and KVAL(P) $\neq k$, go to S3.

S2. [Combine with buddy.] Set

$$\text{LINKF(LINKB(P))} \leftarrow \text{LINKF(P)}, \qquad \text{LINKB(LINKF(P))} \leftarrow \text{LINKB(P)}.$$

(This removes block P from the AVAIL[k] list.) Then set $k \leftarrow k + 1$, and if P < L set L ← P. Return to S1.

S3. [Put on list.] Set TAG(L) ← 1, P ← AVAILF[k], LINKF(L) ← P, LINKB(P) ← L, KVAL(L) ← k, LINKB(L) ← LOC(AVAIL[k]), AVAILF[k] ← L. (This puts block L on the AVAIL[k] list.) ∎

D. Comparison of the methods. The mathematical analysis of these dynamic storage-allocation algorithms has proved to be quite difficult, but there is one interesting phenomenon that is fairly easy to analyze, namely the "fifty-percent rule":

> *If Algorithms A and B are used continually in such a way that the system tends to an equilibrium condition, where there are N reserved blocks in the system, on the average, each equally likely to be the next one freed, and where the quantity K in Algorithm A takes on nonzero values (or, more generally, values $\geq c$ as in step A4') with probability p, then the average number of available blocks tends to be approximately $\frac{1}{2}pN$.*

This rule tells us approximately how long the AVAIL list will be. When the quantity p is near 1 — this will happen if c is very small and if the block sizes are infrequently equal to each other — we have about half as many available blocks as unavailable ones; hence the name "fifty-percent rule."

It is not hard to derive this rule. Consider the following memory map:

This shows the reserved blocks divided into three categories:

A: when freed, the number of available blocks will decrease by one;
B: when freed, the number of available blocks will not change;
C: when freed, the number of available blocks will increase by one.

Now let N be the number of reserved blocks, and let M be the number of available ones; let A, B, and C be the number of blocks of the types identified above. We have

$$N = A + B + C$$
$$M = \tfrac{1}{2}(2A + B + \epsilon) \tag{15}$$

where $\epsilon = 0$, 1, or 2 depending on conditions at the lower and upper boundaries.

Let us assume that N is essentially constant, but that A, B, C, and ϵ are random quantities that reach a stationary distribution after a block is freed and a (slightly different) stationary distribution after a block is allocated. The average change in M when a block is freed is the average value of $(C - A)/N$; the average change in M when a block is allocated is $-1 + p$. So the equilibrium assumption tells us that the average value of $C - A - N + pN$ is zero. But then the average value of $2M$ is pN plus the average value of ϵ, since $2M = N + A - C + \epsilon$ by (15). The fifty-percent rule follows.

Our assumption that each deletion applies to a random reserved block will be valid if the lifetime of a block is an exponentially distributed random variable. On the other hand, if all blocks have roughly the same lifetime, this assumption is false; John E. Shore has pointed out that type A blocks tend to be "older" than type C blocks when allocations and liberations tend to have a somewhat first-in-first-out character, since a sequence of adjacent reserved blocks tends to be in order from youngest to oldest and since the most recently allocated block is almost never type A. This tends to produce a smaller number of available blocks, giving even better performance than the fifty-percent rule would predict. [See *CACM* **20** (1977), 812–820.]

For more detailed information about the fifty-percent rule, see D. J. M. Davies, *BIT* **20** (1980), 279–288; C. M. Reeves, *Comp. J.* **26** (1983), 25–35; G. Ch. Pflug, *Comp. J.* **27** (1984), 328–333.

Besides this interesting rule, our knowledge of the performance of dynamic storage allocation algorithms is based almost entirely on Monte Carlo experiments. Readers will find it instructive to conduct their own simulation experiments when they are choosing between storage allocation algorithms for a particular machine and a particular application or class of applications. The author carried out several such experiments just before writing this section (and, indeed, the fifty-percent rule was noticed during those experiments before a proof for it was found); let us briefly examine the methods and results of those experiments here.

The basic simulation program ran as follows, with TIME initially zero and with the memory area initially all available:

P1. [Tick.] Advance TIME by 1.

P2. [Sync.] Free all blocks in the system that are scheduled to be freed at the current value of TIME.

P3. [Get data.] Calculate two quantities S (a random size) and T (a random lifetime), based on some probability distributions, using the methods of Chapter 3.

P4. [Use data.] Reserve a new block of length S, which is due to be freed at (TIME $+ T$). Return to P1. ∎

Whenever TIME was a multiple of 200, detailed statistics about the performance of the reservation and liberation algorithms were printed. The same sequence of values of S and T was used for each pair of algorithms tested. After TIME advanced past 2000, the system usually had reached a more-or-less steady state that gave every indication of being maintained indefinitely thereafter. However, depending on the total amount of storage available and on the distributions of S and T in step P3, the allocation algorithms would occasionally fail to find enough space and the simulation experiment was then terminated.

Let C be the total number of memory locations available, and let $\bar{S}$ and $\bar{T}$ denote the average values of S and T in step P3. It is easy to see that the expected number of unavailable words of memory at any given time is $\bar{S}\bar{T}$, once TIME is sufficiently large. When $\bar{S}\bar{T}$ was greater than about $\frac{2}{3}C$ in the experiments, memory overflow usually occurred, often before C words of memory were actually needed. The memory was able to become over 90 percent filled when the block size was small compared to C, but when the block sizes were allowed to exceed $\frac{1}{3}C$ (as well as taking on much smaller values) the program tended to regard the memory as "full" when fewer than $\frac{1}{2}C$ locations were actually in use. Empirical evidence suggests strongly that *block sizes larger than $\frac{1}{10}C$ should not be used with dynamic storage allocation* if effective operation is expected.

The reason for this behavior can be understood in terms of the fifty-percent rule: If the system reaches an equilibrium condition in which the size f of an average free block is less than the size r of an average block in use, we can expect to get an unfillable request unless a large free block is available for emergencies. Hence $f \geq r$ in a saturated system that doesn't overflow, and we have $C = fM + rN \geq rM + rN \approx (p/2+1)rN$. The total memory in use is therefore $rN \leq C/(p/2+1)$; when $p \approx 1$ we are unable to use more than about 2/3 of the memory cells.

The experiments were conducted with three size distributions for S:

(*S1*) an integer chosen uniformly between 100 and 2000;

(*S2*) sizes (1, 2, 4, 8, 16, 32) chosen with respective probabilities $(\frac{1}{2}, \frac{1}{4}, \frac{1}{8}, \frac{1}{16}, \frac{1}{32}, \frac{1}{32})$;

(*S3*) sizes (10, 12, 14, 16, 18, 20, 30, 40, 50, 60, 70, 80, 90, 100, 150, 200, 250, 500, 1000, 2000, 3000, 4000) selected with equal probability.

The time distribution T was usually a random integer chosen uniformly between 1 and t, for fixed $t = 10$, 100, or 1000.

Experiments were also made in which T was chosen uniformly between 1 and $\min\left(\left\lfloor \frac{5}{4}U \right\rfloor, 12500\right)$ in step P3, where U is the number of time units remaining until the next scheduled freeing of some currently reserved block in the system. This time distribution was meant to simulate an "almost-last-in-first-out" behavior: For if T were always chosen $\leq U$, the storage allocation system would degenerate into simply a stack operation requiring no complex algorithms. (See exercise 1.) The stated distribution causes T to be chosen greater than U about 20 percent of the time, so we have almost, but not quite, a stack operation. When this distribution was used, algorithms such as A, B, and C behaved much better than usual; there were rarely, if ever, more than two items in the entire AVAIL list, while there were about 14 reserved blocks. On the other hand, the buddy system algorithms, R and S, were slower when this distribution was used, because they tend to split and coalesce blocks more frequently in a stack-like operation. The theoretical properties of this time distribution appear to be quite difficult to deduce (see exercise 32).

Figure 42, which appeared near the beginning of this section, was the configuration of memory at TIME = 5000, with size distribution (*S1*) and with

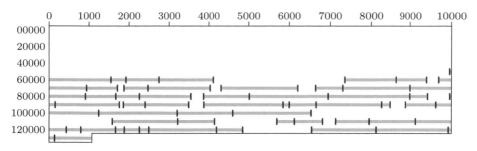

Fig. 43. Memory map obtained with the best-fit method. (Compare this with Fig. 42, which shows the first-fit method, and Fig. 44, which shows the buddy system, for the same sequence of storage requests.)

the times distributed uniformly in $\{1, \ldots, 100\}$, using the first-fit method just as in Algorithms A and B above. For this experiment, the probability p that enters into the "fifty-percent rule" was essentially 1, so we would expect about half as many available blocks as reserved blocks. Actually Fig. 42 shows 21 available and 53 reserved. This does not disprove the fifty-percent rule: For example, at TIME = 4600 there were 25 available and 49 reserved. The configuration in Fig. 42 merely shows how the fifty-percent rule is subject to statistical variations. The number of available blocks generally ranged between 20 and 30, while the number of reserved blocks was generally between 45 and 55.

Figure 43 shows the configuration of memory obtained with *the same data as Fig. 42* but with the best-fit method used instead of the first-fit method. The constant c in step A4′ was set to 16, to eliminate small blocks, and as a result the probability p dropped to about 0.7 and there were fewer available areas.

When the time distribution was changed to vary from 1 to 1000 instead of 1 to 100, situations precisely analogous to those shown in Figs. 42 and 43 were obtained, with all appropriate quantities approximately multiplied by 10. For example, there were 515 reserved blocks; and 240 free blocks in the equivalent of Fig. 42, 176 free blocks in the equivalent of Fig. 43.

In all experiments comparing the best-fit and first-fit methods, the latter always appeared to be superior. When memory size was exhausted, the first-fit method actually stayed in action longer than the best-fit method before memory overflow occurred, in most instances.

The buddy system was also applied to the same data that led to Figs. 42 and 43, and Fig. 44 was the result. Here, all sizes in the range 257 to 512 were treated as 512, those between 513 and 1024 were raised to 1024, etc. On the average this means that more than four thirds as much memory was requested (see exercise 21); the buddy system, of course, works better on size distributions like that of (*S2*) above, instead of (*S1*). Notice that there are available blocks of sizes 2^9, 2^{10}, 2^{11}, 2^{12}, 2^{13}, and 2^{14} in Fig. 44.

Simulation of the buddy system showed that it performs much better than might be expected. It is clear that the buddy system will sometimes allow two adjacent areas of the same size to be available without merging them into one

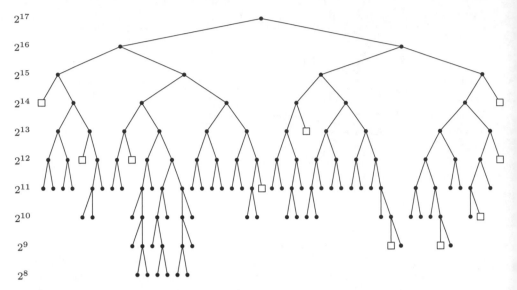

Fig. 44. Memory map obtained with the buddy system. (The tree structure indicates the division of certain large blocks into buddies of half the size. Squares indicate available blocks.)

(if they are not buddies); but this situation is not present in Fig. 44 and, in fact, it is rare in practice. In cases where memory overflow occurred, memory was 95 percent reserved, and this reflects a surprisingly good allocation balance. Furthermore, it was very seldom necessary to split blocks in Algorithm R, or to merge them in Algorithm S; the tree remained much like Fig. 44, with available blocks on the most commonly used levels. Some mathematical results that give insight into this behavior, at the lowest level of the tree, have been obtained by P. W. Purdom, Jr., and S. M. Stigler, *JACM* **17** (1970), 683–697.

Another surprise was the excellent behavior of Algorithm A after the modification described in exercise 6; only 2.8 inspections of available block sizes were necessary on the average (using size distribution (*S1*) and times chosen uniformly between 1 and 1000), and more than half of the time only the minimum value, one iteration, was necessary. This was true in spite of the fact that about 250 available blocks were present. The same experiment with Algorithm A unmodified showed that about 125 iterations were necessary on the average (so about half of the AVAIL list was being examined each time); 200 or more iterations were found to be necessary about 20 percent of the time.

This behavior of Algorithm A unmodified can, in fact, be predicted as a consequence of the fifty-percent rule. At equilibrium, the portion of memory containing the last half of the reserved blocks will also contain the last half of the free blocks; that portion will be involved half of the time when a block is freed, and so it must be involved in half of the allocations in order to maintain equilibrium. The same argument holds when one-half is replaced by any other fraction. (These observations are due to J. M. Robson.)

The exercises below include MIX programs for the two principal methods that are recommended as a consequence of the remarks above: (i) the boundary tag system, as modified in exercises 12 and 16; and (ii) the buddy system. Here are the approximate results:

	Time for reservation	Time for liberation
Boundary tag system:	$33 + 7A$	18, 29, 31, or 34
Buddy system:	$19 + 25R$	$27 + 26S$

Here $A \geq 1$ is the number of iterations necessary when searching for an available block that is large enough; $R \geq 0$ is the number of times a block is split in two (the initial difference of $j - k$ in Algorithm R); and $S \geq 0$ is the number of times buddy blocks are reunited during Algorithm S. The simulation experiments indicate that under the stated assumptions with size distribution $(S1)$ and time chosen between 1 and 1000, we may take $A = 2.8$, $R = S = 0.04$ on the average. (The average values $A = 1.3$, $R = S = 0.9$ were observed when the "almost-last-in-first-out" time distribution was substituted as explained above.) This shows that both methods are quite fast, with the buddy system slightly faster in MIX's case. Remember that the buddy system requires about 44 percent more space when block sizes are not constrained to be powers of 2.

A corresponding time estimate for the garbage collection and compacting algorithm of exercise 33 is about 104 units of time to locate a free node, assuming that garbage collection occurs when the memory is approximately half full, and assuming that the nodes have an average length of 5 words with 2 links per node. The pros and cons of garbage collection are discussed in Section 2.3.5. When the memory is not heavily loaded and when the appropriate restrictions are met, garbage collection and compacting is very efficient; for example, on the MIX computer, the garbage collection method is faster than the other two, if the accessible items never occupy more than about one-third of the total memory space, and if the nodes are relatively small.

If the assumptions underlying garbage collection are met, the best strategy may be to divide the pool of memory into two halves and to do all allocation sequentially within one half. Instead of freeing blocks as they become available, we simply wait until the current active half of memory is full; then we can copy all active data to the other half, simultaneously removing all holes between blocks, with a method like that of exercise 33. The size of each half pool might also be adjusted as we switch from one half to the other.

The simulation techniques mentioned above were applied also to some other storage allocation algorithms. The other methods were so poor by comparison with the algorithms of this section that they will be given only brief mention here:

a) Separate AVAIL lists were kept for each size. A single free block was occasionally split into two smaller blocks when necessary, but no attempt was made to put such blocks together again. The memory map became fragmented into finer and finer parts until it was in terrible shape; a simple scheme like this is almost equivalent to doing separate allocation in disjoint areas, one area for each block size.

b) An attempt was made to do two-level allocation: The memory was divided into 32 large sectors. A brute-force allocation method was used to reserve large blocks of 1, 2, or 3 (rarely more) adjacent sectors; each large block such as this was subdivided to meet storage requests until no more room was left within the current large block, and then another large block was reserved for use in subsequent allocations. Each large block was returned to free storage only when *all* space within it became available. This method almost always ran out of storage space very quickly.

Although this particular method of two-level allocation was a failure for the data considered in the author's simulation experiments, there are other circumstances (which occur not infrequently in practice) when a multiple-level allocation strategy can be beneficial. For example, if a rather large program operates in several stages, we might know that certain types of nodes are needed only within a certain subroutine. Some programs might also find it desirable to use quite different allocation strategies for different classes of nodes. The idea of allocating storage by zones, with possibly different strategies employed in each zone and with the ability to free an entire zone at once, is discussed by Douglas T. Ross in *CACM* **10** (1967), 481–492.

For further empirical results about dynamic storage allocation, see the articles by B. Randell, *CACM* **12** (1969), 365–369, 372; P. W. Purdom, S. M. Stigler, and T. O. Cheam, *BIT* **11** (1971), 187–195; B. H. Margolin, R. P. Parmelee, and M. Schatzoff, *IBM Systems J.* **10** (1971), 283–304; J. A. Campbell, *Comp. J.* **14** (1971), 7–9; John E. Shore, *CACM* **18** (1975), 433–440; Norman R. Nielsen, *CACM* **20** (1977), 864–873.

*E. Distributed fit. If the distribution of block sizes is known in advance, and if each block present is equally likely to be the next one freed regardless of when it was allocated, we can use a technique that has substantially better memory utilization than the general-purpose techniques described so far, by following the suggestions of E. G. Coffman, Jr., and F. T. Leighton [*J. Computer and System Sci.* **38** (1989), 2–35]. Their "distributed-fit method" works by partitioning memory into roughly $N + \sqrt{N} \lg N$ slots, where N is the desired maximum number of blocks to be handled in steady state. Each slot has a fixed size, although different slots may have different sizes; the main point is that any given slot has fixed boundaries, and it will either be empty or contain a single allocated block.

The first N slots in Coffman and Leighton's scheme are laid out according to the assumed distribution of sizes, while the last $\sqrt{N} \lg N$ slots all have the maximum size. For example, if we assume that the block sizes will be uniformly distributed between 1 and 256, and if we expect to handle $N = 2^{14}$ such blocks, we would divide the memory into $N/256 = 2^6$ slots of each size 1, 2, ..., 256, followed by an "overflow area" that contains $\sqrt{N} \lg N = 2^7 \cdot 14 = 1792$ blocks of size 256. When the system is operating at full capacity, we expect it to handle N blocks of average size $\frac{257}{2}$, occupying $\frac{257}{2} N = 2^{21} + 2^{13} = 2{,}105{,}344$ locations; this is the amount of space we have allocated to the first N slots. We have also set aside an additional $1792 \cdot 256 = 458{,}752$ locations to handle the effects of random variations; this additional overhead amounts to $O(N^{-1/2} \log N)$ of the total space, rather than a constant multiple of N as in the buddy system, so it becomes a negligible fraction when $N \to \infty$. In our example, however, it still amounts to about 18% of the total allocation.

The slots should be arranged in order so that the smaller slots precede the larger ones. Given this arrangement, we can allocate blocks by using either the first-fit or the best-fit technique. (Both methods are equivalent in this case, because the slot sizes are ordered.) The effect, under our assumptions, is to start searching at an essentially random place among the first N slots whenever a new allocation request comes in, and to continue until we find an empty slot.

If the starting slot for each search is truly random between 1 and N, we will not have to invade the overflow area very often. Indeed, if we insert exactly N items starting at random slots, overflow will occur only $O(\sqrt{N})$ times, on the average. The reason is that we can compare this algorithm to hashing with linear probing (Algorithm 6.4L), which has the same behavior except that the search for an empty cell wraps around from N to 1 instead of going into an overflow area. The analysis of Algorithm 6.4L in Theorem 6.4K shows that, when N items have been inserted, the average displacement of each item from its hash address is $\frac{1}{2}(Q(N) - 1) \sim \sqrt{\pi N/8}$; by circular symmetry this average is easily seen to be the same as the average number of times a search goes from slot k to slot $k+1$, for each k. Overflows in the distributed-fit method correspond to searches that go from slot N to slot 1, except that our situation is even better because we avoid some congestion by not wrapping around. Therefore fewer than $\sqrt{\pi N/8}$ overflows will occur, on the average. This analysis does not take account of deletions, which preserve the assumptions of Algorithm 6.4L only if we move blocks back when deleting another block that intervened between their starting slots and their allocated slots (see Algorithm 6.4R); again, however, moving them back would only increase the chance of overflow. Our analysis also fails to account for the effect of having more than N blocks present at once; this can happen if we assume only that the arrival time between blocks is about one Nth of the residence time. For the case of more than N blocks we need to extend the analysis of Algorithm 6.4L, but Coffman and Leighton proved that the overflow area will almost never need more than $\sqrt{N} \lg N$ slots; the probability of running off the end is less than $O(N^{-M})$ for all M.

In our example, the starting slot for the search during an allocation is not uniform among slots 1, 2, $\ldots$, N; it is, instead, uniform among slots 1, 65, 129, $\ldots$, $N - 63$, because there are $N/256 = 64$ slots of each size. But this deviation from the random model considered in the previous paragraph makes overflow even less likely than predicted. All bets are off, of course, if the assumptions about block size distribution and occupancy time are violated.

F. Overflow. What do we do when no more room is available? Suppose there is a request for, say, n consecutive words, when all available blocks are too small. The first time this happens, there usually are more than n available locations present, but they are not consecutive; compacting memory (that is, moving some of the locations that are in use, so that all available locations are brought together) would mean that we could continue processing. But compacting is slow, and it requires a disciplined use of pointers; moreover, the vast majority of cases in which the first-fit method runs out of room will soon thereafter run completely out of space anyway, no matter how much compacting and re-compacting is done. Therefore it is generally not worthwhile to write a compacting program, except under special circumstances in connection with garbage collection, as in exercise 33. If overflow is expected to occur, some method for removing items from memory and storing them on an external memory device can be used, with provision for bringing the information back again when it is needed. This implies that all programs referring to the dynamic memory area must be severely restricted with regard to the allowable references they make to other blocks, and special computer hardware (for example, interrupt on absence of data, or automatic "paging") is generally required for efficient operation under these conditions.

Some decision procedure is necessary to decide which blocks are the most likely candidates for removal. One idea is to maintain a doubly linked list of the reserved blocks, in which a block is moved up to the front of the list each time it is accessed; then the blocks are effectively sorted in order of their last access, and the block at the rear of the list is the one to remove first. A similar effect can be achieved more simply by putting the reserved blocks into a circular list and including a "recently used" bit in each block; the latter is set to 1 whenever the block is accessed. When it is time to remove a block, a pointer moves along the circular list, resetting all "recently used" bits to 0 until finding a block that has not been used since the last time the pointer reached this part of the circle.

J. M. Robson has shown [*JACM* **18** (1971), 416–423] that dynamic storage allocation strategies that never relocate reserved blocks cannot possibly be guaranteed to use memory efficiently; there will always be pathological circumstances in which the method breaks down. For example, even when blocks are restricted to be of sizes 1 and 2, overflow might occur with the memory only about $\frac{2}{3}$ full, no matter what allocation algorithm is used! Robson's interesting results are surveyed in exercises 36–40, and in exercises 42–43 where he has shown that the best-fit method has a very bad worst case by comparison with first-fit.

G. For further reading. A comprehensive survey and critical review of dynamic storage allocation techniques, based on many more years of experience than were available to the author when the material above was written, has been compiled by Paul R. Wilson, Mark S. Johnstone, Michael Neely, and David Boles, *Lecture Notes in Computer Science* **986** (1995), 1–116.

EXERCISES

1. [*20*] What simplifications can be made to the reservation and liberation algorithms of this section, if storage requests always appear in a "last-in-first-out" manner, that is, if no reserved block is freed until after all blocks that were reserved subsequently have already been freed?

2. [*HM23*] (E. Wolman.) Suppose that we want to choose a fixed node size for variable-length items, and suppose also that when each node has length k and when an item has length l, it takes $\lceil l/(k - b) \rceil$ nodes to store this item. (Here b is a constant, signifying that b words of each node contain control information, such as a link to the next node.) If the average length l of an item is L, what choice of k minimizes the average amount of storage space required? (Assume that the average value of $(l/(k - b)) \bmod 1$ is equal to $1/2$, for any fixed k, as l varies.)

3. [*40*] By computer simulation, compare the best-fit, first-fit, and *worst-fit* methods of storage allocation; in the latter method, the largest available block is always chosen. Is there any significant difference in the memory usage?

4. [*22*] Write a MIX program for Algorithm A, paying special attention to making the inner loop fast. Assume that the SIZE field is (4:5), the LINK field is (0:2), and $\Lambda < 0$.

▶ **5.** [*18*] Suppose it is known that N is always 100 or more in Algorithm A. Would it be a good idea to set $c = 100$ in the modified step A4′?

▶ **6.** [*23*] (*Next fit.*) After Algorithm A has been used repeatedly, there will be a strong tendency for blocks of small SIZE to remain at the front of the AVAIL list, so that it will often be necessary to search quite far into the list before finding a block of length N or more. For example, notice how the size of the blocks essentially increases in Fig. 42, for both reserved and free blocks, from the beginning of memory to the end. (The AVAIL list used while Fig. 42 was being prepared was kept sorted by order of location, as required by Algorithm B.) Can you suggest a way to modify Algorithm A so that (a) short blocks won't tend to accumulate in a particular area, and (b) the AVAIL list may still be kept in order of increasing memory locations, for purposes of algorithms like Algorithm B?

7. [*10*] The example (1) shows that first-fit can sometimes be definitely superior to best-fit. Give a similar example that shows a case where best-fit is superior to first-fit.

8. [*21*] Show how to modify Algorithm A in a simple way to obtain an algorithm for the best-fit method, instead of first-fit.

▶ **9.** [*26*] In what ways could a reservation algorithm be designed to use the best-fit method, without searching through the whole AVAIL list? (Try to think of ways that cut down the necessary search as much as possible.)

10. [*22*] Show how to modify Algorithm B so that the block of N consecutive cells beginning at location P0 is made available, without assuming that each of these N cells is currently unavailable; assume, in fact, that the area being freed may actually overlap several blocks that are already free.

11. [*M25*] Show that the improvement to Algorithm A suggested in the answer to exercise 6 can also be used to lead to a slight improvement in Algorithm B, which cuts the average length of search from half the length of the AVAIL list to one-third this length. (Assume that the block being freed will be inserted into a random place within the sorted AVAIL list.)

▶ **12.** [*20*] Modify Algorithm A so that it follows the boundary-tag conventions of (7)–(9), uses the modified step A4′ described in the text, and also incorporates the improvement of exercise 6.

13. [*21*] Write a MIX program for the algorithm of exercise 12.

14. [*21*] What difference would it make to Algorithm C and the algorithm of exercise 12, (a) if the SIZE field were not present in the last word of a free block? or (b) if the SIZE field were not present in the first word of a reserved block?

▶ **15.** [*24*] Show how to speed up Algorithm C at the expense of a slightly longer program, by not changing any more links than absolutely necessary in each of four cases depending on whether TAG(PO − 1), TAG(PO + SIZE(PO)) are plus or minus.

16. [*24*] Write a MIX program for Algorithm C, incorporating the ideas of exercise 15.

17. [*10*] What should the contents of LOC(AVAIL) and LOC(AVAIL) + 1 be in (9) when there are no available blocks present?

▶ **18.** [*20*] Figures 42 and 43 were obtained using the same data, and essentially the same algorithms (Algorithms A and B), except that Fig. 43 was prepared by modifying Algorithm A to choose best-fit instead of first-fit. Why did this cause Fig. 42 to have a large available area in the *higher* locations of memory, while in Fig. 43 there is a large available area in the *lower* locations?

▶ **19.** [*24*] Suppose that blocks of memory have the form of (7), but without the TAG or SIZE fields required in the last word of the block. Suppose further that the following simple algorithm is being used to make a reserved block free again: Q ← AVAIL, LINK(PO) ← Q, LINK(PO + 1) ← LOC(AVAIL), LINK(Q + 1) ← PO, AVAIL ← PO, TAG(PO) ← "−". (This algorithm does nothing about collapsing adjacent areas together.)

   Design a reservation algorithm, similar to Algorithm A, that does the necessary collapsing of adjacent free blocks while searching the AVAIL list, and at the same time avoids any unnecessary fragmentation of memory as in (2), (3), and (4).

20. [*00*] Why is it desirable to have the AVAIL[k] lists in the buddy system doubly linked instead of simply having straight linear lists?

21. [*HM25*] Examine the ratio a_n/b_n, where a_n is the sum of the first n terms of $1 + 2 + 4 + 4 + 8 + 8 + 8 + 8 + 16 + 16 + \cdots$, and b_n is the sum of the first n terms of $1 + 2 + 3 + 4 + 5 + 6 + 7 + 8 + 9 + 10 + \cdots$, as n goes to infinity.

▶ **22.** [*21*] The text repeatedly states that the buddy system allows only blocks of size 2^k to be used, and exercise 21 shows this can lead to a substantial increase in the storage required. But if an 11-word block is needed in connection with the buddy system, why couldn't we find a 16-word block and divide it into an 11-word piece together with two free blocks of sizes 4 and 1?

23. [*05*] What is the binary address of the buddy of the block of size 4 whose binary address is 011011110000? What would it be if the block were of size 16 instead of 4?

24. [*20*] According to the algorithm in the text, the largest block (of size 2^m) has no buddy, since it represents all of storage. Would it be correct to define $\text{buddy}_m(0) = 0$ (namely, to make this block its own buddy), and then to avoid testing $k = m$ in step S1?

▶ **25.** [*22*] Criticize the following idea: "Dynamic storage allocation using the buddy system will never reserve a block of size 2^m in practical situations (since this would fill the whole memory), and, in general, there is a maximum size 2^n for which no blocks of greater size will ever be reserved. Therefore it is a waste of time to start with such large blocks available, and to combine buddies in Algorithm S when the combined block has a size larger than 2^n."

▶ **26.** [*21*] Explain how the buddy system could be used for dynamic storage allocation in memory locations 0 through M − 1 even when M does not have the form 2^m as required in the text.

27. [24] Write a MIX program for Algorithm R, and determine its running time.

28. [25] Assume that MIX is a binary computer, with a new operation code XOR defined as follows (using the notation of Section 1.3.1): "C = 5, F = 5. For each bit position in location M that equals 1, the corresponding bit position in register A is complemented (changed from 0 to 1 or 1 to 0); the sign of rA is unaffected. The execution time is $2u$."
Write a MIX program for Algorithm S, and determine its running time.

29. [20] Could the buddy system do without the tag bit in each reserved block?

30. [M48] Analyze the average behavior of Algorithms R and S, given reasonable distributions for the sequence of storage requests.

31. [M40] Can a storage allocation system analogous to the buddy system be designed using the Fibonacci sequence instead of powers of two? (Thus, we might start with F_m available words, and split an available block of F_k words into two buddies of respective lengths F_{k-1} and F_{k-2}.)

32. [HM46] Determine $\lim_{n\to\infty} \alpha_n$, if it exists, where α_n is the mean value of t_n in a random sequence defined as follows: Given the values of t_k for $0 \le k < n$, let t_n be chosen uniformly from $\{1, 2, \ldots, g_n\}$, where

$$g_n = \left\lfloor \tfrac{5}{4} \min\big(10000,\ f(t_{n-1}-1),\ f(t_{n-2}-2),\ \ldots,\ f(t_0-n)\big) \right\rfloor,$$

and $f(x) = x$ if $x > 0$, $f(x) = \infty$ if $x \le 0$. [*Note:* Some limited empirical tests indicate that α_n might be approximately 14, but this is probably not very accurate.]

▶ **33.** [28] (*Garbage collection and compacting.*) Assume that memory locations 1, 2, ..., AVAIL − 1 are being used as a storage pool for nodes of varying sizes, having the following form: The first word of NODE(P) contains the fields

> SIZE(P) = number of words in NODE(P);
> T(P) = number of link fields in NODE(P); T(P) < SIZE(P);
> LINK(P) = special link field for use only during garbage collection.

The node immediately following NODE(P) in memory is NODE(P + SIZE(P)). Assume that the only fields in NODE(P) that are used as links to other nodes are LINK(P + 1), LINK(P + 2), ..., LINK(P + T(P)), and each of these link fields is either Λ or the address of the first word of another node. Finally, assume that there is one further link variable in the program, called USE, and it points to one of the nodes.

Design an algorithm that (i) determines all nodes accessible directly or indirectly from the variable USE, (ii) moves these nodes into memory locations 1 through K − 1, for some K, changing all links so that structural relationships are preserved, and (iii) sets AVAIL ← K.

For example, consider the following contents of memory, where INFO(L) denotes the contents of location L, excluding LINK(L):

1: SIZE = 2, T = 1	6: SIZE = 2, T = 0	AVAIL = 11,
2: LINK = 6, INFO = A	7: CONTENTS = D	USE = 3.
3: SIZE = 3, T = 1	8: SIZE = 3, T = 2	
4: LINK = 8, INFO = B	9: LINK = 8, INFO = E	
5: CONTENTS = C	10: LINK = 3, INFO = F	

Your algorithm should transform this into

1: SIZE = 3, T = 1	4: SIZE = 3, T = 2	AVAIL = 7,
2: LINK = 4, INFO = B	5: LINK = 4, INFO = E	USE = 1.
3: CONTENTS = C	6: LINK = 1, INFO = F	

34. [*29*] Write a MIX program for the algorithm of exercise 33, and determine its running time.

35. [*22*] Contrast the dynamic storage allocation methods of this section with the techniques for variable-size sequential lists discussed at the end of Section 2.2.2.

▶ **36.** [*20*] A certain lunch counter in Hollywood, California, contains 23 seats in a row. Diners enter the shop in groups of one or two, and a glamorous hostess shows them where to sit. Prove that she will always be able to seat people immediately without splitting up any pairs, if no customer who comes alone is assigned to any of the seats numbered 2, 5, 8, ..., 20, provided that there never are more than 16 customers present at a time. (Pairs leave together.)

▶ **37.** [*26*] Continuing exercise 36, prove that the hostess can't always do such a good job when there are only 22 seats at the counter: No matter what strategy she uses, it will be possible to reach a situation where two friends enter and only 14 people are seated, but no two adjacent seats are vacant.

38. [*M21*] (J. M. Robson.) The lunch-counter problem in exercises 36 and 37 can be generalized to establish the worst-case performance of any dynamic storage allocation algorithm that never relocates reserved blocks. Let $N(n, m)$ be the smallest amount of memory such that any series of requests for allocation and liberation can be handled without overflow, provided that all block sizes are $\leq m$ and the total amount of space requested never exceeds n. Exercises 36 and 37 prove that $N(16, 2) = 23$; determine the exact value of $N(n, 2)$ for all n.

39. [*HM23*] (J. M. Robson.) In the notation of exercise 38, show that $N(n_1+n_2, m) \leq N(n_1, m) + N(n_2, m) + N(2m - 2, m)$; hence for fixed m, $\lim_{n \to \infty} N(n, m)/n = N(m)$ exists.

40. [*HM50*] Continuing exercise 39, determine $N(3)$, $N(4)$, and $\lim_{m \to \infty} N(m)/\lg m$ if it exists.

41. [*M27*] The purpose of this exercise is to consider the worst-case memory usage of the buddy system. A particularly bad case occurs, for example, if we start with an empty memory and proceed as follows: First reserve $n = 2^{r+1}$ blocks of length 1, which go into locations 0 through $n - 1$; then for $k = 1, 2, ..., r$, liberate all blocks whose starting location is not divisible by 2^k, and reserve $2^{-k-1}n$ blocks of length 2^k, which go into locations $\frac{1}{2}(1 + k)n$ through $\frac{1}{2}(2 + k)n - 1$. This procedure uses $1 + \frac{1}{2}r$ times as much memory as is ever occupied.

Prove that the worst case cannot be substantially worse than this: When all requests are for block sizes 1, 2, ..., 2^r, and if the total space requested at any time never exceeds n, where n is a multiple of 2^r, the buddy system will never overflow a memory area of size $(r + 1)n$.

42. [*M40*] (J. M. Robson, 1975.) Let $N_{BF}(n, m)$ be the amount of memory needed to guarantee non-overflow when the best-fit method is used for allocation as in exercise 38. Find an attacking strategy to show that $N_{BF}(n, m) \geq mn - O(n + m^2)$.

43. [*HM35*] Continuing exercise 42, let $N_{FF}(n, m)$ be the memory needed when the first-fit method is used. Find a defensive strategy to show that $N_{FF}(n, m) \leq H_m n/\ln 2$. (Hence the worst case of first-fit is not far from the best possible worst case.)

44. [*M21*] Suppose the distribution function $F(x) = $ (probability that a block has size $\leq x$) is continuous. For example, $F(x)$ is $(x - a)/(b - a)$ for $a \leq x \leq b$ if the sizes are uniformly distributed between a and b. Give a formula that expresses the sizes of the first N slots that should be set up when we use the distributed-fit method.

2.6. HISTORY AND BIBLIOGRAPHY

LINEAR LISTS and rectangular arrays of information kept in consecutive memory locations were widely used from the earliest days of stored-program computers, and the earliest treatises on programming gave the basic algorithms for traversing these structures. [For example, see J. von Neumann, *Collected Works* **5**, 113–116 (written 1946); M. V. Wilkes, D. J. Wheeler, S. Gill, *The Preparation of Programs for an Electronic Digital Computer* (Cambridge, Mass.: Addison–Wesley, 1951), subroutine V-1; and see especially also the work of Konrad Zuse, *Berichte der Gesellschaft für Mathematik und Datenverarbeitung* **63** (Bonn: 1972), written in 1945. Zuse was the first to develop nontrivial algorithms that worked with lists of dynamically varying lengths.] Before the days of index registers, operations on sequential linear lists were done by performing arithmetic on the machine language instructions themselves, and the need to do such arithmetic was one of the early motivations for having a computer whose programs share memory space with the data they manipulate.

Techniques that permit variable-length linear lists to share sequential locations, in such a way that they shift back and forth when necessary as described in Section 2.2.2, were apparently a much later invention. J. Dunlap of Digitek Corporation developed such techniques before 1963 in connection with the design of a series of compiler programs; about the same time the idea appeared independently in the design of a COBOL compiler at IBM Corporation, and a collection of related subroutines called CITRUS was subsequently used at various installations. The techniques remained unpublished until after they had been developed independently by Jan Garwick of Norway; see *BIT* **4** (1964), 137–140.

The idea of having linear lists in *non*sequential locations seems to have originated in connection with the design of computers with rotating drum memories. After executing the instruction in location n, such a computer was usually not ready to get its next instruction from location $n + 1$, because the drum had already rotated past that point. Depending on the instruction being performed, the most favorable position for the next instruction might be $n + 7$ or $n + 18$, say, and the machine could operate up to six or seven times faster if its instructions were located optimally rather than consecutively. [For a discussion of the interesting problems concerning the best placement of instructions, see the author's article in *JACM* **8** (1961), 119–150.] Therefore an extra address field was provided in each machine language instruction, to serve as a link to the next command. This idea, called "one-plus-one addressing," was discussed by John Mauchly in 1946 [*Theory and Techniques for the Design of Electronic Computers* **4** (U. of Pennsylvania, 1946), Lecture 37]; it contained the notion of linked lists in embryonic form, although the dynamic insertion and deletion operations that we have used so frequently in this chapter were still unknown. Another early appearance of links in programs was in H. P. Luhn's 1953 memorandum suggesting the use of "chaining" for external searching; see Section 6.4.

Linked memory techniques were really born when A. Newell, J. C. Shaw, and H. A. Simon began their investigations of heuristic problem-solving by machine. As an aid to writing programs that searched for proofs in mathematical logic, they designed the first List-processing language, IPL-II, in the spring of 1956. (IPL was an acronym for Information Processing Language.) This was a system that made use of pointers and included important concepts like the list of available space, but the concept of stacks was not yet well developed. IPL-III, designed a year later, included "push down" and "pop up" for stacks as important basic operations. [For references to IPL-II see *IRE Transactions* **IT-2** (September 1956), 61–79; *Proc. Western Joint Comp. Conf.* **9** (1957), 218–240. Material on IPL-III first appeared in course notes given at the University of Michigan in the summer of 1957.]

The work of Newell, Shaw, and Simon inspired many other people to use linked memory, which was often referred to as NSS memory at the time, but mostly for problems dealing with simulation of human thought processes. Gradually, the techniques became recognized as basic computer-programming tools; the first article describing the usefulness of linked memory for "down-to-earth" problems was published by J. W. Carr, III, in *CACM* **2**, 2 (February 1959), 4–6. Carr pointed out in this article that linked lists can readily be manipulated in ordinary programming languages, without requiring sophisticated subroutines or interpretive systems. See also G. A. Blaauw, "Indexing and control-word techniques," *IBM J. Res. and Dev.* **3** (1959), 288–301.

At first, one-word nodes were used for linked tables, but about 1959 the usefulness of several consecutive words per node and "multilinked" lists was gradually being discovered by several different groups of people. The first article dealing specifically with this idea was published by D. T. Ross, *CACM* **4** (1961), 147–150. At that time he used the term "plex" for what has been called a "node" in this chapter, but he subsequently used the word "plex" in a different sense to denote a class of nodes combined with associated algorithms for their traversal.

Notations for referring to fields within nodes are generally of two kinds: The name of the field either precedes or follows the pointer designation. Thus, while we have written "INFO(P)" in this chapter, some other authors write, for example, "P.INFO". At the time this chapter was prepared, the two notations seemed to be equally prominent. The notation adopted here has the great advantage that it translates immediately into FORTRAN, COBOL, or similar languages, if we define INFO and LINK arrays and use P as the index. Furthermore it seems natural to use mathematical functional notation to describe attributes of a node. Note that "INFO(P)" is pronounced "info of P" in conventional mathematical verbalization, just as $f(x)$ is rendered "f of x." The alternative notation P.INFO has less of a natural flavor, since it tends to put the emphasis on P, although it can be read "P's info"; the reason INFO(P) seems preferable is apparently the fact that P is variable, but INFO has a fixed significance when the notation is employed. By analogy, we could consider a vector $A = (A[1], A[2], \ldots, A[100])$ to be a node having 100 fields named $1, 2, \ldots, 100$. Now the second field would be referred to as "2(P)" in our notation, where P points to the vector A; but if we are referring to the jth element of the vector, we find it more natural to write $A[j]$, putting the variable quantity "j" second. Similarly it seems most appropriate to put the variable quantity "P" second in the notation INFO(P).

Perhaps the first people to recognize that the concepts "stack" (last-in-first-out) and "queue" (first-in-first-out) are important objects of study were cost accountants interested in reducing income tax assessments; for a discussion of the "LIFO" and "FIFO" methods of pricing inventories, see any intermediate accounting textbook, e.g., C. F. and W. J. Schlatter, *Cost Accounting* (New York: Wiley, 1957), Chapter 7. In the mid-1940s, A. M. Turing developed a stack mechanism called Reversion Storage for subroutine linkage, local variables, and parameters. His names for "push" and "pop" were "bury" and "disinter/unbury." (See the references in Section 1.4.5.) No doubt simple uses of stacks kept in sequential memory locations were common in computer programming from the earliest days, since a stack is such an intuitive concept. The programming of stacks in linked form appeared first in IPL, as stated above; the name "stack" stems from IPL terminology (although "pushdown list" was the more official IPL wording), and it was also independently introduced by E. W. Dijkstra [*Numer. Math.* **2** (1960), 312–318]. "Deque" is a term coined by E. J. Schweppe in 1966.

The origin of circular and doubly linked lists is obscure; presumably these ideas occurred naturally to many people. A strong factor in the popularization of such techniques was the existence of general List-processing systems based on them [principally the Knotted List Structures, *CACM* **5** (1962), 161–165, and Symmetric List Processor, *CACM* **6** (1963), 524–544, of J. Weizenbaum]. Ivan Sutherland introduced the use of independent doubly linked lists within larger nodes, in his Sketchpad system [Ph.D. thesis (Mass. Inst. of Technology, 1963)].

Various methods for addressing and traversing multidimensional arrays of information were developed independently by clever programmers since the earliest days of computers, and thus another part of the unpublished computer folklore was born. This subject was first surveyed in print by H. Hellerman, *CACM* **5** (1962), 205–207. See also J. C. Gower, *Comp. J.* **4** (1962), 280–286.

Tree structures represented explicitly in computer memory were originally used for applications to algebraic formula manipulation. The machine language for several early computers used a three-address code to represent the computation of arithmetic expressions; the latter is equivalent to the INFO, LLINK, and RLINK of a binary tree representation. In 1952, H. G. Kahrimanian developed algorithms for differentiating algebraic formulas represented in an extended three-address code; see *Symposium on Automatic Programming* (Washington, D.C.: Office of Naval Research, May 1954), 6–14.

Since then, tree structures in various guises have been studied independently by many people in connection with numerous computer applications, but the basic techniques for tree manipulation (not general List manipulation) have seldom appeared in print except in detailed description of particular algorithms. The first general survey was made in connection with a more general study of all data structures by K. E. Iverson and L. R. Johnson [IBM Corp. research reports RC-390, RC-603 (1961); see Iverson, *A Programming Language* (New York: Wiley, 1962), Chapter 3]. See also G. Salton, *CACM* **5** (1962), 103–114.

The concept of *threaded* trees is due to A. J. Perlis and C. Thornton, *CACM* **3** (1960), 195–204. Their paper also introduced the important idea of traversing trees in various orders, and gave numerous examples of algebraic manipulation algorithms. Unfortunately, this important paper was prepared hastily and it contains many misprints. The threaded lists of Perlis and Thornton were only "right-threaded trees" in our terminology; binary trees that are threaded in *both* directions were independently discovered by A. W. Holt, *A Mathematical and Applied Investigation of Tree Structures* (Thesis, U. of Pennsylvania, 1963). Postorder and preorder for the nodes of trees were called "normal along order" and "dual along order" by Z. Pawlak [*Colloquium on the Foundation of Mathematics*, Tihany, 1962 (Budapest: Akadémiai Kiadó, 1965), 227–238]. Preorder was called "subtree order" by Iverson and Johnson in the references cited above. Graphical ways to represent the connection between tree structures and corresponding linear notations were described by A. G. Oettinger, *Proc. Harvard Symp. on Digital Computers and their Applications* (April 1961), 203–224. The representation of trees in preorder by degrees, with associated algorithms relating this representation to Dewey decimal notation and other properties of trees, was presented by S. Gorn, *Proc. Symp. Math. Theory of Automata* (Brooklyn: Poly. Inst., 1962), 223–240.

The history of tree structures as mathematical entities, together with a bibliography of the subject, is reviewed in Section 2.3.4.6.

At the time this section was first written in 1966, the most widespread knowledge about information structures was due to programmers' exposure to List processing systems, which played a very important part in this history. The first widely used system was IPL-V (a descendant of IPL-III, developed late in 1959); IPL-V was an interpretive system in which a programmer learned a machine-like language for List operations. At about the same time, FLPL (a set of FORTRAN subroutines for List manipulation, also inspired by IPL but using subroutine calls instead of interpretive language) was developed by H. Gelernter and others. A third system, LISP, was designed by J. McCarthy, also in 1959. LISP was quite different from its predecessors: Its programs were (and still are) expressed in mathematical functional notation combined with "conditional expressions," then converted into a List representation. Many List processing systems came into existence during the 1960s; the most prominent among these from a historical standpoint was J. Weizenbaum's SLIP, a set of subroutines that implemented doubly linked Lists in FORTRAN.

An article by Bobrow and Raphael, *CACM* **7** (1964), 231–240, may be read as a brief introduction to IPL-V, LISP, and SLIP; it gives a comparison of these systems. An excellent early introduction to LISP was published by P. M. Woodward and D. P. Jenkins, *Comp. J.* **4** (1961), 47–53. See also the authors' discussions of their own systems, which are articles of considerable historical importance: "An introduction to IPL-V" by A. Newell and F. M. Tonge, *CACM* **3** (1960), 205–211; "A FORTRAN-compiled List Processing Language" by H. Gelernter, J. R. Hansen, and C. L. Gerberich, *JACM* **7** (1960), 87–101; "Recursive functions of symbolic expressions and their computation by machine, I" by John McCarthy, *CACM* **3** (1960), 184–195; "Symmetric List Processor" by J. Weizenbaum, *CACM* **6** (1963), 524–544. Weizenbaum's article included a complete description of all of the algorithms used in SLIP. Of all these early systems, only LISP had the necessary ingredients to survive the ensuing decades of further progress. McCarthy has described LISP's early history in *History of Programming Languages* (Academic Press, 1981), 173–197.

Several *string manipulation* systems also appeared during the 1960s; they were primarily concerned with operations on variable-length strings of alphabetic information — looking for occurrences of certain substrings and replacing them by others, etc. The most important of these from a historical perspective were COMIT [V. H. Yngve, *CACM* **6** (1963), 83–84] and SNOBOL [D. J. Farber, R. E. Griswold, and I. P. Polonsky, *JACM* **11** (1964), 21–30]. String manipulation systems were used widely, and they were composed primarily of algorithms like the ones we have seen in this chapter, but they played a comparatively small role in the history of the techniques of information structure representation; users of such systems were isolated from the details of the actual internal processes carried on by the computer. For a survey of early string manipulation techniques, see S. E. Madnick, *CACM* **10** (1967), 420–424.

The IPL-V and FLPL systems for List-processing did not use either a garbage collection or a reference count technique for the problem of shared Lists; instead, each List was "owned" by one List and "borrowed" by all other Lists that referred to it, and a List was erased when its "owner" allowed it to disappear. Hence, the programmer was enjoined to make sure that no List was still borrowing any Lists that were being erased. The reference counter technique for Lists was introduced by G. E. Collins, *CACM* **3** (1960), 655–657, and explained further in *CACM* **9** (1966), 578–589. Garbage collection was first described in McCarthy's article of 1960; see also Weizenbaum's remarks in *CACM* **7** (1964), 38, and an article by Cohen and Trilling, *BIT* **7** (1967), 22–30.

An increasing realization of the importance of link manipulations led naturally to their inclusion in algebraic programming languages designed after 1965. The new languages allowed programmers to choose suitable forms of data representation without resorting to assembly language or paying the overhead of completely general List structures. Some of the fundamental steps in this development were the work of N. Wirth and H. Weber [*CACM* **9** (1966), 13–23, 25, 89–99]; H. W. Lawson [*CACM* **10** (1967), 358–367]; C. A. R. Hoare [*Symbol Manipulation Languages and Techniques*, ed. by D. G. Bobrow (Amsterdam: North-Holland, 1968), 262–284]; O.-J. Dahl and K. Nygaard [*CACM* **9** (1966), 671–678]; A. van Wijngaarden, B. J. Mailloux, J. E. L. Peck, and C. H. A. Koster [*Numerische Math.* **14** (1969), 79–218]; Dennis M. Ritchie [*History of Programming Languages — II* (ACM Press, 1996), 671–698].

Dynamic storage allocation algorithms were in use several years before they were ever described in print. A very readable discussion was prepared by W. T. Comfort in 1961 and published in *CACM* **7** (1964), 357–362. The boundary-tag method, introduced in Section 2.5, was designed by the author in 1962 for use in an operating system for the Burroughs B5000 computer. The buddy system was first used by H. Markowitz in connection with the SIMSCRIPT programming system in 1963, and it was independently discovered and published by K. Knowlton, *CACM* **8** (1965), 623–625; see also *CACM* **9** (1966), 616–625. For additional early discussions of dynamic storage allocation, see the articles by Iliffe and Jodeit, *Comp. J.* **5** (1962), 200–209; Bailey, Barnett, and Burleson, *CACM* **7** (1964), 339–346; A. T. Berztiss, *CACM* **8** (1965), 512–513; and D. T. Ross, *CACM* **10** (1967), 481–492.

A general discussion of information structures and their relation to programming was prepared by Mary d'Imperio, "Data Structures and their Representation in Storage," *Annual Review in Automatic Programming* **5** (Oxford: Pergamon Press, 1969), 1–75. Her paper is a valuable guide to the history of the topic, since it includes a detailed analysis of the structures used in connection with twelve List processing and string manipulation systems. See also the proceedings of two symposia, *CACM* **3** (1960), 183–234 and *CACM* **9** (1966), 547–643, for further historical details. (Several of the individual papers from those proceedings have already been cited above.)

An excellent annotated bibliography of early work on symbol manipulation and algebraic formula manipulation, having numerous connections with the material of this chapter, was compiled by Jean E. Sammet; see *Computing Reviews* **7** (July–August 1966), B1–B31.

In this chapter we have looked at particular types of information structures in great detail, and (lest we fail to see the forest for the trees) it is perhaps wise to take stock of what we have learned and to summarize briefly the general subject of information structures from a broader perspective. Starting with the basic idea of a *node* as an element of data, we have seen many examples that illustrate convenient ways to represent structural relationships either implicitly (based on the relative order in which nodes are stored in computer memory) or explicitly (by means of links in the nodes, which point to other nodes). The amount of structural information that ought to be represented within the tables of a computer program depends on the operations that are to be performed on the nodes.

For pedagogic reasons, we have largely concentrated on the connections between information structures and their machine representations, instead of discussing those issues separately. However, to gain a deeper understanding it is helpful to consider the subject from a more abstract point of view, distilling off several layers of ideas that can be studied by themselves. Several noteworthy approaches of this kind have been developed, and the following thought-provoking papers are especially recommended from the early literature: G. H. Mealy, "Another look at data," *Proc. AFIPS Fall Joint Computer Conf.* **31** (1967), 525–534; J. Earley, "Toward an understanding of data structures," *CACM* **14** (1971), 617–627; C. A. R. Hoare, "Notes on data structuring," in *Structured Programming* by O.-J. Dahl, E. W. Dijkstra, and C. A. R. Hoare (Academic Press, 1972), 83–174; Robert W. Engles, "A tutorial on data-base organization," *Annual Review in Automatic Programming* **7** (1972), 3–63.

The discussion in this chapter does not cover the entire subject of information structures in full generality; at least three important aspects of the subject have not been treated here:

a) We often want to search through a table to find a node or set of nodes possessing a certain value, and the need for such an operation often has a profound effect on the structure of the table. This situation is explored in detail in Chapter 6.

b) We have primarily been concerned with the internal representation of structure within a computer; but that is obviously only part of the story, since structure must also be represented in the external input and output data. In simple cases, external structure can be treated by essentially the same techniques that we have been considering; but the processes of converting between strings of characters and more complex structures are also very important. Those processes are analyzed in Chapters 9 and 10.

c) We have primarily discussed representations of structures within a high-speed random-access memory. When slower memory devices such as disks or tapes are being used, we find that all of the structural problems are intensified; it becomes much more crucial to have efficient algorithms and efficient schemes for data representation. Nodes that link to each other in such cases ought to go into nearby areas of the memory. Usually the problems are highly dependent on the characteristics of individual machines, so it is difficult to discuss them in general. The simpler examples treated in this chapter should help to prepare the reader for solving the more difficult problems that arise in connection with less ideal memory devices; Chapters 5 and 6 discuss some of these problems in detail.

What are the main implications of the subjects treated in this chapter? Perhaps the most important conclusion we can reach is that the ideas we have encountered are not limited to computer programming alone; they apply more generally to everyday life. A collection of nodes containing fields, some of which point to other nodes, appears to be a very good abstract model for structural relationships of all kinds. This model shows how we can build up complicated structures from simple ones, and we have seen that corresponding algorithms for manipulating the structure can be designed in a natural manner.

Therefore it seems appropriate to develop much more theory about linked sets of nodes than we know at this time. Perhaps the most obvious way to start such a theory is to define a new kind of abstract machine or "automaton" that deals with linked structures. For example, such a device might be defined informally as follows: There are numbers k, l, r, and s, such that the automaton processes nodes containing k link fields and r information fields; it has l link registers and s information registers, which enable it to control the processes it is performing. The information fields and registers may contain any symbols from some given set of information symbols; each of the link fields and link registers either contains Λ or points to a node. The machine can (i) create new nodes (putting a link to the node into a register), (ii) compare information symbols or link values for equality, and (iii) transfer information symbols or link values between registers and nodes. Only nodes pointed to by link registers are immediately accessible. Suitable restrictions on the machine's behavior will make it equivalent to several other species of automata.

A related model of computation was proposed by A. N. Kolmogorov as early as 1952. His machine essentially operates on graphs G, having a specially designated starting vertex v_0. The action at each step depends only on the subgraph G' consisting of all vertices at distance $\leq n$ from v_0 in G, replacing G' in G by another graph $G'' = f(G')$, where G'' includes v_0 and the vertices at distance exactly n from v_0, and possibly other vertices (which are newly created); the remainder of graph G is left unaltered. Here n is a fixed number specified in advance for any particular algorithm, but it can be arbitrarily large. A symbol from a finite alphabet is attached to each vertex, and restrictions are made so that no two vertices with the same symbol can be adjacent to a common vertex. (See A. N. Kolmogorov, *Uspekhi Mat. Nauk* **8**, 4 (1953), 175–176; Kolmogorov and Uspensky, *Uspekhi Mat. Nauk* **13**, 4 (1958), 3–28; *Amer. Math. Soc. Translations*, series 2, **29** (1963), 217–245.)

Linking automata can easily simulate graph machines, taking at most a bounded number of steps per graph step. Conversely, however, it is unlikely that graph machines can simulate arbitrary linking automata without unboundedly increasing the running time, unless the definition is changed from undirected to directed graphs, in view of the restriction to vertices of bounded degree. The linking model is, of course, quite close to the operations available to programmers on real machines, while the graph model is not.

Some of the most interesting problems to solve for such devices would be to determine how fast they can solve certain problems, or how many nodes they need to solve certain problems (for example, to translate certain formal languages). At the time this chapter was first written, several interesting results of this kind had been obtained (notably by J. Hartmanis and R. E. Stearns) but only for special classes of Turing machines having multiple tapes and read/write heads. The Turing machine model is comparatively unrealistic, so these results tended to have little to do with practical problems.

We must admit that, as the number n of nodes created by a linking automaton approaches infinity, we don't know how to build such a device physically, since we want the machine operations to take the same amount of time regardless of the size of n; if linking is represented by using addresses as in a computer memory, it is necessary to put a bound on the number of nodes, since the link fields have a fixed size. A multitape Turing machine is therefore a more realistic model when n approaches infinity. Yet it seems reasonable to believe that a linking automaton as described above leads to a more appropriate theory of the complexity of algorithms than Turing machines do, even when asymptotic formulas for large n are considered, because the theory is more likely to be relevant for practical values of n. Furthermore when n gets bigger than 10^{30} or so, not even a one-tape Turing machine is realistic: It could never be built. Relevance is more important than realism.

Many years have passed since the author wrote most of the comments above, and everybody can be glad that substantial progress has indeed been made on the theory of linking automata (now called *pointer machines*). But of course much still remains to be done.

General rules for programming have been discovered.
Most of them have been used in the
Kansas City freight yards for a long time.

— DERRICK LEHMER (1949)

I must explain, to begin with,
that all the Trees, in this system, grow head-downwards:
the Root is at the top, *and the Branches are* below.
If it be objected that the name "Tree" is a misnomer, my answer
is that I am only following the example of all writers on Genealogy.
A Genealogical *tree always* grows downwards:
then why may not a Logical *"Tree" do likewise?*

— LEWIS CARROLL, in *Symbolic Logic* (1896)

You will, I am sure, agree with me ... that if page
534 finds us only in the second chapter, the length of
the first one must have been really intolerable.

— SHERLOCK HOLMES, in *The Valley of Fear* (1914)

ANSWERS TO EXERCISES

I am not bound to please thee with my answers.

— SHYLOCK, in *The Merchant of Venice* (Act IV, Scene 1, Line 65)

NOTES ON THE EXERCISES

1. An average problem for a mathematically inclined reader.

2. They help you to lodge ideas in your brain.

4. See W. J. LeVeque, *Topics in Number Theory* **2** (Reading, Mass.: Addison–Wesley, 1956), Chapter 3; P. Ribenboim, *13 Lectures on Fermat's Last Theorem* (New York: Springer-Verlag, 1979); A. Wiles, *Annals of Mathematics* (2) **141** (1995), 443–551.

SECTION 1.1

1. $t \leftarrow a$, $a \leftarrow b$, $b \leftarrow c$, $c \leftarrow d$, $d \leftarrow t$.

2. After the first time, the values of the variables m and n are the previous values of n and r, respectively; and $n > r$.

3. Algorithm F (*Euclid's algorithm*). Given two positive integers m and n, find their greatest common divisor.

> **F1.** [Remainder m/n.] Divide m by n and let m be the remainder.
>
> **F2.** [Is it zero?] If $m = 0$, the algorithm terminates with answer n.
>
> **F3.** [Remainder n/m.] Divide n by m and let n be the remainder.
>
> **F4.** [Is it zero?] If $n = 0$, the algorithm terminates with answer m; otherwise go back to step F1. ∎

4. By Algorithm E, $n = 6099$, 2166, 1767, 399, 171, 57. Answer: 57.

5. Not finite nor definite nor effective, perhaps no output; in format, no letter is given before step numbers, no summary phrase appears, and there is no "∎".

6. Trying Algorithm E with $n = 5$ and $m = 5q + (1, 2, 3, 4, 5)$, for any $q \geq 0$, we find that step E1 is executed (2, 3, 4, 3, 1) times, respectively. So the average is $2.6 = T_5$.

7. In all but a finite number of cases, $n > m$. And when $n > m$, the first iteration of Algorithm E merely exchanges these numbers; so $U_m = T_m + 1$. For example, try $m = 5$ and $n = 1, 2, \ldots$: The average of 1, 2, 3, 2, 1, 3, 4, 5, 4, 2, 3, 4, 5, 4, 2, $\ldots$ is 3.6.

8. Let $A = \{a, b, c\}$, $N = 5$. The algorithm will terminate with the string $a^{\gcd(m,n)}$.

j	θ_j	ϕ_j	b_j	a_j	
0	ab	(empty)	1	2	Remove one a and one b, or go to 2.
1	(empty)	c	0	0	Add c at extreme left, go back to 0.
2	a	b	2	3	Change all a's to b's.
3	c	a	3	4	Change all c's to a's.
4	b	b	0	5	If b's remain, repeat.

Each iteration either decreases m or keeps m unchanged and decreases n.

9. For instance we can say C_2 represents C_1 if there is a function g from I_1 into I_2, a function h from Q_2 into Q_1, and a function j from Q_2 into the positive integers, satisfying the following conditions:

a) If x is in I_1 then $h(g(x)) = x$.

b) If q is in Q_2 then $f_1(h(q)) = h(f_2^{[j(q)]}(q))$, where $f_2^{[j(q)]}$ means that the function f_2 is to be iterated $j(q)$ times.

c) If q is in Q_2 then $h(q)$ is in Ω_1 if and only if q is in Ω_2.

For example, let C_1 be as in (2) and let C_2 have $I_2 = \{(m, n)\}$, $\Omega_2 = \{(m, n, d)\}$, $Q_2 = I_2 \cup \Omega_2 \cup \{(m, n, a, b, 1)\} \cup \{(m, n, a, b, r, 2)\} \cup \{(m, n, a, b, r, 3)\} \cup \{(m, n, a, b, r, 4)\} \cup \{(m, n, a, b, 5)\}$. Let $f_2((m, n)) = (m, n, m, n, 1)$; $f_2((m, n, d)) = (m, n, d)$; $f_2((m, n, a, b, 1)) = (m, n, a, b, a \bmod b, 2)$; $f_2((m, n, a, b, r, 2)) = (m, n, b)$ if $r = 0$, otherwise $(m, n, a, b, r, 3)$; $f_2((m, n, a, b, r, 3)) = (m, n, b, b, r, 4)$; $f_2((m, n, a, b, r, 4)) = (m, n, a, r, 5)$; $f_2((m, n, a, b, 5)) = f_2((m, n, a, b, 1))$.

Now let $h((m, n)) = g((m, n)) = (m, n)$; $h((m, n, d)) = (d)$; $h((m, n, a, b, 1)) = (a, b, 0, 1)$; $h((m, n, a, b, r, 2)) = (a, b, r, 2)$; $h((m, n, a, b, r, 3)) = (a, b, r, 3)$; $h((m, n, a, b, r, 4)) = h(f_2((m, n, a, b, r, 4)))$; $h((m, n, a, b, 5)) = (a, b, b, 1)$; $j((m, n, a, b, r, 3)) = j((m, n, a, b, r, 4)) = 2$, otherwise $j(q) = 1$. Then C_2 represents C_1.

Notes: It is tempting to try to define things in a more simple way — for example, to let g map Q_1 into Q_2 and to insist only that when $x_0, x_1, \ldots$ is a computational sequence in C_1 then $g(x_0), g(x_1), \ldots$ is a subsequence of the computational sequence in C_2 that begins with $g(x_0)$. But this is inadequate; in the example above, C_1 forgets the original value of m and n but C_2 does not.

If C_2 represents C_1 by means of functions g, h, j, and if C_3 represents C_2 by means of functions g', h', j', then C_3 represents C_1 by means of functions g'', h'', j'', where

$$g''(x) = g'(g(x)), \qquad h''(x) = h(h'(x)), \qquad \text{and} \qquad j''(q) = \sum_{0 \le k < j(h'(q))} j'(q_k),$$

if $q_0 = q$ and $q_{k+1} = f_3^{[j'(q_k)]}(q_k)$. Hence the relation defined above is transitive. We can say C_2 *directly represents* C_1 if the function j is bounded; this relation is also transitive. The relation "C_2 represents C_1" generates an equivalence relation in which two computational methods apparently are equivalent if and only if they compute isomorphic functions of their inputs; the relation "C_2 directly represents C_1" generates a more interesting equivalence relation that perhaps matches the intuitive idea of being "essentially the same algorithm."

For an alternative approach to simulation, see R. W. Floyd and R. Beigel, *The Language of Machines* (Computer Science Press, 1994), Section 3.3.

SECTION 1.2.1

1. (a) Prove $P(0)$. (b) Prove that $P(0), \ldots, P(n)$ implies $P(n+1)$, for all $n \geq 0$.

2. The formula for b involves division by zero when $n = 1$. Therefore the theorem has not been proved when $n + 1 = 2$.

3. The correct answer is $1 - 1/n$. The mistake occurs in the proof for $n = 1$, when the formula on the left either may be assumed to be meaningless, or it may be assumed to be zero (since there are $n - 1$ terms).

5. If n is prime, it is trivially a product of one or more primes. Otherwise n has factors, so $n = km$ for some k and m with $1 < k, m < n$. Since both k and m are less than n, by induction they can be written as products of primes; hence n is the product of the primes appearing in the representations of k and m.

6. In the notation of Fig. 4, we prove A5 implies A6. This is clear since A5 implies $(a' - qa)m + (b' - qb)n = (a'm + b'n) - q(am + bn) = c - qd = r$.

7. $n^2 - (n-1)^2 + \cdots - (-1)^n 1^2 = 1 + 2 + \cdots + n = n(n+1)/2$.

8. (a) We must show that $(n^2 - n + 1) + (n^2 - n + 3) + \cdots + (n^2 + n - 1)$ equals n^3: And indeed, the sum is $n(n^2 - n) + (1 + 3 + \cdots + (2n-1)) = n^3 - n^2 + n^2$, by Eq. (2). But an inductive proof was requested, so another approach should be taken! For $n = 1$, the result is obvious. Let $n \geq 1$; we have $(n+1)^2 - (n+1) = n^2 - n + 2n$, so the first terms for $n + 1$ are $2n$ larger; thus the sum for $n + 1$ is the sum for n plus

$$\underbrace{2n + \cdots + 2n}_{n \text{ times}} + (n+1)^2 + (n+1) - 1;$$

this equals $n^3 + 2n^2 + n^2 + 3n + 1 = (n+1)^3$. (b) We have shown that the first term for $(n+1)^3$ is two greater than the last term for n^3. Therefore by Eq. (2), $1^3 + 2^3 + \cdots + n^3 = $ sum of consecutive odd numbers starting with unity = (number of terms)$^2 = (1 + 2 + \cdots + n)^2$.

9. It's true when $n = 0$; also whenever it's known to be true for $n + 1$ or $n - 1$.

10. Obvious for $n = 10$. If $n \geq 10$, we have $2^{n+1} = 2 \cdot 2^n > (1 + 1/n)^3 2^n$ and by induction this is greater than $(1 + 1/n)^3 n^3 = (n+1)^3$.

11. $(-1)^n (n+1)/(4(n+1)^2 + 1)$.

12. The only nontrivial part of the extension is the calculation of the integer q in E2. This can be done by repeated subtraction, reducing to the problem of determining whether $u + v\sqrt{2}$ is positive, negative, or zero, and the latter problem is readily solved.

It is easy to show that whenever $u + v\sqrt{2} = u' + v'\sqrt{2}$, we must have $u = u'$ and $v = v'$, since $\sqrt{2}$ is irrational. Now it is clear that 1 and $\sqrt{2}$ have no common divisor, if we define divisor in the sense that $u + v\sqrt{2}$ divides $a(u + v\sqrt{2})$ if and only if a is an integer. The algorithm extended in this way computes the regular continued fraction of the ratio of its inputs; see Section 4.5.3.

[*Note:* If we extend the concept of divisor so that $u + v\sqrt{2}$ divides $a(u + v\sqrt{2})$ if and only if a has the form $u' + v'\sqrt{2}$ for integers u' and v', there *is* a way to extend Algorithm E so that it always will terminate: If in step E2 we have $c = u + v\sqrt{2}$ and $d = u' + v'\sqrt{2}$, compute $c/d = c(u' - v'\sqrt{2})/(u'^2 - 2v'^2) = x + y\sqrt{2}$ where x and y are rational. Now let $q = u'' + v''\sqrt{2}$, where u'' and v'' are the nearest integers to x and y; and let $r = c - qd$. If $r = u''' + v'''\sqrt{2}$, it follows that $|u'''^2 - 2v'''^2| < |u'^2 - 2v'^2|$, hence the computation will terminate. See "quadratic Euclidean domains" in number theory texts.]

13. Add "$T \leq 3(n-d) + k$" to assertions A3, A4, A5, A6, where k takes the respective values 2, 3, 3, 1. Also add "$d > 0$" to A4.

15. (a) Let $A = S$ in (iii); every nonempty well-ordered set has a least element.

(b) Let $x \prec y$ if $|x| < |y|$ or if $|x| = |y|$ and $x < 0 < y$.

(c) No, the subset of all positive reals fails to satisfy (iii). [*Note:* Using the so-called axiom of choice, a rather complicated argument can be given to show that every set can be well-ordered somehow; but nobody has yet been able to define an explicit relation that well-orders the real numbers.]

(d) To prove (iii) for T_n, use induction on n: Let A be a nonempty subset of T_n and consider A_1, the set of first components of A. Since A_1 is a nonempty subset of S, and S is well-ordered, A_1 contains a smallest element x. Now consider A_x, the subset of A in which the first component equals x; A_x may be considered a subset of T_{n-1} if its first component is suppressed, so by induction A_x contains a smallest element $(x, x_2, \ldots, x_n)$ that in fact is the smallest element of A.

(e) No, although properties (i) and (ii) are valid. If S contains at least two distinct elements, $a \prec b$, the set (b), (a, b), (a, a, b), (a, a, a, b), (a, a, a, a, b), $\ldots$ has no least element. On the other hand T can be well-ordered if we define $(x_1, \ldots, x_m) \prec (y_1, \ldots, y_n)$ whenever $m < n$, or $m = n$ and $(x_1, \ldots, x_n) \prec (y_1, \ldots, y_n)$ in T_n.

(f) Let S be well-ordered by $\prec$. If such an infinite sequence exists, the set A consisting of the members of the sequence fails to satisfy property (iii), for no element of the sequence can be smallest. Conversely if $\prec$ is a relation satisfying (i) and (ii) but not (iii), let A be a nonempty subset of S that has no smallest element. Since A is not empty, we can find x_1 in A; since x_1 is not the smallest element of A, there is x_2 in A for which $x_2 \prec x_1$; since x_2 is not the smallest element either, we can find $x_3 \prec x_2$; etc.

(g) Let A be the set of all x for which $P(x)$ is false. If A is not empty, it contains a smallest element x_0. Hence $P(y)$ is true for all $y \prec x_0$. But this implies $P(x_0)$ is true, so x_0 is not in A (a contradiction). Therefore A must be empty: $P(x)$ is always true.

SECTION 1.2.2

1. There is none; if r is a positive rational, $r/2$ is smaller.

2. Not if infinitely many nines appear in a row; in that case the decimal expansion of the number is $1 + .24000000\ldots$, according to Eq. (2).

3. $-1/27$, but the text hasn't defined it.

4. 4.

6. The decimal expansion of a number is unique, so $x = y$ if and only if $m = n$ and $d_i = e_i$ for all $i \geq 1$. If $x \neq y$, one may compare m vs. n, d_1 vs. e_1, d_2 vs. e_2, etc.; when the first inequality occurs, the larger quantity belongs to the larger of $\{x, y\}$.

7. One may use induction on x, first proving the laws for x positive, and then for x negative. Details are omitted here.

8. By trying $n = 0, 1, 2, \ldots$ we find the value of n for which $n^m \leq u < (n+1)^m$. Assuming inductively that $n, d_1, \ldots, d_{k-1}$ have been determined, d_k is the digit such that

$$\left(n + \frac{d_1}{10} + \cdots + \frac{d_k}{10^k}\right)^m \leq u < \left(n + \frac{d_1}{10} + \cdots + \frac{d_k}{10^k} + \frac{1}{10^k}\right)^m.$$

This construction can't make $d_k = 9$ for all $k > l$, because that could happen only if $(n + d_1/10 + \cdots + d_l/10^l + 1/10^l)^m \leq u$.

9. $((b^{p/q})^{u/v})^{qv} = (((b^{p/q})^{u/v})^v)^q = ((b^{p/q})^u)^q = ((b^{p/q})^q)^u = b^{pu}$. using (7) twice. Hence $(b^{p/q})^{u/v} = b^{pu/qv}$. This proves the second law. We prove the first law using the second: $b^{p/q}b^{u/v} = (b^{1/qv})^{pv}(b^{1/qv})^{qu} = (b^{1/qv})^{pv+qu} = b^{p/q+u/v}$.

10. If $\log_{10} 2 = p/q$, with p and q positive, then $2^q = 10^p$, which is absurd since the right-hand side is divisible by 5 but the left-hand side isn't.

11. Infinitely many! No matter how many digits of x are given, we will not know whether 10^x begins with $1.99999\ldots$ or $2.00000\ldots$, if x's digits agree with the digits of $\log_{10} 2$. There is nothing mysterious or paradoxical in this; a similar situation occurs in addition, if we are adding $.444444\ldots$ to $.55555\ldots$.

12. They are the only values of $d_1, \ldots, d_8$ that satisfy Eq. (8).

13. (a) First prove by induction that if $y > 0$, $1 + ny \le (1 + y)^n$. Then set $y = x/n$, and take nth roots. (b) $x = b - 1$, $n = 10^k$.

14. Set $x = \log_b c$ in the second equation of (6), then take logarithms of both sides.

15. Prove it, by transposing "$\log_b y$" to the other side of the equation and using (12).

16. $\ln x / \ln 10$, by (15).

17. 5; 1; 1; 0; undefined.

18. No, $\log_8 x = \lg x / \lg 8 = \frac{1}{3} \lg x$.

19. Yes, since $\lg n < (\log_{10} n)/.301 < 14/.301 < 47$.

20. They are reciprocals.

21. $(\ln \ln x - \ln \ln b)/\ln b$.

22. From the tables in Appendix A, $\lg x \approx 1.442695 \ln x$; $\log_{10} x \approx .4342945 \ln x$. The relative error is $\approx (1.442695 - 1.4342945)/1.442695 \approx 0.582\%$.

23. Take the figure of area $\ln y$, and divide its height by x while multiplying its length by x. This deformation preserves its area and makes it congruent to the piece left when $\ln x$ is removed from $\ln xy$, since the height at point $x + xt$ in the diagram for $\ln xy$ is $1/(x + xt) = (1/(1 + t))/x$.

24. Substitute 2 everywhere 10 appears.

25. Note that $z = 2^{-p} \lfloor 2^{p-k} x \rfloor > 0$, when p is the precision (the number of binary digits after the radix point). The quantity $y + \log_b x$ stays approximately constant.

27. Prove by induction on k that

$$x^{2^k} (1 - \delta)^{2^{k+1}-1} \le 10^{2^k (n + b_1/2 + \cdots + b_k/2^k)} x_k' \le x^{2^k} (1 + \epsilon)^{2^{k+1}-1}$$

and take logarithms.

28. The following solution uses the same auxiliary table as before.

> **E1.** [Initialize.] Set $x \leftarrow 1 - \epsilon - x$, $y \leftarrow y_0$, and $k \leftarrow 1$, where $1 - \epsilon$ is the largest possible value of x, and y_0 is the nearest approximation to $b^{1-\epsilon}$. (The quantity yb^{-x} will remain approximately constant in the following steps.)
>
> **E2.** [Test for end.] If $x = 0$, stop.
>
> **E3.** [Compare.] If $x < \log_b(2^k/(2^k - 1))$, increase k by 1 and repeat this step.
>
> **E4.** [Reduce values.] Set $x \leftarrow x - \log_b(2^k/(2^k - 1))$, $y \leftarrow y - (y$ shifted right $k)$, and go to E2. ∎

If y is set to $b^{1-\epsilon}(1 + \epsilon_0)$ in step E1, the subsequent computational error arises when $x \leftarrow x + \log_b(1 - 2^{-k}) + \delta_j$ and $y \leftarrow y(1 - 2^{-k})(1 + \epsilon_j)$ during the jth execution of step E4, for certain small errors δ_j and ϵ_j. When the algorithm terminates we have computed $y = b^{x - \Sigma \delta_j} \prod_j (1 + \epsilon_j)$. Further analysis depends on b and the computer word size. Notice that both in this case and in exercise 26, it is possible to refine the error estimates somewhat if the base is e, since for most values of k the table entry $\ln(2^k/(2^k - 1))$ can be given with high accuracy: It equals $2^{-k} + \frac{1}{2} 2^{-2k} + \frac{1}{3} 2^{-3k} + \cdots$.

Note: Similar algorithms can be given for trigonometric functions; see J. E. Meggitt, *IBM J. Res. and Dev.* **6** (1962), 210–226; **7** (1963), 237–245. See also T. C. Chen, *IBM J. Res. and Dev.* **16** (1972), 380–388; V. S. Linsky, *Vychisl. Mat.* **2** (1957), 90–119; D. E. Knuth, METAFONT: *The Program* (Addison–Wesley, 1986), §120–§147.

29. e; 3; 4.

30. x.

SECTION 1.2.3

1. $-a_1$; and $a_2 + \cdots + a_1 = 0$. In general, sums with '$\cdots$' are defined so that $(a_p + \cdots + a_q) + (a_{q+1} + \cdots + a_r) = a_p + \cdots + a_r$ for arbitrary integers p, q, and r.

Note: We might also say that $a_2 + \cdots + a_0 = \sum_{j=2}^{0} a_j$, and that $\sum_{j=p}^{q} a_j + \sum_{j=q+1}^{r} a_j = \sum_{j=p}^{r} a_j$, using the left half of (1). On the other hand, we should *not* replace $\cdots$ using the right half of (1)! The sum $\sum_{2 \le j \le 0} a_j$ is 0, by (2).

2. $a_1 + a_2 + a_3$.

3. $\frac{1}{1} + \frac{1}{3} + \frac{1}{5} + \frac{1}{7} + \frac{1}{9} + \frac{1}{11}$; $\frac{1}{9} + \frac{1}{3} + \frac{1}{1} + \frac{1}{3} + \frac{1}{9}$. The rule for $p(j)$ is violated: In the first case $n^2 = 3$ occurs for no n, and in the second case $n^2 = 4$ occurs for *two* n. [See Eq. (18).]

4. $(a_{11}) + (a_{21} + a_{22}) + (a_{31} + a_{32} + a_{33}) = (a_{11} + a_{21} + a_{31}) + (a_{22} + a_{32}) + (a_{33})$.

5. It is only necessary to use the rule $a \sum_{R(i)} x_i = \sum_{R(i)} (ax_i)$:

$$\left(\sum_{R(i)} a_i \right) \left(\sum_{S(j)} b_j \right) = \sum_{R(i)} a_i \left(\sum_{S(j)} b_j \right) = \sum_{R(i)} \left(\sum_{S(j)} a_i b_j \right).$$

7. Use Eq. (3); the two limits are interchanged and the terms between a_0 and a_c must be transferred from one limit to the other.

8. Let $a_{(i+1)i} = +1$, and $a_{i(i+1)} = -1$, for all $i \ge 0$, and all other a_{ij} zero; let $R(i) = S(i) = \text{``}i \ge 0\text{''}$. The left-hand side is -1, the right-hand side is $+1$.

9, 10. No; the applications of rule (d) assume that $n \ge 0$. (The result is correct for $n = -1$ but the derivation isn't.)

11. $(n+1)a$.

12. $\frac{7}{6}(1 - 1/7^{n+1})$.

13. $m(n - m + 1) + \frac{1}{2}(n - m)(n - m + 1)$; or, $\frac{1}{2}(n(n + 1) - m(m - 1))$.

14. $\frac{1}{4}(n(n + 1) - m(m - 1))(s(s + 1) - r(r - 1))$, if $m \le n$ and $r \le s$.

15, 16. Key steps:

$$\sum_{0 \le j \le n} j x^j = x \sum_{1 \le j \le n} j x^{j-1} = x \sum_{0 \le j \le n-1} (j+1) x^j = x \sum_{0 \le j \le n} j x^j - n x^{n+1} + x \sum_{0 \le j \le n-1} x^j.$$

17. The number of elements in S.

18. $S'(j)$ sums over j with "$1 \le j < n$". $R'(i, j)$ sums over i with "n is a multiple of i and $i > j$".

19. $(a_n - a_{m-1})[m \le n]$.

20. $(b - 1) \sum_{k=0}^{n} (n - k)b^k + n + 1 = \sum_{k=0}^{n} b^k$; this formula follows from (14) and the result of exercise 16.

21. $\sum_{R(j)} a_j + \sum_{S(j)} a_j = \sum_j a_j [R(j)] + \sum_j a_j [S(j)] = \sum_j a_j ([R(j)] + [S(j)])$; now use the fact that $[R(j)] + [S(j)] = [R(j) \text{ or } S(j)] + [R(j) \text{ and } S(j)]$. In general, bracket notation gives us the ability to manipulate "on the line" instead of "below the line."

22. For (5) and (7), just change $\sum$ to $\prod$. We also have $\prod_{R(i)} b_i c_i = (\prod_{R(i)} b_i)(\prod_{R(i)} c_i)$ and

$$\left(\prod_{R(j)} a_j\right)\left(\prod_{S(j)} a_j\right) = \left(\prod_{R(j) \text{ or } S(j)} a_j\right)\left(\prod_{R(j) \text{ and } S(j)} a_j\right).$$

23. $0 + x = x$ and $1 \cdot x = x$. This makes many operations and equations simpler, such as rule (d) and its analog in the previous exercise.

25. The first step and last step are OK. The second step uses i for two different purposes at once. The third step should probably be $\sum_{i=1}^{n} n$.

26. Key steps, after transforming the problem as in Example 2:

$$\prod_{i=0}^{n}\left(\prod_{j=0}^{n} a_i a_j\right) = \prod_{i=0}^{n}\left(a_i^{n+1}\prod_{j=0}^{n} a_j\right) = \left(\prod_{i=0}^{n} a_i^{n+1}\right)\left(\prod_{i=0}^{n}\left(\prod_{j=0}^{n} a_j\right)\right) = \left(\prod_{i=0}^{n} a_i\right)^{2n+2}.$$

The answer is $P_1 = (P_1 P_2)^{1/2} = (\prod_{i=0}^{n} a_i)^{n+2}$, because $P_1 = (\prod_{i=0}^{n}\prod_{j=i}^{n} a_i a_j) = P_2$.

28. $(n+1)/2n$.

29. (a) $\sum_{0 \le k \le j \le i \le n} a_i a_j a_k$. (b) Let $S_r = \sum_{i=0}^{n} a_i^r$. Solution: $\frac{1}{3}S_3 + \frac{1}{2}S_1 S_2 + \frac{1}{6}S_1^3$. The general solution to this problem, as the number of indices gets larger, may be found in Section 1.2.9, Eq. (38).

30. Write the left side as $\sum_{1 \le j,k \le n} a_j b_k x_j y_k$, and do a similar thing on the right. (This identity is the special case $m = 2$ of exercise 46. Cauchy's sums were extended to integrals by V. Bouniakowsky [*Mém. Acad. St.-Pétersbourg* (7) **1** (1859), No. 9, 4] and H. A. Schwarz [*Acta Societatis Scientiarum Fennicæ* **15** (1885), 315–362].)

31. Set $a_j = u_j$, $b_j = 1$, $x_j = v_j$, and $y_j = 1$, to obtain the answer $n\sum_{j=1}^{n} u_j v_j - (\sum_{j=1}^{n} u_j)(\sum_{j=1}^{n} v_j)$. Consequently we have $(\sum_{j=1}^{n} u_j)(\sum_{j=1}^{n} v_j) \le n\sum_{j=1}^{n} u_j v_j$ when $u_1 \le u_2 \le \cdots \le u_n$ and $v_1 \le v_2 \le \cdots \le v_n$, a result known as *Chebyshev's monotonic inequality*. [See *Soobshch. mat. obshch. Khar'kovskom Univ.* **4**, 2 (1882), 93–98.]

33. This can be proved by induction on n, if we rewrite the formula as

$$\frac{1}{x_n - x_{n-1}}\left(\sum_{j=1}^{n} \frac{x_j^r(x_j - x_{n-1})}{\prod_{1 \le k \le n,\, k \ne j}(x_j - x_k)} - \sum_{j=1}^{n} \frac{x_j^r(x_j - x_n)}{\prod_{1 \le k \le n,\, k \ne j}(x_j - x_k)}\right).$$

Each of these sums now has the form of the original sum, except on $n-1$ elements, and the values turn out nicely by induction when $0 \le r \le n-1$. When $r = n$, consider the identity

$$0 = \sum_{j=1}^{n} \frac{\prod_{k=1}^{n}(x_j - x_k)}{\prod_{1 \le k \le n,\, k \ne j}(x_j - x_k)} = \sum_{j=1}^{n} \frac{x_j^n - (x_1 + \cdots + x_n)x_j^{n-1} + P(x_j)}{\prod_{1 \le k \le n,\, k \ne j}(x_j - x_k)}$$

where $P(x_j)$ is a polynomial of degree $n-2$ in x_j whose coefficients are symmetric functions of $\{x_1, \ldots, x_n\}$ that don't depend on j. (See exercise 1.2.9–10.) We obtain the desired answer from the solutions for $r = 0, 1, \ldots, n-1$.

Notes: Dr. Matrix was anticipated in this discovery by L. Euler, who wrote to Christian Goldbach about it on 9 November 1762. See Euler's *Institutionum Calculi Integralis* **2** (1769), §1169; and E. Waring, *Phil. Trans.* **69** (1779), 64–67. The following alternative method of proof, using complex variable theory, is less elementary but more elegant: By the residue theorem, the value of the given sum is

$$\frac{1}{2\pi i}\int_{|z|=R} \frac{z^r\, dz}{(z - x_1)\ldots(z - x_n)}$$

where $R > |x_1|, \ldots, |x_n|$. The Laurent expansion of the integrand converges uniformly on $|z| = R$; it is

$$z^{r-n} \left(\frac{1}{1 - x_1/z}\right) \cdots \left(\frac{1}{1 - x_n/z}\right)$$

$$= z^{r-n} + (x_1 + \cdots + x_n)z^{r-n-1} + (x_1^2 + x_1 x_2 + \cdots)z^{r-n-2} + \cdots.$$

Integrating term by term, everything vanishes except the coefficient of z^{-1}. This method gives us the *general formula* for an arbitrary integer $r \geq 0$:

$$\sum_{\substack{j_1 + \cdots + j_n = r-n+1 \\ j_1, \ldots, j_n \geq 0}} x_1^{j_1} \ldots x_n^{j_n} = \sum_{1 \leq j_1 \leq \cdots \leq j_{r-n+1} \leq n} x_{j_1} \ldots x_{j_{r-n+1}};$$

see Eq. 1.2.9–(33). [J. J. Sylvester, *Quart. J. Math.* **1** (1857), 141–152.]

34. If the reader has tried earnestly to solve this problem, *without* getting the answer, perhaps its purpose has been achieved. The temptation to regard the numerators as polynomials in x rather than as polynomials in k is almost overwhelming. It would undoubtedly be easier to prove the considerably more general result

$$\sum_{k=1}^{n} \frac{\prod_{1 \leq r \leq n-1}(y_k - z_r)}{\prod_{1 \leq r \leq n, \, r \neq k}(y_k - y_r)} = 1,$$

which is an identity in $2n - 1$ variables!

35. If $R(j)$ never holds, the value should be $-\infty$. The stated analog of rule (a) is based on the identity $a + \max(b, c) = \max(a+b, \, a+c)$. Similarly if all a_i, b_j are *nonnegative*, we have

$$\sup_{R(i)} a_i \sup_{S(j)} b_j = \sup_{R(i)} \sup_{S(j)} a_i b_j.$$

Rules (b), (c) do not change; for rule (d) we get the simpler form

$$\max\left(\sup_{R(j)} a_j, \sup_{S(j)} a_j\right) = \sup_{R(j) \text{ or } S(j)} a_j.$$

36. Subtract column one from columns $2, \ldots, n$. Add rows $2, \ldots, n$ to row one. The result is a triangular determinant.

37. Subtract column one from columns $2, \ldots, n$. Then subtract x_1 times row $k - 1$ from row k, for $k = n, n-1, \ldots, 2$ (in that order). Now factor x_1 out of the first column and factor $x_k - x_1$ out of columns $k = 2, \ldots, n$, obtaining $x_1(x_2 - x_1) \ldots (x_n - x_1)$ times a Vandermonde determinant of order $n - 1$. The process continues by induction.

Alternative proof, using "higher" mathematics: The determinant is a polynomial in the variables $x_1, \ldots, x_n$ of total degree $1 + 2 + \cdots + n$. It vanishes if $x_j = 0$ or if $x_i = x_j$ ($i < j$), and the coefficient of $x_1^1 x_2^2 \ldots x_n^n$ is $+1$. These facts characterize its value. In general, if two rows of a matrix become equal for $x_i = x_j$, their difference is usually divisible by $x_i - x_j$, and this observation often speeds the evaluation of determinants.

38. Subtract column one from columns $2, \ldots, n$, and factor out

$$(x_1 + y_1)^{-1} \ldots (x_n + y_1)^{-1}(y_1 - y_2) \ldots (y_1 - y_n)$$

from rows and columns. Now subtract row one from rows $2, \ldots, n$ and factor out $(x_1 - x_2) \ldots (x_1 - x_n)(x_1 + y_2)^{-1} \ldots (x_1 + y_n)^{-1}$; we are left with the Cauchy determinant of order $n - 1$.

39. Let I be the identity matrix (δ_{ij}), and J the matrix of all ones. Since $J^2 = nJ$, we have $(xI + yJ)((x + ny)I - yJ) = x(x + ny)I$.

40. [A. de Moivre, *The Doctrine of Chances*, 2nd edition (London: 1738), 197–199.]
We have

$$\sum_{t=1}^{n} b_{it} x_j^t = x_j \prod_{\substack{1 \le k \le n \\ k \ne i}} (x_k - x_j) \Bigg/ x_i \prod_{\substack{1 \le k \le n \\ k \ne i}} (x_k - x_i) = \delta_{ij}.$$

41. This follows immediately from the relation of an inverse matrix to its cofactors. It may also be interesting to give a direct proof here: We have

$$\sum_{t=1}^{n} \frac{1}{x_i + y_t} b_{tj} = \sum_{t=1}^{n} \frac{\prod_{k \ne t}(x_j + y_k - x) \prod_{k \ne i}(x_k + y_t)}{\prod_{k \ne j}(x_j - x_k) \prod_{k \ne t}(y_t - y_k)}$$

when $x = 0$. This is a polynomial of degree at most $n - 1$ in x. If we set $x = x_j + y_s$, $1 \le s \le n$, the terms are zero except when $s = t$, so the value of this polynomial is

$$\prod_{k \ne i}(-x_k - y_s) \Bigg/ \prod_{k \ne j}(x_j - x_k) = \prod_{k \ne i}(x_j - x_k - x) \Bigg/ \prod_{k \ne j}(x_j - x_k).$$

These polynomials of degree at most $n - 1$ agree at n distinct points x, so they agree also for $x = 0$; hence

$$\sum_{t=1}^{n} \frac{1}{x_i + y_t} b_{tj} = \prod_{k \ne i}(x_j - x_k) \Bigg/ \prod_{k \ne j}(x_j - x_k) = \delta_{ij}.$$

42. $n/(x + ny)$.

43. $1 - \prod_{k=1}^{n}(1 - 1/x_k)$. This is easily verified if any $x_i = 1$, since the inverse of any matrix having a row or column all of ones must have elements whose sum is 1. If none of the x_i equals one, sum the elements of row i by setting $x = 1$ in exercise 40 and obtaining $\prod_{k \ne i}(x_k - 1)/x_i \prod_{k \ne i}(x_k - x_i)$. After multiplying numerator and denominator by $x_i - 1$, we can sum on i by applying exercise 33 with $r = 0$ to the $n + 2$ numbers $\{0, 1, x_1, \dots, x_n\}$.

44. We find

$$c_j = \sum_{i=1}^{n} b_{ij} = \prod_{k=1}^{n}(x_j + y_k) \Bigg/ \prod_{\substack{1 \le k \le n \\ k \ne j}}(x_j - x_k),$$

after applying exercise 33. And

$$\sum_{j=1}^{n} c_j = \sum_{j=1}^{n} \frac{(x_j^n + (y_1 + \cdots + y_n)x_j^{n-1} + \cdots)}{\prod_{1 \le k \le n, \, k \ne j}(x_j - x_k)}$$

$$= (x_1 + x_2 + \cdots + x_n) + (y_1 + y_2 + \cdots + y_n).$$

45. Let $x_i = i$, $y_j = j - 1$. From exercise 44, the sum of the elements of the inverse is $(1 + 2 + \cdots + n) + ((n - 1) + (n - 2) + \cdots + 0) = n^2$. From exercise 38, the elements of the inverse are

$$b_{ij} = \frac{(-1)^{i+j}(i + n - 1)! \, (j + n - 1)!}{(i + j - 1)(i - 1)!^2 (j - 1)!^2 (n - i)! \, (n - j)!}.$$

This quantity can be put into several forms involving binomial coefficients, for example

$$\frac{(-1)^{i+j} ij}{i + j - 1} \binom{-i}{n} \binom{n}{i} \binom{-j}{n} \binom{n}{j} = (-1)^{i+j} j \binom{i+j-2}{i-1} \binom{i+n-1}{i-1} \binom{j+n-1}{n-i} \binom{n}{j}.$$

From the latter formula we see that b_{ij} is not only an integer, it is divisible by i, j, n, $i+j-1$, $i+n-1$, $j+n-1$, $n-i+1$, and $n-j+1$. Perhaps the prettiest formula for b_{ij} is

$$(i+j-1)\binom{i+j-2}{i-1}^2\binom{-(i+j)}{n-i}\binom{-(i+j)}{n-j}.$$

The solution to this problem would be extremely difficult if we had not realized that a Hilbert matrix is a special case of a Cauchy matrix; the more general problem is much easier to solve than its special case! It is frequently wise to generalize a problem to its "inductive closure," i.e., to the smallest generalization such that all subproblems that arise in an attempted proof by mathematical induction belong to the same class. In this case, we see that cofactors of a Cauchy matrix are determinants of Cauchy matrices, but cofactors of Hilbert matrices are not determinants of Hilbert matrices. [For further information, see J. Todd, *J. Research Nat. Bur. Stand.* **65** (1961), 19–22; A. Cauchy, *Exercices d'analyse et de physique mathématique* **2** (1841), 151–159.]

46. For any integers $k_1, k_2, \ldots, k_m$, let $\epsilon(k_1, \ldots, k_m) = \text{sign}(\prod_{1 \le i < j \le m}(k_j - k_i))$, where $\text{sign}\, x = [x > 0] - [x < 0]$. If $(l_1, \ldots, l_m)$ is equal to $(k_1, \ldots, k_m)$ except for the fact that k_i and k_j have been interchanged, we have $\epsilon(l_1, \ldots, l_m) = -\epsilon(k_1, \ldots, k_m)$. Therefore we have the equation $\det(B_{k_1 \ldots k_m}) = \epsilon(k_1, \ldots, k_m) \det(B_{j_1 \ldots j_m})$, if $j_1 \le \cdots \le j_m$ are the numbers $k_1, \ldots, k_m$ rearranged into nondecreasing order. Now by definition of the determinant,

$$\det(AB) = \sum_{1 \le l_1, \ldots, l_m \le m} \epsilon(l_1, \ldots, l_m)\left(\sum_{k=1}^n a_{1k}b_{kl_1}\right) \cdots \left(\sum_{k=1}^n a_{mk}b_{kl_m}\right)$$

$$= \sum_{1 \le k_1, \ldots, k_m \le n} a_{1k_1} \ldots a_{mk_m} \sum_{1 \le l_1, \ldots, l_m \le m} \epsilon(l_1, \ldots, l_m)b_{k_1 l_1} \ldots b_{k_m l_m}$$

$$= \sum_{1 \le k_1, \ldots, k_m \le n} a_{1k_1} \ldots a_{mk_m} \det(B_{k_1 \ldots k_m})$$

$$= \sum_{1 \le k_1, \ldots, k_m \le n} \epsilon(k_1, \ldots, k_m)a_{1k_1} \ldots a_{mk_m} \det(B_{j_1 \ldots j_m})$$

$$= \sum_{1 \le j_1 \le \cdots \le j_m \le n} \det(A_{j_1 \ldots j_m}) \det(B_{j_1 \ldots j_m}).$$

Finally, if $j_i = j_{i+1}$, $\det(A_{j_1 \ldots j_m}) = 0$. [*J. de l'École Polytechnique* **9** (1813), 280–354; **10** (1815), 29–112. Binet and Cauchy presented their papers on the same day in 1812.]

47. Let $a_{ij} = (\prod_{k=1}^{j-1}(x_i+p_k))(\prod_{k=j+1}^n(x_i+q_k))$. Subtract column $k-1$ from column k and factor out $p_{k-j} - q_k$, for $k = n$, $n-1$, $\ldots$, $j+1$ (in that order), for $j = 1$, 2, $\ldots$, $n-1$ (in that order). This leaves $\prod_{1 \le i < j \le n}(p_i - q_j)$ times $\det(b_{ij})$ where $b_{ij} = \prod_{k=j+1}^n(x_i + q_k)$. Now subtract q_{k+j} times column $k+1$ from column k for $k = 1$, $\ldots$, $n-j$, and for $j = 1$, $\ldots$, $n-1$; this leaves $\det(c_{ij})$, where $c_{ij} = x_i^{n-j}$ essentially defines a Vandermonde matrix. We can now proceed as in exercise 37, operating on rows instead of columns, obtaining

$$\det(a_{ij}) = \prod_{1 \le i < j \le n} (x_i - x_j)(p_i - q_j).$$

When $p_j = q_j = y_j$ for $1 \le j \le n$, the matrix in this exercise is a Cauchy matrix with row i multiplied by $\prod_{j=1}^n(x_i + y_j)$. Therefore this result generalizes exercise 38 by adding $n-2$ independent parameters. [*Manuscripta Math.* **69** (1990), 177–178.]

SECTION 1.2.4

1. 1, −2, −1, 0, 5.

2. $\lfloor x \rfloor$.

3. By definition, $\lfloor x \rfloor$ is the greatest integer less than or equal to x; therefore $\lfloor x \rfloor$ is an integer, $\lfloor x \rfloor \le x$, and $\lfloor x \rfloor + 1 > x$. The latter properties, plus the fact that when m and n are integers we have $m < n$ if and only if $m \le n - 1$, lead to an easy proof of propositions (a) and (b). Similar arguments prove (c) and (d). Finally, (e) and (f) are just combinations of previous parts of this exercise.

4. By part (f), $x \le \lceil x \rceil < x + 1$; hence $-x - 1 < -\lceil x \rceil \le -x$; use part (e).

5. $\lfloor x + \frac{1}{2} \rfloor$. The value of $(-x$ rounded$)$ will be the same as $-(x$ rounded$)$, *except* when $x \bmod 1 = \frac{1}{2}$. In the latter case, the negative value is rounded towards zero and the positive value is rounded away from zero.

6. (a) is true: $\lfloor \sqrt{x} \rfloor = n \iff n^2 \le x < (n+1)^2 \iff n^2 \le \lfloor x \rfloor < (n+1)^2 \iff \lfloor \sqrt{\lfloor x \rfloor} \rfloor = n$. Similarly, (b) is true. But (c) fails when x is, say, 1.1.

7. $\lfloor x+y \rfloor = \lfloor \lfloor x \rfloor + x \bmod 1 + \lfloor y \rfloor + y \bmod 1 \rfloor = \lfloor x \rfloor + \lfloor y \rfloor + \lfloor x \bmod 1 + y \bmod 1 \rfloor$. The inequality should be $\ge$ for ceilings, and then equality holds if and only if either x or y is an integer or $x \bmod 1 + y \bmod 1 > 1$; that is, if and only if $(-x) \bmod 1 + (-y) \bmod 1 < 1$.

8. 1, 2, 5, −100.

9. −1, 0, −2.

10. 0.1, 0.01, −0.09.

11. $x = y$.

12. All.

13. +1, −1.

14. 8.

15. Multiply both sides of Eq. (1) by z; the result is also easily verified if $y = 0$.

17. As an example, consider the multiplication portion of Law A: We have $a = b + qm$ and $x = y + rm$, for some integers q and r; so $ax = by + (br + yq + qrm)m$.

18. We have $a - b = kr$ for some integer k, and also $kr \equiv 0$ (modulo s). Hence by Law B, $k \equiv 0$ (modulo s), so $a - b = qsr$ for some integer q.

20. Multiply both sides of the congruence by a'.

21. There is at least one such representation, by the previously proved exercise. If there are two representations, $n = p_1 \ldots p_k = q_1 \ldots q_m$, we have $q_1 \ldots q_m \equiv 0$ (modulo p_1); so if none of the q's equals p_1 we could cancel them all by Law B and obtain $1 \equiv 0$ (modulo p_1). The latter is impossible since p_1 is not equal to 1. So some q_j equals p_1, and $n/p_1 = p_2 \ldots p_k = q_1 \ldots q_{j-1} q_{j+1} \ldots q_m$. Either n is prime, when the result is clearly true, or by induction the two factorizations of n/p_1 are the same.

22. Let $m = ax$, where $a > 1$ and $x > 0$. Then $ax \equiv 0$ but $x \not\equiv 0$ (modulo m).

24. Law A is always valid for addition and subtraction; Law C is always valid.

26. If b is not a multiple of p, then $b^2 - 1$ is, so one of the factors must be.

27. A number is relatively prime to p^e if and only if it is not a multiple of p. So we count those that are not multiples of p and get $\varphi(p^e) = p^e - p^{e-1}$.

28. If a and b are relatively prime to m, so is $ab \bmod m$, since any prime dividing the latter and m must divide a or b also. Now simply let $x_1, \ldots, x_{\varphi(m)}$ be the numbers relatively prime to m, and observe that $ax_1 \bmod m, \ldots, ax_{\varphi(m)} \bmod m$ are the same numbers in some order, etc.

29. We prove (b): If $r \perp s$ and if k^2 divides rs, then p^2 divides rs for some prime p, so p divides r (say) and cannot divide s; so p^2 divides r. We see that $f(rs) = 0$ if and only if $f(r) = 0$ or $f(s) = 0$.

30. Suppose $r \perp s$. One idea is to prove that the $\varphi(rs)$ numbers relatively prime to rs are precisely the $\varphi(r)\varphi(s)$ distinct numbers $(sx_i + ry_j) \bmod (rs)$ where $x_1, \ldots, x_{\varphi(r)}$ and $y_1, \ldots, y_{\varphi(s)}$ are the corresponding values for r and s.

Since φ is multiplicative, $\varphi(10^6) = \varphi(2^6)\varphi(5^6) = (2^6 - 2^5)(5^6 - 5^5) = 400000$. And in general when $n = p_1^{e_1} \ldots p_r^{e_r}$, we have $\varphi(n) = (p_1^{e_1} - p_1^{e_1 - 1}) \ldots (p_r^{e_r} - p_r^{e_r - 1}) = n \prod_{p \backslash n, \, p \text{ prime}} (1 - 1/p)$. (Another proof appears in exercise 1.3.3–27.)

31. Use the fact that the divisors of rs may be uniquely written in the form cd where c divides r and d divides s. Similarly, if $f(n) \geq 0$, one can show that the function $\max_{d \backslash n} f(d)$ is multiplicative (see exercise 1.2.3–35).

33. Either $n + m$ or $n - m + 1$ is even, so one of the quantities inside the brackets is an integer; so equality holds in exercise 7, and we obtain (a) n; (b) $n + 1$.

34. b must be an integer ≥ 2. (Set $x = b$.) The sufficiency is proved as in exercise 6. The same condition is necessary and sufficient for $\lceil \log_b x \rceil = \lceil \log_b \lceil x \rceil \rceil$.

Note: R. J. McEliece has pointed out the following generalization: Let f be a continuous, strictly increasing function defined on an interval A, and assume that both $\lfloor x \rfloor$ and $\lceil x \rceil$ are in A whenever x is in A. Then the relation $\lfloor f(x) \rfloor = \lfloor f(\lfloor x \rfloor) \rfloor$ holds for all x in A if and only if the relation $\lceil f(x) \rceil = \lceil f(\lceil x \rceil) \rceil$ holds for all x in A, if and only if the following condition is satisfied for all x in A: "$f(x)$ is an integer implies x is an integer." The condition is obviously necessary, for if $f(x)$ is an integer and it equals $\lfloor f(\lfloor x \rfloor) \rfloor$ or $\lceil f(\lceil x \rceil) \rceil$ then x must equal $\lfloor x \rfloor$ or $\lceil x \rceil$. Conversely if, say, $\lfloor f(\lfloor x \rfloor) \rfloor < \lfloor f(x) \rfloor$ then by continuity there is some y with $\lfloor x \rfloor < y \leq x$ for which $f(y)$ is an integer; but y cannot be an integer.

35. $\dfrac{x+m}{n} - 1 = \dfrac{x+m}{n} - \dfrac{1}{n} - \dfrac{n-1}{n} < \dfrac{\lfloor x \rfloor + m}{n} - \dfrac{n-1}{n} \leq \left\lfloor \dfrac{\lfloor x \rfloor + m}{n} \right\rfloor \leq \dfrac{x+m}{n}$;

apply exercise 3. Use of exercise 4 gives a similar result for the ceiling function. Both identities follow as a special case of McEliece's theorem in exercise 34.

36. Assume first that $n = 2t$. Then

$$\sum_{k=1}^{n} \left\lfloor \frac{k}{2} \right\rfloor = \sum_{k=1}^{n} \left\lfloor \frac{n+1-k}{2} \right\rfloor;$$

hence

$$\sum_{k=1}^{n} \left\lfloor \frac{k}{2} \right\rfloor = \frac{1}{2} \sum_{k=1}^{n} \left(\left\lfloor \frac{k}{2} \right\rfloor + \left\lfloor \frac{n+1-k}{2} \right\rfloor \right) = \frac{1}{2} \sum_{k=1}^{n} \left\lfloor \frac{2t+1}{2} \right\rfloor = t^2 = \frac{n^2}{4},$$

by exercise 33. And if $n = 2t + 1$, we have $t^2 + \lfloor n/2 \rfloor = t^2 + t = n^2/4 - 1/4$. For the second sum we get, similarly, $\lceil n(n+2)/4 \rceil$.

37. $\displaystyle\sum_{0\le k<n} \frac{mk+x}{n} = \frac{m(n-1)}{2} + x$. Let $\{y\}$ denote $y \bmod 1$; we must subtract

$$S = \sum_{0\le k<n} \left\{ \frac{mk+x}{n} \right\}.$$

This quantity S consists of d copies of the same sum, since if $t = n/d$ we have

$$\left\{ \frac{mk+x}{n} \right\} = \left\{ \frac{m(k+t)+x}{n} \right\}.$$

Let $u = m/d$; then

$$\sum_{0\le k<t} \left\{ \frac{mk+x}{n} \right\} = \sum_{0\le k<t} \left\{ \frac{x}{n} + \frac{uk}{t} \right\},$$

and since $t \perp u$ this sum may be rearranged to equal

$$\left\{ \frac{x \bmod d}{n} \right\} + \left\{ \frac{x \bmod d}{n} + \frac{1}{t} \right\} + \cdots + \left\{ \frac{x \bmod d}{n} + \frac{t-1}{t} \right\}.$$

Finally, since $(x \bmod d)/n < 1/t$, the braces in this sum may be removed and we have

$$S = d\left(\frac{t(x \bmod d)}{n} + \frac{t-1}{2} \right).$$

An application of exercise 4 yields the similar identity

$$\sum_{0\le k<n} \left\lceil \frac{mk+x}{n} \right\rceil = \frac{(m+1)(n-1)}{2} - \frac{d-1}{2} + d\lceil x/d \rceil.$$

This formula would become symmetric in m and n if it were extended over the range $0 < k \le n$. (The symmetry can be explained by drawing the graph of the summand as a function of k, then reflecting about the line $y = x$.)

38. Both sides increase by $\lceil y \rceil$ when x increases by 1, so we can assume that $0 \le x < 1$. Then both sides are zero when $x = 0$, and both sides increase by 1 when x increases past the values $1 - k/y$ for $y > k \ge 0$. [*Crelle* **136** (1909), 42; the case $y = n$ is due to C. Hermite, *Acta Math.* **5** (1884), 315.]

39. Proof of part (f): Consider the more general identity $\prod_{0\le k<n} 2\sin\pi(x + k/n) = 2\sin\pi nx$, which can be demonstrated as follows: Since $2\sin\theta = (e^{i\theta} - e^{-i\theta})/i = (1 - e^{-2i\theta})e^{i\theta - i\pi/2}$, the identity is a consequence of the two formulas

$$\prod_{0\le k<n} (1 - e^{-2\pi(x+ik/n)}) = 1 - e^{-2\pi nx} \quad\text{and}\quad \prod_{0\le k<n} e^{\pi(x-(1/2)+(k/n))} = e^{\pi(nx-1/2)}.$$

The latter is true since the function $x - \frac{1}{2}$ is replicative; and the former is true because we may set $z = 1$ in the factorization of the polynomial $z^n - \alpha^n = (z - \alpha)(z - \omega\alpha)\cdots (z - \omega^{n-1}\alpha)$, where $\omega = e^{-2\pi i/n}$.

40. (Note by N. G. de Bruijn.) If f is replicative, $f(nx+1) - f(nx) = f(x+1) - f(x)$ for all $n > 0$. Hence if f is continuous, $f(x+1) - f(x) = c$ for all x, and $g(x) = f(x) - c\lfloor x \rfloor$ is replicative and periodic. Now

$$\int_0^1 e^{2\pi inx} g(x)\, dx = \frac{1}{n} \int_0^1 e^{2\pi iy} g(y)\, dy;$$

expanding in Fourier series shows that $g(x) = (x - \frac{1}{2})a$ for $0 < x < 1$. It follows that $f(x) = (x - \frac{1}{2})a$. In general, this argument shows that any replicative locally Riemann-integrable function has the form $(x-\frac{1}{2})a+b\max(\lfloor x \rfloor,0)+c\min(\lfloor x \rfloor,0)$ almost everywhere. For further results see L. J. Mordell, *J. London Math. Soc.* (2) **33** (1958), 371–375; M. F. Yoder, *Æquationes Mathematicæ* **13** (1975), 251–261.

41. We want $a_n = k$ when $\frac{1}{2}k(k-1) < n \le \frac{1}{2}k(k+1)$. Since n is an integer, this is equivalent to

$$\frac{k(k-1)}{2} + \frac{1}{8} < n < \frac{k(k+1)}{2} + \frac{1}{8},$$

i.e., $k - \frac{1}{2} < \sqrt{2n} < k + \frac{1}{2}$. Hence $a_n = \lfloor \sqrt{2n} + \frac{1}{2} \rfloor$, the nearest integer to $\sqrt{2n}$. Other correct answers are $\lceil \sqrt{2n} - \frac{1}{2} \rceil$, $\lceil (\sqrt{8n+1} - 1)/2 \rceil$, $\lfloor (\sqrt{8n-7}+1)/2 \rfloor$, etc.

42. (a) See exercise 1.2.7–10. (b) The given sum is $n\lfloor \log_b n \rfloor - S$, where

$$S = \sum_{\substack{1 \le k < n \\ k+1 \text{ is a power of } b}} k = \sum_{1 \le t \le \log_b n} (b^t - 1) = (b^{\lfloor \log_b n \rfloor + 1} - b)/(b-1) - \lfloor \log_b n \rfloor.$$

43. $\lfloor \sqrt{n} \rfloor \left(n - \frac{1}{6}(2\lfloor \sqrt{n} \rfloor + 5)(\lfloor \sqrt{n} \rfloor - 1)\right)$.

44. The sum is $n + 1$ when n is negative.

45. $\lfloor mj/n \rfloor = r$ if and only if $\left\lceil \dfrac{rn}{m} \right\rceil \le j < \left\lceil \dfrac{(r+1)n}{m} \right\rceil$, and we find that the given sum is therefore

$$\sum_{0 \le r < m} f(r) \left(\left\lceil \frac{(r+1)n}{m} \right\rceil - \left\lceil \frac{rn}{m} \right\rceil \right).$$

The stated result follows by rearranging the latter sum, grouping the terms with a particular value of $\lceil rn/m \rceil$. The second formula is immediate by the substitution

$$f(x) = \binom{x+1}{k}.$$

46. $\sum_{0 \le j < an} f(\lfloor mj/n \rfloor) = \sum_{0 \le r < am} \lceil rn/m \rceil (f(r-1) - f(r)) + \lceil an \rceil f(\lceil am \rceil - 1)$.

47. (a) The numbers 2, 4, $\ldots$, $p-1$ are the even residues (modulo p); since $2kq = p\lfloor 2kq/p \rfloor + (2kq) \bmod p$, the number $(-1)^{\lfloor 2kq/p \rfloor}((2kq) \bmod p)$ will be an even residue or an even residue minus p, and each even residue clearly occurs just once. Hence $(-1)^\sigma q^{(p-1)/2} 2 \cdot 4 \ldots (p-1) \equiv 2 \cdot 4 \ldots (p-1)$. (b) Let $q = 2$. If $p = 4n+1$, $\sigma = n$; if $p = 4n+3$, $\sigma = n+1$. Hence $\left(\frac{2}{p}\right) = (1,-1,-1,1)$ according as $p \bmod 8 = (1,3,5,7)$, respectively. (c) For $k < p/4$, we have

$$\lfloor (p-1-2k)q/p \rfloor = q - \lceil (2k+1)q/p \rceil = q - 1 - \lfloor (2k+1)q/p \rfloor \equiv \lfloor (2k+1)q/p \rfloor \pmod{2}.$$

Hence we may replace the last terms $\lfloor (p-1)q/p \rfloor$, $\lfloor (p-3)q/p \rfloor, \ldots$ by $\lfloor q/p \rfloor$, $\lfloor 3q/p \rfloor$, etc. (d) $\sum_{0 \le k < p/2} \lfloor kq/p \rfloor + \sum_{0 \le r < q/2} \lceil rp/q \rceil = \lfloor p/2 \rfloor (\lceil q/2 \rceil - 1) = (p+1)(q-1)/4$. Also $\sum_{0 \le r < q/2} \lceil rp/q \rceil = \sum_{0 \le r < q/2} \lfloor rp/q \rfloor + (q-1)/2$. The idea of this proof goes back to G. Eisenstein, *Crelle* **28** (1844), 246–248; Eisenstein also gave several other proofs of this and other reciprocity laws in the same volume.

48. (a) This is clearly not always true when $n < 0$; when $n > 0$ it is easy to verify. (b) $\lfloor (n+2-\lfloor n/25 \rfloor)/3 \rfloor = \lceil (n - \lfloor n/25 \rfloor)/3 \rceil = \lceil (n+\lceil -n/25 \rceil)/3 \rceil = \lceil \lceil 24n/25 \rceil/3 \rceil = \lceil 8n/25 \rceil = \lfloor (8n+24)/25 \rfloor$. The penultimate equality is justified by exercise 35.

49. Since $f(0) = f(f(0)) = f(f(0) + 0) = f(0) + f(0)$, we have $f(n) = n$ for all integers n. If $f(\frac{1}{2}) = k \le 0$, we have $k = f(\frac{1}{1-2k}f(\frac{1}{2} - k)) = f(\frac{1}{1-2k}(f(\frac{1}{2}) - k)) = f(0) = 0$. And if $f(\frac{1}{n-1}) = 0$ we have $f(\frac{1}{n}) = f(\frac{1}{n}f(1 + \frac{1}{n-1})) = f(\frac{1}{n-1}) = 0$; furthermore $1 \le m < n$ implies $f(\frac{m}{n}) = f(\frac{1}{a}f(\frac{am}{n})) = f(\frac{1}{a}) = 0$, for $a = \lceil n/m \rceil$, by induction on m. Thus $f(\frac{1}{2}) \le 0$ implies $f(x) = \lfloor x \rfloor$ for all rational x. On the other hand, if $f(\frac{1}{2}) > 0$ the function $g(x) = -f(-x)$ satisfies (i) and (ii) and has $g(\frac{1}{2}) = 1 - f(\frac{1}{2}) \le 0$; hence $f(x) = -g(-x) = -\lfloor -x \rfloor = \lceil x \rceil$ for all rational x. [P. Eisele and K. P. Hadeler, *AMM* **97** (1990), 475–477.]

It does not follow, however, that $f(x) = \lfloor x \rfloor$ or $\lceil x \rceil$ for all *real* values of x. If, for example, $h(x)$ is any function with $h(1) = 1$ and $h(x + y) = h(x) + h(y)$ for all real x and y, then the function $f(x) = \lfloor h(x) \rfloor$ satisfies (i) and (ii); but $h(x)$ may be unbounded and highly erratic when $0 < x < 1$ [G. Hamel, *Math. Annalen* **60** (1905), 459–462].

50. No: $\lfloor 3143/\pi \rfloor = 1000$. But $\lceil m\alpha \rceil = n$ does imply that $\lfloor n/\alpha \rfloor = m$, whenever $\alpha \ge 1$; and $\lfloor n/\alpha \rfloor = m$ does imply that $\lceil m\alpha \rceil = n$, whenever $0 < \alpha \le 1$.

SECTION 1.2.5

1. 52!. For the curious, this number is 806 58175 17094 38785 71660 63685 64037 66975 28950 54408 83277 82400 00000 00000. (!)

2. $p_{nk} = p_{n(k-1)}(n - k + 1)$. After the first $n - 1$ objects have been placed, there is only one possibility for the last object.

3. $53124, 35124, 31524, 31254, 31245; 42351, 41352, 41253, 31254, 31245$.

4. There are 2568 digits. The leading digit is 4 (since $\log_{10} 4 = 2\log_{10} 2 \approx .602$). The least significant digit is zero, and in fact by Eq. (8) the low order 249 digits are all zero. The exact value of 1000! was calculated by H. S. Uhler using a desk calculator and much patience over a period of several years, and appears in *Scripta Mathematica* **21** (1955), 266–267. It begins with 402 38726 00770 .... (The last step in the calculation, to multiply the two numbers 750! and $\prod_{k=751}^{1000} k$, was performed on UNIVAC I by John W. Wrench, Jr., "in the extraordinary time of $2\frac{1}{2}$ minutes." Nowadays, of course, a desktop machine easily produces 1000! in a fraction of a second, and we can confirm that Uhler's value was 100% correct.)

5. $(39902)(97/96) \approx 416 + 39902 = 40318$.

6. $2^{18} \cdot 3^8 \cdot 5^4 \cdot 7^2 \cdot 11 \cdot 13 \cdot 17 \cdot 19$.

8. It is $\lim_{m\to\infty} m^n m!/((n + m)!/n!) = n! \lim_{m\to\infty} m^n/((m + 1)\ldots(m + n)) = n!$, since $m/(m + k) \to 1$.

9. $\sqrt{\pi}$ and $-2\sqrt{\pi}$. (Exercise 10 used.)

10. Yes, except when x is zero or a negative integer. For we have

$$\Gamma(x + 1) = x \lim_{m\to\infty} \frac{m^x m!}{x(x + 1)\ldots(x + m)} \left(\frac{m}{x + m + 1}\right).$$

11, 12. $\mu = (a_k p^{k-1} + \cdots + a_1) + (a_k p^{k-2} + \cdots + a_2) + \cdots + a_k$

$= a_k(p^{k-1} + \cdots + p + 1) + \cdots + a_1 = (a_k(p^k - 1) + \cdots + a_0(p^0 - 1))/(p - 1)$

$= (n - a_k - \cdots - a_1 - a_0)/(p - 1)$.

13. For each n, $1 \le n < p$, determine n' as in exercise 1.2.4–19. There is exactly one such n', by Law 1.2.4B; and $(n')' = n$. Therefore we can pair off the numbers in groups of two, provided that $n' \ne n$. If $n' = n$, we have $n^2 \equiv 1$ (modulo p); hence, as in exercise 1.2.4–26, $n = 1$ or $n = p-1$. So $(p-1)! \equiv 1 \cdot 1 \ldots 1 \cdot (-1)$, since 1 and $p-1$ are the only unpaired elements.

14. Among the numbers $\{1, 2, \ldots, n\}$ that are *not* multiples of p, there are $\lfloor n/p \rfloor$ complete sets of $p-1$ consecutive elements, each with a product congruent to -1 (modulo p) by Wilson's theorem. There are also a_0 left over, which are congruent to $a_0!$ (modulo p); so the contribution from the factors that are not multiples of p is $(-1)^{\lfloor n/p \rfloor} a_0!$. The contribution from the factors that *are* multiples of p is the same as the contribution in $\lfloor n/p \rfloor!$; this argument can therefore be repeated to get the desired formula.

15. $(n!)^3$. There are $n!$ terms. Each term has one entry from each row and each column, so it has the value $(n!)^2$.

16. The terms do not approach zero, since the coefficients approach $1/e$.

17. Express the gamma functions as limits by Eq. (15).

18. $\displaystyle \prod_{n \geq 1} \frac{n}{n - \frac{1}{2}} \frac{n}{n + \frac{1}{2}} = \frac{\Gamma(\frac{1}{2})\Gamma(\frac{3}{2})}{\Gamma(1)\Gamma(1)} = 2\Gamma(\frac{3}{2})^2.$

[Wallis's own heuristic "proof" can be found in D. J. Struik's *Source Book in Mathematics* (Harvard University Press, 1969), 244–253.]

19. Change of variable $t = mt$, integration by parts, and induction.

20. [For completeness, we prove the stated inequality. Start with the easily verified inequality $1 + x \leq e^x$; set $x = \pm t/n$ and raise to the nth power to get $(1 \pm t/n)^n \leq e^{\pm t}$. Hence $e^{-t} \geq (1-t/n)^n = e^{-t}(1-t/n)^n e^t \geq e^{-t}(1-t/n)^n(1+t/n)^n = e^{-t}(1-t^2/n^2)^n \geq e^{-t}(1-t^2/n)$ by exercise 1.2.1–9.]

Now the given integral minus $\Gamma_m(x)$ is

$$\int_m^\infty e^{-t} t^{x-1}\, dt + \int_0^m \left(e^{-t} - \left(1 - \frac{t}{m}\right)^m\right) t^{x-1}\, dt.$$

As $m \to \infty$, the first of these integrals approaches zero, since $t^{x-1} < e^{t/2}$ for large t; and the second is at most

$$\frac{1}{m} \int_0^m t^{x+1} e^{-t}\, dt < \frac{1}{m} \int_0^\infty t^{x+1} e^{-t}\, dt \to 0.$$

21. If $c(n, j, k_1, k_2, \ldots)$ denotes the appropriate coefficient, we find

$$c(n+1, j, k_1, \ldots) = c(n, j-1, k_1-1, k_2, \ldots) + (k_1+1)c(n, j, k_1+1, k_2-1, k_3, \ldots)$$
$$+ (k_2+1)c(n, j, k_1, k_2+1, k_3-1, k_4, \ldots) + \cdots,$$

by differentiation. The equations $k_1 + k_2 + \cdots = j$ and $k_1 + 2k_2 + \cdots = n$ are preserved in this induction relationship. We can easily factor $n!/(k_1!\,(1!)^{k_1} k_2!\,(2!)^{k_2} \ldots)$ out of each term appearing on the right-hand side of the equation for $c(n+1, j, k_1, \ldots)$, and we are left with $k_1 + 2k_2 + 3k_3 + \cdots = n+1$. (In the proof it is convenient to assume that there are infinitely many k's, although clearly $k_{n+1} = k_{n+2} = \cdots = 0$.)

The solution just given makes use of standard techniques, but it doesn't give a satisfactory explanation of *why* the formula has this form, nor how it could have been discovered in the first place. Let us examine this question using a combinatorial argument suggested by H. S. Wall [*Bull. Amer. Math. Soc.* **44** (1938), 395–398]. Write for convenience $w_j = D_u^j w$, $u_k = D_x^k u$. Then $D_x(w_j) = w_{j+1} u_1$ and $D_x(u_k) = u_{k+1}$.

By these two rules and the rule for derivative of a product we find

$$D_x^1 w = w_1 u_1$$
$$D_x^2 w = (w_2 u_1 u_1 + w_1 u_2)$$
$$D_x^3 w = ((w_3 u_1 u_1 u_1 + w_2 u_2 u_1 + w_2 u_1 u_2) + (w_2 u_1 u_2 + w_1 u_3)), \text{ etc.}$$

Analogously we may set up a corresponding tableau of set partitions thus:

$$\mathcal{D}^1 = \{1\}$$
$$\mathcal{D}^2 = (\{2\}\{1\} + \{2,1\})$$
$$\mathcal{D}^3 = ((\{3\}\{2\}\{1\} + \{3,2\}\{1\} + \{2\}\{3,1\}) + (\{3\}\{2,1\} + \{3,2,1\})), \text{ etc.}$$

Formally, if $a_1 a_2 \ldots a_j$ is a partition of the set $\{1, 2, \ldots, n - 1\}$, define

$$\mathcal{D}a_1 a_2 \ldots a_j = \{n\} a_1 a_2 \ldots a_j + (a_1 \cup \{n\}) a_2 \ldots a_j$$
$$+ a_1 (a_2 \cup \{n\}) \ldots a_j + \cdots + a_1 a_2 \ldots (a_j \cup \{n\}).$$

This rule is an exact parallel of the rule

$$D_x(w_j u_{r_1} u_{r_2} \ldots u_{r_j}) = w_{j+1} u_1 u_{r_1} u_{r_2} \ldots u_{r_j} + w_j u_{r_1+1} u_{r_2} \ldots u_{r_j}$$
$$+ w_j u_{r_1} u_{r_2+1} \ldots u_{r_j} + \cdots + w_j u_{r_1} u_{r_2} \ldots u_{r_j+1},$$

if we let the term $w_j u_{r_1} u_{r_2} \ldots u_{r_j}$ correspond to a partition $a_1 a_2 \ldots a_j$ with r_t elements in a_t, $1 \le t \le j$. So there is a natural mapping from $\mathcal{D}^n$ onto $D_x^n w$, and furthermore it is easy to see that $\mathcal{D}^n$ includes each partition of the set $\{1, 2, \ldots, n\}$ exactly once. (See exercise 1.2.6–64.)

From these observations we find that if we collect like terms in $D_x^n w$, we obtain a sum of terms $c(k_1, k_2, \ldots) w_j u_1^{k_1} u_2^{k_2} \ldots$, where $j = k_1 + k_2 + \cdots$ and $n = k_1 + 2k_2 + \cdots$, and where $c(k_1, k_2, \ldots)$ is *the number of partitions of* $\{1, 2, \ldots, n\}$ *into* j *subsets such that there are* k_t *subsets having* t *elements.*

It remains to count these partitions. Consider an array of k_t boxes of capacity t:

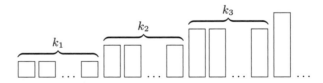

The number of ways to put n different elements into these boxes is the multinomial coefficient

$$\binom{n}{1, 1, \ldots, 1, 2, 2, \ldots, 2, 3, 3, \ldots, 3, 4, \ldots} = \frac{n!}{1!^{k_1} 2!^{k_2} 3!^{k_3} \ldots}.$$

To get $c(k_1, k_2, k_3, \ldots)$ we should divide this by $k_1! \, k_2! \, k_3! \ldots$, since the boxes in each group of k_t are indistinguishable from each other; they may be permuted in $k_t!$ ways without affecting the set partition.

Arbogast's original proof [*Du Calcul des Dérivations* (Strasbourg: 1800), §52] was based on the fact that $D_x^k u / k!$ is the coefficient of z^k in $u(x + z)$ and $D_u^j w / j!$ is the coefficient of y^j in $w(u+y)$, hence the coefficient of z^n in $w(u(x+z))$ is

$$\frac{D_x^n w}{n!} = \sum_{j=0}^{n} \frac{D_u^j w}{j!} \sum_{\substack{k_1+k_2+\cdots+k_n=j \\ k_1+2k_2+\cdots+nk_n=n \\ k_1,k_2,\ldots,k_n \geq 0}} \frac{j!}{k_1!\,k_2!\ldots k_n!} \left(\frac{D_x^1 u}{1!}\right)^{k_1} \left(\frac{D_x^2 u}{2!}\right)^{k_2} \cdots \left(\frac{D_x^n u}{n!}\right)^{k_n}.$$

His formula was forgotten for many years, then rediscovered independently by F. Faà di Bruno [*Quarterly J. Math.* **1** (1857), 359–360], who observed that it can also be expressed as a determinant

$$D_x^n = \det \begin{pmatrix} \binom{n-1}{0}u_1 & \binom{n-1}{1}u_2 & \binom{n-1}{2}u_3 & \cdots & \binom{n-1}{n-2}u_{n-1} & \binom{n-1}{n-1}u_n \\ -1 & \binom{n-2}{0}u_1 & \binom{n-2}{1}u_2 & \cdots & \binom{n-2}{n-3}u_{n-2} & \binom{n-2}{n-2}u_{n-1} \\ 0 & -1 & \binom{n-3}{0}u_1 & \cdots & \binom{n-3}{n-4}u_{n-3} & \binom{n-3}{n-3}u_{n-2} \\ \vdots & \vdots & \vdots & \ddots & \vdots & \vdots \\ 0 & 0 & 0 & \cdots & -1 & \binom{0}{0}u_1 \end{pmatrix}$$

where $u_j = (D_x^j u)\, D_u$; both sides of this equation are differential operators to be applied to w. For a generalization of Arbogast's formula to functions of several variables, and a list of references to other related work, see the paper by I. J. Good, *Annals of Mathematical Statistics* **32** (1961), 540–541.

22. The hypothesis that $\lim_{n\to\infty}(n+x)!/(n!\,n^x) = 1$ is valid for integers x; for example, if x is positive, the quantity is $(1+1/n)(1+2/n)\ldots(1+x/n)$, which certainly approaches unity. If we also assume that $x! = x(x-1)!$, the hypothesis leads us to conclude immediately that

$$1 = \lim_{n\to\infty} \frac{(n+x)!}{n!\,n^x} = x! \lim_{n\to\infty} \frac{(x+1)\ldots(x+n)}{n!\,n^x},$$

which is equivalent to the definition given in the text.

23. $z(-z)!\,\Gamma(z) = \lim_{m\to\infty} \prod_{n=1}^{m}(1-z/n)^{-1}(1+z/n)^{-1}$ by (13) and (15).

24. $n^n/n! = \prod_{k=1}^{n-1}(k+1)^k/k^k \leq \prod_{k=1}^{n-1} e$; $n!/n^{n+1} = \prod_{k=1}^{n-1}k^{k+1}/(k+1)^{k+1} \leq \prod_{k=1}^{n-1} e^{-1}$.

25. $x^{\overline{m+n}} = x^{\underline{m}}(x-m)^{\underline{n}}$; $x^{\overline{m+n}} = x^{\overline{m}}(x+m)^{\overline{n}}$. These laws hold also when m and n are nonintegers, by (21).

SECTION 1.2.6

1. n, since each combination leaves out one item.

2. 1. There's exactly one way to choose nothing from the empty set.

3. $\binom{52}{13}$. The actual number is 635013559600.

4. $2^4 \cdot 5^2 \cdot 7^2 \cdot 17 \cdot 23 \cdot 41 \cdot 43 \cdot 47$.

5. $(10+1)^4 = 10000 + 4(1000) + 6(100) + 4(10) + 1$.

6. $r = -3$: 1 -3 6 -10 15 -21 28 -36 ...
   $r = -2$: 1 -2 3 -4 5 -6 7 -8 ...
   $r = -1$: 1 -1 1 -1 1 -1 1 -1 ...

7. $\lfloor n/2 \rfloor$; or, alternatively, $\lceil n/2 \rceil$. It is clear from (3) that for smaller values the binomial coefficient is strictly increasing, and afterwards it decreases to zero.

8. The nonzero entries in each row are the same from left to right as from right to left.

9. One if n is positive or zero; zero if n is negative.

10. (a), (b), and (f) follow immediately from (e); (c) and (d) follow from (a), (b), and Eq. (9). Thus it suffices to prove (e). Consider $\binom{n}{k}$ as a fraction, given by Eq. (3) with factors in numerator and denominator. The first $k \bmod p$ factors have no p's in the denominator; and in the numerator and denominator those factors are clearly congruent to the corresponding factors of

$$\binom{n \bmod p}{k \bmod p},$$

which differ by multiples of p. (When dealing with non-multiples of p we may work modulo p in both numerator and denominator, since if $a \equiv c$ and $b \equiv d$ and a/b, c/d are integers, then $a/b \equiv c/d$.) There remain $k - k \bmod p$ factors, which fall into $\lfloor k/p \rfloor$ groups of p consecutive values each. Each group contains exactly one multiple of p; the other $p - 1$ factors in a group are congruent (modulo p) to $(p - 1)!$ so they cancel in numerator and denominator. It remains to investigate the $\lfloor k/p \rfloor$ multiples of p in numerator and denominator; we divide each of them by p and are left with the binomial coefficient

$$\binom{\lfloor (n - k \bmod p)/p \rfloor}{\lfloor k/p \rfloor}.$$

If $k \bmod p \le n \bmod p$, this equals

$$\binom{\lfloor n/p \rfloor}{\lfloor k/p \rfloor}$$

as desired; and if $k \bmod p > n \bmod p$, the other factor $\binom{n \bmod p}{k \bmod p}$ is zero, so the formula holds in general. [*American J. Math.* **1** (1878), 229–230; see also L. E. Dickson, *Quart. J. Math.* **33** (1902), 383–384; N. J. Fine, *AMM* **54** (1947), 589–592.]

11. If $a = a_r p^r + \cdots + a_0$, $b = b_r p^r + \cdots + b_0$, and $a + b = c_r p^r + \cdots + c_0$, the value of n (according to exercise 1.2.5–12 and Eq. (5)) is

$$(a_0 + \cdots + a_r + b_0 + \cdots + b_r - c_0 - \cdots - c_r)/(p - 1).$$

A carry decreases c_j by p and increases c_{j+1} by 1, giving a net change of $+1$ in this formula. [Similar results hold for q-nomial and Fibonomial coefficients; see Knuth and Wilf, *Crelle* **396** (1989), 212–219.]

12. By either of the two previous exercises, n must be one less than a power of 2. More generally, $\binom{n}{k}$ is never divisible by the prime p, $0 \le k \le n$, if and only if $n = ap^m - 1$, $1 \le a < p$, $m \ge 0$.

14. $24 \binom{n+1}{5} + 36 \binom{n+1}{4} + 14 \binom{n+1}{3} + \binom{n+1}{2}$

$$= \frac{n^5}{5} + \frac{n^4}{2} + \frac{n^3}{3} - \frac{n}{30} = \frac{n(n+1)(n+\frac{1}{2})(3n^2 + 3n - 1)}{15}.$$

15. Induction and (9).

17. We may assume that r and s are positive integers. Also

$$\sum_n \binom{r+s}{n} x^n = (1+x)^{r+s} = \sum_k \binom{r}{k} x^k \sum_m \binom{s}{m} x^m$$

$$= \sum_k \binom{r}{k} x^k \sum_n \binom{s}{n-k} x^{n-k} = \sum_n \left(\sum_k \binom{r}{k} \binom{s}{n-k} \right) x^n$$

for all x, so the coefficients of x^n must be identical.

21. The left-hand side is a polynomial of degree $\leq n$; the right-hand side is a polynomial of degree $m+n+1$. The polynomials agree at $n+1$ points, but that isn't enough to prove them equal. [In fact, the correct formula in general is

$$\sum_{k=0}^{r}\binom{r-k}{m}\binom{s+k}{n} = \binom{r+s+1}{m+n+1} - \sum_{k=0}^{m}\binom{r+1}{k}\binom{s}{m+n+1-k}$$

when m, n, and r are nonnegative integers.]

22. Assume that $n > 0$. The kth term is $r/(r - tk)$ times

$$\frac{1}{n!}\binom{n}{k} \prod_{0\leq j<k}(r - tk - j) \prod_{0\leq j<n-k}(n - 1 - r + tk - j)$$

$$= \frac{(-1)^k}{n!}\binom{n}{k} \prod_{0\leq j<k}(-r + tk + j) \prod_{k\leq j<n}(-r + tk + j)$$

and the two products give a polynomial of degree $n - 1$ in k after division by $r - tk$. So the sum over k is zero by Eq. (34).

24. The proof is by induction on n. If $n \leq 0$ the identity is obvious. If $n > 0$, we prove it holds for $(r, n - r + nt + m, t, n)$, by induction on the integer $m \geq 0$, using the previous two exercises and the validity for $n-1$. This establishes the identity (r, s, t, n) for infinitely many s, and it holds for all s since both sides are polynomials in s.

25. Using the ratio test and straightforward estimates for large values of k we can prove convergence. When w is sufficiently small, we have

$$1 = \sum_{k,j}(-1)^j\binom{k}{j}\binom{r-jt}{k}\frac{r}{r-jt}w^k = \sum_j(-1)^j\frac{r}{r-jt}\sum_k\binom{k}{j}\binom{r-jt}{k}w^k$$

$$= \sum_j\frac{(-1)^j r}{r-jt}\sum_k\binom{r-jt}{j}\binom{r-jt-j}{k-j}w^k = \sum_j(-1)^j A_j(r,t)(1+w)^{r-jt-j}w^j.$$

Now let $x = 1/(1+w)$, $z = -w/(1+w)^{1+t}$. This proof is due to H. W. Gould [*AMM* **63** (1956), 84–91]. See also the more general formulas in exercises 2.3.4.4–33 and 4.7–22.

26. We could start with identity (35) in the form

$$\sum_j(-1)^j\binom{k}{j}\binom{r-jt}{k} = t^k$$

and proceed as in exercise 25. Another way is to differentiate the formula of that exercise with respect to z; we get

$$\sum_k kA_k(r,t)z^k = z\frac{d(x^r)}{dz} = \frac{(x^{t+1} - x^t)rx^r}{(t+1)x^{t+1} - tx^t},$$

hence we can obtain the value of

$$\sum_k\left(1 - \frac{t}{r}k\right)A_k(r,t)z^k.$$

27. For Eq. (26), multiply the series for $x^{r+1}/((t+1)x - t)$ by the series for x^s, and get a series for $x^{r+s+1}/((t+1)x - t)$ in which coefficients of z may be equated to the coefficients arising from the series for $x^{(r+s)+1}/((t+1)x - t)$.

28. Denoting the left-hand side by $f(r, s, t, n)$, we find

$$\binom{r+s}{n} + t f(r+t-1,\, s-t,\, t,\, n-1) = f(r, s, t, n)$$

by considering the identity

$$\sum_k \binom{r+tk}{k}\binom{s-tk}{n-k}\frac{r}{r+tk} + \sum_k \binom{r+tk}{k}\binom{s-tk}{n-k}\frac{tk}{r+tk} = f(r, s, t, n).$$

29. $(-1)^k \binom{n}{k} \Big/ n! = (-1)^k/(k!\,(n-k)!) = (-1)^n \Big/ \prod_{\substack{0 \le j \le n \\ j \ne k}} (k-j).$

30. Apply (6) and (19) to get

$$\sum_{k \ge 0} \binom{n+k}{n-m-k}\binom{-k-1}{k}\frac{1}{k+1}.$$

Now we can apply Eq. (26) with $(r, s, t, n) = (-1, 2n-m, 1, n-m)$, obtaining

$$\binom{n-1}{n-m}.$$

This result is the same as our previous formula, when n is positive; but when $n = 0$ the answer we have obtained is correct while $\binom{n-1}{m-1}$ is not. Our derivation has a further bonus, since the answer $\binom{n-1}{n-m}$ is valid for $n \ge 0$ and *all* integers m.

31. [This sum was first obtained in closed form by J. F. Pfaff, *Nova Acta Acad. Scient. Petr.* **11** (1797), 37–57.] We have

$$\sum_k \sum_j \binom{m-r+s}{k}\binom{n+r-s}{n-k}\binom{r}{m+n-j}\binom{k}{j}$$

$$= \sum_j \sum_k \binom{m-r+s}{j}\binom{n+r-s}{n-k}\binom{r}{m+n-j}\binom{m-r+s-j}{k-j}$$

$$= \sum_j \binom{m-r+s}{j}\binom{r}{m+n-j}\binom{m+n-j}{n-j}.$$

Changing $\binom{m+n-j}{n-j}$ to $\binom{m+n-j}{m}$ and applying (20) again, we get

$$\sum_j \binom{m-r+s}{j}\binom{r}{m}\binom{r-m}{n-j} = \binom{r}{m}\binom{s}{n}.$$

32. Replace x by $-x$ in (44).

33, 34. [*Mém. Acad. Roy. Sci.* (Paris, 1772), part 1, 492; C. Kramp, *Élémens d'Arith-métique Universelle* (Cologne: 1808), 359; *Giornale di Mat. Battaglini* **33** (1895), 179–182.] Since $x^{\bar{n}} = n!\binom{x+n-1}{n}$, the equation may be transformed into

$$\binom{x+y+n-1}{n} = \sum_k \binom{x+(1-z)k}{k}\binom{y-1+nz+(n-k)(1-z)}{n-k}\frac{x}{x+(1-z)k},$$

which is a case of (26). Similarly, $(x+y)^{\underline{n}} = \sum_k \binom{n}{k}x(x-kz-1)^{\underline{k-1}}(y+kz)^{\underline{n-k}}$, an equivalent formula of Rothe [*Formulæ de Serierum Reversione* (Leipzig: 1793), 18].

35. For example, we prove the first formula:

$$\sum_k (-1)^{n+1-k}\left(n\begin{bmatrix} n \\ k \end{bmatrix} + \begin{bmatrix} n \\ k-1 \end{bmatrix}\right) x^k = -nx^{\underline{n}} + x x^{\underline{n}} = x^{\underline{n+1}}.$$

36. By (13), assuming that n is a nonnegative integer, we get 2^n and δ_{n0}, respectively.

37. When $n > 0$, 2^{n-1}. (The odd and even terms cancel, so each equals half the total sum.)

38. Let $\omega = e^{2\pi i/m}$. Then

$$\sum_{0 \le j < m} (1 + \omega^j)^n \omega^{-jk} = \sum_t \sum_{0 \le j < m} \binom{n}{t} \omega^{j(t-k)}.$$

Now

$$\sum_{0 \le j < m} \omega^{rj} = m\,[r \equiv 0 \;(\text{modulo } m)]$$

(it is the sum of a geometric progression), so the right-hand sum is $m \displaystyle\sum_{t \bmod m = k} \binom{n}{t}$.

The original sum on the left is

$$\sum_{0 \le j < m} (\omega^{-j/2} + \omega^{j/2})^n \omega^{j(n/2-k)} = \sum_{0 \le j < m} \left(2 \cos \frac{j\pi}{m}\right)^n \omega^{j(n/2-k)}.$$

Since the quantity is known to be real, we may take the real part and obtain the stated formula. [See *Crelle* **11** (1834), 353–355.]

The cases $m = 3$ and $m = 5$ have special properties discussed in *CMath*, exercises 5.75 and 6.57.

39. $n!$; $\delta_{n0} - \delta_{n1}$. (The row sums in the second triangle are not so simple; we will find (exercise 64) that $\sum_k \left\{{n \atop k}\right\}$ is the number of ways to partition a set of n elements into disjoint sets, which is the number of equivalence relations on $\{1, 2, \ldots, n\}$.)

40. Proof of (c): By parts,

$$B(x + 1, y) = -\frac{t^x (1 - t)^y}{y}\bigg|_0^1 + \frac{x}{y} \int_0^1 t^{x-1}(1 - t)^y \, dt.$$

Now use (b).

41. $m^x \mathrm{B}(x, m + 1) \to \Gamma(x)$ as $m \to \infty$, regardless of whether m runs through integer values or not (by monotonicity). Hence, $(m + y)^x \mathrm{B}(x, m + y + 1) \to \Gamma(x)$, and $(m/(m + y))^x \to 1$.

42. $1/((r + 1)\mathrm{B}(k + 1, r - k + 1))$, if this is defined according to exercise 41(b). In general when z and w are arbitrary complex numbers we define

$$\binom{z}{w} = \lim_{\zeta \to z} \lim_{\omega \to w} \frac{\zeta!}{\omega!\,(\zeta - \omega)!}, \qquad \text{where } \zeta! = \Gamma(\zeta + 1);$$

the value is infinite when z is a negative integer and w is not an integer.

With this definition, the symmetry condition (6) holds for all complex n and k, except when n is a negative integer and k is an integer; Eqs. (7), (9), and (20) are never false, although they may occasionally take indeterminate forms such as $0 \cdot \infty$ or $\infty + \infty$. Equation (17) becomes

$$\binom{z}{w} = \frac{\sin \pi (w - z - 1)}{\sin \pi z} \binom{w - z - 1}{w}.$$

We can even extend the binomial theorem (13) and Vandermonde's convolution (21), obtaining $\sum_k \binom{r}{\alpha+k} z^{\alpha+k} = (1 + z)^r$ and $\sum_k \binom{r}{\alpha+k}\binom{s}{\beta-k} = \binom{r+s}{\alpha+\beta}$; these formulas hold for all complex r, s, z, α, and β whenever the series converge, provided that complex powers are suitably defined. [See L. Ramshaw, *Inf. Proc. Letters* **6** (1977), 223–226.]

43. $\int_0^1 dt/(t^{1/2}(1-t)^{1/2}) = 2\int_0^1 du/(1-u^2)^{1/2} = 2 \arcsin u\big|_0^1 = \pi.$

45. For large r, $\dfrac{1}{k\Gamma(k)}\sqrt{\dfrac{r}{r-k}}\dfrac{1}{e^k}\dfrac{(1-k/r)^k}{(1-k/r)^r} \to \dfrac{1}{\Gamma(k+1)}.$

46. $\sqrt{\dfrac{1}{2\pi}\left(\dfrac{1}{x}+\dfrac{1}{y}\right)}\left(1+\dfrac{y}{x}\right)^x\left(1+\dfrac{x}{y}\right)^y,$ and $\dbinom{2n}{n} \approx 4^n/\sqrt{\pi n}.$

47. Each quantity is δ_{k0} when $k \le 0$, and is multiplied by $(r-k)(r-\frac{1}{2}-k)/(k+1)^2$ when k is replaced by $k+1$. When $r = -\frac{1}{2}$ this implies $\binom{-1/2}{k} = (-1/4)^k\binom{2k}{k}.$

48. This can be proved by induction, using the fact that

$$0 = \sum_k \binom{n}{k}(-1)^k = \sum_k \binom{n}{k}\frac{(-1)^k k}{k+x} + \sum_k \binom{n}{k}\frac{(-1)^k x}{k+x}$$

when $n > 0$. Alternatively, we have

$$\mathrm{B}(x, n+1) = \int_0^1 t^{x-1}(1-t)^n \, dt = \sum_k \binom{n}{k}(-1)^k \int_0^1 t^{x+k-1} \, dt.$$

(In fact, the stated sum equals $\mathrm{B}(x, n+1)$ for noninteger n also, when the series converges.)

49. $\dbinom{r}{m} = \sum_k \dbinom{r}{k}\dbinom{-r}{m-2k}(-1)^{m+k},$ integer m. (See exercise 17.)

50. The kth summand is $\binom{n}{k}(-1)^{n-k}(x-kz)^{n-1}x$. Apply Eq. (34).

51. The right-hand side is

$$\sum_k \binom{n}{n-k}x(x-kz)^{k-1}\sum_j \binom{n-k}{j}(x+y)^j(-x+kz)^{n-k-j}$$

$$= \sum_j \binom{n}{j}(x+y)^j\sum_k \binom{n-j}{n-j-k}x(x-kz)^{k-1}(-x+kz)^{n-k-j}$$

$$= \sum_{j\le n}\binom{n}{j}(x+y)^j 0^{n-j} = (x+y)^n.$$

The same device may be used to prove Torelli's sum (exercise 34).

Another neat proof of Abel's formula comes from the fact that it is readily transformed into the more symmetric identity derived in exercise 2.3.4.4–29:

$$\sum_k \binom{n}{k}x(x+kz)^{k-1}y(y+(n-k)z)^{n-k-1} = (x+y)(x+y+nz)^{n-1}.$$

Abel's theorem has been generalized even further by A. Hurwitz [*Acta Mathematica* **26** (1902), 199–203] as follows:

$$\sum x(x+\epsilon_1 z_1 + \cdots + \epsilon_n z_n)^{\epsilon_1+\cdots+\epsilon_n-1}(y-\epsilon_1 z_1 - \cdots - \epsilon_n z_n)^{n-\epsilon_1-\cdots-\epsilon_n} = (x+y)^n$$

where the sum is over all 2^n choices of $\epsilon_1, \ldots, \epsilon_n = 0$ or 1 independently. This is an identity in $x, y, z_1, \ldots, z_n$, and Abel's formula is the special case $z_1 = z_2 = \cdots = z_n$. Hurwitz's formula follows from the result in exercise 2.3.4.4–30.

52. $\sum_{k \geq 0}(k+1)^{-2} = \pi^2/6$. [M. L. J. Hautus observes that the sum is absolutely convergent for all complex x, y, z, n whenever $z \neq 0$, since the terms for large k are always of order $1/k^2$. This convergence is uniform in bounded regions, so we may differentiate the series term by term. If $f(x, y, n)$ is the value of the sum when $z = 1$, we find $(\partial/\partial y)f(x, y, n) = nf(x, y, n-1)$ and $(\partial/\partial x)f(x, y, n) = nf(x-1, y+1, n-1)$. These formulas are consistent with $f(x, y, n) = (x+y)^n$; but actually the latter equality seems to hold rarely, if ever, unless the sum is finite. Furthermore the derivative with respect to z is almost always nonzero.]

53. For (b), set $r = \frac{1}{2}$ and $s = -\frac{1}{2}$ in the result of (a).

54. Insert minus signs in a checkerboard pattern as shown.

$$\begin{pmatrix} 1 & -0 & 0 & -0 \\ -1 & 1 & -0 & 0 \\ 1 & -2 & 1 & -0 \\ -1 & 3 & -3 & 1 \end{pmatrix}$$

This is equivalent to multiplying a_{ij} by $(-1)^{i+j}$. The result is the desired inverse, by Eq. (33).

55. Insert minus signs in one triangle, as in the previous exercise, to get the inverse of the other. (Eq. (47).)

56. 210 310 320 321 410 420 421 430 431 432 510 520 521 530 531 532 540 541 542 543 610. With a fixed, b and c run through the combinations of a things two at a time; with a and b fixed, c runs through the combinations of b things one at a time.

    Similarly, we could express all numbers in the form $n = \binom{a}{4} + \binom{b}{3} + \binom{c}{2} + \binom{d}{1}$ with $a > b > c > d \geq 0$; the sequence begins 3210 4210 4310 4320 4321 5210 5310 5320 .... We can find the combinatorial representation by a "greedy" method, first choosing the largest possible a, then the largest possible b for $n - \binom{a}{4}$, etc. [Section 7.2.1.3 discusses further properties of this representation.]

58. [*Systematisches Lehrbuch der Arithmetik 2* (Leipzig: 1811), xxix.] Use induction and

$$\binom{n}{k}_q = \binom{n-1}{k}_q + \binom{n-1}{k-1}_q q^{n-k} = \binom{n-1}{k}_q q^k + \binom{n-1}{k-1}_q.$$

Therefore [F. Schweins, *Analysis* (Heidelberg: 1820), §151] the q-generalization of (21) is

$$\sum_k \binom{r}{k}_q \binom{s}{n-k}_q q^{(r-k)(n-k)} = \sum_k \binom{r}{k}_q \binom{s}{n-k}_q q^{(s-n+k)k} = \binom{r+s}{n}_q.$$

And the identity $1 - q^t = -q^t(1 - q^{-t})$ makes it easy to generalize (17) to

$$\binom{r}{k}_q = (-1)^k \binom{k-r-1}{k}_q q^{kr - k(k-1)/2}.$$

The q-nomial coefficients arise in many diverse applications; see, for example, Section 5.1.2, and the author's note in *J. Combinatorial Theory* **A10** (1971), 178–180.

    Useful facts: When n is a nonnegative integer, $\binom{n}{k}_q$ is a polynomial of degree $k(n-k)$ in q with nonnegative integer coefficients, and it satisfies the reflective laws

$$\binom{n}{k}_q = \binom{n}{n-k}_q = q^{k(n-k)} \binom{n}{k}_{q^{-1}}.$$

If $|q| < 1$ and $|x| < 1$, the q-nomial theorem holds when n is an arbitrary real number, if we replace the left-hand side by $\prod_{k \geq 0}((1 + q^k x)/(1 + q^{n+k}x))$. Properties of power series make it necessary to verify this only when n is a positive integer, because we can set $q^n = y$; the identity has then been verified for infinitely many values of y. Now we can negate the upper index in the q-nomial theorem, obtaining

$$\prod_{k \geq 0} \frac{(1 - q^{k+r+1}x)}{(1 - q^k x)} = \sum_k \binom{-r-1}{k}_q q^{k(k-1)/2}(-q^{r+1}x)^k = \sum_k \binom{k+r}{k}_q x^k.$$

For further information, see G. Gasper and M. Rahman, *Basic Hypergeometric Series* (Cambridge Univ. Press, 1990). The q-nomial coefficients were introduced by Gauss in *Commentationes societatis regiæ scientiarum Gottingensis recentiores* **1** (1808), 147–186; see also Cauchy [*Comptes Rendus Acad. Sci.* **17** (Paris, 1843), 523–531], Jacobi [*Crelle* **32** (1846), 197–204], Heine [*Crelle* **34** (1847), 285–328], and Section 7.2.1.4.

59. $(n+1)\binom{n}{k} - \binom{n}{k+1}$.

60. $\binom{n+k-1}{k}$. This formula can be remembered easily, since it is

$$\frac{n(n+1)\dots(n+k-1)}{k(k-1)\dots 1},$$

like Eq. (2) except that the numbers in the numerator go up instead of down. A slick way to prove it is to note that we want to count the number of integer solutions $(a_1, \dots, a_k)$ to the relations $1 \leq a_1 \leq a_2 \leq \dots \leq a_k \leq n$. This is the same as $0 < a_1 < a_2 + 1 < \dots < a_k + k - 1 < n + k$; and the number of solutions to

$$0 < b_1 < b_2 < \dots < b_k < n + k$$

is the number of choices of k distinct things from the set $\{1, 2, \dots, n+k-1\}$. (This trick is due to H. F. Scherk, *Crelle* **3** (1828), 97; curiously it was also given by W. A. Förstemann in the same journal, **13** (1835), 237, who said "One would almost believe this must have been known long ago, but I have found it nowhere, even though I have consulted many works in this regard.")

61. If a_{mn} is the desired quantity, we have $a_{mn} = na_{m(n-1)} + \delta_{mn}$ by (46) and (47). Hence the answer is $[n \geq m]\, n!/m!$. The same formula is also easily obtained by inversion of (56).

62. Use the identity of exercise 31, with $(m, n, r, s, k) \leftarrow (m+k, l-k, m+n, n+l, j)$:

$$\sum_k (-1)^k \binom{l+m}{l+k}\binom{m+n}{m+k}\binom{n+l}{n+k}$$

$$= \sum_{j,k} (-1)^k \binom{l+m}{l+k}\binom{l+k}{j}\binom{m-k}{l-k-j}\binom{m+n+j}{m+l}$$

$$= \sum_{j,k} (-1)^k \binom{2l-2j}{l-j+k} \frac{(m+n+j)!}{(2l-2j)!\,j!\,(m-l+j)!\,(n+j-l)!},$$

by rearranging the factorial factors. The sum on k now vanishes unless $j = l$.

The case $l = m = n$ of this identity was published by A. C. Dixon [*Messenger of Math.* **20** (1891), 79–80], who established the general case twelve years later [*Proc. London Math. Soc.* **35** (1903), 284–289]. However, L. J. Rogers had already published a much more general formula in the meantime [*Proc. London Math. Soc.* **26** (1895), 15–32, §8]. See also papers by P. A. MacMahon, *Quarterly Journal of Pure and Applied Math.* **33** (1902), 274–288, and John Dougall, *Proc. Edinburgh Math. Society* **25**

(1907), 114–132. The corresponding q-nomial identities are

$$\sum_k \binom{m-r+s}{k}_q \binom{n+r-s}{n-k}_q \binom{r+k}{m+n}_q q^{(m-r+s-k)(n-k)} = \binom{r}{m}_q \binom{s}{n}_q,$$

$$\sum_k (-1)^k \binom{l+m}{l+k}_q \binom{m+n}{m+k}_q \binom{n+l}{n+k}_q q^{(3k^2-k)/2} = \frac{(l+m+n)!_q}{l!_q \, m!_q \, n!_q},$$

where $n!_q = \prod_{k=1}^n (1+q+\cdots+q^{k-1})$.

63. See *CMath*, exercises 5.83 and 5.106.

64. Let $f(n,m)$ be the number of partitions of $\{1,2,\ldots,n\}$ into m parts. Clearly $f(0,m) = \delta_{0m}$. If $n > 0$, the partitionings are of two varieties: (a) The element n alone forms a set of the partition; there are $f(n-1,\, m-1)$ ways to construct partitions like this. (b) The element n appears together with another element; there are m ways to insert n into any m-partition of $\{1,\, 2,\, \ldots,\, n-1\}$, hence there are $mf(n-1,\, m)$ ways to construct partitions like this. We conclude that $f(n,m) = f(n-1,\, m-1) + mf(n-1,\, m)$, and $f(n,m) = \left\{ {n \atop m} \right\}$ by induction.

65. See *AMM* **99** (1992), 410–422.

66. Let $X = \binom{x}{n}$, $\underline{X} = \binom{x}{n-1} = \frac{n}{x-n+1} X$, $\overline{X} = \binom{x}{n+1} = \frac{x-n}{n+1} X$, with similar notations for Y and Z. We may assume that $y \geq n-1$ is fixed, so that x is a function of z.

Let $F(z) = \overline{X} - \overline{Y} - \overline{Z}$, and suppose that $F(z) = 0$ for some $z > n-2$. We will prove that $F'(z) < 0$; therefore $z = y$ must be the only root $> n-2$, proving the second inequality. Since $F(z) = \frac{x-n}{n+1}(Y+Z) - \frac{y-n}{n+1}Y - \frac{z-n+1}{n}Z = 0$ and $x > y$ and $Y, Z > 0$, we must have $\frac{x-n}{n+1} < \frac{z-n+1}{n}$. Setting $X' = dX/dx$ and $Z' = dZ/dz = dX/dz$, we have

$$\frac{X'}{X} = \frac{1}{x} + \frac{1}{x-1} + \cdots + \frac{1}{x-n+1} > \frac{n}{n+1}\left(\frac{1}{z} + \cdots + \frac{1}{z-n+2}\right) = \frac{n}{n+1}\frac{Z'}{Z},$$

since $\frac{x-n+1}{n+1} < \frac{z-n+2}{n}, \ldots, \frac{x-1}{n+1} < \frac{z}{n}$. Thus $dx/dz = Z'/X' < \frac{n+1}{n}(Z/X)$, and

$$F'(z) = \frac{X}{n+1}\frac{dx}{dz} + \frac{x-n}{n+1}Z' - \frac{Z}{n} - \frac{z-n+1}{n}Z' < \left(\frac{x-n}{n+1} - \frac{z-n+1}{n}\right)Z' < 0.$$

To prove the first inequality, we may assume that $n > 2$. Then if $\underline{X} = Y + Z$ for some $z > n-2$, the second inequality tells us that $z = y$.

References: L. Lovász, *Combinatorial Problems and Exercises* (1993), Problem 13.31(a); R. M. Redheffer, *AMM* **103** (1996), 62–64.

67. In fact exercise 1.2.5–24 gives the slightly sharper (but less memorable) upper bounds $\binom{n}{k} = n^{\underline{k}}/k! \leq n^k/k! \leq \frac{1}{e}\left(\frac{ne}{k}\right)^k \leq \left(\frac{ne}{k+1}\right)^k$. The corresponding lower bound is $\binom{n}{k} \geq \left(\frac{(n-k+1)e}{k}\right)^k \frac{1}{ek}$, which is less memorable (but often sharper) than $\binom{n}{k} \geq \left(\frac{n}{k}\right)^k$.

68. Let $t_k = k\binom{n}{k}p^k(1-p)^{n+1-k}$; then $t_k - t_{k+1} = \binom{n}{k}p^k(1-p)^{n-k}(k-np)$. So the stated sum is

$$\sum_{k < \lceil np \rceil} (t_{k+1} - t_k) + \sum_{k \geq \lceil np \rceil} (t_k - t_{k+1}) = 2t_{\lceil np \rceil}.$$

[De Moivre stated this identity in *Miscellanea Analytica* (1730), 101, in the case that np is an integer; H. Poincaré proved the general case in his *Calcul des Probabilités* (1896), 56–60. See P. Diaconis and S. Zabell, *Statistical Science* **6** (1991), 284–302, for the interesting history of this identity and for a variety of similar formulas.]

SECTION 1.2.7

1. 0, 1, and 3/2.

2. Replace each term $1/(2^m + k)$ by the upper bound $1/2^m$.

3. $H_{2^m-1}^{(r)} \leq \sum_{0 \leq k < m} 2^k/2^{kr}$; $2^{r-1}/(2^{r-1} - 1)$ is an upper bound.

4. (b) and (c).

5. 9.78760 60360 44382 ...

6. Induction and Eq. 1.2.6–(46).

7. $T(m+1, n) - T(m, n) = 1/(m+1) - 1/(mn+1) - \cdots - 1/(mn+n) \leq 1/(m+1) - (1/(mn + n) + \cdots + 1/(mn + n)) = 1/(m + 1) - n/(mn + n) = 0$. The maximum value occurs at $m = n = 1$, and the minimum is approached when m and n get very large. By Eq. (3) the greatest lower bound is γ, which is never actually attained. A generalization of this result appears in *AMM* **70** (1963), 575–577.

8. By Stirling's approximation, $\ln n!$ is approximately $(n + \frac{1}{2}) \ln n - n + \ln \sqrt{2\pi}$; also $\sum_{k=1}^n H_k$ is approximately $(n+1) \ln n - n(1-\gamma) + (\gamma + \frac{1}{2})$; the difference is approximately $\gamma n + \frac{1}{2} \ln n + .158$.

9. $(n = 0? \ 0: -1/n)$.

10. Break the left side into two sums; change k to $k + 1$ in the second sum.

11. $2 - H_n/n - 1/n$, for $n > 0$.

12. $1.000 \ldots$ is correct to more than three hundred decimal places.

13. Use induction as in the proof of Theorem A. Or use calculus: Differentiate with respect to x, also evaluate at $x = 1$.

14. See Section 1.2.3, Example 2. The second sum is $\frac{1}{2}(H_{n+1}^2 - H_{n+1}^{(2)})$.

15. $\sum_{j=1}^n (1/j) \sum_{k=j}^n H_k$ can be summed by formulas in the text; the answer comes to $(n + 1)H_n^2 - (2n + 1)H_n + 2n$.

16. $H_{2n} - \frac{1}{2} H_n$.

17. *First solution* (elementary): Taking the denominator to be $(p - 1)!$, which is a multiple of the true denominator but not a multiple of p, we must show only that the corresponding numerator, $(p - 1)!/1 + (p - 1)!/2 + \cdots + (p - 1)!/(p - 1)$, *is* a multiple of p. Modulo p, $(p - 1)!/k \equiv (p - 1)! k'$, where k' can be determined by the relation $kk' \bmod p = 1$. The set $\{1', 2', \ldots, (p - 1)'\}$ is just the set $\{1, 2, \ldots, p - 1\}$; so the numerator is congruent to $(p - 1)! (1 + 2 + \cdots + p - 1) \equiv 0$.

Second solution (advanced): By exercise 4.6.2–6, we have $x^{\bar{p}} \equiv x^p - x$ (modulo p); hence $\begin{bmatrix} p \\ k \end{bmatrix} \equiv \delta_{kp} - \delta_{k1}$, by exercise 1.2.6–32. Now apply exercise 6.

The numerator of H_{p-1} is in fact known to be a multiple of p^2 when $p > 3$; see Hardy and Wright, *An Introduction to the Theory of Numbers*, Section 7.8.

18. If $n = 2^k m$ where m is odd, the sum equals $2^{2k} m_1/m_2$ where m_1 and m_2 are both odd. [*AMM* **67** (1960), 924–925.]

19. Only $n = 0$, $n = 1$. For $n \geq 2$, let $k = \lfloor \lg n \rfloor$. There is precisely one term whose denominator is 2^k, so $2^{k-1} H_n - \frac{1}{2}$ is a sum of terms involving only odd primes in the denominator. If H_n were an integer, $2^{k-1} H_n - \frac{1}{2}$ would have a denominator equal to 2.

20. Expand the integrand term by term. See also *AMM* **69** (1962), 239, and an article by H. W. Gould, *Mathematics Magazine* **34** (1961), 317–321.

21. $H_{n+1}^2 - H_{n+1}^{(2)}$.

22. $(n + 1)(H_n^2 - H_n^{(2)}) - 2n(H_n - 1)$.

23. $\Gamma'(n+1)/\Gamma(n+1) = 1/n + \Gamma'(n)/\Gamma(n)$, since $\Gamma(x+1) = x\Gamma(x)$. Hence $H_n = \gamma + \Gamma'(n+1)/\Gamma(n+1)$. The function $\psi(x) = \Gamma'(x)/\Gamma(x) = H_{x-1} - \gamma$ is called the *psi function* or the *digamma function*. Some values for rational x appear in Appendix A.

24. It is
$$x \lim_{n\to\infty} e^{(H_n - \ln n)x} \prod_{k=1}^{n}\left(\left(1 + \frac{x}{k}\right)e^{-x/k}\right) = \lim_{n\to\infty} \frac{x(x+1)\dots(x+n)}{n^x n!}.$$
Note: The generalization of H_n considered in the previous exercise is therefore equal to $H_x^{(r)} = \sum_{k\geq 0}(1/(k+1)^r - 1/(k+1+x)^r)$, when $r = 1$; the same idea can be used for larger values of r. The infinite product converges for all complex x.

25. $H_n^{(0,v)} = \sum_{k=1}^{n} k^{1-v} = H_n^{(v-1)}$ and $H_n^{(u,0)} = \sum_{k=1}^{n} H_k^{(u)}$; so the identity generalizes (8). [See L. Euler, *Novi Comment. Acad. Sci. Pet.* **20** (1775), 140–186, §2.]

SECTION 1.2.8

1. After k months there are F_{k+2} pairs, so the answer is $F_{14} = 377$ pairs.

2. $\ln(\phi^{1000}/\sqrt{5}) = 1000\ln\phi - \frac{1}{2}\ln 5 = 480.40711$; $\log_{10} F_{1000}$ is $1/(\ln 10)$ times this, or 208.64; F_{1000} is therefore a 209-digit number whose leading digit is 4.

4. 0, 1, 5; afterwards F_n increases too fast.

5. 0, 1, 12.

6. Induction. (The equation holds for *negative* n also; see exercise 8.)

7. If d is a proper divisor of n, F_d divides F_n. Now F_d is greater than one and less than F_n provided d is greater than 2. The only nonprime number greater than 1 that has no proper factor greater than 2 is $n = 4$; $F_4 = 3$ is the only exception.

8. $F_{-1} = 1$; $F_{-2} = -1$; $F_{-n} = (-1)^{n+1}F_n$ by induction on n.

9. Not (15). The others are valid, by an inductive argument that proves something true for $n-1$ assuming it true for n and greater.

10. When n is even, it is greater; when n is odd, it is less. (See Eq. (14).)

11. Induction; see exercise 9. This is a special case of exercise 13(a).

12. If $G(z) = \sum F_n z^n$, $(1 - z - z^2)G(z) = z + F_0 z^2 + F_1 z^3 + \cdots = z + z^2 G(z)$. Hence $G(z) = G(z) + zG(z)^2$; from Eq. (17) we find $F_n = ((3n+3)/5)F_n - (n/5)F_{n+1}$.

13. (a) $a_n = rF_{n-1} + sF_n$. (b) Since $(b_{n+2} + c) = (b_{n+1} + c) + (b_n + c)$, we may consider the new sequence $b'_n = b_n + c$. Applying part (a) to b'_n, we obtain the answer $cF_{n-1} + (c+1)F_n - c$.

14. $a_n = F_{m+n+1} + F_n - \binom{n}{m} - \binom{n+1}{m-1} - \cdots - \binom{n+m}{0}$.

15. $c_n = xa_n + yb_n + (1 - x - y)F_n$.

16. F_{n+1}. Induction, and $\binom{n+1-k}{k} = \binom{n-k}{k} + \binom{(n-1)-(k-1)}{k-1}$.

17. In general, the quantity $(x^{n+k} - y^{n+k})(x^{m-k} - y^{m-k}) - (x^n - y^n)(x^m - y^m)$ is equal to $(xy)^n(x^{m-n-k} - y^{m-n-k})(x^k - y^k)$. Set $x = \phi$, $y = \hat{\phi}$, and divide by $(\sqrt{5})^2$.

18. It is F_{2n+1}.

19. Let $u = \cos 72°$, $v = \cos 36°$. We have $u = 2v^2 - 1$; $v = 1 - 2\sin^2 18° = 1 - 2u^2$. Hence $u + v = 2(v^2 - u^2)$, i.e., $1 = 2(v - u) = 2v - 4v^2 + 2$. We conclude that $v = \frac{1}{2}\phi$. (Also $u = \frac{1}{2}\phi^{-1}$, $\sin 36° = \frac{1}{2}5^{1/4}\phi^{-1/2}$, $\sin 72° = \frac{1}{2}5^{1/4}\phi^{1/2}$. Another interesting angle is $\alpha = \arctan\phi = \frac{\pi}{4} + \frac{1}{2}\arctan\frac{1}{2}$, for which we have $\sin\alpha = 5^{-1/4}\phi^{1/2}$, $\cos\alpha = 5^{-1/4}\phi^{-1/2}$.)

20. $F_{n+2} - 1$.

21. Multiply by $x^2 + x - 1$; the solution is $(x^{n+1} F_{n+1} + x^{n+2} F_n - x)/(x^2 + x - 1)$. If the denominator is zero, x is $1/\phi$ or $1/\hat{\phi}$; then the solution is $(n + 1 - x^n F_{n+1})/(2x + 1)$.

22. F_{m+2n}; set $t = 2$ in the next exercise.

23. $\dfrac{1}{\sqrt{5}} \sum_k \binom{n}{k} (\phi^k F_t^k F_{t-1}^{n-k} \phi^m - \hat{\phi}^k F_t^k F_{t-1}^{n-k} \hat{\phi}^m)$

$$= \frac{1}{\sqrt{5}} (\phi^m (\phi F_t + F_{t-1})^n - \hat{\phi}^m (\hat{\phi} F_t + F_{t-1})^n) = F_{m+tn}.$$

24. F_{n+1} (expand by cofactors in the first row).

25. $2^n \sqrt{5}\, F_n = (1 + \sqrt{5})^n - (1 - \sqrt{5})^n$.

26. By Fermat's theorem, $2^{p-1} \equiv 1$; now apply the previous exercise and exercise 1.2.6–10(b).

27. The statement is true if $p = 2$. Otherwise $F_{p-1} F_{p+1} - F_p^2 = -1$; hence, from the previous exercise and Fermat's theorem, $F_{p-1} F_{p+1} \equiv 0$ (modulo p). Only one of these factors can be a multiple of p, since $F_{p+1} = F_p + F_{p-1}$.

28. $\hat{\phi}^n$. *Note:* The solution to the recurrence $a_{n+1} = Aa_n + B^n$, $a_0 = 0$, is

$$a_n = (A^n - B^n)/(A - B) \text{ if } A \ne B, \qquad a_n = nA^{n-1} \text{ if } A = B.$$

29. (a)

$\binom{n}{0}_{\mathcal{F}}$	$\binom{n}{1}_{\mathcal{F}}$	$\binom{n}{2}_{\mathcal{F}}$	$\binom{n}{3}_{\mathcal{F}}$	$\binom{n}{4}_{\mathcal{F}}$	$\binom{n}{5}_{\mathcal{F}}$	$\binom{n}{6}_{\mathcal{F}}$
1	0	0	0	0	0	0
1	1	0	0	0	0	0
1	1	1	0	0	0	0
1	2	2	1	0	0	0
1	3	6	3	1	0	0
1	5	15	15	5	1	0
1	8	40	60	40	8	1

Part (b) follows from (6). [É. Lucas, *Amer. J. Math.* **1** (1878), 201–204.]

30. We argue by induction on m, the statement being obvious when $m = 1$:

(a) $\displaystyle \sum_k \binom{m}{k}_{\mathcal{F}} (-1)^{\lceil (m-k)/2 \rceil} F_{n+k}^{m-2} F_k = F_m \sum_k \binom{m-1}{k-1}_{\mathcal{F}} (-1)^{\lceil (m-k)/2 \rceil} F_{n+k}^{m-2} = 0.$

(b) $\displaystyle \sum_k \binom{m}{k}_{\mathcal{F}} (-1)^{\lceil (m-k)/2 \rceil} F_{n+k}^{m-2} (-1)^k F_{m-k}$

$$= (-1)^m F_m \sum_k \binom{m-1}{k}_{\mathcal{F}} (-1)^{\lceil (m-1-k)/2 \rceil} F_{n+k}^{m-2} = 0.$$

(c) Since $(-1)^k F_{m-k} = F_{k-1} F_m - F_k F_{m-1}$ and $F_m \ne 0$, we conclude from (a) and (b) that $\sum_k \binom{m}{k}_{\mathcal{F}} (-1)^{\lceil (m-k)/2 \rceil} F_{n+k}^{m-2} F_{k-1} = 0$.

(d) Since $F_{n+k} = F_{k-1} F_n + F_k F_{n+1}$ the result follows from (a) and (c). This result may also be proved in slightly more general form by using the q-nomial theorem of exercise 1.2.6–58. *References:* Dov Jarden, *Recurring Sequences*, 2nd ed. (Jerusalem, 1966), 30–33; J. Riordan, *Duke Math. J.* **29** (1962), 5–12.

31. Use exercise 11.

32. Modulo F_n the Fibonacci sequence is $0, 1, \ldots, F_{n-1}, 0, F_{n-1}, -F_{n-2}, \ldots$.

33. Note that $\cos z = \frac{1}{2}(e^{iz} + e^{-iz}) = -i/2$, for this particular z; then use the fact that $\sin(n+1)z + \sin(n-1)z = 2 \sin nz \cos z$, for all z.

34. Prove that the only possible value for F_{k_1} is the largest Fibonacci number less than or equal to n; hence $n - F_{k_1}$ is less than F_{k_1-1}, and by induction there is a unique representation of $n - F_{k_1}$. The outline of this proof is quite similar to the proof of the unique factorization theorem. The Fibonacci number system is due to E. Zeckendorf [see *Simon Stevin* **29** (1952), 190–195; *Bull. Soc. Royale des Sciences de Liège* **41** (1972), 179–182]; but Section 7.2.1.7 points out that it was implicitly known in 14th-century India. For generalizations, see exercise 4.5.3–52, exercise 5.4.2–10, and Section 7.1.3.

35. See G. M. Bergman, *Mathematics Magazine* **31** (1957), 98–110. To represent $x > 0$, find the largest k with $\phi^k \leq x$ and represent x as ϕ^k plus the representation of $x - \phi^k$.

The representation of nonnegative integers can also be obtained from the following all-integer recursive rules, starting with the trivial representations of 0 and 1: Let $L_n = \phi^n + \hat{\phi}^n = F_{n+1} + F_{n-1}$. The representation of $L_{2n} + m$ for $0 \leq m \leq L_{2n-1}$ and $n \geq 1$ is $\phi^{2n} + \phi^{-2n}$ plus the representation of m. The representation of $L_{2n+1} + m$ for $0 < m < L_{2n}$ and $n \geq 0$ is $\phi^{2n+1} + \phi^{-2n-2}$ plus the representation of $m - \phi^{-2n}$, where the latter is obtained by applying the rule $\phi^k - \phi^{k-2j} = \phi^{k-1} + \phi^{k-3} + \cdots + \phi^{k-2j+1}$. It turns out that all strings α of 0s and 1s, such that α begins with 1 and has no adjacent 1s, occur to the left of the radix point in the representation of exactly one positive integer, except for the strings that end with $10^{2^k}1$; the latter strings never occur in such representations.

36. We may consider the infinite string S_∞, since S_n for $n > 1$ consists of the first F_n letters of S_∞. There are no double a's, no triple b's. The string S_n contains F_{n-2} a's and F_{n-1} b's. If we express $m - 1$ in the Fibonacci number system as in exercise 34, the mth letter of S_∞ is a if and only if $k_r = 2$. The kth letter of S_∞ is b if and only if $\lfloor (k + 1)\phi^{-1} \rfloor - \lfloor k\phi^{-1} \rfloor = 1$; the number of b's in the first k letters is therefore $\lfloor (k + 1)\phi^{-1} \rfloor$. Also, the kth letter is b if and only if $k = \lfloor m\phi \rfloor$ for some positive integer m. This sequence was studied by John Bernoulli III in the 18th century, by A. A. Markov in the 19th, and by many other mathematicians since then; see K. B. Stolarsky, *Canadian Math. Bull.* **19** (1976), 473–482.

37. [*Fibonacci Quarterly* **1**, 4 (December 1963), 9–12.] Consider the Fibonacci number system of exercise 34; if $n = F_{k_1} + \cdots + F_{k_r} > 0$ in that system, let $\mu(n) = F_{k_r}$. Also let $\mu(0) = \infty$. We find that: (A) If $n > 0$, $\mu(n - \mu(n)) > 2\mu(n)$. *Proof:* $\mu(n - \mu(n)) = F_{k_{r-1}} \geq F_{k_r+2} > 2F_{k_r}$ since $k_r \geq 2$. (B) If $0 < m < F_k$, $\mu(m) \leq 2(F_k - m)$. *Proof:* Let $\mu(m) = F_j$; $m \leq F_{k-1} + F_{k-3} + \cdots + F_{j+(k-1-j) \bmod 2} = -F_{j-1+(k-1-j) \bmod 2} + F_k \leq -\frac{1}{2}F_j + F_k$. (C) If $0 < m < \mu(n)$, $\mu(n - \mu(n) + m) \leq 2(\mu(n) - m)$. *Proof:* This follows from (B). (D) If $0 < m < \mu(n)$, $\mu(n - m) \leq 2m$. *Proof:* Set $m = \mu(n) - m$ in (C).

Now we will prove that if there are n chips, and if at most q may be taken in the next turn, there is a winning move if and only if $\mu(n) \leq q$. *Proof:* (a) If $\mu(n) > q$ all moves leave a position n', q' with $\mu(n') \leq q'$. [This follows from (D), above.] (b) If $\mu(n) \leq q$, we can either win on this move (if $q \geq n$) or we can make a move that leaves a position n', q' with $\mu(n') > q'$. [This follows from (A) above: Our move is to take $\mu(n)$ chips.] It can be seen that the set of all winning moves, if $n = F_{k_1} + \cdots + F_{k_r}$, is to remove $F_{k_j} + \cdots + F_{k_r}$, for some j with $1 \leq j \leq r$, provided that $j = 1$ or $F_{k_{j-1}} > 2(F_{k_j} + \cdots + F_{k_r})$.

The Fibonacci representation of 1000 is $987 + 13$; the *only* lucky move to force a victory is to take 13 chips. The first player can always win unless n is a Fibonacci number.

The solution to considerably more general games of this type has been obtained by A. J. Schwenk [*Fibonacci Quarterly* **8** (1970), 225–234, 241].

39. $(3^n - (-2)^n)/5$.

40. We prove, by induction on m, that $f(n) = m$ for $F_m < n \le F_{m+1}$: First, $f(n) \le \max(1 + f(F_m),\, 2 + f(n - F_m)) = m$. Second, if $f(n) < m$ there is some $k < n$ with $1 + f(k) < m$ (hence $k \le F_{m-1}$) and $2 + f(n - k) < m$ (hence $n - k \le F_{m-2}$); but then $n \le F_{m-1} + F_{m-2}$. [Thus the Fibonacci trees defined in Section 6.2.1 minimize the maximum root-to-leaf cost when a right branch costs twice as much as a left branch.]

41. $F_{k_1+1} + \cdots + F_{k_r+1} = \phi n + (\hat\phi^{k_1} + \cdots + \hat\phi^{k_r})$ is an integer, and the parenthesized quantity lies between $\hat\phi^3 + \hat\phi^5 + \cdots = \phi^{-1} - 1$ and $\hat\phi^2 + \hat\phi^4 + \cdots = \phi^{-1}$. Similarly, $F_{k_1-1} + \cdots + F_{k_r-1} = \phi^{-1}n + (\hat\phi^{k_1} + \cdots + \hat\phi^{k_r}) = f(\phi^{-1}n)$. [Such Fibonacci shifting is a convenient way to convert mentally between miles and kilometers; see *CMath*, §6.6.]

42. [*Fibonacci Quarterly* **6** (1968), 235–244.] If such a representation exists, we have

$$mF_{N-1} + nF_N = F_{k_1+N} + F_{k_2+N} + \cdots + F_{k_r+N} \qquad (*)$$

for all integers N; hence two different representations would contradict exercise 34.

Conversely, we can prove the existence of such joint representations for all non-negative m and n by induction. But it is more interesting to use the previous exercise, and to prove that such joint representations exist for possibly negative integers m and n if and only if $m + \phi n \ge 0$: Let N be large enough so that $|m\hat\phi^{N-1} + n\hat\phi^N| < \phi^{-2}$, and represent $mF_{N-1} + nF_N$ as in $(*)$. Then $mF_N + nF_{N+1} = \phi(mF_{N-1} + nF_N) + (m\hat\phi^{N-1} + n\hat\phi^N) = f(\phi(mF_{N-1} + nF_N)) = F_{k_1+N+1} + \cdots + F_{k_r+N+1}$, and it follows that $(*)$ holds for all N. Now set $N = 0$ and $N = 1$.

SECTION 1.2.9

1. $1/(1 - 2z) + 1/(1 - 3z)$.

2. It follows from (6), since $\binom{n}{k} = n!/k!(n-k)!$.

3. $G'(z) = \ln(1/(1 - z))/(1 - z)^2 + 1/(1 - z)^2$. From this and the significance of $G(z)/(1 - z)$, we have $\sum_{k=1}^{n-1} H_k = nH_n - n$; this agrees with Eq. 1.2.7–(8).

4. Put $t = 0$.

5. The coefficient of z^k is, by (11) and (22),

$$\frac{(n-1)!}{k!} \sum_{0 \le j < k} \left\{ {j \atop n-1} \right\} \binom{k}{j}.$$

Now apply Eqs. 1.2.6–(46) and 1.2.6–(52). (Or, differentiate and use 1.2.6–(46).)

6. $(\ln(1/(1 - z)))^2$; the derivative is twice the generating function for the harmonic numbers; the sum is therefore $2H_{n-1}/n$.

8. $1/((1 - z)(1 - z^2)(1 - z^3)\ldots)$. [This is historically one of the first applications of generating functions. For an interesting account of L. Euler's eighteenth-century researches concerning this generating function, see G. Pólya, *Induction and Analogy in Mathematics* (Princeton: Princeton University Press, 1954), Chapter 6.]

9. $\frac{1}{24}S_1^4 + \frac{1}{4}S_1^2 S_2 + \frac{1}{8}S_2^2 + \frac{1}{3}S_1 S_3 + \frac{1}{4}S_4$.

10. $G(z) = (1 + x_1 z)\ldots(1 + x_n z)$. Taking logarithms as in the derivation of Eq. (38), we have the same formulas except that (24) replaces (17), and the answer is exactly the same except that $S_2, S_4, S_6, \ldots$ are replaced by $-S_2, -S_4, -S_6, \ldots$. We have $e_1 = S_1$, $e_2 = \frac{1}{2}S_1^2 - \frac{1}{2}S_2$, $e_3 = \frac{1}{6}S_1^3 - \frac{1}{2}S_1 S_2 + \frac{1}{3}S_3$, $e_4 = \frac{1}{24}S_1^4 - \frac{1}{4}S_1^2 S_2 + \frac{1}{8}S_2^2 + \frac{1}{3}S_1 S_3 - \frac{1}{4}S_4$. (See exercise 9.) The recurrence analogous to (39) is $ne_n = S_1 e_{n-1} - S_2 e_{n-2} + \cdots$.

Note: The equations in this recurrence are called *Newton's identities*, since they were first published in Isaac Newton's *Arithmetica Universalis* (1707); see D. J. Struik's *Source Book in Mathematics* (Harvard University Press, 1969), 94–95.

11. Since $\sum_{m\geq1} S_m z^m/m = \ln G(z) = \sum_{k\geq1}(-1)^{k-1}(h_1 z + h_2 z^2 + \cdots)^k/k$, the desired coefficient is $(-1)^{k_1+k_2+\cdots+k_m-1}m(k_1+k_2+\cdots+k_m-1)!/k_1!\,k_2!\ldots k_m!$. [Multiply by $(-1)^{m-1}$ to get the coefficient of $e_1^{k_1}e_2^{k_2}\ldots e_m^{k_m}$ when S_m is expressed in terms of the e's of exercise 10. Albert Girard stated the formulas for S_1, S_2, S_3, and S_4 in terms of e_1, e_2, e_3, and e_4 near the end of his *Invention Nouvelle en l'Algebre* (Amsterdam: 1629); this was the birth of the theory of symmetric functions.]

12. $\displaystyle\sum_{m,n\geq0} a_{mn}w^m z^n = \sum_{m,n\geq0}\binom{n}{m}w^m z^n = \sum_{n\geq0}(1+w)^n z^n = 1/(1-z-wz).$

13. $\int_n^{n+1} e^{-st} f(t)\,dt = (a_0 + \cdots + a_n)(e^{-sn} - e^{-s(n+1)})/s$. Adding these expressions together for all n, we find $\mathbf{L}f(s) = G(e^{-s})/s$.

14. See exercise 1.2.6–38.

15. $G_n(z) = G_{n-1}(z) + zG_{n-2}(z) + \delta_{n0}$, so we find $H(w) = 1/(1-w-zw^2)$. Hence, ultimately, we find

$$G_n(z) = \left(\left(\frac{1+\sqrt{1+4z}}{2}\right)^{n+1} - \left(\frac{1-\sqrt{1+4z}}{2}\right)^{n+1}\right)\Bigg/\sqrt{1+4z} \quad\text{when } z \neq -\tfrac{1}{4};$$

$G_n(-\tfrac{1}{4}) = (n+1)/2^n$ for $n \geq 0$.

16. $G_{nr}(z) = (1+z+\cdots+z^r)^n = \left(\dfrac{1-z^{r+1}}{1-z}\right)^n.$ [Note the case $r = \infty$.]

17. $\displaystyle\sum_k \binom{-w}{k}(-z)^k = \sum_{k\geq0}\frac{w(w+1)\ldots(w+k-1)}{k(k-1)\ldots1}z^k = \sum_{n,k\geq0}\begin{bmatrix}k\\n\end{bmatrix}z^k w^n/k!.$

(Alternatively, write it as $e^{w\ln(1/(1-z))}$ and expand first by powers of w.)

18. (a) For fixed n and varying r, the generating function is

$$G_n(z) = (1+z)(1+2z)\ldots(1+nz) = z^{n+1}\left(\frac{1}{z}\right)\left(\frac{1}{z}+1\right)\left(\frac{1}{z}+2\right)\ldots\left(\frac{1}{z}+n\right)$$

$$= \sum_k\begin{bmatrix}n+1\\k\end{bmatrix}z^{n+1-k}$$

by Eq. (27). Hence the answer is $\begin{bmatrix}n+1\\n+1-r\end{bmatrix}$. (b) Similarly, the generating function is

$$\frac{1}{1-z}\cdot\frac{1}{1-2z}\cdot\ \cdots\ \cdot\frac{1}{1-nz} = \sum_k\begin{Bmatrix}k\\n\end{Bmatrix}z^{k-n}$$

by Eq. (28), so the answer is $\begin{Bmatrix}n+r\\n\end{Bmatrix}$.

19. $\sum_{n\geq1}(1/n - 1/(n+p/q))x^{p+nq} = \sum_{k=0}^{q-1}\omega^{-kp}\ln(1-\omega^k x) - x^p\ln(1-x^q) + \frac{q}{p}x^p = f(x) + g(x)$, where $\omega = e^{2\pi i/q}$ and

$$f(x) = \sum_{k=1}^{q-1}\omega^{-kp}\ln(1-\omega^k x),\quad g(x) = (1-x^p)\ln(1-x) + \frac{q}{p}x^p - x^p\ln\frac{1-x^q}{1-x}.$$

Now $\lim_{x \to 1-} g(x) = q/p - \ln q$. From the identity

$$\ln(1 - e^{i\theta}) = \ln\left(2e^{i(\theta-\pi)/2}\,\frac{e^{i\theta/2} - e^{-i\theta/2}}{2i}\right) = \ln 2 + \tfrac{1}{2}i(\theta - \pi) + \ln\sin\frac{\theta}{2},$$

we may write $\lim_{x \to 1-} f(x) = f(1) = A + B$ where

$$A = \sum_{k=1}^{q-1} \omega^{-kp}\left(\ln 2 - \frac{i\pi}{2} + \frac{ik\pi}{q}\right) = -\ln 2 + \frac{i\pi}{2} + \frac{i\pi}{(\omega^{-p} - 1)};$$

$$B = \sum_{k=1}^{q-1} \omega^{-kp} \ln\sin\frac{k}{q}\pi = \sum_{0 < k < q/2} (\omega^{-kp} + \omega^{-(q-k)p})\ln\sin\frac{k}{q}\pi$$

$$= 2 \sum_{0 < k < q/2} \cos\frac{2pk}{q}\pi \cdot \ln\sin\frac{k}{q}\pi.$$

Finally,

$$\frac{i}{2} + \frac{i}{(\omega^{-p} - 1)} = \frac{i}{2}\left(\frac{1 + \omega^p}{1 - \omega^p}\right) = -\frac{i}{2}\left(\frac{\omega^{p/2} + \omega^{-p/2}}{\omega^{p/2} - \omega^{-p/2}}\right) = -\frac{1}{2}\cot\frac{p}{q}\pi.$$

[Gauss derived these results in §33 of his monograph on hypergeometric series, Eq. [75], but with insufficient proof; Abel provided a justification in *Crelle* **1** (1826), 314–315.]

20. $c_{mk} = k!\left\{{m \atop k}\right\}$, by Eq. 1.2.6–(45).

21. We find $z^2 G'(z) + zG(z) = G(z) - 1$. The solution to this differential equation is $G(z) = (-1/z)\,e^{-1/z}\big(E_1(-1/z) + C\big)$, where $E_1(z) = \int_z^\infty e^{-t}\,dt/t$ and C is a constant. This function is very ill-behaved in the neighborhood of $z = 0$, and $G(z)$ has no power series expansion. Indeed, since $\sqrt[n]{n!} \approx n/e$ is not bounded, the generating function does not converge in this case; it is, however, an asymptotic expansion for the stated function, when $z < 0$. [See K. Knopp, *Theory and Application of Infinite Series*, 2nd ed. (Glasgow: Blackie, 1951), Section 66.]

22. $G(z) = (1 + z)^r(1 + z^2)^r(1 + z^4)^r(1 + z^8)^r \ldots = (1 - z)^{-r}$. It follows that the stated sum is $\binom{r+n-1}{n}$.

23. (a) When $m = 1$ this is the binomial theorem, with $f_1(z) = z$ and $g_1(z) = 1 + z$. When $m \geq 1$ we can increase m by 1 if we replace z_m by $z_m(1 + z_{m+1}^{-1})$ and let $f_{m+1}(z_1, \ldots, z_{m+1}) = z_{m+1}f_m(z_1, \ldots, z_{m-1}, z_m(1 + z_{m+1}^{-1}))$, $g_{m+1}(z_1, \ldots, z_{m+1}) = z_{m+1}g_m(z_1, \ldots, z_{m-1}, z_m(1 + z_{m+1}^{-1}))$. Thus $g_2(z_1, z_2) = z_1 + z_2 + z_1 z_2$ and

$$\frac{g_m(z_1, \ldots, z_m)}{f_m(z_1, \ldots, z_m)} = 1 + \cfrac{z_1^{-1}}{1 + \cfrac{z_2^{-1}}{1 + \cfrac{\ddots}{1 + z_m^{-1}}}}.$$

Both polynomials f_m and g_m satisfy the same recurrence $f_m = z_m f_{m-1} + z_{m-1}f_{m-2}$, $g_m = z_m g_{m-1} + z_{m-1}g_{m-2}$, with the initial conditions $f_{-1} = 0$, $f_0 = g_{-1} = g_0 = z_0 = 1$. It follows that g_m is the sum of all terms obtainable by starting with $z_1 \ldots z_m$ and striking out zero or more nonadjacent factors; there are F_{m+2} ways to do this. A similar interpretation applies to f_m, except that z_1 must remain. In part (b) we will encounter the polynomial $h_m = z_m g_{m-1} + z_{m-1}f_{m-2}$; this is the sum of all terms obtained from $z_1 \ldots z_m$ by striking out factors that are not *cyclically* adjacent. For example, $h_3 = z_1 z_2 z_3 + z_1 z_2 + z_1 z_3 + z_2 z_3$.

(b) By part (a), $S_n(z_1, \ldots, z_{m-1}, z) = [z_m^n] \sum_{r=0}^{n} z^r z_m^{n-r} f_m^{n-r} g_m^r$; hence

$$S_n(z_1, \ldots, z_m) = \sum_{0 \le s \le r \le n} \binom{r}{s} \binom{n-r}{s} a^{r-s} b^s c^s d^{n-r-s},$$

where $a = z_m g_{m-1}$, $b = z_{m-1} g_{m-2}$, $c = z_m f_{m-1}$, $d = z_{m-1} f_{m-2}$. Multiplying this equation by z^n and summing first on n, then on r, then on s, yields the closed form

$$S_n(z_1, \ldots, z_m) = [z^n] \frac{1}{(1-az)(1-dz) - bcz^2} = \frac{\rho^{n+1} - \sigma^{n+1}}{\rho - \sigma},$$

where $1 - (a+d)z + (ad - bc)z^2 = (1 - \rho z)(1 - \sigma z)$. Here $a + d = h_m$, and $ad - bc$ simplifies to $(-1)^m z_1 \ldots z_m$. [We have, incidentally, established the recurrence $S_n = h_m S_{n-1} - (-1)^m z_1 \ldots z_m S_{n-2}$, a relation that is not easy to derive without the help of generating functions.]

(c) Let $\rho_1 = (z + \sqrt{z^2 + 4z})/2$ and $\sigma_1 = (z - \sqrt{z^2 + 4z})/2$ be the roots when $m = 1$; then $\rho_m = \rho_1^m$ and $\sigma_m = \sigma_1^m$.

Carlitz used this result to deduce a surprising fact: The characteristic polynomial $\det(xI - A)$ of the $n \times n$ matrix

$$A = \begin{pmatrix} 0 & 0 & \cdots & 0 & \binom{0}{0} \\ 0 & 0 & \cdots & \binom{1}{0} & \binom{1}{1} \\ \vdots & \vdots & \ddots & \vdots & \vdots \\ \binom{n-1}{0} & \binom{n-1}{1} & \cdots & \binom{n-1}{n-2} & \binom{n-1}{n-1} \end{pmatrix}$$

of "right justified binomial coefficients" is $\sum_k \binom{n}{k}_{\mathcal{F}} (-1)^{\lceil (n-k)/2 \rceil} x^k$, with Fibonomial coefficients (see exercise 1.2.8–30). He also showed, using similar methods, that

$$\sum_{k_1, \ldots, k_m \ge 0} \binom{k_1 + k_2}{k_1} \binom{k_2 + k_3}{k_2} \cdots \binom{k_m + k_1}{k_m} z_1^{k_1} \ldots z_m^{k_m}$$

$$= \frac{1}{\sqrt{z_1^2 \ldots z_m^2 \, h_m(-z_1^{-1}, \ldots, -z_m^{-1})^2 - 4z_1 \ldots z_m}}.$$

[*Collectanea Mathematica* **17** (1965), 281–296.]

24. Both sides are equal to $\sum_k \binom{m}{k} [z^n](zG(z))^k$. When $G(z) = 1/(1-z)$, the identity becomes $\sum_k \binom{m}{k}\binom{n-1}{n-k} = \binom{m+n-1}{n}$, a case of 1.2.6–(21). When $G(z) = (e^z - 1)/z$, it becomes $\sum_k m^k \{ {n \atop k} \} = m^n$, Eq. 1.2.6–(45).

25. $\sum_k [w^k](1-2w)^n [z^n] z^k (1+z)^{2n-2k} = [z^n] (1+z)^{2n} \sum_k [w^k](1-2w)^n (z/(1+z)^2)^k$, which equals $[z^n] (1+z)^{2n} (1 - 2z/(1+z)^2)^n = [z^n] (1 + z^2)^n = \binom{n}{n/2}[n$ even$]$. Similarly, we find $\sum_k \binom{n}{k}\binom{2n-2k}{n-k}(-4)^k = (-1)^n \binom{2n}{n}$. Many examples of this summation technique can be found in G. P. Egorychev's book *Integral Representation and the Computation of Combinatorial Sums* (Amer. Math. Soc., 1984), translated from the Russian edition of 1977.

26. $[F(z)] G(z)$ denotes the constant term of $F(z^{-1})G(z)$. See the discussion by D. E. Knuth in *A Classical Mind* (Prentice–Hall, 1994), 247–258.

SECTION 1.2.10

1. $G_n(0) = 1/n$; this is the probability that $X[n]$ is the largest.

2. $G''(1) = \sum_k k(k-1)p_k$, $G'(1) = \sum_k kp_k$.

3. (min 0, ave 6.49, max 999, dev 2.42). Note that $H_n^{(2)}$ is approximately $\pi^2/6$; see Eq. 1.2.7–(7).

4. $\binom{n}{k}p^k q^{n-k}$.

5. The mean is $36/5 = 7.2$; the standard deviation is $6\sqrt{2}/5 \approx 1.697$.

6. For (18), the formula

$$\ln(q + pe^t) = \ln\left(1 + pt + \frac{pt^2}{2} + \frac{pt^3}{6} + \cdots\right) = pt + p(1-p)\frac{t^2}{2} + p(1-p)(1-2p)\frac{t^3}{6} + \cdots$$

tells us that $\kappa_3/n = p(1-p)(1-2p) = pq(q-p)$. (This nice pattern does not continue to the coefficient of t^4.) Setting $p = k^{-1}$ gives us $\kappa_3 = \sum_{k=2}^{n} k^{-1}(1-k^{-1})(1-2k^{-1}) = H_n - 3H_n^{(2)} + 2H_n^{(3)}$ in the case of distribution (8). And for (20), we have $\ln G(e^t) = t + H(nt) - H(t)$ where $H(t) = \ln((e^t - 1)/t)$. Since $H'(t) = 1/(1 - e^{-t}) - 1/t$, we have $\kappa_r = (n^r - 1)B_r/r$ for all $r \geq 2$ in this case; in particular, $\kappa_3 = 0$.

7. The probability that $A = k$ is p_{mk}. For we may consider the values to be $1, 2, \ldots, m$. Given any partitioning of the n positions into m disjoint sets, there are $m!$ ways to assign the numbers $1, \ldots, m$ to these sets. Algorithm M treats these values as if only the rightmost element of each set were present; so p_{mk} is the average for any fixed partitioning. For example, if $n = 5$, $m = 3$, one partition is

$$\{X[1], X[4]\} \quad \{X[2], X[5]\} \quad \{X[3]\};$$

the arrangements possible are 12312, 13213, 21321, 23123, 31231, 32132. In every partition we get the same percentage of arrangements with $A = k$.

On the other hand, the probability distribution does change if more information is given. If $n = 3$ and $m = 2$, for example, our argument in the previous paragraph considers the six possibilities 122, 212, 221, 211, 121, 112; if we know that there are two 2s and one 1, then only the first three of these possibilities should be considered. But this interpretation is not consistent with the statement of the exercise.

8. $M^{\underline{n}}/M^n$. The larger M is, the closer this probability gets to one.

9. Let q_{nm} be the probability that exactly m distinct values occur; then from the recurrence

$$q_{nm} = \frac{M - m + 1}{M} q_{(n-1)(m-1)} + \frac{m}{M} q_{(n-1)m}$$

we deduce that

$$q_{nm} = M! \left\{ {n \atop m} \right\} \Big/ (M - m)! \, M^n.$$

See also exercise 1.2.6–64.

10. This is $q_{nm}p_{mk}$ summed over all m, namely $M^{-n} \sum_m \binom{M}{m} \left\{ {n \atop m} \right\} \left[{m \atop k+1} \right]$. There does not appear to be a simple formula for the average, which is one less than

$$H_M - \sum_{m=1}^{M} \left(1 - \frac{m}{M}\right)^n m^{-1} = H_n + \sum_{k=1}^{n} \left(\binom{n}{k} - 1 \right) B_k M^{-k} k^{-1} - \frac{n-1}{M}.$$

11. Since this is a product, we add the semi-invariants of each term. If $H(z) = z^n$, $H(e^t) = e^{nt}$, so we find $\kappa_1 = n$ and all others are zero. Therefore, mean$(F) = n +$

mean(G), and all other semi-invariants are unchanged. (This accounts for the name "semi-invariant.")

12. The first identity is obvious by writing out the power series for e^{kt}. For the second, let $u = 1 + M_1 t + M_2 t^2/2! + \cdots$; when $t = 0$ we have $u = 1$ and $D_t^k u = M_k$. Also, $D_u^j(\ln u) = (-1)^{j-1}(j-1)!/u^j$. By exercise 11, the same formula applies for central moments except that we leave out all terms with $k_1 > 0$; thus $\kappa_2 = m_2$, $\kappa_3 = m_3$, $\kappa_4 = m_4 - 3m_2^2$.

13. $G_n(z) = \dfrac{\Gamma(n+z)}{\Gamma(z+1)n!} = \dfrac{e^{-z}(n+z)^{z-1}}{\Gamma(z+1)}\left(1+\dfrac{z}{n}\right)^n (1+O(n^{-1})) = \dfrac{n^{z-1}}{\Gamma(z+1)}(1+O(n^{-1})).$

Let $z_n = e^{it/\sigma_n}$. When $n \to \infty$ and t is fixed, we have $z_n \to 1$; hence $\Gamma(z_n + 1) \to 1$, and

$$\lim_{n\to\infty} z_n^{-\mu_n} G_n(z_n) = \lim_{n\to\infty} \exp\left(\frac{-it\mu_n}{\sigma_n} + (e^{it/\sigma_n} - 1)\ln n\right)$$

$$= \lim_{n\to\infty} \exp\left(\frac{-t^2 \ln n}{2\sigma_n^2} + O\left(\frac{1}{\sqrt{\log n}}\right)\right) = e^{-t^2/2}.$$

Notes: This is a theorem of Goncharov [*Izv. Akad. Nauk SSSR Ser. Math.* **8** (1944), 3–48]. P. Flajolet and M. Soria [*Disc. Math.* **114** (1993), 159–180] have extended the analysis to show that $G_n(z)$ and a large family of related distributions not only are approximately normal near their mean values, they also have uniformly exponential tails, in the sense that

$$\Pr\left(\left|\frac{X_n - \mu_n}{\sigma_n}\right| > x\right) < e^{-ax}$$

for some positive constant a and for all n and x.

14. $e^{-itpn/\sqrt{pqn}}(q + pe^{it/\sqrt{pqn}})^n = (qe^{-itp/\sqrt{pqn}} + pe^{itq/\sqrt{pqn}})^n$. Expand the exponentials in power series, to get $(1 - t^2/2n + O(n^{-3/2}))^n = \exp(n\ln(1 - t^2/2n + O(n^{-3/2}))) = \exp(-t^2/2 + O(n^{-1/2})) \to \exp(-t^2/2)$.

15. (a) $\sum_{k\geq 0} e^{-\mu}(\mu z)^k/k! = e^{\mu(z-1)}$. (b) $\ln e^{\mu(e^t-1)} = \mu(e^t - 1)$, so all semi-invariants equal μ. (c) $\exp(-itnp/\sqrt{np})\exp(np(it/\sqrt{np} - t^2/(2np) + O(n^{-3/2}))) = \exp(-t^2/2 + O(n^{-1/2}))$.

16. $g(z) = \sum_k p_k g_k(z)$; mean$(g) = \sum_k p_k$ mean(g_k); and var$(g) = \sum_k p_k$ var$(g_k) + \sum_{j<k} p_j p_k (\text{mean}(g_j) - \text{mean}(g_k))^2$.

17. (a) The coefficients of $f(z)$ and $g(z)$ are nonnegative, and $f(1) = g(1) = 1$. Clearly $h(z)$ shares these same characteristics, since $h(1) = g(f(1))$, and the coefficients of h are polynomials in those of f and g, with nonnegative coefficients.

(b) Let $f(z) = \sum p_k z^k$ where p_k is the probability that some event yields a "score" of k. Let $g(z) = \sum q_k z^k$ where q_k is the probability that the event described by f happens exactly k times (each occurrence of the event being independent of the others). Then $h(z) = \sum r_k z^k$, where r_k is the probability that the sum of the scores of the events that occurred is equal to k. (This is easy to see if we observe that $f(z)^k = \sum s_t z^t$, where s_t is the probability that a total score t is obtained in k independent occurrences of the event.) *Example:* If f gives the probabilities that a woman has k female offspring, and if g gives the probabilities that there are k females in the nth generation, then h gives the probabilities that there are k females in the $(n + 1)$st generation, assuming independence.

(c) mean$(h) = \text{mean}(g)\,\text{mean}(f)$; var$(h) = \text{var}(g)\,\text{mean}^2(f) + \text{mean}(g)\,\text{var}(f)$.

18. Consider the choice of $X[1], \ldots, X[n]$ as a process in which we first place all the n's, then place all the $(n-1)$'s among these n's, $\ldots$, finally place the ones among the rest. As we place the r's among the numbers $\{r+1, \ldots, n\}$, the number of local maxima from right to left increases by one if and only if we put an r at the extreme right. This happens with probability $k_r/(k_r + k_{r+1} + \cdots + k_n)$.

19. Let $a_k = l$. Then a_k is a left-to-right max of $a_1 \ldots a_n \iff j < k$ implies $a_j < l \iff a_j > l$ implies $j > k \iff j > l$ implies $b_j > k \iff k$ is a right-to-left min of $b_1 \ldots b_n$.

20. We have $m_L = \max\{a_1 - b_1, \ldots, a_n - b_n\}$. *Proof:* If not, let k be the smallest subscript such that $a_k - b_k > m_L$. Then a_k is not a left-to-right maximum, so there is a $j < k$ with $a_j \geq a_k$. But then $a_j - b_j \geq a_k - b_k > m_L$, contradicting the minimality of k. Similarly, $m_R = \max\{b_1 - a_1, \ldots, b_n - a_n\}$.

21. The result is trivial when $\epsilon \geq q$, so we may assume that $\epsilon < q$. Setting $x = \frac{p+\epsilon}{p} \frac{q}{q-\epsilon}$ in (25) gives $\Pr(X \geq n(p+\epsilon)) \leq ((\frac{p}{p+\epsilon})^{p+\epsilon} (\frac{q}{q-\epsilon})^{q-\epsilon})^n$. Now $(\frac{p}{p+\epsilon})^{p+\epsilon} \leq e^{-\epsilon}$ since $t \leq e^{t-1}$ for all real t. And $(q-\epsilon)\ln \frac{q}{q-\epsilon} = \epsilon - \frac{1}{2\cdot 1}\epsilon^2 q^{-1} - \frac{1}{3\cdot 2}\epsilon^3 q^{-2} - \cdots \leq \epsilon - \frac{1}{2q}\epsilon^2$. (A more detailed analysis yields the slightly stronger estimate $\exp(-\epsilon^2 n/(2pq))$ when $p \geq \frac{1}{2}$. Still further work yields the upper bound $\exp\left(-\sum_{k\geq 1} 2^{2k-1}\epsilon^{2k}/(2k^2 - k)\right) \leq \exp(-2\epsilon^2 n)$, valid for all p.)

By reversing the roles of heads and tails we find

$$\Pr(X \leq n(p-\epsilon)) = \Pr(n - X \geq n(q+\epsilon)) \leq e^{-\epsilon^2 n/(2p)}.$$

(One should not confuse "tails" with the tail of a probability distribution.)

22. (a) Set $x = r$ in (24) and (25), and note that $q_k + p_k r = 1 + (r-1)p_k \leq e^{(r-1)p_k}$. [See H. Chernoff, *Annals of Math. Stat.* **23** (1952), 493–507.]

(b) Let $r = 1 + \delta$ where $|\delta| \leq 1$. Then $r^{-r}e^{r-1} = \exp(-\frac{1}{2\cdot 1}\delta^2 + \frac{1}{3\cdot 2}\delta^3 - \cdots)$, which is $\leq e^{-\delta^2/2}$ when $\delta \leq 0$ and $\leq e^{-\delta^2/3}$ when $\delta \geq 0$. The slightly more complicated bound $e^{-\delta^2/(2+\delta)}$ can be used for all $\delta \geq 0$, because $2\delta/(2+\delta) \leq \ln(1+\delta)$.

(c) The function $r^{-1}e^{1-1/r}$ decreases from 1 to 0 as r increases from 1 to ∞. If $r \geq 2$ it is $\leq e^{1/2}/2 < .825$; if $r \geq 4.32$ it is $< 1/2$.

Incidentally, the tail inequalities with $x = r$ give precisely the same estimate $(r^{-r}e^{r-1})^\mu$ when X has the Poisson distribution of exercise 15.

23. Setting $x = \frac{p-\epsilon}{p} \frac{q}{q-\epsilon}$ in (24) gives $\Pr(X \leq n(p-\epsilon)) \leq ((\frac{p}{p-\epsilon})^{p-\epsilon}(\frac{q-\epsilon}{q})^{q-\epsilon})^n \leq e^{-\epsilon^2 n/(2pq)}$. Similarly, $x = \frac{p+\epsilon}{p}\frac{q}{q+\epsilon}$ yields $\Pr(X \geq n(p+\epsilon)) \leq ((\frac{p}{p+\epsilon})^{p+\epsilon}(\frac{q+\epsilon}{q})^{q+\epsilon})^n$. Let $f(\epsilon) = (q+\epsilon)\ln(1+\frac{\epsilon}{q}) - (p+\epsilon)\ln(1+\frac{\epsilon}{p})$, and note that $f'(\epsilon) = \ln(1+\frac{\epsilon}{q}) - \ln(1+\frac{\epsilon}{p})$. It follows that $f(\epsilon) \leq -\epsilon^2/(6pq)$ if $0 \leq \epsilon \leq p$.

SECTION 1.2.11.1

1. Zero.

2. Each O-symbol represents a different approximate quantity; since the left-hand side might be $f(n) - (-f(n)) = 2f(n)$, the best we can say is $O(f(n)) - O(f(n)) = O(f(n))$, which follows from (6) and (7). To prove (7), note that if $|x_n| \leq M|f(n)|$ for $n \geq n_0$ and $|x'_n| \leq M'|f(n)|$ for $n \geq n'_0$, then $|x_n \pm x'_n| \leq |x_n| + |x'_n| \leq (M+M')|f(n)|$ for $n \geq \max(n_0, n'_0)$. (Signed, J. H. Quick, student.)

3. $n(\ln n) + \gamma n + O(\sqrt{n}\ln n)$.

4. $\ln a + (\ln a)^2/2n + (\ln a)^3/6n^2 + O(n^{-3})$.

5. If $f(n) = n^2$ and $g(n) = 1$, then n belongs to the set $O(f(n) + g(n))$ but not to the set $f(n) + O(g(n))$. So the statement is false.

6. A variable number, n, of O-symbols has been replaced by a single O-symbol, falsely implying that a single value of M will suffice for each term $|kn| \leq Mn$. The given sum is actually $\Theta(n^3)$, as we know. The last equality, $\sum_{k=1}^{n} O(n) = O(n^2)$, is perfectly valid.

7. If x is positive, the power series 1.2.9–(22) tells us that $e^x > x^{m+1}/(m+1)!$; hence the ratio of e^x/x^m is unbounded by any M.

8. Replace n by e^n and apply the method of the previous exercise.

9. If $|f(z)| \leq M|z|^m$ for $|z| \leq r$, then $|e^{f(z)}| \leq e^{M|z|^m} = 1 + |z|^m (M + M^2|z|^m/2! + M^3|z|^{2m}/3! + \cdots) \leq 1 + |z|^m (M + M^2 r^m/2! + M^3 r^{2m}/3! + \cdots)$.

10. $\ln(1 + O(z^m)) = O(z^m)$, if m is a positive integer. *Proof:* If $f(z) = O(z^m)$, there exist positive numbers $r < 1$, $r' < 1$, and a constant M such that $|f(z)| \leq M|z|^m \leq r'$ when $|z| \leq r$. Then $|\ln(1 + f(z))| \leq |f(z)| + \frac{1}{2}|f(z)|^2 + \cdots \leq |z|^m M (1 + \frac{1}{2}r' + \cdots)$.

11. We can apply Eq. (12) with $m = 1$ and $z = \ln n/n$. This is justified since $\ln n/n \leq r$ for any given $r > 0$, when n is sufficiently large.

12. Let $f(z) = (ze^z/(e^z - 1))^{1/2}$. If $\left[\begin{smallmatrix} 1/2 \\ 1/2-k \end{smallmatrix}\right]$ were $O(n^k)$, the stated identity would show that $[z^k] f(z) = O(n^k/(k-1)!)$, so $f(z)$ would converge when $z = 2\pi i$. But $f(2\pi i) = \infty$.

13. *Proof:* We may take $L = 1/M$ in the definitions of O and Ω.

SECTION 1.2.11.2

1. $(B_0 + B_1 z + B_2 z^2/2! + \cdots)e^{-z} = (B_0 + B_1 z + B_2 z^2/2! + \cdots) - z$; use Eq. 1.2.9–(11).

2. The function $B_{m+1}(\{x\})$ must be continuous, for the integration by parts.

3. $|R_{mn}| \leq |B_m/m!| \int_1^n |f^{(m)}(x)| \, dx$. [*Notes:* We have $B_m(x) = (-1)^m B_m(1-x)$, and $B_m(x)$ is $m!$ times the coefficient of z^m in $ze^{xz}/(e^z - 1)$. In particular, since $e^{z/2}/(e^z - 1) = 1/(e^{z/2} - 1) - 1/(e^z - 1)$ we have $B_m(\frac{1}{2}) = (2^{1-m} - 1)B_m$. It is not difficult to prove that the maximum of $|B_m - B_m(x)|$ for $0 \leq x \leq 1$ occurs at $x = \frac{1}{2}$ when m is even. Now when $m = 2k \geq 4$, let us write simply R_m and C_m for the quantities R_{mn} and C_{mn}. We have $R_{m-2} = C_m + R_m = \int_1^n (B_m - B_m(\{x\}))f^{(m)}(x) \, dx/m!$, and $B_m - B_m(\{x\})$ is between 0 and $(2 - 2^{1-m})B_m$; hence R_{m-2} lies between 0 and $(2 - 2^{1-m})C_m$. It follows that R_m lies between $-C_m$ and $(1 - 2^{1-m})C_m$, a slightly stronger result. According to this argument we see that if $f^{(m+2)}(x) f^{(m+4)}(x) > 0$ for $1 < x < n$, the quantities C_{m+2} and C_{m+4} have opposite signs, while R_m has the sign of C_{m+2} and R_{m+2} has the sign of C_{m+4} and $|R_{m+2}| \leq |C_{m+2}|$; this proves (13). See J. F. Steffensen, *Interpolation* (Baltimore: 1927), §14.]

4. $S_m(n) = \dfrac{n^{m+1}}{1+m} + 0^m + \sum_{k=1}^{m} \dfrac{B_k}{k!} m^{\underline{k-1}} n^{m-k+1} = \dfrac{B_{m+1}(n+1) - B_{m+1}}{m+1} + 0^m$.

5. It follows that

$$\kappa = \sqrt{2} \lim_{n \to \infty} \frac{2^{2n}(n!)^2}{\sqrt{n}\,(2n)!};$$

$$\kappa^2 = \lim_{n \to \infty} \frac{2}{n} \frac{n^2(n-1)^2 \ldots (1)^2}{(n-\frac{1}{2})^2(n-\frac{3}{2})^2 \ldots (\frac{1}{2})^2} = 4 \frac{2 \cdot 2 \cdot 4 \cdot 4 \cdot \cdots}{1 \cdot 3 \cdot 3 \cdot 5 \cdot \cdots} = 2\pi.$$

6. Assume that $c > 0$ and consider $\sum_{0 \leq k \leq n} \ln(k + c)$. We find

$$\ln(c(c+1)\ldots(c+n)) = (n+c)\ln(n+c) - c\ln c - n + \tfrac{1}{2}\ln(n+c) + \tfrac{1}{2}\ln c$$

$$+ \sum_{1 < k \leq m} \frac{B_k(-1)^k}{k(k-1)} \left(\frac{1}{(n+c)^{k-1}} - \frac{1}{c^{k-1}} \right) + R_{mn}.$$

Also

$$\ln n! = (n + \tfrac{1}{2}) \ln n - n + \sigma + \sum_{1 < k \le m} \frac{B_k(-1)^k}{k(k-1)} \left(\frac{1}{n^{k-1}}\right) - \frac{1}{m} \int_n^\infty \frac{B_m(\{x\})\,dx}{x^m}.$$

Now let $\Gamma_m(x) = m^x m!/x^{\overline{m+1}}$, so that $\ln \Gamma_n(c) = c \ln n + \ln n! - \ln(c(c+1)\dots(c+n))$; substituting and letting $n \to \infty$, we get

$$\ln \Gamma(c) = -c + (c - \tfrac{1}{2}) \ln c + \sigma + \sum_{1 < k \le m} \frac{B_k(-1)^k}{k(k-1)c^{k-1}} - \frac{1}{m} \int_0^\infty \frac{B_m(\{x\})\,dx}{(x+c)^m}.$$

This shows that $\Gamma(c+1) = ce^{\ln \Gamma(c)}$ has the same expansion we derived for $c!$.

7. $A\,n^{n^2/2+n/2+1/12}e^{-n^2/4}$ where A is a constant. To obtain this result, apply Euler's summation formula to $\sum_{k=1}^n k \ln k$. A more accurate formula is obtained if we multiply the answer above by

$$\exp\bigl(-B_4/(2 \cdot 3 \cdot 4n^2) - \cdots - B_{2t}/((2t-2)(2t-1)(2t)n^{2t-2}) + O(1/n^{2t})\bigr).$$

In these formulas, A is the "Kinkelin–Glaisher constant" $1.2824271\ldots$ [*Crelle* **57** (1860), 122–138; *Messenger of Math.* **7** (1877), 43–47], which can be shown to equal $e^{1/12-\zeta'(-1)} = (2\pi e^{\gamma-\zeta'(2)/\zeta(2)})^{1/12}$ [de Bruijn, *Asymptotic Methods in Analysis*, §3.7].

8. We have, for example, $\ln(an^2 + bn) = 2 \ln n + \ln a + \ln(1 + b/(an))$. Thus the answer to the first question is found to be $2an^2 \ln n + a(\ln a - 1)n^2 + 2bn \ln n + bn \ln a + \ln n + b^2/(2a) + \tfrac{1}{2} \ln a + \sigma + (3a - b^2)b/(6a^2 n) + O(n^{-2})$. Massive cancellation occurs when we compute the quantity $\ln(cn^2)! - \ln(cn^2 - n)! - n \ln c - \ln n^2! + \ln(n^2 - n)! = (c-1)/(2c) - (c-1)(2c-1)/(6c^2 n) + O(n^{-2})$. The answer is therefore

$$e^{(c-1)/(2c)} \left(1 - \frac{(c-1)(2c-1)}{6c^2 n}\right)(1 + O(n^{-2})).$$

Incidentally, $\binom{cn^2}{n}/\bigl(c^n \binom{n^2}{n}\bigr)$ can be written $\prod_{j=1}^{n-1}\bigl(1 + \alpha j/(n^2 - j)\bigr)$ where $\alpha = 1 - 1/c$.

9. (a) We have $\ln(2n)! = (2n + \tfrac{1}{2}) \ln 2n - 2n + \sigma + \frac{1}{24n} + O(n^{-3})$, and $\ln(n!)^2 = (2n+1) \ln n - 2n + 2\sigma + \frac{1}{6n} + O(n^{-3})$; hence $\binom{2n}{n} = \exp(2n \ln 2 - \tfrac{1}{2} \ln \pi n - \frac{1}{8n} + O(n^{-3})) = 2^{2n}(\pi n)^{-1/2}(1 - \tfrac{1}{8}n^{-1} + \frac{1}{128}n^{-2} + O(n^{-3}))$. (b) Since $\binom{2n}{n} = 2^{2n}\binom{n-1/2}{n}$ and $\binom{n-1/2}{n} = \Gamma(n+1/2)/(n\Gamma(n)\Gamma(1/2)) = n^{-1}n^{\overline{1/2}}/\sqrt{\pi}$, we obtain the same result from 1.2.11.1–(16) because

$$\begin{bmatrix} 1/2 \\ 1/2 \end{bmatrix} = 1, \quad \begin{bmatrix} 1/2 \\ -1/2 \end{bmatrix} = \binom{1/2}{2} = -\frac{1}{8}, \quad \begin{bmatrix} 1/2 \\ -3/2 \end{bmatrix} = \binom{1/2}{4} + 2\binom{3/2}{4} = \frac{1}{128}.$$

Method (b) explains why the denominators in

$$\binom{2n}{n} = \frac{2^{2n}}{\sqrt{\pi n}}\left(1 - \frac{n^{-1}}{8} + \frac{n^{-2}}{128} + \frac{5n^{-3}}{1024} - \frac{21n^{-4}}{32768} - \frac{399n^{-5}}{262144} + \frac{869n^{-6}}{4194304} + O(n^{-7})\right)$$

are all powers of 2 [Knuth and Vardi, *AMM* **97** (1990), 629–630].

SECTION 1.2.11.3

1. Integrate by parts.

2. Substitute the series for e^{-t} in the integral.

3. See Eq. 1.2.9–(11) and exercise 1.2.6–48.

4. $1 + 1/u$ is bounded as a function of v, since it goes to zero as v goes from r to infinity. Replace it by M and the resulting integral is Me^{-rx}.

5. $f''(x) = f(x)((n+1/2)(n-1/2)/x^2 - (2n+1)/x + 1)$ changes sign at the point $r = n + 1/2 - \sqrt{n+1/2}$, so $|R| = O(\int_0^r |f''(x)| dx) = O(\int_0^r f''(x) dx - \int_r^n f''(x) dx) = O(f'(n) - 2f'(r) + f'(0)) = O(f(n)/\sqrt{n})$.

6. It is $n^{n+\beta} \exp((n+\beta)(\alpha/n - \alpha^2/2n^2 + O(n^{-3})))$, etc.

7. The integrand as a power series in x^{-1} has the coefficient of x^{-n} as $O(u^{2n})$. After integration, terms in x^{-3} are $Cu^7/x^3 = O(x^{-5/4})$, etc. To get $O(x^{-2})$ in the answer, we can discard terms u^n/x^m with $4m - n \geq 9$. Thus, an expansion of the product $\exp(-u^2/2x) \exp(u^3/3x^2) \dots$ leads ultimately to the answer

$$yx^{1/4} - \frac{y^3}{6}x^{-1/4} + \frac{y^5}{40}x^{-3/4} + \frac{y^4}{12}x^{-1} - \frac{y^7}{336}x^{-5/4} - \frac{y^6}{36}x^{-3/2} + \left(\frac{y^9}{3456} - \frac{y^5}{20}\right)x^{-7/4} + O(x^{-2}).$$

8. (Solution by Miklós Simonovits.) We have $|f(x)| < x$ if x is large enough. Let $R(x) = \int_0^{f(x)} (e^{-g(u,x)} - e^{-h(u,x)}) du$ be the difference between the two given integrals, where $g(u,x) = u - x \ln(1 + u/x)$ and $h(u,x) = u^2/2x - u^3/3x^2 + \dots + (-1)^m u^m/mx^{m-1}$. Notice that $g(u,x) \geq 0$ and $h(u,x) \geq 0$ when $|u| < x$; also $g(u,x) = h(u,x) + O(u^{m+1}/x^m)$.

According to the mean value theorem, $e^a - e^b = (a-b)e^c$ for some c between a and b. Therefore $|e^a - e^b| \leq |a - b|$ when $a, b \leq 0$. It follows that

$$|R(x)| \leq \int_{-|f(x)|}^{|f(x)|} |g(u,x) - h(u,x)| du = O\left(\int_{-Mx^r}^{Mx^r} \frac{u^{m+1} du}{x^m}\right)$$

$$= O(x^{(m+2)r-m}) = O(x^{-s}).$$

9. We may assume that $p \neq 1$, since $p = 1$ is given by Theorem A. We also assume that $p \neq 0$, since the case $p = 0$ is trivial.

Case 1: $p < 1$. Substitute $t = px(1 - u)$ and then $v = -\ln(1 - u) - pu$. We have $dv = ((1 - p + pu)/(1 - u)) du$, so the transformation is monotone for $0 \leq u \leq 1$, and we obtain an integral of the form

$$\int_0^\infty xe^{-xv} dv \left(\frac{1-u}{1 - p + pu}\right).$$

Since the parenthesized quantity is $(1-p)^{-1}(1 - v(1-p)^{-2} + \dots)$, the answer is

$$\frac{p}{1-p}(pe^{1-p})^x \frac{e^{-x}x^x}{\Gamma(x+1)}\left(1 - \frac{1}{(p-1)^2 x} + O(x^{-2})\right).$$

Case 2: $p > 1$. This is $1 - \int_{px}^\infty(\ )$. In the latter integral, substitute $t = px(1+u)$, then $v = pu - \ln(1 + u)$, and proceed as in Case 1. The answer turns out to be the same formula as Case 1, plus one. Notice that $pe^{1-p} < 1$, so $(pe^{1-p})^x$ is *very* small.

The answer to exercise 11 gives another way to solve this problem.

10. $\dfrac{p}{p-1}(pe^{1-p})^x e^{-x}x^x \left(1 - e^{-y} - \dfrac{e^{-y}(e^y - 1 - y - y^2/2)}{x(p-1)^2} + O(x^{-2})\right).$

11. First, $xQ_x(n) + R_{1/x}(n) = n! (x/n)^n e^{n/x}$ generalizes (4). Next, we have $R_x(n) = n! (e^x/nx)^n \gamma(n, nx)/(n-1)!$, generalizing (9). Since $a\gamma(a, x) = \gamma(a+1, x) + e^{-x}x^a$ we can also write $R_x(n) = 1 + (e^x/nx)^n \gamma(n+1, nx)$, relating this problem to exercise 9.

Moreover, we can tackle $Q_x(n)$ and $R_x(n)$ directly by using Eqs. 1.2.9–(27) and (28) to derive series expansions involving Stirling numbers:

$$1 + xQ_x(n) = \sum_{k \geq 0} x^k n^{\underline{k}}/n^k = \sum_{k,m \geq 0} \frac{(-1)^m}{n^m} \begin{bmatrix} k \\ k-m \end{bmatrix} x^k;$$

$$R_x(n) = \sum_{k \geq 0} x^k n^k/(n+1)^{\overline{k}} = \sum_{k,m \geq 0} \frac{(-1)^m}{n^m} \begin{Bmatrix} k+m \\ k \end{Bmatrix} x^k.$$

The sums over k are convergent for fixed m when $|x| < 1$, and when $|x| > 1$ we can use the relation between $Q_x(n)$ and $R_{1/x}(n)$; this leads to the formulas

$$Q_x(n) = \frac{1}{1-x} - \frac{x}{(1-x)^3 n} + \cdots + \frac{(-1)^m q_m(x)}{(1-x)^{2m+1} n^m} + O(n^{-1-m}),$$

$$R_x(n) = \frac{1}{1-x} - \frac{x}{(1-x)^3 n} + \cdots + \frac{(-1)^m r_m(x)}{(1-x)^{2m+1} n^m} + O(n^{-1-m}), \quad \text{if } x < 1;$$

$$Q_x(n) = \frac{n!\, x^{n-1} e^{n/x}}{n^n} + \frac{1}{1-x} - \frac{x}{(1-x)^3 n} + \cdots + \frac{(-1)^m q_m(x)}{(1-x)^{2m+1} n^m} + O(n^{-1-m}),$$

$$R_x(n) = \frac{n!\, e^{nx}}{n^n x^n} + \frac{1}{1-x} - \frac{x}{(1-x)^3 n} + \cdots + \frac{(-1)^m r_m(x)}{(1-x)^{2m+1} n^m} + O(n^{-1-m}), \quad \text{if } x > 1.$$

Here

$$q_m(x) = \left\langle\!\!\left\langle \begin{matrix} m \\ 0 \end{matrix} \right\rangle\!\!\right\rangle x^{2m-1} + \left\langle\!\!\left\langle \begin{matrix} m \\ 1 \end{matrix} \right\rangle\!\!\right\rangle x^{2m-2} + \cdots$$

and

$$r_m(x) = \left\langle\!\!\left\langle \begin{matrix} m \\ 0 \end{matrix} \right\rangle\!\!\right\rangle x + \left\langle\!\!\left\langle \begin{matrix} m \\ 1 \end{matrix} \right\rangle\!\!\right\rangle x^2 + \cdots$$

are polynomials whose coefficients are "second-order Eulerian numbers" [*CMath* §6.2; see L. Carlitz, *Proc. Amer. Math. Soc.* **16** (1965), 248–252]. The case $x = -1$ is somewhat delicate, but it can be handled by continuity, because the bound implied by $O(n^{-1-m})$ is independent of x when $x < 0$. It is interesting to note that $R_{-1}(n) - Q_{-1}(n) = (-1)^n n!/(e^n n^n) \approx (-1)^n \sqrt{2\pi n}/e^{2n}$ is extremely small.

12. $\gamma(\frac{1}{2}, \frac{1}{2}x^2)/\sqrt{2}$.

13. See P. Flajolet, P. Grabner, P. Kirschenhofer, and H. Prodinger, *J. Computational and Applied Math.* **58** (1995), 103–116.

15. Expanding the integrand by the binomial theorem, we obtain $1 + Q(n)$.

16. Write $Q(k)$ as a sum, and interchange the order of summation using Eq. 1.2.6–(53).

17. $S(n) = \sqrt{\pi n/2} + \frac{2}{3} - \frac{1}{24}\sqrt{\pi/2n} - \frac{4}{135}n^{-1} + \frac{49}{1152}\sqrt{\pi/2n^3} + O(n^{-2})$. [Note that $S(n+1) + P(n) = \sum_{k \geq 0} k^{n-k} k!/n!$, while $Q(n) + R(n) = \sum_{k \geq 0} n!/k!\, n^{n-k}$.]

18. Let $S_n(x,y) = \sum_k \binom{n}{k}(x+k)^k(y+n-k)^{n-k}$. Then for $n > 0$ we have $S_n(x,y) = x\sum_k \binom{n}{k}(x+k)^{k-1}(y+n-k)^{n-k} + n\sum_k \binom{n-1}{k}(x+1+k)^k(y+n-1-k)^{n-1-k} = (x+y+n)^n + nS_{n-1}(x+1, y)$ by Abel's formula 1.2.6–(16); consequently $S_n(x,y) = \sum_k \binom{n}{k}k!\,(x+y+n)^{n-k}$. [This formula is due to Cauchy, who proved it using the calculus of residues; see his *Œuvres* (2) **6**, 62–73.] The stated sums are therefore equal respectively to $n^n(1 + Q(n))$ and $(n+1)^n Q(n+1)$.

19. Suppose C_n exists for all $n \geq N$ and $|f(x)| \leq Mx^\alpha$ for $0 \leq x \leq r$. Let $F(x) = \int_r^x e^{-Nt} f(t)\, dt$. Then when $n > N$ we have

$$|C_n| \leq \int_0^r e^{-nx} |f(x)|\, dx + \left| \int_r^\infty e^{-(n-N)x} e^{-Nx} f(x)\, dx \right|$$

$$\leq M \int_0^r e^{-nx} x^\alpha\, dx + (n-N) \left| \int_r^\infty e^{-(n-N)x} F(x)\, dx \right|$$

$$\leq M \int_0^\infty e^{-nx} x^\alpha\, dx + (n-N) \sup_{x \geq r} |F(x)| \int_r^\infty e^{-(n-N)x}\, dx$$

$$= M\Gamma(\alpha+1) n^{-1-\alpha} + \sup_{x \geq r} |F(x)| e^{-(n-N)r} = O(n^{-1-\alpha}).$$

[E. W. Barnes, *Phil. Trans.* **A206** (1906), 249–297; G. N. Watson, *Proc. London Math. Soc.* (2) **17** (1918), 116–148.]

20. [C. C. Rousseau, *Applied Math. Letters* **2** (1989), 159–161.] We have $Q(n) + 1 = n \int_0^\infty e^{-nx} (1+x)^n\, dx = n \int_0^\infty e^{-n(x-\ln(1+x))}\, dx = n \int_0^\infty e^{-nu} g(u)\, du$, by substituting $u = x - \ln(1+x)$ and letting $g(u) = dx/du$. Notice that $x = \sum_{k=1}^\infty c_k (2u)^{k/2}$ when u is sufficiently small. Hence $g(u) = \sum_{k=1}^{m-1} k c_k (2u)^{k/2-1} + O(u^{m/2-1})$, and we can apply Watson's lemma to $Q(n) + 1 - n \int_0^\infty e^{-nu} \sum_{k=1}^{m-1} k c_k (2u)^{k/2-1}\, du$.

SECTION 1.3.1

1. Four; each byte would then contain $3^4 = 81$ different values.

2. Five, since five bytes is always adequate but four is not.

3. (0:2); (3:3); (4:4); (5:5).

4. Presumably index register 4 contains a value greater than or equal to 2000, so that a valid memory address results after indexing.

5. 'DIV -80,3(0:5)' or simply 'DIV -80,3'.

6. (a) rA ← | - | 5 | 1 | 200 | 15 |. (b) rI2 ← −200. (c) rX ← | + | 0 | 0 | 5 | 1 | ? |. (d) Undefined; we can't load such a big value into an index register. (e) rX ← | - | 0 | 0 | 0 | 0 | 0 |.

7. Let $n = |\text{rAX}|$ be the magnitude of registers A and X before the operation, and let $d = |V|$ be the magnitude of the divisor. After the operation the magnitude of rA is $\lfloor n/d \rfloor$, and the magnitude of rX is $n \bmod d$. The sign of rX afterwards is the previous sign of rA; the sign of rA afterwards is + if the previous signs of rA and V were the same, otherwise it is −.

Stating this another way: If the signs of rA and V are the same, rA ← $\lfloor \text{rAX}/V \rfloor$ and rX ← rAX mod V. Otherwise rA ← $\lceil \text{rAX}/V \rceil$ and rX ← rAX mod −V.

8. rA ← | + | 0 | 617 | 0 | 1 |; rX ← | - | 0 | 0 | 0 | 1 | 1 |.

9. ADD, SUB, DIV, NUM, JOV, JNOV, INCA, DECA, INCX, DECX.

10. CMPA, CMP1, CMP2, CMP3, CMP4, CMP5, CMP6, CMPX. (Also FCMP, for floating point.)

11. MOVE, LD1, LD1N, INC1, DEC1, ENT1, ENN1.

12. INC3 0,3.

13. 'JOV 1000' makes no difference except time. 'JNOV 1001' makes a different setting of rJ in most cases. 'JNOV 1000' makes an extraordinary difference, since it may lock the computer in an infinite loop.

14. NOP with anything; ADD, SUB with F = (0:0) or with address equal to * (the location of the instruction) and F = (3:3); HLT (depending on how you interpret the statement of the exercise); any shift with address and index zero; SLC or SRC with index 0 and address a multiple of 10; MOVE with F = 0; STJ *(0:0), STZ *(0:0), and STZ *(3:3); JSJ *+1; any of the INC or DEC instructions with address and index zero. But 'ENT1 0,1' is not always a no-op, because it might change rI1 from −0 to +0.

15. 70; 80; 120. (The block size times 5.)

16. (a) STZ 0; ENT1 1; MOVE 0(49); MOVE 0(50). If the byte size were known to equal 100, only one MOVE instruction would have been necessary, but we are not allowed to make assumptions about the byte size. (b) Use 100 STZ's.

17. (a) STZ 0,2; DEC2 1; J2NN 3000.

```
      (b)     STZ   0
              ENT1  1
              JMP   3004
      (3003)  MOVE  0(63)
      (3004)  DEC2  63
              J2P   3003
              INC2  63
              ST2   3008(4:4)
      (3008)  MOVE  0          ∎
```

(A slightly faster, but quite preposterous, program uses 993 STZ's: JMP 3995; STZ 1,2; STZ 2,2; ...; STZ 993,2; J2N 3999; DEC2 993; J2NN 3001; ENN1 0,2; JMP 3000,1.)

18. (If you have correctly followed the instructions, an overflow will occur on the ADD, with minus zero in register A afterwards.) *Answer:* Overflow is set on, comparison is set EQUAL, rA is set to $\boxed{-\;30\;30\;30\;30\;30}$, rX is set to $\boxed{-\;31\;30\;30\;30\;30}$, rI1 is set to +3, and memory locations 0001, 0002 are set to +0. (Unless the program itself begins in location 0000.)

19. $42u = (2 + 1 + 2 + 2 + 1 + 1 + 1 + 2 + 2 + 1 + 2 + 2 + 3 + 10 + 10)u.$

20. (Solution by H. Fukuoka.)

```
      (3991)  ENT1  0
              MOVE  3995     (standard F for MOVE is 1)
      (3993)  MOVE  0(43)    (3999 = 93 times 43)
              JMP   3993
      (3995)  HLT   0        ∎
```

21. (a) Not unless it can be set to zero by external means (see the "GO button," exercise 26), since a program can set rJ ← N only by jumping from location N − 1.

```
      (b)     LDA   -1,4
              LDX   3004
              STX   -1,4
              JMP   -1,4
      (3004)  JMP   3005
      (3005)  STA   -1,4      ∎
```

22. *Minimum time:* If b is the byte size, the assumption that $|X^{13}| < b^5$ implies that $X^2 < b$, so X^2 can be contained in one byte. The following ingenious solution due to Y. N. Patt makes use of this fact. The sign of rA is the sign of X.

```
(3000) LDA  2000
       MUL  2000(1:5)
       STX  3500(1:1)
```

Instruction	rA					rX				
SRC 1	X^2	0	0	0	0	0	0	0	0	0
MUL 3500	X^4		0	0	0	0	0	0	0	0
STA 3501	X^4		0	0	0	0	0	0	0	0
ADD 2000	X^4		0	0	X	0	0	0	0	0
MUL 3501(1:5)	X^8				0	X^5		0	0	0
STX 3501	X^8				0	X^5		0	0	0
MUL 3501(1:5)	0	X^{13}					0	0	0	0
SLAX 1	X^{13}					0	0	0	0	0

```
       HLT  0
(3500) NOP  0
(3501) NOP  0  ∎
```

space $= 14$; time $= 54u$, not counting the HLT.

At least five multiplications are "necessary," according to the theory developed in Section 4.6.3, yet this program uses only four! And in fact there is an even better solution below.

Minimum space:
```
       (3000) ENT4 12        DEC4 1
              LDA  2000       J4P  3002
       (3002) MUL  2000       HLT  0  ∎
              SLAX 5            space = 7; time = 171u.
```

True minimum time: As R. W. Floyd points out, the conditions imply that $|X| \le 5$, so the minimum execution time is achieved by referring to a table:

```
(3000) LD1  2000
       LDA  3500,1
       HLT  0
(3495) (-5)^13       [This line needed only when b > 65.]
(3496) (-4)^13
       ⋮
(3505) (+5)^13       [This line needed only when b > 65.]  ∎
```

space $= 14$; time $= 4u$.

23. First, by R. D. Dixon: Second, by George Wahid, if rA ≥ 0:

```
(3000) ENT1 4        DEC1 1          (3000) ENT1 5:5      DEC1 1:1
(3001) LDA  200      J1NN 3001       (3001) SLA  1        J1P  3001
       SRA  0,1      SLAX 5                 ST1  3003(4:4) HLT  0  ∎
       SRAX 1        HLT  0  ∎        (3003) ADD  200(*)
```

24. (a) DIV 3500, where 3500 = `+ | 1 | 0 | 0 | 0 | 0`.

(b) SRC 4; SRA 1; SLC 5.

25. Some ideas: (a) Obvious things like faster memory, more input-output devices. (b) The I field could be used for J-register indexing, and/or multiple indexing (to specify two different index registers) and/or "indirect addressing" (exercises 2.2.2–3, 4, 5). (c) Index registers and J register could be extended to a full five bytes; therefore locations with higher addresses could be referred to only by indexing, but that would not be so intolerable if multiple indexing were available as in (b). (d) An interrupt capability could be added, using negative memory addresses as in exercise 1.4.4–18. (e) A "real time clock" could be added, in a negative memory address. (f) Bitwise operations, jumps on register even or odd, and binary shifts could be added to binary versions of MIX (see, for example, exercises 2.5–28, 5.2.2–12, and 6.3–9; also Program 4.5.2B, 6.4–(24), and Section 7.1). (g) An "execute" command, meaning to perform the instruction at location M, could be another variant of C = 5. (h) Another variant of C = 48, . . . , 55 could set CI ← register : M.

26. It is tempting to use a (2:5) field to get at columns 7–10 of the card, but this cannot be done since $2 \cdot 8 + 5 = 21$. To make the program easier to follow, it is presented here in symbolic language, anticipating Section 1.3.2.

					characters punched on card:
	BUFF	EQU	29	Buffer area is 0029–0044	
		ORIG	0		
00	LOC	IN	16(16)	Read in second card.	␣0␣06
01	READ	IN	BUFF(16)	Read next card.	␣Z␣06
02		LD1	0(0:0)	rI1 ← 0.	␣␣␣␣I
03		JBUS	*(16)	Wait for read to finish.	␣C␣04
04		LDA	BUFF+1	rA ← columns 6–10.	␣0␣EH
05	=1=	SLA	1		␣A␣␣F
06		SRAX	6	rAX ← columns 7–10.	␣F␣CF
07	=30=	NUM	30		␣0␣␣E
08		STA	LOC	LOC ← starting location.	␣␣␣EU
09		LDA	BUFF+1(1:1)		␣0␣IH
10		SUB	=30=(0:2)		␣G␣BB
11	LOOP	LD3	LOC	rI3 ← LOC.	␣␣␣EJ
12		JAZ	0,3	Jump, if transfer card.	␣␣CA.
13		STA	BUFF	BUFF ← count.	␣Z␣EU
14		LDA	LOC		␣␣␣EH
15		ADD	=1=(0:2)		␣E␣BA
16		STA	LOC	LOC ← LOC + 1.	␣␣␣EU
17		LDA	BUFF+3,1(5:5)		␣2A–H
18		SUB	=25=(0:2)		␣S␣BB
19		STA	0,3(0:0)	Store the sign.	␣␣C␣U
20		LDA	BUFF+2,1		␣1AEH
21		LDX	BUFF+3,1		␣2AEN
22	=25=	NUM	25		␣V␣␣E
23		STA	0,3(1:5)	Store the magnitude.	␣␣CLU
24		MOVE	0,1(2)	rI1 ← rI1 + 2. (!)	␣␣ABG
25		LDA	BUFF		␣Z␣EH
26		SUB	=1=(0:2)	Decrease the count.	␣E␣BB
27		JAP	LOOP	Repeat until the count is zero.	␣J␣B.
28		JMP	READ	Now read a new card.	␣A␣␣9

SECTION 1.3.2

1. ENTX 1000; STX X.

2. The STJ instruction in line 03 resets this address. (It is conventional to denote the address of such instructions by '*', both because it is simple to write, and because it provides a recognizable test of an error condition in a program, in case a subroutine has not been entered properly because of some oversight. Some people prefer '*-*'.)

3. Read in 100 words from tape unit zero; exchange their maximum with the last of them; exchange the maximum of the remaining 99 with the last of those; etc. Eventually the 100 words will become completely sorted into nondecreasing order. The result is then written onto tape unit one. (Compare with Algorithm 5.2.3S.)

4. Nonzero locations:

3000:	+	0000	00	18	35
3001:	+	2051	00	05	09
3002:	+	2050	00	05	10
3003:	+	0001	00	00	49
3004:	+	0499	01	05	26
3005:	+	3016	00	01	41
3006:	+	0002	00	00	50
3007:	+	0002	00	02	51
3008:	+	0000	00	02	48
3009:	+	0000	02	02	55
3010:	−	0001	03	05	04
3011:	+	3006	00	01	47
3012:	−	0001	03	05	56
3013:	+	0001	00	00	51
3014:	+	3008	00	06	39
3015:	+	3003	00	00	39
3016:	+	1995	00	18	37
3017:	+	2035	00	02	52
3018:	−	0050	00	02	53
3019:	+	0501	00	00	53
3020:	−	0001	05	05	08

3021:	+	0000	00	01	05
3022:	+	0000	04	12	31
3023:	+	0001	00	01	52
3024:	+	0050	00	01	53
3025:	+	3020	00	02	45
3026:	+	0000	04	18	37
3027:	+	0024	04	05	12
3028:	+	3019	00	00	45
3029:	+	0000	00	02	05
0000:	+				2
1995:	+	06	09	19	22	23
1996:	+	00	06	09	25	05
1997:	+	00	08	24	15	04
1998:	+	19	05	04	00	17
1999:	+	19	09	14	05	22
2024:	+				2035
2049:	+				2010
2050:	+				3
2051:	−				499

(the latter two may be interchanged, with corresponding changes to 3001 and 3002)

5. Each OUT waits for the previous printer operation to finish (from the other buffer).

6. (a) If n is not prime, by definition n has a divisor d with $1 < d < n$. If $d > \sqrt{n}$, then n/d is a divisor with $1 < n/d < \sqrt{n}$. (b) If N is not prime, N has a *prime* divisor d with $1 < d \le \sqrt{N}$. The algorithm has verified that N has no prime divisors $\le p = $ PRIME[K]; also $N = pQ + R < pQ + p \le p^2 + p < (p+1)^2$. Any prime divisor of N is therefore greater than $p + 1 > \sqrt{N}$.

We must also prove that there will be a sufficiently large prime less than N when N is prime, namely that the $(k+1)$st prime p_{k+1} is less than $p_k^2 + p_k$; otherwise K would exceed J and PRIME[K] would be zero when we needed it to be large. The necessary proof follows from "Bertrand's postulate": If p is prime there is a larger prime less than $2p$.

7. (a) It refers to the location of line 29. (b) The program would then fail; line 14 would refer to line 15 instead of line 25; line 24 would refer to line 15 instead of line 12.

8. It prints 100 lines. If the 12000 characters on these lines were arranged end to end, they would reach quite far and would consist of five blanks followed by five A's followed by ten blanks followed by five A's followed by fifteen blanks ... followed by $5k$ blanks followed by five A's followed by $5(k+1)$ blanks ... until 12000 characters have been printed. The third-from-last line ends with AAAAA and 35 blanks; the final two lines are entirely blank. The total effect is one of OP art.

9. The $(4:4)$ field of each entry in the following table holds the maximum F setting; the $(1:2)$ field is the location of an appropriate validity-check routine.

```
B     EQU  1(4:4)           BEGIN LDA  INST
BMAX  EQU  B-1                    CMPA VALID(3:3)
UMAX  EQU  20                     JG   BAD          I field > 6?
TABLE NOP  GOOD(BMAX)              LD1  INST(5:5)
      ADD  FLOAT(5:5)             DEC1 64
      SUB  FLOAT(5:5)             J1NN BAD          C field ≥ 64?
      MUL  FLOAT(5:5)             CMPA TABLE+64,1(4:4)
      DIV  FLOAT(5:5)             JG   BAD          F field > F max?
      HLT  GOOD                   LD1  TABLE+64,1(1:2) Jump to special
      SRC  GOOD                   JMP  0,1             routine.
      MOVE MEMORY(BMAX)    FLOAT CMPA VALID(4:4)    F = 6 allowed on
      LDA  FIELD(5:5)            JE   MEMORY           arithmetic op
      ...                 FIELD ENTA 0
      STZ  FIELD(5:5)            LDX  INST(4:4)      This is a tricky
      JBUS MEMORY(UMAX)         DIV  =9=              way to check
      IOC  GOOD(UMAX)           STX  *+1(0:2)         for a valid
      IN   MEMORY(UMAX)         INCA 0                partial field.
      OUT  MEMORY(UMAX)         DECA 5
      JRED MEMORY(UMAX)         JAP  BAD
      JLE  MEMORY         MEMORY LDX  INST(3:3)
      JANP MEMORY                JXNZ GOOD           If I = 0,
      ...                       LDX  INST(0:2)        ensure the
      JXNP MEMORY               JXN  BAD              address is a
      ENNA GOOD                 DECX 3999            valid memory
      ...                       JXNP GOOD            location.
      ENNX GOOD                 JMP  BAD
      CMPA FLOAT(5:5)     VALID CMPX 3999,6(6)       ▌
      CMP1 FIELD(5:5)
      ...
      CMPX FIELD(5:5)
```

10. The catch to this problem is that there may be several places in a row or column where the minimum or maximum occurs, and each is a potential saddle point.

Solution 1: In this solution we run through each row in turn, making a list of all columns in which the row minimum occurs and then checking each column on the list to see if the row minimum is also a column maximum. rX ≡ current min; rI1 traces through the matrix, going from 72 down to zero unless a saddle point is found; rI2 ≡ column index of rI1; rI3 ≡ size of list of minima. Notice that in all cases the terminating condition for a loop is that an index register is ≤ 0.

```
       * SOLUTION 1
A10       EQU   1008        Location of a₁₀
LIST      EQU   1000

START     ENT1  9*8         Begin at the lower right corner.
ROWMIN    ENT2  8           Now rI1 is at column 8 of its row.
2H        LDX   A10,1       Candidate for row minimum
          ENT3  0           List empty
4H        INC3  1
          ST2   LIST,3      Put column index in list.
1H        DEC1  1           Go left one.
          DEC2  1
          J2Z   COLMAX      Done with row?
3H        CMPX  A10,1
          JL    1B          Is rX still minimum?
          JG    2B          New minimum?
          JMP   4B          Remember another minimum.
COLMAX    LD2   LIST,3      Get column from list.
          INC2  9*8-8
1H        CMPX  A10,2
          JL    NO          Is row min < column element?
          DEC2  8
          J2P   1B          Done with column?
YES       INC1  A10+8,2     Yes; rI1 ← address of saddle.
          HLT
NO        DEC3  1           Is list empty?
          J3P   COLMAX      No; try again.
          J1P   ROWMIN      Have all rows been tried?
          HLT               Yes; rI1 = 0, no saddle.  ▮
```

Solution 2: An infusion of mathematics gives a different algorithm.

Theorem. *Let* $R(i) = \min_j a_{ij}$, $C(j) = \max_i a_{ij}$. *The element* $a_{i_0 j_0}$ *is a saddle point if and only if* $R(i_0) = \max_i R(i) = C(j_0) = \min_j C(j)$.

Proof. If $a_{i_0 j_0}$ is a saddle point, then for any fixed i, $R(i_0) = C(j_0) \geq a_{i j_0} \geq R(i)$; so $R(i_0) = \max_i R(i)$. Similarly $C(j_0) = \min_j C(j)$. Conversely, we have $R(i) \leq a_{ij} \leq C(j)$ for all i and j; hence $R(i_0) = C(j_0)$ implies that $a_{i_0 j_0}$ is a saddle point. ▮

(This proof shows that we always have $\max_i R(i) \leq \min_j C(j)$. So there is no saddle point if and only if all the R's are less than all the C's.)

According to the theorem, it suffices to find the smallest column maximum, then to search for an equal row minimum. During Phase 1, rI1 ≡ column index; rI2 runs through the matrix. During Phase 2, rI1 ≡ possible answer; rI2 runs through the matrix; rI3 ≡ row index times 8; rI4 ≡ column index.

```
        * SOLUTION 2
        CMAX    EQU   1000
        A10     EQU   CMAX+8
        PHASE1  ENT1  8            Start at column 8.
        3H      ENT2  9*8-8,1      Start at row 9.
                JMP   2F
        1H      CMPX  A10,2        Is rX still maximum?
                JGE   *+2
        2H      LDX   A10,2        New maximum in column
                DEC2  8
                J2P   1B
                STX   CMAX+8,2     Store column maximum.
                J2Z   1F           First time?
                CMPA  CMAX+8,2     rA still min max?
                JLE   *+2
        1H      LDA   CMAX+8,2
                DEC1  1            Move left a column.
                J1P   3B
        PHASE2  ENT3  9*8          At this point rA = min_j C(j)
        3H      ENT2  0,3          Prepare to search a row.
                ENT4  8
        1H      CMPA  A10,2        Is min_j C(j) > a[i,j]?
                JG    NO           No saddle in this row
                JL    2F
                CMPA  CMAX,4       Is a[i,j] = C(j)?
                JNE   2F
                ENT1  A10,2        Remember a possible saddle point.
        2H      DEC4  1            Move left in row.
                DEC2  1
                J4P   1B
                HLT                A saddle point was found.
        NO      DEC3  8
                J3P   3B           Try another row.
                ENT1  0
                HLT                rI1 = 0; no saddle.    ▮
```

We leave it to the reader to invent a still better solution in which Phase 1 records all possible rows that are candidates for the row search in Phase 2. It is not necessary to search all rows, just those i_0 for which $C(j_0) = \min_j C(j)$ implies $a_{i_0 j_0} = C(j_0)$. Usually there is at most one such row.

In some trial runs with elements selected at random from $\{0, 1, 2, 3, 4\}$, solution 1 required approximately $730u$ to run, while solution 2 took about $530u$. Given a matrix of all zeros, solution 1 found a saddle point in $137u$, solution 2 in $524u$.

If an $m \times n$ matrix has *distinct* elements, and $m \geq n$, we can solve the problem by looking at only $O(m + n)$ of them and doing $O(m \log n)$ auxiliary operations. See Bienstock, Chung, Fredman, Schäffer, Shor, and Suri, *AMM* **98** (1991), 418–419.

11. Assume an $m \times n$ matrix. (a) By the theorem in the answer to exercise 10, all saddle points of a matrix have the same value, so (under our assumption of distinct elements) there is at most one saddle point. By symmetry the desired probability is mn times the probability that a_{11} is a saddle point. This latter is $1/(mn)!$ times the number of permutations with $a_{12} > a_{11}, \ldots, a_{1n} > a_{11}, a_{11} > a_{21}, \ldots, a_{11} > a_{m1}$; this is $1/(m+n-1)!$ times the number of permutations of $m+n-1$ elements in which the first is greater than the next $(m-1)$ and less than the remaining $(n-1)$, namely $(m-1)!\,(n-1)!$. The answer is therefore

$$mn(m-1)!\,(n-1)!/(m+n-1)! = (m+n)\Big/\binom{m+n}{n}.$$

In our case this is $17/\binom{17}{8}$, only one chance in 1430. (b) Under the second assumption, an entirely different method must be used. The probability equals the probability that there is a saddle point with value zero plus the probability that there is a saddle point with value one. The former is the probability that there is at least one column of zeros; the latter is the probability that there is at least one row of ones. The answer is $\left(1 - (1-2^{-m})^n\right) + \left(1 - (1-2^{-n})^m\right)$; in our case it comes to $924744796234036231/18446744073709551616$, about 1 in 19.9. An approximate answer is $n2^{-m} + m2^{-n}$.

12. M. Hofri and P. Jacquet [*Algorithmica* **22** (1998), 516–528] have analyzed the case when the $m \times n$ matrix entries are distinct and in random order. The running times of the two MIX programs are then respectively $(6mn+5mH_n+8m+6+5(m+1)/(n-1))u+O((m+n)^2/\binom{m+n}{m}))$ and $(5mn + 2nH_m + 7m + 7n + 9H_n)u + O(1/n) + O((\log n)^2/m)$, as $m \to \infty$ and $n \to \infty$, assuming that $(\log n)/m \to 0$.

13. * CRYPTANALYST PROBLEM (CLASSIFIED)

```
      TAPE  EQU   20              Input unit number
      TYPE  EQU   19              Output unit number
      SIZE  EQU   14              Input block size
      OSIZE EQU   14              Output block size
      TABLE EQU   1000            Table of counts
            ORIG  TABLE              (initially zero
            CON   -1                 except entries for
            ORIG  TABLE+46           blank space and
            CON   -1                 asterisk)
            ORIG  2000
      BUF1  ORIG  *+SIZE          First buffer area
            CON   -1              "Sentinel" at end of buffer
            CON   *+1             Reference to second buffer
      BUF2  ORIG  *+SIZE          Second buffer
            CON   -1              "Sentinel"
            CON   BUF1            Reference to first buffer
      BEGIN IN    BUF1(TAPE)      Input first block.
            ENT6  BUF2
      1H    IN    0,6(TAPE)       Input next block.
            LD6   SIZE+1,6        During this input, prepare
            ENT5  0,6                to process the previous one.
            JMP   4F
      2H    INCA  1
            STA   TABLE,1         Update table entry.
      3H    SLAX  1
            STA   *+1(2:2)        rI1 ← next char.
            ENT1  0
            LDA   TABLE,1
            JANN  2B              Normal character?
```

> main loop, should run as fast as possible

```
         J1NZ 3F          Asterisk?
         JXP  3B          Skip over a blank.
         INC5 1
4H       LDX  0,5         rX ← five chars.
         JXNN 3B          Jump if not a sentinel.
         JMP  1B          Done with block.
3H       ENT1 1           Begin the endgame: rI1 ← 'A'.
2H       LDA  TABLE,1
         JANP 1F          Skip zero answers.
         CHAR             Convert to decimal.
         JBUS *(TYPE)     Wait till the typewriter is ready.
         ST1  CHAR(1:1)
         STA  CHAR(4:5)
         STX  FREQ
         OUT  ANS(TYPE)   Type one answer.
1H       CMP1 =63=
         INC1 1           Up to 63 character
         JL   2B             codes are counted
         HLT
ANS      ALF              The output buffer
         ALF
CHAR     ALF  C   NN
FREQ     ALF  NNNNN
         ORIG ANS+OSIZE   Rest of buffer is blank
         END  BEGIN       The literal constant =63= comes here.   ▮
```

For this problem, buffering of *output* is not desirable since it could save at most $7u$ of time per line output.

14. To make the problem more challenging, the following solution due in part to J. Petolino uses a lot of *trickery* in order to reduce execution time. Can the reader squeeze out any more microseconds?

```
* DATE OF EASTER
EASTER     STJ   EASTX
           STX   Y
           ENTA  0              E1.
           DIV   =19=
           STX   GMINUS1(0:2)
           LDA   Y              E2.
           MUL   =1//100+1=     (see
           INCA  61                below)
           STA   CPLUS60(1:2)
           MUL   =3//4+1=
           STA   XPLUS57(1:2)
CPLUS60    ENTA  *
           MUL   =8//25+1=      rA ← Z + 24.
GMINUS1    ENT2  *              E5.
           ENT1  1,2            rI1 ← G.
           INC2  1,1
           INC2  0,2
```

```
            INC2  0,1
            INC2  0,2
            INC2  773,1           rI2 ← 11G + 773.
XPLUS57     INCA  -*,2            rA ← 11G + Z - X + 20 + 24 · 30 (≥0).
            SRAX  5
            DIV   =30=            rX ← E.
            DECX  24
            JXN   4F
            DECX  1
            JXP   2F
            JXN   3F
            DEC1  11
            J1NP  2F
3H          INCX  1
2H          DECX  29              E6.
4H          STX   20MINUSN(0:2)
            LDA   Y               E4.
            MUL   =1//4+1=
            ADD   Y
            SUB   XPLUS57(1:2)    rA ← D - 47.
20MINUSN    ENN1  *
            INCA  67,1            E7.
            SRAX  5               rX ← D + N
            DIV   =7=
            SLAX  5
            DECA  -4,1            rA ← 31 - N
            JAN   1F              E8.
            DECA  31
            CHAR
            LDA   MARCH
            JMP   2F
1H          CHAR
            LDA   APRIL
2H          JBUS  *(18)
            STA   MONTH
            STX   DAY(1:2)
            LDA   Y
            CHAR
            STX   YEAR
            OUT   ANS(18)         Print
EASTX       JMP   *
MARCH       ALF   MARCH
APRIL       ALF   APRIL
ANS         ALF
DAY         ALF   DD
MONTH       ALF   MMMMM
            ALF   ,
YEAR        ALF   YYYYY
            ORIG  *+20
```

```
BEGIN     ENTX  1950              "driver"
          ENT6  1950-2000         routine,
          JMP   EASTER            uses the
          INC6  1                 subroutine
          ENTX  2000,6            above.
          J6NP  EASTER+1
          HLT
          END   BEGIN
```

A rigorous justification for the change from division to multiplication in several places can be based on the fact that the number in rA is not too large. The program works with all byte sizes.

[To calculate Easter in years ≤ 1582, see *CACM* **5** (1962), 209–210. The first systematic algorithm for calculating the date of Easter was the *canon paschalis* due to Victorius of Aquitaine (A.D. 457). There are many indications that the sole nontrivial application of arithmetic in Europe during the Middle Ages was the calculation of Easter date, hence such algorithms are historically significant. See *Puzzles and Paradoxes* by T. H. O'Beirne (London: Oxford University Press, 1965), Chapter 10, for further commentary; and see the book *Calendrical Calculations* by E. M. Reingold and N. Dershowitz (Cambridge Univ. Press, 2001) for date-oriented algorithms of all kinds.]

15. The first such year is A.D. 10317, although the error *almost* leads to failure in A.D. $10108 + 19k$ for $0 \leq k \leq 10$.

Incidentally, T. H. O'Beirne pointed out that the date of Easter repeats with a period of exactly 5,700,000 years. Calculations by Robert Hill show that the most common date is April 19 (220400 times per period), while the earliest and least common is March 22 (27550 times); the latest, and next-to-least common, is April 25 (42000 times). Hill found a nice explanation for the curious fact that the number of times any particular day occurs in the period is always a multiple of 25.

16. Work with scaled numbers, $R_n = 10^n r_n$. Then $R_n(1/m) = R$ if and only if $10^n/(R+\frac{1}{2}) < m \leq 10^n/(R-\frac{1}{2})$; thus we find $m_h = \lfloor 2 \cdot 10^n/(2R-1) \rfloor$.

```
* SUM OF HARMONIC SERIES
BUF    ORIG  *+24
START  ENT2  0
       ENT1  3          5 − n
       ENTA  20
OUTER  MUL   =10=
       STX   CONST      2 · 10ⁿ
       DIV   =2=
       ENTX  2
       JMP   1F
INNER  STA   R
       ADD   R
       DECA  1
       STA   TEMP       2R − 1
       LDX   CONST
       ENTA  0
       DIV   TEMP
       INCA  1
       STA   TEMP       m_h + 1
```

```
           SUB   M
           MUL   R
           SLAX  5
           ADD   S
           LDX   TEMP
    1H     STA   S           Partial sum
           STX   M           m = m_e
           LDA   M
           ADD   M
           STA   TEMP
           LDA   CONST
           ADD   M           Compute R = R_n(1/m) =
           SRAX  5               ⌊(2 · 10^n + m)/(2m)⌋.
           DIV   TEMP
           JAP   INNER       R > 0?
           LDA   S           10^n S_n
           CHAR
           SLAX  0,1         Neat formatting
           SLA   1
           INCA  40          Decimal point
           STA   BUF,2
           STX   BUF+1,2
           INC2  3
           DEC1  1
           LDA   CONST
           J1NN  OUTER
           OUT   BUF(18)
           HLT
           END   START       ∎
```

The output is

$$0006.16 \qquad 0008.449 \qquad 0010.7509 \qquad 0013.05363$$

in $65595u$ plus output time. (It would be faster to calculate $R_n(1/m)$ directly when $m < 10^{n/2}\sqrt{2}$, and then to apply the suggested procedure.)

17. Let $N = \lfloor 2 \cdot 10^n/(2m+1) \rfloor$. Then $S_n = H_N + O(N/10^n) + \sum_{k=1}^{m} (\lfloor 2 \cdot 10^n/(2k-1) \rfloor - \lfloor 2 \cdot 10^n/(2k+1) \rfloor)k/10^n = H_N + O(m^{-1}) + O(m/10^n) - 1 + 2H_{2m} - H_m = n \ln 10 + 2\gamma - 1 + 2\ln 2 + O(10^{-n/2})$ if we sum by parts and set $m \approx 10^{n/2}$.

Incidentally, the next several values are $S_6 = 15.356262$, $S_7 = 17.6588276$, $S_8 = 19.96140690$, $S_9 = 22.263991779$, and $S_{10} = 24.5665766353$; our approximation to S_{10} is ≈ 24.566576621, which is closer than predicted.

```
18. FAREY  STJ   9F          Assume that rI1 contains n, where n > 1.
           STZ   X           x_0 ← 0.
           ENTX  1
           STX   Y           y_0 ← 1.
           STX   X+1         x_1 ← 1.
           ST1   Y+1         y_1 ← n.
           ENT2  0           k ← 0.
```

```
1H      LDX   Y,2
        INCX  0,1
        ENTA  0
        DIV   Y+1,2
        STA   TEMP      ⌊(y_k + n)/y_{k+1}⌋
        MUL   Y+1,2
        SLAX  5
        SUB   Y,2
        STA   Y+2,2    y_{k+2}
        LDA   TEMP
        MUL   X+1,2
        SLAX  5
        SUB   X,2
        STA   X+2,2    x_{k+2}
        CMPA  Y+2,2    Test if x_{k+2} < y_{k+2}.
        INC2  1        k ← k + 1.
        JL    1B       If so, continue.
9H      JMP   *        Exit from subroutine.   ∎
```

19. (a) Induction. (b) Let $k \geq 0$ and $X = ax_{k+1} - x_k$, $Y = ay_{k+1} - y_k$, where $a = \lfloor (y_k + n)/y_{k+1} \rfloor$. By part (a) and the fact that $0 < Y \leq n$, we have $X \perp Y$ and $X/Y > x_{k+1}/y_{k+1}$. So if $X/Y \neq x_{k+2}/y_{k+2}$ we have, by definition, $X/Y > x_{k+2}/y_{k+2}$. But this implies that

$$\frac{1}{Y y_{k+1}} = \frac{X y_{k+1} - Y x_{k+1}}{Y y_{k+1}} = \frac{X}{Y} - \frac{x_{k+1}}{y_{k+1}}$$

$$= \left(\frac{X}{Y} - \frac{x_{k+2}}{y_{k+2}} \right) + \left(\frac{x_{k+2}}{y_{k+2}} - \frac{x_{k+1}}{y_{k+1}} \right)$$

$$\geq \frac{1}{Y y_{k+2}} + \frac{1}{y_{k+1} y_{k+2}} = \frac{y_{k+1} + Y}{Y y_{k+1} y_{k+2}} > \frac{n}{Y y_{k+1} y_{k+2}} \geq \frac{1}{Y y_{k+1}}.$$

Historical notes: C. Haros gave a (more complicated) rule for constructing such sequences, in *J. de l'École Polytechnique* **4**, 11 (1802), 364–368; his method was correct, but his proof was inadequate. Several years later, the geologist John Farey independently conjectured that x_k/y_k is always equal to $(x_{k-1} + x_{k+1})/(y_{k-1} + y_{k+1})$ [*Philos. Magazine and Journal* **47** (1816), 385–386]; a proof was supplied shortly afterwards by A. Cauchy [*Bull. Société philomatique de Paris* (3) **3** (1816), 133–135], who attached Farey's name to the series. For more of its interesting properties, see G. H. Hardy and E. M. Wright, *An Introduction to the Theory of Numbers*, Chapter 3.

20.
```
     * TRAFFIC SIGNAL PROBLEM
BSIZE   EQU   1(4:4)              Bytesize
2BSIZE  EQU   2(4:4)              Twice bytesize
DELAY   STJ   1F                  If rA contains n,
        DECA  6                     this subroutine
        DECA  2                     waits max(n, 7)u
        JAP   *-1                   exactly, not including
        JAN   *+2                   the jump to the subroutine
        NOP
1H      JMP   *
```

```
FLASH  STJ   2F          4    This subroutine flashes the
       ENT2  8           5       appropriate DON'T WALK light
1H     LDA   =49991=     7
       JMP   DELAY       8
       DECX  0,1         9    Turn light off.
       LDA   =49996=     2
       JMP   DELAY       3
       INCX  0,1         4    "DON'T WALK"
       DEC2  1           1
       J2Z   1F          2    Repeat eight times.
       LDA   *           4    Waste 2u of time.
       JMP   1B          5    Get back in synch.
1H     LDA   =399992=    4    Set amber 2u after exit.
       JMP   DELAY       5
2H     JMP   *           6
WAIT   JNOV  *           5    Del Mar green until tripped
TRIP   INCX  BSIZE       6    DON'T WALK on Del Mar
       ENT1  2BSIZE      1
       JMP   FLASH       2    Flash Del Mar.
       LDX   BAMBER      8    Amber on boulevard
       LDA   =799995=    2
       JMP   DELAY       3    Wait 8 seconds.
       LDX   AGREEN      5    Green for avenue
       LDA   =799996=    2
       JMP   DELAY       3    Wait 8 seconds.
       INCX  1           4    DON'T WALK on Berkeley
       ENT1  2           1
       JMP   FLASH       2    Flash Berkeley.
       LDX   AAMBER      8    Amber on avenue
       JOV   *+1         1    Cancel redundant trip.
       LDA   =499994=    3
       JMP   DELAY       4    Wait 5 seconds.
BEGIN  LDX   BGREEN      6    Green on boulevard
       LDA   =1799994=   2
       JMP   DELAY       3    Wait at least 18
       JMP   WAIT        4       seconds.
AGREEN ALF   CABA             Green for avenue
AAMBER ALF   CBBB             Amber for avenue
BGREEN ALF   ACAB             Green for boulevard
BAMBER ALF   BCBB             Amber for boulevard
       END   BEGIN        ▌
```

22.
```
     * JOSEPHUS PROBLEM
  N    EQU   24
  M    EQU   11
  X    ORIG  *+N
  OH   ENT1  N-1          1         Set each cell to the
       STZ   X+N-1        1            number of the next man
       ST1   X-1,1        N − 1        in the sequence.
       DEC1  1            N − 1
       J1P   *-2          N − 1
```

```
      ENTA 1                1             (Now rI1 = 0)
1H    ENT2 M-2              N − 1         (Assume M > 2)
      LD1  X,1          (M − 2)(N − 1)    Count around
      DEC2 1            (M − 2)(N − 1)       the circle.
      J2P  *-2          (M − 2)(N − 1)
      LD2  X,1              N − 1         rI1 ≡ lucky man
      LD3  X,2              N − 1         rI2 ≡ doomed man
      CHAR                 N − 1         rI3 ≡ next man
      STX  X,2(4:5)        N − 1         Store execution number.
      NUM                  N − 1
      INCA 1               N − 1
      ST3  X,1             N − 1         Take man from circle.
      ENT1 0,3             N − 1
      CMPA =N=             N − 1
      JL   1B              N − 1
      CHAR                  1            One man left;
      STX  X,1(4:5)         1               he is clobbered too.
      OUT  X(18)            1            Print the answer.
      HLT                   1
      END  OB                          ▮
```

The last man is in position 15. The total time before output is $(4(N−1)(M+7.5)+16)u$. Several improvements are possible, such as D. Ingalls's suggestion to have three-word packets of code 'DEC2 1; J2P NEXT; JMP OUT', where OUT modifies the NEXT field so as to delete a packet. An asymptotically faster method appears in exercise 5.1.1–5.

SECTION 1.3.3

1. $(1\ 2\ 4)(3\ 6\ 5)$.

2. $a \leftrightarrow c,\ c \leftrightarrow f;\ b \leftrightarrow d$. The generalization to arbitrary permutations is clear.

3. $\begin{pmatrix} a & b & c & d & e & f \\ d & b & f & c & a & e \end{pmatrix}$.

4. $(a\,d\,c\,f\,e)$.

5. 12. (See exercise 20.)

6. The total time decreases by $8u$ for every blank word following a "(", because lines 30–32 cost $4u$ while lines 26–28, 33–34, 36–38 cost $12u$. It decreases by $2u$ for every blank word following a name, because lines 68–71 cost $5u$ while 42–46 or 75–79 cost $7u$. Initial blanks and blanks between cycles do not affect the execution time. The position of blanks has no effect whatever on Program B.

7. $X = 2$, $Y = 29$, $M = 5$, $N = 7$, $U = 3$, $V = 1$. Total, by Eq. (18), $2161u$.

8. Yes; we would then keep the inverse of the permutation, so that x_i goes to x_j if and only if $T[j] = i$. (The final cycle form would then be constructed from right to left, using the T table.)

9. No. For example, given (6) as input, Program A will produce '(ADG)(CEB)' as output, while Program B produces '(CEB)(DGA)'. The answers are equivalent but not identical, due to the nonuniqueness of cycle notation. The first element chosen for a cycle is the leftmost available name, in the case of Program A, and the last available distinct name to be encountered from right to left, in Program B.

10. (1) Kirchhoff's law yields $A = 1 + C - D$; $B = A + J + P - 1$; $C = B - (P - L)$; $E = D - L$; $G = E$; $Q = Z$; $W = S$. (2) Interpretations: $B =$ number of words of input $= 16X - 1$; $C =$ number of nonblank words $= Y$; $D = C - M$; $E = D - M$; $F =$ number of comparisons in names table search; $H = N$; $K = M$; $Q = N$; $R = U$; $S = R - V$; $T = N - V$ since each of the other names gets tagged. (3) Summing up, we have $(4F + 16Y + 80X + 21N - 19M + 9U - 16V)u$, which is somewhat better than Program A because F is certainly less than $16NX$. The time in the stated case is $983u$, since $F = 74$.

11. "Reflect" it. For example, the inverse of $(a\,c\,f)(b\,d)$ is $(d\,b)(f\,c\,a)$.

12. (a) The value in cell $L + mn - 1$ is fixed by the transposition, so we may omit it from consideration. Otherwise if $x = n(i - 1) + (j - 1) < mn - 1$, the value in $L + x$ should go to cell $L + mx \bmod N = L + (mn(i-1) + m(j-1)) \bmod N = L + m(j-1) + (i-1)$, since $mn \equiv 1$ (modulo N) and $0 \le m(j-1) + (i-1) < N$. (b) If one bit in each memory cell is available (for example, the sign), we can "tag" elements as we move them, using an algorithm like Algorithm I. [See M. F. Berman, *JACM* **5** (1958), 383–384.] If there is no room for a tag bit, tag bits can be kept in an auxiliary table, or else a list of representatives of all non-singleton cycles can be used: For each divisor d of N, we can transpose those elements that are multiples of d separately, since m is prime to N. The length of the cycle containing x, when $\gcd(x, N) = d$, is the smallest integer $r > 0$ such that $m^r \equiv 1$ (modulo N/d). For each d, we want to find $\varphi(N/d)/r$ representatives, one from each of these cycles. Some number-theoretic methods are available for this purpose, but they are not simple enough to be really satisfactory. An efficient but rather complicated algorithm can be obtained by combining number theory with a small table of tag bits. [See N. Brenner, *CACM* **16** (1973), 692–694.] Finally, there is a method analogous to Algorithm J; it is slower, but needs no auxiliary memory, and it performs *any* desired permutation *in situ*. [See P. F. Windley, *Comp. J.* **2** (1959), 47–48; D. E. Knuth, *Proc. IFIP Congress* (1971), **1**, 19–27; E. G. Cate and D. W. Twigg, *ACM Trans. Math. Software* **3** (1977), 104–110; F. E. Fich, J. I. Munro, and P. V. Poblete, *SICOMP* **24** (1995), 266–278.]

13. Show by induction that, at the beginning of step J2, $X[i] = +j$ if and only if $j > m$ and j goes to i under π; $X[i] = -j$ if and only if no number $> m$ goes to i under π, but i goes to j under π^{k+1}, where k is the smallest nonnegative integer such that π^k takes i into a number $\le m$.

14. Writing the *inverse* of the given permutation in canonical cycle form and dropping parentheses, the quantity $A - N$ is the sum of the number of consecutive elements greater than a given element and immediately to its right. For example, if the original permutation is $(1\,6\,5)(3\,7\,8\,4)$, the canonical form of the inverse is $(3\,4\,8\,7)(2)(1\,5\,6)$; set up the array

$$
\begin{array}{cccccccc}
3 & 4 & 8 & 7 & 2 & 1 & 5 & 6
\end{array}
$$

and the quantity A is the number of "dots," 16. The number of dots below the kth element is the number of right-to-left minima in the first k elements (there are 3 dots below 7 in the example above, since there are 3 right-to-left minima in 3487). Hence the average is $H_1 + H_2 + \cdots + H_n = (n+1)H_n - n$.

15. If the first character of the linear representation is 1, the last character of the canonical representation is 1. If the first character of the linear representation is $m > 1$, then "...$1m$..." appears in the canonical representation. So the only solution is the permutation of a single object. (Well, there's also the permutation of *no* objects.)

16. $1324, 4231, 3214, 4213, 2143, 3412, 2413, 1243, 3421, 1324, \ldots$.

17. (a) The probability p_m that the cycle is an m-cycle is $n!/m$ divided by $n! \, H_n$, so $p_m = 1/(mH_n)$. The average length is $p_1 + 2p_2 + 3p_3 + \cdots = \sum_{m=1}^{n} m/(mH_n) = n/H_n$.

(b) Since the total number of m-cycles is $n!/m$, the total number of appearances of elements in m-cycles is $n!$. Each element appears as often as any other, by symmetry, so k appears $n!/n$ times in m-cycles. In *this* case, therefore, $p_m = 1/n$ for all k and m; the average is $\sum_{m=1}^{n} m/n = (n+1)/2$.

18. See exercise 22(e).

19. $|P_{n0} - n!/e| = n!/(n+1)! - n!/(n+2)! + \cdots$, an alternating series of decreasing magnitudes, which is less than $n!/(n+1)! \le \frac{1}{2}$.

20. There are $\alpha_1 + \alpha_2 + \cdots$ cycles in all, which can be permuted among one another, and each m-cycle can be independently written in m ways. So the answer is

$$(\alpha_1 + \alpha_2 + \cdots)! \, 1^{\alpha_1} 2^{\alpha_2} 3^{\alpha_3} \cdots.$$

21. $1/(\alpha_1! \, 1^{\alpha_1} \alpha_2! \, 2^{\alpha_2} \ldots)$ if $n = \alpha_1 + 2\alpha_2 + \cdots$; zero otherwise.

Proof. Write out α_1 1-cycles, α_2 2-cycles, etc., in a row, with empty positions; for example if $\alpha_1 = 1$, $\alpha_2 = 2$, $\alpha_3 = \alpha_4 = \cdots = 0$, we would have "$(-)(--)(--)$". Fill the empty positions in all $n!$ possible ways; we obtain each permutation of the desired form exactly $\alpha_1! \, 1^{\alpha_1} \alpha_2! \, 2^{\alpha_2} \ldots$ times. (See also answer 1.2.5–21.)

22. (a) If $k_1 + 2k_2 + \cdots = n$, the probability in (ii) is $\prod_{j>0} f(w, j, k_j)$, which is assumed to equal $(1-w)w^n/(k_1! \, 1^{k_1} k_2! \, 2^{k_2} \ldots)$; hence

$$\frac{f(w, m, k_m + 1)}{f(w, m, k_m)} = \left(\prod_{j>0} f(w, j, k_j) \right)^{-1} \prod_{j>0} f(w, j, k_j + \delta_{jm}) = \frac{w^m}{m(k_m + 1)}.$$

Therefore by induction $f(w, m, k) = (w^m/m)^k f(w, m, 0)/k!$, and condition (i) implies that $f(w, m, k) = (w^m/m)^k e^{-w^m/m}/k!$. [In other words, α_m is chosen with a Poisson distribution; see exercise 1.2.10–15.]

(b) $\displaystyle \sum_{\substack{k_1 + 2k_2 + \cdots = n \\ k_1, k_2, \ldots \ge 0}} \left(\prod_{j>0} f(w, j, k_j) \right) = (1-w)w^n \sum_{\substack{k_1 + 2k_2 + \cdots = n \\ k_1, k_2, \ldots \ge 0}} P(n; k_1, k_2, \ldots) = (1-w)w^n.$

Hence the probability that $\alpha_1 + 2\alpha_2 + \cdots \le n$ is $(1-w)(1 + w + \cdots + w^n) = 1 - w^{n+1}$.

(c) The average of ϕ is

$$\sum_{n \ge 0} \left(\sum_{k_1 + 2k_2 + \cdots = n} \phi(k_1, k_2, \ldots) \Pr(\alpha_1 = k_1, \alpha_2 = k_2, \ldots) \right)$$

$$= (1 - w) \sum_{n \ge 0} w^n \left(\sum_{k_1 + 2k_2 + \cdots = n} \phi(k_1, k_2, \ldots)/k_1! \, 1^{k_1} k_2! \, 2^{k_2} \ldots \right).$$

(d) Let $\phi(\alpha_1, \alpha_2, \ldots) = \alpha_2 + \alpha_4 + \alpha_6 + \cdots$. The average value of the linear combination ϕ is the sum of the average values of $\alpha_2, \alpha_4, \alpha_6, \ldots$; and the average value of α_m is

$$\sum_{k \ge 0} k f(w, m, k) = \sum_{k \ge 1} \frac{1}{(k-1)!} \left(\frac{w^m}{m} \right)^k e^{-w^m/m} = \frac{w^m}{m}.$$

Therefore the average value of ϕ is

$$\frac{w^2}{2} + \frac{w^4}{4} + \frac{w^6}{6} + \cdots = \frac{1-w}{2}\left(H_1 w^2 + H_1 w^3 + H_2 w^4 + H_2 w^5 + H_3 w^6 + \cdots\right).$$

The desired answer is $\frac{1}{2}H_{\lfloor n/2\rfloor}$.

(e) Set $\phi(\alpha_1, \alpha_2, \dots) = z^{\alpha_m}$, and observe that the average value of ϕ is

$$\sum_{k\geq 0} f(w, m, k) z^k = \sum_{k\geq 0} \frac{1}{k!}\left(\frac{w^m z}{m}\right)^k e^{-w^m/m} = e^{w^m(z-1)/m} = \sum_{j\geq 0} \frac{w^{mj}}{j!}\left(\frac{z-1}{m}\right)^j$$

$$= (1-w)\sum_{n\geq 0} w^n \left(\sum_{0\leq j\leq n/m} \frac{1}{j!}\left(\frac{z-1}{m}\right)^j\right) = (1-w)\sum_{n\geq 0} w^n G_{nm}(z).$$

Hence

$$G_{nm}(z) = \sum_{0\leq j\leq n/m} \frac{1}{j!}\left(\frac{z-1}{m}\right)^j; \quad p_{nkm} = \frac{1}{m^k k!} \sum_{0\leq j\leq n/m-k} \frac{(-1/m)^j}{j!};$$

the statistics are (min 0, ave $1/m$, max $\lfloor n/m\rfloor$, dev $\sqrt{1/m}$), when $n \geq 2m$.

23. The constant λ is $\int_0^\infty \exp(-t - E_1(t))\,dt$, where $E_1(x) = \int_x^\infty e^{-t}dt/t$. See *Trans. Amer. Math. Soc.* **121** (1966), 340–357, where many other results are proved, in particular that the average length of the *shortest* cycle is approximately $e^{-\gamma}\ln n$. Further terms of the asymptotic representation of l_n have been found by Xavier Gourdon [Ph.D. thesis (Paris: École Polytechnique, 1996)]; the series begins

$$\lambda n + \tfrac{1}{2}\lambda - \tfrac{1}{24}e^\gamma n^{-1} + \left(\tfrac{1}{48}e^\gamma - \tfrac{1}{8}(-1)^n\right)n^{-2} + \left(\tfrac{17}{3840}e^\gamma + \tfrac{1}{8}(-1)^n + \tfrac{1}{6}\omega^{1-n} + \tfrac{1}{6}\omega^{n-1}\right)n^{-3},$$

where $\omega = e^{2\pi i/3}$. William C. Mitchell has calculated a high-precision value of $\lambda = .62432\ 99885\ 43550\ 87099\ 29363\ 83100\ 83724\ 41796+$ [*Math. Comp.* **22** (1968), 411–415]; no relation between λ and classical mathematical constants is known. The same constant had, however, been computed in another context by Karl Dickman in *Arkiv för Matematik, Astronomi och Fysik* **22A**, 10 (1930), 1–14; the coincidence wasn't noticed until many years later [*Theoretical Computer Science* **3** (1976), 343].

24. See D. E. Knuth, *Proc. IFIP Congress* (1971), **1**, 19–27.

25. One proof, by induction on N, is based on the fact that when the Nth element is a member of s of the sets it contributes exactly

$$\binom{s}{0} - \binom{s}{1} + \binom{s}{2} - \cdots = (1-1)^s = \delta_{s0}$$

to the sum. Another proof, by induction on M, is based on the fact that the number of elements that are in S_M but not in $S_1 \cup \cdots \cup S_{M-1}$ is

$$|S_M| - \sum_{1\leq j<M} |S_j \cap S_M| + \sum_{1\leq j<k<M} |S_j \cap S_k \cap S_M| - \cdots.$$

26. Let $N_0 = N$ and let $N_k = \sum_{1\leq j_1<\cdots<j_k\leq M} |S_{j_1} \cap \cdots \cap S_{j_k}|$. Then

$$N_r - \binom{r+1}{r}N_{r+1} + \binom{r+2}{r}N_{r+2} - \cdots$$

is the desired formula. It can be proved from the principle of inclusion and exclusion itself, or by using the method of exercise 25 together with the fact that

$$\binom{r}{r}\binom{s}{r} - \binom{r+1}{r}\binom{s}{r+1} + \cdots = \binom{s}{r}\binom{s-r}{0} - \binom{s}{r}\binom{s-r}{1} + \cdots = \delta_{sr}.$$

27. Let S_j be the multiples of m_j in the stated range and let $N = am_1 \ldots m_t$. Then $|S_j \cap S_k| = N/m_j m_k$, etc., so the answer is

$$N - N \sum_{1 \le j \le t} \frac{1}{m_j} + N \sum_{1 \le j < k \le t} \frac{1}{m_j m_k} - \cdots = N \left(1 - \frac{1}{m_1}\right) \cdots \left(1 - \frac{1}{m_t}\right).$$

This also solves exercise 1.2.4–30, if we let $m_1, \ldots, m_t$ be the primes dividing N.

28. See I. N. Herstein and I. Kaplansky, *Matters Mathematical* (1974), §3.5.

29. When passing over a man, assign him a new number (starting with $n + 1$). Then the kth man executed is number $2k$, and man number j for $j > n$ was previously number $(2j) \bmod (2n + 1)$. Incidentally, the original number of the kth man executed is $2n + 1 - (2n + 1 - 2k) 2^{\lfloor \lg(2n/(2n+1-2k)) \rfloor}$. [Armin Shams, *Proc. Nat. Computer Conf. 2002*, English papers section, **2** (Mashhad, Iran: Ferdowsi University, 2002), 29–33.]

31. See *CMath*, Section 3.3. Let $x_0 = jm$ and $x_{i+1} = (m(x_i - n) - d_i)/(m - 1)$, where $1 \le d_i < m$. Then $x_k = j$ if and only if $a_k j = b_k n + t_k$, where $a_k = m^{k+1} - (m-1)^k$, $b_k = m(m^k - (m-1)^k)$, and $t_k = \sum_{i=0}^{k-1} m^{k-1-i}(m-1)^i d_i$. Since $a_k \perp b_k$ and the $(m-1)^k$ possibilities for t_k are distinct, the average number of k-step fixed elements is $(m-1)^k/a_k$.

32. (a) In fact, $k - 1 \le \pi_k \le k + 2$ when k is even; $k - 2 \le \pi_k \le k + 1$ when k is odd.

(b) Choose the exponents from left to right, setting $e_k = 1$ if and only if k and $k + 1$ are in different cycles of the permutation so far. [Steven Alpern, *J. Combinatorial Theory* **B25** (1978), 62–73.]

33. For $l = 0$, let $(\alpha_{01}, \alpha_{02}; \beta_{01}, \beta_{02}) = (\pi, \rho; \epsilon, \epsilon)$ and $(\alpha_{11}, \alpha_{12}; \beta_{11}, \beta_{12}) = (\epsilon, \epsilon; \pi, \rho)$, where $\pi = (1\,4)(2\,3)$, $\rho = (1\,5)(2\,4)$, and $\epsilon = ()$.

Suppose we have made such a construction for some $l \ge 0$, where $\alpha_{jk}^2 = \beta_{jk}^2 = ()$ for $0 \le j < m$ and $1 \le k \le n$. Let $\pi^\tau = \tau^- \pi \tau$ as in exercise 38. Then the permutations

$$(A_{(jm+j')1}, \ldots, A_{(jm+j')(4n)}; B_{(jm+j')1}, \ldots, B_{(jm+j')(4n)}) =$$
$$(\alpha_{j1}^\sigma, \ldots, \alpha_{jn}^\sigma, \alpha_{j'1}^\tau, \ldots, \alpha_{j'n}^\tau, \beta_{jn}^\sigma, \ldots, \beta_{j1}^\sigma, \beta_{j'n}^\tau, \ldots, \beta_{j'1}^\tau;$$
$$\beta_{j1}^\sigma, \ldots, \beta_{jn}^\sigma, \beta_{j'1}^\tau, \ldots, \beta_{j'n}^\tau, \alpha_{jn}^\sigma, \ldots, \alpha_{j1}^\sigma, \alpha_{j'n}^\tau, \ldots, \alpha_{j'1}^\tau)$$

have the property that

$$A_{(im+i')1} B_{(jm+j')1} \cdots A_{(im+i')(4n)} B_{(jm+j')(4n)} = (1\,2\,3\,4\,5)^\sigma (1\,2\,3\,4\,5)^\tau (5\,4\,3\,2\,1)^\sigma (5\,4\,3\,2\,1)^\tau$$

if $i = j$ and $i' = j'$, otherwise the product is (). Choosing $\sigma = (2\,3)(4\,5)$ and $\tau = (3\,4\,5)$ will make the product $(1\,2\,3\,4\,5)$ as desired, when $im + i' = jm + j'$.

The construction that leads from l to $l+1$ is due to David A. Barrington [*Journal of Computer and System Sciences* **38** (1989), 150–164], who proved a general theorem by which any Boolean function can be represented as a product of permutations of $\{1, 2, 3, 4, 5\}$. With a similar construction we can, for example, find sequences of permutations $(\alpha_{j1}, \ldots, \alpha_{jn}; \beta_{j1}, \ldots, \beta_{jn})$ such that

$$\alpha_{i1} \beta_{j1} \alpha_{i2} \beta_{j2} \ldots \alpha_{in} \beta_{jn} = \begin{cases} (1\,2\,3\,4\,5), & \text{if } i < j; \\ (), & \text{if } i \ge j; \end{cases}$$

for $0 \le i, j < m = 2^{2^l}$ when $n = 6^{l+1} - 4^{l+1}$.

34. Let $N = m + n$. If $m \perp n$ there is only one cycle, because every element can be written in the form $am \bmod N$ for some integer a. And in general if $d = \gcd(m, n)$, there are exactly d cycles $C_0, C_1, \ldots, C_{d-1}$, where C_j contains the elements $\{j, j + d, \ldots, j + N - d\}$ in some order. To carry out the permutation, we can therefore proceed as follows for $0 \le j < d$ (in parallel, if convenient): Set $t \leftarrow x_j$ and $k \leftarrow j$; then while $(k+m) \bmod N \ne j$, set $x_k \leftarrow x_{(k+m) \bmod N}$ and $k \leftarrow (k+m) \bmod N$; finally set $x_k \leftarrow t$. In this algorithm the relation $(k+m) \bmod N \ne j$ will hold if and only if $(k+m) \bmod N \ge d$, so we can use whichever test is more efficient. [W. Fletcher and R. Silver, *CACM* **9** (1966), 326.]

35. Let $M = l+m+n$ and $N = l+2m+n$. The cycles for the desired rearrangement are obtained from the cycles of the permutation on $\{0, 1, \dots, N-1\}$ that takes k to $(k+l+m) \bmod N$, by simply striking out all elements of each cycle that are $\ge M$. (Compare this behavior with the similar situation in exercise 29.) *Proof:* When the hinted interchange sets $x_k \leftarrow x_{k'}$ and $x_{k'} \leftarrow x_{k''}$ for some k with $k' = (k+l+m) \bmod N$ and $k'' = (k'+l+m) \bmod N$ and $k' \ge M$, we know that $x_{k'} = x_{k''}$; hence the rearrangement $\alpha\beta\gamma \to \gamma\beta\alpha$ replaces x_k by $x_{k''}$.

It follows that there are exactly $d = \gcd(l+m, m+n)$ cycles, and we can use an algorithm similar to the one in the previous exercise.

A slightly simpler way to reduce this problem to the special case in exercise 34 is also noteworthy, although it makes a few more references to memory: Suppose $\gamma = \gamma'\gamma''$ where $|\gamma''| = |\alpha|$. Then we can change $\alpha\beta\gamma'\gamma''$ to $\gamma''\beta\gamma'\alpha$, and interchange $\gamma''\beta$ with γ'. A similar approach works if $|\alpha| > |\gamma|$. [See J. L. Mohammed and C. S. Subi, *J. Algorithms* **8** (1987), 113–121.]

37. The result is clear when $n \le 2$. Otherwise we can find $a, b < n$ such that π takes a to b. Then $(n\,a)\,\pi\,(b\,n) = (\alpha\,a)(b\,\beta)$ for $(n-1)$-cycles $(\alpha\,a)$ and $(b\,\beta)$ if and only if $\pi = (n\,\alpha\,a)(b\,\beta\,n)$. [See A. Jacques, C. Lenormand, A. Lentin, and J.-F. Perrot, *Comptes Rendus Acad. Sci.* **266** (Paris, 1968), A446–A448.]

38. (a) Obviously $\pi = \tau^{-}\pi\tau \iff \tau\pi = \pi\tau$. (b) π^{τ} takes $b_{ij} \mapsto a_{ij} \mapsto a_{i(j+1)} \mapsto b_{i(j+1)}$, if we regard $i(l_i+1)$ as $i1$. (c) One of the $6 \cdot 3 \cdot 2$ solutions is $\tau = (1\,8)(2\,7)(3\,6)(4\,5)$. Others are $\tau = (2\,3)(7\,8)$; $\tau = (1\,6\,2\,8\,3\,7)$. (d) None. (c) True. (f) True. [See E. Netto, *The Theory of Substitutions and its Applications to Algebra* (1892), §46.]

SECTION 1.4.1

1. Calling sequence: JMP MAXN; or, JMP MAX100 if $n = 100$.
   Entry conditions: For the MAXN entrance, rI3 $= n$; assume $n \ge 1$.
   Exit conditions: Same as in (4).

2. MAX50 STJ EXIT
           ENT3 50
           JMP 2F

3. Entry conditions: rI1 $= n$.
   Exit conditions: If $n \ge 1$, rA, rI2, and rI3 are as in (4), with rI2 maximal $\le n$; otherwise rA $=$ CONTENTS(X+n), rI2 $= n$, and rI3 $= n-1$; rJ $=$ EXIT $+1$; CI is unchanged if $n \le 1$; otherwise CI is greater, equal, or less, according as the maximum is greater than $X[1]$, equal to $X[1]$ with rI2 > 1, or equal to $X[1]$ with rI2 $= 1$.

(The analogous exercise for (9) would of course be somewhat more complicated.)

4. SMAX1 ENT1 1 $r = 1$
     SMAX STJ EXIT general r
           JMP 2F   continue as before

```
      ...
         DEC3  0,1      decrease by r
         J3P   1B
   EXIT  JMP   *        exit.
```

Calling sequence: `JMP SMAX`; or, `JMP SMAX1` if $r = 1$.

Entry conditions: $rI3 = n$, assumed positive; for the `SMAX` entrance, $rI1 = r$, assumed positive.

Exit conditions: $rA = \max_{0 \le k < n/r} \text{CONTENTS}(X + n - kr) = \text{CONTENTS}(X + rI2)$; and $rI3 = (n - 1) \bmod r + 1 - r = -((-n) \bmod r)$.

5. Any other register can be used. For example,

Calling sequence: `ENTA *+2`

`            JMP    MAX100`

Entry conditions: None.

Exit conditions: Same as in (4).

The code is like (1), but the first instruction becomes '`MAX100 STA EXIT(0:2)`'.

6. (Solution by Joel Goldberg and Roger M. Aarons.)

```
   MOVE STJ   3F
        STA   4F           Save rA and rI2.
        ST2   5F(0:2)
        LD2   3F(0:2)      rI2 ← address of 'NOP A,I(F)'.
        LDA   0,2(0:3)     rA ← 'A,I'.
        STA   *+2(0:3)
        LD2   5F(0:2)      Restore rI2, because I might be 2.
        ENTA  *            rA ← indexed address.
        LD2   3F(0:2)
        LD2N  0,2(4:4)     rI2 ← −F.
        J2Z   1F
        DECA  0,2
        STA   2F(0:2)
        DEC1  0,2          rI1 ← rI1 + F.
        ST1   6F(0:2)
   2H   LDA   *,2
   6H   STA   *,2
        INC2  1            Increase rI2 until it becomes zero.
        J2N   2B
   1H   LDA   4F           Restore rA and rI2.
   5H   ENT2  *
   3H   JMP   *            Exit to the NOP instruction.
   4H   CON   0  ▮
```

7. (1) An operating system can allocate high-speed memory more efficiently if program blocks are known to be "read-only." (2) An instruction cache in hardware will be faster and less expensive if instructions cannot change. (3) Same as (2), with "pipeline" in place of "cache." If an instruction is modified after entering a pipeline, the pipeline needs to be flushed; the circuitry needed to check this condition is complex and time-consuming. (4) Self-modifying code cannot be used by more than one process at once. (5) Self-modifying code can defeat a jump-trace routine (exercise 1.4.3.2–7), which is an important diagnostic tool for "profiling" (that is, for computing the number of times each instruction is executed).

SECTION 1.4.2

1. If one coroutine calls the other only once, it is nothing but a subroutine; so we need an application in which each coroutine calls the other in at least two distinct places. Even then, it is often easy to set some sort of switch or to use some property of the data, so that upon entry to a fixed place within one coroutine it is possible to branch to one of two desired places; again, nothing more than a subroutine would be required. Coroutines become correspondingly more useful as the number of references between them grows larger.

2. The first character found by IN would be lost. [We started OUT first because lines 58–59 do the necessary initialization for IN. If we wanted to start IN first, we'd have to initialize OUT by saying 'ENT4 -16', and clearing the output buffer if it isn't known to be blank. Then we could make line 62 jump first to line 39.]

3. *Almost* true, since 'CMPA =10=' within IN is then the only comparison instruction of the program, and since the code for '.' is 40. (!) But the comparison indicator isn't initialized; and if the final period is preceded by a replication digit, it won't be noticed. [*Note:* The most nitpickingly efficient program would probably remove lines 40, 44, and 48, and would insert 'CMPA PERIOD' between lines 26 and 27, 'CMPX PERIOD' between lines 59 and 60. The state of the comparison indicator should then become part of the coroutine characteristics in the program documentation.]

4. Here are examples from three rather different computers of historic importance: (i) On the IBM 650, using SOAP assembly language, we would have the calling sequences 'LDD   A' and 'LDD   B', and linkage 'A STD BX AX' and 'B STD AX BX' (with the two linkage instructions preferably in core). (ii) On the IBM 709, using common assembly languages, the calling sequences would be 'TSX A,4' and 'TSX B,4'; the linkage instructions would be as follows:

```
A    SXA   BX,4              B    SXA   AX,4
AX   AXT   1-A1,4            BX   AXT   1-B1,4
     TRA   1,4                    TRA   1,4
```

(iii) On the CDC 1604, the calling sequences would be "return jump" (SLJ 4) to A or B, and the linkage would be, for example,

```
A:  SLJ  B1;  ALS  0
B:  SLJ  A1;  SLJ  A
```

in two consecutive 48-bit words.

5. 'STA HOLDAIN; LDA HOLDAOUT' between OUT and OUTX, and 'STA HOLDAOUT; LDA HOLDAIN' between IN and INX.

6. Within A write 'JMP AB' to activate B, 'JMP AC' to activate C. Locations BA, BC, CA, and CB would, similarly, be used within B and C. The linkage is:

```
AB   STJ   AX         BC   STJ   BX         CA   STJ   CX
BX   JMP   B1         CX   JMP   C1         AX   JMP   A1
CB   STJ   CX         AC   STJ   AX         BA   STJ   BX
     JMP   BX              JMP   CX              JMP   AX
```

[*Note:* With n coroutines, $2(n-1)n$ cells would be required for this style of linkage. If n is large, a "centralized" routine for linkage could of course be used; a method with $3n+2$ cells is not hard to invent. But in practice the faster method above requires just $2m$ cells, where m is the number of pairs (i,j) such that coroutine i jumps to coroutine j. When there are many coroutines each independently jumping to others, the sequence of control is usually under external influence, as discussed in Section 2.2.5.]

SECTION 1.4.3.1

1. FCHECK is used only twice, both times immediately followed by a call on MEMORY. So it would be slightly more efficient to make FCHECK a special entrance to the MEMORY subroutine, and also to make it put −R in rI2.

2.

```
     SHIFT J5N   ADDRERROR
           DEC3  5
           J3P   FERROR
           LDA   AREG
           LDX   XREG
           LD1   1F,3(4:5)
           ST1   2F(4:5)
           J5Z   CYCLE
       2H  SLA   1
           DEC5  1
           J5P   2B
           JMP   STOREAX
           SLA   1
           SRA   1
           SLAX  1
           SRAX  1
           SLC   1
       1H  SRC   1   ▌
```

3.

```
     MOVE  J3Z   CYCLE
           JMP   MEMORY
           SRAX  5
           LD1   I1REG
           LDA   SIGN1
           JAP   *+3
           J1NZ  MEMERROR
           STZ   SIGN1(0:0)
           CMP1  =BEGIN=
           JGE   MEMERROR
           STX   0,1
           LDA   CLOCK
           INCA  2
           STA   CLOCK
           INC1  1
           ST1   I1REG
           INC5  1
           DEC3  1
           JMP   MOVE   ▌
```

4. Just insert 'IN 0(16)' and 'JBUS *(16)' between lines 003 and 004. (Of course on another computer this would be considerably different since it would be necessary to convert to MIX character code.)

5. Central control time is $34u$, plus $15u$ if indexing is required; the GETV subroutine takes $52u$, plus $5u$ if L $\neq$ 0; extra time to do the actual loading is $11u$ for LDA or LDX, $13u$ for LDi, $21u$ for ENTA or ENTX, $23u$ for ENTi (add $2u$ to the latter two times if M = 0). Summing up, we have a total time of $97u$ for LDA and $55u$ for ENTA, plus $15u$ for indexing, and plus $5u$ or $2u$ in certain other circumstances. It would seem that simulation in this case is causing roughly a 50:1 ratio in speeds. (Results of a test run that involved $178u$ of simulated time required $8422u$ of actual time, a 47:1 ratio.)

7. Execution of IN or OUT sets a variable associated with the appropriate input device to the time when transmission is desired. The 'CYCLE' control routine interrogates these variables on each cycle, to see if CLOCK has exceeded either (or both) of them; if so, the transmission is carried out and the variable is set to ∞. (When more than two I/O units must be handled in this way, there might be so many variables that it would be preferable to keep them in a sorted list using linked memory techniques; see Section 2.2.5.) We must be careful to complete the I/O when simulating HLT.

8. False; rI6 can equal BEGIN, if we "fall through" from the location BEGIN − 1. But then a MEMERROR will occur, trying to STZ into TIME! On the other hand, we always do have $0 \leq$ rI6 $\leq$ BEGIN, because of line 254.

SECTION 1.4.3.2

1. Change lines 48 and 49 to the following sequence:

```
XREG    ORIG  *+2                           JMP   -1,1
LEAVE   STX   XREG               1H         JMP   *+1
        ST1   XREG+1                         STA   -1,1
        LD1   JREG(0:2)                      LD1   XREG+1
        LDA   -1,1                           LDX   XREG
        LDX   1F                             LDA   AREG
        STX   -1,1            LEAVEX JSJ   *
```

The operator 'JSJ' here is, of course, particularly crucial.

2.
```
    * TRACE ROUTINE                          STA   BUF+1,1(4:5)
        ORIG  *+99                           ENTA  8
BUF     CON   0                              JNOV  1F
        .............lines 02–04             ADD   BIG
        ST1   I1REG              1H JL   1F
        .............lines 05–07             INCA  1
PTR     ENT1  -100                           JE    1F
        JBUS  *(0)                           INCA  1
        STA   BUF+1,1(0:2)       1H STA  BUF+1,1(3:3)
        .............lines 08–11             INC1  10
        STA   BUF+2,1                        J1N   1F
        .............lines 12–13             OUT   BUF-99(0)
        LDA   AREG                           ENT1  -100
        STA   BUF+3,1            1H ST1  PTR(0:2)
        LDA   I1REG                          LD1   I1REG
        STA   BUF+4,1             .............lines 14–35
        ST2   BUF+5,1                        ST1   I1REG
        ST3   BUF+6,1             .............lines 36–48
        ST4   BUF+7,1                        LD1   I1REG
        ST5   BUF+8,1             .............lines 49–50
        ST6   BUF+9,1            B4 EQU  1(1:1)
        STX   BUF+10,1           BIG CON  B4-8,B4-1(1:1)
        LDA   JREG(0:2)
```

A supplementary routine that writes out the final buffer and rewinds tape 0 should be called after all tracing has been performed.

3. Tape is faster; and the editing of this information into characters while tracing would consume far too much space. Furthermore the tape contents can be selectively printed.

4. A true trace, as desired in exercise 6, would not be obtained, since restriction (a) mentioned in the text is violated. The first attempt to trace CYCLE would cause a loop back to tracing ENTER+1, because PREG is clobbered.

6. Suggestion: Keep a table of values of each memory location within the trace area that has been changed by the outer program.

7. The routine should scan the program until finding the first jump (or conditional jump) instruction; after modifying that instruction and the one following, it should restore registers and allow the program to execute all its instructions up to that point, in one burst. [This technique can fail if the program modifies its own jump instructions, or changes non-jumps into jumps. For practical purposes we can outlaw such practices, except for STJ, which we probably ought to handle separately anyway.]

SECTION 1.4.4

1. (a) No; the input operation might not yet be complete. (b) No; the input operation might be going just a little faster than the `MOVE`. This proposal is much too risky.

2.
```
ENT1 2000
JBUS *(6)
MOVE 1000(50)
MOVE 1050(50)
OUT  2000(6)  ▌
```

3.
```
WORDOUT STJ  1F                          DEC5 100
        STA  0,5                         JMP  2B
        INC5 1                   * BUFFER AREAS
2H      CMP5 BUFMAX             OUTBUF1 ORIG *+100
1H      JNE  *                  ENDBUF1 CON  *+101  (ENDBUF2)
        OUT  -100,5(V)          OUTBUF2 ORIG *+100
        LD5  0,5                ENDBUF2 CON  ENDBUF1
        ST5  BUFMAX             BUFMAX  CON  ENDBUF1  ▌
```

At the beginning of the program, give the instruction '`ENT5 OUTBUF1`'. At the end of the program, say

```
LDA  BUFMAX                      INC5 1
DECA 100,5                       CMP5 BUFMAX
JAZ  *+6                         JNE  *-3
STZ  0,5                         OUT  -100,5(V)
```

4. If the calculation time exactly equals the I/O time (which is the most favorable situation), both the computer and the peripheral device running simultaneously will take half as long as if they ran separately. Formally, let C be the calculation time for the entire program, and let T be the total I/O time required; then the best possible running time with buffering is $\max(C, T)$, while the running time without buffering is $C + T$; and of course $\frac{1}{2}(C + T) \leq \max(C, T) \leq C + T$.

However, some devices have a "shutdown penalty" that causes an extra amount of time to be lost if too long an interval occurs between references to that unit; in such a case, better than 2:1 ratios are possible. (See, for example, exercise 19.)

5. The best ratio is $(n + 1)$:1.

6. $\begin{Bmatrix} \text{IN} & \text{INBUF1(U)} \\ \text{ENT6} & \text{INBUF2+99} \end{Bmatrix}$ or $\begin{Bmatrix} \text{IN} & \text{INBUF2(U)} \\ \text{ENT6} & \text{INBUF1+99} \end{Bmatrix}$

(possibly preceded by `IOC 0(U)` to rewind the tape just in case it is necessary).

7. One way is to use coroutines:

```
INBUF1  ORIG *+100                       INC6 1
INBUF2  ORIG *+100                       J6N  2B
1H      LDA  INBUF2+100,6                IN   INBUF1(U)
        JMP  MAIN                        ENN6 100
        INC6 1                           JMP  1B
        J6N  1B                  WORDIN  STJ  MAINX
WORDIN1 IN   INBUF2(U)           WORDINX JMP  WORDIN1
        ENN6 100                 MAIN    STJ  WORDINX
2H      LDA  INBUF1+100,6        MAINX   JMP  *  ▌
        JMP  MAIN
```

Adding a few more instructions to take advantage of special cases will actually make this routine faster than (4).

8. At the time shown in Fig. 23, the two red buffers have been filled with line images, and the one indicated by NEXTR is being printed. At the same time, the program is computing between RELEASE and ASSIGN. When the program ASSIGNs, the green buffer indicated by NEXTG becomes yellow; NEXTG moves clockwise and the program begins to fill the yellow buffer. When the output operation is complete, NEXTR moves clockwise, the buffer that has just been printed turns green, and the remaining red buffer begins to be printed. Finally, the program RELEASEs the yellow buffer and it too is ready for subsequent printing.

9, 10, 11.

time	action $(N = 1)$	action $(N = 2)$	action $(N = 4)$
0	ASSIGN(BUF1)	ASSIGN(BUF1)	ASSIGN(BUF1)
1000	RELEASE, OUT BUF1	RELEASE, OUT BUF1	RELEASE, OUT BUF1
2000	ASSIGN (wait)	ASSIGN(BUF2)	ASSIGN(BUF2)
3000		RELEASE	RELEASE
4000		ASSIGN (wait)	ASSIGN(BUF3)
5000			RELEASE
6000			ASSIGN(BUF4)
7000			RELEASE
8000			ASSIGN (wait)
8500	BUF1 assigned, output stops	BUF1 assigned, OUT BUF2	BUF1 assigned, OUT BUF2
9500	RELEASE, OUT BUF1	RELEASE	
10500	ASSIGN (wait)	ASSIGN (wait)	
15500			RELEASE

and so on. Total time when $N = 1$ is $110000u$; when $N = 2$ it is $89000u$; when $N = 3$ it is $81500u$; and when $N \geq 4$ it is $76000u$.

12. Replace the last three lines of Program B by

```
        STA   2F
        LDA   3F
        CMPA  15,5(5:5)
        LDA   2F
        LD5   -1,5
        DEC6  1
        JNE   1B
        JMP   COMPUTE
        JMP   *-1    (or JMP COMPUTEX)
     2H CON   0
     3H ALF   ␣␣␣␣.    ▌
```

13.   JRED CONTROL(U)
           J6NZ *-1   ▌

14. If $N = 1$ the algorithm breaks down (possibly referring to the buffer while I/O is in progress); otherwise the construction will have the effect that there are two yellow buffers. This can be useful if the computational program wants to refer to two buffers at once, although it ties up buffer space. In general, the excess of ASSIGNs over RELEASEs should be nonnegative and not greater than N.

15.

```
    U          EQU   0
    V          EQU   1
    BUF1       ORIG  *+100
    BUF2       ORIG  *+100
    BUF3       ORIG  *+100
    TAPECPY IN    BUF1(U)
            ENT1  99
    1H      IN    BUF2(U)
            OUT   BUF1(V)
            IN    BUF3(U)
```

```
            OUT   BUF2(V)
            IN    BUF1(U)
            OUT   BUF3(V)
            DEC1  3
            J1P   1B
            JBUS  *(U)
            OUT   BUF1(V)
            HLT
            END   TAPECPY
```

This is a special case of the algorithm indicated in Fig. 26.

18. Partial solution: In the algorithms below, t is a variable that equals 0 when the I/O device is idle, and 1 when it is active.

Algorithm A' (ASSIGN, *a normal state subroutine*).

This algorithm is unchanged from Algorithm 1.4.4A.

Algorithm R' (RELEASE, *a normal state subroutine*).

R1'. Increase n by one.

R2'. If $t = 0$, force an interrupt, going to step B3' (using the INT operator).

Algorithm B' (*Buffer control routine, which processes interrupts*).

B1'. Restart the main program.

B2'. If $n = 0$, set $t \leftarrow 0$ and go to B1'.

B3'. Set $t \leftarrow 1$, and initiate I/O from the buffer area specified by NEXTR.

B4'. Restart the main program; an "I/O complete" condition will interrupt it and lead to step B5'.

B5'. Advance NEXTR to the next clockwise buffer.

B6'. Decrease n by one, and go to step B2'.

19. If $C \leq L$ we can have $t_k = (k-1)L$, $u_k = t_k + T$, and $v_k = u_k + C$ if and only if $NL \geq T + C$. If $C > L$ the situation is more complex; we can have $u_k = (k-1)C + T$ and $v_k = kC + T$ if and only if there are integers $a_1 \leq a_2 \leq \cdots \leq a_n$ such that $t_k = (k-1)L + a_k P$ satisfies $u_k - T \geq t_k \geq v_{k-N}$ for $N < k \leq n$. An equivalent condition is that $NC \geq b_k$ for $N < k \leq n$, where $b_k = C + T + ((k-1)(C-L)) \bmod P$. Let $c_l = \max\{b_{l+1}, \ldots, b_n, 0\}$; then c_l decreases as l increases, and the smallest value of N that keeps the process going steadily is the minimum l such that $c_l/l \leq C$. Since $c_l < C + T + P$ and $c_l \leq L + T + n(C - L)$, this value of N never exceeds $\lceil \min\{C + T + P, L + T + n(C - L)\}/C \rceil$. [See A. Itai and Y. Raz, *CACM* **31** (1988), 1338–1342.]

In the stated example we have therefore (a) $N = 1$; (b) $N = 2$; (c) $N = 3$, $c_N = 2.5$; (d) $N = 35$, $c_N = 51.5$; (e) $N = 51$, $c_N = 101.5$; (f) $N = 41$, $c_N = 102$; (g) $N = 11$, $c_N = 109.5$; (h) $N = 3$, $c_N = 149.5$; (i) $N = 2$, $c_N = 298.5$.

SECTION 2.1

1. (a) SUIT(NEXT(TOP)) = SUIT(NEXT(242)) = SUIT(386) = 4. (b) Λ.

2. Whenever V is a link variable (else CONTENTS(V) makes no sense) whose value is not Λ. It is wise to *avoid* using LOC in contexts like this.

3. Set `NEWCARD ← TOP`, and if `TOP ≠ Λ` set `TOP ← NEXT(TOP)`.

4. C1. Set `X ← LOC(TOP)`. (For convenience we make the reasonable assumption that `TOP ≡ NEXT(LOC(TOP))`, namely that the value of `TOP` appears in the `NEXT` field of the location where it is stored. This assumption is compatible with program (5), and it saves us the bother of writing a special routine for the case of an empty pile.)

  C2. If `NEXT(X) ≠ Λ`, set `X ← NEXT(X)` and repeat this step.

  C3. Set `NEXT(X) ← NEWCARD`, `NEXT(NEWCARD) ← Λ`, `TAG(NEWCARD) ← 1`. ∎

5. D1. Set `X ← LOC(TOP)`, `Y ← TOP`. (See step C1 above. By hypothesis, `Y ≠ Λ`. Throughout the algorithm that follows, `X` trails one step behind `Y` in the sense that `Y = NEXT(X)`.)

  D2. If `NEXT(Y) ≠ Λ`, set `X ← Y`, `Y ← NEXT(Y)`, and repeat this step.

  D3. (Now `NEXT(Y) = Λ`, so `Y` points to the bottom card; also `X` points to the next-to-last card.) Set `NEXT(X) ← Λ`, `NEWCARD ← Y`. ∎

6. Notations (b) and (d). *Not* (a)! `CARD` is a node, not a link to a node.

7. Sequence (a) gives `NEXT(LOC(TOP))`, which in this case is identical to the value of `TOP`; sequence (b) is correct. There is no need for confusion; consider the analogous example when `X` is a numeric variable: To bring `X` into register A, we write `LDA X`, not `ENTA X`, since the latter brings `LOC(X)` into the register.

8. Let `rA ≡ N`, `rI1 ≡ X`.

`ENTA`	`0`	*B1.* `N ← 0.`	`INCA`	`1`	*B3.* `N ← N + 1.`
`LD1`	`TOP`	`X ← TOP.`	`LD1`	`0,1(NEXT)`	`X ← NEXT(X).`
`J1Z`	`*+4`	*B2.* Is `X = Λ`?	`J1NZ`	`*-2`	∎

9. Let `rI2 ≡ X`.

`PRINTER`	`EQU`	`18`	Unit number for line printer
`TAG`	`EQU`	`1:1`	
`NEXT`	`EQU`	`4:5`	Definition of fields
`NAME`	`EQU`	`0:5`	
`PBUF`	`ALF`	`PILE`	Message printed in case
	`ALF`	`EMPTY`	pile is empty
	`ORIG`	`PBUF+24`	
`BEGIN`	`LD2`	`TOP`	Set `X ← TOP`.
	`J2Z`	`2F`	Is the pile empty?
`1H`	`LDA`	`0,2(TAG)`	`rA ← TAG(X).`
	`ENT1`	`PBUF`	Get ready for `MOVE` instruction.
	`JBUS`	`*(PRINTER)`	Wait until printer is ready.
	`JAZ`	`*+3`	Is `TAG = 0` (is card face up)?
	`MOVE`	`PAREN(3)`	No: Copy parentheses.
	`JMP`	`*+2`	
	`MOVE`	`BLANKS(3)`	Yes: Copy blanks.
	`LDA`	`1,2(NAME)`	`rA ← NAME(X).`
	`STA`	`PBUF+1`	
	`LD2`	`0,2(NEXT)`	Set `X ← NEXT(X).`
`2H`	`OUT`	`PBUF(PRINTER)`	Print the line.
	`J2NZ`	`1B`	If `X ≠ Λ`, repeat the print loop.
`DONE`	`HLT`		

```
PAREN    ALF        (
BLANKS   ALF
         ALF    )
         ALF                          ∎
```

SECTION 2.2.1

1. Yes. (Consistently insert all items at one of the two ends.)

2. To obtain 325641, do SSSXXSSXSXXX (in the notation of the following exercise). The order 154623 cannot be achieved, since 2 can precede 3 only if it is removed from the stack before 3 has been inserted.

3. An admissible sequence is one in which the number of X's never exceeds the number of S's if we read from the left to the right.

Two different admissible sequences must give a different result, since if the two sequences agree up to a point where one has S and the other has X, the latter sequence outputs a symbol that cannot possibly be output before the symbol just inserted by the S of the former sequence.

4. This problem is equivalent to many other interesting problems, such as the enumeration of binary trees, the number of ways to insert parentheses into a formula, and the number of ways to divide a convex polygon into triangles, and it appeared as early as 1759 in notes by Euler and von Segner (see Section 2.3.4.6).

The following elegant solution uses a "reflection principle" due to J. Aebly and D. Mirimanoff [*L'Enseignement Math.* **23** (1923), 185–189]: There are obviously $\binom{2n}{n}$ sequences of S's and X's that contain n of each. It remains to evaluate the number of *inadmissible* sequences (those that contain the right number of S's and X's but violate the other condition). In any inadmissible sequence, locate the first X for which the X's outnumber the S's. Then in the partial sequence leading up to and including this X, replace each X by S and each S by X. The result is a sequence with $(n + 1)$ S's and $(n - 1)$ X's. Conversely for every sequence of the latter type we can reverse the process and find the inadmissible sequence of the former type that leads to it. For example, the sequence XXSXSSSXXSSS must have come from SSXSXXXXXSSS. This correspondence shows that the number of inadmissible sequences is $\binom{2n}{n-1}$. Hence $a_n = \binom{2n}{n} - \binom{2n}{n-1}$.

Using the same idea, we can solve the more general "ballot problem" of probability theory, which essentially is the enumeration of all partial admissible sequences with a given number of S's and X's. This problem was actually resolved as early as 1708 by Abraham de Moivre, who showed that the number of sequences containing l A's and m B's, and containing at least one initial substring with n more A's than B's, is $f(l, m, n) = \binom{l+m}{\min(m, l-n)}$. In particular, $a_n = \binom{2n}{n} - f(n, n, 1)$ as above. (De Moivre stated this result without proof [*Philos. Trans.* **27** (1711), 262–263]; but it is clear from other passages in his paper that he knew how to prove it, since the formula is obviously true when $l \geq m + n$, and since his generating-function approach to similar problems yields the symmetry condition $f(l, m, n) = f(m + n, l - n, n)$ by simple algebra.) For the later history of the ballot problem and some generalizations, see the comprehensive survey by D. E. Barton and C. L. Mallows, *Annals of Math. Statistics* **36** (1965), 236–260; see also exercise 2.3.4.4–32 and Section 5.1.4.

We present here a new method for solving the ballot problem with the use of double generating functions, since this method lends itself to the solution of more difficult problems such as the question in exercise 11.

Let g_{nm} be the number of sequences of S's and X's of length n, in which the number of X's never exceeds the number of S's if we count from the left, and in which there are m more S's than X's in all. Then $a_n = g_{(2n)0}$. Obviously g_{nm} is zero unless $m + n$ is even. We see easily that these numbers can be defined by the recurrence relations

$$g_{(n+1)m} = g_{n(m-1)} + g_{n(m+1)}, \quad m \geq 0, \quad n \geq 0; \qquad g_{0m} = \delta_{0m}.$$

Consider the double generating function $G(x, z) = \sum_{n,m} g_{nm} x^m z^n$, and let $g(z) = G(0, z)$. The recurrence above is equivalent to the equation

$$\left(x + \frac{1}{x}\right) G(x, z) = \frac{1}{x} g(z) + \frac{1}{z}(G(x, z) - 1), \quad \text{i.e.,} \quad G(x, z) = \frac{zg(z) - x}{z(x^2 + 1) - x}.$$

This equation unfortunately tells us nothing if we set $x = 0$, but we can proceed by factoring the denominator as $z(1 - r_1(z)x)(1 - r_2(z)x)$ where

$$r_1(z) = \frac{1}{2z}(1 + \sqrt{1 - 4z^2}), \quad r_2(z) = \frac{1}{2z}(1 - \sqrt{1 - 4z^2}).$$

(Note that $r_1 + r_2 = 1/z$; $r_1 r_2 = 1$.) We now proceed heuristically; the problem is to find some value of $g(z)$ such that $G(x, z)$ as given by the formula above has an infinite power series expansion in x and z. The function $r_2(z)$ has a power series, and $r_2(0) = 0$; moreover, for fixed z, the value $x = r_2(z)$ causes the denominator of $G(x, z)$ to vanish. This suggests that we should choose $g(z)$ so that the numerator also vanishes when $x = r_2(z)$; in other words, we probably ought to take $zg(z) = r_2(z)$. With this choice, the equation for $G(x, z)$ simplifies to

$$G(x, z) = \frac{r_2(z)}{z(1 - r_2(z)x)} = \sum_{n \geq 0} (r_2(z))^{n+1} x^n z^{-1}.$$

This is a power series expansion that satisfies the original equation, so we must have found the right function $g(z)$.

The coefficients of $g(z)$ are the solution to our problem. Actually we can go further and derive a simple form for all the coefficients of $G(x, z)$: By the binomial theorem,

$$r_2(z) = \sum_{k \geq 0} z^{2k+1} \binom{2k + 1}{k} \frac{1}{2k + 1}.$$

Let $w = z^2$ and $r_2(z) = zf(w)$. Then $f(w) = \sum_{k \geq 0} A_k(1, -2)w^k$ in the notation of exercise 1.2.6–25; hence

$$f(w)^r = \sum_{k \geq 0} A_k(r, -2)w^k.$$

We now have

$$G(x, z) = \sum_{m,n \geq 0} A_m(n + 1, -2) x^n z^{2m+n},$$

so the general solution is

$$g_{(2n)(2m)} = \binom{2n + 1}{n - m} \frac{2m + 1}{2n + 1} = \binom{2n}{n - m} - \binom{2n}{n - m - 1};$$

$$g_{(2n+1)(2m+1)} = \binom{2n + 2}{n - m} \frac{2m + 2}{2n + 2} = \binom{2n + 1}{n - m} - \binom{2n + 1}{n - m - 1}.$$

5. If $j < k$ and $p_j < p_k$, we must have taken p_j off the stack before p_k was put on; if $p_j > p_k$, we must have left p_k on the stack until after p_j was put on. Combining these two rules, the condition $i < j < k$ and $p_j < p_k < p_i$ is impossible: It means that p_i must go off before p_j is put on, and then p_k, yet p_i appears after p_k.

Conversely, the desired permutation can be obtained by using the following algorithm: "For $j = 1, 2, \ldots, n$, input zero or more items (as many as necessary) until p_j first appears in the stack; then output p_j." This algorithm can fail only if we reach a j for which p_j is not at the top of the stack but it is covered by some element p_k for $k > j$. Since the values on the stack are always monotone increasing, we have $p_j < p_k$. And the element p_k must have gotten there because it was less than p_i for some $i < j$.

P. V. Ramanan [*SICOMP* **13** (1984), 167–169] has shown how to characterize the permutations obtainable when m auxiliary storage locations can be used freely in addition to a stack. (This generalization of the problem is surprisingly difficult.)

6. Only the trivial one, $12 \ldots n$, by the nature of a queue.

7. An input-restricted deque that first outputs n must simply put the values 1, 2, $\ldots, n$ on the deque in order as its first n operations. An output-restricted deque that first outputs n must put the values $p_1 p_2 \ldots p_n$ on its deque as its first n operations. Therefore we find the unique answers (a) 4132, (b) 4213, (c) 4231.

8. When $n \leq 4$, no; when $n = 5$, there are four (see exercise 13).

9. By operating backwards, we can get the reverse of the inverse of the reverse of any input-restricted permutation with an output-restricted deque, and conversely. This rule sets up a one-to-one correspondence between the two sets of permutations.

10. (i) There should be n X's and n combined S's and Q's. (ii) The number of X's must never exceed the combined number of S's and Q's, if we read from the left. (iii) Whenever the number of X's equals the combined number of S's and Q's (reading from the left), the next character must be a Q. (iv) The two operations XQ must never be adjacent in this order.

Clearly rules (i) and (ii) are necessary. The extra rules (iii) and (iv) are added to remove ambiguity, since S is the same as Q when the deque is empty, and since XQ can always be replaced by QX. Thus, any obtainable permutation corresponds to at least one admissible sequence.

To show that two admissible sequences give different permutations, consider sequences that are identical up to a point, and then one sequence has an S while the other has an X or Q. Since by (iii) the deque is not empty, clearly different permutations (relative to the order of the element inserted by S) are obtained by the two sequences. The remaining case is where sequences A, B agree up to a point and then sequence A has Q, sequence B has X. Sequence B may have further X's at this point, and by (iv) they must be followed by an S, so again the permutations are different.

11. Proceeding as in exercise 4, we let g_{nm} be the number of partial admissible sequences of length n, leaving m elements on the deque, *not* ending in the symbol X; h_{nm} is defined analogously, for those sequences that *do* end with X. We have $g_{(n+1)m} = 2g_{n(m-1)} + h_{n(m-1)}[m > 1]$, and $h_{(n+1)m} = g_{n(m+1)} + h_{n(m+1)}$. Define $G(x, z)$ and $H(x, z)$ by analogy with the definition in exercise 4; we have

$$G(x, z) = xz + 2x^2 z^2 + 4x^3 z^3 + (8x^4 + 2x^2)z^4 + (16x^5 + 8x^3)z^5 + \cdots;$$
$$H(x, z) = z^2 + 2xz^3 + (4x^2 + 2)z^4 + (8x^3 + 6x)z^5 + \cdots.$$

Setting $h(z) = H(0, z)$, we find $z^{-1}G(x, z) = 2xG(x, z) + x(H(x, z) - h(z)) + x$, and $z^{-1}H(x, z) = x^{-1}G(x, z) + x^{-1}(H(x, z) - h(z))$; consequently

$$G(x, z) = \frac{xz(x - z - xh(z))}{x - z - 2x^2z + xz^2}.$$

As in exercise 4, we try to choose $h(z)$ so that the numerator cancels with a factor of the denominator. We find $G(x, z) = xz/(1 - 2xr_2(z))$ where

$$r_2(z) = \frac{1}{4z}\left(z^2 + 1 - \sqrt{(z^2 + 1)^2 - 8z^2}\right).$$

Using the convention $b_0 = 1$, the desired generating function comes to

$$\tfrac{1}{2}\left(3 - z - \sqrt{1 - 6z + z^2}\right) = 1 + z + 2z^2 + 6z^3 + 22z^4 + 90z^5 + \cdots.$$

By differentiation we find a recurrence relation that is handy for calculation: $nb_n = 3(2n - 3)b_{n-1} - (n - 3)b_{n-2}$, $n \ge 2$.

Another way to solve this problem, suggested by V. Pratt, is to use context-free grammars for the set of strings (see Chapter 10). The infinite grammar with productions $S \to q^n(Bx)^n$, $B \to sq^n(Bx)^{n+1}B$, for all $n \ge 0$, and $B \to \epsilon$, is unambiguous, and it allows us to count the number of strings with n x's, as in exercise 2.3.4.4–31.

12. We have $a_n = 4^n/\sqrt{\pi n^3} + O(4^n n^{-5/2})$ by Stirling's formula. To analyze b_n, let us first consider the general problem of estimating the coefficient of w^n in the power series for $\sqrt{1 - w}\sqrt{1 - \alpha w}$ when $|\alpha| < 1$. We have, for sufficiently small α,

$$\sqrt{1 - w}\sqrt{1 - \alpha w} = \sqrt{1 - w}\sqrt{1 - \alpha + \alpha(1 - w)} = \sqrt{1 - \alpha}\sum_k \binom{1/2}{k}\beta^k(1 - w)^{k+1/2},$$

where $\beta = \alpha/(1 - \alpha)$; hence the desired coefficient is $(-1)^n\sqrt{1 - \alpha}\sum_k \binom{1/2}{k}\beta^k\binom{k+1/2}{n}$. Now

$$(-1)^n\binom{k+1/2}{n} = \binom{n-k-3/2}{n} = \frac{\Gamma(n-k-1/2)}{\Gamma(n+1)\Gamma(-k-1/2)} = \frac{(-1/2)^{k+1}}{\sqrt{\pi n}}\, n^{-k-1/2},$$

and $n^{-k-1/2} = \sum_{j=0}^m \left[{-k-1/2 \atop -k-1/2-j}\right]n^{-k-1/2-j} + O(n^{-k-3/2-m})$ by Eq. 1.2.11.1–(16). Thus we obtain the asymptotic series $[w^n]\sqrt{1-w}\sqrt{1-\alpha w} = c_0 n^{-3/2} + c_1 n^{-5/2} + \cdots + c_m n^{-m-3/2} + O(n^{-m-5/2})$ where

$$c_j = \sqrt{\frac{1-\alpha}{\pi}}\sum_{k=0}^j \binom{1/2}{k}(-1/2)^{k+1}\left\{{j + 1/2 \atop k + 1/2}\right\}\frac{\alpha^k}{(1-\alpha)^k}.$$

For b_n, we write $1 - 6z + z^2 = (1 - (3+\sqrt{8})z)(1 - (3-\sqrt{8})z)$ and let $w = (3+\sqrt{8})z$, $\alpha = (3-\sqrt{8})/(3+\sqrt{8})$, obtaining the asymptotic formula

$$b_n = \frac{(\sqrt{2}-1)(3+\sqrt{8})^n}{2^{3/4}\pi^{1/2}n^{3/2}}(1 + O(n^{-1})) = \frac{(\sqrt{2}+1)^{2n-1}}{2^{3/4}\pi^{1/2}n^{3/2}}(1 + O(n^{-1})).$$

13. V. Pratt has found that a permutation is unobtainable if and only if it contains a subsequence whose relative magnitudes are respectively

$$5, 2, 7, 4, \ldots, 4k+1, 4k-2, 3, 4k, 1 \quad \text{or} \quad 5, 2, 7, 4, \ldots, 4k+3, 4k, 1, 4k+2, 3$$

for some $k \ge 1$, or the same with the last two elements interchanged, or with the 1 and 2 interchanged, or both. Thus the forbidden patterns for $k = 1$ are 52341, 52314, 51342, 51324, 5274163, 5274136, 5174263, 5174236. [*STOC* **5** (1973), 268–277.]

14. (Solution by R. Melville, 1980.) Let R and S be stacks such that the queue runs from top to bottom of R followed by bottom to top of S. To insert at the rear, push onto S. To delete from the front, pop the top of R — except that if R is empty, first pop the elements of S onto R until S becomes empty. Each element is first pushed onto S, then popped from S and pushed to R, then popped from R when leaving the queue. (But if R and S are both empty, one might prefer to push directly onto R.)

SECTION 2.2.2

1. $M - 1$ (*not* M). If we allowed M items, as (6) and (7) do, it would be impossible to distinguish an empty queue from a full one by examination of R and F, since only M possibilities can be detected. It is better to give up one storage cell than to make the program overly complicated.

2. Delete from rear: If $R = F$ then UNDERFLOW; $Y \leftarrow X[R]$; if $R = 1$ then $R \leftarrow M$, otherwise $R \leftarrow R - 1$. Insert at front: Set $X[F] \leftarrow Y$; if $F = 1$ then $F \leftarrow M$, otherwise $F \leftarrow F - 1$; if $F = R$ then OVERFLOW.

3. (a) LD1 I; LDA BASE,7:1. This takes 5 cycles instead of 4 or 8 as in (8).

(b) *Solution 1:* LDA BASE,2:7 where each base address is stored with $I_1 = 0$, $I_2 = 1$. *Solution 2:* If it is desired to store the base addresses with $I_1 = I_2 = 0$, we could write LDA X2,7:1 where location X2 contains NOP BASE,2:7. The second solution takes one more cycle, but it allows the base table to be used with any index registers.

(c) This is equivalent to 'LD4 X(0:2)', and takes the same execution time, except that rI4 will be set to $+0$ when X(0:2) contains -0.

4. (a) NOP *,7. (b) LDA X,7:7(0:2). (c) This is impossible; the code LDA Y,7:7 where location Y contains NOP X,7:7 breaks the restriction on 7:7. (See exercise 5.) (d) LDA X,7:1 with the auxiliary constants

```
X   NOP   *+1,7:2
    NOP   *+1,7:3
    NOP   *+1,7:4
    NOP   0,5:6
```

The execution time is 6 units. (e) INC6 X,7:6 where X contains NOP 0,6:6.

5. (a) Consider the instruction ENTA 1000,7:7 with the memory configuration

location	ADDRESS	I_1	I_2
1000:	1001	7	7
1001:	1004	7	1
1002:	1002	2	2
1003:	1001	1	1
1004:	1005	1	7
1005:	1006	1	7
1006:	1008	7	7
1007:	1002	7	1
1008:	1003	7	2

and with rI1 = 1, rI2 = 2. We find that $1000,7,7 = 1001,7,7,7 = 1004,7,1,7,7 = 1005,1,7,1,7,7 = 1006,7,1,7,7 = 1008,7,7,1,7,7 = 1003,7,2,7,1,7,7 = 1001,1,1,2,7,1,7,7 = 1002,1,2,7,1,7,7 = 1003,2,7,1,7,7 = 1005,7,1,7,7 = 1006,1,7,1,7,7 = 1007,7,1,7,7 = 1002,7,1,1,7,7 = 1002,2,2,1,1,7,7 = 1004,2,1,1,7,7 = 1006,1,1,7,7 = 1007,1,7,7 = 1008,7,7 = 1003,7,2,7 = 1001,1,1,2,7 = 1002,1,2,7 = 1003,2,7 = 1005,7 = 1006,1,7 = 1007,7 =$

$1002,7,1 = 1002,2,2,1 = 1004,2,1 = 1006,1 = 1007$. (A faster way to do this derivation by hand would be to evaluate successively the addresses specified in locations 1002, 1003, 1007, 1008, 1005, 1006, 1004, 1001, 1000, in this order; but a computer evidently needs to go about the evaluation essentially as shown.) The author tried out several fancy schemes for changing the contents of memory while evaluating the address, with everything to be restored again by the time the final address has been obtained. Similar algorithms appear in Section 2.3.5. However, these attempts were unfruitful and it appears that there is just not enough room to store the necessary information.

(b, c) Let H and C be auxiliary registers and let N be a counter. To get the effective address M, for the instruction in location L, do the following:

A1. [Initialize.] Set $H \leftarrow 0$, $C \leftarrow L$, $N \leftarrow 0$. (In this algorithm, C is the "current" location, H is used to add together the contents of various index registers, and N measures the depth of indirect addressing.)

A2. [Examine address.] Set $M \leftarrow$ ADDRESS(C). If $I_1(C) = j$, $1 \le j \le 6$, set $M \leftarrow M + rIj$. If $I_2(C) = j$, $1 \le j \le 6$, set $H \leftarrow H + rIj$. If $I_1(C) = I_2(C) = 7$, set $N \leftarrow N + 1$, $H \leftarrow 0$.

A3. [Indirect?] If either $I_1(C)$ or $I_2(C)$ equals 7, set $C \leftarrow M$ and go to A2. Otherwise set $M \leftarrow M + H$, $H \leftarrow 0$.

A4. [Reduce depth.] If $N > 0$, set $C \leftarrow M$, $N \leftarrow N - 1$, and go to A2. Otherwise M is the desired answer. ∎

This algorithm will handle any situation correctly except those in which $I_1 = 7$ and $1 \le I_2 \le 6$ *and* the evaluation of the address in ADDRESS involves a case with $I_1 = I_2 = 7$. The effect is as if I_2 were zero. To understand the operation of Algorithm A, consider the notation of part (a); the state "L,7,1,2,5,2,7,7,7,7" is represented by C or $M = L$, $N = 4$ (the number of trailing 7s), and $H = rI1 + rI2 + rI5 + rI2$ (the post-indexing). In a solution to part (b) of this exercise, the counter N will always be either 0 or 1.

6. (c) causes OVERFLOW. (e) causes UNDERFLOW, and if the program resumes it causes OVERFLOW on the final I_2.

7. No, since TOP[i] must be greater than OLDTOP[i].

8. With a stack, the useful information appears at one end with the vacant information at the other:

where $A =$ BASE[j], $B =$ TOP[j], $C =$ BASE[j + 1]. With a queue or deque, the useful information appears at the ends with the vacant information somewhere in the middle:

or in the middle with the vacant information at the ends:

where $A =$ BASE[j], $B =$ REAR[j], $C =$ FRONT[j], $D =$ BASE[j + 1]. The two cases are distinguished by the conditions $B \le C$ and $B > C$, respectively, in a nonempty queue; or, if the queue is known not to have overflowed, the distinguishing conditions are respectively $B < C$ and $B \geq C$. The algorithms should therefore be modified in an obvious way so as to widen or narrow the gaps of vacant information. (Thus in case of overflow, when $B = C$, we make empty space between B and C by moving one part and not the other.) In the calculation of SUM and D[j] in step G2, each queue should be considered to occupy one more cell than it really does (see exercise 1).

9. Given any sequence specification $a_1, a_2, \ldots, a_m$ there is one move operation required for every pair (j, k) such that $j < k$ and $a_j > a_k$. (Such a pair is called an "inversion"; see Section 5.1.1.) The number of such pairs is therefore the number of moves required. Now imagine all n^m specifications written out, and for each of the $\binom{m}{2}$ pairs (j, k) with $j < k$ count how many specifications have $a_j > a_k$. Clearly this equals $\binom{n}{2}$, the number of choices for a_j and a_k, times n^{m-2}, the number of ways to fill in the remaining places. Hence the total number of moves among all specifications is $\binom{m}{2}\binom{n}{2}n^{m-2}$. Divide this by n^m to get the average, Eq. (14).

10. As in exercise 9 we find that the expected value is

$$\binom{m}{2} \sum_{1 \leq j < k \leq n} p_j p_k = \frac{1}{2}\binom{m}{2}\left((p_1 + \cdots + p_n)^2 - (p_1^2 + \cdots + p_n^2)\right)$$

$$= \frac{1}{2}\binom{m}{2}(1 - (p_1^2 + \cdots + p_n^2)).$$

For this model, it makes *absolutely no difference* what the relative order of the lists is! (A moment's reflection explains why; if we consider all possible permutations of a given sequence $a_1, \ldots, a_m$, we find that the total number of moves summed over all these permutations depends only on the number of pairs of distinct elements $a_j \neq a_k$.)

11. Counting as before, we find that the expected number is

$$E_{mnt} = \frac{1}{n^m}\binom{n}{2}\sum_{k=1}^{m}\sum_{r \geq t}(k-1)\binom{k-2}{r}(n-1)^{k-2-r}n^{m-k};$$

here r is the number of entries in $a_1, a_2, \ldots, a_{k-1}$ that equal a_k. This quantity can also be expressed in the simpler form

$$E_{mnt} = \frac{1}{n^m}\binom{n}{2}\sum_{k>t}\binom{m}{k}(n-1)^{m-k}\left(\binom{k}{2} - \binom{t+1}{2}\right), \quad \text{for } t \geq 0.$$

Is there a simpler way yet to give the answer? Apparently not, since the generating function for given n and t is

$$\sum_m E_{mnt}z^m = \frac{n-1}{2n}\frac{z}{(1-z)^3}\left(\frac{z}{n-(n-1)z}\right)^{t+1}(z + (1-z)n(t+1)).$$

12. If $m = 2k$, the average is 2^{-2k} times

$$\binom{2k}{0}2k + \binom{2k}{1}(2k-1) + \cdots + \binom{2k}{k}k + \binom{2k}{k+1}(k+1) + \cdots + \binom{2k}{2k}2k.$$

The latter sum is

$$\binom{2k}{k}k + 2\left(\binom{2k-1}{k}2k + \cdots + \binom{2k-1}{2k-1}2k\right) = \binom{2k}{k}k + 4k \cdot \frac{1}{2} \cdot 2^{2k-1}.$$

A similar argument may be used when $m = 2k + 1$. The answer is

$$\frac{m}{2} + \frac{m}{2^m}\binom{m-1}{\lfloor m/2 \rfloor}.$$

13. A. C. Yao has proved that we have $\mathrm{E}\max(k_1, k_2) = \frac{1}{2}m + (2\pi(1-2p))^{-1/2}\sqrt{m} + O(m^{-1/2}(\log m)^2)$ for large m, when $p < \frac{1}{2}$. [*SICOMP* **10** (1981), 398–403.] And P. Flajolet has extended the analysis, showing in particular that the expected value is asymptotically αm when $p = \frac{1}{2}$, where

$$\alpha = \frac{1}{2} + 8\sum_{n\geq 1}\frac{\sin(n\pi/2)\cosh(n\pi/2)}{n^2\pi^2\sinh n\pi} \approx 0.67531\,44833.$$

Moreover, when $p > \frac{1}{2}$ the final value of k_1 tends to be uniformly distributed as $m \to \infty$, so $\mathrm{E}\max(k_1, k_2) \approx \frac{3}{4}m$. [See *Lecture Notes in Comp. Sci.* **233** (1986), 325–340.]

14. Let $k_j = m/n + \sqrt{m}\,x_j$. (This idea was suggested by N. G. de Bruijn.) Stirling's approximation implies that

$$n^{-m}\frac{m!}{k_1!\ldots k_n!}\max(k_1, \ldots, k_n)$$

$$= (\sqrt{2\pi m})^{1-n}n^{n/2}\left(\frac{m}{n} + \sqrt{m}\max(x_1, \ldots, x_n)\right)$$

$$\times \exp\left(-\frac{n}{2}(x_1^2 + \cdots + x_n^2)\right)(\sqrt{m})^{1-n}\left(1 + O\left(\frac{1}{\sqrt{m}}\right)\right),$$

when $k_1 + \cdots + k_n = m$ and when the x's are uniformly bounded. The sum of the latter quantity over all nonnegative $k_1, \ldots, k_n$ satisfying this condition is an approximation to a Riemann integral; we may deduce that the asymptotic behavior of the sum is $a_n(m/n) + c_n\sqrt{m} + O(1)$, where

$$a_n = (\sqrt{2\pi})^{1-n}n^{n/2}\int_{x_1+\cdots+x_n=0}\exp\left(-\frac{n}{2}(x_1^2 + \cdots + x_n^2)\right)dx_2\ldots dx_n,$$

$$c_n = (\sqrt{2\pi})^{1-n}n^{n/2}\int_{x_1+\cdots+x_n=0}\max(x_1, \ldots, x_n)\exp\left(-\frac{n}{2}(x_1^2 + \cdots + x_n^2)\right)dx_2\ldots dx_n,$$

since it is possible to show that the corresponding sums come within ϵ of a_n and c_n for any ϵ.

We know that $a_n = 1$, since the corresponding sum can be evaluated explicitly. The integral that appears in the expression for c_n equals nI_1, where

$$I_1 = \int_{\substack{x_1+\cdots+x_n=0\\x_1\geq x_2,\ldots,x_n}}x_1\exp\left(-\frac{n}{2}(x_1^2 + \cdots + x_n^2)\right)dx_2\ldots dx_n.$$

We may make the substitution

$$x_1 = \frac{1}{n}(y_2 + \cdots + y_n), \quad x_2 = x_1 - y_2, \quad x_3 = x_1 - y_3, \quad \ldots, \quad x_n = x_1 - y_n;$$

then we find $I_1 = I_2/n^2$, where

$$I_2 = \int_{y_2,\ldots,y_n\geq 0}(y_2 + \cdots + y_n)\exp\left(-\frac{Q}{2}\right)dy_2\ldots dy_n,$$

and $Q = n(y_2^2 + \cdots + y_n^2) - (y_2 + \cdots + y_n)^2$. Now by symmetry, I_2 is $(n-1)$ times the same integral with $(y_2 + \cdots + y_n)$ replaced by y_2; hence $I_2 = (n-1)I_3$, where

$$I_3 = \int_{y_2,\ldots,y_n \geq 0} (ny_2 - (y_2 + \cdots + y_n)) \exp\left(-\frac{Q}{2}\right) dy_2 \ldots dy_n$$

$$= \int_{y_3,\ldots,y_n \geq 0} \exp\left(-\frac{Q_0}{2}\right) dy_3 \ldots dy_n;$$

here Q_0 is Q with y_2 replaced by zero. [When $n = 2$, let $I_3 = 1$.] Now let $z_j = \sqrt{n}\, y_j - (y_3 + \cdots + y_n)/(\sqrt{2} + \sqrt{n})$, $3 \leq j \leq n$. Then $Q_0 = z_3^2 + \cdots + z_n^2$, and we deduce that $I_3 = I_4/n^{(n-3)/2}\sqrt{2}$, where

$$I_4 = \int_{y_3,\ldots,y_n \geq 0} \exp\left(-\frac{z_3^2 + \cdots + z_n^2}{2}\right) dz_3 \ldots dz_n$$

$$= \alpha_n \int \exp\left(-\frac{z_3^2 + \cdots + z_n^2}{2}\right) dz_3 \ldots dz_n = \alpha_n (\sqrt{2\pi})^{n-2},$$

where α_n is the "solid angle" in $(n-2)$-dimensional space spanned by the vectors $(n+\sqrt{2n}, 0, \ldots, 0) - (1, 1, \ldots, 1)$, $\ldots$, $(0, 0, \ldots, n+\sqrt{2n}) - (1, 1, \ldots, 1)$, divided by the total solid angle of the whole space. Hence

$$c_n = \frac{(n-1)\sqrt{n}}{2\sqrt{\pi}} \alpha_n.$$

We have $\alpha_2 = 1$, $\alpha_3 = \frac{1}{2}$, $\alpha_4 = \pi^{-1} \arctan \sqrt{2} \approx .304$, and

$$\alpha_5 = \frac{1}{8} + \frac{3}{4\pi} \arctan \frac{1}{\sqrt{8}} \approx .206.$$

[The value of c_3 was found by Robert M. Kozelka, *Annals of Math. Stat.* **27** (1956), 507–512, but the solution to this problem for higher values of n has apparently never appeared in the literature.]

16. Not unless the queues meet the restrictions that apply to the primitive method of (4) and (5).

17. First show that $\mathtt{BASE[j]}_0 \leq \mathtt{BASE[j]}_1$ at all times. Then observe that each overflow for stack i in $s_0(\sigma)$ that does not also overflow in $s_1(\sigma)$ occurs at a time when stack i has gotten larger than ever before, yet its new size is not more than the original size allocated to stack i in $s_1(\sigma)$.

18. Suppose the cost of an insertion is a, plus $bN + cn$ if repacking is needed, where N is the number of occupied cells; let the deletion cost be d. After a repacking that leaves N cells occupied and $S = M - N$ cells vacant, imagine that each insertion until the next repacking costs $a + b + 10c + 10(b + c)nN/S = O(1 + n\alpha/(1 - \alpha))$, where $\alpha = N/M$. If p insertions and q deletions occur before that repacking, the imagined cost is $p(a+b+10c+10(b+c)nN/S)+qd$, while the actual cost is $pa+bN'+cn+qd \leq pa + pb + bN + cn + qd$. The latter is less than the imagined cost, because $p > .1S/n$; our assumption that $M \geq n^2$ implies that $cS/n + (b+c)N \geq bN + cn$.

19. We could simply decrease all the subscripts by 1; the following solution is slightly nicer. Initially $\mathtt{T = F = R = 0}$.

Push $\mathtt{Y}$ onto stack $\mathtt{X}$: If $\mathtt{T = M}$ then $\mathtt{OVERFLOW}$; $\mathtt{X[T]} \leftarrow \mathtt{Y}$; $\mathtt{T \leftarrow T + 1}$.

Pop $\mathtt{Y}$ from stack $\mathtt{X}$: If $\mathtt{T = 0}$ then $\mathtt{UNDERFLOW}$; $\mathtt{T \leftarrow T - 1}$; $\mathtt{Y \leftarrow X[T]}$.

Insert Y into queue X: $X[R] \leftarrow Y$; $R \leftarrow (R+1) \bmod M$; if $R = F$ then OVERFLOW.

Delete Y from queue X: if $F = R$ then UNDERFLOW; $Y \leftarrow X[F]$; $F \leftarrow (F+1) \bmod M$. As before, T is the number of elements on the stack, and $(R - F) \bmod M$ is the number of elements on the queue. But the top stack element is now $X[T - 1]$, not $X[T]$.

Even though it is almost always better for computer scientists to start counting at 0, the rest of the world will probably never change to 0-origin indexing. Even Edsger Dijkstra counts "1–2–3–4 | 1–2–3–4" when he plays the piano!

SECTION 2.2.3

1. OVERFLOW is implicit in the operation $P \Leftarrow \text{AVAIL}$.

2.

```
   INSERT  STJ   1F              Store location of 'NOP T'.
           STJ   9F              Store exit location.
           LD1   AVAIL           rI1 ⇐ AVAIL.
           J1Z   OVERFLOW
           LD3   0,1(LINK)
           ST3   AVAIL
           STA   0,1(INFO)  INFO(rI1) ← Y.
   1H      LD3   *(0:2)     rI3 ← LOC(T).
           LD2   0,3        rI2 ← T.
           ST2   0,1(LINK)  LINK(rI1) ← T.
           ST1   0,3        T ← rI1.
   9H      JMP   *              ▌
```

3.

```
   DELETE  STJ   1F              Store location of 'NOP T'.
           STJ   9F              Store exit location.
   1H      LD2   *(0:2)     rI2 ← LOC(T).
           LD3   0,2        rI3 ← T.
           J3Z   9F         Is T = Λ?
           LD1   0,3(LINK)  rI1 ← LINK(T).
           ST1   0,2        T ← rI1.
           LDA   0,3(INFO)  rA ← INFO(rI3).
           LD2   AVAIL      AVAIL ⇐ rI3.
           ST2   0,3(LINK)
           ST3   AVAIL
           ENT3  2               Prepare for second exit.
   9H      JMP   *,3            ▌
```

4.

```
 OVERFLOW STJ   9F               Store setting of rJ.
          ST1   8F(0:2)          Save rI1 setting.
          LD1   POOLMAX
          ST1   AVAIL            Set AVAIL to new location.
          INC1  c
          ST1   POOLMAX          Increment POOLMAX.
          CMP1  SEQMIN
          JG    TOOBAD           Has storage been exceeded?
          STZ   -c,1(LINK)       Set LINK(AVAIL) ← Λ.
   9H     ENT1  *                Take rJ setting.
          DEC1  2                Subtract 2.
          ST1   *+2(0:2)         Store exit location.
   8H     ENT1  *                Restore rI1.
          JMP   *                Return.   ▌
```

5. Inserting at the front is essentially like the basic insertion operation (8), with an additional test for empty queue: P $\Leftarrow$ AVAIL, INFO(P) $\leftarrow$ Y, LINK(P) $\leftarrow$ F; if F $= \Lambda$ then R $\leftarrow$ P; F $\leftarrow$ P.

To delete from the rear, we would have to find which node links to NODE(R), and that is necessarily inefficient since we have to search all the way from F. This could be done, for example, as follows:

a) If F $= \Lambda$ then UNDERFLOW, otherwise set P $\leftarrow$ LOC(F).

b) If LINK(P) $\neq$ R then set P $\leftarrow$ LINK(P) and repeat this step until LINK(P) $=$ R.

c) Set Y $\leftarrow$ INFO(R), AVAIL $\Leftarrow$ R, R $\leftarrow$ P, LINK(P) $\leftarrow \Lambda$.

6. We could remove the operation LINK(P) $\leftarrow \Lambda$ from (14), if we delete the commands "F $\leftarrow$ LINK(P)" and "if F $= \Lambda$ then set R $\leftarrow$ LOC(F)" from (17); the latter are to be replaced by "if F $=$ R then F $\leftarrow \Lambda$ and R $\leftarrow$ LOC(F), otherwise set F $\leftarrow$ LINK(P)".

The effect of these changes is that the LINK field of the rear node in the queue will contain spurious information that is never interrogated by the program. A trick like this saves execution time and it is quite useful in practice, although it violates one of the basic assumptions of garbage collection (see Section 2.3.5) so it cannot be used in conjunction with such algorithms.

7. (Make sure that your solution works for empty lists.)

I1. Set P $\leftarrow$ FIRST, Q $\leftarrow \Lambda$.

I2. If P $\neq \Lambda$, set R $\leftarrow$ Q, Q $\leftarrow$ P, P $\leftarrow$ LINK(Q), LINK(Q) $\leftarrow$ R, and repeat this step.

I3. Set FIRST $\leftarrow$ Q. ∎

In essence we are popping nodes off one stack and pushing them onto another.

8.

	LD1	FIRST	1	*I1.* P $\equiv$ rI1 $\leftarrow$ FIRST.
	ENT2	0	1	Q $\equiv$ rI2 $\leftarrow \Lambda$.
	J1Z	2F	1	*I2.* If the list is empty, jump.
1H	ENTA	0,2	n	R $\equiv$ rA $\leftarrow$ Q.
	ENT2	0,1	n	Q $\leftarrow$ P.
	LD1	0,2(LINK)	n	P $\leftarrow$ LINK(Q).
	STA	0,2(LINK)	n	LINK(Q) $\leftarrow$ R.
	J1NZ	1B	n	Is P $\neq \Lambda$?
2H	ST2	FIRST	1	*I3.* FIRST $\leftarrow$ Q. ∎

The time is $(7n + 6)u$. Better speed $(5n + \text{constant})u$ is attainable; see exercise 1.1–3.

9. (a) Yes.   (b) Yes, if biological parenthood is considered; no, if legal parenthood is considered (a man's daughter might marry his father, as in the song "I'm My Own Grampa").   (c) No ($-1 \prec 1$ and $1 \prec -1$).   (d) Let us hope so, or else there is a circular argument.   (e) $1 \prec 3$ and $3 \prec 1$.   (f) The statement is ambiguous. If we take the position that the subroutines called by y are dependent upon which subroutine calls y, we would have to conclude that the transitive law does not necessarily hold. (For example, a general input-output subroutine might call on different processing routines for each I/O device present, but these processing subroutines are usually not all needed in a single program. This is a problem that plagued many automatic programming systems in the old days.)

10. For (i) there are three cases: $x = y$; $x \subset y$ and $y = z$; $x \subset y$ and $y \subset z$. For (ii) there are two cases: $x = y$; $x \neq y$. Each case is handled trivially, as is (iii).

11. "Multiply out" the following to get all 52 solutions: $13749(25 + 52)86 + (1379 + 1397 + 1937 + 9137)(4258 + 4528 + 2458 + 5428 + 2548 + 5248 + 2584 + 5284)6 + (1392 + 1932 + 1923 + 9123 + 9132 + 9213)7(458 + 548 + 584)6$.

12. For example: (a) List all sets with k elements (in any order) before all sets with $k+1$ elements, $0 \le k < n$. (b) Represent a subset by a sequence of 0s and 1s showing which elements are in the set. This gives a correspondence between all subsets and the integers 0 through $2^n - 1$, via the binary number system. The order of correspondence is a topological sequence.

13. Sha and Kleitman [*Discrete Math.* **63** (1987), 271–278] proved that the number is at most $\prod_{k=0}^{n} \binom{n}{k} \binom{n}{k}$; Brightwell and Tetali [*Order* **20** (2003), 333–345] improved this upper bound to $\exp((2en2^n/r)^r \prod_{k=0}^{n} \binom{n}{k}!)$, where $r = (2^{n+1} - 2)/(n+1)$. The obvious lower bound is $\prod_{k=0}^{n} \binom{n}{k}! = 2^{2^n(n+O(\log n))}$. For the initial values $\langle a_n \rangle = \langle 1, 1, 2, 48, 1680384, \dots \rangle$, up to $a_7 \approx 6.305 \times 10^{137}$, see OEIS sequence A046873.

14. If $a_1 a_2 \dots a_n$ and $b_1 b_2 \dots b_n$ are two possible topological sorts, let j be minimal such that $a_j \ne b_j$; then $a_k = b_j$ and $a_j = b_m$ for some $k, m > j$. Now $b_j \not\preceq a_j$ since $k > j$, and $a_j \not\preceq b_j$ since $m > j$, hence (iv) fails. Conversely if there is only one topological sort $a_1 a_2 \dots a_n$, we must have $a_j \preceq a_{j+1}$ for $1 \le j < n$, since otherwise a_j and a_{j+1} could be interchanged. This and transitivity imply (iv).

Note: The following alternative proofs work also for infinite sets. (a) Every partial ordering can be embedded in a linear ordering. For if we have two elements with $x_0 \not\preceq y_0$ and $y_0 \not\preceq x_0$ we can generate another partial ordering by the rule "$x \preceq y$ or ($x \preceq x_0$ and $y_0 \preceq y$)." The latter ordering "includes" the former and has $x_0 \preceq y_0$. Now apply Zorn's lemma or transfinite induction in the usual way to complete the proof. (b) Obviously a linear ordering cannot be embedded in any different linear ordering. (c) A partial ordering that has incomparable elements x_0 and y_0 as in (a) can be extended to two linear orderings in which $x_0 \preceq y_0$ and $y_0 \preceq x_0$, respectively, so at least two linear orderings exist.

15. If S is finite, we can list all relations $a \prec b$ that are true in the given partial ordering. By successively removing, one at a time, any relations that are implied by others, we arrive at an irredundant set. The problem is to show there is just one such set, no matter in what order we go about removing redundant relations. If there were two irredundant sets U and V, in which "$a \prec b$" appears in U but not in V, there are $k+1$ relations $a \prec c_1 \prec \cdots \prec c_k \prec b$ in V for some $k \ge 1$. But it is possible to deduce $a \prec c_1$ and $c_1 \prec b$ from U, *without* using the relation $a \prec b$ (since $b \not\preceq c_1$ and $c_1 \not\preceq a$), hence the relation $a \prec b$ is redundant in U.

The result is false for infinite sets S, when there is *at most* one irredundant set of relations. For example if S denotes the integers plus the element ∞ and we define $n \prec n+1$ and $n \prec \infty$ for all n, there is no irredundant set of relations that characterizes this partial ordering.

16. Let $x_{p_1} x_{p_2} \dots x_{p_n}$ be a topological sorting of S; apply the permutation $p_1 p_2 \dots p_n$ to both rows and columns.

17. If k increases from 1 to n in step T4, the output is 1932745860. If k decreases from n to 1 in step T4, as it does in Program T, the output is 9123745860.

18. They link together the items in sorted order: QLINK[0] first, QLINK[QLINK[0]] second, and so on; QLINK[last] $= 0$.

19. This would fail in certain cases; when the queue contains only one element in step T5, the modified method would set F $= 0$ (thereby emptying the queue), but other entries could be placed in the queue in step T6. The suggested modification would therefore require an additional test of F $= 0$ in step T6.

20. Indeed, a stack *could* be used, in the following way. (Step T7 disappears.)

T4. Set T ← 0. For $1 \leq k \leq n$ if COUNT[k] is zero do the following: Set SLINK[k] ← T, T ← k. (SLINK[k] ≡ QLINK[k].)

T5. Output the value of T. If T=0, go to T8; otherwise, set N ← N − 1, P ← TOP[T], T ← SLINK[T].

T6. Same as before, except go to T5 instead of T7; and when COUNT[SUC(P)] goes down to zero, set SLINK[SUC(P)] ← T and T ← SUC(P).

21. Repeated relations only make the algorithm a little slower and take up more space in the storage pool. A relation "$j \prec j$" would be treated like a loop (an arrow from a box to itself in the corresponding diagram), which violates partial order.

22. To make the program "fail-safe" we should (a) check that $0 < n <$ some appropriate maximum; (b) check each relation $j \prec k$ for the conditions $0 < j, k \leq n$; (c) make sure that the number of relations doesn't overflow the storage pool area.

23. At the end of step T5, add "TOP[F] ← Λ". (Then at all times TOP[1], ..., TOP[n] point to all the relations not yet canceled.) In step T8, if N > 0, print 'LOOP DETECTED IN INPUT:', and set QLINK[k] ← 0 for $1 \leq k \leq n$. Now add the following steps:

T9. For $1 \leq k \leq n$ set P ← TOP[k], TOP[k] ← 0, and perform step T10. (This will set QLINK[j] to one of the predecessors of object j, for each j not yet output.) Then go to T11.

T10. If P ≠ Λ, set QLINK[SUC(P)] ← k, P ← NEXT(P), and repeat this step.

T11. Find a k with QLINK[k] ≠ 0.

T12. Set TOP[k] ← 1 and k ← QLINK[k]. Now if TOP[k] = 0, repeat this step.

T13. (We have found the start of a loop.) Print the value of k, set TOP[k] ← 0, k ← QLINK[k], and if TOP[k] = 1 repeat this step.

T14. Print the value of k (the beginning and end of the loop) and stop. (*Note:* The loop has been printed backwards; if it is desired to print the loop in forward order, an algorithm like that in exercise 7 should be used between steps T12 and T13.) ∎

24. Insert three lines in the program of the text:

```
08a  PRINTER EQU  18
14a          ST6  NO
59a          STZ  X,1(TOP)        TOP[F] ← Λ.
```

Replace lines 74–75 by the following:

```
74          J6Z  DONE
75          OUT  LINE1(PRINTER)   Print indication of loop.
76          LD6  NO
77          STZ  X,6(QLINK)       QLINK[k] ← 0.
78          DEC6 1
79          J6P  *-2              n ≥ k ≥ 1.
80          LD6  NO
81  T9      LD2  X,6(TOP)         P ← TOP[k].
82          STZ  X,6(TOP)         TOP[k] ← 0.
83          J2Z  T9A              Is P = Λ?
84  T10     LD1  0,2(SUC)         rI1 ← SUC(P).
85          ST6  X,1(QLINK)       QLINK[rI1] ← k.
86          LD2  0,2(NEXT)        P ← NEXT(P).
```

87		J2P	T10	Is P $\neq \Lambda$?
88	T9A	DEC6	1	
89		J6P	T9	$n \geq k \geq 1$.
90	T11	INC6	1	
91		LDA	X,6(QLINK)	
92		JAZ	*-2	Find k with QLINK$[k] \neq 0$.
93	T12	ST6	X,6(TOP)	TOP$[k] \leftarrow k$.
94		LD6	X,6(QLINK)	$k \leftarrow$ QLINK$[k]$.
95		LD1	X,6(TOP)	
96		J1Z	T12	Is TOP$[k] = 0$?
97	T13	ENTA	0,6	
98		CHAR		Convert k to alphameric.
99		JBUS	*(PRINTER)	
100		STX	VALUE	Print.
101		OUT	LINE2(PRINTER)	
102		J1Z	DONE	Stop when TOP$[k] = 0$.
103		STZ	X,6(TOP)	TOP$[k] \leftarrow 0$.
104		LD6	X,6(QLINK)	$k \leftarrow$ QLINK$[k]$.
105		LD1	X,6(TOP)	
106		JMP	T13	
107	LINE1	ALF	LOOP	Title line
108		ALF	DETEC	
109		ALF	TED I	
110		ALF	N INP	
111		ALF	UT:	
112	LINE2	ALF		Succeeding lines
113	VALUE	EQU	LINE2+3	
114		ORIG	LINE2+24	
115	DONE	HLT		End of computation
116	X	END	TOPSORT	∎

Note: If the relations $9 \prec 1$ and $6 \prec 9$ are added to the data (18), this program will print "9, 6, 8, 5, 9" as the loop.

26. One solution is to proceed in two phases as follows:

Phase 1. (We use the X table as a (sequential) stack as we mark B = 1 or 2 for each subroutine that needs to be used.)

   A0. For $1 \leq J \leq N$ set B(X[J]) $\leftarrow$ B(X[J]) $+ 2$, if B(X[J]) ≤ 0.

   A1. If N = 0, go to phase 2; otherwise set P $\leftarrow$ X[N] and decrease N by 1.

   A2. If $|$B(P)$| = 1$, go to A1, otherwise set P $\leftarrow$ P $+ 1$.

   A3. If B(SUB1(P)) ≤ 0, set N $\leftarrow$ N $+ 1$, B(SUB1(P)) $\leftarrow$ B(SUB1(P)) $+ 2$, X[N] $\leftarrow$ SUB1(P). If SUB2(P) $\neq 0$ and B(SUB2(P)) ≤ 0, do a similar set of actions with SUB2(P). Go to A2. ∎

Phase 2. (We go through the table and allocate memory.)

   B1. Set P $\leftarrow$ FIRST.

   B2. If P = Λ, set N $\leftarrow$ N$+1$, BASE(LOC(X[N])) $\leftarrow$ MLOC, SUB(LOC(X[N])) $\leftarrow$ 0, and terminate the algorithm.

B3. If $B(P) > 0$, set $N \leftarrow N + 1$, $BASE(LOC(X[N])) \leftarrow MLOC$, $SUB(LOC(X[N])) \leftarrow P$, $MLOC \leftarrow MLOC + SPACE(P)$.

B4. Set $P \leftarrow LINK(P)$ and return to B2. ∎

27. Comments on the following code are left to the reader.

```
B      EQU  0:1        A1 J1Z  B1              INC1 1
SPACE  EQU  2:3           LD2  X,1             INCA 2
LINK   EQU  4:5           DEC1 1               STA  0,3(B)
SUB1   EQU  2:3        A2 LDA  0,2(1:1)        ST3  X,1
SUB2   EQU  4:5           DECA 1               JMP  A2
BASE   EQU  0:3           JAZ  A1           B1 ENT2 FIRST
SUB    EQU  4:5           INC2 1               LDA  MLOC
A0     LD2  N         A3 LD3  0,2(SUB1)        JMP  1F
       J2Z  2F           LDA  0,3(B)        B3 LDX  0,2(B)
1H     LD3  X,2           JAP  9F               JXNP B4
       LDA  0,3(B)        INC1 1               INC1 1
       JAP  *+3           INCA 2               ST2  X,1(SUB)
       INCA 2            STA  0,3(B)           ADD  0,2(SPACE)
       STA  0,3(B)        ST3  X,1         1H STA  X+1,1(BASE)
       DEC2 1         9H LD3  0,2(SUB2)     B4 LD2  0,2(LINK)
       J2P  1B           J3Z  A2           B2 J2NZ B3
2H     LD1  N            LDA  0,3(B)           STZ  X+1,1(SUB)  ∎
                         JAP  A2
```

28. We give here only a few comments related to the military game. Let A be the player with three men whose pieces start on nodes A13; let B be the other player. In this game, A must "trap" B, and if B can cause a position to be repeated for a second time we can consider B the winner. To avoid keeping the entire past history of the game as an integral part of the positions, however, we should modify the algorithm in the following way: Start by marking the positions 157–4, 789–B, 359–6 with B to move as "lost" and apply the suggested algorithm. Now the idea is for player A to move only to B's lost positions. But A must also take precautions against repeating prior moves. A good computer game-playing program will use a random number generator to select between several winning moves when more than one is present, so an obvious technique would be to make the computer, playing A, just choose randomly among those moves that lead to a lost position for B. But there are interesting situations that make this plausible procedure fail! For example, consider position 258–7 with A to move; this is a won position. From position 258–7, player A might try moving to 158–7 (which is a lost position for B, according to the algorithm). But then B plays to 158–B, and this forces A to play to 258–B, after which B plays back to 258–7; B has won, since the former position has been repeated! This example shows that the algorithm must be re-invoked after every move has been made, starting with each position that has previously occurred marked "lost" (if A is to move) or "won" (if B is to move). The military game makes a very satisfactory computer demonstration program.

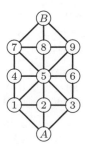

Board for the "military game."

29. (a) If $\text{FIRST} = \Lambda$, do nothing; otherwise set $P \leftarrow \text{FIRST}$, and then repeatedly set $P \leftarrow \text{LINK(P)}$ zero or more times until $\text{LINK(P)} = \Lambda$. Finally set $\text{LINK(P)} \leftarrow \text{AVAIL}$ and $\text{AVAIL} \leftarrow \text{FIRST}$ (and probably also $\text{FIRST} \leftarrow \Lambda$).   (b) If $F = \Lambda$, do nothing; otherwise set $\text{LINK(R)} \leftarrow \text{AVAIL}$ and $\text{AVAIL} \leftarrow F$ (and probably also $F \leftarrow \Lambda$, $R \leftarrow \text{LOC(F)}$).

30. To insert, set $P \Leftarrow \text{AVAIL}$, $\text{INFO(R)} \leftarrow Y$, $\text{LINK(R)} \leftarrow P$, $R \leftarrow P$, $\text{LINK(P)} \leftarrow \Lambda$. (We need not set LINK(P); but that lack of discipline might confuse a garbage collection algorithm, as in exercise 6.) To delete, UNDERFLOW if $F = R$; otherwise set $P \leftarrow F$, $F \leftarrow \text{LINK(P)}$, $Y \leftarrow \text{INFO(P)}$, $\text{AVAIL} \Leftarrow P$.

SECTION 2.2.4

1. No, it does not help; it seems to hinder, if anything. (The stated convention is *not* especially consistent with the circular list philosophy, unless we put NODE(LOC(PTR)) into the list as its list head.)

2. Before:

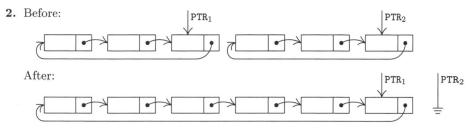

3. If $\text{PTR}_1 = \text{PTR}_2$, the only effect is $\text{PTR}_2 \leftarrow \Lambda$. If $\text{PTR}_1 \neq \text{PTR}_2$, the exchange of links breaks the list into two parts, as if a circle had been broken in two by cutting at two points; the second part of the operation then makes PTR_1 point to a circular list that consists of the nodes that would have been traversed if, in the original list, we followed the links from PTR_1 to PTR_2.

4. The text's operation (a) is unchanged; so is operation (c), but it's now preceded by "if $\text{LINK(PTR)} = \text{PTR}$, then UNDERFLOW." Operation (b) becomes "$\text{INFO(PTR)} \leftarrow Y$, $P \Leftarrow \text{AVAIL}$, $\text{LINK(P)} \leftarrow \text{LINK(PTR)}$, $\text{LINK(PTR)} \leftarrow P$, $\text{PTR} \leftarrow P$."

5. (Compare with exercise 2.2.3–7.) Set $Q \leftarrow \Lambda$, $P \leftarrow \text{PTR}$, and then while $P \neq \Lambda$ repeatedly set $R \leftarrow Q$, $Q \leftarrow P$, $P \leftarrow \text{LINK(Q)}$, $\text{LINK(Q)} \leftarrow R$. (Afterwards $Q = \text{PTR}$.)

6.

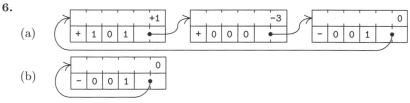

7. Matching terms in the polynomial are located in one pass over the list, so repeated random searches are avoided. Also, *increasing* order would be incompatible with the "−1" sentinel.

8. We must know what node points to the current node of interest, if we are going to delete that node or to insert another one ahead of it. There are alternatives, however: We could delete NODE(Q) by setting $Q2 \leftarrow \text{LINK(Q)}$ and then setting $\text{NODE(Q)} \leftarrow \text{NODE(Q2)}$, $\text{AVAIL} \Leftarrow Q2$; we could insert a NODE(Q2) in front of NODE(Q) by first interchanging $\text{NODE(Q2)} \leftrightarrow \text{NODE(Q)}$, then setting $\text{LINK(Q)} \leftarrow Q2$, $Q \leftarrow Q2$. These clever tricks allow the deletion and insertion *without* knowing which node links to NODE(Q); they were used in early versions of IPL. But they have the disadvantage that the sentinel node at the end of a polynomial will occasionally move, and other link variables may be pointing to this node.

9. Algorithm A with P = Q simply doubles polynomial(Q), as it should — except in the anomalous case that COEF = 0 for some term with ABC $\geq$ 0, when it fails badly. Algorithm M with P = M also gives the expected result. Algorithm M with P = Q sets polynomial(P) $\leftarrow$ polynomial(P) times $(1 + t_1)(1 + t_2)\ldots(1 + t_k)$ if M = $t_1 + t_2 + \cdots + t_k$ (although this is not immediately obvious). When M = Q, Algorithm M surprisingly gives the expected result, polynomial(Q) $\leftarrow$ polynomial(Q) + polynomial(Q) $\times$ polynomial(P), except that the computation blows up when the constant term of polynomial(P) is -1.

10. None. (The only possible difference would be in step M2, removing error checks that A, B, or C might individually overflow; these error checks were not specified because we assumed that they were not necessary.) In other words, the algorithms in this section may be regarded as operations on the polynomial $f(x^{b^2}, x^b, x)$ instead of on $f(x, y, z)$.

11.
```
    COPY STJ  9F        (comments          ST6  1,3(LINK)
         ENT3 9F         are               ENT3 0,6
         LDA  1,1        left              LD1  1,1(LINK)
    1H   LD6  AVAIL      to                LDA  1,1
         J6Z  OVERFLOW   the               JANN 1B
         LDX  1,6(LINK)  reader)           LD2  8F(LINK)
         STX  AVAIL                        ST2  1,3(LINK)
         STA  1,6                     9H  JMP  *
         LDA  0,1                     8H  CON  0    ▌
         STA  0,6
```

12. Let the polynomial copied have p terms. Program A takes $(27p + 13)u$, and to make it a fair comparison we should add the time to create a zero polynomial, say $18u$ with exercise 14. The program of exercise 11 takes $(21p + 31)u$, about 78% as much.

13.
```
    ERASE STJ  9F
          LDX  AVAIL
          LDA  1,1(LINK)
          STA  AVAIL
          STX  1,1(LINK)
    9H    JMP  *   ▌
```

14.
```
    ZERO STJ  9F                     MOVE 1F(2)
         LD1  AVAIL                   ST2  1,2(LINK)
         J1Z  OVERFLOW           9H  JMP  *
         LDX  1,1(LINK)          1H  CON  0
         STX  AVAIL                  CON  -1(ABC)   ▌
         ENT2 0,1
```

15.
```
    MULT STJ  9F        Entrance to subroutine
         LDA  5F        Change settings of switches
         STA  SW1
         LDA  6F
         STA  SW2
         STA  SW3
```

```
        JMP   *+2
2H      JMP   ADD              M2. Multiply cycle.
1H      LD4   1,4(LINK)        M1. Next multiplier. M ← LINK(M).
        LDA   1,4
        JANN  2B               To M2 if ABC(M) ≥ 0.
8H      LDA   7F               Restore settings of switches.
        STA   SW1
        LDA   8F
        STA   SW2
        STA   SW3
9H      JMP   *                Return.
5H      JMP   *+1              New setting of SW1
        LDA   0,1
        MUL   0,4              rX ← COEF(P) × COEF(M).
        LDA   1,1(ABC)         ABC(P)
        JAN   *+2
        ADD   1,4(ABC)          + ABC(M), if ABC(P) ≥ 0.
        SLA   2                Move into 0:3 field of rA.
        STX   OF               Save rX for use in SW2 and SW3.
        JMP   SW1+1
6H      LDA   OF               New setting of SW2 and SW3
7H      LDA   1,1              Usual setting of SW1
8H      LDA   0,1              Usual setting of SW2 and SW3
OH      CON   0                Temp storage ▌
```

16. Let r be the number of terms in polynomial(M). The subroutine requires $21pr + 38r + 29 + 27 \sum m' + 18 \sum m'' + 27 \sum p' + 8 \sum q'$ units of time, where the summations refer to the corresponding quantities during the r activations of Program A. The number of terms in polynomial(Q) goes up by $p' - m'$ each activation of Program A. If we make the not unreasonable assumption that $m' = 0$ and $p' = \alpha p$ where $0 < \alpha < 1$, we get the respective sums equal to 0, $(1 - \alpha)pr$, αpr, and $rq'_0 + \alpha p(r(r-1)/2)$, where q'_0 is the value of q' in the first iteration. The grand total is $4\alpha pr^2 + 40pr + 4\alpha pr + 8q'_0 r + 38r + 29$. This analysis indicates that the multiplier ought to have fewer terms than the multiplicand, since we have to skip over unmatching terms in polynomial(Q) more often. (See exercise 5.2.3–29 for a faster algorithm.)

17. There actually is very little advantage; addition and multiplication routines with either type of list would be virtually the same. The efficiency of the ERASE subroutine (see exercise 13) is apparently the only important difference.

18. Let the link field of node x_i contain LOC(x_{i+1}) ⊕ LOC(x_{i-1}), where "⊕" denotes "exclusive or." Other invertible operations, such as addition or subtraction modulo the pointer field size, could also be used. It is convenient to include two adjacent list heads in the circular list, to help get things started properly. (The origin of this ingenious technique is unknown.)

SECTION 2.2.5

1. Insert Y at the left: P ⇐ AVAIL; INFO(P) ← Y; LLINK(P) ← Λ; RLINK(P) ← LEFT; if LEFT ≠ Λ then LLINK(LEFT) ← P else RIGHT ← P; LEFT ← P. Set Y to leftmost and delete: if LEFT = Λ then UNDERFLOW; P ← LEFT; LEFT ← RLINK(P); if LEFT = Λ then RIGHT ← Λ, else LLINK(LEFT) ← Λ; Y ← INFO(P); AVAIL ⇐ P.

2. Consider the case of several deletions (at the same end) in succession. After each deletion we must know what to delete next, so the links in the list must point away from that end of the list. Deletion at both ends therefore implies that the links must go both ways. On the other hand, exercise 2.2.4–18 explains how to represent two links in a single link field; in that way general deque operations *are* possible.

3. To show the independence of CALLUP from CALLDOWN, notice for example that in Table 1 the elevator did not stop at floors 2 or 3 at time 0393–0444 although there were people waiting; these people had pushed CALLDOWN, but if they had pushed CALLUP the elevator would have stopped.

To show the independence of CALLCAR from the others, notice that in Table 1, when the doors start to open at time 1378, the elevator has already decided to be GOINGUP. Its state would have been NEUTRAL at that point if CALLCAR[1] = CALLCAR[2] = CALLCAR[3] = CALLCAR[4] = 0, according to step E2, but in fact CALLCAR[2] and CALLCAR[3] have been set to 1 by users 7 and 9 in the elevator. (If we envision the same situation with all floor numbers increased by 1, the fact that STATE = NEUTRAL or STATE = GOINGUP when the doors open would affect whether the elevator would perhaps continue to go downward or would unconditionally go upward.)

4. If a dozen or more people were getting out at the same floor, STATE might be NEUTRAL all during this time, and when E9 calls the DECISION subroutine this may set a new state before anyone has gotten in on the current floor. It happens very rarely indeed (and it certainly was the most puzzling phenomenon observed by the author during his elevator experiments).

5. The state from the time the doors start to open at time 1063 until user 7 gets in at time 1183 would have been NEUTRAL, since there would have been no calls to floor 0 and nobody on board the elevator. Then user 7 would set CALLCAR[2] ← 1 and the state would correspondingly change to GOINGUP.

6. Add the condition "if OUT < IN then STATE ≠ GOINGUP; if OUT > IN then STATE ≠ GOINGDOWN" to the condition "FLOOR = IN" in steps U2 and U4. In step E4, accept users from QUEUE[FLOOR] only if they are headed in the elevator's direction, unless STATE = NEUTRAL (when we accept all comers).

[Stanford's math department has just such an elevator, but its users don't actually pay much attention to the indicator lights; people tend to get on as soon as they can, regardless of direction. Why didn't the elevator designers realize this, and design the logic accordingly by clearing both CALLUP and CALLDOWN? The whole process would be faster, since the elevator wouldn't have to stop as often.]

7. In line 227 this user is assumed to be in the WAIT list. Jumping to U4A makes sure that this assumption is valid. It is assumed that GIVEUPTIME is positive, and indeed that it is probably 100 or more.

8. Comments are left to the reader.

```
277  E8  DEC4 1
278      ENTA 61
279      JMP  HOLDC
280      LDA  CALL,4(3:5)
281      JAP  1F
282      ENT1 -2,4
283      J1Z  2F
284      LDA  CALL,4(1:1)
```

285		JAZ	E8
286	2H	LDA	CALL-1,4
287		ADD	CALL-2,4
288		ADD	CALL-3,4
289		ADD	CALL-4,4
290		JANZ	E8
291	1H	ENTA	23
292		JMP	E2A ∎

9.

01	DECISION	STJ	9F	Store exit location.
02		J5NZ	9F	*D1. Decision necessary?*
03		LDX	ELEV1+2(NEXTINST)	
04		DECX	E1	*D2. Should doors open?*
05		JXNZ	1F	Jump if elevator not at E1.
06		LDA	CALL+2	
07		ENT3	E3	Prepare to schedule E3,
08		JANZ	8F	if there is a call on floor 2.
09	1H	ENT1	-4	*D3. Any calls?*
10		LDA	CALL+4,1	Search for a nonzero call variable.
11		JANZ	2F	
12	1H	INC1	1	rI1 $\equiv j - 4$
13		J1NP	*-3	
14		LDA	9F(0:2)	All CALL[j], $j \neq$ FLOOR, are zero.
15		DECA	E6B	Is exit location = line 250?
16		JANZ	9F	
17		ENT1	-2	Set $j \leftarrow 2$.
18	2H	ENT5	4,1	*D4. Set STATE.*
19		DEC5	0,4	STATE $\leftarrow j -$ FLOOR.
20		J5NZ	*+2	
21		JANZ	1B	$j =$ FLOOR not allowed in general.
22		JXNZ	9F	*D5. Elevator dormant?*
23		J5Z	9F	Jump if not at E1 or if $j = 2$.
24		ENT3	E6	Otherwise schedule E6.
25	8H	ENTA	20	Wait 20 units of time.
26		ST6	8F(0:2)	Save rI6.
27		ENT6	ELEV1	
28		ST3	2,6(NEXTINST)	Set NEXTINST to E3 or E6.
29		JMP	HOLD	Schedule the activity.
30	8H	ENT6	*	Restore rI6.
31	9H	JMP	*	Exit from subroutine. ∎

11. Initially let LINK[k] = 0, $1 \leq k \leq n$, and HEAD = -1. During a simulation step that changes V[k], give an error indication if LINK[k] $\neq$ 0; otherwise set LINK[k] $\leftarrow$ HEAD, HEAD $\leftarrow k$ and set NEWV[k] to the new value of V[k]. After each simulation step, set $k \leftarrow$ HEAD, HEAD $\leftarrow -1$, and do the following operation repeatedly zero or more times until $k < 0$: set V[k] $\leftarrow$ NEWV[k], $t \leftarrow$ LINK[k], LINK[k] $\leftarrow$ 0, $k \leftarrow t$.

Clearly this method is readily adapted to the case of scattered variables, if we include a NEWV and LINK field in each node associated with a variable field V.

12. The WAIT list has deletions from the left to the right, but insertions are sorted in from the right to the left (since the search is likely to be shorter from that side).

Also we delete nodes from all three lists in several places when we do not know the predecessor or successor of the node being deleted. Only the ELEVATOR list could be converted to a one-way list, without much loss of efficiency.

Note: It may be preferable to use a nonlinear list as the WAIT list in a discrete simulator, to reduce the time for sorting in. Section 5.2.3 discusses the general problem of maintaining priority queues, or "smallest in, first out" lists, such as this. Several ways are known in which only $O(\log n)$ operations are needed to insert or delete when there are n elements in the list, although there is of course no need for such a fancy method when n is known to be small.

SECTION 2.2.6

1. (Here the indices run from 1 to n, not from 0 to n as in Eq. (6).) $\texttt{LOC(A[J,K])} = \texttt{LOC(A[0,0])} + 2n\texttt{J} + 2\texttt{K}$, where $\texttt{A[0,0]}$ is an assumed node that is actually nonexistent. If we set $\texttt{J} = \texttt{K} = 1$, we get $\texttt{LOC(A[1,1])} = \texttt{LOC(A[0,0])} + 2n + 2$, so the answer can be expressed in several ways. The fact that $\texttt{LOC(A[0,0])}$ might be negative has led to many bugs in compilers and loading routines.

2. $\texttt{LOC(A[I}_1,\ldots,\texttt{I}_k\texttt{])} = \texttt{LOC(A[0,}\ldots\texttt{,0])} + \sum_{1 \le r \le k} a_r \texttt{I}_r = \texttt{LOC(A[}l_1,\ldots,l_k\texttt{])} + \sum_{1 \le r \le k} a_r \texttt{I}_r - \sum_{1 \le r \le k} a_r l_r$, where $a_r = c \prod_{r < s \le k} (u_s - l_s + 1)$.

Note: For a generalization to the structures occurring in programming languages such as C, and a simple algorithm to compute the relevant constants, see P. Deuel, *CACM* **9** (1966), 344–347.

3. $1 \le k \le j \le n$ if and only if $0 \le k - 1 \le j - 1 \le n - 1$; so replace k, j, n respectively by $k - 1$, $j - 1$, $n - 1$ in all formulas derived for lower bound zero.

4. $\texttt{LOC(A[J,K])} = \texttt{LOC(A[0,0])} + n\texttt{J} - \texttt{J(J}-1)/2 + \texttt{K}$.

5. Let $\texttt{AO} = \texttt{LOC(A[0,0])}$. There are at least two solutions, assuming that J is in rI1 and K is in rI2. (i) 'LDA TA2,1:7', where location TA2+j is 'NOP j+1*j/2+AO,2'; (ii) 'LDA C1,7:2', where location C1 contains 'NOP TA,1:7' and location TA+j says 'NOP j+1*j/2+AO'. The latter takes one more cycle but doesn't tie the table down to index register 2.

6. (a) $\texttt{LOC(A[I,J,K])} = \texttt{LOC(A[0,0,0])} + \dbinom{\texttt{I}+2}{3} + \dbinom{\texttt{J}+1}{2} + \dbinom{\texttt{K}}{1}$.

(b) $\texttt{LOC(B[I,J,K])} = \texttt{LOC(B[0,0,0])}$
$$+ \dbinom{n+3}{3} - \dbinom{n+3-\texttt{I}}{3} + \dbinom{n+2-\texttt{I}}{2} - \dbinom{n+2-\texttt{J}}{2} + \texttt{K} - \texttt{J},$$
hence the stated form is possible in this case also.

7. $\texttt{LOC(A[I}_1,\ldots,\texttt{I}_k\texttt{])} = \texttt{LOC(A[0,}\ldots\texttt{,0])} + \displaystyle\sum_{1 \le r \le k} \dbinom{\texttt{I}_r+k-r}{1+k-r}$. See exercise 1.2.6–56.

8. (Solution by P. Nash.) Let $\texttt{X[I,J,K]}$ be defined for $0 \le \texttt{I} \le n$, $0 \le \texttt{J} \le n+1$, $0 \le \texttt{K} \le n+2$. We can let $\texttt{A[I,J,K]} = \texttt{X[I,J,K]}$; $\texttt{B[I,J,K]} = \texttt{X[J,I}+1,\texttt{K]}$; $\texttt{C[I,J,K]} = \texttt{X[I,K,J}+1\texttt{]}$; $\texttt{D[I,J,K]} = \texttt{X[J,K,I}+2\texttt{]}$; $\texttt{E[I,J,K]} = \texttt{X[K,I}+1,\texttt{J}+1\texttt{]}$; $\texttt{F[I,J,K]} = \texttt{X[K,J}+1,\texttt{I}+2\texttt{]}$. This scheme is the best possible, since it packs the $(n+1)(n+2)(n+3)$ elements of the six tetrahedral arrays into consecutive locations with no overlap. *Proof:* A and B exhaust all cells $\texttt{X[}i,j,k\texttt{]}$ with $k = \min(i,j,k)$; C and D exhaust all cells with $j = \min(i,j,k) \ne k$; E and F exhaust all cells with $i = \min(i,j,k) \ne j, k$.

(The construction generalizes to m dimensions, if anybody ever wants to pack the elements of $m!$ generalized tetrahedral arrays into $(n+1)(n+2)\ldots(n+m)$ consecutive locations. Associate a permutation $a_1a_2 \ldots a_m$ with each array, and store its elements in $X[I_{a_1} + B_1, I_{a_2} + B_2, \ldots, I_{a_m} + B_m]$, where $B_1 B_2 \ldots B_m$ is an inversion table for $a_1 a_2 \ldots a_m$ as defined in exercise 5.1.1–7.)

9. G1. Set pointer variables P1, P2, P3, P4, P5, P6 to the first locations of the lists FEMALE, A21, A22, A23, BLOND, BLUE, respectively. Assume in what follows that the end of each list is given by link Λ, and Λ is smaller than any other link. If P6 $= \Lambda$, stop (the list, unfortunately, is empty).

G2. (Many possible orderings of the following actions could be done; we have chosen to examine EYES first, then HAIR, then AGE, then SEX.) Set P5 $\leftarrow$ HAIR(P5) zero or more times until P5 $\leq$ P6. If now P5 $<$ P6, go to step G5.

G3. Set P4 $\leftarrow$ AGE(P4) repeatedly if necessary until P4 $\leq$ P6. Similarly do the same to P3 and P2 until P3 $\leq$ P6 and P2 $\leq$ P6. If now P4, P3, P2 are all smaller than P6, go to G5.

G4. Set P1 $\leftarrow$ SEX(P1) until P1 $\leq$ P6. If P1 $=$ P6, we have found one of the young ladies desired, so output her address, P6. (Her age can be determined from the settings of P2, P3, and P4.)

G5. Set P6 $\leftarrow$ EYES(P6). Now stop if P6 $= \Lambda$; otherwise return to G2. ∎

This algorithm is interesting but not the best way to organize a list for such a search.

10. See Section 6.5.

11. At most $200 + 200 + 3 \cdot 4 \cdot 200 = 2800$ words.

12. VAL(Q0) $= c$, VAL(P0) $= b/a$, VAL(P1) $= d$.

13. It is convenient to have at the end of each list a sentinel that "compares low" in some field on which the list is ordered. A straight one-way list *could* have been used, for example by retaining just the LEFT links in BASEROW[i] and the UP links in BASECOL[j], by modifying Algorithm S thus: In S2, test if P0 $= \Lambda$ before setting J $\leftarrow$ COL(P0); if so, set P0 $\leftarrow$ LOC(BASEROW[I0]) and go to S3. In S3, test if Q0 $= \Lambda$; if so, terminate. Step S4 should change by analogy with step S2. In S5, test if P1 $= \Lambda$; if so, act as if COL(P1) $<$ 0. In S6, test if UP(PTR[J]) $= \Lambda$; if so, act as if its ROW field were negative.

These modifications make the algorithm more complicated and save no storage space except a ROW or COL field in the list heads (which in the case of MIX is no saving at all).

14. One could first link together those columns that have a nonzero element in the pivot row, so that all other columns could be skipped as we pivot on each row. Rows in which the pivot column is zero are skipped over immediately.

15. Let rI1 $\equiv$ PIVOT, J; rI2 $\equiv$ P0; rI3 $\equiv$ Q0; rI4 $\equiv$ P; rI5 $\equiv$ P1, X; LOC(BASEROW[i]) $\equiv$ BROW $+ i$; LOC(BASECOL[j]) $\equiv$ BCOL $+ j$; PTR[j] $\equiv$ BCOL $+ j(1:3)$.

```
01  ROW         EQU   0:3
02  UP          EQU   4:5
03  COL         EQU   0:3
04  LEFT        EQU   4:5
05  PTR         EQU   1:3
06  PIVOTSTEP STJ   9F            Subroutine entrance, rI1 = PIVOT
07  S1          LD2   0,1(ROW)     S1. Initialize.
08              ST2   I0           I0 ← ROW(PIVOT).
09              LD3   1,1(COL)
```

10		ST3	J0	J0 ← COL(PIVOT).
11		LDA	=1.0=	Floating point constant 1
12		FDIV	2,1	
13		STA	ALPHA	ALPHA ← 1/VAL(PIVOT).
14		LDA	=1.0=	
15		STA	2,1	VAL(PIVOT) ← 1.
16		ENT2	BROW,2	P0 ← LOC(BASEROW[I0]).
17		ENT3	BCOL,3	Q0 ← LOC(BASECOL[J0]).
18		JMP	S2	
19	2H	ENTA	BCOL,1	
20		STA	BCOL,1(PTR)	PTR[J] ← LOC(BASECOL[J]).
21		LDA	2,2	
22		FMUL	ALPHA	
23		STA	2,2	VAL(P0) ← ALPHA × VAL(P0).
24	S2	LD2	1,2(LEFT)	_S2. Process pivot row._ P0 ← LEFT(P0).
25		LD1	1,2(COL)	J ← COL(P0).
26		J1NN	2B	If J ≥ 0, process J.
27	S3	LD3	0,3(UP)	_S3. Find new row._ Q0 ← UP(Q0).
28		LD4	0,3(ROW)	rI4 ← ROW(Q0).
29	9H	J4N	*	If rI4 < 0, exit.
30		CMP4	I0	
31		JE	S3	If rI4 = I0, repeat.
32		ST4	I(ROW)	I ← rI4.
33		ENT4	BROW,4	P ← LOC(BASEROW[I]).
34	S4A	LD5	1,4(LEFT)	P1 ← LEFT(P).
35	S4	LD2	1,2(LEFT)	_S4. Find new column._ P0 ← LEFT(P0).
36		LD1	1,2(COL)	J ← COL(P0).
37		CMP1	J0	
38		JE	S4	Repeat if J = J0.
39		ENTA	0,1	
40		SLA	2	rA(0:3) ← J.
41		J1NN	S5	
42		LDAN	2,3	If J < 0,
43		FMUL	ALPHA	set VAL(Q0) ← −ALPHA × VAL(Q0).
44		STA	2,3	
45		JMP	S3	
46	1H	ENT4	0,5	P ← P1.
47		LD5	1,4(LEFT)	P1 ← LEFT(P).
48	S5	CMPA	1,5(COL)	_S5. Find I, J element._
49		JL	1B	Loop until COL(P1) ≤ J.
50		JE	S7	If =, go right to S7.
51	S6	LD5	BCOL,1(PTR)	_S6. Insert I, J element._ rI5 ← PTR[J].
52		LDA	I	rA(0:3) ← I.
53	2H	ENT6	0,5	rI6 ← rI5.
54		LD5	0,6(UP)	rI5 ← UP(rI6).
55		CMPA	0,5(ROW)	
56		JL	2B	Jump if ROW(rI5) > I.
57		LD5	AVAIL	X ⇐ AVAIL.
58		J5Z	OVERFLOW	

```
59              LDA   0,5(UP)
60              STA   AVAIL
61              LDA   0,6(UP)
62              STA   0,5(UP)          UP(X) ← UP(PTR[J]).
63              LDA   1,4(LEFT)
64              STA   1,5(LEFT)        LEFT(X) ← LEFT(P).
65              ST1   1,5(COL)         COL(X) ← J.
66              LDA   I(ROW)
67              STA   0,5(ROW)         ROW(X) ← I.
68              STZ   2,5              VAL(X) ← 0.
69              ST5   1,4(LEFT)        LEFT(P) ← X.
70              ST5   0,6(UP)          UP(PTR[J]) ← X.
71   S7         LDAN  2,3              S7. Pivot. −VAL(Q0)
72              FMUL  2,2                × VAL(P0)
73              FADD  2,5                 + VAL(P1).
74              JAZ   S8               If significance lost, to S8.
75              STA   2,5              Otherwise store in VAL(P1).
76              ST5   BCOL,1(PTR)      PTR[J] ← P1.
77              ENT4  0,5              P ← P1.
78              JMP   S4A              P1 ← LEFT(P), to S4.
79   S8         LD6   BCOL,1(PTR)      S8. Delete I, J element. rI6 ← PTR[J].
80              JMP   *+2
81              LD6   0,6(UP)          rI6 ← UP(rI6).
82              LDA   0,6(UP)
83              DECA  0,5              Is UP(rI6) = P1?
84              JANZ  *-3              Loop until equal.
85              LDA   0,5(UP)
86              STA   0,6(UP)          UP(rI6) ← UP(P1).
87              LDA   1,5(LEFT)
88              STA   1,4(LEFT)        LEFT(P) ← LEFT(P1).
89              LDA   AVAIL            AVAIL ⇐ P1.
90              STA   0,5(UP)
91              ST5   AVAIL
92              JMP   S4A              P1 ← LEFT(P), to S4.   ▌
```

Note: Using the conventions of Chapter 4, lines 71–74 would actually be coded

LDA 2,3; FMUL 2,2; FCMP 2,5; JE S8; STA TEMP; LDA 2,5; FSUB TEMP;

with a suitable parameter EPSILON in location zero.

17. For each row i and each element $A[i,k] \neq 0$, add $A[i,k]$ times row k of B to row i of C. Maintain only the COL links of C while doing this; the ROW links are easily filled in afterwards. [A. Schoor, *Inf. Proc. Letters* **15** (1982), 87–89.]

18. The three pivot steps, in respective columns 3, 1, 2, yield respectively

$$\begin{pmatrix} \frac{1}{3} & \frac{2}{3} & \frac{1}{3} \\ -\frac{2}{3} & -\frac{1}{3} & -\frac{2}{3} \\ -\frac{1}{3} & -\frac{2}{3} & -\frac{1}{3} \end{pmatrix}, \quad \begin{pmatrix} \frac{1}{2} & \frac{1}{2} & 0 \\ -\frac{3}{2} & \frac{1}{2} & 1 \\ -\frac{1}{2} & -\frac{1}{2} & 0 \end{pmatrix}, \quad \begin{pmatrix} 0 & 1 & 0 \\ -2 & 1 & 1 \\ 1 & -2 & 0 \end{pmatrix};$$

after the final permutations, we have the answer

$$\begin{pmatrix} 1 & -2 & 1 \\ 0 & 1 & -2 \\ 0 & 0 & 1 \end{pmatrix}.$$

20. $a_0 = $ LOC(A[1,1]) $- 3$, $a_1 = 1$ or 2, $a_2 = 3 - a_1$.

21. For example, M $\leftarrow$ max(I, J), LOC(A[I,J]) $=$ LOC(A[1,1]) $+$ M(M $-$ 1) $+$ I $-$ J. (Such formulas have been proposed independently by many people. A. L. Rosenberg and H. R. Strong have suggested the following k-dimensional generalization: LOC(A[$I_1, \ldots, I_k$]) $= L_k$ where $L_1 = $ LOC(A[1, $\ldots$,1]) $+ I_1 - 1$, $L_r = L_{r-1} + (M_r - 1)^r +$ ($M_r - I_r$)($M_r^{r-1} - (M_r - 1)^{r-1}$), and $M_r = $ max($I_1, \ldots, I_r$) [*IBM Technical Disclosure Bulletin* **14** (1972), 3026–3028]. See *Current Trends in Programming Methodology* **4** (Prentice–Hall, 1978), 263–311, for further results of this kind.)

22. According to the combinatorial number system (exercise 1.2.6–56), we can let

$$p(i_1, \ldots, i_k) = \binom{i_1}{1} + \binom{i_1 + i_2 + 1}{2} + \cdots + \binom{i_1 + i_2 + \cdots + i_k + k - 1}{k}.$$

[*Det Kongelige Norske Videnskabers Selskabs Forhandlinger* **34** (1961), 8–9.]

23. Let $c[J] = $ LOC(A[0,J]) $= $ LOC(A[0,0]) $+ mJ$, if there were m rows when the matrix grew from J to J$+1$ columns; similarly, let $r[I] = $ LOC(A[I,0]) $= $ LOC(A[0,0]) $+ nI$, if there were n columns when we created row I. Then we can use the allocation function

$$\text{LOC(A[I,J])} = \begin{cases} \text{I} + c[\text{J}], & \text{if } c[\text{J}] \geq r[\text{I}]; \\ \text{J} + r[\text{I}], & \text{otherwise.} \end{cases}$$

It is not hard to prove that $c[J] \geq r[I]$ implies $c[J] \geq r[I] + J$, and $c[J] \leq r[I]$ implies $c[J] + I \leq r[I]$; therefore the relation

$$\text{LOC(A[I,J])} = \max(\text{I} + \text{LOC(A[0,J])}, \text{J} + \text{LOC(A[I,0])})$$

also holds. We need not restrict allocation to mn consecutive locations; the only constraint is that, when the matrix grows, we allocate m or n consecutive new cells in locations greater than those previously used. This construction is due to E. J. Otoo and T. H. Merrett [*Computing* **31** (1983), 1–9], who also generalized it to k dimensions.

24. [Aho, Hopcroft, and Ullman, *The Design and Analysis of Computer Algorithms* (Addison–Wesley, 1974), exercise 2.12.] Besides the array A, maintain also a verification array V of the same size, and a list L of the locations used. Let n be the number of items in L; initially $n = 0$ and the contents of L, A, and V are arbitrary. Whenever you want to access A[k] for a value of k that you might not have used before, first check whether $0 \leq $ V[k] $< n$ and L[V[k]] $= k$. If not, set V[k] $\leftarrow n$, L[n] $\leftarrow k$, A[k] $\leftarrow 0$, and $n \leftarrow n + 1$. Otherwise you can be sure that A[k] already contains legitimate data. (By a slight extension of this method, it is possible to save and eventually restore the contents of all entries of A and V that change during the computation.)

SECTION 2.3

1. There are three ways to choose the root. Once the root has been chosen, say A, there are three ways to partition the other nodes into subtrees: $\{B\}$, $\{C\}$; $\{C\}$, $\{B\}$; $\{B, C\}$. In the latter case there are two ways to make $\{B, C\}$ into a tree, depending

on which is the root. Hence we get
the four trees shown when A is the
root, and 12 in all. This problem is
solved for any number n of nodes
in exercise 2.3.4.4–23.

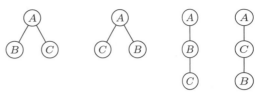

2. The first two trees in the answer to exercise 1 are the same, as oriented trees, so we get only 9 different possibilities in this case. For the general solution, see Section 2.3.4.4, where the formula n^{n-1} is proved.

3. Part 1: To show there is *at least one* such sequence. Let the tree have n nodes. The result is clear when $n = 1$, since X must be the root. If $n > 1$, the definition implies there is a root X_1 and subtrees $T_1, T_2, \ldots, T_m$; either $X = X_1$ or X is a member of a unique T_j. In the latter case, there is by induction a path $X_2, \ldots, X$ where X_2 is the root of T_j, and since X_1 is the parent of X_2 we have a path $X_1, X_2, \ldots, X$.

Part 2: To show there is *at most one* such sequence. We will prove by induction that if X is not the root of the tree, X has a unique parent (so that X_k determines X_{k-1} determines X_{k-2}, etc.) If the tree has one node, there is nothing to prove; otherwise X is in a unique T_j. Either X is the root of T_j, in which case X has a unique parent by definition; or X is not the root of T_j, in which case X has a unique parent in T_j by induction, and no node outside of T_j can be X's parent.

4. True (unfortunately).

5. 4.

6. Let $\text{parent}^{[0]}(X)$ denote X, and let $\text{parent}^{[k+1]}(X) = \text{parent}(\text{parent}^{[k]}(X))$, so that $\text{parent}^{[1]}(X)$ is X's parent, and $\text{parent}^{[2]}(X)$ is X's grandparent; when $k \geq 2$, $\text{parent}^{[k]}(X)$ is X's "(great-)$^{k-2}$grandparent." The requested cousinship condition is that $\text{parent}^{[m+1]}(X) = \text{parent}^{[m+n+1]}(Y)$ but $\text{parent}^{[m]}(X) \neq \text{parent}^{[m+n]}(Y)$. When $n > 0$, this relation is not symmetrical with respect to X and Y, although people usually treat it as symmetrical in everyday conversation.

7. Use the (unsymmetric) condition defined in exercise 6, with the convention that $\text{parent}^{[j]}(X) \neq \text{parent}^{[k]}(Y)$ if either j or k (or both) is -1. To show that this relation is always valid for some unique m and n, consider the Dewey decimal notation for X and Y, namely $1.a_1. \cdots .a_p.b_1. \cdots .b_q$ and $1.a_1. \cdots .a_p.c_1. \cdots .c_r$, where $p \geq 0$, $q \geq 0$, $r \geq 0$ and (if $qr \neq 0$) $b_1 \neq c_1$. The Dewey numbers of any pair of nodes can be written in this form, and clearly we must take $m = q - 1$ and $m + n = r - 1$.

8. *No* binary tree is really a tree; the concepts are quite separate, even though the diagram of a nonempty binary tree may look treelike.

9. A is the root, since we conventionally put the root at the top.

10. Any *finite* collection of nested sets corresponds to a forest as defined in the text, as follows: Let $A_1, \ldots, A_n$ be the sets of the collection that are contained in no other. For fixed j, the sub-collection of all sets contained in A_j is nested; hence we may assume that this sub-collection corresponds to a tree (unordered) with A_j as the root.

11. In a nested collection $\mathcal{C}$ let $X \equiv Y$ if there is some $Z \in \mathcal{C}$ such that $X \cup Y \subseteq Z$. This relation is obviously reflexive and symmetric, and it is in fact an equivalence relation since $W \equiv X$ and $X \equiv Y$ implies that there are Z_1 and Z_2 in $\mathcal{C}$ with $W \subseteq Z_1$, $X \subseteq Z_1 \cap Z_2$, and $Y \subseteq Z_2$. Since $Z_1 \cap Z_2 \neq \emptyset$, either $Z_1 \subseteq Z_2$ or $Z_2 \subseteq Z_1$; hence $W \cup Y \subseteq Z_1 \cup Z_2 \in \mathcal{C}$. Now if $\mathcal{C}$ is a nested collection, define an oriented forest corresponding to C by the rule "X is an ancestor of Y, and Y is a descendant of X (that is, a *proper* ancestor or descendant), if and only if $X \supset Y$." Each equivalence class of C corresponds to an oriented tree, which is an oriented forest with $X \equiv Y$ for all X, Y. (We thereby have generalized the definitions of forest and tree that were given for finite collections.) In these terms, we may define the *level* of X as the cardinal number of ancestors(X). Similarly, the *degree* of X is the cardinal number of equivalence classes in the nested collection descendants(X). We say X is the *parent* of Y, and Y is a *child* of X, if X is an ancestor of Y but there is no Z such that $X \supset Z \supset Y$. (It is possible for X to have descendants but no children, ancestors but no parent.) To get *ordered* trees and forests, order the equivalence classes mentioned above in some ad hoc manner, for example by embedding the relation $\subseteq$ into linear order as in exercise 2.2.3–14.

Example (a): Let $S_{\alpha k} = \{ x \mid x = .d_1 d_2 d_3 \dots$ in decimal notation, where $\alpha = .e_1 e_2 e_3 \dots$ in decimal notation, and $d_j = e_j$ if $j \bmod 2^k \neq 0 \}$. The collection $C = \{ S_{\alpha k} \mid k \geq 0, 0 < \alpha < 1 \}$ is nested, and gives a tree with infinitely many levels and uncountable degree for each node.

Examples (b), (c): It is convenient to define this set in the plane, instead of in terms of real numbers, and this is sufficient since there is a one-to-one correspondence between the plane and the real numbers. Let $S_{\alpha mn} = \{(\alpha, y) \mid m/2^n \leq y < (m+1)/2^n \}$, and let $T_\alpha = \{(x, y) \mid x \leq \alpha \}$. The collection $C = \{ S_{\alpha mn} \mid 0 < \alpha < 1, n \geq 0, 0 \leq m < 2^n \} \cup \{ T_\alpha \mid 0 < \alpha < 1 \}$ is easily seen to be nested. The children of $S_{\alpha mn}$ are $S_{\alpha(2m)(n+1)}$ and $S_{\alpha(2m+1)(n+1)}$, and T_α has the child $S_{\alpha 00}$ plus the subtree $\{ S_{\beta mn} \mid \beta < \alpha \} \cup \{ T_\beta \mid \beta < \alpha \}$. So each node has degree 2, and each node has uncountably many ancestors of the form T_α. This construction is due to R. Bigelow.

Note: If we take a suitable well-ordering of the real numbers, and if we define $T_\alpha = \{(x, y) \mid x \succ \alpha \}$, we can improve this construction slightly, obtaining a nested collection where each node has uncountable level, degree 2, *and* two children.

12. We impose an additional condition on the partial ordering (analogous to that of "nested sets") to ensure that it corresponds to a forest: If $x \preceq y$ and $x \preceq z$ then either $y \preceq z$ or $z \preceq y$. In other words, the elements larger than any given element are linearly ordered. To make a tree, also assert the existence of a largest element r such that $x \preceq r$ for all x. A proof that this gives an unordered tree as defined in the text, when the number of nodes is finite, runs like the proof for nested sets in exercise 10.

13. $a_1.a_2.\cdots.a_k,\ a_1.a_2.\cdots.a_{k-1},\ \dots,\ a_1.a_2,\ a_1$.

14. Since S is nonempty, it contains an element $1.a_1.\cdots.a_k$ where k is as small as possible; if $k > 0$ we also take a_k as small as possible in S, and we immediately see that k must be 0. In other words, S must contain the element 1. Let 1 be the root. All other elements have $k > 0$, and so the remaining elements of S can be partitioned into sets $S_j = \{1.j.a_2.\cdots.a_k\}$, $1 \leq j \leq m$, for some $m \geq 0$. If $m \neq 0$ and S_m is nonempty, we deduce by reasoning as above that $1.j$ is in S_j for each S_j; hence each S_j is nonempty. Then it is easy to see that the sets $S_j' = \{1.a_2.\cdots.a_k \mid 1.j.a_2.\cdots.a_k$ is in $S_j\}$ satisfy the same condition as S did. By induction, each of the S_j forms a tree.

15. Let the root be 1, and let the roots of the left and right subtrees of α be $\alpha.0$ and $\alpha.1$, respectively, when such roots exist. For example, King Christian IX appears in two positions of Fig. 18(a), namely 1.0.0.0.0 and 1.1.0.0.1.0. For brevity we may drop the decimal points and write merely 10000 and 110010. *Note:* This notation is due to Francis Galton; see *Natural Inheritance* (Macmillan, 1889), 249. For pedigrees, it is more mnemonic to use F and M in place of 0 and 1 and to drop the initial 1; thus Christian IX is Charles III's *MFFMF*, his mother's father's father's mother's father.

The 0 and 1 convention is interesting for another reason: It gives us an important correspondence between nodes in a binary tree and positive integers expressed in the binary system (namely, memory addresses in a computer).

16. (a)   (b)   *or*   *or*

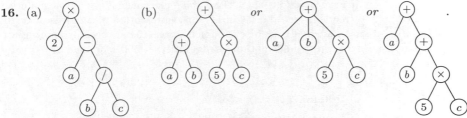

17. $\text{parent}(Z[1]) = A$; $\text{parent}(Z[1,2]) = C$; $\text{parent}(Z[1,2,2]) = E$.

18. $L[5,1,1] = (2)$. $L[3,1]$ is nonsense, since $L[3]$ is an empty List.

19. $*[L]$ $L[2] = (L)$; $L[2,1,1] = a$.

     a $*$

         $[L]$

20. (Intuitively, the correspondence between 0-2-trees and binary trees is obtained by removing all terminal nodes of the 0-2-tree; see the important construction in Section 2.3.4.5.) Let a 0-2-tree with one node correspond to the empty binary tree; and let a 0-2-tree with more than one node, consisting therefore of a root r and 0-2-trees T_1 and T_2, correspond to the binary tree with root r, left subtree T_1', and right subtree T_2', where T_1 and T_2 correspond respectively to T_1' and T_2'.

21. $1 + 0 \cdot n_1 + 1 \cdot n_2 + \cdots + (m-1) \cdot n_m$. *Proof:* The number of nodes in the tree is $n_0 + n_1 + n_2 + \cdots + n_m$, and this also equals $1 +$ (number of children in the tree) $= 1 + 0 \cdot n_0 + 1 \cdot n_1 + 2 \cdot n_2 + \cdots + m \cdot n_m$.

22. The basic idea is to proceed recursively, with the representation of a nonempty binary tree defined to be the representation of its root plus half-size-and-rotated representations of its left and right subtrees. Thus an arbitrarily large binary tree can be represented on a single sheet of paper, if one has a sufficiently powerful magnifying glass.

     Many variations on this theme are possible. For example, one idea is to represent the root by a line from the center of a given landscape-oriented page to the top edge, and to rotate the left-subtree representation by 90° clockwise in the left halfpage, the right-subtree representation by 90° counterclockwise in the right halfpage. Each node is then represented by a line. (When this method is applied to a complete binary tree having $2^k - 1$ nodes on k levels, it yields so-called "H-trees," which are the most efficient layouts of such binary trees on a VLSI chip; see R. P. Brent and H. T. Kung, *Inf. Proc. Letters* **11** (1980), 46–48.)

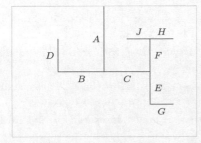

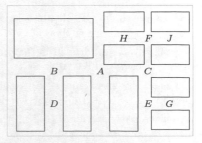

Another idea is to represent an empty binary tree by some sort of box, and to rotate the subtree representations of nonempty binary trees so that left subsubtrees are alternately to the left of or below the corresponding right subsubtrees, depending on whether the depth of recursion is even or odd. Then the boxes correspond to external nodes in an extended binary tree (see Section 2.3.4.5). This representation, which is strongly related to the 2-d trees and quadtrees discussed in Section 6.5, is especially appropriate when the external nodes carry information but the internal nodes do not.

SECTION 2.3.1

1. `INFO(T)` $= A$, `INFO(RLINK(T))` $= C$, etc.; the answer is H.

2. Preorder: 1245367; symmetric order: 4251637; postorder: 4526731.

3. The statement is true; notice, for example, that nodes 4, 5, 6, 7 always appear in this order in exercise 2. The result is immediately proved by induction on the size of the binary tree.

4. It is the reverse of postorder. (This is easily proved by induction.)

5. In the tree of exercise 2, for example, preorder is 1, 10, 100, 101, 11, 110, 111, using binary notation (which is in this case equivalent to the Dewey system). The strings of digits have been sorted, like words in a dictionary.

In general, the nodes will be listed in preorder if they are sorted lexicographically from left to right, with "blank" $< 0 < 1$. The nodes will be listed in postorder if they are sorted lexicographically with $0 < 1 <$ "blank". For inorder, use $0 <$ "blank" < 1.

(Moreover, if we imagine the blanks at the left and treat the Dewey labels as ordinary binary numbers, we get *level order*; see 2.3.3–(8).)

6. The fact that $p_1 p_2 \ldots p_n$ is obtainable with a stack is readily proved by induction on n, or in fact we may observe that Algorithm T does precisely what is required in its stack actions. (The corresponding sequence of S's and X's, as in exercise 2.2.1–3, is the same as the sequence of 1s and 2s as subscripts in double order; see exercise 18.)

Conversely, if $p_1 p_2 \ldots p_n$ is obtainable with a stack and if $p_k = 1$, then $p_1 \ldots p_{k-1}$ is a permutation of $\{2, \ldots, k\}$ and $p_{k+1} \ldots p_n$ is a permutation of $\{k+1, \ldots, n\}$; these are the permutations corresponding to the left and right subtrees, and both are obtainable with a stack. The proof now proceeds by induction.

7. From the preorder, the root is known; then from the inorder, we know the left subtree and the right subtree; and in fact we know the preorder and inorder of the nodes in the latter subtrees. Hence the tree is readily constructed (and indeed it is quite amusing to construct a simple algorithm that links the tree together in the normal fashion, starting with the nodes linked together in preorder in `LLINK` and in inorder in `RLINK`). Similarly, postorder and inorder together characterize the structure. But preorder and postorder do not; there are two binary trees having AB as preorder and BA as postorder. If all nonterminal nodes of a binary tree have *both* branches nonempty, its structure *is* characterized by preorder and postorder.

8. (a) Binary trees with all `LLINK`s null. (b) Binary trees with zero or one nodes. (c) Binary trees with all `RLINK`s null.

9. T1 once, T2 $2n+1$ times, T3 n times, T4 $n+1$ times, T5 n times. These counts can be derived by induction or by Kirchhoff's law, or by examining Program T.

10. A binary tree with all `RLINK`s null will cause all n node addresses to be put in the stack before any are removed.

11. Let a_{nk} be the number of binary trees with n nodes for which the stack in Algorithm T never contains more than k items. If $g_k(z) = \sum_n a_{nk} z^n$, we find $g_1(z) = 1/(1-z)$, $g_2(z) = 1/(1 - z/(1-z)) = (1-z)/(1-2z)$, $\ldots$, $g_k(z) = 1/(1 - zg_{k-1}(z)) = q_{k-1}(z)/q_k(z)$ where $q_{-1}(z) = q_0(z) = 1$, $q_{k+1}(z) = q_k(z) - zq_{k-1}(z)$; hence $g_k(z) = (f_1(z)^{k+1} - f_2(z)^{k+1})/(f_1(z)^{k+2} - f_2(z)^{k+2})$ where $f_j(z) = \frac{1}{2}(1 \pm \sqrt{1 - 4z})$. It can now be shown that $a_{nk} = [u^n](1-u)(1+u)^{2n}(1 - u^{k+1})/(1 - u^{k+2})$; hence $s_n = \sum_{k \geq 1} k(a_{nk} - a_{n(k-1)})$ is $[u^{n+1}](1-u)^2(1+u)^{2n} \sum_{j \geq 1} u^j/(1 - u^j)$, minus a_{nn}. The technique of exercise 5.2.2–52 now yields the asymptotic series

$$s_n/a_{nn} = \sqrt{\pi n} - \frac{3}{2} - \frac{13}{24}\sqrt{\frac{\pi}{n}} + \frac{1}{2n} + O(n^{-3/2}).$$

[N. G. de Bruijn, D. E. Knuth, and S. O. Rice, in *Graph Theory and Computing*, ed. by R. C. Read (New York: Academic Press, 1972), 15–22.]

When the binary tree represents a forest as described in Section 2.3.2, the quantity analyzed here is the *height* of that forest (the furthest distance between a node and a root, plus one). Generalizations to many other varieties of trees have been obtained by Flajolet and Odlyzko [*J. Computer and System Sci.* **25** (1982), 171–213]; the asymptotic distribution of heights, both near the mean and far away, was subsequently analyzed by Flajolet, Gao, Odlyzko, and Richmond [*Combinatorics, Probability and Computing* **2** (1993), 145–156].

12. Visit NODE(P) between steps T2 and T3, instead of in step T5. For the proof, demonstrate the validity of the statement "*Starting at step T2 with $\ldots$ original value* A[1] $\ldots$ A[m]," essentially as in the text.

13. (Solution by S. Araújo, 1976.) Let steps T1 through T4 be unchanged, except that a new variable Q is initialized to Λ in step T1′; Q will point to the last node visited, if any. Step T5 becomes two steps:

    T5′. [Right branch done?] If RLINK(P) $= \Lambda$ or RLINK(P) $=$ Q, go on to T6′; otherwise set A $\Leftarrow$ P, P $\leftarrow$ RLINK(P) and return to T2′.

    T6′. [Visit P.] Visit NODE(P), set Q $\leftarrow$ P, and return to T4′.

A similar proof applies. (Steps T4′ and T5′ can be streamlined so that nodes are not taken off the stack and immediately reinserted.)

14. By induction, there are always exactly $n + 1$ Λ links (counting T when it is null). There are n nonnull links, counting T, so the remark in the text about the majority of null links is justified.

15. There is a thread LLINK or RLINK pointing to a node if and only if it has a nonempty right or left subtree, respectively. (See Fig. 24.)

16. If LTAG(Q) $= 0$, Q∗ is LLINK(Q); thus Q∗ is one step down and to the left. Otherwise Q∗ is obtained by going upwards in the tree (if necessary) repeatedly until the first time it is possible to go down to the right without retracing steps; typical examples are the trips from P to P∗ and from Q to Q∗ in the following tree:

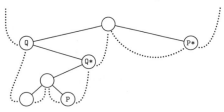

17. If LTAG(P) = 0, set Q ← LLINK(P) and terminate. Otherwise set Q ← P, then set Q ← RLINK(Q) zero or more times until finding RTAG(Q) = 0; finally set Q ← RLINK(Q) once more.

18. Modify Algorithm T by inserting a step T2.5, "Visit NODE(P) the first time"; in step T5, we are visiting NODE(P) the second time.

Given a threaded tree the traversal is extremely simple:

$$(P, 1)^{\triangle} = (\text{LLINK}(P), 1) \text{ if LTAG}(P) = 0, \text{ otherwise } (P, 2);$$

$$(P, 2)^{\triangle} = (\text{RLINK}(P), 1) \text{ if RTAG}(P) = 0, \text{ otherwise } (\text{RLINK}(P), 2).$$

In each case, we move at most one step in the tree; in practice, therefore, double order and the values of d and e are embedded in a program and not explicitly mentioned.

Suppressing all the first visits gives us precisely Algorithms T and S; suppressing all the second visits gives us the solutions to exercises 12 and 17.

19. The basic idea is to start by finding the parent Q of P. Then if P ≠ LLINK(Q) we have P♯ = Q; otherwise we can find P♯ by repeatedly setting Q ← Q$ zero or more times until RTAG(Q) = 1. (See, for example, P and P♯ in the tree shown.)

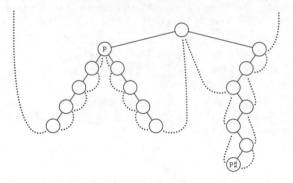

There is no efficient algorithm to find the parent of P in a general right-threaded tree, since a degenerate right-threaded tree in which all left links are null is essentially a circular list in which the links go the wrong way. Therefore we cannot traverse a right-threaded tree in postorder with the same efficiency as the stack method of exercise 13, if we keep no history of how we have reached the current node P.

But if the tree is threaded in both directions, we *can* find P's parent efficiently:

F1. Set Q ← P and R ← P.

F2. If LTAG(Q) = RTAG(R) = 0, set Q ← LLINK(Q) and R ← RLINK(R) and repeat this step. Otherwise go to F4 if RTAG(R) = 1.

F3. Set Q ← LLINK(Q), and terminate if P = RLINK(Q). Otherwise set R ← RLINK(R) zero or more times until RTAG(R) = 1, then set Q ← RLINK(R) and terminate.

F4. Set R ← RLINK(R), and terminate with Q ← R if P = LLINK(R). Otherwise set Q ← LLINK(Q) zero or more times until LTAG(Q) = 1, then set Q ← LLINK(Q) and terminate. ∎

The average running time of Algorithm F is $O(1)$ when P is a random node of the tree. For if we count only the steps Q ← LLINK(Q) when P is a right child, or only the steps R ← RLINK(R) when P is a left child, each link is traversed for exactly one node P.

20. Replace lines 06–09 by: Replace lines 12–13 by:

```
T3   ENT4   0,6                    LD4    0,6(LINK)
     LD6    AVAIL                  LD5    0,6(INFO)
     J6Z    OVERFLOW               LDX    AVAIL
     LDX    0,6(LINK)              STX    0,6(LINK)
     STX    AVAIL                  ST6    AVAIL
     ST5    0,6(INFO)              ENT6   0,4
     ST4    0,6(LINK)
```

If two more lines of code are added at line 06

```
T3   LD3   0,5(LLINK)
     J3Z   T5                         To T5 if LLINK(P) = Λ.
```

with appropriate changes in lines 10 and 11, the running time goes down from $(30n + a + 4)u$ to $(27a + 6n - 22)u$. (This same device would reduce the running time of Program T to $(12a + 6n - 7)u$, which is a slight improvement, if we set $a = (n + 1)/2$.)

21. The following solution by Joseph M. Morris [*Inf. Proc. Letters* **9** (1979), 197–200] traverses also in preorder (see exercise 18).

> **U1.** [Initialize.] Set P ← T and R ← Λ.
>
> **U2.** [Done?] If P = Λ, the algorithm terminates.
>
> **U3.** [Look left.] Set Q ← LLINK(P). If Q = Λ, visit NODE(P) in preorder and go to U6.
>
> **U4.** [Search for thread.] Set Q ← RLINK(Q) zero or more times until either Q = R or RLINK(Q) = Λ.
>
> **U5.** [Insert or remove thread.] If Q ≠ R, set RLINK(Q) ← P and go to U8. Otherwise set RLINK(Q) ← Λ (it had been changed temporarily to P, but we've now traversed P's left subtree).
>
> **U6.** [Inorder visit.] Visit NODE(P) in inorder.
>
> **U7.** [Go to right or up.] Set R ← P, P ← RLINK(P), and return to U2.
>
> **U8.** [Preorder visit.] Visit NODE(P) in preorder.
>
> **U9.** [Go to left.] Set P ← LLINK(P) and return to step U3. ▮

Morris also suggested a slightly more complicated way to traverse in postorder.

A completely different solution was found by J. M. Robson [*Inf. Proc. Letters* **2** (1973), 12–14]. Let's say that a node is "full" if its LLINK and RLINK are nonnull, "empty" if its LLINK and RLINK are both empty. Robson found a way to maintain a stack of pointers to the full nodes whose right subtrees are being visited, using the link fields in empty nodes!

Yet another way to avoid an auxiliary stack was discovered independently by G. Lindstrom and B. Dwyer, *Inf. Proc. Letters* **2** (1973), 47–51, 143–145. Their algorithm traverses in *triple order* — it visits every node exactly three times, once in each of preorder, inorder, and postorder — but it does not know which of the three is currently being done.

> **W1.** [Initialize.] Set P ← T and Q ← S, where S is a sentinel value — any number that is known to be different from any link in the tree (e.g., −1).
>
> **W2.** [Bypass null.] If P = Λ, set P ← Q and Q ← Λ.
>
> **W3.** [Done?] If P = S, terminate the algorithm. (We will have Q = T at termination.)

W4. [Visit.] Visit NODE(P).

W5. [Rotate.] Set R ← LLINK(P), LLINK(P) ← RLINK(P), RLINK(P) ← Q, Q ← P, P ← R, and return to W2. ∎

Correctness follows from the fact that if we start at W2 with P pointing to the root of a binary tree T and Q pointing to X, where X is not a link in that tree, the algorithm will traverse the tree in triple order and reach step W3 with P = X and Q = T.

If $\alpha(\text{T}) = x_1 x_2 \ldots x_{3n}$ is the resulting sequence of nodes in triple order, we have $\alpha(\text{T}) = \text{T}\,\alpha(\text{LLINK(T)})\,\text{T}\,\alpha(\text{RLINK(T)})\,\text{T}$. Therefore, as Lindstrom observed, the three subsequences $x_1 x_4 \ldots x_{3n-2}$, $x_2 x_5 \ldots x_{3n-1}$, $x_3 x_6 \ldots x_{3n}$ each include every tree node just once. (Since x_{j+1} is either the parent or child of x_j, these subsequences visit the nodes in such a way that each is at most three links away from its predecessor. Section 7.2.1.6 describes a general traversal scheme called *prepostorder* that has this property not only for binary trees but for trees in general.)

22. This program uses the conventions of Programs T and S, with Q in rI6 and/or rI4. The old-fashioned MIX computer is not good at comparing index registers for equality, so variable R is omitted and the test "Q = R" is changed to "RLINK(Q) = P".

01	U1	LD5	HEAD(LLINK)	1	*U1. Initialize.* P ← T.
02	U2A	J5Z	DONE	1	Stop if P = Λ.
03	U3	LD6	0,5(LLINK)	$n+a-1$	*U3. Look left.* Q ← LLINK(P).
04		J6Z	U6	$n+a-1$	To U6 if Q = Λ.
05	U4	CMP5	1,6(RLINK)	$2n-2b$	*U4. Search for thread.*
06		JE	5F	$2n-2b$	Jump if RLINK(Q) = P.
07		ENT4	0,6	$2n-2b-a+1$	rI4 ← Q.
08		LD6	1,6(RLINK)	$2n-2b-a+1$	
09		J6NZ	U4	$2n-2b-a+1$	To U4 with Q ← RLINK(Q) if it's ≠ 0.
10	U5	ST5	1,4(RLINK)	$a-1$	*U5a. Insert thread.* RLINK(Q) ← P.
11	U9	LD5	0,5(LLINK)	$a-1$	*U9. Go to left.* P ← LLINK(P).
12		JMP	U3	$a-1$	To U3.
13	5H	STZ	1,6(RLINK)	$a-1$	*U5b. Remove thread.* RLINK(Q) ← Λ.
14	U6	JMP	VISIT	n	*U6. Inorder visit.*
15	U7	LD5	1,5(RLINK)	n	*U7. Go to right or up.* P ← RLINK(P).
16	U2	J5NZ	U3	n	*U2. Done?* To U3 if P ≠ Λ.
17	DONE	...			∎

The total running time is $21n + 6a - 3 - 14b$, where n is the number of nodes, a is the number of null RLINKs (hence $a - 1$ is the number of nonnull LLINKs), and b is the number of nodes on the tree's "right spine" T, RLINK(T), RLINK(RLINK(T)), etc.

23. Insertion to the right: RLINKT(Q) ← RLINKT(P), RLINK(P) ← Q, RTAG(P) ← 0, LLINK(Q) ← Λ. Insertion to the left, assuming LLINK(P) = Λ: Set LLINK(P) ← Q, LLINK(Q) ← Λ, RLINK(Q) ← P, RTAG(Q) ← 1. Insertion to the left, between P and LLINK(P) ≠ Λ: Set R ← LLINK(P), LLINK(Q) ← R, and then set R ← RLINK(R) zero or more times until RTAG(R) = 1; finally set RLINK(R) ← Q, LLINK(P) ← Q, RLINK(Q) ← P, RTAG(Q) ← 1.

(A more efficient algorithm for the last case can be used if we know a node F such that P = LLINK(F) or P = RLINK(F); assuming the latter, for example, we could set INFO(P) ↔ INFO(Q), RLINK(F) ← Q, LLINK(Q) ← P, RLINKT(Q) ← RLINKT(P), RLINK(P) ← Q, RTAG(P) ← 1. This takes a fixed amount of time, but it is generally not recommended because it switches nodes around in memory.)

24. No:

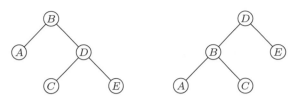

25. We first prove (b), by induction on the number of nodes in T, and similarly (c). Now (a) breaks into several cases; write $T \preceq_1 T'$ if (i) holds, $T \preceq_2 T'$ if (ii) holds, etc. Then $T \preceq_1 T'$ and $T' \preceq T''$ implies $T \preceq_1 T''$; $T \preceq_2 T'$ and $T' \preceq T''$ implies $T \preceq_2 T''$; and the remaining two cases are treated by proving (a) by induction on the number of nodes in T.

26. If the double order of T is $(u_1, d_1), (u_2, d_2), \ldots, (u_{2n}, d_{2n})$ where the u's are nodes and the d's are 1 or 2, form the "trace" of the tree $(v_1, s_1), (v_2, s_2), \ldots, (v_{2n}, s_{2n})$, where $v_j = \mathrm{info}(u_j)$, and $s_j = l(u_j)$ or $r(u_j)$ according as $d_j = 1$ or 2. Now $T \preceq T'$ if and only if the trace of T (as defined here) *lexicographically* precedes or equals the trace of T'. Formally, this means that we have either $n \le n'$ and $(v_j, s_j) = (v'_j, s'_j)$ for $1 \le j \le 2n$, or else there is a k for which $(v_j, s_j) = (v'_j, s'_j)$ for $1 \le j < k$ and either $v_k \prec v'_k$ or $v_k = v'_k$ and $s_k < s'_k$.

27. R1. [Initialize.] Set $\mathtt{P} \leftarrow \mathtt{HEAD}$, $\mathtt{P}' \leftarrow \mathtt{HEAD}'$; these are the respective list heads of the given right-threaded binary trees. Go to R3.

  R2. [Check INFO.] If $\mathtt{INFO(P)} \prec \mathtt{INFO(P')}$, terminate $(T \prec T')$; if $\mathtt{INFO(P)} \succ \mathtt{INFO(P')}$, terminate $(T \succ T')$.

  R3. [Go to left.] If $\mathtt{LLINK(P)} = \Lambda = \mathtt{LLINK(P')}$, go to R4; if $\mathtt{LLINK(P)} = \Lambda \ne \mathtt{LLINK(P')}$, terminate $(T \prec T')$; if $\mathtt{LLINK(P)} \ne \Lambda = \mathtt{LLINK(P')}$, terminate $(T \succ T')$; otherwise set $\mathtt{P} \leftarrow \mathtt{LLINK(P)}$, $\mathtt{P}' \leftarrow \mathtt{LLINK(P')}$, and go to R2.

  R4. [End of tree?] If $\mathtt{P} = \mathtt{HEAD}$ (or, equivalently, if $\mathtt{P}' = \mathtt{HEAD}'$), terminate $(T$ is equivalent to $T')$.

  R5. [Go to right.] If $\mathtt{RTAG(P)} = 1 = \mathtt{RTAG(P')}$, set $\mathtt{P} \leftarrow \mathtt{RLINK(P)}$, $\mathtt{P}' \leftarrow \mathtt{RLINK(P')}$, and go to R4. If $\mathtt{RTAG(P)} = 1 \ne \mathtt{RTAG(P')}$, terminate $(T \prec T')$. If $\mathtt{RTAG(P)} \ne 1 = \mathtt{RTAG(P')}$, terminate $(T \succ T')$. Otherwise, set $\mathtt{P} \leftarrow \mathtt{RLINK(P)}$, $\mathtt{P}' \leftarrow \mathtt{RLINK(P')}$, and go to R2. ∎

To prove the validity of this algorithm (and therefore to understand how it works), one may show by induction on the size of the tree T_0 that the following statement is valid: *Starting at step R2 with P and P' pointing to the roots of two nonempty right-threaded binary trees T_0 and T_0', the algorithm will terminate if T_0 and T_0' are not equivalent, indicating whether $T_0 \prec T_0'$ or $T_0 \succ T_0'$; the algorithm will reach step R4 if T_0 and T_0' are equivalent, with P and P' then pointing respectively to the successor nodes of T_0 and T_0' in symmetric order.*

28. Equivalent *and* similar.

29. Prove by induction on the size of T that the following statement is valid: *Starting at step C2 with P pointing to the root of a nonempty binary tree T and with Q pointing to a node that has empty left and right subtrees, the procedure will ultimately arrive at step C6 after setting $\mathtt{INFO(Q)} \leftarrow \mathtt{INFO(P)}$ and attaching copies of the left and right subtrees of $\mathtt{NODE(P)}$ to $\mathtt{NODE(Q)}$, and with P and Q pointing respectively to the preorder successor nodes of the trees T and $\mathtt{NODE(Q)}$.*

30. Assume that the pointer T in (2) is LLINK(HEAD) in (10). Thus LOC(T) = HEAD, and HEAD$ is the first node of the binary tree in symmetric order.

L1. [Initialize.] Set Q ← HEAD, RLINK(Q) ← Q.

L2. [Advance.] Set P ← Q$. (See below.)

L3. [Thread.] If RLINK(Q) = Λ, set RLINK(Q) ← P, RTAG(Q) ← 1; otherwise set RTAG(Q) ← 0. If LLINK(P) = Λ, set LLINK(P) ← Q, LTAG(P) ← 1; otherwise set LTAG(P) ← 0.

L4. [Done?] If P ≠ HEAD, set Q ← P and return to L2. ∎

Step L2 of this algorithm implies the activation of an inorder traversal coroutine like Algorithm T, with the additional proviso that Algorithm T visits HEAD after it has fully traversed the tree. This notation is a convenient simplification in the description of tree algorithms, since we need not repeat the stack mechanisms of Algorithm T over and over again. Of course Algorithm S cannot be used during step L2, since the tree hasn't been threaded yet. But Algorithm U in answer 21 *can* be used in step L2; it provides us with a very pretty method that threads a tree without using any auxiliary stack.

31. **X1.** Set P ← HEAD.

X2. Set Q ← P$ (using, say, Algorithm S, modified for a right-threaded tree).

X3. If P ≠ HEAD, set AVAIL ⇐ P.

X4. If Q ≠ HEAD, set P ← Q and go back to X2.

X5. Set LLINK(HEAD) ← Λ. ∎

Other solutions that decrease the length of the inner loop are clearly possible, although the order of the basic steps is somewhat critical. The stated procedure works because we never return a node to available storage until after Algorithm S has looked at both its LLINK and its RLINK; as observed in the text, each of these links is used precisely once during a complete tree traversal.

32. RLINK(Q) ← RLINK(P), SUC(Q) ← SUC(P), SUC(P) ← RLINK(P) ← Q, PRED(Q) ← P, PRED(SUC(Q)) ← Q.

33. Inserting NODE(Q) just to the left and below NODE(P) is quite simple: Set LLINKT(Q) ← LLINKT(P), LLINK(P) ← Q, LTAG(P) ← 0, RLINK(Q) ← Λ. Insertion to the right is considerably harder, since it essentially requires finding *Q, which is of comparable difficulty to finding Q♯ (see exercise 19); the node-moving technique discussed in exercise 23 could perhaps be used. So general insertions are more difficult with this type of threading. But the insertions required by Algorithm C are not as difficult as insertions are in general, and in fact the copying process is slightly faster for this kind of threading:

C1. Set P ← HEAD, Q ← U, go to C4. (The assumptions and philosophy of Algorithm C in the text are being used throughout.)

C2. If RLINK(P) ≠ Λ, set R ⇐ AVAIL, LLINK(R) ← LLINK(Q), LTAG(R) ← 1, RLINK(R) ← Λ, RLINK(Q) ← LLINK(Q) ← R.

C3. Set INFO(Q) ← INFO(P).

C4. If LTAG(P) = 0, set R ⇐ AVAIL, LLINK(R) ← LLINK(Q), LTAG(R) ← 1, RLINK(R) ← Λ, LLINK(Q) ← R, LTAG(Q) ← 0.

C5. Set P ← LLINK(P), Q ← LLINK(Q).

C6. If P ≠ HEAD, go to C2. ∎

The algorithm now seems almost too simple to be correct!

Algorithm C for threaded or right-threaded binary trees takes slightly longer due to the extra time to calculate P*, Q* in step C5.

It would be possible to thread RLINKs in the usual way or to put ‡P in RLINK(P), in conjunction with this copying method, by appropriately setting the values of RLINK(R) and RLINKT(Q) in steps C2 and C4.

34. **A1.** Set Q ← P, and then repeatedly set Q ← RLINK(Q) zero or more times until RTAG(Q) = 1.

A2. Set R ← RLINK(Q). If LLINK(R) = P, set LLINK(R) ← Λ. Otherwise set R ← LLINK(R), then repeatedly set R ← RLINK(R) zero or more times until RLINK(R) = P; then finally set RLINKT(R) ← RLINKT(Q). (This step has removed NODE(P) and its subtrees from the original tree.)

A3. Set RLINK(Q) ← HEAD, LLINK(HEAD) ← P. ∎

(The key to inventing and/or understanding this algorithm is the construction of good "before and after" diagrams.)

36. No; see the answer to exercise 1.2.1–15(e).

37. If LLINK(P) = RLINK(P) = Λ in the representation (2), let LINK(P) = Λ; otherwise let LINK(P) = Q where NODE(Q) corresponds to NODE(LLINK(P)) and NODE(Q + 1) to NODE(RLINK(P)). The condition LLINK(P) or RLINK(P) = Λ is represented by a sentinel in NODE(Q) or NODE(Q + 1) respectively. This representation uses between n and $2n − 1$ memory positions; under the stated assumptions, (2) would require 18 words of memory, compared to 11 in the present scheme. Insertion and deletion operations are approximately of equal efficiency in either representation. But this representation is not quite as versatile in combination with other structures.

SECTION 2.3.2

1. If B is empty, $F(B)$ is an empty forest. Otherwise, $F(B)$ consists of a tree T plus the forest $F(\text{right}(B))$, where $\text{root}(T) = \text{root}(B)$ and $\text{subtrees}(T) = F(\text{left}(B))$.

2. The number of zeros in the binary notation is the number of decimal points in the decimal notation; the exact formula for the correspondence is

$$a_1.a_2.\cdots.a_k \leftrightarrow 1^{a_1}01^{a_2-1}0\ldots01^{a_k-1},$$

where 1^a denotes a ones in a row.

3. Sort the Dewey decimal notations for the nodes lexicographically (from left to right, as in a dictionary), placing a shorter sequence $a_1.\cdots.a_k$ in front of its extensions $a_1.\cdots.a_k.\cdots.a_r$ for preorder, and behind its extensions for postorder. Thus, if we were sorting words instead of sequences of numbers, we would place the words *cat*, *cataract* in the usual dictionary order, to get preorder; we would reverse the order of initial subwords (*cataract*, *cat*), to get postorder. These rules are readily proved by induction on the size of the tree.

4. True, by induction on the number of nodes.

5. (a) Inorder. (b) Postorder. It is interesting to formulate rigorous induction proofs of the equivalence of these traversal algorithms.

6. We have $\text{preorder}(T) = \text{preorder}(T')$, and $\text{postorder}(T) = \text{inorder}(T')$, even if T has nodes with only one child. The remaining two orders are not in any simple relation; for example, the root of T comes at the end in one case and about in the middle in the other.

7. (a) Yes; (b) no; (c) no; (d) yes. Note that reverse preorder of a forest equals postorder of the left-right reversed forest (in the sense of mirror reflection).

8. $T \preceq T'$ means that either info$(\text{root}(T)) \prec$ info$(\text{root}(T'))$, or these info's are equal and the following condition holds: Suppose the subtrees of root(T) are $T_1, \ldots, T_n$ and the subtrees of root(T') are $T'_1, \ldots, T'_{n'}$, and let $k \geq 0$ be as large as possible such that T_j is equivalent to T'_j for $1 \leq j \leq k$. Then either $k = n$ or $k < n$ and $T_{k+1} \preceq T'_{k+1}$.

9. The number of nonterminal nodes is one less than the number of right links that are Λ, in a nonempty forest, because the null right links correspond to the rightmost child of each nonterminal node, and also to the root of the rightmost tree in the forest. (This fact gives another proof of exercise 2.3.1–14, since the number of null left links is obviously equal to the number of *terminal* nodes.)

10. The forests are similar if and only if $n = n'$ and $d(u_j) = d(u'_j)$, for $1 \leq j \leq n$; they are equivalent if and only if in addition info$(u_j) =$ info(u'_j), $1 \leq j \leq n$. The proof is similar to the previous proof, by generalizing Lemma 2.3.1P; let $f(u) = d(u) - 1$.

11.

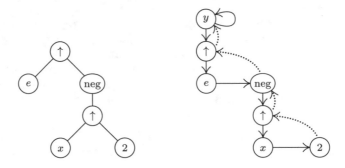

12. If INFO(Q1) $\neq$ 0: Set R $\leftarrow$ COPY(P1); then if TYPE(P2) $= 0$ and INFO(P2) $\neq 2$, set R $\leftarrow$ TREE("↑",R,TREE(INFO(P2) $- 1$)); if TYPE(P2) $\neq 0$, set R $\leftarrow$ TREE("↑",R, TREE("−",COPY(P2),TREE(1))); then set Q1 $\leftarrow$ MULT(Q1,MULT(COPY(P2),R)).

If INFO(Q) $\neq$ 0: Set Q $\leftarrow$ TREE("×",MULT(TREE("ln",COPY(P1)),Q),TREE("↑", COPY(P1),COPY(P2))).

Finally go to DIFF[4].

13. The following program implements Algorithm 2.3.1C with rI1 $\equiv$ P, rI2 $\equiv$ Q, rI3 $\equiv$ R, and with appropriate changes to the initialization and termination conditions:

```
064        ST3   6F(0:2)       Save contents of rI3, rI2.
065        ST2   7F(0:2)       C1. Initialize.
066        ENT2  8F            Start by creating NODE(U) with
067        JMP   1F                RLINK(U) = Λ.
068   8H  CON   0              Zero constant for initialization
069   4H  LD1   0,1(LLINK)     Set P ← LLINK(P) = P*.
070   1H  LD3   AVAIL          R ⇐ AVAIL.
071        J3Z   OVERFLOW
072        LDA   0,3(LLINK)
073        STA   AVAIL
074        ST3   0,2(LLINK)    LLINK(Q) ← R.
075        ENNA  0,2
076        STA   0,3(RLINKT)   RLINK(R) ← Q, RTAG(R) ← 1.
```

```
077      INCA 8B           rA ← LOC(init node) − Q.
078      ENT2 0,3          Set Q ← R = Q*.
079      JAZ  C3           To C3, the first time.
080  C2 LDA  0,1           C2. Anything to right?
081      JAN  C3           Jump if RTAG(P) = 1.
082      LD3  AVAIL        R ⇐ AVAIL.
083      J3Z  OVERFLOW
084      LDA  0,3(LLINK)
085      STA  AVAIL
086      LDA  0,2(RLINKT)
087      STA  0,3(RLINKT)  Set RLINKT(R) ← RLINKT(Q).
088      ST3  0,2(RLINKT)  RLINK(Q) ← R, RTAG(Q) ← 0.
089  C3 LDA  1,1           C3. Copy INFO.
090      STA  1,2          INFO field copied.
091      LDA  0,1(TYPE)
092      STA  0,2(TYPE)    TYPE field copied.
093  C4 LDA  0,1(LLINK)    C4. Anything to left?
094      JANZ 4B           Jump if LLINK(P) ≠ Λ.
095      STZ  0,2(LLINK)   LLINK(Q) ← Λ.
096  C5 LD2N 0,2(RLINKT)   C5. Advance. Q ← −RLINKT(Q).
097      LD1  0,1(RLINK)   P ← RLINK(P).
098      J2P  C5           Jump if RTAG(Q) was 1.
099      ENN2 0,2          Q ← −Q.
100  C6 J2NZ C2            C6. Test if complete.
101      LD1  8B(LLINK)    rI1 ← location of first node created.
102  6H ENT3 *             Restore index registers.
103  7H ENT2 *             ▮
```

14. Let a be the number of nonterminal (operator) nodes copied. The number of executions of the various lines in the previous program is as follows: 064–067, 1; 069, a; 070–079, $a + 1$; 080–081, $n - 1$; 082–088, $n - 1 - a$; 089–094, n; 095, $n - a$; 096–098, $n + 1$; 099–100, $n - a$; 101–103, 1. The total time is $(36n + 22)u$; we use about 20% of the time to get available nodes, 40% to traverse, and 40% to copy the INFO and LINK information.

15. Comments are left to the reader.

```
218 DIV LDA  1,6
219     JAZ  1F
220     JMP  COPYP2
221     ENTA SLASH
222     ENTX 0,6
223     JMP  TREE2
224     ENT6 0,1
225  1H LDA  1,5
226     JAZ  SUB
227     JMP  COPYP2
228     ST1  1F(0:2)
229     ENTA CON2
230     JMP  TREE0
```

```
231     ENTA UPARROW
232  1H ENTX *
233     JMP  TREE2
234     ST1  1F(0:2)
235     JMP  COPYP1
236     ENTA 0,1
237     ENT1 0,5
238     JMP  MULT
239     ENTX 0,1
240  1H ENT1 *
241     ENTA SLASH
242     JMP  TREE2
243     ENT5 0,1
244     JMP  SUB  ▮
```

16. Comments are left to the reader.

```
245 PWR  LDA  1,6        263      JMP  TREE0       281      ENTA LOG
246      JAZ  4F         264  1H  ENTX *          282      JMP  TREE1
247      JMP  COPYP1     265      ENTA MINUS      283      ENTA 0,1
248      ST1  R(0:2)     266      JMP  TREE2      284      ENT1 0,5
249      LDA  0,3(TYPE)  267  5H  LDX  R(0:2)     285      JMP  MULT
250      JANZ 2F         268      ENTA UPARROW    286      ST1  1F(0:2)
251      LDA  1,3        269      JMP  TREE2      287      JMP  COPYP1
252      DECA 2          270      ST1  R(0:2)     288      ST1  2F(0:2)
253      JAZ  3F         271  3H  JMP  COPYP2     289      JMP  COPYP2
254      INCA 1          272      ENTA 0,1        290  2H  ENTX *
255      STA  CON0+1     273  R   ENT1 *          291      ENTA UPARROW
256      ENTA CON0       274      JMP  MULT       292      JMP  TREE2
257      JMP  TREE0      275      ENTA 0,6        293  1H  ENTX *
258      STZ  CON0+1     276      JMP  MULT       294      ENTA TIMES
259      JMP  5F         277      ENT6 0,1        295      JMP  TREE2
260  2H  JMP  COPYP2     278  4H  LDA  1,5        296      ENT5 0,1
261      ST1  1F(0:2)    279      JAZ  ADD        297      JMP  ADD
262      ENTA CON1       280      JMP  COPYP1
```

17. References to early work on such problems can be found in a survey article by J. Sammet, *CACM* **9** (1966), 555–569.

18. First set $\mathtt{LLINK}[j] \leftarrow \mathtt{RLINK}[j] \leftarrow j$ for all j, so that each node is in a circular list of length 1. Then for $j = n, n-1, \ldots, 1$ (in this order), if $\mathtt{PARENT}[j] = 0$ set $r \leftarrow j$, otherwise insert the circular list starting with j into the circular list starting with $\mathtt{PARENT}[j]$ as follows: $k \leftarrow \mathtt{PARENT}[j]$, $l \leftarrow \mathtt{RLINK}[k]$, $i \leftarrow \mathtt{LLINK}[j]$, $\mathtt{LLINK}[j] \leftarrow k$, $\mathtt{RLINK}[k] \leftarrow j$, $\mathtt{LLINK}[l] \leftarrow i$, $\mathtt{RLINK}[i] \leftarrow l$. This works because (a) each nonroot node is always preceded by its parent or by a descendant of its parent; (b) nodes of each family appear in their parent's list, in order of location; (c) preorder is the unique order satisfying (a) and (b).

20. If u is an ancestor of v, it is immediate by induction that u precedes v in preorder and follows v in postorder. Conversely, suppose u precedes v in preorder and follows v in postorder; we must show that u is an ancestor of v. This is clear if u is the root of the first tree. If u is another node of the first tree, v must be also, since u follows v in postorder; so induction applies. Similarly if u is not in the first tree, v must not be either, since u precedes v in preorder. (This exercise also follows easily from the result of exercise 3. It gives us a quick test for ancestorhood, if we know each node's position in preorder and postorder.)

21. If $\mathtt{NODE(P)}$ is a binary operator, pointers to its two operands are $\mathtt{P1} = \mathtt{LLINK(P)}$ and $\mathtt{P2} = \mathtt{RLINK(P1)} = \mathtt{\$P}$. Algorithm D makes use of the fact that $\mathtt{P2\$} = \mathtt{P}$, so that $\mathtt{RLINK(P1)}$ may be changed to $\mathtt{Q1}$, a pointer to the derivative of $\mathtt{NODE(P1)}$; then $\mathtt{RLINK(P1)}$ is reset later in step D3. For ternary operations, we would have, say, $\mathtt{P1} = \mathtt{LLINK(P)}$, $\mathtt{P2} = \mathtt{RLINK(P1)}$, $\mathtt{P3} = \mathtt{RLINK(P2)} = \mathtt{\$P}$, so it is difficult to generalize the binary trick. After computing the derivative $\mathtt{Q1}$, we could set $\mathtt{RLINK(P1)} \leftarrow \mathtt{Q1}$ temporarily, and then after computing the next derivative $\mathtt{Q2}$ we could set $\mathtt{RLINK(Q2)} \leftarrow \mathtt{Q1}$ and $\mathtt{RLINK(P1)} \leftarrow \mathtt{Q2}$ and reset $\mathtt{RLINK(P1)} \leftarrow \mathtt{P2}$. But this is certainly inelegant, and it becomes progressively more so as the degree of the operator becomes higher. Therefore the device of temporarily changing $\mathtt{RLINK(P1)}$ in Algorithm D is definitely a *trick*, not a *technique*. A more aesthetic way to control a differentiation process, because it generalizes to operators of higher degree and does not rely on isolated tricks, can be based on Algorithm 2.3.3F; see exercise 2.3.3–3.

22. From the definition it follows immediately that the relation is transitive; that is, if $T \subseteq T'$ and $T' \subseteq T''$ then $T \subseteq T''$. (In fact the relation is easily seen to be a partial ordering.) If we let f be the function taking nodes into themselves, clearly $l(T) \subseteq T$ and $r(T) \subseteq T$. Therefore if $T \subseteq l(T')$ or $T \subseteq r(T')$ we must have $T \subseteq T'$.

Suppose f_l and f_r are functions that respectively show $l(T) \subseteq l(T')$ and $r(T) \subseteq r(T')$. Let $f(u) = f_l(u)$ if u is in $l(T)$, $f(u) = \text{root}(T')$ if u is $\text{root}(T)$, otherwise $f(u) = f_r(u)$. Now it follows easily that f shows $T \subseteq T'$; for example, if we let $r'(T)$ denote $r(T) \setminus \text{root}(T)$ we have $\text{preorder}(T) = \text{root}(T) \ \text{preorder}(l(T)) \ \text{preorder}(r'(T))$; $\text{preorder}(T') = f(\text{root}(T)) \ \text{preorder}(l(T')) \ \text{preorder}(r'(T'))$.

The converse does not hold: Consider the subtrees with roots b and b' in Fig. 25.

SECTION 2.3.3

1. Yes, we can reconstruct them just as (3) is deduced from (4), but interchanging LTAG and RTAG, LLINK and RLINK, and using a queue instead of a stack.

2. Make the following changes in Algorithm F: Step F1, change to "last node of the forest in preorder." Step F2, change "$f(x_d), \ldots, f(x_1)$" to "$f(x_1), \ldots, f(x_d)$" in two places. Step F4, "If P is the first node in preorder, terminate the algorithm. (Then the stack contains $f(\text{root}(T_1)), \ldots, f(\text{root}(T_m))$, from top to bottom, where $T_1, \ldots, T_m$ are the trees of the given forest, from left to right.) Otherwise set P to its predecessor in preorder (P ← P − c in the given representation), and return to F2."

3. In step D1, also set S ← Λ. (S is a link variable that links to the top of the stack.) Step D2 becomes, for example, "If NODE(P) denotes a unary operator, set Q ← S, S ← RLINK(Q), P1 ← LLINK(P); if it denotes a binary operator, set Q ← S, Q1 ← RLINK(Q), S ← RLINK(Q1), P1 ← LLINK(P), P2 ← RLINK(P1). Then perform DIFF[TYPE(P)]." Step D3 becomes "Set RLINK(Q) ← S, S ← Q." Step D4 becomes "Set P ← P$." The operation LLINK(DY) ← Q may be avoided in step D5 if we assume that S ≡ LLINK(DY). This technique clearly generalizes to ternary and higher-order operators.

4. A representation like (10) takes $n - m$ LLINKs and $n + (n - m)$ RLINKs. The difference in total number of links is $n - 2m$ between the two forms of representation. Arrangement (10) is superior when the LLINK and INFO fields require about the same amount of space in a node and when m is rather large, namely when the nonterminal nodes have rather large degrees.

5. It would certainly be silly to include threaded RLINKs, since an RLINK thread just points to PARENT anyway. Threaded LLINKs as in 2.3.2–(4) would be useful if it is necessary to move leftward in the tree, for example if we wanted to traverse a tree in reverse postorder, or in family order; but these operations are not significantly harder without threaded LLINKs unless the nodes tend to have very high degrees.

6. L1. Set P ← FIRST, FIRST ← Λ.

  L2. If P = Λ, terminate. Otherwise set Q ← RLINK(P).

  L3. If PARENT(P) = Λ, set RLINK(P) ← FIRST, FIRST ← P; otherwise set R ← PARENT(P), RLINK(P) ← LCHILD(R), LCHILD(R) ← P.

  L4. Set P ← Q and return to L2. ∎

7. $\{1,5\}\{2,3,4,7\}\{6,8,9\}$.

8. Perform step E3 of Algorithm E, then test if $j = k$.

9. PARENT[k]:   5   0   2   2   0   8   2   2   8
$\phantom{\textbf{9.} \text{PARENT}}k$:   1   2   3   4   5   6   7   8   9

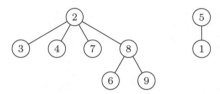

10. One idea is to set PARENT of each *root* node to the negative of the number of nodes in its tree (these values being easily kept up to date); then if $|\text{PARENT}[j]| > |\text{PARENT}[k]|$ in step E4, the roles of j and k are interchanged. This technique (due to M. D. McIlroy) ensures that each operation takes $O(\log n)$ steps.

For still more speed, we can use the following suggestion due to Alan Tritter: In step E4, set PARENT[x] $\leftarrow k$ for all values $x \neq k$ that were encountered in step E3. This makes an extra pass up the trees, but it collapses them so that future searches are faster. (See Section 7.4.1.1.)

11. It suffices to define the transformation that is done for each input (P, j, Q, k):

> **T1.** If PARENT(P) $\neq \Lambda$, set $j \leftarrow j + \text{DELTA(P)}$, P $\leftarrow$ PARENT(P), and repeat this step.
>
> **T2.** If PARENT(Q) $\neq \Lambda$, set $k \leftarrow k + \text{DELTA(Q)}$, Q $\leftarrow$ PARENT(Q), and repeat this step.
>
> **T3.** If P $=$ Q, check that $j = k$ (otherwise the input erroneously contains contradictory equivalences). If P $\neq$ Q, set DELTA(Q) $\leftarrow j - k$, PARENT(Q) $\leftarrow$ P, LBD(P) $\leftarrow$ min(LBD(P), LBD(Q) + DELTA(Q)), and UBD(P) $\leftarrow$ max(UBD(P), UBD(Q) + DELTA(Q)). ∎

Note: It is possible to allow the ARRAY X[l:u] declarations to occur intermixed with equivalences, or to allow assignment of certain addresses of variables before others are equivalenced to them, etc., under suitable conditions that are not difficult to understand. For further development of this algorithm, see *CACM* **7** (1964), 301–303, 506.

12. (a) Yes. (If this condition is not required, it would be possible to avoid the loops on S that appear in steps A2 and A9.) (b) Yes.

13. The crucial fact is that the UP chain leading upward from P always mentions the same variables and the same exponents for these variables as the UP chain leading upward from Q, except that the latter chain may include additional steps for variables with exponent zero. (This condition holds throughout most of the algorithm, except during the execution of steps A9 and A10.) Now we get to step A8 either from A3 or from A10, and in each case it was verified that EXP(Q) $\neq 0$. Therefore EXP(P) $\neq 0$, and in particular it follows that P $\neq \Lambda$, Q $\neq \Lambda$, UP(P) $\neq \Lambda$, UP(Q) $\neq \Lambda$; the result stated in the exercise now follows. Thus the proof depends on showing that the UP chain condition stated above is preserved by the actions of the algorithm.

14, 15. See Martin Ward and Hussain Zedan, "Provably correct derivation of algorithms using FermaT," *Formal Aspects of Computing* **26** (2014), 993–1031.

16. We prove (by induction on the number of nodes in a *single tree* T) that if P is a pointer to T, and if the stack is initially empty, steps F2 through F4 will end with the single value $f(\text{root}(T))$ on the stack. This is true for $n = 1$. If $n > 1$, there are $0 < d = \text{DEGREE}(\text{root}(T))$ subtrees $T_1, \ldots, T_d$; by induction and the nature of a stack, and since postorder consists of $T_1, \ldots, T_d$ followed by $\text{root}(T)$, the algorithm computes $f(T_1), \ldots, f(T_d)$, and then $f(\text{root}(T))$, as desired. The validity of Algorithm F for forests follows.

17. G1. Set the stack empty, and let P point to the root of the tree (the last node in postorder). Evaluate $f(\text{NODE}(\text{P}))$.

    G2. Push DEGREE(P) copies of $f(\text{NODE}(\text{P}))$ onto the stack.

    G3. If P is the first node in postorder, terminate the algorithm. Otherwise set P to its predecessor in postorder (this would be simply P ← P − c in (9)).

    G4. Evaluate $f(\text{NODE}(\text{P}))$ using the value at the top of the stack, which is equal to $f(\text{NODE}(\text{PARENT}(\text{P})))$. Pop this value off the stack, and return to G2. ▮

Note: An algorithm analogous to this one can be based on preorder instead of postorder as in exercise 2. In fact, family order or level order could be used; in the latter case we would use a queue instead of a stack.

18. The INFO1 and RLINK tables, together with the suggestion for computing LTAG in the text, give us the equivalent of a binary tree represented in the usual manner. The idea is to traverse this tree in postorder, counting degrees as we go:

    P1. Let R, D, and I be stacks that are initially empty; then set R $\Leftarrow n + 1$, D $\Leftarrow 0$, $j \leftarrow 0$, $k \leftarrow 0$.

    P2. If top(R) $> j + 1$, go to P5. (If an LTAG field were present, we could have tested LTAG$[j] = 0$ instead of top(R) $> j + 1$.)

    P3. If I is empty, terminate the algorithm; otherwise set $i \Leftarrow$ I, $k \leftarrow k + 1$, INFO2$[k] \leftarrow$ INFO1$[i]$, DEGREE$[k] \Leftarrow$ D.

    P4. If RLINK$[i] = 0$, go to P3; otherwise delete the top of R (which will equal RLINK$[i]$).

    P5. Set top(D) ← top(D) $+ 1$, $j \leftarrow j + 1$, I $\Leftarrow j$, D $\Leftarrow 0$, and if RLINK$[j] \neq 0$ set R $\Leftarrow$ RLINK$[j]$. Go to P2. ▮

19. (a) This property is equivalent to saying that SCOPE links do not cross each other. (b) The first tree of the forest contains $d_1 + 1$ elements, and we can proceed by induction. (c) The condition of (a) is preserved when we take minima.

    Notes: By exercise 2.3.2–20, it follows that $d_1 d_2 \ldots d_n$ can also be interpreted in terms of inversions: If the kth node in postorder is the p_kth node in preorder, then d_k is the number of elements $> k$ that appear to the left of k in $p_1 p_2 \ldots p_n$.

    A similar scheme, in which we list the number of descendants of each node in *postorder* of the forest, leads to sequences of numbers $c_1 c_2 \ldots c_n$ characterized by the properties (i) $0 \leq c_k < k$ and (ii) $k \geq j \geq k - c_k$ implies $j - c_j \geq k - c_k$. Algorithms based on such sequences have been investigated by J. M. Pallo, *Comp. J.* **29** (1986), 171–175. Notice that c_k is the size of the left subtree of the kth node in symmetric order of the corresponding binary tree. We can also interpret d_k as the size of the *right* subtree of the kth node in symmetric order of a suitable binary tree, namely the binary tree that corresponds to the given forest by the dual method of exercise 2.3.2–5.

    The relation $d_k \leq d'_k$ for $1 \leq k \leq n$ defines an interesting lattice ordering of forests and binary trees, first introduced in another way by D. Tamari [Thèse (Paris, 1951)]; see exercise 6.2.3–32.

SECTION 2.3.4.1

1. (B, A, C, D, B), (B, A, C, D, E, B), (B, D, C, A, B), (B, D, E, B), (B, E, D, B), (B, E, D, C, A, B).

2. Let $(V_0, V_1, \ldots, V_n)$ be a walk of smallest possible length from V to V'. If now $V_j = V_k$ for some $j < k$, then $(V_0, \ldots, V_j, V_{k+1}, \ldots, V_n)$ would be a shorter walk.

3. (The fundamental path traverses e_3 and e_4 once, but cycle C_2 traverses them -1 times, giving a net total of zero.) Traverse the following edges: e_1, e_2, e_6, e_7, e_9, e_{10}, e_{11}, e_{12}, e_{14}.

4. If not, let G'' be the subgraph of G' obtained by deleting each edge e_j for which $E_j = 0$. Then G'' is a finite graph that has no cycles and at least one edge, so by the proof of Theorem A there is at least one vertex, V, that is adjacent to exactly one other vertex, V'. Let e_j be the edge joining V to V'; then Kirchhoff's equation (1) at vertex V is $E_j = 0$, contradicting the definition of G''.

5. $A = 1 + E_8$, $B = 1 + E_8 - E_2$, $C = 1 + E_8$, $D = 1 + E_8 - E_5$, $E = 1 + E_{17} - E_{21}$, $F = 1 + E_{13}'' + E_{17} - E_{21}$, $G = 1 + E_{13}''$, $H = E_{17} - E_{21}$, $J = E_{17}$, $K = E_{19}'' + E_{20}$, $L = E_{17} + E_{19}'' + E_{20} - E_{21}$, $P = E_{17} + E_{20} - E_{21}$, $Q = E_{20}$, $R = E_{17} - E_{21}$, $S = E_{25}$.
Note: In this case it is also possible to solve for $E_2, E_5, \ldots, E_{25}$ in terms of $A, B, \ldots, S$; hence there are nine independent solutions, explaining why we eliminated six variables in Eq. 1.3.3–(8).

6. (The following solution is based on the idea that we may print out each edge that does not make a cycle with the preceding edges.) Use Algorithm 2.3.3E, with each pair (a_i, b_i) representing $a_i \equiv b_i$ in the notation of that algorithm. The only change is to print (a_i, b_i) if $j \neq k$ in step E4.

To show that this algorithm is valid, we must prove that (a) the algorithm prints out no edges that form a cycle, and (b) if G contains at least one free subtree, the algorithm prints out $n - 1$ edges. Define $j \equiv k$ if there exists a path from V_j to V_k or if $j = k$. This is clearly an equivalence relation, and moreover $j \equiv k$ if and only if this relation can be deduced from the equivalences $a_1 \equiv b_1, \ldots, a_m \equiv b_m$. Now (a) holds because the algorithm prints out no edges that form a cycle with previously printed edges; (b) is true because $\texttt{PARENT}[k] = 0$ for precisely one k if all vertices are equivalent.

A more efficient algorithm can, however, be based on depth-first search; see Algorithm 2.3.5A and Section 7.4.1.2.

7. Fundamental cycles: $C_0 = e_0 + e_1 + e_4 + e_9$ (fundamental path is $e_1 + e_4 + e_9$); $C_5 = e_5 + e_3 + e_2$; $C_6 = e_6 - e_2 + e_4$; $C_7 = e_7 - e_4 - e_3$; $C_8 = e_8 - e_9 - e_4 - e_3$. Therefore we find $E_1 = 1$, $E_2 = E_5 - E_6$, $E_3 = E_5 - E_7 - E_8$, $E_4 = 1 + E_6 - E_7 - E_8$, $E_9 = 1 - E_8$.

8. Each step in the reduction process combines two arrows e_i and e_j that start at the same box, and it suffices to prove that such steps can be reversed. Thus we are given the value of $e_i + e_j$ after combination, and we must assign consistent values to e_i and e_j before the combination. There are three essentially different situations:

Case 1	Case 2	Case 3

Before

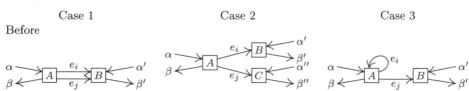

After

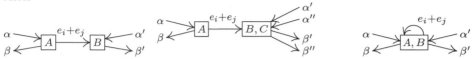

Here A, B, and C stand for vertices or supervertices, and the α's and β's stand for the other given flows besides $e_i + e_j$; these flows may each be distributed among several edges, although only one is shown. In Case 1 (e_i and e_j lead to the same box), we may choose e_i arbitrarily, then $e_j \leftarrow (e_i + e_j) - e_i$. In Case 2 ($e_i$ and e_j lead to different boxes), we must set $e_i \leftarrow \beta' - \alpha'$, $e_j \leftarrow \beta'' - \alpha''$. In Case 3 ($e_i$ is a loop but e_j is not), we must set $e_j \leftarrow \beta' - \alpha'$, $e_i \leftarrow (e_i + e_j) - e_j$. In each case we have reversed the combination step as desired.

The result of this exercise essentially proves that the number of fundamental cycles in the reduced flow chart is the minimum number of vertex flows that must be measured to determine all the others. In the given example, the reduced flow chart reveals that only three vertex flows (e.g., a, c, d) need to be measured, while the original chart of exercise 7 has four independent edge flows. (The unit flow in e_0 needn't be measured.) We save one measurement every time Case 1 occurs during the reduction.

A similar reduction procedure could be based on combining the arrows flowing *into* a given box, instead of those flowing out. It can be shown that this would yield the same reduced flow chart, except that the supervertices would contain different names.

The construction in this exercise is based on ideas due to Armen Nahapetian and F. Stevenson. For further comments, see A. Nahapetian, *Acta Informatica* **3** (1973), 37–41; D. E. Knuth and F. Stevenson, *BIT* **13** (1973), 313–322.

9. Each edge from a vertex to itself becomes a "fundamental cycle" all by itself. If there are $k + 1$ edges $e, e', \ldots, e^{(k)}$ between vertices V and V', make k fundamental cycles $e' \pm e$, $\ldots$, $e^{(k)} \pm e$ (choosing $+$ or $-$ according as the edges go in the opposite or the same direction), and then proceed as if only edge e were present.

Actually this situation would be much simpler conceptually if we had defined a graph in such a way that multiple edges are allowed between vertices, and edges are allowed from a vertex to itself; paths and cycles would be defined in terms of edges instead of vertices. Such a definition is, in fact, made for directed graphs in Section 2.3.4.2.

10. If the terminals have all been connected together, the corresponding graph must be connected in the technical sense. A minimum number of wires will involve no cycles, so we must have a free tree. By Theorem A, a free tree contains $n - 1$ wires, and a graph with n vertices and $n - 1$ edges is a free tree if and only if it is connected.

11. It is sufficient to prove that when $n > 1$ and $c(n - 1, n)$ is the minimum of the $c(i, n)$, there exists at least one minimum cost tree in which T_{n-1} is wired to T_n. (For, any minimum cost tree with $n > 1$ terminals and with T_{n-1} wired to T_n must also be a minimum cost tree with $n - 1$ terminals if we regard T_{n-1} and T_n as "common," using the convention stated in the algorithm.)

To prove the statement above, suppose we have a minimum cost tree in which T_{n-1} is not wired to T_n. If we add the wire $T_{n-1} \!-\!\!- T_n$ we obtain a cycle, and any of the other wires in that cycle may be removed; removing the other wire touching T_n gives us another tree, whose total cost is not greater than the original, and $T_{n-1} \!-\!\!- T_n$ appears in that tree.

References: V. Jarník, *Acta Societatis Scientiarum Naturalium Moravicæ* **6** (1930), 57–61; R. C. Prim, *Bell System Technical Journal* **36** (1957), 1389–1401.

12. Keep two auxiliary tables, $a(i)$ and $b(i)$, for $1 \le i < n$, representing the fact that the cheapest connection from T_i to a chosen terminal is to $T_{b(i)}$, and its cost is $a(i)$; initially $a(i) = c(i,n)$ and $b(i) = n$. Then do the following operation $n-1$ times: Find i such that $a(i) = \min_{1 \le j < n} a(j)$; connect T_i to $T_{b(i)}$; for $1 \le j < n$ if $c(i,j) < a(j) < \infty$ set $a(j) \leftarrow c(i,j)$ and $b(j) \leftarrow i$; and set $a(i) \leftarrow \infty$. Here $c(i,j)$ means $c(j,i)$ when $j < i$.

(It is somewhat more efficient to avoid the use of ∞, keeping instead a one-way linked list of those j that have not yet been chosen. With or without this straight-forward improvement, the algorithm takes $O(n^2)$ operations.) See also E. W. Dijkstra, *Indagationes Mathematicæ* **28** (1960), 196–199; D. E. Knuth, *The Stanford GraphBase* (New York: ACM Press, 1994), 460–497. Significantly better algorithms to find a minimum-cost spanning tree are discussed in Section 7.5.4.

13. If there is no path from V_i to V_j, for some $i \ne j$, then no product of the transpositions will move i to j. So if all permutations are generated, the graph must be connected. Conversely if it is connected, remove edges if necessary until we have a free tree. Then renumber the vertices so that V_n is adjacent to only one other vertex, namely V_{n-1}. (See the proof of Theorem A.) Now the transpositions other than $(n-1\ n)$ form a free tree with $n-1$ vertices; so by induction if π is any permutation of $\{1, 2, \ldots, n\}$ that leaves n fixed, π can be written as a product of those transpositions. If π moves n to j then $\pi(j\ n-1)(n-1\ n) = \rho$ fixes n; hence $\pi = \rho(n-1\ n)(j\ n-1)$ can be written as a product of the given transpositions.

SECTION 2.3.4.2

1. Let $(e_1, \ldots, e_n)$ be an oriented walk of smallest possible length from V to V'. If now $\text{init}(e_j) = \text{init}(e_k)$ for $j < k$, $(e_1, \ldots, e_{j-1}, e_k, \ldots, e_n)$ would be a shorter walk; a similar argument applies if $\text{fin}(e_j) = \text{fin}(e_k)$ for $j < k$. Hence $(e_1, \ldots, e_n)$ is simple.

2. Those cycles in which all signs are the same: C_0, C_8, C''_{13}, C_{17}, C''_{19}, C_{20}.

3. For example, use three vertices A, B, C, with arcs from A to B and A to C.

4. If there are no oriented cycles, Algorithm 2.2.3T topologically sorts G. If there is an oriented cycle, topological sorting is clearly impossible. (Depending on how this exercise is interpreted, oriented cycles of length 1 could be excluded from consideration.)

5. Let k be the smallest integer such that $\text{fin}(e_k) = \text{init}(e_j)$ for some $j \le k$. Then $(e_j, \ldots, e_k)$ is an oriented cycle.

6. False (on a technicality), just because there may be several different arcs from one vertex to another.

7. True for finite directed graphs: If we start at any vertex V and follow the only possible oriented path, we never encounter any vertex twice, so we must eventually reach the vertex R (the only vertex with no successor). For infinite directed graphs the result is obviously false since we might have vertices $R, V_1, V_2, V_3, \ldots$ and arcs from V_j to V_{j+1} for $j \ge 1$.

9. All arcs point upward.

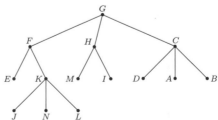

10. G1. Set $k \leftarrow P[j]$, $P[j] \leftarrow 0$.

    G2. If $k = 0$, stop; otherwise set $m \leftarrow P[k]$, $P[k] \leftarrow j$, $j \leftarrow k$, $k \leftarrow m$, and repeat step G2. ∎

11. This algorithm combines Algorithm 2.3.3E with the method of the preceding exercise, so that all oriented trees have arcs that correspond to actual arcs in the directed graph; $S[j]$ is an auxiliary table that tells whether an arc goes from j to $P[j]$ ($S[j] = +1$) or from $P[j]$ to j ($S[j] = -1$). Initially $P[1] = \cdots = P[n] = 0$. The following steps may be used to process each arc (a, b):

    C1. Set $j \leftarrow a$, $k \leftarrow P[j]$, $P[j] \leftarrow 0$, $s \leftarrow S[j]$.

    C2. If $k = 0$, go to C3; otherwise set $m \leftarrow P[k]$, $t \leftarrow S[k]$, $P[k] \leftarrow j$, $S[k] \leftarrow -s$, $s \leftarrow t$, $j \leftarrow k$, $k \leftarrow m$, and repeat step C2.

    C3. (Now a appears as the root of its tree.) Set $j \leftarrow b$, and then if $P[j] \neq 0$ repeatedly set $j \leftarrow P[j]$ until $P[j] = 0$.

    C4. If $j = a$, go to C5; otherwise set $P[a] \leftarrow b$, $S[a] \leftarrow +1$, print (a, b) as an arc belonging to the free subtree, and terminate.

    C5. Print "CYCLE" followed by "(a, b)".

    C6. If $P[b] = 0$ terminate. Otherwise if $S[b] = +1$, print "$+(b, P[b])$", else print "$-(P[b], b)$"; set $b \leftarrow P[b]$ and repeat step C6. ∎

Note: This algorithm will take at most $O(m \log n)$ steps if we incorporate the suggestion of McIlroy in answer 2.3.3–10. But there is a much better solution that needs only $O(m)$ steps: Use depth-first search to construct a "palm tree," with one fundamental cycle for each "frond" [R. E. Tarjan, *SICOMP* **1** (1972), 146–150].

12. It equals the in-degree; the out-degree of each vertex can be only 0 or 1.

13. Define a sequence of oriented subtrees of G as follows: G_0 is the vertex R alone. G_{k+1} is G_k, plus any vertex V of G that is not in G_k but for which there is an arc from V to V' where V' is in G_k, plus one such arc $e[V]$ for each such vertex. It is immediate by induction that G_k is an oriented tree for all $k \geq 0$, and that if there is an oriented path of length k from V to R in G then V is in G_k. Therefore G_∞, the set of all V and $e[V]$ in any of the G_k, is the desired oriented subtree of G.

14. $(e_{12}, e_{20}, e_{00}, e'_{01}, e_{10}, e_{01}, e'_{12}, e_{22}, e_{21})$, $(e_{12}, e_{20}, e_{00}, e'_{01}, e'_{12}, e_{22}, e_{21}, e_{10}, e_{01})$,
$(e_{12}, e_{20}, e'_{01}, e_{10}, e_{00}, e_{01}, e'_{12}, e_{22}, e_{21})$, $(e_{12}, e_{20}, e'_{01}, e'_{12}, e_{22}, e_{21}, e_{10}, e_{00}, e_{01})$,
$(e_{12}, e_{22}, e_{20}, e_{00}, e'_{01}, e_{10}, e_{01}, e'_{12}, e_{21})$, $(e_{12}, e_{22}, e_{20}, e_{00}, e'_{01}, e'_{12}, e_{21}, e_{10}, e_{01})$,
$(e_{12}, e_{22}, e_{20}, e'_{01}, e_{10}, e_{00}, e_{01}, e'_{12}, e_{21})$, $(e_{12}, e_{22}, e_{20}, e'_{01}, e'_{12}, e_{21}, e_{10}, e_{00}, e_{01})$,

in lexicographic order; the eight possibilities come from the independent choices of which of e_{00} or e'_{01}, e_{10} or e'_{12}, e_{20} or e_{22}, should precede the other.

15. True for finite graphs: If it is connected and balanced and has more than one vertex, it has an Eulerian trail that touches all the vertices. (But false in general.)

16. Consider the directed graph G with vertices V_1, ..., V_{13} and with an arc from V_j to V_k for each k in pile j; this graph is balanced. Winning the game is equivalent to tracing out an Eulerian trail in G, because the game ends when the fourth arc to V_{13} is encountered (namely, when the fourth king turns up). Now if the game is won, the stated digraph is an oriented subtree by Lemma E. Conversely if the stated digraph is an oriented tree, the game is won by Theorem D.

17. $\frac{1}{13}$. This answer can be obtained, as the author first obtained it, by laborious enumeration of oriented trees of special types and the application of generating functions, etc., based on the methods of Section 2.3.4.4. But such a simple answer deserves a simple, direct proof, and indeed there is one [see Tor B. Staver, *Norsk Matematisk Tidsskrift* **28** (1946), 88–89]. Define an order for turning up *all* cards of the deck, as follows: Obey the rules of the game until getting stuck, then "cheat" by turning up the first available card (find the first pile that is not empty, going clockwise from pile 1) and continue as before, until eventually all cards have been turned up. The cards *in the order of turning up* are in completely random order (since the value of a card need not be specified until after it is turned up). So the problem is just to calculate the probability that in a randomly shuffled deck the last card is a king. More generally the probability that k cards are still face down when the game is over is the probability that the last king in a random shuffle is followed by k cards, namely $4!\binom{51-k}{3}\frac{48!}{52!}$. Hence a person playing this game without cheating will turn up an average of exactly 42.4 cards per game. *Note:* Similarly, it can be shown that the probability that the player will have to "cheat" k times in the process described above is exactly given by the Stirling number $\left[\begin{smallmatrix}13\\k+1\end{smallmatrix}\right]/13!$. (See Eq. 1.2.10–(9) and exercise 1.2.10–7; the case of a more general card deck is considered in exercise 1.2.10–18.)

18. (a) If there is a cycle $(V_0, V_1, \ldots, V_k)$, where necessarily $3 \le k \le n$, the sum of the k rows of A corresponding to the k edges of this cycle, with appropriate signs, is a row of zeros; so if G is not a free tree the determinant of A_0 is zero.

But if G is a free tree we may regard it as an ordered tree with root V_0, and we can rearrange the rows and columns of A_0 so that columns are in preorder and so that the kth row corresponds to the edge from the kth vertex (column) to its parent. Then the matrix is triangular with ± 1's on the diagonal, so the determinant is ± 1.

(b) By the Binet–Cauchy formula (exercise 1.2.3–46) we have

$$\det A_0^T A_0 = \sum_{1 \le i_1 < \cdots < i_n \le m} \left(\det A_{i_1 \ldots i_n}\right)^2$$

where $A_{i_1 \ldots i_n}$ represents a matrix consisting of rows $i_1, \ldots, i_n$ of A_0 (thus corresponding to a choice of n edges of G). The result now follows from (a).

[See S. Okada and R. Onodera, *Bull. Yamagata Univ.* **2** (1952), 89–117.]

19. (a) The conditions $a_{00} = 0$ and $a_{jj} = 1$ are just conditions (a), (b) of the definition of oriented tree. If G is not an oriented tree there is an oriented cycle (by exercise 7), and the rows of A_0 corresponding to the vertices in this oriented cycle will sum to a row of zeros; hence $\det A_0 = 0$. If G is an oriented tree, assign an arbitrary order to the children of each family and regard G as an ordered tree. Now permute rows and columns of A_0 until they correspond to preorder of the vertices. Since the same permutation has been applied to the rows as to the columns, the determinant is unchanged; and the resulting matrix is triangular with $+1$ in every diagonal position.

(b) We may assume that $a_{0j} = 0$ for all j, since no arc emanating from V_0 can participate in an oriented subtree. We may also assume that $a_{jj} > 0$ for all $j \ge 1$ since otherwise the whole jth row is zero and there obviously are no oriented subtrees. Now use induction on the number of arcs: If $a_{jj} > 1$ let e be some arc leading from V_j; let B_0 be a matrix like A_0 but with arc e deleted, and let C_0 be the matrix like A_0 but with all arcs *except* e that lead from V_j deleted. *Example:* If $A_0 = \left(\begin{smallmatrix} 3 & -2 \\ -1 & 2 \end{smallmatrix}\right)$, $j = 1$, and e is an arc from V_1 to V_0, then $B_0 = \left(\begin{smallmatrix} 2 & -2 \\ -1 & 2 \end{smallmatrix}\right)$, $C_0 = \left(\begin{smallmatrix} 1 & 0 \\ -1 & 2 \end{smallmatrix}\right)$. In general we have $\det A_0 = \det B_0 + \det C_0$, since the matrices agree in all rows except row j, and A_0 is the sum of B_0 and C_0 in that row. Moreover, the number of oriented subtrees of G is the number of subtrees that do *not* use e (namely, $\det B_0$, by induction) plus the number that *do* use e (namely, $\det C_0$).

Notes: The matrix A is often called the *Laplacian* of the graph, by analogy with a similar concept in the theory of partial differential equations. If we delete any set S of rows from the matrix A, and the same set of columns, the determinant of the resulting matrix is the number of oriented forests whose roots are the vertices $\{V_k \mid k \in S\}$ and whose arcs belong to the given digraph. The matrix tree theorem for oriented trees was stated without proof by J. J. Sylvester in 1857 (see exercise 28), then forgotten for many years until it was independently rediscovered by W. T. Tutte [*Proc. Cambridge Phil. Soc.* **44** (1948), 463–482, §3]. The first published proof in the special case of *undirected* graphs, when the matrix A is symmetric, was given by C. W. Borchardt [*Crelle* **57** (1860), 111–121]. Several authors have ascribed the theorem to Kirchhoff, but Kirchhoff proved a quite different (though related) result.

20. Using exercise 18 we find $B = A_0^T A_0$. Or, using exercise 19, B is the matrix A_0 for the directed graph G' with two arcs (one in each direction) in place of each edge of G; each free subtree of G corresponds uniquely to an oriented subtree of G' with root V_0, since the directions of the arcs are determined by the choice of root.

21. Construct the matrices A and A^* as in exercise 19. For the example graphs G and G^* in Figs. 36 and 37,

$$A = \begin{pmatrix} 2 & -2 & 0 \\ -1 & 3 & -2 \\ -1 & -1 & 2 \end{pmatrix}, \quad A^* =$$

	[00]	[10]	[20]	[01]	[01]	[21]	[12]	[12]	[22]
[00]	2	0	0	−1	−1	0	0	0	0
[10]	−1	3	0	−1	−1	0	0	0	0
[20]	−1	0	3	−1	−1	0	0	0	0
[01]	0	−1	0	3	0	0	−1	−1	0
[01]	0	−1	0	0	3	0	−1	−1	0
[21]	0	−1	0	0	0	3	−1	−1	0
[12]	0	0	−1	0	0	−1	3	0	−1
[12]	0	0	−1	0	0	−1	0	3	−1
[22]	0	0	−1	0	0	−1	0	0	2

Add the indeterminate λ to every diagonal element of A and A^*. If $t(G)$ and $t(G^*)$ are the numbers of oriented subtrees of G and G^*, we then have $\det A = \lambda t(G) + O(\lambda^2)$, $\det A^* = \lambda t(G^*) + O(\lambda^2)$. (The number of oriented subtrees of a balanced graph is the same for any given root, by exercise 22, but we do not need that fact.)

If we group vertices V_{jk} for equal k the matrix A^* can be partitioned as shown above. Let $B_{kk'}$ be the submatrix of A^* consisting of the rows for V_{jk} and the columns for $V_{j'k'}$, for all j and j' such that V_{jk} and $V_{j'k'}$ are in G^*. By adding the 2nd, $\ldots$, mth columns of each submatrix to the first column and then subtracting the first row of each submatrix from the 2nd, $\ldots$, mth rows, the matrix A^* is transformed so that

$$B_{kk'} = \begin{pmatrix} a_{kk'} & * & \cdots & * \\ 0 & 0 & \cdots & 0 \\ \vdots & \vdots & \ddots & \vdots \\ 0 & 0 & \cdots & 0 \end{pmatrix} \quad \text{for } k \neq k', \qquad B_{kk} = \begin{pmatrix} \lambda + a_{kk} & * & \cdots & * \\ 0 & \lambda + m & \cdots & 0 \\ \vdots & \vdots & \ddots & \vdots \\ 0 & 0 & \cdots & \lambda + m \end{pmatrix}.$$

The asterisks in the top rows of the transformed submatrices turn out to be irrelevant, because the determinant of A^* is now seen to be $(\lambda + m)^{(m-1)n}$ times

$$\det \begin{pmatrix} \lambda + a_{00} & a_{01} & \cdots & a_{0(n-1)} \\ a_{10} & \lambda + a_{11} & \cdots & a_{1(n-1)} \\ \vdots & \vdots & \ddots & \vdots \\ a_{(n-1)0} & a_{(n-1)1} & \cdots & \lambda + a_{(n-1)(n-1)} \end{pmatrix} = \lambda t(G) + O(\lambda^2).$$

Notice that when $n = 1$ and there are m arcs from V_0 to itself, we find in particular that exactly m^{m-1} oriented trees are possible on m labeled nodes. This result will be obtained by quite different methods in Section 2.3.4.4.

This derivation can be generalized to determine the number of oriented subtrees of G^* when G is an *arbitrary* directed graph; see R. Dawson and I. J. Good, *Ann. Math. Stat.* **28** (1957), 946–956; D. E. Knuth, *Journal of Combinatorial Theory* **3** (1967), 309–314. An alternative, purely combinatorial proof has been given by J. B. Orlin, *Journal of Combinatorial Theory* **B25** (1978), 187–198.

22. The total number is $(\sigma_1 + \cdots + \sigma_n)$ times the number of Eulerian trails starting with a given edge e_1, where $\text{init}(e_1) = V_1$. Each such trail determines an oriented subtree with root V_1 by Lemma E, and for each of the T oriented subtrees there are $\prod_{j=1}^{n}(\sigma_j - 1)!$ walks satisfying the three conditions of Theorem D, corresponding to the different order in which the arcs $\{e \mid \text{init}(e) = V_j, e \neq e[V_j], e \neq e_1\}$ are entered into P. (Exercise 14 provides a simple example.)

23. Construct the directed graph G_k with m^{k-1} vertices as in the hint, and denote by $[x_1, \ldots, x_k]$ the arc mentioned there. For each function that has maximum period length, we can define a unique corresponding Eulerian trail, by letting $f(x_1, \ldots, x_k) = x_{k+1}$ if arc $[x_1, \ldots, x_k]$ is followed by $[x_2, \ldots, x_{k+1}]$. (We regard Eulerian trails as being the same if one is just a cyclic permutation of the other.) Now $G_k = G_{k-1}^*$ in the sense of exercise 21, so G_k has $m^{m^{k-1} - m^{k-2}}$ times as many oriented subtrees as G_{k-1}; by induction G_k has $m^{m^{k-1} - 1}$ oriented subtrees, and $m^{m^{k-1} - k}$ with a given root. Therefore by exercise 22 the number of functions with maximum period, namely the number of Eulerian trails of G_k starting with a given arc, is $m^{-k}(m!)^{m^{k-1}}$. [For $m = 2$ this result is due to C. Flye Sainte-Marie, *L'Intermédiaire des Mathématiciens* **1** (1894), 107–110.]

24. Define a new directed graph having E_j copies of e_j, for $0 \leq j \leq m$. This graph is balanced, hence it contains an Eulerian trail $(e_0, \ldots)$ by Theorem G. The desired oriented walk comes by deleting the edge e_0 from this Eulerian trail.

25. Assign an arbitrary order to all arcs in the sets $I_j = \{e \mid \text{init}(e) = V_j\}$ and $F_j = \{e \mid \text{fin}(e) = V_j\}$. For each arc e in I_j, let $\text{ATAG}(e) = 0$ and $\text{ALINK}(e) = e'$ if e' follows e in the ordering of I_j; also let $\text{ATAG}(e) = 1$ and $\text{ALINK}(e) = e'$ if e is last in I_j and e' is first in F_j. Let $\text{ALINK}(e) = \Lambda$ in the latter case if F_j is empty. Define BLINK and BTAG by the same rules, reversing the roles of init and fin.

Examples (using alphabetic order in each set of arcs):

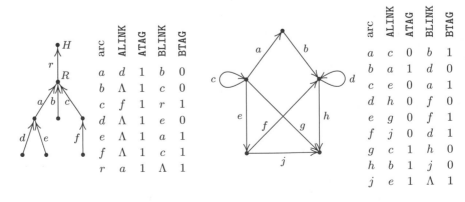

arc	ALINK	ATAG	BLINK	BTAG
a	d	1	b	0
b	Λ	1	c	0
c	f	1	r	1
d	Λ	1	e	0
e	Λ	1	a	1
f	Λ	1	c	1
r	a	1	Λ	1

arc	ALINK	ATAG	BLINK	BTAG
a	c	0	b	1
b	a	1	d	0
c	e	0	a	1
d	h	0	f	0
e	g	0	f	1
f	j	0	d	1
g	c	1	h	0
h	b	1	j	0
j	e	1	Λ	1

Note: If in the oriented tree representation we add another arc from H to itself, we get an interesting situation: Either we get the standard conventions 2.3.1–(8) with LLINK, LTAG, RLINK, RTAG *interchanged* in the list head, or (if the new arc is placed last in the ordering) we get the standard conventions except RTAG $= 0$ in the node associated with the root of the tree.

This exercise is based on an idea communicated to the author by W. C. Lynch. Can tree traversal algorithms like Algorithm 2.3.1S be generalized to classes of digraphs that are not oriented trees, using such a representation?

27. Let a_{ij} be the sum of $p(e)$ over all arcs e from V_i to V_j. We are to prove that $t_j = \sum_i a_{ij} t_i$ for all j. Since $\sum_i a_{ji} = 1$, we must prove that $\sum_i a_{ji} t_j = \sum_i a_{ij} t_i$. But this is not difficult, because both sides of the equation represent the sum of all products $p(e_1) \ldots p(e_n)$ taken over subgraphs $\{e_1, \ldots, e_n\}$ of G such that $\text{init}(e_i) = V_i$ and such that there is a unique oriented cycle contained in $\{e_1, \ldots, e_n\}$, where this cycle includes V_j. Removing any arc of the cycle yields an oriented tree; the left-hand side of the equation is obtained by factoring out the arcs that leave V_j, while the right-hand side corresponds to those that enter V_j.

In a sense, this exercise is a combination of exercises 19 and 26.

28. Every term in the expansion is $a_{1p_1} \ldots a_{mp_m} b_{1q_1} \ldots b_{nq_n}$, where $0 \le p_i \le n$ for $1 \le i \le m$ and $0 \le q_j \le m$ for $1 \le j \le n$, times some integer coefficient. Represent this product as a directed graph on the vertices $\{0, u_1, \ldots, u_m, v_1, \ldots, v_n\}$, with arcs from u_i to v_{p_i} and from v_j to u_{q_j}, where $u_0 = v_0 = 0$.

If the digraph contains a cycle, the integer coefficient is zero. For each cycle corresponds to a factor of the form

$$a_{i_0 j_0} b_{j_0 i_1} a_{i_1 j_1} \ldots a_{i_{k-1} j_{k-1}} b_{j_{k-1} i_0} \qquad (*)$$

where the indices $(i_0, i_1, \ldots, i_{k-1})$ are distinct and so are the indices $(j_0, j_1, \ldots, j_{k-1})$. The sum of all terms containing $(*)$ as a factor is $(*)$ times the determinant obtained by setting $a_{i_l j} \leftarrow [j = j_l]$ for $0 \le j \le n$ and $b_{j_l i} \leftarrow [i = i_{(l+1) \bmod k}]$ for $0 \le i \le m$, for $0 \le l < k$, leaving the variables in the other $m + n - 2k$ rows unchanged. This determinant is identically zero, because the sum of rows $i_0, i_1, \ldots, i_{k-1}$ in the top section equals the sum of rows $j_0, j_1, \ldots, j_{k-1}$ in the bottom section.

On the other hand, if the directed graph contains no cycles, the integer coefficient is $+1$. This follows because each factor $a_{i p_i}$ and $b_{j q_j}$ must have come from the diagonal of the determinant: If any off-diagonal element $a_{i_0 j_0}$ is chosen in row i_0 of the top section, we must choose some off-diagonal $b_{j_0 i_1}$ from row j_0 of the bottom section, hence we must choose some off-diagonal $a_{i_1 j_1}$ from row i_1 of the top section, etc., forcing a cycle.

Thus the coefficient is $+1$ if and only if the corresponding digraph is an oriented tree with root 0. The number of such terms (hence the number of such oriented trees) is obtained by setting each a_{ij} and b_{ji} to 1; for example,

$$\det \begin{pmatrix} 4 & 0 & 1 & 1 & 1 \\ 0 & 4 & 1 & 1 & 1 \\ 1 & 1 & 3 & 0 & 0 \\ 1 & 1 & 0 & 3 & 0 \\ 1 & 1 & 0 & 0 & 3 \end{pmatrix} = \det \begin{pmatrix} 4 & 0 & 1 & 1 & 1 \\ -4 & 4 & 0 & 0 & 0 \\ 1 & 1 & 3 & 0 & 0 \\ 0 & 0 & -3 & 3 & 0 \\ 0 & 0 & -3 & 0 & 3 \end{pmatrix} = \det \begin{pmatrix} 4 & 0 & 3 & 1 & 1 \\ 0 & 4 & 0 & 0 & 0 \\ 2 & 1 & 3 & 0 & 0 \\ 0 & 0 & 0 & 3 & 0 \\ 0 & 0 & 0 & 0 & 3 \end{pmatrix}$$

$$= \det \begin{pmatrix} 4 & 3 \\ 2 & 3 \end{pmatrix} \cdot 4 \cdot 3 \cdot 3.$$

In general we obtain $\det \begin{pmatrix} n+1 & n \\ m & m+1 \end{pmatrix} \cdot (n+1)^{m-1} \cdot (m+1)^{n-1}$.

Notes: J. J. Sylvester considered the special case $m = n$ and $a_{10} = a_{20} = \cdots = a_{m0} = 0$ in *Quarterly J. of Pure and Applied Math.* **1** (1857), 42–56, where he conjectured (correctly) that the total number of terms is then $n^n(n+1)^{n-1}$. He also stated without proof that the $(n+1)^{n-1}$ nonzero terms present when $a_{ij} = \delta_{ij}$ correspond to all connected cycle-free graphs on $\{0, 1, \ldots, n\}$. In that special case, he reduced the determinant to the form in the matrix tree theorem of exercise 19, e.g.,

$$\det \begin{pmatrix} b_{10} + b_{12} + b_{13} & -b_{12} & -b_{13} \\ -b_{21} & b_{20} + b_{21} + b_{23} & -b_{23} \\ -b_{31} & -b_{32} & b_{30} + b_{31} + b_{32} \end{pmatrix}.$$

Cayley quoted this result in *Crelle* **52** (1856), 279, ascribing it to Sylvester; thus it is ironic that the theorem about the number of such graphs is often attributed to Cayley.

By negating the first m rows of the given determinant, then negating the first m columns, we can reduce this exercise to the matrix tree theorem.

[Matrices having the general form considered in this exercise are important in iterative methods for the solution of partial differential equations, and they are said to have "Property $\mathcal{A}$." See, for example, Louis A. Hageman and David M. Young, *Applied Iterative Methods* (Academic Press, 1981), Chapter 9.]

SECTION 2.3.4.3

1. The root is the empty sequence; arcs go from $(x_1, \ldots, x_n)$ to $(x_1, \ldots, x_{n-1})$.

2. Take one tetrad type and rotate it 180° to get another tetrad type; these two types clearly tile the plane (without further rotations), by repeating a 2×2 pattern.

3. Consider the set of tetrad types for all positive integers j. The right half plane can be tiled in uncountably many ways; but whatever square is placed in the center of the plane puts a finite limit on the distance it can be continued to the left.

4. Systematically enumerate all possible ways to tile an $n \times n$ block, for $n = 1, 2, \ldots$, looking for toroidal solutions within these blocks. If there is no way to tile the plane, the infinity lemma tells us there is an n with no $n \times n$ tilings. If there *is* a way to tile the plane, the assumption tells us that there is an n with an $n \times n$ tiling containing a rectangle that yields a toroidal solution. Hence in either case the algorithm will terminate.

[But the stated assumption is false, as shown in the next exercise; and in fact there is no algorithm that will determine in a finite number of steps whether or not there exists a way to tile the plane with a given set of types. On the other hand, if such a tiling does exist, there is always a tiling that is *quasitoroidal*, in the sense that each of its $n \times n$ blocks occurs at least once in every $f(n) \times f(n)$ block, for some function f. See B. Durand, *Theoretical Computer Science* **221** (1999), 61–75.]

5. Start by noticing that we need classes $\begin{smallmatrix} \alpha & \beta \\ \gamma & \delta \end{smallmatrix}$ replicated in 2×2 groups in any solution. Then, step 1: Considering just the α squares, show that the pattern $\begin{smallmatrix} a & b \\ c & d \end{smallmatrix}$ must be replicated in 2×2 groups of α squares. Step $n > 1$: Determine a pattern that must appear in a cross-shaped region of height and width $2^n - 1$. The middle of the crosses has the pattern $\begin{smallmatrix} Na & Nb \\ Nc & Nd \end{smallmatrix}$ replicated throughout the plane.

For example, after step 3 we will know the contents of 7×7 blocks throughout the plane, separated by unit length strips, every eight units. The 7×7 blocks that have types (αa, δNa, αd, δNa, αa, δNd, αd) on the main diagonal have the form

αa	βKQ	αb	βQP	αa	βK	αb
γJP	δNa	γR	δKQ	γJL	δNb	γP
αc	βDS	αd	βYQT	αc	βS	αd
γPQ	δJP	γXP	δNa	γRQ	δR	γR
αa	βKU	αb	βDP	αa	βK	αb
γJT	δNc	γS	δSD	γJS	δNd	γT
αc	βQS	αd	βDT	αc	βS	αd

The middle column and the middle row is the "cross" just filled in during step 3; the other four 3×3 squares were filled in after step 2; the squares just to the right and below this 7×7 square are part of a 15×15 cross to be filled in at step 4.

(Six of the 92 types can actually be omitted; see exercise 7.2.2.1–121.) For a similar construction that leads to a set of only 35 tetrad types having nothing but nontoroidal solutions, see R. M. Robinson, *Inventiones Math.* **12** (1971), 177–209. Robinson also exhibited a set of *six* squarish shapes that tile the plane only nontoroidally, even when rotations and reflections are allowed.

After many decades of improvements, an optimum solution has finally been found: E. Jeandel and M. Rao [*Advances in Combinatorics* (2021) 1:1–1:39] constructed a set of eleven tetrad types, using only four colors, that tiles the plane only nontoroidally. They also proved that no solution with fewer types or fewer colors is possible.

6. Let k and m be fixed. Consider an oriented tree whose vertices each represent, for some n, one of the partitions of $\{1, \ldots, n\}$ into k parts, containing no arithmetic progression of length m. A node that partitions $\{1, \ldots, n+1\}$ is a child of one for $\{1, \ldots, n\}$ if the two partitions agree on $\{1, \ldots, n\}$. If there were an infinite path to the root we would have a way to divide *all* integers into k sets with no arithmetic progression of length m. Hence, by the infinity lemma and van der Waerden's theorem, this tree is finite. (If $k = 2$, $m = 3$, the tree can be rapidly calculated by hand, and the least value of N is 9. See *Studies in Pure Mathematics*, ed. by L. Mirsky (Academic Press, 1971), 251–260, for van der Waerden's interesting account of how the proof of his theorem was discovered.)

7. The positive integers can be partitioned into two sets S_0 and S_1 such that neither set contains any infinite *computable* sequence (see exercise 3.5–32). So in particular there is no infinite arithmetic progression. Theorem K does not apply because there is no way to put partial solutions into a tree with finite degrees at each vertex.

8. Let a "counterexample sequence" be an infinite sequence of trees that violates Kruskal's theorem, if such sequences exist. Assume that the theorem is false; then let T_1 be a tree with the smallest possible number of nodes such that T_1 can be the first tree in a counterexample sequence; if $T_1, \ldots, T_j$ have been chosen, let T_{j+1} be a tree with the smallest possible number of nodes such that $T_1, \ldots, T_j, T_{j+1}$ is the beginning of a counterexample sequence. This process defines a counterexample sequence $\langle T_n \rangle$. None of these T's is just a root. Now, we look at this sequence very carefully:

(a) Suppose there is a subsequence $T_{n_1}, T_{n_2}, \ldots$ for which $l(T_{n_1})$, $l(T_{n_2})$, $\ldots$ is a counterexample sequence. This is impossible; otherwise $T_1, \ldots, T_{n_1-1}, l(T_{n_1})$, $l(T_{n_2}), \ldots$ would be a counterexample sequence, contradicting the definition of T_{n_1}.

(b) Because of (a), there are only finitely many j for which $l(T_j)$ cannot be embedded in $l(T_k)$ for any $k > j$. Therefore by taking n_1 larger than any such j we can find a subsequence for which $l(T_{n_1}) \subseteq l(T_{n_2}) \subseteq l(T_{n_3}) \subseteq \cdots$.

(c) Now by the result of exercise 2.3.2–22, $r(T_{n_j})$ cannot be embedded in $r(T_{n_k})$ for any $k > j$, else $T_{n_j} \subseteq T_{n_k}$. Therefore $T_1, \ldots, T_{n_1-1}, r(T_{n_1}), r(T_{n_2}), \ldots$ is a counterexample sequence. But this contradicts the definition of T_{n_1}.

Notes: Kruskal, in *Trans. Amer. Math. Soc.* **95** (1960), 210–225, actually proved a stronger result, using a weaker notion of embedding. His theorem does not follow directly from the infinity lemma, although the results are vaguely similar. Indeed, Kőnig himself proved a special case of Kruskal's theorem, showing that there is no infinite sequence of pairwise incomparable n-tuples of nonnegative integers, where comparability means that all components of one n-tuple are $\leq$ the corresponding components of the other [*Matematikai és Fizikai Lapok* **39** (1932), 27–29]. For further developments, see *J. Combinatorial Theory* **A13** (1972), 297–305. See also N. Dershowitz, *Inf. Proc. Letters* **9** (1979), 212–215, for applications to termination of algorithms.

SECTION 2.3.4.4

1. $\ln A(z) = \ln z + \sum_{k \geq 1} a_k \ln\left(\frac{1}{1-z^k}\right) = \ln z + \sum_{k,t \geq 1} \frac{a_k z^{kt}}{t} = \ln z + \sum_{t \geq 1} \frac{A(z^t)}{t}$.

2. By differentiation, and equating the coefficients of z^n, we obtain the identity

$$na_{n+1} = \sum_{k \geq 1} \sum_{d \backslash k} d a_d a_{n+1-k}.$$

Now interchange the order of summation.

4. (a) $A(z)$ certainly converges at least for $|z| < \frac{1}{4}$, since a_n is less than the number of *ordered* trees b_{n-1}. Since $A(1)$ is infinite and all coefficients are positive, there is a positive number $\alpha \leq 1$ such that $A(z)$ converges for $|z| < \alpha$, and there is a singularity at $z = \alpha$. (See exercise 7.2.2.2–348.) Let $\psi(z) = A(z)/z$; since $\psi(z) > e^{z\psi(z)}$, we see that $\psi(z) = m$ implies $z < \ln m/m$, so $\psi(z)$ is bounded and $\lim_{z \to \alpha^-} \psi(z)$ exists. Thus $\alpha < 1$, and by Abel's limit theorem $a = \alpha \cdot \exp\left(a + \frac{1}{2}A(\alpha^2) + \frac{1}{3}A(\alpha^3) + \cdots\right)$.

(b) $A(z^2), A(z^3), \ldots$ are analytic for $|z| < \sqrt{\alpha}$, and $\frac{1}{2}A(z^2) + \frac{1}{3}A(z^3) + \cdots$ converges uniformly in a slightly smaller disk.

(c) If $\partial F/\partial w = a - 1 \neq 0$, the implicit function theorem implies that there is an analytic function $f(z)$ in a neighborhood of $(\alpha, a/\alpha)$ such that $F(z, f(z)) = 0$. But this implies $f(z) = A(z)/z$, contradicting the fact that $A(z)$ is singular at α.

(d) Obvious.

(e) $\partial F/\partial w = A(z) - 1$ and $|A(z)| < A(\alpha) = 1$, since the coefficients of $A(z)$ are all positive. Hence, as in (c), $A(z)$ is regular at all such points.

(f) Near $(\alpha, 1/\alpha)$ we have the identity $0 = \beta(z - \alpha) + (\alpha/2)(w - 1/\alpha)^2 + $ higher order terms, where $w = A(z)/z$; so w is an analytic function of $\sqrt{z - \alpha}$ here by the implicit function theorem. Consequently there is a region $|z| < \alpha_1$ minus a cut $[\alpha, \alpha_1]$ in which $A(z)$ has the stated form. (The minus sign is chosen since a plus sign would make the coefficients ultimately negative.)

(g) Any function of the stated form has coefficient asymptotically $\dfrac{\sqrt{2\beta}}{\alpha^n}\dbinom{1/2}{n}$. Note that

$$\binom{3/2}{n} = O\left(\frac{1}{n}\binom{1/2}{n}\right).$$

For further details, and asymptotic values of the number of free trees, see R. Otter, *Annals of Mathematics* (2) **49** (1948), 583–599.

5.
$$c_n = \sum_{j_1 + 2j_2 + \cdots = n} \binom{c_1 + j_1 - 1}{j_1} \cdots \binom{c_n + j_n - 1}{j_n} - c_n, \quad n > 1.$$

Therefore

$$2C(z) + 1 - z = (1-z)^{-c_1}(1-z^2)^{-c_2}(1-z^3)^{-c_3}\cdots = \exp\bigl(C(z) + \tfrac{1}{2}C(z^2) + \cdots\bigr).$$

We find $C(z) = z + z^2 + 2z^3 + 5z^4 + 12z^5 + 33z^6 + 90z^7 + 261z^8 + 766z^9 + \cdots$. When $n > 1$, the number of series-parallel networks with n edges is $2c_n$ [see P. A. MacMahon, *Proc. London Math. Soc.* **22** (1891), 330–339].

6. $zG(z)^2 = 2G(z) - 2 - zG(z^2);$ $G(z) = 1 + z + z^2 + 2z^3 + 3z^4 + 6z^5 + 11z^6 + 23z^7 + 46z^8 + 98z^9 + \cdots$. The function $F(z) = 1 - zG(z)$ satisfies the simpler relation $F(z^2) = 2z + F(z)^2$. [J. H. M. Wedderburn, *Annals of Math.* (2) **24** (1922), 121–140. Incidentally, there are g_{n-1} oriented trees with n *leaves* and in-degree 2 at nonleaves.]

7. $g_n = ca^n n^{-3/2}(1 + O(1/n))$, where $c \approx 0.7916031835775$, and $a \approx 2.483253536173$ satisfies $F(1/a) = 0$.

8.

9. If there are two centroids, by considering a path from one to the other we find that there can't be intermediate points, so any two centroids are adjacent. A tree cannot contain three mutually adjacent vertices, so there are at most two.

10. If X and Y are adjacent, let $s(X, Y)$ be the number of vertices in the Y subtree of X. Then $s(X, Y) + s(Y, X) = n$. The argument in the text shows that if Y is a centroid, weight$(X) = s(X, Y)$. Therefore if both X and Y are centroids, weight$(X) = $ weight$(Y) = n/2$.

In terms of this notation, the argument in the text goes on to show that if $s(X, Y) \geq s(Y, X)$, there is a centroid in the Y subtree of X. So if two free trees with m vertices are joined by an edge between X and Y, we obtain a free tree in which $s(X, Y) = m = s(Y, X)$, and there must be two centroids (namely X and Y).

[It is a nice programming exercise to compute $s(X, Y)$ for all adjacent X and Y in $O(n)$ steps; from this information we can quickly find the centroid(s). An efficient algorithm for centroid location was first given by A. J. Goldman, *Transportation Sci.* **5** (1971), 212–221.]

11. $zT(z)^t = T(z) - 1$; thus $z + T(z)^{-t} = T(z)^{1-t}$. By Eq. 1.2.9–(21), $T(z) = \sum_n A_n(1, -t)z^n$, so the number of t-ary trees is

$$\binom{1+tn}{n}\frac{1}{1+tn} = \binom{tn}{n}\frac{1}{(t-1)n+1}.$$

12. Consider the directed graph that has one arc from V_i to V_j for all $i \neq j$. The matrix A_0 of exercise 2.3.4.2–19 is a combinatorial $(n-1) \times (n-1)$ matrix with $n-1$ on the diagonal and -1 off the diagonal. So its determinant is

$$(n + (n-1)(-1))n^{n-2} = n^{n-2},$$

the number of oriented trees with a given root. (Exercise 2.3.4.2–20 could also be used.)

13.

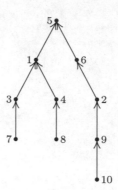

14. True, since the root will not become a leaf until all other branches have been removed.

15. In the canonical representation, $V_1, V_2, \ldots, V_{n-1}, f(V_{n-1})$ is a topological sort of the oriented tree considered as a directed graph, but this order would not in general be output by Algorithm 2.2.3T. Algorithm 2.2.3T can be changed so that it determines the values of $V_1, V_2, \ldots, V_{n-1}$ if the "insert into queue" operation of step T6 is replaced by a procedure that adjusts links so that the entries of the list appear in ascending order from front to rear; then the queue becomes a priority queue.

(However, a general priority queue isn't needed to find the canonical representation; we only need to sweep through the vertices from 1 to n, looking for leaves, while pruning off paths from new leaves less than the sweep pointer; see the following exercise.)

16. **D1.** Set $\texttt{C[1]} \leftarrow \cdots \leftarrow \texttt{C[n]} \leftarrow 0$, then set $\texttt{C[}f(V_j)\texttt{]} \leftarrow \texttt{C[}f(V_j)\texttt{]}+1$ for $1 \leq j < n$. (Thus vertex k is a leaf if and only if $\texttt{C[}k\texttt{]} = 0$.) Set $k \leftarrow 0$ and $j \leftarrow 1$.

D2. Increase k one or more times until $\texttt{C[}k\texttt{]} = 0$, then set $l \leftarrow k$.

D3. Set $\texttt{PARENT[}l\texttt{]} \leftarrow f(V_j)$, $l \leftarrow f(V_j)$, $\texttt{C[}l\texttt{]} \leftarrow \texttt{C[}l\texttt{]} - 1$, and $j \leftarrow j+1$.

D4. If $j = n$, set $\texttt{PARENT[}l\texttt{]} \leftarrow 0$ and terminate the algorithm.

D5. If $\texttt{C[}l\texttt{]} = 0$ and $l < k$, go to D3; otherwise go back to D2. ∎

17. There must be exactly one cycle $x_1, x_2, \ldots, x_k$ where $f(x_j) = x_{j+1}$ and $f(x_k) = x_1$. We will enumerate all f having a cycle of length k such that the iterates of each x ultimately come into this cycle. Define the canonical representation $f(V_1), f(V_2), \ldots, f(V_{m-k})$ as in the text; now $f(V_{m-k})$ is in the cycle, so we continue to get a "canonical representation" by writing down the rest of the cycle $f(f(V_{m-k}))$, $f(f(f(V_{m-k})))$, etc. For example, the function with $m = 13$ whose graph is shown here leads to the representation 3, 1, 8, 8, 1, 12, 12, 2, 3, 4, 5, 1. We obtain a sequence of $m - 1$ numbers in which the last k are distinct. Conversely, from any such sequence we can reverse the construction (assuming that k is known); hence there are precisely $m^{\underline{k}} m^{m-k-1}$ such functions having a k-cycle. (For related results, see exercise 3.1–14. The formula $m^{m-1}Q(m)$ was first obtained by L. Katz, *Annals of Math. Statistics* **26** (1955), 512–517.)

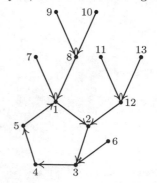

18. To reconstruct the tree from a sequence s_1, s_2, $\ldots$, s_{n-1}, begin with s_1 as the root and successively attach arcs to the tree that point to s_1, s_2, $\ldots$; if vertex s_k has appeared earlier, leave the initial vertex of the arc leading to s_{k-1} nameless, otherwise give this vertex the name s_k. After all $n-1$ arcs have been placed, give names to all vertices that remain nameless by using the numbers that have not yet appeared, assigning names in increasing order to nameless vertices in the order of their creation.

For example, from 3, 1, 4, 1, 5, 9, 2, 6, 5 we would construct the tree shown on the right. There is no simple connection between this method and the one in the text. Several more representations are possible; see the article by E. H. Neville, *Proc. Cambridge Phil. Soc.* **49** (1953), 381–385.

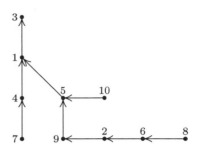

19. The canonical representation will have precisely $n - k$ different values, so we enumerate the sequences of $n-1$ numbers with this property. The answer is $n^{n-k}\left\{{n-1 \atop n-k}\right\}$.

20. Consider the canonical representation of such trees. We are asking how many terms of $(x_1 + \cdots + x_n)^{n-1}$ have k_0 exponents zero, k_1 exponents one, etc. This is plainly the coefficient of such a term times the number of such terms, namely

$$\frac{(n-1)!}{(0!)^{k_0}(1!)^{k_1}\ldots(n!)^{k_n}} \times \frac{n!}{k_0!\,k_1!\ldots k_n!}.$$

21. There are none with $2m$ vertices; if there are $n = 2m + 1$ vertices, the answer is obtained from exercise 20 with $k_0 = m+1$, $k_2 = m$, namely $\binom{2m+1}{m}(2m)!/2^m$.

22. Exactly n^{n-2}; for if X is a particular vertex, the free trees are in one-to-one correspondence with oriented trees having root X.

23. It is possible to put the labels on every unlabeled, ordered tree in $n!$ ways, and each of these labeled, ordered trees is distinct. So the total number is $n!\,b_{n-1} = (2n-2)!/(n-1)!$.

24. There are as many with one given root as with another, so the answer in general is $1/n$ times the answer in exercise 23; and in this particular case the answer is 30.

25. For $0 \le q < n$, $r(n,q) = (n-q)n^{q-1}$. (The special case $s = 1$ in Eq. (24).)

26. ($k = 7$)

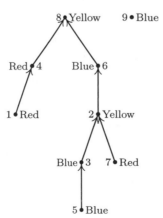

27. Given a function g from $\{1, 2, \ldots, r\}$ to $\{1, 2, \ldots, q\}$ such that adding arcs from V_k to $U_{g(k)}$ introduces no oriented cycles, construct a sequence $a_1, \ldots, a_r$ as follows: Call vertex V_k "free" if there is no oriented path from V_j to V_k for any $j \neq k$. Since there are no oriented cycles, there must be at least one free vertex. Let b_1 be the smallest integer for which V_{b_1} is free; and assuming that $b_1, \ldots, b_t$ have been chosen, let b_{t+1} be the smallest integer different from $b_1, \ldots, b_t$ for which $V_{b_{t+1}}$ is free in the graph obtained by deleting the arcs from V_{b_k} to $U_{g(b_k)}$ for $1 \leq k \leq t$. This rule defines a permutation $b_1 b_2 \ldots b_r$ of the integers $\{1, 2, \ldots, r\}$. Let $a_k = g(b_k)$ for $1 \leq k \leq r$; this defines a sequence such that $1 \leq a_k \leq q$ for $1 \leq k < r$, and $1 \leq a_r \leq p$.

Conversely if such a sequence $a_1, \ldots, a_r$ is given, call a vertex V_k "free" if there is no j for which $a_j > p$ and $f(a_j) = k$. Since $a_r \leq p$ there are at most $r - 1$ non-free vertices. Let b_1 be the smallest integer for which V_{b_1} is free; and assuming that $b_1, \ldots, b_t$ have been chosen, let b_{t+1} be the smallest integer different from $b_1, \ldots, b_t$ for which $V_{b_{t+1}}$ is free with respect to the sequence $a_{t+1}, \ldots, a_r$. This rule defines a permutation $b_1 b_2 \ldots b_r$ of the integers $\{1, 2, \ldots, r\}$. Let $g(b_k) = a_k$ for $1 \leq k \leq r$; this defines a function such that adding arcs from V_k to $U_{g(k)}$ introduces no oriented cycles.

28. Let f be any of the n^{m-1} functions from $\{2, \ldots, m\}$ to $\{1, 2, \ldots, n\}$, and consider the directed graph with vertices $U_1, \ldots, U_m, V_1, \ldots, V_n$ and arcs from U_k to $V_{f(k)}$ for $1 < k \leq m$. Apply exercise 27 with $p = 1$, $q = m$, $r = n$, to show that there are m^{n-1} ways to add further arcs from the V's to the U's to obtain an oriented tree with root U_1. Since there is a one-to-one correspondence between the desired set of free trees and the set of oriented trees with root U_1, the answer is $n^{m-1} m^{n-1}$. [This construction can be extensively generalized; see D. E. Knuth, *Canadian J. Math.* **20** (1968), 1077–1086.]

29. If $y = x^t$, then $(tz)y = \ln y$, and we see that it is sufficient to prove the identity for $t = 1$. Now if $zx = \ln x$ we know by exercise 25 that $x^m = \sum_k E_k(m, 1) z^k$ for nonnegative integers m. Hence

$$x^r = e^{zxr} = \sum_k \frac{(zxr)^k}{k!} = \sum_{j,k} \frac{r^k z^{k+j} E_j(k,1)}{k!} = \sum_k \frac{z^k}{k!} \sum_j \binom{k}{j} j! E_j(k-j,1) r^{k-j}$$

$$= \sum_k \frac{z^k}{k!} \sum_j \binom{k-1}{j} k^j r^{k-j} = \sum_k z^k E_k(r,1).$$

[Exercise 4.7–22 derives considerably more general results.]

30. Each graph described defines a set $C_x \subseteq \{1, \ldots, n\}$, where j is in C_x if and only if there is a path from t_j to r_i for some $i \leq x$. For a given C_x each graph described is composed of two independent parts: one of the $x(x + \epsilon_1 z_1 + \cdots + \epsilon_n z_n)^{\epsilon_1 + \cdots + \epsilon_n - 1}$ graphs on the vertices r_i, s_{jk}, t_j for $i \leq x$ and $j \in C_x$, where $\epsilon_j = [j \in C_x]$, plus one of the $y(y + (1 - \epsilon_1)z_1 + \cdots + (1 - \epsilon_n)z_n)^{(1-\epsilon_1) + \cdots + (1-\epsilon_n) - 1}$ graphs on the other vertices.

31. $G(z) = z + G(z)^2 + G(z)^3 + G(z)^4 + \cdots = z + G(z)^2/(1 - G(z))$. Hence $G(z) = \frac{1}{4}(1 + z - \sqrt{1 - 6z + z^2}) = z + z^2 + 3z^3 + 11z^4 + 45z^5 + \cdots$. [*Notes:* Another problem equivalent to this one was posed and solved by E. Schröder, *Zeitschrift für Mathematik und Physik* **15** (1870), 361–376, who determined the number of ways to insert nonoverlapping diagonals in a convex $(n + 1)$-gon. These numbers for $n > 1$ are just half the values obtained in exercise 2.2.1–11, since Pratt's grammar allows the root node of the associated parse tree to have degree one. The asymptotic value is calculated in exercise 2.2.1–12. Curiously, the value $[z^{10}] G(z) = 103049$ seems to have been calculated already by Hipparchus in the second century B.C., as the number of "affirmative compound propositions that can be made from only ten simple propositions"; see R. P. Stanley, *AMM* **104** (1997), 344–350; F. Acerbi, *Archive for History of Exact Sciences* **57** (2003), 465–502.]

32. Zero if $n_0 \neq 1 + n_2 + 2n_3 + 3n_4 + \cdots$ (see exercise 2.3–21), otherwise

$$(n_0 + n_1 + \cdots + n_m - 1)!/n_0!\,n_1!\ldots n_m!.$$

To prove this result we recall that an unlabeled tree with $n = n_0 + n_1 + \cdots + n_m$ nodes is characterized by the sequence $d_1\,d_2\ldots d_n$ of the degrees of the nodes in postorder (Section 2.3.3). Furthermore such a sequence of degrees corresponds to a tree if and only if $\sum_{j=1}^k (1 - d_j) > 0$ for $0 < k \leq n$. (This important property of Polish postfix notation is readily proved by induction; see Algorithm 2.3.3F with f a function that creates a tree, like the TREE function of Section 2.3.2.) In particular, d_1 must be 0. The answer to our problem is therefore the number of sequences $d_2\ldots d_n$ with n_j occurrences of j for $j > 0$, namely the multinomial coefficient

$$\binom{n-1}{n_0-1,\; n_1,\ldots,\; n_m},$$

minus the number of such sequences $d_2\ldots d_n$ for which $\sum_{j=2}^k (1 - d_j) < 0$ for some $k > 2$.

We may enumerate the latter sequences as follows: Let t be minimal such that $\sum_{j=2}^t (1 - d_j) < 0$; then $\sum_{j=2}^t (1 - d_j) = -s$ where $1 \leq s < d_t$, and we may form the subsequence $d_2'\ldots d_n' = d_{t-1}\ldots d_2 0 d_{t+1}\ldots d_n$, which has n_j occurrences of j for $j \neq d_t$, $n_j - 1$ occurrences of j for $j = d_t$. Now $\sum_{j=2}^k (1 - d_j')$ is equal to d_t when $k = n$, and equal to $d_t - s$ when $k = t$; when $k < t$, it is

$$\sum_{2 \leq j < t} (1 - d_j) - \sum_{2 \leq j \leq t-k} (1 - d_j) \leq \sum_{2 \leq j < t} (1 - d_j) = d_t - s - 1.$$

It follows that, given s and any sequence $d_2'\ldots d_n'$, the construction can be reversed; hence the number of sequences $d_2\ldots d_n$ that have a given value of d_t and s is the multinomial coefficient

$$\binom{n-1}{n_0,\ldots,\; n_{d_t}-1,\ldots,\; n_m}.$$

The number of sequences $d_2\ldots d_n$ that correspond to trees is therefore obtained by summing over the possible values of d_t and s:

$$\sum_{j=0}^m (1 - j)\binom{n-1}{n_0,\ldots,\; n_j-1,\ldots,\; n_m} = \frac{(n-1)!}{n_0!\,n_1!\ldots n_m!}\sum_{j=0}^m (1 - j)n_j$$

and the latter sum is 1.

An even simpler proof of this result has been given by G. N. Raney, *Transactions of the American Math. Society* **94** (1960), 441–451. If $d_1\,d_2\ldots d_n$ is any sequence with n_j appearances of j, there is precisely one cyclic rearrangement $d_k\ldots d_n d_1\ldots d_{k-1}$ that corresponds to a tree, namely the rearrangement where k is maximal such that $\sum_{j=1}^{k-1} (1 - d_j)$ is minimal. [This argument in the case of binary trees was apparently first discovered by C. S. Peirce in an unpublished manuscript; see his *New Elements of Mathematics* **4** (The Hague: Mouton, 1976), 303–304. It was discovered in the case of t-ary trees by Dvoretzky and Motzkin, *Duke Math. J.* **14** (1947), 305–313.]

Still another proof, by G. Bergman, inductively replaces $d_k d_{k+1}$ by $(d_k + d_{k+1} - 1)$ if $d_k > 0$ [*Algebra Universalis* **8** (1978), 129–130].

The methods above can be generalized to show that the number of (ordered, unlabeled) forests having f trees and n_j nodes of degree j is $(n-1)!\,f/n_0!\,n_1!\ldots n_m!$, provided that the condition $n_0 = f + n_2 + 2n_3 + \cdots$ is satisfied.

33. Consider the number of trees with n_1 nodes labeled 1, n_2 nodes labeled 2, $\ldots$, and such that each node labeled j has degree e_j. Let this number be $c(n_1, n_2, \ldots)$, with the specified degrees $e_1, e_2, \ldots$ regarded as fixed. The generating function $G(z_1, z_2, \ldots) = \sum c(n_1, n_2, \ldots)z_1^{n_1} z_2^{n_2} \ldots$ satisfies the identity $G = z_1 G^{e_1} + \cdots + z_r G^{e_r}$, since $z_j G^{e_j}$ enumerates the trees whose root is labeled j. And by the result of the previous exercise,

$$c(n_1, n_2, \ldots) = \begin{cases} \dfrac{(n_1 + n_2 + \cdots - 1)!}{n_1!\,n_2!\ldots}, & \text{if } (1 - e_1)n_1 + (1 - e_2)n_2 + \cdots = 1; \\ 0, & \text{otherwise.} \end{cases}$$

More generally, since G^f enumerates the number of ordered forests having such labels, we have for integer $f > 0$

$$w^f = \sum_{f=(1-e_1)n_1 + (1-e_2)n_2 + \cdots} \frac{(n_1 + n_2 + \cdots - 1)!\,f}{n_1!\,n_2!\ldots} z_1^{n_1} z_2^{n_2} \ldots\,.$$

These formulas are meaningful when $r = \infty$, and they are essentially equivalent to Lagrange's inversion formula.

SECTION 2.3.4.5

1. There are $\binom{8}{5}$ in all, since the nodes numbered 8, 9, 10, 11, 12 may be attached in any of eight positions below 4, 5, 6, and 7.

2.

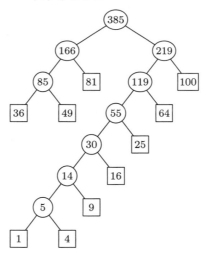

3. By induction on m, the condition is necessary. Conversely if $\sum_{j=1}^{m} 2^{-l_j} = 1$, we want to construct an extended binary tree with path lengths $l_1, \ldots, l_m$. When $m = 1$, we have $l_1 = 0$ and the construction is trivial. Otherwise we may assume that the l's are ordered so that $l_1 = l_2 = \cdots = l_q > l_{q+1} \ge l_{q+2} \ge \cdots \ge l_m > 0$ for some q with $1 \le q \le m$. Now $2^{l_1 - 1} = \sum_{j=1}^{m} 2^{l_1 - l_j - 1} = \frac{1}{2}q + \text{integer}$, hence q is even. By induction on m there is a tree with path lengths $l_1 - 1$, l_3, l_4, $\ldots$, l_m; take such a tree and replace one of the external nodes at level $l_1 - 1$ by an internal node whose children are at level $l_1 = l_2$.

4. First, find a tree by Huffman's method. If $w_j < w_{j+1}$, then $l_j \geq l_{j+1}$, since the tree is optimal. The construction in the answer to exercise 3 now gives us another tree with these same path lengths and with the weights in the proper sequence. For example, the tree (11) becomes

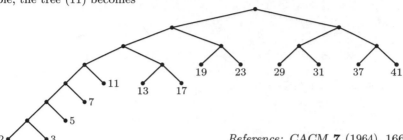

Reference: CACM **7** (1964), 166–169.

5. (a) $b_{np} = \displaystyle\sum_{\substack{k+l=n-1 \\ r+s+n-1=p}} b_{kr} b_{ls}$. Hence $zB(w, wz)^2 = B(w, z) - 1$.

(b) Take the partial derivative with respect to w:

$$2zB(w, wz)\big(B_w(w, wz) + zB_z(w, wz)\big) = B_w(w, z).$$

Therefore if $H(z) = B_w(1, z) = \sum_n h_n z^n$, we find $H(z) = 2zB(z)(H(z) + zB'(z))$; and the known formula for $B(z)$ implies

$$H(z) = \frac{1}{1 - 4z} - \frac{1}{z}\left(\frac{1 - z}{\sqrt{1 - 4z}} - 1\right), \qquad \text{so} \qquad h_n = 4^n - \frac{3n + 1}{n + 1}\binom{2n}{n}.$$

The average value is h_n/b_n. (c) Asymptotically, this comes to $n\sqrt{\pi n} - 3n + O(\sqrt{n})$.

For the solution to similar problems, see John Riordan, *IBM J. Res. and Devel.* **4** (1960), 473–478; A. Rényi and G. Szekeres, *J. Australian Math. Soc.* **7** (1967), 497–507; John Riordan and N. J. A. Sloane, *J. Australian Math. Soc.* **10** (1969), 278–282; and exercise 2.3.1–11.

6. $n + s - 1 = tn$.

7. $E = (t - 1)I + tn$.

8. Summation by parts gives $\sum_{k=1}^{n} \lfloor \log_t((t - 1)k) \rfloor = nq - \sum k$, where the sum on the right is over values of k such that $0 \leq k \leq n$ and $(t - 1)k + 1 = t^j$ for some j. The latter sum may be rewritten $\sum_{j=1}^{q}(t^j - 1)/(t - 1)$.

9. Induction on the size of the tree.

10. By adding extra *zero* weights, if necessary, we may assume that $m \bmod (t - 1) = 1$. To obtain a t-ary tree with minimum weighted path length, combine the smallest t values at each step and replace them by their sum. The proof is essentially the same as the binary case. The desired ternary tree is shown.

F. K. Hwang has observed [*SIAM J. Appl. Math.* **37** (1979), 124–127] that a similar procedure is valid for minimum weighted path length trees having any prescribed multiset of degrees: Combine the smallest t weights at each step, where t is as small as possible.

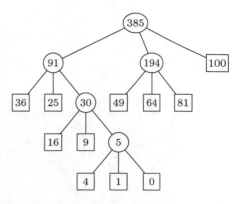

11. The "Dewey" notation is the binary representation of the node number.

12. By exercise 9, it is the internal path length divided by n, plus 1. (This result holds for general trees as well as binary trees.)

13. [See J. van Leeuwen, *Proc. 3rd International Colloq. Automata, Languages and Programming* (Edinburgh University Press, 1976), 382–410.]

> **H1.** [Initialize.] Set $A[m - 1 + i] \leftarrow w_i$ for $1 \leq i \leq m$. Then set $A[2m] \leftarrow \infty$, $x \leftarrow m$, $i \leftarrow m + 1$, $j \leftarrow m - 1$, $k \leftarrow m$. (During this algorithm $A[i] \leq \cdots \leq A[2m - 1]$ is the queue of unused external weights; $A[k] \geq \cdots \geq A[j]$ is the queue of unused internal weights, empty if $j < k$; the current left and right pointers are x and y.)
>
> **H2.** [Find right pointer.] If $j < k$ or $A[i] \leq A[j]$, set $y \leftarrow i$ and $i \leftarrow i+1$; otherwise set $y \leftarrow j$ and $j \leftarrow j - 1$.
>
> **H3.** [Create internal node.] Set $k \leftarrow k-1$, $L[k] \leftarrow x$, $R[k] \leftarrow y$, $A[k] \leftarrow A[x]+A[y]$.
>
> **H4.** [Done?] Terminate the algorithm if $k = 1$.
>
> **H5.** [Find left pointer.] (At this point $j \geq k$ and the queues contain a total of k unused weights. If $A[y] < 0$ we have $j = k$, $i = y + 1$, and $A[i] > A[j]$.) If $A[i] \leq A[j]$, set $x \leftarrow i$ and $i \leftarrow i + 1$; otherwise set $x \leftarrow j$ and $j \leftarrow j - 1$. Return to step H2. ∎

14. The proof for $k = m - 1$ applies with little change. [See *SIAM J. Appl. Math.* **21** (1971), 518.]

15. Use the combined-weight functions (a) $1 + \max(w_1, w_2)$ and (b) $xw_1 + xw_2$, respectively, instead of $w_1 + w_2$ in (9). [Part (a) is due to M. C. Golumbic, *IEEE Trans.* **C-25** (1976), 1164–1167; part (b) to T. C. Hu, D. Kleitman, and J. K. Tamaki, *SIAM J. Appl. Math.* **37** (1979), 246–256. Huffman's problem is the limiting case of (b) as $x \to 1$, since $\sum(1 + \epsilon)^{l_j} w_j = \sum w_j + \epsilon \sum w_j l_j + O(\epsilon^2)$.]

D. Stott Parker, Jr., has pointed out that a Huffman-like algorithm will also find the minimum of $w_1 x^{l_1} + \cdots + w_m x^{l_m}$ when $0 < x < 1$, if the two *maximum* weights are combined at each step as in part (b). In particular, the minimum of $w_1 2^{-l_1} + \cdots + w_m 2^{-l_m}$, when $w_1 \leq \cdots \leq w_m$, is $w_1/2 + \cdots + w_{m-1}/2^{m-1} + w_m/2^{m-1}$. See D. E. Knuth, *J. Comb. Theory* **A32** (1982), 216–224, for further generalizations.

16. Let $l_{m+1} = l'_{m+1} = 0$. Then

$$\sum_{j=1}^{m} w_j l_j \leq \sum_{j=1}^{m} w_j l'_j = \sum_{k=1}^{k}(l'_k - l'_{k+1}) \sum_{j=1}^{m} w_j \leq \sum_{k=1}^{k}(l'_k - l'_{k+1}) \sum_{j=1}^{m} w'_j = \sum_{j=1}^{m} w'_j l'_j ,$$

since $l'_j \geq l'_{j+1}$ as in exercise 4. The same proof holds for many other kinds of optimum trees, including those of exercise 10.

17. (a) This is exercise 14. (b) We can extend $f(n)$ to a concave function $f(x)$, so the stated inequality holds. Now $F(m)$ is the minimum of $\sum_{j=1}^{m-1} f(s_j)$, where the s_j are internal node weights of an extended binary tree on the weights 1, 1, ..., 1. Huffman's algorithm, which constructs the complete binary tree with $m - 1$ internal nodes in this case, yields the optimum tree. The choice $k = 2^{\lceil \lg(n/3) \rceil}$ defines a binary tree with the same internal weights, so it yields the minimum in the recurrence, for each n. [*SIAM J. Appl. Math.* **31** (1976), 368–378.] We can evaluate $F(n)$ in $O(\log n)$ steps; see exercises 5.2.3–20 and 5.2.3–21. If $f(n)$ is convex instead of concave, so that $\Delta^2 f(n) \geq 0$, the solution to the recurrence is obtained when $k = \lfloor n/2 \rfloor$.

SECTION 2.3.4.6

1. Choose one edge of the polygon and call it the base. Given a triangulation, let the triangle on the base correspond to the root of a binary tree, and let the other two sides of that triangle define bases of left and right subpolygons, which correspond to left and right subtrees in the same way. We proceed recursively until reaching "2-sided" polygons, which correspond to empty binary trees.

Stating this correspondence another way, we can label the non-base edges of a triangulated polygon with the integers $0, \ldots, n$; and when two adjacent sides of a triangle are labeled α and β in clockwise order, we can label the third side $(\alpha\beta)$. The label of the base then characterizes the binary tree and the triangulation. For example,

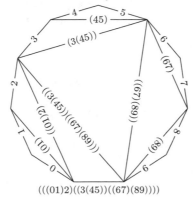

$$(((01)2)((3(45))((67)(89))))$$

corresponds to the binary tree shown in 2.3.1–(1). [See H. G. Forder, *Mathematical Gazette* **45** (1961), 199–201.]

2. (a) Take a base edge as in exercise 1, and give it d descendants if that edge is part of a $(d+1)$-gon in the dissected r-gon. The other d edges are then bases for subtrees. This defines a correspondence between Kirkman's problem and all ordered trees with $r-1$ leaves and $k+1$ nonleaves, having no nodes of degree 1. (When $k = r-3$ we have the situation of exercise 1.)

(b) There are $\binom{r+k}{k+1}\binom{r-3}{k}$ sequences $d_1 d_2 \ldots d_{r+k}$ of nonnegative integers such that $r-1$ of the d's are 0, none of them are 1, and the sum is $r+k-1$. Exactly one of the cyclic permutations $d_1 d_2 \ldots d_{r+k}$, $d_2 \ldots d_{r+k} d_1$, $\ldots$, $d_{r+k} d_1 \ldots d_{r+k-1}$ satisfies the additional property that $\sum_{j=1}^{q}(1-d_j) > 0$ for $1 \le q \le r+k$.

[Kirkman gave evidence for his conjecture in *Philos. Trans.* **147** (1857), 217–272, §22. Cayley proved it in *Proc. London Math. Soc.* **22** (1891), 237–262, without noticing the connection to trees.]

3. (a) Let the vertices be $\{1, 2, \ldots, n\}$. Draw an RLINK from i to j if i and j are consecutive elements of the same part and $i < j$; draw an LLINK from j to $j+1$ if $j+1$ is the smallest of its part. Then there are $k-1$ nonnull LLINKs, $n-k$ nonnull RLINKs, and we have a binary tree whose nodes are $12 \ldots n$ in preorder. Using the natural correspondence of Section 2.3.2, this rule defines a one-to-one correspondence between "partitions of an n-gon's vertices into k noncrossing parts" and "forests with n vertices and $n-k+1$ leaves." Interchanging LLINK with RLINK also gives "forests with n vertices and k leaves."

(b) A forest with n vertices and k leaves also corresponds to a sequence of nested parentheses, containing n left parentheses, n right parentheses, and k occurrences of "()". We can enumerate such sequences as follows:

Say that a string of 0s and 1s is an (m, n, k) string if there are m 0s, n 1s, and k occurrences of "01". Then 0010101001110 is a $(7, 6, 4)$ string. The number of (m, n, k) strings is $\binom{m}{k}\binom{n}{k}$, because we are free to choose which 0s and 1s will form the 01 pairs.

Let $S(\alpha)$ be the number of 0s in α minus the number of 1s. We say that a string σ is *good* if $S(\alpha) \geq 0$ whenever α is a prefix of σ (in other words, if $\sigma = \alpha\beta$ implies that $S(\alpha) \geq 0$); otherwise σ is *bad*. The following alternative to the "reflection principle" of exercise 2.2.1–4 establishes a one-to-one correspondence between bad (n, n, k) strings and arbitrary $(n-1, n+1, k)$ strings:

Any bad (n, n, k) string σ can be written uniquely in the form $\sigma = \alpha 0 \beta$, where $\overline{\alpha}^R$ and β are good. (Here $\overline{\alpha}^R$ is the string obtained from α by reversing it and complementing all the bits.) Then $\sigma' = \alpha 1 \beta$ is an $(n-1, n+1, k)$ string. Conversely, every $(n-1, n+1, k)$ string can be written uniquely in the form $\alpha 1 \beta$ where $\overline{\alpha}^R$ and β are good, and $\alpha 0 \beta$ is then a bad (n, n, k) string.

Thus the number of forests with n vertices and k leaves is $\binom{n}{k}\binom{n}{k} - \binom{n-1}{k}\binom{n+1}{k} = \binom{n-1}{k-1}\binom{n}{k} - \binom{n-1}{k}\binom{n}{k-1} = n!\,(n-1)!/(n-k+1)!\,(n-k)!\,k!\,(k-1)!$, a so-called *Narayana number* [T. V. Narayana, *Comptes Rendus Acad. Sci.* **240** (Paris, 1955), 1188–1189].

Notes: G. Kreweras, *Discrete Math.* **1** (1972), 333–350, enumerated noncrossing partitions in a different way. The partial ordering of partitions by refinement leads to an interesting partial ordering of forests, different from the one discussed in exercise 2.3.3–19; see Y. Poupard, *Cahiers du Bureau Univ. de Recherche Opér.* **16** (1971), Chapter 8; *Discrete Math.* **2** (1972), 279–288; P. Edelman, *Discrete Math.* **31** (1980), 171–180, **40** (1982), 171–179; N. Dershowitz and S. Zaks, *Discrete Math.* **62** (1986), 215–218.

A third way to define a natural lattice ordering of forests was introduced by R. Stanley in *Fibonacci Quarterly* **13** (1975), 215–232: Suppose we represent a forest by a string σ of 0s and 1s representing left and right parentheses as above; then $\sigma \leq \sigma'$ if and only if $S(\sigma_k) \leq S(\sigma'_k)$ for all k, where σ_k denotes the first k bits of σ. Stanley's lattice is *distributive*, unlike the other two. See exercises 7.2.1.6–26 through 7.2.1.6–34.

4. Let $m = n + 2$; by exercise 1, we want a correspondence between triangulated m-gons and $(m-1)$-rowed friezes. First let's look more closely at the previous correspondence, by giving a "top-down" labeling to the edges of a triangulation instead of the "bottom-up" one considered earlier: Assign the empty label ϵ to the base, then recursively give the labels αL and αR to the opposite edges of a triangle whose base is labeled α. For example, the previous diagram becomes

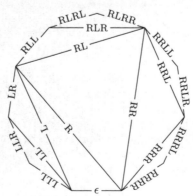

under these new conventions. If the base edge in this example is called 10, while the other edges are 0 to 9 as before, we can write $0 = 10LLL$, $1 = 10LLR$, $2 = 10LR$,

$3 = 10RLL$, etc. Any of the other edges can also be chosen as the base; thus, if 0 is chosen we have $1 = 0L$, $2 = 0RL$, $3 = 0RRLLL$, etc. It is not difficult to verify that if $u = v\alpha$ we have $v = u\alpha^T$, where α^T is obtained by reading α from right to left and interchanging L with R. For example, $10 = 0RRR = 1LRR = 2LR = 3RRL$, etc. If u, v, and w are edges of the polygon with $w = u\alpha L\gamma$ and $w = v\beta R\gamma$, then $u = v\beta L\alpha^T$ and $v = u\alpha R\beta^T$.

Given a triangulation of a polygon whose edges are numbered $0, 1, \ldots, m-1$, we define (u, v) for any pair of distinct edges u and v as follows: Let $u = v\alpha$, and interpret α as a 2×2 matrix by letting $L = \left(\begin{smallmatrix} 1 & 1 \\ 0 & 1 \end{smallmatrix}\right)$ and $R = \left(\begin{smallmatrix} 1 & 0 \\ 1 & 1 \end{smallmatrix}\right)$. Then (u, v) is defined to be the element in the upper left corner of α. Notice that α^T is the transpose of the matrix α, since $R = L^T$; hence we have $(v, u) = (u, v)$. Notice also that $(u, v) = 1$ if and only if u_- and v_- are joined by an edge of the triangulation, where u_- denotes the vertex between edges u and $u - 1$.

Let $(u, u) = 0$ for all polygon edges u. We can now prove that $v = u\alpha$ implies

$$\alpha = \begin{pmatrix} (u, v) & (u, v+1) \\ (u+1, v) & (u+1, v+1) \end{pmatrix} \qquad \text{for all } u \neq v, \qquad (*)$$

where $u+1$ and $v+1$ are the clockwise successors of u and v. The proof is by induction on m: Eq. $(*)$ is trivial when $m = 2$, since the two parallel edges u and v are then related by $u = v\epsilon$, and $\alpha = \epsilon$ is the identity matrix. If any triangulation is augmented by extending some edge v with a triangle $v\, v'\, v''$, then $v = u\alpha$ implies $v' = u\alpha L$ and $v'' = u\alpha R$; hence (u, v') and (u, v'') in the extended polygon are respectively equal to (u, v) and $(u, v) + (u, v+1)$ in the original one. It follows that

$$\alpha L = \begin{pmatrix} (u, v') & (u, v'') \\ (u+1, v') & (u+1, v'') \end{pmatrix} \qquad \text{and} \qquad \alpha R = \begin{pmatrix} (u, v'') & (u, v''+1) \\ (u+1, v'') & (u+1, v''+1) \end{pmatrix},$$

and $(*)$ remains true in the extended polygon.

The frieze pattern corresponding to the given triangulation is now defined to be the periodic sequence

$(0,1)$	$(1,2)$	$(2,3)$	$\ldots$	$(m{-}1,0)$	$(0,1)$	$(1,2)$	$\ldots$	
$(0,2)$	$(1,3)$	$(2,4)$	$\ldots$	$(m{-}1,1)$	$(0,2)$	$(1,3)$	$\ldots$	
$(m{-}1,2)$	$(0,3)$	$(1,4)$	$\ldots$	$(m{-}2,1)$	$(m{-}1,2)$	$(0,3)$	$\ldots$	
$(m{-}1,3)$	$(0,4)$	$(1,5)$	$\ldots$	$(m{-}2,2)$	$(m{-}2,2)$	$(m{-}1,3)$	$(0,4)$	$\ldots$

and so on until $m - 1$ rows have been defined; the final row begins with $(\lceil m/2 \rceil + 1, \lceil m/2 \rceil)$ when $m > 3$. Condition $(*)$ proves that this pattern is a frieze, namely that

$$(u, v)(u+1, v+1) - (u, v+1)(u+1, v) = 1, \qquad (**)$$

because $\det L = \det R = 1$ implies $\det \alpha = 1$. Our example triangulation yields

```
1  1  1  1  1  1  1  1  1  1  1  1  1  1  1  1  1  1  1  1   ...
 1  2  4  2  1  5  1  3  1  4  3  1  2  4  2  1  5  1  3  1  4   ...
2  1  7  7  1  4  4  2  2  3 11  2  1  7  7  1  4  4  2  2  3   ...
 1  3 12  3  3  3  7  1  5  8  7  1  3 12  3  3  3  7  1  5  8   ...
3  2  5  5  8  2  5  3  2 13  5  3  2  5  5  8  2  5  3  2 13   ...
 5  3  2 13  5  3  2  5  5  8  2  5  3  2 13  5  3  2  5  5  8   ...
3  7  1  5  8  7  1  3 12  3  3  3  7  1  5  8  7  1  3 12  3   ...
 4  2  2  3 11  2  1  7  7  1  4  4  2  2  3 11  2  1  7  7  1   ...
5  1  3  1  4  3  1  2  4  2  1  5  1  3  1  4  3  1  2  4  2   ...
 1  1  1  1  1  1  1  1  1  1  1  1  1  1  1  1  1  1  1  1   ...
```

The relation $(u, v) = 1$ defines the edges of the triangulation, hence different triangulations yield different friezes. To complete the proof of one-to-one correspondence, we must show that every $(m - 1)$-rowed frieze pattern of positive integers is obtained in this way from some triangulation.

Given any frieze of $m - 1$ rows, extend it by putting a new row 0 at the top and a new row m at the bottom, both consisting entirely of zeros. Now let the elements of row 0 be called $(0,0)$, $(1,1)$, $(2,2)$, etc., and for all nonnegative integers $u < v \leq u+m$ let (u, v) be the element in the diagonal southeast of (u, u) and in the diagonal southwest of (v, v). By assumption, condition $(**)$ holds for all $u < v < u + m$. We can in fact extend $(**)$ to the considerably more general relation

$$(t, u)(v, w) + (t, w)(u, v) = (t, v)(u, w) \qquad \text{for } t \leq u \leq v \leq w \leq t + m. \qquad (***)$$

For if $(***)$ is false, let (t, u, v, w) be a counterexample with the smallest value of $(w - t)m + u - t + w - v$. Clearly $t \neq u$ and $v \neq w$. *Case 1: $t + 1 < u$.* Then $(***)$ holds for $(t, t + 1, v, w)$, $(t, t + 1, u, v)$, and $(t + 1, u, v, w)$, so we find $((t, u)(v, w) + (t, w)(u, v))(t + 1, v) = (t, v)(u, w)(t + 1, v)$; this implies $(t + 1, v) = 0$, a contradiction. *Case 2: $v+1 < w$.* Then $(***)$ holds for $(t, u, w-1, w)$, $(u, v, w-1, w)$, and $(t, u, v, w-1)$; we obtain a similar contradiction $(u, w - 1) = 0$. *Case 3: $u = t + 1$ and $w = v + 1$.* In this case $(***)$ reduces to $(**)$.

Now we set $u = t + 1$ and $w = t + m$ in $(***)$, obtaining $(t, v) = (v, t + m)$ for $t \leq v \leq t + m$, because $(t + 1, t + m) = 1$ and $(t, t + m) = 0$. We conclude that the entries of any $(m - 1)$-rowed frieze are periodic: $(u, v) = (v, u+m) = (u+m, v+m) = (v + m, u + 2m) = \cdots$.

Every frieze pattern of positive integers contains a 1 in row 2. For if we set $t = 0$, $v = u + 1$, and $w = u + 2$ in $(***)$ we get $(0, u + 1)(u, u + 2) = (0, u) + (0, u + 2)$, hence $(0, u + 2) - (0, u + 1) \geq (0, u + 1) - (0, u)$ if and only if $(u, u + 2) \geq 2$. This cannot hold for all u in the range $0 \leq u \leq m - 2$, because $(0, 1) - (0, 0) = 1$ and $(0, m) - (0, m - 1) = -1$.

Finally, if $m > 3$ we cannot have two consecutive 1s in row 2, because $(u, u + 2) = (u + 1, u + 3) = 1$ implies $(u, u + 3) = 0$. Therefore we can reduce the frieze to another one with m reduced by 1, as illustrated here for 7 rows reduced to 6:

The reduced frieze corresponds to a triangulation, by induction, and the unreduced frieze corresponds to attaching one more triangle. [*Math. Gazette* **57** (1973), 87–94, 175–183; Conway and Guy, *The Book of Numbers* (New York: Copernicus, 1996), 74–76, 96–97, 101–102.]

Notes: This proof demonstrates that the function (u, v), which we defined on any triangulation via 2×2 matrices, satisfies $(***)$ whenever (t, u, v, w) are edges of the polygon in clockwise order. We can express each (u, v) as a polynomial in the numbers $a_j = (j - 1, j + 1)$; these polynomials are essentially identical to the "continuants" discussed in Section 4.5.3, except for the signs of individual terms. In fact, $(j, k) = i^{1-k+j} K_{k-j-1}(ia_{j+1}, ia_{j+2}, \ldots, ia_{k-1})$. Thus $(***)$ is equivalent to Euler's identity for continuants in the answer to exercise 4.5.3–32. The matrices L and R have the interesting property that any 2×2 matrix of nonnegative integers with determinant 1 can be expressed uniquely as a product of L's and R's.

Many other interesting relationships are present; for example, the numbers in row 2 of an integer frieze count the number of triangles touching each vertex of the corresponding triangulated polygon. The total number of occurrences of $(u, v) = 1$ in the basic region $0 \le u < v - 1 < m - 1$ and $(u, v) \ne (0, m - 1)$ is the number of diagonals (chords) of the triangulation, namely $m - 3 = n - 1$. The total number of 2s is also $n - 1$, because $(u, v) = 2$ if and only if u_- and v_- are opposing vertices of the two triangles adjacent to a chord.

Another interpretation of (u, v) was found by D. Broline, D. W. Crowe, and I. M. Isaacs [*Geometriæ Dedicata* **3** (1974), 171–176]: It is the number of ways to match the $v - u - 1$ vertices between edges u and $v - 1$ with distinct triangles adjacent to those vertices.

SECTION 2.3.5

1. A List structure is a directed graph in which the arcs leaving each vertex are ordered, and where some of the vertices that have out-degree 0 are designated "atoms." Furthermore there is a vertex S such that there is an oriented path from S to V for all vertices $V \ne S$. (With directions of arcs reversed, S would be a "root.")

2. Not in the same way, since thread links in the usual representation lead back to "PARENT," which is not unique for sub-Lists. The representation discussed in exercise 2.3.4.2–25, or some similar method, could perhaps be used (but this idea has not yet been exploited at the time of writing).

3. As mentioned in the text, we prove also that P = P0 upon termination. If only P0 is to be marked, the algorithm certainly operates correctly. If $n > 1$ nodes are to be marked, we must have ATOM(P0) = 0. Step E4 then sets ALINK(P0) ← Λ and executes the algorithm with P0 replaced by ALINK(P0) and T replaced by P0. By induction (note that since MARK(P0) is now 1, all links to P0 are equivalent to Λ by steps E4 and E5), we see that ultimately we will mark all nodes on paths that start with ALINK(P0) and do not pass through P0; and we will then get to step E6 with T = P0 and P = ALINK(P0). Now since ATOM(T) = 1, step E6 restores ALINK(P0) and ATOM(P0) and we reach step E5. Step E5 sets BLINK(P0) ← Λ, etc., and a similar argument shows that we will ultimately mark all nodes on paths that start with BLINK(P0) and do not pass through P0 or nodes reachable from ALINK(P0). Then we will get to E6 with T = P0, P = BLINK(P0), and finally we get to E6 with T = Λ, P = P0.

4. The program that follows incorporates the suggested improvements in the speed of processing atoms that appear in the text after the statement of Algorithm E.

In steps E4 and E5 of the algorithm, we want to test if MARK(Q) = 0. If NODE(Q) = +0, this is an unusual case that can be handled properly by setting it to −0 and treating it as if it were originally −0, since it has ALINK and BLINK both Λ. This simplification is not reflected in the timing calculations below.

rI1 ≡ P, rI2 ≡ T, rI3 ≡ Q, and rX ≡ −1 (for setting MARKs).

```
01  MARK   EQU  0:0
02  ATOM   EQU  1:1
03  ALINK  EQU  2:3
04  BLINK  EQU  4:5
```

05	E1	LD1	P0	1	*E1. Initialize.* P ← P0.
06		ENT2	0	1	T ← Λ.
07		ENTX	-1	1	rX ← -1.
08	E2	STX	0,1(MARK)	1	*E2. Mark.* MARK(P) ← 1.
09	E3	LDA	0,1(ATOM)	1	*E3. Atom?*
10		JAZ	E4	1	Jump if ATOM(P) = 0.
11	E6	J2Z	DONE	n	*E6. Up.*
12		ENT3	0,2	$n-1$	Q ← T.
13		LDA	0,3(ATOM)	$n-1$	
14		JANZ	1F	$n-1$	Jump if ATOM(T) = 1.
15		LD2	0,3(BLINK)	t_2	T ← BLINK(Q).
16		ST1	0,3(BLINK)	t_2	BLINK(Q) ← P.
17		ENT1	0,3	t_2	P ← Q.
18		JMP	E6	t_2	
19	1H	STZ	0,2(ATOM)	t_1	ATOM(T) ← 0.
20		LD2	0,3(ALINK)	t_1	T ← ALINK(Q).
21		ST1	0,3(ALINK)	t_1	ALINK(Q) ← P.
22		ENT1	0,3	t_1	P ← Q.
23	E5	LD3	0,1(BLINK)	n	*E5. Down BLINK.* Q ← BLINK(P).
24		J3Z	E6	n	Jump if Q = Λ.
25		LDA	0,3	$n-b_2$	
26		STX	0,3(MARK)	$n-b_2$	MARK(Q) ← 1.
27		JANP	E6	$n-b_2$	Jump if NODE(Q) was already marked.
28		LDA	0,3(ATOM)	t_2+a_2	
29		JANZ	E6	t_2+a_2	Jump if ATOM(Q) = 1.
30		ST2	0,1(BLINK)	t_2	BLINK(P) ← T.
31	E4A	ENT2	0,1	$n-1$	T ← P.
32		ENT1	0,3	$n-1$	P ← Q.
33	E4	LD3	0,1(ALINK)	n	*E4. Down ALINK.* Q ← ALINK(P).
34		J3Z	E5	n	Jump if Q = Λ.
35		LDA	0,3	$n-b_1$	
36		STX	0,3(MARK)	$n-b_1$	MARK(Q) ← 1.
37		JANP	E5	$n-b_1$	Jump if NODE(Q) was already marked.
38		LDA	0,3(ATOM)	t_1+a_1	
39		JANZ	E5	t_1+a_1	Jump if ATOM(Q) = 1.
40		STX	0,1(ATOM)	t_1	ATOM(P) ← 1.
41		ST2	0,1(ALINK)	t_1	ALINK(P) ← T.
42		JMP	E4A	t_1	T ← P, P ← Q, to E4. ∎

By Kirchhoff's law, $t_1 + t_2 + 1 = n$. The total time is $(34n + 4t_1 + 3a - 5b - 8)u$, where n is the number of nonatomic nodes marked, a is the number of atoms marked, b is the number of Λ links encountered in marked nonatomic nodes, and t_1 is the number of times we went down an ALINK ($0 \le t_1 < n$).

   5. (The following is the fastest known marking algorithm for a one-level memory.)

   S1. Set MARK(P0) ← 1. If ATOM(P0) = 1, the algorithm terminates; otherwise set
        S ← 0, R ← P0, T ← Λ.

   S2. Set P ← BLINK(R). If P = Λ or MARK(P) = 1, go to S3. Otherwise set
        MARK(P) ← 1. Now if ATOM(P) = 1, go to S3; otherwise if S < N set S ← S + 1,
        STACK[S] ← P, and go to S3; otherwise go to S5.

S3. Set P ← ALINK(R). If P = Λ or MARK(P) = 1, go to S4. Otherwise set MARK(P) ← 1. Now if ATOM(P) = 1, go to S4; otherwise set R ← P and return to S2.

S4. If S = 0, terminate the algorithm; otherwise set R ← STACK[S], S ← S − 1, and go to S2.

S5. Set Q ← ALINK(P). If Q = Λ or MARK(Q) = 1, go to S6. Otherwise set MARK(Q) ← 1. Now if ATOM(Q) = 1, go to S6; otherwise set ATOM(P) ← 1, ALINK(P) ← T, T ← P, P ← Q, go to S5.

S6. Set Q ← BLINK(P). If Q = Λ or MARK(Q) = 1, go to S7; otherwise set MARK(Q) ← 1. Now if ATOM(Q) = 1, go to S7; otherwise set BLINK(P) ← T, T ← P, P ← Q, go to S5.

S7. If T = Λ, go to S3. Otherwise set Q ← T. If ATOM(Q) = 1, set ATOM(Q) ← 0, T ← ALINK(Q), ALINK(Q) ← P, P ← Q, and return to S6. If ATOM(Q) = 0, set T ← BLINK(Q), BLINK(Q) ← P, P ← Q, and return to S7. ▮

Reference: CACM **10** (1967), 501–506.

6. From the second phase of garbage collection (or perhaps also the initial phase, if all mark bits are set to zero at that time).

7. Delete steps E2 and E3, and delete "ATOM(P) ← 1" in E4. Set MARK(P) ← 1 in step E5 and use "MARK(Q) = 0", "MARK(Q) = 1" in step E6 in place of the present "ATOM(Q) = 1", "ATOM(Q) = 0" respectively. The idea is to set the MARK bit only after the left subtree has been marked. This algorithm works even if the tree has overlapping (shared) subtrees, but it does not work for all recursive List structures such as those with NODE(ALINK(Q)) an ancestor of NODE(Q). (Note that ALINK of a marked node is never changed.)

8. *Solution 1:* Analogous to Algorithm E, but simpler.

F1. Set T ← Λ, P ← P0.

F2. Set MARK(P) ← 1, and set P ← P + SIZE(P).

F3. If MARK(P) = 1, go to F5.

F4. Set Q ← LINK(P). If Q ≠ Λ and MARK(Q) = 0, set LINK(P) ← T, T ← P, P ← Q and go to F2. Otherwise set P ← P − 1 and return to F3.

F5. If T = Λ, stop. Otherwise set Q ← T, T ← LINK(Q), LINK(Q) ← P, P ← Q − 1, and return to F3. ▮

A similar algorithm, which sometimes decreases the storage overhead and which avoids all pointers into the middle of nodes, has been suggested by Lars-Erik Thorelli, *BIT* **12** (1972), 555–568.

Solution 2: Analogous to Algorithm D. For this solution, we assume that the SIZE field is large enough to contain a link address. Such an assumption is probably not justified by the statement of the problem, but it lets us use a slightly faster method than the first solution when it is applicable.

G1. Set T ← Λ, MARK(P0) ← 1, P ← P0 + SIZE(P0).

G2. If MARK(P) = 1, go to G5.

G3. Set Q ← LINK(P), P ← P − 1.

G4. If Q ≠ Λ and MARK(Q) = 0, set MARK(Q) ← 1, S ← SIZE(Q), SIZE(Q) ← T, T ← Q + S. Go back to G2.

G5. If T = Λ, stop. Otherwise set P ← T and find the first value of Q = P, P − 1, P − 2, ... for which MARK(Q) = 1; set T ← SIZE(Q) and SIZE(Q) ← P − Q. Go back to G2. ∎

9. H1. Set L ← 0, K ← M + 1, MARK(0) ← 1, MARK(M + 1) ← 0.

H2. Increase L by one, and if MARK(L) = 1 repeat this step.

H3. Decrease K by one, and if MARK(K) = 0 repeat this step.

H4. If L > K, go to step H5; otherwise set NODE(L) ← NODE(K), ALINK(K) ← L, MARK(K) ← 0, and return to H2.

H5. For L = 1, 2, ..., K do the following: Set MARK(L) ← 0. If ATOM(L) = 0 and ALINK(L) > K, set ALINK(L) ← ALINK(ALINK(L)). If ATOM(L) = 0 and BLINK(L) > K, set BLINK(L) ← ALINK(BLINK(L)). ∎

See also exercise 2.5–33.

10. Z1. [Initialize.] Set F ← P0, R ⇐ AVAIL, NODE(R) ← NODE(F), REF(F) ← R. (Here F and R are pointers for a queue set up in the REF fields of all header nodes encountered.)

Z2. [Begin new List.] Set P ← F, Q ← REF(P).

Z3. [Advance to right.] Set P ← RLINK(P). If P = Λ, go to Z6.

Z4. [Copy one node.] Set Q1 ⇐ AVAIL, RLINK(Q) ← Q1, Q ← Q1, NODE(Q) ← NODE(P).

Z5. [Translate sub-List link.] If T(P) = 1, set P1 ← REF(P), and if REF(P1) = Λ set REF(R) ← P1, R ⇐ AVAIL, REF(P1) ← R, NODE(R) ← NODE(P1), REF(Q) ← R. If T(P) = 1 and REF(P1) ≠ Λ, set REF(Q) ← REF(P1). Go to Z3.

Z6. [Move to next List.] Set RLINK(Q) ← Λ. If REF(F) ≠ R, set F ← REF(REF(F)) and return to Z2. Otherwise set REF(R) ← Λ, P ← P0.

Z7. [Final cleanup.] Set Q ← REF(P). If Q ≠ Λ, set REF(P) ← Λ and P ← Q and repeat step Z7. ∎

Of course, this use of the REF fields makes it impossible to do garbage collection with Algorithm D; moreover, Algorithm D is ruled out by the fact that the Lists aren't well-formed during the copying.

Several elegant List-moving and List-copying algorithms that make substantially weaker assumptions about List representation have been devised. See D. W. Clark, *CACM* **19** (1976), 352–354; J. M. Robson, *CACM* **20** (1977), 431–433.

11. Here is a pencil-and-paper method that can be written out more formally to answer the problem: First attach a unique name (e.g., a capital letter) to each List in the given set; in the example we might have A = (a: C, b, a: F), F = (b: D), B = (a: F, b, a: E), C = (b: G), G = (a: C), D = (a: F), E = (b: G). Now make a list of pairs of List names that must be proved equal. Successively add pairs to this list until either a contradiction is found because we have a pair that disagree on the first level (then the originally given Lists are unequal), or until the list of pairs does not imply any further pairs (then the originally given Lists are equal). In the example, this list of pairs would originally contain only the given pair, *AB*; then it gets the further pairs *CF*, *EF* (by matching A and B), *DG* (from *CF*); and then we have a self-consistent set.

To prove the validity of this method, observe that (i) if it returns the answer "unequal", the given Lists are unequal; (ii) if the given Lists are unequal, it returns the answer "unequal"; (iii) it always terminates.

12. When the `AVAIL` list contains N nodes, where N is a specified constant to be chosen as discussed below, initiate another coroutine that shares computer time with the main routine and does the following: (a) Marks all N nodes on the `AVAIL` list; (b) marks all other nodes that are accessible to the program; (c) links all unmarked nodes together to prepare a new `AVAIL` list for use when the current `AVAIL` list is empty, and (d) resets the mark bits in all nodes. One must choose N and the ratio of time sharing so that operations (a), (b), (c), and (d) are guaranteed to be complete before N nodes are taken from the `AVAIL` list, yet the main routine is running sufficiently fast. It is necessary to use some care in step (b) to make sure that all nodes "accessible to the program" are included, as the program continues to run; details are omitted here. If the list formed in (c) has fewer than N nodes, it may be necessary to stop eventually because memory space might become exhausted. [For further information, see Guy L. Steele Jr., *CACM* **18** (1975), 495–508; P. Wadler, *CACM* **19** (1976), 491–500; E. W. Dijkstra, L. Lamport, A. J. Martin, C. S. Scholten, and E. F. M. Steffens, *CACM* **21** (1978), 966–975; H. G. Baker, Jr., *CACM* **21** (1978), 280–294.]

SECTION 2.4

1. Preorder.

2. It is essentially proportional to the number of Data Table entries created.

3. Change step A5 to:

A5'. [Remove top level.] Remove the top stack entry; and if the new level number at the top of the stack is $\geq$ L, let (L1,P1) be the new entry at the top of the stack and repeat this step. Otherwise set `SIB(P1)` $\leftarrow$ Q and then let (L1,P1) be the new entry at the top of the stack.

4. (Solution by David S. Wise.) Rule (c) is violated if and only if there is a data item whose *complete qualification* A_0 OF ... OF A_n is also a COBOL reference to some other data item. Since the parent A_1 OF ... OF A_n must also satisfy rule (c), we may assume that this other data item is a descendant of the same parent. Therefore Algorithm A would be extended to check, as each new data item is added to the Data Table, whether its parent is an ancestor of any other item of the same name, or if the parent of any other item of the same name is in the stack. (When the parent is Λ, it is everybody's ancestor and always on the stack.)

On the other hand, if we leave Algorithm A as it stands, the COBOL programmer will get an error message from Algorithm B when trying to use an illegal item. Only `MOVE CORRESPONDING` can make use of such items without error.

5. Make these changes:

Step	replace	by
B1.	P $\leftarrow$ LINK(P_0)	P $\leftarrow$ LINK(INFO(T))
B2.	$k \leftarrow 0$	K $\leftarrow$ T
B3.	$k < n$	RLINK(K) $\neq \Lambda$
B4.	$k \leftarrow k + 1$	K $\leftarrow$ RLINK(K)
B6.	NAME(S) $= P_k$	NAME(S) $=$ INFO(K)

6. A simple modification of Algorithm B makes it search only for complete references (if $k = n$ and `PARENT(S)` $\neq \Lambda$ in step B3', or if `NAME(S)` $\neq P_k$ in step B6', set P $\leftarrow$ `PREV(P)` and go to B2'). The idea is to run through this modified Algorithm B first; then, if Q is *still* Λ, to perform the unmodified algorithm.

7. MOVE MONTH OF DATE OF SALES TO MONTH OF DATE OF PURCHASES. MOVE DAY OF DATE OF SALES TO DAY OF DATE OF PURCHASES. MOVE YEAR OF DATE OF SALES TO YEAR OF

DATE OF PURCHASES. MOVE ITEM OF TRANSACTION OF SALES TO ITEM OF TRANSACTION OF PURCHASES. MOVE QUANTITY OF TRANSACTION OF SALES TO QUANTITY OF TRANSACTION OF PURCHASES. MOVE PRICE OF TRANSACTION OF SALES TO PRICE OF TRANSACTION OF PURCHASES. MOVE TAX OF TRANSACTION OF SALES TO TAX OF TRANSACTION OF PURCHASES.

8. If and only if α or β is an elementary item. (It may be of interest to note that the author failed to handle this case properly in his first draft of Algorithm C, and it actually made the algorithm more complicated.)

9. "MOVE CORRESPONDING α TO β", if neither α nor β is elementary, is equivalent to the set of statements "MOVE CORRESPONDING A OF α TO A OF β" taken over all names A common to groups α and β. (This is a more elegant way to state the definition than the more traditional and more cumbersome definition of "MOVE CORRESPONDING" given in the text.) We may verify that Algorithm C satisfies this definition, using an inductive proof that steps C2 through C5 will ultimately terminate with P = P0 and Q = Q0. Further details of the proof are filled in as we have done many times before in a "tree induction" (see, for example, the proof of Algorithm 2.3.1T).

10. (a) Set S1 $\leftarrow$ LINK(P_k). Then repeatedly set S1 $\leftarrow$ PREV(S1) zero or more times until either S1 = Λ (NAME(S) $\neq P_k$) or S1 = S (NAME(S) = P_k). (b) Set P1 $\leftarrow$ P and then set P1 $\leftarrow$ PREV(P1) zero or more times until PREV(P1) = Λ; do a similar operation with variables Q1 and Q; then test if P1 = Q1. Alternatively, if the Data Table entries are ordered so that PREV(P) < P for all P, a faster test can be made in an obvious way depending on whether P > Q or not, following the PREV links of the larger to see if the smaller is encountered.

11. A minuscule improvement in the speed of step C4 would be achieved by adding a new link field SIB1(P) $\equiv$ CHILD(PARENT(P)). More significantly, we could modify the CHILD and SIB links so that NAME(SIB(P)) > NAME(P); this would speed up the search in step C3 considerably because it would require only one pass over each family to find the matching members. This change would therefore remove the only "search" present in Algorithm C. Algorithms A and C are readily modified for this interpretation, and the reader may find it an interesting exercise. (However, if we consider the relative frequency of MOVE CORRESPONDING statements and the usual size of family groups, the resulting speedup will not be terribly significant in the translation of actual COBOL programs.)

12. Leave steps B1, B2, B3 unchanged; change the other steps thus:

B4″. Set $k \leftarrow k + 1$, R $\leftarrow$ LINK(P_k).

B5″. If R = Λ, set P $\leftarrow$ PREV(P) and go to B2″ (we haven't found a match). If R < S $\leq$ SCOPE(R), set S $\leftarrow$ R and go to B3″. Otherwise set R $\leftarrow$ PREV(R) and repeat step B5″. ∎

This algorithm does *not* adapt to the PL/I convention of exercise 6.

13. Use the same algorithm, minus the operations that set NAME, PARENT, CHILD, and SIB. Whenever removing the top stack entry in step A5, set SCOPE(P1) $\leftarrow$ Q − 1. When the input is exhausted in step A2, simply set L $\leftarrow$ 0 and continue, then terminate the algorithm if L = 0 in step A7.

14. The following algorithm, using an auxiliary stack, has steps numbered to show a direct correspondence with the text's algorithm.

C1′. Set P $\leftarrow$ P0, Q $\leftarrow$ Q0, and set the stack contents empty.

C2′. If SCOPE(P) = P or SCOPE(Q) = Q, output (P, Q) as one of the desired pairs and go to C5′. Otherwise put (P, Q) on the stack and set P ← P+1, Q ← Q+1.

C3′. Determine if P and Q point to entries with the same name (see exercise 10(b)). If so, go to C2′. If not, let (P1, Q1) be the entry at the top of the stack; if SCOPE(Q) < SCOPE(Q1), set Q ← SCOPE(Q) + 1 and repeat step C3′.

C4′. Let (P1, Q1) be the entry at the top of the stack. If SCOPE(P) < SCOPE(P1), set P ← SCOPE(P) +1, Q ← Q1+1, and go back to C3′. If SCOPE(P) = SCOPE(P1), set P ← P1, Q ← Q1 and remove the top entry of the stack.

C5′. If the stack is empty, the algorithm terminates. Otherwise go to C4′. ∎

SECTION 2.5

1. In such fortuitous circumstances, a stack-like operation may be used as follows: Let the memory pool area be locations 0 through M − 1, and let AVAIL point to the lowest free location. To reserve N words, report failure if AVAIL + N ≥ M, otherwise set AVAIL ← AVAIL + N. To free these N words, just set AVAIL ← AVAIL − N.

Similarly, cyclic queue-like operation is appropriate for a first-in-first-out discipline.

2. The amount of storage space for an item of length l is $k\lceil l/(k - b)\rceil$, which has the average value $kL/(k - b) + (1 - \alpha)k$, where α is assumed to be $1/2$, independent of k. This expression is a minimum (for real values of k) when $k = b + \sqrt{2bL}$. So choose k to be the integer just above or just below this value, whichever gives the lowest value of $kL/(k - b) + \frac{1}{2}k$. For example, if $b = 1$ and $L = 10$, we would choose $k \approx 1 + \sqrt{20} = 5$ or 6; both are equally good. For much greater detail about this problem, see *JACM* **12** (1965), 53–70.

4. rI1 ≡ Q, rI2 ≡ P.

A1	LDA	N	rA ← N.
	ENT2	AVAIL	P ← LOC(AVAIL).
A2A	ENT1	0,2	Q ← P.
A2	LD2	0,1(LINK)	P ← LINK(Q).
	J2N	OVERFLOW	If P = Λ, no room.
A3	CMPA	0,2(SIZE)	
	JG	A2A	Jump if N > SIZE(P).
A4	SUB	0,2(SIZE)	rA ← N − SIZE(P) ≡ K.
	JANZ	*+3	Jump if K ≠ 0.
	LDX	0,2(LINK)	
	STX	0,1(LINK)	LINK(Q) ← LINK(P).
	STA	0,2(SIZE)	SIZE(P) ← K.
	LD1	0,2(SIZE)	Optional ending,
	INC1	0,2	sets rI1 ← P + K. ∎

5. Probably not. The unavailable storage area just before location P will subsequently become available, and its length will be increased by the amount K; an increase of 99 would not be negligible.

6. The idea is to try to search in different parts of the AVAIL list each time. We can use a "roving pointer," called ROVER for example, which is treated as follows: In step A1, set Q ← ROVER. After step A4, set ROVER ← LINK(Q) if LINK(Q) ≠ Λ, otherwise set ROVER ← LOC(AVAIL). In step A2, when P = Λ the first time during a particular execution of Algorithm A, set Q ← LOC(AVAIL) and repeat step A2. When P = Λ the *second* time, the algorithm terminates unsuccessfully. In this way ROVER will tend to point to a random spot in the AVAIL list, and the sizes will be more balanced. At the beginning of the program, set ROVER ← LOC(AVAIL); it is *also* necessary to set ROVER to LOC(AVAIL) everywhere else in the program where the block whose address equals the current setting of ROVER is taken out of the AVAIL list. (Sometimes, however, it is useful to have small blocks at the beginning, as in the strict first-fit method; for example, we might want to keep a sequential stack at the high end of memory. In such cases we can reduce the search time by using trees as suggested in exercise 6.2.3–30.)

7. 2000, 1000 with requests of sizes 800, 1300. [An example where *worst-fit* succeeds, while best-fit fails, has been constructed by R. J. Weiland.]

8. In step A1″, also set M ← ∞, R ← Λ. In step A2″, if P = Λ go to A6″. In step A3″, go to A5″ instead of to A4″. Add new steps as follows:

A5″. [Better fit?] If M > SIZE(P), set R ← Q and M ← SIZE(P). Then set Q ← P and return to A2″.

A6″. [Any found?] If R = Λ, the algorithm terminates unsuccessfully. Otherwise set Q ← R, P ← LINK(Q), and go to A4″. ∎

9. Obviously if we are so lucky as to find SIZE(P) = N, we have a best fit and it is not necessary to search farther. (When there are only very few different block sizes, this occurs rather often.) If a "boundary tag" method like Algorithm C is being used, it is possible to maintain the AVAIL list in sorted order by size; so the length of search could be cut down to half the length of the list or less, on the average. But the best solution is to make the AVAIL list into a balanced tree structure as described in Section 6.2.3, if it is expected to be long.

10. Make the following changes:
Step B2, for "P > P0" read "P ≥ P0".
At the beginning of step B3, insert "If P0 + N > P and P ≠ Λ, set N ← max(N, P + SIZE(P) − P0), P ← LINK(P), and repeat step B3."
Step B4, for "Q + SIZE(Q) = P0", read "Q + SIZE(Q) ≥ P0"; and for "SIZE(Q) ← SIZE(Q) + N" read "SIZE(Q) ← max(SIZE(Q), P0 + N − Q)".

11. If P0 is greater than ROVER, we can set Q ← ROVER instead of Q ← LOC(AVAIL) in step B1. If there are n entries in the AVAIL list, the average number of iterations of step B2 is $(2n + 3)(n + 2)/(6n + 6) = \frac{1}{3}n + \frac{5}{6} + O\left(\frac{1}{n}\right)$. For example if $n = 2$ we get 9 equally probable situations, where P1 and P2 point to the two existing available blocks:

	P0 < P1	P1 < P0 < P2	P2 < P0
ROVER = P1	1	1	2
ROVER = P2	1	2	1
ROVER = LOC(AVAIL)	1	2	3

This chart shows the number of iterations needed in each case. The average is

$$\frac{1}{9}\left(\binom{2}{2} + \binom{3}{2} + \binom{4}{2} + \binom{3}{2} + \binom{2}{2}\right) = \frac{1}{9}\left(\binom{5}{3} + \binom{4}{3}\right) = \frac{14}{9}.$$

12. A1*. Set P ← ROVER, F ← 0.

A2*. If P = LOC(AVAIL) and F = 0, set P ← AVAIL, F ← 1, and repeat step A2*. If P = LOC(AVAIL) and F ≠ 0, the algorithm terminates unsuccessfully.

A3*. If SIZE(P) ≥ N, go to A4*; otherwise set P ← LINK(P) and return to A2*.

A4*. Set ROVER $\leftarrow$ LINK(P), K $\leftarrow$ SIZE(P) $-$ N. If K $< c$ (where c is a constant ≥ 2), set LINK(LINK(P + 1)) $\leftarrow$ ROVER, LINK(ROVER + 1) $\leftarrow$ LINK(P + 1), L $\leftarrow$ P; otherwise set L $\leftarrow$ P + K, SIZE(P) $\leftarrow$ SIZE(L $-$ 1) $\leftarrow$ K, TAG(L $-$ 1) $\leftarrow$ "$-$", SIZE(L) $\leftarrow$ N. Finally set TAG(L) $\leftarrow$ TAG(L + SIZE(L) $-$ 1) $\leftarrow$ "+".   ∎

13. rI1 $\equiv$ P, rX $\equiv$ F, rI2 $\equiv$ L.

```
LINK  EQU  4:5
SIZE  EQU  1:2
TSIZE EQU  0:2
TAG   EQU  0:0
A1    LDA  N              rA ← N.
      SLA  3              Shift into SIZE field.
      ENTX 0              F ← 0.
      LD1  ROVER          P ← ROVER.
      JMP  A2
A3    CMPA 0,1(SIZE)
      JLE  A4             Jump if N ≤ SIZE(P).
      LD1  0,1(LINK)      P ← LINK(P).
A2    ENT2 -AVAIL,1       rI2 ← P − LOC(AVAIL).
      J2NZ A3
      JXNZ OVERFLOW       Is F ≠ 0?
      ENTX 1              Set F ← 1.
      LD1  AVAIL(LINK)    P ← AVAIL.
      JMP  A2
A4    LD2  0,1(LINK)
      ST2  ROVER          ROVER ← LINK(P).
      LDA  0,1(SIZE)      rA ≡ K ← SIZE(P) − N.
      SUB  N
      CMPA =c=
      JGE  1F             Jump if K ≥ c.
      LD3  1,1(LINK)      rI3 ← LINK(P + 1).
      ST2  0,3(LINK)      LINK(rI3) ← ROVER.
      ST3  1,2(LINK)      LINK(ROVER + 1) ← rI3.
      ENT2 0,1            L ← P.
      LD3  0,1(SIZE)      rI3 ← SIZE(P).
      JMP  2F
1H    STA  0,1(SIZE)      SIZE(P) ← K.
      LD2  0,1(SIZE)
      INC2 0,1            L ← P + K.
      LDAN 0,1(SIZE)      rA ← −K.
      STA  -1,2(TSIZE)    SIZE(L − 1) ← K, TAG(L − 1) ← "−".
      LD3  N              rI3 ← N.
2H    ST3  0,2(TSIZE)     TAG(L) ← "+", also set SIZE(L) ← rI3.
      INC3 0,2
      STZ  -1,3(TAG)      TAG(L + SIZE(L) − 1) ← "+".     ∎
```

14. (a) This field is needed to locate the beginning of the block, in step C2. It could be replaced (perhaps to advantage) by a link to the first word of the block. See also exercise 19. (b) This field is needed because we sometimes need to reserve more than N words (for example if K = 1), and the amount reserved must be known when the block is subsequently freed.

15, 16. $rI1 \equiv P0$, $rI2 \equiv P1$, $rI3 \equiv F$, $rI4 \equiv B$, $rI6 \equiv -N$.

C1	LD1	P0	*C1.*
	LD2	0,1(SIZE)	
	ENN6	0,2	$N \leftarrow SIZE(P0)$.
	INC2	0,1	$P1 \leftarrow P0 + N$.
	LD5	0,2(TSIZE)	
	J5N	C4	To C4 if $TAG(P1) =$ "$-$".
C2	LD5	-1,1(TSIZE)	*C2.*
	J5N	C7	To C7 if $TAG(P0 - 1) =$ "$-$".
C3	LD3	AVAIL(LINK)	*C3.* Set $F \leftarrow AVAIL$.
	ENT4	AVAIL	$B \leftarrow LOC(AVAIL)$.
	JMP	C5	To C5.
C4	INC6	0,5	*C4.* $N \leftarrow N + SIZE(P1)$.
	LD3	0,2(LINK)	$F \leftarrow LINK(P1)$.
	LD4	1,2(LINK)	$B \leftarrow LINK(P1 + 1)$.
	CMP2	ROVER	(New code, because of the ROVER
	JNE	*+3	feature of exercise 12:
	ENTX	AVAIL	If $P1 = ROVER$,
	STX	ROVER	set $ROVER \leftarrow LOC(AVAIL)$.)
	DEC2	0,5	$P1 \leftarrow P1 + SIZE(P1)$.
	LD5	-1,1(TSIZE)	
	J5N	C6	To C6 if $TAG(P0 - 1) =$ "$-$".
C5	ST3	0,1(LINK)	*C5.* $LINK(P0) \leftarrow F$.
	ST4	1,1(LINK)	$LINK(P0 + 1) \leftarrow B$.
	ST1	1,3(LINK)	$LINK(F + 1) \leftarrow P0$.
	ST1	0,4(LINK)	$LINK(B) \leftarrow P0$.
	JMP	C8	To C8.
C6	ST3	0,4(LINK)	*C6.* $LINK(B) \leftarrow F$.
	ST4	1,3(LINK)	$LINK(F + 1) \leftarrow B$.
C7	INC6	0,5	*C7.* $N \leftarrow N + SIZE(P0 - 1)$.
	INC1	0,5	$P0 \leftarrow P0 - SIZE(P0 - 1)$.
C8	ST6	0,1(TSIZE)	*C8.* $SIZE(P0) \leftarrow N$, $TAG(P0) \leftarrow$ "$-$".
	ST6	-1,2(TSIZE)	$SIZE(P1 - 1) \leftarrow N$, $TAG(P1 - 1) \leftarrow$ "$-$". ▌

17. Both LINK fields equal to $LOC(AVAIL)$.

18. Algorithm A reserves the upper end of a large block. When storage is completely available, the first-fit method actually begins by reserving the high-order locations, but once these become available again they are not re-reserved since a fit is usually found already in the lower locations; thus the initial large block at the lower end of memory quickly disappears with first-fit. A large block rarely is the best fit, however, so the best-fit method leaves a large block at the beginning of memory.

19. Use the algorithm of exercise 12, except delete the references to $SIZE(L - 1)$, $TAG(L - 1)$, and $TAG(L + SIZE(L) - 1)$ from step A4*; also insert the following new step between steps A2* and A3*:

A2.5*. Set $P1 \leftarrow P + SIZE(P)$. If $TAG(P1) =$ "$+$", proceed to step A3. Otherwise set $P2 \leftarrow LINK(P1)$, $LINK(P2 + 1) \leftarrow LINK(P1 + 1)$, $LINK(LINK(P1 + 1)) \leftarrow P2$, $SIZE(P) \leftarrow SIZE(P) + SIZE(P1)$. If $ROVER = P1$, set $ROVER \leftarrow P2$. Repeat step A2.5*.

Clearly the situation of (2), (3), (4) can't occur here; the only real effect on storage allocation is that the search here will tend to be longer than in exercise 12, and sometimes K will be less than c although there is really another available block preceding this one that we do not know about.

(An alternative is to take the collapsing out of the inner loop A2.5*, and to do the collapsing only in step A4* before the final allocation or in the inner loop when the algorithm would otherwise have terminated unsuccessfully. This alternative requires a simulation study to see if it is an improvement or not.)

[This method, with a few refinements, has proved to be quite satisfactory in the implementations of TEX and METAFONT. See TEX: The Program (Addison–Wesley, 1986), §125.]

20. When a buddy is found to be available, during the collapsing loop, we want to remove that block from its AVAIL[k] list, but we do not know which links to update unless (i) we do a possibly long search, or (ii) the list is doubly linked.

21. If $n = 2^k\alpha$, where $1 \le \alpha \le 2$, a_n is $2^{2k+1}(\alpha - \frac{2}{3}) + \frac{1}{3}$, and b_n is $2^{2k-1}\alpha^2 + 2^{k-1}\alpha$. The ratio a_n/b_n for large n is essentially $4(\alpha - \frac{2}{3})/\alpha^2$, which takes its minimum value $\frac{4}{3}$ when $\alpha = 1$ and 2, and its maximum value $\frac{3}{2}$ when $\alpha = 1\frac{1}{3}$. So a_n/b_n approaches no limit; it oscillates between these two extremes. The averaging methods of Section 4.2.4 do, however, yield an average ratio of $4(\ln 2)^{-1}\int_1^2 (\alpha - \frac{2}{3})\, d\alpha/\alpha^3 = (\ln 2)^{-1} \approx 1.44$.

22. This idea requires a TAG field in several words of the 11-word block, not only in the first word. It is a workable idea, if those extra TAG bits can be spared, and it would appear to be especially suitable for use in computer hardware.

23. 011011110100; 011011100000.

24. This would introduce a bug in the program; we may get to step S1 when TAG(0) = 1, since S2 may return to S1. To make it work, add "TAG(L) ← 0" after "L ← P" in step S2. (It is easier to assume instead that TAG(2^m) = 0.)

25. The idea is absolutely correct. (Criticism need not be negative.) The list heads AVAIL[k] may be eliminated for $n < k \le m$; the algorithms of the text may be used if "m" is changed to "n" in steps R1, S1. The initial conditions (13) and (14) should be changed to indicate 2^{m-n} blocks of size 2^n instead of one block of size 2^m.

26. Using the binary representation of M, we can easily modify the initial conditions (13), (14) so that all memory locations are divided into blocks whose size is a power of two, with blocks in decreasing order of size. In Algorithm S, TAG(P) should be regarded as 0 whenever $P \ge M - 2^k$.

27. rI1 $\equiv k$, rI2 $\equiv j$, rI3 $\equiv j - k$, rI4 $\equiv$ L, LOC(AVAIL[j]) $=$ AVAIL $+ j$; assume that there is an auxiliary table TWO[j] $= 2^j$, stored in location TWO $+ j$, for $0 \le j \le m$. Assume further that "+" and "−" represent tags of 0 and 1, and that TAG(LOC(AVAIL[j])) $=$ "−"; but TAG(LOC(AVAIL[$m + 1$])) $=$ "+" is a sentinel.

```
00   KVAL  EQU  5:5
01   TAG   EQU  0:0
02   LINKF EQU  1:2
03   LINKB EQU  3:4
04   TLNKF EQU  0:2
05   R1    LD1  K              1   R1. Find block.
06         ENT2 0,1            1   j ← k.
07         ENT3 0              1
08         LD4  AVAIL,2(LINKF) 1
```

```
09   1H    ENT5  AVAIL,2          1 + R
10         DEC5  0,4              1 + R
11         J5NZ  R2               1 + R   Jump if AVAILF[j] ≠ LOC(AVAIL[j]).
12         INC2  1                  R     Increase j.
13         INC3  1                  R
14         LD4N  AVAIL,2(TLNKF)     R
15         J4NN  1B                 R     Is j ≤ m?
16         JMP   OVERFLOW
17   R2    LD5   0,4(LINKB)         1     R2. Remove from list.
18         ST5   AVAIL,2(LINKB)     1     AVAILB[j] ← LINKB(L).
19         ENTA  AVAIL,2            1
20         STA   0,5(LINKF)         1     LINKF(L) ← LOC(AVAIL[j]).
21         STZ   0,4(TAG)           1     TAG(L) ← 0.
22   R3    J3Z   DONE               1     R3. Split required?
23   R4    DEC3  1                  R     R4. Split.
24         DEC2  1                  R     Decrease j.
25         LD5   TWO,2              R     rI5 ≡ P.
26         INC5  0,4                R     P ← L + 2^j.
27         ENNA  AVAIL,2            R
28         STA   0,5(TLNKF)         R     TAG(P) ← 1, LINKF(P) ← LOC(AVAIL[j]).
29         STA   0,5(LINKB)         R     LINKB(P) ← LOC(AVAIL[j]).
30         ST5   AVAIL,2(LINKF)     R     AVAILF[j] ← P.
31         ST5   AVAIL,2(LINKB)     R     AVAILB[j] ← P.
32         ST2   0,5(KVAL)          R     KVAL(P) ← j.
33         J3P   R4                 R     Go to R3.
34   DONE  ...                              ▌
```

28. $rI1 \equiv k$, $rI5 \equiv P$, $rI4 \equiv L$; assume $TAG(2^m) = $ "+".

```
01   S1 LD4   L                    1       S1. Is buddy available?
02      LD1   K                    1
03   1H ENTA  0,4                 1 + S
04      XOR   TWO,1               1 + S    rA ← buddy_k(L).
05      STA   TEMP                1 + S
06      LD5   TEMP                1 + S    P ← rA.
07      LDA   0,5                 1 + S
08      JANN  S3                  1 + S    Jump if TAG(P) = 0.
09      CMP1  0,5(KVAL)           B + S
10      JNE   S3                  B + S    Jump if KVAL(P) ≠ k.
11   S2 LD2   0,5(LINKB)            S      S2. Combine with buddy.
12      LD3   0,5(LINKF)            S
13      ST3   0,2(LINKF)            S      LINKF(LINKB(P)) ← LINKF(P).
14      ST2   0,3(LINKB)            S      LINKB(LINKF(P)) ← LINKB(P).
15      INC1  1                     S      Increase k.
16      CMP4  TEMP                  S
17      JL    1B                    S
18      ENT4  0,5                   A      If L > P, set L ← P.
19      JMP   1B                    A
20   S3 LD2   AVAIL,1(LINKF)        1      S3. Put on list.
21      ENNA  AVAIL,1               1
22      STA   0,4(0:4)              1      TAG(L) ← 1, LINKB(L) ← LOC(AVAIL[k]).
```

23	ST2	0,4(LINKF)	1	LINKF(L) ← AVAILF[k].
24	ST1	0,4(KVAL)	1	KVAL(L) ← k.
25	ST4	0,2(LINKB)	1	LINKB(AVAILF[k]) ← L.
26	ST4	AVAIL,1(LINKF)	1	AVAILF[k] ← L. ∎

29. Yes, but only at the expense of some searching, or (better) an additional table of TAG bits packed somehow. (It is tempting to suggest that buddies not be joined together during Algorithm S, but only in Algorithm R if there is no block large enough to meet the request; but that would probably lead to a badly fragmented memory.)

31. See David L. Russell, *SICOMP* **6** (1977), 607–621.

32. Steven Crain points out that the method always frees all blocks and starts afresh before 16667 units of time have elapsed; hence the stated limit certainly exists. *Proof:* Let $u_n = n + t_n$, so that $g_n = \lfloor \frac{5}{4} \min(10000, f(u_{n-1} - n), f(u_{n-2} - n), \ldots, f(u_0 - n)) \rfloor$. Let $x_0 = 0$ and $x_1 = u_0$, and $x_{k+1} = \max(u_0, \ldots, u_{x_k-1})$ for $k \geq 1$. If $x_k > x_{k-1}$ then

$$u_n \leq n + \frac{5}{4} f(x_k - n) = \frac{5}{4} x_k - \frac{1}{4} n \leq \frac{5}{4} x_k - \frac{1}{4} x_{k-1} \qquad \text{for } x_{k-1} \leq n < x_k;$$

therefore $x_{k+1} - x_k \leq \frac{1}{4}(x_k - x_{k-1})$, and we must have $x_k = x_{k-1}$ before reaching time $12500 + \lfloor 12500/4 \rfloor + \lfloor 12500/4^2 \rfloor + \cdots$.

33. G1. [Clear LINKs.] Set P ← 1, and repeat the operation LINK(P) ← Λ, P ← P + SIZE(P) until P = AVAIL. (This merely sets the LINK field in the first word of each node to Λ; we may assume in most cases that this step is unnecessary, since LINK(P) is set to Λ in step G9 below and it can be set to Λ by the storage allocator.)

G2. [Initialize marking phase.] Set TOP ← USE, LINK(TOP) ← AVAIL, LINK(AVAIL) ← Λ. (TOP points to the top of a stack as in Algorithm 2.3.5D.)

G3. [Pop up stack.] Set P ← TOP, TOP ← LINK(TOP). If TOP = Λ, go to G5.

G4. [Put new links on stack.] For $1 \leq k \leq$ T(P), do the following operations: Set Q ← LINK(P + k); then if Q ≠ Λ and LINK(Q) = Λ, set LINK(Q) ← TOP, TOP ← Q. Then go back to G3.

G5. [Initialize next phase.] (Now P = AVAIL, and the marking phase has been completed so that the first word of each accessible node has a nonnull LINK. Our next goal is to combine adjacent inaccessible nodes, for speed in later steps, and to assign new addresses to the accessible nodes.) Set Q ← 1, LINK(AVAIL) ← Q, SIZE(AVAIL) ← 0, P ← 1. (Location AVAIL is being used as a sentinel to signify the end of a loop in subsequent phases.)

G6. [Assign new addresses.] If LINK(P) = Λ, go to G7. Otherwise if SIZE(P) = 0, go to G8. Otherwise set LINK(P) ← Q, Q ← Q + SIZE(P), P ← P + SIZE(P), and repeat this step.

G7. [Collapse available areas.] If LINK(P + SIZE(P)) = Λ, increase SIZE(P) by SIZE(P + SIZE(P)) and repeat this step. Otherwise set P ← P + SIZE(P) and return to G6.

G8. [Translate all links.] (Now the LINK field in the first word of each accessible node contains the address to which the node will be moved.) Set USE ← LINK(USE), and AVAIL ← Q. Then set P ← 1, and repeat the following operation until SIZE(P) = 0: If LINK(P) ≠ Λ, set LINK(Q) ← LINK(LINK(Q)) for all Q such that P < Q ≤ P + T(P) and LINK(Q) ≠ Λ; then regardless of the value of LINK(P), set P ← P + SIZE(P).

G9. [Move.] Set P ← 1, and repeat the following operation until SIZE(P) = 0: Set Q ← LINK(P), and if Q ≠ Λ set LINK(P) ← Λ and NODE(Q) ← NODE(P); then whether Q = Λ or not, set P ← P + SIZE(P). (The operation NODE(Q) ← NODE(P) implies the movement of SIZE(P) words; we always have Q ≤ P, so it is safe to move the words in order from smallest location to largest.) ∎

[This method is called the "LISP 2 garbage collector." An interesting alternative, which does not require the LINK field at the beginning of a node, can be based on the idea of linking together all pointers that point to each node — see Lars-Erik Thorelli, *BIT* **16** (1976), 426–441; R. B. K. Dewar and A. P. McCann, *Software Practice & Exp.* **7** (1977), 95–113; F. Lockwood Morris, *CACM* **21** (1978), 662–665, **22** (1979), 571; H. B. M. Jonkers, *Inf. Proc. Letters* **9** (1979), 26–30; J. J. Martin, *CACM* **25** (1982), 571–581; F. Lockwood Morris, *Inf. Proc. Letters* **15** (1982), 139–142, **16** (1983), 215. Other methods have been published by B. K. Haddon and W. M. Waite, *Comp. J.* **10** (1967), 162–165; B. Wegbreit, *Comp. J.* **15** (1972), 204–208; D. A. Zave, *Inf. Proc. Letters* **3** (1975), 167–169. J. Cohen and A. Nicolau have analyzed four of these approaches in *ACM Trans. Prog. Languages and Systems* **5** (1983), 532–553.]

34. Let TOP ≡ rI1, Q ≡ rI2, P ≡ rI3, k ≡ rI4, SIZE(P) ≡ rI5. Assume further that Λ = 0, and LINK(0) ≠ 0 to simplify step G4. Step G1 is omitted.

```
01  LINK EQU  4:5
02  INFO EQU  0:3
03  SIZE EQU  1:2
04  T    EQU  3:3
05  G2   LD1  USE            1        G2. Initialize marking phase. TOP ← USE.
06       LD2  AVAIL          1
07       ST2  0,1(LINK)      1        LINK(TOP) ← AVAIL.
08       STZ  0,2(LINK)      1        LINK(AVAIL) ← Λ.
09  G3   ENT3 0,1          a + 1      G3. Pop up stack. P ← TOP.
10       LD1  0,1(LINK)    a + 1      TOP ← LINK(TOP).
11       J1Z  G5           a + 1      To G5 if TOP = Λ.
12  G4   LD4  0,3(T)           a      G4. Put new links on stack. k ← T(P).
13  1H   J4Z  G3           a + b      k = 0?
14       INC3 1                b      P ← P + 1.
15       DEC4 1                b      k ← k − 1.
16       LD2  0,3(LINK)       b      Q ← LINK(P).
17       LDA  0,2(LINK)       b
18       JANZ 1B               b      Jump if LINK(Q) ≠ Λ.
19       ST1  0,2(LINK)    a − 1      Otherwise set LINK(Q) ← TOP,
20       ENT1 0,2          a − 1        TOP ← Q.
21       JMP  1B           a − 1
22  G5   ENT2 1                1      G5. Initialize next phase. Q ← 1.
23       ST2  0,3              1      LINK(AVAIL) ← 1, SIZE(AVAIL) ← 0.
24       ENT3 1                1      P ← 1.
25       JMP  G6               1
26  1H   ST2  0,3(LINK)        a      LINK(P) ← Q.
27       INC2 0,5              a      Q ← Q + SIZE(P).
28       INC3 0,5              a      P ← P + SIZE(P).
29  G6   LDA  0,3(LINK)    a + 1      G6. Assign new addresses.
30  G6A  LD5  0,3(SIZE)  a + c + 1
```

31		JAZ	G7	$a+c+1$	Jump if LINK(P) $= \Lambda$.
32		J5NZ	1B	$a+1$	Jump if SIZE(P) $\neq 0$.
33	G8	LD1	USE	1	*G8. Translate all links.*
34		LDA	0,1(LINK)	1	
35		STA	USE	1	USE $\leftarrow$ LINK(USE).
36		ST2	AVAIL	1	AVAIL $\leftarrow$ Q.
37		ENT3	1	1	P $\leftarrow$ 1.
38		JMP	G8P	1	
39	1H	LD6	0,6(SIZE)	d	
40		INC5	0,6	d	rI5 $\leftarrow$ rI5 $+$ SIZE(P $+$ SIZE(P)).
41	G7	ENT6	0,3	$c+d$	*G7. Collapse available areas.*
42		INC6	0,5	$c+d$	rI6 $\leftarrow$ P $+$ SIZE(P).
43		LDA	0,6(LINK)	$c+d$	
44		JAZ	1B	$c+d$	Jump if LINK(rI6) $\equiv \Lambda$.
45		ST5	0,3(SIZE)	c	SIZE(P) $\leftarrow$ rI5.
46		INC3	0,5	c	P $\leftarrow$ P $+$ SIZE(P).
47		JMP	G6A	c	
48	2H	DEC4	1	b	$k \leftarrow k - 1$.
49		INC2	1	b	$Q \leftarrow Q + 1$.
50		LD6	0,2(LINK)	b	
51		LDA	0,6(LINK)	b	
52		STA	0,2(LINK)	b	LINK(Q) $\leftarrow$ LINK(LINK(Q)).
53	1H	J4NZ	2B	$a+b$	Jump if $k \neq 0$.
54	3H	INC3	0,5	$a+c$	P $\leftarrow$ P $+$ SIZE(P).
55	G8P	LDA	0,3(LINK)	$1+a+c$	
56		LD5	0,3(SIZE)	$1+a+c$	
57		JAZ	3B	$1+a+c$	Is LINK(P) $= \Lambda$?
58		LD4	0,3(T)	$1+a$	$k \leftarrow$ T(P).
59		ENT2	0,3	$1+a$	Q $\leftarrow$ P.
60		J5NZ	1B	$1+a$	Jump unless SIZE(P) $= 0$.
61	G9	ENT3	1	1	*G9. Move.* P $\leftarrow$ 1.
62		ENT1	1	1	Set rI1 for MOVE instructions.
63		JMP	G9P	1	
64	1H	STZ	0,3(LINK)	a	LINK(P) $\leftarrow \Lambda$.
65		ST5	*+1(4:4)	a	
66		MOVE	0,3(*)	a	NODE(rI1) $\leftarrow$ NODE(P), rI1 $\leftarrow$ rI1 $+$ SIZE(P).
67	3H	INC3	0,5	$a+c$	P $\leftarrow$ P $+$ SIZE(P).
68	G9P	LDA	0,3(LINK)	$1+a+c$	
69		LD5	0,3(SIZE)	$1+a+c$	
70		JAZ	3B	$1+a+c$	Jump if LINK(P) $= \Lambda$.
71		J5NZ	1B	$1+a$	Jump unless SIZE(P) $= 0$. ∎

In line 66 we are assuming that the size of each node is sufficiently small that it can be moved with a single MOVE instruction; this seems a fair assumption for most cases when this kind of garbage collection is applicable.

The total running time for this program is $(44a+17b+2w+25c+8d+47)u$, where a is the number of accessible nodes, b is the number of link fields therein, c is the number of inaccessible nodes that are *not* preceded by an inaccessible node, d is the number of inaccessible nodes that *are* preceded by an inaccessible node, and w is the total number of words in the accessible nodes. If the memory contains n nodes, with ρn of them inaccessible, then we may estimate $a = (1 - \rho)n$, $c = (1 - \rho)\rho n$, $d = \rho^2 n$. Example: five-word nodes (on the average), with two link fields per node (on the average), and a memory of 1000 nodes. Then when $\rho = 0.2$, it takes $374u$ per available node recovered; when $\rho = 0.5$, it takes $104u$; and when $\rho = 0.8$, it takes only $33u$.

36. A single customer will be able to sit in one of the sixteen seats 1, 3, 4, 6, ..., 23. If a pair enters, there must be room for them; otherwise there are at least two people in seats $(1, 2, 3)$, at least two in $(4, 5, 6)$, ..., at least two in $(19, 20, 21)$, and at least one in 22 or 23, so at least fifteen people are already seated.

37. First sixteen single males enter, and she seats them. There are 17 gaps of empty seats between the occupied seats, counting one gap at each end, with a gap of length zero assumed between adjacent occupied seats. The total number of empty seats, namely the sum of all seventeen gaps, is 6. Suppose x of the gaps are of odd length; then $6 - x$ spaces are available to seat pairs. (Note that $6 - x$ is even and ≥ 0.) Now each of the customers 1, 3, 5, 7, 9, 11, 13, 15, from left to right, who has an even gap on both sides, finishes his lunch and walks out. Each odd gap prevents at most one of these eight diners from leaving, hence at least $8 - x$ people leave. There *still* are only $6 - x$ spaces available to seat pairs. But now $(8 - x)/2$ pairs enter.

38. The arguments generalize readily; $N(n, 2) = \lfloor (3n - 1)/2 \rfloor$ for $n \geq 1$. [When the hostess uses a first-fit strategy instead of an optimal one, Robson has proved that the necessary and sufficient number of seats is $\lfloor (5n - 2)/3 \rfloor$.]

39. Divide memory into three independent regions of sizes $N(n_1, m)$, $N(n_2, m)$, and $N(2m - 2, m)$. To process a request for space, put each block into the first region for which the stated capacity is not exceeded, using the relevant optimum strategy for that region. This cannot fail, for if we were unable to fill a request for x locations we must have at least $(n_1 - x + 1) + (n_2 - x + 1) + (2m - x - 1) > n_1 + n_2 - x$ locations already occupied.

  Now if $f(n) = N(n, m) + N(2m - 2, m)$, we have the subadditive law $f(n_1 + n_2) \leq f(n_1) + f(n_2)$. Hence $\lim f(n)/n$ exists. (*Proof:* $f(a + bc) \leq f(a) + bf(c)$; hence $\limsup_{n \to \infty} f(n)/n = \max_{0 \leq a < c} \limsup_{b \to \infty} f(a + bc)/(a + bc) \leq f(c)/c$ for all c; hence $\limsup_{n \to \infty} f(n)/n \leq \liminf_{n \to \infty} f(n)/n$.) Therefore $\lim N(n, m)/n$ exists.

  [From exercise 38 we know that $N(2) = \frac{3}{2}$. The value $N(m)$ is not known for any $m > 2$. It is not difficult to show that the multiplicative factor for just two block sizes, 1 and b, is $2 - 1/b$; hence $N(3) \geq 1\frac{2}{3}$. Robson's methods imply that $N(3) \leq 1\frac{11}{12}$, and $2 \leq N(4) \leq 2\frac{1}{6}$.]

40. Robson has proved that $N(2^r) \leq 1 + r$, by using the following strategy: Allocate to each block of size k, where $2^m \leq k < 2^{m+1}$, the first available block of k locations starting at a multiple of 2^m.

  Let $N(\{b_1, b_2, \ldots, b_n\})$ denote the multiplicative factor when all block sizes are constrained to lie in the set $\{b_1, b_2, \ldots, b_n\}$, so that $N(n) = N(\{1, 2, \ldots, n\})$. Robson and S. Krogdahl have discovered that $N(\{b_1, b_2, \ldots, b_n\}) = n - (b_1/b_2 + \cdots + b_{n-1}/b_n)$ whenever b_i is a multiple of b_{i-1} for $1 < i \leq n$; indeed, Robson has established the *exact* formula $N(2^r m, \{1, 2, 4, \ldots, 2^r\}) = 2^r m(1 + \frac{1}{2}r) - 2^r + 1$. Thus in particular, $N(n) \geq 1 + \frac{1}{2}\lfloor \lg n \rfloor$. He also has derived the upper bound $N(n) \leq 1.1825 \ln n + O(1)$, and he conjectures tentatively that $N(n) = H_n$. This conjecture would follow if $N(\{b_1, b_2, \ldots, b_n\})$ were equal to $n - (b_1/b_2 + \cdots + b_{n-1}/b_n)$ in general, but this is unfortunately not the case since Robson has proved that $N(\{3, 4\}) \geq 1\frac{4}{15}$. (See *Inf. Proc. Letters* **2** (1973), 96–99; *JACM* **21** (1974), 491–499.)

41. Consider maintaining the blocks of size 2^k: The requests for sizes 1, 2, 4, ..., 2^{k-1} will periodically call for a new block of size 2^k to be split, or a block of that size will be returned. We can prove by induction on k that the total storage consumed by such split blocks never exceeds kn; for after every request to split a block of size 2^{k+1}, we are using at most kn locations in split 2^k-blocks and at most n locations in unsplit ones.

This argument can be strengthened to show that $a_r n$ cells suffice, where $a_0 = 1$ and $a_k = 1 + a_{k-1}(1 - 2^{-k})$; we have

$k =$	0	1	2	3	4	5
$a_k =$	1	$1\frac{1}{2}$	$2\frac{1}{8}$	$2\frac{55}{64}$	$3\frac{697}{1024}$	$4\frac{18535}{32768}$

Conversely for $r \le 5$ it can be shown that a buddy system sometimes *requires* as many as $a_r n$ cells, if the mechanism of steps R1 and R2 is modified to choose the worst possible available 2^j-block to split instead of the first such block.

Robson's proof that $N(2^r) \le 1 + r$ (see exercise 40) is easily modified to show that such a "leftmost" strategy will never need more than $(1 + \frac{1}{2}r)n$ cells to allocate space for blocks of sizes 1, 2, 4, ..., 2^r, since blocks of size 2^k will never be placed in locations $\ge (1 + \frac{1}{2}k)n$. Although his algorithm seems very much like the buddy system, it turns out that no buddy system will be this good, even if we modify steps R1 and R2 to choose the best possible available 2^j-block to split. For example, consider the following sequence of "snapshots" of the memory, for $n = 16$ and $r = 3$:

```
11111111   11111111   00000000   00000000
10101010   10101010   2-2-2-2-   00000000
11110000   11110000   2-110000   00000000
11111111   11110000   11110000   00000000
10101010   10102-2-   10102-2-   00000000
10001000   10002-00   10002-00   4---4---
10000000   10000000   10000000   4---0000
```

Here 0 denotes an available location and k denotes the beginning of a k-block. In a similar way there is a sequence of operations, whenever n is a multiple of 16, that forces $\frac{3}{16}n$ blocks of size 8 to be $\frac{1}{8}$ full, and another $\frac{1}{16}n$ to be $\frac{1}{2}$ full. If n is a multiple of 128, a subsequent request for $\frac{9}{128}n$ blocks of size 8 will require more than $2.5n$ memory cells. (The buddy system allows unwanted 1s to creep into $\frac{3}{16}n$ of the 8-blocks, since there are no other available 2s to be split at a crucial time; the "leftmost" algorithm keeps all 1s confined.)

42. We can assume that $m \ge 6$. The main idea is to establish the occupancy pattern $R_{m-2}(F_{m-3}R_1)^k$ at the beginning of the memory, for $k = 0, 1, \ldots$, where R_j and F_j denote reserved and free blocks of size j. The transition from k to $k+1$ begins with

$$R_{m-2}(F_{m-3}R_1)^k \to R_{m-2}(F_{m-3}R_1)^k R_{m-2}R_{m-2}$$
$$\to R_{m-2}(F_{m-3}R_1)^{k-1}F_{2m-4}R_{m-2}$$
$$\to R_{m-2}(F_{m-3}R_1)^{k-1}R_m R_{m-5}R_1 R_{m-2}$$
$$\to R_{m-2}(F_{m-3}R_1)^{k-1}F_m R_{m-5}R_1 ;$$

then the commutation sequence $F_{m-3}R_1 F_m R_{m-5}R_1 \to F_{m-3}R_1 R_{m-2}R_2 R_{m-5}R_1 \to F_{2m-4}R_2 R_{m-5}R_1 \to R_m R_{m-5}R_1 R_2 R_{m-5}R_1 \to F_m R_{m-5}R_1 F_{m-3}R_1$ is used k times until we get $F_m R_{m-5}R_1(F_{m-3}R_1)^k \to F_{2m-5}R_1(F_{m-3}R_1)^k \to R_{m-2}(F_{m-3}R_1)^{k+1}$. Finally, when k gets large enough, there is an endgame that forces overflow unless the memory size is at least $(n - 4m + 11)(m - 2)$; details appear in *Comp. J.* **20** (1977),

242–244. [Notice that the worst conceivable worst case, which begins with the pattern $F_{m-1}R_1F_{m-1}R_1F_{m-1}R_1\ldots$, is only slightly worse than this; the next-fit strategy of exercise 6 can produce this pessimal pattern.]

43. We will show that if D_1, D_2, $\ldots$ is any sequence of numbers such that $D_1/m + D_2/(m+1) + \cdots + D_m/(2m-1) \geq 1$ for all $m \geq 1$, and if $C_m = D_1/1 + D_2/2 + \cdots + D_m/m$, then $N_{\mathrm{FF}}(n,m) \leq nC_m$. In particular, since

$$\frac{1}{m} + \frac{1}{m+1} + \cdots + \frac{1}{2m+1} = 1 - \frac{1}{2} + \cdots + \frac{1}{2m-3} - \frac{1}{2m-2} + \frac{1}{2m-1} > \ln 2,$$

the constant sequence $D_m = 1/\ln 2$ satisfies the necessary conditions. The proof is by induction on m. Let $N_j = nC_j$ for $j \geq 1$, and suppose that some request for a block of size m cannot be allocated in the leftmost N_m cells of memory. Then $m > 1$. For $0 \leq j < m$, we let N'_j denote the rightmost position allocated to blocks of sizes $\leq j$, or 0 if all reserved blocks are larger than j; by induction we have $N'_j \leq N_j$. Furthermore we let N'_m be the rightmost occupied position $\leq N_m$, so that $N'_m \geq N_m - m + 1$. Then the interval $(N'_{j-1} . . N'_j]$ contains at least $\lceil j(N'_j - N'_{j-1})/(m+j-1) \rceil$ occupied cells, since its free blocks are of size $< m$ and its reserved blocks are of size $\geq j$. It follows that $n - m \geq$ number of occupied cells $\geq \sum_{j=1}^{m} j(N'_j - N'_{j-1})/(m+j-1) = mN'_m/(2m-1) - (m-1)\sum_{j=1}^{m-1} N'_j/(m+j)(m+j-1) > mN_m/(2m-1) - m - (m-1)\sum_{j=1}^{m-1} N_j(1/(m+j-1) - 1/(m+j)) = \sum_{j=1}^{m} nD_j/(m+j-1) - m \geq n - m$, a contradiction.

[This proof establishes slightly more than was asked. If we define the D's by $D_1/m + \cdots + D_m/(2m-1) = 1$, then the sequence C_1, C_2, $\ldots$ is 1, $\frac{7}{4}$, $\frac{161}{72}$, $\frac{7483}{2880}$, $\ldots$; and the result can be improved further, even in the case $m = 2$, as in exercise 38.]

44. $\lceil F^{-1}(1/N) \rceil$, $\lceil F^{-1}(2/N) \rceil$, $\ldots$, $\lceil F^{-1}(N/N) \rceil$.

TABLES OF NUMERICAL QUANTITIES

Table 1

QUANTITIES THAT ARE FREQUENTLY USED IN STANDARD SUBROUTINES
AND IN ANALYSIS OF COMPUTER PROGRAMS (40 DECIMAL PLACES)

$$\sqrt{2} = 1.41421\ 35623\ 73095\ 04880\ 16887\ 24209\ 69807\ 85697-$$
$$\sqrt{3} = 1.73205\ 08075\ 68877\ 29352\ 74463\ 41505\ 87236\ 69428+$$
$$\sqrt{5} = 2.23606\ 79774\ 99789\ 69640\ 91736\ 68731\ 27623\ 54406+$$
$$\sqrt{10} = 3.16227\ 76601\ 68379\ 33199\ 88935\ 44432\ 71853\ 37196-$$
$$\sqrt[3]{2} = 1.25992\ 10498\ 94873\ 16476\ 72106\ 07278\ 22835\ 05703-$$
$$\sqrt[3]{3} = 1.44224\ 95703\ 07408\ 38232\ 16383\ 10780\ 10958\ 83919-$$
$$\sqrt[4]{2} = 1.18920\ 71150\ 02721\ 06671\ 74999\ 70560\ 47591\ 52930-$$
$$\ln 2 = 0.69314\ 71805\ 59945\ 30941\ 72321\ 21458\ 17656\ 80755+$$
$$\ln 3 = 1.09861\ 22886\ 68109\ 69139\ 52452\ 36922\ 52570\ 46475-$$
$$\ln 10 = 2.30258\ 50929\ 94045\ 68401\ 79914\ 54684\ 36420\ 76011+$$
$$1/\ln 2 = 1.44269\ 50408\ 88963\ 40735\ 99246\ 81001\ 89213\ 74266+$$
$$1/\ln 10 = 0.43429\ 44819\ 03251\ 82765\ 11289\ 18916\ 60508\ 22944-$$
$$\pi = 3.14159\ 26535\ 89793\ 23846\ 26433\ 83279\ 50288\ 41972-$$
$$1° = \pi/180 = 0.01745\ 32925\ 19943\ 29576\ 92369\ 07684\ 88612\ 71344+$$
$$1/\pi = 0.31830\ 98861\ 83790\ 67153\ 77675\ 26745\ 02872\ 40689+$$
$$\pi^2 = 9.86960\ 44010\ 89358\ 61883\ 44909\ 99876\ 15113\ 53137-$$
$$\sqrt{\pi} = \Gamma(1/2) = 1.77245\ 38509\ 05516\ 02729\ 81674\ 83341\ 14518\ 27975+$$
$$\Gamma(1/3) = 2.67893\ 85347\ 07747\ 63365\ 56929\ 40974\ 67764\ 41287-$$
$$\Gamma(2/3) = 1.35411\ 79394\ 26400\ 41694\ 52880\ 28154\ 51378\ 55193+$$
$$e = 2.71828\ 18284\ 59045\ 23536\ 02874\ 71352\ 66249\ 77572+$$
$$1/e = 0.36787\ 94411\ 71442\ 32159\ 55237\ 70161\ 46086\ 74458+$$
$$e^2 = 7.38905\ 60989\ 30650\ 22723\ 04274\ 60575\ 00781\ 31803+$$
$$\gamma = 0.57721\ 56649\ 01532\ 86060\ 65120\ 90082\ 40243\ 10422-$$
$$\ln \pi = 1.14472\ 98858\ 49400\ 17414\ 34273\ 51353\ 05871\ 16473-$$
$$\phi = 1.61803\ 39887\ 49894\ 84820\ 45868\ 34365\ 63811\ 77203+$$
$$e^\gamma = 1.78107\ 24179\ 90197\ 98523\ 65041\ 03107\ 17954\ 91696+$$
$$e^{\pi/4} = 2.19328\ 00507\ 38015\ 45655\ 97696\ 59278\ 73822\ 34616+$$
$$\sin 1 = 0.84147\ 09848\ 07896\ 50665\ 25023\ 21630\ 29899\ 96226-$$
$$\cos 1 = 0.54030\ 23058\ 68139\ 71740\ 09366\ 07442\ 97660\ 37323+$$
$$-\zeta'(2) = 0.93754\ 82543\ 15843\ 75370\ 25740\ 94567\ 86497\ 78979-$$
$$\zeta(3) = 1.20205\ 69031\ 59594\ 28539\ 97381\ 61511\ 44999\ 07650-$$
$$\ln \phi = 0.48121\ 18250\ 59603\ 44749\ 77589\ 13424\ 36842\ 31352-$$
$$1/\ln \phi = 2.07808\ 69212\ 35027\ 53760\ 13226\ 06117\ 79576\ 77422-$$
$$-\ln \ln 2 = 0.36651\ 29205\ 81664\ 32701\ 24391\ 58232\ 66946\ 94543-$$

Table 2

QUANTITIES THAT ARE FREQUENTLY USED IN STANDARD SUBROUTINES
AND IN ANALYSIS OF COMPUTER PROGRAMS (45 OCTAL PLACES)

The names at the left of the "=" signs are given in decimal notation.

$0.1 =$	$0.06314\ 63146\ 31463\ 14631\ 46314\ 63146\ 31463\ 14631\ 46315-$
$0.01 =$	$0.00507\ 53412\ 17270\ 24365\ 60507\ 53412\ 17270\ 24365\ 60510-$
$0.001 =$	$0.00040\ 61115\ 64570\ 65176\ 76355\ 44264\ 16254\ 02030\ 44672+$
$0.0001 =$	$0.00003\ 21556\ 13530\ 70414\ 54512\ 75170\ 33021\ 15002\ 35223-$
$0.00001 =$	$0.00000\ 24761\ 32610\ 70664\ 36041\ 06077\ 17401\ 56063\ 34417-$
$0.000001 =$	$0.00000\ 02061\ 57364\ 05536\ 66151\ 55323\ 07746\ 44470\ 26033+$
$0.0000001 =$	$0.00000\ 00153\ 27745\ 15274\ 53644\ 12741\ 72312\ 20354\ 02151+$
$0.00000001 =$	$0.00000\ 00012\ 57143\ 56106\ 04303\ 47374\ 77341\ 01512\ 63327+$
$0.000000001 =$	$0.00000\ 00001\ 04560\ 27640\ 46655\ 12262\ 71426\ 40124\ 21742+$
$0.0000000001 =$	$0.00000\ 00000\ 06676\ 33766\ 35367\ 55653\ 37265\ 34642\ 01627-$
$\sqrt{2} =$	$1.32404\ 74631\ 77167\ 46220\ 42627\ 66115\ 46725\ 12575\ 17435+$
$\sqrt{3} =$	$1.56663\ 65641\ 30231\ 25163\ 54453\ 50265\ 60361\ 34073\ 42223-$
$\sqrt{5} =$	$2.17067\ 36334\ 57722\ 47602\ 57471\ 63003\ 00563\ 55620\ 32021-$
$\sqrt{10} =$	$3.12305\ 40726\ 64555\ 22444\ 02242\ 57101\ 41466\ 33775\ 22532+$
$\sqrt[3]{2} =$	$1.20505\ 05746\ 15345\ 05342\ 10756\ 65334\ 25574\ 22415\ 03024+$
$\sqrt[3]{3} =$	$1.34233\ 50444\ 22175\ 73134\ 67363\ 76133\ 05334\ 31147\ 60121-$
$\sqrt[4]{2} =$	$1.14067\ 74050\ 61556\ 12455\ 72152\ 64430\ 60271\ 02755\ 73136+$
$\ln 2 =$	$0.54271\ 02775\ 75071\ 73632\ 57117\ 07316\ 30007\ 71366\ 53640+$
$\ln 3 =$	$1.06237\ 24752\ 55006\ 05227\ 32440\ 63065\ 25012\ 35574\ 55337+$
$\ln 10 =$	$2.23273\ 06735\ 52524\ 25405\ 56512\ 66542\ 56026\ 46050\ 50705+$
$1/\ln 2 =$	$1.34252\ 16624\ 53405\ 77027\ 35750\ 37766\ 40644\ 35175\ 04353+$
$1/\ln 10 =$	$0.33626\ 75425\ 11562\ 41614\ 52325\ 33525\ 27655\ 14756\ 06220-$
$\pi =$	$3.11037\ 55242\ 10264\ 30215\ 14230\ 63050\ 56006\ 70163\ 21122+$
$1° = \pi/180 =$	$0.01073\ 72152\ 11224\ 72344\ 25603\ 54276\ 63351\ 22056\ 11544+$
$1/\pi =$	$0.24276\ 30155\ 62344\ 20251\ 23760\ 47257\ 50765\ 15156\ 70067-$
$\pi^2 =$	$11.67517\ 14467\ 62135\ 71322\ 25561\ 15466\ 30021\ 40654\ 34103-$
$\sqrt{\pi} = \Gamma(1/2) =$	$1.61337\ 61106\ 64736\ 65247\ 47035\ 40510\ 15273\ 34470\ 17762-$
$\Gamma(1/3) =$	$2.53347\ 35234\ 51013\ 61316\ 73106\ 47644\ 54653\ 00106\ 66046-$
$\Gamma(2/3) =$	$1.26523\ 57112\ 14154\ 74312\ 54572\ 37655\ 60126\ 23231\ 02452+$
$e =$	$2.55760\ 52130\ 50535\ 51246\ 52773\ 42542\ 00471\ 72363\ 61661+$
$1/e =$	$0.27426\ 53066\ 13167\ 46761\ 52726\ 75436\ 02440\ 52371\ 03355+$
$e^2 =$	$7.30714\ 45615\ 23355\ 33460\ 63507\ 35040\ 32664\ 25356\ 50217+$
$\gamma =$	$0.44742\ 14770\ 67666\ 06172\ 23215\ 74376\ 01002\ 51313\ 25521-$
$\ln \pi =$	$1.11206\ 40443\ 47503\ 36413\ 65374\ 52661\ 52410\ 37511\ 46057+$
$\phi =$	$1.47433\ 57156\ 27751\ 23701\ 27634\ 71401\ 40271\ 66710\ 15010+$
$e^\gamma =$	$1.61772\ 13452\ 61152\ 65761\ 22477\ 36553\ 53327\ 17554\ 21260+$
$e^{\pi/4} =$	$2.14275\ 31512\ 16162\ 52370\ 35530\ 11342\ 53525\ 44307\ 02171-$
$\sin 1 =$	$0.65665\ 24436\ 04414\ 73402\ 03067\ 23644\ 11612\ 07474\ 14505-$
$\cos 1 =$	$0.42450\ 50037\ 32406\ 42711\ 07022\ 14666\ 27320\ 70675\ 12321+$
$-\zeta'(2) =$	$0.74001\ 45144\ 53253\ 42362\ 42107\ 23350\ 50074\ 46100\ 27706+$
$\zeta(3) =$	$1.14735\ 00023\ 60014\ 20470\ 15613\ 42561\ 31715\ 10177\ 06614+$
$\ln \phi =$	$0.36630\ 26256\ 61213\ 01145\ 13700\ 41004\ 52264\ 30700\ 40646+$
$1/\ln \phi =$	$2.04776\ 60111\ 17144\ 41512\ 11436\ 16575\ 00355\ 43630\ 40651+$
$-\ln\ln 2 =$	$0.27351\ 71233\ 67265\ 63650\ 17401\ 56637\ 26334\ 31455\ 57005-$

Several of the 40-digit values in Table 1 were computed on a desk calculator by John W. Wrench, Jr., for the first edition of this book. When computer software for such calculations became available during the 1970s, all of his contributions proved to be correct. See the answer to exercise 1.3.3–23 for the 40-digit value of another fundamental constant.

Table 3

VALUES OF HARMONIC NUMBERS, BERNOULLI NUMBERS,
AND FIBONACCI NUMBERS, FOR SMALL VALUES OF n

n	H_n	B_n	F_n	n
0	0	1	0	0
1	1	1/2	1	1
2	3/2	1/6	1	2
3	11/6	0	2	3
4	25/12	−1/30	3	4
5	137/60	0	5	5
6	49/20	1/42	8	6
7	363/140	0	13	7
8	761/280	−1/30	21	8
9	7129/2520	0	34	9
10	7381/2520	5/66	55	10
11	83711/27720	0	89	11
12	86021/27720	−691/2730	144	12
13	1145993/360360	0	233	13
14	1171733/360360	7/6	377	14
15	1195757/360360	0	610	15
16	2436559/720720	−3617/510	987	16
17	42142223/12252240	0	1597	17
18	14274301/4084080	43867/798	2584	18
19	275295799/77597520	0	4181	19
20	55835135/15519504	−174611/330	6765	20
21	18858053/5173168	0	10946	21
22	19093197/5173168	854513/138	17711	22
23	444316699/118982864	0	28657	23
24	1347822955/356948592	−236364091/2730	46368	24
25	34052522467/8923714800	0	75025	25
26	34395742267/8923714800	8553103/6	121393	26
27	312536252003/80313433200	0	196418	27
28	315404588903/80313433200	−23749461029/870	317811	28
29	9227046511387/2329089562800	0	514229	29
30	9304682830147/2329089562800	8615841276005/14322	832040	30

For any x, let $H_x = \sum_{n \geq 1} \left(\dfrac{1}{n} - \dfrac{1}{n+x} \right)$. Then

$$H_{1/2} = 2 - 2\ln 2,$$
$$H_{1/3} = 3 - \tfrac{1}{2}\pi/\sqrt{3} - \tfrac{3}{2}\ln 3,$$
$$H_{2/3} = \tfrac{3}{2} + \tfrac{1}{2}\pi/\sqrt{3} - \tfrac{3}{2}\ln 3,$$
$$H_{1/4} = 4 - \tfrac{1}{2}\pi - 3\ln 2,$$
$$H_{3/4} = \tfrac{4}{3} + \tfrac{1}{2}\pi - 3\ln 2,$$
$$H_{1/5} = 5 - \tfrac{1}{2}\pi\phi^{3/2}5^{-1/4} - \tfrac{5}{4}\ln 5 - \tfrac{1}{2}\sqrt{5}\ln\phi,$$
$$H_{2/5} = \tfrac{5}{2} - \tfrac{1}{2}\pi\phi^{-3/2}5^{-1/4} - \tfrac{5}{4}\ln 5 + \tfrac{1}{2}\sqrt{5}\ln\phi,$$
$$H_{3/5} = \tfrac{5}{3} + \tfrac{1}{2}\pi\phi^{-3/2}5^{-1/4} - \tfrac{5}{4}\ln 5 + \tfrac{1}{2}\sqrt{5}\ln\phi,$$
$$H_{4/5} = \tfrac{5}{4} + \tfrac{1}{2}\pi\phi^{3/2}5^{-1/4} - \tfrac{5}{4}\ln 5 - \tfrac{1}{2}\sqrt{5}\ln\phi,$$
$$H_{1/6} = 6 - \tfrac{1}{2}\pi\sqrt{3} - 2\ln 2 - \tfrac{3}{2}\ln 3,$$
$$H_{5/6} = \tfrac{6}{5} + \tfrac{1}{2}\pi\sqrt{3} - 2\ln 2 - \tfrac{3}{2}\ln 3,$$

and, in general, when $0 < p < q$ (see exercise 1.2.9–19),

$$H_{p/q} = \frac{q}{p} - \frac{\pi}{2}\cot\frac{p}{q}\pi - \ln 2q + 2 \sum_{1 \leq n < q/2} \cos\frac{2pn}{q}\pi \cdot \ln\sin\frac{n}{q}\pi.$$

INDEX TO NOTATIONS

In the following formulas, letters that are not further qualified have the following significance:

j, k	integer-valued arithmetic expression
m, n	nonnegative integer-valued arithmetic expression
x, y	real-valued arithmetic expression
f	real-valued or complex-valued function
P	pointer-valued expression (either Λ or a computer address)
S, T	set or multiset
α	string of symbols

Formal symbolism	Meaning	Where defined
$V \leftarrow E$	give variable V the value of expression E	1.1
$U \leftrightarrow V$	interchange the values of variables U and V	1.1
A_n or $A[n]$	the nth element of linear array A	1.1
A_{mn} or $A[m, n]$	the element in row m and column n of rectangular array A	1.1
NODE(P)	the node (group of variables that are individually distinguished by their field names) whose address is P, assuming that $P \neq \Lambda$	2.1
F(P)	the variable in NODE(P) whose field name is F	2.1
CONTENTS(P)	contents of computer word whose address is P	2.1
LOC(V)	address of variable V within a computer	2.1
$P \Leftarrow$ AVAIL	set the value of pointer variable P to the address of a new node	2.2.3
AVAIL $\Leftarrow$ P	return NODE(P) to free storage; all its fields lose their identity	2.2.3
top(S)	node at the top of a nonempty stack S	2.2.1
$X \Leftarrow$ S	pop up S to X: set $X \leftarrow$ top(S); then delete top(S) from nonempty stack S	2.2.1
S $\Leftarrow X$	push down X onto S: insert the value X as a new entry on top of stack S	2.2.1

Formal symbolism	Meaning	Where defined
$(R?\ a{:}\ b)$	conditional expression: denotes a if relation R is true, b if R is false	
$[R]$	characteristic function of relation R: $(R?\ 1{:}\ 0)$	1.2.3
δ_{kj}	Kronecker delta: $[j = k]$	1.2.3
$[z^n]\,g(z)$	coefficient of z^n in power series $g(z)$	1.2.9
$\displaystyle\sum_{R(k)} f(k)$	sum of all $f(k)$ such that the variable k is an integer and relation $R(k)$ is true	1.2.3
$\displaystyle\prod_{R(k)} f(k)$	product of all $f(k)$ such that the variable k is an integer and relation $R(k)$ is true	1.2.3
$\displaystyle\min_{R(k)} f(k)$	minimum value of all $f(k)$ such that the variable k is an integer and relation $R(k)$ is true	1.2.3
$\displaystyle\max_{R(k)} f(k)$	maximum value of all $f(k)$ such that the variable k is an integer and relation $R(k)$ is true	1.2.3
$j\backslash k$	j divides k: $k \bmod j = 0$ and $j > 0$	1.2.4
$S \setminus T$	set difference: $\{a \mid a \text{ in } S \text{ and } a \text{ not in } T\}$	
$\gcd(j, k)$	greatest common divisor of j and k: $$\left(j{=}k{=}0?\ 0{:}\ \max_{d\backslash j,\, d\backslash k} d\right)$$	1.1
$j \perp k$	j is relatively prime to k: $\gcd(j,k) = 1$	1.2.4
A^T	transpose of rectangular array A: $A^T[j,k] = A[k,j]$	
α^R	left-right reversal of α	
x^y	x to the y power (when x is positive)	1.2.2
x^k	x to the kth power: $$\left(k \geq 0?\ \prod_{0 \leq j < k} x{:}\ 1/x^{-k}\right)$$	1.2.2
$x^{\overline{k}}$	x to the k rising: $\Gamma(x+k)/\Gamma(x) =$ $$\left(k \geq 0?\ \prod_{0 \leq j < k} (x+j){:}\ 1/(x+k)^{\overline{-k}}\right)$$	1.2.5
$x^{\underline{k}}$	x to the k falling: $x!/(x-k)! =$ $$\left(k \geq 0?\ \prod_{0 \leq j < k} (x-j){:}\ 1/(x-k)^{\underline{-k}}\right)$$	1.2.5

Formal symbolism	Meaning	Where defined
$n!$	n factorial: $\Gamma(n+1) = n^{\underline{n}}$	1.2.5
$\binom{x}{k}$	binomial coefficient: $(k < 0?\ 0:\ x^{\underline{k}}/k!)$	1.2.6
$\binom{n}{n_1, n_2, \ldots, n_m}$	multinomial coefficient (defined only when $n = n_1 + n_2 + \cdots + n_m$)	1.2.6
$\left[\begin{matrix} n \\ m \end{matrix}\right]$	Stirling number of the first kind: $$\sum_{0 < k_1 < k_2 < \cdots < k_{n-m} < n} k_1 k_2 \ldots k_{n-m}$$	1.2.6
$\left\{\begin{matrix} n \\ m \end{matrix}\right\}$	Stirling number of the second kind: $$\sum_{1 \le k_1 \le k_2 \le \cdots \le k_{n-m} \le m} k_1 k_2 \ldots k_{n-m}$$	1.2.6
$\{a \mid R(a)\}$	set of all a such that the relation $R(a)$ is true	
$\{a_1, \ldots, a_n\}$	the set or multiset $\{a_k \mid 1 \le k \le n\}$	
$\{x\}$	fractional part (used in contexts where a real value, not a set, is implied): $x - \lfloor x \rfloor$	1.2.11.2
$a_1 + a_2 + \cdots + a_n$	n-fold sum: $\sum_{j=1}^{n} a_j$	1.2.3
$[a \mathrel{..} b]$	closed interval: $\{x \mid a \le x \le b\}$	1.2.2
$(a \mathrel{..} b)$	open interval: $\{x \mid a < x < b\}$	1.2.2
$[a \mathrel{..} b)$	half-open interval: $\{x \mid a \le x < b\}$	1.2.2
$(a \mathrel{..} b]$	half-closed interval: $\{x \mid a < x \le b\}$	1.2.2
$|S|$	cardinality: the number of elements in set S	
$|x|$	absolute value of x: $(x \ge 0?\ x:\ -x)$	
$|\alpha|$	length of α	
$\lfloor x \rfloor$	floor of x, greatest integer function: $\max_{k \le x} k$	1.2.4
$\lceil x \rceil$	ceiling of x, least integer function: $\min_{k \ge x} k$	1.2.4
$x \bmod y$	mod function: $\big(y = 0?\ x:\ x - y\lfloor x/y \rfloor\big)$	1.2.4
$x \equiv x' \ (\text{modulo } y)$	relation of congruence: $x \bmod y = x' \bmod y$	1.2.4
$O\big(f(n)\big)$	big-oh of $f(n)$, as the variable $n \to \infty$	1.2.11.1
$O\big(f(z)\big)$	big-oh of $f(z)$, as the variable $z \to 0$	1.2.11.1
$\Omega\big(f(n)\big)$	big-omega of $f(n)$, as the variable $n \to \infty$	1.2.11.1
$\Theta\big(f(n)\big)$	big-theta of $f(n)$, as the variable $n \to \infty$	1.2.11.1

Formal symbolism	Meaning	Where defined
$\log_b x$	logarithm, base b, of x (when $x > 0$, $b > 0$, and $b \neq 1$): the y such that $x = b^y$	1.2.2
$\ln x$	natural logarithm: $\log_e x$	1.2.2
$\lg x$	binary logarithm: $\log_2 x$	1.2.2
$\exp x$	exponential of x: e^x	1.2.9
$\langle X_n \rangle$	the infinite sequence X_0, X_1, X_2, ... (here the letter n is part of the symbolism)	1.2.9
$f'(x)$	derivative of f at x	1.2.9
$f''(x)$	second derivative of f at x	1.2.10
$f^{(n)}(x)$	nth derivative: $\big(n = 0?\ f(x)\!: g'(x)\big)$, where $g(x) = f^{(n-1)}(x)$	1.2.11.2
$H_n^{(x)}$	harmonic number of order x: $\displaystyle\sum_{1 \leq k \leq n} 1/k^x$	1.2.7
H_n	harmonic number: $H_n^{(1)}$	1.2.7
F_n	Fibonacci number: $(n \leq 1?\ n\!: F_{n-1} + F_{n-2})$	1.2.8
B_n	Bernoulli number: $n!\,[z^n]\,z/(1 - e^{-z})$	1.2.11.2
$\det(A)$	determinant of square matrix A	1.2.3
$\mathrm{sign}(x)$	sign of x: $[x > 0] - [x < 0]$	
$\zeta(x)$	zeta function: $\lim_{n\to\infty} H_n^{(x)}$ (when $x > 1$)	1.2.7
$\Gamma(x)$	gamma function: $(x - 1)! = \gamma(x, \infty)$	1.2.5
$\gamma(x, y)$	incomplete gamma function: $\int_0^y e^{-t} t^{x-1}\,dt$	1.2.11.3
γ	Euler's constant: $\lim_{n\to\infty}(H_n - \ln n)$	1.2.7
e	base of natural logarithms: $\sum_{n \geq 0} 1/n!$	1.2.2
π	circle ratio: $4\sum_{n \geq 0}(-1)^n/(2n + 1)$	1.2.2
∞	infinity: larger than any number	
Λ	null link (pointer to no address)	2.1
ϵ	empty string (string of length zero)	
$\emptyset$	empty set (set with no elements)	
ϕ	golden ratio: $\frac{1}{2}\big(1 + \sqrt{5}\,\big)$	1.2.8
$\varphi(n)$	Euler's totient function: $\displaystyle\sum_{0 \leq k < n} [k \perp n]$	1.2.4
$x \approx y$	x is approximately equal to y	1.2.5

Formal symbolism	Meaning	Where defined
$\Pr(S(X))$	probability that statement $S(X)$ is true, for random values of X	1.2.10
$\mathrm{E}\,X$	expected value of X: $\sum_x x \Pr(X = x)$	1.2.10
$\mathrm{mean}(g)$	mean value of the probability distribution represented by generating function g: $g'(1)$	1.2.10
$\mathrm{var}(g)$	variance of the probability distribution represented by generating function g: $$g''(1) + g'(1) - g'(1)^2$$	1.2.10
$(\min x_1, \mathrm{ave}\ x_2,$ $\max x_3, \mathrm{dev}\ x_4)$	a random variable having minimum value x_1, average (expected) value x_2, maximum value x_3, standard deviation x_4	1.2.10
P*	address of preorder successor of NODE(P) in a binary tree or tree	2.3.1, 2.3.2
P\$	address of inorder successor of NODE(P) in a binary tree, postorder successor in a tree	2.3.1, 2.3.2
P♯	address of postorder successor of NODE(P) in a binary tree	2.3.1
*P	address of preorder predecessor of NODE(P) in a binary tree or tree	2.3.1, 2.3.2
\$P	address of inorder predecessor of NODE(P) in a binary tree, postorder predecessor in a tree	2.3.1, 2.3.2
♯P	address of postorder predecessor of NODE(P) in a binary tree	2.3.1
▮	end of algorithm, program, or proof	1.1
␣	one blank space	1.3.1
rA	register A (accumulator) of MIX	1.3.1
rX	register X (extension) of MIX	1.3.1
rI1, ..., rI6	(index) registers I1, ..., I6 of MIX	1.3.1
rJ	(jump) register J of MIX	1.3.1
(L:R)	partial field of MIX word, $0 \le L \le R \le 5$	1.3.1
OP ADDRESS,I(F)	notation for MIX instruction	1.3.1, 1.3.2
u	unit of time in MIX	1.3.1
*	"self" in MIXAL	1.3.2
OF, 1F, 2F, ..., 9F	"forward" local symbol in MIXAL	1.3.2
OB, 1B, 2B, ..., 9B	"backward" local symbol in MIXAL	1.3.2
OH, 1H, 2H, ..., 9H	"here" local symbol in MIXAL	1.3.2

APPENDIX C

INDEX TO ALGORITHMS AND THEOREMS

Numerical experimentations are necessary
to fully understand the algorithms and theorems in this book.
— STÉPHANE MALLAT, *A Wavelet Tour of Signal Processing* (1998)

INDEX AND GLOSSARY

When an index entry refers to a page containing a relevant exercise, see also the *answer* to that exercise for further information. An answer page is not indexed here unless it refers to a topic not included in the statement of the exercise.

Roll, 240.
Root of a directed graph, 372.
Root of a number, 22, 25, 110.
Root of a tree, 308, 309, 317, 465.
  changing, in an oriented tree, 377.
Rooting a free tree, 373.
Roots of unity, 89.
Rosenberg, Arnold Leonard, 560.
Rosenstiehl, Pierre, 243.
Ross, Douglas Taylor, 450, 458, 462.
Rotating memory devices, 228, 457.
Rothe, Heinrich August, 63, 71, 486.
Rounding, 41, 83, 160, 183.
Rousseau, Cecil Clyde, 507.
Roving pointer, 607.
Row major order, 159, 182, 299.
RTAG, 322, 332–334, 338, 349–351, 359, 380.
Running time, see Execution time.
Russell, David Lewis, 613.
Russell, Lawford John, 202.

Saddle point, 159.
Salton, Gerard Anton, 351, 459.
Sammet, Jean Elaine, 462, 574.
Satterthwaite, Edwin Hallowell, Jr., 231.
Saving and restoring registers, 188,
  198, 213, 228.
Schäffer, Alejandro Alberto, 514.
Schatzoff, Martin, 450.
Scherk, Heinrich Ferdinand, 490.
Schlatter, Charles Fordemwalt, 459.
Schlatter, William Joseph, 459.
Scholten, Carel Steven, 231, 605.
Schoor, Amir (אמיר שור), 559.
Schorr, Herbert, 418, 422.
Schreiber, Peter, 81.
Schreier, Otto, 385.
Schröder, Friedrich Wilhelm Karl Ernst, 592.
Schwartz, Eugene Sidney, 404.
Schwarz, Karl Hermann Amandus,
  inequality, 36, 472.
Schweins, Franz Ferdinand, 489.
Schwenk, Allen John Carl, 495.
Schweppe, Earl Justin, 459.
SCOPE link, 350, 362, 434.
Scroll, 240.
Segner, Johann Andreas von, 407, 536.
Seki, Takakazu (關孝和), 112, 115.
Self-modifying code, 187, 193.
Selfridge, John Lewis, 78.
Semaphores, 231.
Semi-invariants of a probability distribution,
  103–106.
Sentinel: A special value placed in a table,
  designed to be easily recognizable
  by the accompanying program,
  217–218, 276, 567.

Sequential (consecutive) allocation of
  tables, 244.
  arrays, 158–159, 299–301, 305–307.
  contrasted to linked, 254–256, 296, 433.
  history, 457.
  linear lists, 244–254, 264–266, 325.
  tree structures, 348–352, 359–362, 433.
Series, infinite: An infinite sum.
Series-parallel networks, 589.
Sets, partition of, 74, 482.
Sha, Jichang (沙基昌), 547.
Shakespeare (= Shakspere), William,
  232, 466.
Shams Baragh, Armin (آرمین شمس براق), 526.
Shared subtrees, 326, 603.
Shaw, John Clifford, 230, 457–458.
Shelf, 240.
Shephard, Geoffrey Colin, 384.
Shepp, Lawrence Alan, 183, 184.
Shift operators of MIX, 135, 211.
Shor, Peter Williston, 514.
Shore, John Edward, 445, 450.
Shylock, 466.
Sibling, in a tree structure, 311.
Sibling link, 334, 336, 427–433; see also
  RLINK in trees.
SICOMP: SIAM Journal on Computing,
  published by the Society for Industrial
  and Applied Mathematics since 1972.
Sideways addition, 131, 480.
Sign function (sign x), 475.
Silver, Roland Lazarus, 527.
Similar binary trees, 327–329.
Similar forests, 346.
Simon, Herbert Alexander, 230, 457–458.
Simonovits, Miklós, 505.
Simple oriented path, 372, 376.
Simple path, 363, 369.
SIMSCRIPT language, 461.
SIMULA I language, 229.
Simulated time, 283, 288.
Simulation: Imitation of some process, 445.
  continuous, 282, 298.
  discrete, 203, 282–298.
  of one computer on another, 9, 202–203.
  of one computer on itself, 212–214.
Singh, Parmanand (परमानन्द सिंह), 80.
Singleton cycle of a permutation, 164,
  171, 180–181.
Singular matrix, 307.
Singularity of a function, 396.
Sister, in a tree structure, 311.
SLA (shift left rA), 135, 530.
SLAX (shift left rAX), 135, 530.
SLC (shift left rAX circularly), 135, 530.
Slesvig-Holsteen-Sønderborg-Glücksborg,
  Christian af, see Christian IX.
SLIP system, 460–461.
Sloane, Neil James Alexander, 595.
Smallest in, first out, 556.
SNOBOL language, 461.
SODA: Proceedings of the ACM–SIAM
  Symposia on Discrete Algorithms,
  inaugurated in 1990.

> *We must not ... think that computation,*
> *that is ratiocination, has place only in numbers.*
> — THOMAS HOBBES, *Elementary Philosophy* (1656)

THIS BOOK was composed on a Sun SPARCstation with Computer Modern typefaces, using the TEX and METAFONT software as described in the author's books *Computers & Typesetting* (Reading, Mass.: Addison–Wesley, 1986), Volumes A–E. The illustrations were produced with John Hobby's METAPOST system. Some names in the index were typeset with additional fonts developed by Yannis Haralambous (Greek, Hebrew, Arabic), Olga G. Lapko (Cyrillic), Frans J. Velthuis (Devanagari), Masatoshi Watanabe (Japanese), and Linbo Zhang (Chinese).

01	2	02	2	03	10
$rA \leftarrow rA + V$		$rA \leftarrow rA - V$		$rAX \leftarrow rA \times V$	
ADD(0:5) FADD(6)		SUB(0:5) FSUB(6)		MUL(0:5) FMUL(6)	

	2	09	2	10	2	11	2
V		$rI1 \leftarrow V$		$rI2 \leftarrow V$		$rI3 \leftarrow V$	
(0:5)		LD1(0:5)		LD2(0:5)		LD3(0:5)	

	2	17	2	18	2	19	2
$rA \leftarrow -V$		$rI1 \leftarrow -V$		$rI2 \leftarrow -V$		$rI3 \leftarrow -V$	
LDAN(0:5)		LD1N(0:5)		LD2N(0:5)		LD3N(0:5)	

24	2	25	2	26	2	27	2
$M(F) \leftarrow rA$		$M(F) \leftarrow rI1$		$M(F) \leftarrow rI2$		$M(F) \leftarrow rI3$	
STA(0:5)		ST1(0:5)		ST2(0:5)		ST3(0:5)	

32	2	33	2	34	1	35	$1+T$
$M(F) \leftarrow rJ$		$M(F) \leftarrow 0$		Unit F busy?		Control, unit F	
STJ(0:2)		STZ(0:5)		JBUS(0)		IOC(0)	

40	1	41	1	42	1	43	1
$rA : 0$, jump		$rI1 : 0$, jump		$rI2 : 0$, jump		$rI3 : 0$, jump	
JA[+]		J1[+]		J2[+]		J3[+]	

48	1	49	1	50	1	51	1
$rA \leftarrow [rA]? \pm M$		$rI1 \leftarrow [rI1]? \pm M$		$rI2 \leftarrow [rI2]? \pm M$		$rI3 \leftarrow [rI3]? \pm M$	
INCA(0) DECA(1) ENTA(2) ENNA(3)		INC1(0) DEC1(1) ENT1(2) ENN1(3)		INC2(0) DEC2(1) ENT2(2) ENN2(3)		INC3(0) DEC3(1) ENT3(2) ENN3(3)	

56	2	57	2	58	2	59	2
$CI \leftarrow rA(F) : V$		$CI \leftarrow rI1(F) : V$		$CI \leftarrow rI2(F) : V$		$CI \leftarrow rI3(F) : V$	
CMPA(0:5) FCMP(6)		CMP1(0:5)		CMP2(0:5)		CMP3(0:5)	

General form:

C	t
Description	
OP(F)	

C = operation code, (5 : 5) field of instruction
F = op variant, (4 : 4) field of instruction
M = address of instruction after indexing
$V = M(F)$ = contents of F field of location M
OP = symbolic name for operation
(F) = normal F setting
t = execution time; T = interlock time